2025 EDITION

Greenberg's GUIDES®

LIONEL® TRAINS

POCKET PRICE GUIDE 1901-2025

Edited by Roger Carp

Firecrown
605 Chestnut Street, Suite 800
Chattanooga, TN 37450

Shop.Trains.com

Published in 2024

Forty-fourth Edition

Manufactured in the United States of America

ISBN: 979-8-89491-004-8
EISBN: 979-8-89491-005-5

Front cover photo: Lionel No. 84400 Burlington Northern SD60M diesel engine, courtesy Jack Sommerfeld, Sommerfeld's Trains & Hobbies, Butler, Wis.

Back cover photo: Lionel No. 192 Railroad Control Tower, courtesy Joe Algozzini

We constantly strive to improve Greenberg's Pocket Price Guides. If you find missing items or detect misinformation, please contact us.
Send your comments, new information, or corrections via e-mail to books@firecrown.com or by mail to Lionel Pocket Price Guide Editor at the address above.

CONTENTS

INTRODUCTION

Whether you are a longtime Lionel enthusiast or a newcomer to the toy train hobby, this guide contains the information you need to identify and evaluate thousands of items made by Lionel since 1901. Most of all, you'll have at your fingertips the most up-to-date prices for locomotives, freight cars, passenger cars, stations, tunnels, signals, track sections, transformers, and other items.

What is listed

Almost every Lionel Standard, O, O-27, and OO gauge toy train and accessory produced over the years is listed in the pages that follow.

This edition of the *Lionel Pocket Price Guide* contains information about new additions to the product line as described in Lionel catalogs, press releases, and other sources. Any additions that Lionel makes to its line after this book is printed will be reported in the next edition.

In addition, the *Lionel Pocket Price Guide* provides information about items associated with Lionel yet not mentioned in its catalogs. These uncataloged or promotional items include unique models and specially decorated locomotives and cars that Lionel produces for national and regional toy train collecting and operating groups, museums, local railroad clubs, and other customers.

When to consult this guide

Many readers of the *Lionel Pocket Price Guide* use it after the fact. They already have some trains and accessories and now want to identify and evaluate those items. Maybe someone lucked upon a bridge at a garage sale and wants to know whether it's a No. 300 Hellgate Bridge or a No. 314 Deck Girder Bridge. Somebody else needs to provide his or her insurance agent with a complete list of O gauge locomotives that includes their conditions and current values. This guide contains the information needed to identify that bridge as well as determining present values for that engine roster.

In addition, the *Lionel Pocket Price Guide* can help you think about what to acquire in the future. That's really when the fun begins! You just have to spend some time considering how you want to approach the hobby. Collect, operate, or both? Prewar, postwar, or modern? Particular types of locomotives or cars? Favorite railroads? Promotional items?

Once you have a general idea of how to enjoy this hobby, you can make informed decisions about which trains you want.

UNDERSTANDING VALUES

The values presented here are an averaged reflection of prices for items bought and sold across the country during the year prior to the publication of this edition. These values are offered as guidelines and should be viewed as starting points that buyers and sellers can use to begin informed and reasonable negotiations.

In a listing for a steam locomotive, the value includes a tender, even if the tender is not listed in the description. The value of steam locomotives, particularly prewar items, may be affected significantly by the type of tender included.

Values for individual items may differ from what is listed in this price guide due to a few key factors. Where collectible trains are scarce and demand outruns supply, actual values may exceed what is shown. Values may also rise where certain items are especially popular, often because of their road names. And as with all collectibles, national and local economic conditions will impact values, which tend to drop when times are tough and demand falls.

Original packaging

Items in Like New or better condition require their original packaging to maintain their high level of value. The values given for items in Good and Excellent condition are not based on the expectation that a box and other associated items are present.

Items that do have their original packaging, especially if it is complete and undamaged, command a premium among collectors of prewar and postwar trains. No hard-and-fast rules can be stated as to how much higher their value is over the same items in Excellent condition. Generally speaking, though, boxed items in Like New condition are valued about 50 percent above the same item without a box.

Using the values

The values listed are what a consumer would pay — more or less — to get a particular item in a specific condition. One collector selling that item to another would probably ask the stated value and expect to get something close to it.

However, someone selling that same item to a person or business that intends to resell it (a train dealer) is unlikely to receive the stated value. Experience shows that sellers get about half the amount. Dealers offer less so they can earn a profit when reselling an item.

When buying or selling a toy train, you should learn more about it. Start by consulting this price guide and then look for more about it in a reference guide or website on toy trains. You can also ask more experienced hobbyists for their opinion about the item's condition and value.

FINDING A PRODUCT

The *Lionel Pocket Price Guide* has been divided into eight major sections.

Section 1: Prewar 1901–1942

Section 1 of the *Lionel Pocket Price Guide* is devoted to the pre-World War II period. The entries cover just about every train, accessory, and transformer associated with Lionel's line during its first 42 years.

The only outfits (sets) listed are those of articulated streamlined trains that consist of a powered unit and attached unpowered cars.

In an item's listing, the basic description specifies its gauge (the distance between the inside of the outermost rails). During this time, Lionel catalogued models in four sizes. It is noted in parentheses whether an item is 2⅞-inch, Standard (2⅛ inches), O (1¼ inches), or OO (¾ inches). O gauge models intended to run on tighter 27-inch-diameter track belong to Lionel's O-27 gauge line and are identified as such.

Transformers, rheostats, and many accessories were not limited to a single gauge, so their descriptions do not specify a gauge.

Section 2: Postwar 1945–1969

Section 2 concentrates on the post-World War II period of production. Nearly every train and accessory (except outfits) that Lionel cataloged between 1945 and 1969 has its own listing. By this time, Lionel no longer made trains in 2⅞-inch, Standard, or OO gauge. Instead, it offered trains that ran on track that had a diameter of either 31 inches (O gauge) or 27 inches (O-27 gauge). However, the entries in this section do not distinguish between O and O-27 since only a handful of locomotives and cars could operate solely on the wider curves.

Section 3: Modern Era 1970–2024

Section 3 shows the trains, accessories, transformers, and other items that Lionel has cataloged since 1970. The modern era encompasses the products of three companies: General Mills (Model Products Corp. and Fundimensions divisions), 1970–85; Lionel Trains Inc. (LTI), 1986–95; and Lionel LLC (LLC), 1996–2024.

These incarnations of Lionel are responsible for an enormous inventory of trains, rolling stock, transformers, and accessories. Cataloged and uncataloged O gauge items (ranging from the near-scale Standard O to the toy-like O-27) can be found within the pages of this section. All items in Section 3 are arranged according to their Lionel catalog number (omitting the numeral 6 used as a prefix). The descriptions of products made during the modern era may include information that relates to where in the product line a particular item belongs. Models derived from older designs have been described as traditional. Rolling stock whose dimensions and features approach scale realism may be designated as Standard O (abbreviated as std O). Locomotives equipped with TrainMaster Command Control or its successor, Legacy, are identified with the abbreviation CC.

Section 4: Lionel Corporation Tinplate

Section 4 features 800 products developed jointly by Lionel and MTH Electric Trains since 2009. These Lionel Corporation trains and accessories are reproductions of Lionel (and some American Flyer) tinplate items from the prewar era. You'll find trains here that operate as tinplate trains did prior to 1942 as well as others that have been updated with modern features and technology, such as Proto-Sound. The retail prices are listed for these products.

Section 5: Modern tinplate

Section 4 covers a category of modern-era trains that is referred to as modern tinplate. Here you'll find reissues of Standard and O gauge trains and accessories dating from the prewar period that LTI and LLC brought out for the purpose of satisfying a growing market. Also included in this section are a few Standard gauge trains that Lionel LLC has created, based on new designs.

Section 6: Club Cars and Special Production

Section 5 gathers the various items, principally locomotives and rolling stock, Lionel has made or sponsored for different hobby organizations, museums, and businesses since the 1970s. These uncataloged club cars and special production items are arranged according to the groups that offered them for sale. These groups are listed alphabetically; regional divisions of national organizations follow the parent organization's listing. Within each subordinate section, items are listed in numerical (not chronological) order, with a description similar to that used for cataloged entries.

Section 7: Boxes

Over the past 25 years, original boxes and other forms of packaging have assumed significance for some collectors. These hobbyists insist that the trains they buy come in the boxes and have the paperwork and ancillary pieces (inserts, instruction sheets, and envelopes) that the manufacturer packed with them before offering them for sale.

Cardboard boxes, inserts, and assorted sheets of paper are more fragile than die-cast metal or plastic trains. They were also deemed to be less important to the children playing with toy trains long ago and so were not treated with the same care. Instruction sheets were lost, and boxes were discarded. As a result, fewer boxes and instruction sheets have survived than have the trains and accessories that went with them. In some cases, the box that a particular locomotive, car, or even set came in is now valued more than the item itself. Boxes are evaluated according to standards and conditions established by the Train Collectors Association, similar to those developed for toy trains and accessories:

P-10 **Mint:** Brand new, complete, all original as made, and unused. Flaps appear to never have been opened, and edges are crisp. No tears, fading, or wear marks. Contains original contents and all applicable sealing tape, wrap, and staples.

P-9 **Store New:** Complete, all original, and unused. May have merchant additions such as store stamps and price tags. Must have appropriate inner liners.

P-8 **Like New:** Complete and all original. There is evidence of light use and aging. Box may have notations (discrete) added since leaving the manufacturer.

P-7 **Excellent:** Complete and all original. Box shows moderate signs of being opened and closed including edge and corner wear. All flaps must be intact.

P-6 **Very Good:** Complete and all original. Box shows signs of usage such as minor abrasions, small tears, color changes, and minor soiling. Inner liners may be missing, and inner flaps may require strengthening. The box can still safely store its original contents.

P-5 **Good:** Box shows substantial wear, and edges may be damaged. Box may have extensive color fading but no evident water damage or cardboard deterioration. Exterior flaps are present, but their connection to the box may require repair. Inner liners may be missing. With care, the box can still store contents. (Any box that has been repaired cannot be graded above P-5.)

P-4 **Fair:** Box shows heavy damage and may have been repaired. Inner flaps may be missing. Box cannot store its original contents. Water damage may be present.

Values for postwar boxes in this section are shown for Good (P-5) and Excellent (P-7) conditions.

Lionel used these box types during the postwar years:

Art Deco: Original postwar box with bold orange and blue design and lettering. It was used in 1946 and 1947.

Classic: More understated design than Art Deco. It was the main component box from 1948 through 1958. Boxes can be divided into Early (1948–49), Middle (1949–55), and Late (1956–58) Classic designs, which are marked by minor lettering changes.

Orange Perforated: This was a significant change from the Classic design. The solid orange box features white lettering and a tear-out perforated front panel. It was used in 1959 and 1960.

Orange Picture: Instead of a perforated panel, this version of the Orange Perforated box features an illustration of a steam locomotive and an F3 diesel on the front. It was used from 1961 to 1964.

Hillside Orange Picture: Similar to an Orange Picture box, it is labeled with Hillside, N.J., where Lionel's plant was located. It was used in 1965.

Cellophane: Used in 1966, this box features a clear cellophane window on the front.

Hagerstown Checkerboard: It has a Lionel checkerboard pattern and Hagerstown, Maryland, printed on end flap bottoms. The box was used in 1968.

Hillside Checkerboard: This 1969 box is the same as the Hagerstown Checkerboard box, but with Hillside, New Jersey, printed on it.

Lionel also used brown corrugated and plain white boxes.

Section 8: Sets

This section lists boxed train sets cataloged by Lionel during the postwar years, 1945–69. When collecting sets, it is important that the sets, or outfits, contain all the items, including ancillary ones, that Lionel packed with them. These items include the locomotive (and tender if a steam engine) rolling stock, any accessories, track, transformer, instructions and other paper pieces, component boxes, and the set box.

The listings include the set's catalog number, a short description, and product numbers for the locomotives, rolling stock, and any major accessories. Sets came with O-27 gauge, O gauge, or Super O track. O-27 and Super O track are listed in the set's description. If no track is listed, the set came with O gauge.

Set values are listed for Excellent (C-7) condition. The presence and condition of original component boxes, set boxes, inserts and other packaging materials can have a significant effect on a set's value. The values reflect the inclusion of these materials. Values of individual set and component boxes can be found in Section 7.

Due to space constraints, not every item found in a set is listed in the description. You can find more complete information on a set's contents on various websites and in the third volume of *Greenberg's Guide to Lionel Trains 1945–1969: Cataloged Sets* by Paul Ambrose and Harold J. Lovelock. Even though the book is out of print, copies can be found from booksellers on the internet.

USING THE GUIDE

Number	Description	Good	Exc	
2561	Vista Valley Observation Car, 59–61 *	75	230	___
X6454	NYC Boxcar, 48			
	(A) Brown body	15	35	___
	(B) Orange body	50	140	___
	(C) Tan body	20	60	___
6475	Libby's Crushed Pineapple Vat Car, 63u	35	90	___

Identifying a catalog number

A Lionel catalog number is usually stamped, printed, or painted on an item. However, some products do not contain a catalog number. In these cases, you can match the product with its catalog number using a comprehensive reference book or website, including Lionel.com, which contains current and some past catalogs.

Two-, three-, and four-digit numbers predominated during the prewar (1901–42) and postwar (1945–69) periods. Four- and five-digit numbers, and now seven digit numbers, have been most common during the modern era (1970–2024).

On the models, catalog numbers often double as road numbers, although sometimes separate road numbers were added.

Locating an item

Sections are arranged in numerical order of catalog numbers. Items having one or more zeroes as placeholders are listed before those without placeholders. For example, a 004 4-6-4 Locomotive is listed before a 4 Electric Locomotive.

In the prewar and postwar sections, some items, such as transformers and track pieces, are identified by a letter. These products follow the numbered items.

Reading an entry

Every entry begins with the product's catalog number assigned by Lionel. (Club and special production cars may have numbers that were assigned by the group.)

A basic description of the model follows. It gives the type of product, lists the name of any railroad identified with it, and includes identifying characteristics, such as color or lettering. If the item has a road number that differs from its catalog number, that number is shown in quotation marks. (Most of these are seen in Section 3). Abbreviations used in the descriptions, including those of railroad names, are listed at the back of the price guide.

Next, you'll find the year or years during which that item was part of Lionel's cataloged product line. The years are shown in italics. If a year is followed by a u, this item is considered to be uncataloged. It was not part of the cataloged line but a promotional item that Lionel made or sponsored for an outside business or group.

Entries that show an asterisk (*) after the year have had one or more reissues of the item made.

Many entries feature variations, each indicated by a separate letter (A, B, and so forth). Variations amount to slight yet noteworthy differences in appearance that distinguish models that otherwise seem identical. These differences can relate to color, lettering, and details that were added or deleted. For items having many variations, an entry may not include every variation.

An entry concludes with an indication of the value of the item for several common conditions.

Condition

Lionel enthusiasts should be familiar with the condition and grading standards established by the Train Collectors Association, which are used as the basis for evaluating the condition of toy trains and accessories:

C-10 **Mint:** Brand new—all original, unused, and unblemished.

C-9 **Factory New:** Same condition as Mint but with evidence of factory rubs or slight signs of handling, shipping, and being test run at the factory.

C-8 **Like New:** Complete and all original with no rust or no missing parts; may show effects of being displayed or signs of age and may have been run.

C-7 **Excellent:** All original and may have minute scratches and paint nicks; no rust, no missing parts, and no distortion of component parts.

C-6 **Very Good:** Has minor scratches, paint nicks, or minor spots of surface rust; is free of dents and may have minor parts replaced.

C-5 **Good:** Shows evidence of heavy use and signs of play wear—small dents, scratches, minor paint loss, and minor surface rust.

C-4 **Fair:** Shows evidence of heavy use—scratches and dents, moderate paint loss, missing parts, and surface rust.

C-3 **Poor:** Requires major body repair and is a candidate for restoration; major rust, missing parts, and heavily scratched.

C-2 **Restoration:** Needs to be restored.

C-1 **Junk:** Parts value only.

Values are listed for prewar and postwar trains in Good (C-5) and Excellent (C-7) conditions. For modern-era trains, including special production and club cars, the values for Excellent (C-7) and Mint (C-10) are shown.

You may also see NRS listed as a value. NRS (No Reported Sales) refers to an item with limited pricing data since only a handful of these scarce items may have been reported.

Determining a model's condition

Look over a model carefully to see whether it has suffered serious damage, including warping and breaking. Then note whether any parts are missing. Feel for dents in metal and cracks in plastic. Check for areas marred by rust, mildew, or chipped paint.

The TCA condition standards will assist you in evaluating your model, such as deciding whether a prewar or postwar model falls below Good or above Excellent.

The assessment of a toy train's value is based on the expectations that it has not been modified and that all parts are present and original to it. Repainting or relettering a model seriously undermines a train's value, regardless of how beat-up and scratched it may have been before undergoing modification. Any model that has been altered should be labeled as a restoration; potential buyers deserve to be informed about how it has been modified, so they do not mistake it for an original.

A model that is missing some parts should be sold as is or have those parts replaced by identical originals. A tank car cataloged in 1935 that needs a brake wheel must have a part from 1935 put on it to be considered a true original. Adding a brake wheel from 1936 undermines the car's legitimacy as much as adding one from 2023 does.

The same rule applies to the ancillary items that came with various models. The value of a flatcar may depend largely on the miniature airplane or rocket packed with it; therefore, having a load that is a genuine original is essential to maintaining the value of that flatcar. Similarly, freight loaders must have whatever cargo came with them (coal, logs, trailers, and so forth). Reproductions should be identified as such.

NOTES

Section 1
PREWAR 1901–1942

			Good	Exc
___	**001**	4-6-4 Locomotive (00), 38-42	195	360
___	**1**	Bild-A-Motor (0), 28-31	60	140
___	**1**	Trolley (std), 06-14		
___		(A) Cream body, orange band and roof	1900	4750
___		(B) White body, blue band and roof	1750	4750
___		(C) Cream body, blue band and roof	1300	3150
___		(D) Cream body, blue band and roof, Curtis Bay	2150	5550
___		(E) Blue, cream band, blue roof	1450	3150
___	**1/111**	Trolley Trailer (std), 06-14	1000	2700
___	**002**	4-6-4 Locomotive (00), 39-42	160	285
___	**2**	Bild-A-Motor (std), 28-31	100	180
___	**2**	Trolley (std), 06-16*		
___		(A) Yellow, red band	1200	3575
___		(B) Red, yellow band	1200	2250
___	**2/200**	Trolley Trailer (std), 06-16	1000	1800
___	**003**	4-6-4 Locomotive (00), 39-42		
___		(A) 003W whistling Tender	190	395
___		(B) 003T nonwhistling Tender	175	355
___	**3**	Trolley (std), 06-13		
___		(A) Cream, orange band	1400	3100
___		(B) Cream, dark olive green band	1400	3100
___		(C) Orange, dark olive green band	1400	3100
___		(D) Dark green, cream windows	1400	3100
___		(E) Green, cream windows, Bay Shore	1650	3700
___	**3/300**	Trolley Trailer (std), 06-13	1500	3500
___	**004**	4-6-4 Locomotive (00), 39-42		
___		(A) 004W whistling Tender	210	350
___		(B) 004T nonwhistling Tender	190	310
___	**4**	Electric Locomotive 0-4-0 (0), 28-32*		
___		(A) Orange, black frame	550	875
___		(B) Gray, apple green stripe	580	1050
___	**4**	Trolley (std), 06-12		
___		(A) Cream, dark olive green band	3000	4950
___		(B) Green or olive green, cream roof	3000	4950
___	**4U**	No. 4 Kit Form (0), 28-29	1150	2050
___	**5**	0-4-0 Locomotive, no tender, early (std), 06-07		
___		(A) NYC & HRR	1000	1450
___		(B) Pennsylvania	1400	2300
___		(C) NYC & HRRR (3 Rs)	992	2050
___		(D) B&O RR	1500	6200
___	**5**	0-4-0 Locomotive, tender, early Special (std), 06-09	980	1300
___	**5**	0-4-0 Locomotive, no tender, later (std), 10-11	750	1150
___	**5**	0-4-0 Locomotive, tender, later Special (std), 10-11	920	1200

PREWAR 1901-1942		Good	Exc	
5/51	0-4-0 Locomotive, tender, latest (std), 12-23	800	1100	___
6	4-4-0 Locomotive (std), 06-23	860	2075	___
6	0-4-0 Locomotive Special (std), 08-09	1700	2950	___
7	Steam 4-4-0 Locomotive (std), 10-23*	1850	2550	___
8	Electric Locomotive 0-4-0 (std), 25-32			___
	(A) Maroon or mojave, brass windows and trim	130	250	___
	(B) Olive green, brass windows	155	205	___
	(C) Red, brass or cream windows	136	250	___
	(D) Peacock, orange windows	520	750	___
8	Trolley (std), 08-14*			___
	(A) Cream, orange band and roof	3000	5400	___
	(B) Dark green, cream windows	2825	5400	___
8E	Electric Locomotive 0-4-0 (std), 26-32			___
	(A) Mojave, brass windows and trim	175	250	___
	(B) Red, brass or cream windows	150	225	___
	(C) Peacock, orange windows	370	590	___
	(D) Pea green, cream stripe	465	670	___
9	Electric Locomotive 0-4-0 (std), 29*	1200	2150	___
9	Motor Car (std), 09-12		NRS	___
9	Trolley (std), 09	3000	5400	___
9E	Electric Locomotive (std), 28-35*			___
	(A) 0-4-0, orange	700	1250	___
	(B) 2-4-2, two-tone green	880	2550	___
	(C) 2-4-2, gunmetal gray	514	1100	___
9U	Electric Locomotive 0-4-0 Kit (std), 28-29	817	1975	___
10	Electric Locomotive 0-4-0 (std), 25-29*			___
	(A) Mojave, brass trim	145	215	___
	(B) Gray, brass trim	105	228	___
	(C) Peacock, brass inserts	145	165	___
	(D) Red, cream stripe	580	880	___
10	Interurban (std), 10-16			___
	(A) Maroon	3000	5750	___
	(B) Dark olive green	1200	2150	___
10E	Electric Locomotive 0-4-0 (std), 26-30			___
	(A) Olive green, black frame		NRS	___
	(B) Peacock, dark green or black frame	245	400	___
	(C) State brown, dark green frame	435	630	___
	(D) Gray, black frame	165	220	___
	(E) Red, cream stripe	620	890	___
011	Non derailing switches, 33-37	18	38	___
11	Flatcar, early (std), 06-08	150	360	___
11	Flatcar, later (std), 09-15	45	90	___
11	Flatcar, latest (std), 16-18	50	90	___
11	Flatcar, Lionel Corp. (std), 18-26	50	80	___
012	Switches, pair (O), 27-33	20	40	___
12	Gondola, early (std), 06-08	150	360	___

	No.	Description	Good	Exc
___	**12**	Gondola, later (std), 09-15	50	100
___	**12**	Gondola, latest (std), 16-18	33	70
___	**12**	Gondola, Lionel Corp. (std), 18-26	50	70
___	**013**	012 Switches and 439 panel board, 27-33	120	190
___	**13**	Cattle Car, early (std), 06-08	300	950
___	**13**	Cattle Car, later (std), 09-15	150	225
___	**13**	Cattle Car, latest (std), 16-18	65	115
___	**13**	Cattle Car, Lionel Corp. (std), 18-26	65	115
___	**0014**	Boxcar (OO), 38-42		
___		(A) Yellow, Lionel Lines	80	155
___		(B) Tuscan, Pennsylvania	40	75
___	**14**	Boxcar, early (std), 06-08	195	468
___	**14**	Boxcar, later (std), 09-15	80	105
___	**14**	Boxcar, latest (std), 16-18	75	105
___	**14**	Boxcar, Lionel Corp. (std), 18-26	2090	2153
___	**0015**	Tank Car (OO), 38-42		
___		(A) Silver, Sunoco	40	90
___		(B) Black, Shell	50	83
___	**15**	Oil Car, early (std), 06-08	200	360
___	**15**	Oil Car, later (std), 09-15	75	115
___	**15**	Oil Car, latest (std), 16-18	75	115
___	**15**	Oil Car, Lionel Corp. (std), 18-26	75	115
___	**0016**	Hopper Car (OO), 38-42		
___		(A) Gray	75	160
___		(B) Black	58	115
___	**16**	Ballast Dump Car, early (std), 06-11	400	700
___	**16**	Ballast Dump Car, later (std), 09-15	95	175
___	**16**	Ballast Dump Car, latest (std), 16-18	95	175
___	**16**	Ballast Dump Car, Lionel Corp. (std), 18-26	95	175
___	**0017**	Caboose (OO), 38-42	40	90
___	**17**	Caboose, early (std), 06-08	220	495
___	**17**	Caboose, later (std), 09-15	70	135
___	**17**	Caboose, latest (std), 16-18	75	135
___	**17**	Caboose, Lionel Corp. (std), 18-26	50	90
___	**18**	Pullman Car (std), 08		
___		(A) Dark olive green, nonremovable roof	700	2150
___		(B) Dark olive green, removable roof	88	215
___		(C) Yellow-orange, removable roof	315	870
___		(D) Orange, removable roof	90	205
___		(E) Mojave, removable roof	305	890
___	**18**	Pullman Car (std), 11-13	600	900
___	**18**	Pullman Car (std), 13-15	150	270
___	**18**	Pullman Car (std), 15-18	150	270
___	**18**	Pullman Car (std), 18-22	90	155
___	**18**	Pullman Car (std), 23-26	270	530

PREWAR 1901-1942		Good	Exc
19	Combine Car (std), 08		
	(A) Dark olive green, nonremovable roof	1100	2600
	(B) Dark olive green, removable roof	80	148
	(C) Yellow-orange, removable roof	260	430
	(D) Orange, removable roof	115	205
	(E) Mojave, removable roof	305	890
19	Combine Car (std), 11-13	600	900
19	Combine Car (std), 13-15	200	270
19	Combine Car (std), 15-18	200	270
19	Combine Car (std), 18-22	90	155
19	Combine Car (std), 23-26	265	520
020	90-degree Crossover (O), 15-42	4	13
020X	45-degree Crossover (O), 17-42	3	10
20	90-degree Crossover (std), 09-32	4	10
20	Direct Current Reducer, 06	95	195
20X	45-degree Crossover (std), 28-32	5	10
021	Switches, pair (O), 15-37	20	50
21	90-degree Crossover (std), 06	10	20
21	Switches, pair (std), 15-25	35	70
022	Remote Control Switches, pair (O), 38-42	40	70
22	Manual Switches, pair (std), 06-25	45	75
023	Bumper (O), 15-33	15	35
23	Bumper (std), 06-23	15	40
0024	Pennsylvania Boxcar (OO), 39-42	45	75
24	Open Railway Station (std), 06	300	1500
025	Bumper (O), 28-42	15	54
0025	Tank Car (OO), 39-42		
	(A) Black, Shell	40	90
	(B) Silver, Sunoco	40	80
25	Open Station (std), 06		NRS
25	Bumper (std), 27-42	25	45
26	Passenger Bridge (std), 06	15	40
0027	Caboose (OO), 39-42	40	70
27	Lighting Set, 11-23	15	40
27	Station (std), 09-12		NRS
28	Double Station with dome, 09-12		NRS
29	Day Coach (std), 07-22		
	(A) Dark olive green, 9 windows	1500	3000
	(B) Maroon, 10 windows	1200	1500
	(C) Dark green, 10 windows	3000	4500
	(D) Dark olive green, 10 windows	485	1000
	(E) Dark green, 10 windows	450	900
0031	2-rail 13" Curve Track (OO), 39-42	5	10
31	Combine Car (std), 21-25		
	(A) Maroon	70	90
	(B) Orange	125	195

		PREWAR 1901-1942	Good	Exc
___		(C) Dark olive green	65	90
___		(D) Brown	75	95
___	**0032**	2-rail 12" Straight Track (OO), 39-42	10	15
___	**32**	Mail Car (std), 21-25		
___		(A) Maroon	85	125
___		(B) Orange	120	185
___		(C) Dark olive green	65	85
___		(D) Brown	70	90
___	**32**	Miniature Figures, 09-18	95	250
___	**33**	Electric Locomotive 0-6-0, early (std), 13		
___		(A) Dark olive green, NYC in oval	105	188
___		(B) Black, NYC	320	950
___		(C) Dark olive green, NYC	440	950
___		(D) Pennsylvania RR	580	1250
___	**33**	Electric Locomotive 0-4-0, later (std), 13-24		
___		(A) Dark olive green or black, NYC	105	170
___		(B) Black, lettered C&O	395	720
___		(C) Maroon, red, or peacock	340	620
___	**0034**	2-rail 13" Curve Track, electrical connectors (OO), 39-42	10	15
___	**34**	Electric Locomotive 0-6-0, early (std), 12	520	860
___	**34**	Electric Locomotive 0-4-0 (std), 13	200	385
___	**35**	Pullman Car (std), 12-13		
___		(A) Dark blue	470	900
___		(B) Dark olive green	170	235
___	**35**	Pullman Car (std), 14-16		
___		(A) Dark olive green, maroon windows	35	70
___		(B) Maroon, green windows	75	105
___		(C) Orange, maroon windows	125	195
___	**35**	Pullman Car (std), 15-18	40	70
___	**35**	Pullman Car (std), 18-23		
___		(A) Dark olive green, maroon windows	30	50
___		(B) Maroon, green windows	25	45
___		(C) Orange, maroon windows	120	210
___		(D) Brown, green windows	30	50
___	**35**	Boulevard Street Lamp, 6 1/8" high, 40-42	27	50
___	**35**	Pullman Car (std), 24	40	55
___	**35**	Pullman Car (std), 25-26	40	55
___	**36**	Observation Car (std), 12-13		
___		(A) Dark blue	315	810
___		(B) Dark olive green	145	205
___	**36**	Observation Car (std), 14-16		
___		(A) Dark olive green, maroon windows	60	95
___		(B) Maroon, green windows	50	70
___		(C) Orange, maroon windows	180	290
___		(D) Brown, green windows	50	75
___	**36**	Observation Car (std), 15-18	60	80

		Good	Exc	
36	Observation Car (std), 18-23			___
	(A) Dark olive green, maroon windows	40	55	___
	(B) Maroon, green windows	40	55	___
	(C) Orange, maroon windows	130	215	___
	(D) Brown, green windows	40	55	___
36	Observation Car (std), 24	40	55	___
36	Observation Car (std), 25-26	40	55	___
38	Electric Locomotive 0-4-0 (std), 13-24			___
	(A) Black	100	163	___
	(B) Red	475	680	___
	(C) Mojave or pea green	405	540	___
	(D) Dark green	270	360	___
	(E) Brown	270	315	___
	(F) Red, cream trim	405	540	___
	(G) Maroon	170	270	___
	(H) Gray	70	125	___
41	Accessory Contactor, 37-42	3	12	___
042	Switches, pair (O), 38-42	15	40	___
42	Electric Locomotive 0-4-4-0, square hood, early (std), 12*	760	1650	___
42	Electric Locomotive 0-4-4-0 , round hood, later (std), 13-23			
	(A) Black or gray	300	510	___
	(B) Maroon	1250	2050	___
	(C) Dark gray	388	600	___
	(D) Dark green or mojave	600	800	___
	(E) Peacock	1100	1800	___
	(F) Olive or dark olive green	750	1200	___
043/43	Bild-A-Motor Gear Set, 29	40	85	___
0044	Boxcar (OO), 39-42	40	80	___
0044K	Boxcar Kit (OO), 39-42	75	120	___
0045	Tank Car (OO), 39-42			
	(A) Black, Shell	40	95	___
	(B) Silver, Sunoco	40	80	___
0045K	Tank Car Kit (OO), 39-42	75	120	___
045	Automatic Gateman (O), 35-36	15	149	___
45	Automatic Gateman (std), 35-36	20	45	___
45N	Automatic Gateman (std, O), 37-42	40	159	___
0046	Hopper Car (OO), 39-42	50	90	___
0046K	Hopper Car Kit (OO), 39-42			
	(A) Southern Pacific	75	135	___
	(B) Reading		NRS	___
46	Single Crossing Gate, 39-42	75	120	___
0047	Caboose (OO), 39-42	30	60	___
0047K	Caboose Kit (OO), 39-42	75	135	___
47	Double Crossing Gate, 39-42	55	140	___
48W	Whistle Station, 37-42	20	65	___

	PREWAR 1901-1942		Good	Exc
___	**50**	Electric Locomotive 0-4-0 (std), 24		
___		(A) Dark green or dark gray	133	250
___		(B) Maroon	315	600
___		(C) Mojave	175	345
___	**50**	Cardboard Train, Cars, Accessory (O), 43*	200	360
___	**0051**	7" Curve Track (OO), 39-42	5	15
___	**51**	0-4-0 Locomotive, late, 8-wheel (std), 12-23	638	1150
___	**0052**	7" Straight Track (OO), 39-42	10	15
___	**52**	Lamp Post, 33-41	45	112
___	**53**	Electric Locomotive 0-4-4-0, early (std), 12-14	1200	2450
___	**53**	Electric Locomotive 0-4-0, later (std), 15-19		
___		(A) Maroon	550	950
___		(B) Mojave	670	1350
___		(C) Dark olive green	560	1150
___	**53**	Electric Locomotive 0-4-0, latest (std), 20-21	200	450
___	**53**	Electric Locomotive 0-6-6-0, early (std), 11		NRS
___	**53**	Lamp Post, 31-42	30	65
___	**0054**	7" Curve Track, electrical connectors (OO), 39-42	10	15
___	**54**	Electric Locomotive 0-4-4-0, early (std), 12*	2500	4050
___	**54**	Electric Locomotive 0-4-4-0, late (std), 13-23	1800	2700
___	**54**	Lamp Post, 29-35	60	108
___	**56**	Lamp Post, removable lens and cap, 24-42		
___		(A) Mojave	85	185
___		(B) Dark gray	55	110
___		(C) 45N green	25	45
___		(D) Pea green	30	50
___		(E) Aluminum	30	45
___		(F) Copper	60	160
___		(G) Dark green	30	45
___	**57**	Lamp Post with street names, 22-42		
___		(A) Orange post, Main St. & Broadway	35	55
___		(B) Orange post, Fifth Ave. & 42nd St.	40	95
___		(C) Orange post, Broadway & 21st St.	45	90
___		(D) Orange post, Broadway, 42nd St., Fifth Ave. & 21st St.	70	145
___		(E) Yellow post, Main St. & Broadway	35	89
___	**58**	Lamp Post, 7 3/8" high, 22-42		
___		(A) Cream	28	60
___		(B) Peacock	30	60
___		(C) Pea green	30	60
___		(D) Maroon	33	85
___		(E) Dark green	28	50
___		(F) Orange	30	60
___	**59**	Lamp Post, 8 3/4" high, 20-36	40	100
___	**060**	Telegraph Post (O), 29-42	10	25
___	**60**	Telegraph Post (std), 20-28	10	73
___	**60**	Electric Locomotive 0-4-0, FAO Schwartz (std), 15 u		NRS

PREWAR 1901-1942		Good	Exc	
0061	7" Curve Track, tubular (00), 38	3	10	___
61	Lamp Post, one globe, 14-36	35	65	___
61	Electric Locomotive 0-4-4-0, FAO Schwartz (std), 15 u		NRS	___
0062	7" Straight Track, tubular (00), 38	5	10	___
62	Semaphore, 20-32	30	50	___
62	Electric Locomotive 0-4-0, FAO Schwartz (std), 24-32 u		NRS	___
0063	Half Curve Track, tubular (00), 38-42	8	15	___
63	Semaphore, single arm, 15-21	25	50	___
63	Lamp Post, two globes, 33-42	135	265	___
0064	7" Curve Track, tubular, electrical connectors (00), 38	8	15	___
64	Lamp Post, 40-42	35	70	___
64	Semaphore, double arm, 15-21	30	60	___
0065	Half Straight Track, tubular (00), 38-42	10	15	___
65	Semaphore, one-arm, 15-26	30	60	___
65	Whistle Controller, 35	8	15	___
0066	5 5/8" Straight Track (00), 38-42	10	15	___
66	Semaphore, two-arm, 15-26	35	70	___
66	Whistle Controller, 36-39	5	10	___
67	Lamp Post, 15-32	85	145	___
67	Whistle Controller, 36-39	12	30	___
068	Warning Signal (0), 25-42	107	202	___
68	Warning Signal (std), 20-39	12	30	___
069	Electric Warning Bell Signal (0), 21-35	37	75	___
69	Electric Warning Bell Signal (std), 21-35	40	76	___
69N	Electric Warning Bell Signal (std, 0), 36-42	35	70	___
0070	90-degree Crossing, 38-42	5	10	___
70	Outfit: 62 (2), 59 (1), 68 (1), 21-32	60	130	___
071	060 Telegraph Post Set, 6 pieces (0), 29-42	70	160	___
71	60 Telegraph Post Set, 6 pieces (std), 21-31	35	145	___
0072	Remote Control Switches, pair (00), 38-42	155	290	___
0072L	Remote Control Switch, left hand (00), 38-42	50	95	___
0072R	Remote Control Switch, right hand (00)	50	95	___
0074	Boxcar (00), 39-42	35	85	___
0075	Tank Car (00), 39-42	50	145	___
076	Block Signal (0), 23-28	35	105	___
76	Warning Bell and Shack, 39-42	47	180	___
0077	Caboose (00), 39-42	30	60	___
77/077	Automatic Crossing Gate, 23-35	14	50	___
78/078	Train Signal, 24-32	45	100	___
79	Flashing Signal, 28-42	97	175	___
80/080	Semaphore, 26-35	50	120	___
81	Controlling Rheostat, 27-33	5	17	___
82/082	Semaphore, 27-35	40	120	___
83	Flashing Traffic Signal, 27-42	65	195	___
084	Semaphore (0), 27-32	60	100	___
84	Semaphore (std), 27-32	43	85	___

	PREWAR 1901-1942		Good	Exc
___	**85**	Telegraph Pole (std), 29-42	18	30
___	**86**	Telegraph Poles, 6 pieces, 29-42	60	135
___	**87**	Flashing Crossing Signal, 27-42	168	308
___	**88**	Rheostat, 15-27	3	10
___	**88**	Direction Controller, 33-42	4	12
___	**89**	Flagpole, 23-34	40	132
___	**90**	Flagpole, 27-42	40	98
___	**91**	Circuit Breaker, 30-42	30	50
___	**092**	Signal Tower, 23-27	85	190
___	**92**	Floodlight Tower, 31-42*	110	215
___	**93**	Water Tower, 31-42	55	114
___	**94**	High Tension Tower, 32-42*	150	290
___	**95**	Controlling Rheostat, 34-42	5	15
___	**096**	Telegraph Post (0), 34-35	15	25
___	**96**	Coal Elevator, manual, 38-40	165	390
___	**097**	Telegraph Post and Signal Set (0), 34-35	45	75
___	**97**	Coal Elevator, 38-42	118	558
___	**98**	Coal Bunker, 38-40	107	320
___	**99N**	Train Control Block Signal, 36-42	45	153
___	**100**	Wooden Gondola (2 7/8"), 01		NRS
___	**100**	Bridge Approaches, 2 ramps (std), 20-31	20	40
___	**100**	Electric Locomotive (2 7/8"), 03-05*	2900	5200
___	**100**	Trolley (std), 10-16		
___		(A) Blue, white windows	1300	2700
___		(B) Blue, cream windows	1675	3600
___		(C) Red, cream windows	1300	2700
___	**101**	Bridge, span (104) and 2 approaches (100), 20-31	53	120
___	**101**	Summer Trolley (std), 10-13	1300	2950
___	**102**	Bridge, 2 spans (104) and 2 approaches (100), 20-31	70	175
___	**103**	Bridge (std), 13-16	40	75
___	**103**	Bridge, 3 spans (104) and 2 approaches (100), 20-31	60	145
___	**104**	Bridge Center Span (std), 20-31	20	45
___	**104**	Tunnel, papier mache (std), 09-14	50	135
___	**105**	Bridge (std), 11-14	40	70
___	**105**	Bridge Approaches, 2 ramps (0), 20-31	50	70
___	**106**	Bridge, span (110) and 2 approaches (105), 20-31	30	72
___	**106**	Rheostat, 11-14	3	10
___	**107**	DC Reducer, 110V, 23-32		NRS
___	**108**	Bridge, 2 spans (110) and 2 approaches (105), 20-31	50	90
___	**109**	Bridge, 3 spans, (110) and 2 approaches (105), 20-32	50	115
___	**109**	Tunnel, papier mache (std), 13-14	30	70
___	**110**	Bridge Center Span (0), 20-31	10	25
___	**111**	Box of 50 Bulbs, 20-31	55	105
___	**112**	Gondola, early (std), 10-12	225	400
___	**112**	Gondola, later (std), 12-16	40	65
___	**112**	Gondola, latest (std), 16-18	40	65

PREWAR 1901-1942		Good	Exc	
112	Gondola, Lionel Corp. (std), 18-26	40	65	___
112	Station, 31-35	133	270	___
113	Cattle Car, later (std), 12-16	50	70	___
113	Cattle Car, latest (std), 16-18	50	70	___
113	Cattle Car, Lionel Corp. (std), 18-26	30	55	___
113	Station with light fixtures, 31-34	150	310	___
114	Boxcar, later (std), 12-16	50	90	___
114	Boxcar, latest (std), 16-18	40	70	___
114	Boxcar, Lionel Corp. (std), 18-26	40	70	___
114	Station with light fixtures, 31-34	428	1200	___
115	Station with train control, 35-42*	128	370	___
116	Ballast Car, early and later (std), 10-16	85	115	___
116	Ballast Car, latest (std), 16-18	65	105	___
116	Ballast Car, Lionel Corp. (std), 18-26	55	95	___
116	Station with train control, 35-42*	354	920	___
117	Caboose, early (std), 12	40	75	___
117	Caboose, later (std), 12-16	40	75	___
117	Caboose, latest (std), 16-18	40	75	___
117	Caboose, Lionel Corp. (std), 18-26	30	60	___
117	Station, 36-42	103	235	___
118	Tunnel, metal, 8" long (O), 20-32	23	65	___
118L	Tunnel, metal, lighted, 8" long, 27	20	55	___
119	Tunnel, metal, 12" long, 20-42	25	60	___
119L	Tunnel, metal, lighted, 12" long, 27-33	20	55	___
120	Tunnel, metal, 17" long, 22-27	30	75	___
120L	Tunnel, metal, lighted, 17" long, 27-42	75	165	___
121	Station, lighted (std), 09-16			
	(A) 14" x 10" x 9"		NRS	___
	(B) 13" x 9" x 13"	150	300	___
121	Station (std), 20-26	75	165	___
121X	Station (std), 17-19	110	255	___
122	Station (std), 20-30	55	190	___
123	Station (std), 20-23	75	210	___
123	Tunnel, paperboard base, 18 1/2" long (O), 33-42	105	235	___
124	Lionel City Station, 20-36*			
	(A) Tan or gray base, pea green roof	77	240	___
	(B) Pea green base, red roof	117	360	___
125	Lionelville Station, 23-25	80	185	___
125	Track Template, 38	1	5	___
126	Lionelville Station, 23-36	95	205	___
127	Lionel Town Station, 23-36	95	160	___
128	115 Station and 129 Terrace, 35-42*	900	1900	___
128	124 Station and 129 Terrace, 31-34*	900	1900	___
129	Terrace, 28-42*	425	1100	___
130	Tunnel, 26" long (O), 20-36	100	415	___
130L	Tunnel, lighted, 26" long, 27-33	150	450	___

	PREWAR 1901-1942		Good	Exc
___	**131**	Corner Display, 24-28	125	295
___	**132**	Corner Grass Plot, 24-28	125	295
___	**133**	Heart-shaped Plot, 24-28	125	295
___	**134**	Lionel City Station with stop, 37-42	173	445
___	**134**	Oval-shaped Plot, 24-28	125	300
___	**135**	Circular Plot, 24-28	125	295
___	**136**	Large Elevation, 24-28		NRS
___	**136**	Lionelville Station with stop, 37-42	123	180
___	**137**	Station with stop, 37-42	97	160
___	**140L**	Tunnel, lighted, 37" long, 27-32	460	1050
___	**150**	Electric Locomotive 0-4-0, early (O), 17	93	180
___	**150**	Electric Locomotive 0-4-0, late (O), 18-25		
___		(A) Brown, brown or olive windows	95	225
___		(B) Maroon, dark olive windows	90	135
___	**152**	Electric Locomotive 0-4-0 (O), 17-27		
___		(A) Dark green	90	135
___		(B) Gray	100	160
___		(C) Mojave	340	680
___		(D) Peacock	340	680
___	**152**	Crossing Gate, 40-42	20	40
___	**153**	Block Signal, 40-42	25	45
___	**153**	Electric Locomotive 0-4-0 (O), 24-25		
___		(A) Dark green	100	160
___		(B) Gray	100	160
___		(C) Mojave	100	160
___	**154**	Electric Locomotive 0-4-0 (O), 17-23	100	180
___	**154**	Highway Signal, 40-42		
___		(A) Black base	25	50
___		(B) Orange base	123	245
___	**155**	Freight Shed, 30-42*		
___		(A) Cream base, terra cotta floor	168	320
___		(B) Ivory base, red floor	133	400
___	**156**	Electric Locomotive 0-4-0 (O), 17-23	400	720
___	**156**	Station Platform, 39-42	78	115
___	**156**	Electric Locomotive 4-4-4 (O), 17-23		
___		(A) Dark green	475	810
___		(B) Maroon	540	890
___		(C) Olive green	600	1050
___		(D) Gray	670	1200
___	**156X**	Electric Locomotive 0-4-0 (O), 23-24		
___		(A) Maroon	330	495
___		(B) Olive green	200	400
___		(C) Gray	530	710
___		(D) Brown	420	600
___	**157**	Hand Truck, 30-32	20	40

		Good	Exc	
158	Electric Locomotive 0-4-0 (0), 19-23			
	(A) Gray or red windows	75	205	___
	(B) Black	95	250	___
158	Station Set: 136 Station and 2 platforms (156), 40-42	120	280	___
159	Block Actuator, 40	10	30	___
161	Baggage Truck, 30-32*	40	80	___
162	Dump Truck, 30-32*	40	80	___
163	Freight Accessory Set: 2 hand trucks (157), baggage truck (161), and dump truck (162), 30-42*	220	360	___
164	Log Loader, 40-42	120	743	___
165	Magnetic Crane, 40-42	182	245	___
165-22	Scrap Steel with bag, 40-42	50	125	___
165-83	Steel Blanks with bag, 40-42	50	110	___
166	Whistle Controller, 40-42	3	10	___
167	Whistle Controller, 40-42	8	25	___
167X	Whistle Controller (00), 40-42	5	15	___
168	Magic Electrol Controller, 40-42	25	75	___
169	Controller, 40-42	4	18	___
170	DC Reducer, 220V, 14-38	5	10	___
171	DC to AC Inverter, 110V, 36-42	5	15	___
172	DC to AC Inverter, 229V, 39-42	3	7	___
180	Pullman Car (std), 11-13			
	(A) Maroon body and roof	145	205	___
	(B) Brown body and roof	145	255	___
180	Pullman Car (std), 13-15	80	160	___
180	Pullman Car (std), 15-18	80	160	___
180	Pullman Car (std), 18-22	80	135	___
181	Combine Car (std), 11-13			
	(A) Maroon, dark olive doors	145	205	___
	(B) Brown, dark olive doors	145	205	___
	(C) Yellow-orange, orange doors	350	495	___
181	Combine Car (std), 13-15	80	160	___
181	Combine Car (std), 15-18	80	160	___
181	Combine Car (std), 18-22	80	135	___
182	Observation Car (std), 11-13			
	(A) Maroon, dark olive doors	145	205	___
	(B) Brown, dark olive doors	145	205	___
	(C) Yellow-orange, orange doors	300	495	___
182	Observation Car (std), 13-15	80	160	___
182	Observation Car (std), 15-18	80	160	___
182	Observation Car (std), 18-22	80	135	___
184	Bungalow, illuminated, 23-32*	65	123	___
185	Bungalow, 23-24	50	115	___
186	184 Bungalows, set of 5, 23-32	195	630	___
186	Log Loader Outfit, 40-41	130	340	___
187	185 Bungalows, set of 5, 23-24	170	590	___

			Good	Exc
___	188	Elevator and Car Set, 38-41	115	370
___	189	Villa, illuminated, 23-32*	125	400
___	190	Observation Car (std), 08		
___		(A) Dark olive green, nonremovable roof	1150	2600
___		(B) Dark olive green, removable roof	115	205
___		(C) Yellow-orange, removable roof	320	620
___		(D) Orange, removable roof	115	205
___		(E) Mojave, removable roof	345	870
___	190	Observation Car (std), 11-13	600	900
___	190	Observation Car (std), 13-15	200	295
___	190	Observation Car (std), 15-18	200	295
___	190	Observation Car (std), 18-22	80	135
___	190	Observation Car (std), 23-26	230	475
___	191	Villa, illuminated, 23-32*	114	413
___	192	Illuminated Villa Set: 189, 191, 184 (2), 27-32	388	800
___	193	Automatic Accessory Set (O), 27-29	150	325
___	194	Automatic Accessory Set (std), 27-29	100	325
___	195	Terrace, 27-30	350	2130
___	196	Accessory Set, 27	200	335
___	200	Electric Express (2 7/8"), 03-05*	4000	11400
___	200	Trailer, matches No. 2 Trolley (std), 11-16	1200	2400
___	200	Turntable (std), 28-33*	85	190
___	201	0-6-0 Locomotive (O), 40-42		
___		(A) 2201B Tender, bell	296	760
___		(B) 2201T Tender, no bell	345	690
___	202	Summer Trolley (std), 10-13		
___		(A) Electric Rapid Transit	1300	2700
___		(B) Preston St.	3250	4500
___	203	Armored 0-4-0 (O), 17-21	1100	1800
___	203	0-6-0 Locomotive (O), 40-42		
___		(A) 2203B Tender, bell	400	495
___		(B) 2203T Tender, no bell	325	550
___	204	2-4-2 Locomotive (O), 40-42 u		
___		(A) Black	55	105
___		(B) Gunmetal gray	80	165
___	205	Merchandise Containers, 3 pieces, 30-38*	130	373
___	206	Sack of Coal, 38-42	5	20
___	208	Tool Set: 6 assorted tools, 34-42*	65	150
___	0209	Barrels, wooden, 6 pieces (O), 34-42		
___		(A) Solid barrels	10	25
___		(B) 2-piece barrels	53	153
___	209	Barrels, wooden, 4 pieces (std), 34-42	10	142
___	210	Switches, pair (std), 26, 34-42	40	75
___	211	Flatcar (std), 26-40*	125	248
___	212	Gondola (std), 26-40*		
___		(A) Gray or light green	100	205

		Good	Exc	
	(B) Maroon	69	301	___
213	Cattle Car (std), 26-40*			
	(A) Mojave, maroon roof	160	365	___
	(B) Terra-cotta, pea green roof	130	470	___
	(C) Cream, maroon roof	300	650	___
214	Boxcar (std), 26-40*			
	(A) Terra-cotta, dark green roof	195	458	___
	(B) Cream body, orange roof	138	315	___
	(C) Yellow, brown roof	300	495	___
214R	Refrigerator Car (std), 29-40*			
	(A) Ivory or white, peacock roof	263	548	___
	(B) White, light blue roof	435	790	___
215	Tank Car (std), 26-40*			
	(A) Pea green	153	215	___
	(B) Ivory	220	555	___
	(C) Aluminum	315	798	___
216	Hopper Car (std), 26-38*			
	(A) Dark green, brass plates	125	348	___
	(B) Dark green, nickel plates	445	1100	___
217	Caboose (std), 26-40*			
	(A) Orange, maroon roof	325	510	___
	(B) Red, peacock roof	99	375	___
	(C) Red body and roof, ivory doors	150	360	___
217	Lighting Set, 14-23		NRS	___
218	Dump Car (std), 26-38*	220	365	___
219	Crane Car (std), 26-40*			
	(A) Peacock, red boom	123	385	___
	(B) Yellow, light green or red boom	198	452	___
	(C) Ivory, light green boom	205	685	___
220	Floodlight Car (std), 31-40*			
	(A) Terra-cotta base	217	580	___
	(B) Green base	340	485	
220	Switches, pair (std), 26*	25	90	___
222	Switches, pair (std), 26-32	40	100	___
223	Switches, pair (std), 32-42	35	120	___
224/224E	2-6-2 Locomotive (0), 38-42			
	(A) Black, die-cast 2224 Tender	110	294	___
	(B) Black, plastic 2224 Tender	110	195	___
	(C) Gunmetal, die-cast 2224 Tender	385	950	___
	(D) Gunmetal, sheet-metal 2689 Tender	120	306	___
225	222 Switches and 439 Panel, 29-32	115	260	___
225/225E	2-6-2 Locomotive (0), 38-42			
	(A) Black, 2235 or 2245 Tender	190	372	___
	(B) Black, 2235 plastic Tender	185	320	___
	(C) Gunmetal, 2225 or 2265 Tender	203	360	___
	(D) Gunmetal, 2235 die-cast Tender	285	1040	___

			Good	Exc
___	**226/226E**	2-6-4 Locomotive (O), 38-41	254	654
___	**227**	0-6-0 Locomotive (O), 39-42		
___		(A) 2227B Tender, bell	513	1413
___		(B) 2227T Tender, no bell	577	1200
___	**228**	0-6-0 Locomotive (O), 39-42		
___		(A) 2228B Tender, bell	600	1250
___		(B) 2228T Tender, no bell	600	1150
___	**229**	2-4-2 Locomotive (O), 39-42		
___		(A) Black or gunmetal, 2689W Tender	155	240
___		(B) Black or gunmetal, 2689T Tender	120	200
___		(C) Black, 2666W whistle Tender	155	280
___		(D) Black, 2666T nonwhistling Tender	120	200
___	**230**	0-6-0 Locomotive (O), 39-42	1050	2050
___	**231**	0-6-0 Locomotive (O), 39	1000	1800
___	**232**	0-6-0 Locomotive (O), 40-42	1000	1800
___	**233**	0-6-0 Locomotive (O), 40-42	900	1800
___	**238**	4-4-2 Locomotive (O), 39-40 u	430	710
___	**238E**	4-4-2 Locomotive (O), 36-38		
___		(A) 265W or 2225W whistle Tender	280	345
___		(B) 265 or 2225T nonwhistling Tender	275	360
___	**248**	Electric Locomotive 0-4-0 (O), 27-32	150	240
___	**249/249E**	2-4-2 Locomotive (O), 36-39		
___		(A) Gunmetal, 265T or 265W Tender	100	270
___		(B) Black, 265W Tender	110	210
___	**250**	Electric Locomotive 0-4-0, early (O), 26	125	220
___	**250**	Electric Locomotive 0-4-0, late (O), 34		
___		(A) Yellow-orange body, terra-cotta frame	145	245
___		(B) Terra-cotta body, maroon frame	160	270
___	**250E**	4-4-2 Hiawatha Locomotive (O), 35-42*	400	1100
___	**250W**	Hiawatha Tender (O), 35-42*	125	250
___	**251**	Electric Locomotive 0-4-0 (O), 25-32		
___		(A) Gray body, red windows	190	340
___		(B) Red body, ivory stripe	215	455
___		(C) Red body, no ivory stripe	200	380
___	**251E**	Electric Locomotive 0-4-0 (O), 27-32		
___		(A) Red body, ivory stripe	225	425
___		(B) Red body, no ivory stripe	215	395
___		(C) Gray, red trim	153	513
___	**252**	Electric Locomotive 0-4-0 (O), 26-32		
___		(A) Peacock or olive green	87	187
___		(B) Terra-cotta or yellow-orange	113	560
___	**252E**	Electric Locomotive 0-4-0 (O), 33-35		
___		(A) Terra-cotta	145	250
___		(B) Yellow-orange	125	205
___	**253**	Electric Locomotive 0-4-0 (O), 24-32		
___		(A) Maroon	180	430

		Good	Exc	
	(B) Dark green	105	250	___
	(C) Mojave	105	235	___
	(D) Terra-cotta	180	430	___
	(E) Peacock	95	195	___
	(F) Red	210	475	___
253E	Electric Locomotive 0-4-0 (O), 31-36			
	(A) Green	150	205	___
	(B) Terra-cotta	190	305	___
254	Electric Locomotive 0-4-0 (O), 24-32	210	340	___
254E	Electric Locomotive 0-4-0 (O), 27-34	180	292	___
255E	2-4-2 Locomotive (O), 35-36	485	1000	___
256	Electric Locomotive 0-4-4-0 (O), 24-30*			
	(A) Rubber-stamped lettering	470	1175	___
	(B) no outline around Lionel	338	770	___
	(C) Lionel Lines and No. 256 on brass	388	1050	___
257	2-4-0 Locomotive (O), 30-35 u			
	(A) Black tender	145	300	___
	(B) Black crackle-finish tender	240	435	___
258	2-4-0 Locomotive, early (O), 30-35 u			
	(A) 4-wheel 257 Tender	85	170	___
	(B) 8-wheel 258 Tender	100	195	___
258	2-4-2 Locomotive, late (O), 41 u			
	(A) Black	60	100	___
	(B) Gunmetal	85	135	___
259	2-4-2 Locomotive (O), 32	70	144	___
259E	2-4-2 Locomotive (O), 33-42	80	168	___
259T	Tender	15	30	___
260E	2-4-2 Locomotive (O), 30-35*			
	(A) Black body, green or black frame	362	475	___
	(B) Dark gunmetal body and frame	435	693	___
261	2-4-2 Locomotive (O), 31	125	210	___
261E	2-4-2 Locomotive (O), 35	175	285	___
262	2-4-2 Locomotive (O), 31-32	153	320	___
262E	2-4-2 Locomotive (O), 33-36			
	(A) Gloss black, copper and brass trim	110	270	___
	(B) Satin black, nickel trim	125	260	___
263E	2-4-2 Locomotive (O), 36-39*			
	(A) Gunmetal gray	272	610	___
	(B) 2-tone blue, from Blue Comet	415	950	___
263W	Tender, gunmetal	99	200	___
264E	2-4-2 Locomotive (O), 35-36			
	(A) Red, Red Comet	135	295	___
	(B) Black	200	380	___
265E	2-4-2 Locomotive (O), 35-40			
	(A) Black or gunmetal	160	345	___
	(B) Light blue, Blue Streak	460	800	___

			Good	Exc
___	**265T**	Tender	15	28
___	**267E/W**	Set: 616, 617 (2), 618, 35-41	275	560
___	**270**	Bridge, 10" long (0), 31-42	30	133
___	**270**	Lighting Set, 15-23		NRS
___	**271**	270 Bridges, set of 2, 31-33, 35-40	65	150
___	**271**	Lighting Set, 15-23		NRS
___	**272**	270 Bridges, set of 3, 31-33, 35-40	60	165
___	**280**	Bridge, 14" long (std), 31-42	60	127
___	**281**	280 Bridges, set of 2, 31-33, 35-40	90	205
___	**282**	280 Bridges, set of 3, 31-33, 35-40	105	265
___	**289E**	2-4-2 Locomotive (0), 37 u	120	305
___	**300**	Electric Trolley Car (2 7/8"), 01-05	2000	3600
	300	Hellgate Bridge (std), 28-42*		
___		(A) Cream towers, green truss	613	1350
___		(B) Ivory towers, aluminum truss	658	1600
___	**303**	Summer Trolley, 10-13	1500	3150
___	**308**	Signs, set of 5 (0), 40-42	30	70
___	**309**	Electric Trolley Trailer (2 7/8"), 01-05	2500	4050
	309	Pullman Car (std), 26-39		
___		(A) Maroon body and roof, mojave windows	100	160
___		(B) Mojave body and roof, maroon windows	100	160
___		(C) Light brown body, dark brown roof	120	190
___		(D) Medium blue body, dark blue roof	170	280
___		(E) Apple green body, dark green roof	170	280
___		(F) Pale blue body, silver roof	100	185
___		(G) Maroon body, terra-cotta roof	130	195
___	**310**	Rails and Ties, complete section (2 7/8"), 01-02	5	15
	310	Baggage Car (std), 26-39		
___		(A) Maroon body and roof, mojave windows	100	160
___		(B) Mojave body and roof, maroon windows	85	160
___		(C) Light brown body, dark brown roof	115	185
___		(D) Medium blue body, dark blue roof	170	280
___		(E) Apple green body, dark green roof	170	280
___		(F) Pale blue body, silver roof	100	175
	312	Observation Car (std), 24-39		
___		(A) Maroon body and roof, mojave windows	100	160
___		(B) Mojave body and roof, maroon windows	85	160
___		(C) Light brown body, dark brown roof	120	185
___		(D) Medium blue body, dark blue roof	170	280
___		(E) Apple green body, dark green roof	170	280
___		(F) Pale blue body, silver roof	100	175
___		(G) Maroon body, terra-cotta roof	130	195
	313	Bascule Bridge (0), 40-42		
___		(A) Silver bridge	235	500
___		(B) Gray bridge	180	590
___	**314**	Girder Bridge (0), 40-42	20	40

PREWAR 1901-1942		Good	Exc	
315	Illuminated Trestle Bridge (O), 40-42	30	80	___
316	Trestle Bridge (O), 40-42	25	50	___
318	Electric Locomotive 0-4-0 (std), 24-32			
	(A) Gray, dark gray, or mojave	150	300	___
	(B) Pea green	150	250	___
	(C) State brown	250	395	___
318E	Electric Locomotive 0-4-0, 26-35			
	(A) Gray, mojave, or pea green	150	250	___
	(B) State brown	275	440	___
	(C) Black	550	1275	___
319	Pullman Car (std), 24-27	105	175	___
320	Baggage Car (std), 25-27	100	175	___
320	Switch and Signal (2 7/8"), 02-05		NRS	___
322	Observation Car (std), 24-27, 29-30 u	100	175	___
330	90-degree Crossing (2 7/8"), 02-05		NRS	___
332	Baggage Car (std), 26-33			
	(A) Red body and roof, cream doors	80	120	___
	(B) Peacock body and roof, orange doors	75	115	___
	(C) Gray body and roof, maroon doors	75	115	___
	(D) Olive green body and roof, red doors	90	145	___
	(E) State brown body, dark brown roof	190	430	___
337	Pullman Car (std), 25-32			
	(A) Red body and roof, cream doors	95	190	___
	(B) Mojave body and roof, maroon doors	68	190	___
	(C) Olive green body and roof, red doors	105	225	___
	(D) Olive green body and roof, maroon doors	95	190	___
	(E) Pea green body and roof, cream doors	210	500	___
338	Observation Car (std), 25-32			
	(A) Red body and roof, cream doors	95	190	___
	(B) Mojave body and roof, maroon doors	68	190	___
	(C) Olive green body and roof, red doors	105	225	___
	(D) Olive green body and roof, maroon doors	95	190	___
339	Pullman Car (std), 25-33			
	(A) Peacock body and roof, orange doors	55	90	___
	(B) Gray body and roof, maroon doors	55	100	___
	(C) State brown body, dark brown roof	135	380	___
	(D) Peacock body, dark green roof	75	130	___
	(E) Mojave body, maroon roof and doors	145	230	___
340	Suspension Bridge (2 7/8"), 02-05*		NRS	___
341	Observation Car (std), 25-33			
	(A) Peacock body and roof, orange doors	50	70	___
	(B) Gray body and roof, maroon doors	50	70	___
	(C) State brown body, dark brown roof	75	160	___
	(D) Peacock body, dark green roof	65	95	___
	(E) Mojave body, maroon roof and doors	135	165	___
350	Track Bumper (2 7/8"), 02-05	225	550	___

	PREWAR 1901-1942		Good	Exc
___	**380**	Elevated Pillars (2 7/8"), 04-05*	30	70
___	**380**	Electric Locomotive 0-4-0 (std), 23-27	310	440
	380E	Electric Locomotive 0-4-0 (std), 26-29		
___		(A) Mojave	445	630
___		(B) Maroon	295	400
___		(C) Dark green	370	460
___	**381**	Electric Locomotive 4-4-4 (std), 28-29*	1600	2100
	381E	Electric Locomotive 4-4-4 (std), 28-36*		
___		(A) State green, apple green subframe	1112	2385
___		(B) State green, red subframe	1900	3250
___	**381U**	Electric Locomotive 4-4-4 Kit (std), 28-29	1600	4100
___	**384**	2-4-0 Locomotive (std), 30-32*	415	730
___	**384E**	2-4-0 Locomotive (std), 30-32*	425	650
___	**385E**	2-4-2 Locomotive (std), 33-39*	370	670
___	**390**	2-4-2 Locomotive (std), 29*	460	820
	390E	2-4-2 Locomotive (std), 29-31*		
___		(A) Black, with or without orange stripe	430	690
___		(B) 2-tone blue, cream-orange stripe	650	1050
___		(C) 2-tone green, orange or green stripe	990	2050
	392E	4-4-2 Locomotive (std), 32-39*		
___		(A) Black, 384 Tender	750	1250
___		(B) Black, large 12-wheel tender	838	1850
___		(C) Gunmetal gray	988	1800
___	**400**	Express Trail Car (2 7/8"), 03-05*	3500	5850
	400E	4-4-4 Locomotive (std), 31-39*		
___		(A) Black	1400	2425
___		(B) Blue	1500	2350
___		(C) Gunmetal or light blue	1350	2800
___		(D) Black crackle finish	1600	3500
___	**402**	Electric Locomotive 0-4-4-0 (std), 23-27	342	570
___	**402E**	Electric Locomotive 0-4-4-0 (std), 26-29	337	550
___	**404**	Summer Trolley (std), 10		NRS
	408E	Electric Locomotive 0-4-4-0 (std), 27-36*		
___		(A) Apple green or mojave, red pilots	765	1450
___		(B) State brown, brown pilots	2000	3000
___		(C) State green, red pilots	2000	3800
	412	California Pullman Car (std), 29-35*		
___		(A) Light green body, dark green roof	590	1750
___		(B) Light brown body, dark brown roof	735	2100
	413	Colorado Pullman Car (std), 29-35*		
___		(A) Light green body, dark green roof	590	1750
___		(B) Light brown body, dark brown roof	620	2100
	414	Illinois Pullman Car (std), 29-35*		
___		(A) Light green body, dark green roof	590	1750
___		(B) Light brown body, dark brown roof	620	2050

		Good	Exc	
416	New York Observation Car (std), 29-35*			
	(A) Light green body, dark green roof	590	1750	___
	(B) Light brown body, dark brown roof	620	2100	___
418	Pullman Car (std), 23-32*	225	320	___
419	Combination (std), 23-32*	190	280	___
420	Faye Pullman Car (std), 30-40*			
	(A) Brass trim	555	900	___
	(B) Nickel trim	450	1200	___
421	Westphal Pullman Car (std), 30-40*			
	(A) Brass trim	500	900	___
	(B) Nickel trim	500	1200	___
422	Tempel Observation Car (std), 30-40*			
	(A) Brass trim	555	900	___
	(B) Nickel trim	500	1200	___
424	Liberty Bell Pullman Car (std), 31-40*			
	(A) Brass trim	350	530	___
	(B) Nickel trim	385	650	___
425	Stephen Girard Pullman Car (std), 31-40*			
	(A) Brass trim	350	530	___
	(B) Nickel trim	385	650	___
426	Coral Isle Observation Car (std), 31-40*			
	(A) Brass trim	350	530	___
	(B) Nickel trim	385	650	___
428	Pullman Car (std), 26-30*			
	(A) Dark green body and roof	250	385	___
	(B) Orange body and roof, apple green windows	390	890	___
429	Combine Car (std), 26-30*			
	(A) Dark green body and roof	250	385	___
	(B) Orange body and roof, apple green windows	390	890	___
430	Observation Car (std), 26-30*			
	(A) Dark green body and roof	250	385	___
	(B) Orange body and roof, apple green windows	390	890	___
431	Diner (std), 27-32*			
	(A) Mojave body, screw-mounted roof	350	540	___
	(B) Mojave body, hinged roof	465	720	___
	(C) Dark green body, orange windows	410	720	___
	(D) Orange body, apple green windows	410	720	___
	(E) Apple green body, red windows	410	720	___
435	Power Station, 26-38*	165	400	___
436	Power Station, 26-37*			
	(A) Power Station plate	135	295	___
	(B) Edison Service plate	270	610	___
437	Switch Signal Tower, 26-37*	157	545	___
438	Signal Tower, 27-39*			
	(A) Mojave base, orange house	158	325	___
	(B) Black base, white house	238	640	___

			Good	Exc
___	**439**	Panel Board, 28-42*	85	148
___	**440/0440**	Signal Bridge, 32-35*	180	470
___	**440C**	Panel Board, 32-42	90	145
___	**441**	Weighing Station (std), 32-36	278	1325
___	**442**	Landscaped Diner, 38-42	117	215
___	**444**	Roundhouse (std), 32-35*	1350	2850
___	**444-18**	Roundhouse Clip, 33		NRS
	450	Electric Locomotive 0-4-0, Macy's (O), 30 u		
___		(A) Red, black frame	295	700
___		(B) Apple green, dark green frame	415	880
___	**450**	Set: 450, matching 605, 606 (2), 30 u	750	1800
___	**490**	Observation Car (std), 23-32*	190	255
___	**500**	Electric Derrick Car (2 7/8"), 03-04*	5000	6750
	511	Flatcar (std), 27-40		
___		(A) Dark green	65	95
___		(B) Medium green	75	165
	512	Gondola (std), 27-39		
___		(A) Peacock	30	60
___		(B) Light green	50	95
	513	Cattle Car (std), 27-38		
___		(A) Olive green, orange roof	70	360
___		(B) Orange, pea green roof	60	255
___		(C) Cream, maroon roof	80	250
	514	Boxcar (std), 29-40		
___		(A) Cream, orange roof	90	327
___		(B) Yellow, brown roof	115	285
___	**514**	Refrigerator Car, ivory or white, peacock roof, (std), 27-28	240	400
	514R	Refrigerator Car (std), 29-40		
___		(A) Ivory, peacock roof	113	190
___		(B) White, light blue roof	350	545
	515	Tank Car (std), 27-40		
___		(A) Terra-cotta	90	145
___		(B) Ivory	105	378
___		(C) Aluminum	90	325
___		(D) Orange, red Shell decal	340	750
	516	Hopper Car (std), 28-40		
___		(A) Red	170	280
___		(B) Red, rubber-stamped data	200	300
___		(C) Light red, nickel trim	200	325
	517	Caboose (std), 27-40		
___		(A) Pea green body, red roof	50	133
___		(B) Red body and roof	90	155
___		(C) Red body, black roof, orange windows	355	640
	520	Floodlight Car (std), 31-40		
___		(A) Terra-cotta base	110	210
___		(B) Green base	85	240

		Good	Exc	
529	Pullman Car (0), 26-32			
	(A) Olive green body and roof	25	45	___
	(B) Terra-cotta body and roof	25	60	___
530	Observation Car (0), 26-32			
	(A) Olive green body and roof	25	45	___
	(B) Terra-cotta body and roof	25	60	___
550	Miniature Figures, boxed (std), 32-36*	175	455	___
551	Engineer (std), 32	25	45	___
552	Conductor (std), 32	20	40	___
553	Porter with stool (std), 32	25	50	___
554	Male Passenger (std), 32	25	45	___
555	Female Passenger (std), 32	25	45	___
556	Red Cap with suitcase (std), 32	25	65	___
600	Derrick Trailer (2 7/8"), 03-04*	5000	8550	___
600	Pullman Car, early (0), 15-23			
	(A) Dark green	65	170	___
	(B) Maroon or brown	45	85	___
600	Pullman Car, late (0), 33-42			___
	(A) Light red or gray, red roof	50	90	___
	(B) Light blue, aluminum roof	70	120	___
601	Observation Car, late (0), 33-42			
	(A) Light red body and roof	50	85	___
	(B) Light gray, red roof	50	90	___
	(C) Light blue body, aluminum roof	70	120	___
601	Pullman Car, early (0), 15-23	50	70	___
602	Lionel Lines Baggage Car, late (0), 33-42			
	(A) Light red or gray, red roof	60	110	___
	(B) Light blue, aluminum roof	90	150	___
602	NYC Baggage Car (0), 15-23	33	45	___
602	Observation Car (0), 22 u	30	45	___
603	Pullman Car, early (0), 22 u	40	70	___
603	Pullman Car, later (0), 20-25	20	45	___
603	Pullman Car, latest (0), 31-36			
	(A) Light red body and roof	45	85	___
	(B) Red body, black roof	35	60	___
	(C) Stephen Girard green body, dark green roof	35	60	___
	(D) Maroon body and roof, Macy Special	60	125	___
604	Observation Car, later (0), 20-25	35	60	___
604	Observation Car, latest (0), 31-36			
	(A) Light red body and roof	45	85	___
	(B) Red body, black roof	35	60	___
	(C) Yellow-orange body, terra-cotta roof	35	60	___
	(D) Stephen Girard green body, dark green roof	35	60	___
	(E) Maroon body and roof	70	150	___

			Good	Exc
___	**605**	Pullman Car (O), 25-32		
___		(A) Gray, Lionel Lines	85	170
___		(B) Gray, Illinois Central	85	170
___		(C) Red, Lionel Lines	170	255
___		(D) Red, Illinois Central	255	340
___		(E) Orange, Lionel Lines	170	255
___		(F) Orange, Illinois Central	300	430
___		(G) Olive green, Lionel Lines	255	340
___	**606**	Observation Car (O), 25-32		
___		(A) Gray, Lionel Lines	130	215
___		(B) Gray, Illinois Central	90	170
___		(C) Red, Lionel Lines	170	255
___		(D) Red, Illinois Central	255	340
___		(E) Orange, Lionel Lines	170	255
___		(F) Orange, Illinois Central	170	255
___		(G) Olive green, Lionel Lines	255	340
___	**607**	Pullman Car (O), 26-27		
___		(A) Peacock, Lionel Lines	50	70
___		(B) Peacock, Illinois Central	75	115
___		(C) 2-tone green, Lionel Lines	50	75
___		(D) Red, Lionel Lines	75	110
___	**608**	Observation Car (O), 26-37		
___		(A) Peacock, Lionel Lines	50	70
___		(B) Peacock, Illinois Central	75	115
___		(C) 2-tone green, Lionel Lines	50	75
___		(D) Red, Lionel Lines	75	110
___	**609**	Pullman Car (O), 37	60	85
___	**610**	Pullman Car, early (O), 15-25		
___		(A) Dark green body and roof	50	65
___		(B) Maroon body and roof	60	95
___		(C) Mojave body and roof	60	95
___	**610**	Pullman Car, late (O), 26-30		
___		(A) Olive green body and roof	65	80
___		(B) Mojave body and roof	55	80
___		(C) Terra-cotta body, maroon roof	100	155
___		(D) Pea green body and roof	70	115
___		(E) Light blue body, aluminum roof	130	260
___		(F) Light red body, aluminum-painted roof	100	155
___	**611**	Observation Car (O), 37	55	80
___	**612**	Observation Car, early (O), 15-25		
___		(A) Dark green body and roof	40	60
___		(B) Maroon body and roof	70	90
___		(C) Mojave body and roof	70	90
___	**612**	Observation Car, late (O), 26-30		
___		(A) Olive green body and roof	55	80
___		(B) Mojave body and roof	55	80

		Good	Exc	
	(C) Terra-cotta body, maroon roof	100	155	___
	(D) Pea green body and roof	70	115	___
	(E) Light blue body, aluminum roof	130	260	___
	(F) Light red body, aluminum-painted roof	100	155	___
613	Pullman Car (O), 31-40*			___
	(A) Terra-cotta body, maroon/terra-cotta roof	85	195	___
	(B) Light red body, light red/aluminum roof	175	350	___
	(C) Blue, two-tone blue roof	115	354	___
614	Observation Car (O), 31-40*			___
	(A) Terra-cotta body, maroon/terra-cotta roof	100	190	___
	(B) Light red body, light red/aluminum roof	175	350	___
	(C) Blue, two-tone blue roof	100	228	___
615	Baggage Car (O), 33-40*	150	260	___
616E/W	Diesel only (O), 35-41	90	215	___
616E/W	Set: 616, 617 (2), 618	225	570	___
617	Coach (O), 35-41			___
	(A) Blue and white	55	85	___
	(B) Chrome, gunmetal skirts	55	180	___
	(C) Chrome, chrome skirts	55	85	___
	(D) Silver-painted	55	85	___
618	Observation Car (O), 35-41			___
	(A) Blue and white	55	85	___
	(B) Chrome, gunmetal skirts	55	85	___
	(C) Chrome, chrome skirts	55	85	___
	(D) Silver-painted	55	85	___
619	Combine Car (O), 36-38			___
	(A) Blue, white windows band	100	205	___
	(B) Chrome, chrome skirts	100	205	___
620	Floodlight Car (O), 37-42	39	85	___
629	Pullman Car (O), 24-32			___
	(A) Dark green body and roof	25	40	___
	(B) Orange body and roof	25	40	___
	(C) Red body and roof	20	35	___
	(D) Light red body and roof	30	55	___
630	Observation Car, 24-32			___
	(A) Dark green body and roof	25	40	___
	(B) Orange body and roof	25	40	___
	(C) Red body and roof	20	35	___
	(D) Light red body and roof	30	55	___
636W	Diesel only (O), 36-39	90	175	___
636W	Set: 636W, 637 (2), 638, 36-39	375	640	___
637	Coach (O), 36-39	70	105	___
638	Observation Car (O), 36-39	70	105	___
651	Flatcar (O), 35-40	30	65	___
652	Gondola (O), 35-40	28	55	___
653	Hopper Car (O), 34-40	35	65	___

			Good	Exc
___	**654**	Tank Car (O), 34-42		
___		(A) Orange or aluminum	35	60
___		(B) Gray	40	75
___	**655**	Boxcar (O), 34-42		
___		(A) Cream, maroon roof	35	60
___		(B) Cream, tuscan roof	45	75
___	**656**	Cattle Car (O), 35-40		
___		(A) Light gray, vermilion roof	40	100
___		(B) Burnt orange, tuscan roof	70	125
___	**657**	Caboose (O), 34-42		
___		(A) Red body and roof	20	35
___		(B) Red body, tuscan roof	25	40
___	**659**	Dump Car (O), 35-42	40	82
___	**700**	Electric Locomotive 0-4-0 (O), 15-16	360	690
___	**700E**	4-6-4 NYC Hudson "5344," scale (O), 37-42*	1400	4250
___	**700K**	4-6-4 Locomotive, unbuilt gray primer (O), 38-42	4400	5950
___	**701**	0-6-0 PRR Locomotive "8976," 41	900	2100
___	**701**	Electric Locomotive 0-4-0 (O), 15-16	376	660
___	**702**	Baggage Car (O), 17-21	115	305
___	**703**	Electric Locomotive 4-4-4 (O), 15-16	711	1194
___	**706**	Electric Locomotive 0-4-0 (O), 15-16	375	630
___	**708**	0-6-0 PRR Locomotive "8976" (O), 39-42*	1450	2850
___	**710**	Pullman Car (O), 24-34		
___		(A) Red, Lionel Lines	200	300
___		(B) Orange, Lionel Lines	150	225
___		(C) Orange, New York Central	175	225
___		(D) Orange, Illinois Central	300	450
___		(E) 2-tone blue, Lionel Lines	300	415
___		(F) Orange, New York Central	200	260
___	**711**	Remote Control Switches, pair (072), 35-42	83	236
___	**712**	Observation Car (O), 24-34		
___		(A) Red, Lionel Lines	185	355
___		(B) Orange, Lionel Lines	140	265
___		(C) Orange, New York Central	160	310
___		(D) Orange, Illinois Central	315	530
___		(E) 2-tone blue, Lionel Lines	280	485
___	**714**	Boxcar (O), 40-42*	333	610
___	**714K**	Boxcar, unbuilt (O), 40-42	220	480
___	**715**	Tank Car (O), 40-42*		
___		(A) SEPS 8124 decal	340	610
___		(B) SUNX 715 decal	313	880
___	**715K**	Tank Car, unbuilt (O), 40-42	250	530
___	**716**	Hopper Car (O), 40-42*	290	400
___	**716K**	Hopper Car, unbuilt (O), 40-42	350	730
___	**717**	Caboose (O), 40-42*	340	510
___	**717K**	Caboose, unbuilt (O), 40-42	275	590

		Good	Exc	
720	90-degree Crossing (072), 35-42	20	40	___
721	Manual Switches, pair (072), 35-42	50	105	___
730	90-degree Crossing (072), 35-42	20	40	___
731	Remote Control Switches, pair, T-rail (072), 35-42	80	237	___
751E/W	Set: 752, 753 (2), 754 (0), 34-41*	640	1050	___
752E	Diesel only (0), 34-41*			
	(A) Yellow and brown	170	355	___
	(B) Aluminum	145	340	___
753	Coach (0), 36-41			
	(A) Yellow and brown	85	185	___
	(B) Aluminum	75	180	___
754	Observation Car (0), 36-41			
	(A) Yellow and brown	80	185	___
	(B) Aluminum	75	180	___
760	Curved Track, 16 pieces, (072), 35-42	40	80	___
761	Curved Track (072), 34-42	1	2	___
762	Straight Track (072), 34-42	1	2	___
762S	Insulated Straight Track (072), 34-42	2	5	___
763E	4-6-4 Locomotive (0), 37-42			
	(A) Gunmetal, 263 or 2263W Tender	1125	2385	___
	(B) Gunmetal, 2226X or 2226WX Tender	1150	2950	___
	(C) Black, 2226WX Tender	965	2725	___
771	Curved Track, T-rail (072), 35-42	3	10	___
772	Straight Track, T-rail (072), 35-42	5	25	___
772S	Insulated Straight Track, T-rail (072), 35-42	15	30	___
773	Fishplate Set, 50 plates (072), 36-42	15	67	___
782	Hiawatha Combine Car (0), 35-41*	230	380	___
783	Hiawatha Coach (0), 35-41*	140	290	___
784	Hiawatha Observation Car (0), 35-41*	205	445	___
792	Rail Chief Combine Car (0), 37-41*	215	580	___
793	Rail Chief Coach (0), 37-41*	290	800	___
794	Rail Chief Observation Car (0), 37-41*	250	800	___
800	Boxcar (2 7/8"), 04-05*	2500	7775	___
800	Boxcar (0), 15-26			
	(A) Light orange body, brown-maroon roof	45	70	___
	(B) Orange body and roof, PRR	25	45	___
801	Caboose (0), 15-26	30	50	___
802	Stock Car (0), 15-26	40	60	___
803	Hopper Car, early (0), 23-28	25	55	___
803	Hopper Car, late (0), 29-34	30	55	___
804	Tank Car (0), 23-28	11	45	___
805	Boxcar (0), 27-34			
	(A) Pea green, terra-cotta roof	35	55	___
	(B) Pea green, maroon roof	45	115	___
	(C) Orange, maroon roof	45	95	___

			Good	Exc
	806	Stock Car (O), 27-34		
___		(A) Pea green, terra-cotta roof	40	75
___		(B) Orange, various color roofs	35	50
	807	Caboose (O), 27-40		
___		(A) Peacock body, dark green roof	20	35
___		(B) Red body, peacock roof	20	93
___		(C) Light red body and roof	20	40
	809	Dump Car (O), 31-41		
___		(A) Orange bin	40	136
___		(B) Green bin	40	85
	810	Crane Car (O), 30-42		
___		(A) Terra-cotta cab, maroon roof	170	270
___		(B) Cream cab, vermilion roof	110	205
	811	Flatcar (O), 26-40		
___		(A) Maroon	40	83
___		(B) Aluminum	50	100
___	**812**	Gondola (O), 26-42	40	70
___	**812T**	Tool Set: pick, shovel, hammer, 30-41	40	105
	813	Stock Car (O), 26-42		
___		(A) Orange body, pea green roof	76	145
___		(B) Orange body, maroon roof	55	135
___		(C) Cream body, maroon roof	100	225
___		(D) Tuscan body and roof	650	1600
	814	Boxcar (O), 26-42		
___		(A) Cream, orange roof	50	145
___		(B) Cream, maroon roof	118	140
___		(C) Yellow, brown roof	95	120
	814R	Refrigerator Car (O), 29-42		
___		(A) Ivory, peacock roof	100	213
___		(B) White, light blue roof	103	230
___		(C) Flat white, brown roof	600	900
	815	Tank Car (O), 26-42		
___		(A) Pea green, maroon frame	250	510
___		(B) Pea green, black frame	70	155
___		(C) Aluminum, black frame	50	100
___		(D) Orange-yellow, black frame	150	255
	816	Hopper Car (O), 27-42		
___		(A) Olive green	85	155
___		(B) Red body	65	140
___		(C) Black body	370	680
	817	Caboose (O), 26-42		
___		(A) Peacock body, dark green roof	45	70
___		(B) Red body, peacock roof	45	80
___		(C) Light red body and roof	45	80
	820	Boxcar (O), 15-26		
___		(A) Orange, Illinois Central	40	80

		Good	Exc	
	(B) Orange, Union Pacific	50	105	___
820	Floodlight Car (O), 31-42			
	(A) Terra-cotta	100	180	___
	(B) Green	100	175	___
	(C) Light green	105	180	___
821	Stock Car (O), 15-16, 25-26	45	85	___
822	Caboose (O), 15-26	35	65	___
831	Flatcar (O), 27-34	20	130	___
840	Industrial Power Station, 28-40*	685	3050	___
900	Ammunition Car (O), 17-21	120	340	___
900	Box Trail Car (2 7/8"), 04-05*	2000	4350	___
901	Gondola (O), 19-27	25	50	___
902	Gondola (O), 27-34	25	45	___
910	Grove of Trees, 32-42	70	357	___
911	Country Estate, 32-42	162	533	___
912	Suburban Home	263	620	___
913	Landscaped Bungalow, 40-42	168	348	___
914	Park Landscape, 32-35	160	270	___
915	Tunnel, 65" or 60" long, 32-33, 35	160	435	___
916	Tunnel, 29" long, 35	95	180	___
917	Scenic Hillside, 34" x 15", 32-36	90	205	___
918	Scenic Hillside, 30" x 10", 32-36	90	205	___
919	Park Grass, cloth bag, 32-42	10	20	___
920	Village, 32-33	600	1600	___
921	Scenic Park, 3 pieces, 32-33	980	2600	___
921C	Park Center, 32-33	400	1050	___
922	Terrace, 32-36	90	295	___
923	Tunnel, 40" long, 33-42	125	225	___
924	Tunnel, 30" long (072), 35-42	50	135	___
925	Lubricant, 35-42	25	120	___
927	Flag Plot, 37-42	70	266	___
1000	Passenger Car (2 7/8"), 05*	4500	6750	___
1000	Trolley Trailer (std), 10-16	1400	2250	___
1010	Electric Locomotive 0-4-0, Winner Lines (O), 31-32	90	160	___
1010	Interurban Trailer (std), 10-16	1000	1800	___
1011	Pullman Car, Winner Lines (O), 31-32	45	75	___
1012	Station, 32	40	70	___
1015	0-4-0 Locomotive (O), 31-32	100	205	___
1017	Winner Station, 33	25	70	___
1019	Observation Car (O), 31-32	50	70	___
1020	Baggage Car (O), 31-32	65	110	___
1021	90-degree Crossover (027), 32-42	1	5	___
1022	Tunnel, 18" long (O), 35-42	115	165	___
1023	Tunnel, 19" long, 34-42	20	40	___
1024	Switches, pair (027), 37-42	5	33	___
1025	Bumper (027), 40-42	15	25	___

PREWAR 1901-1942			Good	Exc
___	**1027**	Transformer Station, 34	50	115
___	**1028**	Transformer, 40 watts, 39	3	10
___	**1029**	Transformer, 25 watts, 36	5	20
___	**1030**	Electric Locomotive 0-4-0 (O), 32	75	135
___	**1030**	Transformer, 40 watts, 35-38	6	25
___	**1035**	0-4-0 Locomotive (O), 32	75	115
___	**1037**	Transformer, 40 watts, 40-42	7	25
___	**1038**	Transformer, 30 watts, 40	2	5
___	**1039**	Transformer, 35 watts, 37-40	7	20
___	**1040**	Transformer, 60 watts, 37-39	10	30
___	**1041**	Transformer, 60 watts, 39-42	15	30
___	**1045**	Watchman, 38-42	30	68
___	**1050**	Passenger Car Trailer (2 7/8"), 05*	3900	7200
___	**1100**	Summer Trolley Trailer (std), 10-13		NRS
	1100	Mickey Mouse Handcar, 35-37*		
___		(A) Red base	350	640
___		(B) Apple green base, orange shoes	500	880
___		(C) Orange base	600	1225
___	**1103**	Peter Rabbit Handcar (O), 35-37*	330	820
	1105	Santa Claus Handcar (O), 35-35*		
___		(A) Red base	660	1050
___		(B) Green base	720	1200
___	**1107**	Transformer Station, 33	25	70
	1107	Donald Duck Handcar (O), 36-37*		
___		(A) White dog house, red roof	475	1200
___		(B) White dog house, green roof	380	1100
___		(C) Orange dog house, green roof	640	1850
___	**1121**	Switches, pair (027), 37-42	15	35
___	**1506L**	0-4-0 Locomotive (O), 33-34	95	125
___	**1506M**	0-4-0 Locomotive (O), 35	250	430
___	**1508**	0-4-0 Commodore Vanderbilt with 1509 Mickey Mouse stoker Tender, 35	420	690
___	**1511**	0-4-0 Locomotive (O), 36-37	110	280
___	**1512**	Gondola (O), 31-33, 36-37	25	33
___	**1514**	Boxcar (O), 31-37	25	40
___	**1515**	Tank Car (O), 33-37	25	40
___	**1517**	Caboose (O), 31-37	25	40
___	**1518**	Mickey Mouse Circus Dining Car (O), 35	120	260
___	**1519**	Mickey Mouse Band Car (O), 35	120	260
___	**1520**	Mickey Mouse Circus Car (O), 35	120	260
___	**1536**	Mickey Mouse Circus Set: 1508, 1509, 1518, 1519, 1520, 35	770	1350
___	**1550**	Switches, for windup trains, pair, 33-37	2	5
___	**1555**	90-degree Crossover, for windup trains, 33-37	1	2
___	**1560**	Station, 33-37	15	35
___	**1569**	Accessory Set, 8 pieces, 33-37	35	70

PREWAR 1901-1942		Good	Exc	
1588	0-4-0 Locomotive (O), 36-37	150	250	
1630	Pullman Car (O), 38-42			
	(A) Aluminum windows	35	70	___
	(B) Light gray windows	45	80	___
1631	Observation Car (O), 38-42			
	(A) Aluminum windows	35	70	___
	(B) Light gray windows	45	80	___
1651E	Electric Locomotive 0-4-0 (O), 33	130	240	___
1661E	2-4-0 Locomotive (O), 33	75	160	___
1662	0-4-0 Locomotive (027), 40-42	154	365	___
1663	0-4-0 Locomotive (027), 40-42	200	385	___
1664/E	2-4-2 Locomotive (027), 38-42			
	(A) Gunmetal	60	188	___
	(B) Black	60	95	___
1666/E	2-6-2 Locomotive (027), 38-42			
	(A) Gunmetal	115	170	___
	(B) Black	90	150	___
1668/E	2-6-2 Locomotive (027), 37-41			
	(A) Gunmetal	75	115	___
	(B) Black	75	130	___
1673	Coach (O), 36-37			
	(A) Aluminum windows	35	75	___
	(B) Light gray windows	45	90	___
1674	Pullman Car (O), 36-37	35	75	___
1675	Observation Car (O), 36-37	30	70	___
1677	Gondola (O), 33-35, 39-42			
	(A) Light blue, Ives	40	60	___
	(B) Blue or red, Lionel	20	40	___
1679	Boxcar (O), 33-42			
	(A) Cream, Ives	25	40	___
	(B) Cream, Lionel	25	40	___
	(C) Cream or yellow, Baby Ruth	20	40	___
1680	Tank Car (O), 33-42			
	(A) Aluminum, Ives Tank Lines	60	95	___
	(B) Aluminum, no Ives lettering	11	35	___
	(C) Orange, Shell Oil	15	32	___
1681	2-4-0 Locomotive (O), 34-35			
	(A) Black, red frame	55	120	___
	(B) Red, red frame	110	145	___
1681E	2-4-0 Locomotive (O), 34-35			
	(A) Black, red frame	65	130	___
	(B) Red, red frame	130	165	___
1682	Caboose (O), 33-42			
	(A) Vermilion, Ives	35	70	___
	(B) Red or tuscan, Lionel	6	40	___

			Good	Exc
	1684	2-4-2 Locomotive (027), 41-42		
___		(A) Black	45	70
___		(B) Gunmetal	45	70
	1685	Coach (O), 33-37 u		
___		(A) Gray, maroon roof	240	495
___		(B) Red, maroon roof	170	335
___		(C) Blue, silver roof	170	315
	1686	Baggage Car (O), 33-37 u		
___		(A) Gray, maroon roof	240	495
___		(B) Red, maroon roof	170	335
___		(C) Blue, silver roof	170	315
	1687	Observation Car (O), 33-37 u		
___		(A) Gray, maroon roof	170	315
___		(B) Red, maroon roof	180	315
___		(C) Blue, silver roof	170	315
___	**1688/E**	2-4-2 Locomotive (027), 36-40	50	125
	1689E	2-4-2 Locomotive (027), 36-37		
___		(A) Gunmetal	75	115
___		(B) Black	60	100
___	**1689T**	Tender, black	15	38
___	**1690**	Pullman Car (O), 33-40	35	60
___	**1691**	Observation Car (O), 33-40	35	60
___	**1692**	Pullman Car (027), 39 u	45	70
___	**1693**	Observation Car (027), 39 u	45	70
___	**1700E**	Diesel, power unit only (027), 35-37	45	70
	1700E	Set: 1700, 1701 (2), 1702, 35-37 u		
___		(A) Aluminum and light red	140	250
___		(B) Chrome and light red	140	250
___		(C) Orange and gray	155	285
	1701	Coach (027), 35-37		
___		(A) Chrome sides and roof	20	45
___		(B) Silver sides and roof	30	55
___		(C) Orange and gray	75	150
	1702	Observation Car (027), 35-37		
___		(A) Chrome sides and roof	20	45
___		(B) Silver sides and roof	30	55
___		(C) Orange and gray	75	150
___	**1703**	Observation Car, hooked coupler, 35-37 u	50	110
___	**1717**	Gondola (O), 33-40 u	30	50
___	**1717X**	Gondola (O), 40 u	25	50
___	**1719**	Boxcar (O), 33-40 u	30	50
___	**1719X**	Boxcar (O), 41-42 u	30	50
___	**1722**	Caboose (O), 33-42 u	25	50
___	**1722X**	Caboose (O), 39-40 u	25	40
	1766	Pullman Car (std), 34-40*		
___		(A) Terra-cotta, maroon roof, brass trim	300	650

		Good	Exc	
	(B) Red, maroon roof, nickel trim	300	540	
1767	Baggage Car (std), 34-40*			
	(A) Terra-cotta, maroon roof, brass trim	295	850	___
	(B) Red, maroon roof, nickel trim	295	700	___
1768	Observation Car (std), 34-40*			
	(A) Terra-cotta, maroon roof, brass trim	300	650	___
	(B) Red, maroon roof, nickel trim	300	540	___
1811	Pullman Car (O), 33-37	35	70	___
1812	Observation Car (O), 33-37	30	65	___
1813	Baggage Car (O), 33-37	60	135	___
1816/W	Diesel (O), 35-37	100	240	___
1817	Coach (O), 35-37	25	50	___
1818	Observation Car (O), 35-37	25	50	___
1835E	2-4-2 Locomotive (std), 34-39	448	730	___
1910	Electric Locomotive 0-6-0, early (std), 10-11	920	1550	___
1910	Electric Locomotive 0-6-0, late (std), 12	550	1350	___
1910	Pullman Car (std), 09-10 u	860	1800	___
1911	Electric Locomotive 0-4-0, early (std), 10-12	860	1700	___
1911	Electric Locomotive 0-4-0, late (std), 13	700	1100	___
1911	Electric Locomotive 0-4-4-0 Special (std), 11-12	860	2500	___
1912	Electric Locomotive 0-4-4-0 (std), 10-12*			
	(A) New York, New Haven & Hartford	1550	3200	___
	(B) New York Central Lines	1300	2700	___
1912	Electric Locomotive 0-4-4-0 Special (std), 11*	2500	4500	___
2200	Summer Trolley Trailer (std), 10-13	1100	2250	___
2203B	Tender	40	99	___
2224W	Tender	55	137	___
2225W	Tender	30	60	___
2228B	Tender	140	280	___
2235W	Tender	25	65	___
2600	Pullman Car (O), 38-42	80	155	___
2601	Observation Car (O), 38-42	60	115	___
2602	Baggage Car (O), 38-42	90	185	___
2613	Pullman Car (O), 38-42*			
	(A) Blue, 2-tone blue roof	100	300	___
	(B) State green, 2-tone green roof	200	440	___
2614	Observation Car (O), 38-42*			
	(A) Blue, 2-tone blue roof	100	300	___
	(B) State green, 2-tone green roof	200	440	___
2615	Baggage Car (O), 38-42*			
	(A) Blue, 2-tone blue roof	115	300	___
	(B) State green, 2-tone green roof	200	420	___
2620	Floodlight Car (O), 38-42	65	100	___
2623	Pullman Car (O), 41-42			
	(A) Irvington	175	843	___
	(B) Manhattan	220	310	___

PREWAR 1901-1942			Good	Exc
	2624	Pullman Car (O), 41-42	750	1700
___	2630	Pullman Car (O), 38-42	30	70
___	2631	Observation Car (O), 38-42	30	70
	2640	Pullman Car, illuminated (O), 38-42		
___		(A) Light blue, aluminum roof	30	120
___		(B) State green, dark green roof	30	70
	2641	Observation Car, illuminated (O), 38-42		
___		(A) Light blue, aluminum roof	30	100
___		(B) State green, dark green roof	30	70
___	2642	Pullman Car (O), 41-42	30	70
___	2643	Observation Car (O), 41-42	30	65
___	2651	Flatcar (O), 38-42	30	80
___	2652	Gondola (O), 38-41	25	65
	2653	Hopper Car (O), 38-42		
___		(A) Stephen Girard green	35	70
___		(B) Black	60	130
	2654	Tank Car (O), 38-42		
___		(A) Aluminum, Sunoco	35	60
___		(B) Orange, Shell	35	60
___		(C) Light gray, Sunoco	40	70
	2655	Boxcar (O), 38-42		
___		(A) Cream, maroon roof	35	65
___		(B) Cream, tuscan roof	40	70
	2656	Stock Car (O), 38-41		
___		(A) Light gray, red roof	45	75
___		(B) Burnt orange, tuscan roof	39	67
___	2657	Caboose (O), 40-41	30	45
___	2657X	Caboose (O), 40-41	25	40
___	2659	Dump Car (O), 38-41	40	70
___	2660	Crane Car (O), 38-42	80	266
___	2672	Caboose (027), 41-42	20	50
___	2677	Gondola (027), 39-41	25	40
___	2679	Boxcar (027), 38-42	13	30
	2680	Tank Car (027), 38-42		
___		(A) Aluminum, Sunoco	15	40
___		(B) Orange, Shell	15	40
___	2682	Caboose (027), 38-42	6	30
___	2682X	Caboose (027), 38-42	20	35
___	2689T	Tender	15	35
___	2689W	Tender	35	50
___	2717	Gondola (O), 38-42 u	20	40
___	2719	Boxcar (O), 38-42 u	30	50
___	2722	Caboose (O), 38-42 u	25	50
___	2755	Tank Car (O), 41-42	71	195
___	2757	Caboose (O), 41-42	25	53
___	2757X	Caboose (O), 41-42	25	40

		Good	Exc	
2758	Automobile Boxcar (O), 41-42	35	60	___
2810	Crane Car (O), 38-42	130	160	___
2811	Flatcar (O), 38-42	50	95	___
2812	Gondola (O), 38-42			
	(A) Green	40	143	___
	(B) Dark orange	45	95	___
2813	Stock Car (O), 38-42	120	363	___
2814	Boxcar (O), 38-42			
	(A) Cream, maroon roof	85	150	___
	(B) Orange, brown roof, rubber-stamped lettering	200	825	___
2814R	Refrigerator Car (O), 38-42			
	(A) White, light blue roof, nickel plates	129	260	___
	(B) White, brown roof, no plates	375	660	___
2815	Tank Car (O), 38-42			
	(A) Aluminum	85	165	___
	(B) Orange	113	215	___
2816	Hopper Car (O), 35-42			
	(A) Red	100	320	___
	(B) Black	110	220	___
2817	Caboose (O), 36-42			
	(A) Light red body and roof	78	140	___
	(B) Flat red body, tuscan roof	115	371	___
2820	Floodlight Car (O), 38-42			
	(A) Stamped nickel searchlights	110	205	___
	(B) Gray die-cast searchlights	120	260	___
2954	Boxcar (O), 40-42*	132	375	___
2955	Sunoco Tank Car (O), 40-42*			
	(A) Shell decal	198	500	___
	(B) Sunoco decal	279	690	___
2956	Hopper Car (O), 40-42*	150	400	___
2957	Caboose (O), 40-42*	110	501	___
3300	Summer Trolley Trailer (std), 10-13	1400	2250	___
3651	Operating Lumber Car (O), 39-42	25	55	___
3652	Operating Gondola (O), 39-42	27	75	___
3659	Operating Dump Car (O), 39-42	20	40	___
3811	Operating Lumber Car (O), 39-42	35	88	___
3814	Operating Merchandise Car (O), 39-42	85	195	___
3859	Operating Dump Car (O), 38-42	45	90	___

Other Transformers and Motors

A	Miniature Motor, 04	50	95	___
A	Transformer, 40, 60 watts, 21-37	10	41	___
B	New Departure Motor, 06-16	75	135	___
B	Transformer, 50, 75 watts, 16-38	7	25	___
C	New Departure Motor, 06-16	100	180	___
D	New Departure Motor, 06-14	100	180	___

PREWAR 1901-1942			Good	Exc
___	E	New Departure Motor, 06-14	100	180
___	F	New Departure Motor, 06-14	100	180
___	G	Fan Motor, battery-operated, 06-14	100	180
___	K	Transformer, 150, 200 watts, 13-38	18	73
___	L	Transformer, 50, 75 watts, 13-16, 33-38	10	25
___	M	Peerless Motor, battery-operated, 15-20	30	80
___	N	Transformer, 50 watts, 41-42	7	20
___	Q	Transformer, 50 watts, 14-15	10	21
___	Q	Transformer, 75 watts, 38-42	12	28
___	R	Peerless Motor, battery-operated, reversing, 15-20	30	75
___	R	Transformer, 100 watts, 38-42	20	45
___	S	Transformer, 50 watts, 14-17	13	28
___	T	Transformer, 75, 100, 150 watts, 14-28	8	30
___	U	Transformer, Aladdin, 32-33	5	15
___	V	Transformer, 150 watts, 39-42	40	200
___	W	Transformer, 75 watts, 32-33	10	35
___	Y	Peerless Motor, battery-operated, 3-speed, 15-20	40	80
___	Z	Transformer, 250 watts, 39-42	64	184

Track, Lockons, and Contactors			
___	0 Straight		1
___	0 Curve		1
___	072 Straight	1	3
___	072 Curve	1	3
___	027 Straight		1
___	027 Curve		1
___	Standard Straight	1	3
___	Standard Curve	1	2
___	Standard Insulated Straight, 33-42	2	4
___	Standard Insulated Curve, 33-42	1	2
___	0 Gauge Lockon	0	4
___	Standard Gauge Lockon		1
___	UTC Lockon		1
___	145C Contactor	3	9
___	153C Contactor	3	7
___	Track Clips, dozen (0), 37	5	10

Section 2
POSTWAR 1945–1969

		Good	Exc	
5C	Test Set	784	1512	___
5D	Test Set, 54	1219	2193	___
5E	Electronic Set Tester, 46-49	1295	2873	___
5F	Test Set	854	1703	___
011-11	Fiber Pins, dozen (O), 46-50	1	3	___
011-43	Insulating Pins, dozen (O), 61	1	3	___
20	90-degree Crossover (O), 45-61	2	6	___
020X	45-degree Crossover (O), 46-59	3	8	___
22	Remote Control Switches, pair (O), 45-69	19	67	___
022-500	Adapter Set (O), 57-61	2	7	___
022A	Remote Control Switches, pair (O), 47	21	53	___
022C-1	Switch Controller	5	11	___
25	Bumper (O), 46-47	5	15	___
26	Bumper, 48-50			
	(A) Red, 49-50	5	14	___
	(B) Gray, 48	16	48	___
027C-1	Track Clips, box of 12 (027), 47, 49	4	13	___
027C-1	Track Clips, box of 50 (027)	10	35	___
30	Water Tower, 47-50			___
	(A) Single-walled	17	56	___
	(B) Double-walled	28	82	___
31	Curved Track (Super O), 57-66	1	4	___
31-5	Track Ground Pins, Dozen (Super O), 57-60	2	5	___
31-7	Power Blade Connection, dozen (Super O), 57-60	7	11	___
31-15	Ground Rail Pin, dozen (Super O), 57-66	3	11	___
31-45	Power Blade Connection, dozen (Super O), 61-66	4	10	___
32	Straight Track (Super O), 57-66	2	5	___
32-10	Insulating Pin, dozen (Super O), 57-60	5	11	___
32-20	Power Blade Insulator, dozen (Super O), 57-60	3	10	___
32-25	Insulating Pin (Super O), 57-61		1	___
32-30	Ground Pin (Super O), 57-61		1	___
32-31	Power Pin, Dozen (Super O), 57-61	3	10	___
32-32	Insulating Pin, Dozen (Super O), 57-61	3	8	___
32-33	Ground Pin, Dozen (Super O), 57-61	3	9	___
32-34	Power Pin (Super O), 57-61	3	9	___
32-35	Insulating Pin, dozen (Super O to 027), 57-61	4	8	___
32-45	Power Blade Insulators, dozen (Super O), 61-66	3	11	___
32-55	Insulating Pins, dozen (Super O), 61-66	3	10	___
33	Half Curved Track (Super O), 57-66	2	5	___
34	Half Straight Track (Super O), 57-66	3	6	___
35	Boulevard Lamp, 45-49	11	31	___
36	Operating Car Remote Control Set (Super O), 57-66	10	31	___
37	Uncoupling Track Set (Super O), 57-66	10	18	___

			Good	Exc
___	**38**	Operating Water Tower, 46-47	78	249
___	**38-85**	Accessory Adapter Tracks, pair (Super O), 57-61	9	27
___	**39**	Operating Set (Super O), 57	7	14
___	**39-5**	Operating Set (Super O), 57-58	4	89
___	**39-6**	Operating Set (Super O), 57-58	4	9
___	**39-10**	Operating Set (Super O), 58	4	8
___	**39-15**	Operating Set with blade (Super O), 57-58	4	8
___	**39-20**	Operating Set (Super O), 57-58	4	8
___	**39-25**	Operating Set (Super O), 61-66	8	46
___	**39-35**	Operating Set (Super O), 59	8	24
	40	Hookup Wire, 50-51, 53-63		
___		(A) Single reel, orange or gray, with tape	7	50
___		(B) 8 sealed reels in dealer box	97	397
___	**40-25**	Conductor Wire with envelope, 56-59	9	54
___	**40-50**	Cable Reel with envelope, 60-61	13	49
	41	U.S. Army Switcher, 55-57		
___		(A) Unpainted black body	51	117
___		(B) Black-painted body	286	884
___	**042/42**	Manual Switches, pair (O), 46-59	11	31
___	**42**	Picatinny Arsenal Switcher, 57	89	240
___	**43**	Power Track (Super O), 59-66	5	15
___	**44**	U.S. Army Mobile Launcher, 59-62	141	290
___	**44-80**	Missiles, 59-60	13	30
___	**45**	U.S. Marines Mobile Launcher, 60-62	104	230
___	**45**	Automatic Gateman, 46-49	11	38
___	**45N**	Automatic Gateman, 45	14	37
___	**48**	Insulated Straight Track (Super O), 57-66	5	13
___	**49**	Insulated Curved Track (Super O), 57-66	5	10
	50	Section Gang Car, 54-64		
___		(A) Gray bumpers, rotating blue man and fixed olive men, center horn, 54	286	887
___		(B) Blue bumpers, rotating olive man and fixed blue men, center horn	25	64
___		(C) Blue bumpers, rotating olive man and fixed blue men, off-center horn	25	60
___	**51**	Navy Yard Switcher, 56-57	141	281
___	**52**	Fire Car, 58-61	63	156
	53	Rio Grande Snowplow, 57-60		
___		(A) Backwards "a" in Rio Grande	63	213
___		(B) Correctly printed "a"	145	438
___	**54**	Ballast Tamper, 58-61, 66, 68-69	55	148
	55	PRR Tie-Jector Car, 57-61		
___		(A) Ventilation slot behind motorman	49	133
___		(B) No slot behind motorman	37	98
___	**55-150**	Ties, 24 pieces, 57-60	15	29
___	**56**	Lamp Post, 46-49	16	42
___	**56**	M&StL Mine Transport, 58	165	320

POSTWAR 1945-1969		Good	Exc
57	AEC Switcher, 59-60	190	464 ___
58	GN Snowplow, 59-61	126	477 ___
58	Lamp Post, 46-50	14	97 ___
59	Minuteman Switcher, 62-63	170	579 ___
60	Lionelville Rapid Transit Trolley, 55-58		
	(A) Metal motorman silhouettes	79	230 ___
	(B) No motorman silhouettes	37	115 ___
61	Ground Lockon (Super O), 57-66	3	6 ___
61-25	Super O Ground clips, dozen, with dealer envelope	9	17 ___
62	Power Lockon (Super O), 57-66	3	6 ___
64	Highway Lamp Post, 45-49	14	51 ___
65	Handcar, 62-66		
	(A) Light yellow	71	244 ___
	(B) Dark yellow	65	214 ___
68	Executive Inspection Car, 58-61	55	156 ___
69	Maintenance Car, 60-62	74	187 ___
70	Yard Light, 49-50	10	35 ___
71	Lamp Post, 49-59	6	15 ___
75	Goose Neck Lamps, set of 2, 61-63	13	33 ___
76	Boulevard Street Lamps, set of 3, 59-66, 68-69	18	74 ___
80	Controller, 60	7	18 ___
88	Controller, 46-60	6	20 ___
89	Flagpole, 56-58	16	99 ___
90	Controller, 55-66		
	(A) Metal clip	5	13 ___
	(B) No metal clip	5	10 ___
91	Circuit Breaker, 57-60	10	27 ___
92	Circuit Breaker, 59-66, 68-69	7	20 ___
93	Water Tower, 46-49	16	122 ___
96C	Controller, 45-54	4	8 ___
97	Coal Elevator, 46-50	80	199 ___
108	Trestle Set, 12 black piers,	9	21 ___
109	Partial Trestle Set, 61	5	14 ___
110	Graduated Trestle Set, 22 or 24 piers, 55-69	10	21 ___
110-75	Graduated Trestle Set with 110-78 envelope	10	181 ___
111	Elevated Trestle Set, 10 A piers, 56-69	11	20 ___
111-100	Elevated Trestle Piers, set of 2, 60-63	11	111 ___
112	Remote Control Switches, pair (Super O), 57-66	36	124 ___
114	Newsstand with horn, 57-59	32	84 ___
115	Passenger Station, 46-49	103	265 ___
118	Newsstand with whistle, 57-58	33	85 ___
119	Landscaped Tunnel, 57-58	200	400 ___
120	90-degree Crossing (Super O), 57-66	5	15 ___
121	Landscaped Tunnel, 59-66	70	300 ___
122	Lamp Assortment, 48-52	81	368 ___
123	Lamp Assortment, 55-59	68	334 ___

			Good	Exc
___	**123-60**	Lamp Assortment, 60-63	37	253
	125	Whistle Shack, 50-55		
___		(A) Gray base	14	45
___		(B) Green base	21	56
___	**128**	Animated Newsstand, 57-60	47	93
___	**130**	60-degree Crossing (Super O), 57-66	7	17
___	**131**	Curved Tunnel, 59-66	8	43
___	**132**	Passenger Station, 49-55	25	109
___	**133**	Passenger Station, 57, 61-62, 66	17	41
___	**138**	Water Tower, 53-57	24	94
___	**140**	Automatic Banjo Signal, 54-66	14	62
___	**142**	Manual Switches, pair (Super O), 57-66	22	50
	145	Automatic Gateman, 50-66		
___		(A) Red roof	13	61
___		(B) Maroon roof	10	69
___	**145C**	Contactor, 50-60	4	20
___	**147**	Whistle Controller, 61-66	2	6
___	**148**	Dwarf Trackside Signal, 57-60	19	119
___	**148-100**	Controller (SPDT switch), 57-60	5	19
___	**150**	Telegraph Pole Set, 47-50	18	39
	151	Automatic Semaphore, 47-69		
___		(A) Green base, yellow blade, 47	45	91
___		(B) Black base, yellow blade, 47	15	68
___		(C) Black base, red blade, 47	189	422
___	**152**	Automatic Crossing Gate, 45-49	9	38
___	**153**	Automatic Block Control Signal, 45-59	13	122
___	**153C**	Contactor	3	10
___	**154**	Automatic Highway Signal, 45-69	11	77
___	**154C**	Contactor	4	15
___	**155**	Blinking Light Signal with bell, 55-57	21	83
___	**156**	Station Platform, 46-49	31	85
___	**156-5**	Station Platform Fence with envelope	23	50
	157	Station Platform, 52-59		
___		(A) Maroon base	13	62
___		(B) Red base	26	89
___	**157-23**	Station Platform Fence with envelope	14	43
	160	Unloading Bin, 52-57		
___		(A) Black plastic, long	2	6
___		(B) Black metal, short	39	70
___		(C) Multicolor Bakelite, short	6	28
___		(D) Black Bakelite, short	3	9
___	**161**	Mail Pickup Set, 61-63	25	99
___	**163**	Single Target Block Signal, 61-69	13	48
___	**164**	Log Loader, 46-50	46	137
___	**164-64**	Log Set, 5 pieces, separate sale w/box, 52-58	26	69
___	**167**	Whistle Controller, 45-50, 52-57	3	7

POSTWAR 1945-1969		Good	Exc
175	Rocket Launcher, 58-60	50	340 ___
175-50	Extra Rocket, 59-60	10	23 ___
182	Magnetic Crane, 46-49	91	233 ___
182-22	Steel Scrap with bag, 46-49	48	108 ___
192	Operating Control Tower, 59-60	87	254 ___
193	Industrial Water Tower, 53-55		
	(A) Red	43	84 ___
	(B) Black, 53	67	189 ___
195	Floodlight Tower, 57-69		
	(A) Medium tan base, rubber-stamped lettering	23	74 ___
	(B) All other variations	19	58 ___
195-75	Floodlight Extension, 8-bulb (with box), 58-60	28	88 ___
196	Smoke Pellets, 46-47	38	93 ___
197	Rotating Radar Antenna, 57-59		
	(A) Orange platform	42	170 ___
	(B) Gray platform	29	89 ___
197-75	Separate Sale Radar Head with box	58	150 ___
199	Microwave Relay Tower, 58-59	23	68 ___
202	UP Alco Diesel A Unit, 57	24	67 ___
204	Santa Fe Alco Diesel AA Units, 57	63	273 ___
205	Missouri Pacific Alco Diesel AA Units, 57-58		
	(A) Pilot without support	53	120 ___
	(B) Pilot with painted metal support	71	172 ___
206	Artificial Coal, large bag, 46-68	12	20 ___
207	Artificial Coal, small bag, 46-48	7	14 ___
208	Santa Fe Alco Diesel AA Units, 58-59	79	538 ___
209	New Haven Alco Diesel AA Units, 58	179	694 ___
209	Wooden Barrels, set of 6, 46-50	9	15 ___
210	Texas Special Alco Diesel AA Units, 58	57	121 ___
211	Texas Special Alco Diesel AA Units, 62-66	60	176 ___
212	Santa Fe Alco Diesel AA Units, 64-66		
	(A) With Built Date 8-57, 64-65	43	112 ___
	(B) Without Built Date, 66	61	145 ___
212T	Santa Fe Alco Diesel Dummy A Unit, 64-66		___
	(A) With Built Date 8-57, 64-65	21	46 ___
	(B) Without Built Date, 66	30	64 ___
212	USMC Alco Diesel A Unit, 58-59	56	137 ___
212T	USMC Diesel Dummy A Unit, 58 u	408	1264 ___
213	M&StL Alco Diesel AA Units, 64	72	187 ___
214	Plate Girder Bridge, 53-69	9	25 ___
215	Santa Fe Alco Diesel Units, 65 u		
	(A) AB Units	63	130 ___
	(B) AA Units	77	161 ___
215	Santa Fe Alco Diesel Powered A Unit, 65 u	25	54 ___
216	Burlington Alco Diesel A Unit, 58	119	440 ___
216	M&StL Alco Diesel AA Units (213T dummy A unit), 64 u	67	179 ___

			Good	Exc
___	**217**	B&M Alco Diesel AB Units, 59	77	187
___	**217C**	B&M Alco Diesel B Unit, 59	30	70
	218	Santa Fe Alco Diesel Units, 59-63		
___		(A) AA Units	77	295
___		(B) AB Units	62	197
___		(C) AA Units, solid nose decal	71	200
___	**218C**	Santa Fe Alco B Unit, 61-63	40	90
___	**219**	Missouri Pacific Alco Diesel AA Units, 59 u	65	147
	220	Santa Fe Alco Diesel Units, 60-61		
___		(A) A Unit	39	90
___		(B) AA Units	72	172
	221	2-6-4 Locomotive, 221W Tender, 46-47		
___		(A) Gray body, black drivers	60	141
___		(B) Black body, nickel-rimmed black drivers, 47	60	141
___		(C) Gray body, cast-aluminum drivers, 46	114	319
___	**221**	Rio Grande Alco Diesel A Unit, 63-64	29	58
___	**221**	Santa Fe Alco Diesel A Unit, 63-64 u	245	664
___	**221**	U.S. Marine Corps Alco Diesel A Unit, 63-64 u	286	630
	221T	Tender		
___		(A) Gray	19	41
___		(B) Black	17	42
___	**221W**	Whistle Tender	28	63
___	**222**	Rio Grande Alco Diesel A Unit, 62	28	69
___	**223**	Santa Fe Alco Diesel AB Units, 63	62	173
	224	2-6-2 Locomotive, 2466W or 2466WX Tender, 45-46		
___		(A) Blackened handrails, 45	116	246
___		(B) Silver handrails	61	126
___	**224**	US Navy "B" Unit	39	78
___	**224**	U.S. Navy Alco Diesel AB Units, 60	107	216
___	**225**	C&O Alco Diesel A Unit, 60	30	66
___	**226**	B&M Alco Diesel AB Units, 60 u	79	225
___	**226C**	B&M Alco Diesel B Unit, 60 u	31	73
___	**227**	CN Alco Diesel A Unit, 60 u	59	178
___	**228**	CN Alco Diesel A Unit, 61 u	63	253
	229	M&StL Alco Diesel Units, 61-62		
___		(A) A Unit, 61	44	108
___		(B) AB Units, 62	80	321
___	**229C**	M&StL Alco Diesel B Unit, 61-62	30	84
___	**230**	C&O Alco Diesel A Unit, 61	32	185
	231	Rock Island Alco Diesel A Unit, 61-63		
___		(A) With red stripe	39	98
___		(B) Without red stripe	134	390
___	**232**	New Haven Alco Diesel A Unit, 62	50	140
___	**233**	2-4-2 Scout Locomotive, 233W Tender, 61-62	33	71
___	**233W**	Whistle Tender	17	37

		Good	Exc
234T	Lionel Lines Tender	9	24 ___
234T	Pennsylvania Tender	17	42 ___
234W	Lionel Whistle Tender	22	56 ___
234W	Pennsylvania Whistle Tender	36	92 ___
235	2-4-2 Scout Locomotive, 1130T or 1060T Tender, 60 u	78	298 ___
236	2-4-2 Scout Locomotive, 61-62		
	(A) 1050T Slope-back Tender	15	37 ___
	(B) 1130T Tender	15	36 ___
237	2-4-2 Scout Locomotive, 63-66		
	(A) 1060T Tender	24	51 ___
	(B) 234W Tender	31	72 ___
238	2-4-2 Scout Locomotive, stripe on running board, 234W Tender, 63-64	42	109 ___
239	2-4-2 Scout Locomotive, 234W Tender, 65-66	34	71 ___
240	2-4-2 Scout Locomotive, 242T Tender, 64 u	74	238 ___
241	2-4-2 Scout Locomotive, 65 u		
	(A) Narrow stripe, 234W Tender	31	74 ___
	(B) Wide stripe, 1130T Tender	25	58 ___
242	2-4-2 Scout Locomotive, 1060T or 1062T Tender, 62-66	23	49 ___
243	2-4-2 Scout Locomotive, 243W Tender, 60	32	72 ___
243W	Whistle Tender	19	45 ___
244	2-4-2 Scout Locomotive, 244T or 1130T Tender, 60-61	21	47 ___
244T	Tender	9	27 ___
245	2-4-2 Scout Locomotive, 1130T Tender, 59 u	25	119 ___
246	2-4-2 Scout Locomotive, 244T or 1130T Tender, 59-61	19	67 ___
247	2-4-2 Scout Locomotive, 247T Tender, 59		
	(A) Closed pilot	22	59 ___
	(B) Open pilot	35	107 ___
247T	B&O Tender	15	43 ___
248	2-4-2 Scout Locomotive, 1130T Tender, 58	25	60 ___
249	2-4-2 Scout Locomotive, 250T Tender, 58	21	71 ___
250	2-4-2 Scout Locomotive, 250T Tender, 57	23	120 ___
250T	Tender	13	26 ___
251	2-4-2 Scout Locomotive, 66 u		
	(A) 1062T Slope-back Tender	64	153 ___
	(B) 250T-type Tender	64	152 ___
252	Crossing Gate, 50-62	10	55 ___
253	Block Control Signal, 56-59	11	47 ___
256	Illuminated Freight Station, 50-53		
	(A) Dark green roof	25	83 ___
	(B) Light green roof	40	95 ___
257	Freight Station with Diesel Horn, 56-57		
	(A) Maroon base	28	63 ___
	(B) Brown base	38	81 ___
	(C) Maroon or brown base, light green roof	58	125 ___

	POSTWAR 1945-1969		Good	Exc
	260	Bumper, 51-69		
___		(A) Die-cast	7	30
___		(B) Black plastic	13	45
___	**262**	Highway Crossing Gate, 62-69	10	77
___	**264**	Operating Forklift Platform, 57-60	61	251
___	**282**	Portal Gantry Crane, 54-57	72	165
___	**282R**	Portal Gantry Crane, 56-57	65	171
___	**299**	Code Transmitter Beacon Set, 61-63	31	188
___	**308**	Railroad Sign Set, die-cast, 45-49	16	37
___	**309**	Yard Sign Set, plastic, 50-59	8	17
___	**309-100**	Yard Sign Set in Plastic Packaging, 66-69 u	10	66
___	**310**	Billboard Set, 50-68	8	24
___	**313**	Bascule Bridge, 46-49	71	256
___	**313-82**	Fiber Pins, dozen, 46-60	1	3
___	**313-121**	Fiber Pins, dozen, 61	2	4
___	**314**	Scale Model Girder Bridge, 45-50	10	43
___	**315**	Illuminated Trestle Bridge, 46-48	31	85
___	**316**	Trestle Bridge, 49	16	35
___	**317**	Trestle Bridge, 50-56	15	34
___	**321**	Trestle Bridge, 58-64	15	36
___	**321-100**	Trestle Bridge	21	48
___	**332**	Arch-Under Trestle Bridge, 59-66	16	35
___	**334**	Operating Dispatching Board, 57-60	61	152
___	**342**	Culvert Loader, 56-58	59	176
___	**345**	Culvert Unloader, 57-59	52	280
___	**346**	Culvert Unloader, manual, 65 u	46	157
___	**347**	Cannon Firing Range Set, 64 u	267	708
___	**348**	Culvert Unloader, manual, 66-69	57	138
___	**350**	Engine Transfer Table, 57-60	103	240
___	**350-50**	Transfer Table Extension, 57-60	50	153
___	**352**	Ice Depot with 6352 Ice Car, 55-57	75	109
___	**353**	Trackside Control Signal, 60-61	11	27
	356	Operating Freight Station, 52-57		
___		(A) Dark green roof, 52-57	36	81
___		(B) Light green roof, 57	56	156
	362	Barrel Loader, 52-57		
___		(A) Gold lettering	23	80
___		(B) Red lettering	115	312
	362-78	Wooden Barrels, 6 pieces, 52-57		
___		(A) Brown	8	35
___		(B) Red	96	225
___	**364**	Conveyor Lumber Loader, 48-57	28	75
___	**364C**	On/Off Switch, 48-64	7	26
___	**365**	Dispatching Station, 58-59	37	92
___	**365-35**	Set of Delivery Carts, 52	10	32
___	**375**	Turntable, 62-64	58	152

POSTWAR 1945-1969		Good	Exc
390C	Switch, double-pole, double-throw, 60-64	6	24 ___
394	Rotary Beacon, 49-53		
	(A) Steel tower, red platform	15	45 ___
	(B) Steel tower, green platform	34	328 ___
	(C) Aluminum tower, platform, and base	13	100 ___
	(D) Aluminum tower, red steel base	33	113 ___
	(E) Steel tower, red platform, stick-on nameplate	36	81 ___
395	Floodlight Tower, 49-56		
	(A) Light green, silver, or unpainted aluminum	13	112 ___
	(B) Red	32	313 ___
	(C) Dark green	77	262 ___
	(D) Yellow	44	159 ___
397	Operating Coal Loader, 48-57		
	(A) Yellow generator, 48	114	546 ___
	(B) Blue generator, 49-57	29	90 ___
400	B&O Passenger Rail Diesel Car, 56-58	66	179 ___
404	B&O Baggage-Mail Rail Diesel Car, 57-58	111	262 ___
410	Billboard Blinker, 56-58	15	51 ___
413	Countdown Control Panel, 62	17	87 ___
415	Diesel Fueling Station, 55-57	47	124 ___
419	Heliport Control Tower, 62	137	305 ___
443	Missile Launching Platform with ammo dump, 60-62	27	62 ___
445	Switch Tower, lighted, 52-57	20	65 ___
448	Missile Firing Range Set, 61-63	44	165 ___
450	Operating Signal Bridge, 52-58	21	92 ___
450L	Signal Light Head, 52-58	11	29 ___
452	Overhead Gantry Signal, 61-63	38	109 ___
455	Operating Oil Derrick, 50-54		
	(A) Dark green tower, green top	49	240 ___
	(B) Dark green tower, red top	65	237 ___
	(C) Apple green tower, red top	108	379 ___
456	Coal Ramp with 3456 Hopper, 50-55		
	(A) Light gray ramp	37	104 ___
	(B) Dark gray ramp	55	119 ___
456C	Coal Ramp Controller	13	28 ___
460	Piggyback Transportation Set, 55-57		
	(A) Metal stick-on signs on lift truck	45	84 ___
	(B) Rubber-stamped lettering on lift truck	53	109 ___
460P	Piggyback Platform, 55-57	17	43 ___
460-150	Separate Sale 2 Trailers in Box	54	216 ___
461	Platform with Truck and Trailer, 66	54	142 ___
462	Derrick Platform Set, 61-62	102	271 ___
464	Lumber Mill, 56-60	42	101 ___
465	Sound Dispatching Station, 56-57	36	93 ___
470	Missile Launching Platform with 6470 Exploding Boxcar, 59-62	54	92 ___

			Good	Exc
___	**479-1**	Truck for 6362 Truck Car with envelope, 55-56	23	56
___	**480-25**	Conversion Magnetic Coupler, 50-60	1	5
___	**480-32**	Conversion Magnetic Coupler, 61-69	1	8
	494	Rotary Beacon, 54-66		
___		(A) Painted steel	23	42
___		(B) Unpainted aluminum	17	46
___	**497**	Coaling Station, 53-58	43	101
___	**497C**	Controller, 53-58	11	25
	520	LL Boxcab Electric Locomotive, 56-57		
___		(A) Black pantograph	31	69
___		(B) Copper-colored pantograph	39	81
	600	MKT NW2 Switcher, 55		
___		(A) Black frame, black end rails	48	98
___		(B) Gray frame, yellow or black end rails	74	202
	601	Seaboard NW2 Switcher, 56		
___		(A) Red stripes with square ends	71	194
___		(B) Red stripes with round ends	66	146
___	**602**	Seaboard NW2 Switcher, 57-58	67	175
	610	Erie NW2 Switcher, 55		
___		(A) Black frame, one-axle Magne-Traction	45	72
___		(B) Black frame, two-axle Magne-Traction	97	252
___		(C) Yellow frame, two-axle Magne-Traction	187	563
___		(D) Replacement body with nameplates	87	261
___	**611**	Jersey Central NW2 Switcher, 57-58	63	131
___	**613**	UP NW2 Switcher, 58	92	304
	614	Alaska NW2 Switcher, 59-60		
___		(A) Plastic bell, no brake	71	145
___		(B) No bell, yellow brake	108	369
___		(C) "Built by Lionel" outlined in yellow near nose	139	277
	616	Santa Fe NW2 Switcher, 61-62		
___		(A) Open E-unit slot and bell/horn slots	78	167
___		(B) Plugged E-unit slot and open bell/horn slots	90	197
___		(C) Plugged E-unit slot and bell/horn slots	99	224
___	**617**	Santa Fe NW2 Switcher, 63	106	244
___	**621**	Jersey Central NW2 Switcher, 56-57	56	103
___	**622**	Santa Fe NW2 Switcher, 49-50		
___		(A) Large GM decal on cab	101	211
___		(B) Small GM decal on side	80	174
___	**623**	Santa Fe NW2 Switcher, 52-54	66	223
___	**624**	C&O NW2 Switcher, 52-54	64	166
___	**625**	LV GE 44-ton Switcher, 57-58	41	109
___	**626**	B&O GE 44-ton Switcher, 56-57, 59	116	250
___	**627**	LV GE 44-ton Switcher, 56-57	30	83
___	**628**	NP GE 44-ton Switcher, 56-57	36	252
___	**629**	Burlington GE 44-ton Switcher, 56	132	329
___	**633**	Santa Fe NW2 Switcher, 62	57	143

		Good	Exc
634	Santa Fe NW2 Switcher, 63, 65-66		
	(A) Safety stripes	70	139 ___
	(B) No safety stripes	47	89 ___
635	UP NW2 Switcher, 65 u	55	104 ___
637	2-6-4 Locomotive, 2046 736W Tender, 59-63		
	(A) 2046W Lionel Lines Tender	55	126 ___
	(B) 736W Pennsylvania Tender	69	358 ___
638-2361	Van Camp's Pork & Beans Boxcar, 62 u	15	33 ___
645	Union Pacific NW2 Switcher, 69	67	148 ___
646	4-6-4 Locomotive, 2046W Tender, 54-58	58	472 ___
665	4-6-4 Locomotive, 2046W, 6026W, or 736W Tender, 54-59, 66	73	573 ___
671	6-8-6 Steam Turbine Locomotive, 46-49		
	(A) Bulb smoke unit, 671W Tender, 46	40	147 ___
	(B) E-unit slot, heater smoke unit, 671W Tender, 47	59	163 ___
	(C) Thin nickel rims, 2671WX Tender with functioning backup lights, 48	63	208 ___
	(D) Thin nickel rims, 2671W Tender, nonfunctioning backup lights, 48	56	135 ___
	(E) Thin nickel rims, 2671W Tender, no backup light lenses, 48	52	113 ___
	(F) No rims on drivers, 49	50	110 ___
671-75	Smoke Lamp, 12 volt, 46	11	22 ___
671R	6-8-6 Steam Turbine Locomotive, 4424W or 4671W Tender, 46-49	160	322 ___
671RR	6-8-6 Steam Turbine Locomotive, 2046W-50 Tender, 52	81	223 ___
671S	Smoke Conversion Kit	20	77 ___
671W	Whistle Tender, 46-48	27	67 ___
675	2-6-2 Locomotive, 2466WX or 6466WX Tender, 47-49		
	(A) Aluminum smokestack, 47	67	190 ___
	(B) Black smokestack, 48-49	57	167 ___
675	2-6-4 Locomotive, 2046W Tender, 52	67	207 ___
681	6-8-6 Steam Turbine Locomotive		
	(A) 2671W Tender, 50-51	68	157 ___
	(B) 2046W-50 Tender, 53	48	144 ___
682	6-8-6 Steam Turbine Locomotive, 2046W-50 Tender, 54-55	138	522 ___
685	4-6-4 Hudson Locomotive, 6026W Tender, 53	79	259 ___
703-10	Smoke Lamp, 18 volt, 46	11	26 ___
726	2-8-4 Berkshire, 46-49		
	(A) Turned stanchions, no front coupler, bulb smoke unit, 2426W Tender, 46	271	690 ___
	(B) Cotter pin stanchions, E-unit slot, no front coupler, heater smoke unit, 2426W Tender, 47	206	579 ___
	(C) Simulated front coupler, 2426W Tender, 48-49	105	342 ___
726RR	2-8-4 Berkshire Locomotive, 2046W Tender, 52	108	264 ___
726S	Smoke Conversion Kit	31	93 ___

	POSTWAR 1945-1969		Good	Exc
	736	2-8-4 Berkshire Locomotive, 50-66		
___		(A) No headlight wedge brace, hexagonal flagstaff base, 2671WX Tender , 50-51	120	311
___		(B) Headlight wedge brace, round flagstaff brace, 2046W Tender, 53-54	134	216
___		(C) Sheet metal and plastic trailing truck, 55-56	113	198
___		(D) Smaller typeface on cab number, 57-60	110	169
___		(E) 736W Tender, 61-66	73	184
___	**736W**	PRR Whistle Tender	29	103
	746	N&W 4-8-4 Class J Northern, 57-60		
___		(A) Tender with long stripe	411	998
___		(B) Tender with short stripe	342	1089
	746W	N&W Tender		
___		(A) Short stripe	66	196
___		(B) Long stripe	100	190
___	**760**	Curved Track, 16 sections (072), 54-57	28	77
	773	4-6-4 Hudson Locomotive, 50, 64-66		
___		(A) Valve guides cast in steam chest, 2426W Tender, 50	788	1314
___		(B) No valve guides in steam chest, 736W Pennsylvania Tender, 64	548	955
___		(C) No valve guides in steam chest, 773W New York Central Tender, 64-66	555	1040
	773W	NYC Whistle Tender, 64-66		
___		(A) Closed spaced lettering	250	500
___		(B) Widely spaced lettering	175	350
___	**902**	Elevated Trestle Set, 60, u	33	111
___	**908**	Union Station, 59, u	494	906
	909	Smoke Fluid, large or small bottle, 57-66, 68-69		
___		(A) 1/2-ounce bottle	8	55
___		(B) 2-ounce bottle	15	36
___	**B909**	Smoke Fluid, 2-ounce bottle in blister pack, 66	88	285
___	**919**	Artificial Grass, 46-64	7	18
___	**920**	Scenic Display Set, 57-58	30	85
___	**920-2**	Tunnel Portals, pair, 58-59	12	30
___	**920-3**	Green Grass, 57	5	13
___	**920-4**	Yellow Grass, 57	9	18
___	**920-5**	Artificial Rock, 57-58	7	21
___	**920-6**	Dry Glue, 57-58	4	13
___	**920-8**	Dyed Lichen, 57-58	5	15
___	**925**	Lubricant, 2 ounce tube, 46-69	3	20
___	**925-1**	Lubricant, 1 ounce tube, 50-69	2	6
___	**926**	Lubricant, 1/2 ounce tube, 55	2	3
___	**926-5**	Instruction Booklet, 46-48	1	4
___	**927**	Lubricating Kit, 50-59	10	39
___	**927-3**	Track Cleaner	4	14
___	**928**	Maintenance and Lubricating Kit, 60-63	23	48
___	**943**	Ammo Dump, 59-61	18	39

		Good	Exc	
950	U.S. Railroad Map, 58-66	13	69	___
951	Farm Set, 13 pieces, 58	35	85	___
952	Figure Set, 30 pieces, 58	32	96	___
953	Figure Set, 32 pieces, 59-62	41	80	___
954	Swimming Pool and Playground Set, 30 pieces, 59	45	164	___
955	Highway Set, 22 pieces, 58	30	63	___
956	Stockyard Set, 18 pieces, 59	38	80	___
957	Farm Building and Animal Set, 35 pieces, 58	50	113	___
958	Vehicle Set, 24 pieces, 58	44	194	___
959	Barn Set, 23 pieces, 58	87	179	___
960	Barnyard Set, 29 pieces, 59-61	50	114	___
961	School Set, 36 pieces, 59	39	276	___
962	Turnpike Set, 24 pieces, 58	49	112	___
963	Frontier Set, 18 pieces, 59-60	52	112	___
963-100	Boxed Frontier Set, 60	125	400	___
964	Factory Site Set, 18 pieces, 59	70	191	___
965	Farm Set, 36 pieces, 59	57	196	___
966	Firehouse Set, 45 pieces, 58	68	142	___
967	Post Office Set, 25 pieces, 58	48	230	___
968	TV Transmitter Set, 28 pieces, 58	55	113	___
969	Construction Set, 23 pieces, 60	60	122	___
970	Ticket Booth, 58-60	27	95	___
971	Lichen with box, 60-64	26	100	___
972	Landscape Tree Assortment, 61-64	24	131	___
973	Complete Landscaping Set, 60-64	41	139	___
974	Scenery Set, 58	63	181	___
980	Ranch Set, 14 pieces, 60	45	108	___
981	Freight Yard Set, 10 pieces, 60	47	150	___
982	Suburban Split Level Set, 18 pieces, 60	60	201	___
983	Farm Set, 7 pieces, 60-61	27	140	___
984	Railroad Set, 22 pieces, 61-62	49	118	___
985	Freight Area Set, 32 pieces, 61	37	471	___
986	Farm Set, 20 pieces, 62	131	316	___
987	Town Set, 24 pieces, 62	30	402	___
988	Railroad Structure Set, 16 pieces, 62	40	434	___
1001	2-4-2 Scout Locomotive, plastic body, 1001T Tender, 48			
	(A) Silver rubber-stamped cab number	28	69	___
	(B) White heat-stamped cab number	13	35	___
1001T	Tender	6	15	___
1002	Gondola, 48-52			
	(A) Black, white lettering	4	9	___
	(B) Blue, white lettering	4	9	___
	(C) Silver, black lettering	185	467	___
	(D) Yellow, black lettering	143	620	___
	(E) Red, white lettering	180	471	___
X1004	PRR Baby Ruth Boxcar, 48-52	4	10	___

			Good	Exc
___	**1005**	Sunoco 1-D Tank Car, 48-50	3	9
	1007	LL SP-type Caboose, 48-52		
___		(A) Red body	2	7
___		(B) Red body, raised board on catwalk	8	22
___		(C) Tuscan body	182	462
___	**1008**	Uncoupling Unit (027), 57-62	2	4
___	**1008-50**	Uncoupling Track Section (027), 57-62	1	5
___	**1009**	Manumatic Track Section (027), 48-52	2	4
___	**1010**	Transformer, 35 watts, 61-66	5	11
___	**1011**	Transformer, 25 watts, 48-49	3	10
___	**1012**	Transformer, 35 watts, 50-54	5	10
___	**1013**	Curved Track (027), 45-69		1
___	**1013-17**	Steel Pins, dozen (027), 46-60		1
___	**1013-42**	Steel Pins, dozen (027), 61-68		2
___	**1014**	Transformer, 40 watts, 55	5	11
___	**1015**	Transformer, 45 watts, 56-60	5	10
___	**1016**	Transformer, 35 watts, 59-60	4	8
___	**1018**	Half Straight Track (027), 55-69		1
___	**1018**	Straight Track (027), 45-69		1
___	**1019**	Remote Control Track Set (027), 46-48	2	7
___	**1020**	90-degree Crossing (027), 55-69	2	5
___	**1021**	90-degree Crossing (027), 45-54	2	4
___	**1022**	Manual Switches, pair (027), 53-69	6	11
___	**1023**	45-degree Crossing (027), 56-69	2	5
___	**1024**	Manual Switches, pair (027), 46-52	5	11
___	**1025**	Illuminated Bumper (027), 46-47	5	11
___	**1025**	Transformer, 45 watts, 61-69	4	10
___	**1026**	Transformer, 25 watts, 61-64	2	22
___	**1032**	Transformer, 75 watts, 48	9	23
___	**1033**	Transformer, 90 watts, 48-56	20	33
___	**1034**	Transformer, 75 watts, 48-54	10	43
___	**1035**	Transformer, 60 watts, 47	7	56
___	**1037**	Transformer, 40 watts, 46-47	4	8
___	**1041**	Transformer, 60 watts, 45-46	7	15
___	**1042**	Transformer, 75 watts, 47-48	10	21
___	**1043**	Transformer, 50 watts, 53-57	5	17
___	**1043-500**	Transformer, 60 watts, ivory, 57-58	64	213
___	**1044**	Transformer, 90 watts, 57-69	16	33
___	**1045**	Operating Watchman, 46-50	16	79
___	**1045C**	Contactor	4	9
___	**1047**	Operating Switchman, 59-61	31	123
___	**1050**	0-4-0 Scout Locomotive, 1050T Tender, 59 u	40	98
___	**1050T**	Tender	6	15
___	**1053**	Transformer, 60 watts, 56-60	6	14
___	**1055**	Texas Special Alco Diesel A Unit, 59-60	22	54
___	**1060**	2-4-2 Locomotive, 1050T or 1060T Tender, 60-62	15	30

		Good	Exc	
1060T	Lionel Lines Tender	6	13	___
1060T-50	Southern Pacific Tender, 63-64 u	11	25	___
1061	0-4-0 or 2-4-2 Scout Locomotive, 1061T Tender, 64, 69			
	(A) Slope-back Lionel Lines tender	9	24	___
	(B) Paper number labels	36	99	___
	(C) No number stamped on cab	22	55	___
1061T	Tender	4	16	___
1062	0-4-0 or 2-4-2 Scout Locomotive, 63-64			
	(A) Streamlined Southern Pacific Tender	25	53	___
	(B) Other tenders	15	39	___
1063	Transformer, 75 watts, 60-64	11	26	___
1063	Transformer 75 watt, with green whistle control	90	123	___
1065	Union Pacific Alco Diesel A Unit, 61	26	64	___
1066	Union Pacific Alco Diesel A Unit, 64 u	25	60	___
1073	Transformer, 60 watts, 61-66	6	15	___
1101	Transformer, 25 watts, 48	2	5	___
1101	2-4-2 Scout Locomotive, 1001T Tender, 48 u			
	(A) Cab correctly marked "1101"	15	33	___
	(B) Cab marked "1001"	70	161	___
1110	2-4-2 Locomotive, 1001T Tender, 49, 51-52	15	31	___
1120	2-4-2 Scout Locomotive, 1001T Tender, 50	17	32	___
1121	Remote Control Switches, pair (027), 46-51	11	28	___
1122	Remote Control Switches, pair (027), 52-53	12	24	___
1122-34	Remote Control Switches, pair, 52-53	11	26	___
1122-500	Gauge Adapter (027), 57-66	3	7	___
1122E	Remote Control Switches, pair (027), 53-69	11	26	___
1130	2-4-2 Locomotive, 6066T or 1130T Tender, 53-54			
	(A) Plastic body	15	38	___
	(B) Die-cast body	30	71	___
1130T	Tender			
	(A) Black-painted shell	24	56	___
	(B) Black plastic shell	6	14	___
1130T-500	Tender, pink, from Girls Set	113	276	___
1144	Transformer, 75 watts, 61-66	10	25	___
1232	Transformer, 75 watts, made for export, 48	17	38	___
1615	0-4-0 Locomotive, 1615T Tender, 55-57			
	(A) No grab irons	57	126	___
	(B) Grab irons on locomotive and tender	91	208	___
1615T	Tender	15	30	___
1625	0-4-0 Locomotive, 1625T Tender, 58	145	381	___
1625T	Tender	22	48	___
1640-100	Presidential Kit, 60	45	118	___
1654	2-4-2 Locomotive, 1654W Tender, 46-47	33	71	___
1654T	Tender	10	24	___
1654W	Whistling Tender	15	35	___

			Good	Exc
___	**1655**	2-4-2 Locomotive, 6654W Tender, 48-49	30	70
	1656	0-4-0 Locomotive, 6403B Tender, 48-49		
___		(A) Large silver cab number	105	307
___		(B) Small silver cab number	106	278
___	**1665**	0-4-0 Locomotive, 2403B Tender, 46	147	317
___	**1666**	2-6-2 Locomotive, 2466W or 2466WX Tender, 46-47		
___		(A) Number plate and two-piece bell	58	123
___		(B) Rubber-stamped number and one-piece bell	68	128
___	**1666T**	Tender	10	23
___	**1862**	4-4-0 Civil War General, 1862T Tender, 59-62		
___		(A) Gray smokestack	73	142
___		(B) Black smokestack	79	154
___	**1862T**	Tender	21	43
___	**1865**	Western & Atlantic Coach, 59-62	22	46
___	**1866**	Western & Atlantic Mail-Baggage Car, 59-62	21	47
___	**1872**	4-4-0 Civil War General, 1872T Tender, 59-62	102	301
___	**1872T**	Tender	29	57
___	**1875**	Western & Atlantic Coach, 59-62	80	266
___	**1875W**	Western & Atlantic Coach, whistle, 59-62	51	122
___	**1876**	Western & Atlantic Baggage Car, 59-62	36	107
___	**1877**	Flatcar with fence and horses, 59-62	47	105
___	**1882**	4-4-0 Civil War General, 1882T Tender, 60 u	186	368
___	**1882T**	Tender, 60 u	41	91
___	**1885**	Western & Atlantic Coach, 60 u	90	223
___	**1887**	Flatcar with fences and horses, 60 u	85	174
___	**2001**	Track Make-up Kit (027), 63	288	760
___	**2002**	Track Make-up Kit (027), 63	495	1181
___	**2003**	Track Make-up Kit (027), 63	600	3267
___	**2016**	2-6-4 Locomotive, 6026W Tender, 55-56	42	93
	2018	2-6-4 Locomotive, 56-59, 61		
___		(A) 6026T Tender	32	58
___		(B) 6026W Tender	42	89
___		(C) 1130T Tender	34	154
___	**2020**	6-8-6 Steam Turbine Locomotive, 2020W or 2466WX Tender, smoke lamp, 46	82	213
___	**2020**	6-8-6 Steam Turbine Locomotive, 2020W or 6020W Tender, 47-49	74	176
___	**2020W**	Whistling Tender	31	66
	2023	Union Pacific Alco Diesel AA Units, 50-51		
___		(A) Yellow body	83	276
___		(B) Gray nose and side frames	1239	3622
___		(C) Silver body	77	173
___	**2024**	C&O Alco Diesel A Unit, 69	30	71
	2025	2-6-2 Locomotive, 2466WX or 6466WX Tender, 47-49		
___		(A) Black smokestack, 48-49	70	160
___		(B) Aluminum smokestack, 47	78	183
___	**2025**	2-6-4 Locomotive, 6466W Tender, 52	89	214

		Good	Exc
2026	2-6-2 Locomotive, 6466WX Tender, 48-49	48	117 ___
2026	2-6-4 Locomotive, 6466W, 6466T, or 6066T Tender, 51-53	39	70 ___
2028	Pennsylvania GP7 Diesel, 55		
	(A) Gold lettering	124	255 ___
	(B) Yellow lettering	93	186 ___
	(C) Tan frame	179	380 ___
2029	2-6-4 Locomotive, 64-69		
	(A) 234W Lionel Lines Tender	48	155 ___
	(B) LL Tender with "Hagerstown" on bottom	61	126 ___
	(C) 234W Pennsylvania Tender	71	152 ___
2031	Rock Island Alco Diesel AA Units, 52-54	75	221 ___
2032	Erie Alco Diesel AA Units, 52-54	92	259 ___
2033	Union Pacific Alco Diesel AA Units, 52-54	76	179 ___
2034	2-4-2 Scout Locomotive, 6066T Tender, 52	29	63 ___
2035	2-6-4 Locomotive, 6466W Tender, 50-51	55	117 ___
2036	2-6-4 Locomotive, 6466W Tender, 50	41	1474 ___
2037	2-6-4 Locomotive, 54-55, 57-63		
	(A) 6026T or 1130T Tender	35	74 ___
	(B) 6026W, 233W, or 234W whistle Tender	53	238 ___
2037-500	2-6-4 Locomotive, pink, 1130T-500 Tender, 57-58	346	942 ___
2041	Rock Island Alco Diesel AA Units, 69	61	140 ___
2046	4-6-4 Locomotive, 2046W Tender, 50-51, 53	90	279 ___
2046T	Tender, for export	62	201 ___
2046W	Whistle Tender	27	152 ___
2046W-50	PRR Whistle Tender	33	126 ___
2055	4-6-4 Locomotive, 2046W or 6026W Tender, 53-55	83	212 ___
2056	4-6-4 Locomotive, 2046W Tender, 52	72	223 ___
2065	4-6-4 Locomotive, 2046W or 6026W Tender, 54-56	75	265 ___
2203B	Tender with bell	54	120 ___
2203T	Tender, 45-46	36	54 ___
2224W	Whistle Tender	28	66 ___
2240	Wabash F3 AB Units, 56	189	419 ___
2242	New Haven F3 AB Units, 58-59	263	939 ___
2242C	New Haven F3 B Unit, 58-59	101	323 ___
2243	Santa Fe F3 AB Units, 55-57		
	(A) Gray body mold, raised molded cab door ladder	100	250 ___
	(B) Typical molded cab door ladder	80	388 ___
2243C	Santa Fe F3 B Unit, 55-57	51	162 ___
2245	Texas Special F3 AB Units, 54-55	133	260 ___
	(A) B Unit with portholes, 54	207	720 ___
	(B) B Unit without portholes, 55	227	539 ___
2257	SP-type caboose, 47		
	(A) Red body, no smokestack	5	15 ___
	(B) Tuscan body and smokestack	107	287 ___
	(C) Red body and smokestack	153	373 ___

			Good	Exc
	2321	Lackawanna FM Train Master Diesel, 54-56		
___		(A) Gray roof	168	379
___		(B) Maroon roof	295	611
	2322	Virginian FM Train Master Diesel, 65-66		
___		(A) Unpainted blue body, yellow stripes	222	425
___		(B) Blue or black body, painted blue and yellow stripes	237	593
___	**2328**	Burlington GP7 Diesel, 55-56	83	298
___	**2329**	Virginian GE E-33/EL-C Electric Locomotive, 58-59	164	412
___	**2330**	Pennsylvania GG1 Electric Locomotive, green, 50	327	954
	2331	Virginian FM Train Master Diesel, 55-58		
___		(A) Black and yellow stripes, gray mold, 55	306	729
___		(B) Yellow stripes, blue mold, 56-58	272	654
___		(C) Blue and yellow stripes, gray mold	324	964
	2332	Pennsylvania GG1 Electric Locomotive, 47-49		
___		(A) Black	530	1970
___		(B) Dark green	218	697
	2333	NYC F3 Diesel AA Units, 48-49		
___		(A) Rubber-stamped lettering	220	675
___		(B) Heat-stamped lettering	159	471
___	**2333**	Santa Fe F3 Diesel AA Units, 48-49	169	392
___	**2337**	Wabash GP7 Diesel, 58	116	212
	2338	Milwaukee Road GP7 Diesel, 55-56		
___		(A) Orange band around shell	447	1633
___		(B) Interrupted orange band	104	210
___	**2339**	Wabash GP7 Diesel, 57	136	255
	2340	Pennsylvania GG1 Electric Locomotive, 55		
___		(A) Tuscan	410	1084
___		(B) Dark green	279	702
	2341	Jersey Central FM Train Master Diesel, 56		
___		(A) High-gloss orange	869	2673
___		(B) Dull orange	831	2041
___	**2343**	Santa Fe F3 Diesel AA Units, 50-52	159	429
	2343C	Santa Fe F3 Diesel B Unit, 50-55		
___		(A) Screen roof vents	89	244
___		(B) Louver roof vents	67	184
___	**2344**	NYC F3 Diesel AA Units, 50-52	186	431
	2344C	NYC F3 Diesel B Unit, 50-55		
___		(A) Screen roof vents	89	244
___		(B) Louver roof vents	67	184
___	**2345**	Western Pacific F3 Diesel AA Units, 52	435	1120
___	**2346**	B&M GP9 Diesel, 65-66	116	264
___	**2347**	C&O GP7 Diesel, 65 u	1568	4190
___	**2348**	M&StL GP9 Diesel, 58-59	151	338
___	**2349**	Northern Pacific GP9 Diesel, 59-60	138	455

		Good	Exc
2350	New Haven EP-5 Electric Locomotive, 56-58		
	(A) Painted nose trim, white N and orange H	187	449 ___
	(B) Decaled nose trim, white N and orange H	101	267 ___
	(C) Painted nose trim, orange N and black H	757	2796 ___
	(D) Decaled nose trim, orange N and black H	386	858 ___
	(E) Orange and white stripes go through doorjambs	296	917 ___
2351	Milwaukee Road EP-5 Electric Locomotive, 57-58	145	432 ___
2352	Pennsylvania EP-5 Electric Locomotive, 58-59		
	(A) Tuscan body	167	384 ___
	(B) Chocolate brown body	214	404 ___
2353	Santa Fe F3 Diesel AA Units, 53-55	153	414 ___
2354	NYC F3 Diesel AA Units, 53-55	186	419 ___
2355	Western Pacific F3 Diesel AA Units, 53	411	1662 ___
2356	Southern F3 Diesel AA Units, 54-56	319	775 ___
2356C	Southern F3 Diesel B Unit, 54-56	131	325 ___
2357	SP-type Caboose, 47-48		
	(A) Red body and smokestack	231	550 ___
	(B) Tuscan body and smokestack	12	40 ___
	(C) Tile red, no smokestack, "6357" stamped on bottom	56	148 ___
2358	Great Northern EP-5 Electric Locomotive, 59-60	211	580 ___
2359	Boston & Maine GP9 Diesel, 61-62	102	331 ___
2360	Pennsylvania GG1 Electric Locomotive, 56-58, 61-63		
	(A) Tuscan, 5 gold stripes	491	1521 ___
	(B) Dark green, 5 gold stripes	395	771 ___
	(C) Tuscan, 1 gold stripe, heat-stamped letters	361	736 ___
	(D) Tuscan, 1 gold stripe, decaled lettering	364	665 ___
2363	Illinois Central F3 Diesel AB Units, 55-56		
	(A) Black lettering	334	938 ___
	(B) Brown lettering	372	918 ___
2363C	Illinois Central F3 Diesel B Unit	47	210 ___
2365	C&O GP7 Diesel, 62-63	128	409 ___
2367	Wabash F3 Diesel AB Units, 55	306	1129 ___
2367C	Wabash F3 Diesel B Unit, 55	80	213 ___
2368	B&O F3 Diesel AB Units, 56	557	1907 ___
2368C	B&O F3 Diesel B Unit, 56	145	510 ___
2373	CP F3 Diesel AA Units, 57	718	1684 ___
2378	Milwaukee Road F3 Diesel AB Units, 56		
	(A) Yellow roof line stripes	456	1087 ___
	(B) No roof line stripes	423	918 ___
2378C	Milwaukee Road F3 Diesel B Unit, yellow roof line stripe, 56	224	514 ___
2379	Denver & Rio Grande Western F3 Diesel AB Units, 57-58	351	959 ___
2379C	Denver & Rio Grande Western F3 Diesel B Unit	88	275 ___
2383	Santa Fe F3 Diesel AA Units, 58-66	167	449 ___
2400	Maplewood Pullman Car, green, 48-49	42	82 ___
2401	Hillside Observation Car, green, 48-49	27	70 ___

			Good	Exc
___	**2402**	Chatham Pullman Car, green, 48-49	34	82
___	**2403B**	Tender, 46	20	47
___	**2404**	Santa Fe Vista Dome Car, 64-65	26	59
___	**2405**	Santa Fe Pullman Car, 64-65	26	60
___	**2406**	Santa Fe Observation Car, 64-65	21	52
___	**2408**	Santa Fe Vista Dome Car, 66	32	67
___	**2409**	Santa Fe Pullman Car, 66	34	68
___	**2410**	Santa Fe Observation Car, 66	27	58
	2411	Lionel Lines Flatcar, 46-48		
___		(A) With pipes, 46	33	68
___		(B) With logs, 47-48	18	36
___	**2412**	Santa Fe Vista Dome Car, 59-63	31	115
___	**2414**	Santa Fe Pullman Car, 59-63	39	116
___	**2416**	Santa Fe Observation Car, 59-63	28	88
___	**2419**	DL&W Work Caboose, 46-47	18	43
	2420	DL&W Work Caboose with searchlight, 46-48		
___		(A) Light or dark gray, heat-stamped lettering	39	81
___		(B) Light or dark gray, rubber-stamped lettering	65	137
	2421	Maplewood Pullman Car, 50-53		
___		(A) Gray roof	26	60
___		(B) Silver roof	22	73
	2422	Chatham Pullman Car, 50-53		
___		(A) Gray roof	27	63
___		(B) Silver roof	21	97
	2423	Hillside Observation Car, 50-53		
___		(A) Gray roof	25	60
___		(B) Silver roof	21	48
___	**2426W**	Whistle Tender,46-50	131	334
___	**2429**	Livingston Pullman Car, 52-53	50	134
___	**2430**	Pullman Car, blue, 46-47	22	81
___	**2431**	Observation Car, blue, 46-47	21	72
___	**2432**	Clifton Vista Dome Car, 54-58	27	95
___	**2434**	Newark Pullman Car, 54-58	29	122
___	**2435**	Elizabeth Pullman Car, 54-58	44	123
___	**2436**	Mooseheart Observation Car, 57-58	25	64
___	**2436**	Summit Observation Car, 54-56	23	59
	2440	Pullman Car, green, 46-47		
___		(A) Silver lettering	31	63
___		(B) White lettering	25	53
	2441	Observation Car, green, 46-47		
___		(A) Silver lettering	31	63
___		(B) White lettering	23	48
___	**2442**	Clifton Vista Dome Car, 56	36	91
	2442	Pullman Car, brown, 46-48		
___		(A) Silver lettering	34	70
___		(B) White lettering	27	77

		Good	Exc
2443	Observation Car, brown, 46-48		
	(A) Silver lettering	33	65 ___
	(B) White lettering	28	80 ___
2444	Newark Pullman Car, 56	41	84 ___
2445	Elizabeth Pullman Car, 56	152	179 ___
2446	Summit Observation Car, 56	40	84 ___
2452	Pennsylvania Gondola, 45-47		
	(A) Whirly wheels, 45	22	85 ___
	(B) Regular wheels	7	17 ___
	(C) Early flying shoe trucks, two holes in floor, 45	41	98 ___
2452X	Pennsylvania Gondola, 46-47	10	24 ___
X2454	Baby Ruth Boxcar, PRR logo, 46-47	15	66 ___
X2454	Pennsylvania Boxcar, 46		
	(A) Brown door	62	180 ___
	(B) Orange door	132	385 ___
2456	Lehigh Valley Hopper, 48		
	(A) Flat black, 2 lines of data, 48	11	27 ___
	(B) Flat black, 3 lines of data, 48	73	187 ___
2457	PRR N5-type Caboose 477618, illuminated, 45-47		
	(A) Brown body, white lettering centered, red window frames, 45	15	45 ___
	(B) Brown body, white lettering not centered, 45	88	332 ___
	(C) Red body, red window frames, 46-47	10	28 ___
	(D) Red body, black window frames, 46-47	13	46 ___
	(E) Red body, no "Eastern Division" markings, 46-47	10	20 ___
	(F) Same as E, but black smokejack, 46-47	10	21 ___
X2458	PRR Automobile Boxcar, 46-48	23	207 ___
2460	Bucyrus Erie Crane Car, 12-wheel, 46-50		
	(A) Gray cab	74	225 ___
	(B) Black cab	32	101 ___
2461	Transformer Car, die-cast, 47-48		
	(A) Red transformer	29	78 ___
	(B) Black transformer	25	59 ___
	(C) Red transformer, number rubber-stamped on bottom	52	125 ___
2465	Sunoco 2-D Tank Car, 46-48		___
	(A) "Gas, Sunoco, and Oils" in diamond, centered	181	553 ___
	(B) "Sunoco" in diamond	6	15 ___
	(C) "Sunoco" extends beyond diamond	6	17 ___
	(D) Sunoco in diamond, centered	63	120 ___
2466T	Tender	16	33 ___
2466W	Whistle Tender, 46-48		
	(A) Number heat-stamped on front, 46	64	151 ___
	(B) Number missing from front, 47-48	12	30 ___
2466WX	Whistle Tender, 45-48	25	64 ___
2472	PRR N5-type Caboose, tinplate, 46-47	12	39 ___
2481	Plainfield Pullman Car, yellow, 50	82	215 ___

			Good	Exc
___	**2482**	Westfield Pullman Car, yellow, 50	82	233
___	**2483**	Livingston Observation Car, yellow, 50	72	221
___	**2521**	President McKinley Observation Car, 62-66	64	148
___	**2522**	President Harrison Vista Dome Car, 62-66	69	160
___	**2523**	President Garfield Pullman Car, 62-66	77	160
	2530	REA Baggage Car, 54-60		
___		(A) Large doors	143	403
___		(B) Small doors	61	227
	2531	Silver Dawn Observation Car, 52-60		
___		(A) Ribbed channels, round rivets	29	85
___		(B) Ribbed channels, hex rivets	37	85
___		(C) Ribbed channels, hex rivets, red center taillight	68	137
___		(D) Flat channels, glued nameplates	42	124
	2532	Silver Range Vista Dome Car, 52-60		
___		(A) Ribbed channels, or hex rivets	36	87
___		(B) Flat channels, glued nameplates	40	131
	2533	Silver Cloud Pullman Car, 52-59		
___		(A) Ribbed channels, or hex rivets	33	84
___		(B) Flat channels, glued nameplates	43	98
	2534	Silver Bluff Pullman Car, 52-59		
___		(A) Ribbed channels, or hex rivets	37	89
___		(B) Flat channels, glued nameplates	40	94
___	**2541**	Alexander Hamilton Observation Car, 55-56*	63	132
___	**2542**	Betsy Ross Vista Dome Car, 55-56*	64	137
___	**2543**	William Penn Pullman Car, 55-56*	64	141
___	**2544**	Molly Pitcher Pullman Car, 55-56*	64	139
___	**2550**	B&O Baggage-Mail Rail Diesel Car, 57-58	149	364
___	**2551**	Banff Park Observation Car, 57*	93	210
___	**2552**	Skyline 500 Vista Dome Car, 57*	120	255
___	**2553**	Blair Manor Pullman Car, 57*	155	331
___	**2554**	Craig Manor Pullman Car, 57*	155	333
___	**2555**	Sunoco 1-D Tank Car, 46-48	18	49
___	**2559**	B&O Passenger Rail Diesel Car, 57-58	122	249
	2560	Lionel Lines Crane Car, 8-wheel, 46-47		
___		(A) Black boom	24	75
___		(B) Brown boom	29	69
___		(C) Green boom	34	81
___	**2561**	Vista Valley Observation Car, 59-61*	79	180
___	**2562**	Regal Pass Vista Dome Car, 59-61*	84	220
___	**2563**	Indian Falls Pullman Car, 59-61*	84	211
	2625	Irvington Pullman Car, 46-50*		
___		(A) No silhouettes	64	146
___		(B) Silhouettes	76	202
___	**2625**	Madison Pullman Car, 46-47*	57	152
___	**2625**	Manhattan Pullman Car, 46-47*	58	154
___	**2627**	Madison Pullman Car, 48-50*		

		Good	Exc
	(A) No silhouettes	54	160
	(B) Silhouettes	76	201 ___
2628	Manhattan Pullman Car, 48-50*		
	(A) No silhouettes	58	207 ___
	(B) Silhouettes	79	254 ___
2666T	Tender	9	18 ___
2671T	PRR Tender, for export	53	135 ___
2671W	Whistle Tender	37	109 ___
2671W	PRR Tender with silver letters and back-up light	185	367 ___
2671WX	Whistle Tender	42	269 ___
2755	Sunoco 1-D Tank Car, 45	23	58 ___
X2758	PRR Automobile Boxcar, 45-46	28	56 ___
2855	Sunoco 1-D Tank Car, 46-47		
	(A) Black	62	190 ___
	(B) Black, decal without "Gas" and "Oils"	54	175 ___
	(C) Gray	47	135 ___
3309	Turbo Missile Launch Car, red body, 63-64	16	46 ___
3309-50	Turbo Missile Launch Car, olive body, 63-64	170	478 ___
3330	Flatcar with submarine kit, 60-62	58	263 ___
3330-100	Operating Submarine Kit with box, 60-61	151	370 ___
3349	Turbo Missile Launch Car, red body, 62-65	18	78 ___
3356	Operating Horse Car and Corral Set, 56-60, 64-66	51	363 ___
3356	Operating Horse Car only, 56-60, 64-66		
	(A) Built date, bar-end trucks, 56-60	40	88 ___
	(B) No built date, AAR trucks, 64-66	48	104 ___
3356-100	Black Horses, 9 pieces, 56-59	16	36 ___
3356-150	Horse Car Corral, 57-60	49	264 ___
3357	Hydraulic Maintenance Car, 62-64		
	(A) Blue, 62-64	10	33 ___
	(B) Teal, 62-64	40	91 ___
3357-27	Trestle Components for Cop and Hobo Car, 62	26	50 ___
3359	Lionel Lines Twin-bin Coal Dump Car, 55-58	20	117 ___
3360	Operating Burro Crane, self-propelled, 56-57	61	152 ___
3361	Operating Log Dump Car, 55-58	16	58 ___
3362	Helium Tank Unloading Car, 61-63, 69	23	98 ___
3364	Operating Dump Car with 3 logs, 65-66, 68	17	66 ___
3366	Circus Car Corral Set, 59-62	107	233 ___
3366	Circus Car Corral only, 59-62	18	95 ___
3366	Circus Car only, 59-62	44	95 ___
3366-100	White Horses, 9 pieces, 59-62	34	58 ___
3370	W&A Sheriff and Outlaw Car, 61-64		
	(A) AAR trucks	19	65 ___
	(B) Archbar trucks	25	60 ___
3376	Bronx Zoo Car, 60-66, 69		
	(A) Blue, white lettering	19	104 ___
	(B) Green, yellow lettering	26	53 ___

			Good	Exc
___		(C) Blue, yellow lettering	81	221
___	**3386**	Bronx Zoo Car, 60	23	56
___	**3409**	Helicopter Car, 61	32	80
	3410	Helicopter Car, 61-63		
___		(A) 2 operating couplers, gray Navy helicopter	27	69
___		(B) Single operating coupler, yellow helicopter, 63	51	113
___	**3413**	Mercury Capsule Car, 62-64	44	138
___	**3419**	Helicopter Car, 59-65	32	129
___	**3424**	Wabash Operating Boxcar, 56-58	18	88
___	**3424-75**	Low Bridge Signal, 56-57	63	215
___	**3424-100**	Low Bridge Signal Set, 56-58	20	133
___	**3428**	U.S. Mail Operating Boxcar, 59-60	38	108
___	**3429**	USMC Helicopter Car, 60	220	608
	3434	Poultry Dispatch Car, 59-60, 64-66		
___		(A) Gray man	58	149
___		(B) Blue man	48	99
	3435	Traveling Aquarium Car, 59-62		
___		(A) Gold lettering, tank designations, and circle around L	375	888
___		(B) Gold lettering, tank designations, no circle around L	243	533
___		(C) Gold lettering, no tank designations, no circle around L	95	203
___		(D) Yellow lettering, no tank designations, no circle around L	50	175
___	**3444**	Erie Operating Gondola, 57-59	31	75
	3451	Operating Log Dump Car, 46-48		
___		(A) Heat-stamped lettering	13	33
___		(B) Rubber-stamped lettering	23	60
	3454	PRR Operating Merchandise Car, 46-47		
___		(A) Red lettering	1005	3646
___		(B) Blue lettering	38	151
___	**3456**	N&W Operating Hopper, 50-55	21	57
	3459	LL Operating Coal Dump Car, 46-48		
___		(A) Aluminum bin	115	301
___		(B) Black bin	17	41
___		(C) Green bin	23	64
___	**3460**	Flatcar with trailers, 55-57	30	70
	3461	LL Operating Log Car, 49-55		
___		(A) Black car, heat-stamped lettering	18	87
___		(B) Black car, rubber-stamped lettering	135	390
___	**3461-25**	LL Operating Log Car, green	23	75
	3462	Automatic Milk Car, 47-48		
___		(A) Flat white or cream, steel base mechanism	11	45
___		(B) Flat white or cream, brass base mechanism	22	58
___		(C) Glossy cream	64	199
___	**3462-70**	Magnetic Milk Cans, 52-59	11	17
___	**3462P**	Milk Car Platform, 47-48	6	19
___	**X3464**	ATSF Operating Boxcar, 49-52		

		Good	Exc	
	(A) Orange body, corner steps, 49	8	14	
	(B) Orange body, no steps, 50-52	8	35	___
	(C) Tan body	444	1088	___
X3464	NYC Operating Boxcar, 49-52			
	(A) Corner steps, 49	8	15	___
	(B) No steps, 50-52	6	13	___
3469	LL Operating Coal Dump Car, 49-55	20	71	___
3470	Target Launching Car, dark blue, 62-64	27	137	___
3470-100	Target Launching Car, light blue, 63	56	162	___
3472	Automatic Milk Car, 49-53	23	60	___
3474	Western Pacific Operating Boxcar, 52-53	22	115	___
3482	Automatic Milk Car, 54-55			
	(A) "RT3472" on right	38	88	___
	(B) "RT3482" on right	18	50	___
3484	Pennsylvania Operating Boxcar, 53	21	58	___
3484-25	ATSF Operating Boxcar, 54			
	(A) White lettering	29	67	___
	(B) Black lettering	508	1197	___
3494-1	NYC Operating Boxcar, 55	34	95	___
3494-150	MP Operating Boxcar, 56	45	112	___
3494-275	State of Maine Operating Boxcar, 56-58			
	(A) "3494275" on side	38	107	___
	(B) No number on side	60	177	___
3494-550	Monon Operating Boxcar, 57-58	214	446	___
3494-625	Soo Line Operating Boxcar, 57-58	202	427	___
3509	Satellite Launching Car, 61			
	(A) Chrome satellite cover	28	69	___
	(B) Gray satellite cover	80	192	___
3510	Satellite Launching Car, 62	35	81	___
3512	Fireman and Ladder Car, 59-61			
	(A) Black extension ladder	36	85	___
	(B) Silver extension ladder	65	177	___
3519	Satellite Launching Car, 61-64	22	62	___
3520	Searchlight Car, 52-53			
	(A) Serif lettering	17	40	___
	(B) Sans serif lettering	15	85	___
3530	GM Generator Car, 56-58			
	(A) Blue fuel tank	45	138	___
	(B) Black fuel tank	38	105	___
	(C) 3530 underscored	664	1880	___
3530-50	Searchlight with pole and base, 56-56	21	76	___
3535	Security Car with searchlight, 60-61	45	110	___
3540	Operating Radar Car, 59-60	38	102	___
3545	Operating TV Monitor Car, 61-62	50	138	___
3559	Operating Coal Dump Car, 46-48			___

			Good	Exc
___		(A) Black coil housing	15	53
___		(B) Brown coil housing	29	76
	3562-1	ATSF Operating Barrel Car, 54		
___		(A) Black, black unloading trough	69	215
___		(B) Black, yellow unloading trough	65	177
___		(C) Gray, red lettering	1150	2643
	3562-25	ATSF Operating Barrel Car, gray, 54		
___		(A) Red lettering, no bracket tab	189	452
___		(B) Blue lettering, no bracket tab	19	74
___		(C) Blue lettering, bracket tab	25	73
	3562-50	ATSF Operating Barrel Car, yellow, 55-56		
___		(A) Painted	37	81
___		(B) Unpainted	26	68
___	**3562-75**	ATSF Operating Barrel Car, orange, 57-58	35	144
	3619	Helicopter Reconnaissance Car, 62-64		
___		(A) Light yellow	46	139
___		(B) Dark yellow	63	153
	3620	Searchlight Car, orange generator, 54-56		
___		(A) Unpainted gray plastic searchlight	19	37
___		(B) Gray-painted gray plastic searchlight	26	51
___		(C) Unpainted orange plastic searchlight	56	114
___		(D) Gray-painted orange plastic searchlight	72	200
	3650	Extension Searchlight Car, 56-59		
___		(A) Light gray	28	102
___		(B) Dark gray	50	172
___		(C) Olive gray	111	260
	3656	Armour Operating Cattle Car, some with an open coil, 49-55		
___		(A) Black letters, Armour sticker	126	295
___		(B) White letters, Armour sticker	22	50
___		(C) Black letters, no Armour sticker	94	204
___		(D) White letters, no Armour sticker	17	46
___	**3656**	Stockyard with cattle, 49-55	17	44
	3656-34	Cattle, black, 9 pieces, 49-58		
___		(A) Rounded ridge on base, 49	60	92
___		(B) Plain base	15	27
___	**3656-150**	Corral Platform, yellow tray	225	622
___	**3662**	Automatic Milk Car, 55-60, 64-66	30	123
___	**3662-79**	Nonmagnetic Milk Cans, 7 pieces, white envelope	18	34
___	**3662-80**	Nonmagnetic Milk Cans, 7 pieces, manila envelope	16	32
	3665	Minuteman Operating Car, 61-64		
___		(A) Medium blue roof	75	215
___		(B) Dark blue roof	34	75
___	**3666**	Minuteman Boxcar with cannon, 64 u	189	485
	3672	Bosco Operating Milk Car, 59-60		
___		(A) Unpainted yellow body	78	168

		Good	Exc
	(B) Painted yellow body	122	269 ___
3672-79	Bosco Can Set, 7 pieces in envelope, 59-60	32	66 ___
3820	USMC Operating Submarine Car, 60-62	117	255 ___
3830	Operating Submarine Car, 60-63	38	102 ___
3854	Automatic Merchandise Car, 46-47	173	501 ___
3927	Lionel Lines Track Cleaning Car, 56-60	26	123 ___
3927-38	Track Cleaning Fluid Bottle	8	15 ___
3927-50	Track Wiping Cylinders, 25 pieces, 57-60	16	31 ___
3927-75	Track-Clean Detergent, can, 56-69	5	12 ___
4357	SP-type Caboose, electronic, 48-49		
	(A) Die-cast metal smokestack	75	180 ___
	(B) Matching plastic smokestack	104	237 ___
	(C) Matching plastic smokestack, raised board on catwalk	110	255 ___
4452	PRR Gondola, electronic, 46-49	57	133 ___
4454	Baby Ruth PRR Boxcar, electronic, 46-49	60	142 ___
4457	PRR N5-type Caboose, tinplate, electronic, 46-47	53	147 ___
4671W	Whistle Tender	92	217 ___
5102	Railroad and Roadway Crossing	10	45 ___
5159-50	Maintenance and Lube Kit, 66-69	23	54 ___
5160	Viewing Stand, 63	40	209 ___
5459	LL Coal Dump Car, electronic, 46-49	57	137 ___
6001T	Tender	7	15 ___
6002	NYC Gondola, 50	4	7 ___
X6004	Baby Ruth PRR Boxcar, 50	4	8 ___
6007	Lionel Lines SP-type Caboose, 50	3	6 ___
6009	Remote Control Uncoupling Track, 53-54	2	5 ___
6012	Gondola, 51-56	2	31 ___
6014	Bosco PRR Boxcar, 58		
	(A) White body	18	39 ___
	(B) Red body	4	11 ___
	(C) Orange body	5	16 ___
6014	Chun King Boxcar, 56 u	44	123 ___
6014	Frisco Boxcar, 57, 63-69		
	(A) White body	8	34 ___
	(B) Red body	5	9 ___
	(C) White body, coin slot	16	40 ___
	(D) Orange body, 57	14	36 ___
	(E) Orange body, 69	9	20 ___
X6014	Baby Ruth PRR Boxcar, 51-56		
	(A) White body	5	9 ___
	(B) Red body	4	8 ___
6014-100	Airex Boxcar, 60 u	13	62 ___
6014-150	Wix Boxcar, 59 u	98	211 ___
6015	Sunoco 1-D Tank Car, 54-55		
	(A) Painted tank	73	314 ___

			Good	Exc
___		(B) Unpainted tank	8	16
	6017	Lionel Lines SP-type Caboose, 51-62		
___		(A) Common unpainted red or Tuscan-red body	4	14
___		(B) Glossy Tuscan-painted, orange mold	22	58
___		(C) Semi-glossy Tuscan-painted, orange mold	12	30
___		(D) Light or dark tile red-painted, blue mold	14	35
___		(E) Common-brown painted body	2	8
___	**6017**	Lionel SP-type Caboose, unpainted maroon, 56	9	24
___	**6017-50**	U.S. Marine Corps SP-type Caboose, 58	28	74
___	**6017-85**	Lionel Lines SP-type Caboose, gray-painted, 58	23	75
	6017-100	B&M SP-type Caboose, 59, 62, 65-66		
___		(A) Dark purple-blue	95	357
___		(B) Medium or light blue	13	45
___	**6017-185**	ATSF SP-type Caboose, gray-painted, 59-60	13	35
___	**6017-200**	U.S. Navy SP-type Caboose, 60	53	157
___	**6017-235**	ATSF SP-type Caboose, red-painted, 62	18	48
___	**6019**	Remote Control Track (027), 48-66	2	9
___	**6020W**	Whistle Tender	27	63
___	**6024**	Nabisco Shredded Wheat Boxcar, 57	10	28
___	**6024**	RCA Whirlpool Boxcar, 57 u	20	185
	6025	Gulf 1-D Tank Car, 56-58		
___		(A) Gray body, blue lettering	5	15
___		(B) Orange body, blue lettering	10	23
___		(C) Black body, red-orange Gulf emblem	5	14
___	**6026T**	Tender	14	35
___	**6026W**	Whistle Tender	24	103
___	**6027**	Alaska SP-type Caboose, 59	32	72
___	**6029**	Remote Control Uncoupling Track, 55-63	2	10
___	**6032**	Short Gondola, black (027), 52-54	3	7
	X6034	Baby Ruth PRR Boxcar, 53-54		
___		(A) Orange, blue lettering	5	13
___		(B) Orange, black lettering	6	11
___	**6035**	Sunoco 1-D Tank Car, 52-53	4	10
	6037	Lionel Lines SP-type Caboose, 52-54		
___		(A) Tuscan	3	6
___		(B) Red	4	8
___	**6042**	Short Gondola, 59-61, 62-64	4	8
	6044	Airex Boxcar, orange lettering, 59-60 u		
___		(A) Medium blue	9	22
___		(B) Teal blue	26	63
___		(C) Purple-blue	130	247
___	**6044-1X**	Nestles/McCall's Boxcar, 62-63 u	393	1324
	6045	Lionel Lines 2-D Tank Car, 59-64		
___		(A) Gray	10	21
___		(B) Orange	14	29

		Good	Exc
	(C) Beige	10	21
6045	Cities Service 2-D Tank, 60 u	14	31 ___
6047	Lionel Lines SP-type Caboose, 62		
	(A) Unpainted, medium red	2	7 ___
	(B) Painted, brown	164	466 ___
	(C) Unpainted, coral pink	17	43 ___
6050	Lionel Savings Bank Boxcar, 61		
	(A) Type I body, Blt by Lionel	17	41 ___
	(B) Type I body, Built by Lionel	39	124 ___
	(C) Type IIa body, Blt by Lionel	125	260 ___
6050-110	Swift Boxcar, 62-63		
	(A) Red body	9	27 ___
	(B) Dark red body, 2 open holes in roof walk	40	93 ___
6050-175	Libby's Tomato Juice Boxcar, 63 u		
	(A) Green stems on tomatoes	15	50 ___
	(B) Green stems missing	25	59 ___
	(C) No white lines between glass and tomatoes	25	66 ___
6057	LL SP-type Caboose, 59-62		
	(A) Unpainted red plastic	6	19 ___
	(B) Red-painted	24	102 ___
	(C) Unpainted coral pink plastic	20	50 ___
6057-50	LL SP-type Caboose, orange, 62	18	68 ___
6058	C&O SP-type Caboose, 61		
	(A) Blue lettering	17	43 ___
	(B) Black lettering	25	59 ___
6059	M&StL SP-type Caboose, 61-69		
	(A) Painted, red	15	31 ___
	(B) Unpainted, red	6	16 ___
	(C) Unpainted, maroon	6	12 ___
6062	NYC Gondola with 3 cable reels, 59-62		
	(A) No metal undercarriage	11	25 ___
	(B) Metal undercarriage	20	49 ___
	(C) No metal undercarriage, no paint on bottom	34	69 ___
6062-50	NYC Gondola with 2 canisters, 69	10	20 ___
6066T	Tender	10	20 ___
6067	SP-type Caboose, unmarked, 61-62		
	(A) Red	3	7 ___
	(B) Yellow	6	13 ___
	(C) Brown	7	17 ___
6076	ATSF Hopper, 63 u	8	18 ___
6076	Lehigh Valley Hopper, short, 61-63		
	(A) Gray body	7	16 ___
	(B) Black body	6	12 ___
	(C) Red body	7	13 ___
	(D) Yellow body, painted	391	1103 ___

			Good	Exc
___	**6076-100**	Hopper, gray, unmarked, 63	7	24
___	**6110**	2-4-2 Locomotive, 6001T Tender, 50-51	17	36
	6111	Flatcar with logs, 55-57		
___		(A) Yellow with black lettering	10	35
___		(B) Yellow with white lettering	105	373
	6112	Short Gondola with 4 canisters, 56-58		
___		(A) Black body	5	17
___		(B) Blue body	6	15
___		(C) White body	16	43
	6112-5	Canister, 56-58		
___		(A) Red or white	2	4
___		(B) Red with black letters	20	46
___	**6112-25**	Canister Set, 4 pieces, red or white, with box, 56-58	28	182
___	**6119**	DL&W Work Caboose, red, 55-56	11	22
___	**6119-25**	DL&W Work Caboose, orange, 56-59	18	69
___	**6119-50**	DL&W Work Caboose, brown, 56	22	76
	6119-75	DL&W Work Caboose, 57		
___		(A) Heat-stamped letters on frame	15	45
___		(B) Closely spaced rubber-stamped letters on frame	70	221
___		(C) Widely spaced rubber-stamped letters on frame	67	218
	6119-100	DL&W Work Caboose, red cab, gray tool tray, 57-66, 69		
___		(A) Black frame, white letters	10	23
___		(B) "Built By Lionel" builders plate, 66	22	69
___		(C) Black frame, red-painted cab	53	136
___		(D) Santa Fe cab, gray tool box	10	30
	6119-125	Rescue Caboose, unpainted olive tray, black frame, white lettering, 64	72	241
___	**6120**	Work Caboose, yellow, unmarked, 61-62	6	12
	6121	Flatcar with pipes, 56-57		
___		(A) Yellow, red, or gray	12	43
___		(B) Maroon	17	55
	6130	ATSF Work Caboose, 61, 65-69		
___		(A) Red painted, no builders plate	13	35
___		(B) Red unpainted, builders plate	10	26
___		(C) Red painted, builders plate	63	236
___	**6139**	Remote Control Uncoupling Track (027), 63	1	4
___	**6142**	Short Gondola, green, blue, or black, with 2 canisters, 63-66, 69	5	18
	6142-175	Short Gondola, olive drab, with 2 canisters	75	210
___	**6149**	Remote Control Uncoupling Track (027), 64-69	1	4
	6151	Flatcar with Range Patrol Truck, 58		
___		(A) Yellow frame	35	170
___		(B) Orange frame	27	87
___		(C) Cream frame	35	82
	6162	NYC Gondola with 3 white canisters, 59-68		
___		(A) Blue body	9	38

		Good	Exc
	(B) Red body	72	271 ___
	(C) Teal or green body	28	58 ___
6162-60	Alaska Gondola with 3 red canisters, 59	34	83 ___
6162-100	NYC Gondola		
	(A) Red body with 3 red canisters	80	160 ___
	(B) Teal or green body with 3 white canisters	15	33 ___
6167	LL SP-type Caboose, red, 63-64		
	(A) Unpainted	6	11 ___
	(B) Painted	33	88 ___
6167	SP-type Caboose, unmarked, no end rails, 63-64		
	(A) Red body	5	8 ___
	(B) Brown body	8	17 ___
6167-50	SP-type Caboose, unmarked, yellow	5	14 ___
6167-85	Union Pacific SP-type Caboose, 69	10	27 ___
6167-175	SP-type Caboose, unmarked, olive	116	287 ___
6175	Flatcar with rocket, 58-61		
	(A) Black frame	26	96 ___
	(B) Red frame	26	62 ___
6176	Hopper, unmarked, 63-69		
	(A) Dark yellow	11	26 ___
	(B) Gray	8	15 ___
	(C) Red	9	19 ___
	(D) Bright yellow	22	52 ___
6176-75	Lehigh Valley Hopper, 64-66, 69		
	(A) Dark yellow	5	15 ___
	(B) Gray	6	11 ___
	(C) Black	4	10 ___
	(D) Red	11	24 ___
	(E) Bright yellow	19	41 ___
6176-100	Olive Drab Hopper, unmarked	53	130 ___
6219	C&O Work Caboose, 60	18	41 ___
6220	Santa Fe NW2 Switcher, 49-50		
	(A) Large GM decal on cab	109	259 ___
	(B) Small GM decal on side	78	175 ___
6250	Seaboard NW2 Switcher, 54-55		
	(A) Seaboard decal	77	289 ___
	(B) Widely spaced rubber-stamped letters	103	276 ___
	(C) Closely spaced rubber-stamped letters	134	364 ___
6257	SP-type Caboose, 48-52		
	(A) Dark red, matching plastic smokestack	163	461 ___
	(B) All other variations	8	15 ___
6257-25	SP-type Caboose, circle-L logo, 53-55		
	(A) Red painted	7	16 ___
	(B) Unpainted red plastic	5	11 ___
6257-50	SP-type Caboose, 56	8	20 ___
6257-100	Lionel Lines SP-type Caboose, smokestack, 63-64	12	25 ___

		POSTWAR 1945-1969	Good	Exc
___	**6257X**	SP-type Caboose, red, 2 couplers, with box, 48	24	117
	6262	Flatcar with wheel load, 56-57		
___		(A) Black frame, 56-57	27	72
___		(B) Red frame, 56	364	849
	6264	Flatcar with lumber for 264 Fork Lift Platform, 57-60		
___		(A) Bar-end trucks	28	62
___		(B) Plastic trucks	32	67
___		(C) Separate-sale box and envelope	129	357
___	**6311**	Flatcar with 3 pipes, 55	20	44
	6315	Gulf 1-D Chemical Tank Car, 56-59, 68-69		
___		(A) Early, painted	33	79
___		(B) Late, unpainted	24	52
___		(C) Late, unpainted, built date	46	141
	6315	Lionel Lines 1-D Tank Car, 63-66		
___		(A) Unpainted orange body	15	34
___		(B) Painted orange body	88	297
___	**6342**	NYC Gondola with culvert channel and 7 pipes, 56-58, 64-66	19	60
___	**6343**	Barrel Ramp Car with 6 barrels, 61-62	18	59
___	**6346**	Alcoa Quad Hopper, 56	34	88
	6352-1	PFE Ice Car from 352 Ice Depot, 55-57		
___		(A) 3 lines of data	54	108
___		(B) 4 lines of data	32	86
___		(C) Separate-sale box	524	2521
	6356	NYC Stock Car, 2-level, 54-55		
___		(A) Heat-stamped lettering	22	44
___		(B) Rubber-stamped lettering	29	73
	6357	SP-type Caboose, SP logo, 48-53		
___		(A) Tile red, tuscan, or maroon	12	27
___		(B) Tile red, extra board on catwalk	105	367
	6357	SP-type Caboose, no logo, 57-61		
___		(A) Number to left	12	25
___		(B) Number to right	19	96
	6357-25	SP-type Caboose, circle-L logo, 53-56		
___		(A) Maroon or tuscan body, black metal smokestack	12	25
___		(B) Maroon body, maroon metal smokestack	89	317
___	**6357-50**	ATSF SP-type Caboose, lighted, 60	486	974
	6361	Timber Transport Car, 60-61, 64-69		
___		(A) White lettering	34	93
___		(B) No lettering	51	144
	6362	Rail Truck Car with 3 trucks, 55-56		
___		(A) Shiny orange	19	43
___		(B) Dull orange	33	217
___	**6376**	LL Circus Stock Car, 56-57	26	67
___	**6401**	Flatcar, no load, gray, 60	4	8
	6401-25	Gray flatcar with load, 64-67		

		Good	Exc
	(A) Jeep and cannon	119	235 ___
	(B) Tank	100	212 ___
	(C) Payton automobile	24	52 ___
	(D) Logs	12	26 ___
6402	Flatcar with 2 Cable Reels, 62, 64-66, 69		
	(A) Gray car with orange reels	5	13 ___
	(B) Maroon car with orange reels	6	13 ___
	(C) Brown car with gray or orange reels	8	15 ___
	(D) Gray car with gray reels	8	15 ___
	(E) Gray car with green reels	10	25 ___
6402	Flatcar with blue boat, 69	27	61 ___
6402-25	Flatcar with 2 cable reels (gray or orange), 62, 64-66	12	25 ___
6402-150	Maroon Flatcar with white trailer	18	35 ___
6403B	Tender	40	87 ___
6404	Black Flatcar with auto, 60 u		
	(A) Red auto	33	64 ___
	(B) Yellow auto	58	112 ___
	(C) Brown auto	104	203 ___
	(D) Green auto	110	222 ___
6405	Flatcar with piggyback van, 61	23	51 ___
6406	Flatcar with auto, 61		
	(A) Maroon frame, red auto	34	58 ___
	(B) Maroon frame, yellow auto	71	121 ___
	(C) Gray frame, dark brown auto	116	249 ___
	(D) Gray frame, green auto	130	244 ___
	(E) Gray frame, yellow auto	50	97 ___
	(F) Gray frame, red auto	26	50 ___
6407	Flatcar with rocket, 63	235	410 ___
6408	Flatcar with pipes, 63 u	20	37 ___
6408-50	Flatcar with 2 orange cable reels, 67 u	16	33 ___
6409-25	Flatcar with pipes, 63 u	17	43 ___
6410-25	Flatcar with 2 automobiles, 63 u		
	(A) Yellow autos	152	378 ___
	(B) Brown autos	160	403 ___
6411	Flatcar with logs, 48-50	17	58 ___
6413	Mercury Capsule Carrying Car, 62-63		
	(A) Medium blue frame	69	190 ___
	(B) Aquamarine frame	84	184 ___
	(C) Teal frame	93	345 ___
6414	Evans Auto Loader with 4 cars, 55-66		
	(A) Premium cars (chrome bumpers, windows, rubber wheels): red, yellow, blue-green, and white	40	143 ___
	(B) Cheapie cars (no wheels): 2 red and 2 yellow	153	271 ___
	(C) Red cars with gray bumpers	79	253 ___
	(D) Yellow cars with gray bumpers	261	467 ___

			Good	Exc
___		(E) Brown cars with gray bumpers	270	881
___		(F) Green cars with gray bumpers	463	905
___		(G) Metal trucks, number right of Lionel without nubs on axle	73	147
___		(H) Metal trucks, number right of Lionel, premium cars with nubs on axle first run	54	127
___	**6414-25**	Sct of 4 Automobiles, separate sale box, 55-58	131	338
	6415	Sunoco 3-D Tank Car, 53-55, 64-66, 69	14	38
___	**6416**	Boat Transport Car, 4 boats, 61-63	114	347
	6417	PRR N5c Porthole Caboose, 53-57		
___		(A) New York Zone	17	36
___		(B) Without New York Zone	116	235
___	**6417-25**	Lionel Lines N5c Porthole Caboose, 54	18	54
	6417-50	LV N5c Porthole Caboose, 54		
___		(A) Gray	54	319
___		(B) Tuscan	452	1535
	6418	Machinery Car with 2 steel girders, 55-57		
___		(A) Black girders, "Lionel" in raised letters	51	105
___		(B) Orange girders, "Lionel" in raised letters	43	91
___		(C) Pinkish orange girders, U.S. Steel	62	246
___		(D) Black girders, U.S. Steel	58	117
___	**6419**	DL&W Work Caboose, 48-50, 52-55	15	42
___	**6419-25**	DL&W Work Caboose, one coupler, 54-55	17	38
___	**6419-50**	DL&W Work Caboose, short smokestack, 56-57	16	41
___	**6419-75**	DL&W Work Caboose, one coupler, 56-57	15	40
___	**6419-100**	N&W Work Caboose, 57-58	51	173
	6420	DL&W Work Caboose with searchlight, 48-50		
___		(A) Heat-stamped serif lettering	38	78
___		(B) Rubber-stamped sans serif lettering	60	126
	6424	Twin Auto Flatcar, 56-59		
___		(A) Black frame, premium cars	28	202
___		(B) 6805 slots, no rail stops	46	104
___		(C) AAR trucks, number on right	31	64
___	**6424-110**	Twin Auto Flatcar, 6805 slots and rail stops, 58-59	75	164
___	**6425**	Gulf 3-D Tank Car, 56-58	14	76
___	**6427**	Lionel Lines N5c Porthole Caboose, 54-60	18	49
___	**6427-60**	Virginian N5c Porthole Caboose, 58	234	460
___	**6427-500**	PRR N5c Porthole Caboose, sky blue, from Girls Set, 57-58*	164	338
___	**6428**	U.S. Mail Boxcar, 60-61, 65-66	20	73
___	**6429**	DL&W Work Caboose, AAR trucks, 63	104	256
	6430	Flatcar with 2 trailers, 56-58		
___		(A) Gray Cooper-Jarrett trailers	30	81
___		(B) White Cooper-Jarrett trailers	34	105
___		(C) Green Fruehauf trailers	26	53
___		(D) Gray Cooper-Jarrett trailers with Fruehauf stickers	35	76

POSTWAR 1945-1969		Good	Exc
6431	Flatcar with 2 vans and Midgetoy tractor, 66		
	(A) White vans, 66	57	125 ___
	(B) Yellow vans, 66	137	309 ___
6434	Poultry Dispatch Stock Car, 58-59	30	141 ___
6436-1	LV Open Quad Hopper, black, 55-56, 66		
	(A) No spreader brace holes	48	106 ___
	(B) Spreader brace with holes	11	36 ___
6436-25	LV Open Quad Hopper, maroon, 55-57		
	(A) No spreader brace holes	78	184 ___
	(B) Spreader brace with holes	23	71 ___
6436-110	LV Quad Hopper, red, 63-68		
	(A) No built date	18	42 ___
	(B) Built date "New 3-55"	35	77 ___
6436-500	LV Open Quad Hopper, lilac, from Girls Set, 57-58*		___
	(A) No spreader brace holes	149	383 ___
	(B) Spreader brace with holes	119	285 ___
6436-1969	TCA (Train Collectors Association) Open Quad Hopper, 69 u	47	110 ___
6437	PRR N5c Porthole Caboose, 61-68	18	51 ___
6440	Flatcar with gray vans, 61-63	32	75 ___
6440	Green Pullman Car, 48-49	32	70 ___
6441	Green Observation Car, 48-49	27	67 ___
6442	Brown Pullman Car, 49	33	71 ___
6443	Brown Observation Car, 49	26	61 ___
6445	Fort Knox Gold Reserve Boxcar with coin slot, 61-63	43	148 ___
6446	N&W Covered Quad Hopper, black or gray, 54-55	28	78 ___
6446-25	N&W Covered Quad Hopper, 55-57		
	(A) Black, white lettering	26	67 ___
	(B) Gray, black lettering	31	66 ___
	(C) Gray, AAR truck, spreader brace holes	60	128 ___
6446-60	LV Covered Quad Hopper, 63	76	182 ___
6447	PRR N5c Porthole Caboose, 63	117	304 ___
6448	Exploding Target Range Boxcar, 61-64		
	(A) Red sides, white roof and ends	13	68 ___
	(B) White sides, red roof and ends	12	33 ___
6452	Pennsylvania Gondola, black, 48-49		
	(A) Numbered "6462", 48	18	43 ___
	(B) Numbered "6452", 49	8	17 ___
X6454	Baby Ruth PRR Boxcar, 48	80	250 ___
X6454	Santa Fe Boxcar, 48	15	47 ___
X6454	NYC Boxcar, 48		
	(A) Brown body	18	40 ___
	(B) Orange body	52	129 ___
	(C) Tan body	18	51 ___
X6454	Erie Boxcar, 49-52		
	(A) Corner steps, 49	14	34 ___

			Good	Exc
___		(B) No steps, 50-52	10	26
	X6454	PRR Boxcar, 49-52		
___		(A) Corner steps, 49	15	32
___		(B) No steps, 50-52	10	26
	X6454	SP Boxcar, 49-52		
___		(A) Corner steps, break in herald circle between R and N, 49	27	76
___		(B) No steps, full circle in herald, 50	16	48
___		(C) No steps, red-brown body, 51-52	16	37
	6456	Lehigh Valley Short Hopper, 48-55		
___		(A) Black	11	21
___		(B) Maroon	10	32
___	**6456-25**	Lehigh Valley Short Hopper, gray, 54-55	18	82
___	**6456-50**	Lehigh Valley Short Hopper, enamel red, white lettering, 54	243	740
___	**6456-75**	Lehigh Valley Short Hopper, enamel red, yellow lettering, 54	76	195
	6457	SP-type Caboose, 49-52		
___		(A) Tuscan body and plastic smokejack	14	25
___		(B) Tuscan body and brown metal smokejack	9	15
___		(C) Tuscan body and black metal smokejack	12	22
___		(D) Maroon body and black metal smokejack	12	20
___	**6460**	Bucyrus Erie Crane Car, black cab, 8-wheel, 52-54	20	38
___	**6460-25**	Bucyrus Erie Crane Car, red cab, 8-wheel, 54	38	94
___	**6461**	Transformer Car, 49-50	30	61
___	**6462**	NYC Gondola, black or red, with 6 barrels, 49-54	10	27
	6462-25	NYC Gondola, green, with 6 barrels, 54-57		
___		(A) N in second panel, 2 lines of data	13	32
___		(B) N in third panel, 3 lines of data	15	38
___	**6462-75**	NYC Gondola, red-painted, with 6 barrels, 52-55	13	29
___	**6462-125**	NYC Gondola, red plastic, with 6 barrels, 55-57	9	21
___	**6462-500**	NYC Gondola, pink, from Girls Set, with 4 canisters, 57-58*	97	273
___	**6463**	Rocket Fuel 2-D Tank Car, 62-63	20	56
	6464-1	WP Boxcar, 53-54		
___		(A) Blue lettering	25	100
___		(B) Red lettering	540	1604
___	**6464-25**	GN Boxcar, 53-54	37	77
___	**6464-50**	M&StL Boxcar, 53-56	35	99
	6464-75	RI Boxcar, green, 53-54, 69		
___		(A) Built date, 53-54	29	91
___		(B) No built date, 69	37	121
	6464-100	Western Pacific Boxcar, 54-55		
___		(A) Silver body, yellow feather	42	222
___		(B) Orange body, blue feather	271	862
___	**6464-125**	NYC Pacemaker Boxcar, 54-56	35	101

		Good	Exc
6464-150	MP Boxcar, 54-55, 57		
	(A) Unpainted royal blue or navy blue body	42	94
	(B) Painted royal blue or navy blue body	40	92
	(C) Herald in fifth panel (first panel to left of door)	500	1200
	(D) New 3 54 on left and XME on lower right	45	98
6464-175	Rock Island Boxcar, 54-55		
	(A) Blue lettering	36	170
	(B) Black lettering	385	958
6464-200	Pennsylvania Boxcar, 54-55, 69		
	(A) Built date NEW 5-53	60	130
	(B) No built date	56	127
6464-225	SP Boxcar, 54-56	42	104
6464-250	WP Boxcar, 66	71	222
6464-275	State of Maine Boxcar, 55, 57-59		
	(A) Striped doors	38	94
	(B) Solid doors	58	218
	(C) Striped doors, AAR trucks, 59	22	46
6464-300	Rutland Boxcar, 55-56		
	(A) Rubber-stamped lettering	43	99
	(B) Split door with bottom painted green	368	1108
	(C) Rubber-stamped lettering with solid shield	1858	3767
	(D) Heat-stamped lettering	67	180
	(E) Painted yellow body, rubber-stamped lettering	500	1500
	(F) Painted yellow body, heat-stamped lettering	1350	4150
6464-325	B&O Sentinel Boxcar, 56	163	472
6464-350	MKT Boxcar, 56	152	266
6464-375	Central of Georgia Boxcar, 56-57, 66		
	(A) Unpainted maroon body	42	109
	(B) Painted red body	725	2861
6464-400	B&O Time-Saver Boxcar, 56-57, 69		
	(A) BLT 5-54	41	87
	(B) BLT 2-56	100	264
	(C) No built date	43	116
	(D) 54 built date on one side/56 built date on other	500	975
6464-425	New Haven Boxcar, 56-58, 69	28	70
6464-450	Great Northern Boxcar, 56-57, 66	57	132
6464-475	B&M Boxcar, 57-60, 65-66, 68		
	(A) Medium blue-painted or unpainted plastic	28	92
	(B) Dark purple-painted, gray or blue mold	71	207
	(C) Dark blue-painted, yellow mold	151	397
6464-500	Timken Boxcar, white side band and charcoal lettering, 57-59, 69		
	(A) Unpainted yellow body	45	131
	(B) Painted yellow body, Type II	137	388
	(C) Painted yellow body, Type IV	65	168
6464-510	NYC Pacemaker Boxcar (pastel blue), 57-58	313	569

			Good	Exc
___	**6464-515**	MKT Boxcar (pastel yellow), 57-58	310	596
	6464-525	M&StL Boxcar, 57-58, 64-66		
___		(A) Red, white lettering	34	110
___		(B) Maroon, white lettering	103	287
	6464-650	D&RGW Boxcar, 57-58, 66		
___		(A) Yellow body, silver roof, black stripe	65	138
___		(B) Yellow body, type II, silver roof, no black stripe	549	1304
___		(C) Painted yellow body and yellow roof	738	2102
___		(D) Yellow body, silver roof, no black stripe on one side only	400	1100
___		(E) Yellow body, type IV, silver roof, black stripe on one side only	400	1100
___	**6464-700**	Santa Fe Boxcar, 61, 66	49	144
	6464-725	New Haven Boxcar, 62-66, 68		
___		(A) Orange body	31	65
___		(B) Black body	72	342
___	**6464-825**	Alaska Boxcar, 59-60	134	315
	6464-900	NYC Boxcar, 60-63, 65-66		
___		(A) Green Doors	33	65
___		(B) Black Doors	30	62
	6465	Gulf 2-D Tank Car, 58		
___		(A) Black tank	15	41
___		(B) Gray tank	11	24
	6465	Sunoco 2-D Tank Car, 48-56		
___		(A) Silver tank, rubber-stamped "6465"	8	15
___		(B) Silver tank, rubber-stamped "6455"	17	49
___		(C) Silver tank, no number on frame	7	16
___		(D) Glossy gray tank	10	30
___	**6465-85**	LL 2-D Tank Car, black, 59	17	155
___	**6465-110**	Cities Service 2-D Tank, 60-62	21	61
___	**6465-160**	LL 2-D Tank Car, orange with black ends, 63-64	13	35
___	**6466T**	Tender, 49-53	15	30
___	**6466W**	Whistle Tender, 49-53	23	51
___	**6466WX**	Whistle Tender, 49-53	25	53
___	**6467**	Miscellaneous Car, 56	22	53
___	**6468**	B&O Auto Boxcar, blue, 53-55	18	42
___	**6468X**	B&O Auto Boxcar, Tuscan, 53-55	128	281
	6468-25	NH Auto Boxcar, 56-58		
___		(A) Black N over white H, black doors	24	100
___		(B) White N over black H, black doors	84	297
___		(C) Black N over white H, painted Tuscan doors	53	122
___	**6469**	Liquified Gas Tank Car, 63	37	81
___	**6470**	Explosives Boxcar, 59-60	14	33
___	**6472**	Refrigerator Car, 50-53	14	30
___	**6473**	Horse Transport Car, 62-69	15	67
___	**6475**	Libby's Crushed Pineapple Vat Car, 63 u	51	162
___	**6475**	Pickles Vat Car, 60-62	23	66

		Good	Exc
6476	LV Short Hopper, 57-63		
	(A) Red body	6	16
	(B) Gray body	8	20
	(C) Black body	6	16
6476-75	LV Short Hopper, black, Type VI body, 63	7	16
6476-135	LV Short Hopper, yellow, 64-66, 68	6	75
6476-160	LV Short Hopper, black, 69	6	16
6476-185	LV Short Hopper, yellow, 69	6	16
6477	Miscellaneous Car with pipes, 57-58	25	57
6480	Explosives Boxcar, red, 61	16	33
6482	Refrigerator Car, 57	17	35
6500	Flatcar with Bonanza airplane, 62, 65		
	(A) Plane, red top and wings	344	608
	(B) Plane, white top and wings	405	806
6501	Flatcar with jet boat, 62-63	58	140
6502	Flatcar with Girder, 62		
	(A) Black flatcar	21	58
	(B) Red flatcar	28	74
6502-50	Flatcar, blue or teal, no lettering, with bridge girder, 62	17	53
6511	Flatcar with pipes, 53-56		
	(A) Die-cast metal truck plates, 53	17	48
	(B) Red car, stamped metal truck plates	15	76
	(C) Brown car, stamped metal truck plates	7	25
6511-24	Set of 6 pipes with box, 55-58	59	145
6512	Cherry Picker Car, 62-63	30	73
6517	LL Bay Window Caboose, 55-59		
	(A) Built date underscored	26	63
	(B) Built date not underscored	20	91
	(C) Built date not underscored, lettering higher	21	52
6517-75	Erie Bay Window Caboose, 66	166	443
6518	Transformer Car, 56-58	24	63
6519	Allis-Chalmers Flatcar, 58-61		
	(A) Dark or medium orange base	27	113
	(B) Dull light orange base	43	155
6520	Searchlight Car, 49-51		
	(A) Tan generator	722	1534
	(B) Green generator	144	271
	(C) Maroon generator	19	64
	(D) Orange generator	15	37
	(E) Green generator, black searchlight housing	141	294
6530	Firefighting Instruction Car, 60-61		
	(A) Red body, white lettering	27	84
	(B) Black body, white lettering	122	292
6536	M&StL Open Quad Hopper, 58-59, 63		
	(A) AAR trucks, 59, 63	26	58
	(B) Bar-end trucks, 58	43	99

			Good	Exc
___	**6544**	Missile Firing Car, 4 missiles, 60-64		
___		(A) White-lettered console	44	149
___		(B) Black-lettered console	106	417
___	**6555**	Sunoco 1-D Tank Car, 49-50	13	58
___	**6556**	MKT Stock Car, 58	171	276
	6557	SP-type Smoking Caboose, 58-59		
___		(A) Tuscan, with non-reverse lettering	106	290
___		(B) Brown, with reverse lettering	517	1267
	6560	Bucyrus Erie Crane Car, smokestack, 55-58, 68-69		
___		(A) Black frame, unpainted red-orange cab	32	84
___		(B) Black frame, painted red cab, no "6560"	45	168
___		(C) Black frame, unpainted gray cab	22	55
___		(D) Black frame, unpainted red cab, closed crank spokes	11	21
___		(E) Black frame, unpainted red cab, no "6560" on frame	13	24
___		(F) Black frame, unpainted red cab, open crank spokes	10	20
___		(G) Black frame, black cab	57	129
___		(H) Dark blue frame, bronze hook	19	56
___	**6560-25**	Bucyrus Erie Crane Car, 8-wheel, marked "656025", 56	33	119
	6561	Cable Car, 2 reels, 53-56		
___		(A) Orange reels	16	68
___		(B) Gray reels	28	90
	6562	NYC Gondola with 4 red canisters, 56-58		
___		(A) Gray body, 56	17	115
___		(B) Red body, 56, 58	12	53
___		(C) Black body, 57	12	27
	6572	REA Refrigerator Car, 58-59, 63		
___		(A) Passenger trucks	71	167
___		(B) Bar-end trucks	39	91
___		(C) AAR trucks, 63	32	72
___	**6630**	Missile Launching Car, 61	25	58
___	**6636**	Alaska Open Quad Hopper, 59-60	36	113
___	**6640**	USMC Missile Launching Car, 60	120	204
___	**6646**	Lionel Lines Stock Car, 57	15	38
	6650	IRBM Rocket Launcher, 59-63		
___		(A) "6650" stamped on left	22	64
___		(B) "6650" stamped on right	87	218
___	**6650-80**	Missile, 60	3	15
___	**6651**	USMC Cannon Car, 64 u	99	201
___	**6654W**	Whistle Tender	17	39
	6656	Lionel Lines Stock Car, 49-55		
___		(A) Brown Armour decal	21	47
___		(B) No decal	10	34
	6657	Denver & Rio Grande Wstern SP-type Caboose, 57-58		
___		(A) With ladder slots	52	139
___		(B) Without ladder slots	135	347
___	**6660**	Boom Car, 58	28	104

		Good	Exc
6670	Derrick Car, 59-60		
	(A) "6670" stamped on left	28	66 ____
	(B) "6670" stamped on right	66	183 ____
6672	Santa Fe Refrigerator Car, 54-56		
	(A) Blue lettering, 2 lines of data	20	46 ____
	(B) Black lettering, 2 lines of data	23	80 ____
	(C) Blue lettering, 3 lines of data	81	212 ____
6736	Detroit & Mackinac Open Quad Hopper, 60-62	19	99 ____
6800	Flatcar with airplane, 57-60		
	(A) Plane, black top and wings	40	82 ____
	(B) Plane, yellow top and wings	48	123 ____
6800-60	Airplane, separate sale w/box, 57-58	76	208 ____
6801	Flatcar with boat, white hull, brown deck, 57	28	64 ____
6801-50	Flatcar with boat, yellow hull, white deck, 58-60	35	113 ____
6801-60	Boat, separate sale w/box, 57-58	47	127 ____
6801-75	Flatcar with boat, blue hull, white deck, 58-60	32	78 ____
6802	Flatcar with 2 U.S. Steel girders, 58-59	25	65 ____
6803	Flatcar with USMC tank and sound truck, 58-59	109	230 ____
6804	Flatcar with USMC antiaircraft and sound trucks, 58-59	112	229 ____
6805	Atomic Energy Disposal Flatcar, 58-59	49	281 ____
6806	Flatcar with USMC radar and medical trucks, 58-59	100	216 ____
6807	Flatcar with amphibious vehicle, 58-59	69	184 ____
6808	Flatcar with USMC tank and searchlight truck, 58-59	115	261 ____
6809	Flatcar with USMC antiaircraft and medical trucks, 58-59	101	232 ____
6810	Flatcar with trailer, 58	21	43 ____
6812	Track Maintenance Car, 59		
	(A) Dark yellow superstructure	21	251 ____
	(B) Black base, gray platform and crank handle	20	60 ____
	(C) Gray base, black platform and crank handle	20	64 ____
	(D) Cream superstructure	55	187 ____
	(E) Light yellow superstructure	21	65 ____
6814	Rescue Caboose, 59-61	43	116 ____
6816	Flatcar with Allis-Chalmers bulldozer, 59-60		
	(A) Red car	160	536 ____
	(B) Black car	655	1318 ____
6816-100	Allis-Chalmers Bulldozer, 59-60		
	(A) No box	73	211 ____
	(B) Separate-sale box	252	699 ____
6817	Flatcar with Allis-Chalmers motor scraper, 59-60		
	(A) Red car	165	402 ____
	(B) Black car	689	1213 ____
6817-100	Allis-Chalmers motor scraper, 59-60		
	(A) No box	115	281 ____
	(B) Separate-sale box	225	921 ____
6818	Flatcar with transformer, 58	20	51 ____
6819	Flatcar with helicopter, 59-60	24	58 ____

			Good	Exc
	6820	Aerial Missile Transport Car with helicopter, 60-61		
___		(A) Light blue frame	84	222
___		(B) Medium blue frame	72	189
___	**6821**	Flatcar with crates, 59-60	18	53
	6822	Searchlight Car, 61-69		
___		(A) Black base, gray light	18	43
___		(B) Gray base, black light	24	42
___	**6823**	Flatcar with 2 IRBM missiles, 59-60	30	108
___	**6824**	USMC Work Caboose, 60	87	222
___	**6824-50**	Rescue Caboose, white, 64	37	93
___	**6825**	Flatcar with arch trestle bridge, 59-62	16	44
___	**6826**	Flatcar with Christmas trees, 59-60	35	100
___	**6827**	Flatcar with Harnischfeger power shovel, 60-63	95	250
	6827-100	Harnischfeger Power Shovel, 60		
___		(A) No box	54	130
___		(B) Separate-sale box	95	261
	6828	Flatcar with Harnischfeger crane, 60-63, 66		
___		(A) Black flatcar, light yellow crane cab	73	235
___		(B) Black flatcar, dark yellow crane cab	82	258
___		(C) Red flatcar, dark yellow crane cab	485	1150
	6828-100	Harnischfeger Construction Crane, 60		
___		(A) No box	43	118
___		(B) Separate-sale box	86	249
___	**6830**	Flatcar with submarine, 60-61	52	112
	6844	Missile Carrying Car, 6 missiles, 59-60		
___		(A) Black frame	30	73
___		(B) Red frame	468	1123

Other Track, Transformers, and Assorted Items

			Good	Exc
___	**CO-1**	Track Clips, dozen, with envelope (O), 49	15	44
___	**CO-1**	Track Clips, box of 50 (O), 49	27	69
___	**CO-1**	Track Clips, box of 100 (O), 49	39	98
___	**CTC**	Lockon (O and 027), 47-69	1	4
___	**CTC-14**	Lockons, dozen, with envelope	13	60
___	**ECU-1**	Electronic Control Unit, 46	30	83
___	**KW**	Transformer, 190 watts, 50-65	46	84
___	**LTC**	Lockon (O and 027), 50-69	4	15
___	**LW**	Transformer, 125 watts, 55-56	37	64
___	**OC**	Curved Track (O), 45-61	1	3
___	**OC1/2**	Half Section Curved Track (O), 45-66	1	3
___	**OCS**	Curved Insulated Track (O), 46-50	5	13
___	**OS**	Straight Track (O), 45-61	1	3
___	**OSS**	Straight Insulated Track, 46-50	5	17
___	**OTC**	Lockon Track (O and 027)	2	4
___	**Q**	Transformer, 75 watts, 46	11	24
___	**R**	Transformer, 110 watts, 46-47	16	33

POSTWAR 1945-1969		Good	Exc	
RCS	Remote Control Track (O), 45-48	3	9	___
RW	Transformer, 110 watts, 48-54	18	33	___
RX	Transformer, 100 watts, 47-48	13	27	___
S	Transformer, 80 watts, 47	10	23	___
SP	Smoke Pellets, bottle, 48-69			
	(A) Tall, light amber bottle	11	33	___
	(B) Tall, dark amber bottle	11	33	___
	(C) Short, light amber bottle	14	35	___
	(D) All other bottles	9	23	___
	(E) Bottle on blister pack, 65	23	58	___
SP-12	Dealer Display Box with 12 full smoke bottles	133	300	___
ST-295	Nut Driver, 5/32-inch		29	___
ST-296	Nut Driver, 3/16-inch		43	___
ST-297	Nut Driver, 7/32-inch		58	___
ST-300	Nut Driver Set with holder, service station item	604	911	___
ST-301	Wheel Puller, service station item	72	146	___
ST-302	Spring Adjusting Tool	108	169	___
ST-303	E Unit Spreader, service station item	48	84	___
ST-311	Wheel Puller, service station item	109	183	___
ST-320	Phillips Screwdriver, service station item	136	214	___
ST-321	Flathead Screwdriver, short, service station item	166	261	___
ST-322	Flathead Screwdriver, long, service station item	77	128	___
ST-325	Screwdriver Set, service station item	575	938	___
ST-342	Track Pliers, service station item	86	150	___
ST-343	0 Gauge Track Pliers, service station item	273	451	___
ST-350	Rivet Press, service station item	424	767	___
ST-350-6	Rivet Press Tool Block with tools, service station item	362	503	___
ST-350-17	Sliding Shoe Anvil, service station item	21	34	___
ST-375	Wheel Cup Tool Set, service station item	556	829	___
ST-378	E Unit Vice, service station item	174	348	___
ST-384	Track Pliers, service station item	154	222	___
SW	Transformer, 130 watts, 61-66	24	70	___
TW	Transformer, 175 watts, 53-60	35	69	___
TOC	Curved Track (O), 62-66, 68-69	1	2	___
TOC1/2	Half Section Straight Track (O), 62-66	1	3	___
TOS	Straight Track (O), 62-69	1	3	___
UCS	Remote Control Track (O), 45-69	5	15	___
UTC	Lockon (O, 027, Standard), 45	2	4	___
V	Transformer, 150 watts, 46-47	35	66	___
VW	Transformer, 150 watts, 48-49	39	77	___
Z	Transformer, 250 watts, 45-47	59	105	___
ZW	Transformer, 250 watts, 48-49	63	198	___
ZW	Transformer, 275 watts, 50-56	79	169	___
ZW	Transformer, 275 watts, R type, 57-66	90	182	___

Section 3
MODERN 1970–2023

			Exc	Mint
____	79C95204C	Sears Santa Fe Diesel Freight Set, 71 u	150	165
____	79C9715C	Sears 4-unit Diesel Freight Set, 75 u	50	65
____	79C9717C	Sears 7-unit Steam Freight Set, 75 u	150	165
____	79N95223C	Sears 6-unit Diesel Freight Set, 74 u	150	165
____	79N9552C	Sears 6-unit Steam Freight Set, 72 u	150	165
____	79N9553C	Sears 6-unit Diesel Freight Set, 72 u	150	165
____	79N96178C	Sears 4-unit Steam Freight Set, 74 u	50	65
____	79N97082C	Sears Steam Freight Set, 70 u		NRS
____	79N97101C	Sears 5-unit Steam Freight Set, 72 u	150	165
____	79N98765C	Sears Logging Empire Set, 78 u	100	115
____	**366**	Menards C&NW 4-4-2 Locomotive with tender, 09	45	75
____	**400**	Menards C&NW Chicago Combine Car, 09	25	40
____	**403**	Menards C&NW Lake Superior Observation Car, 09	25	40
____	**410**	Menards C&NW Lake Michigan Coach, 09	40	65
____	**0512**	Toy Fair Reefer, 81 u	60	70
____	**550C**	31" Diameter Curved Track (O), 70	1	2
____	**550S**	Straight Track (O), 70	1	2
____	**665E**	Johnny Cash Blue Train 4-6-4 Locomotive, 71 u		NRS
____	**1050**	New Englander Set, 80-81	155	205
____	**1051**	Texas & Pacific Diesel Set, 80	150	175
____	**1052**	Chesapeake Flyer Set, 80	140	150
____	**1053**	James Gang Set, 80-82	145	195
____	**1070**	Royal Limited Set, 80	238	350
____	**1071**	Mid Atlantic Limited Set, 80	225	230
____	**1072**	Cross Country Express Set, 80-81	197	385
____	**1081**	Wabash Cannonball Set, 70-72	105	120
____	**1082**	Yard Boss Set, 70	110	165
____	**1083**	Pacemaker Set, 70	105	120
____	**1084**	Grand Trunk Western Freight Set, 70	120	140
____	**1085**	Santa Fe Express Diesel Freight Set, 70	175	190
____	**1086**	Mountaineer Train Set, 70	120	145
____	**1087**	Midnight Express Train Set, 70	125	150
____	**1091**	Sears Special Steam Freight Set, 70 u	150	165
____	**1092**	Sears GTW Steam Freight Set, 70 u	150	165
____	**1100**	Happy Huff n' Puff, 74-75 u	55	70
____	**1150**	L.A.S.E.R. Train Set, 81-82	152	203
____	**1151**	Union Pacific Thunder Freight Set, 81-82	150	175
____	**1153**	JCPenney Thunderball Freight Set, 81 u	165	180
____	**1154**	Reading Yard King Set, 81-82	170	190
____	**1155**	Cannonball Freight Set, 82	75	85
____	**1157**	Lionel Leisure Wabash Cannonball Set, 81 u		250
____	**1158**	Maple Leaf Limited Set, 81	298	435
____	**1159**	Toys "R" Us Midnight Flyer Set, 81 u	135	145
____	**1160**	Great Lakes Limited Set, 81	178	330
____	**T-1171**	CN Locomotive Set, 71 u	240	275
____	**T-1172**	Yardmaster Set, 71 u		200
____	**T-1173**	Grand Trunk Western Freight Set, 71-73 u	175	195
____	**T-1174**	Canadian National Set, 71-73 u	265	300
____	**1182**	Yardmaster Set, 71-72	85	105
____	**1183**	Silver Star Set, 71-72	65	80

		Exc	Mint	
1184	Allegheny Set, 71	120	150	___
1186	Cross Country Express Set, 71-72	210	260	___
1187	Illinois Central Set (SSS), 71	363	485	___
1190	Sears Special #1 Set, 71 u	88	103	___
1195	JCPenney Special Set, 71 u	150	165	___
1198	Unnamed Set, 71 u		175	___
1199	Ford-Autolite Allegheny Set, 71 u	187	207	___
1200	Gravel Gus, 75 u	75	100	___
1223	Seattle & North Coast Hi-Cube Boxcar, 86	25	225	___
1250	New York Central Set (SSS), 72	345	380	___
1252	Heavy Iron Set, 82-83	90	130	___
1253	Quicksilver Express Set, 82-83	265	340	___
1254	Black Cave Flyer Set, 82	75	105	___
1260	Continental Limited Set, 82	183	388	___
1261	Sears Black Cave Flyer Set, 82 u	165	195	___
1262	Toys 'R' Us Heavy Iron Set, 82 u	150	165	___
1263	JCPenney Overland Freight Set, 82 u	150	165	___
1264	NIBCO Express Set, 82 u	190	215	___
1265	Tappan Special Set, 82 u	130	155	___
T-1272	Yardmaster Set, 72-73 u	150	165	___
T-1273	Silver Star Set, 72-73 u	90	115	___
1280	Kickapoo Valley & Northern Set, 72	55	75	___
1284	Allegheny Set, 72	140	165	___
1285	Santa Fe Twin Diesel Set, 72	95	140	___
1287	Pioneer Dockside Switcher Set, 72	95	100	___
1290	Sears Steam Freight Set, 72 u	150	165	___
1291	Sears Steam Freight Set, 72 u	150	165	___
1300	Gravel Gus Junior, 75 u	70	90	___
1350	Canadian Pacific Set (SSS), 73	405	620	___
1351	Baltimore & Ohio Set, 83-84	205	280	___
1352	Rocky Mountain Freight Set, 83-84	75	95	___
1353	Southern Streak Set, 83-85	75	95	___
1354	Northern Freight Flyer Set, 83-85	230	280	___
1355	Commando Assault Train, 83-84	158	270	___
1359	Display Case for Set 1355, 83 u	75	95	___
1361	Gold Coast Limited Set, 83	233	400	___
1362	Lionel Leisure BN Express Set, 83 u	200	300	___
1380	U.S. Steel Industrial Switcher Set, 73-75	55	83	___
1381	Cannonball Set, 73-75	70	75	___
1382	Yardmaster Set, 73-74	110	135	___
1383	Santa Fe Freight Set, 73-75	100	125	___
1384	Southern Express Set, 73-76	75	120	___
1385	Blue Streak Freight Set, 73-74	100	120	___
1386	Rock Island Express Set, 73-74	120	140	___
1387	Milwaukee Road Special Set, 73	146	285	___
1388	Golden State Arrow Set, 73-75	215	240	___
1390	Sears 7-unit Steam Freight Set, 73 u	170	190	___
1392	Sears 8-unit Steam Freight Set, 73 u	150	165	___
1393	Sears 6-unit Diesel Freight Set, 73 u	150	165	___
1395	JCPenney Set, 73 u	150	165	___
1400	Happy Huff n' Puff Junior, 75 u	130	140	___
1402	Chessie System Set, 84-85	125	150	___
1403	Redwood Valley Express Set, 84-85	170	205	___
1450	D&RGW Set (SSS), 74	217	394	___

		MODERN 1970-2024	Exc	Mint
___	**1451**	Erie-Lackawanna Limited Set, 84	293	443
___	**1460**	Grand National Set, 74	180	330
___	**1461**	Black Diamond Set, 74 u, 75	100	120
___	**1463**	Coca-Cola Special Set, 74 u, 75	170	284
___	**1487**	Broadway Limited Set, 74-75	160	255
___	**1489**	Santa Fe Double Diesel Set, 74-76	140	165
___	**1492**	Sears 7-unit Steam Freight Set, 74 u	150	165
___	**1493**	Sears 7-unit Steam Freight Set, 74 u	150	165
___	**1499**	JCPenney Great Express Set, 74 u	150	165
___	**1501**	Midland Freight Set, 85-86	75	95
___	**1502**	Yard Chief Set, 85-86	153	230
___	**1506**	Sears Centennial Chessie System Set, 85 u	165	195
___	**1512**	JCPenney Midland Freight Set, 85 u	90	115
___	**1549**	Toys 'R' Us Heavy Iron Set, 85-89 u	160	218
___	**1552**	Burlington Northern Limited Set, 85	338	570
___	**1560**	North American Express Set, 75	275	365
___	**1562**	Fast Freight Flyer Set, 85 u	120	140
___	**1577**	Liberty Special Set, 75 u	212	275
___	**1579**	Milwaukee Road Set (SSS), 75	253	410
___	**1581**	Thunderball Freight Set, 75-76	90	100
___	**1582**	Yard Chief Set, 75-76	115	155
___	**1584**	N&W "Spirit of America" Set, 75	140	180
___	**1585**	75th Anniversary Special Set, 75-77	192	239
___	**1586**	Chesapeake Flyer Set, 75-77	160	190
___	**1587**	Capitol Limited Set, 75	248	300
___	**1593**	Sears Set, 75 u		100
___	**1595**	Sears 6-unit Diesel Freight Set, 75 u	150	165
___	**1602**	Nickel Plate Special Set, 86-91	120	125
___	**1606**	Sears Centennial Nickel Plate Set, 86 u	165	195
___	**1608**	American Express General Set, 86 u	205	320
___	**1615**	Cannonball Express Set, 86-90	65	75
___	**1632**	Santa Fe Work Train (SSS), 86	152	210
___	**1652**	B&O Freight Set, 86	135	185
___	**1658**	Town House TV and Appliances Set, 86 u	80	95
___	**1660**	Yard Boss Set, 76	100	115
___	**1661**	Rock Island Line Set, 76-77	80	100
___	**1662**	Black River Freight Set, 76-78	75	95
___	**1663**	Amtrak Lake Shore Limited Set, 76-77	193	265
___	**1664**	Illinois Central Freight Set, 76-77	265	355
___	**1665**	NYC Empire State Express Set, 76	229	417
___	**1672**	Northern Pacific Set (SSS), 76	215	280
___	**1685**	True Value Freight Flyer Set, 86-87 u	60	75
___	**1686**	Kay Bee Toys Freight Flyer Set, 86 u	150	165
___	**1687**	Freight Flyer Set, 87-90	39	47
___	**1693**	Toys 'R' Us Rock Island Line Set, 76 u	110	130
___	**1694**	Toys 'R' Us Black River Freight Set, 76 u	115	135
___	**1696**	Sears Steam Freight Set, 76 u	110	130
___	**1698**	True Value Rock Island Line Set, 76 u	125	145
___	**1760**	Trains n' Truckin' Steel Hauler Set, 77-78	105	110
___	**1761**	Trains n' Truckin' Cargo King Set, 77-78	95	165
___	**1762**	Wabash Cannonball Set, 77	135	190
___	**1764**	Heartland Express Set, 77	185	240
___	**1765**	Rocky Mountain Special Set, 77	210	315

MODERN 1970-2024		Exc	Mint	
1766	B&O Budd Car Set (SSS), 77	335	390	___
1776	Seaboard U36B Diesel w/wo printing on chassis, 74-76	74	123	___
1790	Lionel Leisure Steel Hauler Set, 77 u	150	200	___
1791	Toys 'R' Us Steel Hauler Set, 77 u	130	175	___
1792	True Value Rock Island Line Set, 77 u	100	135	___
1793	Toys 'R' Us Black River Freight Set, 77 u	120	155	___
1796	JCPenney Cargo Master Set, 77 u		200	___
1860	"Workin' on the Railroad" Timberline Set, 78	65	85	___
1862	"Workin' on the Railroad" Logging Empire Set, 78	85	110	___
1864	Santa Fe Double Diesel Set, 78-79	155	190	___
1865	Chesapeake Flyer Set, 78-79	155	180	___
1866	Great Plains Express Set, 78-79	172	285	___
1867	Milwaukee Road Limited Set, 78	153	275	___
1868	M&StL Set (SSS), 78	215	255	___
1892	JCPenney Logging Empire Set, 78 u	95	125	___
1893	Toys 'R' Us Logging Empire Set, 78 u	175	225	___
1960	Midnight Flyer Set, 79-81	55	75	___
1962	Wabash Cannonball Set, 79	90	105	___
1963	Black River Freight Set, 79-81	75	85	___
1965	Smokey Mountain Line Set, 79	65	85	___
1970	Southern Pacific Limited Set, 79 u	172	365	___
1971	Quaker City Limited Set, 79	156	335	___
1990	Mystery Glow Midnight Flyer Set, 79 u	75	90	___
1991	JCPenney Wabash Cannonball Deluxe Express Set, 79 u	150	165	___
1993	Toys 'R' Us Midnight Flyer Set, 79 u	115	135	___
2110	Graduated Trestle Set, 22 pieces, 70-88	9	13	___
2111	Elevated Trestle Set, 10 pieces, 70-88	8	11	___
2113	Tunnel Portals, pair, 84-87	11	16	___
2115	Dwarf Signal, 84-87	9	13	___
2117	Block Target Signal, 84-87	23	29	___
2122	Extension Bridge, rock piers, 76-87	24	34	___
2125	Whistling Freight Shed, 71	36	43	___
2126	Whistling Freight Shed, 76-87	18	26	___
2127	Diesel Horn Shed, 76-87	25	30	___
2128	Operating Switchman, 83-86	26	29	___
2129	Illuminated Freight Station, 83-86	30	33	___
2133	Lighted Freight Station, 72-78, 80-84	34	38	___
2140	Automatic Banjo Signal, 70-84	17	21	___
2145	Automatic Gateman, 72-84	31	48	___
2151	Operating Semaphore, 78-82	15	19	___
2152	Automatic Crossing Gate, 70-84	21	25	___
2154	Automatic Highway Flasher, 70-87	19	24	___
2156	Illuminated Station Platform, 70-71	26	34	___
2162	Automatic Crossing Gate and Signal "262", 70-87, 94, 96-98, 05	16	27	___
2163	Block Target Signal, 70-78	14	19	___
2170	Street Lamps, set of 3, 70-87	13	19	___
2171	Gooseneck Street Lamps, set of 2, 80-81, 83-84	15	18	___
2175	"Sandy Andy" Gravel Loader Kit, 76-79	34	55	___
2180	Road Signs, 16 pieces, 77-98		6	___
2181	Telephone Pole Set "150", 77-98		5	___
2195	Floodlight Tower, 70-71	38	50	___
2199	Microwave Tower, 72-75	30	39	___

	MODERN 1970-2024		Exc	Mint
___	**2214**	Girder Bridge, 70-71, 72 u, 73-87	5	9
___	**2256**	Station Platform, 73-81	12	18
___	**2260**	Illuminated Bumper, 70-71, 72 u, 73	23	35
___	**2280**	Nonilluminated Bumpers, set of 3, 73-84	2	4
___	**2282**	Die-cast Bumpers, pair, 83 u	12	18
___	**2283**	Die-cast Illuminated Bumpers "260", 84-99	10	16
___	**2290**	Illuminated Bumpers, pair, 75 u, 76-86	7	11
___	**2292**	Station Platform, 85-87	5	9
___	**2300**	Operating Oil Drum Loader, 83-87	80	90
___	**2301**	Operating Sawmill, 80-84	60	65
___	**2302**	Union Pacific Manual Gantry Crane, 80-82	24	31
___	**2303**	Santa Fe Manual Gantry Crane, 80-81, 83 u	17	21
___	**2305**	Getty Operating Oil Derrick, 81-84	105	115
___	**2306**	Operating Ice Station with 6700 Ice Car, 82-83	90	125
___	**2307**	Lighted Billboard, 82-86	12	13
___	**2308**	Animated Newsstand, 82-83	82	120
___	**2309**	Mechanical Crossing Gate, 82-92	4	7
___	**2310**	Mechanical Crossing Gate, 73-77	2	4
___	**2311**	Mechanical Semaphore, 82-92	4	7
___	**2312**	Mechanical Semaphore, 73-77	2	4
___	**2313**	Floodlight Tower, 75-86	22	27
___	**2314**	Searchlight Tower, 75-84	22	27
___	**2315**	Operating Coaling Station, 83-84	80	89
___	**2316**	N&W Operating Gantry Crane, 83-84	90	125
___	**2317**	Operating Drawbridge, 75 u, 76-81	100	130
___	**2318**	Operating Control Tower, 83-86	40	52
___	**2319**	Illuminated Watchtower, 75-78, 80	29	56
___	**2320**	Flagpole Kit, 83-87	10	14
___	**2321**	Operating Sawmill, 84, 86-87	115	133
___	**2323**	Operating Freight Station, 84-87	43	47
___	**2324**	Operating Switch Tower, 84-87	60	65
___	**2390**	Lionel Mirror, 82 u	97	130
___	**2494**	Rotary Beacon, 72-74	37	44
___	**2709**	Rico Station Kit, 81-98		42
___	**2710**	Billboards, set of 5, 70-84	4	10
___	**2714**	Tunnel, 75 u, 76-77	36	43
___	**2716**	Short Extension Bridge, 88-98	3	8
___	**2717**	Short Extension Bridge, 77-87	2	4
___	**2718**	Barrel Platform Kit, 77-84	3	5
___	**2719**	Watchman's Shanty Kit, 77-87	3	5
___	**2720**	Lumber Shed Kit, 77-84, 87	3	5
___	**2721**	Operating Log Mill Kit, 78	2	4
___	**2722**	Barrel Loader Kit, 78	2	4
___	**2783**	Freight Station Kit, 84	6	10
___	**2784**	Freight Platform Kit, 81-90	5	8
___	**2785**	Engine House Kit, 73-77	31	39
___	**2786**	Freight Platform Kit, 73-77	4	6
___	**2787**	Freight Station Kit, 73-77, 83	7	10
___	**2788**	Coal Station Kit, 75 u, 76-77	18	30
___	**2789**	Water Tower Kit, 75-77, 80	19	24
___	**2791**	Cross Country Set, 70-71	22	30
___	**2792**	Whistle Stop Set, 70-71	24	34
___	**2792**	Layout Starter Pack, 80-84	9	21
___	**2793**	Alamo Junction Set, 70-71	22	30

MODERN 1970-2024		Exc	Mint	
2796	Grain Elevator Kit, 76 u, 77	43	47	___
2797	Rico Station Kit, 76-77	23	37	___
2900	Lockon, 70-98	3	8	___
2901	Track Clips, dozen (027), 71-98		8	___
2905	Lockon and Wire, 74-00		3	___
2909	Smoke Fluid, 70-98		8	___
2910	OTC Contactor, 84-86, 88	4	7	___
2911	Smoke Pellets, 70-73	18	35	___
2925	Lubricant, 70-71, 72 u, 73-75		2	___
2927	Maintenance Kit, 70, 78-98		11	___
2928	Oil, 71		2	___
2951	Track Layout Book, 70-86	1	2	___
2952	Train and Accessory Manual, 70-74	1	2	___
2953	Train and Accessory Manual, 75-86	1	2	___
2960	Lionel 75th Anniversary Book, 75 u, 76	15	30	___
2980	Magnetic Conversion Coupler, 70-71	1	2	___
2985	The Lionel Train Book, 86-98		18	___
3100	Great Northern 4-8-4 (FARR 3), 81	238	388	___
4044	Transformer, 45-watt, 70-71	2	7	___
4045	Safety Transformer, 70-71	2	3	___
4050	Safety Transformer, 72-79	2	3	___
4060	Power Master Transformer, 80-93	4	13	___
4090	Power Master Transformer, 70-84	50	65	___
4125	Transformer, 25-watt, 72	2	3	___
4150	Trainmaster Transformer, 72-73, 75-77	6	15	___
4250	Trainmaster Transformer, 74	5	10	___
4651	Trainmaster Transformer, 78-79	1	2	___
4690	MW Transformer, 86-89	60	80	___
4851	AC Transformer, red or black, 85-91, 94-96	5	10	___
5012	27" Diameter Curved Track, card of 4 (027), 70-96		17	___
5013	27" Diameter Curved Track (027), 70-78		1	___
5014	Half Curved Track (027), 70-98		1	___
5016	36" Straight Track (027), 87-88	1	2	___
5017	Straight Track, card of 4 (027), 70-96		4	___
5018	Straight Track (027), 70-78		1	___
5019	Half Straight Track (027), 70-98		1	___
5020	90-degree Crossover (027), 70-98		7	___
5021	27" Manual Switch, left hand (027), 70-98		15	___
5022	27" Manual Switch, right hand (027), 70-98		15	___
5023	45-degree Crossover (027), 70-98		6	___
5024	35" Straight Track (027), 88-98, 05		3	___
5025	Manumatic Uncoupler, 71-72	1	2	___
5027	27" Manual Switches, pair (027), 74-84	13	21	___
5030	Track Expander Set (027), 71-84	18	26	___
5031	Ford-Autolite Layout Expander Set, 71 u	50	65	___
5033	27" Diameter Curved Track (027), 79-98		1	___
5038	Straight Track (027), 79-98		1	___
5041	Insulator Pins, dozen (027), 70-98		1	___
5042	Steel Pins, dozen (027), 70-98		1	___
5045	54" Diameter Curved Track Ballast (027), 87-88	1	2	___
5046	27" Diameter Curved Track Ballast (027), 87-88	1	2	___
5047	Straight Track Ballast (027), 87-88	1	2	___
5049	42" Diameter Curved Track (027), 88-98	1	2	___

			Exc	Mint
___	**5090**	27" Manual Switches, 3 pair (027), 78-84	55	70
___	**5113**	54" Diameter Curved Track (027), 79-98	1	2
___	**5121**	27" Remote Switch, left hand (027), 70-98	18	22
___	**5122**	27" Remote Switch, right hand (027), 70-98	20	22
___	**5125**	27" Remote Switches, pair (027), 71-83	20	30
___	**5132**	31" Remote Switch, right hand (0), 80-94	29	30
___	**5133**	31" Remote Switch, left hand (0), 80-94	22	30
___	**5149**	Remote Uncoupling Section (027), 70-98		15
___	**5165**	72" Remote Switch, right hand (0), 87-98	23	65
___	**5166**	72" Remote Switch, left hand (0), 87-98	23	75
___	**5167**	42" Remote Switch, right hand (027), 88-98	25	37
___	**5168**	42" Remote Switch, left hand (027), 88-98	25	37
___	**5193**	27" Remote Switches, 3 pair (027), 78-83	80	95
___	**5500**	10" Straight Track (0), 71-98		1
___	**5501**	31" Diameter Curved Track (0), 71-98		1
___	**5502**	Remote Uncoupling Section (0), 71-72	7	9
___	**5504**	Half Curved Track (0), 83-98		1
___	**5505**	Half Straight Track (0), 83-98		1
___	**5520**	90-degree Crossover (0), 71-72	6	9
___	**5522**	36" Straight, 87-88		3
___	**5523**	40" Straight Track (0), 88-98		4
___	**5530**	Remote Uncoupling Section (0), 81-98	10	19
___	**5540**	90-degree Crossover (0), 81-98		10
___	**5543**	Insulator Pins, dozen (0), 70-98		1
___	**5545**	45-degree Crossover (0), 83-98		11
___	**5551**	Steel Pins, dozen (0), 70-98		1
___	**5554**	54" Diameter Curved Track (0), 90-98		2
___	**5560**	72" Diameter Curved Track Ballast (0), 87-88	1	2
___	**5561**	31" Diameter Curved Track Ballast (0), 87-88	1	2
___	**5562**	Straight Track Ballast (0), 87-88	1	2
___	**5572**	72" Diameter Curved Track (0), 79-98	2	3
___	**5600**	Curved Track (Trutrack), 73-74	1	2
___	**5601**	Curved Track, card of 4 (Trutrack), 73-74	6	10
___	**5602**	Curved Track Ballast, card of 4 (Trutrack), 73-74	5	9
___	**5605**	Straight Track (Trutrack), 73-74	1	2
___	**5606**	Straight Track, card of 4 (Trutrack), 73-74	5	9
___	**5607**	Straight Track Ballast, card of 4 (Trutrack), 73-74	5	9
___	**5620**	Manual Switch, left hand (Trutrack), 73-74	4	13
___	**5625**	Remote Switch, left hand (Trutrack), 73-74	9	17
___	**5630**	Manual Switch, right hand (Trutrack), 73-74	4	13
___	**5635**	Remote Switch, right hand (Trutrack), 73-74	9	17
___	**5640**	Left Switch Ballast, card of 2 (Trutrack), 73-74	5	9
___	**5650**	Right Switch Ballast, card of 2 (Trutrack), 73-74	5	9
___	**5655**	Lockon (Trutrack), 73-74	1	2
___	**5660**	Terminal Track with lockon (Trutrack), 74	1	3
___	**5700**	Oppenheimer Reefer, 81	32	39
___	**5701**	Dairymen's League Reefer, 81	21	23
___	**5702**	National Dairy Despatch Reefer, 81	16	21
___	**5703**	North American Despatch Reefer, 81	22	26
___	**5704**	Budweiser Reefer, 81-82	69	78
___	**5705**	Ball Glass Jars Reefer, 81-82	30	35
___	**5706**	Lindsay Brothers Reefer, 81-82	26	29
___	**5707**	American Refrigerator Transit Reefer, 81-82	17	20

MODERN 1970-2024		Exc	Mint	
5708	Armour Reefer, 82-83	16	21	___
5709	REA Reefer, 82-83	22	26	___
5710	Canadian Pacific Reefer, 82-83	22	25	___
5711	Commercial Express Reefer, 82-83	13	15	___
5712	Lionel Lines Reefer, 82 u	47	75	___
5713	Cotton Belt Reefer, 83-84	19	22	___
5714	Michigan Central Reefer, 83-84	17	24	___
5715	Santa Fe Reefer, 83-84	19	26	___
5716	Vermont Central Reefer, 83-84	20	23	___
5717	Santa Fe Bunk Car, 83	22	30	___
5719	Canadian National Reefer, 84	11	17	___
5720	Great Northern Reefer, 84	75	90	___
5721	Soo Line Reefer, 84	21	23	___
5722	NKP Reefer, 84	16	18	___
5724	PRR Bunk Car, 84	15	23	___
5726	Southern Bunk Car, 84 u	22	27	___
5727	USMC Bunk Car, 84-85	25	30	___
5728	Canadian Pacific Bunk Car, 86	17	24	___
5730	Strasburg Reefer, 85-86	20	27	___
5731	L&N Reefer, 85-86	19	24	___
5732	Jersey Central Reefer, 85-86		24	___
5733	Lionel Lines Bunk Car, 86 u	18	24	___
5735	NYC Bunk Car, 85-86	33	35	___
5739	B&O Tool Car, 86	32	37	___
5745	Santa Fe Bunk Car (SSS), 86	39	45	___
5760	Santa Fe Tool Car (SSS), 86	30	35	___
5900	AC/DC Converter, 79-83	3	10	___
6076	LV Hopper (027), 70 u	17	21	___
6100	Ontario Northland Covered Quad Hopper, 81-82	30	34	___
6101	BN Covered Quad Hopper, 81-82	17	31	___
6102	GN Covered Quad Hopper (FARR 3), 81	26	28	___
6103	Canadian National Covered Quad Hopper, 81	35	39	___
6104	Southern Quad Hopper with coal (FARR 4), 83	39	60	___
6105	Reading Operating Hopper, 82	34	40	___
6106	N&W Covered Quad Hopper, 82	30	40	___
6107	Shell Covered Quad Hopper, 82	13	26	___
6109	C&O Operating Hopper, 83	29	41	___
6110	MP Covered Quad Hopper, 83-84	17	27	___
6111	L&N Covered Quad Hopper, 83-84	13	20	___
6113	Illinois Central Hopper (027), 83-85	15	25	___
6114	C&NW Covered Quad Hopper, 83	54	80	___
6115	Southern Hopper (027), 83-86	15	19	___
6116	Soo Line Ore Car, 84	21	27	___
6117	Erie Operating Hopper, 84	29	39	___
6118	Erie Covered Quad Hopper, 84	31	45	___
6122	Penn Central Ore Car, 84	20	25	___
6123	PRR Covered Quad Hopper (FARR 5), 84-85	55	105	___
6124	D&H Covered Quad Hopper, 84	19	32	___
6126	Canadian National Ore Car, 86	18	24	___
6127	Northern Pacific Ore Car, 86	20	24	___
6131	Illinois Terminal Covered Quad Hopper, 85-86	15	21	___
6134	BN 2-bay ACF Hopper (std 0), 86 u	95	115	___
6135	C&NW 2-bay ACF Hopper (std 0), 86 u	65	80	___

MODERN 1970-2024		Exc	Mint
6137	NKP Hopper (027), 86-91	13	17
6138	B&O Quad Hopper with coal, 86	21	28
6142	Gondola, black, 70	20	33
6150	Santa Fe Hopper (027), 85-86, 92 u	10	15
6177	Reading Hopper (027), 86-90	14	19
6200	FEC Gondola with canisters, 81-82	13	24
6201	Union Pacific Animated Gondola, 82-83	19	25
6202	WM Gondola with coal, 82	34	36
6203	Black Cave Gondola (027), 82	2	4
6205	CP Gondola with canisters, 83	18	26
6206	C&IM Gondola with canisters, 83-85	18	26
6207	Southern Gondola with canisters (027), 83-85	6	8
6208	Chessie System Gondola with canisters, 83 u	21	24
6209	NYC Gondola with coal (std 0), 84-85	42	46
6210	Erie-Lackawanna Gondola with canisters, 84	21	30
6211	C&O Gondola with canisters, 84-85		10
6214	Lionel Lines Gondola with canisters, 84 u	38	45
6230	Erie-Lackawanna Reefer (std 0), 86 u	95	120
6231	Railgon Gondola with coal (std 0), 86 u	46	76
6232	Illinois Central Boxcar (std 0), 86 u	65	80
6233	CP Flatcar with stakes (std 0), 86 u	36	43
6234	Burlington Northern Boxcar (std 0), 85	55	75
6235	Burlington Northern Boxcar (std 0), 85	33	43
6236	Burlington Northern Boxcar (std 0), 85	33	43
6237	Burlington Northern Boxcar (std 0), 85	33	49
6238	Burlington Northern Boxcar (std 0), 85	33	43
6239	Burlington Northern Boxcar (std 0), 86 u	38	55
6251	NYC Coal Dump Car, 85	25	42
6254	NKP Gondola with canisters, 86-91	6	11
6258	Santa Fe Gondola with canisters (027), 85-86, 92 u	3	5
X6260	NYC Gondola with canisters, 85-86	13	15
6272	Santa Fe Gondola with cable reels (SSS), 86	20	25
6300	Corn Products 3-D Tank Car, 81-82	19	25
6301	Gulf 1-D Tank Car, 81	20	26
6302	Quaker State 3-D Tank Car, 81	42	46
6304	GN 1-D Tank Car (FARR 3), 81	32	53
6305	British Columbia 1-D Tank Car, 81	46	64
6306	Southern 1-D Tank Car (FARR 4), 83	45	50
6307	PRR 1-D Tank Car (FARR 5), 84-85	70	75
6308	Alaska 1-D Tank Car (027), 82-83	27	35
6310	Shell 2-D Tank Car (027), 83-84	19	24
6312	C&O 2-D Tank Car (027), 84-85	18	26
6313	Lionel Lines 1-D Tank Car, 84 u	40	50
6314	B&O 3-D Tank Car, 86	31	38
6317	Gulf 2-D Tank Car (027), 84-85	18	22
6357	Frisco 1-D Tank Car, 83	42	50
6401	Virginian Bay Window Caboose, 81	37	47
6403	Amtrak Vista Dome Car (027), 76-77	24	31
6404	Amtrak Passenger Coach (027), 76-77	24	31
6405	Amtrak Passenger Coach (027), 76-77	24	31
6406	Amtrak Observation Car (027), 76-77	22	29
6410	Amtrak Passenger Coach (027), 77	28	48
6411	Amtrak Passenger Coach (027), 77	24	35

		Exc	Mint	
6412	Amtrak Vista Dome Car (027), 77	22	33	___
6420	Reading Transfer Caboose, 81-82	20	28	___
6421	Joshua L. Cowen Bay Window Caboose, 82	34	40	___
6422	DM&IR Bay Window Caboose, 81	32	38	___
6425	Erie-Lackawanna Bay Window Caboose, 83-84	35	43	___
6426	Reading Transfer Caboose, 82-83	14	24	___
6427	BN Transfer Caboose, 83-84	12	21	___
6428	C&NW Transfer Caboose, 83-85	22	25	___
6430	Santa Fe SP-type Caboose, 83-89	4	14	___
6431	Southern Bay Window Caboose (FARR 4), 83	42	55	___
6432	Union Pacific SP-type Caboose, 81-82	6	10	___
6433	Canadian Pacific Bay Window Caboose, 81	50	70	___
6435	U.S. Marines Transfer Caboose, 83-84	9	17	___
6438	GN Bay Window Caboose (FARR 3), 81	48	65	___
6439	Reading Bay Window Caboose, 84-85	22	30	___
6441	Alaska Bay Window Caboose, 82-83	45	50	___
6446-25	N&W Covered Quad Hopper, 70 u	212	317	___
6449	Wendy's N5c Caboose, 81-82	64	74	___
6464-500	Timken Boxcar, orange, 70 u	225	319	___
6464-500	Timken Boxcar, yellow, 70 u	210	358	___
6476-135	LV Hopper "25000" (027), 70-71 u	6	11	___
6478	Black Cave SP-type Caboose, 82	5	9	___
6482	Nibco Express SP-type Caboose, 82 u	26	34	___
6485	Chessie System SP-type Caboose, 84-85	6	10	___
6486	Southern SP-type Caboose, 83-85	5	7	___
6490	NKP N5c Caboose, 84 u		NRS	___
6491	Erie-Lackawanna Transfer Caboose, 85-86	9	17	___
6493	L&C Bay Window Caboose, 86-87	21	36	___
6494	Santa Fe Bobber Caboose, 85-86	7	9	___
6496	Santa Fe Work Caboose (SSS), 86	21	29	___
6504	L.A.S.E.R. Flatcar with helicopter (027), 81-82	18	26	___
6505	L.A.S.E.R. Radar Car, 81-82	17	25	___
6506	L.A.S.E.R. Security Car, 81-82	18	26	___
6507	L.A.S.E.R. Flatcar with cruise missile, 81-82	21	30	___
6508	Canadian Pacific Crane Car, 81	50	70	___
6509	Depressed Center Flatcar with girders, 81	60	85	___
6510	Union Pacific Crane Car, 82	55	60	___
6515	Union Pacific Flatcar (027), 83-84, 86	5	13	___
6521	NYC Flatcar with stakes (std 0), 84-85	29	35	___
6522	C&NW Searchlight Car, 83-85	27	30	___
6524	Erie Crane Car, 84	55	60	___
6526	Searchlight Car, 84-85	23	25	___
6529	NYC Searchlight Car, 85-86	21	27	___
6531	Express Mail Flatcar with trailers, 85-86	23	32	___
6560	Bucyrus Erie Crane Car, 71	100	130	___
6561	Flatcar with cruise missile (027), 83-84	13	26	___
6562	Flatcar with fences (027), 83-84	13	21	___
6564	U.S. Marines Flatcar with 2 tanks (027), 83-84	13	21	___
6573	Redwood Valley Express Log Dump Car (027), 84-85	8	13	___
6574	Redwood Valley Express Crane Car (027), 84-85	7	13	___
6575	Redwood Valley Express Flatcar with fences (027), 84-85	7	13	___

			Exc	Mint
___	**6576**	Santa Fe Crane Car (027), 85-86, 92 u	7	10
___	**6579**	NYC Crane Car, 85-86	36	44
___	**6585**	PRR Flatcar with fences (027), 86-90	5	9
___	**6587**	W&ARR Flatcar with horses, 86 u	18	26
___	**6593**	Santa Fe Crane Car (SSS), 86	41	48
___	**6700**	PFE Ice Car, 82-83		70
___	**6900**	N&W Extended Vision Caboose, 82	60	65
___	**6901**	Ontario Northland Extended Vision Caboose, 82 u	44	55
___	**6903**	Santa Fe Extended Vision Caboose, 83	80	95
___	**6904**	Union Pacific Extended Vision Caboose, 83	115	135
___	**6905**	NKP Extended Vision Caboose, 83 u	50	65
___	**6906**	Erie-Lack. Extended Vision Caboose, 84	75	90
___	**6907**	NYC Wood-sided Caboose (std 0), 86 u	90	92
___	**6908**	PRR N5c Caboose (FARR 5), 84-85	43	47
___	**6910**	NYC Extended Vision Caboose, 84 u	55	60
___	**6912**	Redwood Valley Express SP-type Caboose, 84-85	9	16
___	**6913**	Burlington Northern Extended Vision Caboose, 85	60	90
___	**6916**	NYC Work Caboose, 85-86	16	22
___	**6917**	Jersey Central Extended Vision Caboose, 86	36	50
___	**6918**	B&O SP-type Caboose, 86	10	15
___	**6919**	Nickel Plate Road SP-type Caboose, 86-91	5	9
___	**6920**	B&A Wood-sided Caboose (std 0), 86 u	65	80
___	**6921**	PRR SP-type Caboose, 86-90	5	9
___	**7200**	Quicksilver Passenger Coach (027), 82-83	26	34
___	**7201**	Quicksilver Passenger Coach (027), 82-83	26	34
___	**7202**	Quicksilver Observation Car (027), 82-83	26	34
___	**7203**	N&W Diner "491", 82 u	130	180
___	**7204**	Southern Pacific Diner, 82 u	190	235
___	**7207**	NYC Diner, 83 u	70	140
___	**7208**	PRR Diner, 83 u	80	90
___	**7210**	Union Pacific Diner, 84	85	110
___	**7211**	Southern Pacific Vista Dome Car, 83 u	145	185
___	**7215**	B&O Passenger Coach, 83-84	43	50
___	**7216**	B&O Passenger Coach, 83-84	43	50
___	**7217**	B&O Baggage Car, 83-84	43	50
___	**7220**	Illinois Central Baggage Car, 85, 87	105	135
___	**7221**	Illinois Central Combination Car, 85, 87	85	105
___	**7222**	Illinois Central Passenger Coach, 85, 87	85	105
___	**7223**	Illinois Central Passenger Coach, 85, 87	85	105
___	**7224**	Illinois Central Diner, 85, 87	75	90
___	**7225**	Illinois Central Observation Car, 85, 87	95	115
___	**7227**	Wabash Diner (FF 1), 86-87	115	130
___	**7228**	Wabash Baggage Car (FF 1), 86-87	90	100
___	**7229**	Wabash Combination Car (FF 1), 86-87	90	100
___	**7230**	Wabash Passenger Coach (FF 1), 86-87	90	100
___	**7231**	Wabash Passenger Coach (FF 1), 86-87	90	100
___	**7232**	Wabash Observation Car (FF 1), 86-87	88	98
___	**7241**	W&ARR Passenger Coach, 86 u	43	50
___	**7242**	W&ARR Baggage Car, 86 u	43	50
___	**7301**	Norfolk & Western Stock Car, 82	34	45
___	**7302**	Texas & Pacific Stock Car (027), 83-84	9	14
___	**7303**	Erie Stock Car, 84	41	50
___	**7304**	Southern Stock Car (FARR 4), 83 u	41	45

		Exc	Mint	
7309	Southern Stock Car (027), 85-86	12	16	___
7312	W&ARR Stock Car (027), 86 u	25	30	___
7401	Chessie System Stock Car (027), 84-85	13	17	___
7404	Jersey Central Boxcar, 86	26	40	___
7500	Lionel 75th Anniversary U36B Diesel, 75-77	153	181	___
7501	Lionel 75th Anniversary Boxcar, 75-77	28	39	___
7502	Lionel 75th Anniversary Reefer, 75-77	30	41	___
7503	Lionel 75th Anniversary Reefer, 75-77	41	47	___
7504	Lionel 75th Anniversary Covered Quad Hopper, 75-77	28	40	___
7505	Lionel 75th Anniversary Boxcar, 75-77	41	50	___
7506	Lionel 75th Anniversary Boxcar, 75-77	20	25	___
7507	Lionel 75th Anniversary Reefer, 75-77	27	39	___
7508	Lionel 75th Anniversary N5c Caboose, 75-77	24	29	___
7509	Kentucky Fried Chicken Reefer, 81-82	88	98	___
7510	Red Lobster Reefer, 81-82	79	88	___
7511	Pizza Hut Reefer, 81-82	70	81	___
7512	Arthur Treacher's Reefer, 82	69	76	___
7513	Bonanza Reefer, 82	70	78	___
7514	Taco Bell Reefer, 82	80	438	___
7515	Denver Mint Car, 81	64	81	___
7517	Philadelphia Mint Car, 82	38	39	___
7518	Carson City Mint Car, 83	34	43	___
7519	Toy Fair Reefer, 82 u	35	42	___
7520	Nibco Express Boxcar, 82 u	265	440	___
7521	Toy Fair Reefer, 83 u	50	65	___
7522	New Orleans Mint Car, 84	33	38	___
7523	Toy Fair Reefer, 84 u	44	49	___
7524	Toy Fair Reefer, 85 u	55	60	___
7525	Toy Fair Boxcar, 86 u	65	80	___
7530	Dahlonega Mint Car, 86	37	48	___
7600	Frisco Spirit of '76 N5c Caboose, 74-76	33	39	___
7601	Delaware Boxcar, 74-76	11	22	___
7602	Pennsylvania Boxcar, 74-76	11	27	___
7603	New Jersey Boxcar, 74-76	13	24	___
7604	Georgia Boxcar, 74 u, 75-76	22	26	___
7605	Connecticut Boxcar, 74 u, 75-76	11	32	___
7606	Massachusetts Boxcar, 74 u, 75-76	25	29	___
7607	Maryland Boxcar, 74 u, 75-76	13	34	___
7608	South Carolina Boxcar, 75 u, 76	38	50	___
7609	New Hampshire Boxcar, 75 u, 76	38	46	___
7610	Virginia Boxcar, 75 u, 76	155	200	___
7611	New York Boxcar, 75 u, 76	50	65	___
7612	North Carolina Boxcar, 75 u, 76	35	60	___
7613	Rhode Island Boxcar, 75 u, 76	36	50	___
7700	Uncle Sam Boxcar, 75 u	44	51	___
7701	Camel Boxcar, 76-77	73	83	___
7702	Prince Albert Boxcar, 76-77	65	84	___
7703	Beechnut Boxcar, 76-77	39	58	___
7704	Toy Fair Boxcar, 76 u	110	120	___
7705	Canadian Toy Fair Boxcar, 76 u	130	145	___
7706	Sir Walter Raleigh Boxcar, 77-78	56	88	___
7707	White Owl Boxcar, 77-78	71	80	___
7708	Winston Boxcar, 77-78	70	85	___

			Exc	Mint
___	**7709**	Salem Boxcar, 78	70	78
___	**7710**	Mail Pouch Boxcar, 78	69	79
___	**7711**	El Producto Boxcar, 78	44	75
___	**7712**	Santa Fe Boxcar (FARR 1), 79	30	50
___	**7800**	Pepsi Boxcar, 76 u, 77	83	93
___	**7801**	A&W Boxcar, 76 u, 77	54	67
___	**7802**	Canada Dry Boxcar, 76 u, 77	44	57
___	**7803**	Trains n' Truckin' Boxcar, 77 u	20	26
___	**7806**	Season's Greetings Boxcar, 76 u	70	95
___	**7807**	Toy Fair Boxcar, 77 u	70	95
___	**7808**	Northern Pacific Stock Car, 77	37	43
___	**7809**	Vernors Boxcar, 77 u, 78	50	65
___	**7810**	Orange Crush Boxcar, 77 u, 78	45	60
___	**7811**	Dr Pepper Boxcar, 77 u, 78	51	65
___	**7813**	Season's Greetings Boxcar, 77 u	65	90
___	**7814**	Season's Greetings Boxcar, 78 u	70	95
___	**7815**	Toy Fair Boxcar, 78 u	65	85
___	**7816**	Toy Fair Boxcar, 79 u	65	85
___	**7817**	Toy Fair Boxcar, 80 u	95	105
___	**7900**	D&RGW Operating Cowboy Car (027), 82-83	22	26
___	**7901**	LL Cop and Hobo Car (027), 82-83	24	27
___	**7902**	Santa Fe Boxcar (027), 82-85	5	9
___	**7903**	Rock Island Boxcar (027), 83	8	13
___	**7904**	San Diego Zoo Giraffe Car (027), 83-84	44	55
___	**7905**	Black Cave Boxcar (027), 82	6	9
___	**7908**	Tappan Boxcar (027), 82 u	39	55
___	**7909**	L&N Boxcar (027), 83-84	40	49
___	**7910**	Chessie System Boxcar (027), 84-85	18	23
___	**7912**	Toys 'R' Us Giraffe Car (027), 82-84 u	70	80
___	**7913**	Turtleback Zoo Giraffe Car (027), 85-86	50	60
___	**7914**	Toys 'R' Us Giraffe Car (027), 85-89 u	70	90
___	**7920**	Sears Centennial Boxcar (027), 85-86 u	39	44
___	**7925**	Erie-Lackawanna Boxcar (027), 86-90	10	18
___	**7926**	NKP Boxcar (027), 86-91	8	10
___	**7930**	True Value Boxcar (027), 86-87 u	34	50
___	**7931**	Town House TV and Appliances Boxcar (027), 86 u	31	39
___	**7932**	Kay Bee Toys Boxcar (027), 86-87 u	40	49
___	**8001**	NKP 2-6-4 Locomotive, 80 u	55	65
___	**8002**	Union Pacific 2-8-4 Locomotive (FARR 2), 80	210	345
___	**8003**	Chessie System 2-8-4 Locomotive, 80	333	542
___	**8004**	Rock Island 4-4-0 Locomotive, 80-82	190	220
___	**8005**	Santa Fe 4-4-0 Locomotive, 80-82	65	75
___	**8006**	ACL 4-6-4 Locomotive, 80 u	202	340
___	**8007**	NYNH&H 2-6-4 Locomotive, 80-81	65	75
___	**8008**	Chessie System 4-4-2 Locomotive, 80	65	75
___	**8010**	Santa Fe NW2 Switcher, 70, 71 u	48	79
___	**8020**	Santa Fe Alco Diesel A Unit, dummy, 70	45	60
___	**8020**	Santa Fe Alco Diesel A Unit, 70-72, 74-76	65	85
___	**8021**	Santa Fe Alco Diesel B Unit, 71-72, 74-76	49	67
___	**8022**	Santa Fe Alco Diesel A Unit, 71 u	80	105
___	**8025**	CN Alco Diesel A Unit, 71-73 u	85	105
___	**8025**	CN Alco Diesel A Unit, dummy, 71-73 u	45	65
___	**8030**	Illinois Central GP9 Diesel, 70-72	75	140

MODERN 1970-2024		Exc	Mint	
8031	Canadian National GP7 Diesel, 71-73 u	80	150	___
8031	Illinois Central GP9 Diesel, unpowered, 70	40	127	___
8040	Canadian National 2-4-2 Locomotive, 71 u	43	85	___
8040	NKP 2-4-2 Locomotive, 70-72	26	34	___
8041	NYC 2-4-2 Locomotive, 70	55	65	___
8041	PRR 2-4-2 Locomotive, 71 u	55	65	___
8042	GTW 2-4-2 Locomotive, 70, 71-73 u	26	34	___
8043	NKP 2-4-2 Locomotive, 70 u	45	65	___
8050	D&H U36C Diesel, 80	105	220	___
8051	D&H U36C Diesel Dummy Unit, 80	95	115	___
8054/55	Burlington F3 Diesel AA Set, 80	330	385	___
8056	C&NW FM Train Master Diesel, 80	137	202	___
8057	Burlington NW2 Switcher, 80	100	115	___
8059	Pennsylvania F3 Diesel B Unit, 80 u	190	290	___
8060	Pennsylvania F3 Diesel B Unit, 80 u	335	420	___
8061	Chessie System U36C Diesel, 80	93	140	___
8062	Burlington F3 Diesel B Unit, 80 u	205	255	___
8063	Seaboard SD9 Diesel, 80	80	100	___
8064	Florida East Coast GP9 Diesel, 80	150	200	___
8065	Florida East Coast GP9 Diesel Dummy Unit, 80	95	120	___
8066	TP&W GP20 Diesel, 80-81, 83 u	65	80	___
8071	Virginian SD18 Diesel, 80 u	135	155	___
8072	Virginian SD18 Diesel Dummy Unit, 80 u	75	110	___
8100	Norfolk & Western 4-8-4 "611", 81	290	402	___
8101	Chicago & Alton 4-6-4 Locomotive "659", 81	275	445	___
8102	Union Pacific 4-4-2 Locomotive, 81-82	49	65	___
8104	Union Pacific 4-4-0 Locomotive "3", 81 u	180	235	___
8111	DT&I NW2 Switcher, 71-74	55	65	___
8140	Southern 2-4-0 Locomotive, 71 u	22	30	___
8141	PRR 2-4-2 Locomotive, 71-72	41	43	___
8142	C&O 4-4-2 Locomotive, 71-72		55	___
8150	PRR GG1 Electric Locomotive "4935", 81	220	395	___
8151	Burlington SD28 Diesel, 81	120	145	___
8152	Canadian Pacific SD24 Diesel, 81	155	185	___
8153	Reading NW2 Switcher, 81-82	100	155	___
8154	Alaska NW2 Switcher, 81-82	120	160	___
8155	Monon U36B Diesel, 81-82	110	135	___
8156	Monon U36B Diesel Dummy Unit, 81-82		65	___
8157	Santa Fe FM Train Master, 81	230	325	___
8158	DM&IR GP35 Diesel, 81-82	90	150	___
8159	DM&IR GP35 Diesel Dummy Unit, 81-82	55	75	___
8160	Burger King GP20 Diesel, 81-82	106	128	___
8161	L.A.S.E.R. Switcher, 81-82	23	55	___
8162	Ontario Northland SD18 Diesel, 81 u	150	210	___
8163	Ontario Northland SD18 Diesel Dummy Unit, 81 u	95	140	___
8164	Pennsylvania F3 Diesel B Unit, 81 u	340	370	___
8182	Nibco Express NW2 Switcher, 82 u	90	130	___
8190	Diesel Horn Kit, 81 u		30	___
8200	Kickapoo Dockside 0-4-0T, 72	28	39	___
8203	PRR 2-4-2 Locomotive, 72, 74 u, 75	26	34	___
8204	C&O 4-4-2 Locomotive, 72	55	60	___
8206	NYC 4-6-4 Locomotive, 72-75	140	155	___
8209	Pioneer Dockside 0-4-0T with tender, 72	45	65	___

			Exc	Mint
___	**8209**	Pioneer Dockside 0-4-0T, no tender, 73-76	42	55
___	**8210**	Joshua L. Cowen 4-6-4 Locomotive, 82	245	350
___	**8212**	Black Cave 0-4-0 Locomotive, 82	30	49
___	**8213**	D&RGW 2-4-2 Locomotive, 82-83, 84-91 u	65	70
___	**8214**	Pennsylvania 2-4-2 Locomotive, 82-83	55	65
___	**8215**	Nickel Plate Road 2-8-4 Locomotive "779", 82 u	245	285
___	**8250**	Santa Fe GP9 Diesel, 72, 74-75	120	145
___	**8251-50**	Horn/Whistle Controller, 72-74	1	2
___	**8252**	D&H Alco Diesel A Unit, 72	85	125
___	**8253**	D&H Alco Diesel B Unit, 72	50	70
___	**8254**	Illinois Central GP9 Diesel Dummy Unit, 72	60	65
___	**8255**	Santa Fe GP9 Diesel Dummy Unit, 72	60	65
___	**8258**	Canadian National GP7 Diesel Dummy Unit, 72-73 u	65	85
___	**8260/62**	Southern Pacific F3 Diesel AA Set, 82	358	520
___	**8261**	Southern Pacific F3 Diesel B Unit, 82 u	330	395
___	**8263**	Santa Fe GP7 Diesel, 82	65	80
___	**8264**	CP Vulcan Switcher Snowplow, 82	80	100
___	**8265**	Santa Fe SD40 Diesel, 82	165	225
___	**8266**	Norfolk & Western SD24 Diesel, 82	113	225
___	**8268**	Quicksilver Alco Diesel A Unit, 82-83	85	105
___	**8269**	Quicksilver Alco Diesel A Unit, dummy, 82-83	55	65
___	**8272**	Pennsylvania EP-5 Electric Locomotive, 82 u	205	265
___	**8300**	Santa Fe 2-4-0 Locomotive, 73-74	22	25
___	**8302**	Southern 2-4-0 Locomotive, 73-76	29	30
___	**8303**	Jersey Central 2-4-2 Locomotive, 73-74	55	59
___	**8304**	B&O 4-4-2 Locomotive, 75	75	105
___	**8304**	Rock Island 4-4-2 Locomotive, 73-75	85	105
___	**8304**	Pennsylvania 4-4-2 Locomotive, 74-75	75	105
___	**8304**	C&O 4-4-2 Locomotive, 75-77	75	105
___	**8305**	Milwaukee Road 4-4-2 Locomotive, 73	95	120
___	**8307**	Southern Pacific 4-8-4 Locomotive "4449", 83	305	560
___	**8308**	Jersey Central 2-4-2 Locomotive, 73-74 u	36	43
___	**8309**	Southern 2-8-2 Locomotive "4501" (FARR 4), 83	385	495
___	**8310**	Nickel Plate Road 2-4-0 Locomotive, 73 u	26	50
___	**8310**	Santa Fe 2-4-0 Locomotive, 74-75 u	26	34
___	**8310**	Jersey Central 2-4-0 Locomotive, 74-75 u	26	50
___	**8311**	Southern 0-4-0 Locomotive, 73 u	26	34
___	**8313**	Santa Fe 0-4-0 Locomotive, 83-84	13	17
___	**8314**	Southern 2-4-0 Locomotive, 83-85	17	21
___	**8315**	B&O 4-4-0 Locomotive, 83-84	85	120
___	**8341**	ACL SP-type Caboose, 86 u, 87-90	6	8
___	**8350**	U.S. Steel Switcher, 73-75	18	26
___	**8351**	Santa Fe Alco Diesel A Unit, 73-75	60	65
___	**8352**	Santa Fe GP20 Diesel, 73-75	65	105
___	**8353**	Grand Trunk Western GP7 Diesel, 73-75	90	120
___	**8354**	Erie NW2 Switcher, 73, 75	80	105
___	**8355**	Santa Fe GP20 Diesel Dummy Unit, 73-74	65	90
___	**8356**	Grand Trunk Western GP7 Diesel Dummy Unit, 73-75	65	75
___	**8357**	PRR GP9 Diesel, 73-75	108	120
___	**8358**	PRR GP9 Diesel Dummy Unit, 73-75	55	100
___	**8359**	Chessie System GP7 Diesel "GM50", 73	95	120
___	**8360**	Long Island GP20 Diesel, 73-74	70	105
___	**8361**	Western Pacific Alco Diesel A Unit, 73-75	50	70

MODERN 1970-2024		Exc	Mint	
8362	Western Pacific Alco Diesel B Unit, 73-75	45	65	___
8363	B&O F3 Diesel A Unit, 73-75	280	310	___
8364	B&O F3 Diesel A Unit, dummy, 73-75	120	160	___
8365/66	CP F3 Diesel AA Set (SSS), 73	355	405	___
8367	Long Island GP20 Diesel Dummy Unit, 73-75	80	100	___
8368	Alaska Vulcan Switcher, 83	120	129	___
8369	Erie-Lackawanna GP20 Diesel, 83-85	125	140	___
8370/72	NYC F3 Diesel AA Set, 83	330	435	___
8371	NYC F3 Diesel B Unit, 83	105	150	___
8374	Burlington Northern NW2 Switcher, 83-85	105	120	___
8375	C&NW GP7 Diesel, 83-85	135	165	___
8376	Union Pacific SD40 Diesel, 83	175	200	___
8377	U.S. Marines Switcher, 83-84	55	65	___
8378	Wabash FM Train Master Diesel "550", 83 u	500	690	___
8379	PRR Fire Car, 83 u	80	100	___
8380	Lionel Lines SD28 Diesel, 83 u	235	315	___
8402	Reading 4-4-2 Locomotive, 84-85	47	55	___
8403	Chessie System 4-4-2 Locomotive, 84-85	55	65	___
8404	PRR 6-8-6 Turbine "6200" (FARR 5), 84-85	250	460	___
8406	NYC 4-6-4 Locomotive "783", 84	309	571	___
8410	Redwood Valley Express 4-4-0 Locomotive, 84-85	34	50	___
8452	Erie Alco Diesel A Unit, 74-75	75	95	___
8453	Erie Alco Diesel B Unit, 74-75	55	75	___
8454	D&RGW GP7 Diesel, 74-75	80	110	___
8455	D&RGW GP7 Diesel Dummy Unit, 74-75	50	85	___
8458	Erie-Lackawanna SD40 Diesel, 84	145	190	___
8459	D&RGW Vulcan Rotary Snowplow, 84	125	146	___
8460	MKT NW2 Switcher, 74-75	45	65	___
8463	Chessie System GP20 Diesel, 74 u	130	200	___
8464/65	D&RGW F3 Diesel AA Set (SSS), 74	220	325	___
8466	Amtrak F3 Diesel A Unit, 74-76	225	250	___
8467	Amtrak F3 Diesel A Unit, dummy, 74-76	80	90	___
8468	B&O F3 Diesel B Unit, 74-75	95	100	___
8469	CP F3 Diesel B Unit (SSS), 74	85	110	___
8470	Chessie System U36B Diesel, 74	80	110	___
8471	Pennsylvania NW2 Switcher, 74-76	170	195	___
8473	Coca-Cola NW2 Switcher, 74 u, 75	120	130	___
8474	D&RGW F3 Diesel B Unit (SSS), 74	110	125	___
8475	Amtrak F3 Diesel B Unit, 74	85	105	___
8477	NYC GP9 Diesel, 84 u	150	205	___
8480/82	Union Pacific F3 Diesel AA Set, 84	280	365	___
8481	Union Pacific F3 Diesel B Unit, 84	150	155	___
8485	USMC NW2 Switcher, 84-85	105	135	___
8500	Pennsylvania 2-4-0 Locomotive, 75-76	17	21	___
8502	Santa Fe 2-4-0 Locomotive, 75	17	21	___
8506	PRR 0-4-0 Locomotive, 75-77	75	90	___
8507	Santa Fe 2-4-0 Locomotive, 75 u	25	30	___
8512	Santa Fe 0-4-0T Locomotive, 85-86	22	30	___
8516	NYC 0-4-0 Locomotive, 85-86	115	140	___
8550	Jersey Central GP9 Diesel, 75-76	120	163	___
8551	Pennsylvania EP-5 Electric Locomotive, 75-76	108	120	___
8552/3/4	SP Alco Diesel ABA Set, 75-76	170	245	___
8555/57	Milwaukee Road F3 Diesel AA Set (SSS), 75	240	315	___

			Exc	Mint
___	**8556**	Chessie System NW2 Switcher, 75-76	115	160
___	**8558**	Milwaukee Road EP-5 Electric Locomotive, 76-77	128	185
___	**8559**	N&W GP9 Diesel "1776", 75	115	145
___	**8560**	Chessie System U36B Diesel Dummy Unit, 75	75	115
___	**8561**	Jersey Central GP9 Diesel Dummy Unit, 75-76	70	95
___	**8562**	Missouri Pacific GP20 Diesel, 75-76	95	138
___	**8563**	Rock Island Alco Diesel A Unit, 75-76 u	65	90
___	**8564**	Union Pacific U36B Diesel, 75	110	155
___	**8565**	Missouri Pacific GP20 Diesel Dummy Unit, 75-76	48	70
___	**8566**	Southern F3 Diesel A Unit, 75-77	220	370
___	**8567**	Southern F3 Diesel A Unit, dummy, 75-77	105	135
___	**8568**	Preamble Express F3 Diesel A Unit, 75 u	90	115
___	**8569**	Soo Line NW2 Switcher, 75-77	60	65
___	**8570**	Liberty Special Alco Diesel A Unit, 75 u	75	90
___	**8571**	Frisco U36B Diesel, 75-76	58	95
___	**8572**	Frisco U36B Diesel Dummy Unit, 75-76	23	55
___	**8573**	Union Pacific U36B Diesel Dummy Unit, 75 u	103	138
___	**8575**	Milwaukee Road F3 Diesel B Unit (SSS), 75	105	160
___	**8576**	Penn Central GP7 Diesel, 75 u, 76-77	90	120
___	**8578**	NYC Ballast Tamper, 85, 87	85	90
___	**8580/82**	Illinois Central F3 Diesel AA Set, 85, 87	420	485
___	**8581**	Illinois Central F3 Diesel B Unit, 85, 87	130	155
___	**8585**	Burlington Northern SD40 Diesel, 85	355	385
___	**8587**	Wabash GP9 Diesel "484", 85 u	250	280
___	**8600**	NYC 4-6-4 Locomotive, 76	175	195
___	**8601**	Rock Island 0-4-0 Locomotive, 76-77	13	33
___	**8602**	D&RGW 2-4-0 Locomotive, 76-78	16	26
___	**8603**	C&O 4-6-4 Locomotive, 76-77	135	190
___	**8604**	Jersey Central 2-4-2 Locomotive, 76 u	39	44
___	**8606**	B&A 4-6-4 Locomotive "784", 86 u	720	760
___	**8610**	Wabash 4-6-2 "672" (FF 1), 86-87	324	610
___	**8615**	L&N 2-8-4 Locomotive "1970", 86 u	540	630
___	**8616**	Santa Fe 4-4-2 Locomotive, 86	60	65
___	**8617**	Nickel Plate Road 4-4-2 Locomotive, 86-91	60	65
___	**8625**	Pennsylvania 2-4-0 Locomotive, 86-90	21	34
___	**8630**	W&ARR 4-4-0 Locomotive "3", 86 u	125	150
___	**8635**	Santa Fe 0-4-0 (SSS), 86	80	100
___	**8650**	Burlington Northern U36B Diesel, 76-77	100	145
___	**8651**	Burlington Northern U36B Diesel Dummy Unit, 76-77	60	93
___	**8652**	Santa Fe F3 Diesel A Unit, 76-77	260	510
___	**8653**	Santa Fe F3 Diesel A Unit, dummy, 76-77	135	160
___	**8654**	Boston & Maine GP9 Diesel, 76-77	143	178
___	**8655**	Boston & Maine GP9 Diesel Dummy Unit, 76-77	90	115
___	**8656**	Canadian National Alco Diesel A Unit, 76	150	193
___	**8657**	Canadian National Alco Diesel B Unit, 76	60	75
___	**8658**	CN Alco Diesel A Unit, dummy, 76	85	170
___	**8659**	Virginian Electric Locomotive, 76-77	113	134
___	**8660**	CP Rail NW2 Switcher, 76-77	112	138
___	**8661**	Southern F3 Diesel B Unit, 76	145	165
___	**8662**	B&O GP7 Diesel, 86	120	130
___	**8664**	Amtrak Alco Diesel A Unit, 76-77	85	120
___	**8665**	BAR Jeremiah O'Brien GP9 Diesel "1776", 76 u	100	170
___	**8666**	Northern Pacific GP9 Diesel (SSS), 76	128	183

		Exc	Mint	
8667	Amtrak Alco Diesel B Unit, 76-77	60	80	___
8668	Northern Pacific GP9 Diesel Dummy Unit (SSS), 76	100	130	___
8669	Illinois Central Gulf U36B Diesel, 76-77	118	153	___
8670	Chessie System Switcher, 76	30	55	___
8679	Northern Pacific GP20 Diesel, 86	90	105	___
8687	Jersey Central FM Train Master Diesel, 86	189	258	___
8690	Lionel Lines Trolley, 86	105	115	___
8701	W&ARR 4-4-0 Locomotive "3", 77-79	157	210	___
8702	Southern 4-6-4 Locomotive, 77-78	280	398	___
8703	Wabash 2-4-2 Locomotive, 77	22	30	___
8750	Rock Island GP7 Diesel, 77-78	110	125	___
8751	Rock Island GP7 Diesel Dummy Unit, 77-78	50	70	___
8753	Pennsylvania GG1 Electric Locomotive, 77 u	290	315	___
8754	New Haven Electric Locomotive, 77-78	100	115	___
8755	Santa Fe U36B Diesel, 77-78	130	150	___
8756	Santa Fe U36B Diesel Dummy Unit, 77-78	75	95	___
8757	Conrail GP9 Diesel, 76 u, 77-78	111	138	___
8758	Southern GP7 Diesel Dummy Unit, 77 u, 78	75	95	___
8759	Erie-Lackawanna GP9 Diesel, 77-79	117	175	___
8760	Erie-Lackawanna GP9 Diesel Dummy Unit, 77-79	95	115	___
8761	GTW NW2 Switcher, 77-78	95	130	___
8762	Great Northern EP-5 Electric Locomotive, 77-78	130	140	___
8763	Norfolk & Western GP9 Diesel, 76 u, 77-78	110	120	___
8764	B&O Budd RDC Passenger (SSS), 77	110	135	___
8765	B&O Budd RDC Baggage Dummy Unit (SSS), 77	80	100	___
8766	B&O Budd RDC Baggage (SSS), 77		310	___
8767	B&O Budd RDC Passenger Dummy Unit (SSS), 77	85	105	___
8768	B&O Budd RDC Passenger Dummy Unit (SSS), 77	85	105	___
8769	Republic Steel Switcher, 77-78	22	39	___
8770	NW2 Switcher, 77-78		65	___
8771	Great Northern U36B Diesel, 77	110	130	___
8772	GM&O GP20 Diesel, 77	85	95	___
8773	Mickey Mouse U36B Diesel, 77-78	497	655	___
8774	Southern GP7 Diesel, 77 u, 78	115	135	___
8775	Lehigh Valley GP9 Diesel, 77 u, 78	85	105	___
8776	C&NW GP20 Diesel, 77 u, 78	87	129	___
8777	Santa Fe F3 Diesel B Unit (SSS), 77	160	175	___
8778	Lehigh Valley GP9 Diesel Dummy Unit, 77 u, 78	90	110	___
8779	C&NW GP20 Diesel Dummy Unit, 77 u, 78	73	109	___
8800	Lionel Lines 4-4-2 Locomotive, 78-81	58	105	___
8801	Blue Comet 4-6-4 Locomotive, 78-80	385	505	___
8803	Santa Fe 0-4-0 Locomotive, 78	14	24	___
8850	Penn Central GG1 Electric Locomotive, 78 u, 79	178	305	___
8851/52	New Haven F3 Diesel AA Set, 78 u, 79	320	430	___
8854	CP Rail GP9 Diesel, 78-79	100	120	___
8855	Milwaukee Road SD18 Diesel, 78		115	___
8857	Northern Pacific U36B Diesel, 78-80	140	180	___
8858	Northern Pacific U36B Diesel Dummy Unit, 78-80	55	85	___
8859	Conrail Electric Locomotive, 78-82	105	150	___
8860	Rock Island NW2 Switcher, 78-79	85	100	___
8861	Santa Fe Alco Diesel A Unit, 78-79	65	85	___
8862	Santa Fe Alco Diesel B Unit, 78-79	36	43	___
8864	New Haven F3 Diesel B Unit, 78	85	105	___

			Exc	Mint
___	**8866**	M&StL GP9 Diesel (SSS), 78	85	120
___	**8867**	M&StL GP9 Diesel Dummy Unit (SSS), 78	65	95
___	**8868**	Amtrak Budd RDC Baggage, 78, 80	195	235
___	**8869**	Amtrak Budd RDC Passenger Dummy Unit, 78, 80	75	95
___	**8870**	Amtrak Budd RDC Passenger Dummy Unit, 78, 80	85	115
___	**8871**	Amtrak Budd RDC Baggage Dummy Unit, 78, 80	85	105
___	**8872**	Santa Fe SD18 Diesel, 78 u	125	155
___	**8873**	Santa Fe SD18 Diesel Dummy Unit, 78 u	60	85
___	**8900**	Santa Fe 4-6-4 Locomotive (FARR 1), 79	270	310
___	**8902**	ACL 2-4-0 Locomotive, 79-82, 86 u, 87-90	13	17
___	**8903**	D&RGW 2-4-2 Locomotive, 79-81	17	21
___	**8904**	Wabash 2-4-2 Locomotive, 79, 81 u	30	34
___	**8905**	Smokey Mountain Dockside 0-4-0T Locomotive, 79	9	17
___	**8950**	Virginian FM Train Master Diesel, 79	185	285
___	**8951**	Southern Pacific FM Train Master Diesel, 79	185	335
___	**8952/53**	PRR F3 Diesel AA Set, 79	350	500
___	**8955**	Southern U36B Diesel, 79	120	195
___	**8956**	Southern U36B Diesel Dummy Unit, 79	80	125
___	**8957**	Burlington Northern GP20 Diesel, 79	120	150
___	**8958**	Burlington Northern GP20 Diesel Dummy Unit, 79	85	90
___	**8960**	Southern Pacific U36C Diesel, 79 u	130	180
___	**8961**	Southern Pacific U36C Diesel Dummy Unit, 79 u	70	80
___	**8962**	Reading U36B Diesel, 79	115	130
___	**8970/71**	PRR F3 Diesel AA Set, 79 u, 80	330	425
___	**9001**	Conrail Boxcar (027), 86-87 u, 88-90	5	10
___	**9010**	GN Hopper (027), 70-71	6	8
___	**9011**	GN Hopper (027), 70 u, 75-76, 78-83	8	10
___	**9012**	TA&G Hopper (027), 71-72	7	8
___	**9013**	Canadian National Hopper (027), 72-76	5	8
___	**9015**	Reading Hopper (027), 73-75	17	21
___	**9016**	Chessie System Hopper (027), 75-79, 87-88, 89 u	4	6
___	**9017**	Wabash Gondola with canisters (027), 78-82	3	5
___	**9018**	DT&I Hopper (027), 78-79, 81-82	6	7
___	**9019**	Flatcar (027), 78	2	3
___	**9020**	Union Pacific Flatcar (027), 70-78	3	5
___	**9021**	Santa Fe Work Caboose, 70-71, 73-75	20	72
___	**9022**	Santa Fe Bulkhead Flatcar (027), 70-72, 75-79	7	13
___	**9023**	MKT Bulkhead Flatcar (027), 73-74	7	10
___	**9024**	C&O Flatcar (027), 73-75	3	6
___	**9025**	DT&I Work Caboose, 71-74, 77-78	8	10
___	**9026**	Republic Steel Flatcar (027), 75-82	5	7
___	**9027**	Soo Line Work Caboose, 75-76	7	9
___	**9030**	Kickapoo Gondola (027), 72, 79	5	9
___	**9031**	NKP Gondola with canisters (027), 73-75, 82-83, 84-91 u	5	8
___	**9032**	SP Gondola with canisters (027), 75-78	3	5
___	**9033**	PC Gondola w/canisters (027), 76-78, 82, 86 u, 87-90, 92 u	3	5
___	**9034**	Lionel Leisure Hopper (027), 77 u	30	34
___	**9035**	Conrail Boxcar (027), 78-82	5	12
___	**9036**	Mobilgas 1-D Tank Car (027), 78-82	7	19
___	**9037**	Conrail Boxcar (027), 78 u, 80	7	10
___	**9038**	Chessie System Hopper (027), 78 u, 80	15	19
___	**9039**	Mobilgas 1-D Tank Car (027), 78 u, 80	10	15
___	**9040**	General Mills Wheaties Boxcar (027), 70-72	9	13

		Exc	Mint	
9041	Hershey's Boxcar (027), 70-71, 73-76	18	28	___
9042	Ford-Autolite Boxcar (027), 71 u, 72 74-76	13	21	___
9043	Erie-Lackawanna Boxcar (027), 73-75	13	20	___
9044	D&RGW Boxcar (027), 75-76	5	8	___
9045	Toys 'R' Us Boxcar (027), 75 u	35	42	___
9046	True Value Boxcar (027), 76 u	26	34	___
9047	Toys 'R' Us Boxcar (027), 76 u	40	43	___
9048	Toys 'R' Us Boxcar (027), 76 u	33	41	___
9049	Toys 'R' Us Boxcar (027), 78 u		87	___
9050	Sunoco 1-D Tank Car (027), 70-71	17	23	___
9051	Firestone 1-D Tank Car (027), 74-75, 78	15	19	___
9052	Toys 'R' Us Boxcar (027), 77 u	26	34	___
9053	True Value Boxcar (027), 77 u	28	40	___
9054	JCPenney Boxcar (027), 77 u	14	19	___
9055	Republic Steel Gondola with canisters, 78 u	9	10	___
9057	CP Rail SP-type Caboose, 78-79	10	15	___
9058	Lionel Lines SP-type Caboose, 78-79, 83	5	7	___
9059	Lionel Lines SP-type Caboose, 79 u, 81 u	7	9	___
9060	Nickel Plate Road SP-type Caboose, 70-72	5	7	___
9061	Santa Fe SP-type Caboose, 70-76	5	8	___
9062	Penn Central SP-type Caboose, 70-72, 74-76	7	9	___
9063	GTW SP-type Caboose, 70, 71-73 u	15	19	___
9064	C&O SP-type Caboose, 71-72, 75-77	7	10	___
9065	Canadian National SP-type Caboose, 71-73 u	19	24	___
9066	Southern SP-type Caboose, 73-76	7	9	___
9067	Kickapoo Valley Bobber Caboose, 72	6	9	___
9068	Reading Bobber Caboose, 73-76	5	7	___
9069	Jersey Central SP-type Caboose, 73-74, 75-76 u	5	8	___
9070	Rock Island SP-type Caboose, 73-74	13	17	___
9071	Santa Fe Bobber Caboose, 74 u, 77-78	7	9	___
9073	Coca-Cola SP-type Caboose, 74 u, 75	33	38	___
9075	Rock Island SP-type Caboose, 75-76 u	13	17	___
9076	"We The People" SP-type Caboose, 75 u	19	28	___
9077	D&RGW SP-type Caboose, 76-83, 84-91 u	7	8	___
9078	Rock Island Bobber Caboose, 76-77	5	7	___
9079	GTW Hopper (027), 77	28	32	___
9080	Wabash SP-type Caboose, 77	9	10	___
9085	Santa Fe Work Caboose, 79-82	4	5	___
9090	General Mills Mini-Max Car, 71	27	32	___
9106	Miller Vat Car, 84-85	33	52	___
9107	Dr Pepper Vat Car, 86-87	30	36	___
9110	B&O Quad Hopper, 71			
	(A) White Lettering	25	30	___
	(B) Gray Lettering	25	35	___
	(C) Yellow Lettering	50	70	___
9111	N&W Quad Hopper, 72-75	15	20	___
9112	D&RGW Covered Quad Hopper, 73-75	20	23	___
9113	Norfolk & Western Quad Hopper (SSS), 73	27	32	___
9114	Morton Salt Covered Quad Hopper, 74-76	18	27	___
9115	Planter's Covered Quad Hopper, 74-76	21	33	___
9116	Domino Sugar Covered Quad Hopper, 74-76	22	29	___
9117	Alaska Covered Quad Hopper (SSS), 74-76	29	33	___
9118	Corning 4-Bay Covered Hopper, 74 u		45	___

			Exc	Mint
___	**9119**	Detroit & Mackinac Covered Hopper, 75 u		20
___	**9120**	Northern Pacific Flatcar with trailers, 70-71	33	38
___	**9121**	L&N Flatcar with bulldozer and scraper, 71-79	47	54
___	**9122**	Northern Pacific Flatcar with trailers, 72-75	19	32
___	**9123**	C&O Auto Carrier, 3-tier, 72 u, 73-74	18	46
___	**9124**	P&LE Flatcar with logs, 73-74	18	25
___	**9125**	Norfolk & Western Auto Carrier, 2-tier, 73-77	23	28
___	**9126**	C&O Auto Carrier, 3-tier, 73-75	23	34
___	**9128**	Heinz Vat Car, 74-76	19	36
___	**9129**	N&W Auto Carrier, 3-tier, 75-76	17	19
___	**9130**	B&O Quad Hopper, 70	23	24
___	**9131**	D&RGW Gondola with canisters, 73-77	5	8
___	**9132**	Libby's Vat Car (SSS), 75-77	16	23
___	**9133**	BN Flatcar with trailers, 76-77, 80	20	28
___	**9134**	Virginian Covered Quad Hopper, 76-77		32
___	**9135**	N&W Covered Quad Hopper, 70 u, 71, 75	12	26
___	**9136**	Republic Steel Gondola with canisters, 72-76, 79	9	11
___	**9138**	Sunoco 3-D Tank Car (SSS), 78	33	37
___	**9139**	PC Auto Carrier, 3-tier, 76-77	21	29
___	**9140**	Burlington Gondola with canisters, 70, 73-82, 87-89	7	9
___	**9141**	BN Gondola with canisters, 70-72	8	10
___	**9142**	Republic Steel Gondola w/2 canisters, 77 u	15	23
___	**9143**	CN Gondola with canisters, 71-73 u	30	34
___	**9144**	D&RGW Gondola with canisters (SSS), 74-76	9	13
___	**9145**	ICG Auto Carrier, 3-tier, 77-80	21	29
___	**9146**	Mogen David Vat Car, 77-81	21	26
___	**9147**	Texaco 1-D Tank Car, 77-78	46	63
___	**9148**	Du Pont 3-D Tank Car, 77-81	25	28
___	**9149**	CP Rail Flatcar with trailers, 77-78	22	35
___	**9150**	Gulf 1-D Tank Car, 70 u, 71	22	28
___	**9151**	Shell 1-D Tank Car, 72	27	31
___	**9152**	Shell 1-D Tank Car, 73-76	25	34
___	**9153**	Chevron 1-D Tank Car, 74-76	33	39
___	**9154**	Borden 1-D Tank Car, 75-76	33	47
___	**9155**	Monsanto 1-D Tank Car, 75 u	38	47
___	**9156**	Mobilgas 1-D Tank Car, 76-77	30	40
___	**9157**	C&O Crane Car, 76-78, 81-82	35	44
___	**9158**	PC Flatcar with shovel, 76-77, 80	40	55
___	**9159**	Sunoco 1-D Tank Car, 76	35	50
___	**9160**	Illinois Central N5c Caboose, 70-72	17	23
___	**9161**	CN N5c Caboose, 72-74	14	25
___	**9162**	PRR N5c Caboose, 72-76	25	30
___	**9163**	Santa Fe N5c Caboose, 73-76	17	24
___	**9165**	Canadian Pacific N5c Caboose (SSS), 73	21	30
___	**9166**	D&RGW SP-type Caboose (SSS), 74-75	20	25
___	**9167**	Chessie System N5c Caboose, 74-76	24	31
___	**9168**	Union Pacific N5c Caboose, 75-77	17	19
___	**9169**	Milwaukee Road SP-type Caboose (SSS), 75	18	35
___	**9170**	N&W N5c Caboose "1776", 75	27	30
___	**9171**	MP SP-type Caboose, 75 u, 76-77	19	20
___	**9172**	Penn Central SP-type Caboose, 75 u, 76-77	23	31
___	**9173**	Jersey Central SP-type Caboose, 75 u, 76-77	22	33
___	**9174**	NYC (P&E) Bay Window Caboose, 76	65	70

MODERN 1970-2024		Exc	Mint	
9175	Virginian N5c Caboose, 76-77	24	26	___
9176	BAR N5c Caboose, 76 u	16	30	___
9177	Northern Pacific Bay Window Caboose (SSS), 76	20	35	___
9178	ICG SP-type Caboose, 76-77	19	24	___
9179	Chessie System Bobber Caboose, 76	7	11	___
9180	Rock Island N5c Caboose, 77-78	12	23	___
9181	B&M N5c Caboose, 76 u, 77	28	49	___
9182	N&W N5c Caboose, 76 u, 77-80	20	26	___
9183	Mickey Mouse N5c Caboose, 77-78	32	54	___
9184	Erie Bay Window Caboose, 77-78	24	30	___
9185	GTW N5c Caboose, 77	21	28	___
9186	Conrail N5c Caboose, 76 u, 77-78	27	29	___
9187	Gulf, Mobile & Ohio SP-type Caboose, 77	10	16	___
9188	GN Bay Window Caboose, 77	22	27	___
9189	Gulf 1-D Tank Car, 77	40	60	___
9193	Budweiser Vat Car, 83-84	92	121	___
9200	Illinois Central Boxcar, 70-71	19	25	___
9201	Penn Central Boxcar, 70	17	25	___
9202	Santa Fe Boxcar, 70	20	24	___
9203	Union Pacific Boxcar, 70		21	___
9204	Northern Pacific Boxcar, 70		21	___
9205	Norfolk & Western Boxcar, 70	22	25	___
9206	Great Northern Boxcar, 70-71		20	___
9207	Soo Line Boxcar, 71	11	18	___
9208	CP Rail Boxcar, 71	21	23	___
9209	Burlington Northern Boxcar, 71-72	16	25	___
9210	B&O DD Boxcar, 71	16	20	___
9211	Penn Central Boxcar, 71	17	28	___
9212	Seaboard Coast Line Flatcar with trailers, 76 u	22	31	___
9213	M&StL Covered Quad Hopper (SSS), 78	20	29	___
9214	Northern Pacific Boxcar, 71-72	16	21	___
9215	Norfolk & Western Boxcar, 71	19	24	___
9216	Great Northern Auto Carrier, 3-tier, 78	25	39	___
9217	Soo Line Operating Boxcar, 82-84	29	36	___
9218	Monon Operating Boxcar, 81	23	33	___
9219	Missouri Pacific Operating Boxcar, 83	29	37	___
9220	Borden Operating Milk Car, 83-86	95	113	___
9221	Poultry Dispatch Operating Chicken Car, 83-85	45	50	___
9222	L&N Flatcar with trailers, 83-84	38	60	___
9223	Reading Operating Boxcar, 84	33	40	___
9224	Churchill Downs Operating Horse Car, 84-86	85	110	___
9225	Conrail Operating Barrel Car, 84	42	55	___
9226	Delaware & Hudson Flatcar with trailers, 84-85	31	34	___
9228	Canadian Pacific Operating Boxcar, 86	23	42	___
9229	Express Mail Operating Boxcar, 85-86	21	27	___
9230	Monon Boxcar (SSS), 71, 72 u	17	24	___
9231	Reading Bay Window Caboose, 79	24	32	___
9232	Allis-Chalmers Condenser Car, 80-81, 83 u	42	50	___
9233	Depressed Center Flatcar with transformer, 80	55	65	___
9234	Radioactive Waste Car, 80	53	78	___
9235	Union Pacific Derrick Car, 83-84	16	22	___
9236	C&NW Derrick Car, 83-85	22	30	___
9237	UPS Express Operating Boxcar, 84	32	99	___

			Exc	Mint
___	**9238**	Northern Pacific Log Dump Car, 84	16	24
___	**9239**	Lionel Lines N5c Caboose, 83 u	50	60
___	**9240**	NYC Operating Hopper, 86	32	39
___	**9240**	NYC Hopper (O27), 87 u	20	29
___	**9241**	PRR Log Dump Car, 85-86	21	27
___	**9250**	WaterPoxy 3-D Tank Car, 70-71	23	34
___	**9260**	Reynolds Aluminum Covered Quad Hopper, 75-77	19	22
___	**9261**	Sun-Maid Raisins Covered Quad Hopper, 75 u, 76	25	31
___	**9262**	Ralston Purina Covered Quad Hopper, 75 u, 76	36	58
___	**9263**	PRR Covered Quad Hopper, 75 u, 76-77	23	30
___	**9264**	Illinois Central Covered Quad Hopper, 75 u, 76-77	28	39
___	**9265**	Chessie System Covered Quad Hopper, 75 u, 76-77	21	27
___	**9266**	Southern "Big John" Covered Quad Hopper, 76	46	65
___	**9267**	Alcoa Covered Quad Hopper (SSS), 76	20	25
___	**9268**	Northern Pacific Bay Window Caboose, 77 u	30	40
___	**9269**	Milwaukee Road Bay Window Caboose, 78	37	59
___	**9270**	Northern Pacific N5c Caboose, 78	14	27
___	**9271**	M&StL Bay Window Caboose (SSS), 78-79	18	30
___	**9272**	New Haven Bay Window Caboose, 78-80	20	34
___	**9273**	Southern Bay Window Caboose, 78 u	36	45
___	**9274**	Santa Fe Bay Window Caboose, 78 u	40	47
___	**9276**	Peabody Quad Hopper, 78	19	28
___	**9277**	Cities Service 1-D Tank Car, 78	41	45
___	**9278**	Life Savers 1-D Tank Car, 78-79	80	156
___	**9279**	Magnolia 3-D Tank Car, 78, 79 u	13	19
___	**9280**	Santa Fe Operating Stock Car (O27), 77-81	16	24
___	**9281**	Santa Fe Auto Carrier, 3-tier, 78-80	21	27
___	**9282**	GN Flatcar with trailers, 78-79, 81-82	22	28
___	**9283**	Union Pacific Gondola with canisters, 77	15	21
___	**9284**	Santa Fe Gondola with canisters, 77	16	27
___	**9285**	ICG Flatcar with trailers, 77	47	48
___		Unpainted yellow	20	39
___	**9286**	B&LE Covered Quad Hopper, 77	14	26
___	**9287**	Southern N5c Caboose, 77 u, 78	18	30
___	**9288**	Lehigh Valley N5c Caboose, 77 u, 78, 80	25	31
___	**9289**	C&NW N5c Caboose, 77 u, 78, 80	25	36
___	**9290**	Union Pacific Operating Barrel Car, 83	65	75
___	**9300**	PC Log Dump Car, 70-75, 77	18	24
___	**9301**	U.S. Mail Operating Boxcar, 73-84	32	42
___	**9302**	L&N Searchlight Car, 72 u, 73-78	21	24
___	**9303**	Union Pacific Log Dump Car, 74-78, 80	17	22
___	**9304**	C&O Coal Dump Car, 74-78	11	25
___	**9305**	Santa Fe Operating Cowboy Car (O27), 80-82	16	23
___	**9306**	Santa Fe Flatcar with horses, 80-82	18	26
___	**9307**	Erie Animated Gondola, 80-84	55	70
___	**9308**	Aquarium Car, 81-84	125	129
___	**9309**	TP&W Bay Window Caboose, 80-81, 83 u	19	25
___	**9310**	Santa Fe Log Dump Car, 78 u, 79-83	13	24
___	**9311**	Union Pacific Coal Dump Car, 78 u, 79-82	13	24
___	**9312**	Conrail Searchlight Car, 78 u, 79-83	18	27
___	**9313**	Gulf 3-D Tank Car, 79 u	43	50
___	**9315**	Southern Pacific Gondola with canisters, 79 u	16	23
___	**9316**	Southern Pacific Bay Window Caboose, 79 u	47	50

		Exc	Mint	
9317	Santa Fe Bay Window Caboose, 79	21	36	___
9320	Fort Knox Mint Car, 79 u	110	135	___
9321	Santa Fe 1-D Tank Car (FARR 1), 79	25	31	___
9322	Santa Fe Covered Quad Hopper (FARR 1), 79	30	38	___
9323	Santa Fe Bay Window Caboose (FARR 1), 79	39	49	___
9324	Tootsie Roll 1-D Tank Car, 79-81	69	98	___
9325	Norfolk & Western Flatcar with fences, 79-81 u	6	10	___
9326	Burlington Northern Bay Window Caboose, 79-80	34	44	___
9327	Bakelite 3-D Tank Car, 80	19	29	___
9328	Chessie System Bay Window Caboose, 80	33	42	___
9329	Chessie System Crane Car, 80	40	47	___
9330	Kickapoo Dump Car, 72, 79	3	7	___
9331	Union 76 1-D Tank Car, 79	39	44	___
9332	Reading Crane Car, 79	37	50	___
9333	Southern Pacific Flatcar with trailers, 79-80	33	47	___
9334	Humble 1-D Tank Car, 79	21	26	___
9335	B&O Log Dump Car, 86	16	22	___
9336	CP Rail Gondola with canisters, 79	16	29	___
9338	Pennsylvania Power & Light Quad Hopper, 79	60	75	___
9339	GN Boxcar (027), 79-83, 85 u, 86	8	10	___
9340	Illinois Central Gondola with canisters (027), 79-81, 82 u, 83	5	9	___
9341	ACL SP-type Caboose, 79-82, 86 u 87-90	6	8	___
9344	Citgo 3-D Tank Car, 80	23	38	___
9345	Reading Searchlight Car, 84-85	20	25	___
9346	Wabash SP-type Caboose, 79	6	10	___
9347	NIagara Falls 3-D Tank Car, 79 u	38	46	___
9348	Santa Fe Crane Car (FARR 1), 79 u	60	70	___
9349	San Francisco Mint Car, 80	55	70	___
9351	PRR Auto Carrier, 3-tier, 80	23	40	___
9352	Trailer Train Flatcar with C&NW trailers, 80	29	55	___
9353	Crystal Line 3-D Tank Car, 80	18	26	___
9354	Pennzoil 1-D Tank Car, 80, 81 u	60	85	___
9355	Delaware & Hudson Bay Window Caboose, 80	37	45	___
9357	Smokey Mountain Bobber Caboose, 79	8	10	___
9359	National Basketball Association Boxcar (027), 79-80 u	19	24	___
9360	National Hockey League Boxcar (027), 79-80 u	21	26	___
9361	C&NW Bay Window Caboose, 80	47	50	___
9362	Major League Baseball Boxcar (027), 79-80 u	17	21	___
9363	N&W Log Dump Car "9325" (027), 79	4	7	___
9364	N&W Crane Car "9325" (027), 79	7	9	___
9365	Toys 'R' Us Boxcar (027), 79 u	30	37	___
9366	UP Covered Quad Hopper (FARR 2), 80	19	23	___
9367	Union Pacific 1-D Tank Car (FARR 2), 80	21	30	___
9368	Union Pacific Bay Window Caboose (FARR 2), 80	30	36	___
9369	Sinclair 1-D Tank Car, 80	60	85	___
9370	Seaboard Gondola with canisters, 80	19	21	___
9371	Atlantic Sugar Covered Quad Hopper, 80	19	22	___
9372	Seaboard Bay Window Caboose, 80	35	40	___
9373	Getty 1-D Tank Car, 80-81, 83 u	31	42	___
9374	Reading Covered Quad Hopper, 80-81, 83 u	39	40	___
9376	Soo Line Boxcar (027), 81 u	40	50	___
9378	Derrick Car, 80-82	18	22	___
9379	Santa Fe Gondola with canisters, 80-81, 83 u	22	30	___

			Exc	Mint
___	**9380**	NYNH&H SP-type Caboose, 80-81	7	10
___	**9381**	Chessie System SP-type Caboose, 80	7	9
___	**9382**	Florida East Coast Bay Window Caboose, 80	34	48
___	**9383**	UP Flatcar with trailers (FARR 2), 80 u	27	34
___	**9384**	Great Northern Operating Hopper, 81	50	55
___	**9385**	Alaska Gondola with canisters, 81	27	34
___	**9386**	Pure Oil 1-D Tank Car, 81	38	50
___	**9387**	Burlington Bay Window Caboose, 81	46	52
___	**9388**	Toys 'R' Us Boxcar (027), 81 u	38	45
___	**9389**	Radioactive Waste Car, 81-82	65	78
___	**9398**	PRR Coal Dump Car, 83-84	28	38
___	**9399**	C&NW Coal Dump Car, 83-85	17	22
___	**9400**	Conrail Boxcar, 78	14	20
___	**9401**	Great Northern Boxcar, 78	18	23
___	**9402**	Susquehanna Boxcar, 78	30	36
___	**9403**	Seaboard Coast Line Boxcar, 78	12	17
___	**9404**	NKP Boxcar, 78	19	21
___	**9405**	Chattahoochee Boxcar, 78	14	19
___	**9406**	D&RGW Boxcar, 78-79	17	21
___	**9407**	Union Pacific Stock Car, 78	18	25
___	**9408**	Lionel Lines Circus Stock Car (SSS), 78	31	40
___	**9411**	Lackawanna Phoebe Snow Boxcar, 78	35	43
___	**9412**	RF&P Boxcar, 79	21	27
___	**9413**	Napierville Junction Boxcar, 79	18	24
___	**9414**	Cotton Belt Boxcar, 79	19	23
___	**9415**	Providence & Worcester Boxcar, 79	17	25
___	**9416**	MD&W Boxcar, 79, 81	13	19
___	**9417**	CP Rail Boxcar, 79	45	50
___	**9418**	FARR Boxcar, 79 u	50	60
___	**9419**	Union Pacific Boxcar (FARR 2), 80	22	31
___	**9420**	B&O Sentinel Boxcar, 80	21	26
___	**9421**	Maine Central Boxcar, 80	10	17
___	**9422**	EJ&E Boxcar, 80	12	20
___	**9423**	NYNH&H Boxcar, 80	14	22
___	**9424**	TP&W Boxcar, 80	17	21
___	**9425**	British Columbia DD Boxcar, 80	26	35
___	**9426**	Chesapeake & Ohio Boxcar, 80	19	30
___	**9427**	Bay Line Boxcar, 80-81	12	17
___	**9428**	TP&W Boxcar, 80-81, 83 u		23
___	**9429**	"The Early Years" Boxcar, 80	13	27
___	**9430**	"The Standard Gauge Years" Boxcar, 80	12	25
___	**9431**	"The Prewar Years" Boxcar, 80	13	25
___	**9432**	"The Postwar Years" Boxcar, 80	22	55
___	**9433**	"The Golden Years" Boxcar, 80	33	43
___	**9434**	Joshua Lionel Cowen "The Man" Boxcar, 80 u	29	37
___	**9436**	Burlington Boxcar, 81	25	30
___	**9437**	Northern Pacific Stock Car, 81	22	36
___	**9438**	Ontario Northland Boxcar, 81	25	31
___	**9439**	Ashley Drew & Northern Boxcar, 81	11	19
___	**9440**	Reading Boxcar, 81	50	65
___	**9441**	Pennsylvania Boxcar, 81	32	42
___	**9442**	Canadian Pacific Boxcar, 81	12	31
___	**9443**	Florida East Coast Boxcar, 81	19	24

MODERN 1970-2024		Exc	Mint	
9444	Louisiana Midland Boxcar, 81	14	18	___
9445	Vermont Northern Boxcar, 81	14	17	___
9446	Sabine River & Northern Boxcar, 81	15	21	___
9447	Pullman Standard Boxcar, 81	16	21	___
9448	Santa Fe Stock Car, 81-82	34	40	___
9449	Great Northern Boxcar (FARR 3), 81	22	35	___
9450	Great Northern Stock Car (FARR 3), 81 u	50	60	___
9451	Southern Boxcar (FARR 4), 83	26	32	___
9452	Western Pacific Boxcar, 82-83	12	16	___
9453	MPA Boxcar, 82-83	14	19	___
9454	New Hope & Ivyland Boxcar, 82-83	21	27	___
9455	Milwaukee Road Boxcar, 82-83	15	29	___
9456	PRR DD Boxcar (FARR 5), 84-85	24	30	___
9461	Norfolk & Southern Boxcar, 82	25	43	___
9462	Southern Pacific Boxcar, 83-84	18	23	___
9463	Texas & Pacific Boxcar, 83-84	15	19	___
9464	NC&StL Boxcar, 83-84	16	22	___
9465	Santa Fe Boxcar, 83-84	12	19	___
9466	Wanamaker Boxcar, 82 u	60	70	___
9467	Tennessee World's Fair Boxcar, 82 u	26	31	___
9468	Union Pacific DD Boxcar, 83	31	34	___
9469	NYC Pacemaker Boxcar (std O), 84-85	37	53	___
9470	Chicago Beltline Boxcar, 84	15	20	___
9471	Atlantic Coast Line Boxcar, 84	13	20	___
9472	Detroit & Mackinac Boxcar, 84	22	26	___
9473	Lehigh Valley Boxcar, 84	13	28	___
9474	Erie-Lackawanna Boxcar, 84	31	35	___
9475	D&H "I Love NY" Boxcar, 84 u	28	37	___
9476	PRR Boxcar (FARR 5), 84-85	27	36	___
9480	MN&S Boxcar, 85-86	15	18	___
9481	Seaboard System Boxcar, 85-86	15	18	___
9482	Norfolk & Southern Boxcar, 85-86	13	17	___
9483	Manufacturers Railway Boxcar, 85-86	14	19	___
9484	Lionel 85th Anniversary Boxcar, 85	22	26	___
9486	GTW "I Love Michigan" Boxcar, 86	23	34	___
9490	Christmas Boxcar for Lionel Employees, 85 u	140	300	___
9491	Christmas Boxcar, 86 u	26	37	___
9492	Lionel Lines Boxcar, 86	23	29	___
9500	Milwaukee Road Passenger Coach, 73	28	75	___
9501	Milwaukee Road Passenger Coach, 73 u, 74-76	33	37	___
9502	Milwaukee Road Observation Car, 73	30	48	___
9503	Milwaukee Road Passenger Coach, 73	33	48	___
9504	Milwaukee Road Passenger Coach, 73 u, 74-76	33	37	___
9505	Milwaukee Road Passenger Coach, 73 u, 74-76	35	38	___
9506	Milwaukee Road Combination Car, 74 u, 75-76	32	37	___
9507	PRR Passenger Coach, 74-75	34	55	___
9508	PRR Passenger Coach, 74-75	32	50	___
9509	PRR Observation Car, 74-75	41	60	___
9510	PRR Combination Car, 74 u, 75-76	30	47	___
9511	Milwaukee Road Passenger Coach, 74 u	33	48	___
9513	PRR Passenger Coach, 75-76	25	44	___
9514	PRR Passenger Coach, 75-76	23	36	___
9515	PRR Passenger Coach, 75-76	22	34	___

			Exc	Mint
___	**9516**	B&O Passenger Coach, 76	27	42
___	**9517**	B&O Passenger Coach, 75	45	65
___	**9518**	B&O Observation Car, 75	45	65
___	**9519**	B&O Combination Car, 75	55	85
___	**9521**	PRR Baggage Car, 75 u, 76	65	95
___	**9522**	Milwaukee Road Baggage Car, 75 u, 76	65	80
___	**9523**	B&O Baggage Car, 75 u, 76	60	70
___	**9524**	B&O Passenger Coach, 76	27	37
___	**9525**	B&O Passenger Coach, 76	30	43
___	**9527**	Milwaukee Road Campaign Observation Car, 76 u	38	60
___	**9528**	PRR Campaign Observation Car, 76 u	48	75
___	**9529**	B&O Campaign Observation Car, 76 u	35	59
___	**9530**	Southern Baggage Car, 77-78	45	65
___	**9531**	Southern Combination Car, 77-78	29	37
___	**9532**	Southern Passenger Coach, 77-78	33	47
___	**9533**	Southern Passenger Coach, 77-78	27	38
___	**9534**	Southern Observation Car, 77-78	31	47
___	**9536**	Blue Comet Baggage Car, 78-80	39	55
___	**9537**	Blue Comet Combination Car, 78-80	35	50
___	**9538**	Blue Comet Passenger Coach, 78-80	35	47
___	**9539**	Blue Comet Passenger Coach, 78-80	35	48
___	**9540**	Blue Comet Observation Car, 78-80	16	40
___	**9541**	Santa Fe Baggage Car, 80-82	21	30
___	**9545**	Union Pacific Baggage Car, 84	135	200
___	**9546**	Union Pacific Combination Car, 84	85	105
___	**9547**	Union Pacific Observation Car, 84	85	105
___	**9548**	UP Placid Bay Passenger Coach, 84	90	110
___	**9549**	UP Ocean Sunset Passenger Coach, 84	85	105
___	**9551**	W&ARR Baggage Car, 77 u, 78-80	36	48
___	**9552**	W&ARR Passenger Coach, 77 u, 78-80	46	60
___	**9553**	W&ARR Flatcar with horses, 77 u, 78-80	32	50
___	**9554**	Chicago & Alton Baggage Car, 81	55	85
___	**9555**	Chicago & Alton Combination Car, 81	50	75
___	**9556**	Chicago & Alton Wilson Passenger Coach, 81	50	75
___	**9557**	Chicago & Alton Webster Groves Passenger Coach, 81	45	65
___	**9558**	Chicago & Alton Observation Car, 81	50	75
___	**9559**	Rock Island Baggage Car, 81-82	42	65
___	**9560**	Rock Island Passenger Coach, 81-82	43	65
___	**9561**	Rock Island Passenger Coach, 81-82	42	65
___	**9562**	N&W Baggage Car "577", 81	80	110
___	**9563**	N&W Combination Car "578", 81	80	105
___	**9564**	N&W Passenger Coach "579", 81	90	100
___	**9565**	N&W Passenger Coach "580", 81	85	100
___	**9566**	N&W Observation Car "581", 81	90	95
___	**9567**	N&W Vista Dome Car "582", 81 u	160	255
___	**9569**	PRR Combination Car, 81 u	115	160
___	**9570**	PRR Baggage Car, 79	85	115
___	**9571**	PRR Passenger Coach, 79	125	145
___	**9572**	PRR Passenger Coach, 79	110	125
___	**9573**	PRR Vista Dome Car, 79	95	120
___	**9574**	PRR Observation Car, 79	75	100
___	**9575**	PRR Passenger Coach, 79-80 u	100	135
___	**9576**	Burlington Baggage Car, 80	145	175

MODERN 1970-2024		Exc	Mint	
9577	Burlington Passenger Coach, 80	95	105	___
9578	Burlington Passenger Coach, 80	105	110	___
9579	Burlington Vista Dome Car, 80	95	110	___
9580	Burlington Observation Car, 80	95	110	___
9581	Chessie System Baggage Car, 80	55	64	___
9582	Chessie System Combination Car, 80	47	53	___
9583	Chessie System Passenger Coach, 80	40	50	___
9584	Chessie System Passenger Coach, 80	34	43	___
9585	Chessie System Observation Car, 80	57	68	___
9586	Chessie System Diner, 86 u	85	93	___
9588	Burlington Vista Dome Car, 80 u	110	120	___
9589	Southern Pacific Baggage Car, 82-83	110	135	___
9590	Southern Pacific Combination Car, 82-83	90	105	___
9591	Southern Pacific Pullman Passenger Coach, 82-83	85	105	___
9592	Southern Pacific Pullman Passenger Coach, 82-83	85	105	___
9593	Southern Pacific Observation Car, 82-83	100	130	___
9594	NYC Baggage Car, 83-84	76	130	___
9595	NYC Combination Car, 83-84	75	85	___
9596	NYC Wayne County Passenger Coach, 83-84	80	95	___
9597	NYC Hudson River Passenger Coach, 83-84	70	85	___
9598	NYC Observation Car, 83-84	75	85	___
9599	Chicago & Alton Diner, 86 u	80	90	___
9600	Chessie System Hi-Cube Boxcar, 75 u, 76-77	19	25	___
9601	ICG Hi-Cube Boxcar, 75 u, 76-77	20	21	___
9602	Santa Fe Hi-Cube Boxcar, 75 u, 76-77	17	20	___
9603	Penn Central Hi-Cube Boxcar, 76-77	12	18	___
9604	Norfolk & Western Hi-Cube Boxcar, 76-77	23	26	___
9605	NH Hi-Cube Boxcar, 76-77	17	21	___
9606	Union Pacific Hi-Cube Boxcar, 76 u, 77	10	17	___
9607	Southern Pacific Hi-Cube Boxcar, 76 u, 77	12	15	___
9608	Burlington Northern Hi-Cube Boxcar, 76 u, 77	21	23	___
9610	Frisco Hi-Cube Boxcar, 77	25	34	___
9620	NHL Wales Boxcar, 80	27	35	___
9621	NHL Campbell Boxcar, 80	27	34	___
9622	NBA Western Boxcar, 80	24	30	___
9623	NBA Eastern Boxcar, 80	26	34	___
9624	National League Baseball Boxcar, 80	27	34	___
9625	American League Baseball Boxcar, 80	27	35	___
9626	Santa Fe Hi-Cube Boxcar, 82-84	10	14	___
9627	Union Pacific Hi-Cube Boxcar, 82-83	15	21	___
9628	Burlington Northern Hi-Cube Boxcar, 82-84	14	19	___
9629	Chessie System Hi-Cube Boxcar, 83-84	24	36	___
9660	Mickey Mouse Hi-Cube Boxcar, 77-78	34	46	___
9661	Goofy Hi-Cube Boxcar, 77-78	57	66	___
9662	Donald Duck Hi-Cube Boxcar, 77-78	38	49	___
9663	Dumbo Hi-Cube Boxcar, 77 u, 78	43	52	___
9664	Cinderella Hi-Cube Boxcar, 77 u, 78	56	63	___
9665	Peter Pan Hi-Cube Boxcar, 77 u, 78	49	77	___
9666	Pinocchio Hi-Cube Boxcar, 78	120	175	___
9667	Snow White Hi-Cube Boxcar, 78	365	473	___
9668	Pluto Hi-Cube Boxcar, 78	149	193	___
9669	Bambi Hi-Cube Boxcar, 78 u	67	105	___
9670	Alice In Wonderland Hi-Cube Boxcar, 78 u	61	91	___

			Exc	Mint
___	**9671**	Fantasia Hi-Cube Boxcar, 78 u	56	91
___	**9672**	Mickey Mouse 50th Anniversary Hi-Cube Boxcar, 78 u	384	484
___	**9700**	Southern Boxcar, 72-73	22	30
___	**9700**	Hoboken Shore RR Boxcar "1029", 98 u		20
___	**9701**	B&O DD Boxcar, 72	14	19
___	**9702**	Soo Line Boxcar, 72-73	15	21
___	**9703**	CP Rail Boxcar, 72	30	40
___	**9704**	Norfolk & Western Boxcar, 72	10	17
___	**9705**	D&RGW Boxcar, 72	13	20
___	**9706**	C&O Boxcar, 72	11	19
___	**9707**	MKT Stock Car, 72-75	14	22
___	**9708**	U.S. Mail Toy Fair Boxcar, 73 u	85	95
___	**9708**	U.S. Mail Boxcar, 72-75	18	23
___	**9709**	BAR State of Maine Boxcar (SSS), 72-74	29	32
___	**9710**	Rutland Boxcar (SSS), 72-74	24	28
___	**9711**	Southern Boxcar, 74-75	19	25
___	**9712**	B&O DD Boxcar, 73-74	31	34
___	**9713**	CP Rail "Season's Greetings" Boxcar, 74 u	95	120
___	**9713**	CP Rail Boxcar, 73-74	24	30
___	**9714**	D&RGW Boxcar, 73-74	16	20
___	**9715**	C&O Boxcar, 73-74	17	22
___	**9716**	Penn Central Boxcar, 73-74	15	20
___	**9717**	Union Pacific Boxcar, 73-74	18	28
___	**9718**	Canadian National Boxcar, 73-74	23	31
___	**9719**	New Haven DD Boxcar, 73 u	23	32
___	**9723**	Western Pacific Toy Fair Boxcar, 74 u	20	60
___	**9723**	Western Pacific Boxcar (SSS), 73-74	27	29
___	**9724**	Missouri Pacific Boxcar (SSS), 73-74	21	24
___	**9725**	MKT Stock Car (SSS), 73-75	15	18
___	**9726**	Erie-Lackawanna Boxcar (SSS), 78	25	30
___	**9729**	CP Rail Boxcar, black, 78		34
___	**9730**	CP Rail Boxcar, silver, 74-75	23	27
___	**9731**	Milwaukee Road Boxcar, 74-75	18	28
___	**9732**	Southern Pacific Boxcar, 79 u	24	31
___	**9734**	Bangor & Aroostook Boxcar, 79	30	38
___	**9735**	Grand Trunk Western Boxcar, 74-75	15	21
___	**9737**	Vermont Central Boxcar, 74-76	27	34
___	**9738**	Illinois Terminal Boxcar, 82	33	45
___	**9739**	D&RGW Boxcar (SSS), 74-76	17	25
___	**9740**	Chessie System Boxcar, 74-75	15	19
___	**9742**	M&StL Boxcar, 73 u	12	19
___	**9742**	M&StL "Season's Greetings" Boxcar, 73 u	85	105
___	**9743**	Sprite Boxcar, 74 u, 75	19	27
___	**9744**	Tab Boxcar, 74 u, 75	17	24
___	**9745**	Fanta Boxcar, 74 u, 75	19	29
___	**9747**	Chessie System DD Boxcar, 75-76	24	28
___	**9748**	CP Rail Boxcar, 75-76	16	20
___	**9749**	Penn Central Boxcar, 75-76	16	21
___	**9750**	DT&I Boxcar, 75-76	13	20
___	**9751**	Frisco Boxcar, 75-76	15	23
___	**9752**	L&N Boxcar, 75-76	20	23
___	**9753**	Maine Central Boxcar, 75-76	16	22
___	**9754**	NYC Pacemaker Boxcar (SSS), 75-77	20	30

		Exc	Mint	
9755	Union Pacific Boxcar, 75-76	20	24	___
9757	Central of Georgia Boxcar, 74 u	16	17	___
9758	Alaska Boxcar (SSS), 75-77	24	31	___
9759	Paul Revere Boxcar, 75 u	36	43	___
9760	Liberty Bell Boxcar, 75 u	30	40	___
9761	George Washington Boxcar, 75 u	36	43	___
9762	Toy Fair Boxcar, 75 u	125	170	___
9763	D&RGW Stock Car, 76-77	15	20	___
9764	GTW DD Boxcar, 76-77	40	63	___
9767	Railbox Boxcar, 76-77	15	20	___
9768	B&M Boxcar, 76-77	18	27	___
9769	B&LE Boxcar, 76-77	13	21	___
9770	Northern Pacific Boxcar, 76-77	14	18	___
9771	Norfolk & Western Boxcar, 76-77	16	24	___
9772	Great Northern Boxcar, 76	49	81	___
9773	NYC Stock Car, 76	32	39	___
9775	M&StL Boxcar (SSS), 76	19	23	___
9776	SP Overnight Boxcar (SSS), 76	32	34	___
9777	Virginian Boxcar, 76-77	19	25	___
9778	"Season's Greetings" Boxcar, 75 u	165	185	___
9780	Johnny Cash Boxcar, 76 u	50	61	___
9781	Delaware & Hudson Boxcar, 77-78	19	23	___
9782	Rock Island Boxcar, 77-78	14	17	___
9783	B&O Time-Saver Boxcar, 77-78	18	27	___
9784	Santa Fe Boxcar, 77-78	13	17	___
9785	Conrail Boxcar, 77-78	20	23	___
9786	C&NW Boxcar, 77-79	18	27	___
9787	Jersey Central Boxcar, 77-79	12	19	___
9788	Lehigh Valley Boxcar, 77-79	17	21	___
9789	Pickens Boxcar, 77	25	33	___
9801	B&O Sentinel Boxcar (std O), 73-75	18	26	___
9802	Miller High Life Reefer (std O), 73-75	30	38	___
9803	Johnson Wax Boxcar (std O), 73-75	27	33	___
9805	Grand Trunk Western Reefer (std O), 73-75	20	31	___
9806	Rock Island Boxcar (std O), 74-75	38	46	___
9807	Stroh's Beer Reefer (std O), 74-76	72	90	___
9808	Union Pacific Boxcar (std O), 75-76	36	50	___
9809	Clark Reefer (std O), 75-76	33	41	___
9811	Pacific Fruit Express Reefer (FARR 2), 80	26	33	___
9812	Arm & Hammer Reefer, 80	24	30	___
9813	Ruffles Reefer, 80	20	28	___
9814	Perrier Reefer, 80	21	30	___
9815	NYC "Early Bird" Reefer (std O), 84-85	34	40	___
9816	Brach's Candy Reefer, 80	21	26	___
9817	Bazooka Bubble Gum Reefer, 80	24	31	___
9818	Western Maryland Reefer, 80	18	23	___
9819	Western Fruit Express Reefer (FARR 3), 81	22	29	___
9820	Wabash Gondola with coal (std O), 73-74	24	38	___
9821	SP Gondola with coal (std O), 73-75	28	32	___
9822	GTW Gondola with coal (std O), 74-75	24	29	___
9823	Santa Fe Flatcar with crates (std O), 75-76	34	44	___
9824	NYC Gondola with coal (std O), 75-76	41	56	___
9825	Schaefer Reefer (std O), 76-77	45	60	___

	No.	Item	Exc	Mint
___	**9826**	P&LE Boxcar (std 0), 76-77	34	39
___	**9827**	Cutty Sark Reefer, 84	45	55
___	**9828**	J&B Reefer, 84	37	49
___	**9829**	Dewar's White Label Reefer, 84	45	51
___	**9830**	Johnnie Walker Red Label Reefer, 84	36	44
___	**9831**	Pepsi Cola Reefer, 82	93	103
___	**9832**	Cheerios Reefer, 82	171	197
___	**9833**	Vlasic Pickles Reefer, 82	23	29
___	**9834**	Southern Comfort Reefer, 83-84	34	47
___	**9835**	Jim Beam Reefer, 83-84	48	62
___	**9836**	Old Grand-Dad Reefer, 83-84	44	54
___	**9837**	Wild Turkey Reefer, 83-84	76	110
___	**9840**	Fleischmann's Gin Reefer, 85	39	44
___	**9841**	Calvert Gin Reefer, 85	44	49
___	**9842**	Seagram's Gin Reefer, 85	44	49
___	**9843**	Tanqueray Gin Reefer, 85	45	50
___	**9844**	Sambuca Reefer, 86	37	49
___	**9845**	Baileys Irish Cream Reefer, 86	62	86
___	**9846**	Seagram's Vodka Reefer, 86	41	49
___	**9847**	Wolfschmidt Vodka Reefer, 86	38	43
___	**9849**	Lionel Lines Reefer, 83 u	20	32
___	**9850**	Budweiser Reefer, 72 u, 73-75	58	70
___	**9851**	Schlitz Reefer, 72 u, 73-75	30	36
___	**9852**	Miller Reefer, 72 u, 73-77	32	38
	9853	Cracker Jack Reefer, 72 u, 73-75		
___		(A) White body, black border on logo	24	34
___		(B) Caramel body, clear background logo	23	28
___		(C) Caramel body, white background logo	23	28
___	**9854**	Baby Ruth Reefer, 72 u, 73-76	22	26
___	**9855**	Swift Reefer, 72 u, 73-77	16	28
___	**9856**	Old Milwaukee Reefer, 75-76	33	40
___	**9858**	Butterfinger Reefer, 73 u, 74-76	22	28
___	**9859**	Pabst Reefer, 73 u, 74-75	43	50
___	**9860**	Gold Medal Reefer, 73 u, 74-76	12	21
___	**9861**	Tropicana Reefer, 75-77	23	35
___	**9862**	Hamm's Reefer, 75-76	35	42
___	**9863**	REA Reefer (SSS), 74-76	24	28
___	**9866**	Coors Reefer, 76-77	42	58
___	**9867**	Hershey's Reefer, 76-77	80	93
___	**9869**	Santa Fe Reefer (SSS), 76	32	37
___	**9870**	Old Dutch Cleanser Reefer, 77-78, 80	15	21
___	**9871**	Carling Black Label Reefer, 77-78, 80	33	45
___	**9872**	Pacific Fruit Express Reefer, 77-79	24	28
___	**9873**	Ralston Purina Reefer, 78	25	38
___	**9874**	Miller Lite Beer Reefer, 78-79	58	63
___	**9875**	A&P Reefer, 78-79	23	31
___	**9876**	Vermont Central Reefer, 78	26	31
___	**9877**	Gerber Reefer, 79-80	68	78
___	**9878**	Good and Plenty Reefer, 79	24	31
___	**9879**	Hills Bros. Reefer, 79-80	24	29
___	**9880**	Santa Fe Reefer (FARR 1), 79	27	31
___	**9881**	Rath Packing Reefer, 79 u	22	31
___	**9882**	NYC "Early Bird" Reefer, 79	25	29

MODERN 1970-2024		Exc	Mint	
9883	Nabisco Oreo Reefer, 79	95	104	___
9884	Fritos Reefer, 81-82	26	34	___
9885	Lipton Tea Reefer, 81-82	30	38	___
9886	Mounds Reefer, 81-82	24	30	___
9887	Fruit Growers Express Reefer (FARR 4), 83	29	38	___
9888	Green Bay & Western Reefer, 83	42	49	___
11000	Holiday Express Freight Set, 08		280	___
11004	NASCAR Diesel Freight Set, 06-07	150	325	___
11005	Dale Earnhardt Jr. Diesel Freight Set, 06-07	65	240	___
11006	Lionel Lion Set, 03 u		230	___
11006	Kasey Kahne Expansion Pack, 06-07		130	___
11007	Dale Earnhardt Sr. Expansion Pack, 06-07		130	___
11008	Dale Earnhardt Jr. Expansion Pack, 06-07		130	___
11009	Tony Stewart Expansion Pack, 06-07		130	___
11010	Jimmie Johnson Expansion Pack, 06-07		130	___
11011	Jeff Gordon Expansion Pack, 06-07		130	___
11020	Harry Potter Hogwarts Express Steam Passenger Set, 08-13	80	330	___
11025	Jimmie Johnson 2006 Champion Boxcar, 07		45	___
11038	Snow-covered Straight Track 4-pack, 08		14	___
11041	Holiday Calliope Car, 08		45	___
11067	Lionel Bear, 08		25	___
11077	Harry Potter Figures, 08		27	___
11096	Engineer Hat, 08		20	___
11098	Holiday Toy Soldier Car, 08		50	___
11099	Pennsylvania Flyer Steam Freight Set, 08	136	210	___
11100	PRR 2-8-2 Mikado Locomotive "9631", CC, 07		370	___
11101	LL 2-8-4 Berkshire Locomotive "737," CC, 06		350	___
11103	Southern PS4 4-6-2 Pacific Locomotive "1403," CC, 06		1000	___
11104	UP Big Boy Locomotive "4014," CC, 06		1800	___
11105	NYC L-2A 4-8-2 Mohawk Locomotive "2770," CC, 06		1100	___
11106	N&W 4-8-4 Northern Locomotive "746," CC, 06-07	610	750	___
11107	LionMaster SP Cab Forward "4276," RailSounds, 06-07		850	___
11108	C&O F19 4-6-2 Pacific Locomotive "494," CC, 06-07		1160	___
11109	C&O 0-8-0 Locomotive "79", TrainSounds, 06		420	___
11110	NYC 0-8-0 Locomotive "7805", TrainSounds, 06		420	___
11114	NYC 4-8-2 Mohawk Locomotive "2795," CC, 06		1000	___
11116	UP 4-8-4 FEF-3 Locomotive "844," gray, CC, 08-09		1160	___
11117	Santa Fe E6 4-4-2 Atlantic Locomotive "1484," CC, 07-09		600	___
11119	Southern 0-8-0 Locomotive "6535," TrainSounds, 07	113	420	___
11122	UP Big Boy Locomotive "4024," CC, 06		1700	___
11123	UP Big Boy Locomotive "4023," CC, 06		1700	___
11126	UP Big Boy Locomotive "4012," CC, 06		1700	___
11127	SP GS-4 4-8-4 Northern Locomotive "4436," CC, 07-09		1200	___
11128	C&O F19 4-6-2 Pacific Locomotive "490", CC, 07		1160	___
11129	C&O 2-8-4 Berkshire Locomotive "2696," CC, 07		1160	___
11129	C&O 2-8-4 Berkshire Locomotive "2699," CC, 07-09		1200	___
11130	Postwar "736" 2-8-4 Berkshire Locomotive, 07		300	___
11131	UP 4-8-4 FEF-3 Locomotive "844," black, CC, 08-09		1160	___
11132	Reading 2-8-0 Consolidation Locomotive "1914," RailSounds, 08		450	___
11133	NYC 2-8-0 Consolidation Locomotive "1149," RailSounds, 08		450	___
11134	WM 2-8-0 Consolidation Locomotive "729," RailSounds, 08		450	___

			Exc	Mint
___	**11135**	B&O 2-8-0 Consolidation Locomotive "2784," RailSounds, 08		450
___	**11136**	WP 2-8-2 Mikado Locomotive "322," CC, 08		800
___	**11137**	UP 2-8-2 Mikado Locomotive "1925," CC, 08		800
___	**11138**	ATSF 2-8-2 Mikado Locomotive "3156," CC, 08		800
___	**11139**	MILW 2-8-2 Mikado Locomotive "462," CC, 08		800
___	**11140**	Cass Scenic Shay Locomotive "7," CC, 07		800
___	**11141**	Birch Valley Lumber Shay Locomotive "5," CC, 07		800
___	**11142**	Hogwarts Express Add-on 2-pack, 09-10		120
___	**11143**	SP AC-4 Cab Forward Locomotive "4100," CC, 08		1670
___	**11145**	CNJ G3s 4-6-2 Pacific Locomotive "835," CC, 08		1290
___	**11145**	CNJ G3s 4-6-2 Pacific Locomotive "835," CC, 08		1290
___	**11146**	Pere Marquette 2-8-4 Berkshire Locomotive "1225," CC, 08		1290
___	**11147**	PRR 4-8-2 Mib Locomotive "6750," CC, 08		1290
___	**11148**	NYC Dreyfuss J-3a 4-6-4 Hudson Locomotive "5448," CC, 08		1130
___	**11149**	LionMaster UP Big Boy 4-8-8-4 Locomotive "4006," CC, 08		860
___	**11150**	NYC F-12e 4-6-0 10-wheel Locomotive "827," CC, 08		700
___	**11151**	Polar Express Tender, RailSounds, 08-10		440
___	**11152**	D&RGW LionMaster 4-6-6-4 Challenger Locomotive "3805," CC, 09		900
___	**11153**	Stourbridge Lion Steam Locomotive, 09-10		430
___	**11154**	PRR CC2s 0-8-8-0 Mallet Locomotive "8183," CC, 09-10		2000
___	**11155**	ATSF 2-10-10-2 Mallet Locomotive "3000," CC, 09-10		2500
___	**11156**	C&O 4-6-0 Ten-Wheeler Locomotive, CC, 10	213	740
___	**11157**	WM Shay Locomotive "6," CC, 10		800
___	**11162**	Lone Ranger Add-on 3-pack, 10		165
___	**11164**	Dewitt Clinton Passenger Set, 10		630
___	**11165**	Dewitt Clinton Add-on Coach, 10		70
___	**11166**	CSX Merger Freight 2-pack #1, 10-11		130
___	**11167**	CSX Merger Freight 2-pack #2, 10-11		105
___	**11168**	CSX Merger Freight 2-pack #3, 10-11		130
___	**11169**	Strasburg Freight Add-on 2-pack, 10		100
___	**11170**	Three Rivers Fast Freight Set, 10-12		400
___	**11172**	Santa Fe 4-4-2 Steam Freight Set, 13		200
___	**11173**	Texan Freight Add-on 2-pack, 10-11		130
___	**11174**	Maple Leaf Freight Add-on 2-pack, 10-11		110
___	**11175**	Operation Eagle Justice Add-on 2-pack, 10-11		125
___	**11180**	Motor City Express Diesel Freight Train Set, CC, 12-13		1175
___	**11181**	CN GP9 Diesel Piggyback Train Set, CC, 12		850
___	**11182**	Dixie Special FT Diesel Freight Set, 11		700
___	**11183**	Lincoln Funeral Train, 13		1140
___	**11194**	Texas Special Diesel Passenger Set, CC, 13-14		1110
___	**11195**	PRR Diesel Passenger Set, CC, 13-14		1110
___	**11196**	BNSF Gondola "670591", 13		35
___	**11197**	ATSF Caboose "999471", 13		48
___	**11199**	UP NW2 Diesel Switcher Work Train Set, CC, 12		600
___	**11200**	UP LionMaster Challenger Locomotive "3985," CC, 10		900
___	**11201**	WM LionMaster Challenger Locomotive "1204," CC, 10		900
___	**11202**	CP 4-6-0 Ten-Wheeler Locomotive "914," CC, 10		740
___	**11203**	Pere Marquette Berkshire Locomotive "1225," CC, 09		980
___	**11204**	Pere Marquette Tender, RailSounds, 09-10		440
___	**11206**	DeWitt Clinton Locomotive and Tender, 11		800
___	**11207**	PRR LionMaster T1 Duplex Locomotive "5511," CC, 10		800

MODERN 1970-2024		Exc	Mint	
11208	UP LionMaster Big Boy Locomotive "4011," CC, 10		900	___
11209	Vision NYC Hudson Locomotive "5344," CC, 10		1600	___
11210	UP Challenger Locomotive "3967," CC, 10		1825	___
11211	UP 4-6-6-4 Challenger Locomotive "3976," CC, 10		1825	___
11212	NKP Berkshire Locomotive "765," CC, 10		1350	___
11215	LV 4-6-0 Camelback Locomotive "1598," CC, 10		550	___
11216	Jersey Central 4-6-0 Camelback Locomotive, CC, 10		550	___
11217	PRR 4-6-0 Camelback Locomotive "822," CC, 10		550	___
11218	Vision NYC Hudson Locomotive "5331," CC, 10		1600	___
11219	Clinchfield Challenger Locomotive "672," CC, 10		1825	___
11220	UP Challenger Locomotive "3989," CC, 10		1825	___
11221	UP Challenger Locomotive "3983," CC, 10		1825	___
11224	PRR Atlantic Locomotive "460," CC, 10-11		700	___
11225	B&O Atlantic Locomotive "1440," CC		700	___
11226	UP Water Tender, black, CC, 11		300	___
11227	UP Water Tender, gray, CC, 11		300	___
11228	Clinchfield Water Tender, CC, 11		300	___
11229	MILW 4-8-4 Northern Locomotive "261," CC, 11		995	___
11230	MILW 4-8-4 Northern Locomotive "267," CC, 11		995	___
11232	Reading Atlantic Locomotive "351," CC, 11		700	___
11233	Pennsylvania Power & Light 2-Truck Shay Locomotive, CC, 11	263	900	___
11234	Pennsylvania Power & Light 2-Truck Shay Locomotive, 11		750	___
11235	West Side Lumber 2-Truck Shay Steam Locomotive, CC, 11		900	___
11236	West Side Lumber 2-Truck Shay Steam Locomotive, 11		750	___
11237	Sugar Pine Lumber Shay Locomotive "4," CC, 11		900	___
11238	Sugar Pine Lumber Shay Locomotive "5," 11		750	___
11239	Merrill & Ring Lumber 2-Truck Shay Steam Locomotive, CC, 11		900	___
11240	Merrill & Ring Lumber 2-Truck Shay Steam Locomotive, 11		750	___
11247	Erie USRA 0-8-0 Steam Switcher "121," CC, 11-12		700	___
11248	Erie USRA 0-8-0 Steam Switcher "1270", 11-12		550	___
11249	L&N USRA 0-8-0 Steam Switcher "2119," CC, 11-12		700	___
11250	L&N USRA 0-8-0 Steam Switcher "2121," 11-12	155	550	___
11251	Pere Marquette USRA 0-8-0 Steam Switcher "1300," CC, 11-12		700	___
11252	Pere Marquette USRA 0-8-0 Steam Switcher "1307", 11-12		550	___
11253	NH 0-8-0 Steam Switcher "3603," CC, 11-13		700	___
11254	NH 0-8-0 Steam Switcher "3606," 11-13		550	___
11255	C&O 2-8-2 Mikado Steam Locomotive "1062," CC, 12		900	___
11256	NH 2-8-2 Mikado Steam Locomotive "3021," CC, 12		900	___
11257	PRR 2-8-2 Mikado Steam Locomotive "8631," CC, 12		900	___
11258	Southern 2-8-2 Mikado Steam Locomotive "4501," CC, 12		900	___
11259	UP 2-8-2 Mikado Steam Locomotive "2840," CC, 12		900	___
11260	Rio Grande 2-8-2 Mikado Steam Locomotive "1207," CC, 12		900	___
11261	DM&I 2-8-2 Mikado Steam Locomotive "1305," CC, 12		900	___
11262	Erie 2-8-2 Mikado Steam Locomotive "3007," CC, 12		900	___
11264	PRR K4 4-6-2 Pacific Steam Locomotive "1361," CC, 11		900	___
11265	PRR K4 4-6-2 Pacific Steam Locomotive '1330," CC, 11		900	___
11266	PRR K4 4-6-2 Pacific Locomotive "1361," 11		750	___
11267	Undecorated S-3 4-8-4 Northern Locomotive, CC, 11		995	___
11268	Strasburg 2-6-0 Mogul Steam Locomotive "89," 11		550	___
11269	RI 2-6-0 Mogul Steam Locomotive "750," 11-13		550	___
11270	GN 2-6-0 Mogul Steam Locomotive "453," 11		550	___

			Exc	Mint
___	**11271**	C&O 2-6-0 Mogul Steam Locomotive "49," 11-12		550
___	**11272**	ATSF 2-6-0 Mogul Steam Locomotive "573," 11		550
___	**11273**	Central Pacific 2-6-0 Mogul Locomotive "1470," 11-13		550
___	**11274**	MKT USRA 0-8-0 Steam Switcher "46," CC, 11-12		700
___	**11275**	MKT 0-8-0 Steam Switcher "51," CC, 11		550
___	**11276**	Lionelville & Western 0-8-0 Steam Switcher "1," CC, 11-13		700
___	**11277**	Lionelville & Western 0-8-0 Steam Switcher "2," 11-13		550
___	**11278**	WP 2-8-2 Mikado Steam Locomotive "322," CC, 11		900
___	**11279**	WP 2-8-2 Mikado Steam Locomotive "327," 11		750
___	**11280**	B&O 2-8-2 Mikado Steam Locomotive "4507," CC, 11		900
___	**11281**	B&O 2-8-2 Mikado Steam Locomotive "451," 11		750
___	**11282**	GN 2-8-2 Mikado Locomotive "3125," CC, 11		900
___	**11283**	GN 2i-8-2 Mikado Locomotive "3130," traditional, 11		750
___	**11284**	MP 2-8-2 Mikado Locomotive "1310," CC, 11		900
___	**11285**	MP 2-8-2 Mikado Locomotive "1312," traditional, 11		750
___	**11286**	RI 2-8-2 Mikado Steam Locomotive "2302," CC, 11		900
___	**11287**	RI 2-8-2 Mikado Steam Locomotive "2305," 11		750
___	**11288**	T&P 2-8-2 Mikado Steam Locomotive "552," CC, 11		900
___	**11289**	T&P 2-8-2 Mikado Steam Locomotive "557," 11		750
___	**11290**	Bethlehem Steel 2-6-0 Mogul Steam Locomotive "28," 11		550
___	**11291**	Weyerhaeuser 2-6-0 Mogul Locomotive "288," 11-13		550
___	**11292**	Nashville 4-4-0 General Locomotive, 13		500
___	**11295**	Elk River Lumber 2-Truck Shay Locomotive "1," CC, 11		900
___	**11296**	Elk River Lumber 2-Truck Shay Locomotive "2", 11		750
___	**11297**	P. Bunyan Lumber 2-Truck Shay Locomotive "18," CC, 11		900
___	**11298**	P. Bunyan Lumber 2-Truck Shay Locomotive "23," 11		750
___	**11299**	C&O 2-6-6-2 Mallet Steam Locomotive "875," CC, 12		1300
___	**11300**	PRR 2-10-4 Texas Steam Locomotive "6479," CC, 11		1300
___	**11301**	PRR 2-10-4 Texas Steam Locomotive "6498," CC, 11		1300
___	**11303**	C&O 2-10-4 Texas Steam Locomotive "3011," CC, 11		1300
___	**11304**	C&O 2-10-4 Texas Steam Locomotive "3025," CC, 11		1300
___	**11306**	NKP 2-10-4 Texas Steam Locomotive "801," CC, 11		1300
___	**11308**	Erie 2-10-4 Texas Steam Locomotive "3405," CC, 11		1300
___	**11310**	Pere Marquette 2-10-4 Texas Locomotive "1241," CC, 11		1300
___	**11312**	MILW S3 4-8-4 Northern Steam Locomotive "265," CC, 11		995
___	**11315**	Pennsylvania-Reading Seashore Atlantic Locomotive, 11		550
___	**11316**	PRR 4-4-2 Atlantic Steam Locomotive "272," 11		550
___	**11317**	Southern 4-4-2 Atlantic Steam Locomotive"1910," 11		550
___	**11318**	CN 4-4-2 Atlantic Steam Locomotive "1630", 11		550
___	**11319**	PRR K4 4-6-2 Pacific Locomotive "5409", 13		900
___	**11320**	PRR K4 4-6-2 Pacific Locomotive, "5436," 13		750
___	**11321**	C&O 2-6-6-2 Mallet Steam Locomotive "1525," CC, 12		1300
___	**11322**	NKP 2-6-6-2 Mallet Steam Locomotive "943," CC, 12		1300
___	**11323**	W&LE 2-6-6-2 Mallet Steam Locomotive "8002," CC, 12		1300
___	**11327**	PRR Prewar K4 4-6-2 Pacific Locomotive "3667," CC, 11		900
___	**11328**	PRR Prewar K4 4-6-2 Pacific Locomotive "3672," CC, 11		900
___	**11329**	PRR Prewar K4 4-6-2 Pacific Locomotive "3678," 11	113	750
___	**11330**	Polar K4 4-6-2 Pacific Locomotive, CC, 11-14		900
___	**11331**	Polar K4 4-6-2 Pacific Locomotive, 11		750
___	**11332**	ATSF 4-8-4 Northern Steam Locomotive "3751," CC, 12	432	1300
___	**11333**	ATSF 4-8-4 Northern Steam Locomotive "3759," CC, 12		1300
___	**11334**	Southern Crescent Limited 4-6-2 Pacific Locomotive, CC, 12		1100
___	**11335**	Blue Comet 4-6-2 Pacific Locomotive "832," CC, 12		1100

		Exc	Mint
11336	Undecorated EM-1 2-8-8-4 Pilot Locomotive, CC, 12		1300 ___
11337	B&O 2-8-8-4 Steam Locomotive "7621," CC, 12		1300 ___
11338	Alton Limited 4-6-2 Pacific Steam Locomotive "657," CC, 12		1100 ___
11339	N&W 2-6-6-2 Mallet Steam Locomotive "1409," CC, 12		1300 ___
11340	B&O 2-8-8-4 Steam Locomotive "659," CC, 12		1300 ___
11341	Pilot 4-12-2 Locomotive, CC, 13		1300 ___
11342	UP 4-12-2 Steam Locomotive "9004," CC, 12-13		1300 ___
11343	UP 4-12-2 Steam Locomotive, black, "9000," CC, 12-13		1300 ___
11344	UP 4-12-2 Steam Locomotive, greyhound, "9000," CC, 12		1300 ___
11363	Cass Scenic RR 2-Truck Shay Steam Locomotive "3," CC, 12		900 ___
11364	Meadow River 2-Truck Shay Locomotive "1," CC, 12-13		900 ___
11365	Weyerhaeuser 2-Truck Shay Locomotive "3," CC, 12-13		900 ___
11366	Pickering Lumber 2-Truck Shay Locomotive "3," CC, 12-13		900 ___
11367	CP 2-Truck Shay Steam Locomotive "111," CC, 12-13		900 ___
11368	WM 2-Truck Shay Steam Locomotive "2," CC, 12		900 ___
11369	Bethlehem Steel 2-Truck Shay Locomotive "5," CC, 12-13		900 ___
11374	DM&I 2-8-8-4 Steam Locomotive "223," CC, 12		1300 ___
11375	WP 2-8-8-4 Steam Locomotive "258," CC, 12		1300 ___
11376	NP 2-8-8-4 Steam Locomotive "5000," CC, 12		1300 ___
11377	GN 2-8-8-4 Steam Locomotive "2060," CC, 12		1300 ___
11379	PRR 0-4-0 Shifter Steam Locomotive "112", 12		450 ___
11380	PRR 0-4-0 Shifter Steam Locomotive "94" , 12		450 ___
11381	North Pole Central 0-4-0 Switcher (std 0), 12		450 ___
11382	Transylvania 0-4-0 Shifter Steam Locomotive "13", 12		450 ___
11383	Bethlehem Steel 0-4-0 Shifter Steam Locomotive "134", 12		450 ___
11384	ATSF 0-4-0 Shifter Steam Locomotive "2301", 13		450 ___
11385	UP 0-4-0 Shifter Steam Locomotive "206", 13		450 ___
11386	B&M 2-8-4 Berkshire Steam Locomotive "4018," CC, 12-13		1250 ___
11387	ATSF 2-8-4 Berkshire Steam Locomotive "4199," CC, 12-13		1250 ___
11388	SP 2-8-4 Berkshire Steam Locomotive "3505," CC, 12-13		1250 ___
11389	B&A 2-8-4 Berkshire Steam Locomotive "1404," CC, 12-13		1250 ___
11390	Lima Demonstrator 2-8-4 Berkshire "1," CC, 12-13		1250 ___
11391	IC 2-8-4 Berkshire Steam Locomotive "7020," CC, 12-13		1250 ___
11392	Michigan Central 2-8-4 Berkshire "1420," CC, 12-13		1250 ___
11399	UP H7 Class 2-8-8-2 Steam Locomotive "3595," CC, 13-14		1350 ___
11400	C&O H7 Class 2-8-8-2 Steam Locomotive "1578" CC, 13-14		1350 ___
11401	Pilot H7 Class 2-8-8-2 Locomotive, CC, 14-15		1350 ___
11402	Virginian USRA Y3 2-8-8-2 Locomotive, CC, 13-14		1350 ___
11403	Pilot USRA 2-8-8-2 Locomotive, CC, 13-15		1350 ___
11404	ATSF USRA Y3 2-8-8-2 Locomotive, CC, 13-14		1350 ___
11405	N&W USRA Y3 2-8-8-2 Locomotive, CC, 13-14		1350 ___
11410	Pilot 4-8-2 Mohawk Locomotive, CC, 13-15		1300 ___
11411	NYC 4-8-2 Mohawk Locomotive "2854," CC, 12-13		1300 ___
11412	NYC 4-8-2 Mohawk Locomotive "2867," CC, 12-13		1300 ___
11413	Pilot 4-8-4 J-Class Locomotive, CC, 13-15		1300 ___
11414	N&W 4-8-4 Steam Locomotive "612," CC, 12-13		1300 ___
11415	Pilot S2 6-8-6 Turbine Locomotive, CC, 14-15		1300 ___
11416	PRR S2 6-8-6 Steam Turbine Locomotive "6200," CC, 12-14		1300 ___
11417	PRR S2 6-8-6 Steam Turbine Locomotive "6200," CC, 12-13		1300 ___
11418	Pilot GS-6 Locomotive, CC, 13-14		1300 ___
11419	SP 4-8-4 GS-2 Locomotive, black, CC, 12-13		1300 ___
11420	SP 4-8-4 GS-2 Locomotive, Daylight, CC, 12		1300 ___
11421	SP 4-8-4 GS-6 Locomotive, black, CC, 12		1300 ___

			Exc	Mint
___	**11422**	WP 4-8-4 GS-64 Locomotive "482," CC, 12		1300
___	**11423**	CNJ Blue Comet Locomotive "833," CC, 12-13		1100
___	**11425**	Alaska 0-4-0 Locomotive, RailSounds, 12-13		1100
___	**11426**	Rio Grande 0-4-0 Locomotive, RailSounds, 12-13		450
___	**11427**	SP 0-4-0 Locomotive "14," RailSounds, 12-13		450
___	**11428**	MILW 0-4-0 Locomotive, RailSounds, 12-13		450
___	**11429**	Southern 0-4-0 Locomotive, RailSounds, 12-13		450
___	**11430**	GN 0-4-0 Locomotive "1066," RailSounds, 12-13		450
___	**11431**	N&W 4-8-4 Locomotive "611," CC, 12		1300
___	**11432**	LL S2 6-8-6 Steam Turbine Locomotive, CC, 13-14		1300
___	**11433**	PRR S2 6-8-6 Steam Turbine Locomotive CC, 13-14		1300
___	**11434**	UP Big Boy Locomotive "4006," CC, 14		2700
___	**11435**	UP Big Boy Locomotive "4018," CC, 14		2700
___	**11436**	UP Big Boy Locomotive "4005," CC, 14		2700
___	**11437**	UP Big Boy Locomotive "4014," CC, 14		2992
___	**11438**	UP Big Boy Locomotive "4017," CC, 14		2700
___	**11446**	UP USRA Y3 2-8-8-2 Locomotive "3671," CC, 13-14		1350
___	**11447**	PRR USRA Y3 2-8-8-2 Locomotive "376," CC, 13-14		1350
___	**11448**	UP Big Boy Locomotive "4012," CC, 14		2700
___	**11449**	UP Big Boy Locomotive "4004," CC, 14		2700
___	**11450**	Polar Express Berkshire Scale Locomotive, gold, CC, 14		1500
___	**11451**	Polar Express Berkshire Scale Locomotive, black, CC, 14	1000	1835
___	**11452**	C&O 2-8-4 Berkshire Locomotive "2687," CC, 14		1500
___	**11453**	Erie 2-8-4 Berkshire Locomotive "3321," CC, 14		1500
___	**11454**	NKP 2-8-4 Berkshire Locomotive "765," CC, 14		1500
___	**11455**	Pere Marquette 2-8-4 Berkshire Locomotive "1225," CC, 14		1500
___	**11456**	Pere Marquette 2-8-4 Berkshire Locomotive "1227," CC, 14		1500
___	**11462**	SP AC-12 Cab-Forward Locomotive "4291," CC, 14		1700
___	**11463**	SP AC-12 Cab-Forward Locomotive "4286," CC, 14		1700
___	**11464**	SP AC-12 Cab-Forward Locomotive "4294," CC, 14		1700
___	**11465**	SP AC-12 Cab-Forward Locomotive "4275," CC, 14		1700
___	**11469**	Pilot AC-12 Cab-Forward Locomotive, CC, 14-15		1700
___	**11528**	Frosty the Snowman Figure Pack, 14, 16		30
___	**11650**	Alderney Dairy General American Milk Car 2-pack (std O), 07		130
___	**11651**	Freeport General American Milk Car 2-pack (std O), 07		130
___	**11652**	BNSF Mechanical Reefer 2-pack (std O), 07-09		140
___	**11653**	SPFE Mechanical Reefer 2-pack (std O), 07		140
___	**11654**	UPFE Mechanical Reefer 2-pack (std O), 07		140
___	**11655**	GN WFE Mechanical Reefer 2-pack (std O), 07		140
___	**11657**	PFE Wood-sided Reefer 3-pack (std O), 06		190
___	**11658**	John Bull Add-on Coach, 08		80
___	**11700**	Conrail Limited Set, 87	203	370
___	**11701**	Rail Blazer Set, 87-88	30	114
___	**11702**	Black Diamond Set, 87	168	265
___	**11703**	Iron Horse Freight Set, 88-91	100	105
___	**11704**	Southern Freight Runner Set (SSS), 87	150	285
___	**11705**	Chessie System Unit Train, 88	218	450
___	**11706**	Dry Gulch Line Set (SSS), 88	195	260
___	**11707**	Silver Spike Set, 88-89	175	245
___	**11708**	Midnight Shift Set, 88 u, 89	60	83
___	**11710**	CP Rail Freight Set, 89	321	415
___	**11711**	Santa Fe F3 Diesel ABA Set, 91	415	745
___	**11712**	Great Lakes Express Set (SSS), 90	205	340

		Exc	Mint	
11713	Santa Fe Dash 8-40B Set, 90	235	480	___
11714	Badlands Express Set, 90-91	49	60	___
11715	Lionel 90th Anniversary Set, 90	163	378	___
11716	Lionelville Circus Special Set, 90-91	155	190	___
11717	CSX Freight Set, 90	230	240	___
11718	Norfolk Southern Dash 8-40C Unit Train, 92	398	481	___
11719	Coastal Freight Set (SSS), 91	165	215	___
11720	Santa Fe Special Set, 91	49	60	___
11721	Mickey's World Tour Train Set, 91, 92 u	105	154	___
11722	Girls Train Set, 91	643	903	___
11723	Amtrak Maintenance Train, 91, 92 u	210	245	___
11724	GN F3 Diesel ABA Set, 92	515	840	___
11726	Erie-Lackawanna Freight Set, 91 u	225	275	___
11727	Coastal Limited Set, 92	90	110	___
11728	High Plains Runner Set, 92	120	130	___
11733	Feather River Set (SSS), 92	210	330	___
11734	Erie Alco Diesel ABA Set (FF 7), 93	200	305	___
11735	NYC Flyer Freight Set "1735WS", 93-99	99	160	___
11736	Union Pacific Express Set, 93-95	110	130	___
11738	Soo Line Set (SSS), 93	205	280	___
11739	Super Chief Set, 93-94	138	165	___
11740	Conrail Consolidated Set, 93	200	240	___
11741	Northwest Express Set, 93	130	155	___
11742	Coastal Limited Set, 93 u	90	115	___
11743	Chesapeake & Ohio Freight Set, 94	240	280	___
11744	NYC Passenger/Freight Set (SSS), 94	221	335	___
11745	U.S. Navy Set, 94-95	173	248	___
11746	Seaboard Freight Set, 94, 95 u	90	183	___
11747	Lionel Lines Steam Set, 95	310	340	___
11748	Amtrak Alco Diesel Passenger Set, 95-96	145	235	___
11749	Western Maryland Set (SSS), 95	167	300	___
11750	McDonald's Nickel Plate Special Set, 87 u	143	153	___
11751	Sears PRR Passenger Set, 87 u	120	155	___
11752	JCPenney Timber Master Set, 87 u	75	115	___
11753	Kay Bee Toys Rail Blazer Set, 87 u	80	100	___
11754	Key America Set, 87 u	150	165	___
11755	Timber Master Set, 87 u	150	165	___
11756	Hawthorne Freight Flyer Set, 87-88 u	65	85	___
11757	Chrysler Mopar Express Set, 88 u	327	387	___
11758	Desert King Set (SSS), 89	195	250	___
11759	JCPenney Silver Spike Set, 88 u	175	250	___
11761	JCPenney Iron Horse Freight Set, 88 u	120	125	___
11762	True Value Cannonball Express Set, 89 u	95	145	___
11763	United Model Freight Hauler Set, 88 u	135	145	___
11764	Sears Iron Horse Freight Set, 88 u	155	190	___
11765	Spiegel Silver Spike Set, 88 u	175	250	___
11767	Shoprite Freight Flyer Set, 88 u	80	125	___
11769	JCPenney Midnight Shift Set, 89 u	100	175	___
11770	Sears Circus Set, 89 u	185	220	___
11771	K-Mart Microracers Set, 89 u	80	110	___
11772	Macy's Freight Flyer Set, 89 u	170	220	___
11773	Sears NYC Passenger Set, 89 u	175	200	___
11774	Ace Hardware Cannonball Express Set, 89 u	145	175	___

			Exc	Mint
___	**11775**	Anheuser-Busch Set, 89-92 u	261	355
___	**11776**	Pace Iron Horse Freight Set, 89 u	115	135
___	**11777**	Sears Lionelville Circus Set, 90 u	175	190
___	**11778**	Sears Badlands Express Set, 90 u	49	60
___	**11779**	Sears CSX Freight Set, 90 u	190	230
___	**11780**	Sears NP Passenger Set, 90 u	155	190
___	**11781**	True Value Cannonball Express Set, 90 u	75	115
___	**11783**	Toys 'R' Us Heavy Iron Set, 90-91 u	138	165
___	**11784**	Pace Iron Horse Freight Set, 90 u	115	135
___	**11785**	Costco Union Pacific Express Set, 90 u	200	230
___	**11789**	Sears Illinois Central Passenger Set, 91 u	170	200
___	**11793**	Santa Fe Set, 91 u	49	60
___	**11794**	Mickey's World Tour Set, 91 u	80	100
___	**11796**	Union Pacific Express Set, 91 u	150	160
___	**11797**	Sears Coastal Limited Set, 92 u	80	100
___	**11800**	Toys 'R' Us Heavy Iron Thunder Limited Set, 92-93 u	238	298
___	**11803**	Nickel Plate Special Set, 92 u	135	145
___	**11804**	K-Mart Coastal Limited Set, 92 u	80	100
___	**11809**	Village Trolley Set, 95-97	55	85
___	**11810**	Budweiser Modern Era Set, 93-94 u	220	231
___	**11811**	United Auto Workers Set, 93 u	189	447
___	**11812**	Coastal Limited Special Set, 93 u	95	115
___	**11813**	Crayola Activity Train Set, 94 u, 95	133	153
___	**11814**	Ford Limited Edition Set, 94 u	196	266
___	**11818**	Chrysler Mopar Set, 94 u	173	268
___	**11819**	Georgia Power Set, 95 u	540	563
___	**11820**	Red Wing Shoes NYC Flyer Set, 95 u	264	324
___	**11821**	Sears Zenith Set, 95 u	368	807
___	**11822**	Chevrolet Set, 96 u	287	337
___	**11825**	Bloomingdale's Set, 96 u	150	333
___	**11826**	Sears NYC Zenith Express Freight Set, 95-96 u	380	776
___	**11827**	Zenith Employees Set, 96 u	340	823
___	**11828**	NJ Transit Passenger Set, 96 u	70	180
___	**11833**	NJ Transit GP38 Diesel Passenger Set, 97	275	300
___	**11837**	Union Pacific GP9 Diesel Set, 97	113	520
___	**11838**	ATSF Warhorse Hudson Freight Set, 97	397	810
___	**11839**	SP&S 4-6-2 Steam Freight Set, 97	95	280
___	**11841**	Bloomingdale's Set, 97 u	157	332
___	**11843**	Boston & Maine GP9 Diesel ABA Set, 98		510
___	**11844**	Union Pacific Die-cast Ore Cars 4-pack, 98		225
___	**11846**	Kal Kan Pet Care Train Set, 97 u	271	879
___	**11849**	Lionel Centennial Series Reefer 4-pack, 98	80	123
___	**11850**	Rice A Roni Trolley Set, 02 u		271
___	**11851**	PFE Reefer 6-pack (std O), 02	225	255
___	**11852**	Clinchfield PS-2 2-bay Hopper, 04		70
___	**11853**	B&M PS-2 2-bay Hopper 2-pack, 05		128
___	**11854**	N&W PS-2 Covered Hopper 2-pack, 04		70
___	**11855**	GN Offset Hopper with coal, 2-pack, 05		120
___	**11856**	Green Bay & Western Offset Hopper 2-pack, 05		120
___	**11857**	Baltimore & Ohio Offset Hopper 2-pack, 05		120
___	**11858**	PRR PS-4 Flatcar with trailers, 2-pack (std O), 05		160
___	**11859**	GN PS-4 Flatcar with trailers (std O), 05		160
___	**11860**	SP PS-4 Flatcar with trailers (std O), 05		160

		Exc	Mint	
11861	C&O PS-4 Flatcar with trailers (std O), 05		160	___
11863	Southern Pacific GP9 Diesel "2383", 98		225	___
11864	New York Central GP9 Diesel "2383", 98		275	___
11865	Alaska GP7 Diesel "1802", 98-99		90	___
11866	Govt. of Canada Cylindrical Hopper 2-pack (std O), 05		120	___
11867	CN Cylindrical Hopper 2-pack (std O), 05		120	___
11868	BN Husky Stack Car 2-pack (std O), 05		160	___
11869	SP Husky Stack Car 2-pack (std O), 05		160	___
11870	CSX Husky Stack Car 2-pack (std O), 05		220	___
11871	TTX Trailer Train Stack Car 2-pack (std O), 05		160	___
11872	PFE Orange Steel-sided Reefer 3-pack (std O), 05		130	___
11873	C&O Offset Hopper 3-pack (std O), 05		130	___
11874	PFE Orange Steel-sided Reefer 3-pack (std O), 05		130	___
11875	NP Steel-sided Reefer 3-pack (std O), 05	68	131	___
11876	PFE Silver Steel-sided Reefer 3-pack (std O), 05		130	___
11877	C&NW Steel-sided Reefer 3-pack (std O), 05		130	___
11878	Santa Fe PS-2 2-bay Covered Hopper 3-pack (std O), 06		125	___
11879	MKT PS-2 2-bay Covered Hopper 3-pack (std O), 06		125	___
11880	Boraxo PS-2 2-bay Covered Hopper 3-pack (std O), 06		125	___
11881	PRR PS-2 2-bay Covered Hopper 3-pack (std O), 06		125	___
11882	RI Offset Hopper with gravel, 3-pack (std O), 06		125	___
11883	CNJ Offset Hopper 3-pack (std O), 06		145	___
11884	Maine Central Offset Hopper 3-pack (std O), 06		145	___
11891	Pennsylvania 3-bay Hopper 3-pack (std O), 06		155	___
11892	Conrail ACF 3-bay Hopper 3-pack (std O), 06		155	___
11893	N&W 3-bay Hopper 3-pack (std O), 06		155	___
11894	UP 3-bay Hopper 3-pack (std O), 06		155	___
11895	GN Steel-sided Reefer 3-pack (std O), 06		145	___
11896	Santa Fe Steel-sided Reefer 3-pack (std O), 06		145	___
11897	Pepper Packing Steel-sided Reefer 3-pack (std O), 06		145	___
11900	SF Steam Freight Set, 96-01		130	___
11903	ACL F3 Diesel ABA Set, 96	125	716	___
11905	U.S. Coast Guard Set, 96	148	205	___
11906	Factory Selection Special Set, 95 u	43	93	___
11909	N&W J 4-8-4 Warhorse Set, 96	415	720	___
11910	Lionel Lines Set (O27), 96	100	160	___
11912	"57" Switcher Service Exclusive, 96	129	310	___
11913	SP GP9 Diesel Freight Set, 97	100	440	___
11914	NYC GP9 Diesel Freight Set, 97		370	___
11918	Conrail SD20 Service Exclusive "X1144" (SSS), 97	117	255	___
11919	Docksider Set, 97		70	___
11920	Port of Lionel City Dive Team Set, 97		185	___
11921	Lionel Lines Freight Set, 97		130	___
11929	ATSF Warbonnet Passenger Set, 97-99		132	___
11930	ATSF Warbonnet Passenger Car 2-pack, 97-99		80	___
11931	Chessie Flyer Freight Set "1931S", 97-99	105	185	___
11933	Dodge Motorsports Freight Set, 96 u	189	323	___
11934	Virginian Electric Locomotive Freight Set, 97-99		260	___
11935	NYC Flyer Freight Set, 97		155	___
11936	Little League Baseball Steam Set, 97	250	321	___
11939	SP&S 4-6-2 Steam Freight Set, 97		220	___
11940	Southern Pacific SD40 Warhorse Coal Set, 98		600	___
11944	Lionel Lines 4-4-2 Steam Freight Set, 98		175	___

			Exc	Mint
___	**11956**	UP GP9 Diesel Set, 97	330	380
___	**11957**	Mobil Oil Steam Special Set, 97	100	458
___	**11971**	D&H 4-4-2 Steam Freight Set, 98	125	155
___	**11972**	Alaska GP7 Diesel Set, 98-99	165	215
___	**11974**	Station Accessory Set, 98		22
___	**11975**	Freight Accessory Pack, 98		23
___	**11977**	NP Freight Cars 4-pack, 98	60	185
___	**11979**	N&W 4-4-2 Steam Freight Set, 98	38	120
___	**11981**	1998 Holiday Trolley Set, 98		75
___	**11982**	New Jersey Transit Ore Car Set, 98		250
___	**11983**	Farmrail GP7 Agricultural Freight Set, 99	195	493
___	**11984**	Corvette GP7 Diesel Set, 99	138	424
___	**11988**	NYC Firecar "18444" and Instruction Car "19853", 99		210
___	**12000**	NY Yankees Berkshire Passenger Set, 13		380
___	**12004**	Philadelphia Phillies Berkshire Passenger Set, 13	188	388
___	**12008**	Boston Red Sox Berkshire Passenger Set , 13		380
___	**12012**	Chicago Cubs Berkshire Passenger Set, 13	175	380
___	**12013**	NY Mets and Yankees Subway Series Set, 13		400
___	**12014**	FasTrack 10" Straight Track, 03-24		6
___	**12015**	FasTrack 036 Curved Track, 03-24		6
___	**12016**	FasTrack 10" Terminal Track, 03-24		10
___	**12017**	FasTrack 036 Manual Switch, left hand, 03-24		55
___	**12018**	FasTrack 036 Manual Switch, right-hand, 03-24		55
___	**12019**	FasTrack 90-degree Crossover, 03-24		29
___	**12020**	FasTrack 5" Uncoupling Track, 03-24		46
___	**12022**	FasTrack 036 Half Curved Track, 03-24		5
___	**12023**	FasTrack 036 Quarter Curved Track, 03-24		5
___	**12024**	FasTrack 5" Straight Track, 03-24		5
___	**12025**	FasTrack 4½" Straight Track, 03-24		5
___	**12026**	FasTrack 1¾" Straight Track, 03-24		5
___	**12027**	FasTrack 10" Insulated Track, 03-24		5
___	**12028**	FasTrack Inner Passing Loop Track Pack, 03-24		127
___	**12029**	FasTrack Accessory Activator Pack, 03-24		23
___	**12030**	FasTrack Figure 8 Track Pack, 03-24		83
___	**12031**	FasTrack Outer Passing Loop Track Pack, 03-24	63	160
___	**12032**	FasTrack 10" Straight Track,4-pack, 03-23		25
___	**12033**	FasTrack 036 Curved Track, 4-pack, 03-24		25
___	**12035**	FasTrack Lighted Bumper, 2-pack, 05-24		37
___	**12036**	FasTrack 10" Grade Crossing, 2-pack, 05-24		22
___	**12037**	FasTrack Graduated Trestle Set, 05-24		94
___	**12038**	FasTrack Elevated Trestle Set, 05-24		50
___	**12039**	FasTrack Railer, 04-24		11
___	**12040**	FasTrack 5" O Gauge Transition Piece, 04-24		11
___	**12041**	FasTrack 072 Curved Track, 04-24		8
___	**12042**	FasTrack 30" Straight Track, 04-24		19
___	**12043**	FasTrack 048 Curved Track, 04-24		7
___	**12044**	FasTrack Siding Track Add-on Track Pack, 04-24		132
___	**12045**	036 Remote Switch, left hand (FasTrack), 04-17		95
___	**12046**	036 Remote Switch, right hand (FasTrack), 04-17		95
___	**12047**	072 Wye Remote Switch (FasTrack), 04-14		97
___	**12048**	072 Remote Switch, left hand (FasTrack), 04-14		104
___	**12049**	072 Remote Switch, right hand (FasTrack), 04-14		104
___	**12050**	FasTrack 22.5-degree Crossover, 04-24		55

MODERN 1970-2024		Exc	Mint	
12051	FasTrack 45-degree Crossover, 04-24		33	___
12052	FasTrack Grade Crossing w/Flashers, 05-24	45	110	___
12053	FasTrack Accessory Power Wire, 04-24		4	___
12054	FasTrack 10" Straight Uncoupling Track, 05-24		50	___
12055	FasTrack 072 Half Curved Track , 04-24		7	___
12056	FasTrack 060 Curved Track, 05-24		8	___
12057	060 Remote Switch, left hand, 05-14		110	___
12058	060 Remote Switch, right hand (FasTrack), 05-14		110	___
12059	FasTrack Earthen Bumper, 04-24		15	___
12060	FasTrack 5" Insulated Block Section, 05-24		13	___
12061	FasTrack 084 Curved Track, 05-24		8	___
12062	FasTrack Grade Crossing w/Gates and Flashers, 06-24		187	___
12065	048 Remote Switch, left hand (FasTrack), 07-14		104	___
12066	048 Remote Switch, right hand (FasTrack), 07-14		104	___
12073	FasTrack 1 3/8" Track Section, 07-24		5	___
12074	FasTrack 1 3/8" Track Section, no roadbed, 07-24		5	___
12080	42" Path Remote Switch, right hand, 07-12		80	___
12081	42" Path Remote Switch, left hand, 07-12		80	___
12700	Erie Magnetic Gantry Crane, 87	125	150	___
12701	Operating Fueling Station, 87	60	74	___
12702	Control Tower, 87	60	75	___
12703	Icing Station, 88-89	60	65	___
12704	Dwarf Signal, 88-93	9	11	___
12705	Lumber Shed Kit, 88-99		9	___
12706	Barrel Loader Building Kit, 87-99		10	___
12707	Billboards, set of 3, 87-99		5	___
12708	Street Lamps, set of 3, 88-93	6	9	___
12709	Banjo Signal, 87-91, 95-00		29	___
12710	Engine House Kit, 87-91	21	25	___
12711	Water Tower Kit, 87-99		13	___
12712	Automatic Ore Loader, 87-88	17	21	___
12713	Automatic Gateman, 87-88, 94-00	30	40	___
12714	No. 252 Automatic Crossing Gate, 87-24		55	___
12715	Illuminated Bumpers, set of 2, 87-15		18	___
12716	Searchlight Tower, 87-89, 91-92	15	22	___
12717	Nonilluminated Bumpers, set of 3, 87-17		7	___
12718	Barrel Shed Kit, 87-99		10	___
12719	Animated Refreshment Stand, 88-89	65	70	___
12720	Rotary Beacon, 88-89	40	45	___
12721	Illuminated Extension Bridge, rock piers, 89	26	38	___
12722	Roadside Diner, smoke, 88-89	27	38	___
12723	Microwave Tower, 88-91, 94-95	14	19	___
12724	Double Signal Bridge, 88-90	39	50	___
12725	Lionel Tractor and Trailer, 88-89	10	18	___
12726	Grain Elevator Kit, 88-91, 94-99		31	___
12727	Operating Semaphore, 89-99		26	___
12728	Illuminated Freight Station, 89	29	38	___
12729	Mail Pickup Set, 88-91, 95	12	16	___
12730	Lionel Girder Bridge, 88-03, 08-24		21	___
12731	Station Platform, 88-00		8	___
12732	Coal Bag, 88-24		8	___
12733	Watchman Shanty Kit, 88-99		5	___
12734	Passenger/Freight Station Kit, 89-99	16	39	___

	MODERN 1970-2024		Exc	Mint
___	12735	Diesel Horn Shed, 88-91	19	24
___	12736	Coaling Station Kit, 88-91	21	31
___	12737	Whistling Freight Shed, 88-99		28
___	12739	Lionel Gas Company Tractor and Tanker, 89	20	25
___	12740	Genuine Wood Logs, set of 3, 88-92, 94-95, 97-99		5
___	12741	Union Pacific Intermodal Crane, 89	138	185
___	12742	Gooseneck Lamps, set of 2, 89-00		21
___	12743	Track Clips, dozen (O), 89-16		12
___	12744	Rock Piers, set of 2, 89-24		19
___	12745	Barrel Pack, set of 6, 89-23		10
___	12746	Operating/Uncoupling Track (027), 89-16		10
___	12748	Illuminated Passenger Platform, 89-99		18
___	12749	Rotary Radar Antenna, 89-92, 95	28	38
___	12750	Crane Kit, 89-91	8	10
___	12751	Shovel Kit, 89-91	8	10
___	12752	History of Lionel Trains Video, 89-92, 94	19	21
___	12753	Ore Load, set of 2, 89-91, 95	1	2
___	12754	Graduated Trestle Set, 22 pieces, 89-15		27
___	12755	Elevated Trestle Set, 10 pieces, 89-15	20	34
___	12756	The Making of the Scale Hudson Video, 91-94	20	22
___	12759	Floodlight Tower, 90-00		25
___	12760	Automatic Highway Flasher, 90-91	23	27
___	12761	Animated Billboard, 90-91, 93, 95	12	23
___	12763	Single Signal Bridge, 90-91, 93	31	35
___	12767	Steam Clean and Wheel Grind Shop, 92-93, 95	240	290
___	12768	Burning Switch Tower, 90, 93	85	94
___	12770	Arch-Under Bridge, 90-03, 08-24		30
___	12771	Mom's Roadside Diner, smoke, 90-91	40	68
___	12772	Truss Bridge, flasher and piers, 90-16, 18, 20		70
___	12773	Freight Platform Kit, 90-98		32
___	12774	Lumber Loader Kit, 90-99		19
___	12777	Chevron Tractor and Tanker, 90-91	9	15
___	12778	Conrail Tractor and Trailer, 90	9	16
___	12779	Lionelville Grain Company Tractor and Trailer, 90	11	19
___	12780	RS-1 50-watt Transformer, 90-93	95	130
___	12781	N&W Intermodal Crane, 90-91	145	160
___	12782	Lift Bridge, 91-92	428	518
___	12783	Monon Tractor and Trailer, 91	11	19
___	12784	Intermodal Containers, set of 3, 91	12	17
___	12785	Lionel Gravel Company Tractor and Trailer, 91	9	15
___	12786	Lionel Steel Company Tractor and Trailer, 91	10	16
___	12791	Animated Passenger Station, 91	45	60
___	12794	Lionel Tractor, 91	7	13
___	12795	Cable Reels, pair, 91-98	3	5
___	12798	Forklift Loader Station, 92-95	33	44
___	12800	Scale Hudson Replacement Pilot Truck, 91 u	13	17
___	12802	Chat & Chew Roadside Diner, smoke and lights, 92-95	41	50
___	12804	Highway Lights, 4-pack, 92-04, 13-24	9	35
___	12805	Intermodal Containers, set of 3, 92	10	14
___	12806	Lionel Lumber Company Tractor and Trailer, 92	10	15
___	12807	Little Caesars Tractor and Trailer, 92	9	14
___	12808	Mobil Tractor and Tanker, 92	8	13
___	12809	Animated Billboard, 92-93	12	22

		Exc	Mint	
12810	American Flyer Tractor and Trailer, 94	12	18	___
12811	Alka Seltzer Tractor and Trailer, 92	11	19	___
12812	Illuminated Freight Station, 93-00		27	___
12818	Animated Freight Station, 92, 94-95	50	60	___
12819	Inland Steel Tractor and Trailer, 92	9	16	___
12821	Lionel Catalog Video, 92	13	17	___
12826	Intermodal Containers, set of 3, 93	10	16	___
12831	Rotary Beacon, 93-95	20	41	___
12832	Block Target Signal, 93-98		25	___
12833	RoadRailer Tractor and Trailer, 93	9	15	___
12834	Pennsylvania Magnetic Gantry Crane, 93	130	170	___
12835	Operating Fueling Station, 93	55	60	___
12836	Santa Fe Quantum Tractor and Trailer, 93	8	14	___
12837	Humble Oil Tractor and Tanker, 93	9	16	___
12838	Crate Load, set of 2, 93-97		3	___
12839	Grade Crossings, set of 2, 93-16		7	___
12840	Insulated Straight Track (O), 93-16		8	___
12841	Insulated Straight Track (O27), 93-16		5	___
12842	Dunkin' Donuts Tractor and Trailer, 92 u	13	25	___
12843	Die-cast Sprung Trucks, pair, 93-99		10	___
12844	Coil Covers, pair (O), 93-98		3	___
12847	Animated Ice Depot, 94-99		65	___
12848	Lionel Oil Company Derrick, 94	55	75	___
12849	Lionel Controller with wall pack, 94, 95 u	22	40	___
12852	Die-cast Intermodal Trailer Frame, 94-01		6	___
12853	Coil Covers, pair (std O), 94-98		7	___
12854	U.S. Navy Tractor and Tanker, 94-95		33	___
12855	Intermodal Containers, set of 3, 94-95	9	13	___
12860	Lionel Visitor's Center Tractor and Trailer, 94 u	10	14	___
12861	Lionel Leasing Company Tractor, 94	8	13	___
12862	Oil Drum Loader, 94-95	75	85	___
12864	Little Caesars Tractor and Trailer, 94	8	14	___
12865	Wisk Tractor and Trailer, 94	12	55	___
12866	TMCC 135-watt PowerHouse Power Supply, 94 u, 95-03	15	46	___
12867	TMCC 135 PowerMaster Power Distribution Center, 94 u, 95-04		49	___
12868	TMCC CAB-1 Remote Controller, 94 u, 95-09		115	___
12869	Marathon Oil Tractor and Tanker, 94	15	22	___
12873	Operating Sawmill, 95-97	40	95	___
12874	Classic Street Lamps, set of 3, 94-00		13	___
12877	Operating Fueling Station, 95	75	85	___
12878	Control Tower, 95	49	60	___
12881	Chrysler Mopar Tractor and Trailer, 94 u	51	62	___
12882	Lighted Billboard, 95	9	14	___
12883	No. 148 Dwarf Signal, 95-24		30	___
12884	Truck Loading Dock Kit, 95-98		16	___
12885	40-watt Control System, 94 u, 95-05		35	___
12886	Floodlight Tower, 95-98		31	___
12888	No. 154 Railroad Crossing Flasher, 95-24		60	___
12889	Operating Windmill, 95-98	15	47	___
12890	Big Red Control Button, 94 u, 95-00		43	___
12891	Lionel Refrigerator Lines Tractor and Trailer, 95	12	16	___
12892	Automatic Flagman, 95-96		25	___

			Exc	Mint
___	**12893**	TMCC PowerMaster Adapter Cable, 94 u, 95-24		25
___	**12894**	Signal Bridge, 95-01		22
___	**12895**	Double-track Signal Bridge, 95-00	13	49
___	**12896**	Tunnel Portals, set of 2, 95-24		22
___	**12897**	Engine House Kit, 96-98		29
___	**12898**	Flagpole, 95-97		9
___	**12899**	Searchlight Tower, 95-98	10	25
___	**12900**	Crane Kit, 95-98		9
___	**12901**	Shovel Kit, 95-98		7
___	**12902**	Marathon Oil Derrick, 94 u, 95	109	161
___	**12903**	Diesel Horn Shed, 95-98		29
___	**12904**	Coaling Station Kit, 95-98		19
___	**12905**	Factory Kit, 95-98		20
___	**12906**	Maintenance Shed Kit, 95-98		20
___	**12907**	Intermodal Containers, set of 3, 95	9	14
___	**12911**	TMCC Command Base, 95-09		80
___	**12912**	Oil Pumping Station, 95-98	38	65
___	**12914**	SC-1 Switch and Accessory Controller, 95-98		35
___	**12915**	Log Loader, 96	40	120
___	**12916**	Water Tower, 96-97		56
___	**12917**	Animated Switch Tower, 96-98		29
___	**12922**	NYC Operating Gantry Crane, coil covers, 96	78	90
___	**12923**	Red Wing Shoes Tractor and Trailer, 95 u	34	38
___	**12925**	42" Diameter Curved Track Section (O), 96-16		4
___	**12926**	Black Globe Street Lamps, 3-pack, 96-03, 08-09, 16-24		30
___	**12927**	No. 65 Yard Light, 3-pack, 96-24		35
___	**12929**	Rail-truck Loading Dock, 96		44
___	**12930**	Lionelville Oil Company Derrick, 95 u, 96	55	75
___	**12931**	Electrical Substation, 96		22
___	**12932**	Laimbeer Packaging Tractor and Trailer Set, 96		14
___	**12933**	GM Parts Tractor and Trailer, 95	17	29
___	**12935**	Zenith Tractor and Trailer, 96		25
___	**12936**	SP Intermodal Crane, 97		195
___	**12937**	NS Intermodal Crane, 97		200
___	**12938**	PowerStation Controller/PowerHouse 135-watt Supply, 97-00		150
___	**12943**	Illuminated Station Platform, 97-00		24
___	**12944**	Sunoco Oil Derrick, 97		85
___	**12945**	Sunoco Pumping Oil Station, 97		80
___	**12948**	Bascule Bridge, 97	121	315
___	**12949**	Billboards, set of 3, 97-00		7
___	**12951**	Airplane Hangar Kit, 97-98		29
___	**12952**	Big L Diner Kit, 97		24
___	**12953**	Linex Gas Tall Oil Tank, 97		9
___	**12954**	Linex Gas Wide Oil Tank, 97		10
___	**12955**	Road Runner and Wile E. Coyote Ambush Shack, 97		100
___	**12958**	Industrial Water Tower, 97-98		50
___	**12960**	Rotary Radar Antenna, 97		26
___	**12961**	Newsstand with diesel horn, 97		30
___	**12962**	LL Passenger Service Train Whistle, 97-99		30
___	**12964**	Donald Duck Radar Antenna, 97		77
___	**12965**	Goofy Rotary Beacon, 97		58
___	**12966**	Rotary Aircraft Beacon, 97-00		35

MODERN 1970-2024		Exc	Mint	
12968	Girder Bridge Building Kit, 97		22	___
12969	TMCC Command Set, 97-09		199	___
12974	Blinking Light Billboard, 97-00		15	___
12975	Steiner Victorian Building Kit, 97-98		33	___
12976	Dobson Victorian Building Kit, 97-98		24	___
12977	Kindler Victorian Building Kit, 97-98		35	___
12982	Culvert Loader, conventional, 98-00	38	170	___
12983	Culvert Unloader, conventional, 99		185	___
12987	Intermodal Containers, set of 3, 98		15	___
12989	Lionel Tractor and Trailer, 98		16	___
12991	Linex Gas Tractor-Tanker, 98		16	___
14000	Operating Forklift Platform, 00		160	___
14001	Operating Belt Lumber Loader, 00		95	___
14002	ZW Amp/Volt Meter, 00-04		80	___
14003	80-watt Transformer/Controller, 00-03		70	___
14004	Operating Coal Loader, 00		135	___
14005	Operating Coal Ramp, 00	50	165	___
14018	ElectroCoupler Kit for Command Upgradeable GP9s, 00		20	___
14062	31" Path Remote Switch, left hand, 01-14		55	___
14063	31" Path Remote Switch, right hand, 01-14		75	___
14065	Nuclear Reactor, 00	110	233	___
14071	Yard Light 3-pack, 00-18		35	___
14072	Haunted House, 01		181	___
14073	History of Lionel, The First 90 Years Video, 00		15	___
14075	A Century of Lionel, 1900-1969 Video, 00		15	___
14076	A Century of Lionel, 1970-2000 Video, 00		15	___
14077	ZW Amp/Volt Meter, 00-03		70	___
14078	Die-cast Sprung Trucks, 2-pack, 00-24		35	___
14079	Operating North Pole Pylon, 01		70	___
14080	Hobo Hotel, 01	30	65	___
14081	Shell Oil Derrick, 01		100	___
14082	Pedestrian Walkover, speed sensor, 01-03		50	___
14083	Pedestrian Walkover, 01-03, 08, 12-16		55	___
14084	Lionel Heliport, 01		85	___
14085	Newsstand, 01		75	___
14086	Water Tower, 00		105	___
14087	Lighthouse, 01		95	___
14090	No. 140 Banjo Signal, 01-24		60	___
14091	Automatic Gateman, 01-03, 07-09		38	___
14092	Floodlight Tower, 01-05, 08-16		48	___
14093	Single Signal Bridge, 01-04, 08		22	___
14094	Double Signal Bridge, 01-04, 08		30	___
14095	Illuminated Station Platform, 01-04		20	___
14096	Station Platform, 01-04		10	___
14097	Rotary Aircraft Beacon, 01-04, 07-10	15	50	___
14098	Auto Crossing Gate 2-pack, 01-24		120	___
14099	Block Target Signal, 01-04, 07-08		22	___
14100	Blinking Light Billboard, 01-03		23	___
14101	Red Baron Pylon, 01		85	___
14102	Rocket Launcher, 01	160	280	___
14104	Burning Switch Tower, 00		70	___
14105	Aquarium, 01		175	___
14106	Operating Freight Station, 00	25	85	___

			Exc	Mint
___	**14107**	Coaling Station, 01-03		95
___	**14109**	Carousel, 01		230
___	**14110**	Operating Ferris Wheel, 01-02, 04	85	279
___	**14111**	1531R Controller, 00-24	20	53
___	**14112**	Lighted Lockon, 01-10, 13-16		6
___	**14113**	Engine Transfer Table, 01	90	210
___	**14114**	Engine Transfer Table Extension, 01		75
___	**14116**	PRR Die-cast Girder Bridge, 01		20
___	**14117**	NYC Die-cast Girder Bridge, 01		20
___	**14119**	Gooseneck Lamps, set of 2, 01-04, 07		22
___	**14121**	Classic Billboards, set of 3, 01-03		10
___	**14124**	ZW Controller with 2 transformers, 01		300
___	**14125**	Christmas Tree with 400E Train, 00		65
___	**14126**	Exploding Ammo Dump		55
___	**14133**	Madison Hobby Shop, 01	223	368
___	**14134**	Triple Action Magnetic Crane, 01		230
___	**14135**	NS Black Die-cast Girder Bridge, 02		15
___	**14137**	Die-cast Girder Bridge, 01-07		25
___	**14138**	Snap-On Tool Animated Billboard, 01 u	27	40
___	**14142**	Industrial Smokestack, 02-04		50
___	**14143**	Industrial Tank, 02-04		40
___	**14145**	Operating Lumberjacks, 02-03		65
___	**14147**	Die-cast Old Style Clock Tower, 02-04, 08-24		30
___	**14148**	Operating Billboard Signmen, 02-03		60
___	**14149**	Scale-sized Banjo Signal, 02-05		40
___	**14151**	Mainline Dwarf Signal, 02-08		43
___	**14152**	Passenger Station, 02-04		37
___	**14153**	Lion Oil Derrick, 02-03		50
___	**14154**	Water Tower, 01-02		65
___	**14155**	Floodlight Tower, 02-03		55
___	**14156**	Lion Oil Diesel Fueling Station, 02-03		70
___	**14157**	Coal Loader, 01-03		120
___	**14158**	Icing Station, 01-02		75
___	**14159**	Animated Billboard, 02-04		20
___	**14160**	Frank's Hotdog Stand, 03-04		55
___	**14161**	Smoking Hobo Shack, 02		60
___	**14162**	Missile Launching Platform, 02-03		48
___	**14163**	Industrial Power Station, 02-03		550
___	**14164**	Lionelville Bandstand, 02		140
___	**14166**	Train Orders Building, 04-05		49
___	**14167**	Operating Lift Bridge, 02	190	410
___	**14168**	Operating Harry's Barber Shop, 02-04		100
___	**14170**	Amusement Park Swing Ride, 03-04		150
___	**14171**	Pirate Ship Ride, 02-04		177
___	**14172**	NYC Railroad Tugboat, 02		215
___	**14173**	Drawbridge, 02-04		70
___	**14175**	Santa Fe Die-cast Girder Bridge, 01-03		17
___	**14176**	Norfolk Southern Die-cast Girder Bridge, 02-03		18
___	**14178**	TMCC Direct Lockon, 02-03		25
___	**14179**	TMCC Track Power Controller, 02-13		230
___	**14180**	B&O Railroad Tugboat, 02-03		155
___	**14181**	TMCC Action Recorder Controller, 02-13	60	115
___	**14182**	TMCC Accessory Switch Controller, 02-13		115

		Exc	Mint	
14183	TMCC Accessory Motor Controller, 02-13		115	___
14184	TMCC Block Power Controller, 02-12		90	___
14185	TMCC Operating Track Controller, 02-13		100	___
14186	TMCC Accessory Voltage Controller, 02-13		160	___
14187	TMCC How-to Video, 02-04		11	___
14189	TMCC Track Power Controller, 02-13		175	___
14190	The Lionel Train Book, 04-14		30	___
14191	TMCC Command Base Cable, 6 feet, 02-13		14	___
14192	TMCC 3-wire Command Base Cable, 02-13		15	___
14193	TMCC Controller to Controller Cable, 1 foot, 02-13		6	___
14194	TMCC TPC Cable Set, 02-13		16	___
14195	TMCC Command Base Cable, 20 feet, 02-07		12	___
14196	TMCC Controller to Controller Cable, 6 feet, 02-13		9	___
14197	TMCC Controller to Controller Cable, 20 feet, 02-07		9	___
14198	CW-80 80-watt Transformer, 03-18	65	150	___
14199	Playground Swings, 03-04, 08-09		50	___
14201	Burning Switch Tower, 05-06		70	___
14202	Water Tower, 05		140	___
14203	Amusement Park Swing Ride, 06-07		230	___
14209	U.S. Steel Gantry Crane, 05		180	___
14210	Pony Ride, 06-07		70	___
14211	Road Crew, 06-08		90	___
14214	Lionelville Mini Golf, 06		80	___
14215	Tug-of-War, 06-08		60	___
14217	Helicopter Pylon, 06-09		140	___
14218	Downtown People Pack, 05-19		27	___
14219	Ice Rink, 06-08		80	___
14220	Lionelville Water Tower, 06-08		21	___
14221	Witches Cauldron, 06-08		70	___
14222	Die-cast Girder Bridge, 06-09		30	___
14225	Sunoco Industrial Tank, 06-09		70	___
14227	Yard Tower, 06-08		45	___
14229	Crossing Shanty, 06-09		20	___
14230	Milk Bottle Toss Midway Game, 06		20	___
14231	Cotton Candy Midway Booth, 06		20	___
14236	Operating Freight Station, 06-07		105	___
14237	Rocket Launcher, 06-07		320	___
14240	Ice Block 10-Pack, 06-24		7	___
14241	Work Crew People Pack, 05-19		27	___
14242	Hard Rock Cafe, 06		50	___
14243	U.S. Army Water Tower, 06-08		95	___
14244	Ammo Loader, 06-07		105	___
14251	Die-cast Sprung Trucks, rotating bearing caps, set of 2, 07-24		40	___
14255	Sand Tower, 06-18		35	___
14257	Passenger Station, 06-13		60	___
14258	North Pole Passenger Station, 06-10		53	___
14259	Christmas People Pack, 06-12		23	___
14260	Christmas Tractor and Trailer, 06-08		25	___
14261	Christmas Tree Lot, 06		70	___
14262	Elevated Tank, 07		70	___
14265	Sawmill with sound, 08		130	___
14267	Sir Topham Hatt Gateman, 07-12		80	___

			Exc	Mint
___	**14273**	Polar Express Add-on Figures, 06-07, 12-24		30
___	**14289**	Operating Santa Gateman, 08		80
___	**14290**	UPS Store, 06		30
___	**14291**	Operating Milk Loading Depot, K-Line, 08		100
___	**14294**	993 Legacy Expansion Set, 07-16, 18-20		335
___	**14295**	990 Legacy Command Set, 07-16, 18-20	175	567
___	**14297**	Halloween Witch Pylon, 07-08	80	150
___	**14500**	KCS F3 Diesel AA Set, Railsounds, CC, 01	380	660
___	**14512**	F3 Diesel ABA Demonstrator "291," CC, 01	360	425
___	**14517**	Santa Fe F3 Diesel B Unit "2343C," powered, 01		280
___	**14518**	CP F3 Diesel B Unit "2373C," RailSounds, CC, 01		345
___	**14520**	Texas Special F3 Diesel B Unit, RailSounds, 01		360
___	**14521**	Rock Island E6 Diesel AA Set, 01	435	612
___	**14524**	Atlantic Coast Line E6 Diesel AA Set, 01	213	630
___	**14536**	Santa Fe F3 Diesel AA Set, RailSounds, CC, 03-04	217	800
___	**14539**	Santa Fe F3 Diesel B Unit, 03		300
___	**14540**	D&RGW F3 Diesel B Unit, RailSounds, CC, 01		315
___	**14541**	C&O F3 Diesel B Unit, RailSounds, CC, 01		300
___	**14542**	KCS F3 Diesel B Unit "2388C," RailSounds, CC, 01		375
___	**14543**	SP F3 Diesel B Unit, RailSounds, CC, 01		282
___	**14544**	Southern E6 AA Diesel Set, CC, 02	275	560
___	**14547**	Burlington E5 AA Diesel Set, CC, 02		570
___	**14552**	NYC F3 Diesel AA Set, RailSounds, CC, 03-04		740
___	**14555**	NYC F3 Diesel B Unit, 03		200
___	**14557**	WP F3 Diesel B Unit, nonpowered, 03-04		190
___	**14558**	B&O F3 Diesel B Unit, nonpowered, 03-04		155
___	**14559**	D&RGW F3 Diesel AA Set, 01		620
___	**14560**	NP F3 Diesel A Unit "2390B," freight, 02		200
___	**14561**	NP F3 Diesel A Unit "2390B," passenger, 02		190
___	**14562**	Milwaukee Road F3 Diesel A Unit "75C", 02	80	190
___	**14563**	Erie-Lackawanna F3 Diesel A Unit "7094", 02		175
___	**14564**	CP F3 Diesel B Unit "237C," CC, 02		350
___	**14565**	B&O F3 Diesel AA Set, 03-04		650
___	**14568**	WP F3 Diesel AA Set, 03-04		780
___	**14571**	Santa Fe PA Diesel AA Set, CC, 03		660
___	**14574**	D&H PA Diesel AA Set, CC, 03		580
___	**14579**	UP Alco PA-1 Diesel A Unit "600," powered, 03		450
___	**14580**	UP Alco PA-1 Diesel B Unit "600B," unpowered, 03		150
___	**14581**	UP Alco PA-1 Diesel A Unit "601," unpowered, 03		150
___	**14584**	Wabash F3 Diesel A Unit, nonpowered, 03		180
___	**14586**	D&H PB Unit, 03		125
___	**14587**	Santa Fe PB Unit, 03		125
___	**14588**	Santa Fe F3 Diesel ABA Set, CC, 04-05		980
___	**14592**	PRR F3 Diesel ABA Set, CC, 04-05		750
___	**14596**	NH Alco PA Diesel AA Set, 04-05		700
___	**14599**	NH Alco PB Diesel B Unit "0767-B", 04-05		150
___	**15000**	D&RGW Waffle-sided Boxcar, 95	12	18
___	**15001**	Seaboard Waffle-sided Boxcar, 95	14	19
___	**15002**	Chesapeake & Ohio Waffle-sided Boxcar, 96	16	20
___	**15003**	Green Bay & Western Waffle-sided Boxcar, 96	16	20
___	**15004**	Bloomingdale's Boxcar, 97 u		40
___	**15005**	"I Love NY" Boxcar, 97 u		65
___	**15008**	CP Rail Boxcar		30

No.	Description	Exc	Mint
15013	L&N Waffle-sided Boxcar "102402", 00		29
15014	Seaboard Waffle-sided Boxcar "125925", 00		25
15015	C&NW Waffle-sided Boxcar "161013", 03		18
15016	IC Waffle-sided Boxcar "12981", 04		20
15017	CSX Waffle-sided Boxcar, 05		27
15018	D&H Waffle-sided Boxcar "24052", 06		30
15020	NH Waffle-sided Boxcar, 07		30
15021	MKT Waffle-sided Boxcar, 08		35
15024	UP Waffle Boxcar "960860", 09-11		40
15028	Southern Waffle-sided Boxcar "539889", 10		40
15029	Western & Atlantic Wood-sided Reefer, 10		53
15033	MTK Stock Car, 10		65
15036	NPC Bass Pro Shops Boxcar, 11		22
15038	CSX Hi-Cube Boxcar, 11-12		40
15039	NS Waffle-sided Boxcar, 11-12		40
15041	BNSF Hi-Cube Boxcar, 10		50
15042	CSX Waffle-sided Boxcar, 11		40
15051	Lionel Lines Boxcar, 11-12		40
15052	Amtrak Hi-Cube Boxcar, 11-12		40
15053	REA Waffle-sided Boxcar, 11-12		40
15054	C&NW Wood-sided Reefer, 11-12		40
15060	K-Line Boxcar, 06		40
15063	U.S.A.F. Minuteman Boxcar, 11		55
15069	Coke Wood-sided Reefer #1, 09-16		65
15071	Coca-Cola Christmas Boxcar, 12		70
15072	Halloween Boxcar, 09-11		55
15074	Mr. Goodbar Wood-sided Reefer, 09-11		55
15075	Boy Scouts of America Eagle Scout Boxcar, 11-14		60
15077	ATSF Stock Car , 11		55
15078	Pabst Wood-sided Reefer, 11		65
15079	Schlitz Wood-sided Reefer, 11		58
15080	C&O 40' Boxcar , 11		55
15083	CP Rail Waffle-sided Boxcar, 13		43
15084	GN Hi-Cube Boxcar, 13-14		43
15086	Alaska Wood-Sided Reefer, 12		40
15091	Angela Trotta Thomas "High Hopes" Hi-Cube Boxcar, 12		55
15094	Sleepy Hollow Halloween Reefer, 14-15		60
15095	1953 Lionel Catalog Art Reefer, 13		55
15096	Hershey's Kisses Christmas Boxcar, 12		70
15097	Peanuts Christmas Boxcar, 12-13		70
15098	Lone Ranger Boxcar, 12-14		60
15100	Amtrak Passenger Coach, 95-97		35
15101	Reading Baggage Car (027), 96		34
15102	Reading Combination Car (027), 96		23
15103	Reading Passenger Coach (027), 96		23
15104	Reading Vista Dome Car (027), 96		26
15105	Reading Full Vista Dome Car (027), 96		26
15106	Reading Observation Car (027), 96		23
15107	Amtrak Vista Dome Car, 96		38
15108	Northern Pacific Vista Dome Car, 96		34
15109	ATSF Combine Car "2407", 97		35
15110	ATSF Vista Dome Car 2404", 97		35
15111	ATSF Observation Car "2406", 97		35

			Exc	Mint
___	**15112**	ATSF Albuquerque Coach "2405", 97		34
___	**15113**	ATSF Culebra Vista Dome Car "2404", 97		34
___	**15114**	NJ Transit Coach "5610", 96 u		45
___	**15115**	NJ Transit Coach "5611", 96 u		45
___	**15116**	NJ Transit Coach "5612", 96 u		45
___	**15117**	Annie Passenger Coach, 97		26
___	**15118**	Clarabel Passenger Coach, 97		26
___	**15122**	NJ Transit Passenger Coach "5613", 97 u		45
___	**15123**	NJ Transit Passenger Coach "5614", 97 u		45
___	**15124**	NJ Transit Passenger Coach "5615", 97 u		45
___	**15125**	Amtrak Observation Car, 97 u		50
___	**15126**	Stars & Stripes Abraham Lincoln General Coach, 99		60
___	**15127**	Stars & Stripes Ulysses S. Grant General Coach, 99		60
___	**15128**	Pride of Richmond Robert E. Lee General Coach, 99		60
___	**15129**	Pride of Richmond Jefferson Davis General Coach, 99		60
___	**15136**	Custom Series Short Observation Car, blue, 99		40
___	**15137**	Custom Series Short Observation Car, red, 99		34
___	**15138**	Pratt's Hollow Baggage Car, 98		100
___	**15139**	Pratt's Hollow Vista Dome Car, 98		100
___	**15140**	Pratt's Hollow Coach, 98		100
___	**15141**	Pratt's Hollow Observation, 98		100
___	**15142**	U.S. Army Baby Heavyweight Coach, 00		50
___	**15143**	U.S. Army Baby Heavyweight Coach, 00		50
___	**15153**	Pullman Baby Madison Set 4-pack, 01		190
___	**15163**	T&P Baby Heavyweight Coach, 01		30
___	**15166**	Union Pacific Whistling Baggage Car, 04		41
___	**15169**	C&O Streamliner Car 4-pack, 03	55	140
___	**15170**	L&N Streamliner Car 4-pack, 03		140
___	**15180**	NYC Streamliner Car 4-pack, 04		340
___	**15185**	UP Streamliner Car 4-pack, 04		340
___	**15300**	NYC Superliner Aluminum Passenger Car 4-pack, 02		360
___	**15301**	NYC Manhattan Superliner Passenger Coach, 02		90
___	**15302**	NYC Queens Superliner Passenger Coach, 02		90
___	**15304**	NYC Staten Island Superliner Passenger Coach, 02		90
___	**15305**	NYC Brooklyn Superliner Passenger Coach, 02		90
___	**15311**	CB&Q California Zephyr Aluminum Passenger Car 4-pack, 03		350
___	**15312**	Santa Fe Super Chief Aluminum Passenger Car 4-pack, 03		275
___	**15313**	D&H Aluminum Passenger Car 4-pack, 03		415
___	**15314**	Amtrak Superliner 2-pack, 03		220
___	**15315**	Santa Fe Superliner 2-pack, 03		200
___	**15316**	NYC Superliner 2-pack, 03		195
___	**15317**	Southern Aluminum Passenger Car 4-pack, 03		350
___	**15318**	Lionel Lines Aluminum Passenger Car 2-pack, 03		125
___	**15319**	Santa Fe Superliner Aluminum Passenger Car 2-pack, 03	50	145
___	**15326**	NYC 20th Century Limited Aluminum Passenger Car 6-pack, 02	243	564
___	**15333**	N&W Powhatan Arrow Aluminum Passenger Car 6-pack, 02-03		435
___	**15334**	N&W Powhatan Arrow Aluminum Baggage Car "117", 02-03		70
___	**15335**	N&W Powhatan Arrow Aluminum Combine, 02-03		70
___	**15336**	N&W Powhatan Arrow Aluminum Coach "537", 02-03		70
___	**15337**	N&W Powhatan Arrow Aluminum Coach "553", 02-03		70
___	**15338**	N&W Powhatan Arrow Aluminum Coach "641", 02-03		70
___	**15339**	N&W Powhatan Arrow Aluminum Observation, 02-03		70

		Exc	Mint	
15340	PRR South Wind Aluminum Passenger Car 6-pack, 02-03	218	525	___
15341	PRR South Wind Aluminum Baggage Car "6529", 02-03		100	___
15342	PRR South Wind Aluminum Combine "6700", 02-03		100	___
15343	PRR South Wind Aluminum Coach "4021", 02-03		100	___
15344	PRR South Wind Aluminum Coach "4022", 02-03		100	___
15345	PRR South Wind Aluminum Coach "4022", 02-03		100	___
15346	PRR South Wind Aluminum Observation "1126", 02-03		100	___
15350	Amtrak Superliner Aluminum Sleeper, 02-03		100	___
15351	Amtrak Superliner Aluminum Lounge Car, 02-03		100	___
15352	ATSF Superliner Hi-Level Sleeper "712", 03		100	___
15353	ATSF Superliner Hi-Level Lounge Car "575", 03		100	___
15364	ATSF Super Chief Aluminum Baggage Car "3425", 03		100	___
15365	ATSF Super Chief Aluminum Sleeper "Palm Leaf", 03		100	___
15366	ATSF Super Chief Aluminum Vista Dome, 03		100	___
15368	UP Streamlined Aluminum Baggage Car "5608", 03		100	___
15369	UP Streamlined Aluminum Combination Car "Clifton", 03		100	___
15370	UP Streamlined Aluminum Diner w/StationSounds, 03		230	___
15371	UP Streamlined Aluminum Coach "Chatham", 03		100	___
15372	UP Streamlined Aluminum Offset Dome Car "Plainfield", 03		100	___
15373	UP Streamlined Aluminum Offset Dome Car "Westfield"		100	___
15374	UP Streamlined Aluminum Observation "Elizabeth", 03		100	___
15375	Southern Aluminum Combination Car "Mississippi", 03		100	___
15376	Southern Aluminum Coach "North Carolina", 03		100	___
15377	Southern Aluminum Coach "Maryland", 03		100	___
15378	Southern Aluminum Observation "Louisiana", 03		100	___
15379	Lionel Lines Silver Valley Aluminum Combination Car, 03		100	___
15380	Lionel Lines Silver Spoon Aluminum Diner, 03		100	___
15381	Santa Fe Aluminum Baggage Car "2571", 03		100	___
15382	Santa Fe Regal Dome Aluminum Vista Dome Car, 03		100	___
15383	NYC 20th Century Limited Diner, StationSounds, 03		195	___
15384	N&W Powhatan Arrow Diner, StationSounds, 03		190	___
15385	Pennsylvania South Wind Diner, StationSounds, 03		190	___
15394	Amtrak Streamliner Car 4-pack, 03-04		450	___
15395	Alaska Streamliner Car 4-pack, 03-04		365	___
15396	Amtrak Superliner Diner, StationSounds, 03		220	___
15397	Santa Fe Superliner Diner, StationSounds, 03	80	200	___
15398	NYC Superliner Diner, StationSounds, 03		225	___
15405	50th Anniversary Hillside Heavyweight Diner, StationSounds, 02		195	___
15406	Blue Comet Giacobini Heavyweight Diner, StationSounds, 02		300	___
15504	Alton Limited Diner, StationSounds, 03		230	___
15506	Alton Limited Heavyweight Baggage Car "R.S. Brauer", 03		115	___
15506	Alton Limited Heavyweight Coach "Oak Park", 03		115	___
15507	Phantom III Passenger Car 4-pack, 02		245	___
15508	Phantom III Baggage Car, 02		65	___
15509	Phantom II Vista Dome, 02		65	___
15510	Phantom III Coach, 02		65	___
15512	Phantom III Observation, 02		65	___
15512	Phantom II Passenger Car 4-pack, 02		250	___
15517	Southern Crescent Limited Heavyweight Car 2-pack, 03-04		205	___
15520	Southern Crescent Limited Diner, StationSounds, 03-04		220	___

			Exc	Mint
____	**15521**	NYC 20th Century Limited Heavyweight Passenger Car 4-pack, 04		345
____	**15526**	Santa Fe Chief Heavyweight Passenger Car 4-pack, 04		370
____	**15538**	NYC 20th Century Limited Heavyweight Passenger Car 2-pack, 04		200
____	**15541**	NYC 20th Century Limited Diner, StationSounds, 04		200
____	**15542**	Santa Fe Chief Heavyweight Passenger Car 2-pack, 04		195
____	**15545**	Santa Fe Chief Heavyweight Diner, StationSounds, 04		200
____	**15546**	Napa Valley Wine Train Heavyweight 2-pack, 05		250
____	**15547**	Napa Valley Wine Train Heavyweight Coach "1015", 05		125
____	**15548**	Napa Valley Wine Train Heavyweight Coach "1100", 05		125
____	**15549**	Napa Valley Wine Train Diner, StationSounds, 05		280
____	**15550**	Napa Valley Wine Train Heavyweight Combination Car "1052", 05		100
____	**15551**	Napa Valley Wine Train Heavyweight Coach "1017", 05		100
____	**15552**	Napa Valley Wine Train Heavyweight Coach "1014", 05		100
____	**15553**	Napa Valley Wine Train Heavyweight Observation "1011", 05		100
____	**15554**	Pennsylvania Heavyweight Car 3-pack (std O), 05		375
____	**15558**	Pennsylvania Heavyweight Add-on Coach (std O), 05		140
____	**15559**	PRR Reading Seashore Heavyweight Car 3-pack (std O), 05		370
____	**15563**	PRR Reading Seashore Heavyweight Add-on Coach, 05		130
____	**15564**	LIRR Heavyweight Car 3-pack (std O), 05		370
____	**15568**	LIRR Heavyweight Add-on Coach (std O), 05		130
____	**15570**	LIRR Heavyweight Car 3-pack (std O), 06		230
____	**15574**	LIRR Heavyweight Car Add-on (std O), 06		140
____	**15575**	C&O Heavyweight Diner, StationSounds (std O), 06-07		295
____	**15576**	C&O Heavyweight Passenger Car 2-pack (std O), 06-07		265
____	**15577**	NYC Heavyweight 3-pack (std O), 05-06		370
____	**15581**	NYC Heavyweight Add-on Coach (std O), 05-06		130
____	**15584**	Amtrak Acela Passenger Car 3-pack (std O), 06		670
____	**15588**	Southern Heavyweight Passenger Car 4-pack, 06		495
____	**15593**	Southern Heavyweight Passenger Car 2-pack, 06		265
____	**15596**	Southern Heavyweight Diner, StationSounds, 06		295
____	**15597**	C&O Heavyweight Passenger Car 4-pack (std O), 06-07		495
____	**15906**	RailSounds Trigger Button, 90-95		12
____	**16000**	PRR Vista Dome Car (027), 87-88	37	55
____	**16001**	PRR Passenger Coach (027), 87-88	33	41
____	**16002**	PRR Passenger Coach (027), 87-88	24	29
____	**16003**	PRR Observation Car (027), 87-88	24	29
____	**16009**	PRR Combination Car (027), 88	36	38
____	**16010**	Virginia & Truckee Passenger Coach (SSS), 88	36	47
____	**16010**	Railbox Modern Boxcar 6-pack, LionScale, 16		360
____	**16011**	Virginia & Truckee Passenger Coach (SSS), 88	36	47
____	**16012**	Virginia & Truckee Baggage Car (SSS), 88	36	47
____	**16013**	Amtrak Combination Car (027), 88-89	21	34
____	**16014**	Amtrak Vista Dome Car (027), 88-89	21	34
____	**16015**	Amtrak Observation Car (027), 88-89	21	34
____	**16016**	NYC Baggage Car (027), 89	36	55
____	**16017**	NYC Combination Car (027), 89	21	29
____	**16018**	NYC Passenger Coach (027), 89	21	29
____	**16019**	NYC Vista Dome Car (027), 89	21	29
____	**16020**	NYC Passenger Coach (027), 89	23	33
____	**16020**	BNSF Modern Boxcar 6-pack, LionScale, 16		360

		Exc	Mint	
16021	NYC Observation Car (027), 89	20	28	___
16022	Pennsylvania Baggage Car (027), 89	27	38	___
16023	Amtrak Passenger Coach (027), 89	21	30	___
16024	Northern Pacific Diner (027), 92	39	44	___
16027	LL Combination Car (027, SSS), 90	39	48	___
16028	LL Passenger Coach (SSS, 027), 90	32	42	___
16029	LL Passenger Coach (SSS, 027), 90	35	42	___
16030	LL Observation Car (SSS, 027), 90	35	42	___
16030	CSX Modern Boxcar 6-pack, LionScale, 16		360	___
16031	Pennsylvania Diner (027), 90	35	39	___
16033	Amtrak Baggage Car (027), 90	28	38	___
16034	NP Baggage Car (027), 90-91	30	45	___
16035	NP Combination Car (027), 90-91	18	26	___
16036	NP Passenger Coach (027), 90-91	21	30	___
16037	NP Vista Dome Car (027), 90-91	18	26	___
16038	NP Passenger Coach (027), 90-91	17	25	___
16039	NP Observation Car (027), 90-91	21	30	___
16040	Southern Pacific Baggage Car, 90-91	22	30	___
16040	NS Modern Boxcar 6-pack, LionScale, 16		360	___
16041	NYC Diner (027), 91	37	47	___
16042	Illinois Central Baggage Car (027), 91	24	34	___
16043	Illinois Central Combination Car (027), 91	22	30	___
16044	Illinois Central Passenger Coach (027), 91	24	34	___
16045	Illinois Central Vista Dome Car (027), 91	22	30	___
16046	Illinois Central Passenger Coach (027), 91	24	34	___
16047	Illinois Central Observation Car (027), 91	24	34	___
16048	Amtrak Diner (027), 91-92	33	40	___
16049	Illinois Central Diner (027), 92	27	38	___
16050	C&NW Baggage Car "6620", 93	44	55	___
16050	AT&SF 3-bay Offset Hopper 6-pack, LionScale, 16		330	___
16051	C&NW Combination Car "6630", 93	40	50	___
16052	C&NW Passenger Coach "6616", 93	34	42	___
16053	C&NW Passenger Coach "6602", 93	37	46	___
16054	C&NW Observation Car "6603", 93	38	47	___
16055	Santa Fe Passenger Coach (027), 93-94	29	38	___
16056	Santa Fe Vista Dome Car (027), 93-94	25	32	___
16057	Santa Fe Passenger Coach (027), 93-94	30	40	___
16058	Santa Fe Combination Car (027), 93-94	27	35	___
16059	Santa Fe Vista Dome Car (027), 93-94	26	34	___
16060	Santa Fe Observation Car (027), 93-94	25	31	___
16060	B&O 3-bay Offset Hopper 6-pack, LionScale, 16		330	___
16061	N&W Baggage Car "6061", 94	60	85	___
16062	N&W Combination Car "6062", 94	38	50	___
16063	N&W Passenger Coach "6063", 94	43	55	___
16064	N&W Passenger Coach "6064", 94	43	55	___
16065	N&W Observation Car "6065", 94	36	48	___
16066	NYC Combination Car "6066" (SSS), 94	55	70	___
16067	NYC Passenger Coach "6067" (SSS), 94	38	47	___
16068	UP Baggage Car "6068" (027), 94	50	65	___
16069	UP Combination Car "6069" (027), 94	36	43	___
16070	UP Passenger Coach "6070" (027), 94	36	43	___
16070	B&M 3-bay Offset Hopper 6-pack, LionScale, 16		330	___
16071	UP Diner "6071" (027), 94	36	46	___

		MODERN 1970-2024	Exc	Mint
___	**16072**	UP Vista Dome Car "6072" (027), 94	36	43
___	**16073**	UP Passenger Coach "6073" (027), 94	36	42
___	**16074**	UP Observation Car "6074" (027), 94	36	43
___	**16075**	Missouri Pacific Baggage Car "6620", 95	44	55
___	**16076**	Missouri Pacific Combination Car "6630", 95	34	41
___	**16077**	Missouri Pacific Passenger Coach "6616", 95	34	41
___	**16078**	Missouri Pacific Passenger Coach "7805", 95	34	39
___	**16079**	Missouri Pacific Observation Car "6609", 95	34	41
___	**16080**	New Haven Baggage Car "6080" (027), 95	35	44
___	**16080**	C&O 3-bay Offset Hopper 6-pack #1, LionScale , 16		330
___	**16081**	New Haven Combination Car "6081" (027), 95	28	37
___	**16082**	New Haven Passenger Coach "6082" (027), 95	28	37
___	**16083**	New Haven Vista Dome Car "6083" (027), 95	30	39
___	**16084**	New Haven Full Vista Dome Car "6084" (027), 95	33	39
___	**16086**	New Haven Observation Car "6086" (027), 95	31	40
___	**16087**	NYC Baggage Car "6087" (SSS), 95	48	65
___	**16088**	NYC Passenger Coach "6088" (SSS), 95	36	43
___	**16089**	NYC Diner "6089" (SSS), 95	36	43
___	**16090**	NYC Observation Car "6090" (SSS), 95	38	46
___	**16090**	C&O 3-bay Offset Hopper 6-pack #2, LionScale, 16		330
___	**16091**	NYC Passenger Cars, set of 4 (SSS), 95	140	165
___	**16092**	Santa Fe Full Vista Dome Car (027), 95	30	38
___	**16093**	Illinois Central Full Vista Dome Car (027), 95	29	38
___	**16094**	Pennsylvania Full Vista Dome Car (027), 95	30	39
___	**16095**	Amtrak Combination Car (027), 95	19	23
___	**16096**	Amtrak Vista Dome Car (027), 95	19	23
___	**16097**	Amtrak Observation Car (027), 95	19	23
___	**16098**	Amtrak Passenger Coach, 95-97	20	33
___	**16099**	Amtrak Vista Dome Car, 95-97	20	33
___	**16100**	Alaska RR 3-bay 9-panel Hopper 6-pack, LionScale, 16		330
___	**16102**	Southern 3-D Tank Car (SSS), 87	23	30
___	**16103**	Lehigh Valley 2-D Tank Car (027), 88	19	25
___	**16104**	Santa Fe 2-D Tank Car (027), 89	19	23
___	**16105**	D&RGW 3-D Tank Car (SSS), 89	48	65
___	**16106**	Mopar Express 3-D Tank Car, 88 u	105	156
___	**16107**	Sunoco 2-D Tank Car (027), 90	16	20
___	**16108**	Racing Fuel 1-D Tank Car "6108" (027), 89 u, 92 u	9	13
___	**16109**	B&O 1-D Tank Car (SSS), 91	29	34
___	**16110**	Circus Animals Operating Stock Car "1989" (027), 89 u	24	34
___	**16110**	Chessie 3-bay 9-panel Hopper 6-pack, LionScale, 16		330
___	**16111**	Alaska 1-D Tank Car (027), 90-91	22	27
___	**16112**	Dow Chemical 3-D Tank Car, 90	20	26
___	**16113**	Diamond Shamrock 2-D Tank Car (027), 91	20	25
___	**16114**	Hooker Chemicals 1-D Tank Car (027), 91	13	17
___	**16115**	MKT 3-D Tank Car, 92	13	16
___	**16116**	U.S. Army 1-D Tank Car, 91 u	36	42
___	**16119**	MKT 2-D Tank Car (027), 92, 93 u	14	19
___	**16120**	Southern 3-bay 9-panel Hopper 6-pack, LionScale, 16		330
___	**16121**	C&NW Stock Car (SSS), 92	33	43
___	**16123**	Union Pacific 3-D Tank Car, 93-95	16	22
___	**16124**	Penn Salt 3-D Tank Car, 93	21	26
___	**16125**	Virginian Stock Car, 93	19	24
___	**16126**	Jefferson Lake 3-D Tank Car, 93	22	26

		Exc	Mint
16127	Mobil 1-D Tank Car, 93	28	33
16128	Alaska 1-D Tank Car, 94	24	29
16129	Alaska 1-D Tank Car (027), 93 u, 94	21	28
16130	SP Stock Car (027), 93 u, 94	10	13
16130	WM 3-bay 9-panel Hopper 6-pack, LionScale, 16		330
16131	T&P Reefer, 94	19	24
16132	Deep Rock 3-D Tank Car, 94	25	30
16133	Santa Fe Reefer, 94	22	28
16134	Reading Reefer, 94	17	21
16135	C&O Stock Car, 94	23	27
16136	B&O 1-D Tank Car, 94	28	32
16137	Ford 1-D Tank Car "12", 94 u	34	39
16138	Goodyear 1-D Tank Car, 95	28	34
16140	Domino Sugar 1-D Tank Car, 95	17	29
16140	Klemme Coop PS-2CD Covered Hopper 6-pack, LionScale, 16		360
16141	Erie Stock Car, 95	22	30
16142	Santa Fe 1-D Tank Car, 95	26	30
16143	Reading Reefer, 95	18	23
16144	San Angelo 3-D Tank Car, 95	22	25
16146	Dairy Despatch Reefer, 95	15	20
16147	Clearly Canadian 1-D Tank Car (027), 94 u	25	40
16149	Zep Chemical 1-D Tank Car (027), 95 u	68	81
16150	Sunoco 1-D Tank Car "6315", 97	35	39
16150	D&RGW PS-2CD Covered Hopper 6-pack, LionScale, 16		360
16152	Sunoco 3-D Tank Car "6415", 97		26
16153	AEC Reactor Fluid 1-D Tank Car "6515-1", 97		94
16154	AEC Reactor Fluid 1-D Tank Car "6515-2", 97	39	107
16155	AEC Reactor Fluid 1-D Tank Car "6515-3", 97	60	109
16157	Gatorade Little League Baseball 1-D Tank Car "6315", 97 u	30	64
16160	AEC Tank Car "6515" with reactor fluid, 98		85
16160	MILW PS-2CD Covered Hopper 6-pack, LionScale, 16		360
16162	Hooker 1-D Tank Car "6315-1", 97		50
16163	Hooker 1-D Tank Car "6315-2", 97		50
16164	Hooker 1-D Tank Car "6315-3", 97		50
16165	Mobilfuel 3-D Tank Car "6415", 97 u		50
16170	RFMX PS-2CD Covered Hopper 6-pack, LionScale, 16		360
16171	Alaska 1-D Tank Car "6171", 98-99		33
16173	Harold the Helicopter Flatcar, 98	45	60
16175	NJ Transit Port Morris Ore Car "9125", 98		45
16176	NJ Transit Raritan Yard Ore Car "9126", 98 u		45
16177	NJ Transit Gladstone Yard Ore Car "9127", 98 u		45
16178	NJ Transit Bay Head Yard Ore Car "9128", 98 u	7	45
16179	NJ Transit Dover Yard Ore Car "9129", 98 u		45
16180	Tabasco 1-D Tank Car, 98	67	84
16181	Biohazard Tank Car with Lights, 98	50	90
16182	Gatorade 1-D Tank Car "6315", 98 u		64
16187	Linex 3-D Tank Car "6425", 99		30
16188	Kodak 1-D Tank Car "6515", 99	74	93
16199	UP 1-D Tank Car "6035", 99-00		25
16200	Rock Island Boxcar (027), 87-88	5	10
16201	Wabash Boxcar (027), 88-91	7	10
16203	Key America Boxcar (027), 87 u	45	65
16204	Hawthorne Boxcar (027), 87 u	50	85

			Exc	Mint
___	**16205**	Mopar Express Boxcar "1987" (027), 87-88 u	55	65
___	**16206**	D&RGW Boxcar (SSS), 89	37	42
___	**16207**	True Value Boxcar (027), 88 u	32	115
___	**16208**	PRR Auto Carrier, 3-tier, 89	24	41
___	**16209**	Disney Magic Boxcar (027), 88 u	90	110
___	**16211**	Hawthorne Boxcar (027), 88 u	45	65
___	**16213**	Shoprite Boxcar (027), 88 u	55	80
___	**16214**	D&RGW Auto Carrier, 90	22	37
___	**16215**	Conrail Auto Carrier, 90	27	38
___	**16217**	Burlington Northern Auto Carrier, 92	24	36
___	**16219**	True Value Boxcar (027), 89 u	55	75
___	**16220**	Ace Hardware Boxcar (027), 89 u	58	81
___	**16221**	Macy's Boxcar (027), 89 u	55	80
___	**16222**	Great Northern Boxcar (027), 90-91	8	15
___	**16223**	Budweiser Reefer, 89-92 u	73	93
___	**16224**	True Value "Lawn Chief" Boxcar (027), 90 u	45	60
___	**16225**	Budweiser Vat Car, 90-91 u	61	105
___	**16226**	Union Pacific Boxcar "6226" (027), 90-91 u	15	19
___	**16227**	Santa Fe Boxcar (027), 91	13	17
___	**16228**	Union Pacific Auto Carrier, 92	26	33
___	**16229**	Erie-Lackawanna Auto Carrier, 91 u	45	55
___	**16232**	Chessie System Boxcar, 92, 93 u, 94, 95 u	25	30
___	**16233**	MKT DD Boxcar, 92	20	29
___	**16234**	ACY Boxcar (SSS), 92	34	41
___	**16235**	Railway Express Agency Reefer, 92	19	23
___	**16236**	NYC Pacemaker Boxcar, 92 u	18	24
___	**16237**	Railway Express Agency Boxcar, 92 u	21	23
___	**16238**	NYNH&H Boxcar, 93-95	10	14
___	**16239**	Union Pacific Boxcar, 93-95	15	20
___	**16241**	Toys 'R' Us Boxcar, 92-93 u	35	45
___	**16242**	Grand Trunk Western Auto Carrier, 93	35	40
___	**16243**	Conrail Boxcar, 93	26	34
___	**16244**	Duluth, South Shore & Atlantic Boxcar, 93	20	24
___	**16245**	Contadina Boxcar, 93	16	20
___	**16247**	ACL Boxcar, 94	15	19
___	**16248**	Budweiser Boxcar, 93-94 u	52	70
___	**16249**	United Auto Workers Boxcar, 93 u		55
___	**16250**	Santa Fe Boxcar (027), 93 u, 94	8	10
___	**16251**	Columbus & Greenville Boxcar, 94	8	15
___	**16252**	U.S. Navy Boxcar "6106888", 94-95		30
___	**16253**	Santa Fe Auto Carrier, 94	32	38
___	**16255**	Wabash DD Boxcar, 95	20	26
___	**16256**	Ford DD Boxcar, 94 u	30	34
___	**16257**	Crayola Boxcar, 94 u, 95	17	23
___	**16258**	Lehigh Valley Boxcar, 95	17	22
___	**16259**	Chrysler Mopar Boxcar, 97 u	33	43
___	**16260**	Chrysler Mopar Auto Carrier, 96 u	59	69
___	**16261**	Union Pacific DD Boxcar, 95	26	29
___	**16263**	ATSF Boxcar, 96-99		25
___	**16264**	Red Wing Shoes Boxcar, 95	26	32
___	**16265**	Georgia Power "Atlanta '96" Boxcar, 95 u	213	241
___	**16266**	Crayola Boxcar, 95	17	23
___	**16267**	Sears Zenith Boxcar, 95-96 u		55

		Exc	Mint
16268	GM/AC Delco Boxcar, 95 u		51
16269	Lionel Lines Boxcar, 96		10
16272	Christmas Boxcar, 97		36
16273	Lionel Employee Christmas Boxcar, 97		55
16274	Marvin the Martian Boxcar, 97		60
16279	Dodge Motorsports Boxcar, 96 u	153	197
16280	Rawlings Little League Boxcar, 97	25	30
16281	MacGregor Little League Boxcar, 97	25	30
16282	Wisk Detergent Boxcar, 97	25	30
16284	Galveston Wharves Boxcar, 98		28
16285	Savannah State Docks Boxcar, 98		26
16291	Christmas Boxcar, 98		34
16292	Lionel Employee Christmas Boxcar, 98	309	369
16293	JCPenney Boxcar, 97		100
16294	Pedigree Boxcar, 97	148	168
16295	Kal Kan Boxcar, 97	159	180
16296	Whiskas Boxcar, 97	142	168
16297	Sheba Boxcar, 97	136	160
16298	Mobil Boxcar, 97		50
16300	Rock Island Flatcar with fences (027), 87-88	8	10
16301	Lionel Barrel Ramp Car, 87	14	19
16303	PRR Flatcar with trailers, 87	26	33
16304	RI Gondola with cable reels (027), 87-88	5	9
16305	Lehigh Valley Ore Car, 87	80	130
16306	Santa Fe Barrel Ramp Car, 88	13	18
16307	NKP Flatcar with trailers, 88	30	40
16308	Burlington Northern Flatcar with trailer, 88-89	20	25
16309	Wabash Gondola with canisters, 88-91	9	13
16310	Mopar Express Gondola with canisters, 87-88 u	35	39
16311	Mopar Express Flatcar with trailers, 87-88 u	117	162
16313	PRR Gondola with cable reels (027), 88 u, 89	5	10
16314	Wabash Flatcar with trailers, 89	26	30
16315	PRR Flatcar with fences (027), 88 u, 89	7	9
16317	PRR Barrel Ramp Car, 89	18	22
16318	LL Depressed Center Flatcar with cable reels, 89	22	26
16320	Great Northern Barrel Ramp Car, 90	13	19
16321/22	Sealand TTUX Flatcar Set with trailers, 90	65	73
16323	Lionel Lines Flatcar with trailers, 90	21	25
16324	PRR Depressed Center Flatcar with cable reels, 90	16	20
16325	Microracers Exhibition Ramp Car, 89 u	21	28
16326	Santa Fe Depressed Center Flatcar with cable reels, 91	16	21
16327	The Big Top Circus Gondola with canisters, 89 u	19	24
16328	NKP Gondola with cable reels, 90-91	17	23
16329	SP Flatcar with horses (027), 90-91	19	24
16330	MKT Flatcar with trailers, 91	25	30
16332	LL Depressed Center Flatcar with transformer, 91	28	33
16333	Frisco Bulkhead Flatcar with lumber, 91	17	22
16334	C&NW Flatcar Set (16337, 16338) with trailers, 91	55	60
16335	NYC Pacemaker Flatcar with trailer (SSS), 91	46	65
16336	UP Gondola "6336" with canisters, 90-91 u	17	21
16337	C&NW Flatcar w/trailer, 91	28	30
16338	C&NW Flatcar w/trailer, 91	28	30
16339	Mickey's World Tour Gondola with canisters (027), 91, 92 u	17	21

			Exc	Mint
___	**16341**	NYC Depressed Center Flatcar with transformer, 92	29	32
___	**16342**	CSX Gondola with coil covers, 92	18	23
___	**16343**	Burlington Gondola with coil covers, 92	20	23
___	**16345/46**	SP TTUX Flatcar Set with trailers, 92	55	65
___	**16347**	Ontario Northland Bulkhead Flatcar with pulp load, 92	22	26
___	**16348**	Erie Liquefied Petroleum Car, 92	23	25
___	**16349**	Allis Chalmers Condenser Car, 92	28	35
___	**16350**	CP Rail Bulkhead Flatcar with lumber, 91 u	20	29
___	**16351**	Flatcar with U.S. Navy submarine, 92	27	39
___	**16352**	U.S. Military Flatcar with cruise missile, 92	33	43
___	**16353**	B&M Gondola with coil covers, 91 u	33	39
___	**16355**	Burlington Gondola, 92, 93 u, 94-95	11	17
___	**16356**	MKT Depressed Center Flatcar with cable reels, 92	17	21
___	**16357**	L&N Flatcar with trailer, 92	24	31
___	**16358**	L&N Gondola with coil covers, 92	17	21
___	**16359**	Pacific Coast Gondola with coil covers (SSS), 92	33	38
___	**16360**	N&W Maxi-Stack Flatcar Set w/containers, 93	44	55
___	**16361**	N&W Maxi-Stack Flatcar w/containers, 93	22	28
___	**16362**	N&W Maxi-Stack Flatcar w/containers, 93	22	28
___	**16363**	Southern TTUX Flatcar Set w/trailers, 93	38	49
___	**16364**	Southern TTUX Flatcar w/trailer, 93	19	25
___	**16365**	Southern TTUX Flatcar w/trailer, 93	19	25
___	**16367**	Clinchfield Gondola with coil covers, 93	18	21
___	**16368**	MKT Liquid Oxygen Car, 93	21	22
___	**16369**	Amtrak Flatcar with wheel load, 92 u	19	28
___	**16370**	Amtrak Flatcar with rail load, 92 u	19	28
___	**16371**	BN I-Beam Flatcar with load, 92 u	23	30
___	**16372**	Southern I-Beam Flatcar with load, 92 u	24	34
___	**16373**	Erie-Lackawanna Flatcar with stakes, 93	19	23
___	**16374**	D&RGW Flatcar with trailer, 93	25	28
___	**16375**	NYC Bulkhead Flatcar, 93-95	21	25
___	**16376**	UP Flatcar with trailer, 93-95	31	37
___	**16378**	Toys 'R' Us Flatcar with trailer, 92-93 u	60	95
___	**16379**	NP Bulkhead Flatcar with pulp load, 93	16	23
___	**16380**	UP I-Beam Flatcar with load, 93	20	26
___	**16381**	CSX I-Beam Flatcar with load, 93	20	30
___	**16382**	Kansas City Southern Bulkhead Flatcar, 93	14	18
___	**16383**	Conrail Flatcar with trailer, 93	50	58
___	**16384**	Soo Line Gondola with cable reels, 93	14	19
___	**16385**	Soo Line Ore Car, 93	65	75
___	**16386**	SP Flatcar with lumber, 94	15	19
___	**16387**	KCS Gondola with coil covers, 94	13	16
___	**16388**	LV Gondola with canisters, 94	16	20
___	**16389**	PRR Flatcar with wheel load, 94	27	32
___	**16390**	Flatcar with water tank, 94	24	27
___	**16391**	Lionel Lines Gondola, 93 u		15
___	**16392**	Wabash Gondola with canisters (027), 93 u, 94	7	9
___	**16393**	Wisconsin Central Bulkhead Flatcar, 94	13	19
___	**16394**	Vermont Central Bulkhead Flatcar, 94	20	30
___	**16395**	CP Flatcar with rail load, 94	19	29
___	**16396**	Alaska Bulkhead Flatcar, 94	17	22
___	**16397**	Milwaukee Road I-Beam Flatcar with load, 94	30	34
___	**16398**	C&O Flatcar with trailer, 94	80	85

		Exc	Mint	
16399	Western Pacific I-Beam Flatcar with load, 94	31	35	___
16400	PRR Hopper (027), 88 u, 89	15	18	___
16402	Southern Quad Hopper with coal (SSS), 87	30	42	___
16406	CSX Quad Hopper with coal, 90	29	34	___
16407	B&M Covered Quad Hopper (SSS), 91	28	37	___
16408	UP Hopper "6408" (027), 90-91 u	17	21	___
16410	MKT Hopper (027), 92, 93 u	19	24	___
16411	L&N Quad Hopper with coal, 92	28	32	___
16412	C&NW Covered Quad Hopper, 94	16	21	___
16413	Clinchfield Quad Hopper with coal, 94	16	22	___
16414	CCC&StL Hopper (027), 94	16	23	___
16416	D&RGW Covered Quad Hopper, 95	16	20	___
16417	Wabash Quad Hopper with coal, 95	19	21	___
16418	C&NW Hopper with coal (027), 95	15	21	___
16419	Tennessee Central Hopper, 96		17	___
16420	WM Quad Hopper with coal (SSS), 95	30	34	___
16421	WM Quad Hopper with coal (SSS), 95	30	33	___
16422	WM Quad Hopper with coal (SSS), 95		33	___
16423	WM Quad Hopper with coal (SSS), 95		30	___
16424	WM Covered Quad Hopper (SSS), 95	34	39	___
16425	WM Covered Quad Hopper (SSS), 95	25	29	___
16426	WM Covered Quad Hopper (SSS), 95	24	27	___
16427	WM Covered Quad Hopper (SSS), 95	27	30	___
16429	WM Quad Hopper with coal, set of 2		70	___
16430	Georgia Power Quad Hopper "82947" with coal, 95 u		109	___
16431	Lionel Corporation 2-bay Hopper "6456-1", 96		30	___
16432	Lionel Corporation 2-bay Hopper "6456-2", 96		64	___
16433	Lionel Corporation 2-bay Hopper "6456-3", 96		18	___
16434	LV 2-bay Hopper "6456", "TLDX", 97		25	___
16435	Virginian 2-bay Hopper "6456-1", 97		30	___
16436	N&W 2-bay Hopper "6456-2", 97		33	___
16437	C&O 2-bay Hopper "6456-3", 97		33	___
16438	Frisco 4-bay Covered Hopper "87538", 98		34	___
16439	Southern 4-bay Covered Hopper "77836", 98		34	___
16440	Alaska 2-bay Hopper "7100", 98-99		35	___
16441	New York Central 4-bay Hopper, 99		26	___
16442	Bethlehem Gondola "6462" (SSS), 99		40	___
16443	GN 2-bay Hopper "172364", 99-00		20	___
16444	CNJ 2-bay Hopper "643", 00		20	___
16445	Frisco 2-bay Hopper "93108", 00		20	___
16446	Burlington 2-bay Hopper, 00		20	___
16447	PRR Tuscan 2-bay Hopper, 00 u		30	___
16448	PRR Gray 2-bay Hopper, 00 u		30	___
16449	PRR Black 2-bay Hopper, 00 u		30	___
16450	PRR Green 2-bay Hopper, 00 u		30	___
16451	Lionel Mines 2-bay Hopper, 00 u		50	___
16453	SP 2-bay Hopper "460604", 01		15	___
16454	Bethlehem Steel Hopper "41025", 01		37	___
16455	Pioneer Seed 2-bay Hopper, 00 u		50	___
16456	B&O 2-bay Hopper, 01		20	___
16459	LV 2-bay Hopper "51102", 01		23	___
16460	Reading 2-bay Hopper "79636", 02		25	___
16463	Rio Grande Icebreaker Tunnel Car "18936", 02		32	___

			Exc	Mint
___	**16464**	NYC Icebreaker Tunnel Car "X3200", 02		32
___	**16465**	WP 2-bay Hopper "100340", 03		19
___	**16466**	Pennsylvania Icebreaker Tunnel Car, 03		33
___	**16467**	Naughty and Nice Hopper 2-pack, 02		60
___	**16468**	ACL Wood-chip Hopper, 02		20
___	**16469**	B&O Hopper "435351", 02		22
___	**16470**	Naughty and Nice Ore Car 2-pack, 03		43
___	**16473**	Rock Island Ore Car "99122", 03		18
___	**16474**	Alaska Ore Car "16474", 04		21
___	**16475**	Santa Fe Hopper "16475", 04		18
___	**16480**	Lionelville Snow Transport Quad Hopper, 04		45
___	**16482**	Norfolk Southern Hopper, traditional, 05		27
___	**16487**	Alaska 2-bay Hopper, 05		35
___	**16489**	BNSF Ore Car, traditional, 05		15
___	**16490**	Sodor Mining Hopper, 05, 13		35
___	**16491**	CNJ Hopper "60714", 06		30
___	**16492**	C&NW Ore Car "114023", 06		30
___	**16493**	Christmas Ice Breaker Car, 06		55
___	**16500**	Rock Island Bobber Caboose, 87-88	9	13
___	**16501**	Lehigh Valley SP-type Caboose, 87	19	24
___	**16503**	NYC Transfer Caboose, 87	16	22
___	**16504**	Southern N5c Caboose (SSS), 87	17	30
___	**16505**	Wabash SP-type Caboose, 88-91	10	15
___	**16506**	Santa Fe Bay Window Caboose, 88	18	28
___	**16507**	Mopar Express SP-type Caboose, 87-88 u	42	54
___	**16508**	Lionel Lines SP-type Caboose "6508", 89 u	13	17
___	**16509**	D&RGW SP-type Caboose (SSS), 89	19	24
___	**16510**	New Haven Bay Window Caboose, 89	25	30
___	**16511**	PRR Bobber Caboose, 88 u, 89	9	13
___	**16513**	Union Pacific SP-type Caboose, 89	14	21
___	**16515**	Lionel Lines SP-type Caboose, RailScope, 89	20	23
___	**16516**	Lehigh Valley SP-type Caboose, 90	15	26
___	**16517**	Atlantic Coast Line Bay Window Caboose, 90	21	26
___	**16518**	Chessie System Bay Window Caboose, 90	41	50
___	**16519**	Rock Island Transfer Caboose, 90	13	17
___	**16520**	Welcome to the Show Circus SP-type Caboose, 89 u	13	21
___	**16521**	PRR SP-type Caboose, 90-91	8	11
___	**16522**	Chills & Thrills Circus N5c Caboose, 90-91	10	15
___	**16523**	Alaska SP-type Caboose, 91	24	31
___	**16524**	Anheuser-Busch SP-type Caboose, 89-92 u	36	47
___	**16525**	D&H Bay Window Caboose (SSS), 91	30	39
___	**16526**	Kansas City Southern SP-type Caboose, 91	17	21
___	**16528**	UP SP-type Caboose "6528", 90-91 u	17	21
___	**16529**	Santa Fe SP-type Caboose "16829", 91	9	13
___	**16530**	Mickey's World Tour SP-type Caboose "16830", 91, 92 u	13	17
___	**16531**	Texas & Pacific SP-type Caboose, 92	18	23
___	**16533**	C&NW Bay Window Caboose, 92	22	30
___	**16534**	Delaware & Hudson SP-type Caboose, 92	14	19
___	**16535**	Erie-Lackawanna Bay Window Caboose, 91 u	42	50
___	**16536**	Chessie System SP-type Caboose, 92, 93 u, 94, 95 u		23
___	**16537**	MKT SP-type Caboose, 92, 93 u	17	21
___	**16538**	L&N Bay Window Caboose "1041", 92 u	29	33
___	**16539**	WP Steelside Caboose "539," smoke, SSS (std O), 92	50	55

		Exc	Mint	
16541	Montana Rail Link Extended Vision Caboose "10131" with smoke, 93	50	73	___
16543	NYC SP-type Caboose, 93-95		20	___
16544	Union Pacific SP-type Caboose, 93-95	22	26	___
16546	Clinchfield SP-type Caboose, 93	22	26	___
16547	Happy Holidays SP-type Caboose, 93-95	46	55	___
16548	Conrail SP-type Caboose, 93	15	20	___
16549	Soo Line Work Caboose, 93	18	26	___
16550	U.S. Navy Searchlight Caboose, 94-95	16	21	___
16551	Budweiser SP-type Caboose, 93-94 u	30	33	___
16552	Frisco Searchlight Caboose, 94	23	26	___
16553	United Auto Workers SP-type Caboose, 93 u		40	___
16554	GT Extended Vision Caboose "79052," smoke, 94	40	47	___
16555	C&O SP-type Caboose, 94	22	26	___
16557	Ford SP-type Caboose, 94 u	19	24	___
16558	Crayola SP-type Caboose, 94 u, 95	17	21	___
16559	Seaboard Center Cupola Caboose "5658", 95	23	24	___
16560	Chrysler Mopar Caboose, 94 u	24	26	___
16561	UP Center Cupola Caboose "25766", 95	27	31	___
16562	Reading Center Cupola Caboose, 95	25	29	___
16563	Lionel Lines SP-type Caboose, 95	22	26	___
16564	Western Maryland Center Cupola Caboose (SSS), 95	30	34	___
16565	Milwaukee Road Bay Window Caboose, 95	45	70	___
16566	U.S. Army SP-type Caboose "907", 95		28	___
16568	ATSF SP-type Caboose, 96-99		23	___
16571	Georgia Power SP-type Caboose "52789", 95 u		68	___
16575	Sears Zenith SP-type Caboose, 95		38	___
16577	U.S. Coast Guard Work Caboose, 96		26	___
16578	Lionel Lines SP-type Caboose, 95 u		20	___
16579	GM/AC Delco, SP-type Caboose, 95		35	___
16580	SP-type Caboose, 96-99		11	___
16581	UP Illuminated Caboose, 96		30	___
16586	SP Illuminated Caboose "6357", 97		42	___
16589	Zenith SP-type Caboose, 97	20	45	___
16590	Dodge Motorsports SP-type Caboose "6950", 96		58	___
16591	Little League Baseball SP-type Caboose "6397", 97		45	___
16593	Lionel Belt Line Caboose "6257", 98		32	___
16594	Caboose "6357", 98		29	___
16600	Illinois Central Coal Dump Car, 88	14	23	___
16601	Canadian National Searchlight Car, 88	19	24	___
16602	Erie-Lackawanna Coal Dump Car, 87	16	26	___
16603	Detroit Zoo Giraffe Car (027), 87	40	49	___
16604	NYC Log Dump Car, 87	15	27	___
16605	Bronx Zoo Giraffe Car (027), 88	39	44	___
16606	Southern Searchlight Car, 87	13	21	___
16607	Southern Coal Dump Car "16707" (SSS), 87	18	26	___
16608	Lehigh Valley Searchlight Car, 87	11	30	___
16609	Lehigh Valley Derrick Car, 87	22	30	___
16610	Track Maintenance Car, 87-88	15	25	___
16611	Santa Fe Log Dump Car, 88	15	23	___
16612	Soo Line Log Dump Car, 89	14	24	___
16613	MKT Coal Dump Car, 89	17	26	___
16614	Reading Cop and Hobo Car (027), 89	24	25	___

			Exc	Mint
___	**16615**	Lionel Lines Extension Searchlight Car, 89	20	28
___	**16616**	D&RGW Searchlight Car (SSS), 89	22	30
___	**16617**	C&NW Boxcar with ETD, 89	23	34
___	**16618**	Santa Fe Track Maintenance Car, 89	11	19
___	**16619**	Wabash Coal Dump Car, 90	14	25
___	**16620**	C&O Track Maintenance Car, 90-91	16	19
___	**16621**	Alaska Log Dump Car, 90	24	31
___	**16622**	CSX Boxcar with ETD, 90-91	20	28
___	**16623**	MKT DD Boxcar with ETD, 91	16	23
___	**16624**	NH Cop and Hobo Car (027), 90-91	23	31
___	**16625**	NYC Extension Searchlight Car, 90	22	30
___	**16626**	CSX Searchlight Car, 90	18	26
___	**16627**	CSX Log Dump Car, 90	19	23
___	**16628**	Cop and Hobo Circus Gondola, 90-91	36	43
___	**16629**	Operating Circus Elephant Car (027), 90-91	38	50
___	**16630**	SP Operating Cowboy Car (027), 90-91	22	26
___	**16631**	RI Boxcar, steam RailSounds, 90	110	130
___	**16632**	BN Boxcar, diesel RailSounds, 90	82	98
___	**16634**	WM Coal Dump Car, 91	26	31
___	**16636**	D&RGW Log Dump Car, 91	19	25
___	**16637**	WP Extension Searchlight Car, 91	27	30
___	**16638**	Operating Circus Animal Car (027), 91	50	55
___	**16639**	B&O Boxcar, steam RailSounds, 91	100	120
___	**16640**	Rutland Boxcar, diesel RailSounds, 91	100	120
___	**16641**	Toys 'R' Us Giraffe Car (027), 90-91 u	48	68
___	**16642**	Mickey's World Tour Goofy Car (027), 91, 92 u	33	41
___	**16644**	Amtrak Crane Car, 91, 92 u	36	42
___	**16645**	Amtrak Searchlight Caboose, 91	27	30
___	**16649**	Railway Express Agency Boxcar, steam RailSounds, 92	110	140
___	**16650**	NYC Pacemaker Boxcar, diesel RailSounds, 92	100	135
___	**16651**	Operating Circus Clown Car (027), 92	24	30
___	**16652**	Radar Car, 92	25	29
___	**16653**	Western Pacific Crane Car (SSS), 92	44	60
___	**16655**	Steam Tender "1993," RailSounds, 93	115	140
___	**16656**	Burlington Log Dump Car, 92 u	18	25
___	**16657**	Lehigh Valley Coal Dump Car, 92 u	22	29
___	**16658**	Erie-Lackawanna Crane Car, 93	47	65
___	**16659**	Union Pacific Searchlight Car, 93-95	15	18
___	**16660**	Fire Car with ladders, 93-94	28	33
___	**16661**	Flatcar with boat, 93	20	22
___	**16662**	Bugs Bunny and Yosemite Sam Outlaw Car (027), 93-94	25	34
___	**16663**	Missouri Pacific Searchlight Car, 93	16	19
___	**16664**	L&N Coal Dump Car, 93	22	25
___	**16665**	Maine Central Log Dump Car, 93	23	27
___	**16666**	Toxic Waste Car, 93-94	25	32
___	**16667**	Conrail Searchlight Car, 93	27	30
___	**16668**	Ontario Northland Log Dump Car, 93	20	24
___	**16669**	Soo Line Searchlight Car, 93	17	21
___	**16670**	TV Car, 93-94	12	22
___	**16673**	Lionel Lines Tender, whistle, 94-97	33	42
___	**16674**	Pinkerton Animated Gondola, 94	28	32
___	**16675**	Great Northern Log Dump Car, 94	21	25
___	**16676**	Burlington Coal Dump Car, 94	23	28

No.	Description	Exc	Mint	
16677	NATO Flatcar with Royal Navy submarine, 94	34	44	___
16678	Rock Island Searchlight Car, 94	12	23	___
16679	U.S. Mail Operating Boxcar, 94	45	50	___
16680	Cherry Picker Car, 94	25	28	___
16681	Aquarium Car, 95	35	44	___
16682	Lionelville Farms Operating Stock Car (027), 94	23	27	___
16683	Los Angeles Zoo Elephant Car (027), 94	22	26	___
16684	U.S. Navy Crane Car, 94-95	35	40	___
16685	Erie Extension Searchlight Car, 95	30	34	___
16686	Mickey Mouse Animated Boxcar, 95	32	38	___
16687	U.S. Mail Operating Boxcar, 94	29	37	___
16688	Fire Car with ladders, 94	35	43	___
16689	Toxic Waste Car, 94	29	32	___
16690	Bugs Bunny and Yosemite Sam Outlaw Car (027), 94	30	34	___
16701	Southern Tool Car (SSS), 87	43	55	___
16702	Amtrak Bunk Car, 91, 92 u	25	27	___
16703	NYC Tool Car, 92	24	31	___
16704	TV Car, 94	27	29	___
16705	Chesapeake & Ohio Cop and Hobo Car, 95	28	34	___
16706	Animal Transport Service Giraffe Car, 95	27	30	___
16708	C&NW Track Maintenance Car, 95	24	31	___
16709	New York Central Derrick Car, 95	22	28	___
16710	U.S. Army Operating Missile Car, 95	40	46	___
16711	Pennsylvania Searchlight Car, 95	27	31	___
16712	Pinkerton Animated Gondola, 95	34	39	___
16715	ATSF Log Dump Car, 96-99		24	___
16717	Jersey Central Crane Car, 96		41	___
16718	USMC Missile Launching Flatcar, 96	26	31	___
16719	Exploding Boxcar, 96		38	___
16720	Lionel Lines Searchlight Car "3650", 96-97		50	___
16724	Mickey and Friends Submarine Car, 96		39	___
16725	Rhino Transport Car, 97		31	___
16726	U.S. Army Fire Ladder Car, 96		43	___
16734	U.S. Coast Guard Searchlight Car, 96		30	___
16735	U.S. Coast Guard Flatcar with radar, 96	28	35	___
16736	U.S. Coast Guard Derrick Car, 96		34	___
16737	Road Runner and Wile E. Coyote Gondola "3444", 96		66	___
16738	Pepe LePew Boxcar "3370", 96		40	___
16739	Foghorn Leghorn Animated Poultry Car "3434", 96		44	___
16740	Lionel Corporation Mail Car "3428", 96		37	___
16741	Union Pacific Illuminated Bunk Car, 97		25	___
16742	Trout Ranch Aquarium Car "3435", 96		32	___
16744	Port of Lionel City Searchlight Car, 97		30	___
16745	Port of Lionel City Flatcar with radar, 97		30	___
16746	Port of Lionel City Derrick Car, 97		30	___
16747	Breyer Animated Horse Car "6473", 97		34	___
16748	U.S. Forest Service Log-Dump Car "3361", 97		30	___
16749	Midget Mines Ore-Dump Car "3479", 97		36	___
16750	Lionel City Aquarium Car "3436", 97		32	___
16751	AIREX Sports Channel TV Car "3545", 97		25	___
16752	Marvin the Martian Missile Launching Flatcar "6655", 97	149	167	___
16754	Porky Pig and Instant Martians Flatcar "6805", 97	100	147	___
16755	Daffy Duck Animated Balloon Car "3470", 97	149	187	___

			Exc	Mint
___	**16760**	Pluto and Cats Animated Gondola "3444", 97		55
___	**16765**	Bureau of Land Management Log Car "3351", 98		30
___	**16766**	Bureau of Land Management Ore Car "3479", 98		31
___	**16767**	New York Central Ice Docks Ice Car "6352", 98		47
___	**16776**	Holiday Boxcar, RailSounds, 98		68
___	**16777**	Animated Cola Car and Platform, 98		100
___	**16782**	Bethlehem Ore Dump Car "3479", 99	24	95
___	**16783**	Westside Lumber Log Dump Car "3351", 99		32
___	**16784**	Pratt's Hollow Seed Dump Car "3479", 99		36
___	**16785**	Happy Holidays Music Reefer "5700", 99	23	100
___	**16789**	Easter Operating Boxcar, 99		39
___	**16790**	UP Stock Car "3356," Crowsounds, 99		90
___	**16791**	New York City Lights Boxcar, 99		44
___	**16792**	Constellation Boxcar "9600", 99		37
___	**16793**	Animated Glow-in-the-Dark Alien Boxcar, 99		44
___	**16794**	Wicked Witch Halloween Boxcar, 99		46
___	**16795**	Elf Chasing Rudolph Gondola "6462", 99		55
___	**16796**	Snowman Loading Ice Car "6352", 99		55
___	**16805**	Budweiser Malt Nutrine Reefer "3285", 91-92 u	82	109
___	**16806**	Toys 'R' Us Boxcar, 92 u	21	26
___	**16807**	H.J. Heinz Reefer "301", 93	23	27
___	**16808**	Toys 'R' Us Boxcar, 93 u	28	30
___	**16817**	Ambassador 1-D Tank Car, 00 u		184
___	**16818**	Engineer Award Tank Car, 00 u		715
___	**16819**	JLC Award Tank Car, 00 u		760
___	**16820**	Ambassador Boxcar, 00 u	322	523
___	**16822**	CSX Water Tower, 08		23
___	**16824**	036 Command Control Switch, left hand (FasTrack), 09-14		110
___	**16825**	036 Command Control Switch, right hand (FasTrack), 09-14		110
___	**16826**	072 Command Control Switch, left hand (FasTrack), 09-14		120
___	**16827**	072 Command Control Switch, right hand (FasTrack), 09-14		120
___	**16828**	060 Command Control Switch, left hand (FasTrack), 09-14		120
___	**16829**	060 Command Control Switch, right hand (FasTrack), 09-14		120
___	**16830**	048 Command Control Switch, left hand (FasTrack), 09-14		120
___	**16831**	048 Command Control Switch, right hand (FasTrack), 09-14		120
___	**16832**	072 Command Control Wye Switch (FasTrack), 09-14		115
___	**16834**	FasTrack 048 Half-Curved Track, 09-24		7
___	**16835**	FasTrack 048 Quarter-Curved Track, 09-24		5
___	**16836**	Christmas Girder Bridge, 09		21
___	**16837**	Christmas Operating Billboard, 09		45
___	**16841**	Halloween Gateman, 09		80
___	**16842**	Big Moe Crane, 10		70
___	**16843**	City and Western Diorama, 10-11		15
___	**16845**	Bookstore, 09-10		60
___	**16846**	Burning Hobo Depot, 09		90
___	**16847**	Legacy Hotel, 10-11		70
___	**16848**	Creature Comforts Pet Store, sound, 09-10		80
___	**16849**	Rotary Dumper with coal conveyor, CC, 10		600
___	**16850**	Operating Wind Turbine, 3-pack, 09-11		225
___	**16851**	Sunoco Cylindrical Oil Tank, gray, 10-11		100
___	**16852**	Sunoco Cylindrical Oil Tank, yellow, 10-11		90
___	**16853**	Polar Express Diorama, 09-11, 13		18
___	**16854**	MTA LIRR Blinking Billboard, 09		30

		Exc	Mint	
16855	MTA LIRR Illuminated Station Platform, 09		37	___
16856	MTA LIRR Passenger Station, 09		60	___
16857	Thomas & Friends Diorama, 10-16, 20		18	___
16859	Grand Central Terminal, 09		1500	___
16861	50,000-gallon Water Tank, 09-11		150	___
16863	Santa's Christmas Wish Station, 09-11		125	___
16868	Straight O Gauge Tunnel, 09-17		55	___
16871	Winter Wonderland Diorama, 09-11		15	___
16872	Illuminated Christmas Station Platform, 09		35	___
16873	Bathtub Gondola Coal Load 3-pack, 10-19		20	___
16874	Coaling Station, 10-11		80	___
16880	Freight Platform, 10-12		30	___
16881	Barrel Shed, 10-11		30	___
16882	12" Covered Bridge, 10-18		60	___
16883	Neil's Guitar Shop, 10-11		60	___
16889	Coal Tipple Pack, 11-20		15	___
16891	Tank Car Accident, 10-11		130	___
16896	Flagpole with lights, 10-16		28	___
16897	75th Anniversary Gateman, 10		80	___
16903	CP Bulkhead Flatcar with pulp load (SSS), 94	22	25	___
16904	NYC Pacemaker Flatcar Set with trailers, 94	55	60	___
16907	Flatcar with farm tractors, 94	27	33	___
16908	U.S. Navy Flatcar "04039" with submarine, 94-95	39	46	___
16909	U.S. Navy Gondola "16556" with canisters, 94-95	16	22	___
16910	Missouri Pacific Flatcar with trailer, 94	22	27	___
16911	B&M Flatcar with trailer, 94	28	34	___
16912	CN Maxi-Stack Flatcar Set with containers, 94	70	75	___
16915	Lionel Lines Gondola (O27), 93-94 u	7	10	___
16916	Ford Flatcar with trailer, 94 u	38	45	___
16917	Crayola Gondola with crayons, 94 u, 95	8	9	___
16919	Chrysler Mopar Gondola with coil covers, 94-96	33	36	___
16922	Chesapeake & Ohio Flatcar with trailer, 95	25	31	___
16923	Intermodal Service Flatcar with wheel chocks, 95	15	22	___
16924	Lionel Corporation Flatcar "6424" with trailer, 96		24	___
16925	New York Central Flatcar with trailer, 95	65	85	___
16926	Frisco Flatcar with trailers, 95	24	31	___
16927	New York Central Flatcar with gondola, 95	17	22	___
16928	Soo Line Flatcar with dump bin (O27), 95	12	15	___
16929	BC Rail Gondola with cable reels, 95	21	25	___
16930	Santa Fe Flatcar with wheel load, 95	20	25	___
16932	Erie Flatcar with rail load, 95	17	22	___
16933	Lionel Lines Flatcar with autos, 95	23	25	___
16934	Pennsylvania Flatcar with Ertl road grader, 95	28	39	___
16935	UP Depressed Center Flatcar with Ertl bulldozer, 95	22	35	___
16936	Sealand Maxi-Stack Flatcar Set with containers, 95	61	85	___
16939	U.S. Navy Flatcar "04040" with boat, 95	25	30	___
16940	ATSF Flatcar with trailer, 96-99		40	___
16941	ATSF Flatcar with autos, 96-99		25	___
16943	Jersey Central Gondola, 96		18	___
16944	Georgia Power Flatcar "31438" with transformer, 95 u		50	___
16945	Georgia Power Flatcar "31950" with cable reels, 95 u		53	___
16946	C&O F9 Well Car "3840", 96		31	___
16951	Southern I-Beam Flatcar "9823" with load, 97		25	___

			Exc	Mint
___	**16952**	U.S. Navy Flatcar with Ertl helicopter, 96		25
___	**16953**	NYC Flatcar with Red Wing Shoes trailer, 95 u	39	45
___	**16954**	NYC Flatcar "6424" with Ertl scraper, 96		30
___	**16955**	ATSF Flatcar with Ertl Challenger, 96		30
___	**16956**	Zenith Flatcar with trailer, 95 u	50	141
___	**16957**	Depressed Center Flatcar "6461" with Ertl Case tractor, 96		29
___	**16958**	Flatcar with Ertl New Holland loader, 96		26
___	**16960**	U.S. Coast Guard Flatcar with boat, 96		40
___	**16961**	GM/AC Delco Flatcar with trailer, 95		73
___	**16963**	Lionel Corporation Flatcar "6411", 96-97		34
___	**16964**	Lionel Corporation Gondola "6462", 97		22
___	**16965**	Scout Flatcar "6424" with stakes, 96-97		20
___	**16967**	Depressed Center Flatcar "6461" with transformer, 96		21
___	**16968**	Depressed Center Flatcar "6461" with Ertl Helicopter, 96	10	40
___	**16969**	Flatcar "6411" with Beechcraft Bonanza, 96		33
___	**16970**	LA County Flatcar "6424" with motorized powerboat, 96	11	20
___	**16971**	Port of Lionel City Flatcar with boat, 97		35
___	**16972**	P&LE Gondola "6462", 97		22
___	**16975**	Well Car Doublestack Set, 97		75
___	**16978**	MILW Flatcar "6424" with P&H shovel, 97		43
___	**16980**	Speedy Gonzales Missile Flatcar "6823", 97	30	56
___	**16982**	BC Rail Bulkhead Flatcar "9823" with lumber, 97		28
___	**16983**	PRR F9 Well Car "6983" with cable reels, 97		39
___	**16986**	Sears Zenith Bulkhead Flatcar, 96 u		45
___	**16987**	Musco Lighting Bulkhead Flatcar, 97 u		35
___	**16997**	Lionel Lines Recovery Crane Car, 99		50
___	**17002**	Conrail 2-bay ACF Hopper (std 0), 87	42	47
___	**17003**	Du Pont 2-bay ACF Hopper (std 0), 90	39	45
___	**17004**	MKT 2-bay ACF Hopper (std 0), 91	23	27
___	**17005**	Cargill 2-bay ACF Hopper (std 0), 92	26	37
___	**17006**	Soo Line 2-bay ACF Hopper (std 0, SSS), 93	31	36
___	**17007**	GN 2-bay ACF Hopper "173872" (std 0), 94	26	31
___	**17008**	D&RGW 2-bay ACF Hopper "10009" (std 0), 95		31
___	**17009**	New York Central 2-bay ACF Hopper, 96		35
___	**17010**	Govt. of Canada ACF 2-bay Covered Hopper "7000", 98	23	35
___	**17010**	NP PS-1 Boxcar 6-pack, LionScale, 17		360
___	**17011**	NP ACF 2-bay Covered Hopper "75052", 98		44
___	**17012**	Govt. of Canada ACF 2-bay Covered Hopper "7001", 98	15	36
___	**17013**	NYC Graffiti 2-bay Covered Hopper "7000", 99		55
___	**17014**	Graffiti 2-bay Covered Hopper "7000" (std 0), 99		45
___	**17015**	Corning 2-bay Hopper "90409" (std 0), 01		40
___	**17016**	C&NW 2-bay Hopper "96644" (std 0), 01		46
___	**17017**	Chessie System 2-bay Hopper "605527" (std 0), 02		32
___	**17018**	Nickel Plate Road Offset Hopper "33074", 02		43
___	**17019**	Santa Fe Offset Hopper "78299", 02		43
___	**17020**	Frisco Offset Hopper "92092", 02		43
___	**17020**	UP PS-1 Boxcar 6-pack, LionScale, 17		360
___	**17021**	NYC Offset Hopper "867999", 02		43
___	**17022**	Burlington 2-bay ACF Hopper "183925" (std 0), 03		30
___	**17023**	BNSF 2-bay Hopper "409038" (std 0), 04		30
___	**17024**	Reading Offset Hopper "81089" (std 0), 03-04		43
___	**17025**	C&O Offset Hopper "300027" (std 0), 03-04		43
___	**17026**	D&H Offset Hopper "7215" (std 0), 03-04		41

		Exc	Mint	
17027	IC Offset Hopper "92142" (std O), 03-04		49	___
17028	GE PS-2 2-bay Covered Hopper "326" (std O), 03-04		35	___
17029	CNJ PS-2 2-bay Covered Hopper "803" (std O), 03-04		35	___
17030	MILW PS-2 2-bay Covered Hopper "99708" (std O), 03-04	18	43	___
17030	Reading PS-1 Boxcar 6-pack, LionScale, 17		360	___
17031	SP PS-2 2-bay Covered Hopper "401306" (std O), 03-04		38	___
17038	Clinchfield PS-2 Covered Hopper, 05		70	___
17039	Boston & Maine PS-2 2-bay Covered Hopper, 05		55	___
17040	Norfolk & Western PS-2 2-bay Covered Hopper, 05		55	___
17040	NYC PS-1 Boxcar 6-pack, LionScale, 17		360	___
17041	Great Northern Offset Hopper, 05		60	___
17042	Green Bay & Western Offset Hopper, 05		60	___
17043	Baltimore & Ohio Offset Hopper, 05		60	___
17044	DT&I PS-2 Covered Hopper (std O), 05-06	15	38	___
17050	NYC 14-panel Hopper 6-pack, LionScale, 17		330	___
17060	D&RGW 14-panel Hopper 6-pack, LionScale, 17		330	___
17063	Santa Fe PS-2 2-bay Covered Hopper "82297" (std O), 06		55	___
17064	MKT PS-2 2-bay Covered Hopper "1311" (std O), 06		55	___
17065	Boraxo PS-2 2-bay Covered Hopper "31062" (std O), 06		55	___
17066	PRR PS-2 2-bay Covered Hopper "256177" (std O), 06		55	___
17067	Rock Island Offset Hopper "89500" with gravel (std O), 06		65	___
17068	CNJ Offset Hopper "61261" (std O), 06		65	___
17069	Maine Central Offset Hopper "3785" (std O), 06		65	___
17070	P&LE Offset Hopper "4990" (std O), 06		65	___
17070	Conrail 14-panel Hopper 6-pack, LionScale, 17		330	___
17075	MKT PS-2 2-bay Covered Hopper "1314" (std O), 06		55	___
17080	EL 14-panel Hopper 6-pack, LionScale, 17		330	___
17083	C&O Offset Hopper "47386" (std O), 05		40	___
17090	Trailer Train 50' Flatcar 6-pack, 17		330	___
17100	Chessie System 3-bay ACF Hopper	49	85	___
17100	BN 50' Flatcar 6-pack, 17		330	___
17101	Chessie System 3-bay ACF Hopper (std O), 88	37	45	___
17102	Chessie System 3-bay ACF Hopper (std O), 88	35	41	___
17103	Chessie System 3-bay ACF Hopper (std O), 88	31	34	___
17104	Chessie System 3-bay ACF Hopper (std O), 88	38	46	___
17105	Chessie System 3-bay ACF Hopper (std O), 88	39	46	___
17107	Sinclair 3-bay ACF Hopper (std O), 89	40	48	___
17108	Santa Fe 3-bay ACF Hopper (std O), 90	42	48	___
17109	N&W 3-bay ACF Hopper (std O), 91	24	31	___
17110	UP Hopper with coal (std O), 91	24	30	___
17110	AT&SF 50' Flatcar 6-pack, 17		330	___
17111	Reading Hopper with coal (std O), 91	23	28	___
17112	Erie-Lack. 3-bay ACF Hopper (std O), 92	24	34	___
17113	LV Hopper with coal (std O), 92-93	25	32	___
17114	Peabody Hopper with coal (std O), 92-93	26	30	___
17118	Archer Daniels Midland 3-bay ACF Hopper "60029" (std O), 93	28	35	___
17120	CSX Hopper "295110" with coal (std O), 94	28	30	___
17120	PRR 50' Flatcar 6-pack, 17		330	___
17121	ICG Hopper "72867" with coal (std O), 94	26	33	___
17122	RI 3-bay ACF Hopper "800200" (std O), 94	32	39	___
17123	Cargill Covered Grain Hopper "844304" (std O), 95	26	37	___
17124	Archer Daniels Midland 3-bay ACF Hopper "50224" (std O), 95	24	30	___
17127	Delaware & Hudson 3-bay Hopper, 96	11	34	___

			Exc	Mint
____	**17128**	Chesapeake & Ohio 3-bay Hopper, 96		30
____	**17129**	WM 3-bay Hopper "9300" with coal (std O), 97		34
____	**17130**	ACFX ACF 4-bay Covered Hopper 6-pack, LionScale, 17		360
____	**17132**	PRR 3-bay ACF Hopper "260815", 98		40
____	**17133**	BNSF ACF 3-bay Covered Hopper "403698", 98	16	39
____	**17134**	BNSF 3-bay Covered Hopper "403698" (std O), 01		38
____	**17135**	BNSF ACF 3-bay Covered Hopper with ETD, 98	16	39
____	**17137**	Cargill 3-bay Covered Hopper "1219" (std O), 99		45
____	**17138**	Farmers Elevator 3-bay Covered Hopper (std O), 99		45
____	**17139**	Grain Train 3-bay Hopper "BLMR 1025", 99-00	29	52
____	**17140**	Virginian 3-bay Hopper 6-pack, "5260-5265", 99		230
____	**17140**	GN ACF 4-bay Covered Hopper 6-pack, LionScale, 17		360
____	**17147**	C&O 3-bay Hopper 6-pack, "156330-156335", 99		230
____	**17150**	AT&SF ACF 4-bay Covered Hopper 6-pack, LionScale, 17		360
____	**17154**	Alberta Cylindrical Hopper "628373" (std O), 01		40
____	**17155**	Shell Cylindrical Hopper "3527" (std O), 01		40
____	**17156**	ACF Pressureaide 3-bay Hopper "59267" (std O), 01		27
____	**17157**	Wonder Bread "56670" 3-bay Hopper (std O), 01		45
____	**17158**	Conrail Coal Hopper "487739" (std O), 01		42
____	**17159**	N&W Coal Hopper "1776" (std O), 01		45
____	**17160**	C&NW (UP) B145ACF 4-bay Covered Hopper 6-pack, LionScale, 17		360
____	**17163**	C&O 3-bay Hopper (std O), 01		30
____	**17170**	General Mills 3-bay Covered Hopper (std O), 00 u		60
____	**17170**	PFE 57' Mechanical Reefer, 6-pack, LionScale, 17		390
____	**17171**	Lionel Lion Cylindrical Hopper (std O), 01		45
____	**17172**	CP Rail Cylindrical Hopper "385206" (std O), 02		37
____	**17173**	Govt. of Canada Cylindrical Hopper "111031" (std O), 02		33
____	**17174**	GN 3-bay Hopper "171250" (std O), 02		29
____	**17175**	IC PS-2CD 4427 Covered Hopper "57031" (std O), 02		40
____	**17176**	Cargill PS-2CD 4427 Covered Hopper "2514" (std O), 02		46
____	**17177**	PS-2CD 4427 Covered Hopper "2500" (std O), 02		40
____	**17178**	Santa Fe PS-2CD 4427 Covered Hopper "304774" (std O), 02		40
____	**17179**	Indianapolis Power & Light Coal Hopper "10074" (std O), 02		40
____	**17180**	Rock Island Coal Hopper "700665" (std O), 02		40
____	**17180**	SPFE 57' Mechanical Reefer 6-pack, LionScale, 17		390
____	**17181**	NYC 4-bay ACF Centerflow Hopper "892138" (std O), 03		45
____	**17182**	Sigco Hybrids 4-bay ACF Centerflow Hopper "1100" (std O), 03		46
____	**17183**	C&O Hopper "156341" (std O), 01		30
____	**17184**	Virginian Hopper "5271" (std O), 01		30
____	**17185**	LLCX Bathtub Gondola "877900" (std O), 01		36
____	**17186**	Cannonaide 4-bay ACF Centerflow Hopper "96169" (std O), 03		40
____	**17187**	Rio Grande 4-bay ACF Centerflow Hopper "15521" (std O), 03		40
____	**17188**	Govt. of Canada 3-bay Cylindrical Hopper (std O), 03		48
____	**17189**	Saskatchewan Grain 3-bay Cylindrical Hopper (std O), 03		48
____	**17190**	Soo/CP 3-bay ACF Hopper "119303" (std O), 03		37
____	**17190**	UPFE 57' Mechanical Reefer 6-pack, LionScale, 17		390
____	**17191**	BN PS-2CD 4427 Hopper "450669" (std O), 03-04		45
____	**17192**	Lehigh Valley PS-2CD 4427 Hopper "51118" (std O), 03-04		40
____	**17193**	Chessie System/WM PS-2CD 4427 Hopper "4673" (std O), 03-04		30
____	**17194**	MKT PS-2CD 4427 Hopper "1122" (std O), 03-04		40

		Exc	Mint	
17195	L&N 3-bay Hopper "240850" (std O), 04		40	___
17196	Firestone 4-bay Hopper "53240" (std O), 04		40	___
17197	Diamond Chemicals 4-bay Hopper "53286" (std O), 04		40	___
17198	Hercules 4-bay Hopper "50503" (std O), 04		40	___
17199	Conrail 4-bay Hopper "888367" (std O), 04		46	___
17200	Canadian Pacific Boxcar (std O), 89	26	32	___
17200	BNFE 57' Mechanical Reefer 6-pack, LionScale, 17		390	___
17201	Conrail Boxcar (std O), 87	33	38	___
17202	Santa Fe Boxcar (std O), diesel RailSounds, 90	80	85	___
17203	Cotton Belt DD Boxcar (std O), 91	34	38	___
17204	Missouri Pacific DD Boxcar (std O), 91	27	30	___
17207	C&IM DD Boxcar (std O), 92	36	42	___
17208	Union Pacific DD Boxcar (std O), 92	32	40	___
17209	B&O DD Boxcar "296000" (std O), 93	37	43	___
17210	Chicago & Illinois Midland Boxcar "16021" (std O), 92 u	30	39	___
17210	BN 100-Ton, 4-Bay Hopper 6-pack, 17		330	___
17211	Chicago & Illinois Midland Boxcar "16022" (std O), 92 u	30	39	___
17212	Chicago & Illinois Midland Boxcar "16023" (std O), 92 u	24	31	___
17213	Susquehanna Boxcar "501" (std O), 93	28	31	___
17214	Railbox Boxcar (std O), diesel RailSounds, 93	75	85	___
17216	PRR DD Boxcar "60155" (std O), 94	34	38	___
17217	New Haven State of Maine Boxcar "45003" (std O), 95	28	35	___
17218	BAR State of Maine Boxcar "2184" (std O), 95	23	36	___
17219	Tazmanian Devil 40th Birthday Boxcar (std O), 95	40	50	___
17220	Pennsylvania Boxcar (std O), 96		23	___
17220	CSX 100-Ton, 4-Bay Hopper 6-pack, 17		330	___
17221	NYC Boxcar (std O), 96	19	33	___
17222	Western Pacific Boxcar (std O), 96	28	34	___
17223	Milwaukee Road DD Boxcar (std O), 96		34	___
17224	Central of Georgia Boxcar "9464-197" (std O), 97	15	29	___
17225	Penn Central Boxcar "9464-297" (std O), 97	13	26	___
17226	Milwaukee Road Boxcar "9464-397" (std O), 97	13	27	___
17227	UP DD Boxcar "9200" (std O), 97		35	___
17230	NS 100-Ton, 4-Bay Hopper 6-pack, 17		330	___
17231	Wisconsin Central DD Boxcar "9200" with auto frames, 98		40	___
17232	SP/UP Merger DD Boxcar "9200", 98		33	___
17233	Western Pacific Boxcar "9464-198", 98		27	___
17234	Port Huron & Detroit Boxcar "9464-298", 98		33	___
17235	Boston & Maine Boxcar "9464-398", 98		41	___
17239	ATSF Texas Chief Boxcar "9464-1", 97		50	___
17240	ATSF Super Chief Boxcar "9464-2", 97		50	___
17240	UP 100-Ton, 4-Bay Hopper 6-pack, 17		330	___
17241	ATSF El Capitan Boxcar "9464-3", 97		50	___
17242	ATSF Grand Canyon Boxcar "9464-4", 97		60	___
17243	NP Boxcar "8722", 98		48	___
17244	Santa Fe Chief Boxcar, 98		37	___
17245	C&O Boxcar with Chessie kitten, 98		44	___
17246	NYC Pacemaker Rolling Stock 4-pack, 98		200	___
17247	NYC 9464 Boxcar "174940", 98		135	___
17248	NYC 9464 Boxcar "174945", 98	50	115	___
17249	NYC 9464 Boxcar "174949", 98		60	___
17250	UP Boxcar "507406" (std O), 99		45	___
17250	AT&SF Stockcar 6-pack, 17		360	___

			Exc	Mint
___	**17251**	BNSF Boxcar "103277", 99		41
___	**17252**	NS Boxcar "564824" (std O), 99		41
___	**17253**	CSX Boxcar "141756" (std O), 99		35
___	**17254**	UP Boxcar "551967" (std O), 99		42
___	**17255**	Chevy DD Boxcar "9200" (std O), 99		38
___	**17257**	Atlantic Coast Line Boxcar "28809" (std O), 99		36
___	**17258**	D&H 9464 Boxcar "29055" std O, 99		41
___	**17259**	MKT 9464 Boxcar "1422" (std O), 99		34
___	**17260**	CP Rail 9464 Boxcar "286138" (std O), silver, 00		45
___	**17260**	PRR Stockcar 6-pack, 17		360
___	**17261**	CP Rail 9464 Boxcar "85154", green, 00	20	45
___	**17262**	CP Rail 9464 Boxcar "56776," red (std O), 00		48
___	**17263**	NYC Boxcar "45725" (std O), 00		46
___	**17264**	C&O Boxcar "6054" (std O), 00		44
___	**17265**	U.S. Army Boxcar (std O), 00		35
___	**17266**	Monon Boxcar "911" (std O), 00		45
___	**17268**	C&O 9464 Boxcar "12700" (std O), 01		44
___	**17269**	Western Maryland 9464 Boxcar "29140" (std O), 01		44
___	**17270**	B&O Time-Saver 9464 Boxcar "467439" (std O), 01		42
___	**17270**	Nickel Plate Road Stockcar 6-pack, 17		360
___	**17271**	The Rock Boxcar "300324" (std O), 01		37
___	**17272**	Railbox Boxcar "15150" (std O), 01		27
___	**17273**	DT&I DD Boxcar "26852" (std O), 01		44
___	**17274**	Soo Line DD Boxcar "177587" (std O), 01		42
___	**17275**	NYC PS-1 Boxcar "175008" (std O), 02		43
___	**17276**	Cotton Belt PS-1 Boxcar "75000" (std O), 02		44
___	**17277**	Rio Grande PS-1 Boxcar "69676" (std O), 02		40
___	**17278**	WP PS-1 Boxcar "1953" (std O), 02		44
___	**17279**	Ontario Northland Boxcar "7428" (std O), 02		40
___	**17280**	Santa Fe Boxcar "600194" with auto frames (std O), 02		45
___	**17280**	UP Stockcar 6-pack, 17		360
___	**17281**	PRR DD Boxcar "83158" (std O), 04		42
___	**17282**	UP DD Boxcar "160300" (std O), 04		42
___	**17283**	GM&O DD Boxcar "9077" (std O), 04		41
___	**17284**	Erie DD Boxcar "66000" (std O), 04		41
___	**17285**	CSX Big Blue Boxcar "151296" (std O), 03		36
___	**17287**	BAR Boxcar "5976" (std O), 03		35
___	**17288**	NYC PS-1 Boxcar "175012" (std O), 03-04		38
___	**17289**	GN PS-1 Boxcar "18485" (std O), 03	29	43
___	**17290**	Seaboard PS-1 Boxcar "24452" (std O), 03-04		42
___	**17290**	Portland Terminal Wood-chip Hopper 6-pack, 17		360
___	**17291**	RI PS-1 Boxcar "21110" (std O), 03-04		42
___	**17292**	B&M PS-1 Boxcar "76182" (std O), 04		34
___	**17293**	IC PS-1 Boxcar "400666" (std O), 04		40
___	**17294**	TP&W PS-1 Boxcar "5036" (std O), 04	18	47
___	**17295**	Santa Fe PS-1 Boxcar "276749" (std O), 04		40
___	**17296**	C&O PS-1 Boxcar (std O), 04		40
___	**17297**	UP PS-1 Boxcar, 03		100
___	**17298**	Southern PS-1 Boxcar w/box load (std O), 05-06	18	42
___	**17300**	Canadian Pacific Reefer (std O), 89	28	33
___	**17300**	Chessie System Wood-chip Hopper 6-pack, 17		360
___	**17301**	Conrail Reefer (std O), 87	35	42
___	**17302**	Santa Fe Reefer with ETD (std O), 90	27	41

		Exc	Mint	
17303	C&O Reefer "7890" (std O), 93	23	30	___
17304	Wabash Reefer "26269" (std O), 94	29	37	___
17305	Pacific Fruit Express Reefer "459400" (std O), 94	27	40	___
17306	Pacific Fruit Express Reefer "459401" (std O), 94	19	27	___
17307	Tropicana Reefer "300" (std O), 95	44	65	___
17308	Tropicana Reefer "301" (std O), 95	22	35	___
17309	Tropicana Reefer "302" (std O), 95	21	29	___
17310	Tropicana Reefer "303" (std O), 95	20	27	___
17310	GM&O Wood-chip Hopper 6-pack, 17		360	___
17311	REA Reefer (std O), 96	28	30	___
17314	PFE Reefer "9800-198", 98		42	___
17315	PFE Reefer "9800-298", 98		39	___
17316	NP Reefer "98583", 98		50	___
17317	PRR Reefer FGE "91904", 98		36	___
17318	UP Reefer "170650" (std O), 99		47	___
17319	PFE Reefer 6-pack (std O), 01	240	300	___
17320	WM Wood-chip Hopper 6-pack, 17		360	___
17331	Hood's General American Milk Car "802" (std O), 02	33	88	___
17332	Pfaudler General American Milk Car "501" (std O), 02	33	70	___
17334	REA General American Milk Car "1741" (std O), 02	21	77	___
17335	New Haven General American Milk Car "102" (std O), 02	25	69	___
17336	PFE Steel-sided Reefer "17760" (std O), 03		45	___
17337	CN Steel-sided Reefer "209712" (std O), 03		38	___
17338	Merchants Dispatch Transit Steel-sided Reefer "12322" (std O), 03		39	___
17339	Burlington Steel-sided Reefer "74825" (std O), 03		45	___
17340	White Bros. General American Milk Car "891" (std O), 03		44	___
17341	Dairymen's League General American Milk Car "779" (std O), 03		43	___
17342	Miller Beer Steel-sided Reefer American Eagle (std O), 03 u	40	63	___
17343	Miller Beer Steel-sided Reefer Lady and Moon (std O), 03 u	40	64	___
17349	NYC General American Milk Car "6581" (std O), 03 u		42	___
17350	Hood's General American Milk Car "503" (std O), 03 u		45	___
17351	Santa Fe Steel-sided Reefer "3526" (std O), 04		43	___
17352	PFE Steel-sided Reefer "20043" (std O), 04		41	___
17353	Needham Packing Steel-sided Reefer "60507" (std O), 04		44	___
17354	Swift Steel-sided Reefer "15392" (std O), 04		42	___
17355	Hood's Steel-sided Reefer "550" (std O), 04	15	40	___
17356	Nestle Nesquik Steel-sided Reefer (std O), 04		44	___
17357	Borden's Steel-sided Reefer "522" (std O), 04		47	___
17358	Fairfield Farms Steel-sided Reefer (std O), 04		44	___
17360	Hood's General American Milk Car "810" (std O), 03	25	53	___
17361	Hood's General American Milk Car "811" (std O), 03		43	___
17362	Pfaudler General American Milk Car "502" (std O), 03		47	___
17363	Pfaudler General American Milk Car "503" (std O), 03		40	___
17364	REA General American Milk Car "1742" (std O), 03		38	___
17365	REA General American Milk Car "1743" (std O), 03		44	___
17366	NH General American Milk Car "103" (std O), 03	25	50	___
17367	NH General American Milk Car "104" (std O), 03		47	___
17368	White Brothers General American Milk Car "892" (std O), 03		43	___
17369	White Brothers General American Milk Car "893" (std O), 03		47	___
17370	Dairymen's League General American Milk Car "780" (std O), 03		47	___
17371	Dairymen's League Milk Car "781" (std O), 03		47	___

			Exc	Mint
___	**17372**	NYC General American Milk Car "6582" (std 0), 03		47
___	**17373**	NYC General American Milk Car "6583" (std 0), 03		40
___	**17374**	Hood's General American Milk Car "504" (std 0), 03	28	54
___	**17375**	Hood's General American Milk Car "505" (std 0), 03	25	54
___	**17377**	Railway Express General American Milk Car "302" (std 0), 05	69	163
___	**17378**	Supplee General American Milk Car (std 0), 05		63
___	**17379**	NP Steel-sided Reefer "91353" (std 0), 05	33	60
___	**17380**	PFE Silver Steel-sided Reefer "45698" (std 0), 05		60
___	**17381**	North Western Steel-sided Reefer "751" (std 0), 05		40
___	**17397**	PFE Steel-sided Reefer "47767" (std 0), 05		45
___	**17398**	A&P General American Milk Car "737" (std 0), 06		65
___	**17399**	Bowman Dairy General American Milk Car "117" (std 0), 06		65
___	**17400**	CP Rail Gondola with coal (std 0), 89	30	34
___	**17401**	Conrail Gondola with coal (std 0), 87	24	26
___	**17402**	Santa Fe Gondola with coal (std 0), 90	19	25
___	**17403**	Chessie System Gondola "371629" with coil covers (std 0), 93	18	25
___	**17404**	ICG Gondola "245998" with coil covers (std 0), 93	26	32
___	**17405**	Reading Gondola "24876" with coil covers (std 0), 94	27	31
___	**17406**	PRR Gondola "385405" with coil covers (std 0), 95	37	42
___	**17407**	NKP Gondola with scrap load, 96		24
___	**17408**	Cotton Belt Gondola "9820" with scrap load (std 0), 97		32
___	**17410**	UP Gondola "903004" with scrap load (std 0), 99		30
___	**17412**	Gondola, blue, online store, 98		20
___	**17413**	Service Center Gondola with parts load (SSS), 00		24
___	**17414**	Nickel Plate PS-5 Gondola "44801" (std 0), 01-02		40
___	**17415**	Frisco PS-5 Gondola "61878" (std 0), 01-02		35
___	**17416**	D&H Gondola "14011" with scrap load (std 0), 01		33
___	**17417**	BN Rotary Bathtub Gondola 3-pack, 01		140
___	**17421**	CSX Rotary Bathtub Gondola 3-pack, 01		135
___	**17425**	Western Maryland PS-5 Gondola "354903" (std 0), 01-02		36
___	**17426**	Maine Central PS-5 Gondola "1116" (std 0), 01-02		40
___	**17427**	CSX Rotary Bathtub Gondola Add-on Unit (std 0), 02		47
___	**17428**	BN Rotary Bathtub Gondola Add-on Unit (std 0), 02		42
___	**17429**	Conrail Rotary Bathtub Gondola 3-pack (std 0), 02-03		115
___	**17433**	BNSF Rotary Bathtub Gondola 3-pack (std 0), 02-03		145
___	**17439**	UP PS-5 Gondola "229606" (std 0), 03		35
___	**17440**	Algoma Central PS-5 Gondola "801" (std 0), 03		32
___	**17441**	Conrail Rotary Bathtub Gondola "507673" (std 0), 03		39
___	**17442**	BNSF Rotary Bathtub Gondola "668330" (std 0), 03		46
___	**17443**	NS Rotary Bathtub Gondola 3-pack (std 0), 03		90
___	**17447**	UP Rotary Bathtub Gondola 3-pack (std 0), 03		100
___	**17457**	GN PS-5 Gondola "72839" (std 0), 03		35
___	**17458**	Reading PS-5 Gondola "33267" (std 0), 03		35
___	**17459**	CP Rail PS-5 Gondola "338966" (std 0), 04		35
___	**17460**	NYC PS-5 Gondola "749592" (std 0), 04		40
___	**17461**	Pennsylvania PS-5 Gondola "374256" (std 0), 04		36
___	**17462**	Santa Fe PS-5 Gondola "167340" (std 0), 04		35
___	**17463**	NS Bathtub Gondola "10303" (std 0), 04		40
___	**17464**	UP Bathtub Gondola "28100" (std 0), 04		35
___	**17465**	CP Rail Bathtub Gondola 3-pack (std 0), 04		105
___	**17469**	B&O/Chessie System PS-5 Drop-end Gondola (std 0), 05-06	15	38
___	**17470**	CP Rail Bathtub Gondola, 05		50

		Exc	Mint	
17471	Burlington PS-5 Gondola with covers (std O), 05		44	___
17472	New Haven PS-5 Gondola with covers (std O), 05		53	___
17473	NYC PS-5 Gondola "502351" (std O), 06-07		65	___
17474	D&H PS-5 Gondola "13816" (std O), 06-07		65	___
17475	Koppers PS-5 Gondola "213" (std O), 06-07		65	___
17477	L&N PS-5 Gondola "170012" (std O), 06-07		46	___
17478	N&W PS-5 Gondola "275005" with containers (std O), 08		70	___
17479	LV PS-5 Gondola "33455" with containers (std O), 08		70	___
17480	RI PS-5 Gondola with coke containers (std O), 08-09		70	___
17488	UP Bathtub Gondola 3-pack (std O), 09		190	___
17500	CP Flatcar with logs (std O), 89	22	37	___
17501	Conrail Flatcar with stakes (std O), 87	37	45	___
17502	Santa Fe Flatcar with trailer (std O), 90	70	75	___
17503	NS Flatcar with trailer (std O), 92	55	65	___
17504	NS Flatcar with trailer (std O), 92	55	65	___
17505	NS Flatcar with trailer (std O), 92	50	55	___
17506	NS Flatcar with trailer (std O), 92	46	55	___
17507	NS Flatcar with trailer (std O), 92	50	55	___
17510	NP Flatcar "61200" with logs (std O), 94	28	35	___
17511	WM Flatcar with logs, set of 3 (std O), 95	60	145	___
17512	WM Flatcar with logs (std O), 95	35	41	___
17513	WM Flatcar with logs (std O), 95	43	50	___
17514	WM Flatcar with logs (std O), 95	39	45	___
17515	Norfolk Southern Flatcar with tractors (std O), 95	24	42	___
17516	T&P Flatcar "9823" with 2 Beechcraft Bonanzas (std O), 97		50	___
17517	WP Flatcar "9823" with Ertl Caterpillar frontloader (std O), 97		39	___
17518	PRR Flatcar "9823" with 2 Corgi Mack trucks (std O), 97	32	53	___
17522	Flatcar with Plymouth Prowler, 98		41	___
17522	Lake Superior & Ishpeming PS-1 Boxcar, 98u		45	___
17524	Lake Superior & Ishpeming PS-1 Boxcar, 98u		45	___
17527	Flatcar with 2 Dodge Vipers, 98		38	___
17529	ATSF Flatcar "90010" with Ford milk truck, 99		55	___
17533	MTTX Ford Flatcar with auto frames, 99		38	___
17534	Diamond T Flatcar with Mack trucks "9823", 99		55	___
17536	Route 66 Flatcar "9823-3" with 2 luxury coupes, 99		37	___
17537	Route 66 Flatcar "9823-4" with 2 touring coupes, 99		32	___
17538	NYC Flatcar with Ford tow truck, 99		43	___
17539	Flatcar "9823" with 2 Corvettes (std O), 99		70	___
17540	Flatcar "9823" with 2 Corvettes (std O), 99		70	___
17546	LL Recovery Flatcar "6424" with rail load, 99		50	___
17547	Lionel Lines Recovery Flatcar "6429" with machinery, 99		50	___
17548	Route 66 Flatcar "9823-6" with 2 luxury coupes, 99		42	___
17549	Route 66 Flatcar "9823-5" with station wagon and trailer, 99		42	___
17550	BN Center Beam Flatcar "6216" with lumber (std O), 99		39	___
17551	NYC Flatcar with NYC pickups "499", 99		49	___
17553	Trailer Train Flatcar "98102" with combine (std O), 99		125	___
17554	GN Flatcar "61042" with logs, 00		32	___
17555	Ford Mustang Flatcar with 2 cars (std O), 01		NRS	___
17556	Ford Mustang Flatcar with 2 cars (std O), 01		NRS	___
17557	Route 66 Flatcar "9823-7" with black sedans, 99-00		39	___
17558	Route 66 Flatcar "9823-8" with brown sedans, 99		39	___
17559	Route 66 Flatcar "9823-9" with 2 wagons (std O), 01		40	___
17560	Route 66 Flatcar "9823-10" with 2 sedans (std O), 01		40	___

			Exc	Mint
___	**17563**	Santa Fe Flatcar "90011" with pickup trucks (std 0), 01		49
___	**17564**	West Side Lumber Shay Log Car 3-pack #2 (std 0), 01		95
___	**17568**	PRR Flatcar "470333" with pickup trucks (std 0), 02		50
___	**17571**	UP Flatcar "909231" with pickup trucks (std 0), 03		50
___	**17572**	Pioneer Seed Flatcar with pedal cars, 02 u		220
___	**17573**	WM PS-4 Flatcar "2631" (std 0), 03		35
___	**17574**	Santa Fe PS-4 Flatcar "90081" (std 0), 03		35
___	**17575**	NYC PS-4 Flatcar "506098" (std 0), 03		40
___	**17576**	Ontario Northland PS-4 Flatcar "2020" (std 0), 03		35
___	**17577**	B&O PS-4 Flatcar "8651" (std 0), 04		35
___	**17578**	B&M PS-4 Flatcar "34007" (std 0), 04		35
___	**17579**	Milwaukee Road PS-4 Flatcar "64073" (std 0), 04		35
___	**17580**	UP PS-4 Flatcar "54603" (std 0), 04		35
___	**17581**	GN Flatcar "X4168" with pickup trucks (std 0), 04		42
___	**17582**	PRR PS-4 Flatcar "469617" with trailers (std 0), 05		110
___	**17583**	GN PS-4 Flatcar with trailers, 05	43	90
___	**17584**	SP PS-4 Flatcar with trailers, 05		80
___	**17585**	C&O PS-4 Flatcar "81000" with trailers (std 0), 05		80
___	**17586**	BN Husky Stack Car "63322" (std 0), 05		80
___	**17587**	SP Husky Stack Car "513915" (std 0), 05		80
___	**17588**	CSX Husky Stack Car "620350" (std 0), 05		80
___	**17589**	TTX Trailer Train Husky Stack Car "456249" (std 0), 05		65
___	**17590**	Penn Central PS-4 Flatcar w/stakes (std 0), 05-06	15	38
___	**17600**	NYC Wood-sided Caboose (std 0), 87 u	35	45
___	**17601**	Southern Wood-sided Caboose (std 0), 88	35	44
___	**17602**	Conrail Wood-sided Caboose (std 0), 87	65	75
___	**17603**	RI Wood-sided Caboose (std 0), 88	19	34
___	**17604**	Lackawanna Wood-sided Caboose (std 0), 88	42	53
___	**17605**	Reading Wood-sided Caboose (std 0), 89	34	37
___	**17606**	NYC Steel-sided Caboose, smoke (std 0), 90	49	65
___	**17607**	Reading Steel-sided Caboose, smoke (std 0), 90	55	65
___	**17608**	C&O Steel-sided Caboose, smoke (std 0), 91	46	55
___	**17610**	Wabash Steel-sided Caboose, smoke (std 0), 91	39	55
___	**17611**	NYC Wood-sided Caboose "6003" (std 0), 90 u	40	55
___	**17612**	NKP Steel-sided Caboose, smoke (FF 6), 92	60	65
___	**17613**	Southern Steel-sided Caboose "7613", smoke (std 0), 92	60	65
___	**17615**	NP Wood-sided Caboose, smoke (std 0), 92	65	70
___	**17617**	D&RGW Steel-sided Caboose (std 0), 95	43	63
___	**17618**	Frisco Wood-sided Caboose (std 0), 95	65	75
___	**17620**	NP Wood-sided Caboose "1746", 98		70
___	**17623**	Farmrail Extended Vision Caboose, 99		74
___	**17624**	Conrail Extended Vision Caboose "6900", 99		43
___	**17625**	Burlington Northern Steel-sided Caboose "7606", 99		65
___	**17626**	Service Center Extended Vision Caboose (SSS), 00		29
___	**17627**	C&O Extended Vision Caboose, 01		65
___	**17628**	BNSF Extended Vision Caboose, 01		65
___	**17629**	Santa Fe Extended Vision Caboose, 01		80
___	**17630**	UP Extended Vision Caboose, 01	25	85
___	**17631**	Virginian Bay Window Caboose, 01	0	90
___	**17632**	CSX Bay Window Caboose, 01		75
___	**17633**	NYC Bay Window Caboose, 01	25	90
___	**17634**	Delaware & Hudson Bay Window Caboose, 01		75
___	**17635**	100th Anniversary Die-cast Gold Caboose, 00	195	597

		Exc	Mint	
17636	NYC Die-cast Caboose "18096", 00-01		100	___
17637	NYC "Quicker via Peoria" Die-cast Caboose, 00		135	___
17638	RI Extended Vision Caboose "17011" (std O), 02		83	___
17639	Chessie Extended Vision Caboose "3322" (std O), 02		55	___
17640	CP Extended Vision Caboose "434604" (std O), 02		57	___
17641	Soo Line Extended Vision Caboose "2" (std O), 02		55	___
17642	Conrail Bay Window Caboose "21023" (std O), 02		65	___
17643	NKP Bay Window Caboose "480" (std O), 02		60	___
17644	Erie Bay Window Caboose "C307", (std O), 02		55	___
17645	N&W Bay Window Caboose "C-6", (std O), 02		55	___
17646	UP Bay Window Caboose "24555", (std O), 02		65	___
17647	B&O Caboose "C-2820" (std O), 03-04		65	___
17648	Chessie System Caboose "C-2800" (std O), 03-04		75	___
17649	Lionel Lines Caboose "7649" (std O), 03-04		65	___
17650	Rio Grande Extended Vision Caboose "01500" (std O), 03		65	___
17651	BN Extended Vision Caboose "10531" (std O), 03-05		80	___
17652	NYC Bay Window Caboose "20200" (std O), 03		75	___
17653	SP Bay Window Caboose "1337" (std O), 03		65	___
17654	Alaska Extended Vision Caboose "989" (std O), 03		75	___
17655	WP Bay Window Caboose "448" (std O), 03-04		75	___
17657	Norman Rockwell Holiday Caboose, 03		30	___
17658	Burlington Extended Vision Caboose "13611" (std O), 04		70	___
17659	CN Extended Vision Caboose "79646" (std O), 04	33	85	___
17660	Seaboard Extended Vision Caboose "5700" (std O), 04		65	___
17661	C&NW Bay Window Caboose "10871" (std O), 04		65	___
17662	PC Bay Window Caboose "21001" (std O), 04		65	___
17663	Southern Bay Window Caboose "X546" (std O), 04		65	___
17664	B&O Caboose "C-2824" (std O), 03-04		65	___
17665	Chessie System Caboose "C-2802" (std O), 03-04		75	___
17669	NYC Bay Window Caboose, smoke, 05		85	___
17670	CP Rail Bay Window Caboose, smoke, 05		85	___
17671	BN Extended Vision Caboose, 05		85	___
17672	GN Extended Vision Caboose "X-106" (std O), 05		85	___
17673	Santa Fe Extended Vision Caboose, 05		85	___
17674	Reading Extended Vision Caboose "94119" (std O), 05		75	___
17675	Rio Grande Extended Vision Caboose "01507" (std O), 06		90	___
17676	NYC Bay Window Caboose "20300", 07		60	___
17677	Erie-Lack. Bay Window Caboose "C359" (std O), 06		90	___
17678	B&O I-12 Caboose "C2421" (std O), 06		90	___
17679	Long Island Bay Window Caboose "C-62" (std O), 06		90	___
17682	Reading Northeastern Caboose "92841" (std O), 06-07		85	___
17683	Chessie System Northeastern Caboose "1893" (std O), 07		85	___
17684	Conrail Northeastern Caboose "18873" (std O), 07		85	___
17685	Jersey Central Northeastern Caboose "91533" (std O), 07		85	___
17687	B&O/Chessie System Smoking Caboose (std O), 05-06	45	92	___
17690	UP CA-4 Caboose "3826" (std O), 06	21	90	___
17691	UP CA-4 Caboose "25103" (std O), 06		90	___
17692	LL CA-4 Caboose "7629" (std O), 06		90	___
17693	Chessie Extended Vision Caboose "3285" (std O), 06		90	___
17694	NS Extended Vision Caboose "555582" (std O), 06		90	___
17695	Alaska I-12 Caboose "1001" (std O), 06		90	___
17696	CP Bay Window Caboose "437266" (std O), 06		90	___
17697	CN Extended Vision Caboose "78128" (std O), 06		90	___

			Exc	Mint
___	**17699**	UP Ca-4 Caboose "25193" (std O), 07		90
___	**17700**	UP ACF 40-ton Stock Car "47456" (std O), 01-02		85
___	**17701**	Rio Grande ACF 40-ton Stock Car "39269" (std O), 01-02		60
___	**17702**	CP ACF 40-ton Stock Car "277083" (std O), 01-02		75
___	**17703**	NYC ACF 40-ton Stock Car "23334" (std O), 01-02		85
___	**17703**	Crayola 2-bay Hopper, LionScale, 17-18		70
___	**17704**	B&O ACF 40-ton Stock Car "110234" (std O), 02		40
___	**17705**	CB&Q ACF 40-ton Stock Car "52886" (std O), 02		40
___	**17707**	PRR ARF 40-ton Stock Car "128994" (std O), 03		35
___	**17708**	CP Rail ACF 40-ton Stock Car "277313" (std O), 03	12	47
___	**17709**	UP Stock Car "48154" (std O), 04		45
___	**17710**	Great Northern Stock Car "56385" (std O), 04		40
___	**17711**	C&O ACF 40-ton Stock Car "95237" (std O), 06		60
___	**17712**	N&W ACF 40-ton Stock Car "33000" (std O), 06		60
___	**17713**	MKT ACF 40-ton Stock Car "47150" (std O), 06		60
___	**17714**	CN 40-ton Stock Car "172755" (std O), 06		60
___	**17715**	MP 40-ton Stock Car "52428" (std O), 06		60
___	**17716**	CGW 40-ton Stock Car "838", 08		60
___	**17717**	UP 40-ton Stock Car "48217", 08		60
___	**17718**	NS Heritage 3-bay Hopper 2-pack (std O), 12		160
___	**17719**	C&BQ ACF Stock Car "52925" (std O), 09	30	70
___	**17720**	UP ACF Stock Car (std O), 10		70
___	**17721**	Postwar Scale Stock Car 2-pack, 10-11		140
___	**17724**	CN Scale Steel-sided Reefer "210552," (std O), 11		80
___	**17725**	NP Scale Steel-sided Reefer "98528," (std O), 11		80
___	**17726**	IC Scale Steel-sided Reefer "16644," (std O), 11		80
___	**17727**	Mopac/Wabash Scale Steel-sided Reefer "30790," (std O), 11		80
___	**17729**	C&O Scale PS-1 Boxcar "2992" (std O), 12		70
___	**17730**	Seaboard Scale Round-roof Boxcar "19293" (std O), 11		70
___	**17731**	Pere Marquette Scale Boxcar "81805" (std O), 12		70
___	**17732**	L&N Scale PS-1 Boxcar "4798" (std O) , 12		70
___	**17733**	PRR Scale Round-roof Boxcar "78948" (std O), 11		70
___	**17734**	PRR Scale Round-roof Boxcar "76644" (std O), 11		70
___	**17735**	PRR Round-roof DD Boxcar "77851" (std O), 12		70
___	**17736**	PRR Round-roof DD Boxcar "60156" (std O), 12		70
___	**17737**	N&W Scale Round-roof Boxcar "46494" (std O), 11		70
___	**17738**	NP Round-roof DD Boxcar "39300" (std O), 12		70
___	**17739**	DT&I Round-roof DD Boxcar "12250" (std O), 12		70
___	**17740**	Alaska Scale Round-roof Boxcar "27781" (std O), 11		70
___	**17741**	Santa Fe Scale Slogan Reefer 5-car Set (std O), 12		320
___	**17747**	Santa Fe Scale Boxcar "39009" (std O), 12		70
___	**17748**	Grave's Mortuary Supply Scale PS-1 Boxcar (std O), 12-13		70
___	**17749**	Erie Scale PS-1 Boxcar "90300" (std O), 12		70
___	**17750**	NYC Round-roof DD Boxcar "77147" (std O), 12		70
___	**17751**	NKP Scale PS-1 Boxcar "6605" (std O), 12		70
___	**17752**	Polar Round-roof Boxcar "1202" (std O), 12-13, 16-17		70
___	**17753**	LV Scale PS-1 Boxcar "65124" (std O), 12		70
___	**17754**	EL DD Boxcar "65000" (std O), 12		75
___	**17755**	D&H DD Boxcar "25025" (std O), 12		75
___	**17756**	CP Rail DD Boxcar "42630" (std O), 12		75
___	**17757**	Milwaukee Road DD Boxcar "13441" (std O), 12		75
___	**17758**	ATSF Map and Slogan Reefer 3-pack, 12		190
___	**17762**	BN 57' Mechanical Reefer "9618" (std O), 12		85

Item	Description	Exc	Mint	
17763	NYC 57' Mechanical Reefer "6762" (std O), 12		85	___
17764	ATSF 57' Mechanical Reefer "56244" (std O), 12		85	___
17765	Virginian Round-roof DD Boxcar "3131" (std O), 13-14		80	___
17766	NH Round-roof Boxcar "39303" (std O), 13		70	___
17767	SP Round-roof DD Boxcar "166052" (std O), 13-14		80	___
17768	Grave's Mortuary Supply Round-roof Boxcar (std O), 13		70	___
17769	D&RGW PS-1 Boxcar "60046" (std O), 13		70	___
17770	MILW PS-1 Boxcar "8777" (std O), 13		70	___
17771	CNJ PS-1 Boxcar "23522" (std O), 13-14		80	___
17772	Central of Georgia PS-1 Boxcar (std O), 13		70	___
17773	D&M Round-roof Boxcar "3148" (std O), 13-14		80	___
17774	D&M PS-1 Boxcar "2833" (std O), 13		70	___
17775	NS Heritage 3-bay Hopper 3-pack (std O), 13-15		240	___
17779	NS Heritage 3-bay Hopper 3-pack (std O), 13-15		240	___
17783	NS Heritage 3-bay Hopper 3-pack (std O), 13-15		240	___
17787	NS Heritage 3-bay Hopper 3-pack (std O), 13		240	___
17791	NS Heritage 3-bay Hopper 3-pack (std O), 13		240	___
17795	NS Heritage 3-bay Hopper 3-pack (std O), 13		240	___
17800	Ontario Northland Ore Car "6126", 00		30	___
17801	CN Ore Car "345165", 00		37	___
17802	CP Ore Car "377249", 00		28	___
17803	DMIR Ore Car "31456", 00		30	___
17804	UP Ore Car "8023", 01		29	___
17805	CP Rail Ore Car "377238", 01		29	___
17806	UP Ore Car "27250", 03		30	___
17807	BN Ore Car "95887", 02		28	___
17900	Santa Fe Unibody Tank Car (std O), 90	37	46	___
17901	Chevron Unibody Tank Car (std O), 90	26	32	___
17902	NJ Zinc Unibody Tank Car (std O), 91	26	34	___
17903	Conoco Unibody Tank Car (std O), 91	24	30	___
17904	Texaco Unibody Tank Car (std O), 92	39	48	___
17905	Archer Daniels Midland Unibody Tank Car (std O), 92	24	33	___
17906	SCM Unibody Tank Car "78286" (std O), 93	47	55	___
17908	Marathon Oil Unibody Tank Car (std O), 95	55	60	___
17909	Hooker Chemicals Unibody Tank Car (std O), 96	25	55	___
17910	Sunoco Unibody Tank Car "7900", 97		37	___
17913	J.M. Huber Tank Car, 98		29	___
17914	Englehard Tank Car, 98		36	___
17915	Gulf Unibody Tank Car "8438", 00		43	___
17916	Burlington Unibody Tank Car "130000", 00	24	38	___
17918	Southern Unibody Tank Car, 01		32	___
17919	Koppers Unibody Tank Car, 01		39	___
17924	Safety Kleen Unibody Tank Car "77603" (std O), 02	20	55	___
17925	Beefmaster Unibody Tank Car "120021" (std O), 02		38	___
17926	Cargill Unibody 1-D Tank Car "5836" (std O), 03		40	___
17927	Union Starch Unibody 1-D Tank Car "59137" (std O), 03		35	___
17928	Merck 1-D Tank Car "25421" (std O), 03		35	___
17929	Wyandotte Chemicals 1-D Tank Car "1325" (std O), 03		34	___
17930	CSX Unibody Tank Car "993369" (std O), 04		35	___
17931	UP Unibody Tank Car "6" (std O), 04		35	___
17932	CIBRO TankTrain Intermediate Car "26263" (std O), 04		35	___
17933	GATX TankTrain Intermediate Car 3-pack (std O), 04		100	___
17946	Candy Cane Unibody Tank Car (std O), 04		60	___

			Exc	Mint
___	**17947**	Domino Sugar Unibody Tank Car (std O), 04		50
___	**17948**	Philadelphia Quartz 1-D Tank Car "806" (std O), 06		55
___	**17949**	Skelly Oil 1-D Tank Car "2293" (std O), 06		55
___	**17950**	ADM Unibody Tank Car "19020" (std O), 06		60
___	**17951**	Cerestar Unibody Tank Car "190177" (std O), 06		60
___	**17959**	Dow 1-D Tank Car "310101" (std O), 07		55
___	**17960**	Amaizo 1-D Tank Car "15440" (std O), 07		55
___	**17962**	Domino Sugar 1-D Tank Car "3008" (std O), 07		60
___	**17966**	Procor 1-D Tank Car "82607" (std O), 07		60
___	**17971**	Simonin's 1-D Tank Car "9569" (std O), 07		60
___	**17972**	Union Starch 1-D Tank Car "724" (std O), 08		60
___	**17973**	UP 1-D Tank Car "907838" (std O), 08		60
___	**17975**	Cargill Foods Unibody Tank Car 3-pack (std O), 08-09		195
___	**17976**	Huber Unibody Tank Car 3-pack (std O), 08-09		195
___	**17983**	GATX TankTrain Intermediate Car 3-pack, 08		195
___	**18000**	PRR 0-6-0 Locomotive "8977", 89, 91	150	405
___	**18001**	Rock Island 4-8-4 Locomotive "5100", 87	208	315
___	**18002**	NYC 4-6-4 Locomotive "785", 87 u	268	421
___	**18003**	DL&W 4-8-4 Locomotive "1501", 88	162	278
___	**18004**	Reading 4-6-2 Locomotive "8004", 89	159	205
___	**18005**	NYC 4-6-4 Locomotive "5340," display case, 90	387	724
___	**18006**	Reading 4-8-4 Locomotive "2100", 89 u	408	528
___	**18007**	Southern Pacific 4-8-4 Locomotive "4410", 91	291	379
___	**18008**	Disneyland 35th Anniversary 4-4-0 Locomotive, display case, 90	266	315
___	**18009**	NYC 4-8-2 Locomotive "3000", 90 u, 91	283	561
___	**18010**	PRR 6-8-6 Steam Turbine Locomotive "6200", 91-92	900	1041
___	**18010**	L&NE AC-2 Covered Hopper 6-pack, 18		360
___	**18011**	Chessie System 4-8-4 Locomotive "2101", 91	402	533
___	**18012**	NYC 4-6-4 Locomotive "5340", 90	615	750
___	**18013**	Disneyland 35th Anniversary 4-4-0 Locomotive, 90	255	296
___	**18014**	Lionel Lines 2-6-4 Locomotive "8014", 91	145	190
___	**18016**	Northern Pacific 4-8-4 Locomotive "2626", 92	293	440
___	**18018**	Southern 2-8-2 Locomotive "4501", 92	523	650
___	**18020**	N&W AC-2 Covered Hopper 6-pack, 18		360
___	**18021**	Frisco 2-8-2 Mikado Locomotive, 93	530	640
___	**18022**	Pere Marquette 2-8-4 Locomotive "1201", 93	550	650
___	**18023**	Western Maryland Shay Locomotive "6", 92	519	1350
___	**18024**	Sears T&P 4-8-2 Locomotive "907," display case, 92 u	750	790
___	**18025**	T&P 4-8-2 Locomotive "907", 92 u		640
___	**18026**	NYC 4-6-4 Dreyfuss Hudson Locomotive, 2-rail, 92 u		2350
___	**18027**	NYC 4-6-4 Dreyfuss Hudson Locomotive, 3-rail, 93 u		1450
___	**18028**	Smithsonian PRR 4-6-2 Locomotive "3768," 2-rail, 93 u		2150
___	**18029**	NYC 4-6-4 Dreyfuss Hudson Locomotive, 3-rail, 93 u	1900	2150
___	**18030**	Frisco 2-8-2 Locomotive "4100", 93 u	530	625
___	**18030**	Pere Marquette AC-2 Covered Hopper 6-pack, 18		360
___	**18031**	2-10-0 Bundesbahn BR-50 Locomotive, 2-rail, 93 u		1500
___	**18034**	Santa Fe 2-8-2 Locomotive "3158", 94	540	620
___	**18035**	2-10-0 Reichsbahn BR-50 Locomotive, 2-rail, 93 u		1500
___	**18036**	2-10-0 French BR-50 Locomotive, 2-rail, 93 u		1500
___	**18040**	N&W 4-8-4 Locomotive "612", 95	362	710
___	**18040**	WM AC-2 Covered Hopper 6-pack, 18		360
___	**18041**	WM AC-2 Covered Hopper "5125", 18		60
___	**18042**	Boston & Albany 4-6-4 Locomotive "618", 95		250

		Exc	Mint	
18043	Chesapeake & Ohio 4-6-4 Locomotive "490", 95	580	750	___
18044	Southern 4-6-2 Locomotive "1390", 96		242	___
18045	Commodore Vanderbilt Locomotive "777", 96	328	678	___
18046	Wabash 4-6-4 Locomotive "700", 96	175	375	___
18049	N&W Warhorse 4-8-4 Locomotive "600", 96		490	___
18050	JCPenney 4-6-2 Pacific Locomotive "2055", 96	235	245	___
18050	Continental Grain ACF 3-Bay Covered Hopper 6-pack, 18		360	___
18051	Continental Grain ACF 3-Bay Covered Hopper "46611", 18		60	___
18052	Pennsylvania Torpedo Locomotive "238E", 97	90	455	___
18053	LL 2-8-4 Berkshire Locomotive "726", 96-97	310	400	___
18054	NYC 0-4-0 Switcher "1665," black, 97		145	___
18055	Continental Grain ACF 3-Bay Covered Hopper "46615", 18		60	___
18056	NYC J1-e Hudson Locomotive "763E," Vanderbilt tender, 97	384	603	___
18057	PRR 6-8-6 Turbine Locomotive "671", 96-98	280	450	___
18058	NYC 4-6-4 Hudson Locomotive "773", 96-97	300	550	___
18060	PRR ACF 3-Bay Covered Hopper 6-pack, 18		360	___
18062	ATSF 4-6-4 Hudson Locomotive "3447", 97		680	___
18063	NYC 4-6-4 Commodore Vanderbilt Locomotive, 99	483	952	___
18064	NYC 4-8-2 Mohawk L-3A Locomotive "3005," tender, 98	275	450	___
18067	NYC Weathered Commodore Vanderbilt Scale Hudson, 97	275	840	___
18068	PRR S2 Steam Tender, 99	145	250	___
18070	Tenneco ACF 3-Bay Covered Hopper 6-pack, 18		360	___
18071	SP Daylight Locomotive "4449", 98	60	680	___
18072	Lionel Lines Torpedo Locomotive, tender, 98		360	___
18079	NYC 2-8-2 Mikado Locomotive "1967", 99		710	___
18080	D&RGW 2-8-2 Mikado Locomotive "1210", 99		720	___
18080	BN ACF 3-Bay Covered Hopper 6-pack, 18		360	___
18082	NYC 4-6-4 Hudson Locomotive "5404", 99		230	___
18083	C&O 4-6-4 Hudson Locomotive "305", 99		205	___
18084	Santa Fe 4-6-4 Hudson Locomotive "305", 99		225	___
18085	NH 4-6-2 Pacific Locomotive "1334", 99		275	___
18086	NYC 4-6-2 Pacific Locomotive "4929", 99		235	___
18087	Santa Fe 4-6-2 Pacific Locomotive "3448", 99		265	___
18088	SP 4-6-2 Pacific Locomotive "1407", 99		350	___
18089	CNJ 4-6-0 Camelback Locomotive "771", 99		405	___
18090	Vesuvius Crucible PS-1 Boxcar 6-pack, 18		360	___
18091	PRR 4-6-0 Camelback Locomotive "821", 99		405	___
18092	SP 4-6-0 Camelback Locomotive "2283", 99	113	395	___
18093	C&NW 4-6-0 Camelback Locomotive "3006", 99		285	___
18094	B&O 4-4-2 E6 Atlantic Locomotive, CC, 99-00		345	___
18095	PRR 4-4-2 E6 Atlantic Locomotive, CC, 99-00	275	455	___
18096	ATSF 4-4-2 E6 Atlantic Locomotive, CC, 99-00		370	___
18097	CNJ 4-6-0 Camelback Locomotive "770", 99		330	___
18098	PRR 4-6-0 Camelback Locomotive "820", 99		355	___
18099	SP 4-6-0 Camelback Locomotive "2282", 99		360	___
18100	Santa Fe F3 Diesel A Unit "8100," powered, 91		300	___
18100	EJ&E PS-1 Boxcar 6-pack, 18		360	___
18101	Santa Fe F3 Diesel B Unit "8101," powered, 91		250	___
18102	Santa Fe F3 Diesel A Unit "8102," unpowered, 91		200	___
18103	Santa Fe F3 Diesel B Unit "8103," unpowered, 91 u	180	190	___
18104	GN F3 Diesel A Unit "366A," powered, 92		500	___
18105	GN F3 Diesel B Unit "370B," unpowered, 92		220	___
18106	GN F3 Diesel A Unit "351C," unpowered, 92		260	___

			Exc	Mint
___	**18107**	D&RGW Alco PA1 Diesel ABA Set, 92	445	740
___	**18108**	Great Northern F3 Diesel B Unit "371B", 93	85	105
___	**18109**	Erie Alco Diesel A Unit "725A," powered, 93		250
___	**18110**	Erie Alco Diesel B Unit "725B," unpowered, 93		160
___	**18110**	Monon PS-1 Boxcar 6-pack, 18		360
___	**18111**	Erie Alco Diesel A Unit "736A," unpowered, 93		170
___	**18115**	Santa Fe F3 Diesel B Unit, 93	90	115
___	**18116**	Erie-Lackawanna Alco PA1 Diesel AA Set, 93	450	490
___	**18117**	ATSF F3 Diesel AA Set, 93		375
___	**18117/18**	Santa Fe F3 Diesel AA Set "200", 93	290	410
___	**18118**	ATSF F3 Diesel A Unit, unpowered, 93		200
___	**18119/20**	UP Alco Diesel AA Set, 94	250	350
___	**18119**	UP Alco FA-2 Diesel AA Set, 94	150	300
___	**18120**	UP Alco FA-2 Diesel A Unit, 94		120
___	**18120**	Rutland PS-1 Boxcar 6-pack, 18		360
___	**18121**	Santa Fe F3 Diesel B Unit "200A", 94	75	95
___	**18122**	Santa Fe F3 Diesel B Unit "200B", 95	140	150
___	**18123**	ACL F3 Diesel A Unit "342," powered, 96		250
___	**18124**	ACL F3 Diesel B Unit "342B," unpowered, 96		185
___	**18125**	ACL F3 Diesel A Unit "343," unpowered, 96		190
___	**18128**	Santa Fe F3 Diesel A Unit "2343", 96		435
___	**18129**	Santa Fe F3 Diesel B Unit "2343C", 96		245
___	**18130**	Santa Fe F3 Diesel AB Set, 96	237	600
___	**18130**	NYC AAR 3-Bay Hopper 6-pack, 18		360
___	**18131**	NP F3 Diesel AB Set, "2390A, 2390C", 97	323	480
___	**18132**	NP F3 Diesel A Unit, powered		300
___	**18133**	NP F3 Diesel B Unit, dummy		150
___	**18134**	Santa Fe F3 Diesel A Unit "2343," dummy, 97	75	195
___	**18135**	NYC F3 AA Diesel Set "2333", 99		650
___	**18135**	NYC F3 Diesel AA Set "2333", 96-99	300	520
___	**18136**	Santa Fe F3 Diesel B Unit "2343C", 97	135	240
___	**18138**	Milwaukee Road F3 Diesel A Unit "75A", 98		400
___	**18139**	Milwaukee Road F3 Diesel B Unit "2378B", 98		250
___	**18140**	Milwaukee Road F3 Diesel AB Set, 98	380	600
___	**18140**	Nickel Plate Road AAR 3-Bay Hopper 6-pack, 18		360
___	**18145**	NP F3 Diesel A Unit "2390A," powered, 97	300	360
___	**18146**	NP F3 Diesel B Unit "2390C", 97		170
___	**18147**	NP F3 Diesel AB Set, 97	438	580
___	**18149**	UP Veranda Gas Turbine Locomotive "61", 98	860	900
___	**18150**	LG Everist AAR 3-Bay Hopper 6-pack, 18		360
___	**18154**	Deluxe Santa Fe FT Diesel AA Set, 98-00		375
___	**18155**	Deluxe Santa Fe FT Diesel A Unit, powered, 98-00		200
___	**18156**	Deluxe Santa Fe FT Diesel A Unit, unpowered, 98-00		160
___	**18157**	Santa Fe FT Diesel AA Set, 98-00		240
___	**18158**	Santa Fe FT Diesel A Unit, powered, 98-00		220
___	**18159**	Santa Fe FT Diesel A Unit, unpowered, 98-00		120
___	**18160**	NYC Deluxe FT Diesel AA Set, "1602"/"1603", 98-00		500
___	**18160**	UP AAR 3-Bay Hopper 6-pack, 18		360
___	**18161**	NYC Deluxe FT Diesel A Unit "1603," powered, 98-00		350
___	**18162**	NYC Deluxe FT Diesel A Unit "1602," unpowered, 98-00		120
___	**18163**	NYC FT Diesel AA Set, "1600, 2400", 98-00		300
___	**18164**	NYC FT Diesel A Unit "1600," powered, 98-00		200
___	**18165**	NYC FT Diesel A Unit "2400," unpowered, 98-00		110

		Exc	Mint
18166	B&O FT Diesel AA Set, CC, 99-00		340
18167	B&O FT Diesel A Unit "8167," CC, 99-00		230
18168	B&O FT Diesel A Unit "8168," unpowered, 99-00		110
18169	B&O FT Diesel AA Set, traditional, 99-00		240
18170	B&O FT Diesel A Unit, traditional, 99-00		140
18171	B&O FT Diesel A Unit, unpowered, 99-00		90
18178	NYC F3 Diesel B Unit, unpowered, 99		275
18189	Army of Potomac Operating Stock Car, 99		45
18190	McNeil's Rangers Operating Stock Car "2", 99		45
18191	WP F3 Diesel AA Set, 98	153	570
18192	WP F3 Diesel A Unit, powered, 98		485
18193	WP F3 Diesel A Unit, unpowered, 98		495
18194	EL F3 Diesel AB Set, 99		450
18195	EL F3 Diesel A Unit "7091, powered", 99		300
18196	EL F3 B Unit, nonpowered, 99		150
18197	WP F3 Diesel B Unit "2355C", 99	88	255
18198	WP F3 Diesel B Unit "2345C" CC, 99		360
18200	Conrail SD40 Diesel "8200", 87	180	200
18201	Chessie System SD40 Diesel "8201", 88	245	340
18202	Erie-Lack. SD40 Diesel Unit "8459," dummy, 89 u	90	140
18203	CP Rail SD40 Diesel "8203", 89	195	250
18204	Chessie SD40 Diesel Unit "8204," dummy, 90 u	135	190
18205	Union Pacific Dash 8-40C Diesel "9100", 89	275	335
18206	Santa Fe Dash 8-40B Diesel "8206", 90	195	293
18207	Norfolk Southern Dash 8-40C Diesel "8689", 92	230	270
18208	BN SD40 Diesel Dummy Unit "8586", 91 u	115	165
18209	CP Rail SD40 Diesel Dummy Unit "8209", 92 u	118	165
18210	Illinois Central SD40 "6006", 93	220	250
18210	Northwestern Refrigerated Wood-sided Reefer 6-pack, 18		360
18211	Susquehanna Dash 8-40B Diesel "4002", 93	145	165
18212	Santa Fe Dash 8-40B Diesel Dummy Unit "8212", 93	155	180
18213	Norfolk Southern Dash 8-40C Diesel "8688", 94	168	240
18214	CSX Dash 8-40C Diesel "7500", 94	235	255
18215	CSX Dash 8-40C Diesel "7643", 94	240	260
18216	Conrail SD-60M Diesel "5500", 94	233	380
18217	Illinois Central SD40 Diesel "6007", 94	170	175
18218	Susquehanna Dash 8-40B Diesel "4004", 94	205	225
18219	C&NW Dash 8-40C Diesel "8501", 95	325	330
18220	C&NW Dash 8-40C Diesel "8502", 95	215	315
18220	PFE Wood-sided Refrigerator Car 6-pack, 18		360
18221	D&RGW SD50 Diesel "5512", 95	455	520
18222	D&RGW SD50 Diesel "5517", 95	280	325
18223	Milwaukee Road SD40 Diesel "154", 95	375	380
18224	Milwaukee Road SD40 Diesel "155", 95	190	265
18226	GE Dash 9 Diesel, 97	70	295
18228	SP Dash 9 Diesel "8228", gray with red nose, 97		340
18229	SP SD40 Diesel "7333", 98	300	425
18230	Swift Wood-sided Refrigerator Car 6-pack, 18		360
18231	BNSF Dash 9 Diesel "739", 98		435
18232	Soo Line SD60 Diesel "5500", 97		350
18233	BNSF Dash 9 Diesel "745", 98		330
18234	BNSF Dash 9 Diesel "740," CC, 98-99		405
18235	BNSF Dash 9 Diesel 2-pack, "739, 740", 98		710

			Exc	Mint
___	**18238**	Conrail SD70 Diesel "4145", 99-00		300
___	**18239**	SP SD40 Diesel "7340", 98		300
___	**18240**	Conrail Dash 8-40B Diesel "5065" CC, 98		260
___	**18240**	Rath Wood-sided Refrigerator Car 6-pack, 18		360
___	**18241**	BN SD70 Diesel "9413", 99-00		345
___	**18245**	PRR Alco PA1 Diesel AA Set, 99		495
___	**18246**	PRR Alco PA1 Diesel A Unit "5750A," powered, 99		350
___	**18247**	PRR Alco PA-1 A Unit, unpowered, 99		240
___	**18248**	PRR Alco PB-1 Diesel "5750B", 99	93	215
___	**18249**	Erie Alco PB-1 Diesel "850B", 00		250
___	**18250**	BNSF SD70 Diesel "9870", 99-00		365
___	**18251**	CSX SD60 Diesel "8701", 99-00	113	300
___	**18252**	Amtrak Dash 9 Diesel, CC, 99	85	285
___	**18253**	BNSF Dash 9 Diesel, CC, 99		305
___	**18254**	ATSF Dash 9 Diesel, CC, 99		340
___	**18255**	NS Dash 9 Diesel, CC, 99		315
___	**18256**	Amtrak Dash 9 Diesel, traditional, 99		200
___	**18257**	BNSF Dash 9 Diesel, traditional, 99		190
___	**18258**	ATSF Dash 9 Diesel, traditional, 99		205
___	**18259**	NS Dash 9 Diesel, traditional, 99		215
___	**18260**	Conrail SD70 Diesel "4144", 99-00		280
___	**18261**	BN SD60 Diesel "9412", 99-00		255
___	**18262**	BNSF SD70 Diesel "9869", 99-00		250
___	**18263**	CSX SD60 Diesel "8700", 99-00		255
___	**18264**	Southern Pacific SD70M Diesel "8238", 99-00		245
___	**18265**	Southern Pacific SD70M Diesel "9803", 99-00		340
___	**18266**	Norfolk Southern SD60 Diesel "6552," CC, 01-02		400
___	**18268**	Lionel Centennial SD90MAC Diesel, CC, 00		428
___	**18269**	UP SD90MAC Diesel "8006," CC, 00		405
___	**18270**	UP SD90MAC Diesel "8004," traditional, 00		330
___	**18271**	CP SD90MAC Diesel "9129," CC, 00		440
___	**18272**	CP SD90MAC Diesel "9127," traditional, 00		330
___	**18273**	UP SD40 Diesel "8071", 99-00		330
___	**18274**	Burlington U30C Diesel "891", CC, 01		370
___	**18276**	Seaboard U30C Diesel "7274", CC, 01		325
___	**18278**	UP U30C Diesel "2938", CC, 01		330
___	**18280**	Maersk SD70 Diesel, CC, 00		345
___	**18281**	BNSF Dash 9-44CW Diesel "788", CC, 00		340
___	**18282**	BNSF Dash 9-44CW Diesel "789", traditional, 00		225
___	**18283**	CSX Dash 9-44CW Diesel "9019", CC, 00		340
___	**18284**	CSX Dash 9-44CW Diesel "9020", traditional, 00		300
___	**18285**	UP Dash 9-44C Diesel "9659", CC, 01		325
___	**18286**	UP Dash 9-44CW Diesel "9717", CC, 01		355
___	**18287**	CN Dash 9-44C Diesel "2529", CC, 01		460
___	**18288**	Odyssey System SD70 Diesel, CC, 00 u		400
___	**18289**	CN Dash 9-44C Diesel "2528," traditional, 01		220
___	**18290**	Amtrak Dash 8-32BWH Diesel "509", CC, 01		325
___	**18291**	BNSF Dash 8-32BWH Diesel "580", CC, 02		340
___	**18292**	Chessie GE U30C Diesel "3312", CC, 02		340
___	**18293**	Santa Fe U30C Diesel, CC, 03		395
___	**18294**	Alaska SD70MAC Diesel "4005", CC, 01-02		435
___	**18295**	Conrail SD80MAC Diesel "7200", CC, 02-03		365
___	**18296**	CSX SD80MAC Diesel "801", CC, 02-03		405

MODERN 1970-2024		Exc	Mint	
18297	NYC SD80MAC Diesel "9914", CC, 02-03		405	___
18298	UP "Desert Victory" SD40-2 Diesel "3593," CC, 02-03		380	___
18299	CP Rail SD40-2 Diesel "5420," CC, 02-03		375	___
18300	PRR GG1 Electric Locomotive "8300", 87	285	335	___
18301	Southern FM Train Master Diesel "8301", 88	140	204	___
18302	GN EP-5 Electric Locomotive "8302" (FF 3), 88	140	260	___
18303	Amtrak GG1 Electric Locomotive "8303", 89	178	338	___
18304	Lackawanna MU Commuter Car Set, 91	278	435	___
18305	Lackawanna MU Commuter Car Dummy Set, 92	165	255	___
18306	PRR MU Commuter Car Set, 92	218	330	___
18307	PRR FM Train Master Diesel "8699", 94	150	202	___
18308	PRR GG1 Electric Locomotive "4866", 92	148	264	___
18309	Reading FM Train Master Diesel "863", 93	173	212	___
18310	PRR MU Commuter Car Dummy Set, 93	265	345	___
18311	Disney EP-5 Electric Locomotive "8311", 94	202	412	___
18313	Pennsylvania GG1 Electric Locomotive "4907", 96	177	271	___
18314	PRR GG1 Electric Locomotive "2332", 5 gold stripes, 97	185	507	___
18315	Virginian E33 Electric Locomotive "2329", 97		240	___
18319	New Haven EP-5 Electric Locomotive, 99	200	365	___
18321	CNJ Train Master Diesel "2341", 99	85	405	___
18322	Lackawanna Train Master Diesel "2321", 99	163	435	___
18323	Amtrak HHP-8 Diesel "656F," CC, 09		500	___
18326	PRR Congressional GG1 Electric Locomotive, 00		600	___
18327	Virginian FM Train Master Diesel "2331", 99-00		410	___
18328	NH MU Commuter Car Set, CC, 00		385	___
18329	NH MU Commuter Car "4082," powered, 00		240	___
18330	NH MU Commuter Car "4083," unpowered, 00		140	___
18331	Reading MU Commuter Car Set, CC, 00		460	___
18332	Reading MU Commuter Car "9109," powered, 00		340	___
18333	Reading MU Commuter Car "9110," unpowered		140	___
18334	NH MU Commuter Car Set, unpowered, 01		180	___
18335	NH MU Commuter Car "4084," unpowered, 01		90	___
18336	NH MU Commuter Car "4085," unpowered, 01		90	___
18337	Reading MU Commuter Car Set, unpowered, 01		200	___
18338	Reading MU Commuter Car "9111," unpowered, 01		100	___
18339	Reading MU Commuter Car "9112," unpowered, 01		100	___
18340	Train Master Demonstrator AA Set, CC, 00		650	___
18341	Train Master Demonstrator A Unit "TM-1," CC, 00		350	___
18342	Train Master Demonstrator A Unit "TM-2," CC, 00		350	___
18343	PRR GG1 Electric Locomotive "2332", CC, 01		610	___
18344	LIRR MU Commuter Car Set, CC, 01		470	___
18345	LIRR MU Commuter Car "1163," CC, 01		360	___
18346	LIRR MU Commuter Car "1163," unpowered, 01		120	___
18347	IC MU Commuter Car Set, CC, 01		470	___
18348	IC MU Commuter Car "1204," CC, 01		360	___
18349	IC MU Commuter Car "1204," unpowered, 01		120	___
18350	Archive No. 2350 NH EP-5 electric, 01		375	___
18351	NYC S1 Electric Locomotive, 03		400	___
18352	JCPenney SP MU Commuter Car, display case, 02		140	___
18353	Pennsylvania E33 Electric Locomotive "4403," CC, 02		280	___
18354	PRR GG1 Electric Locomotive "4918", tuscan, CC, 04	188	790	___
18355	PRR GG1 Electric Locomotive "4876", green, CC, 04	385	900	___
18356	Penn Central GG1 Electric Locomotive "4901", CC, 04		1050	___

			Exc	Mint
___	**18357**	Amtrak Acela Power Unit "2026," CC, 04-05		530
___	**18358**	Amtrak Acela Power Unit "2029," unpowered, 04-05		270
___	**18359**	PRR GG1 Electric Locomotive "2360," CC, 04		430
___	**18360**	New York City R27 Subway Power Unit "8026," CC, 06-07		220
___	**18361**	New York City R27 Subway Power Unit "8027," unpowered, 04		120
___	**18362**	New York City R27 Subway Power Unit "8028," unpowered, 06-07		120
___	**18363**	New York City R27 Subway End Car "8029," unpowered, 06-07		120
___	**18364**	PRR BB1 Electric Locomotive Set "3900, 3901," CC, 05-07	150	530
___	**18365**	PRR BB1 Electric Locomotive "3900", CC, 05-07		370
___	**18366**	PRR BB1 Electric Locomotive "3901," unpowered, 05-07		160
___	**18367**	LIRR BB3 Electric Locomotive Set "328A, 329B," CC, 05		530
___	**18368**	LIRR BB3 Electric Locomotive "328 A," CC, 05		360
___	**18369**	LIRR BB3 Electric Locomotive "329B," unpowered, 05		160
___	**18370**	Postwar Virginian Train Master Diesel "2331," CC, 05-07		340
___	**18371**	PRR GG1 Electric "4912," Tuscan, 5 stripes, CC, 05-07	225	780
___	**18372**	PRR GG1 Electric Locomotive "4925", green, 1 stripe, CC, 05-07		780
___	**18373**	NYC S2 Electric Locomotive "125," CC, 05-07	93	410
___	**18374**	PRR GG1 Electric Locomotive "4866," silver, CC, 06-08		900
___	**18375**	Lackawanna FM Train Master Diesel "850," CC, 06		400
___	**18376**	Lackawanna FM Train Master Diesel "851," nonpowered (std O), 06		130
___	**18378**	New York City R27 Subway Car 2-pack, 07		360
___	**18379**	New York City R27 Subway Car "8030," unpowered, 06-07		100
___	**18380**	New York City R27 Subway Car "8031," unpowered, 06-07		100
___	**18381**	PRR BB1 Electric Locomotive "4751," CC, 06		500
___	**18383**	Postwar GN EP-5 Electric "2358," CC, 06-08		740
___	**18384**	MILW EP-2 Electric Locomotive, CC, 07-08		950
___	**18385**	NYC H-16-44 Diesel "7001", 07-09		202
___	**18386**	NYC H-16-44 Diesel "7002," nonpowered (std O), 07-09		123
___	**18388**	CNJ Train Master Diesel "2341," CC, 08-09		500
___	**18389**	MILW EP-2 Electric Locomotive "E-1," CC, 07-08		950
___	**18399**	NH EF-4 Rectifier Locomotive "306," CC, 09		360
___	**18400**	Santa Fe Vulcan Rotary Snowplow "8400", 87	135	170
___	**18401**	Workmen Handcar, 87-88	30	37
___	**18402**	Lionel Lines Burro Crane, 88	65	87
___	**18403**	Santa Claus Handcar, 88	26	33
___	**18404**	San Francisco Trolley "8404", 88	55	85
___	**18405**	Santa Fe Burro Crane, 89	70	83
___	**18406**	Track Maintenance Car, 89, 91	34	49
___	**18407**	Snoopy and Woodstock Handcar, 90-91	96	115
___	**18408**	Santa Claus Handcar, 89	26	35
___	**18410**	PRR Burro Crane, 90	100	115
___	**18411**	Canadian Pacific Fire Car, 90	70	98
___	**18412**	UP Fire Car, 91	70	100
___	**18413**	Charlie Brown and Lucy Handcar, 91	40	61
___	**18416**	Bugs Bunny and Daffy Duck Handcar, 92-93	129	179
___	**18417**	Section Gang Car, 93	65	80
___	**18419**	Lionelville Electric Trolley "8419", 94	75	90
___	**18421**	Sylvester and Tweety Handcar, 94	44	50
___	**18422**	Santa and Snowman Handcar, 94	32	37
___	**18423**	On-track Step Van, 95	23	28

		Exc	Mint	
18424	On-track Pickup Truck, 95	20	32	___
18425	Goofy and Pluto Handcar, 95	45	58	___
18426	Santa and Snowman Handcar, 95	25	30	___
18427	Tie-Jector Car "55", 97		60	___
18429	Workmen Handcar, 96	28	34	___
18430	Crew Car, 96		28	___
18431	Trolley Car, 96-97		46	___
18433	Mickey and Minnie Handcar, 96-97	48	87	___
18434	Porky and Petunia Handcar, 96		35	___
18436	Dodge Ram Track Inspection Vehicle, 97	20	40	___
18438	PRR High-rail Inspection Vehicle, 98		50	___
18439	Union Pacific High-rail Inspection Vehicle, 98		42	___
18440	NJ Transit High-rail Inspection Vehicle, 98		50	___
18444	Lionelville Fire Car (SSS), 98		150	___
18445	NYC Fire Car, 98		90	___
18446	Postwar "58" GN Rotary Snowplow, 99		181	___
18447	Executive Inspection Vehicle, 99		125	___
18452	Boston Trolley "3321", 99-00		65	___
18454	Executive Inspection Vehicle, blue, 00	48	118	___
18455	NYC Tie-Jector Car "X-2", 00-01		74	___
18456	Postwar "59" Minuteman Motorized Unit, 01-02		290	___
18457	Postwar "65" Handcar, 00-01		45	___
18458	Postwar "53" D&RGW Snowplow, 00		160	___
18459	Christmas Handcar, 01		35	___
18461	Track Cleaning Car, 02-03		90	___
18463	Hot Rod Inspection Vehicle, 01-02		100	___
18464	Postwar "54" Track Ballast Tamper, 02-03		170	___
18465	Postwar "50" Gang Car, 03		78	___
18466	UP Rotary Snow Plow, 01-02		150	___
18467	Train Robbery Handcar, 02		45	___
18468	CN Railroad Speeder, 03-04		49	___
18469	Chessie System Railroad Speeder, 03-04		49	___
18470	Postwar "52" Fire Car, 02		105	___
18471	UP GP20 Diesel "1977", 03		105	___
18473	Lehigh Valley GP38 Diesel "310", 03		160	___
18474	Postwar "41" U.S. Army Switcher, 03-04		145	___
18475	Toy Story Handcar, 03		55	___
18476	Mickey and Minnie Mouse Handcar, 03-04	30	60	___
18477	UP Burro Crane "MOW 10166", 03		95	___
18479	Postwar "45" USMC Mobile Missile Launcher, 03-04		125	___
18480	Hobo Motorized Handcar, 03-04		35	___
18481	Christmas Yuletide Trolley, 03		50	___
18482	New Haven Rail Bonder "16", 04		35	___
18483	C&O Ballast Tamper "48", 04		55	___
18484	NS Dodge Inspection Vehicle, 04-05		55	___
18485	NYC Gang Car, 04-05		100	___
18486	Donald and Daisy Duck Handcar, 04-05		63	___
18487	Postwar "56" M&StL Mine Transport Car, 04-05		230	___
18488	CP Rotary Snow Plow, 03-05		160	___
18489	Great Northern Rail Bonder "HR-73", 04		35	___
18490	UP Ballast Tamper, 04-05		150	___
18491	MOW Ballast Tamper "325", 04		44	___
18492	MOW Rail Bonder "58", 04		35	___

			Exc	Mint
___	**18493**	Santa's Speeder, 05		60
___	**18497**	N&W Speeder "541005", traditional, 05		65
___	**18498**	New York Central Rotary Snowplow, 05		210
___	**18500**	Milwaukee Road GP9 Diesel "8500" (FF 2), 87	155	198
___	**18501**	WM NW2 Switcher "8501" (FF 4), 89	185	215
___	**18502**	LL 90th Anniversary GP9 Diesel "1900", 90	148	173
___	**18503**	Southern Pacific NW2 Switcher "8503", 90	165	280
___	**18504**	Frisco GP7 Diesel "504" (FF 5), 91	155	240
___	**18505**	NKP GP7 Diesel Set "400, 401" (FF 6), 92	295	365
___	**18506**	CN Budd RDC Set, "D202, D203", 92	180	261
___	**18507**	CN Budd RDC Baggage Car "D202," powered, 92	50	75
___	**18508**	CN Budd RDC Passenger Dummy Unit "D203", 92	125	150
___	**18510**	CN Budd RDC Passenger Dummy Unit "D200", 93	50	75
___	**18511**	CN Budd RDC Passenger Dummy Unit "D250", 93	50	75
___	**18512**	CN Budd RDC Dummy Set, "D200, D250", 93	125	195
___	**18513**	NYC GP7 Diesel "7420", 94	90	130
___	**18514**	Missouri Pacific GP7 Diesel "4124", 95	213	310
___	**18515**	Lionel Steel Vulcan Diesel "57" (SSS), 96		190
___	**18516**	Phantom III Locomotive, CC, 02		345
___	**18517**	Phantom IV Locomotive, CC, 08		390
___	**18550**	JCPenney MILW GP9 Diesel "8500," display case, 87 u	180	245
___	**18551**	JCPenney Susquehanna RS3 Diesel "8809," display case, 89 u	180	195
___	**18552**	JCPenney DM&IR SD18 Diesel "8813," display case, 90 u	170	195
___	**18553**	Sears UP GP9 Diesel "150," display case, 91 u	100	150
___	**18554**	JCPenney GM&O RS3 "721," display case, 92-93 u	160	180
___	**18555**	Sears C&IM SD9 Diesel "52", 92 u	165	190
___	**18556**	Sears Chicago & Illinois Midland Freight Car Set, 92 u	110	120
___	**18557**	Chessie System 4-8-4 Locomotive "2101," display case, export, 92 u		NRS
___	**18558**	JCPenney MKT GP9 Diesel "91," display case, 94 u	160	180
___	**18562**	SP GP9 Diesel "2380", 96		195
___	**18563**	NYC GP9 Diesel "2380", 96		230
___	**18564**	CP GP9 Diesel "2380", 97		265
___	**18565**	Milwaukee Road GP9 Diesel "2338", 97	93	220
___	**18566**	CR SD20 Diesel "8495" (SSS), 97		150
___	**18567**	PRR GP9 Diesel "2028", 97	60	225
___	**18569**	CB&Q GP9 Diesel "2380", 98		190
___	**18570**	B&M GP7 Diesel "2380," CC, 98		190
___	**18571**	B&M GP7 Diesel "2381," unpowered, 98		135
___	**18572**	B&M GP7 Diesel "2389," CC, 98		190
___	**18573**	Santa Fe GP9 Diesel "2380", 98	49	155
___	**18574**	Milwaukee Road GP20 Diesel "975", 98	110	270
___	**18575**	Custom Series I GP9 Diesel "2398", 98		350
___	**18576**	SP GP9 Diesel B Unit "2385," nonpowered, 98		135
___	**18577**	NYC GP9 Diesel B Unit "2385," nonpowered, 98		145
___	**18578**	NYC Ballast Tamper "8578", 98		150
___	**18579**	MILW GP9 Diesel "2384," nonpowered, 99		135
___	**18580**	Pennsylvania GP9 Diesel B Unit "2027", 98		165
___	**18582**	Seaboard NW2 Switcher, 98	250	455
___	**18583**	AEC Switcher "57", 98	75	214
___	**18585**	Centennial SD40 Diesel, 99	0	463
___	**18587**	NKP Alco C420 Switcher "577," CC, 99-01	215	255
___	**18588**	D&H Alco C420 Switcher "412," CC, 99-01	250	275
___	**18589**	LV Alco C420 Switcher "409," CC, 99-01	255	300

		Exc	Mint	
18590	NKP Alco C420 Switcher "578," traditional, 99-01		170	___
18591	D&H Alco C420 Switcher "411," traditional, 99-01		215	___
18592	LV Alco C420 Switcher "410," traditional, 99-01		175	___
18594	Farmrail GP7 Diesel "8252," traditional, 99		155	___
18595	D&H RS11 Diesel "5002," traditional, 99-00		160	___
18596	D&H Alco RS11 Diesel "5001," CC, 99-01		370	___
18597	NYC RS11 Diesel "8011," traditional, 99-00		160	___
18598	NYC Alco RS11 Switcher "8010," CC, 99-01		380	___
18599	C&O GP38 Diesel "3855", 99-00		145	___
18600	ACL 4-4-2 Locomotive "8600", 87 u	65	75	___
18601	Great Northern 4-4-2 Locomotive "8601", 88	80	95	___
18602	PRR 4-4-2 Locomotive "8602", 87	75	85	___
18604	Wabash 4-4-2 Locomotive "8604", 88-91	65	75	___
18605	Mopar Express 4-4-2 Locomotive "1987", 87-88 u	75	120	___
18606	NYC 2-6-4 Locomotive "8606", 89	170	190	___
18607	Union Pacific 2-6-4 Locomotive "8607", 89	130	155	___
18608	D&RGW 2-6-4 Locomotive "8608" (SSS), 89	90	105	___
18609	Northern Pacific 2-6-4 Locomotive "8609", 90	170	195	___
18610	Rock Island 0-4-0 Locomotive "8610", 90	105	115	___
18611	Lionel Lines 2-6-4 Locomotive (SSS), 90	125	140	___
18612	C&NW 4-4-2 Locomotive "8612", 89	75	100	___
18613	NYC 4-4-2 Locomotive "8613", 89 u	75	95	___
18614	Circus Train 4-4-2 Locomotive "1989", 89 u	95	125	___
18615	GTW 4-4-2 Locomotive "8615", 90	70	85	___
18616	Northern Pacific 4-4-2 Locomotive "8616", 90 u	85	110	___
18617	Adolphus III 4-4-2 Locomotive, 89-92 u	100	125	___
18618	B&O 4-4-2 Atlantic Locomotive, 91	105	125	___
18620	Illinois Central 2-6-2 Locomotive "8620", 91	165	190	___
18622	Union Pacific 4-4-2 Locomotive "8622", 90-91 u	65	80	___
18623	Texas & Pacific 4-4-2 Locomotive "8623", 92	80	110	___
18625	Illinois Central 4-4-2 Locomotive "8625", 91 u	70	95	___
18626	Delaware & Hudson 2-6-2 Locomotive "8626", 92	105	115	___
18627	C&O 4-4-2 Locomotive "8627" or "8633", 92, 93 u, 94, 95 u	75	95	___
18628	MKT 4-4-2 Locomotive "8628", 92, 93 u	70	85	___
18630	C&NW 4-6-2 Locomotive "2903", 93	325	370	___
18632	NYC 4-4-2 Locomotive "8632", 93-95	75	95	___
18632	C&O Columbia 4-4-2 Locomotive "8632", 97-99	75	95	___
18633	C&O 4-4-2 Locomotive "8633", 94-95	65	85	___
18633	UP 4-4-2 Locomotive "8633", 93-95	65	85	___
18635	Santa Fe 2-6-4 Locomotive "8625", 93	135	155	___
18636	B&O 4-6-2 Locomotive "5300", 94	215	315	___
18637	United Auto Workers 4-4-2 Locomotive "8633", 93 u		90	___
18638	Norfolk & Western 2-6-4 Locomotive "638", 94	150	220	___
18639	Reading 4-6-2 Locomotive "639", 95	145	170	___
18640	Union Pacific 4-6-2 Locomotive "8640", 95	110	130	___
18641	Ford 4-4-2 Locomotive "8641", 94 u	65	85	___
18642	Lionel Lines 4-6-2 Locomotive, 95	110	130	___
18644	ATSF 4-4-2 Columbia Locomotive "8644", 96-99	75	90	___
18648	Sears Zenith 4-4-2 Locomotive "8632", 96 u		140	___
18649	Chevrolet 4-4-2 Locomotive "USA-1", 96 u		150	___
18650	LL 4-4-2 Columbia Locomotive "X-1110", 96-99	95	120	___
18653	B&A 4-6-2 Pacific Locomotive "2044", 97		140	___
18654	SP 4-6-2 Pacific Locomotive "2044", 97		140	___

			Exc	Mint
___	**18656**	Bloomingdale's 4-4-2 Columbia Locomotive "8632", 96		112
___	**18657**	Sears Zenith 4-4-2 Columbia Locomotive "8632", 96		120
___	**18658**	LL Little League 4-4-2 Columbia Locomotive "X-1110", 97		90
___	**18660**	CN 4-6-2 Locomotive "2044," tender, 98		175
___	**18661**	N&W 4-6-2 Locomotive "2044," tender, 98		160
___	**18662**	Pennsylvania 0-4-0 Switcher, 98	165	230
___	**18666**	SP&S 4-6-2 Pacific Locomotive "2044", 97		200
___	**18668**	Bloomingdale's 4-4-2 Columbia Locomotive "8632", 97		130
___	**18669**	JCPenney IC 4-6-2 Pacific Locomotive "2099", 98		205
___	**18670**	D&H Columbia 4-4-2 Locomotive "1400", 98		80
___	**18671**	N&W Columbia 4-4-2 Locomotive "1201", 98		70
___	**18673**	N&W 0-4-0 Locomotive "203", 99		110
___	**18676**	Safari RR 0-4-0 Locomotive, 99		110
___	**18678**	Quaker Oats Columbia 4-4-2 Locomotive "8632", 98		162
___	**18679**	JCPenney T&P 4-6-2 Locomotive "2000", traditional, 99, 00 u		250
___	**18680**	LRRC Century Club 4-6-4 Hudson "2000", 00		200
___	**18681**	PRR 4-4-2 Locomotive "460", 99		75
___	**18682**	Santa Fe 4-4-2 Columbia Locomotive "524," traditional, 00-01		70
___	**18683**	Mickey's Holiday Express 4-4-2 Atlantic, 99		90
___	**18684**	LRRC Inside Track Special Edition 4-6-2 Pacific, 99		185
___	**18685**	NYC 4-4-2 Atlantic "8632", 99		100
___	**18686**	Tinsel Town Express 4-4-2 Atlantic "3766", 00-01		95
___	**18689**	NS Dash 8-40C Diesel "8689", 92		200
___	**18690**	Centennial Express 4-4-2 Atlantic "100", 00		90
___	**18691**	PRR -4-4-2 Atlantic "201", 00		70
___	**18692**	PRR 4-6-4 Hudson, 00		80
___	**18693**	Lionel Mines 4-6-4 Hudson "49", 00		80
___	**18694**	Whirlpool Limited 4-4-2 Atlantic "201", 00		75
___	**18695**	Mickey's Millennium Express 2000, 00		250
___	**18696**	ACL 4-6-4 Locomotive "1800", 01		120
___	**18697**	Santa Fe 4-6-4 Locomotive "3465", 01		100
___	**18698**	Wabash 4-4-2 Atlantic , 07		85
___	**18699**	Alaska 4-4-2 Locomotive "64", 01		105
___	**18700**	Rock Island 0-4-0T Locomotive "8700", 87-88	36	43
___	**18701**	Polar Express LionScale 3-Bay Covered Hopper, 18		65
___	**18702**	V&TRR 4-4-0 Locomotive "8702" (SSS), 88	160	195
___	**18703**	Merry Christmas LionScale 3-Bay Covered Hopper, 18		60
___	**18704**	Lionel Lines 2-4-0 Locomotive, 89 u	36	43
___	**18704**	Halloween ELX 3-Bay Hopper, LionScale, 18		65
___	**18705**	Neptune 0-4-0T Locomotive "8705", 90-91	35	42
___	**18706**	Santa Fe 2-4-0 Locomotive "8706", 91	36	43
___	**18707**	Mickey's World Tour 2-4-0 Locomotive "8707", 91, 92 u	58	68
___	**18709**	Lionel Employee Learning Center 0-4-0T Locomotive, 92 u		140
___	**18710**	SP 2-4-0 Locomotive "2000", 93	30	38
___	**18711**	Southern 2-4-0 Locomotive "2000", 93	30	38
___	**18712**	Jersey Central 2-4-0 Locomotive "2000", 93	30	38
___	**18713**	Chessie System 2-4-0 Locomotive "1993", 94-95	30	38
___	**18716**	Lionelville Circus 4-4-0 Locomotive, 90-91	90	110
___	**18718**	LL 0-4-0 Dockside Switcher "8200", 97-98		40
___	**18719**	Thomas the Tank Engine "1", 97		158
___	**18720**	Union 4-4-0 General Locomotive "1865", 99		175
___	**18721**	Confederate 4-4-0 General Locomotive "1861", 99		175
___	**18722**	Percy the Tank Engine "6", 99		170

MODERN 1970-2024		Exc	Mint
18723	Union Pacific 4-4-0 General Locomotive, 05		100 ___
18725	World of Disney General Locomotive, 03		100 ___
18728	Thomas the Tank Engine "1", 04-07		120 ___
18730	Transylvania RR 4-4-0 Locomotive "13", traditional, 05		105 ___
18731	PH-1 PowerHouse Transformer, 97	75	120 ___
18732	North Pole Central 4-4-0 Locomotive "25", 06		110 ___
18733	Percy the Tank Engine "6", 05-12		120 ___
18734	James the Tank Engine "5", 06-12		120 ___
18736	PRR 4-4-2 Atlantic "1645", 06-07		60 ___
18738	North Pole Central 4-4-2 Atlantic "25", 08-09		90 ___
18739	Great Western 4-4-0 General Locomotive, traditional, 07-09		80 ___
18740	Walter E. Disney 4-4-0 General Locomotive, traditional, 06		90 ___
18741	Thomas the Tank Engine, 08-13		120 ___
18742	Nutcracker 4-4-0 General Locomotive, 08		140 ___
18744	PRR 0-8-0 Locomotive "565", 08		125 ___
18745	Hallow's Eve 4-6-0 Steam Locomotive, 11-12		190 ___
18749	Rio Grande General Locomotive "346", 11-12		145 ___
17850	SP 0-8-0 Locomotive w/Vanderbilt tender "4508", 12		140 ___
18751	Santa Flyer 0-8-0 Locomotive, 11-13		120 ___
18753	Route of the Reindeer RS3 Diesel, 11		190 ___
18754	Polar Express 2-8-4 Berkshire Steam Locomotive, 11, 13		300 ___
18755	C&O Berkshire Steam Locomotive "2751," TrainSounds, 11		290 ___
18756	Coca-Cola 4-4-0 General Locomotive "125", 11-12		175 ___
18765	PRR 2-8-4 Berkshire Locomotive "2331", 12-13		190 ___
18769	Thomas, remote system, 12		140 ___
18770	Christmas Thomas the Tank Engine "1", 13-15		90 ___
18771	Percy, remote system, 13-16		140 ___
18773	UP 0-8-0 Locomotive "4500", 12-13		105 ___
18774	James, remote system, 13-16		140 ___
18775	Diesel, remote system, 13-16		140 ___
18776	Hershey's 0-8-0 Locomotive, 12-13		140 ___
18778	GN 0-8-0 Locomotive w/Vanderbilt Tender '819", 12-13		130 ___
18780	NYC 0-8-0 Locomotive "7794", 11-13		150 ___
18783	Menard's C&NW 0-8-0 Locomotive "1009", 12 u		135 ___
18784	Silver Bells 2-4-2 Columbia Locomotive, 13-15		110 ___
18787	PRR 4-4-0 General Locomotive "1510", 94-95		125 ___
18788	U.S. Military 4-4-0 General Locomotive, 13-14		300 ___
18789	Peanuts LC 2-4-2 Columbia Locomotive "1031", 13-16		155 ___
18790	Gingerbread Junction 0-6-0 Docksider "1226", 13-15		130 ___
18791	PRR 0-8-0 LC Locomotive, 13-17		140 ___
18799	Bethlehem Steel Switcher "44", 99		100 ___
18800	Lehigh Valley GP9 Diesel "8800", 87	80	95 ___
18801	Santa Fe U36B Diesel "8801", 87	100	120 ___
18802	Southern GP9 Diesel "8802" (SSS), 87	100	115 ___
18803	Santa Fe RS3 Diesel "8803", 88	90	105 ___
18804	Soo Line RS3 Diesel "8804", 88	95	115 ___
18805	Union Pacific RS3 Diesel "8805", 89	100	123 ___
18806	New Haven SD18 Diesel "8806", 89	100	115 ___
18807	Lehigh Valley RS3 Diesel "8807", 90	90	120 ___
18808	ACL SD18 Diesel "8808", 90	85	105 ___
18809	Susquehanna RS3 Diesel "8809", 89 u		130 ___
18810	CSX SD18 Diesel "8810", 90	95	130 ___
18811	Alaska SD9 Diesel "8811", 91	95	135 ___

	MODERN 1970-2024		Exc	Mint
___	**18812**	Kansas City Southern GP38 Diesel "4000", 91	120	140
___	**18813**	DM&IR SD18 Diesel "8813", 90 u	90	145
___	**18814**	D&H RS3 Diesel "8814" (SSS), 91	90	120
___	**18815**	Amtrak RS3 Diesel "1815", 91, 92 u	100	130
___	**18816**	C&NW GP38-2 Diesel "4600", 92	105	135
___	**18817**	UP GP9 Diesel "150" (see 18553), 91 u		135
___	**18818**	LRRC GP38-2 Diesel, 92 u	100	117
___	**18819**	L&N GP38-2 Diesel "4136", 92	115	145
___	**18820**	WP GP9 Diesel "8820" (SSS), 92	120	140
___	**18821**	Clinchfield GP38-2 Diesel "6005", 93	125	150
___	**18822**	Gulf, Mobile & Ohio RS3 Diesel "721", 92-93 u		NRS
___	**18823**	Chicago & Illinois Midland SD9 Diesel "52", 92 u		235
___	**18824**	Montana Rail Link SD9 Diesel "600", 93	185	230
___	**18825**	Soo Line GP38-2 Diesel "4000" (SSS), 93	120	145
___	**18826**	Conrail GP7 Diesel "5808", 93	100	120
___	**18827**	Happy Holidays RS3 Diesel "8827", 93	165	220
___	**18830**	Budweiser GP9 Diesel "1947", 93-94 u	125	165
___	**18831**	SP GP20 Diesel "4060", 94	105	120
___	**18832**	PRR RSD4 Diesel "8446", 95	110	135
___	**18833**	Milwaukee Road RS3 Diesel "2487", 94	100	110
___	**18834**	C&O SD28 Diesel "8834", 94	110	140
___	**18835**	NYC RS3 Diesel "8223" (SSS), 94	135	195
___	**18836**	CN (Grand Trunk) GP38-2 Diesel "5800", 94	135	160
___	**18837**	Happy Holidays RS3 Diesel "8837", 94-95	150	190
___	**18838**	Seaboard RSC3 Diesel "1538", 95	110	140
___	**18840**	U.S. Army GP7 Diesel "1821", 95	85	124
___	**18841**	Western Maryland GP20 Diesel "27" (SSS), 95	120	150
___	**18842**	JCPenney B&LE SD38 Diesel "868", 95 u	80	265
___	**18843**	Great Northern RS3 Diesel "197", 96		145
___	**18844**	Nacionales de Mexico GP38 Diesel, 96		150
___	**18845**	D&RGW RS3 Diesel "5204", 97		100
___	**18846**	Lionel Centennial Series GP9 Diesel, 98	265	426
___	**18847**	Santa Fe H-12-44 Switcher "602", 99	118	385
___	**18848**	PRR H-12-44 Switcher "9087", 99	113	420
___	**18853**	JCPenney Santa Fe GP9 Diesel "2370", 97 u		150
___	**18854**	UP GP9 Diesel Dummy Set, "2380, 2387", 97		450
___	**18855**	UP GP9 Diesel "2381," unpowered, 97		210
___	**18856**	NJ Transit GP38-2 Diesel "4303", 99		315
___	**18857**	Union Pacific GP9 Diesel "2397", 97		240
___	**18858**	Lionel Centennial GP20 Diesel, 98		450
___	**18859**	Phantom II Locomotive, 99		360
___	**18860**	Pratt's Hollow Collection I: Phantom, 98	150	400
___	**18864**	Southern Pacific GP9 Diesel B Unit, 98		140
___	**18865**	New York Central GP9 Diesel B Unit, 98		170
___	**18866**	Milwaukee Road GP7 Diesel "2383", 98		205
___	**18868**	NJ Transit GP38-2 Diesel "4300", 98 u		140
___	**18870**	Pennsylvania GP9 Diesel "2029", 98		180
___	**18872**	Wabash GP7 Diesel Set, "453, 454, 455", 99	213	560
___	**18873**	Wabash GP7 Diesel "454," unpowered, 99		125
___	**18874**	Wabash GP7 Diesel "455," CC, 99		260
___	**18876**	C&NW H-12-44 Switcher "1053", 99	125	319
___	**18877**	Union Pacific GP9 Diesel "2399," nonpowered, 99		175
___	**18878**	Alaska GP7 Diesel "1803", 99	55	115

MODERN 1970-2024		Exc	Mint	
18879	B&O GP9 Diesel "5616", 99	90	260	___
18881	Custom GP9 Diesel "5616", 99		350	___
18890	UP RS3 Diesel "8805", 89		85	___
18892	Burlington GP9 Diesel "2328", 99	75	205	___
18893	Corvette GP7 Diesel, traditional, 99		230	___
18897	Christmas GP7 Diesel "1999", 99	66	200	___
18900	PRR Switcher "8900", 88 u, 89	26	34	___
18901	PRR Alco Diesel AA Set "8901, 8902", 88		320	___
18901/02	PRR Alco Diesel AA Set, 88	110	130	___
18902	PRR Alco Diesel FA-2 Unit, unpowered, 88		80	___
18903	Amtrak "Mopar Express", 99		500	___
18904	Amtrak Alco Diesel FA-2, unpowered, 88-89		80	___
18903/04	Amtrak Alco Diesel AA Set, 88-89	90	130	___
18905	PRR 44-ton Switcher "9312", 92	80	116	___
18906	Erie-Lackawanna RS3 Diesel "8906", 91 u	70	90	___
18907	Rock Island 44-ton Switcher "371", 93	95	110	___
18908	NYC Alco Diesel AA Units "8908, 8909", 93	60	150	___
18908/09	NYC Alco Diesel AA Set, 93	105	115	___
18909	NYC Alco FA-2 Diesel "8909," unpowered, 93	50	80	___
18910	CSX Switcher "8910", 93	40	46	___
18911	UP Switcher "8911", 93	33	37	___
18912	Amtrak Switcher "8912", 93	37	43	___
18913	Santa Fe Alco Diesel A Unit "8913", 93-94	55	65	___
18915	WM Alco Diesel A Unit "8915", 93	65	80	___
18916	WM Alco Diesel A Unit "8916," dummy, 93	38	42	___
18917	Soo Line NW2 Switcher, 93	65	75	___
18918	B&M NW2 Switcher "8918", 93	75	90	___
18919	Santa Fe Alco Diesel A Unit "8919," dummy, 93-94	36	55	___
18920	Frisco NW2 Switcher "254", 94	70	75	___
18921	C&NW NW2 Switcher "1017", 94	60	80	___
18922	New Haven Alco Diesel A Unit "8922", 94	75	120	___
18923	New Haven Alco Diesel A Unit "8923," dummy, 94	50	55	___
18924	IC Industrial Switcher "8924", 94-95	37	44	___
18925	D&RGW Industrial Switcher "8925", 94-95	32	37	___
18926	Reading Industrial Switcher "8926", 94-95	31	39	___
18927	U.S. Navy NW2 Switcher "65-00637", 94-95	65	85	___
18928	C&NW NW2 Switcher Calf Unit, 95	50	55	___
18929	B&M NW2 Switcher Calf Unit, 95	44	48	___
18930	Crayola Switcher, 94 u, 95	27	30	___
18931	Chrysler Mopar NW2 Switcher "1818", 94 u	76	88	___
18932	Jersey Central NW2 Switcher "8932", 96		65	___
18933	Jersey Central NW2 Switcher Calf Unit "8933", 96		55	___
18934/35	Reading Alco Diesel AA Set, 95	75	95	___
18934	Reading Alco Diesel A-A Set, 95		220	___
18935	Reading Alco FA-2 Diesel "8935," unpowered, 95		80	___
18936	Amtrak Alco Diesel A Unit "8936", 95		65	___
18937	Amtrak FA2 Alco Diesel, nonpowered, 95-97		50	___
18938	U.S. Navy NW2 Switcher Calf Unit, 95	55	65	___
18939	Union Pacific NW2 Switcher Set, 96		145	___
18940	UP NW2 Switcher, unpowered, 96		75	___
18943	Georgia Power NW2 Switcher "1960", 95 u		170	___
18945	MP NW2 Switcher, 96		168	___
18946	U.S. Coast Guard NW2 Switcher "8946", 96		80	___

			Exc	Mint
___	**18947**	Port of Lionel City Alco FA2 Diesel "2030", 97		70
___	**18948**	Port of Lionel City Alco FB-2 Diesel "2030B", 97		45
___	**18949**	NYC NW2 Switcher, 97		170
___	**18951**	Erie NW2 Switcher "6220", 97		165
___	**18952**	ATSF Alco PA1 Diesel "2000", 97	138	345
___	**18953**	NYC Alco PA1 Diesel "2000", 97		260
___	**18954**	ATSF Alco FA2 Diesel "212," powered, 97-99		80
___	**18955**	NJ Transit NW2 Switcher "500", 96 u		110
___	**18956**	Dodge Motorsports NW2 Switcher "8956", 96 u		172
___	**18959**	New York Central NW2 Switcher "622", 97		475
___	**18961**	Erie Alco PA1 Diesel "850", 98		315
___	**18965**	Santa Fe Alco PB1 Diesel, 98	150	235
___	**18966**	New York Central Alco BP1 Diesel "2008", 98		250
___	**18971**	Alco Diesel A Unit, nonpowered, 98		60
___	**18972**	RI Alco FA Diesel AA Set, 98		180
___	**18973**	RI Alco FA2 Diesel "2031," powered, 98-99		165
___	**18974**	RI Alco FA2 Diesel Dummy Unit, 98-99		80
___	**18975**	Southern 44-ton Switcher "1955", 99		190
___	**18978**	C&O NW2 Switcher "624", 99-00		410
___	**18979**	Area 51 Groom Lake RR Alco FA-2 Diesel, 02		170
___	**18981**	Pennsylvania Railroad Speeder "16", 04		45
___	**18982**	Santa Fe Railroad Speeder "122", 04-05		65
___	**18988**	MP15 Diesel, K-Line, 06		140
___	**18989**	Bethlehem Steel Plymouth Switcher, traditional, K-Line, 06		100
___	**18992**	SP S2 Diesel Switcher "1440," CC, 08		410
___	**18993**	C&NW S2 Diesel Switcher "1031," CC, 08		410
___	**18994**	Lionel Lines FA Diesel, traditional, 08-09		90
___	**19000**	Blue Comet Diner, 87 u	60	75
___	**19001**	Southern Diner, 87 u	55	65
___	**19002**	Pennsylvania Diner, 88 u	29	41
___	**19003**	Milwaukee Road Diner, 88 u	29	44
___	**19010**	B&O Diner, 89 u	36	55
___	**19011**	Lionel Lines Baggage Car, 93	164	290
___	**19015**	Lionel Lines Passenger Coach, 91	108	164
___	**19016**	Lionel Lines Passenger Coach, 91	95	135
___	**19017**	Lionel Lines Passenger Coach, 91	88	118
___	**19018**	Lionel Lines Observation Car, 91	90	117
___	**19019**	SP Baggage Car "9019", 93	120	153
___	**19023**	SP Passenger Coach "9023", 92	125	160
___	**19024**	SP Passenger Coach "9024", 92	85	100
___	**19025**	SP Passenger Coach "9025", 92	100	115
___	**19026**	SP Observation Car "9026", 92	85	100
___	**19038**	Adolphus Busch Observation Car, 92-93 u		85
___	**19039**	Pere Marquette Baggage Car, 93		75
___	**19040**	Pere Marquette Passenger Coach "1115", 93		75
___	**19041**	Pere Marquette Passenger Coach "1116", 93		75
___	**19042**	Pere Marquette Observation Car "36", 93		75
___	**19047**	Baltimore & Ohio Combination Car "9047", 96		55
___	**19048**	Baltimore & Ohio Passenger Coach "9048", 96		50
___	**19049**	Baltimore & Ohio Diner "9049", 96		42
___	**19050**	Baltimore & Ohio Observation Car "9050", 96		42
___	**19056**	NYC Heavyweight Baggage Car, 96		105
___	**19057**	NYC Willow Run Heavyweight Coach, 96		95

		Exc	Mint	
19058	NYC Willow Trail Heavyweight Coach, 96		90	___
19059	NYC Seneca Valley Heavyweight Observation Car, 96		100	___
19060	Pullman Heavyweight Set, 96		473	___
19061	Wabash Passenger Set, 97		235	___
19062	Wabash City of Columbia Coach "2361", 97		90	___
19063	Wabash City of Danville Coach "2362", 97		75	___
19064	Wabash REA Baggage Car "2360", 97		47	___
19065	Wabash Windy City Observation Car "2363", 97		90	___
19066	Commodore Vanderbilt Pullman Heavyweight 2-pack, 97		190	___
19067	Commodore Vanderbilt Willow River Pullman "2543", 97		115	___
19068	Commodore Vanderbilt Willow Valley Pullman "2544", 97		100	___
19069	Pullman Baby Madison Set "9500-02", 97		155	___
19070	Baby Madison Combination Car "9501", 97		40	___
19071	Laurel Gap Baby Madison Coach "9500", 97		34	___
19072	Laurel Summit Baby Madison Coach "9500", 97		40	___
19073	Catskill Valley Baby Madison Observation Car "9502", 97		34	___
19074	Legends of Lionel Madison Set, 97	65	385	___
19075	Mazzone Lionel Legends Coach "2621", 97		105	___
19076	Caruso Lionel Legends Coach "2624", 97		90	___
19077	Raphael Lionel Legends Coach "2652", 97		90	___
19078	Cowen Lionel Legends Observation Car "2600", 97		95	___
19079	NYC Heavyweight Passenger Car Set, 97		275	___
19080	NYC Heavyweight REA Baggage Car "2564", 97		100	___
19081	NYC Park Place Heavyweight Coach "2565", 97		100	___
19082	NYC Star Beam Heavyweight Coach "2566", 97		100	___
19083	NYC Hudson Valley Heavyweight Observation "2567", 97		100	___
19085	N&W Operating Hopper, 97		84	___
19087	C&O Heavyweight Passenger Car 4-pack, "2571-74", 97	80	290	___
19088	C&O Heavyweight Baggage Car "2571", 97		100	___
19089	C&O Heavyweight Sleeper Car "2572", 97		100	___
19090	C&O Heavyweight Diner "2573", 97		110	___
19091	C&O Heavyweight Observation Car "2574", 97		100	___
19093	Commodore Vanderbilt Heavyweight Sleeper Car 2-pack, 98		170	___
19094	Commodore Vanderbilt Niagara Falls Sleeper, 98		75	___
19095	Commodore Vanderbilt Highland Falls Sleeper, 98		75	___
19096	Legends of Lionel Madison Car 2-pack, 98		130	___
19097	Bonnano Lionel Legends Coach "2653", 98		80	___
19098	Pagano Lionel Legends Coach "2654", 98		105	___
19099	PRR Liberty Gap Baggage Car "2623", 99		80	___
19100	Amtrak Baggage Car "9100", 89	125	165	___
19101	Amtrak Combination Car "9101", 89	75	85	___
19102	Amtrak Passenger Coach "9102", 89	75	85	___
19103	Amtrak Vista Dome Car "9103", 89	70	90	___
19104	Amtrak Diner "9104", 89	65	80	___
19105	Amtrak Full Vista Dome Car "9105", 89 u	70	80	___
19106	Amtrak Observation Car "9106", 89	75	90	___
19107	SP Full Vista Dome Car, 90 u	70	88	___
19108	N&W Full Vista Dome Car "576", 91 u	75	85	___
19109	Santa Fe Baggage Car "3400", 91	168	263	___
19110	Santa Fe Combination Car "3500", 91	70	108	___
19111	Santa Fe Diner "601", 91	85	123	___
19112	Santa Fe Passenger Coach, 91	90	135	___
19113	Santa Fe Vista Dome Car, 91	100	135	___

			Exc	Mint
___	**19116**	Great Northern Baggage Car "1200", 92	135	165
___	**19117**	Great Northern Combination Car "1240", 92	65	80
___	**19118**	Great Northern Passenger Coach "1212", 92	75	95
___	**19119**	Great Northern Vista Dome Car "1322", 92	75	95
___	**19120**	Great Northern Observation Car "1192", 92	75	95
___	**19121**	Union Pacific Vista Dome Car "9121", 92 u	90	100
___	**19122**	D&RGW California Zephyr Baggage Car, 93	170	210
___	**19123**	D&RGW California Zephyr Silver Bronco Vista Dome Car, 93	95	115
___	**19124**	D&RGW California Zephyr Silver Colt Vista Dome Car, 93	95	115
___	**19125**	D&RGW California Zephyr Silver Mustang Vista Dome Car, 93	100	125
___	**19126**	D&RGW California Zephyr Silver Pony Vista Dome Car, 93	95	115
___	**19127**	D&RGW California Zephyr Vista Dome Car, 93	85	100
___	**19128**	Santa Fe Full Vista Dome Car "507", 92 u	143	163
___	**19129**	IC Full Vista Dome Car "9129", 93	75	85
___	**19130**	Lackawanna Passenger Cars, set of 4, 94	280	350
___	**19131**	Lackawanna Baggage Car "2000" (see 19130)		150
___	**19132**	Lackawanna Diner "469" (see 19130)		100
___	**19133**	Lackawanna Passenger Coach "260" (see 19130)		100
___	**19134**	Lackawanna Observation Car "789" (see 19130)		85
___	**19135**	Lackawanna Combination Car "425", 94	85	100
___	**19136**	Lackawanna Passenger Coach "211", 94	65	75
___	**19137**	New York Central Roomette Car, 95	71	105
___	**19138**	Santa Fe Roomette Car, 95	75	95
___	**19139**	N&W Baggage Car "577", 95	150	200
___	**19140**	N&W Combination Car "494", 95	60	80
___	**19141**	N&W Diner "495", 95	105	135
___	**19142**	N&W Passenger Coach "538", 95	75	95
___	**19143**	N&W Passenger Coach "537", 95	75	95
___	**19144**	N&W Observation Car "582", 95	80	95
___	**19145**	C&O Combination Car "1403", 96		65
___	**19146**	C&O Passenger Coach "1623", 96		60
___	**19147**	C&O Passenger Coach "1803", 96		55
___	**19148**	C&O Chessie Club Coach "1903", 96		55
___	**19149**	C&O Coach/Diner "1950", 96		50
___	**19150**	C&O Observation Car "2504", 96		55
___	**19151**	Norfolk & Western Duplex Roomette car, 96		108
___	**19152**	Union Pacific Duplex Roomette Car, 96		75
___	**19153**	C&O Passenger Cars, set of 4, 96	60	340
___	**19154**	Atlantic Coast Line Passenger Car Set, 96	90	340
___	**19155**	ACL Combination Car "101", 96		90
___	**19156**	ACL Talladega Diner, 96		90
___	**19157**	ACL Moultrie Coach, 96		95
___	**19158**	ACL Observation Car "256", 96		90
___	**19159**	N&W Passenger Cars, set of 4, 95 u	300	385
___	**19160**	LL REA Baggage Car, 96		90
___	**19161**	LL Silver Mesa Coach, 96		80
___	**19162**	LL Silver Sky Vista Dome Car, 96		75
___	**19163**	LL Silver Rail Observation Car, 96		75
___	**19164**	C&O Passenger Car Add-on, 2-pack, 96		160
___	**19165**	ATSF Super Chief Set, 96		305
___	**19166**	NP Vista Dome Car Set, 97	113	323
___	**19167**	NP Pullman Coach "2571", 97		105
___	**19168**	NP Pullman Coach "2571", 97		105

		Exc	Mint
19169	NP Pullman Coach "2570", 97		95
19170	NP Pullman Coach "2571", 97		100
19171	NYC Streamliner Car 4-pack, 97		290
19172	NYC Aluminum Passenger/Baggage Car "2570", 97		95
19173	NYC Manhattan Island Aluminum Passenger Diner, 97		100
19174	NYC Queensboro Bridge Aluminum Passenger Coach, 97		100
19175	NYC Windgate Brook Aluminum Observation Car, 97		90
19176	ATSF Indian Arrow Diner "2572", 97		90
19177	ATSF Grass Valley Coach "2573", 97		90
19178	ATSF Citrus Valley Coach "2574", 97		90
19179	ATSF Vista Heights Coach "2575", 97		90
19180	ATSF Surfliner Passenger Car 4-pack, 97		250
19181	GN Empire Builder Prairie View Full Vista Dome Car, 98	33	78
19182	GN Empire Builder River View Full Vista Dome Car, 98	38	93
19183	GN Empire Builder Vista Dome Car 2-pack, 98	75	163
19184	Milwaukee Road Passenger Car 4-pack, 99		390
19185	MILW Red River Valley Aluminum Passenger Coach "194", 99		125
19186	MILW Aluminum Coach/Diner "170", 99		110
19187	MILW Cedar Rapids Aluminum Observation Car "186 ", 99		120
19188	MILW Aluminum REA Passenger/Baggage Car "1336", 99		95
19194	KCS Aluminum Passenger Car 4-pack, 00		380
19195	KCS Aluminum Baggage Car "19195", 00-01		95
19196	KCS Aluminum Coach "Texarkana", 00-01		95
19197	KCS Aluminum Coach "Joplin", 00-01		95
19198	KCS Aluminum Observation "New Orleans", 00-01		95
19200	Tidewater Southern Boxcar, 87	14	21
19201	Lancaster & Chester Boxcar, 87	23	37
19202	PRR Boxcar, 87	22	30
19203	D&TS Boxcar, 87	11	18
19204	Milwaukee Road Boxcar (FF 2), 87	30	43
19205	Great Northern DD Boxcar (FF 3), 88	19	24
19206	Seaboard System Boxcar, 88	18	23
19207	CP Rail DD Boxcar, 88	17	22
19208	Southern DD Boxcar, 88	11	13
19209	Florida East Coast Boxcar, 88	15	19
19210	Soo Line Boxcar, 89	19	23
19211	Vermont Railway Boxcar, 89	18	21
19212	PRR Boxcar, 89	21	25
19213	SP&S DD Boxcar, 89	17	25
19214	Western Maryland Boxcar (FF 4), 89	23	27
19215	Union Pacific DD Boxcar, 90	17	21
19216	Santa Fe Boxcar, 90	17	22
19217	Burlington Boxcar, 90	16	21
19218	New Haven Boxcar, 90	16	20
19219	Lionel Lines 1900-1906 Boxcar, diesel RailSounds, 90	120	145
19220	Lionel Lines 1926-1934 Boxcar, 90	27	30
19221	Lionel Lines 1935-1937 Boxcar, 90	27	30
19222	Lionel Lines 1948-1950 Boxcar, 90	27	30
19223	Lionel Lines 1979-1989 Boxcar, 90	18	25
19228	Cotton Belt Boxcar, 91	16	22
19229	Frisco Boxcar, diesel RailSounds (FF 5), 91	75	90
19230	Frisco DD Boxcar (FF 5), 91	21	26
19231	TA&G DD Boxcar, 91	13	16

			Exc	Mint
___	**19232**	Rock Island DD Boxcar, 91	17	20
___	**19233**	Southern Pacific Boxcar, 91	15	19
___	**19234**	NYC Boxcar, 91	60	65
___	**19235**	MKT Boxcar, 91	55	65
___	**19236**	NKP DD Boxcar (FF 6), 92	21	30
___	**19237**	C&IM Boxcar, 92	17	24
___	**19238**	Kansas City Southern Boxcar, 92	17	24
___	**19239**	Toronto, Hamilton & Buffalo DD Boxcar, 92	15	20
___	**19240**	Great Northern DD Boxcar, 92	17	23
___	**19241**	Mickey Mouse 60th Anniversary Hi-Cube Boxcar, 91 u	135	180
___	**19242**	Donald Duck 50th Anniversary Hi-Cube Boxcar, 91 u	143	152
___	**19243**	Clinchfield Boxcar "9790", 91 u	35	41
___	**19244**	L&N Boxcar "9791", 92	35	38
___	**19245**	Mickey's World Tour Hi-Cube Boxcar, 92 u	35	40
___	**19246**	Disney World 20th Anniversary Hi-Cube Boxcar, 92 u	33	40
___	**19247**	Postwar "6464" Series Boxcar Set I, 3 cars, 93	323	550
___	**19248**	Western Pacific Boxcar "6464", 93	75	95
___	**19249**	Great Northern Boxcar "6464", 93	75	95
___	**19250**	M&StL Boxcar "6464", 93	80	105
___	**19251**	Montana Rail Link DD Boxcar "10001", 93	21	34
___	**19254**	Erie Boxcar (FF 7), 93	21	25
___	**19255**	Erie DD Boxcar (FF 7), 93	22	26
___	**19256**	Goofy Hi-Cube Boxcar, 93	23	26
___	**19257**	Postwar "6464" Series Boxcar Set II, 3 cars, 94	73	116
___	**19258**	Rock Island Boxcar "6464", 94	25	34
___	**19259**	Western Pacific Boxcar "6464100", 94	33	46
___	**19260**	Western Pacific Boxcar "6464100", 94	35	49
___	**19261**	Perils of Mickey Hi-Cube Boxcar #1, 93	20	30
___	**19262**	Perils of Mickey Hi-Cube Boxcar #2, 93	20	28
___	**19263**	NYC DD Boxcar (SSS), 94	36	42
___	**19264**	Perils of Mickey Hi-Cube Boxcar #3, 94	28	31
___	**19265**	Mickey Mouse 65th Anniversary Hi-Cube Boxcar, 94	22	44
___	**19266**	Postwar "6464" Series Boxcar Set III, 3 cars, 95	66	98
___	**19267**	NYC Pacemaker Boxcar "6464125", 95	37	42
___	**19268**	Missouri Pacific Boxcar "6464150", 95	25	29
___	**19269**	Rock Island Boxcar "6464", 95	25	26
___	**19270**	Donald Duck 60th Anniversary Hi-Cube Boxcar, 95	30	34
___	**19271**	Minnie Mouse Hi-Cube Boxcar, 95	21	43
___	**19272**	Postwar "6464" Series Boxcar Set IV, 3 cars, 96	73	103
___	**19273**	BAR State of Maine Boxcar "6464275", 96		35
___	**19274**	SP Overnight Boxcar "6464225", 96		28
___	**19275**	Pennsylvania Boxcar "6464", 96		44
___	**19276**	Postwar "6464" Series Boxcar Set V, 3 cars, 96	56	103
___	**19277**	Rutland Boxcar "6464-300", 96		26
___	**19278**	B&O Boxcar "6464-325", 96		30
___	**19279**	Central of Georgia Boxcar "6464-375", 96		29
___	**19280**	Mickey's Wheat Hi-Cube Boxcar, 96		32
___	**19281**	Mickey's Carrots Hi-Cube Boxcar, 96		40
___	**19282**	Santa Fe "Super Chief" Boxcar "6464-196", 96		24
___	**19283**	Erie Boxcar "6464-296", 96		22
___	**19284**	Northern Pacific Boxcar "6464-396", 96	10	35
___	**19285**	B&A State of Maine Boxcar "6464-275", 96	10	30
___	**19286**	Tweety and Sylvester Boxcar, 96		46

		Exc	Mint	
19287	NYC/PC Merger Boxcar "6464-125X" (SSS), 97	50	75	___
19288	PRR/CR Merger Boxcar "6464-200X" (SSS), 97	43	56	___
19289	Monon "Hoosier Line" Boxcar "6464", 97		27	___
19290	Seaboard "Silver Meteor" Boxcar "6464", 97		24	___
19291	GN Boxcar "6464-397", 97	14	33	___
19292	Postwar "6464" Series Boxcar Set VI, 3 cars, 97	25	70	___
19293	MKT Boxcar "6464-350", 97	28	32	___
19294	B&O Boxcar "6464-400", 97	27	34	___
19295	NH Boxcar "6464-425", 97	25	34	___
19300	PRR Ore Car, 87	15	23	___
19301	Milwaukee Road Ore Car, 87	19	26	___
19302	Milwaukee Road Quad Hopper with coal (FF 2), 87	23	35	___
19303	Lionel Lines Quad Hopper with coal, 87 u	20	36	___
19304	GN Covered Quad Hopper (FF 3), 88	17	27	___
19305	Chessie System Ore Car, 88	18	23	___
19307	B&LE Ore Car with load, 89	19	25	___
19308	GN Ore Car with load, 89	18	23	___
19309	Seaboard Covered Quad Hopper, 89	16	19	___
19310	L&C Quad Hopper with coal, 89	16	30	___
19311	SP Covered Quad Hopper, 90	15	18	___
19312	Reading Quad Hopper with coal, 90	21	36	___
19313	B&O Ore Car with load, 90-91	20	25	___
19315	Amtrak Ore Car with load, 91	22	30	___
19316	Wabash Covered Quad Hopper, 91	18	23	___
19317	Lehigh Valley Quad Hopper with coal, 91	47	55	___
19318	NKP Quad Hopper with coal (FF 6), 92	29	32	___
19319	Union Pacific Covered Quad Hopper, 92	19	23	___
19320	PRR Ore Car with load, 92	21	30	___
19321	B&LE Ore Car with load, 92	21	30	___
19322	C&NW Ore Car with load, 93	27	34	___
19323	Detroit & Mackinac Ore Car with load, 93	20	29	___
19324	Erie Quad Hopper with coal (FF 7), 93	25	33	___
19325	N&W 4-bay Hopper "6446-1" with coal, 97		65	___
19326	N&W 4-bay Hopper "6446-2" with coal, 96		60	___
19327	N&W 4-bay Hopper "6446-3" with coal, 96		60	___
19328	N&W 4-bay Hopper "6446-4" with coal, 96		60	___
19329	N&W 4-bay Hopper "6436" with coal, 97		55	___
19330	Cotton Belt 4-bay Hopper "64661" with coal, 98		45	___
19331	Cotton Belt 4-bay Hopper "64662" with coal, 98		45	___
19332	Cotton Belt 4-bay Hopper "64663" with coal, 98		45	___
19333	Cotton Belt 4-bay Hopper "64664" with coal, 98		45	___
19338	Cotton Belt 4-bay Hopper 2-pack, 99		120	___
19339	Cotton Belt 4-bay Hopper "64469", 99		60	___
19340	Cotton Belt 4-bay Hopper "64470", 99		60	___
19341	LV 2-bay Hopper "6456", 99		30	___
19344	D&RGW 3-bay Cylindrical Hopper "15990", 99-00		42	___
19345	CN 3-bay Cylindrical Hopper "370708", 99-00	35	98	___
19346	PRR 4-bay Hopper with coal "744433", 01		40	___
19347	LV 2-bay Hopper "643657", 01		40	___
19348	Duluth, Missabe & Iron Range Ore Car "28000", 03		25	___
19349	U.S. Steel Ore Car "19349", 03		29	___
19350	Postwar "6636" Alaska Quad Hopper, 03		34	___
19357	N&W Hopper "6446-25," Archive Collection, 07		50	___

			Exc	Mint
___	**19361**	Twizzlers Quad Hopper, 10		55
___	**19362**	Coursers Christmas Hopper with gifts, 10		60
___	**19364**	Milk Duds Covered Hopper, 11		55
___	**19365**	Coca-Cola Quad Hopper, 10		60
___	**19366**	Santa's Little Hopper, 10-11		55
___	**19367**	ATSF Quad Hopper, 11		60
___	**19368**	Southern Offset Hopper "106723," (std 0), 11		70
___	**19369**	Alaska Quad Hopper "20756," 12		60
___	**19371**	Burlington Northern I-Beam Car, 04		60
___	**19374**	NS Bathtub Gondola 2-pack (std 0), 15		140
___	**19377**	DETX Bathtub Gondola 2-pack (std 0), 15		140
___	**19380**	CSX Bathtub Gondola 2-pack (std 0), 15		140
___	**19383**	UP PS-4 Flatcar "57125" (std 0), 13		70
___	**19384**	ATSF PS-4 Flatcar "90088" (std 0), 13		70
___	**19385**	CNJ PS-4 Flatcar "339" (std 0), 13		70
___	**19386**	BN PS-4 Flatcar "613200" (std 0), 13		70
___	**19388**	BN 89' Auto Carrier (std 0), 13-14		110
___	**19389**	SP 89' Auto Carrier (std 0), 13-14		110
___	**19390**	CP 89' Auto Carrier (std 0), 13-14, 16		110
___	**19391**	Soo Line 89' Auto Carrier (std 0), 13-14, 16		110
___	**19393**	BNSF Auto Carrier 2-pack (std 0), 12		220
___	**19394**	UP Auto Carrier 2-pack (std 0), 12		220
___	**19395**	Grand Trunk Auto Carrier 2-pack (std 0), 12		220
___	**19396**	CSX Auto Carrier 2-pack (std 0), 12		220
___	**19397**	CN Auto Carrier 2-pack (std 0), 12		220
___	**19398**	Conrail Auto Carrier 2-pack (std 0), 12		220
___	**19400**	Milwaukee Road Gondola with cable reels (FF 2), 87	21	33
___	**19401**	GN Gondola with coal (FF 3), 88	19	25
___	**19402**	GN Crane Car (FF 3), 88	47	65
___	**19403**	WM Gondola with coal (FF 4), 89	20	25
___	**19404**	Trailer Train Flatcar with WM trailers (FF 4), 89	29	33
___	**19405**	Southern Crane Car, 91	42	65
___	**19406**	West Point Mint Car, 91	38	50
___	**19408**	Frisco Gondola with coil covers (FF 5), 91	26	31
___	**19409**	Southern Flatcar with stakes, 91	18	22
___	**19410**	NYC Gondola with canisters, 91	47	55
___	**19411**	NKP Flatcar with Sears trailer (FF 6), 92	30	59
___	**19412**	Frisco Crane Car, 92	49	65
___	**19413**	Frisco Flatcar with stakes, 92	16	21
___	**19414**	Union Pacific Flatcar with stakes (SSS), 92	19	26
___	**19415**	Erie Flatcar with trailer "7200" (FF 7), 93	28	39
___	**19416**	ICG TTUX Flatcar Set with trailers (SSS), 93	70	75
___	**19419**	Charlotte Mint Car, 93	25	32
___	**19420**	Lionel Lines Vat Car, 94	18	22
___	**19421**	Hirsch Brothers Vat Car, 95	16	21
___	**19423**	Circle L Racing Flatcar "6424" with stock cars, 96		27
___	**19424**	Edison Electric Flatcar "6461" w/transformer, 97		31
___	**19427**	Evans Auto Loader "6414", 99		55
___	**19428**	Evans Boat Loader "6414", 99		70
___	**19429**	Culvert Gondola "6342", 98-99		48
___	**19430**	ATSF Flatcar "6411" with Beechcraft Bonanza, 98		47
___	**19438**	Christmas Gondola (std 0), 98		42
___	**19439**	Flatcar with safes, 98		35

		Exc	Mint	
19440	Flatcar with FedEx trailer, 98		34	___
19441	Lobster Vat Car, 98		35	___
19442	Water Supply Flatcar with tank (SSS), 98		31	___
19444	Flatcar with VW Bug, 98		38	___
19445	Borden Milk Tank Car "520", 99		38	___
19446	Pittsburgh Paint Vat Car, 99		43	___
19447	Mama's Baked Beans Vat Car, 99		35	___
19448	Easter Gondola "6462" with candy, 99		27	___
19449	Liquified Gas Tank Car "6469", 99		31	___
19450	Barrel Ramp Car "6343", 99		31	___
19451	Wheel Car "6262", 99		32	___
19454	PRR Flatcar "6424" with gondola, 99		25	___
19455	Lionel Lines Flatcar "6430" with Cooper-Jarrett trailers, 99		60	___
19457	Lionel Lines Extension Searchlight Car, 99		40	___
19459	Valentine Gondola "6462" with candy, 99		50	___
19471	Mobil Flatcar with 2 trailers, 00 u		96	___
19472	Mobil Bulkhead Flatcar with tank, 00 u		68	___
19474	L&N Flatcar "6424" with trailer frames, 99		26	___
19476	Zoo Gondola "6462" with animals, 99-00		43	___
19477	Monday Night Football Flatcar with trailer, 01		30	___
19478	Culvert Gondola "6342", 99		45	___
19479	Borden Milk Car "521", 00		38	___
19480	Valentine's Vat Car "6475", 99-00		30	___
19481	Easter Vat Car, 99-00		38	___
19482	NYC Flat with trailer "6424", 00		50	___
19483	VW Beetle Flatcar, 00		48	___
19484	Flatcar "6264" with timber, 00		34	___
19485	PRR Culvert Gondola "347004", 01		41	___
19486	NYC Lumber Flatcar, 01		34	___
19487	Flatcar "6800" with airplane, 00		41	___
19489	Evans Auto Loader "500085", 00		50	___
19490	Postwar "6475" Libby's Vat Car, 01-02		36	___
19491	Christmas Vat Car, 01		30	___
19492	WM Skeleton Log Car 3-pack, 01		95	___
19496	Westside Lumber Skeleton Log Car 3-pack, 01		112	___
19500	Milwaukee Road Reefer (FF 2), 87	30	44	___
19502	C&NW Reefer, 87	30	33	___
19503	Bangor & Aroostook Reefer, 87	22	25	___
19504	Northern Pacific Reefer, 87	16	22	___
19505	Great Northern Reefer (FF 3), 88	29	35	___
19506	Thomas Newcomen Reefer, 88	18	23	___
19507	Thomas Edison Reefer, 88	21	27	___
19508	Leonardo da Vinci Reefer, 89	19	27	___
19509	Alexander Graham Bell Reefer, 89	17	20	___
19510	PRR Stock Car (FARR 5), 89 u	18	26	___
19511	WM Reefer (FF 4), 89	22	28	___
19512	Wright Brothers Reefer, 90	17	21	___
19513	Ben Franklin Reefer, 90	17	20	___
19515	Milwaukee Road Stock Car (FF 2), 90 u	31	43	___
19516	George Washington Reefer, 89 u, 91	14	19	___
19517	Civil War Reefer, 89 u, 91	14	19	___
19518	Man on the Moon Reefer, 89 u, 91	13	17	___
19519	Frisco Stock Car (FF 5), 91	26	31	___

			Exc	Mint
___	**19520**	CSX Reefer, 91	18	23
___	**19522**	Guglielmo Marconi Reefer, 91	19	23
___	**19523**	Dr. Robert Goddard Reefer, 91	19	23
___	**19524**	Delaware & Hudson Reefer (SSS), 91	29	32
___	**19525**	Speedy Alka Seltzer Reefer, 91 u	31	32
___	**19526**	Jolly Green Giant Reefer, 91 u	21	33
___	**19527**	Nickel Plate Road Reefer (FF 6), 92	20	29
___	**19528**	Joshua L. Cowen Reefer, 92	23	28
___	**19529**	A.C. Gilbert Reefer, 92	18	23
___	**19530**	Rock Island Stock Car, 92 u	34	38
___	**19531**	Rice Krispies Reefer, 92 u	23	33
___	**19532**	Hormel Reefer "901", 92 u	18	24
___	**19535**	Erie Reefer (FF 7), 93	23	26
___	**19536**	Soo Line REA Reefer (SSS), 93	25	30
___	**19537**	Kellogg's Corn Flakes Refrigerator Car, 93 u		NRS
___	**19538**	Hormel Reefer "102", 94	22	25
___	**19539**	Heinz Reefer, 94	33	47
___	**19540**	Broken Arrow Ranch Stock Car "3356", 97		28
___	**19552**	Rutland Reefer "395" (std O), 00		32
___	**19553**	ATSF Stock Car "23003", 00		37
___	**19554**	Postwar Celebration Milk Car "36621", 00		125
___	**19555**	Swift Reefer "5839", red, 01		33
___	**19556**	Swift Reefer "1020", silver, 01		31
___	**19557**	Circus Stock Car "6376", 00		32
___	**19558**	Postwar "6556" MKT Stock Car, 02	0	126
___	**19559**	MKT Stock Car, girls set add-on, 02	30	95
___	**19560**	NP 2-door Stock Car "6356," Archive Collection, 02		33
___	**19561**	Norman Rockwell Holiday Reefer, 03		25
___	**19562**	Norman Rockwell Holiday Reefer, 03		25
___	**19563**	Norman Rockwell Holiday Reefer, 03		25
___	**19564**	Postwar "6672" Santa Fe Reefer, 03		35
___	**19565**	Burlington Reefer "6672," Archive Collection, 03		35
___	**19567**	Postwar "6572" Railway Express Agency Reefer, 05		45
___	**19568**	GN Reefer, Archive Collection, 05	18	45
___	**19569**	Pillsbury Reefer, traditional, 05		53
___	**19570**	Nestle Nesquik Reefer, traditional, 05		53
___	**19572**	NYC Reefer "6672," Archive Collection, 06		45
___	**19573**	Postwar "6356" NYC Stock Car, 06-07		50
___	**19574**	GN Stock Car, 08		50
___	**19575**	REA Reefer "6721", 08-09		50
___	**19576**	Alaska Reefer, 08		50
___	**19577**	Krey's Reefer, 10-11		60
___	**19578**	Granny Smith Apples Wood-sided Reefer, 10-11		53
___	**19580**	Nicholas Smith Wood-side Refrigerator Car, 09u	17	30
___	**19582**	Nicholas Smith Wood-side Refrigerator Car, 09u	17	30
___	**19583**	Nicholas Smith Wood-side Refrigerator Car, 09u	17	30
___	**19584**	Nicholas Smith Wood-side Refrigerator Car, 09u	17	30
___	**19585**	NS Transparent Instruction Car, 10-11		75
___	**19586**	Alaska Husky Transport Car, 10-11		75
___	**19587**	Hershey's Chocolate Wood-sided Reefer, 10		75
___	**19588**	Santa's Wish Transparent Gift Car, 10		75
___	**19589**	Blood Transfusion Bunk Car, 10-11		60
___	**19590**	Wood-sided Reefer 2-pack, 10		110

MODERN 1970-2024		Exc.	Mint	
19593	Hershey's Kisses Wood-sided Reefer, 11-15		60	___
19594	York Peppermint Patty Wood-sided Reefer, 10-11		55	___
19595	AT&SF Warbonnet Refrigerator Car, 10-11	30	55	___
19599	Old Glory Reefers, set of 3, 89 u, 91	37	47	___
19600	Milwaukee Road 1-D Tank Car (FF 2), 87	30	45	___
19601	North American 1-D Tank Car (FF 4), 89	21	32	___
19602	Johnson 1-D Tank Car (FF 5), 91	24	30	___
19603	GATX 1-D Tank Car (FF 6), 92	32	41	___
19604	Goodyear 1-D Tank Car (SSS), 93	33	36	___
19605	Hudson's Bay 1-D Tank Car (SSS), 94	25	29	___
19607	Sunoco 1-D Tank Car "6315", 96	10	31	___
19608	Sunoco Aviation Services 1-D Tank Car "6315" (SSS), 97		38	___
19611	Gulf Oil 1-D Tank Car "6315", 98		33	___
19612	Gulf Oil 3-D Tank Car "6425", 98		30	___
19614	BASF 1-D Tank Car "UTLX 78252", 99-00		25	___
19615	Vulcan Chemicals 1-D Tank Car, 99-00		25	___
19621	Centennial 1-D Tank Car "6015-1", 99		55	___
19622	Centennial 1-D Tank Car "6015-2", 99		62	___
19623	Centennial 1-D Tank Car "6015-3", 99		62	___
19624	Centennial 1-D Tank Car "6015-4", 99		58	___
19625	Ethyl Tank Car "6236", 01		31	___
19626	Diamond Chemical Tank Car "19419", 01		29	___
19627	Shell 1-D Tank Car "1227", 01		37	___
19628	Lion Oil 1-D Tank Car "2256", 01		35	___
19634	General American 1-D Tank Car, 01		30	___
19635	U.S. Army 1-D Tank Car "10936", 01		31	___
19636	Hooker Chemicals 1-D Tank Car "6180", 01		36	___
19637	GATX TankTrain Intermediate Car "44589" (std 0), 02		55	___
19638	CN TankTrain Intermediate Car "75571" (std 0), 02		65	___
19639	GATX TankTrain Intermediate Car 3-pack (std 0), 02		140	___
19644	Union Texas 1-D Tank Car "9922", 02		33	___
19645	Penn Salt 1-D Tank Car "4730", 02		33	___
19646	CN TankTrain Intermediate Car "75571" (std 0), 03		45	___
19647	GATX TankTrain Intermediate Car "44589" (std 0), 03		45	___
19649	Scrooge McDuck Mint Car, 05	90	207	___
19651	Santa Fe Tool Car, 87	30	35	___
19652	Jersey Central Bunk Car, 88	25	33	___
19653	Jersey Central Tool Car, 88	26	28	___
19654	Amtrak Bunk Car, 89	22	25	___
19655	Amtrak Tool Car, 90-91	23	30	___
19656	Milwaukee Road Bunk Car, smoke, 90	38	44	___
19657	Wabash Bunk Car, smoke, 91-92	36	42	___
19658	Norfolk & Western Tool Car, 91	24	29	___
19660	Mint Car, 98		40	___
19663	Pratt's Hollow Bunk Car "5717", 99		40	___
19664	Ambassador Award Bunk Car, bronze, 99 u	213	463	___
19665	Ambassador Engineer Bunk Car, silver, 99 u		630	___
19666	Ambassador Cowen Bunk Car, gold, 99 u		443	___
19667	Wellspring Gold Bullion Car, 99		58	___
19669	King Tut Museum Car "9660", 99		70	___
19670	NY Federal Reserve Bullion Car "6445", 00		44	___
19671	Lionel Model Shop Display Car "6445-01", 99-00		50	___
19672	Lionel Mines Mint Car, 00 u		250	___

			Exc	Mint
___	**19673**	Wellspring Capital Management Mint Car, 99 u		220
___	**19674**	Lionel Lines Platinum Car, 00		43
___	**19675**	Lionel Model Shop Display "6445-2", 01		42
___	**19676**	Philadelphia Mint Car, 01		40
___	**19677**	Fort Knox Mint Car "6445", 00	15	50
___	**19678**	U.S. Army Bunk Car, 02		45
___	**19679**	St. Louis Federal Reserve Mint Car, 02		38
___	**19681**	Area 51 Alien Suspension Car, 02		47
___	**19682**	Alaska Klondike Mining Mint Car, 02		40
___	**19683**	Pony Express Mint Car, 02	13	50
___	**19686**	Chicago Federal Reserve Mint Car "6445", 03-04		45
___	**19687**	UP Bunk Car "3887," smoke, 03		40
___	**19688**	Postwar "6445" Fort Knox Mint Car, 02-03		39
___	**19689**	CIBRO TankTrain Intermediate Car 3-pack (std O), 03		100
___	**19694**	Pony Express Mint Car, 03		50
___	**19696**	U.S. Savings Bond Mint Car, 00		150
___	**19697**	U.S. Bureau of Engraving and Printing Mint Car "19697", 04		40
___	**19698**	San Francisco Federal Reserve Mint Car, 04		40
___	**19700**	Chessie System Extended Vision Caboose, 88	43	50
___	**19701**	Milwaukee Road N5c Caboose (FF 2), 88	50	65
___	**19702**	PRR N5c Caboose, 87	44	55
___	**19703**	GN Extended Vision Caboose (FF 3), 88	41	51
___	**19704**	WM Extended Vision Caboose, smoke (FF 4), 89	42	49
___	**19705**	CP Rail Extended Vision Caboose, smoke, 89	44	64
___	**19706**	UP Extended Vision Caboose "9706," smoke, 89	40	56
___	**19707**	SP Work Caboose with searchlight, smoke, 90	55	60
___	**19708**	Lionel Lines Bay Window Caboose, 90	43	46
___	**19709**	PRR Work Caboose, smoke, 89, 91	49	70
___	**19710**	Frisco Extended Vision Caboose, smoke (FF 5), 91	43	47
___	**19711**	NS Extended Vision Caboose, smoke, 92	47	65
___	**19712**	PRR N5c Caboose, 91	44	47
___	**19714**	NYC Work Caboose with searchlight, smoke, 92	70	110
___	**19715**	DM&IR Extended Vision Caboose "C-217", 92 u	50	60
___	**19716**	IC Extended Vision Caboose "9405," smoke, 93	105	135
___	**19717**	Susquehanna Bay Window Caboose "0121", 93	44	55
___	**19718**	C&IM Extended Vision Caboose "74", 92 u	38	45
___	**19719**	Erie Bay Window Caboose "C-300" (FF 7), 93	47	55
___	**19720**	Soo Line Extended Vision Caboose (SSS), 93	32	41
___	**19721**	GM&O Extended Vision Caboose "2956", 93 u	47	50
___	**19723**	Disney Extended Vision Caboose, 94	36	45
___	**19724**	JCPenney MKT Extended Vision Caboose "125", 94 u	38	43
___	**19726**	NYC Bay Window Caboose (SSS), 95	50	60
___	**19727**	Pennsylvania N5c Caboose "477938", 96		30
___	**19728**	N&W Bay Window Caboose, 96		70
___	**19732**	ATSF Bay Window Caboose "6517", 96		43
___	**19733**	New York Central Caboose "6357", 96		30
___	**19734**	Southern Pacific Caboose "6357", 96		26
___	**19736**	PRR N5c Caboose "6417", 97		27
___	**19737**	Lackawanna Searchlight Caboose "2420", 97		75
___	**19738**	Conrail N5c Caboose "6417" (SSS), 97		55
___	**19739**	NYC Wood-sided Caboose "6907", 97	20	60
___	**19740**	Virginian N5c Caboose "6427", 97 u		65
___	**19741**	Pennsylvania N5c Caboose "6417", 98		50

MODERN 1970-2024		Exc	Mint
19742	Erie Bay Window Caboose "C301," Caboose Talk, 98		95
19748	SP&S Bay Window Caboose "6517", 97 u		50
19749	SP Bay Window Caboose "6517", 98		100
19750	Holiday Music Bay Window Caboose, 98		160
19751	PRR N5c Caboose "492418", 98		30
19752	NP Bay Window Caboose "407", 98		50
19753	UP Extended Vision Caboose "25641", 98		55
19754	NYC Caboose "20112", 98		55
19755	Centennial Porthole Caboose, 99		68
19756	Lionel Lines Bay Window Caboose, 99		50
19758	DL&W Work Caboose "6419", 99		55
19759	Corvette N5c Caboose, 99		60
19772	Lionel Visitor's Center Vat Car, 99 u		40
19773	Lionel Kids Club Barrel Ramp Car "6343", 96 u		48
19778	Case Cutlery Wood-sided Caboose "1889" (std O), 99 u		30
19779	SP Bay Window Caboose "1908", 99		65
19780	LV Porthole Caboose "641751", 99-00		43
19781	Vapor Records Holiday Porthole Caboose "6417", 99-00	12	63
19782	NYC Bay Window Caboose "21719", 00		65
19783	Ford Mustang Extended Vision Caboose, 01		50
19785	SP Bay Window Caboose "6517", 00		55
19786	PRR Extended Vision Caboose, 00 u		40
19787	PRR Porthole Caboose "477927", 01		40
19790	Postwar "6417" Lehigh Valley Caboose, 02		41
19792	Postwar "C301" Erie Bay Window Caboose, 03		45
19796	C&O Bay Window Caboose, 03		50
19800	Circle L Ranch Operating Cattle Car, 88	75	95
19801	Poultry Dispatch Chicken Car, 87	20	27
19802	Carnation Milk Car, 87	87	102
19803	Reading Ice Car, 87	38	44
19804	Wabash Operating Hopper, 87	25	34
19805	Santa Fe Operating Boxcar, 87	28	36
19806	PRR Operating Hopper, 88	28	38
19807	PRR Extended Vision Caboose, smoke, 88	39	53
19808	NYC Ice Car, 88	38	49
19809	Erie-Lackawanna Operating Boxcar, 88	27	35
19810	Bosco Milk Car, 88	80	89
19811	Monon Brakeman Car, 90	43	55
19813	Northern Pacific Ice Car, 89 u	41	46
19815	Delaware & Hudson Brakeman Car, 92	49	60
19816	Madison Hardware Operating Boxcar "190991", 91 u	90	105
19817	Virginian Ice Car, 94	31	35
19818	Dairymen's League Milk Car "788", 94	65	80
19819	Poultry Dispatch Car (SSS), 94	36	43
19820	Die-cast Tender, RailSounds II, 95-96		175
19821	UP Operating Boxcar, 95	27	36
19822	Pork Dispatch Car, 95	29	44
19823	Burlington Ice Car, 94 u, 95	39	49
19824	U.S. Army Target Launcher, 96		32
19825	Generator Car, 96		50
19827	NYC Operating Boxcar, 97		37
19828	C&NW Animated Stock Car "3356" and Stockyard, 96-97	50	125
19830	U.S. Mail Operating Boxcar "3428", 97		39

		MODERN 1970-2024	Exc	Mint
___	**19831**	GM Generator Car "3530," power pole and wire, 97	30	50
___	**19832**	Cola Ice Car "6352", 97		47
___	**19833**	Tender "2426RS," RailSounds II, 97	65	240
___	**19834**	LL 6-wheel Crane Car "2460", 97	30	61
___	**19835**	FedEx Animated Boxcar "3464X", 97		40
___	**19837**	Bucyrus 6-wheel Crane Car "2460", 99	30	54
___	**19845**	Aquarium Car "3435," CC, 98		151
___	**19846**	Animated Giraffe Car "3376C", 98		105
___	**19850**	Stock Car "33760," RailSounds, 00		130
___	**19853**	Firefighting Instruction Generator Car (SSS), 98		60
___	**19854**	Lionelville Fire Car (SSS), 98		55
___	**19855**	Christmas Aquarium Car, 98	15	60
___	**19856**	Mermaid Transport, 98		65
___	**19857**	NYC Firefighting Instruction Car "19853", 98-99		175
___	**19858**	Lionelville Operating Searchlight Car "19854", 99		65
___	**19859**	REA Boxcar "6267," steam RailSounds, 99		170
___	**19860**	Conrail Boxcar "169671," diesel RailSounds, 99		140
___	**19864**	Animated Ostrich Boxcar, 99		37
___	**19867**	Operating Poultry Dispatch Car "3434", 99		48
___	**19868**	Shark Aquarium Car "3435", 99		190
___	**19869**	Alien Aquarium Car "3435", 99		49
___	**19877**	ATSF Operating Barrel Car, 99		55
___	**19878**	Operating Helium Tank Flatcar "3362", 99		40
___	**19880**	Lionel Lines Extension Searchlight Car, 00		50
___	**19882**	Sanderson Farms Poultry Car "3434", 99		41
___	**19883**	LL Bucyrus Erie Crane Car "64608", 99		45
___	**19884**	Atlantis Travel Aquarium Car, 00 u		95
___	**19885**	N&W Operating Hopper Car, 00		31
___	**19886**	Seaboard Boxcar "16126", steam RailSounds, 00		140
___	**19887**	SP Boxcar "651663", diesel RailSounds, 00		140
___	**19888**	Christmas Music Boxcar, 01		65
___	**19889**	PRR Bay Window Caboose "477719," Crewtalk, 00		140
___	**19890**	Santa Fe Bay Window Caboose "999211," Crewtalk, 00		100
___	**19894**	Hood's Operating Milk Car with platform, 03-04		95
___	**19895**	3356 Santa Fe Horse Car with corral, 04		120
___	**19896**	USMC Missile Launch Sound Car "45", 03-04		165
___	**19897**	NYC Crane Car, TMCC, 04	159	263
___	**19898**	Nestle Nesquik Operating Milk Car with platform, 04-05		95
___	**19899**	Pennsylvania Crane Car "19899" CC, 03-05		260
___	**19900**	Toy Fair Boxcar, 87 u	65	80
___	**19901**	"I Love Virginia" Boxcar, 87	25	35
___	**19902**	Toy Fair Boxcar, 88 u	55	80
___	**19903**	Christmas Boxcar, 87 u	22	34
___	**19904**	Christmas Boxcar, 88 u	32	43
___	**19905**	"I Love California" Boxcar, 88	20	24
___	**19906**	"I Love Pennsylvania" Boxcar, 89	26	32
___	**19907**	Toy Fair Boxcar, 89 u	38	55
___	**19908**	Christmas Boxcar, 89 u	30	39
___	**19909**	"I Love New Jersey" Boxcar, 90	19	25
___	**19910**	Christmas Boxcar, 90 u	35	38
___	**19911**	Toy Fair Boxcar, 90 u	75	95
___	**19912**	"I Love Ohio" Boxcar, 91	21	28
___	**19913**	Christmas Boxcar, 91	34	52

		Exc	Mint	
19913	Lionel Employee Christmas Boxcar, 91 u	150	200	___
19914	Toy Fair Boxcar, 91 u	38	50	___
19915	"I Love Texas" Boxcar, 92	35	60	___
19916	Lionel Employee Christmas Boxcar, 92 u	190	220	___
19917	Toy Fair Boxcar, 92 u	45	53	___
19918	Christmas Boxcar, 92 u	49	70	___
19919	"I Love Minnesota" Boxcar, 93	40	60	___
19920	Lionel Visitor's Center Boxcar, 92 u	16	28	___
19921	Lionel Employee Christmas Boxcar, 93 u	93	185	___
19922	Christmas Boxcar, 93	33	41	___
19923	Toy Fair Boxcar, 93 u	65	95	___
19925	Lionel Employee Learning Center Boxcar, 93 u	55	63	___
19926	"I Love Nevada" Boxcar, 94	21	26	___
19927	Lionel Visitor's Center Boxcar, 93 u	26	33	___
19928	Lionel Employee Christmas Boxcar, 94 u	205	230	___
19929	Christmas Boxcar, 94	30	40	___
19931	Toy Fair Boxcar, 94 u	49	65	___
19932	Lionel Visitor's Center Boxcar, 94 u	26	33	___
19933	"I Love Illinois" Boxcar, 95	21	27	___
19934	Lionel Visitor's Center Boxcar, 95 u	18	22	___
19937	Toy Fair Boxcar, 95 u	55	75	___
19938	Christmas Boxcar, 95	19	34	___
19939	Lionel Employee Christmas Boxcar, 95 u	100	128	___
19941	"I Love Colorado" Boxcar, 95	23	30	___
19942	"I Love Florida" Boxcar, 96	19	27	___
19943	"I Love Arizona" Boxcar, 96	20	25	___
19944	Lionel Visitor's Center Tank Car, 96 u		35	___
19945	Holiday Boxcar, 96		29	___
19946	Lionel Employee Christmas Boxcar, 96 u		195	___
19947	Lionel Toy Fair Boxcar, 96 u		200	___
19948	Visitor's Center Flatcar with trailer, 96 u		34	___
19949	"I Love NY" Boxcar, 97		50	___
19950	"I Love Montana" Boxcar, 97		30	___
19951	"I Love Massachusetts" Boxcar, 98		26	___
19952	"I Love Indiana" Boxcar, 98		31	___
19955	Lionel Visitor's Center Gondola with coil covers, 98 u		20	___
19956	Toy Fair Boxcar "777", 98 u		65	___
19957	Ambassador Caboose, 97 u		512	___
19958	Ambassador Caboose, silver (std O), 98 u		558	___
19959	Ambassador Caboose, gold (std O), 98 u	518	778	___
19964	U.S. JCI Senate Boxcar, 92 u	55	63	___
19968	"I Love Maine" Boxcar, 99		40	___
19969	"I Love Vermont" Boxcar, 99		40	___
19970	"I Love New Hampshire" Boxcar, 99		34	___
19971	"I Love Rhode Island" Boxcar, 99		34	___
19976	Lionel Employee Holiday Boxcar, 99 u	23	150	___
19977	Toy Fair Boxcar, 99 u		50	___
19981	Lionel Centennial Boxcar, 99		36	___
19982	Lionel Centennial Boxcar, 99		36	___
19983	Lionel Centennial Boxcar, 99		36	___
19984	Lionel Centennial Boxcar, 99		36	___
19985	"I Love Georgia" Boxcar, 99-00		45	___
19986	"I Love North Carolina" Boxcar, 99-00		40	___

			Exc	Mint
___	**19987**	"I Love South Carolina" Boxcar, 99-00		40
___	**19988**	"I Love Tennessee" Boxcar, 99-00		55
___	**19989**	Toy Fair Boxcar, 00 u		55
___	**19996**	Toy Fair Boxcar, 01 u		50
___	**19997**	Lionel Employee Boxcar, 01 u		125
___	**19998**	Christmas Boxcar, 01		33
___	**19999**	Lionel Visitor's Center 4-bay Hopper, 02 u		153
___	**20000**	PRR Senator Coach 4-pack (std O), 13, 15		640
___	**20005**	SP Sunset Limited Coach 4-pack (std O), 13, 15		640
___	**20010**	UP City of Los Angeles Coach 4-pack (std O), 13, 15		640
___	**20015**	B&O Capitol Limited Coach 4-pack (std O), 13		640
___	**20020**	FEC City of Miami Coach 4-pack (std O), 13		640
___	**20025**	KCS Southern Belle Coach 4-pack (std O), 13		640
___	**20030**	MILW Olympian Coach 4-pack (std O), 13, 15		640
___	**21029**	World of Little Choo Choo Set, 94u, 95	36	43
___	**21141**	North Dakota State Quarter Gondola Bank, 07		60
___	**21142**	South Dakota State Quarter Hopper Bank, 07		60
___	**21163**	SuperStreets FasTrack Grade Crossing, 08-10		20
___	**21164**	SuperStreets 10" Transition to FasTrack, 08-10		9
___	**21165**	SuperStreets Transition to FasTrack, 2 pieces, 08-10		17
___	**21168**	City Traction Trolley Add-on, 08		75
___	**21169**	City Traction Speeder Add-on, 08		75
___	**21170**	NYC 15" Heavyweight Passenger Car 4-pack, 07		250
___	**21175**	NYC 15" Heavyweight Passenger Car 2-pack, 07		125
___	**21198**	ATSF Alco Diesel AA Set, horn, 08		200
___	**21199**	ATSF Midnight Chief Streamliner Car 4-pack, 08		200
___	**21204**	ATSF Midnight Chief Streamliner Car 2-pack, 08		100
___	**21207**	SP Diesel Work Train, 07		175
___	**21212**	NH Diesel Freight Set, 07		250
___	**21217**	Southern Diesel Executive Inspection Train, 07		175
___	**21229**	Ringling Bros. S2 Diesel Switcher, horn, 07		80
___	**21230**	Ringling Bros. Porter Locomotive, 07		105
___	**21231**	Ringling Bros. Streamliner Car 4-pack, 07		210
___	**21234**	Ringling Bros. Streamliner Car 2-pack, 07		105
___	**21237**	Ringling Bros. Flatcar with 3 wagons, 07		50
___	**21238**	Ringling Bros. Flatcar with 3 wagons, 07		50
___	**21239**	Ringling Bros. Flatcar with crates, 07		45
___	**21240**	Ringling Bros. Flatcar with front end loader and poles, 07		45
___	**21252**	Boy Flying Kite, 08		60
___	**21253**	Operating Bunk Car Yard Office, 07		80
___	**21261**	SuperStreets 2.5" Straight-to-Curve Connector, 4 pieces, 08-10		9
___	**21265**	Operating Voltmeter Car, 07		75
___	**21266**	SuperStreets Intersection, 4 pieces, 08-10		40
___	**21267**	PRR Boxcab Electric Locomotive, horn, 07		77
___	**21271**	WP Operating Coal Dump Car with vehicle, 07		33
___	**21276**	Congressional Diner, smoke, 07		110
___	**21277**	Operating Flagman's Shanty, 08		70
___	**21279**	Roach Wranglers Pest Control Van, 08		30
___	**21281**	SuperStreets D21 Curve, 08-10		3
___	**21282**	SuperStreets 2.5" Curve-to-Curve Connector, 4 pieces, 08-10		9
___	**21283**	SuperStreets Tubular Track Grade Crossing, 08-10		18
___	**21284**	SuperStreets 10" Tubular Transition, 08-10		8

MODERN 1970-2024		Exc	Mint	
21285	SuperStreets 10" Tubular Transition, 2 pieces, 08-10		14	___
21286	SuperStreets Intersection, 08-10		10	___
21287	SuperStreets Y Roadway, 08-10		12	___
21288	SuperStreets O Gauge Conversion Pins, 08-10		2	___
21289	SuperStreets Connector Pins, 08-10		2	___
21290	SuperStreets Hookup Wires, 2 pieces, 08-10		3	___
21291	Dogbone Expander pack, 08-10		25	___
21296	City Traction Classic Truck, 07		30	___
21298	NYC 4-6-4 Hudson Locomotive "5279," CC, 07		500	___
21316	Pacific Electric Alco RS3 Diesel "2815," CC, 07		350	___
21324	Acrobats and Clowns Figures, 10 pieces, 08-10		12	___
21325	Ringmaster Circus Figures, 5, with accessories, 08-10		12	___
21326	PRR 15" Interurban Car 2-pack, 07		200	___
21354	Fresh Never Frozen Fish Transport Car, 07		80	___
21355	Dump Bin, 08-10		20	___
21358	Special Addition Boxcar, Girl, 08-10		25	___
21359	Special Addition Boxcar, Boy, 08-10		25	___
21368	Passenger Coach Figures, 9 pieces, 08-10		11	___
21369	Walking Figures, 8 pieces, 08-10		11	___
21370	Sitting Figures, 6, with benches, 08-10		11	___
21371	Standing Figures, 8 pieces, 08-10		11	___
21372	Railroad Station Figures, 6, with accessories, 08-10		11	___
21373	School Figures, 7, with accessories, 08-10		11	___
21374	Service Station Figures, 5, with accessories, 08-10		11	___
21375	Police Figures, 10, with dog, 08		20	___
21376	Seated Passenger Figures, 40 pieces, 08		27	___
21377	Mounted Police, 3, with horses, 08-10		11	___
21378	Factory, 08-10		18	___
21379	Police Station, 08-10		16	___
21380	Colonial House, 08-10		16	___
21381	Suburban Station, 08-10		16	___
21382	School, 08-10		17	___
21383	Suburban Ranch House, 08-10		15	___
21384	Service Station with gas pumps, 08-10		17	___
21385	Barn and Chicken Coop, 08-10		20	___
21386	Firehouse, 08-10		17	___
21387	Church, 08-10		15	___
21388	Country L-shaped Ranch House, 08-10		16	___
21389	Supermarket, 08-10		12	___
21390	Diner, 08-10		15	___
21394	Rotating Beacon, 08-09		31	___
21396	Single Tunnel Portals, pair, 08-10		15	___
21397	SuperSnap 31" Remote Switch, left hand, 08-09		55	___
21398	SuperSnap 31" Remote Switch, right hand, 08-09		55	___
21399	SuperSnap 72" Remote Switch, left hand, 08-09		70	___
21400	SuperSnap 72" Remote Switch, right hand, 08-09		70	___
21412	NYC Plymouth Switcher Freight Set, 07		155	___
21430	SuperStreets D16 Curve, 08-10		2	___
21431	SuperStreets 10" Straight Track, 08-10		2	___
21432	SuperStreets D16 Curved Track, 8 pieces, 08-10		18	___
21433	SuperStreets 5" Straight Track, 4 pieces, 08-10		14	___
21434	SuperStreets 10" Straight Track, 8 pieces, 08-10		19	___
21435	World War II Seated Soldiers, 9, with benches, 08-09		20	___

			Exc	Mint
___	**21436**	Rings and Things Circus Accessories, 08-09		10
___	**21438**	Remote Controller, 07-10		35
___	**21442**	City Figures, 7, with scooter, 08-10		11
___	**21443**	Factory Figures, 6, with accessories, 08-10		11
___	**21444**	Church Figures, 5, with accessories, 08-10		11
___	**21445**	Firefighting Figures, 11, with accessories, 08-10		20
___	**21449**	Operating Loading Platform with flatcar, 07-08		80
___	**21450**	Unloading Station with dump bins, 07		100
___	**21451**	Girder Bridge with stone piers, 07		40
___	**21452**	Graduated Trestle Set, 26 pieces, 07		50
___	**21453**	Elevated Trestle Set, 10 pieces, 07		40
___	**21454**	Double Tunnel Portals, 2 pieces, 08-10		20
___	**21456**	UPS Step Van, 07		30
___	**21466**	Ringling Bros. 15" Aluminum Advertising Car, 07		110
___	**21469**	Ringling Bros. Flatcar, white, with container, 07		45
___	**21470**	Ringling Bros. Flatcar, blue, with container, 07		45
___	**21471**	Ringling Bros. Flatcar with 2 trailers, 08-10		60
___	**21472**	Ringling Bros. Flatcar with 2 trailers, 08-10		60
___	**21476**	Strasburg Plymouth Diesel Switcher, 07		100
___	**21494**	WM RS3 Diesel "189," CC, 07		350
___	**21529**	Montana State Quarter Boxcar Bank, 08		45
___	**21542**	Washington State Quarter Tank Car Bank, 08		45
___	**21543**	Boyd Bros. Ford Classic Truck, 08		33
___	**21549**	Ringling Bros. Crew Bus, 08		33
___	**21552**	S.W.A.T. Team Step Van, 08		30
___	**21560**	Reading Flatcar with rail load, 07		25
___	**21567**	School Bus SuperStreets Set, 08		110
___	**21568**	Dirty Dogz Van SuperStreets Set, 08		100
___	**21569**	Angelo's Pizza Delivery Van, 08		30
___	**21570**	Flying Colors Painting Van, 08		30
___	**21571**	SuperStreets 10" Insulated Roadway, 2 pieces, 08-10		8
___	**21572**	SuperStreets 5" Straight School, 2 pieces, 08-10		8
___	**21573**	SuperStreets 5" Straight Stop Ahead, 2 pieces, 08-10		8
___	**21574**	SuperStreets 5" Straight Crosswalk, 2 pieces, 08-10		8
___	**21575**	SuperStreets 10" Crossing, 2 pieces, 08-10		10
___	**21576**	SuperStreets Skid Mark Roadway Pack, 08-10		13
___	**21577**	Snack-On Step Van, 08		30
___	**21582**	Keystone Coal Porter Locomotive, 08		100
___	**21583**	Keystone Coal Freight Car 4-pack, 08		100
___	**21590**	ATSF "Midnight Chief" 2-bay Hopper "162277", 08		25
___	**21591**	ATSF "Midnight Chief" Flatcar "94468" with trailer, 08		43
___	**21592**	ATSF "Midnight Chief" Caboose, 08		25
___	**21593**	ATSF "Midnight Chief" Boxcar "621593", 08		35
___	**21594**	NYC Empire State Express 15" Aluminum Car 4-pack, 08-09		420
___	**21599**	SP flatcar with wheel load, 07		35
___	**21600**	B&M RS3 Diesel "1538," CC, 08-09	113	350
___	**21607**	Jack Frost Hopper "327" with sugar load, 08		25
___	**21609**	Elephants and Giraffes, 2 pair, 08-10		13
___	**21610**	Lions and Tigers, 2 pair, 08-10		13
___	**21611**	Horses, 4 pieces, 08		13
___	**21621**	ATSF Operating Boxcar "22658", 08-09		90
___	**21623**	Rutland Operating Milk Car with platform, 08-10		150
___	**21626**	Rath Wood-sided Reefer "622", 09		45

		Exc	Mint
21627	Greenlee Packing Wood-sided Reefer "3862", 10		45
21628	CNJ Reefer "1438", 08-09		35
21629	C&O Reefer "7783", 08-09		35
21630	UP Stock Car "42005", 09		45
21631	Reading Boxcar "107984", 08-09		35
21632	GN Boxcar "34285", 08-09		35
21633	RI "Route of the Rockets" Boxcar "21110", 09-10		40
21634	Tidewater Flying A 1-D Tank Car "1367", 09		40
21635	Southern Depressed Center Flatcar, 2 transformers, 09		43
21636	NS Flatcar with bulkheads and stakes, 08-09		35
21637	Ontario Northland Ribbed Hopper with coal, 09		40
21639	Pan Am Boxcar "32126", 08-09		55
21640	UP Modern Steel-sided Reefer "499030", 08-09		55
21641	Ringling Bros. Merchandise Flatcar, 08		50
21643	PRR Die-cast Gondola with covers, 09		73
21644	PRR 16-wheel Flatcar with transformer, 08-09		80
21646	DT&I Work Crane and Boom Car, 09		85
21649	City Traction Trolley with Ringling Bros. banner, 08-09		80
21651	Moo-Town Creamery Step Van, 08-09		38
21656	Quikrete Step Van, 08-09		42
21658	Ringling Bros. Vintage Truck, 08-09		42
21659	DT&I Flatcar "90059" with Ford trailer, 08-09		60
21662	Moo-Town Creamery Vending Machine, 08-09		13
21663	Moo-Town Creamery Bunk Car Ice Cream Shop, 08-09		115
21664	RI Operating Coal Dump Car with vehicle, 08-09		40
21665	Alaska Operating Log Dump Car with vehicle, 09		40
21667	Red River Lumber Boxcab Diesel with horn, 08-09		100
21668	CP Operating Hopper "9628", 08-09		45
21675	Mountain View Creamery Loading Depot, 08-10		130
21676	Beaver Creek Logging Die-cast Porter Locomotive, 08-09		120
21677	Ford Factory, 09		22
21679	Assured Comfort HVAC Van, 08-09		38
21680	Division of Prisons Bus SuperStreets Set, 08-09		150
21688	Ringling Bros. Heavyweight Coach 2-pack, 08-11		240
21691	Ringling Bros. Flatcar with 2 trailers, 08-10		60
21692	C&NW MP15 Diesel with Ringling Bros. banner, 08-09		140
21693	Southern MP15 Diesel Pair, powered and dummy, 10		200
21696	Ford Flatcar with 2 trucks, 08-09		53
21698	Lionel Van SuperStreets Set, 08-10		130
21701	Star Spangled GG1 Electric Locomotive "4837", 08-10		260
21702	Milwaukee Road Girder Bridge, 08-09	8	20
21703	ATSF Black Mesa Aluminum Business Car, 09-10		160
21704	C&O Double Searchlight Car with vehicle, 08-09		50
21706	Chatham Police Van, 08-09		38
21707	NYC Aluminum Business Car, 09		160
21708	CN Operating Log Dump Car, 10		120
21709	PRR Girder Bridge, 08-09		15
21715	Ringling Bros. Stock Car, 08-09		60
21717	Pullman-Standard 1-D Tank Car, 08-09		35
21719	NYC Bay Window Caboose, 99		70
21720	Ringling Bros. Billboard Set #2, 08-09		10
21721	Warning Sign Pack, 12 pieces, 08-10		25
21730	Regulatory Sign Pack, 12 pieces, 08-10		25

			Exc	Mint
___	**21738**	Railroad Crossing Sign Pack, 6 pieces, 08-10		21
___	**21750**	NKP Rolling Stock 4-pack, 98		160
___	**21751**	PRR Rolling Stock 4-pack, 98		145
___	**21752**	Conrail Unit Trailer Train, 98		285
___	**21753**	Service Station Fire Rescue Train, 98	365	590
___	**21754**	BNSF 3-bay Covered Hopper 2-pack (std O), 98	30	73
___	**21755**	4-bay Covered Hoppers 2-pack, 98		65
___	**21756**	Conrail Overstamped Boxcars 2-pack, 98		65
___	**21757**	UP Freight Car Set, 98	117	188
___	**21758**	Bethlehem Steel "44" (SSS), 99	169	375
___	**21759**	Canadian Pacific F3 Diesel Passenger Set, 99	413	985
___	**21761**	B&M Boxcar Set, 4-pack, 99		180
___	**21763**	New Haven Freight Set, 99		265
___	**21766**	ACL Passenger Car 2-pack, 99		385
___	**21769**	Centennial 1-D Tank Car Set, 4-pack, 99		260
___	**21770**	NYC Reefer Set, 4-pack, 99	88	225
___	**21771**	D&RGW Stock Car Set, 4-pack, 99		230
___	**21774**	Custom Series Consist I, 3-pack, 99		150
___	**21775**	Train Wreck Recovery Set, 99	95	220
___	**21778**	ATSF Train Master Diesel Freight Set, 99		950
___	**21779**	Seaboard Freight Car Set, 99	143	280
___	**21780**	NYC Aluminum Passenger Car 2-pack, 99		160
___	**21781**	Case Cutlery Freight Set, 99 u	725	1038
___	**21782**	PRR Congressional Set, 00	238	930
___	**21783**	Monday Night Football 2-pack, 01-02		50
___	**21784**	QVC PRR Coal Freight Steam Set, 00 u		360
___	**21785**	QVC Gold Mine Freight Steam Set, 00 u		300
___	**21786**	Santa Fe F3 Diesel ABBA Passenger Set, 00	742	1693
___	**21787**	Blue Comet Steam Passenger Set, 01-02		1525
___	**21788**	Postwar Missile Launch Freight Set, 02-03	130	350
___	**21789**	Norfolk Southern Piggyback Set, CC (SSS), 01		370
___	**21790**	CN TankTrain Dash 9 Diesel Freight Set, 02	200	630
___	**21791**	Freedom Train Diesel Passenger Set, RailSounds, 03	175	645
___	**21792**	C&O Coal Hopper 6-pack #2 (std O), 01		145
___	**21793**	Virginian Coal Hopper 6-pack #2 (std O), 01		160
___	**21794**	Pioneer Seed GP7 Diesel Freight Set, 01 u	630	925
___	**21795**	Case Farmall Freight Set, 01 u	540	750
___	**21796**	NJ Medical Steam Freight Set, 01 u		487
___	**21797**	SP Daylight Passenger Set, 01		670
___	**21852**	MILW PS-2CD Hopper 3-pack (std O), 06		155
___	**21853**	BNSF PS-2CD Hopper 3-pack (std O), 06		155
___	**21854**	N&W PS-2CD Hopper 3-pack (std O), 06		155
___	**21855**	A&P Milk Car 3-pack, 06		150
___	**21856**	Bowman Dairy Milk Car 3-pack (std O), 06		150
___	**21857**	Western Dairy Milk Car 3-pack (std O), 06		150
___	**21858**	NP PS-4 Flatcar with trailers, 2-pack (std O), 06		170
___	**21859**	C&NW PS-4 Flatcar with trailers, 2-pack (std O), 06		170
___	**21860**	UP PS-4 Flatcar with trailers, 2-pack (std O), 06		170
___	**21861**	PRR PS-4 Flatcar with trailers (std O), 06		170
___	**21863**	ADM Unibody Tank Car 3-pack (std O), 06		135
___	**21864**	Cerestar Unibody Tank Car 3-pack (std O), 06		135
___	**21865**	Coe Rail Husky Stack Car 2-pack (std O), 06		170
___	**21866**	Santa Fe Husky Stack Car 2-pack (std O), 06		170

		Exc	Mint	
21872	C&O Offset Hopper 3-pack (std O), 05		130	___
21873	P&LE Offset Hopper 3-pack (std O), 06		145	___
21874	TTX Trailer Train 2-pack (std O), 06		170	___
21875	CSX Husky Stack Car 2-pack (std O), 06		170	___
21876	Disney Villain Hi-Cube Boxcar 3-pack, 05-06		135	___
21877	Domino Sugar 1-D Tank Car 3-pack (std O), 07		135	___
21878	Procor 1-D Tank Car 3-pack (std O), 07		135	___
21879	C&EI Offset Hopper 3-pack (std O), 07		145	___
21880	Erie Offset Hopper 3-pack (std O), 07		145	___
21881	Frisco Offset Hopper 3-pack (std O), 07-08		200	___
21882	Chessie System Offset Hopper 3-pack (std O), 07		145	___
21883	C&O 3-bay Hopper 2-pack (std O), 07-08		140	___
21884	Pennsylvania Power & Light 3-bay Hopper 2-pack (std O), 07		140	___
21885	Santa Fe 3-bay Hopper 2-pack (std O), 07		140	___
21886	C&NW 3-bay Hopper 2-pack (std O), 07-08		140	___
21888	IMC Canada Cylindrical Hopper 2-pack, 06		130	___
21893	Greenbrier Husky Stack Car 2-pack (std O), 07		170	___
21894	CSX Husky Stack Car 2-pack (std O), 07		170	___
21895	BN Husky Stack Car 2-pack (std O), 07		170	___
21896	Arizona & California Husky Stack Car 2-pack (std O), 07		170	___
21897	REA PS-4 Flatcar with trailers, 2-pack (std O), 07-08		170	___
21898	NYC PS-4 Flatcar with trailers, 2-pack (std O), 07-08		170	___
21899	Lackawanna PS-4 Flatcar with trailers, 2-pack (std O), 07		170	___
21900	Civil War Union Train Set, 99	138	375	___
21901	Civil War Confederate Train Set, 99	158	375	___
21902	MILW PS-4 Flatcar with trailers, 2-pack (std O), 07-08		170	___
21902	Construction Zone Set, 99 u		87	___
21904	UP PS-2 Covered Hopper 2-pack (std O), 07		120	___
21904	Safari Adventure Set, 99 u		90	___
21905	NYC Flyer Set, 99 u		100	___
21909	AGFA Film Steam Freight Set, 98 u		1464	___
21914	Lionel Lines Freight Set, 99		120	___
21916	Lionel Village Trolley, 99		75	___
21917	N&W Freight Set, 99		70	___
21918	PC PS-2 Covered Hopper 2-pack (std O), 07		120	___
21918	Thomas Circus Play Set, 00		100	___
21921	Imco PS-2 Covered Hopper 2-pack (std O), 07-08		120	___
21924	Holiday Trolley Set, 99		65	___
21925	Thomas the Tank Engine Island of Sodor Train Set, 99-00		150	___
21930	NYC PS-2 Covered Hopper 2-pack (std O), 07		120	___
21932	JCPenney NYC Freight Flyer Steam Set, 00 u		170	___
21934	Custom Series Consist II, 3-pack, 99		140	___
21936	Looney Tunes Train Set, 00 u		413	___
21937	NYC Steel-sided Reefer 2-pack (std O), 07		130	___
21939	Dubuque Steel-sided Reefer 2-pack (std O), 07-08		130	___
21940	ADM Steel-sided Reefer 2-pack (std O), 07		130	___
21941	National Car Steel-sided Reefer 2-pack (std O), 07		130	___
21944	Celebrate a Lionel Christmas Steam Set, 00-01		165	___
21945	Christmas Trolley Set, 00		100	___
21948	NYC Freight Flyer Set, air whistle, 00		240	___
21950	Maersk SD70 Diesel Maxi-Stack Set, 00	523	900	___
21951	World War II Troop Train, 00	100	410	___
21952	Lionel Lines Service Station Special Set, 00	125	294	___

			Exc	Mint
___	21953	Ford Mustang GP7 Diesel Set, CC, 01		345
___	21955	D&RGW F3 Diesel AA Passenger Set, CC, 01	163	740
___	21956	New York Central Freight Set, 99-00	152	355
___	21969	Lionel Village Trolley Set, 00		85
___	21970	SP RS3 Diesel Freight Set, horn, 00-01		110
___	21971	Pennsylvania Flyer Steam Set, 00	75	195
___	21972	Frisco GP7 Diesel Freight Set, horn, 00		150
___	21973	ATSF Passenger Set, RailSounds, 00-01		375
___	21974	ATSF Passenger Set, SignalSounds, 00-01	75	240
___	21975	Burlington Steam Freight Set, SignalSounds, 00		275
___	21976	Centennial Steam Freight Starter Set, 00	292	709
___	21977	NYC Train Master Steam Freight Set, 99-00		620
___	21978	ATSF Train Master Diesel Freight Set, 99-00		500
___	21981	JCPenney NYC Flyer Set, 00 u		150
___	21988	NYC Freight Set, RailSounds, 00		325
___	21989	Burlington Steam Freight Set, RailSounds, 00		338
___	21990	NYC Flyer Freight Set, RailSounds, 00		175
___	21999	Whirlpool Steam Freight Set, 00 u	513	745
___	22103	PRR A5 Scale Switcher "411," CC, 08-09		330
___	22104	PRR Freight Car 3-pack, 08		135
___	22105	NYC Empire State Express 4-6-4 Hudson Locomotive "5429," CC, 08-09		420
___	22113	NYC Empire State Express 15" Aluminum Car 2-pack, 08-10		210
___	22116	Ringling Bros. Diesel Freight Set, 08-10		245
___	22121	Ringling Bros. Freight Set, 08-10		390
___	22126	Ringling Bros. Expansion Pack, 08-10		135
___	22131	NH Streamliner Car 3-pack, 07		150
___	22135	CB&Q S2 Diesel Switcher "9305," horn, 07		80
___	22136	Erie S2 Diesel Switcher "522," horn, 07		80
___	22137	Alaska MP15 Diesel "1552," horn, 07		100
___	22138	Astoria Heat & Power Porter Locomotive "4", 07		100
___	22139	LIRR Speeder, 08		50
___	22140	CNJ Boxcab Diesel "1000," horn, 08		90
___	22141	Lackawanna 15" Interurban Car 2-pack, 07		200
___	22142	FEC Operating Dump Car, 07		70
___	22143	B&A Operating Log Dump Car, 08-09		70
___	22144	Alaska Operating Coal Dump Car with vehicle, 08		33
___	22145	WM Operating Log Dump Car with vehicle, 08		33
___	22146	PFE Operating Boxcar, 08		80
___	22147	B&O Operating Hopper with coal, 08		35
___	22148	GN Operating Hopper with coal, 08		35
___	22149	Dairymen's League Operating Milk Car, green, with platform, 08		140
___	22150	D&RGW Bunk Car, smoke, 08		65
___	22151	Alaska Searchlight Car with vehicle, 08		45
___	22152	NKP 2-bay Outside-braced Hopper "31299", 08		50
___	22153	L&N 2-bay Offset Hopper "78660", 08		50
___	22154	D&H 2-bay Rib Side Hopper "5737", 07		50
___	22155	Erie-Lack. 2-bay Aluminum Hopper "21353", 08		60
___	22156	ACF Demonstrator 2-bay Aluminum Hopper "44586", 07		60
___	22157	GN Aluminum Tank Car "74787", 08		60
___	22158	MILW Bulkhead Flatcar "967116" with wood, 08-09		43
___	22159	BNSF Flatcar "585011" with trailer, 08		43
___	22160	UP Flatcar "58059" with container, 08		43

MODERN 1970-2024		Exc	Mint
22161	Conrail Flatcar “705910”" with NS container, 08		43
22162	Foppiano Wine 3-D Tank Car “1112”, 08		45
22163	PRR Weed Control Car “6321226”, 07		45
22166	PRR Reefer “19492”, 08		25
22167	Seaboard Reefer “16622”, 08		25
22168	N&W Boxcar “645772”, 08		25
22169	ATSF Reefer “11744”, 07		25
22170	P&LE Reefer “22300”, 07		25
22171	B&O DD Boxcar “495289”, 08		25
22172	CB&Q Stock Car “52731”, 08		25
22174	Erie-Lackawanna Transfer Caboose, 07		25
22176	PRR Caboose “478884”, 07		25
22177	L&N Caboose “100”, 07		25
22179	NYC Depressed Center Flatcar “66256” with 2 girders, 08		25
22180	IC Depressed Center Flatcar with 2 transformers, 07		25
22182	RI Gondola “180043” with coils, 08		25
22184	B&O Covered Hopper “604321”, 08		25
22185	UP Covered Hopper “53186”, 08		25
22186	P&LE (NYC) Gondola “17243”, 08-09		35
22187	PRR 2-D Tank Car “6351815”, 07		25
22188	Deep Rock 3-D Tank Car “2152”, 08		25
22189	NP Java Diner, smoke, 08		110
22190	C&O Operating Billboard, 08		65
22191	Operating Passenger Station, 08-09		105
22192	Hot Box Operating BBQ Shack, 07		80
22193	Cold Drinks Vending Machine, 08		12
22194	Water Tower with light, 08-09		20
22199	City Traction Trolley Barn, 08-09		65
22202	Loading Ramp, 08-10		20
22203	Dairymen’s League Operating Milk Car, white, with platform, 07		140
22204	Snacks Vending Machine, 08		12
22205	Soup and Sandwich Vending Machine, 08		12
22206	PRR Crew Bus, 08		30
22222	Ringling Bros. Speeder Chase Set, 08-10		92
22225	Ringling Bros. Jomar Heavyweight Private Car, 08-11		120
22226	Ringling Bros. 18" Caledonia Heavyweight Private Car, 08		100
22227	Ringling Bros. 18" Advertising Car, 08		100
22228	Ringling Bros. Flatcar with 3 wagons, 08		50
22231	Ringling Bros. Flatcar with 3 wagons, 08		50
22235	Ringling Bros. Flatcar with pole wagon and truck, 08		75
22238	Ringling Bros. Work Caboose with calliope wagon, 08		40
22240	Ringling Bros. Flatcar/Stock Car with wagon, 08		50
22243	Ringling Bros. Human Cannonball Car, 08		45
22244	Ringling Bros. Operating Searchlight Car with 3 spotlights, 08		60
22247	Ringling Bros. Stock Car “54”, 08		50
22248	Ringling Bros. Stock Car “47”, 08		50
22249	Ringling Bros. Dining Dept. Billboard Reefer, 08		80
22250	Ringling Bros. Dining Dept. Wood-sided Reefer, 08-09		90
22251	Ringling Bros. Dormitory Bunk Car "22", 08		75
22252	Ringling Bros. Operating Billboard, 08-09		75
22253	Ringling Bros. Vintage Billboard Set #1, 08		9
22255	Ringling Bros. Aluminum Coach “40010”, 08-10		165

			Exc	Mint
___	22257	Ringling Bros. Aluminum Shop Car "63002", 08-10		165
___	22258	Ringling Bros. 18" Aluminum Large Animal Car, 08-10		165
___	22259	Ringling Bros. Flatcar with trailer, 08		53
___	22260	Ringling Bros. Tractor Trailer, 08		30
___	22261	Idaho State Quarter Hopper Bank, 08		65
___	22262	Wyoming State Quarter Tank Car Bank, 08		50
___	22263	Utah State Quarter Boxcar Bank, 08		45
___	22264	SuperStreets Figure-8 Expander Pack, 08-10		35
___	22267	Mulligan Spring Water Step Van, 08		30
___	22270	Quikrete Classic Truck with 2 pallets, 08		33
___	22271	MILW EP-5 Electric Locomotive "E20," CC, 08-09		460
___	22272	MILW Olympian Hiawatha 18" Aluminum Car 4-pack, 08		480
___	22277	MILW Olympian Hiawatha 18" Aluminum Car 2-pack, 08		250
___	22280	Erie-Lackawanna RS3 Diesel "933," CC, 08-09		350
___	22281	Southern Train Master Diesel "6300," CC, 08-09		420
___	22282	Southern Bay Window Caboose "X270", 08-09		70
___	22283	UP S2 Diesel Switcher "1103" and Caboose "25384", 08		130
___	22286	GN Boxcab Electric Locomotive "5008-A," horn, 08		90
___	22287	North Shore Line 15" Interurban Car 2-pack, 08		230
___	22288	Commuter Train Station, 6 road name stickers, 09		25
___	22289	Ringling Bros. 18" Aluminum Passenger Car 2-pack, 08		270
___	22290	Erie Boxcar "86448" with graffiti, 08		46
___	22291	C&NW Stock Car "14303", 08		46
___	22292	Land o' Lakes Butter Billboard Reefer, 08		75
___	22293	PRR 4-bay Hopper "253776", 08		65
___	22294	Montana Rail Link 3-bay Aluminum Hopper "50049", 08		70
___	22295	Canada Wheat 4-bay Aluminum Hopper "60641", 08		73
___	22296	Eaglebrook Aluminum Tank Car "19039", 08		70
___	22297	Petri Wine 3-D Tank Car "904", 08-09		45
___	22298	Cotton Belt Offset Cupola Wood-sided Caboose "2230", 08		80
___	22299	MILW Bay Window Caboose "980502", 08-09		70
___	22300	Detroit, Toledo & Ironton Coil Car "1352", 08		60
___	22301	NYC Flatcar "506090" with freight kit, 08		35
___	22302	C&O Flatcar "80951" with freight kit, 08		35
___	22303	Extruded Aluminum I-Beam, 3 pieces, 08-09		6
___	22304	Rails, 12 pieces, 08-09		6
___	22305	Small Transformer Load, pair, 08-09		15
___	22306	Large Transformer Load, 08		19
___	22307	Forklifts, 3, with pallets, 08-09		27
___	22308	Loaders with crates, pair, 08-09		13
___	22309	Loaders with logs, pair, 08-09		13
___	22310	KBL Logistics Container 2-pack, 08		40
___	22312	Commemorative Quarter Extended Vision Caboose, 09		80
___	22313	ATSF Boxcar "137460", 08		25
___	22314	Coastal King Seafood Wood-sided Reefer, 08		25
___	22315	Wisconsin & Southern "God Bless America" Boxcar, 09		43
___	22316	NP Depressed Center Flatcar "6613" with water tank, 08		25
___	22317	U.S. Air Force Hopper "55175" with ballast load, 08		25
___	22318	DM&IR Ore Car "29991", 08		25
___	22319	Celanese Chemicals 1-D Tank Car "12730", 08		25
___	22320	Baldwin Locomotives Works 1-D Tank Car "6809", 08		25
___	22321	B&O Operating Boxcar, 08		45
___	22322	PRR Operating Ballast Dump Car, 08		75

		Exc	Mint
22323	FEMA Voltmeter Car, 08		75
22324	C&NW Cop and Robber Chase Gondola, 08-09		55
22325	White Milk Cans, 10 pieces, 08-10		8
22326	Twin Searchlight Tower, 08-10		33
22327	Tommy's Bunk Car Grill, 08-09		100
22328	Santa Fe Operating Freight Transfer Platform, 08-09		130
22329	Dual Track Signal Bridge, 08-10		45
22330	Stella's Heavyweight Diner, smoke, 08-09		140
22331	Coffee Vending Machine, 08		12
22332	Spring Water Vending Machine, 08		12
22333	Candy Vending Machine, 08		12
22334	Ford Plymouth Diesel Switcher and Ore Car 6-pack, 08		200
22335	NS Operating Paint Shop with boxcar, 08-09		140
22344	KBL Logistics ISO Tank, 08		19
22346	Tableau Circus Wagons, 08		13
22349	Forklift with 6 pallets, 08-09		23
22350	Twin Lamp Posts, 3 pieces, 08-09		22
22352	Lamp Posts, 4 pieces, 08-09		20
22354	Portable Spotlights, 3 pieces, 08-09		15
22356	High Tension Poles, 4 pieces, 08-09		8
22358	Rail Yard Signs, 12 pieces, 08-09		10
22360	Telephone Poles, 6 pieces, 08-09		7
22362	Girder Bridge, 08-09		8
22363	Stone Bridge Piers, pair, 08-10		27
22365	Heavyweight Passenger Coach 6-wheel Scale Trucks, pair, 08-09		25
22366	Aluminum Passenger Coach 4-wheel Scale Trucks, pair, 08-09		25
22367	Timkin Scale Sprung Trucks, pair, 08-09		19
22368	Bettendorf Scale Sprung Trucks, pair, 08-09		19
22369	Scale Couplers, pair, 08-09		6
22379	SuperStreets Barricade, 2 pieces, 08-10		11
22387	Kiosk with 3 vending machines, 08-09		40
22391	Ford MP15 Diesel "10021," horn, 08		115
22392	Ford Farming Boxcar "1681", 08		30
22393	Ford Stampings DD Boxcar "101', 08		35
22394	Ford 2-bay Covered Hopper "1667", 08		30
22395	Ford Speeder "14", 08		65
22396	Ford Water Tower, 08		25
22397	Ford Rotating Sign Tower, 08		55
22398	Boyd Bros. and Ford Barn and Chicken Coop, 08		25
22399	Ford ISO Tank, 08-09		21
22402	PRR Streamlined K4 4-6-2 Pacific Locomotive, tender, 09-10		500
22408	Ringling Bros. Tractor Trailer #1, 08-09		35
22411	Tableau Wagon Set #2, 08-10		18
22412	PRR Operating Flagman's Shanty, 08-09		90
22414	Linde Union Carbide Boxcar with aluminum tank, 08-09		70
22415	Ringling Bros. Flatcar with circus wagon, 08		50
22417	Ringling Bros. Flatcar with container, 09		55
22420	PRR Broadway Limited Aluminum Passenger Car 2-pack, 09-10		300
22423	GN Aluminum Passenger Car 2-pack, 09-10		360
22426	Ford Gondola "13447" with coils, 08-09		43
22427	Ford Operating Billboard, 08-09		75
22428	Ford Tin Sign Replica 4-pack, 08-09		17

			Exc	Mint
___	**22433**	PRR Broadway Limited Aluminum Passenger Car 4-pack, 09-10		600
___	**22438**	Mail Crane, 08-10		30
___	**22439**	Milwaukee Road Aluminum Passenger Car 2-pack, 09-11		360
___	**22447**	Wabash Die-cast 2-bay Ribbed Hopper "37751", 08-09		60
___	**22449**	UP Crew Bus, 08-09		38
___	**22450**	Seaboard Die-cast Hopper with gravel, 10		80
___	**22454**	Oklahoma State Quarter Die-cast Hopper Bank, 08-09		75
___	**22455**	New Mexico State Quarter Die-cast Gondola Bank, 08-09		74
___	**22456**	Arizona State Quarter Tank Car Bank, 08-09		55
___	**22457**	Alaska State Quarter Boxcar Bank, 09		55
___	**22458**	Hawaii State Quarter Die-cast Hopper Bank, 09		75
___	**22459**	Southern Aluminum Passenger Car 2-pack #1, 09		300
___	**22460**	Southern Aluminum Passenger Car 2-pack #2, 09		300
___	**22461**	Scale Skeleton Log Car 4-pack, 08-09		160
___	**22467**	Railroad Water Tower, 08-09		23
___	**22468**	Fast Eddie's Used Car Lot with 2 die-cast vehicles, 08-09		50
___	**22469**	Cola Illuminated Vending Machine, 08-09		13
___	**22470**	SuperStreets Guard Rails, 08-10		20
___	**22472**	Ringling Bros. Tin Sign Replica 4-pack, 08-09		17
___	**22477**	Lionel Tin Sign Replica 4-pack, 08-09		15
___	**22482**	Vintage Tin Sign Replica 4-pack, 08-09		15
___	**22487**	Scooter Gang with scooters, 09-10		13
___	**22492**	Airport Revolving Searchlight, 10		40
___	**22493**	Ringling Bros. Lighted Clown Wood-sided Reefer, 09		75
___	**22494**	Ford Flatcar with 2 Thunderbird convertibles, 09		53
___	**22496**	Vita O Flavored Water Vending Machine, 09		13
___	**22497**	Top Pop Soda Illuminated Vending Machine, 09		13
___	**22498**	Ringling Bros. Flatcar with 3 circus wagons, 09-10		55
___	**22500**	Defense Dept. Flatcar with 2 jeeps and soldier, 09		50
___	**22501**	C&NW Railroad Van, CC, 09-10		100
___	**22502**	Ringling Bros. Flatcar with 3 circus wagons, 09-10		55
___	**22504**	Ford Water Tower with vintage Ford logo, 09-10		25
___	**22505**	Sparkling Springs Beverage Truck, 09		45
___	**22506**	SuperStreets Fishtail Roadway, 09		25
___	**22507**	Ringling Bros. Flatcar with boxcar and ticket wagon, 09		60
___	**22509**	Pallet Pack with banded loads, 09		20
___	**22510**	Lionel Step Van, CC, 09-10		100
___	**22511**	BNSF Flatcar with helicopter, 09		50
___	**22513**	Ringling Bros. Heavyweight Advertising Car, 09		120
___	**22514**	NYC Girder Bridge, 09-10		15
___	**22515**	Milwaukee Road/REA Scale Boxcar "6436", 09		55
___	**22516**	BNSF MP15 Diesel "3704" with horn, 09		120
___	**22517**	Quick Lane Ford Motorcraft Auto Parts Van, 09-10		42
___	**22518**	Lionel Tank Container Leasing ISO Tank, 09-10		23
___	**22519**	Roma Wine Wood-sided Billboard Reefer, 09-10		70
___	**22520**	WWII Soldiers in Action, 10 pieces, 09-10		20
___	**22521**	1959 Ford Billboard Set, 09		10
___	**22523**	American Flyer Vintage Truck, 09		38
___	**22524**	Ford Coil Car "749772", 09		73
___	**22525**	Vermont Railway Operating Boxcar "177", 09		50
___	**22526**	Crabby Matt's Smoking Heavyweight Diner, 09		150
___	**22527**	Toledo, Peoria & Western Boxcar "5067", 09-10		55

		Exc	Mint
22528	GN Stock Car "55973", 09-10		55
22529	U.S. Army 1-D Tank Car "11278", 09		35
22530	Milwaukee Road Aluminum Coach "627", 09-11		180
22531	Southern Girder Bridge, 09		15
22532	Montana Rail Link 1-D Tank Car "100017", 09		35
22533	GN Aluminum Coach "1377", 09-10		180
22534	SuperStreets D16 Curve Guard Rails, 09-10		20
22536	SuperStreets D21 Curve Guard Rails, 09-10		22
22538	Ford Modern Aluminum Tank Car "3016", 09		90
22539	BNSF Flatcar "922267" with Ford trailer, 09-10		60
22542	PRR Flatcar "480227" with freight kit, 09		40
22543	Biodiesel 2-D Tank Car "1544", 09		40
22544	Ringling Bros. Wood-sided Gondola with equipment, 09		63
22548	Kiosk #2 with 3 illuminated vending machines, 09		40
22553	Convenience Mart, 09-10		25
22554	Auto Parts Store, 09-10		20
22555	Ringling Bros. Tractor with Gold Tour container, 09-10		55
22558	PRR Flatcar "469301" with milk containers, 09		50
22559	UP Gondola "229794" with freight kit, 09-10		80
22560	CB&Q Wood-sided Gondola "85150" with spools, 09-10		60
22561	Gondola Scrap Load, 09		9
22562	Operation Lifesaver Boxcar with flashing LEDs, 09		65
22563	Ringling Bros. Handcar and Trailer Set, 10-11		70
22566	SuperStreets 2.5" Straight Roadway, 4 pieces, 10		12
22568	Generators, 2 pieces, 09		9
22570	Large transformer, 09		22
22571	Cage Wagon Set, 09-10		18
22573	Display Base, 09		20
22574	Ringling Bros. Flatcar "39" with trailer, 09		60
22577	Biodiesel Storage Tank with 2 figures, 09-10		40
22578	Ringling Bros. Heavyweight Coach "70", 09		120
22579	Circus Horses, 4 pieces, 09-10		15
22580	Bollards and Chains, 09-10		20
22582	Pipe Stack Load, 09		30
22583	KBL Operating Wind Turbine, 09-10		75
22584	KBL Die-cast 16-wheel Flatcar "34807", 09		85
22587	Old Reading Flatcar Foot Bridge with stone piers, 09-10		50
22590	Roadside Fender Bender, 09-10		75
22592	SuperStreets D16 Turn Roadways, left and right, 10		35
22595	SuperStreets D21 Turn Roadways, left and right, 10		39
22598	SuperStreets Adjustable Straight Kit, 09-10		20
22600	Wire Spool Load, 6 pieces, 09		20
22610	Napa Valley Wine Train Alco FA Diesel AA Set, 10		230
22611	Napa Valley Wine Train Alco FA Diesel "71," powered, 10		150
22612	Napa Valley Wine Train Alco FA Diesel "72," unpowered, 10		80
22613	Napa Valley Wine Train 15" Passenger Car 4-pack, 10		450
22614	Napa Valley Wine Train Heavyweight Observation "1018", 10		110
22615	Napa Valley Wine Train Heavyweight Observation "1011", 10		110
22616	Napa Valley Wine Train Heavyweight Diner "1090", 10		115
22617	Napa Valley Wine Train Heavyweight Diner "1015", 10		115
22618	Signal Oil Co. 1-D Tank Car, 10		40
22619	PRR Paoli MU Commuter Train 2-pack, 10		290
22622	RR Paoli Motorized Combine, 10		200

			Exc	Mint
___	**22623**	PRR Commuter Train Station, 10		35
___	**22624**	NH Die-cast Plymouth Switcher with snowplow, 10		160
___	**22625**	Ringling Bros. 18" Aluminum Generator Car, 10-11		180
___	**22627**	Ringling Bros. Lighted Clown Wood-sided Reefer, 10-11		90
___	**22628**	Ringling Bros. 18" Aluminum Advertising Car, 10-11		180
___	**22629**	Ringling Bros. Stock Car, 10-11		60
___	**22630**	Ringling Bros. Tractor and Trailer, 10-11		35
___	**22633**	Ringling Bros. 18" Aluminum Coach, 10-11		180
___	**22634**	Ringling Bros. 18" Heavyweight Advertising Car, 10-11		146
___	**22635**	Ringling Bros. Operating Dual Searchlight Car, 10-11		60
___	**22637**	Quikrete Step Van, 10		48
___	**22638**	PRR Crew Bus, 10		45
___	**22639**	B&O Boxcab Diesel "195", 10		100
___	**22640**	Central of Georgia Boxcar "5823", 10		45
___	**22641**	New Haven Boxcar "36438", 10		45
___	**22642**	Ringling Bros. Operating Large Animal Feed Car, 10-11		150
___	**22643**	Ford MP15 Diesel "10022", 10-11		135
___	**22644**	Ford Motorcraft 48' Aluminum Tank Car, 10-11		95
___	**22645**	Ringling Bros. Operating Tent Pole Dump Car, 10-11		130
___	**22646**	Ford Speeder, 10-11		75
___	**22647**	Rock Island Gondola "180044", 10		35
___	**22648**	PRR Gondola "353381", 10		35
___	**22651**	Central Vermont Operating Milk Car with platform, 10		175
___	**22653**	Starlite Diner with parking lot, 10		200
___	**22654**	Ringling Bros. Flatcar with 3 circus wagons, 10-11		60
___	**22656**	Ringling Bros. Flatcar with 3 circus wagons, 10-11		60
___	**22658**	Operating Flagman's Shanty, 10		100
___	**22659**	Union 76 1-D Tank Car "6322", 10		40
___	**22660**	Moose Pond Creamery Operating Loading Depot, 10		140
___	**22661**	WM 2-Bay Covered Hopper "5051", 10		35
___	**22662**	PRR Reefer "19494", 10		45
___	**22663**	New Haven Illuminated Caboose, 10		40
___	**22667**	Acme Scrap Platform Crane, 10		60
___	**22670**	ATSF Operating Boxcar, 10		140
___	**22671**	Smoking Southern Bay Window Caboose, 10		90
___	**22672**	Ringling Bros. 18" Sarasota Observation Car, 10-11		146
___	**22673**	Ford Water Tower with light, 10		27
___	**22674**	MILW 21" Aluminum Passenger Car 2-pack, 10-11		400
___	**22679**	Ringling Bros. Operating Billboard, 10-11		100
___	**22902**	Quonset Hut, 98-99	30	45
___	**22907**	Die-cast Girder Bridge, 98-01		10
___	**22910**	Gilbert Tractor Trailer, 98		20
___	**22914**	PowerHouse Lockon, 98-01		24
___	**22915**	Municipal Building, 98-99		28
___	**22916**	190-watt Power Accessory System, 98		425
___	**22918**	Locomotive Backshop, 98	288	460
___	**22919**	ElectroCouplers Kit for GP9 Diesel, 98-00		20
___	**22922**	Intermodal Crane, 98		195
___	**22931**	Die-cast Cantilever Signal Bridge, 98-06		35
___	**22934**	Walkout Cantilever Signal, 98-03		42
___	**22936**	Coaling Tower, 3 pieces, 98		85
___	**22940**	Mast Signal, 98-00		37
___	**22942**	Accessories Box, 98-01		20

	MODERN 1970-2024	Exc	Mint	
22944	Automatic Operating Semaphore, 98-03, 08	17	35	___
22945	Block Target Signal, 98-00		39	___
22946	Automatic Crossing Gate and Signal, 98-99		45	___
22947	Auto Crossing Gate, 98-00		36	___
22948	Gooseneck Street Lamps, set of 2, 98-00		30	___
22949	Highway Lights, set of 4, 98-99		20	___
22950	Classic Street Lamps, set of 3, 98-02		20	___
22951	Dwarf Signal, 98-00		24	___
22952	Classic Billboards, set of 3, 98-00		15	___
22953	Linex Gasoline Tall Oil Tank, 98-99		6	___
22954	Linex Gasoline Wide Oil Tank, 98-99		6	___
22955	ElectroCouplers Kit for J Class and B&A tenders, 98-00		20	___
22956	ElectroCouplers Kit for NW2 Switcher, 98		20	___
22957	ElectroCouplers Kit for F3 Diesel, 98-01		20	___
22958	ElectroCouplers Kit for Dash 9 Diesel, 98-01		20	___
22959	ElectroCoupler Conversion Kit for Atlantic Locomotive, 98-01		13	___
22960	Trainmaster Command Basic Upgrade Kit, 98-01		34	___
22961	Standard GP9 Diesel B Unit Upgrade Kit, 98-01		30	___
22962	Deluxe GP9 Diesel B Unit Upgrade Kit, black trucks, 98-01		44	___
22963	RailSounds Upgrade Kit, steam RailSounds, 98-01		55	___
22964	RailSounds Upgrade Kit, diesel RailSounds, 98-01		55	___
22965	Culvert Loader, CC, 98-01	160	255	___
22966	Figure-8 Add-on Track Pack (027), 98-16	10	17	___
22967	Double Loop Add-on Track Pack (027), 98-16		62	___
22968	Double Loop Track Pack (027), 98-03		65	___
22969	Deluxe Complete Track Pack (O), 98-16		120	___
22972	Bascule Bridge, 98-99	67	337	___
22973	Lionel Corporation Tractor and Trailer, 98		15	___
22975	Culvert Unloader, CC, 99-00		225	___
22979	GP9 Diesel B-Unit Deluxe Upgrade Kit, silver trucks, 98-01		34	___
22980	TMCC SC-2 Switch Controller, 99-16		130	___
22982	Postwar ZW Controller and Transformer Set, 98		265	___
22983	180-watt PowerHouse Power Supply, 99-16. 18		125	___
22990	Flatcar with Route 66 autos, 4-pack, 99		37	___
22991	Christmas Tree and Blue Comet Train, 99-00		60	___
22993	Route 66 Sinclair Dino Cafe, 99-00		210	___
22997	Oil Drum Loader, 99-00		100	___
22998	Triple Action Magnetic Crane, 99		220	___
22999	Sound Dispatching Station, 99-00		90	___
23000	NYC Dreyfuss Hudson Operating Base, 2-rail, 92 u		190	___
23001	NYC Dreyfuss Hudson Operating Base, 3-rail, 93 u		190	___
23002	NYC Hudson Operating Base, 92 u, 93-94		190	___
23003	PRR B-6 Switcher Operating Base, 92 u, 93-94		190	___
23004	NP 4-8-4 Operating Base, 92 u, 93-94		190	___
23005	Reading T-1 Operating Base, 92 u, 93-94		190	___
23006	Chessie System T-1 Operating Base, 92 u, 93-94		190	___
23007	SP Daylight Operating Base, 92 u, 93-94		190	___
23008	NYC L-3 Mohawk Operating Base, 92 u, 93-94		190	___
23009	PRR S2 Turbine Locomotive Operating Base, 92 u, 93-94		190	___
23010	31" Remote Switch, left hand (O), 95-99	30	37	___
23011	31" Remote Switch, right hand (O), 95-99	20	30	___
23012	F3 Diesel ABA Operating Base, 92 u, 93-94		190	___
24018	PRR Boxcar, 05		25	___

			Exc	Mint
___	**24101**	Mainline Color Position Signal, 04-08		25
___	**24102**	Industrial Water Tower, 03		55
___	**24103**	Double Floodlight Tower, 03, 05-09		42
___	**24104**	Hobo Tower, 03-05		70
___	**24105**	Track Gang, 03-06		70
___	**24106**	Exploding Ammunition Dump, 02		25
___	**24107**	Missile Firing Range Set, 02		60
___	**24108**	World War II Pylon, 03		80
___	**24109**	Santa Fe Railroad Tugboat, 03	60	125
___	**24110**	Pennsylvania Railroad Tugboat, 03		118
___	**24111**	Swing Bridge, 03		215
___	**24112**	Oil Field with bubble tubes, 03		44
___	**24113**	Lionelville Ford Auto Dealership, 03		225
___	**24114**	AMC/ARC Gantry Crane, CC, 03		195
___	**24115**	AMC/ARC Log Loader, CC, 03, 06-07		140
___	**24117**	Illuminated Covered Bridge, 02-24		100
___	**24119**	Big Bay Lighthouse, 04-05		170
___	**24122**	Lionelville People Pack, 03, 08-09, 15-17		27
___	**24123**	Passenger Station People Pack, 03, 08-09, 15-20		27
___	**24124**	Carnival People Pack, 03, 08-11, 13-16, 18-20	5	27
___	**24130**	TMCC 135/180 PowerMaster, 04-12		79
___	**24131**	Dumbo Pylon, 03		70
___	**24134**	Bethlehem Steel Gantry Crane, 02		200
___	**24135**	Lionel Lighthouse, 02-03		100
___	**24137**	Mr. Spiff and Puddles, 03, 08		34
___	**24138**	Playtime Playground, 03, 08		50
___	**24139**	Duck Shooting Gallery, 03		110
___	**24140**	Charles Bowdish Homestead, 03		60
___	**24147**	Lionel Sawmill, 03		90
___	**24148**	Coal Tipple Coal Pack, 02, 08-10, 13-20		15
___	**24149**	NYC Hobo Hotel, 02		42
___	**24151**	Hobo Campfire, 03		25
___	**24152**	Conveyor Lumber Loader, 03		65
___	**24153**	Railroad Control Tower, 03, 08-10	30	63
___	**24154**	Maiden Rescue, 03		35
___	**24155**	Blinking Light Billboard, 04-10		21
___	**24156**	Lionelville Street Lamps, 4-pack, 04-23		35
___	**24159**	Illuminated Station Platform, 04-08		32
___	**24160**	Rub-a-Dub-Dub, 04		42
___	**24161**	Test O' Strength, 04-06		70
___	**24164**	Summer Vacation, 04-05		80
___	**24168**	Tire Swing, 04-05		70
___	**24170**	Rover's Revenge, 04-05		70
___	**24171**	Campbell's Soup Water Tower, 04		45
___	**24172**	Balancing Man, 04-05		70
___	**24173**	Derrick Platform, 03-05		60
___	**24174**	Icing Station, 04-06		100
___	**24176**	Irene's Diner, 06-07		65
___	**24177**	Hot Air Balloon Ride, 04-06		95
___	**24179**	Scrambler Amusement Ride, 04-07	87	165
___	**24180**	Choo Choo Barn Lionelville Zoo, 04-05	53	222
___	**24182**	Lionelville Firehouse, 04		100
___	**24183**	Lionelville Gas Station, 04, 06-09		115

MODERN 1970-2024		Exc	Mint	
24187	Classic Billboard Set: 3 stands and 5 inserts, 04-08		10	___
24190	Station Platform, 05-09		17	___
24191	Park People Pack, 04-18		27	___
24192	Park Benches People Pack, 04-09		23	___
24193	Railroad Yard People Pack, 04-08, 14-18	10	19	___
24194	Civil Servants People Pack, 04-18		27	___
24196	Farm People Pack, 04-09		23	___
24197	City Accessory Pack, 04-17		27	___
24200	Lionel FasTrack Book, 07-10, 13-15		35	___
24201	UPS Centennial Operating Billboard Signmen, 07		100	___
24203	Polar Express Original Figures, 4 pieces, 08-24		30	___
24204	Christmas Tractor Trailer with trees, 08		25	___
24205	Classic Billboard Set, 08-10		20	___
24206	MOW Gantry Crane, 08		280	___
24212	Lionel Art Blinking Billboard, 08-09		23	___
24213	Universal Lockon, 12-16		4	___
24214	Postwar "395" Floodlight Tower, 08		75	___
24215	MTA Metro-North Passenger Station, 07		53	___
24218	Sunoco Elevated Tank, 08-09		75	___
24219	PRR Plastic Girder Bridge, 08		18	___
24220	ATSF Girder Bridge, 08-09		18	___
24221	UP Die-cast Girder Bridge, 08		30	___
24222	UPS Die-cast Girder Bridge, 08		30	___
24223	Santa's Sleigh Pylon, 08		150	___
24224	Postwar "38" Water Tower, 08-09		150	___
24226	Christmas Toy Store, 08		52	___
24227	Halloween Animated Billboard, 08-09		54	___
24228	Christmas Operating Billboard, 08		38	___
24229	Pennsylvania Water Tower, 08-09		23	___
24230	Maiden Rescue, 08		60	___
24232	Burning Switch Tower, 08		80	___
24233	Exploding Ammunition Dump, 08		36	___
24234	Missile Firing Range, 08		43	___
24235	UPS Water Tower, 08		80	___
24236	Wimpy's All-Star Burger Stand, 08		97	___
24238	Sunoco Oil Derrick, 08		90	___
24240	MTA Metro-North Blinking Billboard, 07		21	___
24242	Postwar "352" Icing Station, 08		100	___
24243	Rosie's Roadside Diner, 08		85	___
24244	Commuter People, 08, 13-18		27	___
24245	MTA Metro-North Illuminated Station Platform, 07		32	___
24248	Manual Crossing Gate, 08-23		20	___
24250	Mainline Gooseneck Lamps, pair, 08-09		32	___
24251	Polar Express Caribou Pack, 08-24		30	___
24252	Polar Express Wolves and Rabbits Figures, 08-24		30	___
24264	Halloween People, 08-12		23	___
24265	Trick or Treat People, 08-13		23	___
24270	Operating Forklift Platform, 08-09		280	___
24272	Train Orders Building, 08		80	___
24273	Christmas Water Tower, 08-10		23	___
24274	Christmas Girder Bridge, 08		18	___
24279	PowerMaster Bridge, 08-13		55	___
24283	NYC Girder Bridge, 09-10		21	___

			Exc	Mint
___	24284	Halloween Girder Bridge, 09-11		21
___	24285	CP Rail Girder Bridge, 08-09		30
___	24286	Polar Express Girder Bridge, 09-14		21
___	24287	ATSF Blinking Light Water Tower, 09		30
___	24288	NYC Blinking Light Water Tower, 09		30
___	24293	Legacy Module Garage, 08-09		50
___	24294	AEC Nuclear Reactor, 09-10		338
___	24295	Cowen's Corner Hobby Shop, 09		420
___	24296	Engine House, 09-12, 14		70
___	24298	Franklin Mutual Bank, 08		60
___	24299	Main Street Ice Cream Parlor, 08		37
___	24500	D&RGW Alco PA Diesel AA Set, 04-05		530
___	24503	D&RGW Alco PB Diesel, 04-05		150
___	24504	Santa Fe E6 Diesel AA Set, CC, 03		530
___	24507	Milwaukee Road E6 Diesel AA Set, CC, 03		530
___	24511	Burlington FT Diesel AA Set, RailSounds, 03		225
___	24516	Santa Fe F3 Diesel B Unit, 03		235
___	24517	NYC F3 Diesel B Unit "2404," powered, CC, 03		250
___	24518	WP F3 Diesel B Unit, 03		275
___	24519	B&O F3 Diesel B Unit, 03		270
___	24520	Alaska F3 Diesel AA Set, 03		650
___	24521	Alaska F3 Diesel B Unit, nonpowered, 03		200
___	24522	Alaska F3 Diesel B Unit "1519," powered, CC, 03		300
___	24528	Postwar "2379T" Rio Grande F3 Diesel A Unit, nonpowered, 04		175
___	24529	Santa Fe F3 Diesel AA Set, CC, 04	213	690
___	24532	Santa Fe F3 Diesel B Unit "18A," nonpowered, 04		150
___	24533	Santa Fe F3 Diesel B Unit "18B", 04		200
___	24534	Erie-Lack. F3 Diesel ABA Set, CC, 05		900
___	24538	Erie-Lack. F3 Diesel B Unit "8042," powered, CC, 05	60	225
___	24544	NYC FA2 Diesel AA Set, CC, 05		600
___	24547	NYC FB2 Diesel B Unit "3330" (std O), 05		150
___	24548	CN FPA-4 Diesel AA Set, CC, 05		600
___	24551	CN FPB-4 Diesel B Unit "6865" (std O), 05		150
___	24552	UP F3 Diesel ABA Set, CC, 05	340	895
___	24556	UP F3 Diesel B Unit "900C," powered, CC, 05		285
___	24562	Santa Fe F3 Diesel B Unit, powered, 04-05	100	300
___	24563	PRR F3 Diesel B Unit, powered, 04-05		195
___	24566	Napa Valley Wine Train FPA-4 A Unit "71," powered, 05		400
___	24567	Napa Valley Wine Train FPA-4 B Unit "72," nonpowered, 05		100
___	24570	Santa Fe FT Diesel B Unit, nonpowered, 05		85
___	24571	Postwar "2383" ATSF F3 Diesel A Unit, powered, 05		400
___	24572	Postwar "2383" ATSF F3 Diesel A Unit, nonpowered, 05		100
___	24573	Postwar "2383C" Santa Fe F3 Diesel B Unit, nonpowered, 05		180
___	24574	UP E7 Diesel AA Set '988/989," CC, 06		700
___	24577	UP E7 Diesel B Unit "990," nonpowered (std O), 06		150
___	24578	UP E7 Diesel B Unit "988," powered, 06		300
___	24579	NYC E7 Diesel AA Set "4008/4009," CC, 06		700
___	24582	NYC E7 Diesel B Unit "4105," nonpowered (std O), 06		150
___	24583	NYC E7 Diesel B Unit "4104," powered, 06		300
___	24584	Pennsylvania F7 Diesel ABA Set "9642/9643," CC, 06		900
___	24588	Pennsylvania F7 Diesel B Unit "9643B," powered, 06-07		300
___	24589	Santa Fe F7 Diesel ABA Set "332/333," CC, 06-07		900
___	24593	Santa Fe F7 Diesel B Unit "332B," powered, 06-07		300

MODERN 1970-2024		Exc	Mint
24594	PRR F7 Diesel Breakdown B Unit, RailSounds, 06-07		160 ___
24595	Santa Fe F7 Diesel Breakdown B Unit, RailSounds, 06-07		270 ___
24596	UP E7 Diesel Breakdown B Unit, RailSounds, 06		270 ___
24597	NYC E7 Diesel Breakdown B Unit, RailSounds, 06		270 ___
25002	P&LE Boxcar "20982", 05	20	25 ___
25003	WP Boxcar, orange with silver feather, 05		30 ___
25008	Holiday Boxcar, 06		50 ___
25009	Santa Fe Hi-Cube Boxcar "14064", 06		30 ___
25010	NP Boxcar "48189", 06		30 ___
25011	Angela Trotta Thomas "Santa's Break" Boxcar, 06		50 ___
25014	PRR Boxcar, silver, 10		30 ___
25016	ATSF Boxcar, 10		35 ___
25022	NYC Boxcar, 06		35 ___
25024	GM&O Boxcar, 07		30 ___
25025	Reading Boxcar "106502", 07-08		35 ___
25026	RI Hi-Cube Boxcar, 07-08		35 ___
25030	Billboard Boxcar with catalog art, 06		20 ___
25033	Holiday Boxcar, 07	15	50 ___
25034	Angela Trotta Thomas "Santa's Workshop" Boxcar, 07		50 ___
25035	Disney Holiday Boxcar, 06		50 ___
25041	UPS Centennial Boxcar #1, 06		60 ___
25042	UPS Centennial Boxcar #2, 07		60 ___
25043	Macy's Parade Boxcar, 06		40 ___
25047	It's a Wonderful Life Bedford Falls Boxcar, 07 u		75 ___
25048	It's a Wonderful Life Happy Holidays Boxcar, 07 u		75 ___
25050	British Columbia Hi-Cube Boxcar "8008", 08		35 ___
25051	Seaboard Boxcar, 08		35 ___
25052	Disney Holiday Boxcar, 07		75 ___
25053	NYC DD Boxcar "75500", 08		55 ___
25054	Angela Trotta Thomas "Christmas Memories" Boxcar, 08		55 ___
25057	PRR Boxcar "19751", 08		20 ___
25058	Santa Fe Boxcar, 10		30 ___
25059	Democrat 2008 Election Boxcar, 08		50 ___
25060	Republican 2008 Election Boxcar, 08		50 ___
25061	Holiday Boxcar, 08		55 ___
25063	Conrail Boxcar "25063", 09		40 ___
25064	CP Rail Hi-Cube Boxcar, 09-10	18	40 ___
25065	Disney Holiday Boxcar, 08		40 ___
25066	Holiday Boxcar, 09		65 ___
25067	Angela Trotta Thomas "General Delivery" Boxcar, 09	33	84 ___
25068	D&H Boxcar, 08 u		60 ___
25077	Milwaukee Road Boxcar "8484", 09-10	13	40 ___
25083	Wizard of Oz Boxcar, 1, 09		50 ___
25084	Wizard of Oz Boxcar, 2, 09		50 ___
25087	Wabash Boxcar "6439", 10-11		40 ___
25088	Georgia Power Boxcar, 10		40 ___
25093	Seaboard Boxcar, 10		30 ___
25095	Texas Special Boxcar, 10		100 ___
25096	CN Boxcar, 10		45 ___
25103	Chessie "Steam Special" Madison Car 2-pack, 05		100 ___
25106	Pennsylvania Madison Car 4-pack, 05		210 ___
25111	Pennsylvania Madison Car 2-pack, 05		120 ___
25114	Lionel Lines Passenger Car 3-pack, 05		120 ___

			Exc	Mint
___	**25118**	Lionel Lines Passenger Car 2-pack, 05		80
___	**25121**	Southern Streamliner Car 4-pack, 05		210
___	**25126**	Southern Streamliner Car 2-pack, 05-06		120
___	**25134**	Polar Express Add-on Diner, 05-17		70
___	**25135**	Polar Express Add-on Baggage Car, 05-17		70
___	**25142**	NYC Combination Car, "5018", 05		40
___	**25143**	NYC Coach, "3807", 05		45
___	**25144**	NYC Observation, "4152", 05		40
___	**25148**	B&O Madison Car 4-pack, 06-07		220
___	**25153**	B&O Madison Car 2-pack, 06-07		125
___	**25156**	California Zephyr Streamliner Car 4-pack (std O), 06-07		220
___	**25161**	California Zephyr Streamliner Car 2-pack, 06-07		125
___	**25164**	UP Madison Car 4-pack, 06-07		220
___	**25169**	UP Madison Car 2-pack, 06-07		125
___	**25176**	B&O Baggage Car, TrainSounds, 06-07		160
___	**25177**	UP Baggage Car, TrainSounds, 06-07		160
___	**25178**	California Zephyr Streamliner Baggage Car, TrainSounds, 06-07		160
___	**25186**	Polar Express Hot Chocolate Car Add-on, 06-14, 16-17	40	72
___	**25187**	GN Streamliner Car 4-pack, 07		220
___	**25188**	GN Streamliner Car 2-pack, 07		125
___	**25189**	GN Streamliner Baggage Car, TrainSounds, 07		160
___	**25196**	North Pole Central Vista Dome Car, 07-08		45
___	**25197**	North Pole Central Baggage Car, 07-10		45
___	**25198**	PRR Vista Dome Car "4058", 07-08		45
___	**25199**	PRR Baggage Car "9359", 07-09		45
___	**25307**	B&M Operating Boxcar, 07		55
___	**25404**	FEC Champion Aluminum Passenger Car 2-pack, 04-05		290
___	**25407**	FEC Champion Aluminum Diner, StationSounds, 04-05		290
___	**25408**	Santa Fe El Capitan Aluminum Passenger Car 2-pack, 05		290
___	**25411**	Santa Fe El Capitan Aluminum Diner, StationSounds, 05		290
___	**25412**	B&O Columbian Aluminum Passenger Car 2-pack, 05		275
___	**25415**	B&O Columbian Aluminum Diner, StationSounds, 05		290
___	**25416**	SP Daylight Aluminum Passenger Car 2-pack, 04-05		290
___	**25419**	SP Daylight Aluminum Diner, StationSounds, 04-05		290
___	**25420**	PRR Trail Blazer Aluminum Passenger Car 2-pack, 04-05		290
___	**25423**	PRR Trail Blazer Aluminum Diner, StationSounds, 04-05		290
___	**25433**	UP City of Denver Aluminum Passenger Car 4-pack (std O), 05		1000
___	**25438**	Union Pacific Aluminum Passenger Car 2-pack, 05		250
___	**25441**	UP City of Denver 18" Aluminum Diner, StationSounds, 05		290
___	**25442**	REA Baggage Car, 05		60
___	**25443**	Santa Fe Super Chief Vista Dome "Regal Pass", 05		60
___	**25444**	Santa Fe Super Chief Coach "Indian Falls", 05		60
___	**24445**	Santa Fe Super Chief Observation "Vista Valley", 05		60
___	**25446**	Santa Fe Super Chief Streamliner Car 2-pack, 05		150
___	**25447**	Santa Fe Super Chief Vista Dome "Royal Gorge", 05		70
___	**25448**	Santa Fe Super Chief Coach "Indian Arrow", 05		70
___	**25450**	PRR Congressional Aluminum Passenger Car 4-pack (std O), 06-07		580
___	**25455**	PRR Congressional Aluminum Passenger Car 2-pack (std O), 06-07		300
___	**25458**	PRR Congressional Diner, StationSounds (std O), 06-07		300
___	**25473**	NYC Commodore Vanderbilt Aluminum Passenger Car 2-pack (std O), 06		300
___	**25476**	NYC Commodore Vanderbilt Diner, StationSounds (std O), 06		300

Item	Description	Exc	Mint
25496	Texas Special 21" Streamliner Diner, StationSounds (std O), 07		300
25503	Santa Fe Heavyweight Passenger Car 4-pack (std O), 07-09		495
25504	Santa Fe Heavyweight Passenger Car 2-pack (std O), 07-09		265
25505	Santa Fe Heavyweight Diner, StationSounds (std O), 07-09		295
25506	SP Heavyweight Passenger Car 4-pack (std O), 07		495
25507	SP Heavyweight Passenger Car 2-pack (std O), 07-08		265
25508	SP Heavyweight Diner, StationSounds (std O), 07-08	50	295
25512	Texas Special Streamliner Car 2-pack (std O), 07		300
25514	Best Friend of Charleston Coach, 08		125
25515	MILW Heavyweight Passenger Car 4-pack (std O), 07		495
25516	MILW Heavyweight Passenger Car 2-pack (std O), 07		265
25517	MILW Heavyweight Diner, StationSounds (std O), 07-08		295
25518	PRR Heavyweight Passenger Car 4-pack (std O), 07		495
25519	PRR Heavyweight Passenger Car 2-pack (std O), 07		265
25520	PRR Heavyweight Diner, StationSounds (std O), 07-08		295
25521	B&O Heavyweight Passenger Car 4-pack (std O), 07		495
25522	B&O Heavyweight Passenger Car 2-pack (std O), 07		265
25523	B&O Heavyweight Diner, StationSounds (std O), 07-08		295
25559	Phantom IV Passenger Car 4-pack, 08		380
25574	UP Streamlined Diner, StationSounds (std O), 08		325
25575	Polar Express Heavyweight Car 2-pack, 09		400
25576	Polar Express Scale Observation Car, 14, 16		210
25578	Polar Express Heavyweight Add-on Coach, 09		200
25582	New York City Transit R30 Subway 2-pack, 10		400
25586	Polar Express Heavyweight Baggage Car, 10, 12-14		210
25587	Polar Express Abandoned Toy Car, 10, 13		200
25595	New York City Transit R16 Subway 2-pack, 10		400
25598	Polar Express Heavyweight Combination Car, 12-14		210
25600	Postwar Scale CP 18" Aluminum Passenger Car 4-pack , 11		640
25605	Postwar Scale CP 18" Aluminum Passenger Car 2-pack , 11		320
25608	ATSF Super Chief 18" Aluminum Passenger Cars 4-pack, 11		640
25613	ATSF Super Chief 18" Aluminum Passenger Cars 2-pack, 11		320
25616	UP 18" Passenger Car 2-pack (std O), 11		320
25619	PRR "Lindbergh Special" Passenger Car 2-pack, 11		280
25622	Milwaukee Road 18" Passenger Car 4-pack, 11		640
25623	Milwaukee Road 18" Passenger Car 2-pack, 11		320
25630	Polar Express Scale Heavyweight Diner, 12-14, 16		210
25631	Lionel Funeral Set Add-on 2-pack (std O), 13		300
25635	PRR Red Arrow Heavyweight Coach 3-pack (std O), 13		430
25639	PRR Red Arrow Heavyweight Diner (std O), 13		150
25646	ATSF Scout Heavyweight Coach 4-pack (std O), 12-14		550
25651	ATSF Scout Heavyweight Coach 2-pack (std O), 12-14		280
25654	Southern Crescent Limited Heavyweight Passenger Car 2-pack, 12		550
25655	Blue Comet Heavyweight Passenger Car 2-pack, 12-13		550
25656	Alton Limited Heavyweight Passenger Car 2-pack, 12-14	113	550
25665	Amtrak Acela Passenger Car 2-pack, 12		500
25713	NYC 20th Century Limited Heavyweight 4-pack (std O), 12-14		550
25714	NYC 20th Century Limited Van Twiller Combo Car (std O), 12		140
25715	NYC 20th Century Limited Schuyler Mansion Sleeper Car (std O), 12		140
25716	NYC 20th Century Limited Macomb House Sleeper Car (std O), 12		140

			Exc	Mint
___	25717	NYC 20th Century Limited Catskill Valley Observation Car (std O), 12		140
___	25718	NYC 20th Century Limited Heavyweight Passenger Car 2-pack, 12-14		280
___	25719	NYC 20th Century Limited Baggage Car "4857" (std O), 12		140
___	25720	NYC 20th Century Limited Poplar Highlands Sleeper Car (std O), 12		140
___	25721	NYC 20th Century Limited Heavyweight Diner "655" (std O), 12		280
___	25722	D&RGW California Zephyr 18" Aluminum Passenger Car 4-pack, 12		640
___	25727	WP California Zephyr 18" Aluminum Passenger Car 2-pack, 12		320
___	25731	CB&Q California Zephyr 18" Aluminum Passenger Car 2-pack, 12		320
___	25757	Texas Special Passenger Car 2-pack, 13-14		400
___	25760	PRR Passenger Car 2-pack, 13-14		400
___	25773	SAL Round-roof Boxcar "19297" (std O), 14		80
___	25790	NYC 20th Century Limited Heavyweight Diner (std O), 12		140
___	25795	Polar Express 10th Anniversary Scale Coach, 14		215
___	25795	Polar Express Gold Coach, 17		200
___	25796	Polar Express 10th Anniversary Scale Observation Car, 14, 16		215
___	25922	NS Caboose, 13-14	10	25
___	25923	Interstate 1-D Tank Car, 13-14	12	30
___	25930	John Adams Presidential Boxcar, 13, 15-16		70
___	25931	Andrew Johnson Presidential Boxcar, 13, 15-16		70
___	25932	Calvin Coolidge Presidential Boxcar, 13, 15-16		70
___	25933	Harry S. Truman Presidential Boxcar, 13, 15-16		70
___	25934	Santa Fe Reefer 3-pack, 14-17		145
___	25938	PRR Freight Expansion 3-pack, 13		155
___	25942	Western Freight Expansion 3-pack, 13-16		155
___	25946	SP Hi-Cube Boxcar "128132", 13, 15		50
___	25947	North Pole Express Jack Frost Reefer, 13		43
___	25958	Gingerbread Dough Vat Car, 13-14		60
___	25959	Gingerbread 3-D Tank Car, 13		55
___	25960	Christmas Tree Transparent Boxcar, 13-14		75
___	25961	Thanksgiving on Parade Boxcar, 13		60
___	25962	Thanksgiving Poultry Car, 13		70
___	25963	A Christmas Story 30th Anniversary Boxcar, 13-14		65
___	25964	Silver Bell Casting Co. Ore Car, 13		55
___	25965	Polar Express 10th Anniversary Boxcar, 13		65
___	25972	MILW Scale Round-roof Boxcar "714305" (std O), 15	35	61
___	25973	Seaboard Round-roof Boxcar "19297" (std O), 14		80
___	25977	A Christmas Story Leg Lamp Mint Car, 13		80
___	26000	C&O Flatcar with pipes, 01		20
___	26001	BP Flatcar "6424" with trailers, 01 u		150
___	26002	Monopoly Pennsylvania Ave. Flatcar w/Airplane, 00 u		60
___	26003	Lackawanna Flatcar with NH trailer, 01		60
___	26004	Conrail Flatcar "71693" with trailer, 01		50
___	26005	Nickel Plate Flatcar with trailer, 01		55
___	26006	Southern Flatcar "50126" with trailer, 01		50
___	26007	NW Flatcar "203029" with trailer, 01		50
___	26008	Farmall Flatcar, 01 u		100
___	26011	B&M Bulkhead Flatcar, 01 u	20	30
___	26013	CN Flatcar with Zamboni ice resurfacing machine, 01		48
___	26014	JCPenney Flatcar, 01 u		145
___	26016	Soo Line Flatcar with trucks, 01 u		120

		Exc	Mint
26017	Soo Line Flatcar with trailer, 01 u		120
26018	Soo Line Flatcar with trailer, 01 u		120
26019	Alaska Gondola "13801", 02		30
26020	Postwar "3830" Flatcar with submarine, 02		46
26021	CN Flatcar with trailer, 02		44
26022	PFE Flatcar with trailer, 02		32
26023	Postwar "6816" Flatcar with bulldozer, 02		65
26024	Postwar "6817" Flatcar with scraper, 02		65
26025	Postwar "6407" Flatcar with rocket, 02		42
26026	Postwar "6413" Flatcar with Mercury capsules, 02		95
26027	Flatcar "6425" with U.S. Army boat, 02		30
26028	Conrail Well Car "768121", 02		40
26030	NYC Flatcar "601172" with stakes and bulkheads, 02		22
26033	NYC Gondola "6462", 01		30
26035	LL Flatcar with traffic helicopter, 01		50
26039	Lionel Lions Flatcar with Zamboni ice resurfacing machines, 02		39
26042	B&O Gondola "601272" with canisters, 03		19
26043	Seaboard Flatcar "48109" with trailer, 03		30
26044	NYC Flatcar "506089" with trailers, 03		35
26045	Postwar "2411" Flatcar with pipes, 03		40
26046	Postwar "6561" Flatcar with cable reels, 03		30
26047	Postwar "2461" Flatcar with transformer, 03		25
26048	Postwar "6801" Flatcar with boat, 02		29
26049	Speedboat Willie Flatcar with boat, 03		29
26053	PRR Gondola with canisters, 04,àí05		20
26055	C&O Flatcar "475227" w/Trailer Train Truck, 03		50
26056	Southern Bulkhead Flatcar "50125", 02		19
26057	SP Flatcar "599365" w/Tractors, 02		37
26058	SP Flatcar "599366" w/Trailer Frames, 02		35
26060	Postwar "6467" Flatcar w/Bulkheads, 03		42
26061	Lionelville Tree Transport Gondola, 03		40
26062	NYC Gondola "26062" with cable reels, 03		19
26063	Pennsylvania Bulkhead Flatcar "26063", 03		19
26064	Rock Island Flatcar "90088" with trailer, 04		34
26065	REA Flatcar with trailers "TLCX2", 04		35
26066	Great Northern Bulkhead Flatcar "26066", 04		20
26067	Southern Gondola "60141" with cable reels, 04		20
26070	Nestle Nesquik Flatcar "26070" with trailer, 03		70
26077	LL Flatcar "6424" with autos, girls set add-on, 03		44
26078	LL Flatcar "6801" with boat, boys set add-on, 03		40
26080	NJ Medical School Flatcar with handcar, 03		80
26082	Frisco Auto Carrier, 2-tier, 04		20
26085	New York Auto Carrier, 2-tier, 05		27
26086	Alaska Flatcar with bulkheads, 05		25
26087	Rock Island Gondola with canisters, traditional, 05		27
26089	LRRC Western Union Telegraph Gondola w/Handcar, 10		70
26090	Elvis Presley Flatcar w/Billboards, 05		45
26091	Elvis Flatcar with tractor and trailer, traditional, 05		60
26092	WC Gondola "54214" w/Canisters, 04		50
26093	Hobby Town USA Gondola w/Canisters, 04 u		45
26094	UP Screened Auto Carrier, 04		55
26095	CSX Screened Auto Carrier, 04		55
26096	BNSF Screened Auto Carrier, 04		55

			Exc	Mint
____	**26097**	ATSF Screened Auto Carrier "89474" (std O), 04	26	45
____	**26099**	PRR Auto Carrier "500423," 3-tier, 07		30
____	**26100**	PRR 1-D Tank Car, 00		27
____	**26101**	Lenoil 1-D Tank Car "6015", 00		34
____	**26102**	AEC Glow-in-Dark 1-D Tank Car, 00		58
____	**26103**	GATX Tank Train 1-D Tank Car "44588", 00		34
____	**26107**	BP Petroleum 3-D Tank Car, 00 u		105
____	**26108**	Lionel Visitor's Center Reefer "206482", 00 u		38
____	**26109**	NYC (P&LE) 1-D Tank Car, 00		42
____	**26110**	SP 3-D Tank Car "6415", 00-01		15
____	**26111**	Frisco Tank Car, 00		29
____	**26112**	Gulf Oil Tank Car, 00		40
____	**26113**	U.S. Army 1-D Tank Car, 00		35
____	**26114**	Service Station 1-D Tank Car (SSS), 00		32
____	**26115**	Lionel Centennial Tank Car, 00 u	50	95
____	**26116**	Pepe LePew 1-D Tank Car, 00 u		85
____	**26118**	NYC Tank Car "101900", 01		23
____	**26119**	Protex 3-D Tank Car "1054", 00		29
____	**26120**	KCS Tank Car "1229", 00		32
____	**26122**	Pioneer Seed Tank Car, 00 u		60
____	**26123**	Santa Fe Stock Car "23002", 01		35
____	**26124**	C&O 1-D Tank Car "X1019", 01		30
____	**26125**	Winter Wonderland Clear Tank Car with confetti, 00		50
____	**26126**	Cheerios Boxcar, 98		70
____	**26127**	Wellspring Capital Management Tank Car with confetti, 00 u	115	239
____	**26131**	Santa Fe 1-D Tank Car "335268", 02		22
____	**26132**	UP 1-D Tank Car "69015, 02		40
____	**26133**	Tootsie Roll 1-D Tank Car "26133", 02		40
____	**26135**	Whirlpool Tank Car, 01		60
____	**26136**	Southern 1-D Tank Car "8790011", 03		20
____	**26137**	Jack Frost 1-D Tank Car "106", 03		32
____	**26138**	Nestle Nesquik 1-D Tank Car "26138", 03		40
____	**26139**	Lionel Lines Stock Car "26139" with horses, 03		39
____	**26141**	Whirlpool 1-D Tank Car, 03 u		97
____	**26143**	Airco 1-D Tank Car "1137", 03		45
____	**26144**	Chessie System 1-D Tank Car "2233", 02		22
____	**26145**	Do It Best 1-D Tank Car, 03 u		82
____	**26146**	Valspar 1-D Tank Car, 03 u		95
____	**26147**	Diamond Chemicals 1-D Tank Car "6315," Archive Collection, 02		33
____	**26149**	Egg Nog 1-D Tank Car, 03		43
____	**26150**	Alaska 3-D Tank Car "26150", 03		23
____	**26151**	NP Wood-sided Reefer "26151", 03	13	29
____	**26152**	Morton Salt 1-D Tank Car "26152", 04		40
____	**26153**	Pillsbury 1-D Tank Car "26153", 04		40
____	**26154**	NYC 3-D Tank Car "26154", 04		25
____	**26155**	Pennsylvania 1-D Tank Car "26155", 04		20
____	**26156**	North Western Wood-sided Reefer "15356", 04		20
____	**26157**	Ballyhoo Brothers Circus Stock Car "26157", 04		35
____	**26158**	Campbell's Soup 1-D Tank Car, 04		35
____	**26164**	LL 1-D Tank Car "6315," girls set add-on, 03		43
____	**26167**	New Haven 1-D Tank Car, traditional, 05		27
____	**26168**	Conrail 3-D Tank Car, traditional, 05		27
____	**26169**	Santa Fe Wood-sided Reefer, traditional, 05		27

		Exc	Mint	
26170	Atlanta States Gas 1-D Tank Car, 05	20	25	___
26171	Alaska 1-D Tank Car, 05		30	___
26176	Tidmouth Milk 1-D Tank Car, 05		35	___
26179	GN 3-D Tank Car, 06	15	35	___
26180	DM&IR 1-D Tank Car "S15", 06		30	___
26181	NYC Wood-sided Reefer, 06		30	___
26193	UP 1-D Tank Car, 07		20	___
26194	Hooker Chemical 1-D Tank Car, 06		45	___
26195	PRR 3-D Tank Car "2280", 06		20	___
26196	Candy Cane 1-D Tank Car, 06		60	___
26197	D&H 1-D Tank Car "55", 07-08		35	___
26198	D&RGW 3-D Tank Car, 07		30	___
26199	WP PFE Wood-sided Reefer "55327", 07		30	___
26200	NKP Boxcar "18211", 98		35	___
26201	Operation Lifesaver Boxcar, 98		29	___
26203	D&H Boxcar "1829", 98		25	___
26204	Alaska Boxcar "10806", 98-99		35	___
26205	Rocky & Bullwinkle Boxcar, 99		36	___
26206	Curious George Boxcar, 99		40	___
26208	Vapor Records Boxcar #2, 98		60	___
26214	Celebrate the Century Stamp Boxcar, 98 u		97	___
26215	AEC Glow-in-the-Dark Boxcar, 98		105	___
26216	Cheerios Boxcar, 98 u		83	___
26218	Quaker Oats Boxcar, 98 u		475	___
26219	Ace Hardware Boxcar, 98 u		NRS	___
26220	Smuckers Boxcar, 98 u	50	99	___
26222	Penn Central Boxcar "125962", 99		31	___
26223	FEC Boxcar "5027", 99		31	___
26224	D&H Boxcar, 99		24	___
26228	Vapor Records Holiday Boxcar, 99 u		135	___
26230	AEC Glow-in-the-Dark Boxcar #2, 99		59	___
26232	Martin Guitar Lumber Boxcar "9823", 99		50	___
26234	NYC Boxcar, 99		29	___
26235	Valentine Boxcar, 99		40	___
26236	Aircraft Boxcar, 99		28	___
26237	Boy Scout Boxcar, 99		85	___
26238	Detroit Historical Museum Boxcar, 99		29	___
26239	M.A.D.D. Boxcar, 99		19	___
26240	RailBox Boxcar, 99-00		24	___
26241	Norfolk & Western Boxcar, 99-00		17	___
26242	D.A.R.E. Boxcar, 99		30	___
26243	Christmas Boxcar, 99		35	___
26244	Woody Woodpecker Boxcar, 99		43	___
26247	Lionel Lines Boxcar, 99		38	___
26253	Acme Explosives Boxcar, 99 u		NRS	___
26254	Keebler Boxcar, 99 u		NRS	___
26255	NYC Boxcar "200495", 99 u		30	___
26256	Salvation Army Charity Boxcar, 99		29	___
26257	Wheaties Boxcar, 99	50	91	___
26264	Lionel Station Boxcar, 99		44	___
26265	NYC Pacemaker Boxcar, 00		30	___
26271	AEC Glow-in-the-Dark Boxcar, 99		62	___
26272	Christmas Boxcar, 00	26	42	___

			Exc	Mint
___	**26275**	Boy Scout Boxcar, 00		55
___	**26276**	C&O Boxcar "23296", 99-00		23
___	**26277**	UP Boxcar "491050", 00		20
___	**26278**	Cap'n Crunch Christmas Boxcar, 99 u		694
___	**26280**	Tinsel Town Express Boxcar, music, 00		50
___	**26284**	Toy Fair Preview Boxcar, 99 u		725
___	**26285**	NYC Pacemaker Boxcar, 00		40
___	**26288**	AEC Glow-in-Dark Boxcar, 99		55
___	**26290**	SP Boxcar, 00		20
___	**26291**	Pennsylvania Boxcar "47158", 00		20
___	**26292**	Frisco Boxcar "22015", 00		20
___	**26293**	Burlington Boxcar, 00		30
___	**26294**	Centennial Express Boxcar, 00		NRS
___	**26295**	Trainmaster Boxcar, 99 u		55
___	**26296**	Service Station Boxcar Set (SSS), 00		105
___	**26298**	Taz Bobbing Boxcar, 00		70
___	**26300**	UPS Flatcar with trailers, 04		50
___	**26301**	UPS Flatcar with airplane, traditional, 05		53
___	**26302**	Troublesome Truck #1, 05		35
___	**26303**	Troublesome Truck #2, 05		35
___	**26305**	SP Auto Carrier, 2-tier, 06		30
___	**26306**	D&RGW Gondola "56135" with canisters, 06		30
___	**26307**	Chessie System Bulkhead Flatcar, 06		30
___	**26308**	Hard Rock Cafe Flatcar with billboards, 06		55
___	**26309**	Alaska Depressed Center Flatcar with cable reels, 06		50
___	**26310**	CGW Flatcar "3707" with trailer, 06		55
___	**26311**	Santa Fe Flatcar with pickups, 06		60
___	**26317**	AEC Gondola with toxic waste containers (red), 06		30
___	**26318**	AEC Gondola with toxic waste containers (white), 06		30
___	**26327**	NYC Gondola w/Canisters, 06	10	15
___	**26330**	Gondola with trees and presents, 06		60
___	**26331**	Lionel Lines Bulkhead Flatcar, 07		30
___	**26332**	CP Rail Gondola "337061" with canisters, 07		30
___	**26335**	Domino Sugar Flatcar with trailer, 07-08		60
___	**26355**	Kasey Kahne Auto Loader w/2 Autos, 07	25	80
___	**26357**	CSX Flatcar "600514" with pipes , 07-08		50
___	**26366**	REA Flatcar with trailers, 07		60
___	**26367**	Santa's Egg Nog Flatcar with container, 07		60
___	**26368**	Gondola with trees and presents, 07		60
___	**26378**	Conrail Auto Carrier "786414," 2-tier, 08		35
___	**26379**	PRR Gondola with cable reels, 08-09		35
___	**26380**	NYC Bulkhead Flatcar, 08		35
___	**26389**	ATSF Flatcar "108477" with 2 pickups, 08		60
___	**26390**	ATSF Flatcar with bulkheads, 09-10		40
___	**26391**	NYC Gondola "263910" with containers, 09		40
___	**26392**	BNSF Auto Carrier, 09		40
___	**26400**	C&NW Hopper, 07-08		35
___	**26401**	NP Ore Car "78540", 08		35
___	**26410**	Chessie System Hopper "47806", 08		35
___	**26411**	Lionel Lines Ore Car "2026", 08-09		35
___	**26412**	Chessie System 4-bay Hopper "60573", 08		35
___	**26418**	B&M Hopper, 09		40
___	**26421**	PRR Ore Car, 11		40

MODERN 1970-2024		Exc	Mint	
26422	White Pass Ice Breaker Car, 09		50	___
26423	Soo Line Ore Car, 10		40	___
26424	LV Hopper, 11		30	___
26425	UP Hopper, 11		40	___
26429	PRR Hopper, 11		40	___
26430	CP Hopper w/Coal, 11		60	___
26431	CN ACF 2-Bay Hopper "370088", 10-11		40	___
26435	B&M Ice Breaker Hopper , 11		50	___
26437	CSX Hopper, 11		40	___
26439	Central of Georgia Hopper, 11-12		40	___
26443	M&StL Ore Car "6700", 11		40	___
26445	Polar Hopper with presents, 11-14		60	___
26446	Thomas & Friends Troublesome Trucks Christmas 2-pack, 11-15		70	___
26448	U.S. Army Gondola with reels, 11		40	___
26449	CN Hi-Cube Boxcar "799346", 13		55	___
26451	DM&IR Ore Car "28003", 13		43	___
26452	PRR Hopper "153935", 13		43	___
26457	PRR Ore Car, 12		40	___
26467	Central of Georgia 2-Bay Grain Hopper, 13-14	12	30	___
26473	Lackawanna NS Heritage 2-bay Hopper, 13		55	___
26474	NYC NS Heritage Quad Hopper, 13		55	___
26477	Monopoly Electric Company Hopper, 13		65	___
26481	Boy Scouts of America Christmas Gondola, 13		65	___
26488	Hershey's Ice Breakers Hopper, 13		66	___
26489	Hershey's Christmas Bells Boxcar, 13		65	___
26491	Pennsylvania Power & Light Gondola with canisters, 13		43	___
26492	Area 51 3-D Tank Car, 13		43	___
26493	Monopoly Water Works 3-D Tank Car, 13		65	___
26494	PRR Truss Rod Gondola with vats, 13		60	___
26495	C&NW Poultry Car, 13		60	___
26496	Lionelville Aquarium Co. Fish Food Vat Car, 13-16		65	___
26497	Bethlehem Steel Depressed Flatcar with reels, 13		43	___
26499	CN Hi-Cube Boxcar "799346", 14		55	___
26502	UP Bay Window Caboose "6517", 97		47	___
26503	ATSF High-Cupola Caboose "7606R", 97		85	___
26504	Mobil Oil Square Window Caboose "6257", 97 u		37	___
26505	Rescue Unit Caboose, 98		50	___
26506	N&W Square Window Caboose "562748", 98		15	___
26507	D&H Square Window Caboose "35707", 98		20	___
26508	Alaska Square Window Caboose "1081", 98		28	___
26509	ATSF Square Window Caboose, 98	15	20	___
26511	Quaker Oats Square Window Caboose, 98 u		52	___
26513	NYC Emergency Caboose "26505", 99		47	___
26515	Lionel Lines Bobber Caboose, 99		10	___
26516	Safari Bobber Caboose, 99 u		10	___
26519	Christmas Work Caboose "6496", 99		41	___
26520	Bethlehem Steel Work Caboose "6130" (SSS), 99		55	___
26523	Keebler Cheezit Square Window Caboose, 99 u		NRS	___
26524	NYC Square Window Caboose "295", 99 u		20	___
26526	Santa Fe Square Window Caboose "999471", 01		30	___
26527	Christmas Work Caboose with presents, 02		27	___
26528	PRR Square Window Caboose "6257", 99		21	___
26530	LL Square Window Caboose "6257", 99		22	___

			Exc	Mint
____	**26532**	NYC Square Window Caboose "296", 00		20
____	**26533**	SP Square Window Caboose, 00		20
____	**26534**	PRR Square Window Caboose "6257", 00		20
____	**26535**	Frisco Square Window Caboose "1700", 00		20
____	**26536**	Centennial Express Square Window Caboose, 00		NRS
____	**26537**	Lionel Mines Square Window Caboose, 00 u		45
____	**26539**	Whirlpool Square Window Caboose, 00 u		NRS
____	**26542**	ACL Square Window Caboose "069", 01		31
____	**26543**	GN Square Window Caboose "X66", 00-01		28
____	**26544**	Alaska Square Window Caboose "1084", 01		25
____	**26545**	Snap-On Square Window Caboose, 00 u		NRS
____	**26548**	Pioneer Seed Square Window Caboose, 00 u		NRS
____	**26549**	PRR Square Window Caboose "4977947", 01		20
____	**26550**	NYC Square Window Caboose "19293", 01		20
____	**26551**	Chessie System Center Cupola Caboose, 01		25
____	**26552**	Santa Fe Square Window Caboose "999472", 01		25
____	**26553**	C&O Center Cupola Caboose "A918", 01		30
____	**26554**	Monopoly Short Line Square Window Caboose, 00 u		65
____	**26556**	NH Center Cupola Caboose, 01		35
____	**26557**	Farmall Square Window Caboose, 01 u		NRS
____	**26559**	N&W Center Cupola Caboose "518408", 01		20
____	**26560**	B&M Square Window Caboose, 01 u		20
____	**26564**	Soo Line Center Cupola Caboose, 01 u		20
____	**26565**	Lionel Employee Square Window Caboose, 01 u		165
____	**26566**	WP Square Window Caboose "731", 02		25
____	**26568**	NKP Square Window Caboose "1155", 02		25
____	**26569**	Southern Square Window Caboose "252", 02		25
____	**26570**	B&O Square Window Caboose "295", 02		25
____	**26572**	Lionel 20th Century Square Window Caboose, 00 u		25
____	**26580**	Wabash Square Window Caboose "2805", 03		22
____	**26581**	C&O Square Window Caboose "C-1831", 03		20
____	**26582**	L&N Square Window Caboose "318", 03		20
____	**26583**	PRR Square Window Caboose "477814", 03		25
____	**26584**	World of Disney Caboose, 03		40
____	**26589**	PRR Square Window Caboose "982234", 03-05	15	20
____	**26590**	Southern Square Window Caboose "X250", 04		50
____	**26591**	Indiana RR Caboose "2001", 01		79
____	**26592**	GN Caboose "X-242", 03-04		30
____	**26593**	Erie Square Window Caboose "C-101", 03	25	40
____	**26594**	Ontario Northland Work Caboose "26594", 03		25
____	**26595**	UP Caboose "26595", 03		18
____	**26596**	NYC Caboose "17716", 04		25
____	**26597**	Great Northern Caboose "X295", 04		25
____	**26598**	UP Caboose "26598", 04		25
____	**26599**	DM&IR Work Caboose "26599", 04		25
____	**26600**	American Fire and Rescue Water Tank Car, 09-11		55
____	**26603**	LV Depressed Flatcar with reels, 09		40
____	**26604**	Halloween Spooky Grave Gondola, 09		58
____	**26609**	NYC Gondola with Pacemaker canisters		40
____	**26612**	Christmas Gifts Gondola, 09		60
____	**26614**	Tupelo Dairy Farms Milk Car, 10-11		60
____	**26616**	UP Bulkhead Flatcar with pipes, 10		40
____	**26617**	B&O Depressed Center Flatcar with generator, 10		40

MODERN 1970-2024		Exc	Mint	
26629	PRR Flatcar w/Generators, 10		35	___
26630	Soo Flatcar w/Menards trailer, 10		40	___
26631	CP Flatcar w/Log, 11		65	___
26632	CN Boat Loader, 10-11		65	___
26633	CP Flatcar w/Generators, 10-11		35	___
26634	Texas Special Flatcar w/Navajo trailers, 10		40	___
26635	US Army Flatcar w/Helicopter, 11		23	___
26636	Postwar "6830" Flatcar w/Submarine, 10 u		120	___
26637	Postwar "6640" Missile Launching Car, 10 u		65	___
26638	Pennsylvania Power & Light Flatcar w/Reels, 11		40	___
26639	Cities Service 3-Tier Auto Carrier, 11-12		40	___
26640	CN Maple Syrup Barrel Ramp Car, 11-12		40	___
26641	Coca-Cola Flatcar with trailer, 11		78	___
26642	CN Jet Snowblower, 11-12		65	___
26643	D&RGW Jet Snowblower, 11-13		65	___
26644	BNSF Flatcar with generator, 11		40	___
26645	BNSF Flatcar with trailer, 11		40	___
26646	Pennsylvania Power & Light Flatcar with transformer, 11-12		40	___
26647	IC Bulkhead Flatcar with pipes, 11		40	___
26649	Erie-Lack. Gondola with canisters, 11		40	___
26650	M&StL Flatcar with pipes, 11		40	___
26651	ATSF Scout Heavyweight Passenger Car 2-pack (std O), 12		280	___
26652	NYC Gondola with canisters, 11		40	___
26653	PC Flatcar with generator, 11		35	___
26654	Boy Scouts Flatcar with Pinewood Derby Kit, 11-13	33	75	___
26660	Coca-Cola Vat Car, 11-16		75	___
26661	Reindeer Feed Barrel Ramp Car, 09		60	___
26665	Hershey's Special Dark Flatcar with trailer, 11		60	___
26666	Boy Scouts Flatcar with trailer, 11		70	___
26667	Flatcar with Santa's sleigh, 12		70	___
26668	Strasburg Flatcar with wheels, 11		55	___
26669	U.S. Navy Flatcar with Shark submarine, 12-13		60	___
26673	B&M Flatcar with Milk Tank, 12	33	60	___
26674	AT&SF Barrel Ramp Car, 10-11	10	20	___
26675	Monopoly Auto Loader, 12		80	___
26676	Heinz Baked Beans Vat Car, 12		60	___
26677	LIRR Gondola with canisters, 12		40	___
26679	ATSF Gondola with reels, 12-13		55	___
26683	Christmas Track Maintenance Car, 12-13		67	___
26684	Georgia Power Flatcar w/Generator, 12		45	___
26685	Flatcar with Santa's plane, 12		55	___
26686	Hershey's Cocoa Vat Car, 12-13		63	___
26687	Lone Ranger Gondola with gunpowder vats, 12-14		65	___
26691	UP Flatcar w/Trailers, 12-13	39	66	___
26692	UP Gondola w/Coil Covers, 12-13	28	40	___
26693	Hershey's Krackel Piggyback Flatcar with trailer, 12-13		78	___
26694	Carnegie Science Center Flatcar with submarine, 13	50	73	___
26695	NJ Transit Flatcar "9907" w/Trailer, 12	36	55	___
26696	NJ Transit Gondola "9412" w/Wood ties, 12	40	75	___
26699	PRR Flatcar with wheel load, 12-14		55	___
26706	Lighted Christmas Boxcar, 00		47	___
26707	Lionel Steel Operating Welding Flatcar "1108", 00		90	___
26708	ABC Monday Night Football TV Car, 01		50	___

	MODERN 1970-2024		Exc	Mint
___	26709	Postwar "6511" Flatcar w/Psychedelic submarine, 99		32
___	26710	Southern Stock Car, Carsounds, 99		95
___	26712	Churchill Downs Horse Car "6473", 99-00		38
___	26713	Shay Log Car 3-pack, 99		113
___	26714	Westside Lumber Flatcar with logs (std 0), 99		45
___	26715	Westside Lumber Flatcar with logs (std 0), 99		45
___	26716	Westside Lumber Flatcar with logs (std 0), 99		45
___	26717	Orion Star Boxcar 9600, 00		30
___	26718	Christmas Boxcar, RailSounds, 00		160
___	26719	Bobbing Ghost Halloween Boxcar, 00		46
___	26721	Lionel Lines Coal Dump Car "3379", 00		31
___	26722	Lionel Lines Log Dump Car "3351", 00		31
___	26723	Lion Chasing Trainer Gondola "3444", 00		49
___	26724	Veterans Day Boxcar, 00		70
___	26725	NYC Jumping Hobo Boxcar "88160", 00		38
___	26726	T. Rex Bobbing Boxcar, 00		41
___	26727	San Francisco City Lights Boxcar, 00		50
___	26736	Lionel Birthday Boxcar, 02 u		40
___	26737	Operating Santa Gondola "6462", 00 u		65
___	26738	Lionel Mines Animated Gondola, 00 u		90
___	26739	Santa and Snowman Boxcar, 00		46
___	26740	Reindeer Car, 00		43
___	26741	Operating Santa Boxcar, 00		50
___	26743	Christmas Reindeer Car, 01		55
___	26745	Traveling Aquarium Car "506", 01		70
___	26746	Bobbing Vampire Boxcar, 01		46
___	26747	Halloween Bats Aquarium Car, 01		75
___	26748	T&P Operating Hopper Car "9699", 01		38
___	26749	Alaska Log Dump Car, 01		29
___	26751	Chessie Coal Dump Car, 01		27
___	26752	Christmas Aquarium Car, 01	20	55
___	26753	Christmas Operating Dump Car, 01		43
___	26757	Operating Barrel Car "35621", 00		55
___	26758	AEC Nuclear Gondola "719766", 01		95
___	26759	Postwar "3459" Coal Dump Car, 02		60
___	26760	Postwar "3461" Log Dump Car, 02		60
___	26761	AEC Security Caboose 3535, 01		64
___	26762	Postwar "3665" Minuteman Car, 01		55
___	26763	Postwar "6448" Exploding Boxcar, 01		40
___	26764	Bethlehem Steel Operating Welding Car, 01		75
___	26765	Postwar "3370" Sheriff and Outlaw Car, 01-02	40	49
___	26766	Priority Mail Operating Boxcar, 01-02		32
___	26768	Postwar "6520" Searchlight Car, 02		49
___	26769	Santa Fe Crane Car "199793", CC, 03		255
___	26770	Wabash Brakeman Car "3424", 01		70
___	26773	Chessie Searchlight Car, 01		20
___	26774	Santa Fe Log Dump Car, 01		25
___	26775	U.S. Army Searchlight Car, 00		50
___	26776	U.S. Army Operating Boxcar "26413", 00		55
___	26777	U.S. Flag Boxcar, 01 u		250
___	26779	Burlington Operating Hopper "189312", 02		40
___	26780	Postwar "3376" Bronx Zoo Giraffe Car, 02	25	36
___	26781	Postwar "3540" Operating Radar Car, 02		35

MODERN 1970-2024		Exc	Mint	
26782	Lenny the Lion Bobbing Head Car, 02		38	___
26784	Stingray Express Aquarium Car, 02		35	___
26785	Flatcar with powerboat, 02		31	___
26786	Lionelville Operating Parade Car, 02		40	___
26787	Erie Jumping Hobo Boxcar, 01-02		43	___
26788	Christmas Music Boxcar, 02		46	___
26789	Kiss Kringle Chase Gondola, 02		35	___
26790	Lighted Christmas Boxcar, 02		34	___
26791	UP Animated Gondola, 02	40	50	___
26792	REA Operating Boxcar "6299", 03		39	___
26793	Alaska Extension Searchlight Car, 01		44	___
26794	Postwar "6352" PFE Ice Car, 01-02		85	___
26795	NYC Stock Car "3121," Cattle Sounds, 02		50	___
26796	Lionel Farms Poultry Dispatch Car, 01		55	___
26797	GN Log Dump Car "60011", 02		48	___
26798	Bethlehem Steel Coal Dump Car "26798", 02		70	___
26801	Jumping Bart Simpson Boxcar, 04		44	___
26802	Simpsons Animated Gondola, 04		46	___
26803	Santa Fe Derrick Car "26803", 04		25	___
26804	NYC Coal Dump Car "26804", 04		36	___
26805	Pennsylvania Log Dump Car "26805", 04		24	___
26806	Pillsbury Operating Boxcar "3428," Archive Collection, 04		40	___
26807	Blue Chip Line Motorized Animated Gondola, 04		40	___
26808	Egg Nog Barrel Car, 04		55	___
26809	Santa's Extension Searchlight Car, 04		42	___
26810	NYC Operating Searchlight Car, 05		33	___
26811	Pennsylvania Coal Dump Car, 05		33	___
26812	Santa Fe Log Dump Car, 05		33	___
26813	Lionel Lines Derrick Car, 05	17	39	___
26814	NYC Walking Brakeman Car "174226", 05		40	___
26815	PRR "Workin' on the Railroad" Boxcar "24255", 05		42	___
26816	REA Boxcar, steam TrainSounds, 05		105	___
26817	Alaska Boxcar, diesel TrainSounds, 05		145	___
26818	Christmas Music Boxcar, 05		63	___
26819	Holiday Animated Gondola, 05		55	___
26820	Penguin Transport Aquarium Car, 05		60	___
26821	NP Moe & Joe Lumber Flatcar, 05		75	___
26824	Elvis Presley Searchlight Car, 04		40	___
26825	GN Log Dump Car, 04		35	___
26826	Alaska Searchlight Car, 05		40	___
26827	UPS Operating Boxcar "9237," Archive Collection, 05		62	___
26828	Tornado Chaser Radar Tracking Car, 05		63	___
26829	UPS Holiday Operating Boxcar, 05	30	66	___
26832	Lionel Lines Tender, TrainSounds, 07-08		105	___
26833	Wellspring Radar Car, 04	40	75	___
26834	PFE Ice Car "20042" (std O), 05-06		63	___
26835	MOW Track Cleaning Car, 05		140	___
26836	Halloween Boxcar, SpookySounds, 05		105	___
26841	PRR Log Dump Car, 05		27	___
26842	NYC Coal Dump Car, 05		27	___
26843	Christmas Flatcar w/Handcar, 06		60	___
26844	Christmas Reindeer Transport Car, 06		30	___
26845	Southern Derrick Car, 06		35	___

			Exc	Mint
___	**26846**	GN Coal Dump Car, 06		38
___	**26847**	C&O Coal Dump Car, 06-07		80
___	**26848**	Lionel Lines Moe & Joe Flatcar, 06		80
___	**26849**	SP Log Dump Car, 06-07		80
___	**26850**	D&RGW Searchlight Car, 06		75
___	**26851**	WM Log Dump Car, 06		35
___	**26852**	Postwar "3562-25" Santa Fe Barrel Car, 06		75
___	**26853**	SeaWorld Aquarium Car, 06		75
___	**26854**	UP Walking Brakeman Car, 06-07		75
___	**26855**	Halloween Animated Gondola, 06		65
___	**26856**	Christmas Chase Gondola, 06		65
___	**26857**	Alien Radar Tracking Car, 06		65
___	**26858**	Christmas Music Boxcar, 06		65
___	**26859**	Christmas Parade Boxcar, 06		75
___	**26860**	B&O Boxcar "466035," steam TrainSounds (std O), 06-07		75
___	**26861**	Santa Fe Boxcar, diesel TrainSounds (std O), 06-07		110
___	**26862**	Hard Rock Cafe Boxcar, 06		35
___	**26863**	Railway Express Operating Milk Car with platform, 06		140
___	**26864**	Domino Sugar Operating Boxcar, 06-07		40
___	**26865**	CP Animated Caboose, 06-07	35	80
___	**26866**	BN Searchlight Car, 06		35
___	**26867**	Groom Lake Boxcar, AlienSounds, 06-07		110
___	**26868**	U.S. Steel Operating Welding Car, 06		75
___	**26869**	REA Jumping Hobo Boxcar, 06-07		70
___	**26870**	Christmas Dump Car with presents, 06		80
___	**26871**	PRR Tender, steam TrainSounds (std O), 06		105
___	**26872**	U.S. Army Security Car, 06		75
___	**26876**	Missile Firing Trail Car, 06		75
___	**26877**	U.S. Army Missile Launch Sound Car, 06-07		190
___	**26881**	Neiman Marcus Holiday Musical Boxcar, 05		90
___	**26882**	NYC Animated Caboose "17719", 06		120
___	**26883**	Weyerhaeuser Timber Co. Log Dump Car "117", 06		25
___	**26884**	Hammacher Schlemmer Music Boxcar, 08		45
___	**26885**	WC Log Dump Car, 06		50
___	**26886**	Lionel Lines Log Dump Car, 06		50
___	**26887**	Postwar "6470" Exploding Target Car, 06		120
___	**26888**	Weyerhaeuser Timber Co. Log Dump Car "115", 06	11	40
___	**26889**	Weyerhaeuser Timber Co. Log Dump Car "116", 06		40
___	**26891**	PRR Coal Dump Car, 05		30
___	**26897**	Great Western Flatcar with handcar, 07		65
___	**26898**	NYC Log Dump Car, 05		25
___	**26905**	Bethlehem Steel Gondola "6462" with canisters, 98		29
___	**26906**	SP Flatcar "9823" with Corgi '57 Chevy, 98		40
___	**26908**	TTUX Flatcar "6300" with Apple trailers, 98		70
___	**26913**	East St. Louis Gondola "9820", 98		29
___	**26920**	Union Pacific Die-cast Ore Car "64861", 97		70
___	**26921**	Union Pacific Die-cast Ore Car "64862", 97		55
___	**26922**	Union Pacific Die-cast Ore Car "64863", 97		65
___	**26923**	Union Pacific Die-cast Ore Car "64864", 97		55
___	**26924**	Union Pacific Die-cast Ore Car "64865", 97		55
___	**26925**	Union Pacific Die-cast Ore Car "64866", 97		60
___	**26926**	Union Pacific Die-cast Ore Car, 98		55
___	**26927**	Union Pacific Die-cast Ore Car, 98		55

Item	Description	Exc	Mint
26928	Union Pacific Die-cast Ore Car, 98		55
26929	Union Pacific Die-cast Ore Car, 98		40
26936	Die-cast Tank Car 4-pack, 98		335
26937	Die-cast Hopper 4-pack, 98	75	325
26938	NYC Reefer, 99		80
26940	Rio Grande Stock Car "37710", 99		80
26946	D&H Semi-Scale Hopper "9642"		85
26947	Gulf Die-cast Tank Car, 98		120
26948	P&LE Die-cast Hopper, 98		65
26949	NP Flatcar with trailer "6424-2017", 98		47
26950	NP Flatcar with trailer "6424-2016", 98		47
26951	TTX Flatcar "475185" with PRR trailer, 98		55
26952	J.B. Hunt Flatcar with trailer, 98		40
26953	J.B. Hunt Flatcar with trailer, 98		40
26954	J.B. Hunt Flatcar with trailer, 98		40
26955	J.B. Hunt Flatcar with trailer, 98		40
26956	C&O Gondola (027), 98-99		15
26957	Delaware & Hudson Flatcar with stakes, 98		20
26971	Lionel Steel 16-wheel Depressed Center Flatcar, 98		135
26972	Pony Express Animated Gondola, 98		36
26973	Getty Die-cast Tank Car 3-pack, 98		270
26974	Getty Die-cast 1-D Tank Car "4003", 98		80
26975	Getty Die-cast 1-D Tank Car "4004", 98	45	125
26976	Getty Die-cast 1-D Tank Car "4005", 98		80
26977	Sinclair Die-cast Tank Car 3-pack, 98		275
26978	Sinclair Tank Car UTLX "64026", 98		105
26979	Sinclair Tank Car UTLX "64027", 98		85
26980	Sinclair Tank UTLX "64028", 98		90
26981	Gulf Die-cast Tank Car 2-pack, 99		165
26985	B&O Die-cast Hopper 2-pack, 99		160
26987	Chessie System (B&O) Die-cast 4-bay Hopper "235154", 99		90
26991	Lionelville Ladder Fire Car, 99		47
26992	NYC Reefer, 99		75
26993	NYC Reefer, 99		85
26994	NYC Reefer, 99		135
26995	Rio Grande Stock Car "37714", 99		80
26996	Rio Grande Stock Car "37715", 99		80
26997	Rio Grande Stock Car "37716", 99		80
27000	C&EI Offset Hopper "97393" (std 0), 07		65
27001	Erie Offset Hopper "28001" (std 0), 07		65
27002	Frisco Offset Hopper "92399" (std 0), 07		65
27003	Chessie System Offset Hopper "234355" (std 0), 07		65
27016	UP PS-2 Covered Hopper "1312" (std 0), 07-08		60
27019	Imco PS-2 Covered Hopper "41001" (std 0), 07-08		60
27022	PC PS-2 Covered Hopper "74217" (std 0), 07		60
27025	NYC PS-2 Covered Hopper "883180" (std 0), 07		60
27026	NYC PS-2 Covered Hopper "883181" (std 0), 07		60
27027	NYC PS-2 Covered Hopper "883182" (std 0), 07		60
27028	C&O Offset Hopper "27028" (std 0), 07		65
27029	ATSF Offset Hopper 3-pack (std 0), 08-09		200
27030	Monon Offset Hopper 3-pack (std 0), 08-09		200
27031	MoPac Offset Hopper 3-pack (std 0), 08-09		200
27032	NYC Offset Hopper 3-pack (std 0), 08-09		200

			Exc	Mint
____	**27033**	Chessie System PS-2 Hopper 3-pack (std O), 08-09		180
____	**27034**	Nickel Plate Road PS-2 Hopper 3-pack (std O), 08-09		180
____	**27053**	CB&Q ACF 2-bay Covered Hopper "183925" (std O), 08-09		55
____	**27059**	Bakelite Plastics PS-2 Hopper "61445" (std O), 10-11		70
____	**27061**	Clinchfield Freight Car 2-pack (std O), 10		150
____	**27064**	PRR Flatcar with PRR piggyback trailers (std O), 12		98
____	**27065**	SP Flatcar with SP piggyback trailers (std O), 12		98
____	**27066**	IC Flatcar with IC piggyback trailers (std O), 12		98
____	**27067**	C&O Flatcar with REA piggyback trailers (std O), 12		98
____	**27068**	ATSF Flatcar with Santa Fe piggyback trailers (std O), 12		98
____	**27069**	Conrail PS-2 Hopper "878330" (std O), 12-13		70
____	**27070**	N&W Scale Offset Hopper "279850" (std O), 12		70
____	**27071**	CSX 4-Bay Covered Hopper "256300" (std O), 12		90
____	**27072**	C&NW Scale PS-1 Boxcar "7" (std O), 12-13		70
____	**27073**	PRR Scale Offset Hopper 3-pack (std O), 12		200
____	**27077**	L&N Scale Offset Hopper "88494" (std O), 12-13		70
____	**27078**	Frisco Scale 3-Bay Open Hopper "88299" (std O), 12-14		75
____	**27079**	NYC Boxcar, 09		30
____	**27080**	Lionel Vision Boxcar, 14-15		60
____	**27081**	BN PS-2 Hopper "424796" (std O), 12-13		70
____	**27082**	Grand Trunk 4-Bay Covered Hopper "38111" (std O), 12		90
____	**27083**	RI PS-2 Hopper "500751" (std O), 12-13		70
____	**27084**	Seaboard 8000-gallon 1-D Tank Car "27084" (std O), 12		70
____	**27085**	Wabash PS-2 Hopper "30425" (std O), 12-13		70
____	**27086**	Grand Trunk 60' Boxcar "383575" (std O), 12, 14		85
____	**27087**	CN 60' Boxcar "799424" (std O), 12, 14		85
____	**27088**	MKT PS-5 Gondola "12447" (std O), 12-13		65
____	**27089**	LIRR PS-5 Gondola "6053" (std O), 12		65
____	**27090**	NP 8000-gallon 1-D Tank Car "27090" (std O), 12		70
____	**27091**	WM Scale 3-Bay Open Hopper "85125" (std O), 12		80
____	**27092**	CSX Heritage 60' Boxcar "176740" (std O), 12		85
____	**27093**	Boy Scouts PS-2 Hopper "2013" (std O), 13		70
____	**27094**	BNSF PS-2 Hopper 2-pack (std O), 13-14		130
____	**27095**	KCS PS-2 Hopper 2-pack (std O), 13		130
____	**27096**	C&NW PS-2 Hopper 2-pack (std O), 13		130
____	**27099**	North Pole Central PS-1 Boxcar "125025" (std O), 13		70
____	**27100**	C&NW PS-2CD 4427 Hopper "450669" (std O), 04		40
____	**27101**	Morton Salt PS-2CD 4427 Hopper "504" (std O), 04		43
____	**27102**	Pillsbury PS-2CD 4427 Hopper "3980" (std O), 04		42
____	**27103**	Soo Line PS-2CD 4427 Hopper "70207" (std O), 04		49
____	**27104**	Wabash Cylindrical Hopper "33007" (std O), 03		43
____	**27105**	PC Cylindrical Hopper "884312" (std O), 03		42
____	**27113**	Govt. of Canada Cylindrical Hopper, 04-05		60
____	**27114**	Canadian National Cylindrical Hopper, 04-05		60
____	**27115**	D&H 3-bay ACF Hopper "3454" (std O), 05-06		65
____	**27116**	NYC 3-bay ACF Hopper "886270" (std O), 05-06		65
____	**27117**	DM&IR 3-bay ACF Hopper "5017" (std O), 05		65
____	**27118**	WP 3-bay ACF Hopper "11774" (std O), 05-06		65
____	**27119**	Firestone 3-Bay ACF Hopper (std O), 05	35	45
____	**27129**	N&W 3-bay ACF Hopper "10717" (std O), 06		70
____	**27130**	PRR 3-bay ACF Hopper "180658" (std O), 06		70
____	**27131**	Conrail 3-bay ACF Hopper "473877" (std O), 06		70
____	**27132**	UP 3-bay ACF Hopper "18137" (std O), 06		70

MODERN 1970-2024		Exc	Mint	
27133	MILW PS-2CD Hopper "98606" (std O), 06		70	___
27134	BNSF PS-2CD Hopper "414367" (std O), 06		70	___
27135	N&W PS-2CD Hopper "71573" (std O), 06		70	___
27142	CP Rail 3-bay Hopper, 06		48	___
27146	CP Soo 3-bay Hopper, 06		48	___
27165	C&O 3-bay Hopper "86912" (std O), 07		70	___
27166	Pennsylvania Power & Light 3-bay Hopper "347" (std O), 07		70	___
27167	Santa Fe 3-bay Hopper "178558" (std O), 07-08		70	___
27168	C&NW 3-bay Hopper "135000" (std O), 07		70	___
27169	CN Cylindrical Hopper "370708" (std O), 06		65	___
27172	IMC Canada Cylindrical Hopper "45726" (std O), 06		65	___
27177	Union Starch Cylindrical Hopper 3-pack (std O), 08		210	___
27186	PRR Cylindrical Hopper 3-pack (std O), 08		210	___
27187	TH&B Cylindrical Hopper 3-pack (std O), 08		210	___
27188	KCS 3-bay Covered Hopper 3-pack, 08		225	___
27189	BNSF 3-bay Aluminum Covered Hopper 3-pack, 08		225	___
27190	C&NW PS-2CD Covered Hopper 3-pack (std O), 08		225	___
27191	RI PS-2CD Covered Hopper 3-pack, 08		225	___
27192	NP PS-2CD Covered Hopper 3-pack (std O), 08		225	___
27203	NYC DD Boxcar "75509" (std O), 05		63	___
27204	Grand Trunk Western DD Boxcar "596377" (std O), 05		63	___
27205	D&RGW DD Boxcar "63798" (std O), 05		40	___
27206	UP PS 60' Boxcar "960342" (std O), 08		75	___
27207	IC PS 60' Boxcar "44295" (std O), 08		75	___
27208	ATSF PS 60' Boxcar "37287" (std O), 08		75	___
27209	D&RGW PS 60' Boxcar "63835" (std O), 08		75	___
27210	PRR PS-1 Boxcar "47009" (std O), 05		60	___
27211	MKT PS-1 Boxcar "948" (std O), 05		60	___
27212	Rutland PS-1 Boxcar "358" (std O), 05		60	___
27213	N&W DD Boxcar, 05		35	___
27214	Chessie System PS-1 Boxcar "23770" (std O), 06		60	___
27215	Rock Island PS-1 Boxcar "57607" (std O), 06		60	___
27216	Erie-Lack. PS-1 Boxcar "84433" (std O), 06		60	___
27217	Frisco PS-1 Boxcar "17826" (std O), 06		59	___
27218	Santa Fe DD Boxcar "9870" (std O), 06-07		70	___
27219	GN DD Boxcar "35449" (std O), 06-07		70	___
27220	L&N DD Boxcar "41237" (std O), 06-07		70	___
27221	CB&Q DD Boxcar "48500" (std O), 06-07		70	___
27224	CGW PS-1 Boxcar "5180" (std O), 06		60	___
27225	WP PS-1 Boxcar "19528" (std O), 06		60	___
27226	NH PS-1 Boxcar "32196" (std O), 06		60	___
27227	UP PS-1 Boxcar "100306" (std O), 06		60	___
27228	UP DD Boxcar "454400" (std O), 07		70	___
27229	Nickel Plate Road DD Boxcar "87100" (std O), 08		70	___
27230	LV DD Boxcar "8505" (std O), 08	21	70	___
27231	GN USRA Double-sheathed Boxcar (std O), 07		65	___
27232	UP USRA Double-sheathed Boxcar (std O), 07		65	___
27233	Cotton Belt USRA Double-sheathed Boxcar (std O), 07		65	___
27234	C&NW USRA Double-sheathed Boxcar (std O), 07		65	___
27235	Railbox Boxcar "10011" (std O), 07		55	___
27236	D&RGW DD Boxcar "63799" (std O), 07		35	___
27237	MP USRA Double-sheathed Boxcar (std O), 07		65	___
27238	Nickel Plate DD Boxcar "87101" (std O), 07		35	___

			Exc	Mint
___	**27239**	SP DD Boxcar "232852" with auto rack (std O), 08		75
___	**27240**	Pere Marquette DD Boxcar with auto rack (std O), 08		75
___	**27241**	C&O PS-1 Boxcar "18719", 08		60
___	**27242**	LV PS-1 Boxcar "62080", 08		60
___	**27243**	SP PS-1 Boxcar "128131", 08		60
___	**27244**	GN PS-1 Boxcar "39404", 08	36	60
___	**27246**	SP Double-sheathed Boxcar "133" (std O), 08		70
___	**27247**	MP Double-sheathed Boxcar '45111" (std O), 08		70
___	**27249**	GN Express Boxcar '2500' (std O), 08		65
___	**27250**	CN Express Boxcar "11061" (std O), 08-09		65
___	**27251**	WP Express Boxcar '220116", 08-09		65
___	**27254**	Western Pacific UP Heritage Boxcar (std O), 09-11, 13		85
___	**27259**	PRR ACF Stock Car "128988" (std O), 10		70
___	**27260**	ATSF Tool Car "190021" (std O), 09-10		80
___	**27261**	D&RGW Double-sheathed Boxcar "3282", 09		80
___	**27263**	Polar Railroad PS-1 Boxcar, 09		70
___	**27264**	C&O Double-sheathed Boxcar "3502", 10		80
___	**27265**	Virginian PS-1 Boxcar "63300" (std O), 10		70
___	**27266**	PRR Express Boxcar "504141" (std O), 10		70
___	**27267**	SP UP Heritage 60' Boxcar "6991" (std O), 10		85
___	**27268**	NYC DD Boxcar "47100" (std O), 10		70
___	**27270**	B&O PS-1 Boxcar 2-pack (std O), 10-11		140
___	**27273**	Ann Arbor PS-1 Boxcar "1314" (std O), 11		70
___	**27274**	Polar Railroad Double-sheathed Boxcar "1201", 10		70
___	**27275**	SP Overnight PS-1 Boxcar "97938" (std O), 10		70
___	**27276**	NKP Double-sheathed Boxcar "10580" (std O), 10-11		70
___	**27277**	WP Scale PS-1 Boxcar "192" (std O), 11		70
___	**27278**	Cryo-Trans Trans-Mechanical Reefer (std O), 10		95
___	**27282**	UP DD Boxcar "163100" (std O), 10		70
___	**27283**	Postwar Scale Boxcar 2-pack, 10		140
___	**27286**	Postwar Scale 6464 Boxcar 2-pack #2, 11-13		140
___	**27287**	LV Boxcar and Caboose Set (std O), 10-11		160
___	**27289**	Jersey Central Boxcar and Caboose Set (std O), 10-11		160
___	**27291**	PRR Double-sheathed Boxcar "539335" (std O), 10-11		70
___	**27294**	ATSF 57' Mechanical Reefer "3006" (std O), 10		85
___	**27296**	Cryo-Trans 57' Mechanical Reefer (std O), 11		85
___	**27299**	WM Steel-sided Reefer (std O), 11		80
___	**27300**	Western Dairy General American Milk Car (std O), 06		65
___	**27305**	GN Steel-sided Reefer "70290" (std O), 06		65
___	**27306**	Santa Fe Steel-sided Reefer "3494" (std O), 06		42
___	**27307**	Pepper Packing Steel-sided Reefer "2330" (std O), 06		65
___	**27327**	BNSF Mechanical Reefer "798870" (std O), 07		70
___	**27328**	SP Fruit Express Reefer "456465" (std O), 07-09		70
___	**27329**	UP Fruit Express Reefer "55962" (std O), 07		70
___	**27330**	Great Northern WFE Reefer "8873" (std O), 07-08		70
___	**27331**	Alderney Dairy General American Milk Car (std O), 07		65
___	**27332**	Freeport General American Milk Car (std O), 07		65
___	**27345**	Milwaukee Road 40' Steel-sided Reefer "5317" (std O), 12	54	80
___	**27349**	ADM Steel-sided Reefer "7019" (std O), 07		65
___	**27350**	National Car Steel-sided Reefer "2430" (std O), 07		48
___	**27355**	NYC Steel-sided Reefer "2570" (std O), 07-08		65
___	**27358**	Dubuque Steel-sided Reefer "63648" (std O), 07		65
___	**27361**	PFE Wood-sided Reefer "97680" (std O), 06		65

MODERN 1970-2024		Exc	Mint
27364	Erie URTX Steel-sided Reefer (std O), 11		80 ___
27365	Sheffield Farms Milk Car 2-pack (std O), 08		140 ___
27368	CNJ 40' Steel-sided Reefer "1443" (std O), 12		80 ___
27369	Borden's Milk Car 2-pack (std O), 08		140 ___
27372	PFE Steel-sided Reefer 3-pack (std O), 08		210 ___
27373	MILW Reefer 3-pack (std O), 08-09		225 ___
27374	Alaska Reefer 3-pack (std O), 08-09		225 ___
27375	NP Reefer 3-pack (std O), 08-09		225 ___
27394	Detroit, Toledo & Ironton Steel-sided Reefer (std O), 09-10		80 ___
27395	Amtrak ExpressTrak Baggage Car, 10		75 ___
27396	C&NW UP Heritage Mechanical Reefer (std O), 10		85 ___
27409	ATSF Water Tank Car "100844" (std O), 09-10		70 ___
27410	30,000-gallon Ethanol Tank Car 3-pack, sound, 09		270 ___
27411	30,000-gallon Ethanol Tank Car 3-pack, 09		210 ___
27412	GATX TankTrain Car "53782" (std O), 10		70 ___
27418	PRR NS Heritage Unibody Tank Car (std O), 10		70 ___
27419	Pennsylvania Power & Light 3-bay Open Hopper, 08		80 ___
27421	MoPac UP Heritage Cylindrical Hopper (std O), 09-11		80 ___
27422	N&W 3-bay Open Hopper "1776" (std O), 09		80 ___
27424	Penn Central PS-2 Hopper "440774" (std O), 10-11		80 ___
27425	Saskatchewan Cylindrical Hopper "397015' (std O), 09		80 ___
27426	Stourbridge Lion Anthracite Coal Car 2-pack, 09-10		130 ___
27429	MKT UP Heritage PS2-CD Hopper (std O), 09		80 ___
27431	CSX B&O Quad Hopper, 11		50 ___
27432	UP 3-bay Open Hopper "78123" (std O), 10		80 ___
27433	Conrail NS Heritage Cylindrical Hopper (std O), 10-11		80 ___
27434	D&RGW UP Heritage PS2-CD Hopper (std O), 10		80 ___
27435	Polar Railroad Tank Car, 09		70 ___
27436	Alberta Cylindrical Hopper "396363" (std O), 10		80 ___
27438	Virginian NS Heritage 3-bay Open Hopper (std O), 10		80 ___
27439	NS Heritage Unibody Tank Car "14098" (std O), 10		70 ___
27440	BN Cylindrical Hopper "458456" (std O), 10		80 ___
27441	D&M PS-2 Hopper "6133" (std O), 11		70 ___
27445	N&W NS Heritage PS-2CD Hopper (std O), 10		80 ___
27446	Southern NS Heritage Cylindrical Hopper (std O), 10		80 ___
27448	PRR NS Heritage 3-Bay Open Hopper (std O), 11		80 ___
27449	UP Boy Scouts 100th Anniversary Cylindrical Hopper (std O), 11		80 ___
27450	NW NS Heritage 3-Bay Open Hopper (std O), 11		80 ___
27451	Conrail NS Heritage Unibody 1-D Tank Car (std O), 11		70 ___
27452	PRR NS Heritage PS-1 Boxcar "45540" (std O), 11		70 ___
27453	NS Heritage PS-1 Boxcar "67850" (std O), 11		70 ___
27454	CP Cylindrical Hopper (std O), 11	48	77 ___
27455	Amtrak 57' Mechanical Reefer (std O), 11		85 ___
27456	Soo Line PS2 Covered Hopper "70702" (std O), 11		70 ___
27457	NS 3-Bay Open Hopper "148028" (std O), 11		80 ___
27458	UP Mechanical Reefer "457244" (std O), 11		85 ___
27459	WP DD Boxcar "19404"" (std O), 11		70 ___
27460	M&StL Double-sheathed Boxcar "26002" (std O), 11		70 ___
27461	UP ACF 4-Bay Covered Hopper "91341" (std O), 11		85 ___
27462	Chessie ACF 4-Bay Covered Hopper "601878" (std O), 11		85 ___
27463	PRR ACF 3-Bay Covered Hopper "259900" (std O), 11-12		80 ___
27464	BNSF ACF 3-Bay Covered Hopper "453403" (std O), 11		80 ___
27465	CSX 89' Auto Rack Car "604540" (std O), 12-13		150 ___

	No.	Description	Exc	Mint
___	**27466**	UP 89' Auto Rack Car (std O), 12-13		150
___	**27467**	ATSF 89' Auto Rack Car (std O), 12-13		150
___	**27468**	Grand Truck 89' Auto Rack Car (std O), 12-13		150
___	**27469**	Frisco Cylindrical Hopper "81021" (std O), 11		80
___	**27470**	MKT Scale 1-D Tank Car (std O), 11		70
___	**27471**	DT&I 3-Bay Hopper "2070" (std O), 11		80
___	**27472**	CP Scale 1-D Tank Car "9943" (std O), 11		70
___	**27473**	Conrail 89' Auto Rack Car "456249" (std O), 12		150
___	**27474**	SP Cylindrical Hopper "491020" (std O), 11		80
___	**27475**	Lionelville & Western Scale 1-D Tank Car "2747" (std O), 11		80
___	**27476**	U.S. Army Scale 1-D Tank Car (std O), 11		70
___	**27477**	D&RGW 3-Bay Hopper "14901" (std O), 11		80
___	**27478**	NYC 3-Bay Hopper "922158" (std O), 11		80
___	**27479**	BN Scale 3-Bay Open Hopper "516400" (std O), 12		80
___	**27480**	NKP Scale Offset Hopper "33060" (std O), 12		70
___	**27481**	W&LE Scale Offset Hopper "62240" (std O), 12		70
___	**27482**	CP Scale Offset Hopper "354000" (std O), 12	33	69
___	**27483**	SP Unibody 1-D Tank Car "67200" (std O), 12		70
___	**27484**	D&H Unibody 1-D Tank Car "59" (std O), 12		70
___	**27485**	KCS Unibody 1-D Tank Car "996" (std O), 12		70
___	**27488**	Clinchfield CSX Heritage 3-Bay Open Hopper (std O), 12		80
___	**27489**	Chessie System CSX Heritage 3-Bay Open Hopper (std O), 12		80
___	**27490**	ATSF 3-Bay Covered Hopper "314000" (std O), 12-13		85
___	**27491**	GN 3-Bay Covered Hopper "171400" (std O), 12		85
___	**27492**	CN 89' Auto Rack Car "710833" (std O), 12		150
___	**27493**	CN PS-4 Flatcar with piggyback trailers (std O), 12		98
___	**27494**	CN PS-4 Flatcar with piggyback trailers (std O), 12		98
___	**27495**	CN PS-4 Flatcar with piggyback trailers (std O), 12		98
___	**27496**	Polar PS-2 Covered Hopper "124" (std O), 12, 14		70
___	**27497**	UP Offset Hopper "74556" (std O), 12		80
___	**27498**	DM&I 8000-gallon 1-D Tank Car "S19" (std O), 12		70
___	**27499**	Monon Scale PS-1 Boxcar "916" (std O), 12		70
___	**27510**	WP PS-4 Flatcar "2001" (std O), 05-06		53
___	**27511**	P&LE PS-4 Flatcar "1154" (std O), 05-06		35
___	**27512**	Reading PS-4 Flatcar "9314" (std O), 05		53
___	**27513**	UP 40' Flatcar "51219" (std O), 06		55
___	**27514**	CP 40' Flatcar "307401" (std O), 06		55
___	**27515**	Pennsylvania 40' Flatcar "473567" (std O), 06		55
___	**27516**	N&W 40' Flatcar "32900" (std O), 06		55
___	**27517**	NP PS-4 Flatcar "62829" with trailers (std O), 06		85
___	**27518**	C&NW PS-4 Flatcar "44503" with trailers (std O), 06		85
___	**27519**	UP PS-4 Flatcar "53007" with trailers (std O), 06		85
___	**27520**	Coe Rail Husky Stack Car "5540" (std O), 06		85
___	**27521**	Santa Fe Husky Stack Car "254220" (std O), 06		85
___	**27535**	UP PS-4 Flatcar "53008" with trailers (std O), 07		65
___	**27536**	UP PS-4 Flatcar "53009" with trailers (std O), 08		65
___	**27537**	UP Flatcar with wood load, 06		39
___	**27541**	NYC 40' Flatcar "496299" with load (std O), 07		63
___	**27542**	NH 40' Flatcar "17808" with load (std O), 07-08		70
___	**27543**	ATSF 40' Flatcar "191549" with load (std O), 07-08		70
___	**27544**	GT 40' Flatcar "64301" with load (std O), 07-08		70
___	**27545**	REA PS-4 Flatcar "81003" with trailers (std O), 07-08		85
___	**27546**	Greenbrier Husky Stack Car "1993" (std O), 07		85

MODERN 1970-2024		Exc	Mint
27552	Arizona & California Husky Stack Car (std O), 07		85
27562	NYC PS-4 Flatcar "506075" with trailers (std O), 07-08		85
27563	Lackawanna PS-4 Flatcar "16540" with trailers (std O), 07		85
27564	Milwaukee Road PS-4 Flatcar with trailers "64074" (std O), 07-08		85
27583	UP 40' Flatcar "59292" with load (std O), 08		70
27584	Reading Flatcar with covered load (std O), 08-09		70
27585	B&M 40' Flatcar "33773" with stakes (std O), 08-09		65
27586	Cass Scenic Skeleton Log Car 3-pack, 07		170
27587	Birch Valley Lumber Skeleton Log Car 3-pack, 07		170
27594	Wabash PS-4 Flatcar with stakes (std O), 08-09		65
27600	RI Bay Window Caboose "17070" (std O), 07		90
27601	MILW Extended Vision Caboose "992300" (std O), 07		90
27602	C&O Wood-side Caboose "90332" (std O), 07		90
27603	MP UP Heritage Ca-4 Caboose "2891" (std O), 08		95
27604	UP Caboose "3881" (std O), 08		90
27605	Pere Marquette Northeastern Caboose "A986" (std O), 08		90
27606	LL Northeastern Caboose "4679" (std O), 08		90
27607	Monongahela NS Heritage Caboose (std O), 12		95
27608	WM Caboose "1863" (std O), 08		85
27609	B&O Caboose "C-2445" (std O), 07		90
27612	WP Bay Window Caboose "446" (std O), 08		90
27615	NYC Bay Window Caboose "20383" (std O), 07		90
27617	D&H Bay Window Caboose "35725" (std O), 08		90
27618	MKT UP Heritage Ca-4 Caboose "8891" (std O), 08		95
27619	WP UP Heritage Ca-4 Caboose "3891" (std O), 08		95
27623	N&W Northeastern Caboose "500837" (std O), 09		90
27624	D&RGW UP Heritage CA-4 Caboose (std O), 09		95
27625	C&NW UP Heritage CA-4 Caboose (std O), 09		95
27626	SP UP Heritage CA-4 Caboose (std O), 09		95
27628	Wabash Northeastern Caboose "02222" (std O), 09-10		90
27629	C&O Northeastern Caboose (std O), 10		90
27630	Virginian NS Heritage CA-4 Caboose (std O), 10		95
27631	NS Heritage CA-4 Caboose (std O), 10		95
27633	UP CA-3 Caboose (std O), 10		95
27634	ATSF Extended Vision Caboose (std O), 10		85
27635	B&O I-12 Caboose (std O), 10		85
27636	NKP Northeastern Caboose (std O), 10-11		85
27638	Southern NS Heritage CA-4 Caboose (std O), 10-11		95
27639	N&W NS Heritage CA-4 Caboose (std O), 10		95
27640	Clinchfield Northeastern CA-3 Caboose, 10-11		90
27642	Virginian Scale Caboose with smoke, 10-13		90
27645	UP Boy Scouts 100th Anniversary Ca-3 Caboose (std O), 11		95
27648	PRR NS Heritage Ca-3 Caboose (std O), 11	40	105
27649	Baldwin Locomotive Works I-12 Caboose "6000" (std O), 12-13		85
27650	CSX Heritage Scale Bay Window Caboose "2510" (std O), 12		90
27651	B&O CSX Heritage I-12 Caboose (std O), 11		90
27652	CSX Heritage Chessie System Scale Caboose (std O), 12		90
27653	Family Lines CSX Heritage Ca-4 Caboose (std O), 11		90
27654	CSX/Clinchfield Scale Bay-Window Caboose (std O), 12		90
27655	WM CSX Heritage Extended Vision Caboose (std O), 11		90
27656	Polar Express I-12 Caboose, 11		85
27657	Central of Georgia NE Caboose "X 17" (std O), 10		90

			Exc	Mint
____	**27658**	Pennsylvania Power & Light Work Caboose (std 0), 11		80
____	**27659**	Bethlehem Steel Work Caboose (std 0), 11		80
____	**27660**	UP George Bush Extended Vision Caboose (std 0), 11		90
____	**27661**	KCS Extended Vision Caboose (std 0), 11		90
____	**27662**	GTW Northeastern Caboose (std 0), 11		90
____	**27663**	IC Extended Vision Caboose (std 0), 11		90
____	**27664**	Lionel & Western Northeastern Caboose (std 0), 11-12		90
____	**27665**	BN Bicentennial Extended Vision Caboose (std 0), 11		90
____	**27666**	NH Scale Northeastern Caboose "C-66" (std 0), 12		90
____	**27667**	UP Scale Ca-4 Caboose "3857" (std 0), 12-13		95
____	**27668**	UP Scale Ca-3 Caboose "3779" (std 0), 12-13		95
____	**27669**	PC Scale Northeastern Caboose "18420" with smoke (std 0), 12-13		90
____	**27670**	CP Scale Northeastern Caboose "400501" (std 0), 12-13		90
____	**27671**	West Side Lumber Scale Work Caboose "8" (std 0), 12		80
____	**27672**	Weyerhaeuser Timber Scale Work Caboose "12" (std 0), 12-13		80
____	**27673**	NYC Scale Northeastern Caboose "20090" (std 0), 12		90
____	**27674**	Elk River Lumber Work Caboose "6" (std 0), 12, 14, 17		80
____	**27676**	CN Wood-Sided Caboose (std 0), 12		90
____	**27677**	UP Work Caboose "907306" (std 0), 12		80
____	**27678**	ATSF Wood-Sided Caboose "1790" (std 0), 12		85
____	**27679**	NP Wood-Sided Caboose "1282" (std 0), 12		85
____	**27680**	GN Wood-Sided Caboose "X499" (std 0), 12		85
____	**27681**	Southern NS Heritage Caboose (std 0), 12		95
____	**27682**	Conrail NS Heritage Caboose (std 0), 12		95
____	**27683**	Erie NS Heritage Caboose (std 0), 12, 14-15		95
____	**27684**	Illinois Terminal NS Heritage Caboose (std 0), 12, 14-15		95
____	**27685**	Central of Georgia NS Heritage Caboose (std 0), 12		95
____	**27686**	LV NS Heritage Caboose (std 0), 12		95
____	**27687**	Reading NS Heritage Caboose (std 0), 13-15		95
____	**27688**	NYC NS Heritage Caboose (std 0), 13		95
____	**27689**	Wabash NS Heritage Caboose (std 0), 13-15		95
____	**27690**	Virginian NS Heritage Caboose (std 0), 13		95
____	**27691**	PRR NS Heritage Caboose (std 0), 12		95
____	**27692**	N&W NS Heritage Caboose (std 0), 12		95
____	**27693**	CNJ NS Heritage Caboose (std 0), 13-14		95
____	**27694**	NS Heritage Caboose (std 0), 12		95
____	**27695**	DL&W NS Heritage Caboose (std 0), 13-15		95
____	**27696**	Savannah & Atlanta NS Heritage Caboose (std 0), 13-15		95
____	**27697**	Nickel Plate Road NS Heritage Caboose (std 0), 12		95
____	**27698**	Interstate NS Heritage Caboose (std 0), 12		95
____	**27699**	PC NS Heritage Caboose (std 0), 13		95
____	**27702**	Maersk Husky Stack Car 2-pack (std 0), 09		225
____	**27705**	ATSF Wedge Plow Flatcar "191369" (std 0), 09		90
____	**27706**	ATSF Idler Flatcar "191852" with load (std 0), 09		75
____	**27707**	UP Husky Stack Car 2-pack (std 0), 09-10		225
____	**27710**	No. 6464 Variation Boxcar 2-pack #2, 09		110
____	**27767**	Santa Fe Passenger 4-pack, 11-12		240
____	**27771**	Postwar "6572" REA Reefer, 11-13		60
____	**27772**	Santa Fe Baggage Car and Diner 2-pack, 11-12		120
____	**27775**	Postwar "2414" Santa Fe Blue-stripe Coach, 11-13		60
____	**27776**	No. 6464 Variation Boxcar 2-pack #3, 11		105
____	**27779**	Postwar Archive UP Caboose "8561", 11-12		48

		Exc	Mint
27791	Archive 6464-50 M&StL Boxcar, 12		55
27792	Archive Pastel Freight Car 3-pack, 12		170
27800	B&M Gondola with coke containers, 09-11		80
27816	D&RGW Flatcar "22177" with pipes, 09-10		80
27820	Wabash PS-4 Flatcar with piggyback trailers (std 0), 09-10		98
27824	MILW 40' Flatcar with metal pipes (std 0), 10		80
27825	West Side Lumber Skeleton Log Car, 11		70
27826	CP Skeleton Log Car 2-pack (std 0), 10		133
27827	UP Bathtub Gondola "28081" (std 0), 10		65
27828	CN Bathtub Gondola "193140" (std 0), 10		65
27829	WM Skeleton Log Car 2-pack, 10		133
27834	Pere Marquette PS-5 Gondola "18400", 11		70
27835	P. Bunyan Lumber Skeleton Log Car, 11-12		70
27836	Elk River Lumber Skeleton Log Car "11203" (std 0), 11		70
27837	B&M PS-4 Flatcar with bulkheads (std 0), 10-11		80
27838	PRR PS-4 Flatcar with bulkheads (std 0), 10		80
27840	Polar Railroad PS-4 Flatcar with trailers, 10		98
27841	CSX Bathtub Gondola 2-pack (std 0), 11		130
27842	UP Scale Flatcar with bulkheads "15775" (std 0), 11		70
27843	WP Scale PS-5 Gondola "6774" (std 0), 11		70
27844	BNSF Bathtub Gondola 3-pack (std 0), 10		200
27848	Virginian NS Heritage 60' Boxcar (std 0), 11		85
27849	Southern NS Heritage 60' Boxcar (std 0), 11		85
27850	CSX 60' Boxcar "196911" (std 0), 11		85
27851	BNSF Bathtub Gondola 2-pack, 11		130
27854	B&O Double-sheathed Boxcar "196500" (std 0), 11		70
27855	NYC 60' DD Boxcar "53423" (std 0), 11		85
27856	KCS PS-1 Boxcar "18741" (std 0), 11		70
27857	PRR DD Boxcar "81919" (std 0), 11, 14		75
27858	MP DD Boxcar "90103" (std 0), 11		70
27860	Sugar Creek Lumber Skeleton Log Car "1749" (std 0), 11		70
27863	Merrill & Ring Lumber Skeleton Log Car, 11-12		70
27868	NS Bathtub Gondola 2-pack (std 0), 11		130
27871	NS 60' Boxcar "499646" (std 0), 11		85
27872	Polar Hot Cocoa Milk Car, 11, 13		70
27873	Polar Reindeer Stock Car, 11, 13		70
27874	Grove's Mortuary Double-sheathed Boxcar (std 0), 11		70
27875	NYC DD Boxcar "45395" (std 0), 11		70
27876	State of Maine PS-1 Boxcar "51" (std 0), 11		70
27877	NH DD Boxcar "40510" (std 0), 11		70
27882	Southern ACF 40-ton Stock Car "4565" (std 0), 11		70
27883	T&P ACF 40-ton Stock Car "24042" (std 0), 11		70
27884	RI ACF 40-ton Stock Car "77601" (std 0), 11		70
27885	ATSF ACF 40-ton Stock Car "6039" (std 0), 11		70
27886	GN PS-1 Boxcar "11310" (std 0), 11		70
27887	D&RGW PS-5 Gondola "56316" with covers (std 0), 11		65
27888	LIRR 40' Flatcar with wheels (std 0), 11		70
27889	Erie 40' Flatcar "6361" with wheels (std 0), 11		70
27890	L&N 40' Flatcar "22269" with wheels (std 0), 11		70
27891	NKP Heritage PS-4 Flatcar with trailers (std 0), 11		98
27892	Conrail PS-5 Gondola "612690" with covers (std 0), 11		65
27893	GTW PS-1 Boxcar "516650" (std 0), 11		70
27894	C&O PS-5 Gondola "362600" with covers (std 0), 11		65

			Exc	Mint
____	**27895**	ATSF PS-4 Bulkhead Flatcar "90085" (std O), 11		80
____	**27896**	CP 40' Flatcar with pipe load (std O), 11		80
____	**27899**	UP Scale PS-1 Boxcar "196889" (std O), 12		70
____	**27903**	Sager Place Observation Car, 09	23	74
____	**27912**	Postwar "2445" Elizabeth Coach, 08		60
____	**27917**	Postwar "2550" Baggage-Mail Rail Diesel Car, nonpowered, 13-14		83
____	**27928**	UP Boy Scouts 100th Anniversary PS-1 Boxcar (std O), 11		70
____	**27929**	Postwar Nos. 2484/2485 UP Passenger Car 2-pack, 12-13		120
____	**27935**	Postwar "6820" Aerial Missile Transport Car, 13		60
____	**27941**	Postwar "3854" Merchandise Car, 12	25	75
____	**27946**	Postwar "6050-25" Christmas Savings Boxcar, 13-14		55
____	**27947**	Postwar "6473-25" Reindeer Transport Car, 13		60
____	**27948**	Postwar "6464-25" Great Northern Christmas Boxcar, 13		60
____	**27949**	Postwar "3854-25" PRR Christmas Merchandise Car, 13-14		75
____	**27953**	Reading PS-2 Hopper 2-pack (std O), 13-14		140
____	**27962**	L&N PS-2 Hopper 2-pack (std O), 13-14		140
____	**27965**	P&WV Offset Hopper 3-pack (std O), 13-15		210
____	**27969**	N&W Offset Hopper 3-pack (std O), 13-15		210
____	**27973**	C&O Offset Hopper 3-pack (std O), 13-15		210
____	**27977**	GN Offset Hopper 3-pack (std O), 13-15	90	210
____	**27981**	PRR USRA Double-sheathed Boxcar (std O), 13		70
____	**27982**	SP USRA Double-sheathed Boxcar (std O), 13-14		80
____	**27983**	UP USRA Double-sheathed Boxcar (std O), 13-14		70
____	**27984**	Procor 30,000-gallon 1-D Tank Car 3-pack (std O), 13		240
____	**27988**	UTLX 30,000-gallon 1-D Tank Car 3-pack (std O), 13	255	400
____	**27992**	ADM 30,000-gallon 1-D Tank Car 3-pack (std O), 13		240
____	**27996**	ACFX 30,000-gallon 1-D Tank Car 3-pack (std O), 13		240
____	**28000**	C&NW 4-6-4 Hudson Locomotive "3005", 99		205
____	**28004**	B&O 4-4-2 E6 Atlantic Locomotive, traditional, 99-00		410
____	**28005**	PRR 4-4-2 E6 Atlantic Locomotive, traditional, 99-00		345
____	**28006**	ATSF 4-4-2 E6 Atlantic Locomotive, traditional, 99-00		285
____	**28007**	NYC 4-6-4 Hudson Locomotive "5406", 99		380
____	**28008**	C&O 4-6-4 Hudson Locomotive "306", 99		345
____	**28009**	Santa Fe 4-6-4 Hudson Locomotive "3463", 99		330
____	**28011**	C&O 2-6-6-6 Allegheny Locomotive "1601", 99		1800
____	**28012**	4-6-4 Commodore Vanderbilt Locomotive, red, 00 u	717	1700
____	**28013**	NH 4-6-2 Pacific Locomotive "1335", 99		325
____	**28014**	NYC 4-6-2 Pacific Locomotive "4930", 99		305
____	**28015**	Santa Fe Pacific 4-6-2 Pacific Locomotive "3449", 99		340
____	**28016**	Southern 4-6-2 Pacific Locomotive "1407", 99		345
____	**28017**	Case Cutlery 4-6-2 Pacific Locomotive, 99 u		313
____	**28018**	Reading 4-6-0 Camelback Locomotive "571," CC, 01		495
____	**28020**	Lionel Lines 4-6-2 Pacific Locomotive "3344", 99		250
____	**28022**	West Side Lumber Shay Locomotive "800", 99		810
____	**28023**	PRR K4 4-6-2 Pacific Locomotive "3755," CC, 99		375
____	**28024**	4-6-4 Commodore Vanderbilt Locomotive, blue, 00 u	500	1663
____	**28025**	PRR K4 4-6-2 Pacific Locomotive, traditional, 99		330
____	**28026**	LL 4-6-2 Pacific Locomotive, CC, 99		325
____	**28027**	NYC 4-6-4 Hudson Locomotive "5413", 00		590
____	**28028**	Virginian 2-6-6-6 Allegheny Locomotive "1601", 99	213	1318
____	**28029**	UP 4-8-8-4 Big Boy Locomotive "4006", 99-00	375	1500
____	**28030**	NYC 4-6-4 Hudson Locomotive "5450," gray, CC, 00		315

Item	Description	Exc	Mint
28032	B&O 4-6-2 Pacific Locomotive, CC, 00		315
28033	B&O 4-6-2 Pacific Locomotive, traditional, 00		195
28034	UP 4-6-2 Pacific Locomotive, CC, 00		310
28035	UP 4-6-2 Pacific Locomotive, traditional, 00		210
28036	SP 2-8-0 Consolidation Locomotive "2685," CC, 00-01	113	270
28037	SP 2-8-0 Consolidation Locomotive "2686," traditional, 00-01		295
28038	UP 2-8-0 Consolidation Locomotive "324," CC, 00-01		315
28039	UP 2-8-0 Consolidation Locomotive "326," traditional, 00-01	0	308
28044	NYC 4-6-4 Hudson Locomotive, 04		250
28051	B&O 2-8-8-4 EM-1 Articulated Locomotive "7617", 00	375	970
28052	N&W 2-6-6-4 Class A Locomotive "1218", 00		870
28055	GN 4-6-4 Hudson Locomotive "1725," traditional, 00-01		170
28057	Southern 4-8-2 Mountain Locomotive "1491," CC, 00		690
28058	NH 4-8-2 Mountain Locomotive "3310," CC, 00		670
28059	WP 4-8-2 Mountain Locomotive "179," CC, 00		630
28062	LL Gold-plated 700E J-1E 4-6-4 Hudson Locomotive, display case, 00	217	1067
28063	PRR T-1 4-4-4-4 Duplex Locomotive "5511", CC, 00	415	952
28064	UP Challenger Coal Tender "3985", CC, 00 u	1000	1800
28065	NYC Hudson 4-6-4 Locomotive "5412," RailSounds, 00		290
28066	B&O President Polk 4-6-2 Locomotive, CC, 01	375	826
28067	Erie 4-6-2 Locomotive "2934", CC, 01	138	570
28068	D&RGW 4-6-4 Hudson Locomotive, traditional, 01 u		300
28070	SP Daylight 4-4-2 Atlantic Locomotive "3000," CC, 01		425
28071	NP 4-4-2 Atlantic Locomotive "604," CC, 01		415
28072	NYC 4-6-4 Hudson J3a Locomotive "5444," CC, 01	81	788
28074	NP 2-8-4 Berkshire Locomotive "759", CC, 01	150	640
28075	C&O 2-6-6-2 Locomotive "1521", CC, 01		930
28076	NKP 2-6-6-2 Locomotive "921", CC, 01		960
28077	UP 4-6-6-4 Challenger Locomotive "3983", CC, 01		680
28078	PRR 2-10-4 J1a Locomotive "6496", CC, 01	213	880
28079	C&O 2-10-4 Class T Locomotive "3004", CC, 01		882
28080	NYC 0-8-0 Locomotive "7745," CC, 01-02		540
28081	C&O 0-8-0 Locomotive "75," CC, 01-02		520
28084	NYC Dreyfuss Hudson 4-6-4 Locomotive "5452," CC, 01-02	250	790
28085	N&W 2-8-8-2 Y6b Class Locomotive "2200," CC, 03		1207
28086	PRR H9 Consolidation Locomotive "1111", CC, 01		480
28087	UP Auxiliary Tender, yellow, CC, 01		210
28088	N&W Auxiliary Water Tender, CC, 01-02		200
28089	PRR 4-4-4-4 T-1 Duplex Locomotive "5511", 2-rail, 00		1150
28090	UP Challenger Oil Tender "3977," 2-rail, 00 u		1800
28095	PRR K4 4-6-2 Pacific Locomotive w/RailSounds, 01-02		350
28098	NYC 4-6-0 10-wheel Locomotive "1916," CC, 01-02		520
28099	UP Challenger Oil Tender "3977", CC, 00 u		1700
28200	D&H U30C Diesel "702", CC (SSS), 02		375
28201	UP SD90MAC Diesel "8049", 03		345
28202	Conrail SD80MAC Diesel "7203", 03		325
28203	CSX SD80MAC Diesel "803", 03		325
28204	NS SD80MAC Diesel "7201", 03		345
28205	Chessie System SD9 Diesel "1833", CC, 03		230
28207	Erie-Lackawanna U33C Diesel "3304", CC, 02	113	355
28208	BN U33C Diesel "5734", CC, 02		355
28211	CP SD90MAC Diesel "9107", 03		300

			Exc	Mint
___	**28213**	Amtrak GE Dash 8 Diesel "516", CC, 02		300
___	**28214**	BNSF GE Dash 8 Diesel "582", CC, 02		325
___	**28215**	B&O GP30 Diesel "6939", CC, 02		315
___	**28216**	Reading GP30 Diesel "5518", CC, 02		315
___	**28217**	Rio Grande GP30 Diesel "3013", CC, 02		315
___	**28218**	Lehigh Valley Alco C420 Switcher "407," CC, 04		325
___	**28219**	Seaboard Alco C420 Switcher "136," CC, 04		300
___	**28220**	CSX SD60 Diesel "3329", 05		250
___	**28222**	Santa Fe Dash 9 Diesel "605", CC, 05		250
___	**28223**	BNSF SD70MAC Diesel "9433," CC, 05		250
___	**28224**	Jersey Central SD40-2 Diesel "3067," CC, 04		350
___	**28225**	SPSF SD40T-2 Diesel "8521," CC, 04-05		430
___	**28226**	NS SD80MAC Diesel "7204," CC, 04-05		430
___	**28227**	UP SD70MAC Diesel "4979", CC, 04		375
___	**28228**	C&NW Dash 9-44CW Diesel "8669", CC, 03		350
___	**28229**	SP Dash 9-44CW Diesel "8132", CC, 03		350
___	**28230**	Amtrak Dash 8 Diesel "505", CC, 04		295
___	**28235**	Great Northern U33C Diesel "2543," CC, 05		455
___	**28237**	Reading U30C Diesel "6301," CC, 05		455
___	**28239**	Union Pacific SD70 Diesel, TMCC, 04		360
___	**28241**	C&NW U30C Diesel "935," CC, 06		455
___	**28242**	SP U33C Diesel "8773", CC, 06		475
___	**28243**	LIRR Alco C420 Hi-nose Switcher "206," CC, 06		420
___	**28244**	N&W Alco C420 Hi-nose Switcher "417," CC, 06-07		420
___	**28245**	Chessie System SD40T-2 Diesel "7617," RailSounds, 06		265
___	**28246**	Chessie System SD40T-2 Diesel "7618," nonpowered (std O), 06		168
___	**28247**	Rio Grande SD40T-2 Diesel "5348," RailSounds, 06		265
___	**28248**	Rio Grande SD40T-2 Diesel "5349," nonpowered (std O), 06		160
___	**28250**	N&W Alco C420 Hi-nose Switcher "416," nonpowered (std O), 06-07		160
___	**28251**	LIRR Alco C420 Hi-nose Switcher "206," nonpowered (std O), 06		160
___	**28252**	SP U33C Diesel "8771," nonpowered (std O), 06		160
___	**28253**	C&NW U30C Diesel "936," nonpowered (std O), 06		160
___	**28255**	UP SD40T-2 Diesel "4551," traditional, CC, 07-08		265
___	**28256**	UP SD40T-2 Diesel "4596," nonpowered (std O), 07		170
___	**28257**	NS SD40-2 Diesel "3340," CC, 06		430
___	**28258**	NS SD40-2 Diesel "3341," nonpowered (std O), 06		450
___	**28259**	CN SD40-2 Diesel "5383," CC, 06		430
___	**28260**	CN SD40-2 Diesel "5384," nonpowered (std O), 06		170
___	**28261**	UP (MP) SD70ACe Diesel "1982," CC, 07		450
___	**28262**	UP (WP) SD70ACe Diesel "1983," CC, 07	163	450
___	**28263**	UP (MKT) SD70ACe Diesel "1988," CC, 07		450
___	**28264**	UP "Building America" SD70ACe Diesel "8348", CC, 07		450
___	**28265**	MILW U30C Diesel "5657", CC, 07		455
___	**28266**	MILW U30C Diesel "5657," nonpowered (std O), 07-08		170
___	**28267**	Conrail U30C Diesel "6837," CC, 07		455
___	**28268**	Conrail U30C Diesel "6838," nonpowered (std O), 07-08		170
___	**28269**	ATSF Dash 8-40BW Diesel "562," CC, 08		500
___	**28270**	ATSF Dash 8-40CW Diesel "563," nonpowered, 08		220
___	**28272**	"I Love USA" SD60 Diesel "1776," traditional, 06	80	250
___	**28279**	UP SD70ACe Diesel "1989," CC, 07		450
___	**28280**	UP (C&NW) SD70ACe Diesel "1995," CC, 07		450
___	**28281**	UP (SP) SD70ACe Diesel "1996," CC, 07		450

		Exc	Mint
28283	UP "Building America" SD70AC3 Diesel, nonpowered (std O), 07		170
28284	Ferromex SD70ACe Diesel "4011," CC, 08		495
28287	KCS SD70ACe Diesel "4050," CC, 08		495
28292	Chessie System U30C Diesel "3312", CC, 02		300
28293	Santa Fe U28CG Diesel "354", CC, 02		375
28295	Conrail LionMaster SD80MAC Diesel, nonpowered, 08		200
28296	UP AC6000 Diesel "7526," CC, 08		660
28297	SP GP9 Diesel "446," CC, 10		390
28298	CSX AC6000 Diesel "608," CC, 08		660
28299	CSX AC6000 Diesel "609," nonpowered, 08		370
28300	NS Dash 9 Diesel "9607," nonpowered, 08		220
28302	BNSF SD70ACe Diesel "9380," CC, 08		495
28305	CSX AC6000 Diesel "610," nonpowered, RailSounds, 08		430
28306	GE ES44AC Evolution Hybrid Diesel "2010," CC, 09-10	699	1349
28307	Wabash Train Master Diesel "550," CC, 09-10		495
28311	UP DD35A Diesel "70," CC, 11		600
28312	BN SD60 Diesel "8301," CC, 09		800
28314	UP 3GS21B Genset Switcher "2701," CC, 10		675
28316	PRR NS Heritage SD70ACe Diesel "1854," CC, 10	188	500
28318	Conrail NS Heritage SD70ACe Diesel "1209," CC, 10		500
28320	CP Evolution Hybrid Diesel, 10		1320
28323	NS Genset Switcher, CC, 11		800
28327	UP AC6000 Diesel "7050," CC, 10		700
28328	UPAC6000 Diesel "7055," nonpowered, CC, 10		350
28330	UP SD70ACe Diesel "8444," CC, 10		500
28331	CSX AC6000 Diesel "618," CC, 10		700
28333	Virginian NS Heritage SD70ACe Diesel, CC, 10		500
28334	NS Heritage SD70ACe Diesel "1982," CC, 10		500
28338	PRR NS Heritage SD70ACe Diesel, CC, 11		500
28339	ATSF AC6000 Diesel "9876," CC, 10		550
28340	WP GP7 Diesel "705," CC, 10	138	450
28343	Amtrak Dash 9 Diesel "519," CC, 10		500
28344	Southern NS Heritage SD70ACe Diesel, CC, 10		500
28345	N&W NS Heritage SD70ACe Diesel "247," CC, 10		500
28347	UP Boy Scouts 100th Anniversary ES44AC Diesel, CC, 11	0	1538
28350	BNSF ES44AC Diesel, CC, 11		850
28351	KCS ES44AC Diesel "4655," CC, 11		850
28353	Erie GP7 Diesel, CC, 11		450
28354	CSX Genset Switcher "1303," CC, 11		800
28355	BNSF Genset Switcher "1249," CC, 11		800
28356	CSX SD60 Diesel, CC, 11		500
28357	CSX SD60 Diesel, CC, 11		500
28358	Soo Line SD60 Diesel, CC, 11		500
28359	Soo Line SD60 Diesel, CC, 11		500
28360	WP GP7 Diesel "707," CC, 11		450
28361	WM GP7 Diesel "21," CC, 11		450
28362	WM GP7 Diesel "23," CC, 11		450
28363	BN SD60 Diesel "8302," CC, 11		500
28364	BNSF Dash-9 Diesel "4081," CC, 11		500
28365	BNSF Dash-9 Diesel "5121," CC, 11		500
28366	CN Dash-9 Diesel "2643," CC, 11		500
28367	CN Dash-9 Diesel "2692," CC, 11		500
28368	Amtrak Dash-9 Diesel, CC, 11		500

			Exc	Mint
___	**28369**	NYC DD35A Diesel "9950," CC, 11		600
___	**28370**	UP DD35 Diesel "84," CC, 12		600
___	**28371**	UP DD35A Diesel "72," CC, 11		600
___	**28372**	NYC DD35A Diesel "9955," CC, 11		600
___	**28373**	C&NW UP Heritage SD70ACe Diesel, CC, 11		500
___	**28374**	SP UP Heritage SD70ACe Diesel, CC, 11	188	500
___	**28375**	Katy UP Heritage SD70ACe Diesel, CC, 11		500
___	**28376**	MoPac UP Heritage SD70ACe Diesel, CC, 11		500
___	**28377**	Rio Grande UP Heritage SD70ACe Diesel, CC, 11		500
___	**28378**	WP UP Heritage SD70ACe Diesel, CC, 11		500
___	**28380**	NYC DD35A Diesel, nonpowered, 11		440
___	**28381**	ATSF GP30 Diesel, CC, 11		500
___	**28382**	U.S. Army Genset Switcher, CC, 11		800
___	**28383**	Conrail Genset Switcher, CC, 11		800
___	**28384**	CN Genset Switcher "7990," CC, 11-12		800
___	**28385**	ATSF GP30 Diesel "1214," CC, 11		500
___	**28386**	ATSF GP30 Diesel "2710", 11		380
___	**28387**	ATSF GP30 Diesel "2715," nonpowered, 11		240
___	**28388**	ICG GP30 Diesel "2268," CC, 11		500
___	**28389**	ICG GP30 Diesel "2271," CC, 11		500
___	**28390**	UP DD35 Diesel "79," nonpowered, 12		440
___	**28394**	ICG GP30 Diesel "2277", 11		380
___	**28395**	ICG GP30 Diesel "2279," nonpowered, 11		240
___	**28396**	UP ES44AC Diesel "7454," CC, 11		850
___	**28397**	UP ES44AC Diesel "7459," CC, 11		850
___	**28398**	BNSF ES44AC Diesel "6436," CC, 11		850
___	**28399**	KCS ES44AC Diesel "4682," CC, 11		850
___	**28400**	Amtrak Rail Bonder, 05		65
___	**28403**	Pennsylvania Ballast Tamper, traditional, 05-06		105
___	**28404**	Maintenance Car, 05		105
___	**28405**	Picatinny Arsenal Switcher, CC, 05		290
___	**28406**	CSX Rail Bonder "92794," traditional, 05		65
___	**28407**	UP Speeder, 05		65
___	**28408**	CNJ Speeder "MW840," traditional, 06		70
___	**28409**	Conrail Rail Bonder "X409," traditional, 06		70
___	**28411**	U.S. Army Missile Launcher Locomotive, 06-07		300
___	**28412**	Santa's Speeder, 06		70
___	**28413**	Milwaukee Road Snowplow "X903," traditional, 06		210
___	**28414**	Lionel Lines Burro Crane, traditional, 06		160
___	**28415**	Third Avenue Trolley "1651," traditional, 06		70
___	**28416**	Hobo Handcar, traditional, 06		70
___	**28417**	Christmas Rotary Snowplow, 06		180
___	**28418**	Christmas Trolley, 06		70
___	**28419**	Lionel Lines Speeder, 07-08		70
___	**28420**	D&RGW Handcar, 07-08		70
___	**28421**	Fort Collins Trolley, 07		73
___	**28422**	PRR Burro Crane, 07-08		160
___	**28423**	Alaska Rotary Snowplow, 06-07		220
___	**28424**	Postwar "51" Navy Switcher, 07		210
___	**28425**	Polar Express Elf Handcar, 06-23		120
___	**28427**	Christmas Snowplow, 08-10	67	210
___	**28428**	Halloween Handcar, 07		70
___	**28430**	Wellspring Capital Management Trolley, 06	50	85

		Exc	Mint	
28432	Bethlehem Steel Switcher, traditional, 07		210	____
28434	Christmas Trolley, 07		70	____
28438	Portland Birney Trolley, 08-09		65	____
28440	PRR Inspection Vehicle, 08-09		170	____
28441	Transylvania Trolley, 08	60	72	____
28442	Postwar "50" Gang Car, 08		120	____
28444	NH Handcar, 08-09		75	____
28445	AEC Burro Crane Car		100	____
28446	Silver Bell Trolley, 09		90	____
28447	4850TM Factory Trackmobile, CC, 10		300	____
28448	CSX 4850TM Trackmobile, CC, 10		300	____
28449	UP 4850TM Trackmobile, CC, 10		300	____
28450	CP Rail Trackmobile, CC, 11		300	____
28451	Christmas Track Cleaning Car, 10-13		150	____
28452	MOW Early Era Inspection Vehicle, 10		130	____
28453	PRR Early Era Inspection Vehicle, 10		130	____
28454	CP Early Era Inspection Vehicle, 10		130	____
28455	NYC Trackmobile, CC, 11-13		300	____
28456	Coca-Cola Trolley, 10		90	____
28457	B&M Rotary Snowplow "8457", 11		250	____
28466	U.S. Army Trackmobile, CC, 11		300	____
28467	PRR Trackmobile, CC, 11		300	____
28468	Amtrak Trackmobile, CC, 11		300	____
28469	BNSF Trackmobile, CC, 11		300	____
28470	NYC Early Era Inspection Vehicle, 11		130	____
28471	ATSF Early Era Inspection Vehicle, CC, 11		130	____
28472	Southern Early Era Inspection Vehicle, 11		130	____
28473	GN Early Era Inspection Vehicle, CC, 11		130	____
28474	North Pole Central Elf Handcar, 11		80	____
28475	UP Early Era Insprection Vehicle, 11		130	____
28476	IC Early Era Inspection Vehicle, 11		130	____
28478	Frisco Early Era Inspection Vehicle, CC, 11		130	____
28479	Christmas Early Era Inspection Vehicle, 11		130	____
28480	Grand Trunk Early Era Inspection Vehicle, CC, 11		130	____
28500	Mopac GP20 Diesel "2274", 99-00	100	205	____
28501	ATSF GP9 Diesel "2924," traditional, 99		200	____
28502	ATSF GP9 Diesel "2925," CC, 99-00		255	____
28503	ACL GP7 Diesel, CC, 00		245	____
28504	ACL GP7 Diesel, traditional, 00		170	____
28505	Monon Alco C420 Switcher "505," CC, 00-01		230	____
28506	Monon Alco C420 Switcher "506," traditional, 00-01	70	170	____
28507	NH Alco C420 Switcher "2556," CC, 00-01		275	____
28508	NH Alco C420 Switcher "2557," traditional, 00-01		290	____
28509	FEC GP7 Diesel Set, 99		560	____
28514	B&O GP9 Diesel "6590", 00		85	____
28515	Lionel Service Station Alco C420 Switcher, CC, 00		205	____
28516	Lehigh & Hudson River Alco C420 Diesel, 00		160	____
28517	C&NW GP7 Diesel "1518," CC, 00-01		275	____
28518	PRR EP-5 Electric Locomotive "2352," CC, 00		410	____
28519	NP GP9 Diesel "2349," CC, 01	98	270	____
28521	SP Alco RS11 Switcher "5725," CC, 01-02		280	____
28522	MP Alco RS11 Switcher "4611," CC, 01-02		305	____
28523	Soo SD40-2 Diesel "6622", CC, 01		375	____

			Exc	Mint
___	**28524**	Chessie SD40-2 Diesel "7616", CC, 01		355
___	**28527**	AEC GP9 Diesel "2001," CC, 01		413
___	**28528**	NH Alco RS11 Diesel "1406", 01-02	150	300
___	**28529**	Norfolk Southern GP9 Diesel, CC, 02		200
___	**28530**	NP Alco S4 Diesel "722," CC, 02		285
___	**28531**	Santa Fe Alco S2 Switcher "2337," CC, 02		285
___	**28532**	LV Alco S2 Switcher "150," CC, 02		280
___	**28533**	Seaboard Air Line Alco S4 Diesel "1489," CC, 02		290
___	**28536**	Rock Island GP7 Diesel "1274," CC, 02-03		230
___	**28538**	WP Alco S2 Switcher "553," CC, 03		340
___	**28539**	B&O Alco S2 Switcher "9045," CC, 03	163	320
___	**28540**	UP SD40T-2 Diesel "4455," CC, 03		390
___	**28541**	SP SD40T-2 Diesel "8239," CC, 03		400
___	**28542**	Rio Grande SD40T-2 Diesel "5350," CC, 03		400
___	**28543**	Ontario Northland RS3 Diesel "1308", 03		80
___	**28544**	Pennsylvania Alco RS11 Switcher "8618," CC, 04		350
___	**28545**	NP Alco RS11 Switcher "900," CC, 03		325
___	**28547**	SP SD40T-2 Diesel "8232," CC, 04		400
___	**28548**	Chessie System Alco S-4 Diesel "9009," CC, 05		400
___	**28553**	PRR Alco RS11 Switcher "8620," traditional, 07-08	90	285
___	**28554**	PRR Alco RS11 Diesel "8621," nonpowered, 08		170
___	**28555**	Alaska GP38-2 Diesel "2001," CC, 06		400
___	**28556**	Alaska GP38-2 Diesel "2002," nonpowered (std O), 06		160
___	**28557**	CP GP30 Diesel "5000," CC, 06-07		400
___	**28558**	CP GP30 Diesel "5001," nonpowered (std O), 06-07		150
___	**28559**	Chessie System GP30 Diesel "3044," CC, 06-07		400
___	**28560**	Chessie System GP30 Diesel "3045," nonpowered (std O), 06-07		150
___	**28561**	NYC GP7 Diesel "5628," CC, 07-08		340
___	**28562**	NYC GP7 Diesel "5629," nonpowered (std O), 07		170
___	**28563**	GN GP7 Diesel "626," CC, 07	138	400
___	**28564**	GN GP7 Diesel "627," nonpowered (std O), 07		170
___	**28565**	RI GP7 Diesel "1265," CC, 07		400
___	**28566**	RI GP7 Diesel "1266," nonpowered (std O), 07		170
___	**28567**	UP GP7 Diesel "105," CC, 07		400
___	**28568**	UP GP7 Diesel "106," nonpowered (std O), 07		170
___	**28570**	D&RGW GP7 Diesel "5101," CC, 08		440
___	**28573**	PRR GP7 Diesel "8512," CC, 08		440
___	**28578**	D&H GP38-2 Diesel "7307," CC, 08		440
___	**28587**	PRR GP7 Diesel "8510," CC, 10		450
___	**28592**	N&W GP7 Diesel "2446," CC, 09		500
___	**28594**	White Pass & Yukon NW2 Diesel Switcher, traditional, 09-10	100	300
___	**28595**	ATSF SD40 Diesel "5004," CC, 09		380
___	**28596**	Erie GP7 Diesel "1210," CC, 11		450
___	**28598**	ATSF GP7 Diesel "2791," CC, 10		450
___	**28599**	Erie GP9 Diesel "1261," CC, 10		390
___	**28601**	Winter Wonderland 4-4-2 Atlantic Locomotive "34", 02		85
___	**28602**	PRR 4-4-2 Atlantic Locomotive, 01-02		90
___	**28603**	NYC 4-4-2 Atlantic Locomotive, 01-02		90
___	**28604**	ATSF 4-6-4 Hudson Locomotive "3458", 02		150
___	**28606**	Monopoly 4-4-2 Atlantic Locomotive, 00 u		200
___	**28611**	ATSF 4-6-4 Hudson Locomotive "3459", 02		100
___	**28612**	WP 4-4-2 Atlantic Locomotive, traditional, 02		80

MODERN 1970-2024		Exc	Mint
28613	Reading 0-6-0 Dockside Switcher "1251", traditional, 04		100 ____
28615	B&O 4-6-4 Hudson Locomotive, traditional, 02		225 ____
28616	Nickel Plate 2-8-4 Berkshire Locomotive, traditional, 02		190 ____
28617	Southern 2-8-4 Berkshire Locomotive, traditional, 02		235 ____
28624	Santa Fe 0-6-0 Dockside Switcher "2174", traditional, 04		175 ____
28625	Wabash 4-4-2 Atlantic Locomotive "8625," traditional, 03		85 ____
28626	PRR 4-6-4 Hudson Locomotive "626," traditional, 03		175 ____
28627	C&O 2-8-4 Berkshire Locomotive "2755", traditional, 03		200 ____
28628	L&N 2-8-4 Berkshire Locomotive "1970," traditional, 03	150	200 ____
28633	JCPenney B&O 2-8-4 Berkshire Locomotive, 07		135 ____
28636	D&RGW 4-4-2 Atlantic Locomotive "8636," traditional, 04		95 ____
28637	UP 4-6-4 Hudson Locomotive "673," traditional, 04		160 ____
28638	GN 2-8-4 Berkshire Locomotive "3414," traditional, 04		200 ____
28639	NYC 2-8-4 Berkshire Locomotive "9401," traditional, 04		200 ____
28646	North Pole Central 2-8-4 Berkshire "1900," traditional, 04		315 ____
28649	Polar Express 2-8-4 Berkshire Locomotive, 03,àí10		120 ____
28650	NYC 0-6-0 Dockside Switcher "X-8688," traditional, 05		80 ____
28651	Bethlehem Steel 0-6-0 Dockside Switcher "72," traditional, 05		80 ____
28652	LL 4-4-2 Locomotive "8652," traditional, 05		105 ____
28655	Erie 2-8-4 Berkshire Locomotive "3338," traditional, 05		240 ____
28656	PRR 2-8-4 Berkshire Locomotive "56," traditional, 05		240 ____
28660	North Pole Central 0-6-0 Dockside Switcher "25," traditional, 05		105 ____
28661	Santa Fe 0-4-0 Locomotive "2300" traditional, 05		160 ____
28662	C&O 0-4-0 Locomotive "39," traditional, 05		160 ____
28663	Nieman Marcus 4-4-2 Atlantic Locomotive, traditional, 06 u		125 ____
28665	LRRC Western Union 2-8-4 Berkshire Locomotive "665", 10 u		200 ____
28667	Elvis "He Dared to Rock" 2-8-4 Berkshire Locomotive, 04		200 ____
28669	Copper Range 0-6-0 Locomotive "194", 05		155 ____
28671	ATSF 2-8-4 Berkshire Locomotive "4193", 06-07		225 ____
28674	C&O 0-6-0 Dockside Switcher "67," traditional, 06-07		110 ____
28675	SP 0-6-0 Dockside Switcher "675," traditional, 06-07		110 ____
28676	U.S. Steel 0-6-0 Dockside Switcher "76," traditional, 06-07		110 ____
28677	WM 4-4-2 Atlantic Locomotive "103," traditional, 06		110 ____
28678	Rio Grande 0-4-0 Locomotive "55," traditional, 06-07		170 ____
28679	U.S. Army Transportation Corps 0-4-0 Locomotive "40," traditional, 06		170 ____
28680	Reading 0-4-0 Locomotive "1152," traditional, 06		170 ____
28681	Virginian 2-8-4 Berkshire Locomotive "509," traditional, 06		260 ____
28683	B&O 2-8-2 Mikado Locomotive "1520," TrainSounds, 06-07		260 ____
28684	UP 2-8-2 Mikado Locomotive "2498," TrainSounds, 06-07		260 ____
28693	B&O 4-4-2 Locomotive "28," traditional, 05		105 ____
28694	NYC 4-4-2 Atlantic Locomotive "8637," traditional, 06		100 ____
28695	Halloween 0-6-0 Dockside Switcher "X-131", traditional, 06-07		85 ____
28699	Holiday 2-8-2 Mikado Locomotive "25," red, RailSounds, 08		260 ____
28700	CB&Q 0-8-0 Locomotive "543," RailSounds, 05		650 ____
28701	NP 0-8-0 Locomotive "1178," RailSounds, 05	138	650 ____
28702	Boston & Albany 0-8-0 Locomotive "53," RailSounds, 05		650 ____
28704	PRR 4-4-2 Atlantic Locomotive "68," CC, 05		550 ____
28706	PRR Reading Seashore 4-4-2 Atlantic Locomotive "6064," CC, 05		550 ____
28742	B&O 4-6-0 Camelback Locomotive "1630," CC, 03		335 ____
28743	B&O 4-6-0 Camelback Locomotive "1632," traditional, 03		300 ____
28744	D&H 4-6-0 Camelback Locomotive "548," CC, 03		325 ____

MODERN 1970-2024			Exc	Mint
___	**28745**	D&H 4-6-0 Camelback Locomotive "555," traditional, 03		300
___	**28746**	Erie 4-6-0 Camelback Locomotive "860," CC, 03	113	375
___	**28747**	Erie 4-6-0 Camelback Locomotive "878," traditional, 03		300
___	**28748**	Jersey Central 4-6-0 Camelback Locomotive "772," CC, 03		300
___	**28749**	Jersey Central 4-6-0 Camelback Locomotive "773," traditional, 03		300
___	**28750**	Lackawanna 4-6-0 Camelback Locomotive "690," CC, 03	125	375
___	**28751**	Lackawanna 4-6-0 Camelback Locomotive "1031," traditional, 03		300
___	**28752**	LIRR 4-6-0 Camelback Locomotive "126," CC, 03		300
___	**28753**	LIRR 4-6-0 Camelback Locomotive "127," traditional, 03		300
___	**28754**	NYO&W 4-6-0 Camelback Locomotive "249," CC, 03		300
___	**28755**	NYO&W 4-6-0 Camelback "253" Locomotive, traditional, 03		300
___	**28756**	PRR Reading Seashore 4-6-0 Camelback Locomotive "6000," CC, 03		325
___	**28757**	PRR Reading Seashore 4-6-0 Camelback "6001", 03		300
___	**28758**	Susquehanna 4-6-0 Camelback Locomotive "30," CC, 03		365
___	**28759**	Susquehanna 4-6-0 Camelback Locomotive "36," traditional, 03		300
___	**28800**	N&W GP7 Diesel "507", 99-00		80
___	**28801**	Lionel Lines 44-ton Switcher, 99		135
___	**28806**	Jersey Central FM H16-44 Diesel "1516," CC, 01		335
___	**28811**	Santa Fe FM H16-44 Diesel "3003," CC, 01		290
___	**28813**	Milwaukee Road FM H16-44 Diesel "406," CC, 01		315
___	**28815**	B&O GP30 Diesel "6935", CC, 02		295
___	**28817**	Reading GP30 Diesel "5513", CC, 02		310
___	**28819**	Rio Grande GP30 Diesel "3013", CC, 02		310
___	**28821**	GT GP7 Diesel "4438", 01		100
___	**28822**	Southern RS3 Diesel "2127", 01		70
___	**28823**	Virginian Electric Locomotive "234", 01		122
___	**28826**	Pioneer Seed GP7 Diesel "2001," traditional, 00 u		NRS
___	**28827**	Chessie GP38 Diesel, traditional, 01		100
___	**28830**	Soo Line GP9 Diesel, traditional, 01 u	95	270
___	**28831**	Conrail U36B Diesel "2971", traditional, 02	40	100
___	**28832**	Santa Fe RS3 Diesel "2099", traditional, 02		70
___	**28836**	NYC FM H-16-44 Diesel "7000", CC, 02		330
___	**28837**	NH FM H-16-44 Diesel "591", CC, 02		325
___	**28838**	UP FM H-16-44 Diesel "1340", CC, 02		325
___	**28839**	Alaska GP 30 Diesel "2000", CC, 04		315
___	**28840**	Burlington GP30 Diesel "945", CC, 03		325
___	**28841**	Seaboard GP30 Diesel "1315", CC, 03		220
___	**28842**	C&O GP9 Diesel, horn, 04		160
___	**28843**	Southern GP38 Diesel, horn, 04		140
___	**28845**	Amtrak RS3 Diesel "106", 03		70
___	**28846**	Western Pacific U36B Diesel "3067," traditional, 04		100
___	**28847**	DM & IR GP38 Diesel "203", traditional, 04		170
___	**28848**	JCPenney Santa Fe GP38 Diesel, 04		125
___	**28849**	Western Maryland GP7 Diesel, horn, 04		185
___	**28850**	NYC GP30 Diesel "6115" CC, 04		360
___	**28851**	Pennsylvania RS3 Diesel, 04-05		75
___	**28852**	CSX U36B Diesel "1976," traditional, 05		140
___	**28853**	Santa Fe GP38 Diesel "2371," traditional, 05		210
___	**28855**	B&O/Chessie System GP30 Diesel "6945," CC, 05-06	225	425
___	**28857**	Alaska GP9 Diesel, 05		125

		Exc	Mint
28859	Pennsylvania GP30 Diesel "2206," nonpowered, 06		160 ___
28860	UP GP30 Diesel "844", CC, 06		360 ___
28861	UP GP30 Diesel "845," nonpowered (std O), 06		150 ___
28862	CSX GP30 Diesel "4249", CC, 06		400 ___
28863	CSX GP30 Diesel "4250," nonpowered (std O), 06		150 ___
28864	UP RS3 Diesel "1195," traditional, 06		85 ___
28865	GN GP9 Diesel "688," traditional, 06		160 ___
28866	NYC GP20 Diesel "6110", traditional, 06		140 ___
28868	ATSF GP38 Diesel		140 ___
28873	NYC RS3 Diesel "8226," traditional, 06		85 ___
28874	UP GP9 Diesel "178," traditional, 06-07		210 ___
28875	Santa Fe GP20 "1107", traditional, 06		140 ___
28876	GN FT Diesel "418", traditional, 07-08	75	245 ___
28879	UPS Centennial GP38 Diesel, traditional, 06		210 ___
28881	Conrail GP20 Diesel "2107", traditional, 07		140 ___
28882	Alaska RS3 Diesel "1079," traditional, 07		85 ___
28883	Thomas the Tank Engine Diesel, 07-13		120 ___
28884	PRR GP38 Diesel "2389," traditional, 08-09		210 ___
28886	RI RS3 Diesel "492," traditional, 08		95 ___
28887	Southern RS3 Diesel "2028," traditional, 08		95 ___
28890	CN GP9 Diesel "4573," traditional, 08		210 ___
28897	Seaboard U36B Diesel "1762," traditional, 08		140 ___
28900	Iron 'Arry and Iron Bert 2-pack, 08-09		240 ___
28905	ATSF FT Diesel "160," nonpowered, 09-10		120 ___
29000	PRR Caleb Strong Madison Coach "2622", 99		80 ___
29001	PRR Villa Royal Madison Coach "2621", 99		80 ___
29002	PRR Philadelphia Madison Coach "2624", 99	30	80 ___
29003	PRR Madison Car 4-pack, 98		220 ___
29004	NYC Heavyweight Passenger Car 2-pack, 99		170 ___
29007	NYC Pullman Passenger Car 2-pack, 98 u		143 ___
29008	NYC Heavyweight Diner "383", 98		95 ___
29009	NYC Van Twiller Heavyweight Combination Car, 98		95 ___
29010	C&O Heavyweight Passenger Car 2-pack, 99		150 ___
29039	Lionel Lines Recovery Combination Car "9501", 99	65	85 ___
29041	Alaska Streamliner Car 4-pack, 99-00	59	230 ___
29042	Alaska Streamliner Baggage Car "6310", 99-00		50 ___
29043	Alaska Streamliner Coach "5408", 99-00		65 ___
29044	Alaska Streamliner Vista Dome Car "7014", 99-00		65 ___
29046	B&O Streamliner Car 4-pack, 99-00		165 ___
29047	B&O Streamliner Baggage Car, 99-00		35 ___
29048	B&O Streamliner Coach, 99-00		50 ___
29049	B&O Streamliner Vista Dome Car, 99-00		50 ___
29050	B&O Streamliner Observation Car, 99-00		40 ___
29051	ATSF Streamliner Car 4-pack, 99-00		200 ___
29052	ATSF Streamliner Baggage Car, 99-00		40 ___
29053	ATSF Streamliner Coach, 99-00		60 ___
29054	ATSF Streamliner Vista Dome Car, 99-00		60 ___
29055	ATSF Streamliner Observation Car, 99-00		40 ___
29056	NYC Streamliner Car 4-pack, 99-00		180 ___
29057	NYC Streamliner Baggage Car, 99-00		40 ___
29058	NYC Streamliner Coach, 99-00		50 ___
29059	NYC Streamliner Vista Dome Car, 99-00		50 ___
29060	NYC Streamliner Observation Car, 99-00		45 ___

			Exc	Mint
___	**29061**	PRR Madison Passenger Car 4-pack, 99-00		190
___	**29062**	PRR Indian Point Madison Baggage Car, 99-00		50
___	**29063**	PRR Christopher Columbus Madison Coach, 99-00		50
___	**29064**	PRR Andrew Jackson Madison Coach, 99-00		50
___	**29065**	PRR Broussard Madison Observation Car, 99-00		50
___	**29066**	CNJ Madison Passenger Car 4-pack, 99-00		210
___	**29067**	CNJ Madison Baggage Car "420", 99-00		50
___	**29068**	CNJ Beachcomber Madison Coach, 99-00		50
___	**29069**	CNJ Echo Lake Madison Coach, 99-00		50
___	**29070**	CNJ Madison Observation Car "1178", 99-00		50
___	**29071**	NYC Baby Madison Car 4-pack, 00	78	203
___	**29072**	NYC Baby Madison Baggage Car "1001", 00		50
___	**29073**	NYC Baby Madison Coach "1005", 00		50
___	**29074**	NYC Baby Madison Coach "1006", 00		50
___	**29075**	NYC Detroit Baby Madison Observation Car "1019", 00		40
___	**29076**	Southern Baby Madison Car 4-pack, 00		155
___	**29077**	Southern Delaware Madison Baggage Car "702", 00		30
___	**29078**	Southern North Carolina Madison Coach "800", 00		50
___	**29079**	Southern Maryland Madison Coach "801", 00		50
___	**29080**	Southern Madison Observation Car "1100", 00		40
___	**29081**	ATSF Baby Madison Car 4-pack, 00		160
___	**29082**	ATSF Baby Madison Baggage Car "1765", 00		30
___	**29083**	ATSF Baby Madison Coach "3040", 00		50
___	**29084**	ATSF Baby Madison Coach "1535", 00		50
___	**29085**	ATSF Baby Madison Observation Car "10", 00		45
___	**29086**	Madison Car 3-pack, 99		280
___	**29090**	Lionel Liontech Madison Car "2656", 99		75
___	**29091**	Lawrence Cowen Lionel Legends Madison Coach "2657", 99-00		75
___	**29105**	PRR Trail Blazer Aluminum Passenger Car 4-pack, 04-05		550
___	**29108**	Searchlight Car, 00		30
___	**29110**	B&O Columbian Aluminum Passenger Car 4-pack, 04		425
___	**29115**	SP Daylight Aluminum Passenger Car 4-pack, 04-05		550
___	**29122**	EL F3 Diesel Passenger Set, 99		840
___	**29123**	Erie-Lack. Aluminum Coach/Baggage Car "203", 99		100
___	**29124**	Erie-Lack. Aluminum Coach/Diner "770", 99		100
___	**29125**	Erie-Lack. Eleanor Lord Aluminum Coach, 99		100
___	**29126**	Erie-Lack. Tavern Lounge Aluminum Observation Car "789", 99		125
___	**29127**	ACL Aluminum Baggage Car "152", 99		100
___	**29128**	ACL North Hampton Aluminum Coach, 99		100
___	**29129**	Texas Special Passenger Car 4-pack, 99	650	700
___	**29130**	Texas Special Edward Burleson Aluminum Coach "1200", 99	58	125
___	**29131**	Texas Special David G. Burnett Aluminum Coach "1201", 99	58	125
___	**29132**	Texas Special J. Pinckney Henderson Aluminum Coach "1202", 99	38	122
___	**29133**	Texas Special Stephen F. Austin Aluminum Observation Car "1203", 99	50	118
___	**29135**	California Zephyr Silver Poplar Aluminum Vista Dome Car, 99		150
___	**29136**	California Zephyr Silver Palm Aluminum Vista Dome Car, 99		150
___	**29137**	California Zephyr Silver Tavern Aluminum Vista Dome Car, 99		150
___	**29138**	California Zephyr Silver Planet Aluminum Vista Dome Car, 99		150
___	**29139**	Kughn Lionel Legends Madison Car "2655", 99		113
___	**29140**	NYC Castleton Bridge Aluminum Sleeper Car, 99		120

		Exc	Mint
29141	NYC Martin Van Buren Aluminum Combination Car, 99		120
29142	CP Skyline Aluminum Vista Dome Car "596", 99		125
29143	CP Banff Park Aluminum Observation Car, 99		125
29144	Santa Fe El Capitan Aluminum Passenger Car 4-pack, 04		400
29149	CB&Q California Zephyr Aluminum Passenger Car 2-pack, 03		300
29152	Santa Fe Super Chief Aluminum Passenger Car 2-pack, 03		190
29155	D&H Aluminum Passenger Car 2-pack, 03		190
29158	Southern Aluminum Passenger Car 2-pack, 03		205
29165	Amtrak Superliner Passenger Car 2-pack, Phase IV, 04		195
29168	Amtrak Superliner Diner, StationSounds, Phase IV, 04		200
29169	Alaska Superliner Passenger Car 2-pack, 04		200
29172	Alaska Superliner Diner, StationSounds, 04		200
29182	N&W Powhatan Arrow Aluminum Passenger Car 4-pack (std O), 05		550
29187	N&W Powhatan Arrow Aluminum Passenger Car 2-pack (std O), 05		290
29190	N&W Powhatan Arrow Aluminum Diner, StationSounds, 05		290
29191	MILW Hiawatha Passenger Car 4-pack, 06		370
29192	MILW Hiawatha Combination Car "153", 06		95
29193	MILW Hiawatha Coach "437", 06		95
29194	MILW Hiawatha Coach "438", 06		95
29195	MILW Hiawatha Observation "Miller", 06		95
29196	MILW Hiawatha Passenger Car 2-pack, 06		190
29197	MILW Hiawatha Baggage Car "1305", 06		95
29198	MILW Hiawatha Coach "439", 06		95
29199	MILW Hiawatha Diner, StationSounds, 06		190
29202	Santa Fe Map Boxcar "6464", 97 u		53
29203	Maine Central Boxcar "6464-597", 97 u	10	35
29205	Mickey Mouse Hi-Cube Boxcar "9555", 97		70
29206	Vapor Records Boxcar #1, 97		90
29209	Postwar "6464" Boxcar Series VII, 3 cars, 98	23	97
29210	GN Boxcar "6464-450", 98		33
29211	B&M Boxcar "6464-475", 98		27
29212	Timken Boxcar "6464-500", 98		28
29213	ATSF Grand Canyon Route 6464 Boxcar "6464-198", 98		26
29214	Southern 6464 Boxcar "6464-298", 98	32	86
29215	Canadian Pacific 6464 Boxcar "6464-398", 98	9	28
29217	1997 Toy Fair Airex Boxcar, 97		78
29218	Vapor Records Boxcar "6464-496", 97 u	20	49
29220	Lionel Centennial Series Hi-Cube Boxcar Set, 4 cars, 97	200	243
29221	Centennial Series Hi-Cube Boxcar "9697-1", 97		65
29222	Centennial Series Hi-Cube Boxcar "9697-2", 97		72
29223	Centennial Series Hi-Cube Boxcar "9697-3", 97		65
29224	Centennial Series Hi-Cube Boxcar "9697-4", 97		62
29225	H.O.R.D.E. Music Festival Boxcar, 97	48	70
29229	Vapor Records Holiday Car, 98	100	165
29231	Halloween Animated Boxcar, 98		42
29233	Conrail PC Overstamped Boxcar "6464-598", 98		38
29234	Conrail Erie Overstamped Boxcar "6464-698", 98		32
29235	NYC Boxcar "6464-510", 99		47
29236	MKT Boxcar "6464-515", 99		40
29237	M&StL Boxcar "6464-525", 99	13	35
12926	Green Mainline Classic Street Lamps, 3-pack, 08-24		40

			Exc	Mint
___	**29250**	Phoebe Snow Boxcar "6464-199", 99		41
___	**29251**	BN Boxcar "6464-299", 99	13	36
___	**29252**	CP Boxcar "6464-399", 99	13	37
___	**29253**	B&M Boxcar "76032", 99		50
___	**29254**	B&M Boxcar "76033", 99		50
___	**29255**	B&M Boxcar "76034", 99		50
___	**29256**	B&M Boxcar "76035", 99		50
___	**29257**	Southern Boxcar "9464-199", 99		38
___	**29258**	Reading Boxcar "9464-299", 99		36
___	**29259**	NP Bicentennial Boxcar "9464-399", 99		34
___	**29265**	Maine Central Boxcar "8661", 99	10	36
___	**29266**	Frisco Boxcar "8722", 99	15	38
___	**29267**	No. 6464 Boxcar 3-pack, Series VIII, 99	38	86
___	**29268**	Rio Grande Boxcar "63067", 99		40
___	**29271**	Lionel Cola Tractor and Trailer, 98		12
___	**29279**	Conrail Jersey Central Overstamped Boxcar "6464-28X", 99		40
___	**29280**	Conrail LV Overstamped Boxcar "6464-31X", 99		41
___	**29281**	Conrail Overstamped Boxcar 2-pack, 99		70
___	**29282**	Postwar "6464" Boxcar 3-pack, 99	43	125
___	**29283**	NYC Boxcar, 99		55
___	**29284**	GN Boxcar, 99	14	39
___	**29285**	Seaboard Boxcar, 99		36
___	**29286**	Overstamped Boxcar 2-pack, 99		65
___	**29287**	NH PC Overstamped Boxcar "6464-29X", 99	18	34
___	**29288**	Conrail Reading Overstamped Boxcar "6464-32X", 99		38
___	**29289**	Postwar "6464" Series IX, 3 cars, 99-00	35	85
___	**29290**	D&RGW Boxcar "6464-650", 00		41
___	**29291**	ATSF Boxcar "6464-700", 00		38
___	**29292**	NH Boxcar "6464-725", 00		39
___	**29293**	NH Boxcar "6464-425", 99		95
___	**29294**	Hellgate Bridge Boxcar "1900-2000", 99 u		38
___	**29295**	PRR "Don't Stand Me Still" Boxcar "24018", 99-00		65
___	**29296**	PRR "Merchandise" Boxcar "29296", 99-00		65
___	**29297**	PRR "No Damage" Boxcar "47158", 99-00		65
___	**29298**	Lionel Boxcar "6464-2000", 00		46
___	**29300**	50th Anniversary Clear Shell Aquarium Car, 10		85
___	**29301**	Postwar "3662" Transparent Milk Car with platform, 11, 13		155
___	**29302**	Christmas Music Reefer, 10		75
___	**29303**	North Pole Central Crane Car, 10-11		65
___	**29305**	UP Chisholm Trail Stock Car, Cattle Sounds, 11, 13		200
___	**29306**	PRR Hi-Cube Lighted Garland Boxcar, 10-11		70
___	**29309**	GN Pullman-Standard Diesel Freight Set, CC, 13		830
___	**29310**	Marine Science Deep Sea Exhibition Aquarium Car, 11		75
___	**29311**	Strasburg Derrick Car, 11		45
___	**29312**	Santa's Operating Boxcar, 11-12		75
___	**29314**	SP DD Boxcar "214051" (std O), 13-14		75
___	**29317**	CN DD Boxcar "551334" (std O), 13-14	40	80
___	**29318**	NJ Transit Gondola "9422" w/Ballast Load, 12-13		35
___	**29319**	NJ Transit BW Caboose "905", 12-13	70	90
___	**29320**	CNJ DD Boxcar "25031" (std O), 13-14	40	75
___	**29320**	UP Walking Brakeman Car "454400", 12	52	70
___	**29321**	Ice Skating Aquarium Car, 12		80
___	**29322**	Koi Aquarium Car, 13-14		80

		Exc	Mint
29323	UP DD Boxcar "500019" (std O), 13-14		75
29324	Walking Zombie Brakeman Car, 12		80
29326	NP "Pig Palace" Operating Stock Car "84144", 12		200
29327	Bethlehem Steel Operating Hopper "2025", 12		60
29328	Beatles "Nothing is Real" Aquarium Car, 12-13		85
29329	Peanuts Halloween Aquarium Car, 12-13		85
29333	ATSF 89' Auto Carrier 2-pack (std O), 13-16		220
29338	BN 89' Auto Carrier 2-pack (std O), 13-14		220
29344	C&NW DD Boxcar "57766" (std O), 13		75
29345	ATSF 89' Auto Carrier (std O), 13-14		110
29346	Soo Line 89' Auto Carrier 2-pack (std O), 13-16		220
29349	SP 89' Auto Carrier 2-pack (std O), 13-16		220
29364	NYC Water Level Steam Freight Set, CC, 12-13		1600
29365	N&W Pocahontas Steam Passenger Set, CC, 12		1950
29366	SP TankSet Diesel Set, CC, 12		850
29372	BNSF 89' Auto Carrier "300267" (std O), 13		110
29373	CN 89' Auto Carrier "710771" (std O), 13, 16		110
29376	Conrail 89' Auto Carrier "964444" (std O), 13		110
29377	CP 89' Auto Carrier 2-pack (std O), 13-16		220
29380	CSX 89' Auto Carrier "604544" (std O), 13		110
29381	GTW 89' Auto Carrier "50450" (std O), 14-15		110
29382	UP 89' Auto Carrier "604545" (std O), 13		110
29384	DL&W USRA Double-sheathed Boxcar "44153" (std O), 13		70
29385	ATSF USRA Double-sheathed Boxcar "39012" (std O), 13		70
29386	PRR PS-4 Flatcar with stakes "469614" (std O), 13		70
29387	GN PS-4 Flatcar with stakes "629387" (std O), 13		70
29400	Bethlehem Steel Slag Car 3-pack (std O), 03		185
29404	Bethlehem Steel Hot Metal Car 3-pack (std O), 03	60	210
29408	PRR Coil Car, 01		40
29411	Sherwin-Williams Vat Car, 02		35
29412	Tabasco Brand Vat Car, 02		36
29413	Airex Boat Loader Car "29413", 02		42
29414	PRR Evans Auto Loader "480123", 01		56
29415	WM Skeleton Log Car 3-pack #2 (std O), 02		90
29419	West Side Lumber Skeleton Log Car 3-pack #2 (std O), 02		90
29423	Wellspring Capital Management Happy Holidays Vat Car, 03 u		255
29424	Meadow River Lumber Skeleton Log Car 3-pack (std O), 03		90
29429	Campbell's Soup Vat Car "29429", 03		38
29430	Meadow River Lumber Skeleton Log Car 3-pack #2 (std O), 03		90
29434	Weyerhauser Skeleton Log Car 3-pack, 05		108
29438	Trailer Train Flatcar with 2 UP trailers, 03		60
29439	Postwar "6414" Evans Auto Loader, 02		43
29441	UP Flatcar "53471" with grader, 02		43
29442	CSX Flatcar "600513" with backhoe, 02		43
29449	Weyerhaeuser Timber Skeleton Log Car 3-pack #2 (std O), 03		90
29453	Elk River Lumber Skeleton Log Car 3-pack #2 (std O), 03		90
29457	NS Flatcar "157590" with Caterpillar loader, 03		42
29458	BNSF Flatcar "922268" with Caterpillar truck, 03		44
29459	Water Barrel Car "1878," Archive Collection, 03		40
29460	LL Flatcar "3460" with trailers, Archive Collection, 03		39
29461	Postwar "6500" Flatcar with red-and-white airplane, 03		32
29462	Postwar "6500" Flatcar with white-and-red airplane, 03		31

			Exc	Mint
___	**29463**	Postwar "6414" Evans Auto Loader, 03		30
___	**29464**	U.S. Army Vat Car "29464", 04		35
___	**29465**	U.S. Steel Slag Car 3-pack (std O), 04-05		160
___	**29469**	U.S. Steel Hot Metal Car 3-pack (std O), 04-05	70	190
___	**29473**	Youngstown Sheet & Tube Slag Car 3-pack (std O), 03		150
___	**29477**	Youngstown Sheet & Tube Hot Metal Car 3-pack (std O), 03		170
___	**29481**	Cass Scenic Railroad Skeleton Log Car 3-pack (std O), 03		80
___	**29487**	Boat-loader with 4 boats, 04		65
___	**29488**	Cass Scenic Railroad Skeleton Log Car 3-pack #2 (std O), 04		90
___	**29492**	Pickering Lumber Skeleton Log Car 3-pack #1 (std O), 04		100
___	**29496**	Pickering Lumber Skeleton Log Car 3-pack #2 (std O), 04		90
___	**29602**	Celanese Chemicals 1-D Tank Car, 05		45
___	**29603**	Comet 1-D Tank Car, traditional, 05		53
___	**29604**	Meadow Brook Molasses 1-D Tank Car, traditional, 05		53
___	**29606**	Elvis Presley Gold Record Transport Car, 04		120
___	**29607**	Las Vegas Mint Car, traditional, 05		58
___	**29609**	Alien Suspension Car, 06		60
___	**29610**	Dixie Honey 1-D Tank Car, 06		60
___	**29611**	Sunoco 1-D Tank Car, 06	30	63
___	**29612**	Las Vegas Poker Chip Car, 06		40
___	**29613**	Postwar "6463" Rocket Fuel 2-D Tank Car, 06		75
___	**29614**	Postwar "6315" Gulf Chemical Tank Car, 06		48
___	**29617**	Postwar "6465" Cities Service 2-D Tank Car, 06-07		48
___	**29618**	Hooker Chemicals 3-D Tank Car, 07		60
___	**29619**	Grave's Formaldehyde 1-D Tank Car, 07		60
___	**29622**	Fort Knox Mint Car, lilac, Archive Collection, 07		60
___	**29624**	Monopoly Mint Car with money, 08		65
___	**29626**	"Case Closed" Mint Car with shredded documents, 08		109
___	**29628**	Poinsettia Mint Car, 09		70
___	**29629**	AEC Glow-in-the-Dark Tank Car, 09-10		65
___	**29633**	Christmas Ornament Lighted Mint Car, 10		70
___	**29634**	Federal Reserve Bailout Mint Car, 10		70
___	**29635**	Monopoly "Go To Jail" Mint Car, 10		70
___	**29636**	Vampire Transport Mint Car, 10-11		70
___	**29637**	Candy Cane 2-D Tank Car, 10-11		55
___	**29638**	Fort Knox Mint Car, 10-11	40	65
___	**29640**	Coca-Cola Tank Car, 10		65
___	**29642**	Jolly Rancher 1-D Tank Car, 11		55
___	**29643**	Hershey's Syrup 1-D Tank Car, 11		58
___	**29644**	ATSF 1-D Tank Car, 11		55
___	**29645**	Atlantic City Casino Mint Car, 11		70
___	**29646**	Alaska Oil 2-D Tank Car, 11		50
___	**29647**	Gingerbread Man Mint Car, 11		70
___	**29648**	Kansas City Federal Reserve Mint Car, 11		70
___	**29649**	Lionel SP Smoke Pellets Mint Car, 12-13		70
___	**29650**	Cleveland Federal Reserve Mint Car, 11		70
___	**29651**	Richmond Federal Reserve Mint Car, 12		70
___	**29654**	Boston Federal Reserve Mint Car, 13		70
___	**29655**	PRR 16-wheel Flatcar with girders "469846", 12		75
___	**29656**	ATSF 16-wheel Flatcar with transformer "90096", 12		75
___	**29671**	Smoke Pellet Mint Car #2, 13-15		70
___	**29694**	Hershey's Mint Car, 14	64	95
___	**29695**	Trailer Set Maxi-Stack Pair "48", 13		120

		Exc	Mint
29697	Santa's Flatcar with submarine, 13		70
29698	Tree Topper Star Transport Car, 13-14		80
29699	Silver and Gold Christmas Mint Car, 13-14		70
29703	Postwar "6427-500" Girl's PRR Porthole Caboose, 01		45
29704	Postwar "6427" Boy's Set PRR Porthole Caboose, 02		50
29705	PRR Porthole Caboose "477951" (std O), 04		40
29706	Postwar "6437" PRR Porthole Caboose, 04		40
29707	NIckel Plate BW Caboose "408" (std O), 04		80
29708	C&O Bay Window Caboose "8315", 04		45
29709	PRR Porthole Caboose "477938", 04		40
29710	Postwar "6657" D&RGW Caboose, 04-05		33
29711	ATSF Bay Window Caboose, 04-05		60
29712	Postwar "2420" Searchlight Caboose, 04		50
29713	Postwar "6437" PRR Porthole Caboose, 05		20
29714	Postwar "6557" Lionel Lines Smoking Caboose, 05-07		120
29715	PRR Porthole Caboose "477953", 05		45
29716	UP EV Caboose "25462", 04		40
29717	NS EV Caboose "555533", 05	40	50
29718	Postwar "6419-100" N&W Work Caboose, 05-06		48
29719	ATSF Porthole Caboose "6427," Archive Collection, 05-06		48
29720	PRR Porthole Caboose "477861", 06		45
29721	PRR Work Caboose "491064", 06		50
29722	Postwar "6517" LL BW Caboose w/Strobe light, 06		49
29723	LL Porthole Caboose "64273" Archive Collection, 06-08	27	50
29724	Postwar "6517" LL BW Caboose, 06-07		50
29725	CP EV Caboose "43615", 06		50
29726	Virginian Porthole Caboose "6427-60," Archive Collection, 06-07		50
29727	"I Love U.S.A." Bay Window Caboose "1985", 06		60
29728	UP Smoking EV Caboose, 07		60
29729	Bethlehem Steel Searchlight Caboose, 06		90
29730	Postwar "6427-3" LL Porthole Caboose, 07		45
29732	PRR Porthole Caboose "477871", 08		45
29733	White Pass & Yukon EV Caboose, 09-10		90
29734	PRR NS Heritage CA-4 Caboose (std O), 09-10		95
29735	Conrail NS Heritage CA-4 Caboose (std O), 10		95
29736	NYC Smoking NE Caboose "20883", 09-10		55
29737	ATSF Bay Window Caboose, traditional, 10-11		70
29738	Postwar "6517" Transparent Smoking BW Caboose, 10-11		80
29739	B&M Transfer Caboose, 10-11		50
29761	GATX TankTrain A-End "44570", 12		100
29762	GATX TankTrain Intermediate Car "44559", 12		80
29763	GATX TankTrain Intermediate Car "44580", 12		80
29764	GATX TankTrain B-End "44575", 12		100
29765	GATX TankSet Add-on 3-pack (std O), 12		240
29766	GATX TankTrain Intermediate Car "44598", 12		80
29767	GATX TankTrain Intermediate Car "44581", 12		80
29768	GATX TankTrain Intermediate Car "44578", 12		80
29769	NYC/MC Double-sheathed Boxcar "51071", 12-13		100
29770	B&M Offset Hopper "7168", 12-13		40
29771	CN TankSet 2-pack (std O), 12		160
29772	CN TankTrain Intermediate Car "75565", 12		80
29773	CN TankTrain Intermediate Car "75561", 12		80

			Exc	Mint
___	**29774**	GATX TankSet 2-pack (std O), 12		160
___	**29775**	GATX TankTrain Intermediate Car "57009", 12		80
___	**29776**	GATX TankTrain Intermediate Car "48671", 12		80
___	**29777**	CIBRO TankSet 2-pack (std O), 12		160
___	**29778**	CIBRO TankTrain Intermediate Car "26251", 12		80
___	**29779**	CIBRO TankTrain Intermediate Car "26255", 12		80
___	**29780**	NYC 1-D Tank Car, 12-13		90
___	**29781**	NYC Smoking Wood-sided Caboose, 12-13		200
___	**29786**	Bethlehem Steel PS-2 3-bay Hopper (std O), 13		80
___	**29787**	PRR PS-2 3-bay Hopper (std O), 13		80
___	**29788**	PRR Porthole Caboose "477939", 13-17		35
___	**27789**	Penn Salt Chemicals 3-D Tank Car "4727", 13-17		35
___	**29790**	PRR Boxcar "539339", 13-17		36
___	**29791**	Wizard of Oz Anniversary Boxcar, 13-15		70
___	**29792**	Angela Trotta Thomas "Toyland Express" Boxcar, 13		65
___	**29793**	"Where the Wild Things Are" Boxcar, 13-15		70
___	**29800**	MOW Crane Car, TMCC, 04	200	300
___	**29801**	ATSF Operating Barrel Ramp Car, 04-05		89
___	**29802**	Postwar "3530" EMD Generator Car, 04-05		89
___	**29803**	Postwar "3444" Erie Animated Gondola, 04-05		89
___	**29804**	UP Crane Car "JPX 250", CC, 05		320
___	**29805**	Conrail Crane Car "50202", CC, 05		320
___	**29806**	Weyerhaeuser Log Dump Car, 05		75
___	**29807**	DM&IR Coal Dump Car, 05		75
___	**29808**	Candy Cane Dump Car, 05		55
___	**29809**	Santa's Delivery Service Dump Car w/Presents, 05		60
___	**29810**	Operating Egg Nog Car with platform, 05		140
___	**29811**	NYC Merchant's Despatch Transit Hot Box Reefer, 05-06	85	110
___	**29812**	Santa Fe Hot Box Reefer "20699", 05-06		90
___	**29813**	Santa Fe Boom Car "19144," Crane Sounds, 05		270
___	**29814**	Pennsylvania Boom Car "491063," Crane Sounds, 05		210
___	**29815**	NYC Boom Car "X923," Crane Sounds, 05		210
___	**29816**	MOW Boom Car "X-816," Crane Sounds, 05		210
___	**29817**	UP Boom Car "909438," Crane Sounds, 05		210
___	**29818**	Conrail Boom Car, Crane Sounds, 05		210
___	**29820**	Postwar "3356" Operating Horse Car and Corral, 05		75
___	**29821**	Postwar "2460" Lionel Lines Crane Car, gray cab, 05		45
___	**29822**	Postwar "773W" NYC Tender, whistle, 05		48
___	**29823**	Postwar "3484" Pennsylvania Operating Boxcar, 05		38
___	**29824**	Postwar "3662" Operating Milk Car and Platform, 05		59
___	**29825**	Postwar "3434" Poultry Dispatch Car, 05		60
___	**29826**	Postwar "3530" Generator Car and Light Pole, 05		48
___	**29827**	Postwar "3419" Helicopter Launching Car, 06		49
___	**29828**	Postwar "3666" Minuteman Car with cannon, 06		85
___	**29829**	Postwar "6805" Radioactive Waste Car, 06		85
___	**29830**	PFE Hot Box Reefer "5890" (std O), 06		105
___	**29831**	Swift Hot Box Reefer "15342" (std O), 06		150
___	**29832**	Chessie System Crane Car "940504", CC, 06		320
___	**29833**	Chessie System Boom Car "940561", CC, 06		210
___	**29834**	LL Bay Window Caboose "834," TrainSounds (std O), 06-07		110
___	**29835**	SP Bay Window Caboose "4667," TrainSounds (std O), 06-07		160
___	**29838**	Postwar "3666" Cannon Firing Boxcar, 05		149
___	**29839**	Postwar "6512" Cherry Picker Car, 06		63

		Exc	Mint
29841	PRR Ballast Dump Car, 06		28 ___
29842	REA Express Hot Box Refrigerator Car w/Smoke, 06-07		125 ___
29843	Postwar "3356" ATSF Operating Horse Car and Corral, 06-07		110 ___
29844	Postwar "3512" Fireman and Ladder Car, 06-08		50 ___
29845	Postwar "6812" Track Maintenance Car, 06-08		50 ___
29846	Postwar "6650" Operating Missile Launching Car, 06-07		30 ___
29847	Postwar "3419" Helicopter Launching Car, 06-07		60 ___
29648	Postwar "3540" Operating Radar Car, 06-07		50 ___
29849	Lionel Lines Crane Car, silver cab, 05-06		60 ___
29850	N&W J Class Tender, air whistle, 06-07		73 ___
29851	NYC Operating Crane Car "X-15," CC, 06		180 ___
29852	NYC Boom Car w/Sounds, 06		220 ___
29853	Postwar "6651" Big John Cannon Car, 08		75 ___
29854	Satellite Launching Car, 07		70 ___
29855	Lionel Lines Operating Milk Car with platform, 07		140 ___
29856	Postwar "3494-550" Monon Operating Boxcar, 06-07		65 ___
29857	Postwar "6660" Lionel Lines Boom Car, 06-07		55 ___
29858	CP Rail Crane Car "414475," CC, 07		320 ___
29859	CP Rail Boom Car "412567", CC, 07		210 ___
29865	Southern Operating Barrel Car, 07-08		75 ___
29866	Pirates Aquarium Car, 07		75 ___
29867	NYC Jet Snow Blower "X27207", 07		120 ___
29868	Alaska Jet Snow Blower, 07		120 ___
29869	Bethlehem Steel Crane Car, 06		60 ___
29870	MOW Jet Snow Blower "MWX-16", 07		120 ___
29871	Postwar "3359" Twin Bin Dump Car, 07		40 ___
29872	Postwar "3494-275" State of Maine Operating Boxcar, 07		55 ___
29873	Postwar "3361" LL Log Dump Car, 07		40 ___
29874	Peanuts Halloween Aquarium Car, 12		85 ___
29877	Southern Crane Car "D76," CC, 08		350 ___
29878	Southern Boom Car "T-193," CC, 08		230 ___
29882	Witches Operating Brew Car, 08		150 ___
29883	C&NW Operating Crane Car, CC, 10 u		340 ___
29884	CNJ Twin Dump Car, 08		85 ___
29885	BN Crane Car "S-104," CC, 10		340 ___
29886	BN Boom Car "S-1040," CC, 10		220 ___
29888	Postwar "3494-625" Soo Line Operating Boxcar, 08		70 ___
29891	ATSF Operating Crane Car, CC, 09-10		340 ___
29892	ATSF Boom Car, CC, 09-10		220 ___
29893	PRR Operating Stock Car "129893," RailSounds, 09		150 ___
29894	Christmas Chase Gondola, 09		65 ___
29895	Christmas Operating Snow Globe Car, 10		75 ___
29897	CSX Chessie System Research Car "3440", 11		65 ___
29900	"I Love Wisconsin" Boxcar, 01		35 ___
29901	"I Love Kentucky" Boxcar, 01		30 ___
29902	"I Love Iowa" Boxcar, 01		31 ___
29903	"I Love Missouri" Boxcar, 01		31 ___
29904	2002 Toy Fair Boxcar, 02		22 ___
29905	2002 Lionel Employee Christmas Boxcar, 02		80 ___
29906	"I Love Connecticut" Boxcar, 02		33 ___
29907	"I Love West Virginia" Boxcar, 02		33 ___
29908	"I Love Delaware" Boxcar, 02		33 ___

			Exc	Mint
___	**29909**	"I Love Maryland" Boxcar, 02		65
___	**29910**	Toy Fair Centennial Boxcar, 03		40
___	**29911**	2003 Lionel Employee Christmas Boxcar, 03 u		90
___	**29912**	"I Love Alabama" Boxcar, 03		30
___	**29913**	"I Love Mississippi" Boxcar, 03		35
___	**29914**	"I Love Louisiana" Boxcar, 03		35
___	**29915**	"I Love Arkansas" Boxcar, 03		30
___	**29918**	2003 Toy Fair Boxcar, 03 u		48
___	**29919**	2004 Toy Fair Boxcar, 04 u		37
___	**29920**	"I Love North Dakota" Boxcar, 03		35
___	**29921**	"I Love South Dakota" Boxcar, 03		40
___	**29922**	"I Love Nebraska" Boxcar, 03		30
___	**29923**	"I Love Kansas" Boxcar, 03		30
___	**29924**	2004 Lionel Employee Christmas Boxcar, 04 u	23	110
___	**29925**	Toy Fair Polar Express Boxcar, 05 u		250
___	**29926**	2005 Lionel Employee Christmas Boxcar, 05 u		90
___	**29927**	"I Love Washington" Boxcar, 05		45
___	**29928**	"I Love Oregon" Boxcar, 05		40
___	**29929**	"I Love Idaho" Boxcar, 05		45
___	**29930**	"I Love Utah" Boxcar, 05		45
___	**29931**	LRRC Season's Greetings Boxcar, 05 u		40
___	**29932**	"I Love Oklahoma" Boxcar, 06		45
___	**29933**	"I Love New Mexico" Boxcar, 06		45
___	**29934**	"I Love Hawaii" Boxcar, 06		45
___	**29935**	"I Love Alaska" Boxcar, 06		45
___	**29936**	"I Love Wyoming" Boxcar, 06		45
___	**29937**	2006 Toy Fair Boxcar, 06		38
___	**29938**	2006 Lionel Employee Christmas Boxcar, 06 u		25
___	**29939**	LRRC Anniversary Boxcar, 06 u		26
___	**29941**	LRRC 2006 Christmas Boxcar, 06 u		40
___	**29942**	Santa Fe Railroad Art Boxcar, 06		50
___	**29943**	Texas Special Railroad Art Boxcar, 06		50
___	**29944**	1957 Lionel Art Boxcar, 06	10	50
___	**29945**	1947 Lionel Art Boxcar, 06		50
___	**29946**	LRRC 2007 Christmas Boxcar, 07 u		40
___	**29947**	LRRC 2007 Commemorative Boxcar, 07 u		42
___	**29949**	2007 Lionel Employee Christmas Boxcar, 07 u		60
___	**29950**	1948 Lionel Art Boxcar, 08		50
___	**29951**	1954 Lionel Art Boxcar, 08	18	50
___	**29952**	GN Art Boxcar, 08		50
___	**29953**	SP Art Boxcar, 08		50
___	**29954**	2007 Lionel Dealer Christmas Boxcar, 07 u		50
___	**29955**	2008 Lionel Dealer Appreciation Boxcar, 08 u		70
___	**29956**	2008 Lionel Employee Christmas Boxcar, 08 u		60
___	**29957**	LRRC 2008 Christmas Boxcar, 08 u		42
___	**29958**	2009 Lionel Dealer Appreciation Boxcar, 09 u		40
___	**29959**	1952 Lionel Art Boxcar, 09	33	58
___	**29960**	Rock Island Art Boxcar, 09-10		58
___	**29961**	Meet the Beatles Boxcar 2-pack, 10-14		130
___	**29962**	Meet the Beatles Boxcar, 10-14		65
___	**29963**	The Beatles' Second Album Boxcar, 10-14		65
___	**29964**	2009 Lionel Employee Christmas Boxcar, 09 u		25
___	**29965**	Lionel Art Boxcar 2-pack, 10-11		116

MODERN 1970-2024		Exc	Mint	
29966	Lionel Art Boxcar, 12	45	55	___
29967	Lionel Santa Fe Art Boxcar, 10-11		35	___
29968	Beatles "A Hard Day's Night" Boxcar, 11-14		65	___
29969	Beatles "Something New" Boxcar, 11-14		65	___
29970	2010 Lionel Employee Christmas Boxcar, 10 u		25	___
29971	2011 Lionel Employee Christmas Boxcar, 11 u		25	___
29972	2012 Lionel Employee Christmas Boxcar, 12 u		25	___
29973	NYC Pacemaker Boxcar "175005", 10-11		60	___
29974	SP Boxcar "128133", 11		60	___
29975	Holiday Boxcar, 11		60	___
29976	Holiday Boxcar, 12-13		65	___
29977	2011 LRRC Holiday Boxcar, 11 u		60	___
29978	Railroad Museum of Pennsylvania Boxcar, 12		65	___
29979	Angela Trotta Thomas "Christmas Morning" Boxcar, 12-13		60	___
29980	Elvis Presley 35th Anniversary Boxcar, 12		70	___
29982	CV Milk Car "575" (std O), 15-16		80	___
29985	B&M Milk Car "1903" (std O), 15-16		80	___
29989	PFE Steel-sided Refrigerator Car 3-pack (std O), 14-15		240	___
29990	PFE Steel-sided Refrigerator Car "8383" (std O), 14-15		80	___
29991	PFE Steel-sided Refrigerator Car "8171" (std O), 14-15		80	___
29992	PFE Steel-sided Refrigerator Car "8080" (std O), 14-15		80	___
29994	U.S. Army Boxcar, 13-15		70	___
29995	U.S. Navy Boxcar, 13-15		70	___
29996	U.S. Marines Boxcar, 13-15		70	___
29997	U.S. Air Force Boxcar, 13-15		70	___
29998	U.S. National Guard Boxcar, 13-16		70	___
29999	U.S. Coast Guard Boxcar, 13-16		70	___
30000	PRR Keystone Super Freight Steam Train, TMCC, 05		450	___
30001	Santa Fe El Capitan Passenger Set, TrainSounds, 05-10	150	370	___
30002	Neil Young's Greendale Diesel Freight Set, 04		420	___
30003	Pennsylvania Flyer Operating Freight Expansion Pack, 05		99	___
30004	Pennsylvania Flyer Passenger Expansion Pack, 05-08		120	___
30005	Disney Passenger Train, 05		190	___
30007	NYC Flyer Operating Freight Expansion Pack, 05		99	___
30008	NYC Flyer Passenger Expansion Pack, 05-08		120	___
30011	Holiday Expansion Pack, 05		100	___
30012	Thomas the Tank Engine Expansion Pack, 05-13, 16		150	___
30016	NYC Flyer Steam Freight Set, 06-08		290	___
30018	Pennsylvania Flyer Steam Freight Set, 06-07	100	240	___
30020	North Pole Central Christmas Steam Train, 06-07		208	___
30021	Cascade Range Steam Logging Train, 06-08		190	___
30022	Southwest Diesel Freight Set, TrainSounds, 06	80	295	___
30024	UP Fast Freight Steam Set, TrainSounds, 06-07		340	___
30025	Chesapeake Super Freight Steam Set, TMCC, 06-07	238	488	___
30026	CP Diesel Freight Set, TMCC, 06		540	___
30034	Great Western Train Set with Lincoln Logs, 07-09	115	315	___
30035	Sodor Freight Expansion Pack, 06-09		120	___
30036	Great Western Expansion Pack, 07-08		120	___
30037	Pennsylvania Flyer Operating Freight Expansion Pack, 06-08		120	___
30038	NYC Flyer Operating Freight Expansion Pack, 06-08		120	___
30039	North Pole Central Passenger Expansion Pack, 06-11	55	155	___
30040	North Pole Central Freight Expansion Pack, 06-11		110	___
30041	Southwest Diesel Freight Expansion Pack, 06		110	___

		MODERN 1970-2024	Exc	Mint
___	30042	Cascade Range Expansion Pack, 06		110
___	30044	NYC Empire Builder Steam Freight Set, TMCC, 06	1073	2800
___	30045	Alaska Steam Work Train, 07-09	80	270
___	30046	Alaska Work Train Expansion Pack, 07-08		110
___	30047	Northwest Special Diesel Freight Set, TrainSounds, 07-08		295
___	30048	Northwest Special Freight Expansion Pack, 07-08		110
___	30049	D&RGW Fast Freight Set, TrainSounds, 08-09		320
___	30050	Pennsylvania Super Freight Set, CC, 08		450
___	30051	UP Diesel Freight Set, TMCC, 07		500
___	30056	Halloween Steam Freight Set, 07-10	85	225
___	30061	UPS Centennial Stream Freight Set, 07-08	100	230
___	30063	It's a Wonderful Life Christmas Steam Freight Set, 07 u	375	450
___	30064	Pennsylvania Speeder Set, traditional, K-Line, 06		75
___	30065	Best Friend of Charleston Locomotive, 07		425
___	30066/67	C&O Empire Builder Steam Freight Set, CC, 07-09		2700
___	30068	North Pole Central Christmas Freight Set, 08		220
___	30069	Thomas & Friends Passenger Train, 08-12		170
___	30070	Lionel Lines 4-4-2 Steam Freight Set, 07		300
___	30076	Disney Christmas Train, 07		400
___	30081	UP Merger Special GP38 Freight Set, 08	83	300
___	30082	UP Heritage Freight Car 3-pack, 08		100
___	30084	British Great Western Shakespeare Express Passenger Train, 08		300
___	30085	MTA Metro-North M-7 Commuter Car Set, 07-08	140	536
___	30087	Alien Spaceship Recovery Freight Set, 08-09	85	230
___	30088	John Bull Passenger Train, 08		430
___	30089	Pennsylvania Flyer Freight Set, 08-10		200
___	30091	ATSF Steam Freight Set, 08-09		270
___	30094	Chicago & North Western Passenger Set, 08		150
___	30096	Pennsylvania Keystone Special Steam Freight Set, 09		260
___	30103	NYC 0-8-0 Steam Freight Set, 09-10	167	291
___	30108	American Fire and Rescue GP20 Freight Set, 09-10		400
___	30109	Nutcracker Route Christmas Train Set, 10-11		270
___	30111	Pullman Passenger Expansion Pack, 09-16		155
___	30112	Eastern Freight Expansion Pack, 09-17		155
___	30114	MTA LIRR M-7 Commuter Set, 09		320
___	30116	Lone Ranger Wild West Freight Set, 09-13		400
___	30118	A Christmas Story Steam Freight Set, 09-12		340
___	30120	Menards C&NW Steam Passenger Set, 09		250
___	30121	ATSF Baby Madison Car 3-pack, 10-11		190
___	30122	Wizard of Oz Steam Freight Set, 10-12		310
___	30123	Boy Scouts of America Steam Freight Set, 10		310
___	30124	Thunder Valley Quarry Steam Freight Set, 10-11		300
___	30125	Rio Grande Ski Train, TrainSounds, 10-11		340
___	30126	Pennsylvania Flyer Steam Freight Set, 10		230
___	30127	Scout Steam Freight Set, 10-12		200
___	30128	Western Freight Expansion Pack, 10-12		138
___	30131	Chessie System Merger Diesel Freight Set, 10		300
___	30133	Strasburg Steam Passenger Set, 10-13		330
___	30135	Scout Freight Expansion Pack, 11-15		115
___	30136	Thunder Valley Quarry Freight Car Add-on 2-pack, 10-11		110
___	30138	Chessie System Merger Freight Car Add-on 2-pack, 10-11		120
___	30139	Santa Fe Flyer Steam Freight Set, 10		270

		Exc	Mint	
30141	Sodor Tank and Wagon Expansion Pack, 10-16		150	___
30142	Texas Special Freight Set, TrainSounds, 10-11		700	___
30144	Operation Eagle Justice Diesel Freight Set, 10-11	138	500	___
30145	Maple Leaf Diesel Freight Set, 10-11		550	___
30146	Menards Soo Line Freight Set, 10	175	275	___
30147	MTA Long Island M-7 Commuter Set, 11		320	___
30149	Bass Pro Shops North Pole Central Christmas Set, 08 u		220	___
30153	CSX Diesel Freight Set, 11		330	___
30154	BNSF Diesel Freight Set, 11		340	___
30155	M&StL Diesel Freight Set, 11-12		230	___
30156	NYC Flyer Freight Set, TrainSounds, 11		300	___
30157	M&StL Flatcar and Erie-Lack. Gondola 2-pack, 11-15		110	___
30158	Norfolk Southern GP38 Diesel Freight Train Set, 11		320	___
30159	Wabash Blue Bird Passenger Set, 11-12		360	___
30161	Boy Scouts Steam Freight Set, 11-13		320	___
30162	Thomas & Friends Christmas Set, 13-15		200	___
30164	Santa's Flyer Steam Freight Set, 11-13		250	___
30165	Candy Cane Transit Commuter 2-pack, 11-13		180	___
30166	Coca-Cola 125th Anniversary Steam Set, 11-12		355	___
30167	SP Merger Steam Freight Train Set , 12		400	___
30168	Rio Grande General Set, TrainSounds, 11-12		325	___
30169	NJ Transit Train Set, 11		350	___
30170	Sodor Freight 3-pack, 11-13		100	___
30171	GG1 Electric Freight Train Set, 11-13		550	___
30173	Santa Fe Flyer Freight Set, 11-12		270	___
30174	Pennsylvania Flyer Freight Set, 11-13	80	290	___
30176	Wegmans Steam Freight Train Set, 11 u		300	___
30177	Menards Milwaukee Road Steam Freight Set, 11 u		175	___
30178	ATSF Super Chief Diesel Passenger Train Set, 12-13		400	___
30179	RI Rocket Diesel Freight Train Set, 12-13	175	400	___
30180	Horseshoe Curve Steam Freight Train Set, 12-13		440	___
30181	CP Diesel Passenger Set, RailSounds, 13, 15		450	___
30183	Scout Remote Steam Freight Set, 13, 15		220	___
30184	Polar Express Steam Freight Set, 13		420	___
30185	NJ Transit Diesel MOW Train Set, 12-13		350	___
30186	KCS Southern Belle Diesel Freight Train Set, 12-13		350	___
30187	Titanic Centennial Diesel Freight Train Set, 12-13		450	___
30188	UP Flyer Steam Freight Train Set, 12-13		330	___
30189	LIRR Diesel Passenger Train Set, 12-13		330	___
30190	Thomas & Friends Set, LionChief, 12-16		200	___
30191	Sodor Work Set 3-pack, 12-15		100	___
30193	Peanuts Christmas Steam Freight Set, 12-15		370	___
30194	North Pole Express Steam Freight Set, 12-13		290	___
30195	Grand Central Express Diesel Passenger Train Set, 12-14		440	___
30196	Hershey's Steam Freight Train Set, 12-13		312	___
30200	NYC Flyer Steam Freight Train Set, 12-13		350	___
30205	Silver Bells Christmas Steam Freight Set, 513-14		240	___
30206	Area 51 RS3 Diesel Freight Set, 13		250	___
30207	Santa Fe RS3 Diesel Freight Set, 13		200	___
30210	CP Rail Grain SetDiesel Freight Set, 13		390	___
30211	BNSF Maxi Stack Diesel Freight Set, 13		440	___
30213	Northeast NS Heritage Diesel Freight Set, 13		410	___
30214	Peanuts Halloween Steam Freight Set, 13, 15-16		320	___

			Exc	Mint
____	**30217**	SP Black Widow Diesel Freight Set, 13, 15		460
____	**30218**	Polar Express Steam Passenger Set, 13-16		400
____	**30218**	Polar Express Steam Passenger Set w/Personalized Tender, LionChief, 18		440
____	**30219**	Gingerbread Junction Steam Freight Set, 13-14		290
____	**30220**	Polar Express 10th Anniversary Passenger Set, 13-14, 16		500
____	**30221**	Diesel Remote Control Set, 13-16		200
____	**30222**	Percy Remote Control Set, 13-15		200
____	**30223**	James Remote Control Set, 13-15		200
____	**30224**	Pennsylvania Limited Steam Passenger Set, 13		340
____	**30225**	Medal of Honor Train, 13	113	430
____	**30226**	NS Diesel Freight Set, RailSounds, 13		410
____	**30228**	Chattanooga Express Steam Passenger Set, 13		250
____	**30233**	Pennsylvania Flyer Remote Steam Freight Set, 13-17		280
____	**31569**	Western & Atlantic Passenger Car 2-pack, 08		100
____	**31700**	Postwar Girls Freight Set, 01	350	570
____	**31701**	Postwar Boys Freight Set, 02	46	373
____	**31704**	Alton Limited Steam Passenger Set, 02		870
____	**31705**	50th Anniversary Hudson Passenger Set, 02		910
____	**31706**	UP Burro Crane Set, 02	60	210
____	**31707**	C&O Diesel Freight Set, 03	80	280
____	**31708**	Postwar "1805" Marines Missile Launch Train, 03	300	419
____	**31710**	BN Diesel Coal Train, RailSounds, 03	345	745
____	**31711**	Postwar "1563W" Wabash Diesel Freight Set, RailSounds, 03	200	570
____	**31712**	UP Alco PA Diesel Passenger Set, RailSounds, 03	475	1495
____	**31713**	Southern Crescent Limited Steam Passenger Set, RailSounds, 03		1195
____	**31714**	Amtrak Acela Diesel Passenger Set, RailSounds, 04-05	800	2000
____	**31715**	Fire Rescue Steam Freight Set, 02		300
____	**31716**	Fire Rescue Steam Freight Set, 03		280
____	**31717**	CP Rail Snow Removal Train, 03	90	255
____	**31718**	SP "Oil Can" Tank Train Freight Set, 03		1600
____	**31719**	Western Maryland Fireball Diesel Freight Set, 04	193	363
____	**31720**	FEC Champion Diesel Passenger Set, RailSounds, 04	400	900
____	**31721**	Postwar "13138" Majestic Electric Freight Set, RailSounds, 04	277	580
____	**31724**	Nabisco 3-car Passenger Set, 03		110
____	**31727**	Postwar "2291W" D&RGW Diesel Freight Set, RailSounds, 04	421	640
____	**31728**	Elvis "He Dared to Rock" Steam Freight Set, 04		325
____	**31730**	Norman Rockwell Boxcar 4-pack, 05		95
____	**31733**	Jones & Laughlin Steel Slag Train, 05		338
____	**31734**	Chessie Steam Special Passenger Set, TMCC, 05		405
____	**31735**	Chessie Diesel Freight Set, TMCC, 05-06		670
____	**31736**	CP Diesel Grain Train, TMCC, 05	457	813
____	**31737**	Napa Valley Diesel Wine Train, CC, 05		1000
____	**31739**	Postwar "13150" Hudson Steam Freight Set, Super O, 05	350	940
____	**31740**	Postwar "2519W" Virginian Diesel Freight Set, TMCC, 05-07	456	710
____	**31742**	Postwar "2544W" ATSF Super Chief Passenger Set, 05	288	700
____	**31746**	GN Mountain Mover Steam Freight Set, 12-13		430
____	**31747**	Pennsylvania Electric Ballast Train, TMCC, 06	205	550
____	**31748**	Santa Fe U28CG Diesel Freight Set (std O), TMCC, 06-07		770
____	**31749**	Pennsylvania Diesel Coal Train, TMCC, 06	231	770

		Exc	Mint	
31750	NYC Hotbox Reefer Steam Freight Set, TMCC, 06-07		530	___
31751	New York City Transit Authority R27 Subway Train, CC, 07		700	___
31752	Postwar 2269W B&O Diesel Freight Set, TMCC, 06-07	233	740	___
31753	Postwar 2551W GN Diesel Freight Set, TMCC, 06-08	219	740	___
31754	Postwar "2545WS" N&W Space Freight Set, TMCC, 06-07	250	957	___
31755	Texas Special Diesel Passenger Set, CC, 07-08	640	1550	___
31757	Postwar "2289WS" Berkshire Freight Set, CC, 07	225	750	___
31758	Postwar "2270W" JC Diesel Passenger Set, CC, 08		750	___
31760	CSX SD40-2 Diesel Husky Stack Car Set, CC, 07-08		770	___
31765	Postwar "11268" C&O Diesel Freight Set, 08		580	___
31767	Bethlehem Steel Rolling Stock Set, K-Line, 06		100	___
31768	B&O Rolling Stock Set, K-Line, 06		100	___
31772	Conrail LionMaster Diesel Freight Set, CC, 08-09		535	___
31773	NS Dash 9 Diesel TankTrain Set, CC, 08	167	798	___
31774	AEC Burro Crane Set, traditional, 09-11		605	___
31775	Postwar "1562" Burlington GP Passenger Set, 08	113	470	___
31776	"2219W" Lackawanna Train Master Freight Set, 08		415	___
31777	"2124W" GG1 Passenger Set, 08	238	452	___
31778	"1484WS" Steam Passenger Set, 08		610	___
31779	Amtrak HHP-8 Amfleet Passenger Set, CC, 09		500	___
31782	ATSF Crane Car and Boom Car, CC (std O), 09-10		560	___
31783	BNSF Ice Cold Express Diesel Freight Set, CC, 10		1000	___
31784	No. 1593 UP Work Train Set, 09	128	470	___
31787	CN SD70M-2 Diesel Coal Train, CC, 09		800	___
31790	PRR GG1 Passenger Set, 10		500	___
31791	NYC LionMaster Diesel Freight Set, CC, 10	150	700	___
31793	White Pass & Yukon Freight Car Add-on 3-pack, 10-11, 13		195	___
31794	New York City Transit R30 Subway 4-pack, 10	375	700	___
31795	Pere Marquette Freight Car 3-pack (std O), 10-11		210	___
31796	Feather Route Freight Car 3-pack (std O), 10-11		210	___
31797	New York City Transit R16 Subway Set, CC, 10	1050	1460	___
31799	GN Empire Steam Freight Express Set, 10		430	___
31901	Christmas Steam Freight Set, 02		145	___
31902	PRR K4 Freight Set, 01-02		580	___
31904	C&O Steam Freight Set, RailSounds, 01		400	___
31905	NH Diesel Freight Set, CC, 01		660	___
31907	PRR Atlantic Freight Set, 01 u		400	___
31908	Reading Hobo Express Freight Set, 01 u		365	___
31909	Santa Fe Shell Tank Car Freight Set, 01 u		320	___
31910	Soo Line Diesel Freight Set, 01 u		365	___
31911	Snap-On Anniversary Steam Freight Set, 00 u	113	615	___
31913	PRR Flyer Steam Freight Set, 01		126	___
31914	NYC Flyer Steam Freight Set, RailSounds, 01-02		170	___
31915	Chessie GP38 Diesel Freight Set, 01-02	70	155	___
31916	Santa Fe Steam Freight Set, 01		300	___
31918	C&O Steam Freight Set, SignalSounds, 01		315	___
31919	T&P Steam Passenger Set, RailSounds, 01		210	___
31920	L.L. Bean Freight Set, 01 u		270	___
31922	Snap-On Tool Diesel Freight Set, 01 u	90	356	___
31923	PRR Flyer Freight Set, 01 u		130	___
31924	Union Pacific RS3 Diesel Freight Set, 02		95	___
31926	Area 51 FA Diesel Freight Set, 02		160	___
31928	Great Train Robbery Set, 02	70	180	___

MODERN 1970-2024			Exc	Mint
___	31931	Ballyhoo Brothers Circus Train, 02		190
___	31932	NYC Limited Passenger Set, RailSounds, 02		285
___	31933	Santa Fe Steam Freight Set, RailSounds, 02		320
___	31934	Lionel 20th Century Express Steam Freight Set, 00 u		285
___	31936	Pennsylvania Flyer Steam Freight Set, 03-05		158
___	31938	Southern Diesel Freight Set, 03-04	75	160
___	31939	Great Train Robbery Steam Freight Set, 03		185
___	31940	NYC Flyer Steam Freight Set, RailSounds, 03		225
___	31941	Winter Wonderland Railroad Christmas Train, 03		150
___	31942	Norman Rockwell Christmas Train, 03	70	330
___	31944	NYC Limited Diesel Passenger Set, RailSounds, 03		250
___	31945	Santa Fe Steam Super Freight Set, RailSounds, 03		350
___	31946	Disney Christmas Steam Train, 04-05		310
___	31947	World of Disney Steam Freight Set, 03		215
___	31950	Kraft Holiday UP RS3 Diesel Freight Set, 02 u	35	149
___	31952	Great Northern Glacier Route Diesel Freight Set, 03-04		110
___	31953	"Riding the Rails" Hobo Train Set, 03-04		225
___	31956	Thomas the Tank Engine Set, 04-07	88	195
___	31958	Santa Fe Flyer Steam Freight Set, RailSounds, 04		205
___	31960	Polar Express Steam Passenger Set, 04-13	180	420
___	31961	Bloomingdale's Pennsylvania Flyer Steam Freight Set, 02 u		160
___	31962	Nickel Plate Road Super Freight Set, RailSounds, 04		350
___	31963	Southern Pacific Overnight Steam Freight Set, 04		340
___	31966	Holiday Tradition Steam Freight Set, 04-05		210
___	31969	NYC Flyer Steam Freight Set, RailSounds, 04		205
___	31976	Yukon Special Diesel Freight Set, 05		225
___	31977	New York Central Flyer Steam Freight Set, 05		250
___	31985	Santa Fe Steam Fast Freight Set, TrainSounds, 05		320
___	31987	Mickey's Holiday Express Train, 04		280
___	31989	UP Overland Freight Express Set, 04		880
___	31990	Copper Range Steam Freight Mine Set, 05		175
___	31993	NS Black Diamond Diesel Freight Set, TMCC, 05		500
___	32900	DC Billboard, 99		24
___	32902	Construction Zone Signs, set of 6, 99-19		10
___	32904	Hellgate Bridge, 99	213	427
___	32905	Irvington Factory, 99-00		295
___	32910	Rotary Coal Tipple with bathtub gondola, 02	147	575
___	32919	Animated Maiden Rescue, 99		65
___	32920	Animated Pylon with airplane, 99	50	130
___	32921	Electric Coaling Station, 99-01		125
___	32922	Orange Highway Barrels, set of 6, 99-24		10
___	32923	Accessory Transformer, 99-03, 06-16		46
___	32929	Icing Station with Santa, 99		90
___	32930	Power Supply Set w/ZW controller, 99-02, 06-09	240	425
___	32933	Christmas Stocking Hanger Set, 4-piece, 99-00		50
___	32934	Stocking Hanger, gondola, 99-00		15
___	32935	Stocking Hanger, boxcar, 99-00		15
___	32960	Hindenburger Cafe, 99		210
___	32961	Route 66 UFO Cafe, 99		213
___	32987	Hobo Campfire, 99-00	25	45
___	32988	Postwar "192" Railroad Control Tower, 99-00		75
___	32989	Postwar "464" Sawmill, 99-00		75
___	32990	Linex Oil Derrick, 99-00		55

		Exc	Mint	
32991	WLLC Radio Station, 99		75	___
32996	Postwar "362" Barrel Loader, 00		125	___
32997	Aluminum Rico Station, 00		300	___
32998	Hobby Shop, 99-00	80	300	___
32999	Hellgate Bridge, 99-00	113	400	___
33000	GP9 Diesel "3000," RailScope video camera system, 88-90	130	175	___
33002	RailScope Television Monitor, 88-90	53	78	___
34102	Amtrak Shelter, 04-08		25	___
34108	Lionelville Suburban House, 03		20	___
34109	Lionelville Large Suburban House, 03		15	___
34110	Lionelville Estate House, 03		30	___
34111	Lionelville Deluxe Fieldstone House, 03		17	___
34112	Lionelville Fieldstone House, 03		17	___
34113	Lionelville Large Suburban House, 03		17	___
34114	Late Illuminated Station and Terrace, red trim, 03		475	___
34117	Early Illuminated Station and Terrace, green trim, 03		475	___
34120	TMCC Direct Lockon, 04-24		60	___
34121	Lionelville Bungalow, 04		20	___
34122	Lionelville Bungalow with garage, 04		20	___
34123	Lionelville Bungalow with addition, 04		20	___
34124	Lionelville Anastasia's Bakery, 04		20	___
34125	Lionelville Cotton's Candy, 04		20	___
34126	Lionelville Market, 04		20	___
34127	Lionelville O'Grady's Tavern, 04		22	___
34128	Lionelville Pharmacy, 04		15	___
34129	Lionelville Kiddie City Toy Store, 04		20	___
34130	Lionelville Jim's 5&10, 04		25	___
34131	Lionelville Al's Hardware, 04		30	___
34144	Santa Fe Scrap Yard, 05-06		80	___
34145	New Haven Scrap Yard, 06		100	___
34149	Sly Fox and the Hunter, 05-07		80	___
34150	Reading Room, 05-06		70	___
34158	Ring Toss Midway Game, 05-06		20	___
34159	Camel Race Midway Game, 05-06		20	___
34162	Operating Oil Pump, 04-09		53	___
34163	Speeder Shed, 04-06		30	___
34164	Nutcracker Operating Gateman, 05-08		80	___
34190	Carousel, 04-06		165	___
34191	Hobo Depot, 04-05		70	___
34192	Operating Lumberjacks, 04-06		60	___
34193	UPS Animated Billboard, 04		30	___
34194	UPS Package Station, 05		120	___
34195	UPS People Pack, 05-11		27	___
34210	TMCC Direct Lockon, 09		52	___
34359	2011 Lionel Dealer Appreciation Boxcar, 11 u		40	___
34360	2012 Lionel Dealer Appreciation Boxcar, 12 u		40	___
34500	Rio Grande FT Diesel "5484", traditional, 06		245	___
34501	Southern FT Diesel "4102", traditional, 06		400	___
34504	B&O F3 Diesel A Unit "2368," nonpowered, 06-07	100	250	___
34505	B&O E7 Diesel AA Set, CC, 07		700	___
34508	PRR E7 Diesel AA Set, CC, 07		700	___
34509	PRR E7 Diesel B Unit, nonpowered (std O), 07		170	___
34510	PRR E7 Diesel B Unit, powered, CC, 07		300	___

			Exc	Mint
___	**34511**	NYC F7 Diesel ABA Set, CC, 07-08		900
___	**34512**	NYC F7 Diesel B Unit "2439," powered, CC, 07-08		300
___	**34513**	WP F7 Diesel ABA Set, CC, 07-08		900
___	**34514**	WP F7 Diesel B Unit "918C," powered, CC, 07-08		300
___	**34515**	NYC F7 Diesel Breakdown B Unit "2440," RailSounds, 07		270
___	**34518**	PRR E7 Diesel Breakdown B Unit, RailSounds, 07		270
___	**34519**	NYC Sharknose RF-16 Diesel AA Set, CC, 07-08		630
___	**34520**	NYC Sharknose Diesel B Unit "3818," nonpowered (std O), 07-08		160
___	**34521**	Santa Fe F3 Diesel A Unit "17", traditional, 07		265
___	**34522**	Santa Fe F3 Diesel B Unit "17," nonpowered (std O), 07		150
___	**34544**	ATSF F3 Diesel B Unit, CC, 08		270
___	**34545**	D&RGW F3 Diesel B Unit, CC, 08		270
___	**34546**	Southern F3 Diesel B Unit, CC, 08		270
___	**34547**	Texas Special F3 Diesel B Unit, CC, 08		270
___	**34559**	Archive New Haven F3 Diesel AA Set, 10		500
___	**34564**	SP Alco PA Diesel AA Set, CC, 10-11		750
___	**34567**	SP Alco PB B Unit, CC, 10-11		400
___	**34568**	ATSF Alco PA AA Diesel Set, CC, 11		750
___	**34569**	ATSF Alco PB Diesel, CC, 11		400
___	**34570**	B&O FA Diesel AA Set, CC, 10		650
___	**34573**	Postwar Scale ATSF F3 AA Diesel Set, CC, 11		700
___	**34576**	Postwar Scale NYC F3 AA Diesel Set, CC, 11		700
___	**34579**	Postwar Scale ATSF F3 B Unit, CC, 11		380
___	**34580**	Postwar Scale NYC F3 B Unit, CC, 11		380
___	**34581**	Postwar "2331" Virginian Train Master Diesel, CC, 10		495
___	**34582**	Postwar "2373" CP F3 Diesel AA Set, CC, 10		673
___	**34585**	Postwar "2375" CP F3 B Unit, CC, 10		350
___	**34586**	Postwar "2378" MILW F3 Diesel AB Set, CC, 10		700
___	**34589**	Postwar "2377" MILW F3 A, powered, CC, 10		425
___	**34594**	UP Alco PA AA Diesel Set, CC, 11		750
___	**34597**	UP Alco PB Diesel, CC, 11		400
___	**34600**	SP GP30 Diesel "5010," CC, 11		500
___	**34601**	SP GP30 Diesel "5012," CC, 11		500
___	**34602**	SP GP30 Diesel "5014", 11		380
___	**34603**	SP GP30 Diesel "5017," nonpowered, 11		240
___	**34604**	Conrail GP30 Diesel "2178," CC, 11		500
___	**34605**	Conrail GP30 Diesel "2180," CC, 11		500
___	**34606**	Conrail GP30 Diesel "2182", 11		380
___	**34607**	Conrail GP30 Diesel "2185," nonpowered, 11		240
___	**34608**	Lionelville & Western GP30 Diesel "1100," CC, 11		450
___	**34609**	Lionelville & Western GP30 Diesel "1103," CC, 11		450
___	**34610**	Lionelville & Western GP30 Diesel "1107", 11		330
___	**34611**	Lionelville & Western GP30 Diesel "1112," nonpowered, 11		190
___	**34612**	NS SD70M-2 Diesel "2658," CC, 11		550
___	**34613**	NS SD70M-2 Diesel "2663," CC, 11		550
___	**34614**	CN SD70M-2 Diesel "8020," CC, 11		550
___	**34615**	CN SD70M-2 Diesel "8024," CC, 11		550
___	**34616**	FEC SD70M-2 Diesel "101," CC, 11		550
___	**34617**	FEC SD70M-2 Diesel "103," CC, 11		550
___	**34618**	George Bush SD70ACe Diesel "4141," CC, 11	219	611
___	**34619**	NH SD70ACe Diesel "8696," CC, 11		550
___	**34620**	NH SD70ACe Diesel "8699," CC, 11		550

		Exc	Mint
34623	Texas Special SD70ACe Diesel "6340," CC, 11		550 ___
34624	Texas Special SD70ACe Diesel "6344," CC, 11		550 ___
34625	NP F3 AA Diesel Set, CC, 11		700 ___
34628	NP F3 Diesel B Unit "6005C," CC, 11		380 ___
34629	NP F3 Diesel B Unit "6006C," nonpowered, 11		240 ___
34630	Frisco F3 AA Diesel Set, CC, 11		700 ___
34633	Frisco F3 Diesel B Unit, CC, 11		380 ___
34634	Frisco F3 Diesel B Unit, nonpowered, 11		260 ___
34635	ATSF F3 AA Diesel Set, CC, 11		700 ___
34638	ATSF F3 Diesel B Unit, CC, 11		380 ___
34639	ATSF F3 Diesel B Unit, nonpowered, 11		240 ___
34640	GTW F3 AA Diesel Set, CC, 11		700 ___
34643	GTW F3 Diesel B Unit, CC, 11		380 ___
34644	GTW F3 Diesel B Unit, nonpowered, 11		260 ___
34645	CN F3 AA Diesel Set, CC, 11		700 ___
34648	CN F3 Diesel B Unit, CC, 11		380 ___
34649	CN F3 Diesel B Unit, nonpowered, 11		260 ___
34650	MILW DD35A Diesel "1535," CC, 11		600 ___
34651	MILW DD35A Diesel "1537," nonpowered, 11		440 ___
34662	RI GP9 Diesel "1331," CC, 12-13		480 ___
34663	RI GP9 Diesel "1327," CC, 12-13		480 ___
34664	GN GP9 Diesel "688," CC, 12-13		480 ___
34665	GN GP9 Diesel "695," CC, 12-13		480 ___
34666	L&N GP9 Diesel "504," CC, 12-13		480 ___
34667	L&N GP9 Diesel "525," CC, 12-13		480 ___
34668	CN GP90 Diesel "4463" CC, 12		480 ___
34669	CN GP90 Diesel "4455," CC, 12		480 ___
34670	C&O GP9 Diesel "6240," CC, 12-13		480 ___
34671	C&O GP9 Diesel "6243," CC, 12		480 ___
34672	PRR Baldwin Centipede Diesel AA, CC, 12-13		2200 ___
34673	UP Baldwin Centipede Diesel AA, CC, 12		2200 ___
34676	PRR Baldwin Centipede Diesel "5821," CC, 12-14		1100 ___
34677	Seaboard Baldwin Centipede Diesel "4503," CC, 12-14		1100 ___
34680	NdeM Baldwin Centipede Diesel "6402," CC, 12-14		1100 ___
34681	UP GP9 Diesel "256," CC, 12		480 ___
34682	UP GP9 Diesel "261," CC, 12		480 ___
34683	PRR Baldwin Centipede Diesel AA, CC, 12-13		2200 ___
34686	Baldwin Demonstrator Centipede AA, CC, 12		2200 ___
34689	WM F7 AA Diesel Set, CC, 12-13		730 ___
34692	WM F7 B Unit "410," CC, 12-13		400 ___
34693	WM F7 B Unit, 12-13		250 ___
34694	L&N F7 AA Diesel Set, CC, 12		730 ___
34697	L&N F7 B Unit "900," CC, 12-13		400 ___
34698	L&N F7 B Unit, 12-13		250 ___
34701	PRR Baldwin RF-16 Diesel AA Set, CC, 12-14		730 ___
34704	PRR Baldwin RF-16 Diesel B Unit, CC, 12-14		400 ___
34705	PRR Baldwin RF-16 Diesel B Unit, nonpowered, 12-14		250 ___
34731	NH Alco RS-11 Diesel "1413," nonpowered, 12		240 ___
34732	LV Alco RS-11 Diesel "7640," CC, 12		480 ___
34733	LV Alco RS-11 Diesel "7642," CC, 12		480 ___
34734	LV Alco RS-11 Diesel "7643," nonpowered, 12		240 ___
34735	ATSF GP9 Diesel "726," CC, 12		480 ___
34736	ATSF GP9 Diesel "741," CC, 12		480 ___

			Exc	Mint
___	**34737**	NP GP9 Diesel "202," CC, 12		480
___	**34738**	NP GP9 Diesel "317," CC, 12-13		480
___	**34739**	RI GP9 Diesel "1325," nonpowered, 12		240
___	**34740**	GN GP9 Diesel "668," nonpowered, 12		240
___	**34741**	L&N GP9 Diesel "531," nonpowered, 12		240
___	**34742**	CN GP90 Diesel "4527," nonpowered, 12		240
___	**34743**	C&O GP9 Diesel "6249," nonpowered, 12		240
___	**34744**	UP GP9 Diesel "268," nonpowered, 12		240
___	**34745**	Monon Alco C-420 Diesel "509," CC, 12-13		530
___	**34746**	Monon Alco C-420 Diesel "512," CC, 12-13		530
___	**34747**	Monon Alco C-420 Diesel "514," nonpowered, 12-13		260
___	**34748**	LV Alco C-420 Diesel "404," CC, 12		530
___	**34749**	LV Alco C-420 Diesel "412," CC, 12		530
___	**34750**	LV Alco C-420 Diesel "414," nonpowered, 12		260
___	**34754**	Alaska Alco C-420 Diesel "1210," CC, 12		530
___	**34755**	Alaska Alco C-420 Diesel "1214," CC, 12		530
___	**34756**	Alaska Alco C-420 Diesel "1217," nonpowered, 12		260
___	**34757**	Seaboard Alco C-420 Diesel "127," CC, 12-13		530
___	**34758**	Seaboard Alco C-420 Diesel "129," CC, 12-13		530
___	**34759**	Seaboard Alco C-420 Diesel "134," nonpowered, 12-13		260
___	**34760**	NKP Alco C-420 Diesel "578," CC, 12-13		530
___	**34761**	NKP Alco C-420 Diesel "575," CC, 12-13		530
___	**34762**	NKP Alco C-420 Diesel "572," nonpowered, 12-13		260
___	**34763**	CNJ Scale NW2 Diesel Switcher "1060," CC, 12		470
___	**34764**	CNJ Scale NW2 Diesel Switcher "1061," CC, 12		470
___	**34765**	KCS Scale NW2 Diesel Switcher "1221," CC, 12		470
___	**34766**	KCS Scale NW2 Diesel Switcher "1224," CC, 12		470
___	**34767**	L&N Scale NW2 Diesel Switcher "2203," CC, 12		470
___	**34768**	L&N Scale NW2 Diesel Switcher "2206," CC, 12		470
___	**34769**	MKT Scale NW2 Diesel Switcher "8," CC, 12		470
___	**34770**	MKT Scale NW2 Diesel Switcher "12," CC, 12		470
___	**34771**	Reading Scale NW2 Diesel Switcher "102," CC, 12		470
___	**34772**	Reading Scale NW2 Diesel Switcher "104," CC, 12		470
___	**34773**	PRR Scale NW2 Diesel Switcher "9163," CC, 12		470
___	**34774**	PRR Scale NW2 Diesel Switcher "9171," CC, 12		470
___	**34775**	N&W SD40-2 Diesel "6106," nonpowered, 12-13		240
___	**34776**	N&W SD40-2 Diesel "6121," CC, 12-13		530
___	**34777**	N&W SD40-2 Diesel "6109," CC, 12-14		530
___	**34778**	CSX SD40-2 Diesel "8023," nonpowered, 12-13		240
___	**34779**	CSX SD40-2 Diesel "8028," CC, 12-13		530
___	**34780**	CSX SD40-2 Diesel "8033," CC, 12-13		530
___	**34781**	BN SD40-2 Diesel "7140," nonpowered, 12-13		240
___	**34782**	BN SD40-2 Diesel "7153," CC, 12-13		530
___	**34783**	BN SD40-2 Diesel "7162," CC, 12-13		530
___	**34784**	Frisco SD40-2 Diesel "957," CC, 12-13		530
___	**34785**	Frisco SD40-2 Diesel "950" nonpowered, 12-13		240
___	**34786**	Frisco SD40-2 Diesel "952," CC, 12-13		530
___	**34787**	C&NW SD40-2 Diesel "6816," nonpowered, 12-13		240
___	**34788**	C&NW SD40-2 Diesel "6820," CC, 12-13		530
___	**34789**	C&NW SD40-2 Diesel "6832," CC, 12-13		530
___	**34790**	MKT SD40-2 Diesel "602," nonpowered, 12-13		240
___	**34791**	MKT SD40-2 Diesel "609," CC, 12-13		530
___	**34792**	MKT SD40-2 Diesel "620," CC, 12-13		530

MODERN 1970-2024		Exc	Mint
35100	NYC Vista Dome Car "7012", 07-09		45
35101	NYC Baggage Car "5028", 07		40
35102	Santa Fe El Capitan Streamliner Diner, 07		65
35124	Alton Limited Madison Passenger Car 4-pack, 08-10		240
35128	ATSF El Capitan Baggage Car "2103", 08		70
35129	ATSF El Capitan Vista Dome Car "3153", 08		70
35130	Polar Express Disappearing Hobo Car, 08-14, 16-17	45	77
35133	MTA Metro-North M-7 Commuter Add-on 2-pack, 07-08		85
35134	North Pole Central Vista Dome Car, 08	23	182
35135	North Pole Central Diner, 08-10		45
35136	Alaska Heavyweight Passenger Car 4-pack, 08		240
35137	Alaska Baggage Car w/TrainSounds, 08		200
35138	Alton Limited Baggage Car w/TrainSounds, 08		200
35144	Alton Limited Heavyweight Coach "Webster Groves", 08		60
35145	Alton Limited Heavyweight Combination Car "Missouri", 08		60
35146	Alton Limited Heavyweight Diner "Bloomington", 08		60
35147	Alton Limited Heavyweight Observation "Chicago", 08		60
35167	PRR Diner "2044", 10		52
35168	PRR Coach "4046", 09		52
35173	North Pole Central Blitzen Coach, 09	23	133
35174	MTA LIRR M-7 Add-on 2-pack, 09		98
35184	Western & Atlantic Baggage Car, 09		60
35185	Great Western Passenger Car 2-pack, 09		100
35193	PRR Streamliner 4-pack, 10-11		250
35200	Strasburg Observation Car, 10		60
35202	Rio Grande Ski Train Vista Dome "California", 10-11		80
35203	Rio Grande Ski Train Baggage Car "1230", 10-11		75
35204	Rio Grande Ski Train Observation "Kansas", 10-11		75
35205	D&RGW Pikes Peak Add-on Coach, 10-11		70
35211	Strasburg Passenger Car Add-on 2-pack, 10		100
35214	Rio Grande Winter Park Diner, 11		70
35219	Hallow's Eve Express Passenger Car 2-pack, 11		120
35229	Hogwarts Express Dementors Coach, 11-15		60
35239	NJ Transit 2-pack Passenger Car Add-on, 11-14		100
35247	Grand Central Express Passenger Car 2-pack, 12-13		140
35250	North Pole Coach 2-pack, 12-13		120
35256	Hallow's Eve Express Passenger Car 2-pack #2, 12		120
35257	ATSF Vista Dome, 12		70
35258	ATSF Baggage Car, 12-13		70
35259	LIRR Passenger Car 2-pack, 12-15		110
35281	ATSF Super Chief Diner "1495", 13		70
35282	LIRR Jamaica Coach, 13-15		60
35283	CP Baggage Car and Diner 2-pack, 13		130
35286	Peanuts Coach 3-pack, 13		165
35290	Polar Express Passenger Car Add-on 2-pack, 13-14, 16		150
35293	Angela Trotta Thomas "Toyland Express" Boxcar, 13		45
35294	Polar Express Snow Tower, 13-14		28
35295	Christmas Billboard Set, 13-14, 16		13
35403	NYC 20th Century Limited 18" Aluminum Passenger Car 4-pack (std O), 08		625
35408	NYC 20th Century Limited 18" Aluminum Passenger Car 2-pack (std O), 08		325
35411	NYC 20th Century Limited Diner, StationSounds (std O), 08		325

			Exc	Mint
___	**35412**	Lenny Dean Passenger Coach, 08		100
___	**35413**	LL Streamliner Car 2-pack, 08		270
___	**35415**	UP 18" Streamliner Car 4-pack (std O), 08		625
___	**35423**	UP 18" Streamliner Car 2-pack (std O), 08		325
___	**35430**	Amtrak Coach		45
___	**35431**	Amtrak Coach		45
___	**35432**	Amtrak Coach		45
___	**35433**	Amfleet Phase IVB Coach 2-pack (std O), 10		140
___	**35445**	SP Shasta Daylight 18" Passenger Car 4-pack (std O), 11		640
___	**35446**	SP Shasta Daylight 18" Passenger Car 2-pack (std O), 11		320
___	**35454**	Amfleet Cab Control End Car (std O), 10		250
___	**35473**	Amfleet Capstone Coach 3-pack (std O), 10		180
___	**35481**	NYC Add-on Passenger Car "M-498", 11		120
___	**35490**	Alaska Budd RDC Combination Car "702," nonpowered, 11		130
___	**35497**	RI Budd RDC Combination Car "751," nonpowered, 11		130
___	**35498**	RI Budd RDC Coach "750," nonpowered, 11		130
___	**35499**	Alaska Budd RDC Coach "712," nonpowered, 11		130
___	**36000**	Route 66 Flatcar with 2 red sedans, 98		44
___	**36001**	Route 66 Flatcar with 2 wagons, 98		42
___	**36002**	Pratt's Hollow Passenger Car 4-pack, 98		445
___	**36006**	Uranium Flatcar "6508", 99		60
___	**36016**	Flatcar with propellers, 98		45
___	**36020**	Flatcar "TT-6424" with auto frames, 99		32
___	**36021**	Alaska Flatcar "6424" with airplane, 99		44
___	**36024**	J.B. Hunt Flatcar "64245" with trailer, 99		44
___	**36025**	J.B. Hunt Flatcar "64246" with trailer, 99		50
___	**36026**	Flatcar with J.B. Hunt trailers 2-pack, 99		85
___	**36027**	Tredegar Iron Works Flatcar with cannon, 99		45
___	**36028**	Heavy Artillery Flatcar with cannon, 99		45
___	**36029**	SP Auto Carrier "516712", 99		44
___	**36030**	Troublesome Truck #1, 99		35
___	**36031**	Troublesome Truck #2, 99		35
___	**36032**	Christmas Gondola "6462" with presents, 99		35
___	**36036**	C&O Gondola, 99		20
___	**36038**	Construction Zone Gondola, 99 u	11	20
___	**36040**	Bethlehem Flatcar with block (SSS), 99		75
___	**36041**	Bethlehem Ore Car (SSS), 99		40
___	**36043**	Custom Consist Flatcar with pickup truck, 99		40
___	**36044**	Custom Consist Flatcar with dragster, 99		40
___	**36045**	Flatcar with dragster, 04		30
___	**36046**	Flatcar with custom truck, 04		30
___	**36047**	Construction Zone Gondola, 99 u	11	20
___	**36048**	Construction Zone Gondola, 99 u	11	20
___	**36051**	NYC Flatcar w/Bulkhead, 04	8	20
___	**36054**	Archaeological Expedition Gondola with eggs, 00 u		55
___	**36055**	Flatcar with dragster, 01 u		30
___	**36056**	Flatcar with roadster, 01 u		30
___	**36059**	"Season's Greetings" Gondola, 99 u		50
___	**36062**	NYC 6462 Gondola, 99-00		22
___	**36063**	Conrail Gondola "604768", 99-00		20
___	**36064**	Billboard Flatcar "6424", 00		41
___	**36065**	Wabash Flatcar "25536" with trailer, 00		35
___	**36066**	Christmas Gondola with presents, 00		32

		Exc	Mint
36067	King Auto Sales Flatcar "6424" with pink Cadillac, 00		40
36068	Pine Peak Tree Transport Gondola, 00	38	55
36079	Service Station Ltd. Flatcar with trailer, 00		34
36082	D&H Flatcar "16533" w/Whirlpool trailer, 00	27	45
36083	Santa Fe Gondola "168998", 01		17
36084	Grand Trunk Western Coil Car, 00		32
36085	FEC Coil Car, 00		29
36086	SP Flatcar with trailer, 01	34	35
36087	Flatcar "6424" with wooden whistle, 01		25
36088	Allis Chalmers Condenser Car "6519", 00		43
36089	Frisco Flatcar with airplane, 00		35
36090	TT Flatcar "6424" with Pepsi truck, 01		44
36091	Maersk Flatcar "250129" with die-cast tractors, 00		55
36092	Maersk Flatcar "250130" with die-cast frames, 00		55
36093	Soo TT Auto Carrier "906760", 00		49
36094	PC F9 Well Car "768122", 01		41
36095	Christmas Chase Gondola, 01		37
36098	PRR Gondola "385186", 01		20
36099	NYC Flatcar with stakes and bulkheads, 01		25
36104	Area 51 3-D Tank Car, 07		60
36105	Skelly Oil 1-D Tank Car, 08		55
36107	WC Wood-sided Refrigerator Car, 08		35
36108	Candy Cane 1-D Tank Car, 07		60
36109	Alaska 3-D Tank Car, 07		40
36110	CP 1-D Tank Car, 07		30
36111	D&RGW 1-D Tank Car, 07		24
36112	NP 3-D Tank Car, 08		35
36113	IC 1-D Tank Car, 08		35
36114	ART Wood-sided Reefer, 08		35
36117	Lionel Lines 2-D Tank Car, 08		50
36118	NYC Pastel Stock Car "63561", 08-09		55
36128	Texas & Pacific 3-D Tank Car, 09		40
36129	British Columbia 1-D Tank Car, 09		38
36130	Jiminy Cricket 1-D Tank Car, 09		70
36131	Lackawanna Wood-sided Reefer "7000", 09-10		40
36132	Southern 1-D Tank Car, 08		35
36145	Philadelphia Quartz 3-D Tank Car "606", 10		40
36146	Cities Service 1-D Tank Car "11800", 10		40
36149	Strasburg Wood-sided Reefer "105", 10		55
36151	Grave's Blood Bank Tank Car, 10		50
36156	Pennsylvania Power & Light 1-D Tank Car, 10		40
36162	Diamond Chemicals 3-D Tank Car, 11		40
36163	Celanese 2-D Tank Car, 11-12		40
36166	Polar Express Reefer, 11-12		55
36169	Coca-Cola 3-D Tank Car, 11		55
36170	Partridge in a Pear Tree Reefer, 11-13		55
36172	Bubble Yum 1-D Tank Car, 11		55
36173	Santa's Flyer Hot Cocoa 3-D Tank Car, 11		40
36176	C&O 1-D Tank Car, 13		43
36177	WP 3-D Tank Car, 12		40
36178	Frisco 2-D Tank Car, 12-13		40
36182	Eggnog Unibody 1-D Tank Car, 12		70
36191	GN Waffle-sided Boxcar, 13		43

			Exc	Mint
___	**36195**	PRR Flatcar with patrol helicopter, 13		60
___	**36200**	Quaker Life Cereal Boxcar, 00		513
___	**36203**	Whirlpool Boxcar, 00 u		150
___	**36205**	eBay Boxcar, 00		288
___	**36206**	REA Boxcar, 01		25
___	**36207**	Vapor Records Christmas Boxcar, 01		80
___	**36208**	Father's Day Boxcar, 00		35
___	**36210**	Burlington Hi-Cube Boxcar "19825", 01		40
___	**36211**	NP Hi-Cube Boxcar "659999", 01	18	40
___	**36212**	Lionel Employee Christmas Boxcar, 00 u		410
___	**36213**	Vapor Records Christmas Boxcar, 00		50
___	**36214**	GN Boxcar (Lionel Service Station), 00 u	49	55
___	**36215**	Train Station 25th Anniversary Boxcar, 00 u		48
___	**36218**	Snap-On Boxcar, 00 u		150
___	**36219**	UP Boxcar "183518", 02		78
___	**36220**	Pioneer Seed Boxcar, 00 u		NRS
___	**36221**	PRR Boxcar "569356", 01		20
___	**36222**	NYC Boxcar "162440", 01		20
___	**36223**	Chessie System Boxcar, 01		20
___	**36224**	Santa Fe Boxcar "16263", 01		20
___	**36225**	C&O Boxcar "250549", 01		20
___	**36226**	E-Hobbies Boxcar, 01 u		227
___	**36227**	Monopoly Community Chest Boxcar, 00 u		50
___	**36228**	Lionel Visitor Center Boxcar, 01 u		34
___	**36229**	Island Trains 20th Anniversary Boxcar, 01 u		29
___	**36232**	Farmall McCormick Boxcar, 01 u		285
___	**36236**	TM Books "I Love Lionel" Boxcar "7474-1", 01 u		43
___	**36238**	Snap-On Tool Team ASE Racing Boxcar, 01 u		NRS
___	**36239**	L.L. Bean Boxcar, 01 u		150
___	**36240**	Do It Best Boxcar, 01 u		100
___	**36242**	Erie-Lackawanna Boxcar "73113", 02		24
___	**36243**	Christmas Boxcar "2002", 02		31
___	**36244**	Teddy Bear Centennial Boxcar, 02		36
___	**36245**	Lionel 20th Century Boxcar "1900-1925", 00 u		30
___	**36246**	Lionel 20th Century Boxcar "1926-1950", 00 u		30
___	**36247**	Lionel 20th Century Boxcar "1951-1975", 00 u		30
___	**36248**	Lionel 20th Century Boxcar "1976-2000", 00 u		30
___	**36250**	NYC Early Bird Boxcar, 04		20
___	**36253**	Christmas Boxcar (O), 03		32
___	**36254**	Goofy Hi-Cube Boxcar, 03		37
___	**36255**	Donald Duck Hi-Cube Boxcar, 03		40
___	**36256**	GN Boxcar "6341", 03		23
___	**36261**	PRR Boxcar, 03-05		15
___	**36262**	Southern Central of Georgia Boxcar, 03,àí04		20
___	**36264**	Santa Fe Boxcar "600196, 02		18
___	**36265**	Angela Trotta Thomas "Window Wishing" Boxcar, 02		38
___	**36267**	Mickey Mouse Hi-Cube Boxcar, 03		50
___	**36270**	Angela Trotta Thomas "Home for the Holidays" Boxcar, 02-03		30
___	**36272**	New Haven Boxcar "6501", 04		20
___	**36273**	Railbox Hi-Cube Boxcar "15000", 04		21
___	**36275**	Christmas Boxcar, 04		35
___	**36276**	Angela Trotta Thomas "Tis the Season" Boxcar, 04		34

		Exc	Mint
36277	Pluto Hi-Cube Boxcar, 04-05		50
36278	Winnie the Pooh Hi-Cube Boxcar, 04-05		50
36281	B&O Boxcar, 04		35
36291	Simpsons Boxcar, 04-05		44
36294	UP Hi-Cube Boxcar, traditional, 05		27
36295	CN Boxcar, traditional, 05		27
36296	2005 Holiday Boxcar, 05		48
36297	Angela Trotta Thomas "Christmas Eve" Boxcar, 05		48
36299	Hammacher Schlemmer Music Boxcar, 04		65
36305	eBay Boxcar, 00 u		120
36339	Caterpillar Caboose	22	50
36500	Western Pacific Caboose "36500", 04		23
36501	D&RGW Caboose "36501", 04		22
36502	Reading Caboose "36502", 04		25
36515	North Pole Central Lines Caboose "36515", 04		36
36519	Lionel Lines Caboose, 04		22
36520	Santa Fe Caboose "36520", 04		22
36525	CSX Work Caboose, lighted, 05		35
36526	Pennsylvania Work Caboose, traditional, 05		27
36527	Santa Fe Work Caboose, traditional, 05		28
36528	Chesapeake & Ohio Work Caboose, traditional, 05		40
36529	North Pole Central Work Caboose with presents, traditional, 05		38
36530	Pennsylvania Caboose, traditional, 05		33
36531	Erie Caboose "C150", traditional, 05		33
36532	SP Caboose "1097", traditional, 05		48
36533	Reading Caboose "92803", traditional, 05		33
36534	NYC Center Cupola Caboose, traditional, 05		40
36535	LL Center Cupola Caboose, traditional, 05		28
36536	Southern Center Cupola Caboose, traditional, 05		40
36539	Elvis Presley Caboose, 04		40
36541	Copper Range Caboose, 05		28
36542	NYC Caboose, 05		28
36543	ATSF Square-Window Caboose, 05		40
36544	Alaska Caboose, 05		35
36547	Bethlehem Steel Transfer Caboose, traditional, 05		38
36548	Transylvania RR Work Caboose, traditional, 05		45
36550	Halloween Transfer Caboose, traditional, 06-07		45
36551	Christmas Caboose, 06		45
36552	U.S. Steel Work Caboose, traditional, 06-07		45
36553	NYC Caboose, 08		20
36554	SP Work Caboose, traditional, 06		45
36555	Pennsylvania Transfer Caboose, 06		45
36556	Lionel Lines Work Caboose, 06-07		30
36557	D&RGW Work Caboose, traditional, 06		29
36558	Virginian Center Cupola Caboose "316", traditional, 06		45
36559	WM Center Cupola Caboose "1863", traditional, 06		45
36560	C&O Center Cupola Caboose "90876", traditional, 06		45
36562	Army Transportation Work Caboose, traditional, 06		45
36563	Reading Work Caboose, traditional, 06		45
36565	UP SP-type Caboose, traditional, 06		48
36566	NYC SP-type Caboose, traditional, 06		48
36567	GN SP-type Caboose, traditional, 06		48

			Exc	Mint
___	**36571**	PRR Caboose, 08		20
___	**36580**	B&O Center Cupola Caboose "C2047", traditional, 05		40
___	**36582**	C&O Caboose, 05		22
___	**36583**	Holiday Caboose, 07		50
___	**36587**	SP Caboose "1121", 07-09		40
___	**36589**	PRR Work Caboose, 07		40
___	**36590**	UP Work Caboose, 07		45
___	**36591**	Southern Caboose "X99", 08		45
___	**36592**	Santa Fe Caboose "999471", 06		48
___	**36593**	NYC Caboose, 06		48
___	**36601**	UP Caboose, 06		48
___	**36602**	UPS Centennial Caboose, 06		45
___	**36604**	Pennsylvania Caboose, 06		25
___	**36607**	K-Line Caboose, 06		40
___	**36611**	Conrail Caboose "19674", 07		40
___	**36612**	Alaska Caboose "1080", 07		40
___	**36613**	NYC Caboose, 07		30
___	**36618**	It's a Wonderful Life Caboose, 07		65
___	**36621**	Marriott Caboose, 07		75
___	**36622**	C&O Caboose "C-1838", 08-09		40
___	**36623**	ATSF Caboose, 07-09		40
___	**36624**	Lionel Lines Caboose, 08-09		40
___	**36625**	B&M Caboose, 08		50
___	**36626**	Erie Caboose "C101", 08-09		45
___	**36632**	PRR Center Cupola Caboose, 08	8	20
___	**36634**	Holiday Porthole Caboose, green, 08		50
___	**36646**	Monopoly Caboose, 10		48
___	**36647**	Strasburg Caboose, 10		48
___	**36648**	Wizard of Oz Caboose, 09		50
___	**36649**	Pennsylvania Power & Light Work Caboose, 10		45
___	**36657**	Western & Atlantic Caboose, 10-11		48
___	**36659**	PRR Illuminated Porthole Caboose, 11		35
___	**36668**	CSX Illuminated Square Window Caboose, 10		35
___	**36672**	NS Caboose, 11		25
___	**36674**	Polar RR Caboose "C-1225", 11-12		53
___	**36690**	UP Overland Freight Caboose, 12		25
___	**36701**	Baldwin Locomotive Works Operating Welding Car "36701", 02		68
___	**36702**	Bosco Operating Milk Car with platform, 02		115
___	**36703**	Circus Horse Car with corral, 06		132
___	**36704**	Animated Reindeer Stock Car and Corral, 02		145
___	**36718**	AEC Security Caboose, 02		45
___	**36719**	Lionel Lion Bobbing Head Car, 02		20
___	**36720**	Aladdin Aquarium Car, 03		40
___	**36721**	101 Dalmatians Animated Gondola, 03		45
___	**36722**	Peter Pan Bobbing Head Boxcar, 03		45
___	**36726**	Santa Fe Searchlight Car "36726", 03		50
___	**36727**	Weyerhaeuser Moe & Joe Flatcar, 03		65
___	**36728**	SP Walking Brakeman Boxcar 163143", 03		42
___	**36729**	Lionel Lines Animated Caboose, 04-05	60	68
___	**36730**	U.S. Army Missile Launch Sound Car "44", 03		175
___	**36731**	Motorized Aquarium Car "3435", 03		83
___	**36732**	C&NW Jumping Hobo Car, 03		41

		Exc	Mint
36733	Christmas Music Boxcar, 03		45
36734	Santa Fe Operating Searchlight Car "20611", 02		25
36735	WP Ice Car "7045", 02		55
36736	D&RGW Stock Car "39268," RailSounds, 04		45
36738	T&P Poultry Dispatch Car "36738", 02		50
36739	Postwar "3461" Lionel Lines Log Dump Car, 03		50
36740	Postwar "3469" Lionel Lines Coal Dump Car, 03		49
36743	Santa Claus Bobbing Head Boxcar, 03		40
36744	Little Mermaid Aquarium Car, 03		55
36745	Toy Story Animated Gondola, 03		70
36753	LFD Firecar with ladder, 02		60
36757	Southern Searchlight Car "51422", 03-04		40
36758	Patriotic Lighted Boxcar, 02		60
36760	B&O Sentinel Brakeman Car "3424," Archive Collection, 02		65
36761	Wellspring Capital Management Lighted Boxcar, 02 u		220
36764	West Side Lumber Log Dump Car "36764", 03		55
36765	Alaska Coal Dump Car "401", 03		50
36766	Erie Chase Gondola, 03		50
36767	Santa's Radar Tracking Car, 03		40
36769	Fourth of July Lighted Boxcar, 03		70
36770	American Refrigerator Transit Ice Car "23701", 04		42
36771	CN Barrel Car "74208", 04		48
36772	Spokane, Portland & Seattle Log Dump Car "36772", 04		46
36773	Jersey Central Coal Dump Car "92926", 04		45
36774	PRR Moe & Joe Lumber Flatcar, 04		50
36775	Santa Fe Animated Caboose "999010", 05		75
36776	Santa Fe Walking Brakeman Car "19938", 04		43
36778	C&O Searchlight Car "216614", 04		30
36780	Sea-Monkeys Motorized Aquarium Car, 04		45
36781	Finding Nemo Aquarium Car, 04		50
36782	Goofy and Pete Jumping Boxcar, 05		70
36783	Disney Operating Boxcar, 04-05		65
36784	Monsters Inc. Bobbing Head Boxcar, 04		40
36786	Postwar "3494-150" MP Operating Boxcar, 03		40
36787	MOW Remote Control Searchlight Car, 04		45
36788	Lionel Lines Tender, TrainSounds, 04		75
36789	Railbox Boxcar, TrainSounds, 04-05		105
36790	Christmas Music Boxcar, 04		70
36791	Kinzua Pine Mills Operating Log Dump Car, 96		40
36793	Pennsylvania Derrick Car, 03		22
36794	NYC Log Dump Car, 03		25
36795	Southern Coal Dump Car, 03		25
36796	GN Searchlight Car, 03		24
36797	"Operation Iraqi Freedom" Minuteman Car, 03		45
36803	Santa Animated Caboose, 06		75
36804	Candy Cane Dump Car, 06		80
36805	Reindeer Jumping Boxcar, 06		70
36809	NYC Derrick Car, 07-08		35
36810	PRR Searchlight Car, 07		35
36811	UP Dump Coal Dump Car, 07		35
36812	British Columbia Log Dump Car, 07-08		35
36813	State of Maine Brakeman Car, 08		80
36814	D&RGW Animated Caboose "01415", 07-09		80

	MODERN 1970-2024		Exc	Mint
___	**36815**	Santa Fe Moe & Joe Flatcar, 07-08		80
___	**36816**	Virginian Coal Dump Car, 08		80
___	**36818**	U.S. Steel Searchlight Car, 07-08		75
___	**36821**	"Naughty or Nice" Dump Car, 07		80
___	**36823**	Halloween SpookySmoke Boxcar, 07		115
___	**36824**	Alien Smoking Boxcar, 07		110
___	**36825**	Lionel Lines Boom w/Crane, 07		35
___	**36826**	Home Depot/Tony Stewart Searchlight Car, 07		30
___	**36829**	Alien Radioactive Car, 07		70
___	**36830**	Trick or Treat Aquarium Car, 07		75
___	**36831**	MOW Welding Car, 07-08		75
___	**36833**	Christmas Music Boxcar, 07	27	65
___	**36834**	Santa Fe Transparent Instruction Car, 07-08		65
___	**36838**	Lionel Power Co. Voltmeter Car, K-Line, 06		75
___	**36839**	Operating Milk Car with platform, K-Line, 06		140
___	**36841**	Visitor Center 15th Anniversary Lighted Boxcar, 06		70
___	**36847**	Polar Express Tender, TrainSounds, 08-14		130
___	**36848**	Candy Cane Dump Car, 07		80
___	**36849**	Tell-Tale Reindeer Car, 07		53
___	**36850**	Santa and Snowman Boxcar, 07		75
___	**36851**	Generator Car with Christmas tree, 07		75
___	**36853**	U.S. Army Exploding Boxcar, 08		60
___	**36855**	GW Horse Car and Corral, 08		160
___	**36856**	W&ARR Sheriff and Outlaw Car, 08		75
___	**36857**	Bobbing Ghost Boxcar, 08		65
___	**36859**	Lionel Lines Aquarium Car, 08		80
___	**36861**	PRR Poultry Dispatch Car, 08-09		80
___	**36863**	Alien Security Car, 08		80
___	**36864**	Bethlehem Steel Searchlight Car, 08		40
___	**36866**	WP Coal Dump Car "52369", 08		40
___	**36868**	NH Barrel Ramp Car, 08		40
___	**36869**	Bobbing Santa Boxcar, 08		65
___	**36870**	Postwar "6812" Track Maintenance Car, 08		65
___	**36874**	PRR Searchlight Car, 09		35
___	**36875**	Polar Express Coach, sound, 08-14, 16		132
___	**36878**	NYC Track Cleaning Car, 08		150
___	**36879**	REA Ice Car "1221", 08		65
___	**36880**	Koi Fish Aquarium Car, 10		75
___	**36881**	Christmas Music Boxcar, 08		70
___	**36887**	Great Western Animated Gondola, 08-09		65
___	**36888**	Casper Aquarium Car, 09-10		90
___	**36889**	PRR Barrel Ramp Car, 09-10		46
___	**36893**	UP Transparent Instruction Car "195220", 09-10		75
___	**36896**	Christmas Music Boxcar, 09		80
___	**36897**	Pennsylvania Power & Light Coal Dump Car, 09-10		46
___	**36898**	Wisconsin Central Log Dump Car, 09		46
___	**36900**	Depressed Center Flatcar with backshop load, 99	30	115
___	**36913**	Allied Chemical 1-D Tank Car 2-pack, 00		150
___	**36914**	Allied Chemical 1-D Tank Car "68075," die-cast, white, 00		90
___	**36915**	Allied Chemical 1-D Tank Car "68076," die-cast, white, 00		90
___	**36916**	Allied Chemical 1-D Tank Car 2-pack, 00		175
___	**36917**	Allied Chemical 1-D Tank Car "65124," die-cast, black, 00		95
___	**36918**	Allied Chemical 1-D Tank Car "65125," die-cast, black, 00		90

		Exc	Mint
36919	Maersk Maxi-Stack Car, 00		33
36927	B&O DC Hopper 6-pack, "435040-45", 01		520
36935	Maersk Maxi-Stack Car 2-pack, "250131-32", 00		135
36937	SP Maxi-Stack Car "513957", 02		65
36998	Gingerbread Man Gateman, 12-13		80
37001	No. 3444 Erie Animated Gondola, 09		70
37002	Operating Plutonium Car 2-pack, 10-11		140
37003	PRR Jet Snow Blower "491252", 09-10		138
37004	Area 51 Searchlight Car, 09		46
37006	Lionel Flatcar with operating LCD billboard, 09		180
37009	Smoking Mount St. Helens Boxcar, 10-11		125
37010	Pennsylvania Power & Light Searchlight Car, 10		46
37011	B&M Operating Milk Car with platform, 10		155
37012	GN Jumping Hobo Boxcar, 10		75
37015	Jack-o-Lantern Flatcar, 11-13		75
37016	Radioactive Plutonium Flatcar, 11		70
37017	Plutonium Boom Car, 11		70
37022	ATSF Blinking Billboard, 12		25
37032	Postwar "3562" Operating Barrel Car, 11		75
37033	Casper Animated Gondola , 11		70
37035	Santa's Operating Snow Globe Car, 11		75
37036	Halloween Operating Globe Car, 11		78
37038	Halloween Searchlight Car, 12-13		45
37039	Minuteman Searchlight Car, 11		45
37040	UP Derrick Car, 11-12		46
37041	Pennsylvania Power & Light Coal Dump Car, 11		80
37042	IC Coal Dump Car, 11		46
37043	Seaboard Log Dump Car, 11		46
37044	CP Rail Log Dump Car, 11, 13		80
37045	Beatles Yellow Submarine Aquarium Car, 11		85
37047	Santa's Flyer Animated Gondola, 11		55
37053	EL Derrick Car, 12		45
37054	CSX Coal Dump Car, 12		46
37055	SP Log Dump Car, 12		46
37056	Zombie Aquarium Car, 12		80
37057	Bethlehem Steel Culvert Car, 12		65
37058	Ghost Globe Halloween Car, 12-15		80
37059	Christmas Snow Globe Car, 12		85
37060	LIRR Derrick Car, 13-14		50
37061	UP Railroad Speeder, CC, 12-14		150
37062	NS Railroad Speeder, CC, 12-14		150
37063	PRR Railroad Speeder, CC, 12-14, 16		150
37064	CSX Railroad Speeder, CC, 12-14		150
37065	BNSF Railroad Speeder, CC, 12-14		150
37066	MOW Railroad Speeder, CC, 12-14		150
37067	NYC Railroad Speeder, CC, 12-14		150
37068	CN Railroad Speeder, CC, 12-14		150
37069	Strasburg RR Crane Car, 12		65
37070	Gingerbread Man and Santa Animated Gondola, 12		55
37071	MOW Searchlight Car, 12		46
37073	U.S. Marine Corps Cannon Car, 12		75
37075	Boy Scouts of America Crane Car, 13		75
37076	Bethlehem Steel Coal Dump Car, 13		50

	MODERN 1970-2024		Exc	Mint
____	**37078**	RI Searchlight Car, 13		50
____	**37079**	Santa Fe Derrick Car, 13		50
____	**37081**	Peanuts Pumpkin Jack-O-Lantern Car, 13		85
____	**37082**	Peanuts Animated Trick or Treat Chase Gondola, 14-16		75
____	**37083**	Strasburg Coal Dump Car, 13		50
____	**37084**	PRR Cop and Hobo Animated Gondola, 13		65
____	**37085**	BN Log Dump Car, 13		50
____	**37086**	Lionelville Aquarium Co. Aquarium Car, 13		80
____	**37087**	NH Walking Brakeman Car, 13-14		75
____	**37089**	Santa's List Snow Globe Car, 13		90
____	**37090**	Polar Express Searchlight Car, 13		60
____	**37094**	Wizard of Oz Aquarium Car, 13-15		85
____	**37095**	North Pole Sleigh Repair Welding Car, 13		85
____	**37097**	Where the Wild Things Are Aquarium Car, 13-15		85
____	**37099**	North Pole Central EV Caboose "2510" (std O), 13		95
____	**37100**	Barrel Loader Building, 12-14		43
____	**37101**	Smiley Water Tower, 12-14		23
____	**37102**	Watchman Shanty, 12-14		30
____	**37103**	FasTrack O31 Curved Track, 13-24		6
____	**37110**	FasTrack Terminal, LionChief, 14-24		10
____	**37112**	Helicopter 2-pack, 13-20		35
____	**37115**	Pedestrian Walkover, green, 16-18		55
____	**37120**	Railroad Crossing Signs, 13-20		10
____	**37121**	Christmas Station Platform, 13		25
____	**37122**	Santa Fe Blinking Billboard, 13		25
____	**37123**	Weyerhaeuser Timber Operating Sawmill, 12-13		140
____	**37124**	West Side Lumber Operating Sawmill, 12-13		140
____	**37125**	Legacy Writable Utility Mobile, 12-16, 20		20
____	**37127**	Angela Trotta Thomas Gallery, 12		75
____	**37129**	Boy Scouts of America Girder Bridge, 13		23
____	**37130**	Boy Scouts of America Covered Bridge, 13		60
____	**37139**	Tis the Season Accessories, 12-13		310
____	**37140**	All Aboard Accessories, 12-13		65
____	**37141**	Rail Yard Accessories, 12-13		277
____	**37142**	Welcome Home Accessories, 12-13		154
____	**37146**	Legacy PowerMaster, 12-24		130
____	**37147**	CAB-1L/Base-1L Command Set, 12-16, 18-20		250
____	**37149**	FasTrack Modular Layout Straight Section Kit, 13		200
____	**37150**	FasTrack Modular Layout Template, 13-16		30
____	**37151**	Red Christmas Classic Street Lamps, 3-pack, 14-24		40
____	**37152**	Operating Coaling Station, 13-14		180
____	**37153**	FasTrack Modular Layout 45-Degree Reversible Corner Kit, 13		225
____	**37154**	FasTrack Modular Layout 45-Degree Corner Kit, 13		225
____	**37155**	CAB-1L Remote Controller, 12-16, 20-23	75	165
____	**37156**	Base-1L, 12-16		125
____	**37158**	Hershey's Water Tower, 13		30
____	**37159**	Peanuts Figure Pack, 13-15		30
____	**37160**	Strasburg Girder Bridge, 13		21
____	**37161**	Container 4-pack, 13		40
____	**37162**	Lionelville Water Tower, 13		25
____	**37163**	LIRR Girder Bridge, 13		21
____	**37164**	NS Girder Bridge, 13		21

MODERN 1970-2024		Exc	Mint
37165	CP Water Tower, 13		25 ___
37166	Crossing Shanty, 13-14, 16		25 ___
37167	Freight Platform, 13		30 ___
37169	Peanuts Psychiatric Booth, 13-16		40 ___
37172	Black Gooseneck Lamps, 2-pack, 13-23	13	35 ___
37173	Globe Lamp 3-pack, 13-14, 16-19		25 ___
37174	Black Classic Street Lamps, 3-pack, 13-24		40 ___
37176	Santa Fe Shanty, 13		25 ___
37183	Polar Express 10th Anniversary Snowman & Children, 13-17		37 ___
37184	Christmas Half Covered Bridge, 13		43 ___
37185	Christmas Railroad Signs, 13-14, 16-18		10 ___
37187	Kris Kringle's Kloseout Shop, 13		50 ___
37191	36-watt Power Supply, LionChief, 14		36 ___
37195	Grand Central Terminal 100th Anniversary, 13-15		280 ___
37196	Christmas Extension Bridge, 13, 16-18		15 ___
37197	North Pole Central Girder Bridge, 13-14, 16-17		30 ___
37530	Santa Animated Caboose, 11		80 ___
37807	Station Platform, 10-15		23 ___
37808	Sunoco Spherical Oil Tank, 10-11		100 ___
37810	Curved O Gauge Tunnel, 11-17		65 ___
37813	Christmas Tractor and Trailer with trees, 10		27 ___
37814	Christmas Crossing Shanty, 10-14		30 ___
37816	Rockville Bridge, 11-12		700 ___
37820	Lionel Auto Loader Cars 4-pack, 12-13, 16-17		25 ___
37821	Smoke Fluid Loader, 11		250 ___
37826	Classic Travel Billboard Set, 11-14		13 ___
37827	Coca-Cola Covered Bridge, 11		45 ___
37828	Vintage Boy Scouts Figure Pack, 11-14		30 ___
37829	Polar Express Station Platform, 11-18		40 ___
37831	NJ Transit Blinking Light Water Tower, 11-12		30 ___
37834	Lionel Boat 4-pack, 11-20		25 ___
37836	Monopoly Auto 4-pack, 12		25 ___
37837	Polar Express Straight Tunnel, 12-14		80 ___
37840	Santa Fe Diorama, 12-17		15 ___
37841	Premium Smoke Fluid, 12-16		7 ___
37842	CN Tractor with piggyback trailer, 12, 15		90 ___
37846	PRR Tractor Trailer, 12		90 ___
37847	SP Tractor Trailer, 12		90 ___
37848	IC Tractor Trailer, 12		90 ___
37849	ATSF Tractor Trailer, 12		90 ___
37850	REA Tractor Trailer, 12		90 ___
37851	Scale Telephone Poles, 6-pack, 12-24		40 ___
37852	Christmas People Pack, 12-14, 16-18		20 ___
37853	Alien Billboard, 13, 15		13 ___
37854	Classic Christmas Billboard , 12		11 ___
37855	Lionel Airplane 2-pack, 12-20		37 ___
37900	Silver Truss Bridge, 11		70 ___
37901	Lehigh Valley Tugboat, 10		270 ___
37902	Illuminated Barge, 10		180 ___
37903	Cell Tower, 10-24		85 ___
37904	Boy Scouts Billboard Set, 10		13 ___
37907	Christmas Street Lamps with wreaths, 10-14		30 ___
37909	North Pole Central Jet Snowblower, 11-14		138 ___

			Exc	Mint
___	**37910**	Operating Lighthouse, 10		180
___	**37911**	D&RGW Blinking Light Water Tower, 10-11		30
___	**37912**	Lighted Coaling Tower, 10-15		180
___	**37913**	Hopper Shed, 10-15		35
___	**37914**	Illuminated Work House, 10-18		40
___	**37916**	Beige Brick Suburban House, 10		80
___	**37917**	Red Brick Suburban House, 10		80
___	**37919**	Operating Sawmill, 10		130
___	**37920**	Bascule Bridge, 10		350
___	**37921**	ZW-L Transformer, 11-24	392	1000
___	**37922**	Coca-Cola Blinking Light Billboard, 10-11		28
___	**37923**	Coca-Cola Blinking Light Water Tower, 11		28
___	**37928**	Passenger Station, sounds, 11		90
___	**37929**	Coca-Cola Diner, 11, 13		75
___	**37930**	Rotary Aircraft Beacon, 11-12		81
___	**37933**	MG Switch Tower, 11-13		300
___	**37935**	Operating Track Gang, 11		100
___	**37939**	Assorted Telephone Poles, 6-pack, 11-24		45
___	**37940**	PRR Hobo Hotel, 12		150
___	**37941**	House Under Construction, 11		90
___	**37942**	Christmas Hobo Hotel, 12-13		150
___	**37944**	Weathered 50,000-gallon Water Tank, 11-12		170
___	**37946**	House Under Construction #2, 12-13		90
___	**37947**	GW-180 180-watt Transformer, 12-24		360
___	**37948**	Boy Scouts Flagpole with lights, 11		30
___	**37951**	Postwar "342" Culvert Loader, 11		165
___	**37952**	Postwar "345" Culvert Unloader, 11		190
___	**37953**	Jacobs Pharmacy, 11		50
___	**37954**	Halloween Station Platform, 11-13		35
___	**37955**	Sodor Station Platform, 11-15		35
___	**37957**	Deluxe Holiday House, 11		85
___	**37958**	SP Scrap Yard, 11-14		110
___	**37959**	Midway Basketball Shot Game, 11-13		21
___	**37960**	Burning Switch Tower, 11-13		100
___	**37961**	NYC Scrap Yard, 11-13		110
___	**37962**	NJ Transit Station Platform, 11		37
___	**37964**	Archive Operating Freight Terminal, 11-14		150
___	**37965**	Christmas Operating Freight Terminal, 11-14, 16-17		150
___	**37966**	Lionel Cylindrical Oil Tank, 11-17		100
___	**37967**	Boy Scouts Troop Cabin, 12-13		80
___	**37971**	Bethlehem Steel Culvert Loader, 11		165
___	**37972**	Bethlehem Steel Culvert Unloader, 11		190
___	**37973**	Coca-Cola Station Platform, 12		37
___	**37975**	PFE Operating Freight Terminal, 11-16		150
___	**37977**	Hooker Tank Car Accident, 11-17		130
___	**37978**	Deluxe Suburban House, 11-13		80
___	**37979**	Rotary Coal Tipple, 12		540
___	**37980**	Operating Coal Conveyor, 12		90
___	**37984**	Santa's Repair Work House, 12-14		40
___	**37985**	Operating Wind Turbine, 12-15		75
___	**37986**	NJ Transit Blinking Billboard, 12-13		28
___	**37989**	Sodor Train Shed, 12-16		60
___	**37993**	Snoopy and the Red Baron Animated Pylon, 12		160

MODERN 1970-2024		Exc	Mint	
37994	Deluxe Holiday House #2, 12-14		120	___
37995	Illuminated Scale Telephone Poles, 6-pack, 12-24		55	___
37996	Postwar 192 Control Tower, 12		70	___
37997	Christmas Lawn Figure Pack, 12-14, 16-18		20	___
37998	Halloween Haunted Passenger Station, 12-13, 15		75	___
38004	Virginian 4-6-0 10-wheel Locomotive "203," CC, 01-02		570	___
38005	Long Island 4-6-0 10-wheel Locomotive "138," CC, 01-02		510	___
38007	UP Auxiliary tender, black, CC, 01		200	___
38008	UP Auxiliary tender, gray, CC, 01		205	___
38009	D&RGW 4-6-6-4 Challenger Locomotive "3803", CC, 01		1550	___
38010	Clinchfield 4-6-6-4 Challenger Locomotive "673", CC, 01	200	1400	___
38012	Wheeling & Lake Erie 2-6-6-2 Locomotive "8005", CC, 01		610	___
38013	D&H 4-6-6-4 Challenger Locomotive "1527", CC, 01		720	___
38014	D&RGW 4-6-6-4 Challenger Locomotive "3800", CC, 01		710	___
38015	NYC 4-6-4 Hudson Locomotive "773," CC, 01		900	___
38016	Southern 0-8-0 Yard Goat Locomotive "6536," CC, 01-02, 05		530	___
38017	CN 2-6-0 Mogul Locomotive "86," CC, 03, 05		600	___
38018	Wabash 2-6-0 Mogul Locomotive "826," CC, 03		485	___
38019	B&M 2-6-0 Mogul Locomotive "1455," CC, 03, 05	150	600	___
38020	PRR 4-4-4-4 T1 Duplex Locomotive "5514", 02-03		630	___
38021	WP 4-6-6-4 Challenger Locomotive "402", CC, 02	235	650	___
38022	WM 4-6-6-4 Challenger Locomotive "1206", CC, 02		690	___
38023	UP 4-6-6-4 Challenger Locomotive "3976", CC, 02		620	___
38024	PRR 6-4-4-6 S-1 Duplex Locomotive "6100," TMCC, 03		1000	___
38025	PRR 4-6-2 K4 Pacific Locomotive "1361," CC, 02		950	___
38026	N&W 4-8-4 J Class Northern Locomotive "606," CC, 02	550	1450	___
38027	Meadow River Lumber Heisler Geared Locomotive "6," CC, 03	367	880	___
38028	PRR 6-8-6 S2 Steam Turbine Locomotive, 01	150	650	___
38029	UP 4-12-2 Locomotive "9000," CC, 03		633	___
38030	Santa Fe 2-8-8-2 Locomotive "1795," CC, 03	175	920	___
38031	SP 2-8-8-4 AC-9 Locomotive "3809," CC, 04		1100	___
38032	Virginian 2-8-8-2 Locomotive "741," CC, 03		928	___
38036	Long Island 2-8-0 Consolidation Locomotive, 01		500	___
38037	PRR Reading Seashore 2-8-0 Consolidation "6072," CC, 01		495	___
38038	D&RGW Auxiliary Water Tender, 01		230	___
38039	Clinchfield Auxiliary Water Tender, 01	75	220	___
38040	LV 4-6-0 Camelback Locomotive, 01		405	___
38042	C&NW 4-6-0 10-wheel Locomotive "361," CC, 02		450	___
38043	Frisco 4-6-0 10-wheel Locomotive "719," CC, 02		525	___
38044	PRR 4-6-2 K4 Pacific Locomotive "5385," CC, 02		920	___
38045	NYC Hudson J-3a 4-6-4 Locomotive "5418," CC, 03		495	___
38046	GN 0-8-0 Locomotive "815," CC, 02	263	530	___
38047	N&W 0-8-0 Locomotive "266," CC, 02		550	___
38048	NPR 0-8-0 Locomotive "303", CC, 02		530	___
38049	N&W 2-6-6-4 Locomotive "1234," CC, 02		690	___
38050	Nickel Plate 2-8-4 Berkshire Locomotive "779," CC, 03		925	___
38051	Erie 2-8-4 Berkshire Locomotive "3315," CC, 03	175	810	___
38052	Pere Marquette 2-8-4 Berkshire Locomotive "1225," CC, 03		1000	___
38053	NYC 4-8-2 Mohawk L-2a Locomotive "2793," CC, 03		915	___
38055	Santa Fe 4-8-4 Northern Locomotive "3751" CC, 04		1100	___
38056	PRR 4-8-2 Mountain M1a Locomotive "6759," CC, 03		850	___
38057	Weyerhaeuser Shay Locomotive, CC, 03		1000	___

MODERN 1970-2024		Exc	Mint
____ **38058**	C&O 2-8-8-2 H7 Locomotive "1580", CC, 04		1200
____ **38060**	UP 2-8-8-2 H7 Locomotive "3590", CC, 04	350	1200
____ **38061**	Cass Scenic Heisler Geared Locomotive "6," CC, 03		940
____ **38062**	Lionel Lines 4-6-2 Pacific Locomotive "8062," CC, 02-03		275
____ **38065**	UP 2-8-8-2 Mallet Locomotive "3672," CC, 02		1002
____ **38066**	Elk River Shay Locomotive, CC, 03		1000
____ **38067**	MILW 4-6-2 Pacific Locomotive "6316," CC, 03		300
____ **38068**	WM 4-6-2 Pacific Locomotive "204," CC, 03		300
____ **38069**	Erie Hudson Locomotive, whistle, 05		150
____ **38070**	C&O 4-6-2 Pacific Locomotive "489", CC, 04		300
____ **38071**	SP Cab Forward AC-12 Locomotive "4294," CC, 05	250	1550
____ **38075**	UP 4-8-8-4 Big Boy Locomotive "4024," LionMaster, 03		800
____ **38076**	C&O 2-8-4 Berkshire Locomotive "2699," CC, 04		860
____ **38077**	Virginian 2-8-4 Berkshire Locomotive "508," CC, 04		1000
____ **38079**	SP 4-8-4 Northern GS-2 Locomotive "4410" CC, 04	225	980
____ **38080**	WP 4-8-4 Northern GS-64 Locomotive "485" CC, 04		1000
____ **38081**	C&O 2-6-6-6 Allegheny Locomotive "1650", CC, 05-07	313	1700
____ **38082**	Pennsylvania 2-8-8-2 Y3 Locomotive "374", CC, 04		1000
____ **38083**	N&W 2-8-8-2 Y3 Locomotive "2009," CC, 04	275	910
____ **38085**	NYC 4-6-4 Hudson J-3a Locomotive "5422," CC, 03		495
____ **38086**	B&A 4-6-4 Hudson Locomotive "607," CC, 03		495
____ **38087**	Nickel Plate 2-8-4 Berkshire Locomotive, RailSounds, 05		190
____ **38088**	NYC 2-6-0 Mogul Locomotive "1924," CC, 03, 05		600
____ **38089**	Pennsylvania 4-6-2 Pacific Locomotive "3678," CC, 04		300
____ **38090**	Clinchfield 4-6-6-4 Challenger Locomotive "672" CC, 04		640
____ **38091**	NP 4-6-6-4 Challenger Locomotive "5121" CC, 04		660
____ **38092**	Pickering Lumber Heisler Locomotive "5," CC, 04		1000
____ **38093**	UP 4-6-6-4 Challenger Locomotive "3980," CC, 04		700
____ **38094**	MILW Hiawatha 4-4-2 Atlantic Locomotive, CC, 06		950
____ **38095**	N&W 4-8-4 J Class Locomotive "611", CC, 05-06	300	1250
____ **38100**	Texas Special F3 Diesel AB Set, 99	860	930
____ **38103**	Texas Special F3 Diesel "2245", 99	435	510
____ **38104**	CP F3 A Unit "2373," powered, 99		400
____ **38105**	CP F3 A Unit "2373," nonpowered, 99		100
____ **38106**	NYC F3 A Unit "2333," powered, 99		400
____ **38107**	NYC F3 A Unit "2333," nonpowered, 99		250
____ **38114**	ATSF FT Diesel B Unit, 99-00		170
____ **38115**	NYC FT Diesel B Unit "2403," nonpowered, 99-00		130
____ **38116**	B&O FT Diesel B Unit, 99-00		130
____ **38144**	C&O F3 Diesel AA Set "7019, 7021", 00	138	700
____ **38147**	GN Alco FA2 AA Diesel Set, CC, 02		405
____ **38150**	Platinum Ghost "2333", 99	198	495
____ **38153**	"Spirit of the Century" F3 Diesel AA Set, 99		800
____ **38160**	Pennsylvania Alco FB2 Diesel, 02		125
____ **38161**	MKT Alco FB2 Diesel, 02		125
____ **38162**	Burlington FT Diesel B Unit, 01		NRS
____ **38167**	Burlington FT Diesel AA Set, 01		225
____ **38176**	Pennsylvania Alco FA2 AA Diesel Set, CC, 02		405
____ **38182**	MKT Alco FA2 AA Diesel Set, CC, 02		360
____ **38188**	Southern F3 Diesel ABA Set, 00	202	557
____ **38194**	GN Alco FB2 Diesel, 02		125
____ **38195**	Santa Fe FT Diesel A Unit "170", 00		125
____ **38196**	Santa Fe FT Diesel A Unit "171", 00		175

		Exc	Mint
38197	SP F3 Diesel ABA Set, 00	209	640
38202	Wild West Handcar, 10		75
38203	Holly Jolly Trolley 2-car Set, 10		160
38204	ATSF FT B Unit, nonpowered, 10		120
38210	PRR Alco Diesel AA Set, CC, 10		400
38213	Rio Grande Ski Train FT A Unit "541," powered, 10-11		200
38214	Rio Grande Ski Train FT B Unit, nonpowered, 11		120
38215	ATSF FT Diesel "165," RailSounds, 10-11		280
38216	Rio Grande Ski Train FT A Unit, nonpowered, 11		120
38219	Texan FT B Unit Diesel, nonpowered, 11, 13-14	25	120
38221	CNJ Alco AA Diesel Set, 11		300
38224	Alaska Alco AA Diesel Set, 11		300
38234	Classic PRR GG1 Electric Locomotive "4866", 12		330
38235	Classic PC GG1 Electric Locomotive "4840", 12		330
38240	Elf Gang Car, 12		120
38241	MOW Gang Car, 12-13		120
38248	NS GP38 Diesel "1030", 13-14	180	300
38252	CP GE U36B Diesel, "4245", 13	155	200
38300	Postwar "2331" Virginian Train Master Diesel, 08	190	230
38303	Postwar "2340" GG1 Electric Locomotive, 08		280
38305	Postwar "2338" Milwaukee Road GP7 Diesel, 08		220
38308	Postwar 2146WS Berkshire Passenger Set, 12		460
38310	Postwar "2185W" NYC F3 Diesel Freight Set, 09	163	600
38311	Postwar "2276W" B&O RDC Commuter Set, 09		470
38312	Postwar "2343" Santa Fe F3 Diesel AA Set, 09	138	500
38313	B&O Budd RDC 2-pack, 09	100	350
38323	Postwar "2348" M&StL GP9 Diesel, CC, 10		390
38324	Postwar 2507W NH F3 Diesel Freight Set, 10	138	600
38328	Postwar 1623W NP GP9 Diesel Freight Set, 10		750
38329	Postwar 2261W Freight Hauler Set, 10	183	610
38334	Postwar 11288 Orbitor Diesel Freight Set, 10		500
38338	Postwar 2129WS Berkshire Freight Set, 12		550
38339	Postwar 2505W Virginian Rectifier Freight Set, 10		470
38340	Postwar 1587S Girl's Steam Freight Set, 10		580
38342	Postwar 1619W Santa Fe Freight Set, 10-11	125	470
38348	Postwar "2339" Transparent Wabash GP7 Diesel, 11		290
38349	Postwar 12885-500 C&O GP7 Freight Set, 11-12		600
38351	Postwar Archive UP GP7 Diesel, 11		290
38353	Postwar X-628 Promotional U.S. Navy Diesel Freight Set, 12-14		600
38354	Postwar 1464W UP Anniversary Alco Diesel Passenger Set, 12-14	230	480
38357	Postwar 221 U.S. Marine Corps Alco Diesel A Unit, 12-14		300
38358	Postwar 2239 IC F3 Freight Set, 12-14		600
38365	Archive ATSF Black Bonnet F3 AA Diesel Set, 12-14	333	727
38368	Archive NYC Red Lightning F3 AA Diesel Set, 12-14		500
38371	Postwar 2031 RI Alco Diesel AA Set, 12-13		400
38374	Postwar 221 U.S. Marine Corps Alco Diesel B Unit, 12-14		120
38377	Postwar 2363T F3 A Unit, nonpowered, 12-14		170
38379	Archive ATSF Black Bonnet F3 B Unit, 12-14		170
38380	Archive NYC Red Lightning F3 B Unit, 12-14		248
38386	Postwar "2367" Wabash F3 Diesel AB Units, 12-14		500
38388	Postwar "2367" Wabash F3 Diesel A Unit, nonpowered, 12-14		170

			Exc	Mint
___	**38389**	Postwar "2362" UP F3 Diesel AA Set, 14		460
___	**38392**	Postwar "2362" F3 Diesel B Unit, nonpowered, 14		170
___	**38393**	PRR Round-roof Boxcar "76648" (std O), 14		80
___	**38401**	NYC M-497 Jet-Powered Rail Car, 10		600
___	**38402**	Amtrak HHP-8 Electric Locomotive, RailSounds, 10		400
___	**38403**	B&O CSX Heritage AC6000 Diesel "6607," CC, 11		550
___	**38404**	B&O CSX Heritage AC6000 Diesel "7812," CC, 11		550
___	**38405**	Chessie System CSX Heritage AC6000 Diesel, CC, 11-14		550
___	**38406**	Chessie System CSX Heritage AC6000 Diesel, CC, 11-14		550
___	**38407**	WM CSX Heritage AC6000 Diesel "2652," CC, 11		550
___	**38408**	WM CSX Heritage AC6000 Diesel "659," CC, 11	200	550
___	**38409**	Clinchfield CSX Heritage AC6000 Diesel, CC, 11-13	188	550
___	**38410**	Clinchfield CSX Heritage AC6000 Diesel, CC, 11-14		550
___	**38411**	Family Lines CSX Heritage AC6000 Diesel "4825," CC, 11		550
___	**38412**	Family Lines CSX Heritage AC6000 Diesel "4837," CC, 11		550
___	**38413**	CSX Heritage AC6000 Diesel "607," CC, 11-13		550
___	**38414**	CSX Heritage AC6000 Diesel "654" CC, 11-13		550
___	**38415**	PRR U28C Diesel "6531," CC, 11-12		530
___	**38416**	PRR U28C Diesel "6534," CC, 11-12		530
___	**38417**	BN Bicentennial U30C Diesel "1776," CC, 11		530
___	**38418**	BN Bicentennial U30C Diesel "1777," CC, 11		530
___	**38419**	UP U30C Diesel "2918," CC, 11-12		530
___	**38420**	UP U30C Diesel "2897," CC, 11-12		530
___	**38421**	NP U33C Diesel "3305," CC, 11-12		530
___	**38422**	NP U33C Diesel "3307," CC, 11-12		530
___	**38423**	Southern U30C Diesel "3801," CC, 11-12		530
___	**38424**	Southern U30C Diesel "3804," CC, 11-12		530
___	**38425**	RI Budd RDC Jet Car, 11		330
___	**38426**	Central of Georgia GP7 Diesel "126," CC, 11		450
___	**38427**	Central of Georgia GP7 Diesel "128," CC, 11		450
___	**38428**	Alaska Budd RDC Coach, 11		300
___	**38429**	NYC Budd RDC M-497 Jet Car, 11		330
___	**38432**	MKT H16-44 Diesel "1591," CC, 11		500
___	**38433**	MKT H16-44 Diesel "1731," CC, 11		500
___	**38434**	MKT H16-44 Diesel "1732", 11		380
___	**38435**	MKT H16-44 Diesel "1733," nonpowered, 11		240
___	**38436**	LIRR H-16-44 Diesel "1501," CC, 11		500
___	**38437**	LIRR H-16-44 Diesel "1504," CC, 11		500
___	**38438**	LIRR H-16-44 Diesel "1507", 11		380
___	**38439**	LIRR H-16-44 Diesel "1509," nonpowered, 11		240
___	**38440**	UP H-16-44 Diesel "1341," CC, 11	113	500
___	**38441**	UP H-16-44 Diesel '1342," CC, 11		500
___	**38442**	UP H-16-44 Diesel "1343", 11		380
___	**38443**	UP H-16-44 Diesel "1344," nonpowered, 11		240
___	**38444**	PRR H16-44 Diesel "8807," CC, 11		500
___	**38445**	PRR H16-44 Diesel "8810," CC, 11		500
___	**38446**	PRR H16-44 Diesel "8812", 11		380
___	**38447**	PRR H16-44 Diesel "8815," nonpowered, 11		240
___	**38452**	PC Alco RS-11 Diesel "7605," CC, 12		480
___	**38453**	PC Alco RS-11 Diesel "7608," CC, 12		480
___	**38454**	PRR Alco RS-11 Diesel "622," CC, 12		480
___	**38455**	PC Alco RS-11 Diesel "7625," nonpowered, 12		240
___	**38456**	N&W Alco RS11 Diesel "308," CC, 12-13		480

		Exc	Mint
38457	N&W Alco RS-11 Diesel "318," CC, 12		480
38458	PRR Alco RS-11 Diesel "8631," CC, 12		480
38459	N&W Alco RS-11 Diesel "330," nonpowered, 12		240
38460	NKP Alco RS-11 Diesel ""855," CC, 12		480
38461	NKP Alco RS-11 Diesel "859," CC, 12		480
38462	PRR Alco RS-11 Diesel "8639," nonpowered, 12		240
38463	NKP Alco RS-11 Diesel "863," nonpowered, 12		240
38464	Alaska Alco RS-11 Diesel "3602," CC, 12		480
38465	Alaska Alco RS-11 Diesel "3604," CC, 12		480
38466	NH Alco RS-11 Diesel "1403," CC, 12		480
38467	Alaska Alco RS-11 Diesel "3607," nonpowered, 12		240
38468	Seaboard Alco RS-11 Diesel "101," CC, 12-13		480
38469	Seaboard Alco RS-11 Diesel "102," CC, 12		480
38470	NH Alco RS-11 Diesel "1405," CC, 12		480
38471	Seaboard Alco RS-11 Diesel "104," nonpowered, 12		240
38472	C&O Alco S2 Diesel Switcher "5001," CC, 11		470
38473	C&O Alco S2 Diesel Switcher "5505," CC, 11		480
38474	C&O Alco S2 Diesel Switcher "5020", 11		360
38475	C&O Alco S2 Diesel Switcher "5027," nonpowered, 11		220
38476	CN Alco S2 Diesel Switcher "7946," CC, 11		480
38477	CN Alco S2 Diesel Switcher "7949," CC, 11		480
38478	CN Alco S2 Diesel Switcher "7951", 11		360
38479	CN Alco S2 Diesel Switcher "7954", 11		360
38480	NYC Alco S2 Diesel Switcher "8504," CC, 11		480
38481	NYC Alco S2 Diesel Switcher "8507," CC, 11		480
38482	NYC Alco S2 Diesel Switcher "8514", 11		360
38483	NYC Alco S2 Diesel Switcher "8521," nonpowered, 11		220
38484	Southern Alco S2 Diesel Switcher "2209," CC, 11		480
38485	Southern Alco S2 Diesel Switcher "2211," CC, 11		480
38486	Southern Alco S2 Diesel Switcher "2215", 11		360
38487	Southern Alco S2 Diesel Switcher "2218," nonpowered, 11		220
38488	MP Alco S2 Diesel Switcher "9108," CC, 11		480
38489	MP Alco S2 Diesel Switcher "9113," CC, 11		480
38490	MP Alco S2 Diesel Switcher "9116", 11		360
38491	MP Alco S2 Diesel Switcher ""9131," nonpowered, 11		220
38493	ATSF Early Era Inspection Vehicle, CC, 12		150
38494	CP DD35 Diesel "9864," CC, 12		600
38495	CP DD35 Diesel "9868" nonpowered, 12		440
38496	SP DD35A Diesel "9903," CC, 11		600
38497	SP DD35A Diesel "9914," nonpowered , 11		440
38498	PRR DD35A Diesel "2380," CC, 11		600
38499	PRR DD35A Diesel "2383" nonpowered, 11		440
38505	CSX GP-38 Diesel, 11		140
38521	PRR GG1 Electric "4839", 11		330
38522	Amtrak GG1 Electric "926", 11		330
38524	NYC GP35 Diesel "6131," CC, 12		500
38525	NYC GP35 Diesel "6138," CC, 12		500
38526	NYC GP35 Diesel "6147," nonpowered, 12		260
38527	UP GP35 Diesel "742," CC, 12		500
38528	UP GP35 Diesel "753," CC, 12		500
38529	UP GP35 Diesel "760," nonpowered, 12		260
38530	SP GP35 Diesel "7465," CC, 12		500
38531	SP GP35 Diesel "7474," CC, 12		500

			Exc	Mint
___	**38532**	SP GP35 Diesel "7481," nonpowered, 12		260
___	**38533**	CP GP35 Diesel "5014," CC, 12		500
___	**38534**	CP GP35 Diesel "5018," CC, 12		500
___	**38535**	CP GP35 Diesel "5023," nonpowered, 12		260
___	**38536**	PRR GP35 Diesel "2297," CC, 12		500
___	**38537**	PRR GP35 Diesel "2302," CC, 12		500
___	**38538**	PRR GP35 Diesel "2305," nonpowered, 12		260
___	**38539**	N&W Alco RS-11 Diesel "308," CC, 12		480
___	**38539**	Conrail GP35 Diesel "2297," CC, 12		500
___	**38540**	Conrail GP35 Diesel "2302," CC, 12		500
___	**38541**	Conrail GP35 Diesel "2305," nonpowered, 12		260
___	**38542**	Milwaukee Road GP35 Diesel "361," CC, 12		500
___	**38543**	Milwaukee Road GP35 Diesel "363," CC, 12		500
___	**38544**	Milwaukee Road GP35 Diesel '366," nonpowered, 12		260
___	**38545**	Pacific Harbor Line Genset Switcher "31," CC, 11		800
___	**38546**	KCS Genset Switcher "1404," CC, 11-12	225	800
___	**38547**	Santa Fe Genset Switcher "9910," CC, 11		800
___	**38548**	EL GP35 Diesel "2555," CC, 12		500
___	**38549**	EL GP35 Diesel "2558," CC, 12		500
___	**38550**	EL GP35 Diesel "2561," nonpowered, 12		260
___	**38558**	D&H Baldwin RF-16 Diesel AA Set, CC, 12		730
___	**38561**	D&H Baldwin RF-16 Diesel B Unit, CC, 12		400
___	**38562**	D&H Baldwin RF-16 Diesel B Unit, nonpowered, 12		250
___	**38563**	B&O Baldwin RF-16 Diesel AA Set, CC, 12-14		730
___	**38566**	B&O Baldwin RF-16 Diesel B Unit, CC, 12-14		400
___	**38567**	B&O Baldwin RF-16 Diesel B Unit, nonpowered, 12-14		250
___	**38568**	NYC Baldwin RF-16 Diesel AA Set "3806-3808,"" CC, 12-14		730
___	**38571**	NYC Baldwin RF-16 Diesel B Unit, CC, 12-14		400
___	**38572**	NYC Baldwin RF-16 Diesel B Unit, nonpowered, 12-14		250
___	**38573**	SP Baldwin RF-16 Diesel AA Set, CC, 12-14		730
___	**38576**	SP Baldwin RF-16 Diesel B Unit, CC, 12-14		400
___	**38577**	SP Baldwin RF-16 Diesel B Unit, nonpowered, 12-14		250
___	**38579**	ATSF GP9 Diesel "744," nonpowered, 12		240
___	**38580**	NP GP9 Diesel "324," nonpowered, 12		240
___	**38581**	CSX SD80MAC Diesel "809," CC, 12-13		530
___	**38582**	CSX SD80MAC Diesel "812," CC, 12		530
___	**38583**	CSX SD80MAC Diesel "804," nonpowered, 12		260
___	**38584**	NS SD80MAC Diesel "7207," CC, 12		530
___	**38585**	NS SD80MAC Diesel "7203," CC, 12		530
___	**38586**	NS SD80MAC Diesel "7209," nonpowered, 12		260
___	**38587**	Conrail SD80MAC Diesel "4126," CC, 12		530
___	**38588**	Conrail SD80MAC Diesel "4129," CC, 12		530
___	**38589**	Conrail SD80MAC Diesel "4103," nonpowered, 12		260
___	**38593**	UP NW2 Diesel Switcher Locomotive "1028" CC, 12		470
___	**38594**	UP NW2 Diesel Switcher Locomotive "1043," CC, 12		470
___	**38595**	CB&Q Scale NW2 Diesel Switcher "9227," CC, 12		470
___	**38596**	CB&Q Scale NW2 Diesel Switcher "9245," CC, 12		470
___	**38597**	CB&Q F3 AA Diesel Set ""9962A-9962C" CC, 12-13		730
___	**38600**	UP 0-6-0 Dockside Switcher "87," traditional, 07-09		110
___	**38601**	Lionel Lines 0-6-0 Dockside Switcher, traditional, 07-09		110
___	**38605**	PRR 0-4-0 Locomotive "94," traditional, 07		170
___	**38606**	SP 0-4-0 Locomotive "71," traditional, 07-08		170

		Exc	Mint
38607	Southern 2-8-4 Berkshire Locomotive "2718," RailSounds, 07-08		175
38608	LL 2-8-2 Mikado Locomotive "57," RailSounds, 07	95	251
38609	NYC 2-8-2 Mikado Locomotive "1843", CC, 07		370
38610	NKP 2-8-4 Berkshire Locomotive "779," CC, 07-08		370
38619	Santa Fe 4-6-2 Pacific Locomotive "2037", traditional, K-Line, 06		260
38620	B&O Porter Locomotive "16," traditional, K-Line, 06		100
38621	4-6-2 Pacific Locomotive, traditional, K-Line, 06		260
38626	Holiday 2-8-2 Mikado Locomotive "25," green, RailSounds, 08		260
38627	GN 4-4-2 Atlantic Locomotive"1702" traditional, 08-09		110
38630	U.S. Army 0-6-0 Switcher "486," traditional, 08-09		110
38634	NYC 4-6-4 Hudson Locomotive "5417" TrainSounds, 07		200
38635	C&O 4-6-4 Hudson Locomotive "309," TrainSounds, 08		200
38636	ATSF 4-6-4 Hudson Locomotive "3459," TrainSounds, 07		200
38637	LL 4-6-4 Hudson Locomotive "5242," TrainSounds, 08		200
38638	UP 4-6-2 Pacific Locomotive "2888," RailSounds, 08		300
38639	Erie 4-6-2 Pacific Locomotive "2939," RailSounds, 08		300
38640	Southern 4-6-2 Pacific Locomotive "1317," RailSounds, 08		300
38641	B&M 4-6-2 Pacific Locomotive "3713," RailSounds, 08		300
38642	PRR 4-6-2 Pacific Locomotive "5385," RailSounds, 08		300
38643	Alaska Mikado 2-8-2 Locomotive "701," CC, 08-09		280
38644	T&P Mikado 2-8-2 Locomotive "810," CC, 08-09		400
38649	Christmas 4-6-4 Hudson Locomotive, traditional, 08		210
38651	Lionel Lines 0-8-0 Locomotive "100," traditional, 08-09		120
38654	Bethlehem Steel 0-4-0 Locomotive, traditional, 08-09		170
38657	Alton Limited Pacific 4-6-2 Locomotive "659" traditional, 08		300
38658	W&ARR 4-4-0 General "1892" TrainSounds, 08-09		165
38664	LL 4-4-2 Atlantic Locomotive "1058," traditional, 08-09		110
38671	Santa Flyer 4-6-0 Locomotive, 09	100	210
38677	Strasburg 0-6-0 Dockside Switcher '1252", 10		130
38678	Monopoly Hudson Locomotive, TrainSounds, 10		240
38679	ATSF 0-4-0 Switcher "1387", 10-11		190
38684	Pennsylvania Power & Light Docksider Switcher, 10		110
38687	Western & Atlantic 0-4-0 Locomotive "1897", 10-11		190
38689	AT&SF 0-8-0 Steam Locomotive "8689", 10-11	140	255
38691	North Pole Central Santa Flyer "2", 10-11		190
38692	Angela Trotta Thomas Signature Express, 10-11		190
38700	CB&Q F3 B Unit "9962B," CC, 12-13		400
38701	CB&Q F3 B Unit, 12-13		250
38702	D&RGW F3 AA Diesel Set "5531-5533," CC, 12-14		730
38705	D&RGW F3 B Unit "5532," CC, 12-14		400
38706	D&RGW F3 B Unit, 12-14		250
38707	WP F3 AB Diesel Set "803A-803B," CC, 12-14		730
38710	WP F3 A Unit, nonpowered, 12-14		380
38711	WP F3 B Unit "803C,"" CC, 12-14		400
38712	Wabash F7 AA Diesel Set "102A-1102C," CC, 12-13		730
38715	Wabash F7 B Unit "1102B," CC, 12-13		400
38716	Wabash F7 B Unit, 12-13		250
38717	Milwaukee Road F7 AA Diesel Set, CC, 12		730
38720	Milwaukee Road F7 B Unit "109B," CC, 12		400
38721	Milwaukee Road F7 B Unit, 12		250
38722	Grand Trunk SD80MAC Diesel "9085," CC, 12		530
38723	Grand Trunk SD80MAC Diesel "9088," CC, 12		530

			Exc	Mint
____	**38724**	Grand Trunk SD80MAC Diesel "9079," nonpowered, 12		260
____	**38725**	CB&Q SD80MAC Diesel "9654," CC, 12		530
____	**38726**	CB&Q SD80MAC Diesel "9651," CC, 12		530
____	**38727**	CB&Q SD80MAC Diesel "9660," nonpowered, 12		260
____	**38728**	PRR SD80MAC Diesel "9942," CC, 12	175	530
____	**38729**	PRR SD80MAC Diesel "9945," CC, 12		530
____	**38730**	PRR SD80MAC Diesel "9947," nonpowered, 12-13	85	260
____	**38731**	Polar SD80MAC Diesel, CC, 12		530
____	**38732**	CB&Q BNSF Heritage SD70ACe Diesel "1848," CC, 12-13		530
____	**38733**	CB&Q BNSF Heritage SD70ACe Diesel "1852," CC, 12-13	188	530
____	**38734**	CB&Q BNSF Heritage SD70ACe Diesel "1856," nonpowered, 12-13		260
____	**38735**	ATSF BNSF Heritage SD70ACe Diesel "1996," CC, 12-13		530
____	**38736**	ATSF BNSF Heritage SD70ACe Diesel "1997" CC, 12-13		530
____	**38737**	ATSF BNSF Heritage SD70ACe Diesel "1999," nonpowered, 12-13		260
____	**38738**	Frisco BNSF Heritage SD70ACe Diesel "1876," CC, 12-13		530
____	**38739**	Frisco BNSF Heritage SD70ACe Diesel "1896," CC, 12-14		530
____	**38740**	Frisco BNSF Heritage SD70ACe Diesel "1916," nonpowered, 12-13		260
____	**38741**	BN BNSF Heritage SD70ACe Diesel "1970," CC, 12-13		530
____	**38742**	BN BNSF Heritage SD70ACe Diesel "1975," CC, 12-13		530
____	**38743**	BN BNSF Heritage SD70ACe Diesel "1980," nonpowered, 12-13		260
____	**38744**	GN BNSF Heritage SD70ACe Diesel "1889," CC, 12-13		530
____	**38745**	GN BNSF Heritage SD70ACe Diesel "1891," CC, 12-13		530
____	**38746**	GN BNSF Heritage SD70ACe Diesel "1893," nonpowered, 12-13		260
____	**38747**	NP BNSF Heritage SD70ACe Diesel "1870," CC, 12-13		530
____	**38748**	NP BNSF Heritage SD70ACe Diesel "1872," CC, 12-13		530
____	**38749**	NP BNSF Heritage SD70ACe Diesel "1875," nonpowered, 12-13		260
____	**38750**	EMD Demonstrator SD70ACe Diesel "2012" CC, 12-13		530
____	**38751**	CNJ F3 AA Diesel Set, CC, 13-14		730
____	**38752**	Vision Centipede AA Pilot Diesels, CC, 13		2200
____	**38754**	C&NW F7 AA Diesel Set, CC, 13-14		730
____	**38757**	SP F7 AA Diesel Set, CC, 13-14		730
____	**38760**	CNJ F3 B Unit, CC, 13-14		400
____	**38761**	CNJ F3 B Unit, 13-14		250
____	**38762**	C&NW F7 B Unit "410," CC, 13-14		400
____	**38763**	C&NW F7 B Unit, 13-14		250
____	**38764**	SP F7 B Unit "8219," CC, 13		400
____	**38765**	SP F7 B Unit, 13		250
____	**38768**	N&W GP35 Diesel "1306," CC, 13-14		500
____	**38769**	N&W GP35 Diesel "1308," nonpowered, 13-14		260
____	**38770**	RI GP35 Diesel "307," CC, 13-14		500
____	**38771**	RI GP35 Diesel "309," CC, 13-14		500
____	**38772**	RI GP35 Diesel "323," nonpowered, 13-14		260
____	**38773**	WP GP35 Diesel "3002," CC, 13-14		500
____	**38774**	WP GP35 Diesel "3009," CC, 13-14		500
____	**38775**	WP GP35 Diesel "3014," nonpowered, 13-14		260
____	**38778**	C&NW RS3 Diesel '1621," LionChief, 14-16		330
____	**38779**	NYC RS3 Diesel "8244," LionChief, 14-16		330
____	**38782**	C&BQ GP35 Diesel "990," CC, 13		500
____	**38783**	C&BQ GP35 Diesel "996," nonpowered, 13		500

MODERN 1970-2024		Exc	Mint
38784	CN GP35 Diesel "4000," CC, 13		500 ___
38785	CN GP35 Diesel "4005," CC, 13		500 ___
38786	CN GP35 Diesel "4001," nonpowered, 13		260 ___
38787	D&RGW GP35 Diesel "3031," CC, 13		500 ___
38788	D&RGW GP35 Diesel "3034," CC, 13		500 ___
38789	D&RGW GP35 Diesel '3038," nonpowered, 13		260 ___
38790	DT&I GP35 Diesel "351," CC, 13		500 ___
38791	DT&I GP35 Diesel "353," CC, 13	470	900 ___
38792	DT&I GP35 Diesel "355," nonpowered, 13		260 ___
38794	GN GP35 Diesel "3018," CC, 13-14		500 ___
38795	GN GP35 Diesel "3036," nonpowered, 13-14		260 ___
38796	Chessie System GP35 Diesel "1125," CC, 13		500 ___
38797	Chessie System GP35 Diesel "1128," CC, 13		500 ___
38798	Chessie System GP35 Diesel"1113" nonpowered, 13		260 ___
38799	N&W GP35 Diesel "1302," CC, 13-14		500 ___
38800	B&M Early Era Inspection Vehicle, CC, 12		150 ___
38801	KCS Trackmobile, CC, 12-13		300 ___
38802	North Pole Central Trackmobile, CC, 12		300 ___
38803	MOW Trackmobile, CC, 12		300 ___
38804	LIRR Trackmobile, CC, 12		300 ___
38805	Conrail Trackmobile, CC, 12		300 ___
38806	NS Trackmobile, CC, 12		300 ___
38807	NP Trackmobile, CC, 12-13		300 ___
38808	Chessie System Trackmobile, CC, 12		300 ___
38809	CN Trackmobile, CC, 12		300 ___
38810	PRR Early Era Inspection Vehicle, CC, 12		150 ___
38811	D&RGW Early Era Inspection Vehicle, CC, 12		150 ___
38812	SP Early Era Inspection Vehicle, CC, 12-13		150 ___
38813	C&O Early Era Inspection Vehicle, CC, 12-13		150 ___
38814	Milwaukee Road Early Era Inspection Vehicle, CC, 12		150 ___
38815	Transylvania Early Era Inspection Vehicle, CC, 12		150 ___
38816	PRR RS3 Diesel "5620," LionChief, 14-16		330 ___
38819	D&RGW RS3 Diesel "5202," LionChief, 14-16		330 ___
38821	AT&SF GP7 Diesel ""2656," LionChief, 14-15		330 ___
38824	NP GP7 Diesel "563," LionChief, 14-15		330 ___
38825	UP GP7 Diesel "121," LionChief, 14-15		330 ___
38827	CB&Q GP7 Diesel "1596," LionChief, 14-15		330 ___
38848	Christmas Pioneer Zephyr Set, CC, 13-14		1100 ___
38853	Santa and Mrs. Claus Handcar, 13		90 ___
38855	GN GP35 Diesel "2519," CC, 13-14		500 ___
38856	CB&Q Mark Twain Zephyr, CC, 13-14		1100 ___
38860	CB&Q Pioneer Zephyr, CC, 13-14		1100 ___
38864	Lionel Lines Zephyr, CC, 13-14		1100 ___
38865	L&N GP35 Diesel "1105," CC, 13		500 ___
38866	L&N GP35 Diesel "1109," CC, 13		500 ___
38867	L&N GP35 Diesel "1114," nonpowered, 13		260 ___
38868	C&BQ GP35 Diesel "978," CC, 13		500 ___

			Exc	Mint
___	**38874**	B&O GP9 Diesel "6448," CC, 13-14		480
___	**38875**	B&O GP9 Diesel "6456," CC, 13-14		480
___	**38876**	B&O GP9 Diesel "6461," nonpowered, 13-14		240
___	**38877**	B&M GP9 Diesel "1705," CC, 13		480
___	**38878**	B&M GP9 Diesel "1714," CC, 13		480
___	**38879**	B&M GP9 Diesel "1722," nonpowered, 13		240
___	**38883**	C&NW GP9 Diesel "701," CC, 13		480
___	**38884**	C&NW GP9 Diesel "704," CC, 13		480
___	**38885**	C&NW GP9 Diesel "712," nonpowered, 13		240
___	**38886**	Erie GP9 Diesel "1260," CC, 13		480
___	**38887**	Erie GP9 Diesel "1263," CC, 13		480
___	**38888**	Erie GP9 Diesel "1265," nonpowered, 13		240
___	**38889**	Nickel Plate Road GP9 Diesel "514," CC, 13		480
___	**38890**	Nickel Plate Road GP9 Diesel "452," CC, 13		480
___	**38891**	Nickel Plate Road GP9 Diesel ""457," nonpowered, 13		240
___	**38892**	SP GP9 Diesel "3411," CC, 13		480
___	**38893**	SP GP9 Diesel "3415," CC, 13		480
___	**38894**	SP GP9 Diesel "3419," nonpowered, 13		240
___	**38895**	Wabash GP9 Diesel "484," CC, 13		480
___	**38896**	Wabash GP9 Diesel "488," CC, 13		480
___	**38897**	Wabash GP9 Diesel "491," nonpowered, 13		240
___	**38918**	Chessie System SD40-2 Diesel "7609," CC, 13		530
___	**38919**	Chessie System SD40-2 Diesel "7611," CC, 13		530
___	**38920**	Chessie System SD40-2 Diesel "7614," nonpowered, 13		240
___	**38921**	SP SD40T-2 Diesel Locomotive "8322," CC, 13		530
___	**38922**	SP SD40T-2 Diesel Locomotive "8326," CC, 13		530
___	**38923**	SP SD40T-2 Diesel, nonpowered, 13		260
___	**38924**	B&O SD40-2 Diesel "7602," CC, 13		530
___	**38925**	B&O SD40-2 Diesel "7607," CC, 13		530
___	**38926**	B&O SD40-2 Diesel "7611," nonpowered, 13		240
___	**38933**	Conrail SD40-2 Diesel "6424," CC, 13		530
___	**38934**	Conrail SD40-2 Diesel "6437," CC, 13		530
___	**38935**	Conrail SD40-2 Diesel "6468," nonpowered, 13		240
___	**38936**	UP SD40-2 Diesel "2929," CC, 13		530
___	**38937**	UP SD40-2 Diesel "2932," CC, 13		530
___	**38938**	UP SD40-2 Diesel "2947," nonpowered, 13		240
___	**38939**	NS SD40-2 Diesel "3355," CC, 13		530
___	**38940**	NS SD40-2 Diesel "3365," CC, 13		530
___	**38941**	NS SD40-2 Diesel "3379," nonpowered, 13		240
___	**38942**	Central of Georgia NS Heritage ES44AC Diesel, CC, 12		550
___	**38943**	Central of Georgia NS Heritage ES44AC Diesel, CC, 12		550
___	**38944**	Central of Georgia NS Heritage ES44AC Diesel, nonpowered, 12		280
___	**38945**	Conrail NS Heritage ES44AC Diesel, CC, 12		550
___	**38946**	Conrail NS Heritage ES44AC Diesel, CC, 12		550
___	**38947**	Conrail NS Heritage ES44AC Diesel, nonpowered, 12		280
___	**38948**	Interstate NS Heritage ES44AC Diesel Locomotive "8105," CC, 12		550
___	**38949**	Interstate NS Heritage ES44AC Diesel, CC, 12		550
___	**38950**	Interstate NS Heritage ES44AC Diesel, nonpowered, 12		280
___	**38951**	LV NS Heritage ES44AC Diesel, CC, 12		550
___	**38952**	LV NS Heritage ES44AC Diesel, CC, 12		550
___	**38953**	LV NS Heritage ES44AC Diesel, nonpowered, 12		280
___	**38954**	Nickel Plate Road NS Heritage ES44AC Diesel, CC, 12		550

		Exc	Mint
38955	Nickel Plate Road NS Heritage ES44AC Diesel, CC, 12		550
38956	Nickel Plate Road NS Heritage ES44AC Diesel, nonpowered, 12		280
38957	N&W NS Heritage ES44AC Diesel, CC, 12		550
38958	N&W NS Heritage ES44AC Diesel, CC, 12		550
38959	N&W NS Heritage ES44AC Diesel, nonpowered, 12		280
38960	PRR NS Heritage ES44AC Diesel, CC, 12		550
38961	PRR NS Heritage ES44AC Diesel, CC, 12		550
38962	PRR NS Heritage ES44AC Diesel, nonpowered, 12		280
38963	Southern NS Heritage ES44AC Diesel, CC, 12		550
38964	Southern NS Heritage ES44AC Diesel, CC, 12		550
38965	Southern NS Heritage ES44AC Diesel, nonpowered, 12		280
38966	NS Heritage ES44AC Diesel, CC, 12		550
38967	NS Heritage ES44AC Diesel, CC, 12		550
38968	NS Heritage ES44AC Diesel, nonpowered, 12		280
38969	North Pole Central GP35 Diesel "2525," CC, 13		500
38970	North Pole Central GP35 Diesel "2512," CC, 13		500
38971	North Pole Central GP35 Diesel "2513," nonpowered, 13		260
38972	Reading GP35 Diesel "3625," CC, 13		500
38973	Reading GP35 Diesel "3630," CC, 13		500
38974	Reading GP35 Diesel "3633," nonpowered, 13		260
38975	AT&SF GP35 Diesel "3312," CC, 13		500
38976	AT&SF GP35 Diesel "3318," CC, 13		500
38977	AT&SF GP35 Diesel "3329," nonpowered, 13		260
38978	Alaska GP35 Diesel "2501," CC, 13		500
38979	Alaska GP35 Diesel "2503," CC, 13		500
38980	Alaska GP35 Diesel "2502," nonpowered, 13		260
38981	B&O GP35 Diesel "2506," CC, 13-14		500
38982	B&O GP35 Diesel "2511," CC, 13-14		500
38983	B&O GP35 Diesel "2517," nonpowered, 13-14		260
38984	C&O GP35 Diesel "3515," CC, 13-14		500
38985	C&O GP35 Diesel "3521," CC, 13-14		500
38986	C&O GP35 Diesel "3526," nonpowered, 13-14		260
38987	MP GP35 Diesel "603," CC, 13		500
38988	MP GP35 Diesel "607," CC, 13		500
38989	MP GP35 Diesel "611," nonpowered, 13		260
38990	GM&O GP35 Diesel "603," CC, 13-14		500
38991	GM&O GP35 Diesel "607," CC, 13-14		500
38992	GM&O GP35 Diesel "611," nonpowered, 13-14		260
38993	WM GP35 Diesel "3576," CC, 13		500
38994	WM GP35 Diesel "3578," CC, 13		500
38995	WM GP35 Diesel "3580," nonpowered, 13		260
38996	CSX GP35 Diesel "4355," CC, 13		500
38997	CSX GP35 Diesel "4363," CC, 13		500
38998	CSX GP35 Diesel "4390," nonpowered, 13		260
38999	NS GP35 Diesel "2916," CC, 13		500
39008	PRR Heavyweight Passenger Car 4-pack, 00		225
39009	PRR Indian Rock Heavyweight Combination Car, 00		50
39010	PRR Andrew Carnegie Heavyweight Passenger Coach, 00		60
39011	PRR Solomon P. Chase Heavyweight Passenger Coach, 00		60
39012	PRR Skyline View Heavyweight Observation Car, 00		50
39013	B&O Heavyweight Passenger Car 4-pack, 00		400
39014	B&O Harper's Ferry Heavyweight Combination Car, 00		50
39015	B&O Youngstown Heavyweight Passenger Coach, 00		50

			Exc	Mint
___	**39016**	B&O New Castle Heavyweight Passenger Coach, 00		50
___	**39017**	B&O Chicago Heavyweight Observation Car, 00		50
___	**39028**	LL Heavyweight Passenger Car 3-pack, 00		195
___	**39029**	LL Irvington Heavyweight Coach "2625", 00		60
___	**39030**	LL Madison Heavyweight Coach "2627", 00		60
___	**39031**	LL Manhattan Heavyweight Coach "2628", 00		60
___	**39032**	UP Madison Passenger Car 4-pack, 00		275
___	**39038**	SP Madison Baggage Car "6015", 01		100
___	**39039**	SP Madison Coach Car "1978", 01		100
___	**39040**	SP Madison Coach "1975", 01		NRS
___	**39041**	SP Madison Observation Car "2951", 01		100
___	**39042**	N&W Heavyweight Passenger Car 4-pack, 00		325
___	**39047**	B&O Heavyweight Passenger Car 2-pack, 01		160
___	**39050**	PRR Heavyweight Passenger Car 2-pack, 01		215
___	**39053**	Alaska Streamliner Car 2-pack, 01		90
___	**39056**	NYC Streamliner Car 2-pack, 01		75
___	**39059**	Santa Fe Streamliner Car 2-pack, 01		100
___	**39062**	B&O Streamliner Car 2-pack, 01		75
___	**39065**	PRR Streamliner Car 4-pack, 01	63	165
___	**39082**	Blue Comet Heavyweight Passenger Car 2-pack, 02		325
___	**39085**	Freedom Train Heavyweight Passenger Car 3-pack, 03		260
___	**39092**	PRR Streamliner Car 2-pack, 01		70
___	**39099**	Alton Limited Heavyweight Passenger Car 2-pack, 03		230
___	**39100**	William Penn Congressional Coach, 00		115
___	**39101**	Molly Pitcher Congressional Coach, 00		100
___	**39102**	Betsy Ross Congressional Vista Dome Car, 00		100
___	**39103**	Alexander Hamilton Congressional Observation Car, 00		100
___	**39104**	Phoebe Snow Car, StationSounds, 99		255
___	**39105**	Milwaukee Road Hiawatha Car, StationSounds, 99		235
___	**39106**	CP Aluminum Passenger Car 2-pack, 00		185
___	**39107**	CP Blair Manor Aluminum Passenger Coach "2553", 00		115
___	**39108**	CP Craig Manor Aluminum Passenger Coach "2554", 00		110
___	**39109**	"Spirit of the Century" Aluminum Passenger Car 4-pack, 99		520
___	**39110**	"Spirit of the Century" Full Vista Dome Car, 99-00		100
___	**39111**	"Spirit of the Century" Full Vista Dome Car, 99-00		100
___	**39112**	"Spirit of the Century" Full Vista Dome Car, 99-00		100
___	**39113**	"Spirit of the Century" Skytop Observation Car, 99-00		100
___	**39118**	Texas Special Garland Coach "1203," w/StationSounds, 99-00		220
___	**39119**	Southern Aluminum Passenger Car 4-pack, 00		335
___	**39120**	Southern Grand Junction Aluminum Passenger/Baggage Car, 00		280
___	**39121**	Southern Charlottesville Aluminum Passenger Coach "812", 00		90
___	**39122**	Southern Roanoke Aluminum Passenger Coach "814", 00		250
___	**39123**	Southern Memphis Aluminum Observation Car "1152", 00		90
___	**39124**	Amtrak Superliner Aluminum Passenger Car 4-pack, 02		405
___	**39129**	Santa Fe Superliner Aluminum Passenger Car 4-pack, 02		305
___	**39141**	RI Aluminum Passenger Car 4-pack, 01		400
___	**39146**	UP Aluminum Passenger Car 4-pack, 01		285
___	**39151**	CP Aluminum Passenger Car 2-pack, 01		315
___	**39154**	PRR Congressional Aluminum Passenger Car 2-pack, 02		195
___	**39155**	PRR Congressional Baggage Car, 02		105
___	**39156**	PRR Robert Morris Congressional Coach, 02		100

		Exc	Mint
39157	Southern Aluminum Passenger Car 2-pack, 01		290
39160	KCS Aluminum Passenger Car 2-pack, 01	170	260
39163	Erie-Lack. Aluminum Passenger Car 2-pack, 01		230
39166	Texas Special Aluminum Passenger Car 2-pack, 01	300	430
39169	ACL Aluminum Passenger Car 4-pack, 01		360
39170	ACL Aluminum Baggage Car "1634", 01		90
39171	ACL Aluminum Coach "1090", 01		90
39172	ACL Aluminum Coach "1111", 01		90
39173	ACL Aluminum Observation "1115", 01		90
39179	NP Aluminum Passenger Car 2-pack, 02	118	298
39182	WP Aluminum Passenger Car 2-pack, 02		280
39185	Rio Grande Aluminum Passenger Car 2-pack, 02		290
39194	UP Aluminum Passenger Car 2-pack, 02		220
39197	CP Aluminum Passenger Coach, StationSounds, 02		225
39198	PRR Aluminum Passenger Coach, StationSounds, 02		210
39200	Hellgate Bridge Boxcar #2 "1900-2000", 00 u		55
39202	Lionel Centennial Boxcar "1900-2000", 00		46
39203	Postwar "6464" Series X, 3 cars, 01	38	105
39204	New Haven Boxcar "6464-725", 01		44
39205	Alaska Boxcar "6464-825", 01		55
39206	NYC Boxcar "6464-900", 01		40
39207	UP Boxcar "508500," red, 00	23	55
39208	UP Boxcar "903658," silver, 00		42
39209	UP Boxcar "500200," yellow, 00		40
39210	6530 Fire Fighting Car, 00		37
39211	Postwar "6464" Boxcar 3-pack #2, 00	28	88
39212	Postwar "6464" SP&S Boxcar, 00		30
39213	Postwar "6464" Wabash Boxcar, 00		30
39214	Postwar "6464" Kansas, Oklahoma & Gulf Boxcar, 00		30
39216	PRR DD Boxcar "47211", 01		46
39220	B&LE Heavyweight Boxcar "82101", 01		41
39221	L&N Heavyweight Boxcar "109829", 01		41
39222	Conrail Heavyweight Boxcar "269198", 01		44
39223	Postwar "6464" Archive Boxcar Set, 3-pack, 02		125
39224	Postwar "6464" Monon Boxcar, 02		45
39225	Postwar "6464" Tidewater Southern Boxcar, 02		40
39226	Postwar "6464" SP Boxcar, 02		45
39227	Postwar "6468" Automobile Boxcar 3-pack, 01		95
39228	Postwar "6468" B&O DD Boxcar, Blue, 01		30
39229	Postwar "6468" B&O DD Boxcar, Tuscan, 01		40
39230	Postwar "6468" NH DD Boxcar, 01		30
39236	WP Boxcar "6464-250", 01		55
39238	Elvis Boxcar, 03		36
39239	P&LE Boxcar "22300, 02		35
39240	Pennsylvania Boxcar "118747", 02		32
39241	PC Boxcar "252455", 02		28
39242	Postwar "6464" Boxcar 3-pack #1, Archive Collection, 03-04	50	105
39243	Soo Line Boxcar, Archive Collection, 03-04		35
39244	D&RGW Cookie Box Boxcar, Archive Collection, 03-04		35
39245	Duluth, South Shore & Atlantic Boxcar, Archive Collection, 03-04		30
39246	Century Club PRR Sharknose Diesel Boxcar, 00		50
39247	NYC DD Boxcar "6468", 02-03		32

			Exc	Mint
___	**39248**	Lackawanna DD Boxcar w/Hobo, 03		45
___	**39249**	LRRC 2003 Christmas Boxcar, 03 u		40
___	**39250**	Campbell's Kids Centennial Boxcar, 03-04		40
___	**39252**	Lenny Dean 60th Anniversary Boxcar, 04		38
___	**39253**	No. 6464 Boxcar 3-pack #2, Archive Collection, 04		100
___	**39254**	Detroit & Mackinac Boxcar, Archive Collection, 04		35
___	**39255**	NS Boxcar, Archive Collection, 04		35
___	**39256**	L&N Boxcar, Archive Collection, 04		35
___	**39257**	WP Boxcar "6464-100," boys set add-on, 03		50
___	**39258**	Elvis Presley "All Shook Up" Boxcar, 03-04		40
___	**39259**	Buick Centennial Boxcar, 03		40
___	**39260**	New Haven Boxcar, 04		40
___	**39262**	Elvis Presley "Elvis Has Left the Building" Boxcar, 04		38
___	**39263**	M&StL Boxcar, Postwar Celebration Series, 05		35
___	**39267**	No. 6464 Boxcar 3-pack #3, Archive Collection, 05		100
___	**39271**	State of Maine Boxcar, 04		35
___	**39273**	No. 6464 Boxcar 3-pack #4, Archive Collection, 06		100
___	**39274**	NP Boxcar, Archive Collection, 06		35
___	**39275**	US Air Force Boxcar, Archive Collection, 06		35
___	**39276**	Lilly Paper Cup Boxcar, Archive Collection, 06		35
___	**39281**	Florida State University Boxcar, 07	32	50
___	**39282**	Purdue University Boxcar, 08		50
___	**39283**	University of Virginia Boxcar, 08		50
___	**39284**	Penn State University Boxcar, 06-07		45
___	**39285**	U.S. Military Academy at West Point Boxcar, 08		50
___	**39286**	University of Illinois Boxcar, 06-07		45
___	**39287**	University of Alabama Boxcar, 06-07		45
___	**39289**	University of Oklahoma Boxcar, 06-08		50
___	**39290**	Postwar "6464" Boxcar 2-pack, rare variations, 08	50	108
___	**39291**	University of Michigan Boxcar, 06-07		45
___	**39292**	Monopoly Boxcar 3-pack, 08		135
___	**39296**	UPS Centennial Boxcar #3, 08-09		55
___	**39297**	Macy's Parade Boxcar, 07		55
___	**39298**	Monopoly Boxcar 3-pack #2, 08		145
___	**39299**	Lenny Dean Commemorative Boxcar, 08		50
___	**39300**	Postwar "6464-1" WP Boxcar, red lettering, 08		70
___	**39301**	Postwar "6464-300" Rutland Boxcar, 08		80
___	**39302**	University of Maryland Boxcar, 08		50
___	**39303**	Villanova University Boxcar, 08		50
___	**39304**	Auburn University Boxcar, 08		50
___	**39305**	Monopoly Virginia Ave. Boxcar, 08		50
___	**39306**	Monopoly Connecticut Ave. Boxcar, 08		50
___	**39307**	Monopoly Marvin Gardens Boxcar, 08		50
___	**39308**	CP Rail "6565" Boxcar "58700", 08-10		55
___	**39309**	Macy's Parade Boxcar, 08		50
___	**39310**	Monopoly Boxcar 3-pack #3, 09-10		170
___	**39316**	New Haven Automobile Boxcar, 09-10		60
___	**39317**	Wizard of Oz Boxcar #1, 09-10		60
___	**39318**	Wizard of Oz Boxcar #2, 09-10		60
___	**39319**	Boy Scouts "Scout Law" Add-on Boxcar, 10		60
___	**39321**	Lionel Art Boxcar 2-pack, 10		116
___	**39325**	Macy's Parade Boxcar, 09		45
___	**39326**	UPS Centennial Boxcar #4, 10-11		60

MODERN 1970-2024		Exc	Mint	
39328	Monopoly Boxcar 3-pack #4, 10-11		220	___
39332	Holiday Boxcar, 10		60	___
39334	Coca-Cola Christmas Boxcar, 10		70	___
39335	Thomas Kinkade Boxcar, 10, 12		60	___
39336	Angela Trotta Thomas "My Turn Yet, Dad?" Boxcar, 10		60	___
39337	George Washington Boxcar, 11-12		60	___
39338	Abraham Lincoln Boxcar, 11-12		60	___
39339	Theodore Roosevelt Boxcar, 11-12		60	___
39340	Thomas Jefferson Boxcar, 11-12		60	___
39341	2010 Lionel Dealer Appreciation Boxcar, 10 u		40	___
39342	Strasburg Boxcar, 11		55	___
39343	New Jersey Central Boxcar, 10		45	___
39344	Monopoly Boxcar 3-pack #5, 11-12		165	___
39345	Monopoly Tennessee Avenue Boxcar, 11		55	___
39346	Monopoly Atlantic Avenue Boxcar, 11		55	___
39347	Monopoly Illinois Avenue Boxcar, 11		55	___
39348	Lionel NASCAR Collectables Boxcar, 11-12		60	___
39350	Thomas Kinkade "All Aboard for Christmas" Boxcar, 12-13		60	___
39351	Peanuts Thanksgiving Boxcar, 12		70	___
39354	Monopoly North Carolina Avenue Boxcar, 12		70	___
39358	Boy Scouts "Prepared For Life" Boxcar, 12		60	___
39359	Thanksgiving Boxcar, 12		60	___
39360	Boy Scouts Cub Scout Boxcar, 12-13		60	___
39361	Coca-Cola Polar Bear Boxcar, 14		70	___
39362	Thomas Kinkade "Emerald City" Boxcar, 12-15		75	___
39363	Peanuts Halloween Boxcar, 12		65	___
39364	2013 Lionel Employee Christmas Boxcar, 13		60	___
39372	Southern Hi-Cube Boxcar, 13-14	12	30	___
39376	Monopoly Boxcar 2-pack, States and Vermont Avenues, 13-15		140	___
39379	Monopoly Boxcar 2-pack, Med. and St. James Ave, 13-15		140	___
39383	Prewar "2719" Boxcar, 13		65	___
39385	U.S. Navy 1-D Tank Car, 13-15		70	___
39386	U.S. Marines 1-D Tank Car, 13-15		70	___
39387	U.S. Air Force 1-D Tank Car, 13-15		70	___
39388	U.S. National Guard 1-D Tank Car, 13-16		70	___
39389	U.S. Coast Guard 1-D Tank Car, 13-16		70	___
39391	U.S. Army Flatcar, 13-16		70	___
39392	U.S. Navy Flatcar, 13-16		70	___
39393	U.S. Marines Flatcar, 13-16		70	___
39394	U.S. Air Force Flatcar, 13-16		70	___
39395	U.S. National Guard Flatcar, 13-16		70	___
39396	U.S. Coast Guard Flatcar, 13-16	33	70	___
39398	Santa's Flyer Reefer, 13		43	___
39399	U.S. Army 1-D Tank Car, 13-15		70	___
39400	Republic Steel Slag Car 3-pack (std O), 04		100	___
39404	Republic Steel Hot Metal Car 3-pack (std O), 04		130	___
39411	Jones & Laughlin Hot Metal Car 3-pack (std O), 05	80	190	___
39423	Postwar "3460" LL Flatcar with trailers, 05		45	___
39424	U.S. Steel 16-wheel Flatcar with girders, 05		70	___
39425	Hood's Flatcar with milk container, traditional, 05		55	___
39426	Nestle Nesquik Flatcar with milk container, traditional, 05		55	___
39428	Bethlehem Steel Slag Car #4 (std O), 05		60	___
39429	Bethlehem Steel Hot Metal Car #8 (std O), 05		70	___

			Exc	Mint
____	**39430**	Youngstown Sheet & Tube Slag Car #7 (std O), 05		60
____	**39431**	Youngstown Sheet & Tube Hot Metal Car #11 (std O), 05		70
____	**39435**	Postwar "6477" Flatcar with pipes, 06		50
____	**39436**	Postwar "6262" Wheel Car, 06		50
____	**39437**	Supplee Flatcar with milk container, 06		60
____	**39439**	6827 Flatcar with P&H power shovel, 04		50
____	**39440**	6828 Flatcar with P&H truck crane, 04		50
____	**39443**	U.S. Steel Slag Car 3-pack #2 (std O), 06		170
____	**39447**	Postwar "6561" LL Cable Reel Car, Archive Collection, 06-07		55
____	**39450**	Postwar "6414" Evans Auto Loader, Archive Collection, 06		70
____	**39452**	White Bros. Flatcar with milk container, 07		60
____	**39457**	Postwar "6175" Flatcar with rocket, 08		55
____	**39458**	Postwar "6844" Flatcar with missiles, 08		55
____	**39463**	Postwar "6430" Flatcar with trailers, 08		55
____	**39468**	Allis-Chalmers Car "52369", 08-09	28	60
____	**39469**	Christmas Egg Nog Barrel Car, 08		50
____	**39470**	UP Well Car "147128", 08		65
____	**39471**	Postwar "6264" Flatcar, 08		60
____	**39472**	ATSF Culvert Gondola, 08		60
____	**39473**	Play-Doh Vat Car, 08		55
____	**39475**	UPS Flatcar with trailer, 08		65
____	**39476**	Bethlehem Steel 16-wheel Flatcar, 08		75
____	**39477**	Christmas Flatcar with reindeer trailers, 08		60
____	**39478**	Postwar "6475" Pickles Vat Car, 08		55
____	**39479**	Postwar "6404" Flatcar with brown automobile, 08		50
____	**39480**	Western & Atlantic Cannon Flatcar, 09		60
____	**39482**	CSX WM Track Maintenance Car "6812", 11		65
____	**39483**	CSX P&LE Gondola "69812", 11		65
____	**39484**	Cocoa Marsh Vat Car, 10-12		60
____	**39486**	Deep Sea Challenger Submarine Car, 11		60
____	**39487**	BN I-Beam Flatcar "870798", 11		60
____	**39488**	Reese's Vat Car, 10		60
____	**39490**	Western & Atlantic Cannonball Flatcar, 10		55
____	**39497**	Christmas Reindeer Stock Car, 10-11		60
____	**39498**	CNJ Gondola with culvert pipes, 11		55
____	**39499**	Alaska Oil Barrel Ramp Car, 11		50
____	**39502**	Monongahela NS Heritage ES44AC Diesel, nonpowered, 13		280
____	**39530**	PRR 1955 Pickup Truck, CC, 13		180
____	**39531**	UP 1955 Pickup Truck, CC, 13		180
____	**39532**	ATSF 1955 Pickup Truck, CC, 13-14		180
____	**39533**	CP 1955 Pickup Truck, CC, 13-14		180
____	**39534**	D&RGW 1955 Pickup Truck, CC, 13		180
____	**39535**	GN 1955 Pickup Truck, CC, 13		180
____	**39536**	MKT 1955 Pickup Truck, CC, 13-14		180
____	**39537**	NYC 1955 Pickup Truck, CC, 13		180
____	**39538**	Nickel Plate Road 1955 Pickup Truck, CC, 13		180
____	**39539**	NP1955 Pickup Truck, CC, 13-14		180
____	**39540**	Southern 1955 Pickup Truck, CC, 13		180
____	**39541**	SP 1955 Pickup Truck, CC, 13-14		180
____	**39542**	Weyerhaueser 1955 Pickup Truck, CC, 13-14		180
____	**39543**	Texas Special F3 B Unit, 13-14		230
____	**39544**	Texas Special F3 B Unit, CC, 13-14		380
____	**39547**	PRR F3 B Unit, 13-14		230

		Exc	Mint
39548	PRR F3 B Unit, CC, 13-14		380 ___
39554	NS GP35 Diesel "3918," CC, 13		500 ___
39555	NS GP35 Diesel "2915," nonpowered, 13		260 ___
39556	CP GP35 Diesel "5004," CC, 13-14		500 ___
39557	CP GP35 Diesel "5007," CC, 13-14		500 ___
39558	CP GP35 Diesel "5009," nonpowered, 13-14		260 ___
39562	BN GP35 Diesel "2533," CC, 13-14		500 ___
39563	BN GP35 Diesel "2509," CC, 13-14		500 ___
39564	BN GP35 Diesel "2523," nonpowered, 13-14		260 ___
39565	ATSF Dash-9 Diesel "612," CC, 13		530 ___
39566	ATSF Dash-9 Diesel "623," CC, 13		530 ___
39567	ATSF Dash-9 Diesel "631," nonpowered, 13		260 ___
39568	BC Rail Dash-9 Diesel "4641," CC, 13		530 ___
39569	BC Rail Dash-9 Diesel "4647," CC, 13		530 ___
39570	BC Rail Dash-9 Diesel "4652," nonpowered, 13		260 ___
39571	BNSF Dash-9 Diesel "4023," CC, 13		530 ___
39572	BNSF Dash-9 Diesel "4037," CC, 13		530 ___
39573	BNSF Dash-9 Diesel "4046," nonpowered, 13		260 ___
39574	C&NW Dash-9 Diesel "8605," CC, 13		530 ___
39575	C&NW Dash-9 Diesel "8610," CC, 13		530 ___
39576	C&NW Dash-9 Diesel "8622," nonpowered, 13		260 ___
39577	SP Dash-9 Diesel "8112," CC, 13		530 ___
39578	SP Dash-9 Diesel "8123," CC, 13		530 ___
39579	SP Dash-9 Diesel "8129," nonpowered, 13		260 ___
39580	UP Dash-9 Diesel "9599," CC, 13		530 ___
39581	UP Dash-9 Diesel "9714," CC, 13		530 ___
39582	UP Dash-9 Diesel "9717," nonpowered, 13		260 ___
39583	CSX Dash-9 Diesel "9036," CC, 13		530 ___
39584	CSX Dash-9 Diesel "9048," CC, 13		530 ___
39585	CSX Dash-9 Diesel "9051," nonpowered, 13		260 ___
39586	NS Dash-9 Diesel "9310," CC, 13		530 ___
39587	NS Dash-9 Diesel "9322," CC, 13		530 ___
39588	NS Dash-9 Diesel "9334," nonpowered, 13		260 ___
39589	CN Dash-9 Diesel "2534," CC, 13		530 ___
39590	CN Dash-9 Diesel "2547," CC, 13		530 ___
39591	CN Dash-9 Diesel "2570," nonpowered, 13		260 ___
39592	CNJ NS Heritage SD70ACe Diesel "1071," CC, 13		530 ___
39593	CNJ NS Heritage SD70ACe Diesel "1831," CC, 13		530 ___
39594	CNJ NS Heritage SD70ACe Diesel "1834," nonpowered, 13		260 ___
39595	DL&W NS Heritage SD70ACe Diesel "1074," CC, 13		530 ___
39596	DL&W NS Heritage SD70ACe Diesel "1853," CC, 13		530 ___
39597	DL&W NS Heritage SD70ACe Diesel "1856," nonpowered, 13		260 ___
39598	Monongahela NS Heritage ES44AC Diesel "8025," CC, 12		550 ___
39599	Monongahela NS Heritage ES44AC Diesel "1901," CC, 12		550 ___
39600	PRR E8 AA Diesel Set, CC, 13		930 ___
39603	B&O E9 AA Diesel Set, CC, 13		930 ___
39606	FEC E9 AA Diesel Set, CC, 13		930 ___
39609	SP E9 AA Diesel Set, CC, 13		930 ___
39612	UP E9 AA Diesel Set, CC, 13		930 ___
39615	CB&Q E9 AA Diesel Set, CC, 13		930 ___
39618	MILW E9 AA Diesel Set, CC, 13		930 ___
39621	KCS E9 AA Diesel Set, CC, 13		930 ___
39624	Erie NS Heritage SD70ACe Diesel "1068," CC, 13		530 ___

			Exc	Mint
____	**39625**	Erie NS Heritage SD70ACe Diesel "1832," CC, 13		530
____	**39626**	Erie NS Heritage SD70ACe Diesel "1835," nonpowered, 13		260
____	**39627**	Illinois Terminal NS Heritage SD70ACe Diesel "1072," CC, 13		530
____	**39628**	Illinois Terminal NS Heritage SD70ACe Diesel "1896," CC, 13		530
____	**39629**	Illinois Terminal NS Heritage SD70ACe Diesel "1899," nonpowered, 13		260
____	**39630**	NYC NS Heritage SD70ACe Diesel "1066," CC, 13		530
____	**39631**	NYC NS Heritage SD70ACe Diesel "1831," CC, 13		530
____	**39632**	NYC NS Heritage SD70ACe Diesel "1834," nonpowered, 13		260
____	**39633**	Reading NS Heritage SD70ACe Diesel "1067," CC, 13		530
____	**39634**	Reading NS Heritage SD70ACe Diesel "1833," CC, 13		530
____	**39635**	Reading NS Heritage SD70ACe Diesel "1836," nonpowered, 13		260
____	**39636**	Savannah & Atlanta NS Heritage SD70ACe Diesel "1065," CC, 13		530
____	**39637**	Savannah & Atlanta NS Heritage SD70ACe Diesel "1915," CC, 13		530
____	**39638**	Savannah & Atlanta NS Heritage SD70ACe "1918," nonpowered, 13		260
____	**39639**	Virginian NS Heritage SD70ACe Diesel "1069," CC, 13		530
____	**39640**	Virginian NS Heritage SD70ACe Diesel "1907," CC, 13		530
____	**39641**	Virginian NS Heritage SD70ACe Diesel "1910," nonpowered, 13		260
____	**39642**	Wabash NS Heritage SD70ACe Diesel "1070," CC, 13		530
____	**39643**	Wabash NS Heritage SD70ACe Diesel "1877," CC, 13		530
____	**39644**	Wabash NS Heritage SD70ACe Diesel "1880," nonpowered, 13		260
____	**39645**	PC NS Heritage SD70ACe Diesel "1073," CC, 13		530
____	**39646**	PC NS Heritage SD70ACe Diesel "1968," CC, 13		530
____	**39647**	PC NS Heritage SD70ACe Diesel "1971," nonpowered, 13		260
____	**39680**	Wizard of Oz 4-4-2 Atlantic Locomotive, 09		150
____	**51000**	MILW Hiawatha Streamlined Steam Passenger Set, 88		700
____	**51008**	Burlington Pioneer Zephyr Diesel Passenger Set, RailSounds, 04	350	863
____	**51009**	Prewar "269E" Steam Freight Set, TrainSounds, 06		630
____	**51010**	Prewar "246E" Steam Passenger Set, TrainSounds, 07-08	150	630
____	**51012**	Christmas Tinplate Freight Set, 08		675
____	**51014**	Prewar "291W" Red Comet Passenger Car Set, 08	410	675
____	**51220**	NYC Imperial Castle Passenger Coach, 93 u		500
____	**51221**	NYC Niagara County Passenger Coach, 93 u		500
____	**51222**	NYC Cascade Glory Passenger Coach, 93 u		500
____	**51223**	NYC City of Detroit Passenger Coach, 93 u		500
____	**51224**	NYC Imperial Falls Passenger Coach, 93 u		500
____	**51225**	NYC Westchester County Passenger Coach, 93 u		500
____	**51226**	NYC Cascade Grotto Passenger Coach, 93 u		500
____	**51227**	NYC City of Indianapolis Passenger Coach, 93 u		500
____	**51228**	NYC Manhattan Island Observation Car, 93 u		500
____	**51229**	NYC Diner "680", 93 u		500
____	**51230**	NYC Baggage Car "5017", 93 u		500
____	**51231**	NYC Century Club Passenger Coach, 93 u		500
____	**51232**	NYC Thousand Islands Observation Car, 93 u		500
____	**51233**	NYC Diner "684", 93 u		500
____	**51234**	NYC Baggage Car "5020", 93 u		500
____	**51235**	NYC Century Tavern Passenger Coach, 93 u		500
____	**51236**	NYC City of Toledo Passenger Coach, 93 u		500
____	**51237**	NYC Imperial Mansion Passenger Coach, 93 u		500
____	**51238**	NYC Imperial Palace Passenger Coach, 93 u		500

		Exc	Mint
51239	NYC Cascade Spirit Passenger Coach, 93 u		500
51240	NYC Diner "681", 93 u		500
51241	NYC City of Chicago Passenger Coach, 93 u		500
51242	NYC Imperial Garden Passenger Coach, 93 u		500
51243	NYC Imperial Fountain Passenger Coach, 93 u		500
51244	NYC Cascade Valley Passenger Coach, 93 u		500
51245	NYC Diner "685", 93 u		500
51300	Shell Semi-Scale 1-D Tank Car "8124", 91	50	135
51301	Lackawanna Semi-Scale Reefer "7000", 92	119	161
51401	PRR Semi-Scale Boxcar "100800", 91	84	128
51402	C&O Semi-Scale Stock Car "95250", 92	94	138
51422	Southern Searchlight Car, 91-92	15	36
51501	B&O Semi-Scale Hopper "532000", 91	78	108
51502	LL Steel Die-cast Ore Car "6486-3" (SSS), 96		80
51503	LL Steel Die-cast Ore Car "6486-1" (SSS), 96		80
51504	LL Steel Die-cast Ore Car "6486-2" (SSS), 96		70
51600	NYC Depressed Center Flatcar with transformer "6418", 96		105
51701	NYC Semi-Scale Caboose "19400", 91	84	123
51702	PRR N-8 Caboose "478039", 91-92	300	385
52038	Southern Hopper "360794" w/Coal (std 0), 94 u	36	46
52040	GTW Flatcar w/Tractor and trailer, 94 u	42	51
52044	Mogen David Wine Vat Car, 95 u	21	30
52053	TTOS Carail Convention Boxcar, 94	50	55
52054	Carail Boxcar, 94 u		300
52066	Trainmaster Tractor and Trailer, 94 u	80	125
52068	Toy Train Parade Contadina Boxcar "16245", 94	15	28
52069	Carail Tractor and Trailer, 94 u		75
52070	Knoebel's Boxcar #1, 95 u		94
52075	United Auto Workers Boxcar, 95 u		90
52082	Steamtown Lackawanna Boxcar, 95 u		90
52096	Snow Village Boxcar "9756", 95 u	55	85
58032	CTT 30th Anniversary Boxcar "69013", 17 u		50
52132	Knoebel's Boxcar #2, 99 u		95
52133	Knoebel's Boxcar #3, 98 u		108
52134	Knoebel's Boxcar #4, 00 u		105
52136A	Christmas Special Tractor and Trailer, 97 u		100
52136B	Frisco Special Tractor and Trailer, 98 u		100
52137	Red Wing Shoes Boot Oil Tank Car, 98		65
52141	Zep Manufacturing Boxcar, 96	86	132
52158	Monopoly Mint Car "M-0539", 98		340
52159	Monopoly Depressed Center Flatcar with transformer, 98		95
52160	Monopoly Water Works Tank Car, 98		105
52161	Monopoly SP-type Caboose "M-1006", 98		55
52168	Carail Flatcar with Trailer "17455", 99 u		120
52169	Zep Manufacturing Flatcar with trailer "62734", 99 u		90
52181	Monopoly Set #2, 4-pack, 99		295
52182	Monopoly Railroads Boxcar "M0636", 99 u		78
52183	Monopoly Jail Car "M-1131", 99		75
52184	Monopoly Free Parking Flatcar with 2 autos, 99		60
52185	Monopoly Chance Gondola "M-0893", 99		50
52187	Madison Hardware Flatcar with 2 trailers, 99		98
52188	Carail Aquarium with 2 autos, 25th Anniversary, 99		95
52189	Monopoly 4-6-4 Hudson Locomotive, 99	300	555

			Exc	Mint
___	**52200**	TTOS SW SP Overnight Merchandise Service Boxcar, 00 u		40
___	**52207**	Lionel Lines SD40 Diesel, traditional, 00	167	600
___	**52208**	Lionel Lines Extended Vision Caboose, 00 u		200
___	**52218**	Monopoly 4-4-2 Steam Freight Set, 00 u	100	391
___	**52219**	Monopoly 4-6-4 Hudson Locomotive, bronze, 00 u		530
___	**52224A**	SP Flatcar with Navajo tractor and trailer, 01		25
___	**52224B**	SP Flatcar with Trailer Flatcar Service tractor and trailer, 01		25
___	**52225**	Monopoly 4-6-4 Hudson Locomotive, pewter, 01 u		495
___	**52231**	British Columbia 1-D Tank Car, 00 u		65
___	**52249**	Knoebel's Amusement Park 75th Anniversary Boxcar, 01 u		117
___	**52262**	Plasticville Boxcar, 01 u		120
___	**52282**	WP Feather Boxcar, red, 03		365
___	**52315/20**	PRR FM Diesel and Caboose, 04 u		440
___	**52330**	B&O Museum Fundraiser Boxcar, 03 u		100
___	**52334**	TTOS Smokey Bear 60th Anniversary 1-D Tank Car, 04 u		80
___	**52335**	TTOS Smokey Bear 60th Anniversary Boxcar, 04 u		70
___	**52371**	NYC Flatcar with tanker trailer, 05 u		150
___	**52422**	Christmas Festival of Trees Boxcar, 06u		80
___	**52435**	Georgia Power Caboose, 08 u		26
___	**52447**	LCCA NH Alco Diesel and Passenger Cars, 09 u		140
___	**52452**	Grzybowski's Trains 30th Anniversary Boxcar, 07 u		39
___	**52495**	LCCA UP Water Tower, 08 u		30
___	**52597**	U.S. Navy Flatcar w/trailer, "832011", 11		60
___	**55452**	Norscot Caterpillar Steam Freight Set, 08 u	270	325
___	**58213**	LCCA B&M GP7 Diesel "2335," LionChief Plus , 15 u	135	250
___	**58226**	TCA Cumbres & Toltec Boxcar, 16 u		75
___	**58253**	LCCA Lionel 115th Anniversary Trailer, 15 u		25
___	**58255**	LCCA Lionelville Transit Tractor, 15 u	25	40
___	**58262**	U.S. Coast Guard Flatcar w/trailer "832011", 11 u		60
___	**58267**	LCCA KCS Inspection Truck, 16 u	56	90
___	**58269**	LCCA Tacoma Pickup Truck, 17 u		75
___	**58270**	LCCA NP Pickup Truck, 17 u		75
___	**58504**	Lionel Flatcar w/Madison Hardware Trailer, 15 u		120
___	**58510**	Frisco Flatcar w/trailer "100011"		
___	**58513**	LCCA Reading Blue Coal 2-bay Hopper w/ETD, 12 u		75
___	**58515**	LCCA NS Vulcan Switcher, 12 u		50
___	**58517**	NLOE LIRR Alco Diesels, 13 u		300
___	**58522**	TCA Los Alamos Mint Car, 16 u		75
___	**58527**	LCCA Vulcan Switcher, 13 u		80
___	**58528**	LCCA Reading Vulcan Switcher, 14 u		80
___	**58539**	LCCA Texas Special B-W Caboose, 13 u		95
___	**58545**	LCCA Vulcan Switcher, Gold, 12 u		75
___	**58550**	LCCA Texas Special Unibody Tank Car, 13 u	70	95
___	**58585**	LCCA Wabash Auto Loader, white, 14 u		110
___	**58586**	LCCA South Shore Lines Trolley, 14 u		95
___	**58598**	TCA Philly Pretzel Boxcar, 14 u		80
___	**58599**	LCCA UP Cylindrical Hopper, 11 u	28	75
___	**59002**	LCCA TVRM Boxcar, 13 u		150
___	**59015**	LCCA Conway Scenic RR Boxcar, 15 u		200
___	**62162**	Postwar "262" Automatic Crossing Gate and Signal, 99-14		60
___	**37151**	Railroad Signs, set of 14, 99-04, 08-24		10
___	**62181**	Telephone Pole Set, 10-pack, 99-04, 08-24		15
___	**62283**	Die-cast Illuminated Bumpers, 99-17		27

MODERN 1970-2024		Exc	Mint
62709	Rico Station Kit, 99-00		46 ___
62716	Short Extension Bridge, 99-03, 07-24		15 ___
62900	Lockon, 99-13		3 ___
62901	Ives Track Clips, 12 pieces (027), 99-10, 13-16		5 ___
62905	Lockon with wires, 99-10, 13-14		7 ___
62909	Smoke Fluid, 99-12		7 ___
62927	Lubrication/Maintenance Set, 99-23		25 ___
62985	The Lionel Train Book, 99-03		12 ___
65014	Half Curved Track (027), 99-16		1 ___
65019	Half Straight Track (027), 99-16		1 ___
65020	90-degree Crossover (027), 99-16		11 ___
65021	27" Manual Switch, left hand (027), 99-16		17 ___
65022	27" Manual Switch, right hand (027), 99-16		18 ___
65023	45-degree Crossover (027), 99-16		11 ___
65024	35" Straight Track (027), 99-16		5 ___
65033	27" Diameter Curved Track (027), 99-16		2 ___
65038	9" Straight Track (027), 99-16		2 ___
65041	Insulator Pins, dozen (027), 99-04, 06, 13-14		3 ___
65042	Steel Pins, dozen (027), 99-04, 06-09, 13-14		3 ___
65049	42" Diameter Curved Track (027), 99-16		3 ___
65113	54" Diameter Curved Track (027), 99-16		3 ___
65121	27" Path Remote Switch, left hand (027), 99-14		43 ___
65122	27" Path Remote Switch, right hand (027), 99-14		43 ___
65149	Uncoupling Track (027), 99-14		12 ___
65165	72" Path Remote Switch, right hand (0), 99-14		125 ___
65166	72" Path Remote Switch, left hand (0), 99-14		125 ___
65167	42" Remote Switch, right hand (027), 99-14		25 ___
65168	42" Remote Switch, left hand (027), 99-14		25 ___
65500	10" Straight Track (0), 99-16		2 ___
65501	31" Diameter Curved Track (0), 99-16		2 ___
65504	Half Curved Track (0), 99-16		2 ___
65505	Half Straight Track (0), 99-16		2 ___
65514	Half Curved Track (027), 99-03		3 ___
65523	40" Straight Track (0), 99-16		7 ___
65530	Remote Control Track (0), 99-16		38 ___
65540	90-degree Crossover (0), 99-14		16 ___
65543	Insulator Pins, dozen (0), 99-16		3 ___
65545	45-degree Crossover (0), 99-14		27 ___
65551	Steel Pins, dozen (0), 99-16		3 ___
65554	54" Diameter Curved Track (0), 99-16		4 ___
65572	72" Diameter Curved Track (0), 99-16		5 ___
65824	NLOE LIRR Hopper w/Coal load, 17u		95 ___
68677	Frisco Flatcar w/trailer "832013", 98 u		45 ___
71998	LCCA Amtrak Refrigerator Car (Std 0), 10 u		45 ___
81000	BNSF Waffle-sided Boxcar "496464", 14-15		50 ___
81001	SP&S Flatcar with bulkheads, 14-16		50 ___
81002	UP 3-D Tank Car, 14-15		50 ___
81003	CP Bilevel Auto Carrier, 14-16		50 ___
81004	B&O Depressed-Center Flatcar with transformer, 14-15		50 ___
81005	Maine Central 2-bay Hopper "1005", 14-16		50 ___
81006	PRR Hi-Cube Boxcar "31010", 14-16		50 ___
81007	Seaboard Waffle-sided Boxcar "25335", 14-16		50 ___
81008	Central of Georgia Boxcar "5818", 14-17		50 ___

			Exc	Mint
___	**81009**	Southern 2-D Tank Car "951005", 14-16		50
___	**81010**	FEC Gondola "6121" with reels, 14-16		50
___	**81011**	PFE Reefer "33280", 14-16		50
___	**81012**	T&P 1-D Tank Car, 14-16		50
___	**81013**	Frisco Boxcar "700117", 14-16		50
___	**81014**	D&RGW Ore Car "31101", 14-15		50
___	**81015**	B&M Reefer "1878", 14-16		50
___	**81016**	Coaling Station, 14, 16-20		110
___	**81017**	Barrel Loading Building, 14-18		43
___	**81018**	Shell Vat Car, 17		80
___	**81019**	Short Tunnel, 14-16-17		45
___	**81021**	B&M Paul Revere GP9 Diesel Freight Set, 14-15		500
___	**81023**	Jersey Central Yard Boss 0-4-0 Steam Freight Set, 14-15		500
___	**81024**	Christmas Train Set, 02-04		150
___	**81025**	Lackawanna Pocono Berkshire Steam Freight Set, 14-15		480
___	**81027**	Thomas the Tank Engine Set, 01-04		120
___	**81028**	Marquette GP38 Diesel Freight Set, 14-15		430
___	**81029**	C&NW Windy City GP38 Diesel Freight Set, 14-15		400
___	**81030**	UP Gold Coast Flyer Steam Freight Set, 14-15		455
___	**81031**	Dinosaur Diesel Freight Set, LionChief, 14-16		175
___	**81038**	MILW Heavy Mikado Locomotive "8693" CC, 15	588	1300
___	**81063**	Classic Automatic Gateman, 14-24		130
___	**81064**	Construction Zone Signs #2, 14-19		10
___	**81066**	Milwaukee Road Double-sheathed Boxcar "8775" (std O), 14	33	83
___	**81067**	Monopoly Aquarium Car, 14-15		85
___	**81073**	Monopoly Boxcar 2-pack, Ventnor and Indiana Avenues, 14-15		135
___	**81076**	Pennsylvania Salt 8,000-gallon 1-D Tank Car "4724" (std O), 14		73
___	**81077**	Pere Marquette 8,000-gallon 1-D Tank Car "71710" (std O), 14		73
___	**81078**	NYC 8,000-gallon 1-D Tank Car "107898" (std O), 14		73
___	**81079**	NKP 8,000-gallon 1-D Tank Car "50277" (std O), 14		73
___	**81080**	BN 8,000-gallon 1-D Tank Car "977100" (std O), 14		73
___	**81081**	Alaska Steel-sided Reefer "10806" (std O), 14		80
___	**81090**	NS Hi-Cube Boxcar 2-pack (std O), 14-15		190
___	**81093**	2013 Lionel Dealer Appreciation Boxcar, 13 u		40
___	**81094**	Conrail "Big Blue" High-Cube Boxcar Diesel Freight Set, CC, 14-15		970
___	**81095**	Conrail Hi-Cube Boxcar 2-pack (std O), 14-16		190
___	**81101**	Polar Express 10th Anniversary Steam Passenger Set, 14-15		430
___	**81113**	SP 50' DD Boxcar "214051" (std O), 14-15		75
___	**81122**	Christmas 1955 MOW Inspection Truck, CC, 15		180
___	**81126**	WP 1955 MOW Inspection Truck, CC, 15		180
___	**81127**	Alaska 1955 MOW Inspection Truck, CC, 15		180
___	**81129**	MILW 1955 MOW Inspection Truck, CC, 15		180
___	**81130**	CNJ 1955 MOW Inspection Truck, CC, 15		180
___	**81132**	N&W 1955 MOW Inspection Truck, CC, 15		180
___	**81134**	BN SD70MAC Diesel "9424," CC, 14		550
___	**81135**	BN SD70MAC Diesel "9431," CC, 14		550
___	**81137**	BNSF SD70MAC Diesel "9858," CC, 14		550
___	**81138**	BNSF SD70MAC Diesel "9860," CC, 14		550
___	**81141**	Conrail SD70MAC Diesel "4138," CC, 14		550
___	**81142**	PFE Steel-sided Reefers 3-pack (std O), 14		300
___	**81144**	CSX SD70MAC Diesel "781," CC, 14		550

		Exc	Mint
81147	KCS SD7CMAC Diesel "3950," CC, 14		550
81148	KCS SD7CMAC Diesel "3953," CC, 14		550
81151	Alaska SD7CMAC Diesel "4002," CC, 14		550
81152	Alaska SD7CMAC Diesel "4005," CC, 14		550
81153	CSX SD70MAC Diesel "778," CC, 14		550
81154	UP ES44AC Diesel "7361," CC, 14		550
81155	UP ES44AC Diesel "7388," CC, 14		550
81160	CSX ES44AC Diesel "937," CC, 14		550
81161	CSX ES44AC Diesel "944," CC, 14		550
81169	Iowa Interstate ES44AC Diesel "504," CC, 14		550
81170	Iowa Interstate ES44AC Diesel "507," CC, 14		550
81171	Ferromex ES44AC Diesel "4617," CC, 14		550
81172	Ferromex ES44AC Diesel "4626," CC, 14		550
81176	CN ES44AC Diesel "2812," CC, 14		550
81177	CN ES44AC Diesel "2818," CC, 14		550
81179	2-8-2 Heavy Mikado Pilot Locomotive, CC, 14		1300
81180	2-8-2 Heavy Mikado Locomotive, CC, 15		1300
81181	Southern 2-8-2 Heavy Mikado Locomotive "4866," CC, 15		1300
81182	L&N 2-8-2 Heavy Mikado Locomotive "1757," CC, 14		1300
81183	MP 2-8-2 Heavy Mikado Locomotive "1496," CC, 14		1300
81184	P&WV 2-8-2 Heavy Mikado Locomotive "1152," CC, 14		1300
81185	CNJ 2-8-2 Heavy Mikado Locomotive "845," CC, 14		1300
81186	Frisco 2-8-2 Heavy Mikado Locomotive "4126," CC, 14		1300
81187	C&IM 2-8-2 Heavy Mikado Locomotive "551," CC, 14		1300
81188	NYC 2-8-2 Heavy Mikado Locomotive "9506," CC, 14		1300
81189	CB&Q 2-8-2 Heavy Mikado Locomotive "5509," CC, 15		1300
81190	WP 2-8-2 Heavy Mikado Locomotive "334," CC, 15		1300
81191	Erie 2-8-2 Heavy Mikado Locomotive "3207," CC, 15		1300
81192	GN 2-8-2 Heavy Mikado Locomotive "3148," CC, 14		1300
81193	Wheeling & Lake Erie 2-8-2 Heavy Mikado Locomotive "6012," CC, 15		1300
81194	NKP 2-8-2 Heavy Mikado Locomotive "689" CC, 15		1300
81195	PRR Boxcar, 14-15		70
81196	Timken Boxcar, 14-15		70
81197	Santa Fe Boxcar, 14-15		70
81198	GN Boxcar, 14-16		70
81199	PRR 1-D Tank Car, 14-15		70
81200	Timken 1-D Tank Car, 14-16		70
81201	GN 1-D Tank Car, 14-16		70
81202	Santa Fe 1-D Tank Car, 14-15		70
81203	PRR Flatcar, 14-15	24	70
81204	Santa Fe Flatcar, 14-16	37	70
81205	Timken Flatcar, 14-16		70
81206	GN Flatcar, 14-16		70
81207	CP H-24-66 Train Master Diesel "8900," CC, 14		550
81208	CP H-24-66 Train Master Diesel "8903," CC, 14		550
81209	CNJ H-24-66 Train Master Diesel "2401," CC, 14		550
81210	CNJ H-24-66 Train Master Diesel "2406," CC, 14		550
81211	Reading H-24-66 Train Master Diesel "801," CC, 14		550
81212	Reading H-24-66 Train Master Diesel "804," CC, 14		550
81213	SP H-24-66 Train Master Diesel "4803," CC, 14		550
81214	SP H-24-66 Train Master Diesel "4809," CC, 14		550
81215	Southern H-24-66 Train Master Diesel "6300," CC, 14		550

			Exc	Mint
___	**81216**	Southern H-24-66 Train Master Diesel "6303," CC, 14		550
___	**81217**	N&W H-24-66 Train Master Diesel "151," CC, 14		550
___	**81218**	N&W H-24-66 Train Master Diesel "164," CC, 14		550
___	**81219**	Santa Fe E8 Diesel AA Set "84/85," CC, 14		930
___	**81222**	PC E8 Diesel AA Set "4289/4325," CC, 14		930
___	**81225**	RI E8 Diesel AA Set "647/648," CC, 14		930
___	**81228**	C&O E8 Diesel AA Set "4027/4028," CC, 14		930
___	**81231**	Erie E8 Diesel AA Set "822/823," CC, 14		930
___	**81234**	MKT E8 Diesel AA Set "131/132," CC, 14		930
___	**81237**	SAL E8 Diesel AA Set "3051/3055," CC, 14		930
___	**81240**	Wabash E8 Diesel AA Set "1007/1011," CC, 14		930
___	**81243**	Pilot M1a 4-8-2 Locomotive, CC, 14		1500
___	**81245**	PRR M1a 4-8-2 Locomotive "6671," CC, 14		1500
___	**81246**	PRR M1a 4-8-2 Locomotive "6764," CC, 14		1500
___	**81247**	PRR M1a Coal Hauler Twin-hopper Steam Freight Set, CC, 14		1800
___	**81248**	10" Girder Bridge Track, 14-24		25
___	**81249**	Christmas Girder Bridge Track, 14, 16-18		25
___	**81250**	FasTrack 0-96 Curve, 14-24		8
___	**81251**	FasTrack 0-31 Manual Switch, right-hand, 14-24		55
___	**81252**	FasTrack 0-31 Manual Switch, left-hand, 14-24	25	55
___	**81253**	FasTrack 0-31 Remote Switch, right-hand, 14-24		130
___	**81254**	FasTrack 0-31 Remote Switch, left-hand, 14-24		130
___	**81256**	Personalized Birthday Message Boxcar, 14-15		85
___	**81257**	Amtrak Water Tower, 14-18		35
___	**81259**	PRR Broadway Limited Steam Passenger Set, 14		370
___	**81261**	NYC Early Bird Special Steam Freight Set, 16-17		380
___	**81262**	UP Steam Freight Set, LionChief, 15		400
___	**81263**	CNJ Diesel Passenger Set, LionChief, 14-16		390
___	**81264**	Western Union Telegraph Steam Freight Set, 14-16		390
___	**81266**	Amtrak FT Diesel Passenger Set, LionChief, 14-15		460
___	**81269**	PRR Allegheny Hauler Steam Freight Set, 16-17		420
___	**81270**	Bethlehem Steel Steam Work Train, LionChief, 15		340
___	**81279**	Albert Hall European Steam Passenger Set, LionChief, 14-15		430
___	**81280**	Victorian Christmas Steam Passenger Set, 14		400
___	**81284**	Frosty the Snowman Steam Freight Set, LionChief, 14-16		320
___	**81286**	Lionel Junction "Little Steam" Freight Set, 14-15		175
___	**81287**	Lionel Junction UP Steam Freight Set, 14-15		175
___	**81288**	Pet Shop Diesel Freight Set, 14-16		175
___	**81290**	Thomas Kinkade Holiday Covered Bridge, 14		70
___	**81292**	Valley Central 1-D Tank Car "45003", 14-17		45
___	**81294**	LCS FasTrack IR Sensor Track, 13-24		100
___	**81295**	AT&SF 2-8-2 Locomotive "3158," LionChief, 14-16	138	430
___	**81296**	GN 2-8-2 Locomotive "3123," LionChief, 14-15		430
___	**81297**	PRR 2-8-2 Locomotive "9633," LionChief, 14-15		430
___	**81299**	Chessie System 2-8-2 Locomotive "2103," LionChief, 14-15		430
___	**81301**	NYC 4-6-4 Hudson Locomotive "5421," LionChief, 14-15		430
___	**81302**	C&O 4-6-4 Hudson Locomotive "308," LionChief Plus, 14-17		430
___	**81303**	UP 4-6-4 Hudson Locomotive "674," LionChief Plus, 14-17		430
___	**81304**	CN 4-6-4 Hudson Locomotive "5702," LionChief Plus, 14-17		430
___	**81307**	B&O 4-6-2 Locomotive "5307," LionChief, 14-17		430
___	**81308**	CP 4-6-2 Pacific Locomotive "2469," LionChief Plus, 14-17		430
___	**81309**	SP 4-6-2 Pacific Locomotive "3106," LionChief Plus, 14-17		430
___	**81311**	Alaska 4-6-2 Pacific Locomotive "652," LionChief Plus, 14-17		430

		Exc	Mint
81313	FasTrack Power Lockon, 15-24		25
81314	FasTrack Power Block Lockon, 15-24		44
81315	Coaling Station, 15-17, 19-20		160
81316	Personalized Christmas Message Boxcar, 15		80
81317	FasTrack Plug-Expand-Play Accessory Activator Track Pack, 15-24		27
81325	LCS WiFi Module, 13-16, 18-20		180
81326	LCS Serial Converter #2, 14-24		70
81331	Iron Arry Locomotive with Remote, LionChief, 14-15		140
81332	Iron Bert Locomotive with Remote, LionChief, 14-15		140
81373	Candy Cane Flatcar with bulkheads, 15		60
81395	Thomas Kinkade Christmas Passenger Set, LionChief, 14-15		380
81419	Alien Ooze 1-D Tank Car, 14-15		65
81420	PRR Truss-rod Gondola with tarp, 14-16		65
81422	NS Water Tower, 14		31
81423	Sodor Coal and Scrap Cars 2-pack, 14-16		70
81424	Sodor Crane Car and Work Caboose 2-pack, 14		70
81425	Frosty the Snowman Passenger Station, 14		65
81426	Frosty the Snowman Animated Gondola, 14		75
81427	Frosty the Snowman Aquarium Car, 14		85
81428	Frosty the Snowman Boxcar, 14		65
81430	Lionelville Shanty, 14		22
81432	PRR Girder Bridge, 14-15		21
81433	PRR Crossing Shanty, 14		22
81434	Pennsylvania Station Platform, 14-15		23
81435	N&W NS Heritage Quad Hopper with coal, 14-15		60
81436	Intermodal Container 4-pack, 14		43
81437	York Peppermint Patty Vat Car, 14-15		70
81439	Halloween Pumpkinheads Handcar, 14-16		90
81440	Western Union Handcar, 14-16		100
81441	North Pole Central Snowplow, CC , 15-20		280
81442	PRR Rotary Snowplow “1442,” CC, 15-20		280
81443	D&RGW Rotary Snowplow “443," CC, 15-20		280
81444	PRR Tie-Jector, CC, 14-16		200
81445	MOW Tie-Jector, CC, 14-16		200
81446	Santa Fe Tie-Jector, CC, 14-18		200
81447	NS Tie-Jector, CC, 14-18		200
81448	Amtrak Tie-Jector, CC, 14-18	90	200
81449	Zombie Motorized Trolley, 14		100
81450	Polar Express Trolley, 14		110
81451	St. Louis Motorized Trolley, 14		100
81452	Neil Young Texas Special F3 AA Diesels, CC, 13-14		650
81453	Neil Young PRR F3 AA Diesels, CC, 13-14		650
81462	PRR Broadway Limited Add-on Baggage Car, 14-17		70
81463	CNJ Water Tower, 14-17		31
81464	CNJ Montclair Add-on Passenger Car, 14-16		60
81465	SP Flatcar with piggyback trailers, 14-16		75
81466	BN Maxi-Stack Pair, 14-16		140
81469	GN Bilevel Stock Car “65385”, 14-17		65
81470	DC Comics Batman Phantom Train, 16-17		400
81475	DC Comics Batman M7 Subway Set, LionChief, 14-15		370
81479	Batman Add-on M7 Subway Car 2-pack, 14-15		140
81480	John Deere RS3 Diesel Freight Set, LionChief, 14-16	128	325

			Exc	Mint
___	**81486**	NYC Patrol Flatcar with helicopter, 14-15	28	65
___	**81487**	Ronald Reagan Presidential Boxcar, 14-15		70
___	**81488**	Andrew Jackson Presidential Boxcar, 14-16, 18		70
___	**81489**	Warren G. Harding Presidential Boxcar, 14-16, 18, 20		75
___	**81490**	Dwight D. Eisenhower Presidential Boxcar, 14-16		70
___	**81491**	Jersey Central Coal Dump Car, 14-15		65
___	**81492**	Strasburg RR Searchlight Car, 14		50
___	**81493**	Postwar "6844" U.S.A.F. Missile Carrying Car, 15-16		65
___	**81494**	Santa's Sleigh Rocket Fuel Tank Car, 16		65
___	**81495**	40-watt Power Supply, 15-18		65
___	**81496**	2014 Lionel Dealer Appreciation Boxcar, 14 u		40
___	**81497**	2015 Lionel Dealer Appreciation Boxcar, 15 u		40
___	**81499**	LCS Power Supply with DB9 cable, 13-16, 18-20		37
___	**81500**	LCS PDI Sensor Track 1' Cable, 13-24		15
___	**81501**	LCS PDI Sensor Track 3' Cable, 13-24		16
___	**81502**	LCS PDI Sensor Track 10' Cable, 13-24		20
___	**81503**	LCS PDI Sensor Track 20' Cable, 13-24		20
___	**81504**	Ann Arbor FA-2 Diesel AA Set "53/53A," CC, 14		750
___	**81507**	B&O FA-2 Diesel AA Set "817/827," CC, 14-15		750
___	**81510**	Erie FA-2 Diesel AA Set "736A/736D," CC, 14-15		750
___	**81513**	MKT FA-2 Diesel AA Set "331A/331C," CC, 14		750
___	**81516**	NYC FA-2 Diesel AA Set "1075/1078," CC, 14-15		750
___	**81519**	PRR FA-2 Diesel AA Set "9608/9609," CC, 14-15		750
___	**81522**	Ann Arbor FB2 Diesel "53B", CC, 14	80	450
___	**81523**	B&O FB2 Diesel "817B," CC, 14-15		450
___	**81524**	Erie FB2 Diesel "736B," CC, 14-15		450
___	**81525**	MKT FB2 Diesel "331B," CC, 14		450
___	**81526**	NYC FB2 Diesel "3327," CC, 14-15		450
___	**81527**	PRR FB2 Diesel "9608B," CC, 14		450
___	**81528**	Ann Arbor FB2 Diesel, nonpowered, 14		350
___	**81529**	B&O FB2 Diesel, nonpowered, 14-15		350
___	**81530**	Erie FB2 Diesel, nonpowered, 14-15		350
___	**81531**	MKT FB2 Diesel, nonpowered, 14		350
___	**81532**	NYC FB2 Diesel, nonpowered, 14-15		350
___	**81533**	PRR FB2 Diesel, nonpowered, 14-15		350
___	**81534**	Christmas Toys Stock Car, 14		70
___	**81545**	Operation Eagle Missile Launcher Car, CC, 15		350
___	**81546**	Operation Eagle Sound Car, CC, 15		240
___	**81568**	4th of July Parade Boxcar, 14-16		80
___	**81596**	Weathered UP 4-12-2 Locomotive "9000," CC, 13		1400
___	**81597**	Weathered B&O RF-16 Sharknose AA Diesels "855-857," CC, 13		830
___	**81600**	Weathered PRR RF-16 Sharknose AA Diesels "2020A-2021A," CC, 13		830
___	**81603**	72-watt Power Supply, LionChief, 14-24		60
___	**81605**	Santa Fe PS-1 Boxcar 5-pack (std O), 14		380
___	**81615**	UP 1-D Tank Car, 14		45
___	**81617**	Pet Shop 1-D Tank Car, 14-16		45
___	**81619**	Reading PS-1 Boxcar "109448" (std O), 14		80
___	**81620**	Zombie Figure Pack, 14-15		23
___	**81621**	John Deere Billboard Set, 15		25
___	**81622**	John Deere Water Tower, 15		40
___	**81625**	Amtrak Add-on Baggage Car, 14-16		85

MODERN 1970-2024		Exc	Mint
81626	Barrel Shed, 14-16, 18-20		40
81627	Christmas Hopper Shed, 14, 16-17		45
81628	Grain Elevator, 15		80
81629	Lumber Shed Kit, 14-24		35
81635	Water Tower, 14		35
81639	LCS Accessory Switch Controller #2, 14-24		130
81640	LCS Block Power Controller #2, 14-24		130
81641	LCS Accessory Motor Controller, 17-24		130
81644	Chessie System Baby Madison Passenger Car 3-pack, 14-16		270
81649	SP Baby Madison Passenger Car 3-pack, 14-16		270
81654	Philadelphia Energy Solutions 1-D Tank Car "0765", 15-18	25	60
81662	FasTrack O-31 Quarter Curved Track, 14-24		5
81668	Philadelphia Energy Solutions 1-D Tank Car "0771", 15-16, 18		60
81680	Dinosaur 1-D Tank Car, 14-16		45
81686	PRR GL-a 2-bay Hopper 3-pack (std O), 14		220
81687	LV GL-a 2-bay Hopper 2-pack (std O), 14-15		146
81688	CB&Q GL-a 2-bay Hopper 3-pack (std O), 14-16		220
81689	C&O GL-a 2-bay Hopper 3-pack (std O), 14-16		220
81693	Aerial Target Launcher, 15-16		90
81699	Polar Express Scale Twin Hopper, 15		80
81703	Santa Fe Hi-Cube Boxcar 2-pack (std O), 14-16		190
81704	Grand Trunk Hi-Cube Boxcar 2-pack (std O), 14-16		190
81705	Milwaukee Road Hi-Cube Boxcar 2-pack (std O), 14-16		190
81706	Frisco Hi-Cube Boxcar 2-pack (std O), 14-16		190
81707	NYC Hi-Cube Boxcar 2-pack (std O), 14-16		190
81708	Santa Fe Hi-Cube Boxcar "36715" (std O), 14-15		95
81710	Milwaukee Road Hi-Cube Boxcar "4980" (std O), 14-15		95
81711	Frisco Hi-Cube Boxcar "9125" (std O), 14-15		95
81712	NYC Hi-Cube Boxcar "67282" (std O), 14-15		95
81723	Postwar "3413" Mercury Capsule Launcher Car, 15		80
81725	UP Operating Merchandise Car, 14-15		68
81726	REA Operating Merchandise Car, 14-15		80
81729	Great Western Passenger Car Add-on 2-pack, 14		130
81733	Christmas Boxcar, 14	38	65
81734	FasTrack Oval Track and Power Pack, 14-17		200
81735	FasTrack Figure-8 Track and Power Pack, 14-17		250
81736	Classic Lionel Catalogs Billboard Pack, 14-15		13
81737	Passenger Station, 14-15		60
81738	Lionel Auto Loader Cars 4-pack, 14-15, 17		25
81739	Santa Fe Baby Madison Passenger Car 3-pack, 14-16		270
81744	CP Baby Madison Passenger Car 3-pack, 14-16		270
81749	Pullman Baby Madison Passenger Car 3-pack, 14-16		270
81754	NYC Baby Madison Passenger Car 3-pack, 14-16		270
81759	NYC Coach/Diner 2-pack, 14-16		180
81760	NYC Coach/Baggage Car 2-pack, 14-16		180
81763	Pullman Baby Madison Passenger Car 3-pack, 14-16		180
81764	Pullman Coach/Baggage Car 2-pack, 14, 16		180
81768	Chessie System Coach/Diner 2-pack, 14-16		180
81769	Chessie System Coach/Baggage Car 2-pack, 14-16		180
81773	SP Coach/Diner 2-pack, 14-16		180
81774	SP Coach/Baggage Car 2-pack, 14-16		180
81778	Santa Fe Coach/Diner 2-pack, 14-16		180
81779	Santa Fe Coach/Baggage Car 2-pack, 14-16		180

			Exc	Mint
___	**81783**	CP Coach/Diner 2-pack, 14-16		180
___	**81784**	CP Coach/Baggage Car 2-pack, 14-16		180
___	**81789**	NH GL-a 2-bay Hopper 2-pack (std O), 14-16		146
___	**81793**	Berwind GL-a 2-bay Hopper 3-pack (std O), 14-15		220
___	**81800**	Southern 18" Aluminum Observation/Coach Car, 2-pack (std O), 14		320
___	**81801**	Southern 18" Combination/Vista Dome Car, 2-pack (std O), 14		320
___	**81806**	PRR N5b Caboose "477814" (std O), 14		95
___	**81807**	Conrail N5b Caboose "22882" (std O), 14-15		95
___	**81808**	PC N5b Caboose "22802" (std O), 14-16		95
___	**81809**	LIRR N5b Caboose "2" (std O), 14-15		95
___	**81810**	Lionel Lines N5b Caboose "1402" (std O), 14-16		95
___	**81811**	Polar Express N5b Caboose, 16		95
___	**81812**	RI 18" Aluminum Observation/Coach Car, 2-pack (std O), 14		320
___	**81813**	RI 18" Aluminum Combination/Vista Dome Car, 2-pack (std O), 14		320
___	**81818**	C&O 18" Aluminum Observation/Coach Car, 2-pack (std O), 14		320
___	**81819**	C&O 18" Aluminum Combination/Vista Dome Car, 2-pack (std O), 14		320
___	**81824**	P&WV GL-a 2-bay Hopper 2-pack (std O), 14-16		146
___	**81827**	PC Round-roof Boxcar "100104" (std O), 14		80
___	**81828**	GN Round-roof Boxcar "5885" (std O), 14		80
___	**81829**	WP Round-roof Boxcar "10211" (std O), 14-15		80
___	**81830**	MKT 18" Aluminum Observation/Coach Car, 2-pack (std O), 14		320
___	**81831**	MKT 18" Aluminum Baggage/Diner Car, 2-pack (std O), 14		320
___	**81836**	Erie Double-sheathed Boxcar "71107" (std O), 14-15		80
___	**81837**	Frisco Double-sheathed Boxcar "128528" (std O), 14-15		80
___	**81838**	CNJ Double-sheathed Boxcar "14014" (std O), 14-15		80
___	**81839**	Pacific Fright Express Steel-sided Reefer (std O), 14		80
___	**81840**	UP Ca-4 Caboose with smoke "3880" (std O), 14		90
___	**81841**	UP MOW Caboose "903224" (std O), 14		90
___	**81842**	Wabash 18" Dome-Observation/Coach Car, 2-pack (std O), 14		320
___	**81843**	Wabash 18" Aluminum Combination/Vista Dome Car, 2-pack (std O), 14		320
___	**81858**	PRR GL-a 2-bay Hopper 3-pack (std O), 14		220
___	**81862**	FasTrack O-31 Curved Track 4-pack, 14-24		25
___	**81866**	RI 18" Aluminum Baggage/Diner Car, 2-pack (std O), 14		320
___	**81869**	C&O 18" Aluminum Baggage/Diner Car, 2-pack (std O), 14		320
___	**81871**	Loggers Figure Pack, 15-23		30
___	**81872**	Wabash 18" Aluminum Baggage/Diner Car, 2-pack (std O), 14		320
___	**81875**	MKT 18" Aluminum Combination/Vista Dome Car, 2-pack (std O), 14		320
___	**81878**	Southern 18" Aluminum Baggage/Diner Car, 2-pack (std O), 14		320
___	**81881**	SP Crane Car, CC, 14-16		500
___	**81882**	DT&I Crane Car, CC, 14-16		500
___	**81883**	CSX Crane Car, CC, 14-16		500
___	**81884**	Bethlehem Steel Crane Car, CC, 14		500
___	**81885**	MOW Crane Car, CC, 14-16		500
___	**81886**	SP Boom Car, RailSounds, CC, 14-16		240
___	**81887**	DT&I Boom Car, RailSounds, CC, 14-16		240
___	**81888**	CSX Boom Car, RailSounds, CC, 14-16		240
___	**81889**	MOW Boom Car, RailSounds, CC, 14-16		240
___	**81890**	Bethlehem Steel Boom Car, RailSounds, CC, 14		240
___	**81891**	BNSF 52' Gondola "523300" with 3-piece covers (std O), 14		80

Item	Description	Exc	Mint
81892	Bethlehem Steel 52' Gondola "303022" with 3-piece covers (std O), 14		80 ___
81893	GTW 52' Gondola "145391" with 3-piece covers (std O), 14		80 ___
81894	CSX 52' Gondola "709190" with 3-piece covers (std O), 14		80 ___
81895	North Pole Central 52' Gondola "128925" w/covers (std O), 14		80 ___
81896	NYC PS-5 Flatcar "506266" with piggyback trailers (std O), 14		100 ___
81897	Milwaukee Road PS-5 Flatcar "64660" with piggyback trailers (std O), 14	43	108 ___
81898	Lionel PS-5 Flatcar with piggyback trailers (std O), 14		100 ___
81899	CP PS-5 Flatcar "301000" with piggyback trailers (std O), 14		100 ___
81900	UP PS-5 Flatcar "258255" with piggyback trailers (std O), 14		100 ___
81901	NYC Tractor and Piggyback Trailer, 14, 17		90 ___
81902	Milwaukee Road Tractor and Piggyback Trailer, 14		90 ___
81903	Lionel Tractor and Piggyback Trailer, 14		90 ___
81904	CP Tractor and Piggyback Trailer, 14-15, 17		90 ___
81905	UP Tractor and Piggyback Trailer, 14		90 ___
81908	PFE Steel-sided Reefers 3-pack (std O), 14		240 ___
81912	New York Yankees Boxcar, 14		70 ___
81913	St. Louis Cardinals Boxcar, 14		70 ___
81914	Oakland Athletics Boxcar, 14		70 ___
81915	San Francisco Giants Boxcar, 14		70 ___
81916	Boston Red Sox Boxcar, 14		70 ___
81917	Los Angeles Dodgers Boxcar, 14		70 ___
81918	Cincinnati Reds Boxcar, 14		70 ___
81919	San Diego Padres Boxcar, 14		70 ___
81920	Detroit Tigers Boxcar, 14		70 ___
81921	Atlanta Braves Boxcar, 14		70 ___
81922	Baltimore Orioles Boxcar, 14		70 ___
81923	Minnesota Twins Boxcar, 14		70 ___
81924	Chicago White Sox Boxcar, 14		70 ___
81925	Chicago Cubs Boxcar, 14		70 ___
81926	Philadelphia Phillies Boxcar, 14		70 ___
81927	Cleveland Indians Boxcar, 14		70 ___
81928	New York Mets Boxcar, 14		70 ___
81929	Toronto Blue Jays Boxcar, 14		70 ___
81930	Miami Marlins Boxcar, 14		70 ___
81931	Angels Baseball Boxcar, 14		70 ___
81932	Pittsburgh Pirates Boxcar, 14		70 ___
81933	Texas Rangers Boxcar, 14		70 ___
81934	Milwaukee Brewers Boxcar, 14		70 ___
81935	Houston Astros Boxcar, 14		70 ___
81936	Colorado Rockies Boxcar, 14		70 ___
81937	Tampa Bay Rays Boxcar, 14		70 ___
81938	Seattle Mariners Boxcar, 14		70 ___
81939	Washington Nationals Boxcar, 14		70 ___
81940	Arizona Diamondbacks Boxcar, 14		70 ___
81941	Kansas City Royals Boxcar, 14		70 ___
81944	Rotary Beacon, yellow, 14-19		85 ___
81945	Polar Express Scale Coach, 14		210 ___
81946	FasTrack O-36 Remote Switch, right-hand, 14-24		130 ___
81947	FasTrack O-36 Remote Switch, left-hand, 14-24		130 ___
81948	FasTrack O-48 Remote Switch, right-hand, 14-24	60	140 ___
81949	FasTrack O-48 Remote Switch, left-hand, 14-24	60	140 ___
81950	FasTrack O-60 Remote Switch, right-hand, 14-24	60	140 ___

	MODERN 1970-2024		Exc	Mint
____	**81951**	FasTrack O-60 Remote Switch, left-hand, 14-24	65	140
____	**81952**	FasTrack O-72 Remote Switch, right-hand, 14-24	45	130
____	**81953**	FasTrack O-72 Remote Switch, left-hand, 14-24		140
____	**81954**	FasTrack O-72 Remote Switch, wye, 14-24		140
____	**81968**	Halloween Pacific Fright Express Caboose (std O), 14		90
____	**81969**	PRR 18" Aluminum Parlor/Coach Car, 2-pack (std O), 14-15		320
____	**81972**	B&O 18" Aluminum Baggage/Sleeper Car, 2-pack (std O), 14		320
____	**81975**	SP 18" Aluminum Sleeper/Coach Car, 2-pack (std O), 14-15		320
____	**81978**	UP 18" Aluminum Sleeper/Coach Car, 2-pack (std O), 14-15		320
____	**81981**	KCS 18" Aluminum Sleeper/Coach Car, 2-pack (std O), 14		320
____	**81984**	Postwar "1887" Christmas Flatcar with reindeer, 14		70
____	**81985**	Postwar "6428" Christmas Mail Car, 14		60
____	**81986**	Christmas Wish 1-D Tank Car, 14		60
____	**81987**	Angela Trotta Thomas "Santa's Letter" Boxcar, 14		65
____	**81988**	Angela Trotta Thomas Christmas Billboard Pack, 14		15
____	**81990**	Christmas Gondola with reindeer feed vats, 14		65
____	**81992**	Santa Claus Bobbing Head Boxcar, 14		65
____	**81993**	North Pole Central Santa Finder Searchlight Car, 14		55
____	**81999**	PRR Gondola with Christmas gifts and trees, 14		65
____	**82000**	PRR Christmas Crane Car, 14		75
____	**82001**	Merry & Bright Hot Cocoa Car, 14		70
____	**82002**	Old St. Nick Operating Billboard, 14, 16		60
____	**82003**	Christmas Blinking Water Tower, 14		35
____	**82005**	Christmas Wreath Clock Tower, 14, 16-17		43
____	**82008**	Bungalow House, 15-17		80
____	**82009**	Suburban House, 15-16		80
____	**82010**	Joe's Bait & Tackle Shop, 15-16		65
____	**82011**	Keystone Cafe, 15-16		80
____	**82012**	Single Floodlight Tower, 15-23		80
____	**82013**	Double Floodlight Tower, 15-24		90
____	**82014**	Postwar "192" Control Tower, 15-16		100
____	**82015**	Wind Turbine, 15-18		80
____	**82016**	Oil Pump, 15-24		120
____	**82017**	Lionel Art Operating Billboard, 15-20		70
____	**82018**	Track Gang, 15-16		100
____	**82020**	Burning Switch Tower, 15-17		130
____	**82021**	Bascule Bridge, 15		450
____	**82022**	Lionel Steel Gantry Crane, CC, 15-19		400
____	**82023**	Operating Sawmill w/Sounds, CC, 15-17		350
____	**82024**	Postwar "164" Log Loader, 15		340
____	**82026**	Postwar "497" Coaling Station, 15-17		300
____	**82028**	Postwar "352" Icing Station, 15-17		150
____	**82029**	Culvert Loader, CC, 15-20		300
____	**82030**	Culvert Unloader, CC, 15-20		300
____	**82033**	MOW Trackside Crane, CC, 16-19		600
____	**82034**	Loading Station, 16		350
____	**82035**	Work House, crane sounds, 15-19		150
____	**82036**	Luxury Diner, 15-17		80
____	**82038**	8" Female Pigtail Power Cable, 15-24		11
____	**82039**	36" Male Pigtail Power Cable, 15-24		12
____	**82043**	Plug-n-Play 6' 3-position Power Cable Extension, 15-24		18
____	**82045**	Plug-n-Play 6' 6-position Power Cable Extension, 15-24		22
____	**82046**	36" Power Tap Cable, 15-24		18

		Exc	Mint
82047	Lionel Lines Log Dump Car, 15-16		65
82048	AT&SF Ice Car, 15-17		75
82049	Santa's Work Shoppe Log Dump Car, 16		65
82050	Santa's Work Shoppe Sawmill, 16-20		240
82051	North Pole Central Icing Station, 16-17		150
82052	PFE Ice Car, 15-17		75
82053	North Pole Central Icing Car, 16-17		75
82054	Weyerhaeuser Log Dump Car, 15-17		65
82055	Bethlehem Steel Trackside Crane, CC, 16-19		600
82056	Operating Freight Station, 18-19		110
82064	Halloween Operating Billboard , 15-19		80
82066	PRR Log Dump Car, 15		65
82067	Lionel Lines Coal Dump Car, 15-17		65
82068	NS Coal Dump Car, 15		65
82069	Conrail Coal Dump Car, 15-17		65
82072	Philadelphia Quartz Hopper "755", 15-18		50
82073	CN Ore Car, 15-17		50
82074	SP 1-D Tank Car, 15-17		50
82075	NYC Waffle-sided Boxcar, 15-17		50
82076	Chessie System Gondola with containers, 16-18		50
82077	D&H Hi-Cube Boxcar, 16		50
82078	NP 1-D Tank Car, 16		50
82079	UP Wood-sided Reefer, 16		50
82080	C&NW 3-D Tank Car , 16-18		50
82081	CSX Auto Carrier, 16-18		50
82082	NS Flatcar with pipes, 16-18		50
82083	Central of Georgia Gondola with cable reels, 16		50
82084	Virginian Boxcar, 16-18		50
82085	AT&SF Waffle-sided Boxcar, 16-17		50
82086	MKT Reefer, 16		50
82087	WP Depressed Flatcar with generator, 16-18		50
82088	Log Pack, 15-20		10
82091	PRR Tie Work Car "82091", 14-16		75
82092	MOW Tie Work Car "77", 14-16		75
82093	AT&SF Tie Work Car "82093", 14-16		75
82094	NS Tie Work Car "51", 14-16		75
82095	Amtrak Tie Work Car "67", 14-16		75
82096	Lionel Steel Culvert Gondola, 15-16		65
82097	Bucyrus-Erie Gantry Crane, CC, 15-19		400
82098	Bucyrus-Erie Culvert Gondola, 15		65
82099	Zombie Apocalypse Survivors GP38 Diesel Freight Set, LionChief, 15		415
82100	Polar Express Hero Boy's Home, 16-17		90
82101	Postwar "6512" Mercury Capsule Astronaut Car, 15-16		80
82102	Lumberjacks, 15-16		65
82103	Playground Swing, 15-16		75
82104	Playground Playtime, 15-16		100
82105	Tire Swing, 15-16		100
82106	Pony Ride, 15-17		75
82107	Tug-of-War, 15-17		65
82108	Hobo Campfire, 15		100
82110	FasTrack 30" Truss Bridge, 15-24		330
82111	Lionel Industrial Coal 2-bay Hopper "28111", 15-17		60

			Exc	Mint
___	**82112**	B&M Alco S2 Diesel Switcher "1260," CC, 15		650
___	**82113**	B&M Alco S2 Diesel Switcher "1263," CC, 15		650
___	**82114**	CB&Q Alco S2 Diesel Switcher "9306," CC, 15		650
___	**82115**	CB&Q Alco S2 Diesel Switcher "9308," CC, 15		650
___	**82116**	CP Alco S2 Diesel Switcher "7020," CC, 15		650
___	**82117**	CP Alco S2 Diesel Switcher "7024," CC, 15		650
___	**82118**	GM&O Alco S2 Diesel Switcher "1001," CC, 15		650
___	**82119**	GM&O Alco S2 Diesel Switcher "1007," CC, 15		650
___	**82120**	GN Alco S2 Diesel Switcher "2," CC, 15		650
___	**82121**	GN Alco S2 Diesel Switcher "5," CC, 15		650
___	**82122**	PRR Alco S2 Diesel Switcher "5648," CC, 15		650
___	**82123**	PRR Alco S2 Diesel Switcher "5652," CC, 15		650
___	**82124**	South Buffalo Alco S2 Diesel Switcher "102," CC, 15		650
___	**82125**	South Buffalo Alco S2 Diesel Switcher "104," CC, 15		650
___	**82126**	UP Alco S2 Diesel Switcher "1111," CC, 15		650
___	**82127**	UP Alco S2 Diesel Switcher "1138," CC, 15		650
___	**82128**	C&O GP30 Diesel Locomotive "3011," CC, 15		650
___	**82129**	C&O GP30 Diesel Locomotive "3018," CC, 15		650
___	**82130**	EMD Demonstrator GP30 Diesel Locomotive "1962," CC, 15		650
___	**82131**	TP&W GP30 Diesel Locomotive "700," CC, 15		650
___	**82132**	PC GP30 Diesel Locomotive "2202," CC, 15		650
___	**82133**	PC GP30 Diesel Locomotive "2246," CC, 15		650
___	**82134**	GM&O GP30 Diesel Locomotive "501," CC, 15		650
___	**82135**	GM&O GP30 Diesel Locomotive "521," CC, 15		650
___	**82136**	N&W GP30 Diesel Locomotive "522," black, CC, 15		650
___	**82137**	N&W GP30 Diesel Locomotive "542," blue, CC, 15		650
___	**82138**	MILW GP30 Diesel Locomotive "344," CC, 15		650
___	**82139**	MILW GP30 Diesel Locomotive "350," CC, 15		650
___	**82140**	Southern GP30 Diesel Locomotive "2594," CC, 15		650
___	**82141**	Southern GP30 Diesel Locomotive "2601," CC, 15		650
___	**82142**	UP GP30 Diesel Locomotive "803" CC, 15		650
___	**82143**	UP GP30 Diesel Locomotive "830" CC, 15		650
___	**82146**	Soo Line PS-1 Boxcar "45025", 15		80
___	**82147**	N&W PS-1 Boxcar "44292", 15		80
___	**82148**	GB&W PS-1 Boxcar "777", 15		80
___	**82150**	Duluth, South Shore & Atlantic PS-1 Boxcar "15091", 15		80
___	**82163**	B&O NW2 Diesel Locomotive "9555," LionChief, 15-16		300
___	**82164**	BN NW2 Diesel Locomotive "546," LionChief, 15-16		300
___	**82165**	CB&Q NW2 Diesel Locomotive "9412A," LionChief, 15-16		300
___	**82166**	Southern NW2 Diesel Locomotive "2401A," LionChief, 15-16		300
___	**82171**	BNSF GP20 Diesel Locomotive "2050," LionChief Plus, 15-17		340
___	**82172**	NYC GP20 Diesel Locomotive "2102," LionChief Plus, 15-17		340
___	**82173**	NS GP20 Diesel Locomotive "10," LionChief Plus, 15-17		340
___	**82174**	NYS&W GP20 Diesel Locomotive "1800," LionChief Plus, 15-17		340
___	**82175**	Virginian Rectifier Locomotive "135," LionChief Plus, 15-17		340
___	**82176**	N&W Rectifier Locomotive "235," LionChief Plus, 15-17		340
___	**82177**	NH Rectifier Locomotive "306," LionChief Plus, 15-17		340
___	**82178**	Conrail Rectifier Locomotive "4605," LionChief Plus, 15-17		340
___	**82179**	PRR Rectifier Locomotive "4466," LionChief Plus, 15-17		340
___	**82180**	Nickel Plate 2-8-0 Consolidation Locomotive "458," CC, 15		800
___	**82181**	WM 2-8-0 Consolidation Locomotive "734," CC, 15		800
___	**82182**	MILW 2-8-0 Consolidation Locomotive "1201," CC, 15		800

		Exc	Mint
82183	UP 2-8-0 Consolidation Locomotive "618," CC, 15		800
82184	PRR B6sb 0-4-0 Locomotive "1670," CC, 15		700
82185	D&RGW Bicentennial Gondola with canisters, 16		50
82186	Patriot Chemicals 1-D Tank Car "2015", 15, 18		60
82187	Bethlehem Steel Water Tower, 15		35
82188	Metro-North M7 Subway Set, LionChief, 15		350
82192	MTA LIRR M7 Set, LionChief, 18-19		400
82196	Metro-North Add-on 2-pack, 15		130
82199	MTA LIRR Add-on Passenger 2-pack, 18		175
82202	UP Big Boy Commemorative CA-4 Caboose, 15		95
82203	Plug-Expand-Play Remote Control Box, 15-24		30
82205	BNSF Golden Swoosh ES44AC Diesel Locomotive "7695," CC, 15		650
82206	N&W 2-6-6-4 Locomotive "1218," CC, 16		1000
82207	Iowa Interstate/Rock Island ES44AC Diesel Locomotive "513," CC, 15		650
82208	N&W 2-6-6-4 Locomotive "1212," CC, 16		1000
82209	NS ES44AC Diesel Locomotive "8056," CC, 15		650
82210	NS ES44AC Diesel Locomotive "8065," CC, 15		650
82213	KCS ES44AC Diesel Locomotive "4696," CC, 15		650
82214	KCS ES44AC Diesel Locomotive "4685," CC, 15		650
82215	AT&SF ES44AC Diesel Locomotive "440," CC, 15		650
82216	AT&SF ES44AC Diesel Locomotive "444," CC, 15		650
82218	FEC ES44AC Diesel Locomotive "802," CC, 15		650
82219	FEC ES44AC Diesel Locomotive "804," CC, 15		650
82220	SP Alco PA AA Diesel Locomotive Set "6006, 6015," CC, 15		1000
82223	D&RGW Alco PA AA Diesel Locomotive Set "6001, 6003," CC, 15		1000
82226	LV Alco PA AA Diesel Locomotive Set "601, 602," CC, 15		1000
82229	MP Alco PA AA Diesel Locomotive Set "8018, 8018," CC, 15		1000
82232	NKP Alco PA AA Diesel Locomotive Set "190, 189," CC, 15		1000
82235	PRR Alco PA AA Diesel Locomotive Set "5070A, 5071A," CC, 15		1000
82238	Southern Alco PA AA Diesel Locomotive Set "6900, 6901," CC, 15		1000
82241	Wabash Alco PA AA Diesel Locomotive Set "1020, 1020A," CC, 15		1000
82244	SP Alco PB Diesel Locomotive, CC, 15		530
82245	B&O 2-6-6-4 Locomotive "7620," CC, 16		1000
82246	D&RGW Alco PB Diesel Locomotive, CC, 15		530
82247	AT&SF 2-6-6-4 Locomotive "1798," CC, 16		1000
82248	LV Alco PB Diesel Locomotive, CC, 15		530
82249	Bethlehem Steel Boom Car, 15		55
82250	MP Alco PB Diesel Locomotive, CC, 15		530
82251	Zombie Animated Gondola, 15		75
82252	Nickel Plate Road Alco PB Diesel Locomotive, CC, 15		530
82253	John Deere 1-D Tank Car, 15		65
82254	PRR Alco PB Diesel Locomotive, CC, 15		530
82256	Southern Alco PB Diesel Locomotive, CC, 15		530
82258	Wabash Alco PB Diesel Locomotive, CC, 15		530
82260	PC 50' DD Boxcar "267210" (std O), 16-17		80
82261	Frisco 50' DD Boxcar "7002" (std O), 16-17		80
82263	PRR Scrapyard, 15-17		130
82265	MOW Welding Car, 15-16		80
82266	CN 4-6-0 Steam Locomotive "1158," CC, 15		900

	MODERN 1970-2024		Exc	Mint
___	82267	C&NW 4-6-0 Steam Locomotive "1385," CC, 15		900
___	82268	Frisco 4-6-0 Steam Locomotive "633," CC, 15		900
___	82269	NP 4-6-0 Steam Locomotive "1382," CC, 15		900
___	82270	SP 4-6-0 Steam Locomotive "2353," CC, 15		900
___	82271	NYC 4-6-0 Steam Locomotive "1258," CC, 15		900
___	82272	NH 4-6-0 Steam Locomotive "816," CC, 15		900
___	82273	ACL 4-6-0 Steam Locomotive "1031," CC, 15		900
___	82274	Chessie SD40 Diesel Locomotive "7500," CC, 15		650
___	82275	Chessie SD40 Diesel Locomotive "7593," CC, 15		650
___	82276	BN SD40 Diesel Locomotive "6314," CC, 15		650
___	82277	BN SD40 Diesel Locomotive "6320," CC, 15		650
___	82278	GT SD40 Diesel Locomotive "5922," CC, 15		650
___	82279	GT SD40 Diesel Locomotive "5927," CC, 15		650
___	82280	MP SD40 Diesel Locomotive ""3007," CC, 15		650
___	82281	MP SD40 Diesel Locomotive "3014," CC, 15		650
___	82282	Conrail SD40 Diesel Locomotive ""6308," CC, 15		650
___	82283	Conrail SD40 Diesel Locomotive "6350," CC, 15		650
___	82284	Conrail SD40 Diesel Locomotive "6300," CC, 15		650
___	82285	SP SD40 Diesel Locomotive "8402," CC, 15		650
___	82286	SP SD40 Diesel Locomotive "8451," CC, 15		650
___	82287	SP Daylight SD40 Diesel Locomotive "7342," CC, 15		650
___	82288	Clinchfield SD40 Diesel Locomotive "3000," CC, 15		650
___	82289	Clinchfield SD40 Diesel Locomotive "3006," CC, 15		650
___	82290	AT&SF FT AA Diesel Locomotive Set, LionChief Plus, 15-17		500
___	82293	ACL FT AA Diesel Locomotive Set, LionChief Plus, 15-17		500
___	82296	Erie FT AA Diesel Locomotive Set, LionChief Plus, 15-17		500
___	82299	D&RGW FT AA Diesel Locomotive Set, LionChief Plus, 15-17		500
___	82302	AT&SF FT B Unit, LionChief Plus, 15-17		280
___	82303	ACL FT B Unit, LionChief Plus, 15-17		280
___	82304	Erie FT B Unit, LionChief Plus, 15-17		280
___	82305	D&RGW FT B Unit, LionChief Plus, 15-17		280
___	82307	PRR B6sb 0-4-0 Locomotive "5244," CC, 15		700
___	82308	PRR B6sb 0-4-0 Locomotive "3233," CC, 15		700
___	82309	PRR-Reading Seashore Lines B6sb 0-4-0 Locomotive "6096," CC, 15		700
___	82310	LIRR B6sb 0-4-0 Locomotive "2015," CC, 15		700
___	82311	Polar RR B6sb 0-4-0 Locomotive "2515," CC, 15		700
___	82312	UP ACF 40-ton Stock Car "48133" , 15		80
___	82313	GN ACF 40-ton Stock Car "55989" , 15		80
___	82314	MILW ACF 40-ton Stock Car "104954" , 15		80
___	82315	NP ACF 40-ton Stock Car "84161" , 15		80
___	82316	NKP ACF 40-ton Stock Car "42040" , 15		80
___	82324	Chessie Diesel Freight Set, LionChief, 15		400
___	82330	U.S.A.F. Minuteman Missile Launcher Car, CC, 15		350
___	82331	U.S.A.F. Missile Launch Sound Car, CC, 15		240
___	82333	Illuminated Hopper Shed, 15-24		45
___	82334	Ulysses S. Grant Presidential Boxcar, 15		70
___	82335	Franklin D. Roosevelt Presidential Boxcar, 15		70
___	82340	N&W Y6b 2-8-8-2 Steam Locomotive "2171", CC, 15		2000
___	82341	N&W Y6b 2-8-8-2 Steam Locomotive "2175," CC, 15		2000
___	82342	N&W Y6b 2-8-8-2 Steam Locomotive "2195," CC, 15		2000
___	82343	Lionel Steel Welding Car, 15		80
___	82344	WM Wood Chip Hopper "2945"", 15-16		65

		Exc	Mint
82349	Friday the 13th Jason Voorhees Boxcar, 16		85
82394	UP Auxiliary Water Tender "907853," CC, 15		380
82395	UP Auxiliary Water Tender ""907856," CC, 15		380
82396	UP Commemorative Auxiliary Water Tender "809," CC, 15		380
82410	Virginian 2-bay Hopper "13168", 15-17		60
82411	N&W 2-bay Hopper "113733", 15-17		60
82412	Reading Birney Trolley, 15, 18		100
82413	Lionel Transit Birney Trolley, 15		100
82414	CNJ 4-6-0 Camelback Locomotive "777," LionChief, 15-16		440
82415	DL&W 4-6-0 Camelback Locomotive "1035," LionChief Plus, 15-17		440
82416	LV 4-6-0 Camelback Locomotive "1602," LionChief Plus, 15-17		440
82417	Philadelphia & Reading 4-6-0 Camelback Locomotive "675," LionChief Plus, 15-17		440
82418	Erie 4-6-0 Camelback Locomotive "861," LionChief Plus, 15-17		440
82419	UP 8-door Hi-Cube Boxcar "980212", 15-16		100
82420	SP 8-door Hi-Cube Boxcar "615270", 15-16		100
82421	B&O 8-door Hi-Cube Boxcar "192021", 15-16		100
82422	PRR 8-door Hi-Cube Boxcar "110125", 15-16		100
82423	C&NW 8-door Hi-Cube Boxcar "92046", 15-16		100
82424	Chessie 8-door Hi-Cube Boxcar "492025", 15-16		100
82425	PC 8-door Hi-Cube Boxcar "295443", 15-16		100
82426	RI 8-door Hi-Cube Boxcar "532591", 15-16		100
82427	Patriot U36B Diesel Freight Set, LionChief, 15-17		360
82436	Pennsylvania Keystone GP38 Diesel Freight Set, LionChief, 15		450
82442	Five-Star General Old-Time Steam Set, LionChief, 17-18		400
82447	Sheriff & Outlaw Car, 17		80
82453	Amtrak F40PH Diesel Phase II "200," CC, 16		550
82454	Amtrak F40PH Diesel Phase II "207," CC, 16		550
82455	Amtrak F40PH Diesel Phase III "364," CC, 16		550
82456	Amtrak F40PH Diesel Phase III "388," CC, 16		550
82460	CSX F40PH Diesel "9998," CC, 16		550
82461	CSX F40PH Diesel "9999," CC, 16		550
82473	N&W Early Era Inspection Vehicle, CC, 15		200
82474	BN Early Era Inspection Vehicle, CC, 15		200
82475	Bethlehem Steel Early Era Inspection Vehicle, CC, 15		200
82476	NH Early Era Inspection Vehicle, CC, 15		200
82477	Virginian Early Era Inspection Vehicle, CC, 15		200
82478	Reading Early Era Inspection Vehicle, CC, 15		200
82486	Weathered Virginian USRA Y-3 2-8-8-2 Locomotive "737," CC, 14		1450
82487	Weathered AT&SF USRA Y-3 2-8-8-2 Locomotive "1797," CC, 14		1450
82488	Weathered N&W USRA Y-3 2-8-8-2 Locomotive "2029," CC, 14		1450
82489	MILW Olympian 18" Aluminum Passenger Car 2-pack , 14-15		320
82494	Turbo Missile Launch Flatcar, 15		60
82495	D&RGW Scrapyard, 15-19		130
82498	Polar Express Mail Car, 16-17		70
82500	Polar Express Covered Bridge, 15		70
82501	Providence & Worcester 89' Auto Carrier "190091" , 15-16		110
82502	C&NW 89' Auto Carrier "962255" , 15-16		110
82503	Chessie 89' Auto Carrier "255798" , 15-16		110

			Exc	Mint
___	**82504**	TFM 89' Auto Carrier "987408", 15-16		110
___	**82505**	BNSF 89' Auto Carrier "212878" , 15-16		110
___	**82506**	UP 89' Auto Carrier "992579" , 15-16		110
___	**82508**	NYC Milk Car "6589" (std O), 15-16		80
___	**82510**	Polar Express Aquarium Car, 16		85
___	**82512**	Polar Express Work Caboose with presents, 15		85
___	**82514**	Polar Express Reindeer Stock Car, 15		90
___	**82518**	Moon Pie Boxcar, 15		85
___	**82528**	NYC Empire State Express Steam Passenger Set, CC, 15		1950
___	**82534**	NYC J3a 4-6-4 Hudson Locomotive "5429," tender, 15		1500
___	**82535**	NYC J3a 4-6-4 Hudson Locomotive "5426," tender, 15		1500
___	**82536**	NYC J3a 4-6-4 Hudson Locomotive "5429," tender, 15		1500
___	**82537**	NYC J3a 4-6-4 Hudson Locomotive "5426," tender, 15		1500
___	**82543**	Postwar "943" Exploding Ammunition Dump, 15-20		50
___	**82544**	Missile Firing Range, 15-16, 19		65
___	**82545**	Santa's Helper Steam Freight Set, 16-17		238
___	**82550**	Wabash 21" Streamlined Passenger Car 4-pack , 15		600
___	**82555**	Wabash 21" Streamlined Passenger Car 2-pack , 15		300
___	**82558**	Southern 21" Streamlined Passenger Car 4-pack , 15		600
___	**82563**	Southern 21" Streamlined Passenger Car 4-pack , 15		300
___	**82566**	RI 21" Streamlined Passenger Car 4-pack , 15		600
___	**82571**	RI 21" Streamlined Passenger Car 4-pack , 15		300
___	**82574**	Texas Special 21" Streamlined Passenger Car 4-pack , 15		600
___	**82579**	Texas Special 21" Streamlined Passenger Car 4-pack , 15		300
___	**82582**	C&O 21" Streamlined Passenger Car 4-pack , 15		600
___	**82587**	C&O 21" Streamlined Passenger Car 4-pack , 15		300
___	**82590**	Amtrak 21" Passenger Car 4-pack, 16		600
___	**82595**	Amtrak 21" Passenger Car 2-pack, 16		300
___	**82598**	NYC Empire State Passenger Car Add-on 2-pack, 15		300
___	**82611**	PRR GL-a 2-bay Hopper 3-pack , 15		220
___	**82615**	B&O GL-a 2-bay Hopper 2-pack , 15		146
___	**82618**	CNJ GL-a 2-bay Hopper 2-pack , 15		146
___	**82621**	Buffalo Creek Flour PS-1 Boxcar "2366" , 15		80
___	**82622**	U.S. Army PS-1 Boxcar "26875" , 15		80
___	**82623**	West India Fruit & Steamship Co. PS-1 Boxcar "321" , 15		80
___	**82624**	Linde Air Products PS-1 Boxcar "3019" , 15		80
___	**82625**	Air Reduction Products PS-1 Boxcar "100" , 15		80
___	**82629**	PRR N5b Caboose "478883" , 15-16		95
___	**82630**	PRR N5b Caboose with trainphone antenna, 15-16		95
___	**82631**	B&M N5b Caboose "C-16" , 15-16		95
___	**82639**	MILW Milk Car "370" (std O), 15-16, 20, 23		100
___	**82640**	UTLX 1-D Tank Car 3-pack , 15		250
___	**82644**	Philadelphia Energy Solutions 1-D Tank Car 3-pack , 15		250
___	**82648**	Midwest Ethanol Transport 1-D Tank Car 3-pack , 15		250
___	**82652**	Global Ethanol Transport 1-D Tank Car 3-pack , 15		250
___	**82656**	Conrail 60' Boxcar "216010" , 15-17		90
___	**82657**	WM 60' Boxcar "38020" , 15-17		90
___	**82658**	BN 60' Boxcar "355145" , 15-17		90
___	**82659**	RI 60' Boxcar "33825" , 15-17		90
___	**82660**	N&W 60' Boxcar "600949" , 15-17		90
___	**82661**	P&LE PS-5 Gondola and PS-4 Flatcar , 15-16		175
___	**82664**	B&LE PS-5 Gondola and PS-4 Flatcar , 15-16		175
___	**82667**	DT&I PS-5 Gondola and PS-4 Flatcar , 15-16		175

		Exc	Mint
82670	Conrail PS-5 Gondola and PS-4 Flatcar , 15-16		175
82674	UP Bathtub Gondola 2-pack , 15		140
82677	Strasburg 3-D Tank Car , 16		656
82678	Angela Trotta Thomas Christmas Boxcar, 16		85
82683	Batman and Flash Justice League Boxcar 2-pack, 15-16		170
82684	Superman and Green Lantern Boxcar 2-pack, 15-16		170
82685	New York Giants Cooperstown Boxcar, 15		85
82686	Washington Senators Cooperstown Boxcar, 15		85
82687	Detroit Tigers Cooperstown Boxcar, 15		85
82688	Pittsburgh Pirates Cooperstown Boxcar, 15		85
82689	Operation Eagle Missile Carrying Car, 15-17		65
82690	Coca-Cola Anniversary Bottle Boxcar, 15		90
82691	Christmas Boxcar, 15		75
82693	Santa's Helper Crane, 15		85
82694	UP LionMaster 4-6-6-4 Challenger Locomotive "3985," CC , 15		1000
82695	UP LionMaster 4-6-6-4 Challenger Locomotive "3977," CC , 15		1000
82696	UP LionMaster 4-6-6-4 Challenger Locomotive "3989," CC , 15		1000
82697	D&RGW LionMaster 4-6-6-4 Challenger Locomotive"3803," CC , 15		1000
82698	WM LionMaster 4-6-6-4 Challenger Locomotive "1201," CC , 15		1000
82699	Angela Trotta Thomas Lionelville Christmas Boxcar, 15	38	89
82701	Escaping Snowmen Handcar, 15		90
82702	Ontario Northland PS-4 Flatcar with covered load , 15		90
82703	BN PS-4 Flatcar with covered load , 15		90
82704	D&RGW PS-4 Flatcar with covered load , 15		90
82705	Reading PS-4 Flatcar with covered load , 15		90
82706	Southern PS-4 Flatcar with covered load , 15		90
82708	Christmas Gingerbread Shanty, 16-19		40
82709	PRR Silver & Gold Ore Car 2-pack, 16-17		130
82710	PRR Ice Breaker Tunnel Car, 16-17		65
82711	Santa's Favorites Transparent Gift Car, 16		85
82713	Christmas Music Boxcar, 15		80
82716	Mickey's Holiday to Remember Freight Set, 16		400
82717	W. E. Disney Girder Bridge, 16-18		33
82718	Disney Villains Hi-Cube Boxcar 2-pack, 16-19		160
82721	Dumbo 75th Anniversary Boxcar, 16-17		85
82726	Postwar Alco FA Diesel Green Passenger Set, 17-19		550
82728	LCS Switch Throw Monitor, 17-24		110
82734	New York Yankees Cooperstown Boxcar, 15	41	85
82735	Polar Express Conductor Gateman, 18-24	70	133
82736	North Pole Central Water Tower, 15		40
82737	Coca-Cola Santa Boxcar, 15		85
82739	North Pole Central Boxcar, 16-18		80
82740	Winter Wonderland Aquarium Car, 15		95
82741	Christmas Tinsel Vat Car, 16		70
82742	Candy Mountain Christmas Quad Hopper, 16-17		65
82743	Santa's Reindeer Station Platform, 15		50
82744	Santa Claus Automatic Gateman, 16-17		100
82745	Christmas Cocoa Barrel Shed, 15		50
82746	Christmas Floodlight Tower, 16		75

			Exc	Mint
___	**82747**	Christmas Red Arch Under Bridge, 16		30
___	**82748**	Silver Bell Casting Co. Hopper, 15		70
___	**82749**	PRR GG1 Electric "4935," CC, 16		1400
___	**82751**	PRR GG1 Electric "4913," CC, 16		1400
___	**82752**	PRR GG1 Electric "4877," CC, 16		1400
___	**82754**	PC GG1 Electric "4828," CC, 16		1400
___	**82755**	Amtrak GG1 Electric "926," CC, 16		1400
___	**82757**	CP SD90MAC Diesel "9116," CC, 16		650
___	**82758**	CP SD90MAC Diesel "9130," CC, 16		650
___	**82759**	"		650
___	**82760**	NS SD90MAC Diesel "7245," CC, 16		650
___	**82761**	UP SD90MAC Diesel "8130," CC, 16		650
___	**82762**	UP SD90MAC Diesel "8133," CC, 16		650
___	**82763**	UP SD90MAC Diesel "8025," CC, 16		650
___	**82764**	UP SD90MAC Diesel "8055," CC, 16		650
___	**82765**	Indiana SD90MAC Diesel "9003," CC, 16		650
___	**82766**	Indiana SD90MAC Diesel "9006," CC, 16		738
___	**82767**	C&O 2-6-6-6 Locomotive "1601," CC, 16		2200
___	**82768**	C&O 2-6-6-6 Locomotive "1604," CC, 16		2200
___	**82769**	C&O 2-6-6-6 Locomotive "1608," CC, 16		2200
___	**82770**	Virginian 2-6-6-6 Locomotive "906," CC, 16		2200
___	**82875**	Southern 2-8-0 Consolidation Locomotive "630," CC, 15		800
___	**82876**	SP 2-8-0 Consolidation Locomotive "2521," CC, 15		800
___	**82798**	DM&IR SD38 Diesel "221," CC, 15		650
___	**82800**	EJ&E SD38 Diesel "650," CC, 15		650
___	**82784**	BN GP9 Diesel "1706,"CC, 15		550
___	**82785**	BN GP9 Diesel "1804,"CC, 15		550
___	**82786**	Chessie System GP9 Diesel "5903,"CC, 15		550
___	**82787**	Chessie System GP9 Diesel "6240,"CC, 15		550
___	**82788**	D&RGW GP9 Diesel "5911," CC, 15		550
___	**82789**	D&RGW GP9 Diesel "5914," CC, 15		550
___	**82790**	NYC GP9 Diesel "5940," CC, 15		550
___	**82791**	NYC GP9 Diesel "5948," CC, 15		550
___	**82792**	PRR GP9 Diesel "7006," CC, 15		550
___	**82793**	PRR GP9 Diesel "7048," CC, 15		550
___	**82794**	Southern GP9 Diesel "6256," CC, 15		550
___	**82795**	Southern GP9 Diesel "6257," CC, 15		550
___	**82796**	Conrail SD38 Diesel "6935," CC, 15		650
___	**82797**	Conrail SD38 Diesel "6953," CC, 15		650
___	**82799**	DM&IR SD38 Diesel "223," CC, 15		650
___	**82801**	EJ&E SD38 Diesel "654," CC, 15		650
___	**82808**	PCI SD38 Diesel "6940," CC, 15		650
___	**82803**	PC SD38 Diesel "6945," CC, 15		650
___	**82804**	Reading & Northern SD38 "2000," CC, 15		650
___	**82805**	Reading & Northern SD38 "2003," CC, 15		650
___	**82806**	UP FEF-3 4-8-4 Northern "844," CC, 15		1700
___	**82807**	UP FEF-3 4-8-4 Northern Greyhound "844," CC, 15		1700
___	**82808**	UP FEF-3 4-8-4 Northern "8444," CC, 15		1700
___	**82809**	UP FEF-3 4-8-4 Northern "838," CC, 15		1700
___	**82810**	UP FEF-3 4-8-4 Northern Greyhound "835," CC, 15		1700
___	**82811**	Meadow River Lumber Heisler Locomotive "6," CC, 15		1300
___	**82812**	Pickering Lumber Heisler Locomotive "10," CC, 15		1300
___	**82813**	Cass Scenic Heisler Locomotive "6," CC, 15		1300

		Exc	Mint
82814	Kinzua Pine Mills Heisler Locomotive "102," CC, 15		1300
82815	Mount Rainier Scenic Heisler Locomotive "91," CC, 15		1300
82816	St. Regis Paper Heisler Locomotive "92," CC, 15		1300
82825	CP GP38 Diesel "3019," LionChief Plus, 16-17		340
82826	CSX GP38 Diesel "2145," LionChief Plus, 16-17		340
82827	SP GP38 Diesel "4846," LionChief Plus, 16-18		340
82828	UP GP38 Diesel "905," LionChief Plus, 16-17		340
82829	B&O E7 Diesel AA Set "1422/1428," CC, 15		1000
82830	CB&Q E7 Diesel AA Set "9917A/9917B," CC, 15		1000
82831	GN E7 Diesel AA Set "501A/501B," CC, 15		1000
82832	MILW E7 Diesel AA Set "17A/17B," CC, 15		1000
82833	Pere Marquette E7 Diesel AA Set "101/102," CC, 15		1000
82834	SAL E7 Diesel AA Set "3019/3020," CC, 15		1000
82840	AT&SF PS-4 Flatcar with trailer (std O), 15-16		110
82841	E-L PS-4 Flatcar with trailer (std O), 15-16		110
82842	GN PS-4 Flatcar with trailer (std O), 15-16		110
82843	WM PS-4 Flatcar with trailer (std O), 15-16		110
82844	PRR PS-4 Flatcar with trailer (std O), 15-16		110
82845	B&O Truck with 40' trailer, 15-16		90
82846	MILW Truck with 40' trailer, 15-17		90
82847	MKT Truck with 40' trailer, 15-17		90
82848	Logging Disconnect with load, 15-16		65
82849	Logging Disconnect with load 2-pack, 15-16		125
82850	MILW 40' Flatcar with lumber (std O), 15-17		90
82851	NP 40' Flatcar with lumber (std O), 15-17		90
82852	Meadow River 40' Flatcar with lumber (std O), 15-17		90
82853	Pickering 40' Flatcar with lumber (std O), 15-17		90
82854	PRR 40' Flatcar with lumber (std O), 15-16		90
82855	ADM Unibody Tank Car "190516" (std O), 16		75
82856	GATX Unibody Tank Car "4415" (std O), 16		75
82857	AFPX Unibody Tank Car "413303" (std O), 16		75
82858	Shell Unibody Tank Car "82858" (std O), 16		85
82859	Engelhard Unibody Tank Car "24586" (std O), 16		75
82860	PC PS-5 Gondola "557065" (std O), 15-16		90
82861	E-L PS-5 Gondola "14552" (std O), 15-16		90
82862	Frisco PS-5 Gondola "61442" (std O), 15-16		90
82863	CB&Q PS-5 Gondola "82050" (std O), 15-16		90
82864	NYC PS-5 Gondola "712603" (std O), 15-16		90
82865	PRR N5b Caboose "5017" (std O), 16		90
82866	PRR N5b Caboose "477746" (std O), 16		90
82867	PRR N5b Caboose "477625" (std O), 16		90
82868	NH N5 Caboose "C-507" (std O), 16		90
82869	IR Sensor Track O Gauge Tubular Compatible, 17-24		100
82870	Loading Ramp, 15-20		25
82872	Loader/Unloader Workers Figure Pack, 15-20		30
82873	Loggers Cabin, sound, 15-16		140
82874	Early Intermodal Work House, sound, 15-19		130
82877	Thomas Kinkade Polar Express Boxcar, 16		85
82878	Smithsonian Boxcar, 15-16		85
82879	Coca-Cola Christmas Boxcar, 16-17		85
82883	Legacy 360-watt PowerMaster, 15-24		240
82884	Wabash 21" Streamlined Dining Car, StationSounds, 15		300
82885	Southern 21" Streamlined Dining Car, StationSounds, 15		300

			Exc	Mint
____	**82886**	RI 21" Streamlined Dining Car, StationSounds, 15		300
____	**82887**	Texas Special 21" Streamlined Dining Car, StationSounds, 15		300
____	**82888**	C&O 21" Streamlined Dining Car, StationSounds, 15		300
____	**82889**	Amtrak 21" Diner, StationSounds, 16		300
____	**82890**	NYC Empire State Express Diner, StationSounds, 15		300
____	**82906**	Pluto Walking Brakeman Car, 16-18		100
____	**82908**	Mickey's Christmas Shanty, 16-18		50
____	**82913**	Winnie the Pooh Boxcar, 16-17		85
____	**82914**	Disney Aquarium Car, 16-18		85
____	**82917**	Disney Station Platform, 17-19		55
____	**82918**	36" Power Cable Extension (3-pin, M/F), 17-24		14
____	**82921**	Evil Queen Hi-Cube Boxcar, 17-19		80
____	**82922**	Scar Hi-Cube Boxcar, 17-19		80
____	**82925**	Scrooge McDuck Mint Car, 17-18		80
____	**82942**	James Monroe Presidential Boxcar, 16, 18		70
____	**82943**	John F. Kennedy Presidential Boxcar, 16		70
____	**82944**	Herbert Hoover Presidential Boxcar, 16		70
____	**82945**	James Madison Presidential Boxcar, 16		70
____	**82947**	Wonder Woman/Green Arrow Boxcar 2-pack, 16		170
____	**82950**	Aquaman/Martian Manhunter Boxcar 2-pack, 16		170
____	**82953**	Joker/Lex Luthor Boxcar 2-pack, 16		170
____	**82954**	Lionel Christmas Boxcar, 16		65
____	**82958**	Christmas Floodlight, 17-18		75
____	**82959**	115th Anniversary 2-8-4 Berkshire Locomotive, 15		2000
____	**82960**	NYC 2-8-2 Mikado Locomotive "1548," LionChief Plus, 15-18		430
____	**82961**	UP 2-8-2 Mikado Locomotive "2537," LionChief Plus, 15-18		430
____	**82962**	Southern 2-8-2 Mikado Locomotive "4501," LionChief Plus, 15-18		430
____	**82963**	Rio Grande 2-8-2 Mikado Locomotive "1208," LionChief Plu, 15-18		430
____	**82964**	MILW 4-6-4 Hudson Locomotive "125," LionChief Plus, 15-18		430
____	**82965**	AT&SF 4-6-4 Hudson Locomotive "3450," LionChief Plus, 15-18		430
____	**82966**	DL&W 4-6-4 Hudson Locomotive "1151," LionChief Plus, 15-18		430
____	**82967**	CB&Q 4-6-4 Hudson Locomotive "3007," LionChief Plus, 15-18		430
____	**82968**	LL 4-6-2 Pacific Locomotive "462," LionChief Plus, 16-17		430
____	**82969**	WM 4-6-2 Pacific Locomotive "202," LionChief Plus, 16-18		430
____	**82970**	Reading & Northern 4-6-2 Pacific Locomotive "425," LionChief Plus, 16-17		450
____	**82971**	C&NW 4-6-2 Pacific Locomotive "600," LionChief Plus, 16-18		300
____	**82972**	Lionel Junction PRR Diesel Freight Set, 16-17		175
____	**82973**	PRR A5 0-4-0 Locomotive "3891", 16-18		450
____	**82974**	SP A5 0-4-0 Locomotive "1040", 16-18		450
____	**82975**	B&O A5 0-4-0 Locomotive "317", 16-18		450
____	**82976**	Bethlehem Steel A5 0-4-0 Locomotive "140," LionChief, 16-18		450
____	**82982**	Christmas Express Steam Freight Set, LionChief, 17-18		320
____	**82984**	NYC RS3 Diesel Freight Set, 16-17		260
____	**82992**	115th Anniversary Boxcar, 16		90
____	**82993**	Weathered UP Y-3 2-8-8-2 Steam Engine, 3595, CC, 15		1450
____	**82994**	Weathered C&O H-7 2-8-8-2 Steam Engine, 1578, CC, 15		1450
____	**82995**	Weathered UP Y-3 2-8-8-2 Steam Engine, 3671, CC, 15		1450
____	**82996**	Weathered PRR Y-3 2-8-8-2 Steam Engine, 376, CC, 15		1450
____	**83002**	PRR Broadway Limited 21" Diner 2-pack, StationSounds, 16		450

		Exc	Mint
83003	PC 21" StationSounds Diner "4552", 16		300
83006	UP 21" Excursion Diner, StationSounds, 16		300
83007	PRR Broadway Limited 21" Passenger Car 2-pack, 16		300
83010	PC 21" Passenger Car 2-pack, 16		300
83019	UP 21" Excursion Passenger Car 2-pack, 16		300
83022	PRR Broadway Limited 21" Passenger Car 4-pack, 16		600
83027	PC 21" Passenger Car 4-pack, 16		600
83042	UP 21" Excursion Passenger Car 4-pack, 16		675
83063	AT&SF Super Chief Boxcar "143093", 16-19		50
83071	LC Universal Remote, 16-23		55
83072	PRR "Keystone Special" Steam Freight Set, LionChief, 17-20		300
83080	Rio Grande 0-4-0 Switcher Freight Set, 16-17		300
83092	Steel City Switcher Freight Set, CC, 16		1300
83102	SP 21" Passenger Car 4-pack, 16		600
83107	SP 21" Passenger Car 2-pack, 16		300
83110	SP 21" Diner "290," StationSounds, 16		300
83111	American Freedom Train 21" Passenger Car 4-pack, 16-17		675
83116	American Freedom Train 21" Passenger Car 2-pack, 16-17		300
83119	American Freedom Train 21" Exhibit Car, StationSounds, 16-17		300
83120	CSX Office Car Special 21" Passenger Car 4-pack, 16-17		600
83125	CSX Office Car Special 21" Passenger Car 2-pack, 16-17		300
83128	CSX Office Car Special 21" Diner, StationSounds, 16-17		300
83147	Lighted Yard Tower, 16		60
83148	Christmas Express Boxcar, 16-17		53
83157	Smithsonian Air & Space Boxcar 2-pack, 16		170
83162	Nightmare on Elm Street Boxcar, 16		85
83163	Thomas Kinkade Christmas Boxcar, 16-17		85
83164	Frosty the Snowman 1-D Tank Car, 16-17		60
83165	PRR GG1 Electric "4899," CC, 16		1400
83166	PRR GG1 Electric "4800" CC, 16		1400
83167	Conrail Bicentennial GG1 Electric "4800," CC, 16		1400
83168	Iron Workers Figure Pack, 16-23		30
83169	NYC Flatcar with piggyback trailers, 16-19		75
83170	Steel Mill Structure, sound, 16-19		130
83171	MOW Workers Figure Pack, 16-22		30
83172	MOW Work Structure, sound, 16-19		130
83173	Single Signal Bridge, 16-24		90
83174	Double Signal Bridge, 16-24		120
83175	Christmas Music Boxcar, 16		80
83176	Lionel Lines Christmas Caboose, 16-17		75
83177	Angela Trotta Thomas Caboose, 16-17		80
83178	Coca-Cola Caboose, 16		75
83179	Conrail Caboose "23878", 16-19		75
83180	PRR Caboose "477100", 16-17		75
83181	AT&SF Caboose "999316", 16-17		75
83182	ACL Caboose "0634", 16-19		75
83183	Erie Caboose "C226", 16-19		75
83184	UP Caboose "25214", 16-18		75
83185	Polar Express Elves Figure Set, 16-24		33
83186	NYC Caboose "21777", 16-18		75
83190	Moon Pie 1-D Tank Car, 16-17		75
83191	Snow Transport Christmas 1-D Tank Car, 16, 19		85
83192	Smithsonian Dinosaur Aquarium Car, 16-17		85

			Exc	Mint
___	**83193**	SP GS-4 4-8-4 Locomotive "4449," CC, 16		1700
___	**83194**	SP GS-4 4-8-4 Locomotive "4449," CC, 16		1700
___	**83195**	SP GS-4 4-8-4 Locomotive "4443," CC, 16		1700
___	**83196**	SP GS-4 4-8-4 Locomotive "4444," CC, 16		1700
___	**83197**	American Freedom Train GS-4 4-8-4 Locomotive, CC, 16		1700
___	**83198**	Reading T1 4-8-4 Locomotive "2100," CC, 16		1700
___	**83199**	Reading T1 4-8-4 Locomotive "2119," CC, 16		1700
___	**83200**	Reading T1 4-8-4 Locomotive "2102," CC, 16		1700
___	**83201**	Reading T1 4-8-4 Locomotive "2124," CC, 16		1700
___	**83202**	American Freedom Train T1 4-8-4 Locomotive, CC, 16		1700
___	**83203**	Chessie T1 4-8-4 Locomotive "2101," CC, 16		1700
___	**83204**	B&O 0-8-0 Locomotive "1695," CC, 16		900
___	**83205**	GTW 0-8-0 Locomotive "8380," CC, 16		900
___	**83206**	Indiana Harbor Belt 0-8-0 Locomotive "312," CC, 16		900
___	**83208**	Wabash 0-8-0 Locomotive "1526," CC, 16		900
___	**83209**	Terminal Railroad 0-8-0 Locomotive, CC, 16		900
___	**83214**	North Pole Central 4-6-2 Locomotive "1225", 16-17		430
___	**83215**	Transformer 2-pack, 16-19		15
___	**83223**	Steel I-Beam 12-pack, 16-20		15
___	**83230**	Amtrak Metal Girder Bridge, 16-20		43
___	**83231**	Polar Express Metal Girder Bridge, 16-17		43
___	**83232**	Bethlehem Steel Metal Girder Bridge, 16-19		40
___	**83233**	CSX Metal Girder Bridge, 16-19		37
___	**83234**	John Deere Plastic Girder Bridge, 16-19		33
___	**83238**	John Deere Flatcar with spreaders, 16-17		80
___	**83239**	Polar Express Bells Mint Car, 16-17		80
___	**83240**	Shell Operating Oil Derrick, 16		120
___	**83241**	Shell Oil Storage Tank with Light, 16		85
___	**83242**	Shell 1-D Tank Car, 15-16		75
___	**83243**	Shell 3-D Tank Car, 16-17		75
___	**83244**	Shell Elevated Oil Tank, 17		100
___	**83246**	Shell Boxcar, 16		85
___	**83247**	Shell Billboard Pack, 16-17		25
___	**83248**	"It's a Boy" Boxcar, 16		90
___	**83249**	Polar Express Combination Car, 16-17		70
___	**83250**	"It's a Girl" Boxcar, 16		90
___	**83251**	Poultry Dispatch Sweep Car, 16-18		120
___	**83252**	Gold Medal Milk Car with platform, 17-19		180
___	**83253**	D&RGW Searchlight Car, 16-17		63
___	**83254**	Western Union Animated Gondola, 16-18		70
___	**83256**	GN Horse Transport , 16		80
___	**83257**	Bobbing Werewolf Boxcar, 16-17		75
___	**83258**	CP Boom Car, 16		63
___	**83266**	Lionel Junction Santa Fe Steam Freight Set, 16		175
___	**83275**	Sugar Cookie Scented Smoke Fluid, 17-24		9
___	**83276**	Peppermint Scented Smoke Fluid, 17-24		9
___	**83277**	Pine Scented Smoke Fluid, 17-24		9
___	**83278**	Hot Chocolate Scented Smoke Fluid, 17-24		9
___	**83279**	Wood Stove Scented Smoke Fluid, 17-24		9
___	**83280**	Unscented Smoke Fluid, 17-24		9
___	**83284**	Peekaboo Reindeer Operating Boxcar, 16-17	35	75
___	**83286**	John Deere Steam Freight Set, 16-17		400
___	**83291**	Christmas Half-covered Bridge, 16-19		70

		Exc	Mint
83292	Christmas Cookies & Candies Store, 16-17		85
83304	North Pole Elves Work Shanty, 16		40
83305	Illuminated Winter Covered Bridge, 16-24		100
83308	North Pole Central Tank Car "122416", 16-17		75
83311	Santa's Favorites Egg Nog Reefer, 16-18		65
83312	Santa's Cookies Vat Car, 16-17		70
83313	Reindeer Express Agency Flatcar with trailer, 16-17		70
83315	Christmas Toys Stock Car, 16-18		70
83316	Santa's Sleigh Aquarium Car, 16-18		80
83317	BNSF 65' Mill Gondola "518357" (std O), 17		80
83318	C&NW 65' Mill Gondola "342036" (std O), 17		80
83319	CSX 65' Mill Gondola "491600" (std O), 17		80
83320	NS 65' Mill Gondola "195015" (std O), 17		80
83321	SP 65' Mill Gondola "365117" (std O), 17		80
83322	UP 65' Mill Gondola "96257" (std O), 17		80
83340	Boxcar Children Boxcar, 16		85
83347	ACL USRA Double-sheathed Boxcar, 16		85
83348	B&M USRA Double-sheathed Boxcar, 16		85
83349	RI USRA Double-sheathed Boxcar, 16		85
83350	Northwestern Pacific USRA Double-sheathed Boxcar, 16		85
83351	Wabash USRA Double-sheathed Boxcar, 16		85
83352	Polar Express USRA Double-sheathed Boxcar, 16		95
83353	D&RGW Flatcar with snowplow (std O), 16		95
83354	NYC Flatcar with snowplow (std O), 16		95
83355	UP Flatcar with snowplow (std O), 16		95
83356	MOW Flatcar with Snowplow (std O), 16		95
83357	Reading NE-style Caboose "92882" (std O), 16		90
83358	Reading NE-style Caboose "92902" (std O), 16		90
83359	Reading & Northern NE-style Caboose "92884" (std O), 16		90
83360	C&O NE-style Caboose "90352" (std O), 16		90
83361	N&W NE-style Caboose "500830" (std O), 16		90
83362	WM NE-style Caboose "1887" (std O), 16		90
83368	EL SD45 Diesel Locomotive "3607," CC, 16		650
83369	EL SD45 Diesel Locomotive "3618," CC, 16		650
83370	EL Bicentennial SD45 Diesel Locomotive "3632," CC, 16		650
83371	GN "Hustle Muscle" SD45 Diesel Locomotive "400," CC, 16		650
83372	GN SD45 Diesel Locomotive "402," CC, 16		650
83373	GN SD45 Diesel Locomotive "407," CC, 16		650
83374	PC SD45 Diesel Locomotive "6235," CC, 16		650
83375	PC SD45 Diesel Locomotive "6237," CC, 16		650
83376	Southern SD45 Diesel Locomotive "3137," CC, 16		650
83377	Southern SD45 Diesel Locomotive "3156," CC, 16		650
83378	SP SD45 Diesel Locomotive "8801," CC, 16		650
83379	SP SD45 Diesel Locomotive "8820," CC, 16		650
83380	UP SD45 Diesel Locomotive "1," CC, 16		650
83381	UP SD45 Diesel Locomotive "21," CC, 16		650
83382	AT&SF NW2 Diesel Locomotive "2405," CC, 16		500
83383	B&M NW2 Diesel Locomotive "1200," CC, 16		500
83384	B&O NW2 Diesel Locomotive "9527," CC, 16		500
83385	CSX NW2 Diesel Locomotive "9565," CC, 16		500
83387	NYO&W NW2 Diesel Locomotive "116," CC, 16	305	500
83388	PRR NW2 Diesel Locomotive "9171," CC, 16		500

			Exc	Mint
___	**83389**	Philadelphia, Bethlehem & New England NW2 Diesel "27," CC, 16		500
___	**83390**	SP NW2 Diesel Locomotive "1423," CC, 16		500
___	**83391**	SP&S NW2 Diesel Locomotive "41," CC, 16		500
___	**83392**	Union NW2 Diesel Locomotive "555," CC, 16		500
___	**83393**	UP NW2 Diesel Locomotive "1011," CC, 16		500
___	**83395**	AC&Y H16-44 Diesel "201," CC, 16		550
___	**83396**	AC&Y H16-44 Diesel "202," CC, 16		550
___	**83397**	AT&SF H16-44 Diesel "2801," CC, 16		550
___	**83398**	AT&SF H16-44 Diesel "2807," CC, 16		550
___	**83399**	B&O H16-44 Diesel "6705," CC, 16		550
___	**83400**	B&O H16-44 Diesel "6708," CC, 16		550
___	**83401**	MILW H16-44 Diesel "402," CC, 16		550
___	**83402**	MILW H16-44 Diesel "404," CC, 16		550
___	**83403**	DL&W H16-44 Diesel "931," CC, 16		550
___	**83404**	DL&W H16-44 Diesel "934," CC, 16		550
___	**83405**	Southern H16-44 Diesel "6547," CC, 16		550
___	**83406**	Southern H16-44 Diesel "6550," CC, 16		550
___	**83420**	NS Honoring Veterans SD60E Diesel "6920," CC, 15		650
___	**83421**	NS Go Rail SD60E Diesel "6963," CC, 15		650
___	**83422**	NS First Responders SD60E Diesel "911," CC, 15		650
___	**83423**	NS SD60E Diesel "6900," CC, 15		650
___	**83424**	NS SD60E Diesel "6916," CC, 15		650
___	**83426**	Johnstown Birney Trolley, 16		100
___	**83434**	Polar Express Passenger Station, 16-17		90
___	**83435**	World War II Pylon, 17		160
___	**83437**	Polar Express Conductor Announcement Car, 16-17, 19		110
___	**83438**	Miller Coors Operating Billboard, 17		80
___	**83440**	Rico Station Kit, 16-24		60
___	**83442**	Large Suburban House, 17-18		95
___	**83443**	Deluxe Bungalow House, 17-18		95
___	**83444**	Illuminated Station Platform, 16-17		43
___	**83445**	Smithsonian Old St. Nick Boxcar, 16-18		85
___	**83455**	Polar Express Operating Billboard, 16-17		85
___	**83462**	Bethlehem Steel Slag Car 3-pack, 16		240
___	**83466**	U.S. Steel Slag Car 3-pack (std O), 16		240
___	**83470**	Slag Car 3-pack (std O), 16		240
___	**83474**	Weathered Slag Car 3-pack (std O), 16		240
___	**83478**	Bethlehem Steel Hot Metal Car 2-pack, 16		200
___	**83481**	U.S. Steel Hot Metal Car 2-pack (std O), 16		200
___	**83484**	Hot Metal Car 2-pack (std O), 16		200
___	**83487**	Weathered Hot Metal Car 2-pack (std O), 16		200
___	**83490**	Lighted Concrete Coaling Tower, 15-18		180
___	**83491**	Boston Red Sox Cooperstown Boxcar, 16		85
___	**83492**	St. Louis Cardinals Cooperstown Boxcar, 16		85
___	**83493**	Philadelphia Phillies Cooperstown Boxcar, 16		85
___	**83494**	Baltimore Orioles Cooperstown Boxcar, 16		85
___	**83496**	Station Platform, 16-18, 21-24		40
___	**83497**	2016 National Train Day Boxcar, 16-17		85
___	**83503**	Thomas with remote, 16-18		120
___	**83504**	Birthday Thomas with remote, 16-18		120
___	**83510**	Thomas & Friends Passenger Set, LionChief, 16-24		250
___	**83511**	Thomas, Sodor Locomotive, LionChief, 18-23		160

		Exc	Mint
83512	Thomas & Friends Christmas Freight Set, 16-17		200
83518	PRR Boxcar "83518" (std O), 16		100
83519	REA SensorCar Steel Reefer "7844" (std O), 16, 19		130
83520	North Pole Central Flatcar with snowplow, 16		95
83527	AT&SF PS-1 Boxcar "142501," sound (std O), 16		130
83528	BAR PS-1 Boxcar "5149," sound (std O), 16		130
83529	B&O PS-1 Boxcar "467931," sound (std O), 16		130
83530	BN PS-1 Boxcar "132909," sound (std O), 16		130
83531	C&NW PS-1 Boxcar "5," sound (std O), 16		130
83532	NYC PS-1 Boxcar "175001," sound (std O), 16		130
83533	PRR PS-1 Boxcar "47005," sound (std O), 16		130
83534	UP PS-1 Boxcar "196883," sound (std O), 16		130
83535	PRR GL-a 2-bay Hopper 3-pack #1 (std O), 16		220
83539	PRR GL-a 2-bay Hopper 3-pack #2 (std O), 16		220
83544	PRR N5b Caboose "477797" (std O), 16		95
83545	PFE Reefer 3-pack (std O), 16		170
83549	AT&SF Reefer 3-pack (std O), 16		300
83553	Heisler Log Train Set, CC, 16		1450
83555	Red Logging Disconnect Caboose "1" (std O), 16		40
83556	Brown Logging Disconnect Caboose "6" (std O), 16		40
83557	Logging Disconnect Boxcar (std O), 16		40
83558	Logging Disconnect Flatcar (std O), 16		35
83559	Logging Disconnect Gondola (std O), 16		40
83560	Logging Disconnect Tank Car (std O), 16		40
83561	ATSF Express 50' DD Boxcar "1342" (std O), 16-17		80
83562	CNJ PS-1 Express Boxcar "22487" (std O), 16-17		80
83563	C&EI PS-1 Express Boxcar "2" (std O), 16-17		80
83564	GN PS-1 Express Boxcar "2538" (std O), 16-17		80
83565	KCS PS-1 Express Boxcar "400" (std O), 16-17		80
83566	SP PS-1 Express Boxcar "5712" (std O), 16-17		80
83567	T&P PS-1 Express Boxcar "1721" (std O), 16-17		80
83568	C&S Grain-door PS-1 Boxcar "1650" (std O), 16-17		80
83569	CP Grain-door PS-1 Boxcar "260293" (std O), 16-17		80
83570	GN Grain-door PS-1 Boxcar "18119" (std O), 16-17		80
83571	CGW Grain-door PS-1 Boxcar "5450" (std O), 16-17		80
83572	IC Grain-door PS-1 Boxcar "19000" (std O), 16-17		80
83573	MKT Grain-door PS-1 Boxcar "92463" (std O), 16-17		80
83574	UP CA-4 Caboose "3824" (std O), 16		90
83575	UP CA-4 Caboose "25121" (std O), 16		90
83576	B&O Milk Car "847" (std O), 16-17, 20		90
83577	Supplee Milk Car "7" (std O), 16-17, 20		90
83578	Hood Milk Car "807" (std O), 16-17, 20		90
83579	Rutland Milk Car "351" (std O), 16-17, 20		90
83580	BAR State of Maine 40' Trailer, 2-pack, 16-17		65
83581	C&NW 40' Trailer, 2-pack, 16-17		65
83582	PFE 40' Trailer, 2-pack, 16-17		65
83583	PC 40' Trailer, 2-pack, 16-17		65
83584	SP 40' Trailer, 2-pack, 16-17		65
83585	UP 40' Trailer, 2-pack, 16-17		65
83586	PRR Broadway Limited 21" Passenger Car 2-pack #2 (std O), 16		300
83589	American Freedom Train Add-On 2-pack #2, 16-17		300
83592	American Freedom Train Add-On 2-pack #3, 16-17		300
83595	Conrail Office Car Special Diesel Passenger Set, CC, 17		1250

			Exc	Mint
___	**83601**	Conrail Office Car Special Add-on 2-pack, 17		310
___	**83604**	Conrail Office Car Special 21" Dome Car "55," StationSounds , 17		320
___	**83605**	Presidents 2-8-2 Mikado Locomotive "1789," LionChief Plus, 16-17		430
___	**83606**	Halloween 2-8-2 Mikado Locomotive "1031," LionChief Plus, 16-17		430
___	**83607**	USRA 2-8-2 Mikado Locomotive "4500," LionChief Plus, 16-18		430
___	**83608**	B&O 2-8-2 Mikado Locomotive "4500," LionChief Plus, 16-17		430
___	**83609**	C&O 2-8-2 Mikado Locomotive "1067," LionChief Plus, 16-17		430
___	**83610**	MKT 2-8-2 Mikado Locomotive "851," LionChief Plus, 16-17		430
___	**83611**	NYC Empire State Express 21" Coach 4-pack #2, 17		620
___	**83616**	NYC Empire State Express 21" Combine/Observation Car 2-pack #2, 17		310
___	**83617**	NYC Empire State Express Martin Van Buren Combine, 19		155
___	**83618**	NYC Empire State Express Franklin Roosevelt Observation, 19		155
___	**83619**	NYC Empire State Express 21" Diner #2, StationSounds, 17		310
___	**83620**	Hogwarts Express Passenger Set, 16-17		400
___	**83624**	UP Sherman Hill Scout RS3 Freight Set, 16-17		500
___	**83633**	Alaska Gold Mint Car, 17		70
___	**83634**	Keystone Smoke Fluid Loader, 16-20		350
___	**83635**	North American Smoke Fluid Loader, 16-19		350
___	**83636**	2015 Contest Winning Boxcar, 15		85
___	**83637**	Mets-Phillies Mascot Aquarium Car, 16		85
___	**83644**	Macy's Dry Goods Boxcar, 15 u		100
___	**83645**	Polar Express Boxcar 2-pack, 16-18		170
___	**83648**	New York Yankees Subway Set, 16		390
___	**83653**	Scale Passenger Car Figures, 24-pack, 16-24		33
___	**83655**	Hamm's Heritage Beer Wood-sided Reefer, 16-17		80
___	**83656**	Coors Heritage Beer Wood-sided Reefer, 16-17		80
___	**83657**	Miller Heritage Beer Wood-sided Reefer, 16-17		80
___	**83658**	Lionelville School Kit, 16-17		60
___	**83659**	PRR Keystone Special Steam Freight Set, 16-17		280
___	**83688**	Trackside Railroad Details Pack, 16-24		33
___	**83689**	Angela Trotta Thomas Christmas Covered Bridge, 17-20		70
___	**83690**	Company Row House, blue, 16-17		60
___	**83691**	Company Row House, yellow, 16-17		60
___	**83692**	Company Row House, white, 16-17		60
___	**83693**	Company Row House, red, 16-17		60
___	**83694**	Toymaker Limited Trolley Set, 18		200
___	**83696**	NYC "Pacemaker" Lionel Junction Diesel Freight Set, 17		175
___	**83701**	Alaska Gold Mine 0-4-0 Steam Freight Set, LionChief, 17		320
___	**83716**	BNSF RS3 Diesel Scout Freight Set, LionChief, 17		280
___	**83733**	Lighted Aquarius Hi-Cube Boxcar, 17		90
___	**83734**	Lighted Pegasus Hi-Cube Boxcar, 17		90
___	**83745**	Lionelville Hospital Kit, 17-18		80
___	**83751**	Illuminated Yard Tower, 18-19, 22-24		65
___	**83752**	W&A Horse Car and Corral, 17-18		180
___	**83762**	Personalized Christmas Boxcar, 16		90
___	**83763**	Personalized Holiday Boxcar, 16		90
___	**83764**	Happy Birthday Boxcar, 16		90
___	**83765**	Anniversary Boxcar, 16-17		90
___	**83766**	Personalized Polar Express Baggage Car, 16-18		95
___	**83779**	Pearl Harbor 75th Anniversary Boxcar, 16-17		85

		Exc	Mint
83783	Rosie the Riveter Boxcar, 17		85
83784	Heavies and Little Friends Boxcar, 17		85
83785	Doolittle Raid Boxcar, 16-17		85
83786	D-Day Boxcar, 17		85
83788	Uncle Sam "Enlist Now" Boxcar, 16-17		85
83790	Mickey Mouse Happy Holidays Boxcar, 17	25	85
83791	Donald Duck Happy Holidays Boxcar, 17		85
83792	Goofy Happy Holidays Boxcar, 17		85
83794	75th Anniversary of Bambi Boxcar, 17		80
83795	50th Anniversary of The Jungle Book Boxcar, 17		80
83796	100th Anniversary Moon Pie Boxcar, 17		85
83800	Happy Thanksgiving Boxcar, 17		80
83801	Happy Hanukkah Boxcar, 17		80
83802	Disney Happy Halloween Boxcar, 17		85
83913	Personalized Halloween Boxcar, 17		95
83918	Smithsonian Boxcar, John Bull, 17		85
83923	Angela Trotta Thomas Santa's Cookies Boxcar, 17		85
83924	Caddyshack Boxcar, 17		80
83925	Frosty the Snowman Boxcar, 17		85
83926	Personalized Polar Express Boxcar, 17-20		95
83927	Lionel Smoke Fluid 1-D Tank Car, 17		75
83928	Lionel Paint 1-D Tank Car, 17		75
83929	Lionel Hydraulic Oil 1-D Tank Car, 17		75
83938	Harry Potter Hogwarts House Gryffindor Boxcar, 17		80
83939	Harry Potter Hogwarts House Ravenclaw Boxcar, 17		80
83940	Harry Potter Hogwarts House Hufflepuff Boxcar, 17		80
83941	Harry Potter Hogwarts House Slytherin Boxcar, 17		80
83943	Polar Express Boxcar, 17-18		85
83944	John Deere Boxcar, 17		85
83945	Richard Nixon Presidential Boxcar, 17		70
83946	Jimmy Carter Presidential Boxcar, 17, 19		70
83947	Woodrow Wilson Presidential Boxcar, 17, 19-20		75
83948	William Howard Taft Presidential Boxcar, 17, 19-20		75
83950	Personalized "It's A Boy" Boxcar, 17-23		100
83951	Personalized "It's A Girl" Boxcar, 17-23		100
83952	Minnie Mouse Happy Holidays Boxcar, 17		85
83959	Macy's Parade 90th Anniversary Boxcar, 16 u		30
83964	Mickey Mouse Christmas Express Steam Freight Set, LionChief, 17-18		420
83972	Harry Potter Hogwarts Steam Passenger Set, LionChief, 17-19		420
83974	CSX Diesel Intermodal Set, LionChief, 17-18		460
83979	Mickey & Friends Express Steam Freight Set, LionChief, 17, 19-20		370
83984	Pennsylvania Flyer 0-8-0 Steam Freight Set, LionChief, 17, 19-20		300
83994	C&NW Boxcar, 17		100
84000	DETX Rotary Gondola 4-pack (std O), 16-17, 20-23		310
84005	CSX Rotary Gondola 4-pack (std O), 16-17, 20-22		310
84010	UP Rotary Gondola 4-pack (std O), 16-17, 20-22		310
84015	NS Rotary Gondola 4-pack (std O), 16-17, 20-22		310
84020	PPLX Rotary Gondola 4-pack (std O), 16-17, 20-23		310
84025	PPLX Rotary Gondola 2-pack (std O), 16-17, 20-23		155
84028	BNSF Rotary Gondola 4-pack (std O), 16-17, 20-22		310

			Exc	Mint
____	**84033**	BNSF Rotary Gondola 2-pack (std 0), 16-17, 20-23		155
____	**84045**	BN 21" Passenger Car 4-pack, 17		620
____	**84050**	BN 21" Coach 2-pack, 17		310
____	**84053**	BN 21" Diner, StationSounds , 17		310
____	**84063**	Weathered N&W Y6B 2-8-8-2 Locomotive "2186," CC, 16		2200
____	**84064**	MILW 4-8-4 Northern Locomotive "261," CC, 17		1700
____	**84065**	MILW 4-8-4 Northern Locomotive "265," CC, 17		1700
____	**84066**	MILW 4-8-4 Northern Locomotive "262," CC, 17		1700
____	**84067**	MILW 4-8-4 Northern Locomotive "260 Hiawatha," CC, 17		1700
____	**84068**	DL&W 4-8-4 Northern Locomotive "1661," CC, 17		1700
____	**84069**	B&M 2-6-0 Mogul Locomotive "1397," CC, 16		700
____	**84070**	CV 2-6-0 Mogul Locomotive "397," CC, 16		700
____	**84071**	DL&W 2-6-0 Mogul Locomotive "565," CC, 16		700
____	**84072**	Everett 2-6-0 Mogul Locomotive "11," CC, 16		700
____	**84073**	GT 2-6-0 Mogul Locomotive "713," CC, 16		700
____	**84074**	Rutland 2-6-0 Mogul Locomotive "145," CC, 16		700
____	**84075**	ACL E8 Diesel AA Set "544, 545," CC , 17		1000
____	**84078**	BN E8 Diesel AA Set "9935, 9940," CC , 17		1000
____	**84081**	Conrail E8 Diesel AA Set "4020, 4021," CC , 17		1000
____	**84084**	EMD Demonstrator E8 Diesel A Unit "950," CC, 17		650
____	**84085**	L&N E8 Diesel AA Set "796, 797," CC , 17		1000
____	**84088**	NYC E8 Diesel AA Set "4036, 4037," CC , 17		1000
____	**84091**	PRR E8 Diesel AA Set "5763, 5764," CC , 17		1000
____	**84094**	Arkansas & Missouri SD70ACe Diesel Locomotive "70," CC, 16		650
____	**84095**	Arkansas & Missouri SD70ACe Diesel Locomotive "71," CC, 16		650
____	**84096**	BNSF SD70ACe Diesel Locomotive "9372," CC, 16		650
____	**84097**	BNSF SD70ACe Diesel Locomotive "9385," CC, 16		650
____	**84098**	CN SD70ACe Diesel Locomotive "8100," CC, 16		650
____	**84099**	CN SD70ACe Diesel Locomotive "8102," CC, 16		650
____	**84100**	CSX SD70ACe Diesel Locomotive "4837," CC, 16		650
____	**84101**	CSX SD70ACe Diesel Locomotive "4843," CC, 16		650
____	**84102**	EMDX SD70ACe Diesel Locomotive "72," CC, 16		650
____	**84103**	EMDX SD70ACe Diesel Locomotive "73," CC, 16		650
____	**84104**	Montana Rail Link SD70ACe Diesel Locomotive "4309" CC, 16		650
____	**84105**	Montana Rail Link SD70ACe Diesel Locomotive "4312" CC, 16		650
____	**84106**	UP SD70ACe Diesel Locomotive "8360," CC, 16		650
____	**84107**	UP SD70ACe Diesel Locomotive "8415," CC, 16		650
____	**84108**	GN GP7 Diesel "601," LionChief Plus, 16-18		330
____	**84109**	L&N GP7 Diesel "405," LionChief Plus, 16-18		330
____	**84110**	Reading GP7 Diesel "619," LionChief Plus, 16-18		330
____	**84111**	WP GP7 Diesel "707," LionChief Plus, 16-18		330
____	**84112**	Cotton Belt 50' DD Boxcar "47509" (std 0), 16-17		80
____	**84113**	D&RGW 50' DD Boxcar "63689" (std 0), 16-17		80
____	**84114**	Seaboard 50' DD Boxcar "10090" (std 0), 16-17		80
____	**84115**	PRR K4s 4-6-2 Pacific Locomotive "5385," CC, 16		1300
____	**84116**	PRR K4s 4-6-2 Pacific Locomotive "5432," CC, 16		1300
____	**84117**	Burlington Refrigerator Express 40' Steel Reefer "76060" (std 0), 17		85
____	**84118**	BAR 40' Steel Reefer "7342" (std 0), 17		85
____	**84119**	BN 40' Steel Reefer "70609" (std 0), 17		85

		Exc	Mint
84120	Eastern States ERDX 40' Steel Reefer "10060" (std 0), 17		85 ___
84121	National Car Co. 40' Steel Reefer "2430" (std 0), 17		85 ___
84122	FGE 40' Steel Reefer "41475" (std 0), 17		85 ___
84123	B&M PS-2CD Covered Hopper "5717" (std 0), 17		90 ___
84124	L&N PS-2CD Covered Hopper "37399" (std 0), 17		90 ___
84125	MILW PS-2CD Covered Hopper "98333" (std 0), 17		90 ___
84126	NP PS-2CD Covered Hopper "75675" (std 0), 17		90 ___
84127	AT&SF PS-2CD Covered Hopper "304713" (std 0), 17		90 ___
84128	TLDX Demonstrator PS-2CD Covered Hopper "91" (std 0), 17, 19		90 ___
84129	AT&SF Wide Vision Caboose "999705" (std 0), 17		95 ___
84130	BN Freedom Train Wide Vision Caboose "12618" (std 0), 17		95 ___
84131	BNSF Wide Vision Caboose "12584" (std 0), 17		95 ___
84132	CSX Wide Vision Caboose "903180" (std 0), 17		95 ___
84133	D&H Wide-Vision Caboose "35712", 18		100 ___
84134	GN Wide-Vision Caboose "X-109", 18		100 ___
84135	C&O Northeast Caboose "A918" (std 0), 17		90 ___
84137	Conrail Northeast Caboose "18866" (std 0), 17		90 ___
84138	Pere Marquette Northeast Caboose "A909" (std 0), 17		90 ___
84139	WM Northeast Caboose circle herald "1874" (std 0), 17		90 ___
84140	WM Northeast Caboose circus herald "1882" (std 0), 17		90 ___
84141	WM USRA 2-bay Hopper 3-pack #1 (std 0), 17		220 ___
84145	WM USRA 2-bay Hopper 3-pack #2 (std 0), 17		220 ___
84149	Reading USRA 2-bay Hopper 3-pack (std 0), 17		220 ___
84153	B&O 1905 2-bay Hopper 3-pack (std 0), 17		220 ___
84157	Bethlehem Steel 1905 2-bay Hopper 3-pack (std 0), 17		220 ___
84161	Logging Disconnect Stock Car, 17		40 ___
84163	Logging Disconnect Christmas 4-pack (std 0), 17		160 ___
84165	Logging Disconnect Dinner Train 4-pack (std 0), 17, 19		160 ___
84166	Logging Disconnect, 1-pair, brown (std 0), 17, 19		65 ___
84167	Logging Disconnect, 2-pair, brown (std 0), 17		125 ___
84187	B&O 18" Heavyweight Coach 2-pack #1, 18		400 ___
84190	B&O 18" Heavyweight Coach 2-pack #2, 18		400 ___
84193	Reading, Blue Mountain & Northern 18" Heavyweight Coach 2-pack #1, 18		400 ___
84196	Reading, Blue Mountain & Northern 18" Heavyweight Coach 2-pack #2, 18		400 ___
84199	MILW 18" Heavyweight Coach 2-pack #1, 18		400 ___
84202	MILW 18" Heavyweight Coach 2-pack #2, 18		400 ___
84205	Nickel Plate Road 18" Heavyweight Coach 2-pack #1, 18		400 ___
84208	Nickel Plate Road 18" Heavyweight Coach 2-pack #2, 18		400 ___
84211	TH&B 18" Heavyweight Coach 2-pack #1, 18		400 ___
84214	TH&B 18" Heavyweight Coach 2-pack #1, 18		400 ___
84217	Wabash 18" Heavyweight Coach 2-pack #1, 18		400 ___
84220	Wabash 18" Heavyweight Coach 2-pack #2, 18		400 ___
84226	American Freedom Train Add-On 2-pack #4, 17		300 ___
84229	Conrail 21" Theater Inspection Car "9", 17		340 ___
84230	NS 21" Theater Inspection Car Buena Vista, 17		340 ___
84231	CSX 21" Theater Inspection Car Alabama, 17		340 ___
84232	UP 21" Theater Inspection Car Fox River, 17		340 ___
84237	Cass Scenic RR 3-Truck Shay Locomotive "6," CC, 17		1500 ___
84238	Elk River Lumber Co. 3-Truck Shay Locomotive "20," CC, 17		1500 ___
84239	WM 3-Truck Shay Locomotive "6," CC, 17		1500 ___
84240	West Side Lumber Co. 3-Truck Shay Locomotive "3," CC, 17		1500 ___

			Exc	Mint
___	**84248**	SP AC-9 2-8-8-4 Locomotive "3800," CC, 17		2000
___	**84249**	SP AC-9 2-8-8-4 Locomotive "3805," CC, 17		2000
___	**84250**	SP AC-9 Daylight 2-8-8-4 Locomotive "3811," CC, 17		2000
___	**84251**	ATSF 2-8-4 Berkshire Locomotive "4103," LionChief Plus, 17-18		450
___	**84252**	Nickel Plate Road 2-8-4 Berkshire Locomotive "767," LionChief Plus, 17-18		450
___	**84253**	Pere Marquette 2-8-4 Berkshire Locomotive "1223," LionChief Plus, 17-18		450
___	**84254**	IC 2-8-4 Berkshire Locomotive "8006," LionChief Plus, 17-18		450
___	**84255**	Lionel Lines 2-8-4 Berkshire "726," LionChief Plus, 17-18		450
___	**84256**	AT&SF SD40 Diesel "5006," CC, 17		650
___	**84257**	AT&SF SD40 Diesel "5018," CC, 17		650
___	**84258**	UP SD40 Diesel "4057," CC, 17		650
___	**84259**	UP SD40 Diesel "4062," CC, 17		650
___	**84260**	CSX SD40 Diesel "4614," CC, 17		650
___	**84261**	CSX SD40 Diesel "4621," CC, 17		650
___	**84262**	PRR SD40 Diesel "6041," CC, 17		650
___	**84263**	PRR SD40 Diesel "6089," CC, 17		650
___	**84264**	Southern SD40 Diesel "3170," CC, 17		650
___	**84265**	Southern SD40 Diesel"3200," CC, 17		650
___	**84267**	SP SD40R Diesel "7372," CC, 17		650
___	**84268**	WM SD40 Diesel "7547," CC, 17		650
___	**84269**	WM SD40 Diesel "7549," CC, 17		650
___	**84270**	B&O EMD Torpedo GP9 Diesel "3414," CC, 18		550
___	**84271**	B&O EMD Torpedo GP9 Diesel "3419," CC, 18		550
___	**84272**	C&NW EMD Torpedo GP9 Diesel "1725," CC, 18		550
___	**84273**	C&NW EMD Torpedo GP9 Diesel "1730," CC, 18		550
___	**84274**	MILW EMD Torpedo GP9 Diesel "202," CC, 18		550
___	**84275**	MILW EMD Torpedo GP9 Diesel "208," CC, 18		550
___	**84276**	Nickel Plate Road EMD Torpedo GP9 Diesel "482," CC, 18		550
___	**84277**	Nickel Plate Road EMD Torpedo GP9 Diesel "484," CC, 18		550
___	**84278**	TH&B EMD Torpedo GP9 Diesel "402," CC, 18		550
___	**84279**	TH&B EMD Torpedo GP9 Diesel "403," CC, 18		550
___	**84280**	Wabash EMD Torpedo GP9 Diesel "484," CC, 18		550
___	**84281**	Wabash EMD Torpedo GP9 Diesel "486," CC, 18		550
___	**84282**	BN GE U33C Diesel "5716," CC, 18		580
___	**84283**	BN GE U33C Diesel "5723," CC, 18		580
___	**84284**	D&H GE U33C Diesel "757," CC, 18		580
___	**84285**	D&H GE U33C Diesel "762," CC, 18		580
___	**84286**	Guilford D&H GE U33C Diesel "650," CC, 18		580
___	**84287**	Guilford D&H GE U33C Diesel "654," CC, 18		580
___	**84288**	GN GE U33C Diesel "2530," CC, 18		580
___	**84289**	GN GE U33C Diesel "2541," CC, 1		580
___	**84290**	IC GE U33C Diesel "5052," CC, 18		580
___	**84291**	IC GE U33C Diesel "5054," CC, 18		580
___	**84292**	PC GE U33C Diesel "6547," CC, 18		580
___	**84293**	PC GE U33C Diesel "6561," CC, 18		580
___	**84294**	Sacramento Trolley, 17-18		100
___	**84295**	Connecticut Trolley, 17-18		100
___	**84296**	SP Salad Bowl Express Diesel Freight Set, CC, 17		900
___	**84297**	Logging Disconnect Steel Tank Car (std O), 17		40
___	**84303**	Bucking Feed and Tack, 17		85
___	**84304**	CB&Q Gondola with covers, 17		55

MODERN 1970-2024		Exc	Mint
84306	Illuminated John Deere Flagpole, 17-18		60
84307	Lionel Illuminated Flagpole, 17-18, 22-24		45
84308	Gray Half-Covered Bridge, 17		60
84309	PRR Blinking Water Tower, 17-18		45
84310	Modular Train Car Repair Facility, 16-17		110
84312	Alaska RR Gondola with canisters, 17, 19		55
84314	BNSF ACF Covered Hopper "405850", 18		60
84315	Branchline Water Tank Kit, 16-24		40
84317	Passenger Station, 17		80
84318	Illuminated Station Platform, 17-23		55
84327	Santa Fe Operating Billboard, 17		70
84328	Polar Express Steam Passenger Set, LionChief, 17-19		420
84328P	Polar Express Steam Passenger Set w/Personalized Tender, 19-20		420
84330	Witches Brew 1-D Tank Car, 17-18		70
84332	Halloween Boxcar, SpookySounds, 17-18		80
84333	Strasburg RR Gondola with vats, 17, 19		65
84334	Strasburg Half-covered Bridge, 17-18		60
84335	PRR Culvert Gondola "374200", 17, 19		65
84336	UP Log Car, 17		65
84337	MKT Wood-chip Hopper, 17		65
84338	CSX Wood-chip Hopper, 17-18		65
84339	SP Jumping Hobo Boxcar, 17		80
84340	Santa and Snowman Operating Boxcar, 17-18		90
84341	Tell-Tale Reindeer Car, 17		80
84366	PRR Wood-chip Hopper, 17-19		65
84367	Christmas Pylon, 17		160
84369	NYC Welding Car "X939", 17		80
84369	L&N Hummingbird 21" Diner w/StationSounds, 18		330
84370	Polar Express Hopper with silver, 17-18		70
84371	Mickey's Holiday Hopper with presents, 17-18		70
84372	Christmas Station Platform, 17-18		43
84373	Special Trolley Announcement Track, 18-24		60
84374	Christmas Music Boxcar, 17		80
84375	Christmas Boxcar, 17		65
84376	Angela Trotta Thomas Signature Express Aquarium Car, 17-18		85
84377	Christmas Peppermint 1-D Tank Car, 17-18		60
84378	Santa's Choice Milk Car with platform, 17-18		180
84380	Reading & Northern Auxiliary Tender "425-A," CC, 18		300
84383	Elevated Oil Tank, 17-18		95
84388	FasTrack 10" Girder Bridge, gray, 17-24		25
84400	BN "Pulling for Freedom" SD60M Diesel "1991," CC, 17		650
84401	BN SD60M Diesel "9200," CC, 17		650
84402	BN SD60M Diesel "9225," CC, 17		650
84403	Soo Line SD60M Diesel "6058," CC, 17		650
84404	Soo Line SD60M Diesel "6061," CC, 17		650
84405	Conrail SD60M Diesel "5504," CC, 17		650
84406	Conrail SD60M Diesel "5510," CC, 17		650
84407	CSX SD60M Diesel "8783," CC, 17		650
84408	CSX SD60M Diesel "8784," CC, 17		650
84409	NS SD60M Diesel "6808," CC, 17		760
84410	NS SD60M Diesel "6815," CC, 17		650
84411	UP SD60M Diesel "6165," CC, 17		650

			Exc	Mint
___	84412	UP SD60M Diesel "6187," CC, 17		650
___	84413	B&O FA A-A Diesel Set, "814, 815," LionChief Plus, 17-18		500
___	84416	GN FA A-A Diesel Set, "278A, 278B," LionChief Plus, 17-18		500
___	84419	NH FA A-A Diesel Set, "417, 418," LionChief Plus, 17-18		500
___	84422	UP FA A-A Diesel Set, "1616, 1617," LionChief Plus, 17-18		500
___	84433	Polar Express 40' Scale Reefer "122517", 17		90
___	84434	NS 30,000-gallon 1-D Tank Car 3-pack (std O), 16		250
___	84438	NS 30,000-gallon 1-D Tank Car "362785" (std O), 16		80
___	84439	UTLX 30,000-gallon 1-D Tank Car 3-pack (std O), 16		250
___	84443	PESX 30,000-gallon 1-D Tank Car 3-pack (std O), 16, 19		250
___	84447	TILX 30,000-gallon 1-D Tank Car 3-pack (std O), 16, 19		250
___	84451	PRR Flatcar 6-pack, 17		120
___	84452	AT&SF Flatcar 6-pack, 17-18		120
___	84453	UP Flatcar 6-pack, 17-18		120
___	84454	Trailer Train Flatcar 6-pack, 17		120
___	84455	Assorted Flatcar 6-pack, 17-18		120
___	84456	B&O Gondola 6-pack, 17-18		120
___	84457	UP Gondola 6-pack, 17-18		120
___	84458	East Assorted Gondola 6-pack, 17		120
___	84459	Midwest Assorted Gondola 6-pack, 17		120
___	84460	West Assorted Gondola 6-pack, 17-18		120
___	84462	2-Rail Conversion Kit, 50-ton Scale Trucks, 16-24		20
___	84463	2-Rail Conversion Kit, 70-ton Scale Trucks, 16-24		20
___	84465	B&O 2-8-2 Light Mikado Locomotive "4500," CC, 17		1300
___	84466	GTW 2-8-2 Light Mikado Locomotive "3734," CC, 17		1300
___	84467	Maine Central 2-8-2 Light Mikado Locomotive "624," CC, 17		1300
___	84468	NYC 2-8-2 Light Mikado Locomotive "5187," CC, 17		1300
___	84469	PRR 2-8-2 Light Mikado Locomotive "9630," CC, 17		1300
___	84470	Southern 2-8-2 Light Mikado Locomotive "4758," CC, 17		1300
___	84471	UP 2-8-2 Light Mikado Locomotive "2537," CC, 17		1300
___	84472	AT&SF 2-8-2 Mikado Locomotive, Brass Hybrid "3222," CC, 17		1300
___	84480	John Deere Covered Bridge, 17-18		70
___	84481	John Deere General Store, 17-18		85
___	84482	John Deere Gondola with hay bales, 17-18		75
___	84483	John Deere Grain Vat Car, 17		75
___	84485	Disney Covered Bridge, 17-18		70
___	84486	MILW NW2 Diesel Locomotive "1649," CC, 16		500
___	84487	Donald Duck Holiday 1-D Tank Car, 17		70
___	84489	Polar Express Covered Bridge, 17-18		70
___	84490	NS First Responders Diesel Freight Set, LionChief, 17-18		450
___	84496	Shell Service Station, 17		150
___	84498	NS Fire Rescue Car, 17-18		75
___	84499	Mickey Mouse & Friends Industrial Water Tower, 17-20		100
___	84500	NS Unibody 1-D Tank Car "490112", 17-18		75
___	84507	New York Central & Hudson River S2 Electric "3207," CC, 17		800
___	84508	NYC S2 Electric "113," CC, 17		800
___	84509	NYC S2 Electric "115," CC, 17		800
___	84510	PC S2 Electric "4710," CC, 17		800
___	84511	NYC "Lightning Stripe" S2 Electric "101," CC, 17		800
___	84512	S2 Electric Scale Tinplate Freight Set, CC, 17		1000
___	84514	Prewar 514 Tinplate Lionel Lines Refrigerator Car, 17		100
___	84515	Prewar 515 Tinplate Lionel Lines Hopper Car, 17		100
___	84516	Prewar 516 Tinplate Lionel Lines Caboose, 17		100

		Exc	Mint
84525	Uptown Apartment Building, 17		100 ___
84526	Leuzure Marble Co. Warehouse, 17		110 ___
84529	NS Veterans Wide Vision Caboose "6920" (std O), 17-18		95 ___
84530	NS First Responders Wide Vision Caboose "9-1-1" (std O), 17-18		95 ___
84532	Nickel Plate Road 2-8-2 Light Mikado Locomotive "587," CC, 17		1300 ___
84538	NS 65' Mill Gondola "195029" (std O), 17		80 ___
84539	NS 65' Mill Gondola "195065" (std O), 17		80 ___
84553	Logging Disconnect Reindeer Train 4-pack A, 17		160 ___
84554	Logging Disconnect Reindeer Train 4-pack B, 17		160 ___
84555	Logging Disconnect Santa Claus Observation (std O), 17		45 ___
84562	BN "Pulling for Freedom" SD60M Diesel "1991," LionChief, 17		500 ___
84563	BN SD60M Diesel "9215," LionChief, 17		500 ___
84564	Soo Line SD60M Diesel "6060," LionChief, 17		500 ___
84565	Conrail SD60M Diesel "5509," LionChief, 17		500 ___
84566	CSX SD60M Diesel "8757," LionChief, 17		500 ___
84567	NS SD60M Diesel "6810," LionChief, 17		500 ___
84568	UP SD60M Diesel "6170," LionChief, 17		500 ___
84570	First Responders EMT Boxcar, 17-22		100 ___
84571	First Responders Personalized Police Boxcar, 17-23		100 ___
84572	First Responders Fire Fighter Boxcar, 17-22		100 ___
84573	Happy Birthday Boxcar, 17		90 ___
84574	Personalized 2017 Merry Christmas Boxcar, 17		90 ___
84575	U.S. Army Boxcar, 17-23		100 ___
84576	U.S. Marine Boxcar, 17-23		100 ___
84577	U.S. Air Force Boxcar, 17-23		100 ___
84578	U.S. Navy Boxcar, 17-23		100 ___
84579	U.S. Coast Guard Boxcar, 17-22		100 ___
84580	From The Home Front Boxcar, blue, 17-22		100 ___
84581	From The Home Front Boxcar, green, 17-22		100 ___
84582	BNSF 65' Mill Gondola "518375" (std O), 17		80 ___
84583	BNSF 65' Mill Gondola "518392" (std O), 17		80 ___
84584	C&NW 65' Mill Gondola "342045" (std O), 17		80 ___
84585	C&NW 65' Mill Gondola "342049" (std O), 17		80 ___
84586	CSX 65' Mill Gondola "491616" (std O), 17		80 ___
84587	CSX 65' Mill Gondola "491638" (std O), 17		80 ___
84590	SP 65' Mill Gondola "365136" (std O), 17		80 ___
84591	SP 65' Mill Gondola "365142" (std O), 17		80 ___
84592	UP 65' Mill Gondola "96267" (std O), 17		80 ___
84593	UP 65' Mill Gondola "96281" (std O), 17		80 ___
84599	Bucking Feed & Tack Building, 18-20		85 ___
84600	Polar Express Combination Car, 18-24		85 ___
84601	Polar Express Letters to Santa Mail Car, 18-24		85 ___
84602	Polar Express Disappearing Hobo Car, 18-24		90 ___
84603	Polar Express Hot Chocolate Car, 18-19, 22-24		85 ___
84604	Polar Express Diner, 18-24		85 ___
84605	Polar Express Baggage Car, 18-24		85 ___
84605P	Personalized Polar Express Baggage Car, 19-20		95 ___
84608	Smithsonian Boxcar, Southern "1401", 17		85 ___
84611	Lionel BlueTooth Radio Tower, 17		100 ___
84616	Wonder Woman Boxcar, 17		80 ___
84621	2017 National Lionel Train Day Boxcar, 17		85 ___

			Exc	Mint
___	**84622**	D&RGW EMD SD40T-2 Diesel "5401," CC, 17		600
___	**84623**	D&RGW EMD SD40T-2 Diesel ""5405," CC, 17		600
___	**84624**	KCS EMD SD40T-2 Diesel "6102," CC, 17		600
___	**84625**	KCS EMD SD40T-2 Diesel "6110," CC, 17		600
___	**84626**	Lancaster & Chester EMD SD40T-2 Diesel "6002," CC, 17		600
___	**84627**	GECX EMD SD40T-2 Diesel "8661," CC, 17		600
___	**84628**	GECX EMD SD40T-2 Diesel "8678," CC, 17		600
___	**84629**	Ohio Central EMD SD40T-2 Diesel "4026," CC, 17		600
___	**84630**	Ohio Central EMD SD40T-2 Diesel "4027," CC, 17		600
___	**84631**	RJ Corman EMD SD40T-2 Diesel "5361 "CC, 17		600
___	**84632**	RJ Corman EMD SD40T-2 Diesel "5409," CC, 17		600
___	**84633**	SP EMD SD40T-2 Diesel "8532," CC, 17		600
___	**84634**	SP EMD SD40T-2 Diesel "8548," CC, 17		600
___	**84635**	UP EMD SD40T-2 Diesel "8593," CC, 17		600
___	**84636**	UP EMD SD40T-2 Diesel "8715," CC, 17		600
___	**84637**	Cotton Belt EMD SD40T-2 Diesel "9389," Bicentennial, CC, 17		600
___	**84638**	ACL EMD E6 A-A Diesel Set "00-501," CC, 17		1000
___	**84641**	AT&SF EMD E6 A-A Diesel Set "12-13," CC, 17		1000
___	**84644**	C&NW EMD E6 A-A Diesel Set "5005A-5005B," CC, 17		1000
___	**84647**	FEC EMD E3 A-A Diesel Set "1001-1002," CC, 17		1000
___	**84650**	IC EMD E6 A-A Diesel Set "4003-4004" CC, 17		1000
___	**84653**	KCS EMD E3 A-A Diesel Set "2-3," CC, 17		1000
___	**84656**	L&N EMD E6 A-A Diesel Set "754-755," CC, 17		1000
___	**84659**	MILW EMD E6 A-A Diesel Set "15A-15B," CC, 17		1000
___	**84662**	UP EMD E6 A-A Diesel Set "996-997," CC, 17		1000
___	**84666**	Battle for Guadalcanal, 17		85
___	**84667**	Battle of the Bulge Boxcar, 17		85
___	**84668**	Silent Service Boxcar, 17		85
___	**84669**	Desert Storm Boxcar, 18, 20		90
___	**84670**	Korean War Boxcar, 18, 20		85
___	**84671**	Vietnam War Boxcar, 18, 20		85
___	**84672**	Memorial Day Boxcar, 18, 20		90
___	**84674**	AT&SF 2-8-2 Mikado , Brass Hybrid, Painted, Unlettered, CC, 17		1300
___	**84675**	AT&SF 2-8-2 Mikado Locomotive, Brass Hybrid, Unpainted, CC, 17		1300
___	**84676**	Peanuts Hilltop Boxcar, 18		90
___	**84677**	Peanuts Meadow Boxcar, 18		90
___	**84678**	Peanuts Winter Boxcar, 18		90
___	**84679**	AT&SF 4-6-2 Pacific Locomotive "1369," LionChief Plus, 17-18		450
___	**84680**	CNJ 4-6-2 Pacific Locomotive "832," LionChief Plus, 17-18		450
___	**84681**	Alton 4-6-2 Pacific Locomotive "5299," LionChief Plus, 17-18		450
___	**84682**	Southern 4-6-2 Pacific Locomotive "1401," LionChief Plus, 17-18		450
___	**84683**	MILW 4-6-2 Pacific Locomotive "810," LionChief Plus, 17-18		450
___	**84685**	Polar Express Scale 2-8-4 Berkshire Locomotive "1225," CC, 17		1500
___	**84686**	Nickel Plate Road 2-8-4 Berkshire Locomotive "759," CC, 17		1500
___	**84687**	Nickel Plate Road 2-8-4 Berkshire Locomotive "765," CC, 17		1500
___	**84688**	Nickel Plate Road 2-8-4 Berkshire Locomotive "767," CC, 17		1500
___	**84689**	Southern 2-8-4 Berkshire Locomotive "2716," CC, 17		1500
___	**84690**	W&LE 2-8-4 Berkshire Locomotive "6401," CC, 17		1500

Item	Description	Exc	Mint
84691	American Railroads 2-8-4 Berkshire Locomotive "759," CC, 17		1500 ___
84692	RF&P 2-8-4 Berkshire Locomotive "752," CC, 17		1500 ___
84693	Pere Marquette 2-8-4 Berkshire Locomotive "1225," CC, 17		1500 ___
84694	Pere Marquette 2-8-4 Berkshire Locomotive "1223," CC, 17		1500 ___
84695	L&N 2-8-4 Berkshire Locomotive "1992," CC, 17		1500 ___
84696	D&H Alco RS3 Diesel "4121," LionChief Plus, 17-18		350 ___
84697	AT&SF Alco RS3 Diesel "2099," LionChief Plus, 17-18		350 ___
84698	Peabody Coal Short Line RS3 Diesel "101," LionChief Plus, 17-19		350 ___
84699	B&M Alco RS3 Diesel "1536," LionChief Plus, 17-18		350 ___
84700	Hot Wheels Diesel Freight Set, LionChief, 17-19		400 ___
84705	Hot Wheels 50th Anniversary Auto Rack, 17-18		85 ___
84706	Hot Wheels 50th Anniversary Auto Loader, 17-18		90 ___
84707	Hot Wheels 50th Anniversary Flatcar w/Piggyback Trailers, 17-18		85 ___
84708	Hot Wheels Auto Rack, 18		85 ___
84709	NH RS3 Diesel Freight Set, LionChief, 18		300 ___
84719	AT&SF Super Chief Diesel Passenger Set, LionChief, 18-22		500 ___
84724	ATSF Add-on Baggage Car "1386", 18-24		100 ___
84725	ATSF Add-on Vista Dome Car "500", 18-24		100 ___
84726	SP Rising Sun 0-8-0 Steam Freight Set, LionChief, 17-18		320 ___
84732	BNSF Tier 4 Modern Freight Set, LionChief, 18-20		400 ___
84737	Construction Railroad Diesel Freight Set, LionChief, 18-19		350 ___
84747	18 Christmas Boxcar, 18		65 ___
84748	Christmas Music Boxcar #18, 18		80 ___
84754	Anheuser-Busch Clydesdale Old-Time Steam Freight Set, 18-19		420 ___
84760	Daisy Duck 1-D Tank Car, 18-20		75 ___
84761	Chip 'n' Dale Chasing Gondola, 18-20		80 ___
84762	SP Daylight 1-D Tank Car, 17-19		60 ___
84763	Disney Villains Ursula Hi-Cube Boxcar, 18, 20		80 ___
84764	Disney Villains Queen of Hearts Hi-Cube Boxcar, 18, 20		80 ___
84765	Angela Trotta Thomas Christmas Passenger Car 2-pack, 18, 20		300 ___
84766	Gondola w/Construction Signs, 18-19		65 ___
84767	Harry Potter Dementors Coach w/Sound, 18-24		95 ___
84768	Moe & Joe Lumber Flatcar, 18-19		90 ___
84769	Wile E. Coyote & Road Runner Ambush Shack, 18-19		120 ___
84770	Peabody Coal Hopper 6-pack, 18-20		150 ___
84771	PRR Hopper 6-pack, 18-19		150 ___
84772	N&W Hopper 6-pack, 18-20		150 ___
84773	UP Hopper 6-pack, 18-20		150 ___
84774	NS Hopper 6-pack, 18-20		150 ___
84775	DM&IR Ore Car 6-pack, 18-19		150 ___
84776	C&NW Ore Car 6-pack, 18-20		150 ___
84777	GN Ore Car 6-pack, 18-20		150 ___
84778	MILW Ore Car 6-pack, 18-19		150 ___
84779	B&LE Ore Car 6-pack, 18-20		150 ___
84780	U.S. Caboose, 18		75 ___
84781	ELX Halloween Caboose, 18-20		75 ___
84782	Presidential Caboose, 18-20		75 ___
84784	John Deere Harvest Dump Car, 18-19		80 ___
84785	Naughty or Nice Ore Car 2-pack, 18		80 ___

			Exc	Mint
___	**84786**	Christmas Essentials Barrel Car, 18-19		70
___	**84787**	Santa Freight Lines Steam Set, LionChief, 18-19		300
___	**84792**	House Under Construction, 18-19		100
___	**84794**	Budweiser Bar & Grille, 18		90
___	**84795**	Deluxe Christmas House, 18, 20		130
___	**84797**	Christmas Industrial Water Tower, 18, 20		85
___	**84798**	Hunting Rabbit Car, 18-19		85
___	**84799**	Marvin the Martian Earth Stomper Flatcar, 18-19		95
___	**84801**	Justice League Boxcar, 17		85
___	**84802**	Gibson Wine 1-D Tank Car "66719", 17		75
___	**84803**	Tidewater 1-D Tank Car "1367", 17		75
___	**84804**	A.E. Staley 1-D Tank Car "704", 17		75
___	**84805**	Mid-Continent Petroleum 1-D Tank Car "1018", 17		75
___	**84806**	Shell 1-D Tank Car "662", 17		75
___	**84807**	John Deere 1-D Tank Car "236", 17		75
___	**84810**	Polar Express 1-D Tank Car "122518", 17		75
___	**84811**	Polar Express Scale Baggage Car, 17, 24	100	213
___	**84812**	Polar Express Scale Combine, 17, 24		200
___	**84813**	Polar Express Scale Coach, 17, 24	100	213
___	**84814**	Polar Express Scale Diner, 17, 24	100	213
___	**84815**	Polar Express Scale Observation, 17		200
___	**84816**	PRR 1930 Broadway Limited Steam Passenger Set, CC, 17		2000
___	**84821**	PRR Heavyweight Combine Liberty Hill, 17-18		200
___	**84822**	PRR Heavyweight Sleeper Cent Fawn, 17-18		200
___	**84823**	PRR Heavyweight Sleeper Central Park, 17-18		200
___	**84824**	PRR Heavyweight Sleeper Lafayette Square, 17-18		200
___	**84825**	PRR Heavyweight Diner "4498", 17-18		200
___	**84826**	PRR Heavyweight Observation Colonel Lindbergh, 17-18		200
___	**84827**	PRR Heavyweight Observation Washington Circle, 17-18		200
___	**84828**	BNSF 66' Mill Gondola "518726," w/Graffiti, 17		80
___	**84829**	BNSF 66' Mill Gondola "518770", 17		80
___	**84830**	BNSF 66' Mill Gondola "518795", 17		80
___	**84831**	GNTX Railgon 66' Mill Gondola "290146," w/Graffiti, 17		80
___	**84832**	GNTX Railgon 66' Mill Gondola "290087", 17		80
___	**84833**	GNTX Railgon 66' Mill Gondola "290102", 17		80
___	**84834**	Atlantic & Western 66' Mill Gondola "400704," w/Graffiti, 17		80
___	**84835**	Atlantic & Western 66' Mill Gondola "400664", 17		80
___	**84836**	Atlantic & Western 66' Mill Gondola "400675", 17		80
___	**84837**	Arkansas & Oklahoma 66' Mill Gondola "35018," w/Graffiti, 17		80
___	**84838**	Arkansas & Oklahoma 66' Mill Gondola "35007", 17		80
___	**84839**	Arkansas & Oklahoma 66' Mill Gondola "35055", 17		80
___	**84840**	Steelton & Highspire 66' Mill Gondola "125," w/Graffiti, 17		80
___	**84841**	Steelton & Highspire 66' Mill Gondola "117", 17		80
___	**84842**	Steelton & Highspire 66' Mill Gondola "118"", 17		80
___	**84843**	Demonstrator GE AC6000 Diesel "6000," CC, 17		650
___	**84844**	Demonstrator GE AC6000 Diesel "6001," CC, 17		650
___	**84845**	Demonstrator GE AC6000 Diesel "6002," CC, 17		650
___	**84846**	CSX GE AC6000 Diesel "691," CC, 17		650
___	**84847**	CSX GE AC6000 Diesel "5014," CC, 17		650
___	**84848**	CSX GE AC6000 Diesel "Diversity 5000," CC, 17		650
___	**84849**	CSX GE AC6000 Diesel "Diversity 5001," CC, 17		650
___	**84850**	SP GE AC6000 Diesel "601," CC, 17		650

		Exc	Mint
84851	SP GE AC6000 Diesel "602," CC, 17		650
84852	UP GE AC6000 Diesel "7566,," CC, 17		650
84853	UP GE AC6000 Diesel "7579,," CC, 17		650
84854	TTX Husky Double-Stack Car "56210," w/Trailers, 17		130
84855	TTX Husky Double-Stack Car "56289," w/Trailers, 17		130
84856	TTX Husky Double-Stack Car "56368," w/Trailers, 17		130
84857	TTX Husky Double-Stack Car "56150," w/Trailers, 17		130
84858	TTX Husky Double-Stack Car "56168," w/Trailers, 17		130
84859	TTX Husky Double-Stack Car "56174," w/Trailers, 17		130
84860	BNSF Husky Double-Stack Car "203003," w/Trailers, 17		130
84861	BNSF Husky Double-Stack Car "203015," w/Trailers, 17		130
84862	BNSF Husky Double-Stack Car "203032," w/Trailers, 17		130
84863	ARZC Husky Double-Stack Car "100000," w/Trailers, 17		130
84864	ARZC Husky Double-Stack Car "100002," w/Trailers, 17		130
84865	ARZC Husky Double-Stack Car "100005," w/Trailers, 17		130
84866	Southwind Husky Double-Stack Car "5003," w/Trailers, 17		130
84867	Southwind Husky Double-Stack Car "5005," w/Trailers, 17		130
84868	Southwind Husky Double-Stack Car "5008," w/Trailers, 17		130
84869	Hot Wheels Boxcar, 18		85
84870	NP 50' Flatcar "65110" w/NPT 40' Trailer, 17		120
84871	NP 50' Flatcar "65126" w/NPT 40' Trailer, 17		120
84872	PRR 50' Flatcar "469615" w/PRRZ 40' Trailer, 17		120
84873	PRR 50' Flatcar "469675" w/PRRZ 40' Trailer, 17		120
84874	Trailer Train 50' Flatcar "475227" w/SOUZ 40' Trailer, 17		120
84875	Trailer Train 50' Flatcar "475274" w/SOUZ 40' Trailer, 17		120
84876	UP 50' Flatcar "53017" w/UPZ 40' Trailer, 17		120
84877	UP 50' Flatcar "53022" w/UPZ 40' Trailer, 17		120
84878	Wabash 50' Flatcar "2553" w/WABZ 40' Trailer, 17		120
84879	Wabash 50' Flatcar "25549" w/WABZ 40' Trailer, 17		120
84880	D&RGW 50' Flatcar "21032" w/RGMW 40' Trailer, 17		120
84881	D&RGW 50' Flatcar "21036" w/RGMW 40' Trailer, 17		120
84882	C&O 40' Trailer 2-pack, 17		65
84883	GM&O 40' Trailer 2-pack, 17		65
84884	L&N 40' Trailer 2-pack, 17		65
84885	SAL 40' Trailer 2-pack, 17		65
84886	Frisco 40' Trailer 2-pack, 17		65
84887	WP 40' Trailer 2-pack, 17		65
84888	PRR X31 Boxcar "78401," w/Circle Keystone, 17		120
84889	PRR X31 Boxcar "78498," w/Circle Keystone, 17		80
84890	PRR X31 Boxcar "68408," w/Shadow Keystone, 17		80
84891	PRR X31 Boxcar "77061," w/Shadow Keystone, 17		80
84892	PRR X31 Boxcar "76803," w/Plain Keystone, 17		80
84893	PRR X31 Boxcar "77734," w/Plain Keystone, 17		80
84894	PRR X31 Boxcar "497310," w/Stores, 17		80
84895	PRR X31 Boxcar "497329," w/Stores, 17		80
84896	N&W X31 Boxcar "46146", 17		80
84897	N&W X31 Boxcar "46340", 17		80
84898	Personalized Man's Best Friend Boxcar, 18-23		100
84899	Personalized World's Best Cat Boxcar, 18-22		100
84904	BNSF Scale Autorack, Orange "965375", 18		120
84905	BNSF Scale Autorack, Orange "965530", 18		120
84906	Ferromex Scale Autorack "705473", 18		120
84907	Ferromex Scale Autorack "953615", 18		120

			Exc	Mint
___	84908	Southern Scale Autorack "159162", 18		120
___	84909	Southern Scale Autorack "159166", 18		120
___	84910	CSX Scale Autorack "156256", 18		120
___	84911	CSX Scale Autorack "973924", 18		120
___	84912	NS Scale Autorack "983818", 18		120
___	84913	NS Scale Autorack "992879", 18		120
___	84914	MKT Scale Autorack "254176", 18		120
___	84915	MKT Scale Autorack "942194", 18		120
___	84916	Union Tank Car Cylindrical Covered Hopper "44072", 18-19		90
___	84917	Union Tank Car Cylindrical Covered Hopper "44094", 18-19		90
___	84918	Davis Industries Cylindrical Covered Hopper "1002", 18-19		90
___	84919	Davis Industries Cylindrical Covered Hopper "1003", 18-19		90
___	84920	Conrail Cylindrical Covered Hopper "884244", 18-19		90
___	84921	Conrail Cylindrical Covered Hopper "884270", 18-19		90
___	84922	CSX Cylindrical Covered Hopper "225370", 18-19		90
___	84923	CSX Cylindrical Covered Hopper "225382", 18-19		90
___	84924	Wilkes-Barre Mining Cylindrical Covered Hopper "104", 18		90
___	84925	Wilkes-Barre Mining Cylindrical Covered Hopper "106", 18		90
___	84926	SP Cylindrical Covered Hopper "1002", 18		90
___	84927	SP Cylindrical Covered Hopper "1027", 18		90
___	84928	John Quincy Adams Presidential Boxcar, 18		70
___	84929	James K. Polk Presidential Boxcar, 18		70
___	84930	Benjamin Harrison Presidential Boxcar, 18		70
___	84934	NYC 4-6-4 Hudson Locomotive "5425," LionChief Plus, 17-18		450
___	84935	B&A 4-6-4 Hudson Locomotive "616," LionChief Plus, 17-18		450
___	84936	Nickel Plate 4-6-4 Hudson "170," LionChief Plus, 17-18		450
___	84937	GN 4-6-4 Hudson Locomotive "171" LionChief Plus, 17-18		450
___	84938	AT&SF EMD GP38 Diesel "441," LionChief Plus, 17-18		350
___	84939	NS First Responders GP38 "5642" LionChief Plus, 17-18		350
___	84940	Seaboard System EMD GP38 Diesel "543," LionChief Plus, 17-18		350
___	84941	FEC EMD GP38 Diesel "506," LionChief Plus, 17-18		350
___	84942	PRR 4-4-2 Atlantic Locomotive "460," CC, 17		800
___	84943	PRR 4-4-2 Atlantic Locomotive "68," CC, 17		800
___	84944	PRR 4-4-2 Atlantic Locomotive "1163," CC, 17		800
___	84945	PRSL 4-4-2 Atlantic Locomotive "6009," CC, 17		800
___	84946	LIRR 4-4-2 Atlantic Locomotive "1611," CC, 17		800
___	84947	GN 4-4-2 Atlantic Locomotive "1707," CC, 17		800
___	84948	PRR 2-8-0 Consolidation Locomotive "1288," CC, 18		750
___	84949	PRSL 2-8-0 Consolidation Locomotive "8072," CC, 18		750
___	84950	LIRR 2-8-0 Consolidation Locomotive "109,"" CC, 18		750
___	84951	Bellefonte Central 2-8-0 Consolidation Locomotive "21," CC, 18		750
___	84952	PRR 2-8-0 Consolidation Locomotive "3529" Weathered, CC, 18		750
___	84953	Pennsylvania Coal Hauler Steam Freight Set, CC, 18		1100
___	84964	Angela Trotta Thomas 4-6-4 Hudson Locomotive, LionChief Plus, 18		450
___	84965	Rio Grande A5 0-4-0 Locomotive "62," LionChief Plus, 18		480
___	84966	NYC A5 0-4-0 Locomotive "1662," LionChief Plus, 18		480
___	84967	PRR A5 0-4-0 Locomotive "577," LionChief Plus, 18		480
___	84968	UP A5 0-4-0 Locomotive "218," LionChief Plus, 18		480
___	84985	LIRR B60 Baggage Car "7715", 17-18		160
___	84986	LIRR B60 Baggage Car "7724", 17-18		160

		Exc	Mint
84987	PRR B60 Baggage Car, Clerestory "7918", 17-18		160 ___
84988	PRR B60 Baggage Car, Clerestory "7941", 17-18		160 ___
84989	PRR B60 Baggage Car, Round Roof "7919", 17-18		160 ___
84990	PRR B60 Baggage Car, Round Roof "7938", 17-18		160 ___
84991	PRR B60 Baggage Car, Round Roof, Messenger "9352", 17-18		160 ___
84992	PRR B60 Baggage Car, Round Roof, Messenger "9379", 17-18		160 ___
84993	PRR B60 Baggage Car, Round Roof, 1960s "9356", 17-18		160 ___
84994	PRR B60 Baggage Car, Round Roof, 1960s "9384", 17-18		160 ___
84995	PRSL Baggage Car "5437", 17-18		160 ___
84996	PRSL B60 Baggage Car "6403", 17-18		160 ___
84997	LIRR 18" Heavyweight Passenger Coach 2-pack, #1, 17-18		400 ___
85000	LIRR 18" Heavyweight Passenger Coach 2-pack, #2, 17-18		400 ___
85003	PRSL 18" Heavyweight Passenger Coach 2-pack, #1, 17-18		400 ___
85006	PRSL 18" Heavyweight Passenger Coach 2-pack, #2, 17-18		400 ___
85009	PRR 18" Heavyweight Passenger Coach 2-pack, #1, 17-18		400 ___
85012	PRR 18" Heavyweight Passenger Coach 2-pack, #2, 17-18		400 ___
85015	ACL/PRR Champion Passenger Car 4-pack, 17-18		620 ___
85016	ACL/PRR Champion Passenger Car 2-pack, 17-18		310 ___
85017	ACL Champion 21" Diner, w/StationSounds, 17-18		310 ___
85018	ACL EMD SW7 Diesel "648," CC, 18		500 ___
85019	BN EMD SW7 Diesel "111," CC, 18		500 ___
85020	Conemaugh & Black Lick EMD SW7 Diesel "106," CC, 18		500 ___
85021	Chessie System EMD SW7 Diesel "5224," CC, 18		500 ___
85022	LV EMD SW7 Diesel "222," CC, 18		500 ___
85023	MEC EMD SW7 Diesel "331," CC, 18		500 ___
85024	NYC EMD SW7 Diesel "8853," CC, 18		500 ___
85025	Frisco EMD SW7 Diesel "303," CC, 18		500 ___
85026	Southern EMD SW7 Diesel "1100," CC, 18		500 ___
85027	UP EMD SW7 Diesel "1808," CC, 18		500 ___
85028	AT&SF EMD SD45 Diesel "5305," CC, 18		600 ___
85029	AT&SF EMD SD45 Diesel "5319," CC, 18		600 ___
85030	B&P EMD SD45 Diesel "453," CC, 18		600 ___
85031	B&P EMD SD45 Diesel "455," CC, 18		600 ___
85032	C&NW EMD SD45 Diesel "6485," CC, 18		600 ___
85033	C&NW EMD SD45 Diesel "6568," CC, 18		600 ___
85034	Montana Rail Link EMD SD45 Diesel "320," CC, 18		600 ___
85035	Montana Rail Link EMD SD45 Dies "331," CC, 18		600 ___
85036	MPI EMD SD45 Diesel "9009" CC, 18		600 ___
85037	MPI EMD SD45 Diesel "9011," CC, 18		600 ___
85038	N&W EMD SD45 Diesel "1776," CC, 18		600 ___
85039	N&W EMD SD45 Diesel "1790," CC, 18		600 ___
85040	NYS&W EMD SD45 Diesel "3612," CC, 18		600 ___
85041	NYS&W EMD SD45 Diesel "3614," CC, 18		600 ___
85042	WC EMD SD45 Diesel "6525," CC, 18		600 ___
85043	WC EMD SD45 Diesel "6580," CC, 18		600 ___
85046	BNSF EMD SD70ACe Diesel "9214," CC, 18		600 ___
85047	BNSF EMD SD70ACe Diesel "9287," CC, 18		600 ___
85048	CN EMD SD70ACe Diesel "8101," CC, 18		600 ___
85049	CN EMD SD70ACe Diesel "8103," CC, 18		600 ___
85050	CSX EMD SD70ACe Diesel "4849," CC, 18		600 ___
85051	Demonstrator EMD SD70ACe Diesel "1201," CC, 18		600 ___
85052	Demonstrator EMD SD70ACe Diesel "1202," CC, 18		600 ___

	MODERN 1970-2024		Exc	Mint
___	**85053**	KCS EMD SD70ACe Diesel "4156," CC, 18		600
___	**85054**	KCS EMD SD70ACe Diesel "4164," CC, 18		600
___	**85055**	NS EMD SD70ACe Diesel "1030," CC, 18		600
___	**85056**	NS EMD SD70ACe Diesel "1111," CC, 18		600
___	**85057**	UP EMD SD70ACe Diesel "8650," CC, 18		600
___	**85058**	UP EMD SD70ACe Diesel "8665," CC, 18		600
___	**85059**	MKT EMD NW2 Diesel "7," LionChief Plus, 18		320
___	**85060**	PRR EMD NW2 Diesel "9172," LionChief Plus, 18		320
___	**85061**	Nickel Plate Road EMD NW2 Diesel "13," LionChief Plus, 18		320
___	**85062**	UP EMD NW2 Diesel "1037," LionChief Plus, 18		320
___	**85063**	MILW EMD NW2 Diesel "1649," LionChief Plus, 18		320
___	**85065**	Hot Wheels 50th Anniversary Boxcar, 17-18		85
___	**85066**	TTX Husky Double-Stack Car "56210," w/EOT Device, 17		150
___	**85067**	TTX Husky Double-Stack Car "56180," w/EOT Device, 17		150
___	**85068**	BNSF Husky Double-Stack Car "203054," w/EOT Device, 17		150
___	**85069**	ARZC Husky Double-Stack Car "100008," w/EOT Device, 17		150
___	**85070**	Southwind Husky Double-Stack Car "5009," w/EOT Device, 17		150
___	**85071**	AT&SF Wide-Vision Caboose w/Camera "999718" 18		125
___	**85072**	BN Wide-Vision Caboose w/Camera "12345", 18		125
___	**85073**	Chessie System Wide-Vision Caboose w/Camera "903118", 18		125
___	**85074**	CSX Wide-Vision Caboose w/Camera "903282", 18		125
___	**85075**	Reading Wide-Vision Caboose w/Camera "94116", 18		125
___	**85076**	UP Wide-Vision Caboose w/Camera "13605", 18		125
___	**85077**	NS Wide-Vision Caboose w/Camera "555059", 18		125
___	**85078**	PRR Wide-Vision Caboose w/Camera "477900", 18		125
___	**85079**	DODX Wide-Vision Caboose "902", 18		100
___	**85080**	Montana Rail Link Wide-Vision Caboose "1005", 18		100
___	**85081**	UTLX 30,000-Gallon 1-D Tank Car "212189" w/ FreightSounds, 18		150
___	**85082**	GATX 30,000-Gallon 1-D Tank Car "36323" w/ FreightSounds, 18		150
___	**85083**	Philadelphia Energy Solutions 30,000-Gallon 1-D Tank Car "56" w/FreightSounds, 18		150
___	**85084**	TILX 30,000-Gallon 1-D Tank Car "254088" w/ FreightSounds, 18		150
___	**85085**	ADM 30,000-Gallon 1-D Tank Car "29248" w/ FreightSounds, 18		150
___	**85086**	Cargill 30,000-Gallon 1-D Tank Car "7964" w/ FreightSounds, 18		150
___	**85087**	UTLX 30,000-Gallon 1-D Tank Car "212187" w/EOT Device, 18		150
___	**85088**	GATX 30,000-Gallon 1-D Tank Car "36328" w/EOT Device, 18		120
___	**85089**	ADM 30,000-Gallon 1-D Tank Car "29252" w/EOT Device, 18		120
___	**85090**	Cargill 30,000-Gallon 1-D Tank Car "7968" w/EOT Device, 18		120
___	**85091**	ACFX 30,000-Gallon 1-D Tank Car "89990" w/EOT Device, 18		120
___	**85092**	Procor 30,000-Gallon 1-D Tank Car "43579" w/EOT Device, 18		120
___	**85093**	American Potash PS-2 Covered Hopper "31259", 17		75
___	**85094**	American Potash PS-2 Covered Hopper "31275", 17		75
___	**85095**	Bucyrus Erie PS-2 Covered Hopper "1114", 17		75
___	**85096**	Bucyrus Erie PS-2 Covered Hopper "1118", 17		75

		Exc	Mint
85097	Georgia Marble PS-2 Covered Hopper "31340", 17		75
85098	Georgia Marble PS-2 Covered Hopper "31341", 17		75
85099	Ready Mixed Concrete PS-2 Covered Hopper "331", 17		75
85100	Ready Mixed Concrete PS-2 Covered Hopper "340", 17		75
85101	Linde PS-2 Covered Hopper "209", 17		75
85102	Linde PS-2 Covered Hopper "211", 17		75
85103	U.S. Borax PS-2 Covered Hopper "31064", 17		75
85104	U.S. Borax PS-2 Covered Hopper "31066", 17	35	75
85105	Tank Train 2-Pack with EOT Device, #1, 17		200
85108	Tank Train 2-Pack with EOT Device, #2, 17		200
85111	Tank Train 2-Pack with EOT Device, #3, 17		200
85114	GATX Tank Train 2-Pack with EOT Device, 17		200
85117	CN Tank Train 2-Pack with EOT Device, 17		200
85120	Cibro Tank Train 2-Pack with EOT Device, 17		200
85126	Tank Train Car #1, 17		90
85127	Tank Train Car #2, 17		90
85128	Tank Train Car #3, 17		90
85129	Tank Train Car #4, 17		90
85130	Tank Train Car #5, 17		88
85131	Tank Train Car #6, 17		90
85132	Tank Train Car #1, 17		90
85133	Tank Train Car #2, 17		90
85134	Tank Train Car #3, 17		90
85135	Tank Train Car #4, 17		90
85136	Tank Train Car #5, 17		90
85137	Tank Train Car #6, 17		90
85138	Tank Train Car #1, 17		90
85139	Tank Train Car #2, 17		90
85140	Tank Train Car #3, 17		90
85141	Tank Train Car #4, 17		93
85142	Tank Train Car #5, 17		90
85143	Tank Train Car #6, 17		90
85144	GATX Tank Train Car #1, 17		90
85145	GATX Tank Train Car #2, 17	35	90
85146	GATX Tank Train Car #3, 17		90
85147	GATX Tank Train Car #4, 17		90
85148	GATX Tank Train Car #5, 17	35	90
85149	GATX Tank Train Car #6, 17		90
85150	CN Tank Train Car #1, 17		90
85151	CN Tank Train Car #2, 17		90
85152	CN Tank Train Car #3, 17		90
85153	CN Tank Train Car #4, 17		90
85154	CN Tank Train Car #5, 17		90
85155	CN Tank Train Car #6, 17		90
85156	Cibro Tank Train Car #1, 17		90
85157	Cibro Tank Train Car #2, 17		90
85158	Cibro Tank Train Car #3, 17		90
85159	Cibro Tank Train Car #4, 17	35	90
85160	Cibro Tank Train Car #5, 17	35	90
85161	Cibro Tank Train Car #6, 17		90
85168	Tacoma Rail EMD SD70ACe Diesel "7001," CC, 18		600
85169	Tacoma Rail EMD SD70ACe Diesel "7002" CC, 18		600

			Exc	Mint
____	**85170**	Atlanta & West Point USRA 4-6-2 Pacific Locomotive "290," CC, 18		1400
____	**85171**	B&O USRA 4-6-2 Pacific Locomotive "5300," CC, 18		1400
____	**85172**	Reading & Northern USRA 4-6-2 Pacific Locomotive "425," CC, 18		1400
____	**85173**	NP USRA 4-6-2 Pacific Locomotive "2256," CC, 18		1400
____	**85174**	Southern USRA 4-6-2 Pacific Locomotive "1372," CC, 18		1400
____	**85175**	Halloween USRA 4-6-2 Pacific Locomotive "1031," CC, 18		1400
____	**85176**	C&O USRA 2-6-6-2 Locomotive "1522," CC, 18		1600
____	**85177**	W&LE USRA 2-6-6-2 Locomotive "8007," CC, 18		1600
____	**85178**	B&O USRA 2-6-6-2 Locomotive "7555," CC, 18		1600
____	**85179**	Buffalo, Rochester & Pittsburgh USRA 2-6-6-2 "755," CC, 18		1600
____	**85180**	GN USRA 2-6-6-2 Locomotive "1855," CC, 18		1600
____	**85181**	MEC USRA 2-6-6-2 Locomotive "1205," CC, 18		1600
____	**85182**	NYC USRA 2-6-6-2 Locomotive "1400," CC, 18		1600
____	**85183**	SP USRA 2-6-6-2 Locomotive "3932," CC, 18		1600
____	**85184**	WM USRA 2-6-6-2 Locomotive "960," CC, 18		1600
____	**85185**	Renz Hobby Shop, 17		300
____	**85186**	AT&SF EMD F3 A-A Diesel Set, CC, 17	275	850
____	**85189**	AT&SF Powered EMD F3 B Diesel, CC, 17		450
____	**85190**	At&SF SuperBass EMD F3 B Diesel, CC, 17		300
____	**85191**	GN EMD F3 A-A Diesel Set, CC, 17		850
____	**85194**	GN Powered EMD F3 B Diesel, CC, 17		450
____	**85195**	GN SuperBass EMD F3 B Diesel, CC, 17		300
____	**85196**	T&P EMD F7 A-A Diesel Set, CC, 17		850
____	**85199**	T&P Powered EMD F7 B Diesel, CC, 17		450
____	**85200**	T&P SuperBass EMD F3 B Diesel, CC, 17		300
____	**85201**	NYO&W EMD F3 A-A Diesel Set, CC, 17		850
____	**85204**	NYO&W Powered EMD F3 B Diesel, CC, 17		450
____	**85205**	NYO&W SuperBass EMD F3 B Diesel, CC, 17		300
____	**85206**	PRR EMD F7 A-A Diesel Set, CC, 17		850
____	**85209**	PRR Powered EMD F7 B Diesel, CC, 17		450
____	**85210**	PRR SuperBass EMD F7 B Diesel, CC, 17		300
____	**85211**	Reading EMD F3 A-A Diesel Set, CC, 17		850
____	**85214**	Reading Powered EMD F3 B Diesel, CC, 17		450
____	**85215**	ReadingSuperBass EMD F3 B Diesel, CC, 17		300
____	**85216**	Conrail EMD F7 A-A Diesel Set "1792-1730," CC, 17		850
____	**85219**	Conrail Powered EMD F7 B Diesel "3861," CC, 17		450
____	**85220**	Conrail SuperBass EMD F7 B Diesel "3872," CC, 17		300
____	**85222**	CSX Maxi-Stack "85222", 17		75
____	**85223**	BNSF Maxi-Stack "237342", 17-C55718		75
____	**85226**	180-Watt PowerHouse Power Supply, 10-amp, 19-24		230
____	**85227**	GN Oriental Ltd Heavyweight Baggage/Coach, 17-18		400
____	**85230**	GN Oriental Ltd Heavyweight Sleeper/Coach, 17-18		400
____	**85233**	GN Oriental Ltd Heavyweight Sleeper/Diner, 17-18		400
____	**85236**	GN Oriental Ltd Heavyweight Sleeper/Observation, 17-18		400
____	**85241**	Mystery Machine FT Diesel Freight Set, Lionchief, 18-20		430
____	**85246**	Anheuser-Busch Vintage Refrigerator Car, 18-20		80
____	**85247**	Budweiser Clydesdale Vintage Refrigerator Car, 18-19		80
____	**85248**	Budweiser Vintage Refrigerator Car, 18-20		80
____	**85253**	End of the Line Express Diesel Freight Set, LionChief, 18-20		330
____	**85258**	AT&SF FT Ranger Diesel Freight Set, LionChief, 18		430
____	**85263**	Tomb of the Unknown Soldier Walking Brakeman Car, 18		100

MODERN 1970-2024		Exc	Mint	
85264	Harry Potter Hogwarts Add-on Coach, 18-24		90	___
85269	Scooby Doo Sam Witches Café, 18-20		100	___
85270	Hot Wheels Checkered Flagpole, 18		45	___
85271	Polar Express Flagpole, 18-24		45	___
85274	PRR Gla Hopper 3-pack #1, 18		225	___
85278	PRR Gla Hopper 3-pack #2, 18		225	___
85282	PRR Coal Goes To War Gla Hopper 3-pack #3, 18		225	___
85286	Berwind Gla Hopper 3-pack, 18		225	___
85290	PRR MOW PRR Gla Hopper 3-pack #4, 18		225	___
85294	Lionelville Hobby Shop, 18		300	___
85295	LCS CSM2, 18-24		120	___
85296	Layout Control System IRV2, 18-20, 24		100	___
85297	PRR N5 Caboose "477819", 18		100	___
85298	PRR N5 Caboose "478884", 18		100	___
85299	Reading & Northern N5 Caboose "477514", 18		100	___
85300	PRSL N5 Caboose "202", 18		100	___
85301	RJ Corman N5 Caboose, 18		100	___
85309	Flight Night Halloween Pylon, 18-19		150	___
85310	Witches Brew Storage Tank, 18-19		85	___
85311	Warehouse Kit, 18-19		60	___
85312	Modular Office Building Kit, 17-19	80	100	___
85314	Hometown Brewery Kit, 19		70	___
85315	UP EMD SD70ACe Diesel "1943," CC, 18		600	___
85316	UP Wide-Vision Caboose, Spirit of Union Pacific "1943", 18		100	___
85317	UP Spirit of the Union Pacific Boxcar, 18		85	___
85318	Personalized Happy Birthday Boxcar, 18		90	___
85319	Personalized 18 Merry Christmas Boxcar, 18		90	___
85320	Personalized Happy Anniversary Boxcar, 18-19		90	___
85321	John Deere Flatcar w/Tractor Load, 18		80	___
85322	Personalized 18 Halloween Boxcar, 18		90	___
85323	Scooby Doo Boxcar, 18		85	___
85324	Thomas & Friends Christmas Freight Set, LionChief, 18-24	100	250	___
85326	NYC Vision Baggage Car "9152", 18		330	___
85327	NYC Baggage Car 2-pack #1, 18		350	___
85330	NYC Baggage Car 2-pack #2, 18		350	___
85333	NYC Baggage/Combine 2-pack, 18		400	___
85336	NYC 18" Heavyweight Baggage Car 2-pack, 18		350	___
85339	SP Scale RPO Passenger Car "5124", 18		160	___
85340	L&N Scale RPO Passenger Car "1099", 18		160	___
85341	LIRR Scale RPO Passenger Car "737", 18		160	___
85342	MILW Scale RPO Passenger Car "2105", 18		160	___
85343	NYC Scale RPO Passenger Car "4819", 18		160	___
85344	PRR Scale RPO Passenger Car "5265", 18		160	___
85345	PRR Scale RPO Passenger Car "5269", 18		160	___
85346	PC Scale RPO Passenger Car "5267", 18		160	___
85347	UP Scale RPO Passenger Car "2060", 18		160	___
85348	MILW 18" Columbian Passenger Car 2-pack #A, 18		400	___
85351	MILW 18" Columbian Passenger Car 2-pack #B, 18		400	___
85354	MILW 18" Columbian Passenger Car 2-pack #C, 18		400	___
85357	MILW 18" Columbian Passenger Car 2-pack #D, 18		400	___
85360	UP Challenger 21" Passenger Car 4-pack, 18		700	___
85361	UP Challenger 21" Passenger Car 2-pack, 18		350	___
85362	UP Challenger 21" Diner w/StationSounds, 18		330	___

	MODERN 1970-2024		Exc	Mint
___	**85367**	L&N Hummingbird 21" Passenger Car 4-pack, 18		700
___	**85368**	L&N Hummingbird 21" Passenger Car 2-pack, 18		350
___	**85370**	R&N 18" Excursion and Business Car 2-pack, A, 18		400
___	**85373**	R&N 18" Excursion and Business Car 2-pack, B, 18		400
___	**85376**	Reading & Northern 21" Dome Car w/StationSounds, 18		350
___	**85377**	MOW Disconnect Work Car 4-pack, 18		160
___	**85378**	PRR Disconnect Work Car 4-pack, 18		160
___	**85379**	AT&SF Disconnect Work Car 4-pack, 18		160
___	**85380**	UP Disconnect Work Car 4-pack, 18		160
___	**85381**	NYC Disconnect Work Car 4-pack, 18		160
___	**85382**	D&RGW Disconnect Work Car 4-pack, 18		160
___	**85383**	Layout Control System IRV2 Sensor Add-on, 18-20, 24		30
___	**85384**	Orange 10" Straight FasTrack 4-pack, 18-20		25
___	**85386**	Pennsylvania Lines 2-8-0 Consolidation Locomotive "7109," CC, 18		750
___	**85387**	Western Allegheny 2-8-0 Consolidation Locomotive "85," CC, 18		750
___	**85389**	FasTrack White 10" Straight, 4-pack, 18-24		28
___	**85390**	FasTrack White O-36 Curve, 4-pack, 18-24		28
___	**85391**	White PEP Activation Track, 18-20		25
___	**85392**	White 10" Terminal FasTrack, 18-20		10
___	**85400**	Polar Express Skiing Hobo Observation w/Snowy Roof, 19-20		90
___	**85401**	UP LED Flag Boxcar, Yellow and Gray "1862", 18		120
___	**85402**	UP LED Flag Boxcar, C&NW Heritage "1995", 18		120
___	**85403**	UP LED Flag Boxcar, MKT Heritage "1988", 18		120
___	**85404**	UP LED Flag Boxcar, MP Heritage "1982", 18		120
___	**85405**	UP LED Flag Boxcar, D&RGW Heritage "1989", 18		120
___	**85406**	UP LED Flag Boxcar, SP Heritage "1996", 18		120
___	**85407**	UP LED Flag Boxcar, WP Heritage "1983", 18		120
___	**85408**	UP LED Flag Boxcar, Spirit of Union Pacific "1943", 18		120
___	**85409**	UP LED Flag Boxcar, Steam Program "4-8-8-4", 18		120
___	**85410**	Polar Express Hero Boy's Home, 18-24		130
___	**85411**	Pylon with World War II Planes, 18		145
___	**85412**	Santa's Sleigh Pylon, 18		135
___	**99000**	Keebler Elf Express Steam Freight Set, 99 u	775	1196
___	**99001**	Mickey's Holiday Express Freight Set, 99 u	163	180
___	**99002**	Looney Tunes Square Window Caboose, 99 u		65
___	**99006**	Keebler Bulkhead Flatcar, 99 u		200
___	**99007**	Smuckers Fudge 1-D Tank Car, 99 u		90
___	**99008**	Mickey's Merry Christmas Boxcar, 99 u		55
___	**99009**	Mickey's Holiday Express Square Window Caboose, 99 u		45
___	**99013**	Case Cutlery Tank Car "1889", 00 u		70
___	**99014**	Case Cutlery Gondola "1889", 00 u		70
___	**99015**	Case Cutlery Boxcar "1889", 00 u		70
___	**99018**	Case Cutlery Rolling Stock 3-pack, 00 u	140	215
___	**1823010**	Thomas' Best Buddies LionChief Set: Percy, 18-19		200
___	**1823011**	Percy, Sodor Locomotive, LionChief, 18-19		120
___	**1823020**	Thomas' Best Buddies LionChief Set: James, 18-19		200
___	**1823021**	James, Sodor Locomotive, LionChief, 18-19		120
___	**1823030**	Sodor Railway Troublemaker Diesel LionChief Set, 18-19		200
___	**1823031**	Thomas & Friends Sodor Diesel Locomotive, LionChief, 18-19, 23		160
___	**1823040**	Thomas Kinkade Christmas LionChief Steam Freight Set, 18, 20		400

		Exc	Mint
1823050	Mickey Mouse Celebration LionChief Steam Freight Set, 18		400 ___
1830010	Polar Express Snowman & Children People Pack, 19-24		30 ___
1831010	N&W Brass Hybrid USRA 4-8-2 K2 Locomotive "118," CC, 18		1400 ___
1831020	N&W Brass Hybrid USRA 4-8-2 K2 Locomotive "123," CC, 18		1400 ___
1831030	N&W Brass Hybrid USRA 4-8-2 K2 Locomotive "116," CC, 18		1400 ___
1831040	N&W Brass Hybrid USRA 4-8-2 K2 Locomotive "125," CC, 18		1400 ___
1831050	N&W Brass Hybrid USRA 4-8-2 K2 Locomotive "9999," CC, 18		1400 ___
1831060	PRR 4-6-2 Pacific K4 w/Long-haul Tender "5453," CC, 18		1300 ___
1904010	58" x 86" Lionel Train Table, 19-24		1000 ___
1908010	LCS CSM2 DZ-2500 Breakout Board, 18-24		30 ___
1908080	Improved CW80 Transformer, 19-24		170 ___
1918210	Anheuser-Busch Malt Tonics Woodside Refrigerator Car, 19		80 ___
1922010	UP Sherman Hill 4-8-8-4 Steam Freight Set, LionChief Plus 2.0, 19		1600 ___
1922020	Nickel Plate 2-8-4 Steam Freight Set, LionChief Plus 2.0, 19, 22		880 ___
1922030	Warren G. Harding Funeral Steam Passenger Train, CC, 18		2000 ___
1922040	AT&SF Gold Bonnet Streamlined Passenger Set, CC, 19		1000 ___
1922050	NYC Pacemaker Steam Passenger Set, CC, 19		2000 ___
1922060	BNSF Diesel Freight Oil Train Set, CC, 19		1000 ___
1922070	Pennsylvania Limited 2-8-4 Steam Passenger Set, 19, 22		880 ___
1922080	Lionel GE Bi-Polar Electric State Set, CC, 19		1800 ___
1922090	Erie Mining Diesel Ore Set, CC, 19		900 ___
1923020	NYC Flyer 0-8-0 Steam Freight Set, LionChief, 18-19		350 ___
1923030	Polar Express 15th Anniversary Steam Passenger Set, LionChief, 19		450 ___
1923040	UP Flyer 0-8-0 Steam Freight Set, LionChief, 19-22		370 ___
1923050	NS Tier 4 GE ET44C4 Diesel Freight Set, LionChief, 19-20		400 ___
1923070	Blue Comet Steam Passenger Set, LionChief, 19-20		370 ___
1923080	Promontory Summit 150th Anniversary Steam Locomotive Set, 19		550 ___
1923090	LV GE U36B Diesel Freight Set, LionChief, 19-20		330 ___
1923100	U.S. Steam 0-8-0 Steam Freight Set, LionChief, 19-20		400 ___
1923110	UP America Proud GP38 Diesel Freight Set, LionChief, 19-20		400 ___
1923130	Polar Express Trolley Set, 19		200 ___
1923140	Disney Christmas Express Steam Freight Set, LionChief, 19-24		400 ___
1923150	Winter Wonderland Steam Freight Set, LionChief, 19-22		400 ___
1925001	FasTrack Screws, 100-pack, 19-20		10 ___
1926011	CSX 86-foot 4-Door High Cube Boxcar (Boxcar Logo) "181032", 18		100 ___
1926012	CSX 86-foot 4-Door High Cube Boxcar (Boxcar Logo) "181056", 18		100 ___
1926013	CSX 86-foot 4-Door High Cube Boxcar "181053", 18		100 ___
1926014	CSX 86-foot 4-Door High Cube Boxcar "180455", 18		100 ___
1926021	DT&I 86-foot 4-Door High Cube Boxcar, Green "26341", 18		100 ___
1926022	DT&I 86-foot 4-Door High Cube Boxcar, Purple/Pink "26888", 18		100 ___
1926023	DT&I 86-foot 4-Door High Cube Boxcar, Blue "26443", 18		100 ___
1926024	DT&I 86-foot 4-Door High Cube Boxcar, Blue w/Graffiti "26834", 18		100 ___
1926031	N&W 86-foot 4-Door High Cube Boxcar "355155", 18		100 ___
1926032	N&W 86-foot 4-Door High Cube Boxcar "355197", 18		100 ___
1926041	Southern 86-foot 4-Door High Cube Boxcar "42954", 18		100 ___
1926042	Southern 86-foot 4-Door High Cube Boxcar "42995", 18		100 ___

			Exc	Mint
___	**1926051**	UP 86-foot 4-Door High Cube Boxcar "980421", 18		100
___	**1926052**	UP 86-foot 4-Door High Cube Boxcar "980434", 18		100
___	**1926053**	UP 86-foot 4-Door High Cube Boxcar w/Graffiti "980455", 18		100
___	**1926061**	Wabash 86-foot 4-Door High Cube Boxcar "55023", 18		100
___	**1926062**	Wabash 86-foot 4-Door High Cube Boxcar "55055", 18		100
___	**1926070**	ART Refrigerator Car w/FreightSounds "31823", 18		150
___	**1926080**	FGE Refrigerator Car w/FreightSounds "38947", 18		150
___	**1926090**	GN Refrigerator Car w/FreightSounds "68112", 18		150
___	**1926100**	NYC (MDT) Refrigerator Car w/FreightSounds "19091", 18		150
___	**1926110**	PFE Refrigerator Car w/FreightSounds "5860", 18		150
___	**1926120**	AT&SF Refrigerator Car w/FreightSounds "3526", 18		150
___	**1926131**	PRR Bunk Car "498393", 18		100
___	**1926132**	PRR Bunk Car "498396", 18		100
___	**1926133**	PRR Bunk Car "498398", 18		100
___	**1926141**	AT&SF Bunk Car "196752", 18		100
___	**1926142**	AT&SF Bunk Car "196754", 18		100
___	**1926143**	AT&SF Bunk Car "196459", 18		100
___	**1926151**	NYC Bunk Car "x19075", 18		100
___	**1926152**	NYC Bunk Car ""x19076", 18		100
___	**1926153**	NYC Bunk Car "x1907", 18		100
___	**1926161**	D&RGW Bunk Car "x2380", 18		100
___	**1926162**	D&RGW Bunk Car "x2384", 18		100
___	**1926163**	D&RGW Bunk Car ""x2387", 18		100
___	**1926171**	UP Bunk Car "906115", 18		100
___	**1926172**	UP Bunk Car "906118", 18		100
___	**1926173**	UP Bunk Car "906121", 18		100
___	**1926181**	MOW Bunk Car "99832", 18		100
___	**1926182**	MOW Bunk Car "99835", 18		100
___	**1926183**	MOW Bunk Car "99837", 18		100
___	**1926190**	PRR Kitchen Car w/Sounds "492774", 18		150
___	**1926200**	AT&SF Kitchen Car w/Sounds "194200", 18		150
___	**1926210**	NYC Kitchen Car w/Sounds "x22483", 18		150
___	**1926220**	D&RGW Kitchen Car w/Sounds "x4013", 18		150
___	**1926230**	UP Kitchen Car w/Sounds "903675", 18		150
___	**1926240**	MOW Kitchen Car w/Sounds "99402", 18		150
___	**1926250**	PRR Tool Car "493551", 18		90
___	**1926260**	AT&SF Tool Car "190455", 18		90
___	**1926270**	NYC Tool Car "x13568", 18		90
___	**1926280**	D&RGW Tool Car "x4510", 18		90
___	**1926290**	UP Tool Car "915129", 18		90
___	**1926300**	MOW Tool Car "99500", 18		90
___	**1926311**	Chessie 52-foot Coil Gondola "305005", 18		90
___	**1926312**	Chessie 52-foot Coil Gondola "305012", 18		90
___	**1926321**	C&SS 52-foot Coil Gondola "3859", 18		90
___	**1926322**	C&SS 52-foot Coil Gondola "3862", 18		90
___	**1926331**	DT&I 52-foot Coil Gondola "9326", 18		90
___	**1926332**	DT&I 52-foot Coil Gondola "9372", 18		90
___	**1926341**	EJ&E 52-foot Coil Gondola "4144", 18		90
___	**1926342**	EJ&E 52-foot Coil Gondola "4156", 18		90
___	**1926351**	P&LE 52-foot Coil Gondola "50062", 18		90
___	**1926352**	P&LE 52-foot Coil Gondola "50086", 18		90
___	**1926361**	Union RR 52-foot Coil Gondola "3021", 18		90

		Exc	Mint
1926362	Union RR 52-foot Coil Gondola "3163", 18		90
1926370	Polar Express 52-foot Coil Gondola "122519" w/Presents, 18		95
1926381	ACL 50-foot Bulkhead Flatcar "78310", 19		100
1926382	ACL 50-foot Bulkhead Flatcar "78348", 19		100
1926391	B&O 50-foot Bulkhead Flatcar "8831", 19		100
1926392	B&O 50-foot Bulkhead Flatcar "8844", 19		100
1926401	D&RGW 50-foot Bulkhead Flatcar "22392", 19		100
1926402	D&RGW 50-foot Bulkhead Flatcar "22420", 19		100
1926411	MKT 50-foot Bulkhead Flatcar "13912", 19		100
1926421	SAL 50-foot Bulkhead Flatcar "48102", 19		100
1926422	SAL 50-foot Bulkhead Flatcar "48124", 19		100
1926431	Frisco 50-foot Bulkhead Flatcar "4052", 19		100
1926432	Frisco 50-foot Bulkhead Flatcar "4058", 19		100
1926441	AT&SF Grand Canyon Line 50-foot Double-Door Boxcar "10206", 18		80
1926442	AT&SF Scout 50-foot Double-Door Boxcar "10295", 18		80
1926443	AT&SF El Capitan 50-foot Double-Door Boxcar "10350", 18		80
1926444	AT&SF Super Chief 50-foot Double-Door Boxcar "10410", 18		80
1926445	AT&SF Chief 50-foot Double-Door Boxcar "10456", 18		80
1926451	KCS 50-foot Double-Door Boxcar "20825", 18		80
1926452	KCS 50-foot Double-Door Boxcar "20856", 18		80
1926461	Monon 50-foot Double-Door Boxcar "1423", 18		80
1926462	Monon 50-foot Double-Door Boxcar "1426", 18		80
1926471	T&P 50-foot Double-Door Boxcar "70707", 18		80
1926472	T&P 50-foot Double-Door Boxcar "70735", 18		80
1926480	ELX Halloween 50-foot Double-Door Boxcar "103119", 18		80
1926491	UP CA-4 Caboose "3830", 18		100
1926492	UP CA-4 Caboose "3830", 18		100
1926493	UP CA-4 Caboose "3859", 18		100
1926501	Bartlett Grain PS-2CD 4427-cu-ft Covered Hopper "5509", 19		100
1926502	Bartlett Grain PS-2CD 4427-cu-ft Covered Hopper "5511", 19		100
1926511	BN PS-2CD 4427-cu-ft Covered Hopper "439397", 19		100
1926512	BN PS-2CD 4427-cu-ft Covered Hopper "450621", 19		100
1926521	Cargill PS-2CD 4427-cu-ft Covered Hopper "2819", 19		100
1926522	Cargill PS-2CD 4427-cu-ft Covered Hopper "2853", 19		100
1926531	Conrail PS-2CD 4427-cu-ft Covered Hopper "886283", 19		100
1926532	Conrail PS-2CD 4427-cu-ft Covered Hopper "886304", 19		100
1926540	Ely Thomas Logging Cars 2-pack A, 19		150
1926550	Ely Thomas Logging Cars 2-pack B, 19		150
1926560	Long Bell Logging Cars 2-pack A, 19		150
1926570	Long Bell Logging Cars 2-pack B, 19		150
1926580	NY&P Logging Cars 2-pack A, 19		150
1926590	NY&P Logging Cars 2-pack B, 19		150
1926600	Unlettered Logging Cars 2-pack A, 19		150
1926610	Unlettered Logging Cars 2-pack B, 19		150
1926620	B&O Sentinel PS-1 Boxcar "466024" w/FreightSounds, 19		135
1926630	GN PS-1 Boxcar "39412" w/FreightSounds, 19		135
1926640	PRR PS-1 Boxcar "24267" w/FreightSounds, 19		135
1926650	D&RGW Cookie Box PS-1 Boxcar "60034" w/FreightSounds, 19		135
1926660	Southern PS-1 Boxcar "330434" w/FreightSounds, 19		135
1926670	SP Overnight PS-1 Boxcar "97945" w/FreightSounds, 19		135

			Exc	Mint
___	**1926680**	NYS&W PS-1 Boxcar “501” w/FreightSounds, 19		135
___	**1926690**	WP PS-1 Boxcar “19531” w/FreightSounds, 19		135
___	**1926701**	B&M 40-foot Flatcar “33700” w/Sherman Tank Load, 19		130
___	**1926702**	B&M 40-foot Flatcar “33745” w/Sherman Tank Load, 19		130
___	**1926711**	NYC 40-foot Flatcar “496250” w/Sherman Tank Load, 19		130
___	**1926712**	NYC 40-foot Flatcar “496271” w/Sherman Tank Load, 19		130
___	**1926721**	PRR 40-foot Flatcar “925148” w/Sherman Tank Load, 19		130
___	**1926722**	PRR 40-foot Flatcar “925164” w/Sherman Tank Load, 19		130
___	**1926731**	SP 40-foot Flatcar “140014” w/Sherman Tank Load, 19		130
___	**1926732**	SP 40-foot Flatcar “140125” w/Sherman Tank Load, 19		130
___	**1926741**	UP 40-foot Flatcar “51125” w/Sherman Tank Load, 19		130
___	**1926742**	UP 40-foot Flatcar “51196" w/Sherman Tank Load, 19		130
___	**1926751**	US Army 40-foot Flatcar “35351” w/Sherman Tank Load, 19		130
___	**1926752**	US Army 40-foot Flatcar “35359” w/Sherman Tank Load, 19		130
___	**1926760**	CTCX 30,000-gallon 1-D Tank Car 3-pack, 19		250
___	**1926770**	GATX 30,000-gallon 1-D Tank Car 3-pack, 19		250
___	**1926780**	SCMX 30,000-gallon 1-D Tank Car 3-pack, 19		250
___	**1926790**	TILX (Black) 30,000-gallon 1-D Tank Car 3-pack, 19		250
___	**1926800**	TILX (White) 30,000-gallon 1-D Tank Car 3-pack, 19		250
___	**1926810**	VMSX 30,000-gallon 1-D Tank Car 3-pack, 19		250
___	**1926820**	Polar Express 15th Anniversary Boxcar w/FreightSounds, 19		145
___	**1926830**	C&NW NE Caboose "10808", 19		100
___	**1926840**	Conrail (RDG patch) NE Caboose “19730”, 19		100
___	**1926850**	D&H NE Caboose “35802”, 19		100
___	**1926860**	L&HR NE Caboose “17”, 19		100
___	**1926870**	LV NE Caboose “95003”, 19		100
___	**1926880**	Halloween (ELX) NE Caboose “1313”, 19		100
___	**1926890**	Alaska RR EV Caboose “1086” w/CupolaCam, 19		130
___	**1926900**	C&O EV Caboose “3160” w/CupolaCam, 19		130
___	**1926910**	Conrail EV Caboose “22137” w/CupolaCam, 19		130
___	**1926920**	D&RGW EV Caboose “01510” w/CupolaCam, 19		130
___	**1926930**	Milwaukee Road EV Caboose “992303” w/CupolaCam, 19		130
___	**1926940**	MKT EV Caboose “100” w/CupolaCam, 19		130
___	**1926950**	N&W EV Caboose “555100” w/CupolaCam, 19		130
___	**1926960**	Lionel Lines EV Caboose "6960" w/CupolaCam, 19		130
___	**1926971**	Detroit Salt PS-2CD 4427-cu-ft Covered Hopper “5436”, 19		100
___	**1926972**	Detroit Salt PS-2CD 4427-cu-ft Covered Hopper "5446”, 19		100
___	**1926981**	Producers Grain PS-2CD Covered Hopper “3926”, 19		100
___	**1926982**	Producers Grain PS-2CD Covered Hopper “3940”, 19		100
___	**1927010**	AT&SF 21-inch Passenger Car 4-pack, 19		700
___	**1927020**	AT&SF 21-inch Passenger Car 2-pack #1, 19		350
___	**1927030**	AT&SF 21-inch Dome Car “550” w/StationSounds, 19		340
___	**1927040**	AT&SF 21-inch Passenger Car 2-pack #2, 19		350
___	**1927050**	UP Excursion 21-inch Passenger Car Expansion Set, 19		350
___	**1927060**	UP Challenger 21-inch Passenger Car Expansion Set, 19		350
___	**1927070**	Midnight Special 18-inch Passenger Car 2-pack #1, 18		400
___	**1927080**	Midnight Special 18-inch Passenger Car 2-pack #2, 18		400
___	**1927090**	Midnight Special 18-inch Passenger Car 2-pack #3, 18		400
___	**1927100**	Midnight Special Diner “1305,” w/StationSounds, 18		330
___	**1927110**	SP 18-inch Passenger Car 2-pack #1, 18-19		400
___	**1927120**	SP 18-inch Passenger Car 2-pack #2, 18-19		400
___	**1927130**	SP 18-inch Passenger Car 2-pack #3, 18-19		400
___	**1927140**	SP 18-inch Passenger Car 2-pack #4, 18-19		400

		Exc	Mint
1927150	NYC Pacemaker 2-car Add-on Set, 19		400 ___
1927160	NYC Pacemaker Diner "617" w/StationSounds, 19		330 ___
1927170	N&W Cavalier 18-inch Passenger Car 2-pack A, 19		400 ___
1927180	N&W Cavalier 18-inch Passenger Car 2-pack B, 19		400 ___
1927190	N&W Cavalier 18-inch Diner "1018" w/StationSounds, 19		330 ___
1927200	611 Excursion Train NS Coach 4-pack, 19		700 ___
1927210	611 Excursion Train Private Car 2-pack A, 19		350 ___
1927220	611 Excursion Train Private Car 2-pack B, 19		350 ___
1927230	611 Excursion Train Dome Car w/StationSounds, 19		340 ___
1927241	611 Excursion Train N&W Tool Car "1407", 19		180 ___
1927242	N&W Cavalier Baggage "110", 19		180 ___
1927243	N&W Cavalier Baggage "114", 19		180 ___
1927251	PC 60-foot Baggage "7533", 19		180 ___
1927252	PC 60-foot Baggage "7551", 19		180 ___
1927261	SP 60-foot Baggage "6340", 19		180 ___
1927262	SP 60-foot Baggage "6344", 19		180 ___
1927271	REA 60-foot Baggage "1631", 19		180 ___
1927272	REA 60-foot Baggage "1650", 19		180 ___
1927281	UP 60-foot Baggage "1830" (Greyhound), 19		180 ___
1927282	UP 60-foot Baggage "1841" (Greyhound), 19		180 ___
1927283	UP 60-foot Baggage "1830" (Yellow), 19		180 ___
1927284	UP 60-foot Baggage "1837" (Yellow), 19		180 ___
1927291	ACL 60-foot Baggage "555", 19		180 ___
1927292	ACL 60-foot Baggage "559", 19		180 ___
1927300	ACL 60-foot Railway Post Office "11", 19		180 ___
1927310	N&W Cavalier Railway Post Office "96", 19		180 ___
1927320	Southern 60-foot Railway Post Office "39", 18-19		160 ___
1927330	AT&SF 60-foot Railway Post Office "65", 19		180 ___
1927340	UP 60-foot Railway Post Office "2062", 19		180 ___
1927351	Polar Express Railway Post Office, White Roof, 19, 22-24		200 ___
1927352	Polar Express Railway Post Office, Black Roof, 19, 22-24		200 ___
1927360	LIRR 21-inch Streamlined Coach 4-pack, 19		700 ___
1927370	LIRR 21-inch Streamlined Coach 2-pack, 19		350 ___
1927380	UP 1860s Wood Coach w/RailSounds, 2-pack, 19		350 ___
1927390	Central Pacific 1860s Wood Coach w/RailSounds, 2-pack, 19		350 ___
1927461	Southern 60-foot Baggage "100", 18-19		160 ___
1927462	Southern 60-foot Baggage "109", 18-19		160 ___
1927470	Southern 18-inch Passenger Car 2-pack #1, 18-19		400 ___
1927480	Southern 18-inch Passenger Car 2-pack #2, 18-19		400 ___
1927490	Southern 18-inch Passenger Car 2-pack #3, 18-19		400 ___
1927500	Southern Diner "3168" w/StationSounds, 18-19		330 ___
1927510	MP Sunshine Special 18-inch Passenger Car 2-pack #1, 18-19		400 ___
1927520	MP Sunshine Special 18-inch Passenger Car 2-pack #2, 18-19		400 ___
1927530	MP Sunshine Special 18-inch Passenger Car 2-pack #3, 18-19		400 ___
1927540	MP Sunshine Special Diner "10042" w/StationSounds, 18-19		330 ___
1927550	MP Sunshine Special 60-foot RPO "45", 18-19		160 ___
1927560	Defense Special Heavyweight Passenger Car 2-pack A, 19		400 ___
1927570	Defense Special Heavyweight Passenger Car 2-pack B, 19		400 ___
1927580	Defense Special Heavyweight Passenger Car 2-pack C, 19		400 ___
1927590	Defense Special Heavyweight Passenger Car 2-pack D, 19		400 ___
1927600	611 Excursion Train NS Coach 2-pack, 19		350 ___

			Exc	Mint
____	**1927610**	CP 21-inch Passenger Car 4-pack, 19		700
____	**1927620**	CP 21-inch Passenger Car 2-pack, 19		350
____	**1927630**	Polar Express Hot Chocolate Car w/StationSounds, 19		330
____	**1927640**	Polar Express Abandoned Toy Car, 19, 24		200
____	**1927650**	Polar Express 15th Anniversary Coach, 19		200
____	**1927660**	Pennsylvania Limited Suetonius Coach, 19		75
____	**1927670**	Lionel State Set Add-on 2-pack, 19		530
____	**1927680**	Northern Central 1860s Wood Coach w/RailSounds, 2-pack, 19		350
____	**1927690**	Woodruff Sleeping and Parlor 1860s Wood Coach, 2-pack, 19		300
____	**1927700**	Blue Comet Heavyweight Coach, 19-20		75
____	**1927710**	CP 21-inch Diner "550" w/StationSounds, 19		330
____	**1927730**	PRR 1860s Wood Coach w/RailSounds, 2-pack, 19		350
____	**1928011**	BN Auto Rack "159173", 18-19		80
____	**1928012**	BN Auto Rack "159433", 18-19		80
____	**1928021**	Conrail Auto Rack "980139", 18-19		80
____	**1928022**	Conrail Auto Rack "456249", 18-19		80
____	**1928031**	GT Auto Rack "50454", 18-19		80
____	**1928032**	GT Auto Rack "50490", 18-19		80
____	**1928041**	SP Auto Rack "518027", 18-19		80
____	**1928042**	SP Auto Rack "518114", 18-19		80
____	**1928051**	TTX Auto Rack "710866", 18-19		80
____	**1928052**	TTX Auto Rack "710877", 18-19		80
____	**1928060**	Mickey Mouse Celebration Aquarium Car, 18		100
____	**1928070**	NYC Flatcar w/Boat "28070", 18-19		70
____	**1928080**	Hot Wheels Fuel 1-Dome Tank Car, 18-19		75
____	**1928091**	Branch Line Passenger Car 2-pack, 18-19		75
____	**1928092**	James Trucks Wagon Car 2-pack, 18-19		75
____	**1928093**	S.C. Ruffey Wagon Car, 18-19		45
____	**1928110**	BN Hopper 6-pack, 19		150
____	**1928120**	C&NW Hopper 6-pack, 19		150
____	**1928130**	CSX Hopper 6-pack, 19-20		150
____	**1928140**	PP&L Hopper 6-pack, 19-20		150
____	**1928150**	Reading Lines Hopper 6-pack, 19-20		150
____	**1928160**	Bethlehem Steel Ore Car 6-pack, 19-20		150
____	**1928170**	CN Ore Car 6-pack, 19-20		150
____	**1928180**	Erie Mining Ore Car 6-pack, 19		150
____	**1928190**	PRR Ore Car 6-pack, 19-20		150
____	**1928200**	UP Ore Car 6-pack, 19-20		150
____	**1928210**	Malt Tonics Refrigerator Car, 19-22		90
____	**1928220**	Anheuser-Busch 1890s Woodside Refrigerator Car, 19		80
____	**1928240**	Anheuser-Busch Uni-Body 1-D Tank Car "4271", 19		75
____	**1928250**	Anheuser-Busch Barrel Car ""28250", 19		80
____	**1928260**	Miller High Life Woodside Refrigerator Car, 19-20		80
____	**1928270**	Coors Golden Beer Woodside Refrigerator Car, 19-20		80
____	**1928280**	Hamm's Beer Woodside Refrigerator Car, 19, 22		90
____	**1928330**	Pez Mint Car, 19		80
____	**1928340**	John Deere Mower Stockcar, 19		80
____	**1928350**	John Deere Flatcar "28350" w/Piggyback Trailers, 19		85
____	**1928360**	Scooby-Doo Aquarium Car, 19-20		100
____	**1928370**	Spy Vs. Spy Challenge Boxcar, 19		85
____	**1928380**	Trick or Treat Boxcar w/HalloweenSounds, 19		80

		Exc	Mint
1928390	Undead Gondola, 19		70
1928400	Polar Express Hero Boy Walking Brakeman Car, 19		100
1928410	Polar Express Reindeer Car, 19		80
1928420	Polar Express Searchlight Car, 19		70
1928430	Polar Express Barrel Car, 19		80
1928440	Sweetest Helper Refrigerator Car, 19-20		80
1928450	Snowball Fight Animated Gondola, 19-20		75
1928460	Santa Mobile Rest Stop Flatcar, 19-20		75
1928470	Santa Freight Lines Christmas Transfer Caboose, 19-20		70
1928480	Santa Freight Lines Santa Finder Searchlight Car, 19-20		65
1928490	Christmas Boxcar 2019, 19		65
1928500	Christmas Music Boxcar, 19		80
1928510	UP Barrel Ramp Car "28510", 19-20		75
1928520	BNSF Maxi-Stack, 18-19		80
1928530	CSX Maxi-Stack, 18-19		80
1928540	TTX Maxi-Stack, 18-19		80
1928550	NPR Flatcar "1937" w/Trailer, 19		70
1928560	Batman & Robin Boxcar, 19-20		80
1928570	Batman Bat-Signal Searchlight Car, 19		70
1928580	Batman The Joker Laughing Gas Missile Car, 19-20		90
1928590	Happy Birthday Scooby-Doo Sound Car, 19-20		85
1928600	Batman Classic Gotham City Villains Boxcar, 19-20		80
1928610	Chevy Auto Rack "1911", 19-20		85
1928620	Chevy Flatcar w/Frames, 19		75
1928630	Looney Tunes Scent-imental Over You Chasing Gondola, 19		80
1928640	Thomas the Tank Engine Boxcar, 19		75
1928650	Percy Boxcar, 19		75
1928660	James Boxcar, 19		75
1928670	Mickey's Wish List Boxcar, 19-20		70
1928680	UP Uni-Body 1-D Tank Car "8665", 19-20		70
1928690	Toyota Auto Rack "1937", 19		85
1928700	Toyota Flatcar w/Frames, 19		75
1929040	Anheuser-Busch Barrel Loader, 19		70
1929050	Polar Express Barrel Loader, 19		70
1929060	Polar Express Station Platform, 19-24		55
1929070	Winter Wonderland Station Platform, 19-23		55
1929080	Hot Wheels Crash City Café, 18-19		100
1929090	Illuminated Christmas Half-Covered Bridge, 19-23		85
1929100	Defect Detector w/Sounds, 18-24		100
1929110	Halloween House, 18		130
1929130	Elf Tug of War Accessory, 19		75
1929160	Sir Topham Hatt Gateman, 19		120
1929170	Haunted House, 19-22		275
1929230	Burning House, 19-20		120
1929804	Peel and Stick Lights, 4-pack, 19-20		10
1929815	Peel and Stick Lights, 15-pack, 19-20		28
1929904	Peel and Stick LED Lights, 4-pack, 19-20		10
1929915	Peel and Stick LED Lights, 15-pack, 19-20		28
1930010	Steel Coil Load Kit, 18-23		20
1930050	Lumber Load Kit, 19		25
1930060	Millennial People Pack, 18-24		30
1930070	Trick or Treat Figures, 18-24		30
1930080	Halloween Lawn Figures, 18-24		30

			Exc	Mint
___	1930120	Mickey Mouse Celebration Billboard 3-pack, 18		20
___	1930130	Thomas & Friends Covered Bridge, 18-19		70
___	1930140	Trolley House, 19		50
___	1930150	Budweiser Billboard 3-pack, 19-22		25
___	1930170	Green Iron Fence, 19-20		20
___	1930180	Benches, 6-pack, 19-20		10
___	1930190	Sitting People with Benches, 6-pack, 19-20		23
___	1930200	Winter Action Figures, 6-pack, 19-20		23
___	1930210	Sled Kids, 3-pack, 19-20		23
___	1930220	Sitting People, 6-pack, 19-20		23
___	1930230	People on Sleigh Figure Pack, 19-20		23
___	1930240	People Waving, 6-pack, 19-20		23
___	1930160	Brown Picket Fence, 19-20		20
___	1930250	People Eating, 6-pack, 19-20		23
___	1930260	Prisoners (striped), 6-pack, 19-20		23
___	1930270	Travelers, 6-pack, 19-20		23
___	1930280	Horses, 4-pack, 19-20		23
___	1930290	Cows and Calves (brown), 6-pack, 19-20		23
___	1930300	Unpainted Figures, 36-pack, 19-20		35
___	1930310	Unpainted Animals, 36-pack, 19-20		35
___	1930320	Smoking Tony Lighted Figure, 19-20		20
___	1930330	Railroad Worker with Lamp Lighted Figure, 19-20		20
___	1930340	Miner with Headlamp Lighted Figure, 19-20		20
___	1930350	Man with Flashlight Lighted Figure, 19-20		20
___	1930360	Man with Flashing Jackhammer Lighted Figure, 19-20		20
___	1930370	Braga House, 19-20		75
___	1930380	Fraser House, 19-20		75
___	1930390	Harwell House, 19-20		75
___	1930400	Olson House Kit, 19-20		22
___	1930410	Morris House Kit, 19-20		22
___	1930420	Bishop House Kit, 19-20		22
___	1930430	Davis House Kit, 19-20		22
___	1930440	Church, 19-20		86
___	1930450	Unpainted Steel Coils 2-Pack, 19-24		10
___	1931060	L&N USRA 4-8-2 Light Mountain Locomotive "404," CC, 18		1300
___	1931070	MP USRA 4-8-2 Light Mountain Locomotive "5307," CC, 18		1300
___	1931080	NC&StL USRA 4-8-2 Light Mountain Locomotive "551," CC, 18		1300
___	1931090	NH USRA 4-8-2 Light Mountain Locomotive "3301," CC, 18		1300
___	1931100	Frisco USRA 4-8-2 Light Mountain Locomotive "1501," CC, 18		1300
___	1931110	Soo Line USRA 4-8-2 Light Mountain Locomotive "4005," CC, 18		1300
___	1931120	Southern USRA 4-8-2 Light Mountain Locomotive "1483," CC, 18		1300
___	1931130	Southern USRA 4-8-2 Light Mountain Locomotive "1495," CC, 18		1300
___	1931140	North Pole Central 4-8-2 Light Mountain "1224," CC, 18		1300
___	1931150	SP 4-4-2 Atlantic A-6 Locomotive "3001," CC, 18		800
___	1931160	SP 4-4-2 Atlantic A-6 Locomotive "3000," CC, 18		800
___	1931170	SP 4-4-2 Atlantic A-6 Locomotive "3002," CC, 18		800
___	1931180	UP 4-4-2 Atlantic Locomotive "3304," CC, 18		800
___	1931190	C&NW 4-4-2 Atlantic Locomotive "394," CC, 18		800
___	1931200	IC 4-4-2 Atlantic Locomotive "1003," CC, 18		800

MODERN 1970-2024		Exc	Mint
1931210	Clinchfield 4-6-6-4 Locomotive "675," CC, 18		2000 ____
1931220	D&RGW 4-6-6-4 Locomotive "3800," CC, 18		2000 ____
1931230	D&RGW 4-6-6-4 Locomotive "3805," CC, 18		2000 ____
1931240	UP 4-6-6-4 Challenger Locomotive "3975," CC, 18		2000 ____
1931250	UP 4-6-6-4 Challenger Locomotive "3977," CC, 18		2000 ____
1931260	UP 4-6-6-4 Challenger Locomotive "3985," CC, 18		2000 ____
1931270	UP 4-6-6-4 Challenger Locomotive "3981," CC, 18		2000 ____
1931280	UP 4-6-6-4 Challenger Locomotive "3717," CC, 18		2000 ____
1931290	UP 4-6-6-4 Challenger Locomotive "3949," CC, 18		2000 ____
1931300	Undecorated 4-6-6-4 Challenger Locomotive "9999," CC, 18		2000 ____
1931311	UP Vision Auxiliary Water Tender "907853," CC, 18		500 ____
1931312	UP Vision Auxiliary Water Tender "907856," CC, 18		500 ____
1931313	UP Vision Auxiliary Water Tender "907857," CC, 18		500 ____
1931314	UP Vision Auxiliary Water Tender "809," CC, 18		500 ____
1931315	UP Vision Auxiliary Water Tender "814" CC, 18		500 ____
1931316	UP Vision Auxiliary Water Tender "903026," CC, 18		500 ____
1931320	Clinchfield Vision Auxiliary Water Tender "X675," CC, 18		500 ____
1931330	D&RGW Vision Auxiliary Water Tender "3800A," CC, 18		500 ____
1931340	N&W 4-8-4 Northern J-Class "600," CC, 19		1500 ____
1931350	N&W 4-8-4 Northern J-Class "603," CC, 19		1500 ____
1931360	N&W 4-8-4 Northern J-Class "611" (c1982)," CC, 19		1500 ____
1931370	N&W 4-8-4 Northern J-Class "611" (c2016)," CC, 19		1500 ____
1931380	American Freedom Train 4-8-4 "611," CC, 19		1500 ____
1931390	N&W 4-8-4 Northern J-Class "746," CC, 19		1500 ____
1931400	C&O 2-10-4 Texas T1 "3001," CC, 19		1500 ____
1931410	C&O 2-10-4 Texas T1 "3039," CC, 19		1500 ____
1931420	PRR 2-10-4 Texas J1a "6174," CC, 19		1500 ____
1931430	PRR 2-10-4 Texas J1a "6434," CC, 19		1500 ____
1931440	PRR 2-10-4 Texas J1a "6500," CC (artist conception), 19		1500 ____
1931450	NYC 4-6-4 Hudson J3a "5405," CC, 19		1400 ____
1931460	NYC 4-6-4 Hudson J3a "5413," CC, 19		1500 ____
1931470	NYC 4-6-4 Hudson J3a "5418," CC, 19		1400 ____
1931480	NYC 4-6-4 Hudson J3a "5452," CC, 19		1500 ____
1931490	Ely Thomas Two-Truck Shay Locomotive "6," CC, 19		1200 ____
1931500	Lima Stone Two-Truck Shay Locomotive "10," CC, 19		1200 ____
1931510	Lima Locomotive Works Two-Truck Shay Locomotive "2," CC, 19		1200 ____
1931520	Long Bell Two-Truck Shay Locomotive "5," CC, 19		1200 ____
1931530	NY&P Two-Truck Shay Locomotive "3," CC, 19		1200 ____
1931540	Roaring Camp Two-Truck Shay Locomotive "1," CC, 19		1200 ____
1931550	North Pole Woodworks Two-Truck Shay Locomotive "25," CC, 19		1200 ____
1931560	Sleepy Hollow Casket, Two-Truck Shay Locomotive "31," CC, 19		1200 ____
1931650	Central Pacific 4-4-0 Hybrid Jupiter, CC (painted), 19		1100 ____
1931660	UP 4-4-0 Hybrid, "119," CC (painted), 19		1100 ____
1931670	Schenectady Locomotive Works 4-4-0 Hybrid, CC (unpainted), 19		1100 ____
1931680	Rogers Locomotive Works 4-4-0 Hybrid, CC (unpainted), 19		1100 ____
1931690	C&O 2-10-4 Texas T1 "3020," CC (weathered), 19		1700 ____
1931700	PRR 2-10-4 Texas J1a "6481," CC (weathered), 19		1700 ____
1931710	B&LE 2-10-4 Texas "643," CC, 19		1500 ____
1931720	CB&Q 2-10-4 Texas "6328," CC, 19		1500 ____
1931730	DM&IR 2-10-4 Texas "717," CC, 19		1500 ____

			Exc	Mint
___	**1931740**	KCS 2-10-4 Texas "905," CC, 19		1500
___	**1931750**	D&RGW 2-10-4 Texas "1450," CC, 19		1500
___	**1931760**	Southern 2-10-4 Texas "5300," CC, 19		1500
___	**1931770**	Central Pacific 4-4-0 Hybrid Leviathan, CC (painted), 19		1100
___	**1931780**	Northern Central 4-4-0 Hybrid York, CC (painted), 19		1100
___	**1931820**	PRR 4-4-0 Hybrid, "573," CC (painted), 19		1100
___	**1932010**	ATSF 2-8-4 Berkshire "4101," LionChief Plus 2.0, 19-20		500
___	**1932020**	C&O 2-8-4 Berkshire Locomotive "2687," LionChief Plus 2.0, 19		500
___	**1932030**	NPR 2-8-4 Berkshire Locomotive "765," LionChief Plus 2.0, 19-20		500
___	**1932040**	Pere Marquette 2-8-4 Berkshire "1225," LionChief Plus 2.0, 19-20		500
___	**1932050**	Southern 2-8-4 Berkshire, "2716," LionChief Plus 2.0, 19-20		500
___	**1932080**	Disney 2-8-4 Berkshire "2019," LionChief Plus 2.0, 19-20		525
___	**1932090**	Polar Express 2-8-4 Berkshire "1225," LionChief Plus 2.0, 19-20		525
___	**1932100**	North Pole Central 2-8-4 Berkshire "1224," LionChief Plus 2.0, 19-20		500
___	**1932110**	Halloween (ELX) 2-8-4 Berkshire "1031," LionChief Plus 2.0, 19-20		500
___	**1932120**	GN 2-4-2 Columbia Locomotive "374," LionChief, 19		200
___	**1932130**	PRR 2-4-2 Columbia Locomotive "619" LionChief, 19		200
___	**1932140**	AT&SF 2-4-2 Columbia Locomotive "3452," LionChief, 19		200
___	**1932150**	Southern 2-4-2 Columbia Locomotive "1412," LionChief, 19		200
___	**1932161**	UP 4-8-8-4 Big Boy Locomotive "4012," LionChief Plus 2.0, 19		1200
___	**1932162**	UP 4-8-8-4 Big Boy Locomotive "4014," LionChief Plus 2.0, 19		1200
___	**1932163**	UP 4-8-8-4 Big Boy Locomotive "4017," LionChief Plus 2.0, 19		1200
___	**1932164**	UP 4-8-8-4 Big Boy Locomotive "4018," LionChief Plus 2.0, 19		1200
___	**1932170**	UP 4-8-8-4 Big Boy "4000" (Greyhound), LionChief Plus 2.0, 19		1200
___	**1933011**	BN Alco RS11 Diesel "4186," CC, 18		500
___	**1933012**	BN Alco RS11 Diesel "4190," CC, 18		500
___	**1933021**	CV Alco RS11 Diesel ""3601," CC, 18		500
___	**1933022**	CV Alco RS11 Diesel "3611," CC, 18		500
___	**1933031**	Conrail Alco RS11 Diesel "7640," CC, 18		500
___	**1933032**	Conrail Alco RS11 Diesel "7651," CC, 18		500
___	**1933041**	Depew, Lancaster & Western Alco RS11 Diesel "1800," CC, 18		500
___	**1933042**	Depew, Lancaster & Western Alco RS11 Diesel "1804," CC, 18		500
___	**1933051**	L&N Alco RS11 Diesel "952," CC, 18		500
___	**1933052**	L&N Alco RS11 Diesel "955," CC, 18		500
___	**1933061**	SCL Alco RS11 Diesel "1202," CC, 18		500
___	**1933062**	SCL Alco RS11 Diesel "1210," CC, 18		500
___	**1933081**	BN EMD SD40-2 Diesel "6702," CC, 18		550
___	**1933082**	BN EMD SD40-2 Diesel "8002," CC, 18		550
___	**1933083**	BN non-powered EMD SD40-2 Diesel "6772", 18		300
___	**1933091**	FEC EMD SD40-2 Diesel "703," CC, 18		550
___	**1933092**	FEC EMD SD40-2 Diesel "713," CC, 18		550
___	**1933093**	FEC non-powered EMD SD40-2 Diesel "714", 18		300
___	**1933101**	FURX EMD SD40-2 Diesel "3012," CC, 18		550
___	**1933102**	FURX EMD SD40-2 Diesel "3021," CC, 18		550

MODERN 1970-2024		Exc	Mint
1933103	FURX non-powered EMD SD40-2 Diesel "3049", 18		300 ___
1933111	Milwaukee Road Bicentennial EMD SD40-2 Diesel "156," CC, 18		550 ___
1933112	Milwaukee Road EMD SD40-2 Diesel "190," CC, 18		550 ___
1933113	Milwaukee Road EMD SD40-2 Diesel "196," CC, 18		550 ___
1933114	Milwaukee Road non-powered EMD SD40-2 Diesel "197", 18		300 ___
1933121	Soo Line "Bandit" EMD SD40-2 Diesel "6301," CC, 18		550 ___
1933122	Soo Line "Bandit" EMD SD40-2 Diesel "6345," CC, 18		550 ___
1933123	Soo Line "Bandit" non-powered EMD SD40-2 Diesel "6362", 18		300 ___
1933131	UP EMD SD40-2 Diesel "3696," CC, 18		550 ___
1933132	UP EMD SD40-2 Diesel "3707," CC, 18		550 ___
1933133	UP non-powered EMD SD40-2 Diesel "B3641", 18		300 ___
1933141	W&LE EMD SD40-2 Diesel "6310," CC, 18		550 ___
1933142	W&LE EMD SD40-2 Diesel "6311," CC, 18		550 ___
1933143	W&LE non-powered EMD SD40-2 Diesel "6347", 18		300 ___
1933151	W&S EMD SD40-2 Diesel "4001," CC, 18		550 ___
1933152	W&S EMD SD40-2 Diesel "4003," CC, 18		550 ___
1933153	W&S non-powered EMD SD40-2 Diesel "4005", 18		300 ___
1933160	AT&SF Alco PA-PA Diesel Set "54-54," CC, 18		1000 ___
1933163	AT&SF Alco PB w/SuperBass Sound "54A," CC, 18		500 ___
1933170	D&RGW Alco PA-PA Diesel Set "6001-6003," CC, 18		1000 ___
1933173	D&RGW Alco PB w/SuperBass Sound "6002," CC, 18		500 ___
1933180	NYC Alco PA-PA Diesel Set "4903-4904," CC, 18		1000 ___
1933183	NYC Alco PB w/SuperBass Sound "4303," CC, 18		500 ___
1933190	PRR Alco PA-PA Diesel Set "5754-5755+B34," CC, 18		1000 ___
1933193	PRR Alco PB w/SuperBass Sound "5754B," CC, 18		500 ___
1933200	SP Alco PA-PA Diesel Set "6034-6039," CC, 18		1000 ___
1933203	SP Alco PB w/SuperBass Sound "5922," CC, 18		500 ___
1933210	UP Alco PA-PA Diesel Set "606-607," CC, 18		1000 ___
1933213	UP Alco PB w/SuperBass Sound "606B," CC, 18		500 ___
1933221	BNSF (ATSF Patch) GE C44-9W Diesel "599," CC, 18		550 ___
1933222	BNSF (ATSF Patch) GE C44-9W Diesel "662," CC, 18		550 ___
1933223	BNSF (ATSF Patch) non-powered GE C44-9W Diesel "604", 18		300 ___
1933231	BNSF GE C44-9W Diesel "703" CC, 18		550 ___
1933232	BNSF GE C44-9W Diesel "4173," CC, 18		550 ___
1933233	BNSF non-powered GE C44-9W Diesel "5282", 18		300 ___
1933241	Pilbara Rail GE C44-9W Diesel "7079," CC, 18		550 ___
1933242	Pilbara Rail GE C44-9W Diesel "7097," CC, 18		550 ___
1933243	Pilbara Rail non-powered GE C44-9W Diesel "7098", 18		300 ___
1933251	Quebec, North Shore & Labrador GE C44-9W Diesel "405," CC, 18		550 ___
1933252	Quebec, North Shore & Labrador GE C44-B141 Diesel "407," CC, 18		550 ___
1933253	Quebec, North Shore & Labrador non-powered GE C44-9W Diesel "413", 18		300 ___
1933261	UP (SP Patch) GE C44-9W Diesel "9615," CC, 18		550 ___
1933262	UP (SP Patch) GE C44-9W Diesel "9617," CC, 18		550 ___
1933263	UP (SP Patch) non-powered GE C44-9W Diesel "9647", 18		300 ___
1933271	UP GE C44-9W Diesel w/Cheyenne Service Unit Plaque "9700," CC, 18		550 ___
1933272	UP GE C44-9W Diesel "9650," CC, 18		550 ___
1933273	UP non-powered GE C44-9W Diesel "9654", 18		300 ___
1933281	BNSF GE ES44AC Diesel "6411," CC, 19		600 ___

			Exc	Mint
___	**1933282**	BNSF GE ES44AC Diesel "6425," CC, 19		600
___	**1933283**	BNSF non-powered GE ES44AC Diesel "6438", 19		350
___	**1933291**	CitiRail GE ES44AC Diesel "201," CC, 19		600
___	**1933292**	CitiRail GE ES44AC Diesel "1210," CC, 19		600
___	**1933293**	CitiRail non-powered GE ES44AC Diesel "1212", 19		350
___	**1933301**	GE Demonstrator ES44AC Diesel "2005," CC, 19		600
___	**1933302**	GE Demonstrator ES44AC Diesel "2012," CC, 19		600
___	**1933310**	Iowa Interstate GE ES44AC Diesel "516," CC+B387, 19		600
___	**1933321**	UP GE ES44AC Diesel "7964," CC, 19		600
___	**1933322**	UP GE ES44AC Diesel "8109," CC, 19		600
___	**1933323**	UP non-powered GE ES44AC Diesel "8140", 19		350
___	**1933324**	UP GE ES44AC Diesel, Fantasy Greyhound scheme, "8044," CC, 19		600
___	**1933325**	UP GE ES44AC Diesel, Fantasy 49er scheme, "8149," CC, 19		600
___	**1933326**	UP GE ES44AC Diesel Fantasy "119," CC, 19		600
___	**1933327**	UP GE ES44AC Diesel Fantasy Jupiter "60," CC, 19		600
___	**1933331**	Allegheny RR EMD GP35 Diesel "305," CC, 19		500
___	**1933332**	Allegheny RR EMD GP35 Diesel "306," CC, 19		500
___	**1933341**	AT&SF EMD GP35 Diesel "2835," CC, 19		500
___	**1933342**	AT&SF EMD GP35 Diesel "2858," CC, 19		500
___	**1933343**	AT&SF non-powered EMD GP35 Diesel "2932", 19		300
___	**1933351**	C&NW EMD GP35 Diesel "826," CC, 19		500
___	**1933352**	C&NW EMD GP35 Diesel "830," CC, 19		500
___	**1933353**	C&NW non-powered EMD GP35 Diesel "841", 19		300
___	**1933361**	Conrail EMD GP35 Diesel "2398," CC, 19		500
___	**1933362**	Conrail EMD GP35 Diesel "3630," CC, 19		500
___	**1933363**	Conrail non-powered EMD GP35 Diesel "3692", 19		300
___	**1933371**	BNSF EMD GP35 Diesel "2570," CC, 19		500
___	**1933372**	BNSF EMD GP35 Diesel "2615," CC, 19		500
___	**1933373**	BNSF non-powered EMD GP35 Diesel "2931", 19		300
___	**1933381**	Lycoming Valley EMD GP35 Diesel "5510," CC, 19		500
___	**1933382**	Lycoming Valley EMD GP35 Diesel "5514," CC, 19		500
___	**1933391**	PRR EMD GP35 Diesel "2298," CC, 19		500
___	**1933392**	PRR EMD GP35 Diesel "2333," CC, 19		500
___	**1933393**	PRR non-powered EMD GP35 Diesel "2356", 19		300
___	**1933401**	RF&P EMD GP35 Diesel "131," CC, 19		500
___	**1933402**	RF&P EMD GP35 Diesel "34," CC, 19		500
___	**1933403**	RF&P non-powered EMD GP35 Diesel "138", 19		300
___	**1933411**	Apache RR Alco C-420 Diesel "81," CC, 19		500
___	**1933412**	Apache RR Alco C-420 Diesel "82," CC, 19		500
___	**1933413**	Apache RR non-powered Alco C-420 Diesel "84", 19		300
___	**1933421**	D&H Alco C-420 Diesel "404," CC, 19		500
___	**1933422**	D&H Alco C-420 Diesel "414," CC, 19		500
___	**1933423**	D&H non-powered Alco C-420 Diesel, "204", 19		300
___	**1933430**	D&M Alco C-420 Diesel "976," CC, 19		500
___	**1933441**	Erie Mining Alco C-420 Diesel "7220," CC, 19		500
___	**1933442**	Erie Mining non-powered Alco C-420 Diesel "7221", 19		300
___	**1933451**	L&HR Alco C-420 Diesel "21," CC, 19		500
___	**1933452**	L&HR Alco C-420 Diesel "23," CC, 19		500
___	**1933453**	L&HR non-powered Alco C-420 Diesel"21," CC, 19		300
___	**1933461**	LIRR Alco C-420 Diesel "202," CC, 19		500
___	**1933462**	LIRR Alco C-420 Diesel "218," CC, 19		500
___	**1933471**	P&N Alco C-420 Diesel "2000," CC, 19		500
___	**1933472**	P&N Alco C-420 Diesel "2001," CC, 19		500

		Exc	Mint
1933480	NYS&W Alco C-420 Diesel "2010," CC, 19		500 ___
1933490	Alco Demonstrator FA A-A Diesel Set, CC, 19		900 ___
1933498	Alco Demonstrator FB-2 Unit, CC, 19		450 ___
1933499	Alco Demonstrator FB-2 Unit w/RailSounds, 19		430 ___
1933500	C&NW Alco FA A-A Diesel Set, CC, 19		900 ___
1933508	C&NW Alco FB-2 Unit, CC, 19		450 ___
1933509	C&NW Alco FB-2 Unit w/RailSounds, 19		430 ___
1933510	CP Alco FA-2 A-A Diesel Set "4082/4083," CC, 19		900 ___
1933518	CP Alco FB-2 "4469," CC, 19		450 ___
1933519	CP Alco FB-2 Unit w/RailSounds, 19		430 ___
1933520	LV Alco FA A-A Diesel Set, CC, 19		900 ___
1933528	LV Alco FB-2 Unit, CC, 19		450 ___
1933529	LV Alco FB-2 Unit w/RailSounds, 19		430 ___
1933530	MP Alco FA A-A Diesel Set, CC, 19		900 ___
1933538	MP Alco FB-2 Unit, CC, 19		450 ___
1933539	MP Alco FB-2 Unit w/RailSounds, 19		430 ___
1933540	NYC Alco FA A-A Diesel Set, CC, 19		900 ___
1933548	NYC Alco FB-2 Unit, CC, 19		450 ___
1933549	NYC Alco FB-2 Unit w/RailSounds, 19		430 ___
1933550	SP&S Alco FA A-A Diesel Set, CC, 19		900 ___
1933558	SP&S Alco FB-2 Unit, CC, 19		450 ___
1933559	SP&S Alco FB-2 Unit w/RailSounds, 19		430 ___
1933561	LIRR Alco FA Cab Car "607," CC, 19		430 ___
1933562	LIRR Alco FA Cab Car "609," CC, 19		430 ___
1933563	LIRR Alco FA Cab Car "608," CC, 19		430 ___
1933564	LIRR Alco FA Cab Car "610," CC, 19		430 ___
1933571	Milwaukee Road GE Bi-Polar Electric "E-1," CC, 19		1300 ___
1933572	Milwaukee Road GE Bi-Polar Electric "E-2," CC, 19		1300 ___
1933573	Milwaukee Road GE Bi-Polar Electric "E-3," CC, 19		1300 ___
1933574	Milwaukee Road GE Bi-Polar Electric "E-4," CC, 19		1300 ___
1933575	Milwaukee Road GE Bi-Polar Electric "E-5," CC, 19		1300 ___
1933580	GN GE Bi-Polar Electric "5020," CC, 19		1300 ___
1933590	NH GE Bi-Polar Electric "380," CC, 19		1300 ___
1933600	NYC GE Bi-Polar Electric "300," CC, 19		1300 ___
1933610	PRR GE Bi-Polar Electric "4501," CC, 19		1300 ___
1933620	Polar Express GE Bi-Polar Electric "E-25," CC, 19		1300 ___
1933630	NS GE C44-9W Diesel "8520," CC, 18		550 ___
1934011	BNSF GE ET44AC Diesel "3738," LionChief Plus 2.0, 19		400 ___
1934012	BNSF GE ET44AC Diesel "3776," LionChief Plus 2.0, 19		400 ___
1934021	CSX GE ET44AC Diesel "3277," LionChief Plus 2.0, 19		400 ___
1934022	CSX GE ET44AC Diesel "3291," LionChief Plus 2.0, 19		400 ___
1934031	NS GE ET44AC Diesel "3600," LionChief Plus 2.0, 19		400 ___
1934032	NS GE ET44AC Diesel "3619," LionChief Plus 2.0, 19		400 ___
1934041	UP GE ET44AC Diesel "2645," LionChief Plus 2.0, 19		400 ___
1934042	UP GE ET44AC Diesel "2727," LionChief Plus 2.0, 19		400 ___
1934050	BN Alco RS3 Diesel "4068," LionChief, 19		200 ___
1934060	CNJ Alco RS3 Diesel "1552," LionChief, 19		200 ___
1934070	Delaware-Lackawanna Alco RS3 Diesel "4103," LionChief, 19		200 ___
1934080	UP Alco RS3 Diesel "1219," LionChief, 19		200 ___
1934090	AT&SF EMD FT Diesel A-A Set "123/124," LionChief Plus 2.0, 19		550 ___

			Exc	Mint
___	**1934098**	AT&SF EMD FT B Unit, LionChief Plus 2.0, 19		300
___	**1934100**	GN EMD FT Diesel A-A Set "400/401," LionChief Plus 2.0, 19		550
___	**1934108**	GN EMD FT B Unit, LionChief Plus 2.0, 19		300
___	**1934110**	NYC EMD FT Diesel A-A Set "1603/1604," LionChief Plus 2.0, 19		550
___	**1934118**	NYC EMD FT B Unit, LionChief Plus 2.0, 19		300
___	**1934120**	Texas Special FT Diesel A-A "219/220," LionChief Plus 2.0, 19		550
___	**1934128**	Texas Special EMD FT B Unit, LionChief Plus 2.0, 19		300
___	**1935010**	Area 51 Motorized Trackmobile "51," CC, 19		350
___	**1935020**	Bethlehem Steel Motorized Trackmobile "12," CC, 19		350
___	**1935030**	BN Motorized Trackmobile, CC, 19		350
___	**1935040**	Granite Run Quarries Motorized Trackmobile, CC, 19		350
___	**1935050**	Milwaukee Road Motorized Trackmobile, CC, 19		350
___	**1935060**	PP&L Motorized Trackmobile "16," CC, 19		350
___	**1935070**	AT&SF Motorized Trackmobile "8," CC, 19		350
___	**1935080**	SP Motorized Trackmobile "5," CC, 19		350
___	**1935090**	WWII U.S. War Bonds Trolley, 19		100
___	**1938010**	Mickey Mouse Celebration True Original Boxcar, 18		85
___	**1938030**	Well-Stocked Angela Trotta Thomas Boxcar, 18		85
___	**1938040**	Jupiter Anniversary Boxcar, 19		85
___	**1938050**	Southern Ry. 125th Anniversary Boxcar, 19		85
___	**1938060**	Westinghouse Air Brake 150th Anniversary Boxcar, 19		85
___	**1938100**	Pez Vintage Boxcar, 19		85
___	**1938110**	Looney Tunes Duck Dodgers Boxcar, 19		90
___	**1938120**	Looney Tunes Rabbit Season Boxcar, 19		90
___	**1938130**	Looney Tunes Road Runner Boxcar, 19		90
___	**1938180**	Martin Van Buren Presidential Boxcar, 19		70
___	**1938190**	James Buchanan Presidential Boxcar, 19		70
___	**1938200**	William McKinley Presidential Boxcar, 19		70
___	**1938210**	WWII Kiss the Way Goodbye Boxcar, 19		85
___	**1938220**	WWII Sherman Tank Boxcar, 19		85
___	**1938240**	WWII Liberty Ships Boxcar, 19		85
___	**1938260**	Wings of Angels--Blonde Boxcar, 19		90
___	**1938270**	Wings of Angels--Redhead Boxcar, 19		90
___	**1938280**	Wings of Angels--Brunette Boxcar, 19		90
___	**1938290**	Happy Birthday 2019 Boxcar, 19		95
___	**1938300**	Merry Christmas 2019 Boxcar, 19		90
___	**1938310**	Angela Trotta Thomas Christmas Boxcar, 19		90
___	**1938320**	Personalized Christmas Caboose, 19-20		90
___	**1938340**	Happy Birthday Caboose, 19-20		90
___	**1938370**	UP Anniversary Boxcar "199", 19		85
___	**1942170**	UP Vision Challenger Boxcar 6-pack #1, 18		390
___	**1942180**	UP Vision Challenger Boxcar 6-pack #2, 18		390
___	**1942190**	UP Vision Challenger Boxcar 6-pack #3, 18		390
___	**1942200**	UP Vision Challenger Boxcar 6-pack #4, 18		390
___	**1942210**	UP Vision Challenger Express Boxcar 6-pack, 18		390
___	**2001090**	LCCA 50th Anniversary Convention Car 2-pack, 20 u		300
___	**2001100**	LCCA 50th Anniversary UP Registration Mint Car, 20 u		75
___	**2001110**	LCCA UP ET44AC Diesel "2020" LionChief Plus 2.0, 20 u		700
___	**2001160**	LCCA 50th Anniversary UP Unibody 1-D Tank Car, 20 u		75
___	**2022010**	Granite Run Quarry Steam Freight Set, LionChief Plus 2.0, 19		350
___	**2022020**	Christmas Candies Steam Freight Set, LionChief Plus 2.0, 19		350

		Exc	Mint
2022030	Easter Eggspress Steam Freight Set, LionChief Plus 2.0, 19	350	___
2022040	Manufacturers Railway Alco S-2 Diesel Freight Set, CC, 19	800	___
2022050	George H.W. Bush Funeral Diesel Passenger Train, CC, 19	1200	___
2022060	Pennsylvania Fast Freight Electric Freight Set, LionChief Plus 2.0, 19	700	___
2022070	B&M E8 Diesel Passenger Set, CC, 20	800	___
2022080	Preamble Express Diesel Passenger Set, CC, 20	800	___
2022090	Polar Express Elf Steam Work Train Set, LionChief, 20	450	___
2022100	Pennsylvania Train Master Diesell Freight Set, CC, 20	900	___
2022110	CNJ Red Baron SD40 Diesel Freight Set, CC, 20	850	___
2022120	Lionel 120th Deluxe LionChief Plus 2.0 F3 Diesel Freight Set, CC, 20	1000	___
2022130	SP Vision Stock Express Steam Freight Train Set, CC, 20	2500	___
2022140	North Pole Central Snowflake Limited Steam Freight Set, CC, 20	1000	___
2023010	Strasburg RR Steam Freight Set, LionChief, 19-20	370	___
2023020	Shark Research & Rescue Diesel Freight Set, LionChief, 19	400	___
2023030	Budweiser Delivery ET44 Diesel Freight Set, LionChief, 20	370	___
2023040	Disney Frozen 2 Steam Freight Set, LionChief, 20-24	450	___
2023050	Area 51 ET44 Diesel Freight Set, LionChief, 20, 23	475	___
2023070	Lionel Junction North Pole Central Steam Freight Set, LionChief, 20	330	___
2023080	Christmas Light Express Steam Freight Set, LionChief, 20	430	___
2023090	Witherslack Hall Steam Passenger Set, LionChief, 20	400	___
2023100	GE Tier 4 ET44 Diesel Freight Set, LionChief, 20	400	___
2023110	Toy Story Steam Freight Set, LionChief, 20-24	450	___
2023120	Lionel Lines LionChief Steam Freight Set, 20	300	___
2023130	Star Trek Diesel Freight Set, LionChief, 20	450	___
2023140	Polar Express Steam Passenger Set, LionChief, 20	400	___
2023150	Alaska GP38 Diesel Freight Set, LionChief, 20	400	___
2023160	Baldwin Locomotive Works Steam Freight Set, LionChief, 20	400	___
2023170	Hogwarts Express Steam Passenger Set, LionChief, 20	400	___
2025010	Lighted FasTrack 10" Straight, 4-pack, 20-24	66	___
2025020	Lighted Fastrack 0-36 Curve, 4-pack, 20-24	66	___
2025050	Merry Christmas FasTrack Girder Bridge, 20-24	35	___
2025070	Lighted FasTrack Terminal Track Pack, 20-24	44	___
2025080	Lighted FasTrack Oval Track Pack , 20-24	165	___
2026010	Side Dump Car 4-pack, 19	160	___
2026020	Christmas Side Dump Car 4-pack, 19	160	___
2026030	Easter Eggspress Side Dump Car 4-pack, 19	160	___
2026040	Ely Thomas Lumber Logging Caboose, "1", 19	45	___
2026050	Safety First Logging Caboose, "3", 19	45	___
2026061	AT&SF 40' Plug-Door Refrigerator Car, "14180", 19	90	___
2026062	AT&SF 40' Plug-Door Refrigerator Car, "14193", 19	90	___
2026071	BAR 40' Plug-Door Refrigerator Car, "7728", 19	90	___
2026072	BAR 40' Plug-Door Refrigerator Car, "7777", 19	90	___
2026081	GB&W 40' Plug-Door Refrigerator Car, "21002", 19	90	___
2026082	GB&W 40' Plug-Door Refrigerator Car, "21038", 19	90	___
2026091	PFE 40' Plug-Door Refrigerator Car, "18015", 19	90	___
2026092	PFE 40' Plug-Door Refrigerator Car, "18118", 19	90	___
2026101	Reading 40' Plug-Door Refrigerator Car, "272", 19	90	___
2026102	Reading 40' Plug-Door Refrigerator Car, "278", 19	90	___
2026111	Therm Ice 40' Plug-Door Refrigerator Car, "8907", 19	90	___
2026112	Therm Ice 40' Plug-Door Refrigerator Car, "8910", 19	90	___

	Item	Description	Exc	Mint
___	**2026120**	AT&SF PS-1 Boxcar, "17819" w/FreightSounds, 19		135
___	**2026130**	DT&I PS-1 Boxcar, "14253" w/FreightSounds, 19		135
___	**2026140**	EL PS-1 Boxcar, B195 "74210" w/FreightSounds, 19		135
___	**2026150**	GN PS-1 Boxcar, "19038" w/FreightSounds, 19		135
___	**2026160**	Illinois Terminal PS-1 Boxcar, "8427" w/FreightSounds, 19		135
___	**2026170**	NYC PS-1 Boxcar, "163194" w/FreightSounds, 19		135
___	**2026180**	PC PS-1 Boxcar, "253321" w/FreightSounds, 19		135
___	**2026190**	UP PS-1 Boxcar, "125404" w/FreightSounds, 19		135
___	**2026200**	B&O I-12 BW Caboose, "C2428", 19		110
___	**2026210**	B&O I-12 BW Caboose, "C2406", 19		110
___	**2026220**	B&O I-12 BW Caboose, "C2822", 19		110
___	**2026230**	B&O I-12 BW Caboose, "C2457", 19		110
___	**2026240**	Chessie System I-12 BW Caboose, "902440", 19		110
___	**2026250**	Polar Express I-12 BW Caboose, "C2425", 19		110
___	**2026260**	Anheuser Busch 8,000-Gallon 1-D Tank Car, "4274", 19		80
___	**2026270**	Deep Rock 8,000-Gallon 1-D Tank Car, "6516", 19		80
___	**2026280**	Everett Distilling 8,000-Gallon 1-D Tank Car, "41", 19		80
___	**2026290**	Hercules Powder 8,000-Gallon 1-D Tank Car, "10673", 19		80
___	**2026300**	Independence Energy 8,000-Gallon 1-D Tank Car, "1776", 19		80
___	**2026310**	Sinclair 8,000-Gallon 1-D Tank Car, "13103", 19		80
___	**2026320**	Amtrak Veterans 60' LED Flag Boxcar, "70042", 19		120
___	**2026330**	I Love USA 60' LED Flag Boxcar, 19		120
___	**2026340**	KCS 60' LED Flag Boxcar, "4006", 19		120
___	**2026350**	NS First Responders 60' LED Flag Boxcar, "9-1-1", 19		120
___	**2026360**	NS Veterans 60' LED Flag Boxcar, "6920", 19		120
___	**2026370**	UP 60" LED Flag Boxcar "4141", 19		120
___	**2026380**	UP Transcontinental 60' LED Flag Boxcar, "150", 19		120
___	**2026391**	AT&SF 60' Boxcar, "37639", 19		100
___	**2026392**	AT&SF 60' Boxcar, "37719", 19		100
___	**2026401**	CP 60' Boxcar, "205502", 19		100
___	**2026402**	CP 60' Boxcar, "205525", 19		100
___	**2026411**	DT&I 60' Boxcar, "25525"", 19		100
___	**2026412**	DT&I 60' Boxcar, "25528", 19		100
___	**2026421**	NYC 60' Boxcar, "56451", 19		100
___	**2026422**	NYC 60' Boxcar, "56516", 19		100
___	**2026431**	PRR 60' Boxcar, "11789", 19		100
___	**2026432**	PRR 60' Boxcar, "11813", 19		100
___	**2026441**	PC 60' Boxcar, "274570", 19		100
___	**2026442**	PC 60' Boxcar, "274584", 19		100
___	**2026450**	Chevrolet 60' Boxcar "26450", 19		100
___	**2026460**	Ford 60' Boxcar, "26460", 19		100
___	**2026470**	Area 51 57' Smoking Mechanical Refrigerator Car w/ FreightSounds, 20		200
___	**2026480**	AT&SF 57' Smoking Mechanical Refrigerator Car w/ FreightSounds, 20		200
___	**2026490**	BNSF 57' Smoking Mechanical Refrigerator Car w/ FreightSounds, 20		200
___	**2026500**	Conrail 57' Smoking Mechanical Refrigerator Car w/ FreightSounds, 20		200
___	**2026510**	Halloween Smoking 57' Mechanical Refrigerator Car, 20		200
___	**2026520**	PFE 57' Smoking Mechanical Refrigerator Car w/ FreightSounds, 20		200
___	**2026530**	UP 57' Smoking Mechanical Refrigerator Car w/ FreightSounds, 20		200

		Exc	Mint
2026541	AT&SF "Beer Car" Insulated Boxcar, "625355", 20		100
2026542	AT&SF "Beer Car" Insulated Boxcar, "625380", 20		100
2026551	BN "Beer Car" Insulated Boxcar, "3069", 20		100
2026552	BN "Beer Car" Insulated Boxcar, "3116", 20		100
2026561	BNSF "Beer Car" Insulated Boxcar, "782403" w/Graffiti, 20		110
2026562	BNSF "Beer Car" Insulated Boxcar, "782425", 20		100
2026563	BNSF "Beer Car" Insulated Boxcar, "782483", 20		100
2026571	Conrail "Beer Car" Insulated Boxcar, "376045", 20		100
2026572	Conrail "Beer Car" Insulated Boxcar, "376142", 20		100
2026581	Coors "Beer Car" Insulated Boxcar, "24", 20		100
2026582	Coors "Beer Car" Insulated Boxcar, "26", 20		100
2026591	Manufacturers Ry. "Beer Car" Insulated Boxcar, "2520", 20		100
2026592	Manufacturers Ry. "Beer Car" Insulated Boxcar, "2540", 20		100
2026601	SP "Beer Car" Insulated Boxcar, "691783" w/Graffiti, 20		110
2026602	SP "Beer Car" Insulated Boxcar, "691729", 20		100
2026603	SP "Beer Car" Insulated Boxcar, "691745", 20		100
2026611	AT&SF 50' Flatcar, "91156" w/20' Trailers, 20		120
2026612	AT&SF 50' Flatcar, "91220" w/20' Trailers, 20		120
2026621	DT&I 50' Flatcar, "911" w/20' Ford Trailers, 20		120
2026622	DT&I 50' Flatcar, "924" w/20' Ford Trailers, 20		120
2026631	PRR 50' Flatcar, "469469" w/Mason Dixon Trailers, 20		120
2026632	PRR 50' Flatcar, "469625" w/Mason Dixon Trailers, 20		120
2026641	Trailer Train 50' Flatcar, "475231" w/Hennis Trailers, 20		120
2026642	Trailer Train 50' Flatcar, "475293" w/Hennis Trailers, 20		120
2026651	UP 50' Flatcar, "53085" w/Merchants Trailers, 20		120
2026652	UP 50' Flatcar, "53091" w/Merchants Trailers, 20		120
2026661	North Pole Central 50' Flatcar, "2024" w/20' Sled-Ex Trailers, 20		120
2026662	North Pole Central 50' Flatcar, "2025" w/20' Sled-Ex Trailers, 20		120
2026671	Polar Express 50' Flatcar, "122420" w/20' Trailers, 20		125
2026672	Polar Express 50' Flatcar, "122520" w/20' Trailers, 20		125
2026680	Polar Express Elf Work Train, 4-pack, 20		200
2026690	Buffalo, Rochester & Pittsburgh 2-bay Hopper, 3-pack, 20		280
2026700	Blue Coal 2-bay Hopper, 3-pack, 20		280
2026710	NYO&W 2-bay Hopper, 3-pack, 20		280
2026720	Rutland 2-bay Hopper, 3-pack, 20		280
2026730	Waddell Coal 2-bay Hopper, 3-pack, 20		280
2026741	CB&Q Friendship Train PS-1 Boxcar, "36262", 0		75
2026742	C&NW Friendship Train PS-1 Boxcar, "143576", 20		75
2026743	L&N Friendship Train PS-1 Boxcar, "16576", 20		75
2026744	NYC Friendship Train PS-1 Boxcar, "161500", 20		75
2026745	SP Friendship Train PS-1 Boxcar, "97994", 20		75
2026746	UP Friendship Train PS-1 Boxcar, "187989", 20		75
2026750	Chateau Martin Wine Car, "132", 20		100
2026760	Cloverland Dairy Milk Car, "101", 20		100
2026770	D&RGW Milk Car, "1612", 20		100
2026780	Frisco Milk Car, "5009", 20		100
2026790	Reid Ice Cream Milk Car, "103", 20		100
2026800	Scenic Citrus Milk Car, "977", 20		100
2026810	Armour Vision Stockcar 3-pack w/Sound Car, 20		400
2026820	AT&SF Vision Stockcar 3-pack w/Sound Car, 20		400
2026830	CP Vision Stockcar 3-pack w/Sound Car, 20		400

			Exc	Mint
___	**2026840**	CB&Q Vision Stockcar 3-pack w/Sound Car, 20		400
___	**2026850**	C&NW Vision Stockcar 3-pack w/Sound Car, 20		400
___	**2026860**	MKT Vision Stockcar 3-pack w/Sound Car, 20		400
___	**2026870**	PRR N5 Caboose, "476998", 20		100
___	**2026880**	PRR N5 Caboose, "477714", 20		100
___	**2026890**	PRR N5 Caboose, "492418", 20		100
___	**2026900**	PC N5 Caboose, "22838", 20		100
___	**2026910**	Lionel Lines NE Caboose, "120", 20		115
___	**2026930**	NYC Wood Caboose, "19020" w/CupolaCam, 20		190
___	**2026940**	NYC Safety Wood Caboose, "18906" w/CupolaCam, 20		190
___	**2026950**	Ford 2-bay Hopper, 3-pack, 20		280
___	**2026960**	AT&SF Vision Refrigerator Car 3-pack, 20		350
___	**2026970**	PFE Vision Refrigerator Car 3-pack, 20		350
___	**2026980**	MDT Vision Refrigerator Car 3-pack, 20		350
___	**2026990**	PRR Vision Refrigerator Car 3-pack, 20		350
___	**2027011**	Christmas Disconnect Passenger Car, Baggage, 19		45
___	**2027012**	Christmas Disconnect Passenger Car, Coach, 19		45
___	**2027013**	Christmas Disconnect Passenger Car, Diner, 19		45
___	**2027014**	Christmas Disconnect Passenger Car, Sleeper, 19		45
___	**2027015**	Christmas Disconnect Passenger Car, Observation, 19		45
___	**2027021**	NYC Disconnect Passenger Car, Baggage, 19		45
___	**2027022**	NYC Disconnect Passenger Car, Coach, 19		45
___	**2027023**	NYC Disconnect Passenger Car, Diner, 19		45
___	**2027024**	NYC Disconnect Passenger Car, Sleeper, 19		45
___	**2027025**	NYC Disconnect Passenger Car, Observation, 19		45
___	**2027031**	PRR Disconnect Passenger Car, Baggage, 19		45
___	**2027032**	PRR Disconnect Passenger Car, Coach, 19		45
___	**2027033**	PRR Disconnect Passenger Car, Diner, 19		45
___	**2027034**	PRR Disconnect Passenger Car, Sleeper, 19		45
___	**2027035**	PRR Disconnect Passenger Car, Observation, 19		45
___	**2027041**	D&RGW Disconnect Passenger Car, Baggage , 19		45
___	**2027042**	D&RGW Disconnect Passenger Car, Coach, 19		45
___	**2027043**	D&RGW Disconnect Passenger Car, Diner, 19		45
___	**2027044**	D&RGW Disconnect Passenger Car, Sleeper, 19		45
___	**2027045**	D&RGW Disconnect Passenger Car, Observation, 19		45
___	**2027051**	AT&SF Disconnect Passenger Car, Baggage , 19		45
___	**2027052**	AT&SF Disconnect Passenger Car, Coach, 19		45
___	**2027053**	AT&SF Disconnect Passenger Car, Diner, 19		45
___	**2027054**	AT&SF Disconnect Passenger Car, Sleeper, 19		45
___	**2027055**	AT&SF Disconnect Passenger Car, Observation, 19		45
___	**2027061**	SP Disconnect Passenger Car, Baggage, 19		45
___	**2027062**	SP Disconnect Passenger Car, Coach, 19		45
___	**2027063**	SP Disconnect Passenger Car, Diner, 19		45
___	**2027064**	SP Disconnect Passenger Car, Sleeper, 19		45
___	**2027065**	SP Disconnect Passenger Car, Observation, 19		45
___	**2027070**	AT&SF California Limited 18" Passenger Car 2-pack, A, 19		400
___	**2027080**	AT&SF California Limited 18" Passenger Car 2-pack, B, 19		400
___	**2027090**	AT&SF California Limited 18" Passenger Car 2-pack, C, 19		400
___	**2027100**	AT&SF California Limited 18" Diner "1406" w/StationSounds, 19		330
___	**2027110**	AT&SF Shadow Line 18" Passenger Car 2-pack, 19		400
___	**2027120**	Alaska RR 21" Passenger Car 4-pack, 19		720
___	**2027130**	Alaska RR 21" Passenger Car 2-pack, 19		420

		Exc	Mint
2027140	Alaska RR 21" Diner, "400" w/StationSounds, 19		330 ___
2027160	Alaska RR VistaVision Camera Dome Car, "501", 19		330 ___
2027170	UP Challenger 21" Passenger Car Expansion 2-pack, 3, 19		360 ___
2027180	NS Executive Train 21" Passenger Car 4-pack, 19		770 ___
2027190	NS Executive Train 21" Passenger Car 2-pack, 19		360 ___
2027200	NS 21" Diner, "Delaware," w/StationSounds, 19		340 ___
2027210	Philadelphia & Reading Observation, 19-20		85 ___
2027220	Ferdinand Magellan Observation, 19		85 ___
2027230	UP Excursion 21" Passenger Car Expansion 2-pack, 3, 19		360 ___
2027240	UP Excursion 21" Passenger Car Expansion 2-pack, 4, 19		360 ___
2027250	Amtrak VistaVision Dome Car, "9463", 19		330 ___
2027260	UP Excursion VistaVision Dome Car, "Colorado Eagl", 19		330 ___
2027270	UP Challenger VistaVision Dome Car, "7005", 19		330 ___
2027280	Auto-Train VistaVision Dome Car, "706", 19		330 ___
2027290	PRR VistaVision Dome Car, "Catenary View", 19		330 ___
2027300	N&W VistaVision Dome Car, "1613", 19		330 ___
2027310	Southern VistaVision Dome Car, "1613", 19		330 ___
2027330	Friendship Train 18" Sleeper 2-pack, 20		400 ___
2027340	American Freedom Train 18" Passenger Car 2-pack, 1, 20		380 ___
2027350	American Freedom Train 18" Passenger Car 2-pack, 2, 20		380 ___
2027360	Chessie Steam Special Passenger Car 2-pack, 1, 20		450 ___
2027370	Chessie Steam Special Passenger Car 2-pack, 2, 20		450 ___
2027380	Chessie Steam Special Passenger Car 2-pack, 3, 20		450 ___
2027390	Chessie Steam Special Passenger Car 2-pack, 4, 20		450 ___
2027400	SP Golden State 21" Passenger Car 4-pack, 20		730 ___
2027410	SP Golden State 21" Passenger Car 2-pack, 20		360 ___
2027420	SP Golden State 21" Diner w/StationSounds, 20		360 ___
2027430	Reading 18" Passsenger Car 2-pack, 1, 20		380 ___
2027440	Reading 18" Passsenger Car 2-pack, 2, 20		380 ___
2027450	Reading 18" Passsenger Car 2-pack, 3, 20		380 ___
2027460	B&M 18" Passenger Car 2-pack, 20		380 ___
2027470	Polar Express 18" Hobo Passenger Car w/Black Roof, 20-24		240 ___
2027480	Polar Express 18" Hobo Passenger Car w/Snowy Roof, 20-22		240 ___
2027490	PRR/AT&SF 21" Passsenger Car 2-pack, 20		400 ___
2027500	PRR/UP 21" Passsenger Car 2-pack, 20		400 ___
2027510	PRR/MP 21" Passsenger Car 2-pack, 20		400 ___
2027520	SP Lark 21" Passenger Car 4-pack, 20		730 ___
2027530	SP Lark 21" Passenger Car 2-pack, 20		360 ___
2027540	SP Lark 21" Diner, w/StationSounds , 20		460 ___
2027550	SP Daylight 18" Heavyweight Passenger Car 2-pack, A, 20		400 ___
2027560	SP Daylight 18" Heavyweight Passenger Car 2-pack, B, 20		400 ___
2027570	SP Daylight 18" Heavyweight Passenger Car 2-pack, C, 20		400 ___
2027580	UP 21" Baggage Car, "Promontory", 19		180 ___
2027590	SP Penn-Golden State 21" Passenger Car 2-pack, 20		360 ___
2027600	PRR/Frisco 21" Passsenger Car 2-pack, 20		400 ___
2027610	SP Daylight 18" Heavyweight Diner w/StationSounds, 20		330 ___
2027620	Chessie Steam Special Dome Car w/StationSounds, 20		400 ___
2027630	Lionel Lines 21" VistaVision Dome Car, "Chesterfield", 20		340 ___
2027640	SP Cities 21" VistaVision Dome Car, "3601", 20		340 ___
2027650	SP Daylight VistaVision Dome Car, 20		340 ___
2027660	SP Golden State 21" VistaVision Dome Car, 20		340 ___
2027670	SP Lark 21" VistaVision Dome Car, 20		340 ___

			Exc	Mint
___	2027680	GN 21" VistaVision Dome Car, "1325", 20		340
___	2027690	Lionel Lines Vision 21" Baggage, "Madison", 20		350
___	2027700	SP Vision Baggage Car, 20		350
___	2027710	SP Vision Baggage Car, Daylight, 20		350
___	2027720	SP Vision Baggage Car, Golden State, 20		350
___	2027730	SP Vision Baggage Car, Lark, 20		350
___	2027740	REA Vision Baggage Car, 20		350
___	2027750	Lionel Lines 21" Passenger Car 4-pack, 20		730
___	2027760	Lionel Lines 21" Diner, "Mount Clemens," w/StationSounds, 20		330
___	2027770	Milwaukee Road 21" VistaVision Dome Car, "60", 20		340
___	2027780	NYC 21" VistaVision Dome Car, "Hudson Vista", 20		340
___	2027790	NS 21" VistaVision Dome Car, "50", 20		340
___	2027800	Polar Express Skiing Hobo Observation w/Black Roof, 20		85
___	2027810	Great Central Pullman Coach, 20		80
___	2028010	George H.W. Bush Funeral Mint Car, 19-22		95
___	2028020	Shark Aquarium Car, "23020", 19		100
___	2028030	PRR Flatcar w/Trailers, "925030", 19		85
___	2028040	PRR Walking Brakeman Car, "24095", 19, 22		110
___	2028060	Ford Auto Rack, "19032020", 20		85
___	2028090	Finding Nemo Aquarium Car, 20		100
___	2028100	Inside Out Memory Ball Transport Car, 20-23		100
___	2028110	Polar Express Elf Bobbing Car, 20-23		90
___	2028120	Polar Express Hot Cocoa Car, 20-22		200
___	2028130	Olaf's Personal Flurry 1-D Tank Car, 20-22		90
___	2028150	Monster Containment Car, 20		80
___	2028160	Jack O' Lantern Flatcar, 20		80
___	2028170	Thomas & Friends Nia Boxcar, 20		75
___	2028180	Thomas & Friends Rebecca Boxcar, 20		75
___	2028190	Thomas & Friends Gordon Boxcar, 20		75
___	2028200	Christmas Boxcar 2020, 20		65
___	2028210	Christmas Music Boxcar 2020, 20		80
___	2028220	Anheuser Busch Brewing Refrigerator Car, 20-23		90
___	2028230	Enjoy Budweiser Refrigerator Car, 20-23		90
___	2028240	Anheuser Busch Cold Storage Car, 20		90
___	2028250	Miller High Life Woodside Refrigerator Car, 20-23		90
___	2028260	Coors Banquet Woodside Refrigerator Car, 20-23		90
___	2028270	Batman vs. The Joker Duel Car, 20-22		90
___	2028280	Batman Shark Repellent Unibody 1-D Tank Car, 20		75
___	2028290	Batman Hi-Cube Boxcar, 20		80
___	2028300	Christmas Light Express Boxcar, "84746", 20-23		100
___	2028310	Best of Lionel Milk Car, 20		180
___	2028320	Alien Radioactive Flatcar, 20		85
___	2028340	Angela Trotta Thomas Gondola w/Presents and Trees, 20		80
___	2028350	Angela Trotta Thomas Christmas Boxcar, 20		75
___	2028360	Mickey & Friends Christmas 1-D Tank Car, 20		70
___	2028380	John Deere Flatcar, "28380" w/3 Tractors, 20		95
___	2028410	National Lampoon's Christmas Vacation 30th Anniversary Lighted Boxcar, 20		90
___	2028430	Thomas & Friends 75th Birthday Music Car, 20		80
___	2028440	A Christmas Story Leg Lamp Boxcar, 20		75
___	2028450	Angela Trotta Thomas Christmas Hopper, 20		65
___	2028460	Winter Wonderland Wintry Mix 1-D Tank Car, 20		80

		Exc	Mint
2028470	Polar Express Present Mint Car, 20-23		100 ___
2028480	Angela Trotta Thomas 120th Anniversary Boxcar, 20		75 ___
2028500	Lionel Ale 1-D Tank Car, 20		75 ___
2028510	Thomas Kinkade Santa's Special Delivery Boxcar, "28510", 20		75 ___
2028520	Romulan Ale 1-D Tank Car, 20		80 ___
2028530	Tribble Transport Car, 20		80 ___
2028540	Captain Kirk Boxcar, 20		75 ___
2028550	Captain Picard Boxcar, 20		75 ___
2028570	Pizza Planet Aquarium Car, 20-23		120 ___
2029010	85th Anniversary Gateman, 20		110 ___
2029020	Bluetooth Speaker Bandstand, 20		275 ___
2029030	Next Stop, Santa Passenger Station, 20		100 ___
2029040	End of the Line Passenger Station, 20-23		110 ___
2029050	Polar Express Passsenger Station, 20-24		140 ___
2029060	Chuga Chuga Brew Thru Bar, 20		90 ___
2029160	J Tower Switch Tower, 20		80 ___
2029170	Halloween Freight Station, 20		125 ___
2029180	Christmas Operating Freight Station, 20		125 ___
2029200	Area 51 Search Tower, 20		100 ___
2029210	Santa Tracker Command Tower, 20		100 ___
2029220	Roasted Chestnuts Retreat, 20		125 ___
2029230	Taco Stand, 20		125 ___
2029240	Fake News Stand, 20, 22	125	160 ___
2029250	Strasburg RR Groffs Grove Pep Platform, 19		45 ___
2029260	Strasburg RR East Strasburg Station, 20		100 ___
2029270	Lionelville Freight Station, 20		125 ___
2029280	Area 1 Souvenir Stand, 20		125 ___
2030010	Strasburg RR Cherry Hill Station, 20		20 ___
2030050	Stars & Stripes Billboard, 3-pack, 19-22		25 ___
2030060	Fun with Puns Billboard, 3-pack, 19		20 ___
2030070	Strasburg RR Billboard 3-pack, 20		20 ___
2030130	Crossing Shanty, 20-22		20 ___
2030140	Polar Express Elf Warming Shack, 3 pack, 20-23		60 ___
2030150	Polar Express Barrel Shed, 20, 23		25 ___
2030160	Winter Wonderland Barrel Shed, 20-24		25 ___
2030170	Anheuser Busch Barrel Shed, 20-22		25 ___
2030180	City Park People, 6-pack, 20		23 ___
2030190	Street People, 6-pack, 20		23 ___
2030200	Walking Figures, 6-pack, 20		23 ___
2030210	City People, 6-pack, 20		23 ___
2030220	Highway Lamp Single, 3-pack, 20		27 ___
2030230	Highway Lamp Double, 2-pack, 20-22		30 ___
2030240	Construction Signs, 5-pack, 20-23		9 ___
2030250	Halloween Signs, 5-pack, 20		8 ___
2030260	Christmas Signs, 5-pack, 20-24		9 ___
2030270	Santa's Elves Houses, 3-pack, 20		60 ___
2031010	B&A 4-6-6T, "400," CC, 19		1100 ___
2031020	NYC 4-6-6T, "1297," CC, 19		1100 ___
2031030	CN 4-6-6T, "51," CC, 19		1100 ___
2031040	CNJ 4-6-6T, "231," CC, 19		1100 ___
2031050	DL&W 4-6-6T, "428," CC, 19		1100 ___
2031060	IC 4-6-6T, "205," CC, 19		1100 ___

			Exc	Mint
___	**2031070**	NH 4-6-6T, "1850," CC, 19		1100
___	**2031080**	US Army Transportation Corps 4-6-6T, "1945," CC, 19		1100
___	**2031090**	B&O 2-8-8-4 EM-1, "7609," CC, 19		1700
___	**2031100**	B&O 2-8-8-4 EM-1, "7600," CC, 19		1700
___	**2031110**	D&RGW 2-8-8-4 EM-1, "224," CC, 19		1700
___	**2031120**	DM&IR 2-8-8-4 EM-1, "220," CC, 19		1700
___	**2031130**	NP 2-8-8-4 EM-1, "5011," CC, 19		1700
___	**2031140**	UP 2-8-8-4 EM-1, "4050," CC, 19		1700
___	**2031150**	WM 2-8-8-4 EM-1, "1213," CC, 19		1700
___	**2031160**	AT&SF 4-8-4 Northern, "3751," CC, 19		1600
___	**2031170**	AT&SF 4-8-4 Northern, "3759," CC, 19		1600
___	**2031180**	AT&SF 4-8-4 Northern, "3757," CC, 19		1600
___	**2031190**	AT&SF 4-8-4 Northern, "3765," CC, 19		1600
___	**2031200**	ACL 4-8-4S Northern, "1800," CC, 19		1600
___	**2031210**	Rock Island 4-8-4S Northern, "5100" CC, 19		1600
___	**2031220**	D&RGW 4-8-4S Northern, "1802," CC, 19		1600
___	**2031230**	MP 4-8-4S Northern, "2202," CC, 19		1600
___	**2031240**	Frisco 4-8-4S Northern, "4500," CC, 19		1600
___	**2031250**	Frisco 4-8-4S Northern, "4524," CC, 19		1600
___	**2031261**	UP 4-8-8-4 Big Boy, "4014," Excursion Version, CC, 19		2200
___	**2031262**	UP 4-8-8-4 Big Boy, "4005," Oil Tender, CC, 19		2200
___	**2031263**	UP 4-8-8-4 Big Boy, "4012," Greyhound, CC, 19		2200
___	**2031271**	Reading 4-8-4 T1, "2107," CC, 20		1700
___	**2031272**	Reading 4-8-4 T1, "2111," CC, 20		1700
___	**2031281**	Reading 4-8-4 T1, Rambles, "2100," CC, 20		1700
___	**2031282**	Reading 4-8-4 T1, Rambles, "2101," CC, 20		1700
___	**2031290**	Reading, Blue Mountain & Northern 4-8-4 T1, "2102," CC, 20		1700
___	**2031300**	Reading, Blue Mountain & Northern 4-8-4 T1, "2102," CC, 20		1700
___	**2031310**	Conrail 4-8-4 T1, "2101," CC, 20		1700
___	**2031320**	American Freedom Train Vision 4-8-4 T1, "1," CC, 20		1700
___	**2031330**	PRR B6sb 0-4-0, "525," CC, 20		700
___	**2031340**	PRR B6sb 0-4-0, "660," CC, 20		700
___	**2031351**	PRR B6sb 0-4-0, "711," CC, 20		700
___	**2031352**	PRR B6sb 0-4-0, "1644," CC, 20		700
___	**2031360**	AT&SF B6sb 0-4-0, "2101," CC, 20		700
___	**2031370**	Bethlehem Steet B6sb 0-4-0, "1904," CC, 20		700
___	**2031380**	Milwaukee Road B6sb 0-4-0, "1534," CC, 20		700
___	**2031390**	GN B6sb 0-4-0, "90," CC, 20		700
___	**2031400**	Lionel Lines Vision 4-8-4 GS-4, "120," CC, 20		2000
___	**2031411**	SP Vision 4-8-4 GS-1 Brass Hybrid, "4470," CC, 20		2200
___	**2031412**	SP Vision 4-8-4 GS-1 Brass Hybrid, "4471," CC, 20		2200
___	**2031421**	SP Vision 4-8-4 GS-1 Brass Hybrid, "708," CC, 20		2200
___	**2031422**	SP Vision 4-8-4 GS-1 Brass Hybrid, "4403," CC, 20		2200
___	**2031430**	Vision 4-8-4 GS-1 Brass Hybrid Pilot, "9999," CC, 20		2200
___	**2031440**	SP Vision 4-8-4 GS-2 Black, "4410," CC, 20		2000
___	**2031450**	SP Vision 4-8-4 GS-2 Black, "4411," CC, 20		2000
___	**2031460**	SP Vision 4-8-4 GS-2 Daylight, "4412," CC, 20		2000
___	**2031470**	SP Vision 4-8-4 GS-2 Lark, "4414," CC, 20		2000
___	**2031480**	SP Vision 4-8-4 GS-3 Daylight, "4416," CC, 20		2000
___	**2031500**	SP Vision 4-8-4 GS-3 Daylight, "4423," CC, 20		2000
___	**2031510**	SP Vision 4-8-4 GS-3 Golden State, "4428," CC, 20		2000
___	**2031520**	SP Lines Vision 4-8-4 GS-4 Daylight, "4449," CC, 20		2000

		Exc	Mint
2031530	SP Vision 4-8-4 GS-4 Daylight, "4449," CC, 20		2000
2031540	American Freedom Train Vision 4-8-4 GS-4, "4449," CC, 20		2000
2031550	BNSF Vision 4-8-4 GS-4, "4449," CC, 20		2000
2031560	SP Vision 4-8-4 GS-4 Daylight, "4439," CC, 20		2000
2031570	SP Lines Vision 4-8-4 GS-5 Daylight, "4458," CC, 20		2000
2031580	SP Vision 4-8-4 GS-5 Daylight, "4459," CC, 20		2000
2031590	SP Lines Vision 4-8-4 GS-6, "4460," CC, 20		2000
2031600	SP Vision 4-8-4 GS-6, "4462," CC, 20		2000
2031610	SP Vision 4-8-4 GS-6, "4467," CC, 20		2000
2031620	WP Vision 4-8-4 GS-6, "481," CC, 20		2000
2031630	WP Vision 4-8-4 GS-6, "486," CC, 20		2000
2031640	Chessie Steam Special Vision GS-4, "4449," CC, 20		2000
2031650	Chessie Steam Special Auxiliary Water Tender w/RailSounds, CC, 20		350
2031660	Conrail Auxiliary Water Tender w/RailSounds, CC, 20		350
2031671	Freedom Train 1975 Auxiliary Water Tender w/RailSounds, CC, 20		350
2031672	Freedom Train 1976 Auxiliary Water Tender w/RailSounds, CC, 20		350
2031673	American Freedom Train Auxiliary Tender, "4449," CC, 20		350
2031680	SP Daylight Auxiliary Water Tender w/RailSounds, CC, 20		350
2031690	Black Auxiliary Water Tender w/RailSounds, CC, 20		350
2031700	UP 4-8-8-4 Big Boy, "4014," First Run Edition, CC, 19		2200
2032010	AT&SF 0-6-0T, "95," LionChief Plus 2.0, 19-20		250
2032020	Brooklyn Eastern District 0-6-0T, "15," LionChief Plus 2.0, 19-20		250
2032030	Bethlehem Steel 0-6-0T, "76," LionChief Plus 2.0, 19-20		250
2032040	D&RGW 0-6-0T, "27," LionChief Plus 2.0, 19-20		250
2032050	PRR 0-6-0T, "2295," LionChief Plus 2.0, 19-20		250
2032100	C&O Lionmaster 2-6-6-6 Allegheny, "1601," CC, 20		1100
2032110	C&O Lionmaster 2-6-6-6 Allegheny, "1607," CC, 20		1100
2032120	C&O Lionmaster 2-6-6-6 Allegheny, "1611," CC, 20		1100
2032130	Virginian Lionmaster 2-6-6-6 Allegheny, "906," CC, 20		1100
2032200	AT&SF 0-8-0, "729," LionChief, 20		220
2032210	GN 0-8-0, "831," LionChief, 20		220
2032220	Reading 0-8-0, "1493," LionChief, 20		220
2032230	SP 0-8-0, "1849," LionChief, 20		220
2033011	B&LE SD38 Diesel, "861," CC, 19		600
2033012	B&LE SD38 Diesel, "863," CC, 19		600
2033021	Conrail SD38 Diesel, "6929," CC, 19		600
2033022	Conrail SD38 Diesel, "6957," CC, 19		600
2033031	CSX SD38 Diesel, "2461," CC, 19		600
2033032	CSX SD38 Diesel, "2463," CC, 19		600
2033041	GTW SD38 Diesel, "6252," CC, 19		600
2033042	GTW SD38 Diesel, "6254," CC, 19		600
2033051	NS SD38 Diesel, "3806," CC, 19		600
2033052	NS SD38 Diesel, "3808," CC, 19		600
2033061	Rail Logix SD38 Diesel, "2001,v CC, 19		600
2033062	Rail Logix SD38 Diesel, "2002," CC, 19		600
2033070	AT&SF Alco S-4 Diesel Switcher, "1527," CC, 19		500
2033080	EL Alco S-4 Diesel Switcher, "513," CC, 19		500
2033090	Ford Alco S-2 Diesel Switcher, "10013," CC, 19		500
2033100	Morristown & Erie Alco S-2 Diesel Switcher, "14," CC, 19		500
2033110	NYS&W Alco S-2 Diesel Switcher, "206," CC, 19		500

			Exc	Mint
___	2033120	Nickel Plate Road Alco S-4 Diesel Switcher, "79," CC, 19		500
___	2033130	NP Alco S-4 Diesel Switcher, "717," CC, 19		500
___	2033140	Northern Pacific Terminal Alco S-2 Diesel Switcher, "40," CC, 19		500
___	2033150	Portland Terminal Alco S-2 Diesel Switcher, "1001," CC, 19		500
___	2033160	SP Alco S-4 Diesel Switcher, "1820," CC, 19		500
___	2033170	Youngstown Sheet & Tube Alco S-2 Diesel Switcher, "1001," CC, 19		500
___	2033181	CITX SD70M-2 Diesel, "140," CC, 19		600
___	2033182	CITX SD70M-2 Diesel, "141," CC, 19		600
___	2033183	CITX SD70M-2 Diesel, "142,"unpowered, 19		300
___	2033191	EMD SD70M-2 Diesel, "74," CC, 19		600
___	2033192	EMD SD70M-2 Diesel, "75," CC, 19		600
___	2033193	EMD SD70M-2 Diesel, "76," unpowered, 19		300
___	2033201	FEC SD70M-2 Diesel, "104," CC, 19		600
___	2033202	FEC SD70M-2 Diesel, "105," CC, 19		600
___	2033203	FEC SD70M-2 Diesel, "106," unpowered, 19		300
___	2033211	NS SD70M-2 Diesel, "2717," CC, 19		600
___	2033212	NS SD70M-2 Diesel, "2731," CC, 19		600
___	2033213	NS SD70M-2 Diesel, "2778," unpowered, 19		300
___	2033221	P&W SD70M-2 Diesel, "4301," CC, 19		600
___	2033222	P&W SD70M-2 Diesel, "4302," CC, 19		600
___	2033231	Vermont Ry. SD70M-2 Diesel, "431," CC, 19		600
___	2033232	Vermont Ry. SD70M-2 Diesel, "432," CC, 19		600
___	2033240	Alaska RR F7 A-A set, CC, 19		900
___	2033248	Alaska RR F7B Diesel, "1503," CC, 19		450
___	2033249	Alaska RR F7B SuperBass Diesel, "1517," CC, 19		440
___	2033250	BN F7 Diesel A-A set, CC, 19		900
___	2033258	BN F7B Diesel, "761," CC, 19		450
___	2033259	BN F7B SuperBass Diesel, "741," CC, 19		440
___	2033260	CGW F7 Diesel A-A set, CC, 19		900
___	2033268	CGW F7B Diesel, "114-B," CC, 19		450
___	2033269	CGW F7B SuperBass Diesel, "114-0," CC, 19		440
___	2033270	D&RGW F7 Diesel A-A set, CC, 19		900
___	2033278	D&RGW F7B Diesel, "5652," CC, 19		450
___	2033279	D&RGW F7B SuperBass Diesel, "5653," CC, 19		440
___	2033280	NS F9 Diesel A-A set, CC, 19		900
___	2033288	NS F7B Diesel, "4275," CC, 19		450
___	2033289	NS F7B SuperBass Diesel, "4276," CC, 19		440
___	2033290	PC F7 Diesel A-A set, CC, 19		900
___	2033298	PC F7B Diesel, "3460," CC, 19		450
___	2033299	PC F7B SuperBass Diesel, "712," CC, 19		440
___	2033300	Cotton Belt F7 Diesel A-A set, CC, 19		900
___	2033308	Cotton Belt F7B Diesel, "926," CC, 19		450
___	2033309	Cotton Belt F7B SuperBass Diesel, "928," CC, 19		440
___	2033310	UP SD70ACe Diesel, "4141," CC, 19		600
___	2033319	UP SD70ACe Diesel, "4141," unpowered, 19		300
___	2033321	UP SD70AH Diesel, "9096," CC, 19		600
___	2033322	UP SD70AH Diesel, "9069," CC, 19		600
___	2033323	UP SD70AH Diesel, "9088," CC, 19		600
___	2033330	KCS SD70ACe Diesel, "4006," CC, 19		600
___	2033340	Amtrak E8 AA Diesel Set, "4316/249," CC, 20		1000
___	2033350	DL&W E8 AA Diesel Set, "810/811," CC, 20		1000

Item	Description	Exc	Mint
2033360	NYC E8 AA Diesel Set, "4038/4041," CC, 20		1000
2033370	PRR E8 AA Diesel Set, "5711/5809," CC, 20		1000
2033380	Southern E8 AA Diesel Set, "6901/6914," CC, 20		1000
2033390	Frisco E8 AA Diesel Set, "2003/2006," CC, 20		1000
2033401	DL&W Train Master Diesel, "853," CC, 20		550
2033402	DL&W Train Master Diesel, "854," CC, 20		550
2033411	FM Demonstrator Train Master Diesel, "TM-3," CC, 20		550
2033412	FM Demonstrator Train Master Diesel, "TM-4," CC, 20		550
2033420	PRR Train Master Diesel, "8703," CC, 20		550
2033430	Donald Trump SD70ACe diesel "4545," CC, 20		550
2033431	Southern Train Master Diesel, "6301," CC, 20		550
2033432	Southern Train Master Diesel, "6302," CC, 20		550
2033441	SP Train Master Diesel, "4800," CC, 20		550
2033442	SP Train Master Diesel, "4812," CC, 20		550
2033451	Virginian Train Master Diesel, "55," CC, 20		550
2033452	Virginian Train Master Diesel, "60," CC, 20		550
2033461	CP SD40 Diesel, "740," CC, 20		550
2033462	CP SD40 Diesel, "752," CC, 20		550
2033471	CNJ SD40 Diesel, "3064," CC, 20		550
2033472	CNJ SD40 Diesel, "3069," CC, 20		550
2033481	C&O SD40 Diesel, "7452," CC, 20		550
2033482	C&O SD40 Diesel, "7464," CC, 20		550
2033490	CSX SD40 Diesel, "4617," CC, 20		550
2033501	C&NW SD40 Diesel, "867," CC, 20		550
2033502	C&NW SD40 Diesel, "876," CC, 20		550
2033520	BNSF GE ES44AC Diesel, "5815," CC, 20		550
2033530	CSX GE ES44AC Diesel, "3010," CC, 20		313
2033539	CSX GE ES44AC Diesel, "3010," unpowered, 20		350
2033541	KCS de Mexico GE ES44AC Diesel, "4748," CC, 20		550
2033542	KCS de Mexico GE ES44AC Diesel, "4762," CC, 20		550
2033549	KCS de Mexico GE ES44AC Diesel, "4764," unpowered, 20		350
2033551	SVTX GE ES44AC Diesel, "1912," CC, 20		550
2033552	SVTX GE ES44AC Diesel, "1982," CC, 20		550
2033559	SVTX GE ES44AC Diesel, "1986," unpowered, 20		350
2033560	UP GE ES44AC Diesel, "8003," CC, 20		550
2033571	Christmas ES44AC Diesel, "1224," CC, 20		550
2033572	Christmas ES44AC Diesel, "1225," CC, 20		550
2033590	UP SD70ACe Diesel, "8937," CC, 19		600
2033600	UP SD70AH+B86 Diesel, "1111," CC, 19		600
2033610	CSX First Responders GE ES44AC Diesel, "911," CC, 20		550
2033619	CSX First Responders GE ES44AC Diesel, "911," unpowered, 20		185
2033620	CSX Veterans GE ES44AC Diesel, "1776," CC, 20		550
2033629	CSX Veterans GE ES44AC Diesel, "1776," unpowered, 20		350
2033630	CSX GE ES44AC Diesel, "3194," CC, 20		550
2033639	CSX GE ES44AC Diesel, "3194," unpowered, 20		350
2034010	PRR GG1 Electric, "4935," LionChief Plus 2.0, 19		500
2034020	PRR GG1 Electric, "4877," LionChief Plus 2.0, 19		500
2034030	PRR GG1 Electric, "4872," LionChief Plus 2.0, 19		500
2034040	PRR GG1 Electric, "4890," LionChief Plus 2.0, 19		500
2034050	PRR GG1 Electric, "4916," LionChief Plus 2.0, 19		500
2034061	Conrail LionMaster SD80MAC Diesel, "4100," LionChief Plus 2.0, 19		450

			Exc	Mint
___	**2034062**	Conrail LionMaster SD80MAC Diesel, "4102," LionChief Plus 2.0, 19		450
___	**2034071**	CSX LionMaster SD80MAC Diesel, "4592," LionChief Plus 2.0, 19		450
___	**2034072**	CSX LionMaster SD80MAC Diesel, "4594," LionChief Plus 2.0, 19		450
___	**2034081**	NS LionMaster SD80MAC Diesel, "7217," LionChief Plus 2.0, 19		450
___	**2034082**	NS LionMaster SD80MAC Diesel, "7219," LionChief Plus 2.0, 19		450
___	**2034091**	UP LionMaster SD90MAC Diesel, "8025," LionChief Plus 2.0, 19		450
___	**2034092**	UP LionMaster SD90MAC Diesel, "8026," LionChief Plus 2.0, 19		450
___	**2034100**	NYC F3 AA Diesel Set, "1620/1621," LionChief Plus 2.0, 20		700
___	**2034110**	PRR F3 AA Diesel Set, "9542/9542A," LionChief Plus 2.0, 20		700
___	**2034120**	UP F3 AA Diesel Set, "1445/1455," LionChief Plus 2.0, 20		700
___	**2034130**	SP F3 AA Diesel Set, "6148/6157," LionChief Plus 2.0, 20		700
___	**2034180**	Conrail GP38 Diesel, "7670," LionChief, 20		220
___	**2034190**	BN GP38 Diesel, "2085," LionChief, 20		220
___	**2034190**	SP Vision 4-8-4 GS-3 LAUPT Special, "4426," CC, 20		2000
___	**2034200**	Chessie System GP38 Diesel, "3847," LionChief, 20		220
___	**2034210**	North Pole Central GP38 Diesel, "1224," LionChief, 20		220
___	**2034220**	Lightning McQueen GP38 Diesel, "95," LionChief, 20		220
___	**2035010**	ELX Trolley, 20		100
___	**2035020**	Fort Collins Trolley, 20		100
___	**2035030**	Toy Story Handcar, 20-23		120
___	**2035050**	Lionelville Trolley, 20		100
___	**2038010**	B&O 190th Anniversary Boxcar, 19		85
___	**2038020**	D&RGW 150th Anniversary Boxcar, 19		85
___	**2038030**	Casey Jones 120th Anniversary MUSA Boxcar, 20		85
___	**2038040**	BN 50th Anniversary MUSA Boxcar, 20		85
___	**2038050**	George H.W. Bush Boxcar, 19-20		80
___	**2038060**	William Henry Harrison Presidential Boxcar, 20, 24		80
___	**2038070**	James Garfield Presidential Boxcar, 20, 24		80
___	**2038080**	Battlefield Honor — Berlin Wall Boxcar, 20-23		95
___	**2038090**	Battlefield Honor — Candy Bombers Boxcar, 20		90
___	**2038110**	Angela Trotta Thomas Stocked Shelves Boxcar, Middle, 19		85
___	**2038120**	2020 Happy Birthday Boxcar, 20		90
___	**2038130**	Happy Anniversary Boxcar, 20		90
___	**2038140**	2020 Merry Christmas Boxcar, 20		90
___	**2038150**	Foghorn Leghorn Crockett-Doodle Do Boxcar, 20-23		95
___	**2038160**	Picnic With Porky Pig Boxcar, 20-23		95
___	**2038170**	Robin Hood Daffy Duck Boxcar, 20-23		95
___	**2038200**	Wings of Angels — Jessamyne Rose Boxcar, 20		90
___	**2038210**	Wings of Angels — Ashten Goodenough Boxcar, 20		90
___	**2038220**	Wings of Angels — Jessie Ray Boxcar, 20		90
___	**2043011**	BN 50' Boxcar, "217552" (std 0), 20-23		50
___	**2043012**	BN 50' Boxcar, "217618" (std 0), 20-23		50
___	**2043013**	BN 50' Boxcar, "217685" (std 0), 20-23		50
___	**2043014**	BN 50' Boxcar, "217741" (std 0), 20-23		50
___	**2043021**	Golden West 50' Boxcar, "767130" (std 0), 20-23		50
___	**2043022**	Golden West 50' Boxcar, "767150" (std 0), 20-23		50
___	**2043023**	Golden West 50' Boxcar, "767167" (std 0), 20-23		50

		Exc	Mint
2043024	Golden West 50' Boxcar, "767193" (std O), 20-23		50 ___
2043031	KCS 50' Boxcar, "117731" (std O), 20-23		50 ___
2043032	KCS 50' Boxcar, "117756" (std O), 20-23		50 ___
2043033	KCS 50' Boxcar, "117782" (std O), 20-23		50 ___
2043034	KCS 50' Boxcar, "117790" (std O), 20-23		50 ___
2043041	Railbox 50' Boxcar, "10051" (std O), 20-22		50 ___
2043042	Railbox 50' Boxcar, "10189" (std O), 20-22		50 ___
2043043	Railbox 50' Boxcar, "10524" (std O), 20-22		50 ___
2043044	Railbox 50' Boxcar, "10582" (std O), 20-22		50 ___
2043051	MILW Road Centerbeam Flatcar, "6300" (std O), 20-23		50 ___
2043052	MILW Centerbeam Flatcar, "6318" (std O), 20-23		50 ___
2043053	MILW Centerbeam Flatcar, "6336" (std O), 20-23		50 ___
2043054	MILW Centerbeam Flatcar, "6354" (std O), 20-23		50 ___
2043061	Trailer Train Centerbeam Flatcar, "83729" (std O), 20-23		50 ___
2043062	Trailer Train Centerbeam Flatcar, "83741" (std O), 20-23		50 ___
2043063	Trailer Train Centerbeam Flatcar, "83754" (std O), 20-23		50 ___
2043064	Trailer Train Centerbeam Flatcar, "83773" (std O), 20-23		50 ___
2043071	UP Centerbeam Flatcar, "217015" (std O), 20-23		50 ___
2043072	UP Centerbeam Flatcar, "217031" (std O), 20-23		50 ___
2043073	UP Centerbeam Flatcar, "217047" (std O), 20-23		50 ___
2043074	UP Centerbeam Flatcar, "217063" (std O), 20-23		50 ___
2043081	WP Centerbeam Flatcar, "1404" (std O), 20-23		50 ___
2043082	WP Centerbeam Flatcar, "1412" (std O), 20-23		50 ___
2043083	WP Centerbeam Flatcar, "1420" (std O), 20-23		50 ___
2043084	WP Centerbeam Flatcar, "1428" (std O), 20-23		50 ___
2043091	BNSF Bulkhead Flatcar, "545475" (std O), 20-23		50 ___
2043092	BNSF Bulkhead Flatcar, "545512" (std O), 20-23		50 ___
2043093	BNSF Bulkhead Flatcar, "545587" (std O), 20-23		50 ___
2043094	BNSF Bulkhead Flatcar, "545628" (std O), 20-23		50 ___
2043101	GN Bulkhead Flatcar, "160325" (std O), 20-23		50 ___
2043102	GN Bulkhead Flatcar, "160331" (std O), 20-23		50 ___
2043103	GN Bulkhead Flatcar, "160350" (std O), 20-23		50 ___
2043104	GN Bulkhead Flatcar, "160374" (std O), 20-23		50 ___
2043111	NS Bulkhead Flatcar, "118024" (std O), 20-23		50 ___
2043112	NS Bulkhead Flatcar, "118033" (std O), 20-23		50 ___
2043113	NS Bulkhead Flatcar, "118045" (std O), 20-23		50 ___
2043114	NS Bulkhead Flatcar, "118068" (std O), 20-23		50 ___
2043121	Trailer Train Bulkhead Flatcar, "81023" (std O), 20-23		50 ___
2043122	Trailer Train Bulkhead Flatcar, "81094" (std O), 20-23		50 ___
2043123	Trailer Train Bulkhead Flatcar, "81118" (std O), 20-23		50 ___
2043124	Trailer Train Bulkhead Flatcar, "81145" (std O), 20-23		50 ___
2043131	Bethlehem Steel Gondola, "3131" (std O), 20-22		50 ___
2043132	Bethlehem Steel Gondola, "3145" (std O), 20-22		50 ___
2043133	Bethlehem Steel Gondola, "3168" (std O), 20-22		50 ___
2043134	Bethlehem Steel Gondola "3192" w/Coil Covers (std O), 20-23		50 ___
2043141	Chessie System Gondola, "305001" (std O), 20		45 ___
2043142	Chessie System Gondola "305014" w/Coil Covers (std O), 20-23		50 ___
2043143	Chessie System Gondola "305036" w/ Coil Covers (std O), 20-23		50 ___
2043144	Chessie System Gondola "305055" w/ Coil Covers (std O), 20-23		50 ___

	MODERN 1970-2024		Exc	Mint
____	**2043151**	MKT Gondola "14025" w/Coil Covers (std O), 20-23		50
____	**2043152**	MKT Gondola "14032" w/Coil Covers (std O), 20-23		50
____	**2043153**	MKT Gondola "14041" w/Coil Covers (std O), 20-23		50
____	**2043154**	MKT Gondola "14049" w/Coil Covers (std O), 20-23		50
____	**2043161**	Reading Gondola "29061" w/ Coil Covers (std O), 20-23		50
____	**2043162**	Reading Gondola "29086" w/Coil Covers std O), 20-23		50
____	**2043163**	Reading Gondola "29169" w/Coil Covers (std O), 20-23		50
____	**2043164**	Reading Gondola "29172" w/Coil Covers (std O), 20-23		50
____	**2043170**	BN Rotary Gondola, 4-pack, A, 20		280
____	**2043180**	BN Rotary Gondola, 4-pack, B, 20		280
____	**2043190**	BN Rotary Gondola, 2-pack, 20		140
____	**2043200**	Conrail Rotary Gondola, 4-pack, A, 20		280
____	**2043210**	Conrail Rotary Gondola, 4-pack, B, 20		280
____	**2043220**	Conrail Rotary Gondola, 2-pack, 20		140
____	**2043230**	CSX Rotary Gondola, 4-pack, A, 20		280
____	**2043240**	CSX Rotary Gondola, 4-pack, B, 20		280
____	**2043250**	CSX Rotary Gondola, 2-pack, 20		140
____	**2043260**	NS Rotary Gondola, 4-pack, A, 20		280
____	**2043270**	NS Rotary Gondola, 4-pack, B, 20		280
____	**2043280**	NS Rotary Gondola, 2-pack, 20		140
____	**2043290**	C&NW NE-5 Caboose "606" (std O), 20		60
____	**2043300**	Monon NE-5 Caboose "81526" (std O), 20		60
____	**2043310**	Monongahela NE-5 Caboose "64" (std O), 20		60
____	**2043320**	NH NE-5 Caboose "C-516" (std O), 20		60
____	**2122010**	Aliquippa Turn P&LE GP7 Diesel Freight Set, CC, 20		850
____	**2122020**	NYC Xplorer Baldwin Sharknose Passenger Set, CC, 20		900
____	**2122030**	Southern GP7 Diesel Freight Set, CC, 20		850
____	**2122040**	PRR John Bull Display Set, 21		800
____	**2122050**	Camden & Amboy John Bull Steam Passenger Set, 21		800
____	**2122060**	Uncle Sam John Bull Steam Passenger Set, 21		800
____	**2122070**	LV Asa Packer 4-6-2 Pacific Steam Passenger Set, CC, 21		2200
____	**2122080**	NYC 1926 Cardinals 4-6-2 Pacific Steam Passenger Set, CC, 21		2100
____	**2122090**	Amtrak Acela High Speed Train Set, CC, 21		2500
____	**2122100**	Amtrak Acela Concept High Speed Train Set, CC, 21		2500
____	**2122110**	MILW High Speed Train Set, CC, 21		2500
____	**2122120**	NH High Speed Train Set, CC, 21		2500
____	**2122130**	PRR High Speed Train Set, CC, 21		2500
____	**2122140**	ATSF High Speed Train Set, CC, 21		2500
____	**2122150**	UP High Speed Train Set, CC, 21		2500
____	**2122160**	New Hope & Ivyland GP30 Diesel Passenger Excursion Set, CC, 21		1000
____	**2122170**	ATSF Valley Flyer 4-6-2 Pacific Steam Passenger Set, CC, 21		2200
____	**2122180**	Nickel Plate Road Work Train Set, CC, 21		1000
____	**2122190**	Polar Express High Speed Train Set, CC, 21		2500
____	**2123010**	C&O Steam Freight Set LionChief, 20-23		450
____	**2123030**	KCS Tier 4 ET44 Diesel Freight Set LionChief, 21		425
____	**2123040**	John Deere GP38 Diesel Freight Set LionChief, 21-24		450
____	**2123060**	Hallow's Eve Limited Steam Freight Set LionChief, 21-23		400
____	**2123070**	Polar Express Steam Freight Set LionChief, 21-24		400
____	**2123080**	Space Launch GP38 Diesel Freight Set LionChief, 21-24		450
____	**2123090**	Lionel Junction North Pole Central Steam Freight Set LionChief, Upgraded, 21		325

		Exc	Mint
2123100	Christmas Light Express Steam Freight Set LionChief, Upgraded, 21-24		500 ___
2123110	Toy Story Steam Freight Set LionChief, Upgraded, 21		425 ___
2123120	Star Trek FT Diesel Freight Set LionChief, Upgraded, 21		480 ___
2123130	Polar Express Steam Passenger Set LionChief, Upgraded, 21-24		480 ___
2123140	Harry Potter Hogwarts Express Steam Passenger Set LionChief, Upgraded, 21-24		480 ___
2123150	Frozen II Steam Freight Set LionChief, Upgraded, 21		425 ___
2123160	Area 51 ET44 Diesel Freight Set LionChief, Upgraded, 21		450 ___
2123200	Pennsylvania Keystone Bluetooth 5.0 Steam Freight Set, 21-24		400 ___
2125010	Halloween FasTrack Girider Bridge, 21-24		35 ___
2126011	B&LE PS-5 Covered Gondola "32001", 20		90 ___
2126012	B&LE PS-5 Covered Gondola "32054", 20		90 ___
2126021	Bethlehem Steel PS-5 Covered Hopper "303025", 20		90 ___
2126022	Bethlehem Steel PS-5 Covered Hopper "303041", 20		90 ___
2126031	BN PS-5 Covered Gondola "577225", 20		90 ___
2126032	BN PS-5 Covered Gondola "577239", 20		90 ___
2126041	DT&I PS-5 Covered Hopper "9502", 20		90 ___
2126042	DT&I PS-5 Covered Hopper "9509", 20		90 ___
2126051	Reading & Northern PS-5 Covered Hopper "3806", 20		90 ___
2126052	Reading & Northern PS-5 Covered Hopper "3810", 20		90 ___
2126061	UP PS-5 Covered Hopper "229812", 20		90 ___
2126062	UP PS-5 Covered Hopper "903044", 20		90 ___
2126071	Central of Georgia Roof-Hatch Boxcar "6161", 20		95 ___
2126072	Central of Georgia Roof-Hatch Boxcar "6165", 20		95 ___
2126081	C&NW Roof-Hatch Boxcar "108610", 20		95 ___
2126082	C&NW Roof-Hatch Boxcar "108614", 20		95 ___
2126091	Monon Roof-Hatch Boxcar "10249", 20		95 ___
2126092	Monon Roof-Hatch Boxcar "10421", 20		95 ___
2126101	Southern Roof-Hatch Boxcar "26922", 20		95 ___
2126102	Southern Roof-Hatch Boxcar "26961", 20		95 ___
2126111	UP Roof-Hatch Boxcar "284225", 20		95 ___
2126112	UP Roof-Hatch Boxcar "284227", 20		95 ___
2126120	B&LE 100-ton Hopper 2-pack, A, 20		250 ___
2126128	B&LE 100-ton Hopper 2-pack, B, 20		250 ___
2126129	B&LE 100-ton Hopper 2-pack, C, 20		250 ___
2126130	CSX 100-ton Hopper 2-pack, A, 20		250 ___
2126138	CSX 100-ton Hopper 2-pack, B, 20		250 ___
2126139	CSX 100-ton Hopper 2-pack, C, 20		250 ___
2126140	PP&L 100-ton Hopper 2-pack, A, 20		250 ___
2126148	PP&L 100-ton Hopper 2-pack, B, 20		250 ___
2126149	PP&L 100-ton Hopper 2-pack, C, 20		250 ___
2126160	P&LE 100-ton Hopper 2-pack, A, 20		250 ___
2126168	P&LE 100-ton Hopper 2-pack, B, 20		250 ___
2126169	P&LE 100-ton Hopper 2-pack, C, 20		250 ___
2126170	Reading & Northern 100-ton Hopper 2-pack, A, 20		250 ___
2126178	Reading & Northern 100-ton Hopper 2-pack, B, 20		250 ___
2126179	Reading & Northern 100-ton Hopper 2-pack, C, 20		250 ___
2126180	Ann Arbor PS-2 Covered Hopper "800", 20		90 ___
2126190	Central Soya PS-2 Covered Hopper "118", 22		90 ___
2126200	Monon PS-2 Covered Hopper "30648", 20		90 ___
2126210	PRR PS-2 Covered Hopper "257808", 20		90 ___

			Exc	Mint
___	**2126220**	T&P PS-2 Covered Hopper "8744", 20		90
___	**2126230**	WM PS-2 Covered Hopper "4940", 20		90
___	**2126240**	Chessie BW Caboose "C-3010", 20		110
___	**2126250**	Conrail BW Caboose "21736", 20		110
___	**2126260**	SLSF BW Caboose "1730", 20		110
___	**2126270**	L&N BW Caboose "1134", 20		110
___	**2126280**	NYC BW Caboose "20284", 20		110
___	**2126290**	SP Railroad Police BW Caboose "4762", 20		110
___	**2126300**	NYC Pacemaker Expansion Set, 21		500
___	**2126310**	American Steel 65' Mill Gondola "1776", 21		100
___	**2126320**	Bethlehem Steel 65' Mill Gondola "206320", 21		100
___	**2126330**	CP 65' Mill Gondola "337185", 21		100
___	**2126340**	Conrail SW8 Diesel Switcher "8657,"" CC, 21		100
___	**2126350**	CSX 65' Mill Gondola "91038", 21		100
___	**2126360**	PRR 65' Mill Gondola "442650", 21		100
___	**2126370**	B&O Boxcar w/FreightSounds "467434", 21		200
___	**2126380**	M&P Boxcar w/FreightSounds "5624", 21		200
___	**2126390**	MP Boxcar w/FreightSounds "41260", 21		200
___	**2126400**	PRR Boxcar w/FreightSounds "26875", 21		200
___	**2126410**	SP Boxcar w/FreightSounds "163285", 21		200
___	**2126420**	WP Boxcar w/FreightSounds "220086", 21		200
___	**2126431**	BNSF Beer Car "782404", 21		100
___	**2126432**	BNSF Beer Car "782480", 21		110
___	**2126441**	D&RGW Beer Car "50816", 21		100
___	**2126442**	D&RGW Beer Car "50871", 21		100
___	**2126451**	Golden West Beer Car "149000", 21		100
___	**2126452**	Golden West Beer Car "149008", 21		110
___	**2126461**	MP Beer Car "793004", 21		100
___	**2126462**	MP Beer Car "793015", 21		100
___	**2126471**	UP Beer Car "465304", 21		100
___	**2126472**	UP Beer Car "465321", 21		100
___	**2126481**	WP Beer Car "67083", 21		100
___	**2126482**	WP Beer Car "67055", 21		100
___	**2126490**	Nickel Plate Road Work Train Expansion Pack, 21		680
___	**2126500**	CP Tool Car "403503", 21		100
___	**2126510**	CNJ Tool Car "92083", 21		100
___	**2126520**	C&O Tool Car "X509", 21		100
___	**2126530**	MKT Tool Car "X-3257", 21		100
___	**2126540**	N&W Tool Car "526544", 21		100
___	**2126550**	WP Tool Car "MW0995", 21		100
___	**2126560**	CP Kitchen Car "410833", 21		150
___	**2126570**	CNJ Kitchen Car "92111", 21		150
___	**2126580**	C&O Kitchen Car "X41", 21		150
___	**2126590**	MKT Kitchen Car "X-3175", 21		150
___	**2126600**	N&W Kitchen Car "526030", 21		150
___	**2126610**	WP Kitchen Car "MW0912", 21		150
___	**2126621**	CP Bunk Car "411213", 21		100
___	**2126622**	CP Bunk Car "411919", 21		100
___	**2126631**	CNJ Bunk Car "92110", 21		100
___	**2126632**	CNJ Bunk Car "92120", 21		100
___	**2126641**	C&O Bunk Car "B575", 21		100
___	**2126642**	C&O Bunk Car "B579", 21		100
___	**2126651**	MKT Bunk Car "X-2121", 21		100

		Exc	Mint
2126652	MKT Bunk Car "X-2122", 21		100
2126661	N&W Bunk Car "525502", 21		100
2126662	N&W Bunk Car "525534", 21		100
2126671	WP Bunk Car "MW0556", 21		100
2126672	WP Bunk Car "MW0761", 21		100
2126680	Polar Express 40' Flatcar w/Bell, 21		100
2127010	NYC Xplorer Coach 2-pack, 20		370
2127020	ATSF WiFi Theater Car "89", 20		340
2127030	BNSF WiFi Theater Car "William Barstow Strong", 20		340
2127040	C&NW WiFi Theater Car "Fox River", 20		340
2127050	KCS WiFi Theater Car "Arthur E. Stilwell", 20		340
2127060	NS WiFi Theater Car "Buena Vista", 20		340
2127070	SP WiFi Theater Car "Harriman", 20		340
2127080	NYC 1926 Cardinals Passenger Train Expansion Pack, 21		400
2127090	NYC 1926 Cardinals "St. Mary of the Lake" Diner w/ StationSounds, 21		370
2127100	D&RGW Ski Train Power Car, 21-22		370
2127110	D&RGW Ski Train Passenger Car 4-pack, 21-22		825
2127120	D&RGW Ski Train Passenger Car 2-pack, 21-22		410
2127130	D&RGW Ski Train Diner w/StationSounds, 21-22		400
2127140	Polar Express High Speed Train Expansion Pack, 21		1000
2127150	ATSF Valley Flyer Passenger Train Expansion 2-pack, 21		400
2127160	PRR South Wind 21" Passenger Car 4-pack, 20		750
2127170	PRR South Wind 21" Passenger Car 2-pack, 20		370
2127180	PRR South Wind Diner w/StationSounds, 20		350
2127190	PRR "Fleet of Modernism" B60 "7900", 20		190
2127200	PC B60 Passenger Car "7705", 20		190
2127210	PC B60 Passenger Car "7630", 20		190
2127220	Reindeer Express B60 Passenger Car "2124", 20		190
2127230	PRR "Fleet of Modernism" 18" Pullman 2-pack, 20		400
2127240	Pullman Pool Service 18" Sleeper, Green 2-pack, 20		400
2127250	Pullman Pool Service 18" Sleeper, Gray 2-pack, 20		400
2127260	PRR South Wind 1947 Expansion Passenger Car 2-pack, 20		370
2127270	PRR "Fleet of Modernism" RPO "5260", 20		190
2127280	NYC Southwestern Limited 60' Baggage Car "2979", 20		190
2127290	NYC Southwestern Limited 60' Baggage Car "8424", 20		190
2127300	NYC Southwestern Limited RPO "4814", 20		190
2127310	NYC Southwestern Limited 21" Passenger Car 4-pack, 20		750
2127320	NYC Southwestern Limited 21" Passenger Car 2-pack, 20		370
2127330	NYC Southwestern Limited 21" Diner w/StationSounds, 20		370
2127341	Polar Express Sleeping Car "Believe," Black roof, 21		210
2127342	Polar Express Sleeping Car North Pole," Black roof, 21		210
2127351	Polar Express Sleeping Car "Believe," White roof, 21, 24		210
2127352	Polar Express Sleeping Car "North Pole," White roof, 21, 24		210
2127360	D&H 21" Passenger Car 4-pack, 21		750
2127370	D&H 21" Passenger Car 2-pack, 21		370
2127380	D&H 21" Diner w/StationSounds, 21		370
2127390	Amtrak Acela High Speed Train Expansion Set, 21		1000
2127400	Amtrak Acela Concept High Speed Train Expansion Set, 21		1000
2127410	MILW High Speed Train Expansion Set, 21		1000

		Exc	Mint
2127420	NH High Speed Train Expansion Set, 21		1000
2127430	PRR Concept High Speed Train Expansion Set, 21		1000
2127440	ATSF High Speed Train Expansion Set, 21		1000
2127450	UP High Speed Train Expansion Set, 21		1000
2127460	E-L 21" Passenger Car 4-pack, 21		750
2127470	E-L 21" Passenger Car 2-pack, 21		370
2127480	E-L 21" Diner w/StationSounds, 21		370
2127490	GM&O 18" Passenger Car 2-pack, A, 21		400
2127500	GM&O 18" Passenger Car 2-pack, B, 21		400
2127510	GM&O 18" Passenger Car 2-pack, C, 21		400
2127520	GM&O 18" Diner w/StationSounds, 21		370
2127530	Texas Special 18" Passenger Car 2-pack, A, 21		400
2127540	Texas Special 18" Passenger Car 2-pack, B, 21		400
2127550	Texas Special 18" Passenger Car 2-pack, C, 21		400
2127560	Texas Special 18" Diner w/StationSounds, 21		370
2128010	C&O Walking Brakeman Car "21299", 20-24		110
2128020	Shark Fin Containment Car, 21-24		110
2128030	Monsters Inc. Chasing Gondola, 21-23		90
2128040	Cars Aquarium Car, 21-23		120
2128050	Candy Cane Flatcar, 21		75
2128060	Christmas Tree Flatcar, 21-23		100
2128070	Dump Car w/Presents, 21-23		90
2128080	LL Flatcar w/Handcar, 21-23		135
2128090	Star Trek Dilithium Crystals Hopper w/illumination, 21		90
2128100	Star Trek Chasing Gondola w/Picard, Riker and Q, 21		85
2128110	This Bud's For You Refrigerator Car, 21-23		90
2128120	Those Who Know Bud Refrigerator Car, 21-23		90
2128130	Vintage High Life Refrigerator Car, 21-23		90
2128140	Vintage Coors Refrigerator Car, 21-23		90
2128150	Ford Vintage Boxcar, 21		75
2128160	Chevy Vintage Boxcar, 21		75
2128170	Halloween Sound Car, 21-22		85
2128180	2021 Christmas Music Car, 21		80
2128190	2021 Christmas Boxcar, 21		65
2128200	PRR Flatcar w/Girder Bridge, 21-23		95
2128210	Polar Express Flatcar w/Girder Bridge, 21-24		95
2128220	Batman Aquarium Car, 21-23		120
2128230	Road Runner Aquarium Car, 21-22		120
2128240	Polar Express Operating Present Car, 21-23		100
2128250	SledEx Present Unloading Car, 21-23		100
2128260	North Pole Central Flatcar w/Handcar, 21-22		135
2128270	John Deere Refrigerator Car, 21-22		90
2128280	Polar Express Boxcar, 21-24		85
2128290	Angela Trotta Thomas Christmas Caboose, 21-22		90
2128300	Angela Trotta Thomas Santa Fe Boxcar, 21-23		85
2128310	Angela Trotta Thomas Hudson Boxcar, 21-23		85
2128320	Star Trek Capt. Janeway Boxcar, 21		75
2128330	Star Trek Capt. Sisko Boxcar, 21		75
2128340	Mickey & Friends Christmas Flatcar w/Girders, 21-23		95
2128350	Mickey & Friends Christmas Present Car, 21-23		100
2128360	Space Launch Allis-Chalmers Car w/Capsules, 21-23		85
2129010	Big Tatz Ink, 20-22		100
2129020	Sofa King Mattresses & Furniture, 20-22		110

MODERN 1970-2024		Exc	Mint
2129030	Sgt. Stumpy's Red, White & Boom Fireworks, 20-24		300 ___
2129050	Track Laying Crew, 20		100 ___
2129060	Road Crew, 20		100 ___
2129070	Polar Express Present Chute Station, 21-23		200 ___
2129080	SledEx Present Chute Station, 21-22		180 ___
2129090	Angela Trotta Thomas Christmastime Hobby Store, 21-22		300 ___
2129100	Batman Rotary Beacon, 21-22		100 ___
2129110	Classic Rotary Beacon, 21-22		90 ___
2129120	Christmas Rotary Beacon, 21-22		90 ___
2129130	Halloween Rotary Beacon, 21-22		90 ___
2129140	Dr. IP Drips & Sons Plumbing, 20-22		100 ___
2129150	Dominant Jeans , 20-22		120 ___
2129160	McCartney's Wings, 20		100 ___
2129180	T Rex Elevated Oil Tank, 21		90 ___
2129190	Polar Express Elevated Hot Chocolate Tank, 21-24		110 ___
2129200	Lionel Ale Elevated Oil Tank, 21-22		110 ___
2129210	Area 51 Elevated Oil Tank, 21-22		110 ___
2129220	Christmas Joy Flagpole, 21-23		45 ___
2129230	Halloween Flagpole, 21-23		45 ___
2129240	Cowens Towing Garage, 21-22		165 ___
2129250	Talking Passenger Station, 21-22		200 ___
2129260	Ford Water Tower, 21		50 ___
2129270	Chevy Water Tower, 21		50 ___
2129280	Halloween Water Tower, 21-22		50 ___
2129290	Christmas Water Tower, 21-24		60 ___
2129300	Area 51 Water Tower, 21-22		60 ___
2129310	John Deere Service Garage, 21-22		180 ___
2129330	Halloween Lighted Half Covered Bridge, 21-22		90 ___
2129340	Chevrolet Flagpole, 21-24		45 ___
2129350	Ford Flagpole, 21-24		45 ___
2129360	Ford Service Station, 21-22		165 ___
2129370	Chevy Service Station, 21-22		165 ___
2129380	Halloween Elevated Oil Tank, 21-23		100 ___
2130010	Frat House, 20		100 ___
2130020	Santa on the Roof House, 21		85 ___
2130030	Cock & Bull Tavern, 21		75 ___
2130040	Russell House, 21		85 ___
2130050	Garage 2-pack, 20		50 ___
2130060	Turner House Kit, 21		50 ___
2130070	Garage Kit, 2-pack, 20		135 ___
2130080	Design-Your-Own-House Kit, 21		60 ___
2130090	Anheuser-Busch Covered Bridge, 21-22		65 ___
2130100	Polar Express Billboard Pack, 21-24		25 ___
2130110	Log Cabin Scented Smoke Fluid, 21-24		9 ___
2130120	Window Shoppers Figures, 21-23		30 ___
2130130	Thru Truss Bridge Kit, 21-24		70 ___
2131010	American Railroads 6-4-4-6 S1 "6100," CC, 20		1600 ___
2131020	PRR 6-4-4-6 S1 "6100," As-Built, CC, 20		1600 ___
2131030	PRR 6-4-4-6 S1 "6100," Calendar, CC, 20		1600 ___
2131040	PRR 6-4-4-6 S1 "6100," Tuscan Red, CC, 20		1600 ___
2131050	B&M 4-6-0 "2074," CC, 20		750 ___
2131060	CP/Railtours 4-6-0 "972," CC, 20		750 ___
2131070	NYC 4-6-0 "1232," CC, 20		750 ___

			Exc	Mint
___	**2131080**	Reading & Northern 4-6-0 "225," CC, 20		750
___	**2131090**	Rutland 4-6-0 "79," CC, 20		750
___	**2131100**	Soo Line 4-6-0 "2645," CC, 20		750
___	**2131110**	Southern 4-6-0 "947," CC, 20		375
___	**2131120**	T&P 4-6-0 "316," CC, 20		750
___	**2131130**	ATSF USRA 2-8-8-2 "1796," CC, 20		1900
___	**2131140**	B&O USRA 2-8-8-2 "7150," CC, 20		1900
___	**2131150**	Clinchfield USRA 2-8-8-2 "730," CC, 20		1900
___	**2131160**	D&RGW USRA 2-8-8-2 "3504," CC, 20		1900
___	**2131170**	N&W USRA 2-8-8-2 "2020," CC, 20		1900
___	**2131180**	N&W USRA 2-8-8-2 "2050," CC, 20		1900
___	**2131190**	N&W USRA 2-8-8-2 "2021," Weathered, CC, 20		2050
___	**2131200**	NP USRA 2-8-8-2 "4501," CC, 20		1900
___	**2131210**	PRR USRA 2-8-8-2 "377," CC, 2		1900
___	**2131220**	UP USRA 2-8-8-2 "3672," CC, 20		1900
___	**2131230**	Virginian USRA 2-8-8-2 "702," CC, 20		1900
___	**2131240**	ACL USRA 4-6-2 Pacific "1504," CC, 21		1500
___	**2131250**	GM&O USRA 4-6-2 Pacific "5296," CC, 21		1500
___	**2131260**	GN USRA 4-6-2 Pacific "1385," CC, 21		1500
___	**2131270**	MKT USRA 4-6-2 Pacific "411," CC, 21		1500
___	**2131280**	Nickel Plate Road USRA 4-6-2 Pacific "168," CC, 21		1500
___	**2131290**	SP USRA 4-6-2 Pacific "611," CC, 21		1500
___	**2131300**	UP USRA 4-6-2 Pacific "3218," CC, 21		1500
___	**2131310**	ACL USRA Light 2-8-2 "823," CC, 20		1300
___	**2131320**	Georgia USRA Light 2-8-2 "300," CC, 20		1300
___	**2131330**	GTW USRA Light 2-8-2 "4070," CC, 20		1300
___	**2131340**	L&HR USRA Light 2-8-2 "83," CC, 20		1300
___	**2131350**	Monon USRA Light 2-8-2 "554," CC, 20		1300
___	**2131360**	SLSF USRA Light 2-8-2 "4003," CC, 20		1300
___	**2131370**	Southern USRA Light 2-8-2 "4501," CC, 20		1300
___	**2131380**	Wabash USRA Light 2-8-2 "2202," CC, 20		1300
___	**2131390**	CNJ Blue Comet 4-6-0 Camelback "770," CC, 21		650
___	**2131400**	CNJ 4-6-0 Camelback "774," CC, 21		650
___	**2131410**	D&H 4-6-0 Camelback "810," CC, 21		650
___	**2131420**	LIRR 4-6-0 Camelback "18," CC, 21		650
___	**2131430**	NYO&W 4-6-0 Camelback "255," CC, 21		650
___	**2131440**	Reading 4-6-0 Camelback "652," CC, 21		650
___	**2131450**	Strasburg 4-6-0 Camelback "771," CC, 21		650
___	**2131460**	Hallows Eve Limited 4-6-0 Camelback "1313," CC, 21		650
___	**2131470**	ATSF 2-10-10-2 "3001," CC, 21		2500
___	**2131480**	ATSF 2-10-10-2 "3009," CC, 21		2500
___	**2131490**	ATSF Black Bonnet 2-10-10-2 "3005," CC, 21		2500
___	**2131500**	ATSF Valley Flyer 2-10-10-2 "3008," CC, 21		2500
___	**2131510**	NYC 4-8-2 L2a Mohawk "2700," CC, 21		1600
___	**2131520**	NYC 4-8-2 L2a Mohawk "2790," CC, 21		1600
___	**2131530**	NYC 4-8-2 L2a Mohawk "2728," CC, 21		1600
___	**2131540**	NYC 4-8-2 L2a Mohawk "2775," CC, 21		1600
___	**2131550**	NYC 4-8-2 L2a Mohawk "2727," Gray, CC, 21		1600
___	**2131560**	NYC 4-8-2 L2a Mohawk "2750," Pacemaker, CC, 21		1600
___	**2131570**	NH 4-8-2 L2a Mohawk "3507," CC, 21		1600
___	**2132010**	SP LionMaster AC-12 4-8-8-2 Cab-Forward "4294," CC, 20		1300
___	**2132020**	SP LionMaster AC-12 4-8-8-2 Cab-Forward "4291," CC, 20		1300
___	**2132030**	SP LionMaster AC-12 4-8-8-2 Cab-Forward "4280," CC, 20		1300

		Exc	Mint
2132040	SP LionMaster AC-12 4-8-8-2 Cab-Forward "4290," Daylight, CC, 20		1300
2132050	Christmas 4-4-0 General "1225" LionChief, 21-22		275
2132060	Halloween 4-4-0 General "1031" LionChief, 21-22		275
2132070	PRR 4-4-0 General "573" LionChief, 21		250
2132080	W&A 4-4-0 General "3" LionChief, 21		250
2132090	PRR Baby K4 4-6-2 Pacific "1361" LionChief Plus 2.0, 21		550
2132100	PRR Baby K4 4-6-2 Pacific "3750" LionChief Plus 2.0, 21		550
2132110	PRR Baby K4 4-6-2 Pacific "5400" LionChief Plus 2.0, 21		550
2132120	PRR Baby K4 4-6-2 Pacific "5409" LionChief Plus 2.0, 21		550
2133010	CRI&P E7 AA Diesel Set "632/635," CC, 20		1000
2133019	CRI&P E7B SuperBass, 20		450
2133020	SP Golden State E7 AB Diesel Set "6000/6000B," CC, 20		1000
2133029	SP Golden State E7B SuperBass "6000C", 20		450
2133030	NYC E7 AA Diesel Set "4004/4005," CC, 20		1000
2133039	NYC E7B SuperBass "4104", 20		450
2133040	PRR E7 AA Diesel Set "5900/5901," CC, 20		1000
2133043	PRR E7B SuperBass "5848B", 20		450
2133049	PRR E7B SuperBass "5900B", 20		450
2133050	ACL E7 AA Diesel Set "540/541," CC, 20		1000
2133059	ACL E7B SuperBass "755", 20		450
2133060	UP E7 AB Diesel Set "927A/928B," CC, 20		1000
2133069	UP E7B SuperBass "929B", 20		450
2133070	SP Lark E7 AB Diesel Set "6004/6004B," CC, 20		1000
2133079	SP Lark E7B SuperBass "6004C", 20		225
2133080	NYC E7 AA Diesel Set "4002/4003," Black, CC, 20		1000
2133089	NYC E7B SuperBass "4102," Black, 20		450
2133090	Bethlehem Steel Genset Diesel Switcher "420," CC, 20		600
2133100	BNSF Genset Diesel Switcher "1228," CC, 20		600
2133110	CSX Genset Diesel Switcher "1300" CC, 20		600
2133120	NS Genset Diesel Switcher "301," CC, 20		600
2133130	PRR Genset Diesel Switcher "9910," CC, 20		600
2133140	UP Genset Diesel Switcher "2706," CC, 20		600
2133151	ATSF GP7 Diesel "2676," CC, 20		500
2133152	ATSF GP7 Diesel "2804," CC, 20		500
2133161	SSW GP7 Diesel "304," CC, 20		500
2133162	SSW GP7 Diesel "320," CC, 20		500
2133171	MEC GP7 Diesel "562," CC, 20		500
2133172	MEC GP7 Diesel "565," CC, 20		500
2133181	NP GP7 Diesel "564," CC, 20		500
2133182	NP GP7 Diesel "566," CC, 20		500
2133191	SAL GP7 Diesel "1700," CC, 20		500
2133192	SAL GP7 Diesel "1760," CC, 20		500
2133201	T&P GP7 Diesel "1110," CC, 20		500
2133202	T&P GP7 Diesel "1118," CC, 20		500
2133210	ATSF Baldwin Sharknose AA Diesel Set "400A/400D," CC, 20		950
2133218	ATSF Baldwin Sharknose Powered B Diesel "400B," CC, 20		430
2133219	ATSF Baldwin Sharknose B Diesel SuperBass "400C", 20		400
2133220	Baldwin Sharknose AA Diesel Set "6000/6001," CC, 20		950
2133228	Baldwin Sharknose Powered B Diesel "6000B," CC, 20		430
2133229	Baldwin Sharknose B Diesel SuperBass "6001B", 20		400
2133230	EJ&E Baldwin Sharknose AA Diesel Set "700A/701A," CC , 20		950

			Exc	Mint
___	2133238	EJ&E Baldwin Sharknose Powered B Diesel "700B," CC, 20		430
___	2133239	EJ&E Baldwin Sharknose B Diesel SuperBass "701B", 20		400
___	2133240	Monongahela Sharknose AA Diesel Set "1207/1216," CC, 20		950
___	2133248	Monongahela Baldwin Sharknose Powered B Diesel "3708," CC, 20		430
___	2133249	Monongahela Sharknose B Diesel SuperBass "3709", 20		400
___	2133250	NYC Baldwin Sharknose AA Diesel Set "1206/1213," CC, 20		950
___	2133258	NYC Baldwin Sharknose Powered B Diesel "3705," CC, 20		430
___	2133259	NYC Baldwin Sharknose B Diesel SuperBass "3706", 20		400
___	2133260	PRR Baldwin Sharknose AA Diesel Set "5780A/5781A," CC, 20		950
___	2133268	PRR Baldwin Sharknose Powered B Diesel "5780B," CC, 20		430
___	2133269	PRR Baldwin Sharknose B Diesel Superbass "5732B", 22		400
___	2133270	PRR Baldwin Sharknose AA Diesel Set "9730A/9731A," CC, 20		950
___	2133278	PRR Baldwin Sharknose Powered B Diesel "9730B," CC, 20		430
___	2133279	PRR Baldwin Sharknose B Diesel SuperBass "9732B", 20		400
___	2133280	US Army Baldwin Sharknose AA Diesel Set "1775/1776," CC, 20		950
___	2133288	US Army Baldwin Sharknose Powered B Diesel "1926," CC, 20		430
___	2133289	US Army Baldwin Sharknose B Diesel SuperBass "1941", 20		400
___	2133290	UP Genset Diesel Switcher "2709," Graffiti, CC, 20		625
___	2133311	ACL SD70ACe Diesel "1840," CC, 21		600
___	2133312	ACL SD70ACe Diesel "1967," CC, 21		600
___	2133321	ATSF SD70ACe Diesel "1859," CC, 21		600
___	2133322	ATSF SD70ACe Diesel "1995," CC, 21		600
___	2133330	KCS SD70ACe Diesel "4409 - Heroes," CC, 21		600
___	2133331	B&O SD70ACe Diesel "1828," CC, 21		600
___	2133332	B&O SD70ACe Diesel "1987," CC, 21		600
___	2133341	B&M SD70ACe Diesel "1835," CC, 21		600
___	2133342	B&M SD70ACe Diesel "1983," CC, 21		600
___	2133351	CP SD70ACe Diesel "1881," CC, 21		600
___	2133352	CP SD70ACe Diesel "2021," CC, 21		600
___	2133361	GN SD70ACe Diesel "1889," CC, 21		600
___	2133362	GN SD70ACe Diesel "1970," CC, 21		600
___	2133371	Monon SD70ACe Diesel "1847," CC, 21		600
___	2133372	Monon SD70ACe Diesel "1971," CC, 21		600
___	2133380	E-L Alco PA AA Diesel Set "862/863," CC, 21		1000
___	2133390	GM&O Alco PA AA Diesel Set "290/291," CC, 21		1000
___	2133400	MKT Alco PA AA Diesel Set "152A/152C," CC, 21		1000
___	2133410	NH Alco PA AA Diesel Set "0760/0761," CC, 21		1000
___	2133420	SSW Alco PA AA Diesel Set "300/301," CC, 21		1000
___	2133430	D&H Alco PA AA Diesel Set "16/17," CC, 21		1000
___	2133441	BNSF GP30 Diesel "2472," CC, 21		530
___	2133442	BNSF GP30 Diesel "2826," CC, 21		530
___	2133451	C&NW GP30 Diesel "818," CC, 21		530
___	2133452	C&NW GP30 Diesel "823," CC, 21		530
___	2133461	CSX (Chessie) GP30 Diesel "4126," CC, 21		530
___	2133462	CSX (B&O) GP30 Diesel "4131," CC, 21		530
___	2133471	KCS GP30 Diesel "4100," CC, 21		530
___	2133472	KCS GP30 Diesel "4109," CC, 21		530
___	2133481	Reading & Northern GP30 Diesel "2530," CC, 21		530
___	2133482	Reading & Northern GP30 Diesel "2531," CC, 21		530
___	2133491	Soo GP30 Diesel "700," CC, 21		530

		Exc	Mint
2133492	Soo GP30 Diesel "703," CC, 21		530 ___
2133501	UP Veranda Turbine w/SuperBass Tender "61," CC, 21		1650 ___
2133502	UP Veranda Turbine w/SuperBass Tender "69," CC, 21		1650 ___
2133510	Alaska Veranda Turbine w/SuperBass Tender "4501," CC, 21		1650 ___
2133520	GN Veranda Turbine w/SuperBass Tender "5020," CC, 21		1650 ___
2133530	PRR Veranda Turbine w/SuperBass Tender "6201," CC, 21		1650 ___
2133540	D&RGW Veranda Turbine w/SuperBass Tender "4010," CC, 21		1650 ___
2133550	SP Veranda Turbine w/SuperBass Tender "8505," CC, 21		1650 ___
2133560	US Dept of Defense Veranda Turbine w/SuperBass Tender "1941," CC, 21		1650 ___
2133570	B&M SW8 Diesel Switcher "801," CC, 21		500 ___
2133580	Coors Brewing SW8 Diesel Switcher "991," CC, 21		500 ___
2133590	Conrail SW8 Diesel Switcher "8657," CC, 21		500 ___
2133600	NYC SW8 Diesel Switcher "9606," CC, 21		500 ___
2133610	CRI&P SW8 Diesel Switcher "818," CC, 21		500 ___
2133620	SCL SW8 Diesel Switcher "19," CC, 21		500 ___
2133630	SP SW8 Diesel Switcher "1102," CC, 21		500 ___
2133640	Strasburg SW8 Diesel Switcher "8618," CC, 21		500 ___
2133730	UP Veranda Turbine w/SuperBass Tender "65," CC, 21		1650 ___
2133740	UP Veranda Turbine w/SuperBass Tender "67," CC, 21		1650 ___
2134010	ACL GP7 Diesel "105" LionChief Plus 2.0, 20-21		375 ___
2134020	MKT GP7 Diesel "93" LionChief Plus 2.0, 20-21		375 ___
2134030	B&O GP7 Diesel "6698" LionChief Plus 2.0, 20-21		375 ___
2134040	CRI&P GP7 Diesel "1274" LionChief Plus 2.0, 20-21		375 ___
2134050	ATSF GE U36B Diesel ""8733" LionChief, 21-22		250 ___
2134060	UP GE U36B Diesel "8573" LionChief, 21-22		250 ___
2134070	Seaboard System GE U36B Diesel "5701" LionChief, 21-24		250 ___
2134080	CSX GE U36B Diesel "5871" LionChief, 21-22		250 ___
2134090	LV Alco RS3 "216" LionChief Plus 2.0, 21		375 ___
2134100	PRR Alco RS3 "4044" LionChief Plus 2.0, 21		375 ___
2134110	ATSF Alco RS3 "2098" LionChief Plus 2.0, 21		375 ___
2134120	Southern Alco RS3 "520" LionChief Plus 2.0, 21		375 ___
2135010	B&O TMCC Speeder, 21		150 ___
2135020	PC TMCC Speeder, 21		150 ___
2135030	ATSF TMCC Speeder, 21		150 ___
2135040	Sperry TMCC Speeder, 21		150 ___
2135050	Polar Express TMCC Speeder, 21-24		165 ___
2135060	Halloween TMCC Speeder, 21-22		165 ___
2135070	Star Trek TMCC Speeder, 21		150 ___
2135080	BNSF TMCC Tamper, 21		200 ___
2135090	BN TMCC Tamper, 21, 24		200 ___
2135100	Conrail TMCC Tamper, 21		200 ___
2135110	CSX TMCC Tamper, 21		200 ___
2135120	NS TMCC Tamper, 21		200 ___
2135130	SP TMCC Tamper, 21		200 ___
2135140	North Pole Central Trolley, 21-23		120 ___
2138010	Kate Shelley Heritage Boxcar, 20		85 ___
2138020	Angela Trotta Thomas Stocked Shelves Boxcar - Bottom, 20		85 ___
2138030	CP 140th Anniversary Boxcar, 20		85 ___
2138040	Amtrak 50th Anniversary Boxcar, 21		85 ___
2138050	Erie Railroad 170th Anniversary Boxcar, 21		85 ___
2138060	Lyndon B. Johnson Presidential Boxcar, 21		80 ___

		Exc	Mint
2138070	Chester A. Arthur Presidential Boxcar, 21		80
2138080	Franklin Pierce Presidential Boxcar, 21		80
2138110	Wings of Angels Kacie Boxcar, 21-22		95
2138120	Wings of Angels Victoria Boxcar, 21-22		95
2138130	World War II Africa Campaign Boxcar, 21		85
2138140	World War II Fletcher Class Destroyer Boxcar, 21		85
2138150	2021 Happy Birthday Boxcar, 21		90
2138160	2021 Christmas Boxcar, 21		90
2138170	2021 Anniversary Boxcar, 21		90
2138190	Wings of Angels Jessie Boxcar, 21-22		95
2143011	ATSF Flatcar w/Stakes "90410" (std O), 20-22		55
2143012	ATSF Flatcar w/Stakes "90411" (std O), 20-22		55
2143021	N&W Flatcar w/Stakes "32900" (std O), 20-23		55
2143022	N&W Flatcar w/Stakes "329019" (std O), 20-22		55
2143031	NP Flatcar w/Stakes "69001" (std O), 20-22		55
2143032	NP Flatcar w/Stakes "69123" (std O), 20-22		55
2143041	PRR Flatcar w/Stakes "497918" (std O), 20-22		55
2143042	PRR Flatcar w/Stakes "491301" (std O), 20-22		55
2143051	ADM RBL Refrigerator Car "7014" (std O), 20-22		55
2143052	ADM RBL Refrigerator Car "7019" (std O), 20-23		55
2143061	CN RBL Refrigerator Car "290403" (std O), 20-22		55
2143062	CN RBL Refrigerator Car "290936" (std O), 20-22		55
2143071	FGE RBL Refrigerator Car "363454" (std O), 20-22		55
2143072	FGE RBL Refrigerator Car "363700" (std O), 20-22		55
2143081	PRR RBL Refrigerator Car "19103" (std O), 20-22		55
2143082	PRR RBL Refrigerator Car "19198" (std O), 20-22		55
2143091	CP< DD Boxcar "7751" (std O), 21		50
2143092	CP< DD Boxcar "7844" (std O), 21		50
2143101	D&M DD Boxcar "2115", 21		50
2143102	D&M DD Boxcar "2127", 21		50
2143111	Port of Tillamook Bay RR DD Boxcar "164" (std O), 21		50
2143112	Port of Tillamook Bay RR DD Boxcar "187" (std O), 21		50
2143121	Sierra RR DD Boxcar "5009" (std O), 21		50
2143122	Sierra RR DD Boxcar "5036" (std O), 21		50
2143131	NYC Gondola w/Ballast Load "632353" (std O), 21		50
2143132	NYC Gondola w/Ballast Load "632361" (std O), 21		50
2143141	N&W Gondola w/Ballast Load "591000" (std O), 21		50
2143142	N&W Gondola w/Ballast Load "591082" (std O), 21		50
2143151	PRR Gondola w/Ballast Load "490075" (std O), 21		50
2143152	PRR Gondola w/Ballast Load "490079" (std O), 21		50
2143161	UP Gondola w/Ballast Load "908467" (std O), 21		50
2143162	UP Gondola w/Ballast Load "908469" (std O), 21		50
2201290	LCCA N&W 2-6-6-4 Class A Locomotive "1222," CC, 22 u		2100
2208010	Legacy Base 3, 22-23		500
2213050	Strasburg RR 2-10-0 Locomotive (1967/2020) "90," CC, 21		1900
2222010	BNSF SD70MAC Diesel Coal Train Set, CC, 21		900
2222020	UP Rocket Booster Diesel Set, CC, 22		1700
2222030	BN SD45 Hustle Muscle Diesel Freight Set, CC, 21		1100
2222040	Cambria & Indiana SW9 Bicentennial Diesel Coal Train Set, CC, 21		1000
2222050	Grand Canyon Ry Steam Passenger Set, CC, 21		1300
2222060	Amtrak Genesis LionChief Plus 2.0 Set, 22		1000
2222070	B&LE Diesel Ore Train Set, CC, 22		1600

		Exc	Mint
2222080	Black River & Western Excursion Diesel Passenger Set, CC, 22-24		1100
2222090	NS 40th Anniversary Diesel Freight Set, CC, 22		1300
2222100	PRR S2 Steam LionChief Plus 2.0 Set, 22		750
2223010	U.S. Army LionChief Bluetooth 5.0 Diesel Freight Set, 21-24		450
2223020	Christmas Celebration LionChief Bluetooth 5.0 Set, 22-24		400
2223040	Emergency Response LionChief Bluetooth 5.0 Set, 22-24		500
2223050	Anheuser Busch LionChief Bluetooth 5.0 Set, 22-24		400
2223060	Lionel Lines LionChief Bluetooth 5.0 Mixed Freight Set, 22-24		360
2223070	Great Locomotive Chase Deluxe LionChief Bluetooth 5.0 Set, 22-24		600
2223110	Graffiti LionChief Bluetooth 5.0 Set, 22-24		500
2226010	Erie Boxcar "82275" w/HoboSounds, 21		190
2226020	RI Boxcar "48582" w/HoboSounds, 21		190
2226030	AT&SF AAR 2-Bay Hopper 2-Pack, 21		200
2226040	Cambria & Indiana Die-cast AAR 2-Bay Hopper 2-Pack, 21		200
2226050	NYC AAR 2-Bay Hopper 2-Pack, 21		200
2226060	NS AAR 2-Bay Hopper 2-Pack, 21		200
2226070	Pittsburg & Shawmut AAR 2-Bay Hopper 2-Pack, 21		200
2226080	Reading AAR 2-Bay Hopper 2-Pack, 21,24		200
2226090	Alaska Cylindrical Covered Hopper "14500", 21		110
2226100	CSX (ex EL) Cylindrical Covered Hopper "884137", 21		110
2226110	EL Cylindrical Covered Hopper "20021", 21		110
2226120	GM Cylindrical Covered Hopper "61113", 21, 24		110
2226130	NYC Cylindrical Covered Hopper "885950", 21		110
2226140	UP Cylindrical Covered Hopper "221000", 21		110
2226150	CP Caboose "434604" w/CupolaCam, 21		220
2226160	SSW Caboose "3" w/CupolaCam, 21		220
2226170	NP Caboose "10401" w/CupolaCam, 21		220
2226180	SAL Caboose "5754" w/CupolaCam, 21		220
2226190	Soo Caboose "1" w/CupolaCam, 21		220
2226200	North Pole Central Caboose "2521" w/CupolaCam, 21		220
2226210	UP CA-1 Caboose "2664" (brown), 21		150
2226220	UP CA-1 Caboose "2535" (brown), 21		150
2226230	UP CA-1 Caboose "2550" (yellow), 21		150
2226240	UP CA-1 Caboose "2654" (white), 21		150
2226250	SP CA-1 Caboose "703", 21		150
2226260	Great Western CA-1 Caboose "1006", 21		150
2226270	AT&SF 50' Flatcar "91090" w/Fire Truck, 21		160
2226280	C&O 50' Flatcar "81001" w/Fire Truck, 21		160
2226290	NYC 50' Flatcar "506261" w/Fire Truck, 21		160
2226300	PRR 50' Flatcar "469660" w/Fire Truck, 21		160
2226310	Southern 50' Flatcar "51819" w/Fire Truck, 21		160
2226320	UP 50' Flatcar "53026" w/Fire Truck, 21		160
2226330	Ann Arbor 4-Door Hi-Cube Boxcar "10009", 21		130
2226340	CN 4-Door Hi-Cube Boxcar "795101", 21		130
2226350	Ford 4-Door Hi-Cube Boxcar "101", 21		130
2226360	N&W 4-Door Hi-Cube Boxcar "355173", 21		130
2226370	PC 4-Door Hi-Cube Boxcar "237544", 21		130
2226380	WP 4-Door Hi-Cube Boxcar "86011", 21		130
2226390	CN 4-Door Hi-Cube Boxcar w/graffiti, 21		140
2226400	Conrail 4-Door Hi-Cube Boxcar w/graffiti, 21		140
2226410	HLMX 4-Door Hi-Cube Boxcar w/graffiti, 21		140

			Exc	Mint
___	2226420	NS 4-Door Hi-Cube Boxcar w/graffiti, 21		140
___	2226430	UP Rocket Booster Flatcar w/Rocket 5-Pack, 22-24		860
___	2226440	UP Rocket Booster Flatcar 5-Pack, 22		750
___	2226451	Bethlehem Steel Coil Car "216451", 22-24		120
___	2226452	Bethlehem Steel Coil Car "216489", 22		120
___	2226461	BNSF Coil Car "534321", 22-24		120
___	2226462	BNSF Coil Car "534354", 22-24		120
___	2226471	Conrail Coil Car "623603", 22-24		120
___	2226472	Conrail Coil Car "623624", 22-24		120
___	2226481	Ferromex Coil Car "918040", 22-24		120
___	2226482	Ferromex Coil Car "918046", 22-24		120
___	2226491	Reading Coil Car "99502", 22-24		120
___	2226492	Reading Coil Car "99561", 22-24		120
___	2226501	UP Coil Car "242081", 22-24		120
___	2226502	UP Coil Car "242118", 22-24		120
___	2226510	Bethlehem Steel Coil Car w/Graffiti "216469", 22-24		130
___	2226520	BNSF Coil Car w/Graffiti "534370", 22		130
___	2226530	Conrail (NYC) Coil Car w/Graffiti "623684", 22-24		130
___	2226540	Ferromex Coil Car w/Graffiti "918032", 22-24		130
___	2226550	NS Coil Car w/Graffiti "167024", 22-24		130
___	2226560	Polar Express End Door Boxcar, 22		115
___	2226571	BN Husky Stack Car "63345", 22-24		170
___	2226572	BN Husky Stack Car w/Graffiti "63361", 22-24		190
___	2226581	CRLE Husky Stack Car "5462", 22-24		170
___	2226582	CRLE Husky Stack Car w/Graffiti "5496", 22-24		190
___	2226591	CSX Husky Stack Car "620360", 22		170
___	2226592	CSX Husky Stack Car w/Graffiti "620365", 22		190
___	2226601	TT Husky Stack Car "56218", 22-24		170
___	2226602	TT Husky Stack Car w/Graffiti "56317", 22-24		190
___	2226611	TTX Husky Stack Car "56295", 22-24		170
___	2226612	TTX Husky Stack Car w/Graffiti "56363", 22-24		190
___	2226621	Pacer Husky Stack Car "6301", 22		170
___	2226622	Pacer Husky Stack Car w/Graffiti "6325", 22-24		190
___	2226630	AT&SF End Door Boxcar "7176", 22		115
___	2226640	CB&Q End Door Boxcar "48520", 22-24		115
___	2226650	Conoco End Door Boxcar "50014", 22-24		115
___	2226660	Southern End Door Boxcar "42000", 22		115
___	2226670	UP End Door Boxcar "161202", 22-24		115
___	2226680	Wabash End Door Boxcar "18023", 22-24		115
___	2226690	B&O Bobber Caboose "1775", 22		120
___	2226700	LV Bobber Caboose "2606""22		120
___	2226710	Maryland & Pennsylvania Bobber Caboose "2003", 22		120
___	2226720	Northern Central Bobber Caboose "200", 22		120
___	2226730	Strasburg Bobber Caboose "1", 22		120
___	2226740	U.S. Military Bobber Caboose "65", 22		120
___	2226750	BNSF Anniversary BW Caboose, 22		145
___	2226760	CSX Fire BW Caboose, 22		145
___	2226770	CSX Police BW Caboose, 22		145
___	2226780	CSX Veterans BW Caboose, 22		145
___	2226790	CN Veterans BW Caboose, 22		145
___	2226800	CP Veterans BW Caboose, 22-24		145
___	2226810	BNSF Illuminated Flag Boxcar, 22		160
___	2226820	CSX Fire Illuminated Flag Boxcar, 22		160

MODERN 1970-2024		Exc	Mint
2226830	CSX Police Illuminated Flag Boxcar, 22		160 ___
2226840	CSX Veterans Illuminated Flag Boxcar, 22		160 ___
2226850	Conrail Veterans Illuminated Flag Boxcar, 22		160 ___
2226860	Montana Rail Link Illuminated Flag Boxcar, 22-24		160 ___
2226870	AT&SF Vision Line Stockcar 3-Pack, 22-24		450 ___
2226880	B&O Vision Line Stockcar 3-Pack, 22-24		450 ___
2226890	NYC Vision Line Stockcar 3-Pack, 22-24		450 ___
2226900	NP Vision Line Stockcar 3-Pack, 22-24		450 ___
2226910	Swift Vision Line Stockcar 3-Pack, 22-24		450 ___
2226920	UP Vision Line Stockcar 3-Pack, 22-24		450 ___
2226930	N&W 2-Bay Hopper 2-Pack, 22		200 ___
2226940	PRR 2-Bay Hopper 2-Pack, 22-24		200 ___
2226950	Pennsylvania Coal & Coke 2-Bay Hopper 2-Pack, 22-24		200 ___
2226960	VGN 2-Bay Hopper 2-Pack, 22-24		200 ___
2226970	Westmoreland Coal 2-Bay Hopper 2-Pack, 22-24		200 ___
2226980	West Penn. Power 2-Bay Hopper 2-Pack, 22		200 ___
2226990	North Pole Central End Door Boxcar, 22-24		115 ___
2226991	UP Desert Victory Illuminated Flag Boxcar, 22-24		160 ___
2227010	Strasburg RR Observation "Paradise", 21		210 ___
2227020	Philadelphia & Reading Observation "10", 21		210 ___
2227030	Strasburg RR Wood Coach 2-Pack #1 (1990s), 21		400 ___
2227040	Strasburg RR Wood Coach 2-Pack #2 (1990s), 21		400 ___
2227050	Strasburg RR Wood Coach 2-Pack #1 (2000s), 21		400 ___
2227060	Strasburg RR Wood Coach 2-Pack #2 (2000s), 21		400 ___
2227070	PRR Wood Coach 2-Pack #1, 21		400 ___
2227080	PRR Wood Coach 2-Pack #2, 21		400 ___
2227090	B&M Wood Coach 2-Pack #1, 21		400 ___
2227100	B&M Wood Coach 2-Pack #2, 21		400 ___
2227110	LIRR 72' Passenger Coach 2-Pack #1, 21, 24		390 ___
2227120	LIRR 72' Passenger Coach 2-Pack #2, 21, 24		390 ___
2227130	NH 18" Passenger Car 2-Pack #1, 21		420 ___
2227140	NH 18" Passenger Car 2-Pack #2, 21		420 ___
2227150	NH 18" Passenger Car 2-Pack #3, 21		420 ___
2227160	NH 18" Diner w/StationSounds, 21		380 ___
2227170	Strasburg RR B380#1 (1990s), 21		400 ___
2227180	Strasburg RR Wood Coach/Combine 2-Pack #2 (2000s), 21		400 ___
2227190	PRR Wood Coach/Combine 2-Pack, 21		400 ___
2227200	B&M Wood Coach/Combine 2-Pack, 21		400 ___
2227210	Grand Canyon Ry Coach 2-Pack, 21		390 ___
2227220	UP Rocket Train Rider Car "Hialeah", 22		225 ___
2227230	AT&SF Chief Add-On Coach, 22-24		100 ___
2227240	AT&SF Chief Add-On Vista-Dome "501", 22-24		100 ___
2227250	NS Excursion Coach 4-Pack, 22-24		900 ___
2227260	Amtrak Phase III 21" Passenger Car 4-Pack, 22		900 ___
2227270	Amtrak Phase III 21" Passenger Car 2-Pack, 22-24		450 ___
2227280	Amtrak Phase III Diner w/StationSounds, 22		400 ___
2227290	Amtrak Amfleet Phase III Coach 2-Pack, 22		400 ___
2227300	Amtrak Amfleet Phase V Coach 2-Pack, 22		400 ___
2227310	Amtrak Amfleet Phase VI Coach 2-Pack, 22		400 ___
2227320	Amtrak Amfleet Phase III Coach/Cab Car 2-Pack, 22		400 ___
2227330	Amtrak Amfleet Phase V Coach 2-Pack, 22-24		400 ___
2227340	Amtrak Amfleet Phase VI Coach/Cab Car 2-Pack, 22		400 ___
2227350	CSX Business Train 21" Passenger Car 4-Pack, 22		900 ___

			Exc	Mint
___	**2227360**	CSX Business Train 18" Passenger Car 2-Pack, 22		500
___	**2227370**	CSX Business Train 21" Diner w/StationSounds, 22		400
___	**2227380**	Aberdeen, Carolina & Western 21" Passenger Car 2-Pack, 22		450
___	**2227390**	Aberdeen, Carolina & Western 18" Passenger Car 2-Pack, 22		500
___	**2227400**	MOW Wood Baggage/Coach 2-Pack, 22-24		450
___	**2227410**	MOW Wood Combine/Coach 2-Pack, 22-24		450
___	**2227420**	MOW Wood Coach/Observation 2-Pack, 22		450
___	**2227430**	NYC&HR Wood Baggage/Coach 2-Pack, 22		450
___	**2227440**	NYC&HR Wood Combine/Coach 2-Pack, 22		450
___	**2227450**	NYC&HR Wood Coach/Observation 2-Pack, 22		450
___	**2227460**	Southern Wood Baggage/Coach 2-Pack, 22		450
___	**2227470**	Southern Wood Combine/Coach 2-Pack, 22-24		450
___	**2227480**	Southern Wood Coach/Observation 2-Pack, 22-24		450
___	**2227490**	Wabash Wood Baggage/Coach 2-Pack, 22		450
___	**2227500**	Wabash Wood Combine/Coach 2-Pack, 22		450
___	**2227510**	Wabash Wood Coach/Observation 2-Pack, 22		450
___	**2227520**	AT&SF Vision Line Horse Car "1995", 22		370
___	**2227530**	CP Vision Line Horse Car "4560", 22		370
___	**2227540**	L&N Vision Line Horse Car "1507", 22		370
___	**2227550**	PRR Vision Line Horse Car "5024", 22		370
___	**2227560**	REA Vision Line Horse Car "812", 22		370
___	**2227570**	SP Vision Line Horse Car "7200", 22		370
___	**2227580**	North Pole Central Vision Reindeer Car, 22-24		370
___	**2227590**	Polar Express Vision Reindeer Car, 22		370
___	**2227600**	Bureau of Mines 18" Passenger Car 2-Pack, 22-24		500
___	**2227610**	Wood Chapel Car "Evangel", 22-24		225
___	**2228020**	Angela Trotta Thomas GG1 Boxcar, 21-24		85
___	**2228030**	U.S. Army Missile Flatcar, 21-24		90
___	**2228040**	Vintage Anheuser Busch Clydesdale Refrigerator Car, 22-23		90
___	**2228050**	Budweiser Holiday Stein Refrigerator Car, 22-24		90
___	**2228060**	Miller Refrigerator Car, 22		90
___	**2228070**	Coors Refrigerator Car, 22		90
___	**2228080**	Polar Express Aquarium Car, 22-24		120
___	**2228090**	Polar Express Illuminated Boxcar, 22-24		120
___	**2228100**	Hallow's Eve Monster Gondola, 22-23		90
___	**2228110**	Hallow's Eve Illuminated Caboose, 22-24		90
___	**2228120**	Christmas Parade Aquarium Car, 22-24		120
___	**2228130**	Christmas Chasing Gondola, 22-23		90
___	**2228140**	Night Before Christmas Illuminated Boxcar, 22-23		120
___	**2228150**	2022 Christmas Boxcar, 22		70
___	**2228160**	Christmas Music Boxcar "22", 22-24		85
___	**2228170**	Angela Trotta Thomas Christmas Aquarium Car, 22-24		120
___	**2228180**	Angela Trotta Thomas Blue Comet Boxcar, 22-24		85
___	**2228190**	Angela Trotta Thomas NYC Boxcar, 22-24		85
___	**2228220**	Mickey & Friends Christmas Caboose, 22-24		90
___	**2228230**	Mickey & Friends Christmas Searchlight Car, 22-23		85
___	**2228250**	U.S. Navy Flatcar w/Submarine, 22-24		90
___	**2228270**	U.S. Air Force Minuteman Car, 22-24		120
___	**2228280**	U.S. Marine Corps Rocket Launcher Car, 22-24		110
___	**2228290**	U.S. Army Big Cannon Car, 22-24		110
___	**2228300**	Polar Express Caboose, 22-24		90
___	**2228310**	North Pole Central Illuminated Hopper, 22-24		100
___	**2228320**	Budweiser Tank Car, 22-23		85

		Exc	Mint
2228350	Monsters Inc. Scare Tank Car w/LEDs, 22-24		120 ___
2228360	Incredibles Operating Car, 22-24		120 ___
2228370	Toy Story Woody Walking Brakeman Car, 22-24		120 ___
2228380	John Deere Refrigerator Car, 22-24		90 ___
2228390	John Deere Work Caboose, 22-24		85 ___
2228400	Fourth of July LED Car w/Sounds, 22-24		150 ___
2228410	American Flag LED Car, 22-24		120 ___
2228440	Chevrolet Boxcar, 22-24		85 ___
2228450	Chevrolet Flatcar w/Piggyback Trailers, 22-24		95 ___
2228460	Ford Boxcar, 22-24		85 ___
2228470	Ford Flatcar w/Piggyback Trailers, 22-24		95 ___
2228480	Hallow's Eve Mint Car, 22-24		120 ___
2228490	Ghoul Searchlight Car, 22-24		85 ___
2228500	Graffiti Hi-Cube Boxcar, 22-24		80 ___
2228510	W&A Freight Expansion Pack, 22-24		220 ___
2228520	2022 National Lionel Train Day Boxcar, 22-24		70 ___
2229010	No. 943 Exploding Ammunition Dump, 21-24		65 ___
2229020	Missile Range, 21-24		80 ___
2229030	Train Orders Building, 21-22		140 ___
2229040	Mission Control Tower, 21-24		130 ___
2229050	Burning House, 21-22		200 ___
2229060	Tough Guy Gym & Fitness, 21-24		160 ___
2229070	Barn, 21-24		180 ___
2229080	Passenger Station, 21-22		150 ___
2229100	Townhouse, 21-24		110 ___
2229110	Thistle Stop Flower Shop, 21-24		160 ___
2229120	Christmas Barn, 21-24		200 ___
2229130	Military Surplus Store, 21-24		160 ___
2229140	Welcome Home Troops Townhouse, 21-24		110 ___
2229150	Fire Station, 22		330 ___
2229160	Private Investigation Building, 22-24		160 ___
2229170	Bail Bonds Building, 22		110 ___
2229170	Bail Bonds Building, 22-24		110 ___
2229180	Donuts & Coffee Shop, 22-24		110 ___
2229190	Budweiser Brewery, 22-24		220 ___
2229200	Operating Transfer Station, 22-24		300 ___
2229210	Deer Dash Transfer Station, 22-24		300 ___
2229220	Grim's Repo Depot Transfer Station, 22-24		300 ___
2229230	Western Mercantile, 22-24		80 ___
2229250	Sheriff's Headquarters Building, 22-24		80 ___
2229260	Firefighter Tank Car Accident Training, 22-24		130 ___
2229270	Industrial Water Tower w/Graffiti Decals, 22-24		80 ___
2229280	Polar Express Hot Chocolate Industrial Tower, 22-24		90 ___
2229290	Up on the Rooftop Christmas House, 22-24		100 ___
2229300	Rocket Launch Pad, 22-23		430 ___
2229310	Illuminated Coaling Station, 22-24		130 ___
2229320	Christmas Coal Works Lighted Coaling Station, 22-23		130 ___
2230010	Vintage Inspired Space Billboards, 21-24		25 ___
2230020	Amtrak Through The Years Billboards, 21-24		25 ___
2230030	Quonset Hut, 21-24		45 ___
2230050	Thomas & Friends Christmas Girder Bridge, 22-24		35 ___
2230060	Red Fire Truck, 21-24		80 ___
2230070	Yellow Fire Truck, 21-24		80 ___

			Exc	Mint
___	**2230080**	White Fire Truck, 21-24		80
___	**2230090**	Black Fire Truck, 21-24		80
___	**2230100**	Smoke Fluid Dropper 2-Pack, 21-24		5
___	**2230110**	Airplane Accessory 2-Pack, 22-23		14
___	**2230120**	Boats 4-Pack, 22-23		14
___	**2230130**	Helicopters 2-Pack, 22-23		14
___	**2230140**	Railroad Signs 5-Pack, 22-24		9
___	**2230150**	Angela Trotta Thomas Christmas Billboards, 22-24		25
___	**2230160**	Halloween Billboards, 22-24		25
___	**2230170**	Unique Railroad Signs 5-Pack, 22-24		9
___	**2230180**	Firefighter Figures and Dog, 22-24		30
___	**2231010**	Great Western 2-10-0 Locomotive "90," CC, 21		1900
___	**2231020**	Strasburg RR 2-10-0 Locomotive (1990s) "90," CC, 21		1900
___	**2231030**	Strasburg RR 2-10-0 Locomotive (2000s) "90," CC, 21		1900
___	**2231040**	Great Western 2-10-0 Locomotive (2000s) "90," CC, 21		1900
___	**2231060**	SAL 2-10-0 Locomotive "525," CC, 21		1900
___	**2231070**	Osage Ry 2-10-0 Locomotive "10," CC, 21		1900
___	**2231080**	AT&SF 2-8-0 Locomotive "2535," CC, 21		750
___	**2231090**	Buffalo Creek & Gauley 2-8-0 Locomotive "4," CC, 21		750
___	**2231100**	C&O 2-8-0 Locomotive "701," CC, 21		750
___	**2231110**	MEC 2-8-0 Locomotive "519," CC, 21		750
___	**2231120**	NYC 2-8-0 Locomotive "960," CC, 21		750
___	**2231130**	WP 2-8-0 Locomotive "26," CC, 21		750
___	**2231141**	AT&SF 2-10-4 Locomotive "5011," CC, 22		1750
___	**2231142**	AT&SF 2-10-4 Locomotive "5022," CC, 22		1750
___	**2231150**	AT&SF 2-10-4 Locomotive "5001," CC, 22		1750
___	**2231160**	KCS 2-10-4 Locomotive "902," CC, 22		1750
___	**2231170**	KCS 2-10-4 Locomotive "905," CC, 22		1750
___	**2231180**	PRR 2-10-4 Locomotive "6510," CC, 22		1750
___	**2231191**	SP AC-12 Cab Forward Locomotive "4294," CC, 21		2000
___	**2231192**	SP AC-12 Cab Forward Locomotive "4281," CC, 21		2000
___	**2231200**	SP AC-12 Cab Forward Locomotive "4278" w/black tender, CC, 21		2000
___	**2231210**	SP AC-12 Cab Forward Locomotive, Daylight scheme, "4290," CC, 21		2000
___	**2231220**	SP AC-12 Cab Forward Locomotive, Lark scheme, "4285," CC, 21		2000
___	**2231230**	SP AC-12 Cab Forward Locomotive "4278" w/gray boiler, CC, 21		2000
___	**2231241**	UP 4-12-2 Locomotive "9000," CC, 21		1700
___	**2231242**	UP 4-12-2 Locomotive "9023," CC, 21		1700
___	**2231250**	UP 4-12-2 Locomotive "9514," CC, 21		1700
___	**2231260**	UP 4-12-2 Locomotive "9002," CC, 21		1700
___	**2231270**	UP 4-12-2 Locomotive "9014," CC, 21		1700
___	**2231280**	C&O 4-12-2 Locomotive "560," CC, 21		1700
___	**2231290**	D&RGW 4-12-2 Locomotive "1420," CC, 21		1700
___	**2231300**	MILW 4-12-2 Locomotive "1500," CC, 21		1700
___	**2231310**	SP 4-12-2 Locomotive "2124," CC, 21		1700
___	**2231320**	SP&S 4-12-2 Locomotive "651," CC, 21		1700
___	**2231340**	B&A 2-8-4 Berkshire Locomotive "1401," CC, 22		1600
___	**2231350**	B&M 2-8-4 Berkshire Locomotive "4019," CC, 22		1600
___	**2231360**	C&NW 2-8-4 Berkshire Locomotive "2803," CC, 22		1600
___	**2231370**	AT&SF 2-8-4 Berkshire Locomotive "4198," CC, 22		1600
___	**2231380**	SP 2-8-4 Berkshire Locomotive "3506," CC, 22		1600

		Exc	Mint
2231390	TA&G 2-8-4 Berkshire Locomotive "602," CC, 22		1600
2231400	B&M 4-4-2 Atlantic Locomotive "3243," CC, 22		900
2231410	MP 4-4-2 Atlantic Locomotive "5521," CC, 22		900
2231420	NH 4-4-2 Atlantic Locomotive "1111," CC, 22		900
2231430	NYC 4-4-2 Atlantic Locomotive "4751," CC, 22		900
2231440	Southern 4-4-2 Atlantic Locomotive "1905," CC, 22		900
2231450	Wabash 4-4-2 Atlantic Locomotive "606," CC, 22		900
2231460	N&W 2-6-6-4 Class A Locomotive "1218," CC, 22		2100
2231470	N&W 2-6-6-4 Class A Locomotive "1238," CC, 22		2100
2231470	N&W 2-6-6-4 Class A Locomotive "1238," CC, 22		2100
2231480	N&W 2-6-6-4 Class A Locomotive "1200," CC, 22		2100
2231490	N&W 2-6-6-4 Class A Locomotive "1210," CC, 22		2100
2231500	N&W 2-6-6-4 Class A Locomotive "1211," CC, 22		2100
2231510	N&W 2-6-6-4 Class A Locomotive "1201," CC, 22		2100
2231520	N&W 2-6-6-4 Class A Locomotive, "Pilot," CC, 22		2100
2231530	Bethlehem Steel 0-6-0 Locomotive "60," CC, 22		800
2231540	SL&SF 0-6-0 Locomotive "3801," CC, 22		800
2231550	NYC 0-6-0 Locomotive "222," CC, 22		800
2231560	PRR 0-6-0 Locomotive "7007," CC, 22		800
2231570	Strasburg 0-6-0 Locomotive "31," CC, 22		800
2231580	Terminal RR of St. Louis 0-6-0 Locomotive "160," CC, 22		800
2231590	Washington Terminal 0-6-0 Locomotive "32," CC, 22		800
2231600	Unpainted brass 2-10-0 Locomotive, CC, 21		1900
2232010	NYC 4-6-4 Hudson Locomotive "5314," LionChief Plus 2.0, 21-22		650
2232020	UP 4-6-4 Hudson Locomotive "675," LionChief Plus 2.0, 21-22		650
2232030	AT&SF 4-6-4 Hudson Locomotive "3463," LionChief Plus 2.0, 21-22		650
2232040	Lionel Lines 4-6-4 Hudson Locomotive "773," LionChief Plus 2.0, 21-22		650
2232050	Bethlehem Steel 0-4-0 Locomotive "76," CC, 22		700
2232060	B&O 0-4-0 Locomotive "37," CC, 22		700
2232070	U.S. Army 0-4-0 Locomotive "491,"" CC, 22		700
2232080	PRR 0-4-0 Locomotive "477," CC, 22		700
2232090	LIRR 0-4-0 Locomotive "175," CC, 22		700
2232100	B&O 4-6-2 Pacific Locomotive "5215," LionChief Plus 2.0, 22		650
2232110	D&RGW 4-6-2 Pacific Locomotive "801," LionChief Plus 2.0, 22		650
2232120	LV 4-6-2 Pacific Locomotive "2101," LionChief Plus 2.0, 22		650
2232130	Reading & Northern 4-6-2 Pacific Locomotive "425," LionChief Plus 2.0, 22		650
2232140	North Pole Central 4-6-2 Pacific Locomotive "1224," LionChief Plus 2.0, 22-24		650
2233010	BNSF SD70MAC Diesel "9647," CC, 21		650
2233021	BNSF SD70MAC Diesel "9718," CC, 21		650
2233028	BNSF SuperBass SD70MAC Diesel "9829", 21		550
2233031	BNSF SD70MAC Diesel "9721," CC, 21		650
2233032	BNSF SD70MAC Diesel "9789," CC, 21		650
2233038	BNSF SuperBass SD70MAC Diesel "9819", 21		550
2233041	Conrail SD70MAC Diesel "777," CC, 21		650
2233042	Conrail SD70MAC Diesel "780," CC, 21		650
2233048	Conrail SuperBass SD70MAC Diesel "782", 21		550
2233051	CSX SD70MAC Diesel "4551," CC, 21		650

			Exc	Mint
___	**2233052**	CSX SD70MAC Diesel "4553," CC, 21		650
___	**2233058**	CSX SuperBass SD70MAC Diesel "4558", 21		550
___	**2233061**	NS SD70MAC Diesel "1800," CC, 21		650
___	**2233062**	NS SuperBass SD70MAC Diesel "1801", 21		550
___	**2233071**	Paducah & Louisville SD70MAC Diesel "4501," CC, 21		650
___	**2233072**	Paducah & Louisville SD70MAC Diesel "4504," CC, 21		650
___	**2233078**	Paducah & Louisville SuperBass SD70MAC "4523", 21		550
___	**2233081**	BN SD45 Diesel "6445," CC, 21		600
___	**2233082**	BN SD45 Diesel "6452," CC, 21		600
___	**2233088**	BN SuperBass SD45 Diesel "6455", 21		500
___	**2233091**	EMD SD45 Diesel "4351," CC, 21		600
___	**2233092**	EMD SD45 Diesel "4352,"" CC, 21, 24		600
___	**2233098**	EMD SuperBass SD45 Diesel "4353", 21		500
___	**2233101**	Guilford/Springfield Terminal SD45 Diesel "681," CC, 21		600
___	**2233102**	Guilford/Springfield Terminal SD45 Diesel "684," CC, 21		600
___	**2233108**	Guilford/Springfield Terminal SuperBass SD45 Diesel "685", 21		500
___	**2233111**	MILW SD45 Diesel "6," CC, 21		600
___	**2233112**	MILW SD45 Diesel "8," CC, 21		600
___	**2233118**	MILW SuperBass SD45 Diesel "10", 21		500
___	**2233121**	NS SD45 Diesel "1716," CC, 21		600
___	**2233122**	NS SD45 Diesel "766," CC, 21		600
___	**2233128**	NS SuperBass SD45 Diesel """1795", 21		500
___	**2233131**	PRR SD45 Diesel "6186," CC, 21		600
___	**2233132**	PRR SD45 Diesel "197," CC, 21		600
___	**2233138**	PRR SuperBass SD45 Diesel "6202", 21		500
___	**2233141**	Alaska DD35 Diesel "5000," CC, 21		700
___	**2233142**	Alaska DD35 Diesel "5001," CC, 21		700
___	**2233151**	AT&SF DD35 Diesel "1650," CC, 21		700
___	**2233152**	AT&SF DD35 Diesel "1652," CC, 21		700
___	**2233160**	UP DD35 Diesel "71" (Dependable Transportation), CC, 21		700
___	**2233170**	UP DD35 Diesel "76" (We Can Handle It), CC, 21		700
___	**2233180**	UP DD35 Diesel "77" (Shield herald), CC, 21		700
___	**2233190**	UP DD35 Diesel "81" (American flag), CC, 21		700
___	**2233200**	AT&SF SW1200 Diesel "1441," CC, 21		550
___	**2233210**	BNSF SW1200 Diesel "3505," CC, 21		550
___	**2233220**	D&RGW SW1200 Diesel "134," CC, 21		550
___	**2233230**	EJ&E SW1200 Diesel "306," CC, 21		550
___	**2233240**	PC SW1200 Diesel "9020," CC, 21		550
___	**2233250**	US Steel SW1200 Diesel "13," CC, 21		550
___	**2233261**	FM Demonstrator C-Liner Diesel "4801," CC, 21		600
___	**2233262**	FM Demonstrator C-Liner Diesel"4802," CC, 21		600
___	**2233271**	CN C-Liner Diesel "6701," CC, 21		600
___	**2233272**	CN C-Liner Diesel "6705," CC, 21		600
___	**2233281**	LIRR C-Liner Diesel "2001," CC, 21		600
___	**2233282**	LIRR C-Liner Diesel "2003," CC, 21		600
___	**2233291**	NH C-Liner Diesel "792," CC, 21		600
___	**2233292**	NH C-Liner Diesel "798," CC, 21		600
___	**2233301**	NYC C-Liner Diesel "4500," CC, 21		600
___	**2233302**	NYC C-Liner Diesel "4502," CC, 21		600
___	**2233311**	PRR C-Liner Diesel "9570," CC, 21		600
___	**2233312**	PRR C-Liner Diesel "9571," CC, 21		600
___	**2233321**	Alco Demonstrator RS27 Diesel "640-2," CC, 22		600
___	**2233322**	Alco Demonstrator RS27 Diesel "640-4," CC, 22		600

		Exc	Mint
2233331	C&NW Alco RS27 Diesel "900," CC, 22	600	___
2233332	C&NW Alco RS27 Diesel "903," CC, 22	600	___
2233341	Conrail Alco RS27 Diesel "2412," CC, 22	600	___
2233342	Conrail Alco RS27 Diesel "2414," CC, 22	600	___
2233351	GB&W Alco RS27 Diesel "316," CC, 22	600	___
2233352	GB&W Alco RS27 Diesel "318," CC, 22	600	___
2233361	PC Alco RS27 Diesel, "2407," CC, 22	600	___
2233362	PC Alco RS27 Diesel, "2409," CC, 22	600	___
2233371	SOO Alco RS27 Diesel "415," CC, 22	600	___
2233372	SOO Alco RS27 Diesel "416," CC, 22	600	___
2233380	B&O EMD SW1 Diesel "8408," CC, 22	550	___
2233390	BN EMD SW1 Diesel "97," CC, 22	550	___
2233400	Conrail EMD SW1 Diesel "8408," CC, 22	550	___
2233410	Flambeau Paper EMD SW1 Diesel "1," CC, 22	550	___
2233420	SP EMD SW1 Diesel "1000," CC, 22	550	___
2233430	Turtle Creek EMD SW1 Diesel "462," CC, 22	550	___
2233441	BNSF Heritage ES44AC Diesel "6075," CC, 22	700	___
2233442	BNSF Heritage ES44AC Diesel "6111," CC, 22	700	___
2233449	BNSF Heritage ES44AC Diesel "6179" (nonpowered), 22	400	___
2233451	BC Rail Heritage ES44AC Diesel "3115," CC, 22	700	___
2233459	BC Rail Heritage ES44AC Diesel "3115," (nonpowered), 22	400	___
2233461	EJ&E Heritage ES44AC Diesel "3023," CC, 22	700	___
2233469	EJ&E Heritage ES44AC Diesel "3023" (unpowered), 22	400	___
2233471	IC Heritage ES44AC Diesel "3008," CC, 22	700	___
2233479	IC Heritage ES44AC Diesel "3008"(unpowered), 22	400	___
2233481	WC Heritage ES44AC Diesel "3069," CC, 22	700	___
2233489	WC Heritage ES44AC Diesel "3069" (unpowered), 22	400	___
2233491	CN Veterans ES44AC Diesel "3015," CC, 22	700	___
2233492	CN Veterans ES44AC Diesel "3233," CC, 22	700	___
2233499	CN Veterans ES44AC Diesel "3015" (unpowered), 22	400	___
2233501	U.S. Armed Forces ES44AC Diesel "1775," CC, 22	700	___
2233502	U.S. Armed Forces ES44AC Diesel "2022," non-powered, 22-24	400	___
2233511	BN EMD SD40-2 Diesel "1876," CC, 22	650	___
2233519	BN EMD SD40-2 Diesel "1876" (unpowered), 22	350	___
2233521	BN EMD SD40-2 Diesel "8002," CC, 22	650	___
2233529	BN EMD SD40-2 Diesel "8002" (unpowered), 22	350	___
2233531	Louisville & Indiana EMD SD40-2 Diesel "3001," CC, 22	650	___
2233539	Louisville & Indiana EMD SD40-2 Diesel "3001" (unpowered), 22	350	___
2233541	Maersk/Sealand EMD SD40-2 Diesel "3329," CC, 22	650	___
2233549	Maersk/Sealand EMD SD40-2 Diesel "3329" (unpowered), 22	350	___
2233551	Savage EMD SD40-2 Diesel "8638," CC, 22	700	___
2233559	Savage EMD SD40-2 Diesel "8638" (unpowered), 22	400	___
2233561	UP Desert Victory EMD SD40-2 Diesel "3593," CC, 22	700	___
2233569	UP Desert Victory EMD SD40-2 Diesel "3593" (unpowered), 22	400	___
2233570	B&LE EMD F7 A-B Set "722A/722B," CC, 22	1150	___
2233580	Aberdeen, Carolina & Western EMD F9 A-B Set "271/276," CC, 22	1150	___
2233590	Reading & Northern EMD F9 A-B Set "270/275," CC, 22	1150	___
2233601	CP Veterans EMD SD90MAC Diesel "7020," CC, 22	650	___
2233609	CP Veterans EMD SD90MAC Diesel "7020"" (unpowered), 22	400	___

			Exc	Mint
___	**2233611**	CP Veterans EMD SD90MAC Diesel "7021," CC, 22		650
___	**2233619**	CP Veterans EMD SD90MAC Diesel "7021" (unpowered), 22		400
___	**2233621**	CP Veterans EMD SD90MAC Diesel "7022," CC, 22		650
___	**2233629**	CP Veterans EMD SD90MAC Diesel "7022" (unpowered), 22		400
___	**2233631**	CP Veterans EMD SD90MAC Diesel "7023," CC, 22		650
___	**2233639**	CP Veterans EMD SD90MAC Diesel "7023" (unpowered), 22		400
___	**2233641**	CP Veterans EMD SD90MAC Diesel "6644," CC, 22		650
___	**2233649**	CP Veterans EMD SD90MAC Diesel "6644" (unpowered), 22		400
___	**2233651**	CP Heritage EMD SD90MAC Diesel "7010," CC, 22		650
___	**2233652**	CP Heritage EMD SD90MAC Diesel "7016," CC, 22		650
___	**2233660**	EMD Demonstrator SD90MAC Diesel "8204," CC, 22		650
___	**2233671**	NS (UP Patch) EMD SD90MAC Diesel "7240," CC, 22		650
___	**2233672**	NS (UP Patch) EMD SD90MAC Diesel "73140," CC, 22		650
___	**2233681**	San Luis & Rio Grande EMD SD90MAC Diesel "115," CC, 22		650
___	**2233682**	San Luis & Rio Grande EMD SD90MAC Diesel "116," CC, 22		650
___	**2233711**	Amtrak F40PH Diesel Phase III "206," CC, 22		630
___	**2233712**	Amtrak F40PH Diesel Phase III "226," CC, 22		630
___	**2233721**	Amtrak F40PH Diesel Phase IV "401," CC, 22		630
___	**2233722**	Amtrak F40PH Diesel Phase IV "404," CC, 22		630
___	**2233730**	Amtrak F40PH Diesel Phase V "410," CC, 22		630
___	**2233740**	Amtrak F40PH Diesel Veterans "208," CC, 22		630
___	**2233751**	CSX Business Train Diesel "CSX-1,"" CC, 22		630
___	**2233752**	CSX Business Train Diesel "CSX-2," CC, 22		630
___	**2233753**	CSX Business Train Diesel "CSX-3," CC, 22		630
___	**2233761**	D&RGW Ski Train Diesel "242," CC, 22		630
___	**2233762**	D&RGW Ski Train Diesel "283," CC, 22		630
___	**2233770**	Amtrak NPCU Diesel Phase IV Downeaster "90214" (unpowered), 22		500
___	**2233780**	Amtrak NPCU Diesel Phase IV "90229" (unpowered), 22		500
___	**2233790**	Amtrak NPCU Diesel Phase V "90413" (unpowered), 22		500
___	**2233800**	Amtrak NPCU Diesel Veterans "90208" (unpowered), 22		500
___	**2233810**	AT&SF EMD F7 A-A Set "341/344," CC, 22		1200
___	**2233818**	AT&SF EMD F7 B Unit "345A," CC, 22		600
___	**2233819**	AT&SF EMD F7 B Unit SuperBass "348A" (unpowered), 22		550
___	**2233820**	LV EMD F7 A-A Set "562/566," CC, 22		1200
___	**2233828**	LV EMD F7 B Unit "519," CC, 22		600
___	**2233829**	LV EMD F7 B Unit SuperBass "521" (unpowered), 22		550
___	**2233830**	SOO EMD F7 A-A Set "2201A/2201B," CC, 22		1200
___	**2233838**	SOO EMD F7 B Unit "2201C," CC, 22		600
___	**2233839**	SOO EMD F7 B Unit SuperBass "2202C" (unpowered), 22		550
___	**2233840**	SP EMD F7 A-A Set "6475/6476," CC, 22		1200
___	**2233848**	SP EMD F7 B Unit "8375," CC, 22		600
___	**2233849**	SP EMD F7 B Unit SuperBass "8376" (unpowered), 22		550
___	**2233850**	UP EMD F7 A-A Set "1468/1469," CC, 22		1200
___	**2233858**	UP EMD F7 B Unit "1468B," CC, 22		600
___	**2233859**	UP EMD F7 B Unit SuperBass "1468C" (unpowered), 22		550
___	**2234010**	Amtrak Genesis Locomotive "100," LionChief Plus 2.0, 22		550
___	**2234020**	Amtrak Genesis Locomotive "108," LionChief Plus 2.0, 22		550
___	**2234030**	Amtrak Genesis Locomotive "160," LionChief Plus 2.0, 22		550
___	**2234040**	Amtrak Genesis Locomotive "161," LionChief Plus 2.0, 22		550
___	**2234050**	Amtrak Genesis Locomotive Phase V "150," LionChief Plus 2.0, 21-22		550
___	**2034060**	Amtrak Genesis Locomotive Phase 1V "111," LionChief Plus 2.0, 21-22		550

		Exc	Mint
2234060	Amtrak Genesis Locomotive Phase IV NEC "111," LionChief Plus 2.0, 21-22		550
2234070	Amtrak Genesis Locomotive Phase III "40," LionChief Plus 2.0, 21-22		550
2234080	Amtrak Genesis Locomotive Phase V 50th Anniversary "46," LionChief Plus 2.0, 21-22		550
2234090	PRR LionChief 44-Tonner Locomotive "8312", 22-24		250
2234100	ATSF LionChief 44-Tonner Locomotive "463", 22-24		250
2234110	Ford LionChief 44-Tonner Locomotive "1000", 22-24		250
2234120	U.S. Marine Corps LionChief 44-Tonner Locomotive "234120", 22-24		250
2234130	Amtrak LionChief 44-Tonner Locomotive "1100", 22-24		250
2234140	ATSF EMD GP20 Diesel "3009," LionChief Plus 2.0, 22-24		500
2234150	MILW EMD GP20 Diesel "962," LionChief Plus 2.0, 22-24		500
2234160	Conrail EMD GP20 Diesel "2108," LionChief Plus 2.0, 22-24		500
2234170	BN EMD GP20 Diesel "2054," LionChief Plus 2.0, 22-24		500
2234180	BNSF LionChief Dash-8 Diesel, 22-23		280
2234190	NS LionChief Dash-8 Diesel, 22-23		280
2234200	CSX LionChief Dash-8 Diesel, 22-23		280
2234210	UP LionChief Dash-8 Diesel, 22-23		280
2234220	Amtrak Genesis Operation Lifesaver LionChief Plus 2.0 Diesel, 22		550
2235010	Polar Express Trolley, 22-24		120
2235020	First Ave Rapid Transit Trolley, 22-23		120
2235030	Trippy Trolley, 22		140
2235040	AT&SF Doodlebug, LionChief Plus 2.0, 22-24		400
2235050	UP Doodlebug, LionChief Plus 2.0, 22-24		400
2235060	PRR Doodlebug, LionChief Plus 2.0, 22-24		400
2235070	Maryland & Pennsylvania Doodlebug, LionChief Plus 2.0, 22-24		400
2235080	Hallows Eve Limited Doodlebug, LionChief Plus 2.0, 22-24		400
2235090	North Pole Central Doodlebug, LionChief Plus 2.0, 22-24		400
2238010	UP 160th Anniversary Boxcar, 21-22		90
2238020	Great Locomotive Chase 160th Anniversary Boxcar, 21-22		90
2238030	Smithsonian 175th Anniversary Boxcar, 21, 24		90
2238040	Rutherford B. Hayes Presidential Boxcar, 22		90
2238050	Grover Cleveland Presidential Boxcar, 22		90
2238060	Gerald Ford Presidential Boxcar, 22		90
2238070	2022 Birthday Personalized Boxcar, 22		100
2238080	2022 Christmas Personalized Boxcar, 22		100
2238090	2022 Anniversary Personalized Boxcar, 22		100
2238100	World War II Generals Boxcar, 22-24		95
2238110	World War II Aircraft Carrier Boxcar, 22		90
2238120	Wings of Angels Sarah Boxcar, 22-24		95
2238130	Wings of Angels Lisa Boxcar, 22-23		95
2238140	Wings of Angels Raquel Boxcar, 22-24		95
2238150	GM Train of Tomorrow Boxcar, 22-24		90
2238160	Rockville Bridge Boxcar, 22		90
2238180	Bazooka Joe 75th Anniversary Boxcar, 22		90
2238210	MILW 175th Anniversary Boxcar, 22-24		90
2238220	Chevrolet Personalized Boxcar , 22-23		100
2238230	Ford Personalized Boxcar, 22-23		100
2243010	BNSF Rotary Gondola 4-Pack (std O), 21		360
2243020	CSX Rotary Gondola 4-Pack (std O), 21, 24		360
2243030	NS Rotary Gondola 4-Pack (std O), 21		360

			Exc	Mint
___	2243040	PRR Rotary Gondola 4-Pack (std O), 21		360
___	2243050	UP Rotary Gondola 4-Pack (std O), 21		360
___	2243060	CSX Rotary Gondola 2-Pack (std O), 21		180
___	2243070	NS Rotary Gondola 2-Pack (std O), 21		180
___	2243080	PRR Rotary Gondola 2-Pack (std O), 21		180
___	2243090	UP Rotary Gondola 2-Pack (std O), 21		180
___	2243101	Ashley, Drew & Northern Modern Boxcar "8134" (std O), 21, 24		60
___	2243102	Ashley, Drew & Northern Modern Boxcar "8145" (std O), 21-24		60
___	2243111	Conrail Modern Boxcar "166255" (std O), 21, 24		60
___	2243112	Conrail Modern Boxcar "166422" (std O), 21, 24		60
___	2243121	RI Modern Boxcar "300032" (std O), 21		60
___	2243122	RI Modern Boxcar "399370" (std O), 21		60
___	2243131	Railbox Modern Boxcar "30284" (std O), 21		60
___	2243132	Railbox Modern Boxcar "30306" (std O), 21		60
___	2243141	UP Modern Boxcar "357416" (std O), 21		60
___	2243142	UP Modern Boxcar "357429" (std O), 21		60
___	2243150	UP Rocket Idler Car 6-Pack, 22		375
___	2243160	B&LE Ore Car 6-Pack #1, 22		200
___	2243170	B&LE Ore Car 6-Pack #2, 22		200
___	2243180	BN Ore Car 6-Pack #1 (std O), 22-24		200
___	2243190	BN Ore Car 6-Pack #2 (std O), 22-24		200
___	2243200	C&NW Ore Car 6-Pack #1 (std O), 22-24		200
___	2243210	C&NW Ore Car 6-Pack #2 (std O), 22-24		200
___	2243220	DM&IR Ore Car 6-Pack #1 (std O), 22		200
___	2243230	DM&IR Ore Car 6-Pack #2 (std O), 22		200
___	2243240	SOO Ore Car 6-Pack #1 (std O), 22-24		200
___	2243250	SOO Ore Car 6-Pack #2 (std O), 22-24		200
___	2243260	UP Ore Car 6-Pack #1 (std O), 22		200
___	2243270	UP Ore Car 6-Pack #2 (std O), 22-24		200
___	2243281	SSW Insulated Boxcar "30043" (std O), 22-24		70
___	2243282	SSW Insulated Boxcar "30049" (std O), 22-24		70
___	2243291	NH State of Maine Insulated Boxcar "45022" (std O), 22		70
___	2243292	NH State of Maine Insulated Boxcar "45064" (std O), 22		70
___	2243301	NP Insulated Boxcar "98583" (std O), 22		70
___	2243302	NP Insulated Boxcar "98621" (std O), 22-24		70
___	2243311	WM Insulated Boxcar "7" (std O), 22		70
___	2243312	WM Insulated Boxcar "14" (std O), 22-24		70
___	2301050	LCCA UP Vision 4-8-8-4 Big Boy Locomotive "4023," CC, 23u		2900
___	2322010	LV Legacy Camelback Steam Freight Set, CC, 23		1100
___	2322020	WM Hagerstown Hotshot Diesel Freight Set, CC, 22		1600
___	2322030	PRR Cumberland Valley Wayfreight Set, CC, 22		1500
___	2322040	UP Vision Big Boy Steam Freight Set, CC, 23		4500
___	2322050	PRR Iron Hippo Legacy Steam Freight Set, CC, 23		2300
___	2322060	Union RR Hot Metal Diesel Freight Set, CC, 23		1300
___	2322070	RI Quad Cities Rocket Legacy Diesel Passenger Set, CC, 23		1000
___	2322080	ATSF Fast Fruit Express Legacy Steam Freight Set, CC, 23		2500
___	2323030	ATSF Dash-8 Diesel Auto Rack Set, 22-24		550
___	2323040	Disney 100 Years of Wonder LionChief Bluetooth 5.0 Steam Passenger Set, CC, 23-24		530
___	2323050	Fast Fright Halloween LionChief Bluetooth 5.0 Diesel Freight Set, CC, 23-24		500

		Exc	Mint
2323060	NYC 2-8-0 Consolidation LionChief Bluetooth 5.0 Steam Freight Set, CC, 23-24		450
2323070	Willy Wonka & the Chocolate Factory LionChief Bluetooth 5.0 Steam Freight Set, CC, 23-24		450
2323080	Texas Special Diesel Passenger LionChief Bluetooth 5.0 Set, CC, 23-24		500
2323090	UP Flyer LionChief Bluetooth 5.0 Steam Freight Set, CC, 23-24		400
2323100	Winter Wonderland LionChief Bluetooth 5.0 Steam Freight Set, CC, 23-24		400
2323110	ATSF Super Chief LionChief Bluetooth 5.0 Diesel Passenger Set, CC, 23-24		500
2323130	Gold Mountain LionChief Bluetooth 5.0 Steam Set, CC, 23-24		470
2325010	Polar Express Ice FasTrack O-36 Curve 4-pack, 23-24		75
2325030	FasTrack 3" Straight, 22-24		5
2326010	UP Heritage C&NW TOFC Flatcar "231995", 22		150
2326020	UP Heritage D&RGW TOFC Flatcar "231989", 22		150
2326030	UP Heritage MKT TOFC Flatcar "231988", 22		150
2326040	UP Heritage MP TOFC Flatcar "231982", 22		150
2326050	UP Heritage SP TOFC Flatcar "231996", 22		150
2326060	UP Heritage WP TOFC Flatcar "231983", 22		150
2326070	BN 100-ton Hopper 2-pack A, 22		300
2326078	BN 100-ton Hopper 2-pack B, 22		300
2326079	BN 100-ton Hopper 2-pack C, 22		300
2326080	Chessie (B&O) 100-ton Hopper 2-pack, 22-24		300
2326088	Chessie (C&O) 100-ton Hopper 2-pack, 22-24		300
2326089	Chessie (WM) 100-ton Hopper 2-pack, 22		300
2326090	D&RGW 100-ton Hopper 2-pack (blue ends), 22-24		300
2326098	D&RGW 100-ton Hopper 2-pack (white ends), 22		300
2326099	D&RGW 100-ton Hopper 2-pack (blue/white ends), 22-24		300
2326100	NS 100-ton Hopper 2-pack A, 22		300
2326108	NS 100-ton Hopper 2-pack B, 22		300
2326109	NS 100-ton Hopper 2-pack C, 22		300
2326110	Reading 100-ton Hopper 2-pack A, 22-24		300
2326118	Reading 100-ton Hopper 2-pack B, 22-24		300
2326119	Reading 100-ton Hopper 2-pack C, 22-24		300
2326120	SP 100-ton Hopper 2-pack A, 22		300
2326128	SP 100-ton Hopper 2-pack B, 22		300
2326129	SP 100-ton Hopper 2-pack C, 22		300
2326130	John Deere 60' Boxcar "1837", 22-24		130
2326140	Chevrolet 60' Boxcar "236140", 22-24		130
2326150	Ford 60' Boxcar "236150", 22-24		130
2326160	Reading & Northern 60' Boxcar "1998", 22-24		130
2326170	USMC 60' Boxcar "1591", 22-24		130
2326181	WCOR 60' Boxcar w/Graffiti "6510", 22-24		140
2326182	WCOR 60' Boxcar w/Graffiti "6521", 22-24		140
2326190	L&NE NE Caboose "583", 22		130
2326200	MC NE Caboose "662", 22-24		130
2326210	RI NE Caboose "17604", 22-24		130
2326220	USMC NE Caboose "601750", 22-24		130
2326230	SSW Hobo Boxcar "35209", 22-24		210
2326240	Frisco Hobo Boxcar "17350", 22		210
2326250	Ann Arbor Hobo Boxcar "1404", 22-24		210
2326260	Western of Alabama Hobo Boxcar "18252", 22-24		210

			Exc	Mint
___	**2326271**	PRR N6b Cabin Car "980781", 22-24		120
___	**2326272**	PRR N6b Cabin Car "981530", 22-24		120
___	**2326273**	PRR N6b Cabin Car "492891", 22-24		120
___	**2326280**	C&O Wood Caboose "98076", 22		120
___	**2326290**	Strasburg RR Wood Caboose "12", 22		120
___	**2326300**	ATSF Vision Refrigerator Car w/RailSounds 3-pack, 23		500
___	**2326310**	FGE Vision Refrigerator Car w/RailSounds 3-pack, 23		500
___	**2326320**	GN Vision Refrigerator Car w/RailSounds 3-pack, 23		500
___	**2326330**	PFE Vision Refrigerator Car w/RailSounds 3-pack, 23		500
___	**2326340**	D&RGW Vision Stock Car w/RailSounds 3-pack, 23		500
___	**2326350**	PRR Vision Stock Car w/RailSounds 3-pack, 23-24		500
___	**2326360**	T&P Vision Stock Car w/RailSounds 3-pack, 23		500
___	**2326370**	UP Vision Stock Car w/RailSounds 3-pack, 23		500
___	**2326380**	CP 50' Flatcar "505571" w/Reimer Trailer, 23		160
___	**2326390**	MILW 50' Flatcar "57500" w/ICX Trailer, 23		160
___	**2326400**	TTX 50' Flatcar "475326" w/Budweiser Trailer, 23-24		170
___	**2326410**	John Deere 50' Flatcar "26410" w/Trailer, 23-24		170
___	**2326420**	Lionel 50' Flatcar "26420" w/Play World Trailer, 23-24		160
___	**2326440**	UP Vision CA-1 Caboose "2551", 23-24		300
___	**2326450**	UP Vision CA-1 Caboose "2527", 23		300
___	**2326460**	Buffalo Creek & Gauley GLA Hopper 2-pack, 23-24		200
___	**2326470**	Interstate GLA Hopper 2-pack, 23-24		200
___	**2326480**	PRR GLA Hopper 2-pack A, 23-24		200
___	**2326490**	PRR GLA Hopper 2-pack B, 23-24		200
___	**2326500**	Westmoreland Coal GLA Hopper 2-pack, 23-24		200
___	**2326510**	PRR N8 Cabin Car "478125", 23-24		150
___	**2326520**	PRR N8 Cabin Car "478172", 23-24		150
___	**2326530**	PRR N8 Cabin Car "478159", 23		150
___	**2326540**	PC N8 Cabin Car "4710", 23		150
___	**2326550**	Conrail N8 Cabin Car "23236", 23		150
___	**2326560**	Union RR Hot Metal Car "14", 23-24		200
___	**2326570**	Area 51 Scale Hot Metal Car "AF-57X", 23-24		200
___	**2326580**	Christmas Hot Chocolate Thermos Car, 23-24		200
___	**2326590**	Polar Express Hot Chocolate Thermos Car, 23-24		200
___	**2326601**	Ann Arbor PS-5 Gondola "2023", 23-24		120
___	**2326602**	Ann Arbor PS-5 Gondola "2058", 23		120
___	**2326611**	CN PS-5 Gondola "143035", 23-24		120
___	**2326612**	CN PS-5 Gondola "143211", 23		120
___	**2326621**	Conrail PS-5 Gondola "67014", 23-24		120
___	**2326622**	Conrail PS-5 Gondola "67435", 23		120
___	**2326631**	Erie PS-5 Gondola "10325", 23		120
___	**2326632**	Erie PS-5 Gondola "10359", 23		120
___	**2326641**	LV PS-5 Gondola "32953", 23-24		120
___	**2326642**	LV PS-5 Gondola "33059", 23		120
___	**2326651**	RI PS-5 Gondola "3050", 23		120
___	**2326652**	RI PS-5 Gondola "3091", 23		120
___	**2326660**	Christmas Bobber Caboose, 23-24		110
___	**2326670**	C&NW Grain Boxcar "24154", 23-24		110
___	**2326680**	M&StL Grain Boxcar "53150", 23		110
___	**2326690**	Soo Grain Boxcar "44968", 23		110
___	**2326700**	T&P Grain Boxcar "40814", 23		110
___	**2326710**	UP Grain Boxcar "196861", 23		110
___	**2326720**	Wabash Grain Boxcar "90090", 23-24		110

		Exc	Mint
2326770	PRR Vision N8 Cabin Car "478166", 23-24		300 ___
2326780	PRR Vision N8 Cabin Car "478044", 23-24		300 ___
2327010	C&O 18" Passenger Car 2-pack A, 22-24		500 ___
2327020	C&O 18" Passenger Car 2-pack B, 22-24		500 ___
2327030	C&O 18" Passenger Car 2-pack C, 22-24		500 ___
2327040	C&O 18" Diner w/StationSounds, 22-24		430 ___
2327050	The Chessie 21" Passenger Car 4-pack, 22		900 ___
2327060	The Chessie 21" Passenger Car 2-pack, 22		450 ___
2327070	The Chessie 21" Diner w/StationSounds "1971", 22		400 ___
2327080	Strasburg RR Coach (1970s) 2-pack A, 22-24		450 ___
2327090	Strasburg RR Coach (1970s) 2-pack B, 22		450 ___
2327100	Strasburg RR 18" Heavyweight "Pequea Valley" (brown), 22-24		250 ___
2327110	Strasburg RR 18" Heavyweight "Pequea Valley" (green), 22-24		250 ___
2327140	US Army 18" Passenger Car 2-pack A, 22		500 ___
2327150	US Army 18" Passenger Car 2-pack B, 22		500 ___
2327160	US Army 18" Passenger Car 2-pack C, 22		500 ___
2327170	US Army 18" Diner w/StationSounds, 22		430 ___
2327180	CN Wood Passenger Car 2-pack A, 22		450 ___
2327190	CN Wood Passenger Car 2-pack B, 22		450 ___
2327200	CN Wood Passenger Car 2-pack C, 22		450 ___
2327210	Strasburg RR 18" Heavyweight "Pequea Valley" (red), 22-24		250 ___
2327220	Strasburg RR 18" Heavyweight "Pequea Valley" (gray), 22-24		250 ___
2327230	Harry Potter "Slytherin House" Coach, 23-24		90 ___
2327240	Harry Potter "Hufflepuff House" Coach, 23-24		90 ___
2327250	Harry Potter "Ravenclaw House" Coach, 23-24		90 ___
2327260	Harry Potter "Gryffindor House" Coach, 23-24		90 ___
2327270	UP Excursion 21" Passenger Car 4-pack, 23		950 ___
2327280	UP Excursion 21" Passenger Car 2-pack, 23		450 ___
2327290	UP Diner w/StationSounds, 23		400 ___
2327300	Aberdeen, Carolina & Western Diner w/StationSounds 2-pack, 23		650 ___
2327310	NYC 20th Century Limited 21" Passenger Car 4-pack, 23-24		950 ___
2327320	NYC 20th Century Limited 21" Passenger Car 2-pack, 23		450 ___
2327330	NYC 20th Century Limited 21" Diner w/StationSounds 2-pack, 23-24		650 ___
2327340	North Pole Central 21" Passenger Car 4-pack, 23		950 ___
2327350	North Pole Central 21" Passenger Car 2-pack, 23		450 ___
2327360	North Pole Central 21" Diner w/StationSounds, 23		400 ___
2327370	Texas Special "Anson B. Jones" Add-on Baggage Car, 23-24		95 ___
2327380	Texas Special "Tulsa" Add-on Coach, 23-24		100 ___
2327390	Aberdeen, Carolina & Western Dome Car, 23		300 ___
2328060	Gold Medal Flour Flatcar w/Milk Container, 22-24		70 ___
2328070	Lionelville Milk Flatcar w/Milk Container, 22-24		70 ___
2328080	Ferromex Auto Rack, 22-24		100 ___
2328090	Southern Auto Rack, 22-23		100 ___
2328100	DC Justice League Lexcorp Kryptonite Hopper, 23-24		110 ___
2328110	DC Justice League The Flash Mint Car, 23-24		120 ___
2328120	DC Justice League Wonder Woman Invisible Jet Flatcar, 23-24		60 ___
2328130	DC Justice League Wayne Enterprises Transport Car, 23-24		90 ___
2328140	John Deere Tractor Co. Refrigerator Car, 23-24		90 ___

MODERN 1970-2024			Exc	Mint
___	2328150	John Deere Flatcar "28230" w/Combine, 23-24		100
___	2328160	Disney 100 Illuminated Boxcar, 23-24		150
___	2328180	Pennywise Peekaboo Car, 23		100
___	2328190	Exorcist Floating Regan Car, 23		120
___	2328220	Anheuser-Busch Budweiser Clydesdale Refrigerator Car, 23-24		90
___	2328230	Anheuser-Busch Budweiser Military Heritage Reefer, 23-24		90
___	2328240	2023 Christmas Boxcar, 23		85
___	2328250	Christmas Music Illuminated Boxcar "23", 23-24		150
___	2328260	Santa's Choice Milk Flatcar w/Milk Carton, 23-24		70
___	2328270	Snow-Covered Christmas Tree Flatcar, 23-24		100
___	2328280	Polar Express Sleigh Bells Mint Car, 23-24		90
___	2328290	Polar Express Flatcar w/Hot Chocolate Container, 23-24		75
___	2328300	Angela Trotta Thomas Texas Special Boxcar, 23-24		85
___	2328310	Angela Trotta Thomas General Boxcar, 23-24		85
___	2328320	TTX Maxi Stack w/Container, 23-24		100
___	2328330	BNSF Maxi Stack w/Container, 23-24		100
___	2328340	Halloween Graffiti Maxi Stack w/Container, 23-24		100
___	2328350	Christmas Graffiti Maxi Stack w/Container, 23-24		100
___	2328360	Dr. Acula Blood Tonic 1-D Tank Car, 23-24		100
___	2328370	Spooky Sounds Illuminated Boxcar, 23-24		150
___	2328380	DC Justice League Boxcar, 23-24		85
___	2328410	Willy Wonka 1-D Tank Car, 23		100
___	2328420	Disney 100 Mickey Mouse Vault Moments Boxcar, 23-24		90
___	2328430	Disney 100 Minnie Mouse Vault Moments Boxcar, 23-24		90
___	2328440	Disney 100 Goofy Vault Moments Boxcar, 23-24		90
___	2328450	Disney 100 Donald Duck Vault Moments Boxcar, 23-24		90
___	2328460	Christmas Olde Tyme Rolling Stock 3-pack, 23		220
___	2328470	Gold Mountain 1-D Tank Car, 23-24		100
___	2328480	NYC Pacemaker Merchandise Boxcar, 23-24		120
___	2328490	Wonka Bar Golden Ticket Boxcar, 23		90
___	2328530	2023 National Lionel Train Day Boxcar, 23-24		80
___	2329010	Roadside Diner, 22-24		150
___	2329020	Christmas Roadside Diner, 23-24		160
___	2329030	Polar Express Illuminated Covered Bridge, 23		80
___	2329050	Billups Crossing Gate, 22-23		200
___	2329060	Amtrak Passenger Station, 22-24		170
___	2329070	Carnival Treats Stand, 22-23		160
___	2329080	St. Nick's Nog Shoppe Driver-In Diner, 23		400
___	2329090	Area 51 Drive-In Diner, 23		400
___	2329100	Franks & Stein's Bar & Ghoul, 23-24		130
___	2329110	Roscoe Flattz Automotive & Tire Store, 22-24		130
___	2329130	Cowen's Family Creamery NE Caboose w/Deck, 22-24		200
___	2329140	Grandpa's Workshop w/Sounds, 22-23		130
___	2329150	She Shed w/Sounds, 22-24		130
___	2329160	Santa's Workshop w/Sounds, 23-24		130
___	2329170	Hot Cocoa NE Caboose w/Deck, 23-24		200
___	2329190	Disney Christmas Station Platform, 23-24		55
___	2329200	Frankenstein's Monster Halloween Gateman, 23-24		130
___	2329230	Area 51 Hazardous Materials Barrel Loader, 23-24		80
___	2329240	Warner Bros. 100th Anniversary Water Tower, 23-24		90
___	2329250	John Deere Nothing Runs Like a Deere Flagpole, 23-24		45
___	2329270	Prankster Flagpole, 23-24		45
___	2329280	Willy Wonka Wonka Bar Packaging Facility, 23		270

		Exc	Mint
2329300	Patriots Salute Gateman, 23		130
2329340	Lionelville Theatre, 23-24		130
2329350	Warner Bros. 100th Anniversary Theatre, 23		130
2329360	Disney 100 Theatre, 23		130
2330010	Unique Road Signs Pack 2, 22-24		9
2330020	Ford Billboard 3-pack, 22-24		25
2330030	Chevrolet Billboard 3-pack, 22-24		25
2330040	Area 51 Glow in the Dark Haz-Mat Barrels, 23		13
2330050	Midway Games 3-pack and Figures, 22-24		120
2330060	Thomas & Friends Billboard Pack, 23-24		25
2330080	Warner Bros. Classic Movie Billboard Pack, 23		25
2330110	Budweiser Brew Hut, 23		45
2330120	Lionel Ale Quonset Hut, 23		45
2330140	Dasher's Buy and Fly Quonset Hut, 23		45
2330160	Winter Wonderland Scented Smoke Fluid, 23-24		9
2330170	American Summer (Apple Pie) Scented Smoke Fluid, 23-24		9
2330180	Happy Birthday Scented Smoke Fluid, 23-24		9
2330190	Vanilla Bourbon Scented Smoke Fluid, 23-24		9
2330200	Maple Syrup Scented Smoke Fluid, 23-24		9
2330210	Bay Leaf and Tobacco Scented Smoke Fluid, 23		9
2331011	PRR 2-8-2 Mikado L1 Locomotive "496," CC, 22		950
2331012	PRR 2-8-2 Mikado L1 Locomotive "4030," CC, 22		950
2331021	PRR 2-8-2 Mikado L1 Locomotive "1343," CC, 22		950
2331022	PRR 2-8-2 Mikado L1 Locomotive "1627," CC, 22		950
2331030	PRR 2-8-2 Mikado L1 Locomotive "1369," CC, 22		950
2331040	ATSF 2-8-2 Mikado L1 Locomotive "882," CC, 22		1000
2331050	DT&I 2-8-2 Mikado L1 Locomotive "496," CC, 22		950
2331060	L&NE 2-8-2 Mikado L1 Locomotive "501," CC, 22		950
2331070	C&O 4-8-4 Greenbrier Locomotive "614," CC, 22		1700
2331080	C&O 4-8-4 Greenbrier Locomotive "611," CC, 22		1700
2331090	C&O 4-8-4 Greenbrier Locomotive "613," CC, 22		1700
2331100	C&O 4-8-4 Greenbrier Locomotive "612," CC, 22		1700
2331110	Chessie System 4-8-4 Greenbrier Locomotive "614," CC, 22		1700
2331120	Family Lines 4-8-4 Greenbrier Locomotive "614," CC, 22		1700
2331130	CN 2-6-0 Mogul Locomotive "89," CC, 22		800
2331140	Middletown & Hummelstown 2-6-0 Mogul Locomotive "91," CC, 22		800
2331150	San Luis & Rio Grande 2-6-0 Mogul Locomotive "89," CC, 22		800
2331160	SP 2-6-0 Mogul Locomotive "1760," CC, 22		800
2331170	Strasburg RR 2-6-0 Mogul Locomotive "89" (1970s) CC, 22		800
2331180	Strasburg RR 2-6-0 Mogul Locomotive "89" (2000s), CC, 22		800
2331191	UP Brass Hybrid 4-6-6-4 Challenger Locomotive "3819," CC, 22		2500
2331192	UP Brass Hybrid 4-6-6-4 Challenger Locomotive "3826," CC, 22		2500
2331193	UP Brass Hybrid 4-6-6-4 Challenger Locomotive, Unnumbered Style 1, CC, 22		2500
2331200	UP Brass Hybrid 4-6-6-4 Challenger Locomotive Pilot, CC, 22		2500
2331211	UP Brass Hybrid 4-6-6-4 Challenger Locomotive "3836," CC, 22		2500
2331212	UP Brass Hybrid 4-6-6-4 Challenger Locomotive "3839," CC, 22		2500
2331213	UP Brass Hybrid 4-6-6-4 Challenger Locomotive, Unnumbered, Style 2, CC, 22		2500

			Exc	Mint
___	**2331220**	UP Brass Hybrid 4-6-6-4 Challenger Locomotive "3835" (Challenger scheme), CC, 22		2500
___	**2331231**	UP Brass Hybrid 4-6-6-4 Challenger Locomotive "3815," CC, 22		2500
___	**2331232**	UP Brass Hybrid 4-6-6-4 Challenger Locomotive "3828," CC, 22		2500
___	**2331233**	UP Brass Hybrid 4-6-6-4 Challenger Locomotive, Unnumbered, Style 3, CC, 22		2500
___	**2331250**	UP Vision 4-8-8-4 Big Boy Locomotive Oil-Burning "4014," CC, 23		2800
___	**2331261**	UP Vision 4-8-8-4 Big Boy Locomotive "4000," CC, 23		2900
___	**2331262**	UP Vision 4-8-8-4 Big Boy Locomotive "4002," CC, 23		2900
___	**2331263**	UP Vision 4-8-8-4 Big Boy Locomotive "4012," CC, 23		2900
___	**2331264**	UP Vision 4-8-8-4 Big Boy Locomotive "4014," CC, 23		2900
___	**2331270**	UP Vision 4-8-8-4 Big Boy Locomotive "4019," CC, 23		2900
___	**2331280**	UP Vision 4-8-8-4 Big Boy Locomotive "4021," CC, 23		2900
___	**2331290**	UP Vision 4-8-8-4 Big Boy Locomotive "4024," CC, 23		2900
___	**2331300**	Erie Russian 2-10-0 Decapod Locomotive "2445," CC, 23-24		1300
___	**2331310**	Frisco Russian 2-10-0 Decapod Locomotive "1630," CC, 23		1300
___	**2331320**	Minneapolis, Northfield & Southern Russian 2-10-0 Decapod Locomotive "505," CC, 23		1300
___	**2331330**	Philadelphia & Reading Russian 2-10-0 Decapod Locomotive "1162," CC, 23		1300
___	**2331340**	SAL Russian 2-10-0 Decapod Locomotive "544," CC, 23		1300
___	**2331350**	USA Russian 2-10-0 Decapod Locomotive "1918," CC, 23		1300
___	**2331361**	PRR I1 2-10-0 Decapod Locomotive "531," CC, 23		1500
___	**2331362**	PRR I1 2-10-0 Decapod Locomotive "4250," CC, 23		1500
___	**2331371**	PRR I1 2-10-0 Decapod Locomotive "4241," CC, 23		1500
___	**2331372**	PRR I1 2-10-0 Decapod Locomotive "4652," CC, 23		1500
___	**2331381**	PRR I1 2-10-0 Decapod Locomotive "4262," CC, 23		1500
___	**2331382**	PRR I1 2-10-0 Decapod Locomotive "4521," CC, 23		1500
___	**2331391**	PRR I1 2-10-0 Decapod Locomotive "4258," CC, 23		1500
___	**2331392**	PRR I1 2-10-0 Decapod Locomotive "4325," CC, 23		1500
___	**2331401**	NYC Dreyfuss J3 4-6-4 Hudson Locomotive "5449," CC, 23-24		1700
___	**2331402**	NYC Dreyfuss J3 4-6-4 Hudson Locomotive "5452," CC, 23		1700
___	**2331411**	NYC Dreyfuss J3 4-6-4 Hudson Locomotive "5445," CC, 23		1800
___	**2331412**	NYC Dreyfuss J3 4-6-4 Hudson Locomotive "5447," CC, 23		1800
___	**2331420**	NYC Dreyfuss J3 4-6-4 Hudson Locomotive "5445" w/short tender, CC, 23		1700
___	**2331430**	NYC Dreyfuss J3 4-6-4 Hudson Locomotive "5454," CC, 23		1800
___	**2331451**	ATSF 4-8-4 Northern Locomotive "2903," CC, 23		1800
___	**2331452**	ATSF 4-8-4 Northern Locomotive "2912," CC, 23		1800
___	**2331453**	ATSF 4-8-4 Northern Locomotive "2926," CC, 23		1800
___	**2331460**	ATSF 4-8-4 Northern Locomotive Blue Goose "2900," CC, 23		1800
___	**2331470**	ATSF 4-8-4 Northern Locomotive Warbonnet "2901," CC, 23		1800
___	**2331480**	ATSF 4-8-4 Northern Locomotive Restoration "2926," CC, 23		1800
___	**2331540**	Fezziwig RR Legacy 4-6-0 Camelback Locomotive "1225," CC, 23		700
___	**2331550**	DL&W 4-6-0 Camelback Locomotive "1052," CC, 23		700
___	**2331560**	Erie 4-6-0 Camelback Locomotive "918," CC, 23		700
___	**2331570**	L&NE 4-6-0 Camelback Locomotive "151," CC, 23		700
___	**2331580**	Atlantic City RR 4-6-0 Camelback Locomotive "610," CC, 23		700
___	**2331590**	PRR 4-6-0 Camelback Locomotive "824," CC, 23		700

		Exc	Mint
2332010	Reading 0-6-0T Locomotive "1251" LionChief Plus 2.0, 22-23		350 ___
2332020	Alaska 0-6-0T Locomotive "1" LionChief Plus 2.0, 22-23		350 ___
2332030	Lehigh Valley Coal 0-6-0T Locomotive "126" LionChief Plus 2.0, 22-23		350 ___
2332040	NH 0-6-0T Locomotive "2305" LionChief Plus 2.0, 22-23		350 ___
2332050	Halloween 2-8-2 Mikado Locomotive "1031," LionChief Plus 2.0, 23-24		700 ___
2332060	CB&Q 2-8-2 Mikado Locomotive "4978," LionChief Plus 2.0, 23-24		700 ___
2332070	MILW 2-8-2 Mikado Locomotive "753," LionChief Plus 2.0, 23-24		700 ___
2332080	UP 2-8-2 Mikado Locomotive "2549," LionChief Plus 2.0, 23-24		700 ___
2332090	PRR 2-8-2 Mikado Locomotive "9631," LionChief Plus 2.0, 23-24		700 ___
2332100	NKP 2-10-0 Consolidation Locomotive "455," LionChief, 23		330 ___
2332110	WM 2-10-0 Consolidation Locomotive "754," LionChief, 23		330 ___
2332120	ATSF 2-10-0 Consolidation Locomotive "2517," LionChief, 23		330 ___
2332130	C&O 2-10-0 Consolidation Locomotive "752," LionChief, 23		330 ___
2333040	SP Alco FA-2 AA set "802A/802D," CC, 22		1100 ___
2333050	USMC Alco FA-2 AA set "212/213," CC, 22		1100 ___
2333080	D&H Alco FA-2 AA set "20/21," CC, 22		1100 ___
2333088	D&H Alco FB-2 "20B," CC, 22		550 ___
2333089	D&H Alco FB-2 SuperBass "21B", 22		500 ___
2333090	EL Alco FA-2 AA set "7371/7374," CC, 22		1100 ___
2333098	EL Alco FB-2 "7382," CC, 22		550 ___
2333099	EL Alco FB-2 SuperBass "7383", 22		500 ___
2333100	Halloween Alco FA-2 AA set "1030A/1031A," CC, 22		1100 ___
2333108	Halloween Alco FB-2 "1030B," CC, 22		550 ___
2333109	Halloween Alco FB-2 SuperBass "1031B", 22		500 ___
2333110	L&N Alco FA-2 AA set "311/314," CC, 22		1100 ___
2333118	L&N Alco FB-2 "392" CC, 22		550 ___
2333119	L&N Alco FB-2 SuperBass "394", 22		500 ___
2333120	NYC Alco FA-2 AA set "1175/1176," CC, 22		1100 ___
2333128	NYC Alco FB-2 "3375," CC, 22		550 ___
2333129	NYC Alco FB-2 SuperBass "3376", 22		500 ___
2333130	PRR Alco FA-2 AA set "5760A/5762A," CC, 22		1100 ___
2333138	PRR Alco FB-2 "5760B," CC, 22		550 ___
2333139	PRR Alco FB-2 SuperBass "5762B", 22		500 ___
2333148	SP Alco FB-2 "802B," CC, 22		550 ___
2333149	SP Alco FB-2 SuperBass "802C", 22		500 ___
2333158	USMC Alco FB-2 "212B," CC, 22		550 ___
2333159	USMC Alco FB-2 SuperBass "213B", 22		500 ___
2333160	Montana Rail Link Essential Workers EMD SD70ACe "4404," CC, 22		650 ___
2333170	Montana Rail Link Veterans EMD SD70ACe "4407," CC, 22		650 ___
2333180	PRLX EMD SD70ACe "4834," CC, 22		650 ___
2333190	UP C&NW Heritage EMD SD70ACe "1995," CC, 22		650 ___
2333200	UP D&RGW Heritage EMD SD70ACe "1989," CC, 22		650 ___
2333210	UP MKT Heritage EMD SD70ACe "1988," CC, 22		650 ___
2333220	UP MP Heritage EMD SD70ACe "1982," CC, 22		650 ___
2333230	UP SP Heritage EMD SD70ACe "1996," CC, 22		650 ___
2333240	UP WP Heritage EMD SD70ACe "1983," CC, 22		650 ___
2333251	Central of Georgia FM H-15-44 Diesel "101," CC, 22		600 ___

			Exc	Mint
___	**2333252**	Central of Georgia FM H-15-44 Diesel "102," CC, 22		600
___	**2333261**	CRI&P FM H-15-44 Diesel "400," CC, 22		600
___	**2333262**	CRI&P FM H-15-44 Diesel "401," CC, 22		600
___	**2333271**	D&RGW FM H-15-44 Diesel "151," CC, 22		600
___	**2333272**	D&RGW FM H-15-44 Diesel "152," CC, 22		600
___	**2333281**	KCS FM H-15-44 Diesel "40," CC, 22		600
___	**2333282**	KCS FM H-15-44 Diesel "41," CC, 22		600
___	**2333291**	Monon FM H-15-44 Diesel "36," CC, 22		600
___	**2333292**	Monon FM H-15-44 Diesel "37," CC, 22		600
___	**2333301**	UP FM H-15-44 Diesel "1325," CC, 22		600
___	**2333302**	UP FM H-15-44 Diesel "1329," CC, 22		600
___	**2333310**	Aberdeen, Carolina & Western EMD E8 AA set, CC, 23		1200
___	**2333320**	North Pole Central EMD E8 AA set, CC, 23		1200
___	**2333330**	Amtrak EMD E8/E9 AA set "410/422," CC, 23		1200
___	**2333340**	NYC EMD E8/E9 AA set "4053/4083," CC, 23		1200
___	**2333350**	Southern EMD E8/E9 AA set "2923/2925," CC, 23		1200
___	**2333360**	SP EMD E8/E9 AA set "6051/6053," CC, 23		1200
___	**2333371**	ATSF EMD SD40T-2 "5215," CC, 22		650
___	**2333372**	EMD SD40T-2 "5226," CC, 22		650
___	**2333379**	ATSF EMD SD40T-2 SuperBass "5238," 22		600
___	**2333381**	SP EMD SD40T-2 "8524," CC, 22		650
___	**2333382**	SP EMD SD40T-2 "8533," CC, 22		650
___	**2333389**	SP EMD SD40T-2 SuperBass "8548" , 22		600
___	**2333391**	SP EMD SD40T-2 Kodachrome "8286," CC, 22		650
___	**2333392**	SP EMD SD40T-2 Kodachrome "8530," CC, 22		650
___	**2333399**	SP EMD SD40T-2 SuperBass Kodachrome "8573", 22		600
___	**2333401**	NYS&W EMD SD40T-2 "3010," CC, 22		650
___	**2333402**	NYS&W EMD SD40T-2 "3012," CC, 22		650
___	**2333409**	NYS&W EMD SD40T-2 SuperBass "3016", 22		600
___	**2333411**	SP EMD SD40T-2 Black Widow "8520," CC, 22		650
___	**2333412**	SP EMD SD40T-2 Black Widow "8525," CC, 22		650
___	**2333419**	SP EMD SD40T-2 SuperBass Black Widow "8529," 22		600
___	**2333421**	WP EMD SD40T-2 "8625," CC, 22		650
___	**2333422**	WP EMD SD40T-2 "8794," CC, 22		650
___	**2333429**	WP EMD SD40T-2 SuperBass "8864", 22		600
___	**2333431**	BN GE ES44AC "9800," CC, 23		750
___	**2333432**	BN GE ES44AC "9810," CC, 23		750
___	**2333439**	BN GE ES44AC SuperBass "9819", 23		550
___	**2333441**	BNSF GE ES44AC "5555," CC, 23		750
___	**2333442**	BNSF GE ES44AC "5570," CC, 23		750
___	**2333449**	BNSF GE ES44AC SuperBass "5586", 23		550
___	**2333451**	C&NW GE ES44AC "8836," CC, 23		750
___	**2333452**	C&NW GE ES44AC "8842," CC, 23		750
___	**2333459**	C&NW GE ES44AC SuperBass "8850", 23		550
___	**2333461**	Conrail GE ES44AC "4145," CC, 23-24		750
___	**2333462**	Conrail GE ES44AC "4152," CC, 23		750
___	**2333469**	Conrail GE ES44AC SuperBass "4163", 23		550
___	**2333471**	KCS GE ES44AC "4859," CC, 23		750
___	**2333479**	KCS non-powered GE ES44AC "4859," CC, 23		400
___	**2333481**	KCS GE ES44AC "4674," CC, 23		750
___	**2333489**	KCS non-powered GE ES44AC "4674," CC, 23		400
___	**2333490**	BN EMD NW2 Switcher "497," CC, 23		600
___	**2333500**	C&O EMD NW2 Switcher "5067," CC, 23		600

		Exc	Mint
2333510	Detroit Terminal EMD NW2 Switcher "115," CC, 23		600 ___
2333520	GN EMD NW2 Switcher "161," CC, 23		600 ___
2333530	Indiana Harbor Belt EMD NW2 Switcher "8827," CC, 23		600 ___
2333540	LV EMD NW2 Switcher "186," CC, 23		600 ___
2333551	ATSF EMD GP20 Diesel "1106," CC, 23		650 ___
2333552	ATSF EMD GP20 Diesel "1171," CC, 23		650 ___
2333561	CB&Q EMD GP20 Diesel "907," CC, 23-24		650 ___
2333562	CB&Q EMD GP20 Diesel "915," CC, 23		650 ___
2333571	Kyle RR EMD GP20 Diesel "2035," CC, 23		650 ___
2333572	Kyle RR EMD GP20 Diesel "2039," CC, 23		650 ___
2333581	PC EMD GP20 Diesel "2108," CC, 23		650 ___
2333582	PC EMD GP20 Diesel "2109," CC, 23		650 ___
2333591	SSW EMD GP20 Diesel "801," CC, 23		650 ___
2333592	SSW EMD GP20 Diesel "815," CC, 23		650 ___
2333600	KC Terminal EMD GP20 Diesel "WAMX 2005," CC, 23		650 ___
2334010	ATSF EMD NW2 Diesel "2404," CC, 22-23		450 ___
2334020	NYC EMD NW2 Diesel "622," CC, 22-23		450 ___
2334030	GN EMD NW2 Diesel "162," CC, 22-23		450 ___
2334040	SAL EMD NW2 Diesel "1410," CC, 22-23		450 ___
2334050	CN GE ERT44AC Diesel "3810," CC, 23		400 ___
2334060	KCS GE ERT44AC Diesel "5002," CC, 23		400 ___
2334070	BNSF GE ERT44AC Diesel "6337," CC, 23		400 ___
2334080	NS GE ERT44AC Diesel "3657," CC, 23		400 ___
2334090	ATSF EMD FT Diesel "127," CC, 23		300 ___
2334100	NYC EMD FT Diesel "1687," CC, 23-24		300 ___
2334110	PRR EMD FT Diesel "5888," CC, 23-24		300 ___
2334120	North Pole Central EMD FT Diesel "1225," CC, 23-24		300 ___
2335010	MOW TMCC Rail Bonder "M-4," CC, 23		150 ___
2335020	NH TMCC Rail Bonder "18," CC, 23-24		150 ___
2335030	PE TMCC Rail Bonder "1202," CC, 23		150 ___
2335040	LIRR TMCC Rail Bonder "35040," CC, 23		150 ___
2335050	North Pole Central TMCC Rail Bonder "1225," CC, 23-24		150 ___
2335060	Angela Trotta Thomas Trolley, 23		120 ___
2335070	Alaska Budd RDC Unit 2-pack "702/712," CC, 23		600 ___
2335080	B&O Budd RDC Unit 2-pack "9902/9917," CC, 23		600 ___
2335090	NH Budd RDC Unit 2-pack "120/42," CC, 23		600 ___
2335100	SP Budd RDC Unit 2-pack "SP-9/SP-11," CC, 23		600 ___
2335110	Polar Express Budd RDC Unit 2-pack "1225/25," CC, 23		600 ___
2335120	Alaska Budd RDC Unit "711," CC, 23		400 ___
2335130	B&O Budd RDC Unit "9918," CC, 23		400 ___
2335140	NH Budd RDC Unit "41," CC, 23		400 ___
2335150	SP Budd RDC Unit "SP-10," CC, 23		400 ___
2335160	Polar Express Budd RDC Unit "24," CC, 23		400 ___
2335190	Disney's Mickey Mouse and Minnie Mouse Handcar, red, 23-24		200 ___
2338010	Chicago Railroad Fair Boxcar, 22		90 ___
2338030	Millard Fillmore Presidential Boxcar, 23-24		90 ___
2338040	Zachary Taylor Presidential Boxcar, 23-24		90 ___
2338050	John Tyler Presidential Boxcar, 23-24		90 ___
2338060	Chessie System 50th Anniversary Boxcar, 23		90 ___
2338070	Santa Fe Super Chief 75th Anniversary Boxcar, 23-24		95 ___
2338080	Battle of Midway Boxcar, 23-24		95 ___
2338090	Boston Tea Party 250th Anniversary Boxcar, 23-24		90 ___

		Exc	Mint
2338100	Personalized Family Boxcar, 23		100
2338110	2023 Happy Birthday Boxcar, 23		100
2338120	2023 Merry Christmas Boxcar, 23		100
2338130	2023 Happy Anniversary Boxcar, 23		100
2338140	Wings of America Ariella Boxcar, 23-24		95
2338150	Wings of America Jen Boxcar, 23-24		95
2338160	Wings of America Sarah Boxcar, 2, 23		95
2338170	Happy Birthday Caboose, 23		90
2338180	Merry Christmas Caboose, 23		90
2338190	Battle of Mogadishu Boxcar, 23-24		95
2338200	Disney 100 Celebration Personalized Boxcar, 23		100
2338210	James Webb Space Telescope Boxcar, 23		90
2338220	Wright Brothers 120th Anniversary Boxcar, 23-24		90
2338260	Gettysburg Address 160th Anniversary Boxcar, 23-24		90
2338290	Thomas Kinkade Studios Christmas Light Express Boxcar, 24		100
2343011	Reading & Northern Unibody 1-D Tank Car "101275" (std 0), 22-24		75
2343012	Reading & Northern Unibody 1-D Tank Car "2382" (std 0), 22-24		75
2343021	US Army Unibody 1-D Tank Car "18599" (std 0), 22-24		75
2343022	US Army Unibody 1-D Tank Car "18601" (std 0), 22-24		75
2343031	Cargill Unibody 1-D Tank Car "6274" (std 0), 22-24		75
2343032	Cargill Unibody 1-D Tank Car "6281" (std 0), 22-24		75
2343041	GATX Unibody 1-D Tank Car "2658" w/Graffiti (std 0), 22-24		75
2343042	GATX Unibody 1-D Tank Car "2696" w/Graffiti (std 0), 22-24		75
2343051	Procor Unibody 1-D Tank Car "28030" (std 0), 22-24		75
2343052	Procor Unibody 1-D Tank Car "28040" (std 0), 22-24		75
2343061	BN Centerbeam Flatcar "624189" (std 0), 23-24		65
2343062	BN Centerbeam Flatcar "624220" (std 0), 23		65
2343071	CSX Centerbeam Flatcar "600700" (std 0), 23-24		65
2343072	CSX Centerbeam Flatcar "600712" (std 0), 23-24		65
2343081	NS Centerbeam Flatcar "120112" (std 0), 23-24		65
2343082	NS Centerbeam Flatcar "120231" (std 0), 23-24		65
2343091	TTX Centerbeam Flatcar "83519" (std 0), 23-24		65
2343092	TTX Centerbeam Flatcar "83593" (std 0), 23		65
2343101	WCRC Centerbeam Flatcar "7319" (std 0), 23-24		65
2343102	WCRC Centerbeam Flatcar "7540" (std 0), 23		65
2422010	Erie Triplex Super Set, CC, 24		4000
2422020	Lehigh Gorge Scenic Ry. Diesel Passenger Set, CC, 23		1200
2422030	WP Feather River Diesel Freight Set, CC, 23		1600
2422040	PRR M1 Middle Division Steam Freight Set, CC, 23		2000
2422050	Nickel Plate Road Fast Freight Steam Set, CC, 24		2500
2422060	Polar Express 20th Anniversary Scale Freight Passenger Set, CC, 24		2400
2422070	North Pole Central Cocoa Steam Milk Train, CC, 24		1200
2422080	Atomic Energy Commission Glow-In-Dark Diesel Freight Set, CC, 24		1000
2422089	Atomic Energy Commission GP9B SuperBass "1946B," CC, 24		500
2422090	IC City of Miami Diesel Passenger Set, CC, 24		1500
2423010	Looney Tunes Diesel Freight Set, LionChief, 23-24		530
2423020	GN 2-8-0 Steam Freight Set, LionChief, 23		470
2423030	Polar Express 20th Anniversary Steam Passenger Set, LionChief, 24		530
2423040	Disney Frozen Olaf Steam Freight Set, LionChief, 24		480

		Exc	Mint
2423050	LL Prairie Steam Freight Set, LionChief, 24		430 ___
2423060	Sleigh Bell Limited Diesel Passenger Set, LionChief, 24		530 ___
2423070	John Deere Steam Freight Set, LionChief, 24		430 ___
2426010	Chessie System PS-1 Boxcar "23764" w/FreightSounds		210 ___
2426020	CB&Q PS-1 Boxcar "17302" w/FreightSounds, 24		210 ___
2426030	DL&W Friendship Train PS-1 Boxcar "51974" w/ FreightSounds, 24		210 ___
2426040	GN PS-1 Boxcar "18588" w/FreightSounds, 24		210 ___
2426050	ICG PS-1 Boxcar "416224" w/FreightSounds, 24		210 ___
2426060	RF&P PS-1 Boxcar "2872" w/FreightSounds, 24		210 ___
2426070	UP PS-1 WWII Boxcar "194407" w/PatriotSounds, 23		210 ___
2426080	UP PS-1 WWII Boxcar "194414" w/PatriotSounds, 23		210 ___
2426090	UP WWII PS-1 Boxcar "194421" w/FreightSounds, 24		210 ___
2426100	U.S. Army PS-1 Boxcar "26884" w/PatriotSounds, 23		210 ___
2426120	U.S.M.C. PS-1 Boxcar "173232" w/PatriotSounds, 23		210 ___
2426130	U.S.A.F. PS-1 Boxcar "26478" w/PatriotSounds, 23		210 ___
2426140	MILW 40' Flatcar "866981," w/John Deere Tractors , 23		170 ___
2426150	PRR 40' Flatcar "925142," w/John Deere Tractors , 23		170 ___
2426160	NP 40' Flatcar "200204," w/John Deere Tractors , 23		170 ___
2426170	John Deere 40' Flatcar "26170," w/Tractors , 23		170 ___
2426180	John Deere Double-sheathed Boxcar "1837", 23		120 ___
2426190	NYC Double-sheathed Boxcar "161525", 23		100 ___
2426200	NP Double-sheathed Boxcar "11237", 23		100 ___
2426200	U.S. Navy PS-1 Boxcar "61-02450" w/PatriotSounds, 23		210 ___
2426210	PRR Double-sheathed Boxcar "96451", 23		100 ___
2426220	SP Friendship Train Double-sheathed Boxcar "300", 23		100 ___
2426230	Strasburg RR Double-sheathed Boxcar "103", 23		100 ___
2426240	Area 51 PS-5 Covered Gondola "X-51-2645N" , 23		125 ___
2426250	Area 51 PS-5 Gondola "X-51-2650N," w/Coke Containers, 23		135 ___
2426260	Bethlehem Steel PS-5 Gondola "18015," w/Coke Containers, 23		130 ___
2426270	LNLX PS-5 Covered Gondola "426270," w/Graffiti, 23		135 ___
2426280	John Deere PS-5 Gondola w/Containers, 23		135 ___
2426290	P&LE PS-5 Gondola "10691," w/Coke Containers, 23		130 ___
2426300	Reading PS-5 Gondola "33079," w/Coke Containers, 23		130 ___
2426310	U.S. Army Transportation Corps PS-5 Covered Gondola "41310", 23		125 ___
2426320	ATSF Refrigerator Car "7599" w/Hot Box, 24		300 ___
2426330	FGE Refrigerator Car "38945" w/Hot Box, 24		300 ___
2426340	NYC MDT Refrigerator Car "6110" w/Hot Box, 24		300 ___
2426350	PFE Refrigerator Car "5845" w/Hot Box, 24		300 ___
2426370	NP CA-1 Caboose "1370", 24		130 ___
2426380	UP WWII CA-1 Caboose "1944", 24		130 ___
2426390	UP CA-1 Caboose "3349", 24		130 ___
2426400	UP CA-1 Caboose "2659", 24		130 ___
2426410	UP CA-1 Caboose "3279", 24		130 ___
2426420	WP CA-1 Caboose "726", 24		130 ___
2426430	D&H N6b Wood-sided Caboose "35701", 24		125 ___
2426440	DT&I N6b Wood-sided Caboose "77", 24		125 ___
2426450	LL N6b Wood-sided Caboose "231901", 24		125 ___
2426460	North Pole Central N6b Wood-sided Caboose "2325", 24		125 ___
2426470	Strasburg RR N6b Wood-sided Caboose "12", 24		125 ___

			Exc	Mint
____	**2426480**	Christmas Egg Nog Milk Car "241225", 24		120
____	**2426490**	Erie Milk Car "65", 24		120
____	**2426500**	Dr. Acula's Blood Tonic Milk Car "1476", 24		120
____	**2426510**	NC&StL Milk Car "3900", 24		120
____	**2426520**	O'Leary Dairies Milk Car "1871", 24		120
____	**2426530**	Strasburg RR Milk Car "17579", 24		120
____	**2426540**	Acme 8,000-Gallon 1-D Tank Car "19491", 24		110
____	**2426550**	Paluxy Asphalt 8,000-Gallon 1-D Tank Car "4021", 24		100
____	**2426560**	Penn Salt 8,000-Gallon 1-D Tank Car "715", 24		100
____	**2426570**	St. Lawrence Starch 8,000-Gallon 1-D Tank Car "49104", 24		100
____	**2426580**	Stauffer Chemical 8,000-Gallon 1-D Tank Car "86", 24		100
____	**2426590**	Union Oil 8,000-Gallon 1-D Tank Car "8085", 24		100
____	**2426620**	C&NW PS-2 Covered Hopper "4110", 24		90
____	**2426621**	C&NW PS-2 Covered Hopper "3995, weathered, 24		100
____	**2426630**	Conrail PS-2 Covered Hopper "877045", 24		90
____	**2426631**	Conrail PS-2 Covered Hopper "8776978," weathered", 24		100
____	**2426640**	GN PS-2 Covered Hopper "71464", 24		90
____	**2426641**	GN PS-2 Covered Hopper "71436," weathered, 24		100
____	**2426650**	IC PS-2 Covered Hopper "55012", 24		90
____	**2426651**	IC PS-2 Covered Hopper "55044," weathered, 24		100
____	**2426660**	SP PS-2 Covered Hopper "402148", 24		90
____	**2426661**	SP PS-2 Covered Hopper "402148," weathered, 24		100
____	**2426670**	Winchester & Western PS-2 Covered Hopper "4013", 24		90
____	**2426671**	Winchester & Western PS-2 Covered Hopper "4006," weathered, 24		100
____	**2426680**	Looney Tunes Acme Mini-Copter PS-1 Boxcar, 24		110
____	**2426690**	Looney Tunes Acme Giant Magnet PS-1 Boxcar, 24		110
____	**2426700**	Looney Tunes Acme 50-foot Flatcar w/Trailers, 24		170
____	**2426710**	Deer Dash 50-foot Flatcar w/Trailers, 24		160
____	**2426720**	MKT 50-foot Flatcar w/Trailers "13458", 24		160
____	**2426730**	REA 50-foot Flatcar w/Trailers "1649", 24		160
____	**2426740**	SP 50-foot Flatcar w/Trailers "563225", 24		160
____	**2426750**	T&P 50-foot Flatcar w/Trailers "99402", 24		160
____	**2426760**	PRR Vision N6b Wood-sided Caboose w/RailSounds "980310", 24		300
____	**2426770**	PRR Vision N6b Wood-sided Caboose w/RailSounds "981827", 24		300
____	**2426780**	Eerie Vision Caboose w/RailSounds "103124", 24		310
____	**2426790**	Polar Express 20th Anniversary PS-1 Boxcar w/BellSounds, 24		220
____	**2426800**	Polar Express 20th Anniversary PS-1 Boxcar, 24		110
____	**2427010**	C&O George Washington 18" Passenger Car 2-pack, A, 23		500
____	**2427020**	C&O George Washington 18" Passenger Car 2-pack, B, 23		500
____	**2427030**	C&O George Washington 18" Passenger Car 2-pack, C, 23		500
____	**2427040**	C&O George Washington 18" Diner w/StationSounds, 23		430
____	**2427050**	WM Scenic 21" Passenger Car 2-pack, A, 23		500
____	**2427060**	WM Scenic 21" Passenger Car 2-pack, B, 23		500
____	**2427070**	WM Scenic Dome Car w/StationSounds, 23		500
____	**2427080**	GN Empire Builder 21" Passenger Car 4-pack, 23		1000
____	**2427090**	GN Empire Builder 21" Passenger Car 2-pack, 23		500
	2427100	GN Empire Builder 21" Diner w/StationSounds, 23		450
	2427110	Lehigh Gorge Scenic Ry. 72' Passenger Car 2-pack, 23		430
	2427120	GN Empire Builder Full Dome Car "1392", 23		300

		Exc	Mint
2427130	UP 18" Passenger Car 2-pack, A, 23		500 ___
2427140	UP 18" Passenger Car 2-pack, B, 23		500 ___
2427150	UP 18" Passenger Car 2-pack, C, 23		500 ___
2427160	UP 18" Diner w/StationSounds, 23		430 ___
2427170	Amtrak Phase III Modern Dome Car "10031," w/ StationSounds, 23		500 ___
2427180	American Orient Express Full Dome Car, 23		300 ___
2427190	American Orient ExpressPassenger Car 4-pack, 23		1000 ___
2427200	American Orient Express Passenger Car 2-pack, 23		500 ___
2427210	American Orient Express Zurich Diner w/StationSounds, 23		450 ___
2427220	Southern MOW RPO "960408", 23		200 ___
2427230	UP MOW RPO "903688", 23		200 ___
2427240	UP 21" Training Car "211", 23		430 ___
2427250	D&RGW 18" Training Car "X201", 23		430 ___
2427260	GN 18" Fire Prevention Car "X1828", 23		430 ___
2427270	MILW 18" Training Car "X711", 23		430 ___
2427280	NYC 18" Training Car "X-23415", 23		430 ___
2427290	PRR 18" Training Car "492443", 23		430 ___
2427300	Polar Express 20th Anniversary 18" Coach, 24		250 ___
2427310	Polar Express Observation w/round end and black roof, 24		270 ___
2427320	Polar Express Observation w/round end and white roof, 24		270 ___
2427330	IC City of Miami Passenger Car 2-pack, 24		500 ___
2427340	IC City of Miami Diner w/StationSounds, 24		450 ___
2427350	NYC Semi-Vestibule Wood Coach 2-pack, 24		500 ___
2427360	PRR Semi-Vestibule Wood Coach 2-pack, 24		500 ___
2427370	MILW Hiawatha No. 2 18" Aluminum Passenger Car 4-pack, 24		1400 ___
2427380	MILW Hiawatha No. 2 18" Aluminum Passenger Car 3-pack, 24		900 ___
2427400	MILW Hiawatha No. 4 18" Aluminum Passenger Car 4-pack, 24		1400 ___
2427410	MILW Hiawatha No. 4 18" Aluminum Passenger Car 3-pack, 24		900 ___
2427430	North Pole Central 18" Aluminum Passenger Car 4-pack, 24		1400 ___
2427440	North Pole Central 18" Aluminum Passenger Car 3-pack, 24		900 ___
2427460	C&NW 18" Aluminum Passenger Car 4-pack, 24		1400 ___
2427470	C&NW 18" Aluminum Passenger Car 3-pack, 24		900 ___
2427490	SAL 18" Aluminum Passenger Car 4-pack, 24		1400 ___
2427500	SAL 18" Aluminum Passenger Car 3-pack, 24		900 ___
2427520	UP 18" Aluminum Passenger Car 4-pack, 24		1400 ___
2427530	UP 18" Aluminum Passenger Car 3-pack, 24		900 ___
2427550	B&O Royal Blue Wood Passenger Car 2-pack, A, 24		500 ___
2427560	B&O Royal Blue Wood Passenger Car 2-pack, B, 24		500 ___
2427570	B&O Royal Blue Wood Passenger Car 2-pack, C, 24		500 ___
2427640	ATSF Full Vista Dome Car Add-on "60", 24		130 ___
2427650	Halloween Wood Passenger Car 2-pack, A, 24		520 ___
2427660	Halloween Wood Passenger Car 2-pack, B, 24		520 ___
2427670	Halloween Wood Passenger Car 2-pack, C, 24		520 ___
2427680	CB&Q 21" Passenger Car 4-pack, 24		1000 ___
2427690	CB&Q 21" Passenger Car 2-pack, 24		500 ___
2427700	CB&Q 21" Diner w/StationSounds, 24		450 ___
2427710	RI Al Capone Coach 4-pack, 24		1000 ___
2427720	Polar Express 20th Anniversary Coach, white roof, 24		100 ___
2427730	LL Coach "2024", 24		110 ___

			Exc	Mint
___	**2427740**	LL Coach "Joshua", 24		110
___	**2427750**	LL Observation Coach "Cowen", 24		110
___	**2427760**	LL Baggage Car "Tradition", 24		100
___	**2427770**	LL Vista Dome Coach "Vision", 24		120
___	**2427780**	PRR Coach "4041", 24		110
___	**2427790**	PRR Coach "4049", 24		110
___	**2427800**	PRR Observation Coach "1126", 24		110
___	**2427810**	PRR Baggage Car "5868", 24		100
___	**2427820**	PRR Vista Dome Coach "7820", 24		120
___	**2427830**	UP Coach "584", 24		110
___	**2427840**	UP Coach "590", 24		110
___	**2427850**	UP Observation "1576", 24		110
___	**2427860**	UP Baggage Car "5715", 24		100
___	**2427870**	UP Vista Dome "Stardust", 24		120
___	**2427880**	Christmas Coach "12023", 24		110
___	**2427890**	Christmas Coach "12024", 24		110
___	**2427900**	Christmas Observation "12025", 24		110
___	**2427910**	Christmas Baggage Car "Noel", 24		100
___	**2427920**	Christmas Vista Dome "Spirit", 24		120
___	**2427930**	Halloween Coach "New Moon", 24		110
___	**2427940**	Halloween Coach "Crescent Moon", 24		110
___	**2427950**	Halloween Observation Coach "Full Moon", 24		110
___	**2427960**	Halloween Baggage Car "Harvest", 24		100
___	**2427970**	Halloween Vista Dome "Hunter", 24		120
___	**2427980**	Sleigh Bell Limited Passenger Car Add-on 2-pack, 24		200
___	**2427990**	Polar Express 20th Anniversary Coach, black roof, 24		100
___	**2428010**	Tasmanian Devil Lenticular Boxcar, 23		130
___	**2428020**	GN Flatcar "65722," w/Bulkheads, 23		70
___	**2428030**	Bethlehem Steel Flatcar "2054," w/Bulkheads, 23		70
___	**2428040**	Harry Potter Dementors Aquarium Car, 24		130
___	**2428050**	Wizard of Oz Red Slippers Illuminated Boxcar, 24		150
___	**2428060**	Batman 85th Anniversary Bat Signal Caboose, 24		160
___	**2428070**	2024 Christmas Boxcar, 24		90
___	**2428080**	2024 Christmas Music Boxcar, 24		120
___	**2428090**	Peppermint RR Transport Bulkhead Flatcar, 24		70
___	**2428100**	Weather Balloon Defense Car 2-pack, 23		230
___	**2428110**	Harry Potter and the Sorcerer's Stone Boxcar, 24		100
___	**2428120**	Harry Potter and the Chamber of Secrets Boxcar, 24		100
___	**2428130**	Harry Potter and the Prisoner of Azkaban Boxcar, 24		100
___	**2428140**	Thomas Kinkade Mickey & Minnie Sweetheart Central Park Boxcar, 24		100
___	**2428150**	Thomas Kinkade Mickey & Minnie Candy Cane Express Boxcar, 24		100
___	**2428160**	Thomas Kinkade Mickey & Minnie Christmas Lodge Boxcar, 24		100
___	**2428170**	Polar Express 20th Anniversary Illuminated Boxcar w/ sounds, 24		160
___	**2428180**	Fright Liner Auto Rack, 24		85
___	**2428190**	Chevrolet Crane Car "8190", 24		120
___	**2428200**	Ford Crane Car "51", 24		120
___	**2428210**	Ichabod Crane Car, 24		120
___	**2428220**	Bob Ross Boxcar w/sounds, 24		120
___	**2428230**	Polar Express Present Transport Car, 24		110

		Exc	Mint
2428240	Lenny Lager 1-D Tank Car, 24		90
2428250	U.S. Army Boxcar "8250", 24		90
2428260	U.S. Army Flatcar "8260" w/tank, 24		100
2428270	U.S. Army 3-D Tank Car "8270", 24		90
2428280	Aquaman Seven Seas 1-D Tank Car, 24		110
2428290	Superman Flatcar w/steel I-beam, 24		100
2428300	Green Lantern Power Ring Searchlight Caboose, 24		160
2428310	NYSW Boxcar "8310", 24		90
2428320	Blue Coal Hopper w/coal load, 24		90
2428330	DL&W Gondola w/canisters, 24		100
2428340	UP Boxcar "960449", 24		90
2428350	WP Gondola "6053", 24		90
2428360	SP 1-D Tank Car "62904", 24		90
2428370	NS Hi-Cube Boxcar "473177" w/graffiti, 24		90
2428380	UTLX Unibody 1-D Tank Car "X-13878" w/graffiti, 24		90
2428390	Ferromex Auto Rack "705176" w/graffiti, 24		100
2428400	Anheuser-Busch Clydesdale Holiday Refrigerator Car, 24		100
2428410	Budweiser Illuminated Bar Sign Refrigerator Car, 24		150
2428420	Barbie 65th Anniversary Boxcar, 1959, 24		100
2428430	Barbie 65th Anniversary Boxcar, 1960s, 24		100
2428440	Barbie 65th Anniversary Boxcar, 1970s, 24		100
2428450	Mister Rogers Aquarium Car, 24		130
2428460	Mister Rogers Boxcar w/sounds, 24		120
2429010	John Deere Showroom, 23		170
2429020	Acme Dynamite Factory, 24		400
2429050	Amtrak Mail & Express Station, 24		150
2429060	Sled-Ex Christmas Operating Freight Station, 24		150
2429070	Angela Trotta Thomas Halloween Covered Bridge, 24		80
2429080	Bob Ross Gallery Building, 24		130
2429090	Polar Express Billy's House, 24		130
2429100	Polar Express Freight Terminal, 24		150
2429110	Haunted Barn w/Blinking lights, 24		160
2429120	Farm Animals Barn w/Sounds, 24		180
2429130	John Deere Barn, 24		170
2429140	Anheuser-Busch Industrial Water Tower, 24		90
2429150	Lenny Lager Industrial Water Tower, 24		90
2429153	PEP 153 IR, 24		80
2429160	Thomas Kinkade Christmas Light Express Covered Bridge, 24		90
2429180	Decorative Street Lamp 3-pack, green, 24		40
2429190	Decorative Street Lamp 3-pack, black, 24		40
2429200	Station Lights 3-pack, green, 24		40
2429210	Station Lights 3-pack, black, 24		40
2429220	Double-Arm Globe Light 3-pack, 24		40
2429230	Double-Arm Highway Light 3-pack, 24		40
2429240	Single-Light Extended Pole Light 3-pack, 24		40
2430010	Acme Dynamite Powder Barrel Pack, 23		16
2430020	Smoke Fluid Bottle w/Needle Dropper 2-pack, 23		10
2430030	Amtrak Passenger Shelter, 24		50
2430040	Lionelville Passenger Shelter, 24		50
2430050	Bob Ross Water Tower, 24		60
2430060	Polar Express 20th Anniversary Water Tower, 24		60
2430070	Halloween Water Tower, 24		60
2431010	Erie Triplex Steam Locomotive "2603," CC, 24		2500

			Exc	Mint
___	2431020	Erie Triplex Steam Locomotive "5014," CC, 24		2500
___	2431030	Erie Triplex Steam Locomotive "5015," CC, 24		2500
___	2431040	Erie Triplex Steam Locomotive "5016," CC, 24		2500
___	2431050	D&RGW Triplex Steam Locomotive "1090," CC, 24		2500
___	2431060	NP Triplex Steam Locomotive "4050," CC, 24		2500
___	2431070	Virginian Triplex Steam Locomotive "701," CC, 24		2500
___	2431080	Pilot Triplex Steam Locomotive "9999," CC, 24		2500
___	2431090	Halloween Triplex Steam Locomotive "3131," CC, 24		2500
___	2431100	C&O F-19 4-6-2 Pacific Locomotive "490," CC, 23		1300
___	2431110	C&O F-19 4-6-2 Pacific, George Washington "491," CC, 23		1300
___	2431120	C&O F-19 4-6-2 Pacific Locomotive "492," ca 1929, CC, 23		1300
___	2431130	C&O F-19 4-6-2 Pacific Locomotive "493," CC, 23		1300
___	2431140	C&O F-19 4-6-2 Pacific Locomotive "494," CC, 23		1300
___	2431150	C&O F-19 4-6-2 Pacific Locomotive "491," CC, 23		1300
___	2431160	C&O F-19 4-6-2 Pacific George Washington "492," CC, 23		1300
___	2431170	Halloween F-19 4-6-2 Pacific Locomotive "310," CC, 23		1300
___	2431180	Pere Marquette F-19 4-6-2 Pacific Locomotive "730," CC, 23		1300
___	2431190	RF&P F-19 4-6-2 Pacific Locomotive "350," CC, 23		1300
___	2431200	D&RGW 2-6-6-2 Locomotive "3302," CC, 23		1800
___	2431210	Nickel Plate 2-6-6-2 Locomotive "942," CC, 23		1800
___	2431220	NP 2-6-6-2 Locomotive "3110," CC, 23		1800
___	2431230	N&W 2-6-6-2 Locomotive "1303," CC, 23		1800
___	2431240	WM 2-6-6-2 Locomotive "1309," CC, 23		1800
___	2431250	Weyerhaeuser Lumber 2-6-6-2 Locomotive "120," CC, 23		1800
___	2431260	UP FEF-3 4-8-4 Locomotive "844," black, CC, 23		1800
___	2431270	UP FEF-3 4-8-4 Locomotive "844," gray/yellow, CC, 23		1800
___	2431280	UP FEF-3 4-8-4 Locomotive "843," gray/silver, CC, 23		1800
___	2431290	UP FEF-3 4-8-4 Locomotive "838," CC, 23		1800
___	2431300	UP FEF-3 4-8-4 Locomotive Challenger "836," CC, 23		1800
___	2431310	UP FEF-3 4-8-4 Locomotive "841," CC, 23		1800
___	2431320	UP Auxiliary Tender "809," CC, 23		500
___	2431329	UP Auxiliary Tender "809", 23		350
___	2431330	UP Auxiliary Tender "814," CC, 23		500
___	2431339	UP Auxiliary Tender "814", 23		350
___	2431340	Black River & Western 2-8-0 Consolidation "60," CC, 23		900
___	2431350	Colorado & Southern 2-8-0 Consolidation "641," CC, 23		900
___	2431360	DM&IR 2-8-0 Consolidation "332," CC, 23		900
___	2431370	GTW 2-8-0 Consolidation "2683," CC, 23		900
___	2431380	LV 2-8-0 Consolidation "911," CC, 23		900
___	2431390	SAL 2-8-0 Consolidation "900," CC, 23		900
___	2431400	PRR M1 4-8-2 Mountain Locomotive "6855," CC, 23		1600
___	2431410	PRR M1 4-8-2 Mountain Locomotive "6810," CC, 23		1600
___	2431420	PRR M1 4-8-2 Mountain Locomotive "6845," CC, 23		1600
___	2431430	PRR M1 4-8-2 Mountain Locomotive "6871," CC, 23		1600
___	2431440	PRR M1 4-8-2 Mountain Locomotive "6918," CC, 23		1600
___	2431450	PRR M1 4-8-2 Mountain Locomotive "6888," CC, 23		1600
___	2431460	Polar Express 2-8-4 Berkshire Locomotive "1225," CC, 24		1700
___	2431470	Polar Express 20th Anniversary 2-8-4 Berkshire Plasma-Coat "1225," CC, 24		1700
___	2431480	Polar Express 2-8-4 Berkshire Special Red "1225," CC, 24		1700
___	2431501	NPR 2-8-4 Berkshire Locomotive "755," CC, 24		1700
___	2431502	NPR 2-8-4 Berkshire Locomotive "765," CC, 24		1700
___	2431510	NPR 2-8-4 Berkshire Locomotive "777," CC, 24		1700

		Exc	Mint
2431520	C&O 2-8-4 Berkshire Locomotive "2765," CC, 24		1700
2431530	DT&I 2-8-4 Berkshire Locomotive "705," CC, 24		1700
2431540	Pere Marquette 2-8-4 Berkshire Locomotive "1225," CC, 24		1700
2431550	C&O H7 2-8-8-2 Mallet Locomotive "1572" w/1926 tender, CC, 24		2000
2431560	C&O H7 2-8-8-2 Mallet Locomotive "1553" w/Vanderbilt tender, CC, 24		2000
2431570	C&O H7 2-8-8-2 Mallet Locomotive "1564" w/Short Vanderbilt tender, CC, 24		2000
2431580	C&O H7 2-8-8-2 Mallet Locomotive "1584" w/Allegheny tender, CC, 24		2000
2431590	D&RGW H7 2-8-8-2 Mallet Locomotive "3605," CC, 24		2000
2431600	RF&P H7 2-8-8-2 Mallet Locomotive "1," CC, 24		2000
2431611	UP H7 2-8-8-2 Mallet Locomotive "3589," CC, 24		2000
2431612	UP H7 2-8-8-2 Mallet Locomotive "3592," CC, 24		2000
2431620	Christmas F-19 4-6-2 Pacific Locomotive "1224," CC, 23		1300
2431630	B&O 4-6-0 Ten-Wheeler Locomotive "1315," CC, 24		800
2431640	CNJ 4-6-0 Ten-Wheeler Locomotive "185," CC, 24		800
2431650	NYC&HR 4-6-0 Ten-Wheeler Locomotive "2140," CC, 24		800
2431660	NYC 4-6-0 Ten-Wheeler Locomotive "1244," CC, 24		800
2431670	NP 4-6-0 Ten-Wheeler Locomotive "1372," CC, 24		800
2431680	WP 4-6-0 Ten-Wheeler Locomotive "110," CC, 24		800
2431690	MILW Hiawatha 4-4-2 Atlantic Locomotive "1," CC, 24		1200
2431700	MILW Hiawatha 4-4-2 Atlantic Locomotive "2," CC, 24		1200
2431710	MILW Hiawatha 4-4-2 Atlantic Locomotive "4," CC, 24		1200
2431720	North Pole Central 4-4-2 Atlantic Locomotive "12," CC, 24		1200
2431730	C&NW 4-4-2 Atlantic Locomotive "400," CC, 24		1200
2431740	SAL 4-4-2 Atlantic Locomotive "850," CC, 24		1200
2431750	UP 4-4-2 Atlantic Locomotive "2800," CC, 24		1200
2431830	Lionel Lines 4-4-2 Atlantic Locomotive "2024," CC, 24		1200
2432010	LL 2-8-4 Berkshire Locomotive "726," LionChief Plus 2.0, 23		700
2432020	American Railroads 2-8-4 Berkshire "759," LionChief Plus 2.0, 23		700
2432030	DT&I 2-8-4 Berkshire Locomotive "704," LionChief Plus 2.0, 23		700
2432040	ATSF 2-8-4 Berkshire Locomotive "4106," LionChief Plus 2.0, 23		700
2432050	Polar Express 20th Anniversary 2-8-4 Berkshire "1225," LionChief Plus 2.0, 24		600
2432060	Polar Express 2-8-4 Berkshire "1225," LionChief Plus 2.0, 24		600
2432070	NKP 2-8-4 Berkshire "759," LionChief Plus 2.0, 24		600
2432080	Pere Marquette 2-8-4 Berkshire "1223," LionChief Plus 2.0, 24		600
2432090	C&O 2-8-4 Berkshire "2696," LionChief Plus 2.0, 24		600
2432100	L&N 2-8-4 Berkshire "1984," LionChief Plus 2.0, 24		600
2432110	Peppermint RR 2-8-4 Berkshire "2524," LionChief Plus 2.0, 24		600
2433010	Trump GE ES44AC Diesel "2024," CC, 24 u		750
2433031	UP EMD SD70ACe Diesel "8518," CC, 23		700
2433032	UP EMD SD70ACe Diesel "8620," CC, 23		700
2433039	UP EMD SD70ACe Diesel "8522" (unpowered), 23		350
2433040	NS Heritage CNJ EMD SD70ACe Diesel "1071," CC, 23		700

			Exc	Mint
___	**2433049**	NS Heritage CNJ EMD SD70ACe Diesel "1071" (unpowered), 23		350
___	**2433050**	NS Heritage DL&W EMD SD70ACe Diesel "1074," CC, 23		700
___	**2433059**	NS Heritage DL&W EMD SD70ACe Diesel "1074" (unpowered), 23		350
___	**2433060**	NS Heritage Erie EMD SD70ACe Diesel "1068," CC, 23		700
___	**2433069**	NS Heritage Erie EMD SD70ACe Diesel "1068" (unpowered), 23		350
___	**2433070**	NS Heritage IT EMD SD70ACe Diesel "1072," CC, 23		700
___	**2433079**	NS Heritage IT EMD SD70ACe Diesel "1072" (unpowered), 23		350
___	**2433080**	NS Heritage NYC EMD SD70ACe Diesel "1066," CC, 23		700
___	**2433089**	NS Heritage NYC EMD SD70ACe Diesel "1066" (unpowered), 23		350
___	**2433111**	Alaska RR EMD GP30 Diesel "2000," CC, 23		600
___	**2433112**	Alaska RR EMD GP30 Diesel "2504," CC, 23		600
___	**2433121**	Conrail EMD GP30 Diesel "2168," CC, 23		600
___	**2433122**	Conrail EMD GP30 Diesel "2196," CC, 23		600
___	**2433131**	NYC EMD GP30 Diesel "6118," CC, 23		600
___	**2433132**	NYC EMD GP30 Diesel "6121," CC, 23		600
___	**2433141**	PRR EMD GP30 Diesel "2211," CC, 23		600
___	**2433142**	PRR EMD GP30 Diesel "2233," CC, 23		600
___	**2433151**	ATSF EMD GP30 Diesel "1203," CC, 23		600
___	**2433152**	ATSF EMD GP30 Diesel "1220," CC, 23		600
___	**2433161**	WC EMD GP30 Diesel "2252," CC, 23		600
___	**2433162**	WC EMD GP30 Diesel "2253," CC, 23		600
___	**2433170**	ATSF EMD F7 AA Diesel Set "332/335," CC, 23		1200
___	**2433178**	ATSF EMD F7 B Unit "337A," CC, 23		600
___	**2433179**	ATSF EMD F7 B Unit SuperBass "338B", 23		550
___	**2433180**	B&M EMD F7 AA Diesel Set "4265/4268," CC, 23		1200
___	**2433188**	B&M EMD F7 B Unit "4267B," CC, 23		600
___	**2433189**	B&M EMD F7 B Unit SuperBass "4268B", 23		550
___	**2433190**	CB&Q EMD F7 AA Diesel Set "167A/167C," CC, 23		1200
___	**2433198**	CB&Q EMD F7 B Unit "167B," CC, 23		600
___	**2433199**	CB&Q EMD F7 B Unit SuperBass "168B", 23		550
___	**2433200**	GN EMD F7 AA Diesel Set "364A/364C," CC, 23		1200
___	**2433208**	GN EMD F7 B Unit "364B," CC, 23		600
___	**2433209**	GN EMD F7 B Unit SuperBass "364B," CC, 23		550
___	**2433210**	RI EMD F7 AA Diesel Set "120/122," CC, 23		1200
___	**2433218**	RI EMD F7 B Unit "22," CC, 23		600
___	**2433219**	RI EMD F7 B Unit SuperBass "10", 23		550
___	**2433220**	Frisco EMD F7 AA Diesel Set "5032/5033," CC, 23		1200
___	**2433228**	Frisco EMD F7 B Unit "5132," CC, 23		600
___	**2433229**	Frisco EMD F7 B Unit SuperBass "5139", 23		550
___	**2433231**	B&O EMD SD50 Diesel "8577," CC, 23		650
___	**2433232**	B&O EMD SD50 Diesel "8584," CC, 23		650
___	**2433239**	B&O EMD SD50 Diesel SuperBass "8593" (unpowered), 23		600
___	**2433241**	Conrail EMD SD50 Diesel "6709" CC, 23		650
___	**2433249**	Conrail EMD SD50 Diesel SuperBass "6720" (unpowered), 23		600
___	**2433250**	Conrail EMD SD50 Diesel "6707" CC, 23		650
___	**2433261**	D&RGW EMD SD50 Diesel "5503," CC, 23		650
___	**2433262**	D&RGW EMD SD50 Diesel "5507," CC, 23		650

		Exc	Mint
2433269	D&RGW EMD SD50 Diesel SuperBass "5515" (unpowered), 23		600
2433271	MP EMD SD50 Diesel "5000," CC, 23		650
2433272	MP EMD SD50 Diesel "5041," CC, 23		650
2433279	MP EMD SD50 Diesel SuperBass "5050" (unpowered), 23		600
2433281	NS EMD SD40E Diesel "6313" CC, 23		650
2433282	NS EMD SD40E Diesel "6319" CC, 23		650
2433289	NS EMD SD40E Diesel SuperBass "6329" (unpowered), 23		600
2433291	Reading & Northern EMD SD50 Diesel "5018" CC, 23		650
2433299	Reading & Northern EMD SD50 SuperBass "5019" (unpowered), 23		600
2433300	ADM Alco S2 Diesel Switcher "1," CC, 23		550
2433310	CP Alco S2 Diesel Switcher "7020," CC, 23		550
2433320	Staten Island RR Alco S2 Diesel Switcher "821," CC, 23		550
2433330	L&NE Alco S2 Diesel Switcher "611," CC, 23		550
2433340	NASA Alco S2 Diesel Switcher "2," CC, 23		550
2433350	U.S. Army Alco S2 Diesel Switcher "7100," CC, 23		550
2433361	BAR EMD GP9 Diesel "76," CC, 24		600
2433362	BAR EMD GP9 Diesel "78," CC, 24		600
2433371	Conrail EMD GP9 Diesel "7020," CC, 24		600
2433372	Conrail EMD GP9 Diesel "7043," CC, 24		600
2433379	Conrail EMD GP9 B unit SuperBass "3812," CC, 24		500
2433381	M&StL EMD GP9 Diesel "702," CC, 24		600
2433382	M&StL EMD GP9 Diesel "705," CC, 24		600
2433391	N&W EMD GP9 Diesel "500," CC, 24		600
2433392	N&W EMD GP9 Diesel "512," CC, 24		600
2433401	PRR EMD GP9 Diesel "7013," CC, 24		600
2433402	PRR EMD GP9 Diesel "7025," CC, 24		600
2433409	PRR EMD GP9 B unit SuperBass "7185B," CC, 24		500
2433411	UP EMD GP9 Diesel "310," CC, 24		600
2433412	UP EMD GP9 Diesel "312," CC, 24		600
2433419	UP EMD GP9 B unit SuperBass "310B," CC, 24		500
2433421	BNSF GE ES44 Diesel "5780," CC, 24		750
2433422	BNSF GE ES44 Diesel "5856," CC, 24		750
2433429	BNSF GE ES44 SuperBass "5909", 24		600
2433431	CP GE ES44 Diesel "8951," CC, 24		750
2433432	CP GE ES44 Diesel "9370," CC, 24		750
2433439	CP GE ES44 SuperBass "9369", 24		600
2433441	CSX GE ES44 Diesel "3000," CC, 24		750
2433442	CSX GE ES44 Diesel "3035," CC, 24		750
2433449	CSX GE ES44 SuperBass "3059", 24		600
2433451	NS GE ES44 Diesel "8034," CC, 24		750
2433452	NS GE ES44 Diesel "8092," CC, 24		750
2433459	NS GE ES44 SuperBass "8159", 24		600
2433461	UP GE ES44 Diesel "5282," CC, 24		750
2433462	UP GE ES44 Diesel "5283," CC, 24		750
2433469	UP GE ES44 SuperBass "5251", 24		600
2433471	NS Heritage Central of Georgia GE ES44 Diesel "8101," CC, 24		750
2433479	NS Heritage Central of Georgia GE ES44 Diesel "8101," non-powered, 24		430
2433481	NS Heritage LV GE ES44 Diesel "8104," CC, 24		750
2433489	NS Heritage LV GE ES44 Diesel "8104," non-powered, 24		430

			Exc	Mint
___	**2433491**	NS Heritage Monongahela GE ES44 Diesel "8025," CC, 24		750
___	**2433499**	NS Heritage Monongahela GE ES44 Diesel "8025," non-powered, 24		430
___	**2433501**	NS Heritage N&W GE ES44 Diesel "8103," CC, 24		750
___	**2433509**	NS Heritage N&W GE ES44 Diesel "8103," non-powered, 24		430
___	**2433511**	NS Heritage PRR GE ES44 Diesel "8102," CC, 24		750
___	**2433512**	NS Heritage PRR GE ES44 Diesel "8102," non-powered, 24		430
___	**2433521**	ATSF EMD SD45 Diesel "5534," CC, 24		650
___	**2433522**	ATSF EMD SD45 Diesel "5543," CC, 24		650
___	**2433529**	ATSF EMD SD45 Diesel SuperBass "5555", 24		600
___	**2433531**	D&H EMD SD45 Diesel "801," CC, 24		650
___	**2433532**	D&H EMD SD45 Diesel "802," CC, 24		650
___	**2433539**	D&H EMD SD45 Diesel SuperBass "803", 24		600
___	**2433541**	D&RGW EMD SD45 Diesel "5315," CC, 24		650
___	**2433542**	D&RGW EMD SD45 Diesel "5326," CC, 24		650
___	**2433549**	D&RGW EMD SD45 Diesel SuperBass "5340", 24		600
___	**2433551**	Reading EMD SD45 Diesel "7601," CC, 24		650
___	**2433552**	Reading EMD SD45 Diesel "7603," CC, 24		650
___	**2433559**	Reading EMD SD45 Diesel SuperBass "7604", 24		600
___	**2433561**	Frisco EMD SD45 Diesel "911," CC, 24		650
___	**2433562**	Frisco EMD SD45 Diesel "916," CC, 24		650
___	**2433569**	Frisco EMD SD45 Diesel SuperBass "929", 24		600
___	**2433571**	SP EMD SD45 Diesel "7400," CC, 24		650
___	**2433572**	SP EMD SD45 Diesel "7437," CC, 24		650
___	**2433579**	SP EMD SD45 Diesel SuperBass "7401", 24		600
___	**2433580**	CSX Heritage B&O GE ES44 Diesel "1827," CC, 24		750
___	**2433589**	CSX Heritage B&O GE ES44 Diesel "1827," non-powered, 24		430
___	**2433590**	B&O EMD E6 Diesel AB Set "57A/57B," CC, 24		1200
___	**2433599**	B&O EMD E6 B Unit SuperBass "588", 24		500
___	**2433600**	CB&Q RI EMD E5 Diesel AB Set, CC, 24		1200
___	**2433609**	CB&Q EMD E5 B Unit SuperBass "9980B", 24		500
___	**2433610**	GM EMD E6 Diesel AB Set "1939/1940," CC, 24		1200
___	**2433619**	GM EMD E6 B Unit SuperBass "1939B", 24		500
___	**2433620**	MILW EMD E6 Diesel AB Set "15A/15B," CC, 24		1200
___	**2433629**	MILW EMD E6 B Unit SuperBass "15C", 24		500
___	**2433630**	RI EMD E6 Diesel AB Set "630/631," CC, 24		1200
___	**2433639**	RI EMD E7 B Unit SuperBass "610", 24		500
___	**2433640**	Southern EMD E6 Diesel AB Set "2902/2952," CC, 24		1200
___	**2433649**	Southern EMD E6 B Unit SuperBass "2953", 24		500
___	**2433650**	UP City of San Francisco EMD E6 Diesel AB Set "SF4/SF5," CC, 24		1200
___	**2433659**	UP City of San Francisco EMD E6 B Unit SuperBass "SF6", 24		500
___	**2433660**	C&NW EMD SW8 Diesel "127," CC, 24		550
___	**2433670**	Detroit Edison EMD SW8 Diesel "214," CC, 24		550
___	**2433680**	EL EMD SW8 Diesel "364," CC, 24		550
___	**2433690**	Reading & Northern EMD SW8 Diesel "800," CC, 24		550
___	**2433700**	T&P EMD SW8 Diesel "812," CC, 24		550
___	**2433710**	USAF EMD SW8 Diesel "2021," CC, 24		550
___	**2433720**	CSX Heritage Chessie System GE ES44 Diesel "1973," CC, 24		750
___	**2433729**	CSX Heritage Chessie System GE ES44 Diesel "1973," non-powered, 24		430
___	**2433731**	Conrail GE U28C Diesel "6521," CC, 24		650

		Exc	Mint
2433732	Conrail GE U28C Diesel "6530," CC, 24		650 ___
2433741	L&N GE U28C Diesel "1527," CC, 24		650 ___
2433742	L&N GE U28C Diesel "1530," CC, 24		650 ___
2433751	PRR GE U28C Diesel "6520," CC, 24		650 ___
2433752	PRR GE U28C Diesel "6528," CC, 24		650 ___
2433761	PC GE U28C Diesel "6526," CC, 24		650 ___
2433762	PC GE U28C Diesel "6533," CC, 24		650 ___
2433771	Seaboard System GE U28C Diesel "1531," CC, 24		650 ___
2433772	Seaboard System GE U28C Diesel "1532," CC, 24		650 ___
2433781	SP GE U28C Diesel "7152," CC, 24		650 ___
2433782	SP GE U28C Diesel "7159," CC, 24		650 ___
2433791	UP GE U28C Diesel "2800," CC, 24		650 ___
2433792	UP GE U28C Diesel "2804," CC, 24		650 ___
2433861	CSX Heritage Seaboard System GE ES44 Diesel "1982," CC, 24		750 ___
2433869	CSX Heritage Seaboard System GE ES44 Diesel "1982," non-powered, 24		430 ___
2433891	CSX Heritage Conrail GE ES44 Diesel "1976," CC, 24		750 ___
2433899	CSX Heritage Conrail GE ES44 Diesel "1976," non-powered, 24		430 ___
2433901	CSX Heritage C&O GE ES44 Diesel "1869," CC, 24		750 ___
2433909	CSX Heritage C&O GE ES44 Diesel "1869," non-powered, 24		430 ___
2434010	D&RGW EMD GP7 Diesel "5102," LionChief Plus 2.0, 23		400 ___
2434020	Aberdeen & Rockfish EMD GP7 Diesel "205," LionChief Plus 2.0, 23		400 ___
2434030	CNJ EMD GP7 Diesel "1522," LionChief Plus 2.0, 23		400 ___
2434040	RI EMD GP7 Diesel "1208," LionChief Plus 2.0, 23		400 ___
2434050	Amtrak Genesis Locomotive Phase III "145," LionChief Plus 2.0, 24		550 ___
2434060	Amtrak Genesis Locomotive Phase I "156," LionChief Plus 2.0, 24		550 ___
2434070	Amtrak Genesis Locomotive Phase II "130," LionChief Plus 2.0, 24		550 ___
2434090	Amtrak Genesis Locomotive Phase IV "164," LionChief Plus 2.0, 24		550 ___
2434100	Metro-North Genesis Locomotive "208," LionChief Plus 2.0, 24		550 ___
2434110	Metro-North Genesis Locomotive "209," LionChief Plus 2.0, 24		550 ___
2434130	Metro-North Heritage Conrail Genesis Locomotive "201," LionChief Plus 2.0, 24		550 ___
2434229	ATSF EMD FT Diesel "157," non-powered, 24		200 ___
2434239	Texas Special EMD FT Diesel "2001," non-powered, 24		200 ___
2434240	Polar Express Genesis Locomotive, LionChief Plus 2.0, 24		550 ___
2435010	Looney Tunes Handcar, 23		120 ___
2435020	Polar Express 20th Anniversary Windup Handcar, 24		200 ___
2435030	Halloween Trolley, LionChief 2.0, 24		150 ___
2435040	B&O Doodlebug "6041," LionChief Plus 2.0, 24		400 ___
2435050	CB&Q Doodlebug "9841," LionChief Plus 2.0, 24		400 ___
2435060	East Broad Top Doodlebug "M-1," LionChief Plus 2.0, 24		400 ___
2435070	GM&O Doodlebug "2506," LionChief Plus 2.0, 24		400 ___
2435080	NYC Doodlebug "X-8015," LionChief Plus 2.0, 24		400 ___
2435090	NP Doodlebug "B-20," LionChief Plus 2.0, 24		400 ___
2435100	RI Doodlebug "9070," LionChief Plus 2.0, 24		400 ___

			Exc	Mint
___	**2435110**	Polar Express Doodlebug "25," LionChief Plus 2.0, 24		400
___	**2435120**	Polar Express TMCC Speeder, 24		200
___	**2435130**	North Pole Central TMCC Speeder, 24		200
___	**2435140**	Chessie System TMCC Speeder "6240", 24		190
___	**2435150**	C&NW TMCC Speeder "400", 24		190
___	**2435160**	RI TMCC Speeder "4351", 24		190
___	**2435170**	US Army Transportation Corps TMCC Speeder, 24		190
___	**2435190**	Area 51 TMCC Speeder "51", 24		190
___	**2435200**	Polar Express 20th Anniversary Windup Handcar, Gold, 24		230
___	**2438010**	Hogwarts Express Boxcar "1", 24		100
___	**2438020**	Hogwarts Express Boxcar "2", 24		100
___	**2438030**	Looney Tunes "Hare Trigger" Boxcar, 23		95
___	**2438040**	Looney Tunes "Devil May Hare" Boxcar, 23		95
___	**2438070**	Polar Express Personalized Boxcar, 24		100
___	**2438090**	2024 Personalized Happy Graduation Boxcar, 24		100
___	**2438100**	2024 Personalized Merry Christmas Boxcar, 24		100
___	**2438110**	2024 Personalized Happy Anniversary Boxcar, 24		100
___	**2438130**	2024 Personalized Happy Father's Day Boxcar, 24		100
___	**2438140**	2024 Personalized Happy Mother's Day Boxcar, 24		100
___	**2438150**	East Broad Top 150th Anniversary Boxcar, 24		100
___	**2438180**	California Zephyr 75th Anniversary Boxcar, 24		100
___	**2438190**	First Continental Congress 250th Anniversary Boxcar, 24		110
___	**2438210**	Angela Trotta Thomas Prairie Steam Engine Boxcar, 24		100
___	**2438220**	Angela Trotta Thomas Diesel Flag Boxcar, 24		100
___	**2438230**	Bob Ross Boxcar, 24		110
___	**2438270**	Wings of Angels Tala Boxcar, 24		110
___	**2438280**	Wings of Angels Nina Boxcar, 24		110
___	**2438290**	Wings of Angels Caitlin Boxcar, 24		110
___	**2438300**	Looney Tunes Acme Boxcar, 1, 24		100
___	**2438310**	Looney Tunes Acme Boxcar, 2, 24		100
___	**2438340**	Fred Rogers Boxcar, 24		100
___	**2442010**	UP World War II PS-1 Boxcar 3-pack, 1, 23		250
___	**2442020**	UP World War II PS-1 Boxcar 3-pack, 2, 23		250
___	**2442030**	UP World War II PS-1 Boxcar 3-pack, 3, 23		250
___	**2442040**	UP World War II PS-1 Boxcar Art 3-pack, 4, 24		250
___	**2442050**	UP World War II PS-1 Boxcar Art 3-pack, 5, 24		250
___	**2442060**	UP World War II PS-1 Boxcar Art 3-pack, 6, 24		250
___	**2442070**	C&O Composite 2-bay Hopper 2-pack, 1, 23		240
___	**2442075**	C&O Composite 2-bay Hopper 2-pack, 2, 23		240
___	**2442079**	C&O Composite 2-bay Hopper "55520", 23		80
___	**2442080**	CB&Q Composite 2-bay Hopper 2-pack, 1, 23		240
___	**2442085**	CB&Q Composite 2-bay Hopper 2-pack, 2, 23		240
___	**2442089**	CB&Q Composite 2-bay Hopper "194501", 23		80
___	**2442090**	LV Composite 2-bay Hopper 2-pack, 1, 23		240
___	**2442095**	LV Composite 2-bay Hopper 2-pack, 2, 23		240
___	**2442099**	LV Composite 2-bay Hopper "14007", 23		80
___	**2442100**	PRR Composite 2-bay Hopper 2-pack, 1, 23		240
___	**2442105**	PRR Composite 2-bay Hopper 2-pack, 2, 23		240
___	**2442109**	PRR Composite 2-bay Hopper "221190", 23		80
___	**2442110**	ADM PS-2CD Covered Hopper 3-pack, 23		250
___	**2442119**	ADM PS-2CD Covered Hopper "7281", 23		85
___	**2442120**	Illinois Terminal PS-2CD Covered Hopper 3-pack, 23		250
___	**2442129**	Illinois Terminal PS-2CD Covered Hopper "2104", 23		85

		Exc	Mint
2442130	Co-op PS-2CD Covered Hopper 3-pack, 1, 23	250	___
2442140	Co-op PS-2CD Covered Hopper 3-pack, 2, 23	250	___
2442150	CSX/Family Lines PS-2CD Covered Hopper 3-pack, 23	250	___
2442159	CSX/Family Lines PS-2CD Covered Hopper "252325", 23	85	___
2442161	B&M Single-sheath Boxcar "70820", 23	80	___
2442162	B&M Single-sheath Boxcar "70919", 23	80	___
2442171	D&H Single-sheath Boxcar "17187", 23	80	___
2442172	D&H Single-sheath Boxcar "17246", 23	80	___
2442181	NP Single-sheath Boxcar "28544", 23	80	___
2442182	NP Single-sheath Boxcar "28531", 23	80	___
2442191	Wellsville, Addison & Galeton Single-sheath Boxcar "5031", 23	80	___
2442192	Wellsville, Addison & Galeton Single-sheath Boxcar "5053", 23	80	___
2442201	Budweiser Wood-sided Refrigerator Car "3601", 24	100	___
2442202	Budweiser Wood-sided Refrigerator Car "3605", 24	100	___
2442211	A&P Wood-sided Refrigerator Car "12000", 24	80	___
2442212	A&P Wood-sided Refrigerator Car "12021", 24	80	___
2442221	Meyer Kornblum Wood-sided Refrigerator Car "241", 24	80	___
2442222	Meyer Kornblum Wood-sided Refrigerator Car "244", 24	80	___
2442231	PFE/WP Wood-sided Refrigerator Car "55001", 24	80	___
2442232	PFE/WP Wood-sided Refrigerator Car "55759", 24	80	___
2442241	Swift's Premium Wood-sided Refrigerator Car "6001", 24	80	___
2442242	Swift's Premium Wood-sided Refrigerator Car "6039", 24	80	___
2442250	UP WWII PS1 Boxcar Art 3-pack, 7, 24	250	___
2442261	BAR Steel-sided Boxcar "65220", 24	80	___
2442262	BAR Steel-sided Boxcar "65500", 24	80	___
2442271	Central of Georgia Steel-sided Boxcar "4095", 24	80	___
2442272	Central of Georgia Steel-sided Boxcar "4112", 24	80	___
2442281	NS Steel-sided Boxcar "25439", 24	80	___
2442282	NS Steel-sided Boxcar "28077", 24	80	___
2442291	SOO Steel-sided Boxcar "42204", 24	80	___
2442292	SOO Steel-sided Boxcar "42430", 24	80	___
2442300	C&O 2-Bay AAR Hopper 3-pack, 1, 24	240	___
2442305	C&O 2-Bay AAR Hopper 3-pack, 2, 24	240	___
2442309	C&O 2-Bay AAR Hopper "49623", 24	80	___
2442310	Erie 2-Bay AAR Hopper 3-pack, 1, 24	240	___
2442315	Erie 2-Bay AAR Hopper 3-pack, 2, 24	240	___
2442319	Erie 2-Bay AAR Hopper "24133", 24	80	___
2442320	NPR 2-Bay AAR Hopper 3-pack, 1, 24	240	___
2442325	NPR 2-Bay AAR Hopper 3-pack, 2, 24	240	___
2442329	NPR 2-Bay AAR Hopper "33737", 24	80	___
2442330	MILW 2-Bay AAR Hopper 3-pack, 1, 24	240	___
2442335	MILW 2-Bay AAR Hopper 3-pack, 2, 24	240	___
2442339	MILW 2-Bay AAR Hopper "96885", 24	80	___
2442340	ADM 50-foot 1-D Tank Car 3-pack, 24	260	___
2442349	ADM 50-foot 1-D Tank Car "29481", 24	90	___
2442350	BNSF 50-foot 1-D Tank Car 3-pack, 24	260	___
2442359	BNSF 50-foot 1-D Tank Car "880302", 24	90	___
2442360	Cargill Foods 50-foot 1-D Tank Car 3-pack, 24	260	___
2442369	Cargill Foods 50-foot 1-D Tank Car "7852", 24	90	___
2442370	GATX 50-foot 1-D Tank Car 3-pack, 24	260	___
2442379	GATX 50-foot 1-D Tank Car "209792", 24	90	___
2443001	BN DD Boxcar "243832" (std O), 23	70	___
2443002	BN DD Boxcar "243859" (std O), 23	70	___

			Exc	Mint
___	**2443011**	SP DD Boxcar "248401" (std 0), 23		70
___	**2443012**	SP DD Boxcar "248515" (std 0), 23		70
___	**2443021**	UP DD Boxcar "38508" (std 0), 23		70
___	**2443022**	UP DD Boxcar "38515" (std 0), 23		70
___	**2443031**	WP DD Boxcar "38291" (std 0), 23		70
___	**2443032**	WP DD Boxcar "38314" (std 0), 23		70
___	**2445010**	LL 2-4-2 Columbia Locomotive "242," LionChief, 24		250
___	**2445020**	ELX 2-4-2 Columbia Locomotive "800," LionChief, 24		250
___	**2445030**	CB&Q 2-4-2 Columbia Locomotive "3007," LionChief, 24		250
___	**2445040**	NYC 2-4-2 Columbia Locomotive "1939," LionChief, 24		250
___	**2445050**	Sleigh Bell Limited 2-4-2 Columbia Locomotive "2424," LionChief, 24		250
___	**2445060**	ATSF 2-6-2 Prairie Locomotive "1819," LionChief, 24		330
___	**2445070**	PRR 2-6-2 Prairie Locomotive "531," LionChief, 24		330
___	**2445080**	U.S. Army 2-6-2 Prairie Locomotive "75," LionChief, 24		330
___	**2445090**	Winter Wonderland 2-6-2 Prairie Locomotive "2424," LionChief, 24		330
___	**2445100**	Justice League The Flash EMD FT Diesel "1940," LionChief, 24		300
___	**2445110**	UP EMD FT Diesel "1468," LionChief, 24		300
___	**2445120**	PRR EMD FT Diesel "9656," LionChief, 24		300
___	**2445130**	LL EMD FT Diesel "1900," LionChief, 24		300
___	**2445140**	Halloween EMD FT Diesel "3124," LionChief, 24		300
___	**2445150**	Justice League Batman GE ET44 Diesel "Dark Knight," LionChief, 24		300
___	**2445160**	CSX GE ET44 Diesel "3398," LionChief, 24		300
___	**2445170**	BNSF GE ET44 Diesel "3970," LionChief, 24		300
___	**2445180**	U.S. Army GE ET44 Diesel "1775," LionChief, 24		300
___	**2445190**	NPC Snowflake Limited GE ET44 Diesel "240," LionChief, 24		300

Unnumbered Items

			Exc	Mint
___		Amtrak Passenger Car Set, 89, 89 u	640	770
___		Baltimore & Ohio Set, 94, 96		NRS
___		Black Cave Flyer Playmat, 82		8
___		Blue Comet Set, 78-80, 87 u	560	620
___		Boston & Albany Hudson and Standard O Car Set, 86 u	1500	1700
___		Burlington Texas Zephyr Set, 80, 80 u	980	1150
___		Cannonball Freight Playmat, 81-82		8
___		Chesapeake & Ohio Set, 95-96		NRS
___		Chessie System Special Set, 80, 86 u	560	620
___		Chicago & Alton Limited Set, 81, 86 u	560	620
___		Chicago & North Western Passenger Car Set, 93	385	460
___		Commando Assault Train Playmat, 83-84		8
___		D&RGW California Zephyr Set, 92, 93		900
___		Erie Set (FF 7), 93	385	460
___		Erie-Lackawanna Passenger Car Set, 93, 94	940	980
___		Favorite Food Freight Set, 81-82	255	355
___		Frisco Set (FF 5), 91	405	425
___		General Set, 77-80	240	285
___		Great Northern Empire Builder Set, 92, 93	620	730
___		Great Northern Set (FARR 3), 81, 81 u	620	690
___		Illinois Central City of New Orleans Set, 85, 87, 93	885	1045
___		Illinois Central Set, 91-92, 95	255	285
___		Jersey Central Set, 86	345	370

MODERN 1970-2024	Exc	Mint	
Joshua Lionel Cowen Set, 80, 80 u, 82	540	580	___
L.A.S.E.R. Playmat, 81-82		8	___
Lionel Lines Madison Car Set, 91, 93	560	620	___
Lionel Lines Set, 82, 84 u, 86, 86 u, 87 u, 94-95	530	620	___
Mickey Mouse Express Set, 77-78, 78 u	1050	1800	___
Milwaukee Road Set (FF 2), 87, 90 u	380	405	___
Mint Set, 79 u, 80-83, 84 u, 86 u, 87, 91 u, 93	940	1073	___
Missouri Pacific Set, 95		390	___
NASCAR Dale Earnhardt Steam Freight Set (TX328RRGMDE), 12-14		300	___
NASCAR Dale Earnhardt Jr. Steam Freight Set (T8828TRAIN), 12-14		300	___
NASCAR Jeff Gordon Steam Freight Set (T2428RRDUJG), 12-14		300	___
NASCAR Jimmy Johnson Steam Freight Set (T4828RRLOJJ), 12-14		300	___
NASCAR Kyle Busch Steam Freight Set (T1828RRMMKB), 12-14		300	___
NASCAR Tony Stewart Steam Freight Set (T1428R-RODTS), 12-14		300	___
New Haven Set, 94-95		400	___
New York Central Set, 89, 91	240	270	___
New York Central 20th Century Limited Set, 83, 83 u, 95	1000	1200	___
Nickel Plate Road Set (FF 6), 92	385	460	___
Norfolk & Western Powhatan Arrow Set, 81, 81 u, 82 u, 91 u	1450	1700	___
Norfolk & Western Powhatan Arrow Passenger Car Set, 95	370	445	___
Northern Pacific Set, 90-92	190	250	___
Pennsylvania Set, 79-80, 79 u, 80 u 81 u, 83 u	1200	1350	___
Pennsylvania Set (FARR 5), 84-85, 89 u	600	660	___
Pennsylvania Set, 87-90, 95	240	270	___
Pere Marquette Set, 93	720	770	___
Rock Island & Peoria Set, 80-82	240	315	___
Rocky Mountain Platform, 83-84		8	___
Santa Fe Set (FARR 1), 79, 79 u	460	580	___
Santa Fe Super Chief Set, 91, 91 u, 92 u, 93, 95	1400	1700	___
Southern Pacific Daylight Diesel Set, 82-83, 82-83 u, 90 u	2150	2300	___
Southern Pacific Daylight Steam Set, 90, 92-93	790	940	___
Southern Ry. Crescent Limited Set, 77-78, 87 u	540	650	___
Southern Ry. Set (FARR 4), 83, 83 u	620	690	___
Spirit of '76 Set, 74-76	600	720	___
Station Platform, 83-84		8	___
Toys 'R' Us Thunderball Freight Set, 75 u		NRS	___
UCS Remote Control Track Section, 70	4	7	___
Union Pacific Overland Route Set, 84, 92 u	770	840	___
Union Pacific Set (FARR 2), 80, 80 u	540	580	___
Union Pacific Set, 94	430	500	___
Wabash Set (FF 1), 86, 87	755	905	___
Western Maryland Set (FF 4), 89	345	405	___

Section 4
LIONEL CORPORATION TINPLATE

			Exc	Mint
___	**11-1001**	No. 400E Locomotive, black, brass trim (std)		900
___	**11-1002**	No. 400E Locomotive, gray, nickel trim (std)		900
___	**11-1003**	No. 400E Locomotive, gray, brass trim (std)		900
___	**11-1005**	No. 390 Locomotive, green		600
___	**11-1006**	No. 400E Locomotive, crackele black, brass trim		900
___	**11-1008**	No. 400E Lionel Lines Locomotive		900
___	**11-1009**	No. 400E Locomotive, blue, brass trim		900
___	**11-1010**	No. 385E Locomotive (std)		700
___	**11-1012**	No. 1835E Locomotive, black, nickel trim		700
___	**11-1013**	AF No. 4694 Warrior Passenger Set		1400
___	**11-1014**	AF No. 4694 Iron Monarch Passenger Set		1250
___	**11-1015**	No. 392E Locomotive, black, brass trim		800
___	**11-1016**	No. 392E Locomotive, gray, nickel trim		800
___	**11-1017**	No. 400E Locomotive, blue, nickel trim (std)		900
___	**11-1018**	No. 7 Lionel Locomotive (std)		900
___	**11-1019**	No. 6 Pennsylvania Locomotive (std)		900
___	**11-1020**	American Flyer No. 4696 Locomotive		1000
___	**11-1021**	No. 400E Presidential Locomotive (std)		1000
___	**11-1022**	No. 400E Red Comet Locomotive (std)		1000
___	**11-1023**	No. 400E Locomotive, blue, brass trim (std)		900
___	**11-1024**	No. 400E Locomotive, black, brass trim (std)		900
___	**11-1025**	No. 400E Lionel Lines Locomotive (std)		900
___	**11-1026**	No. 400E Locomotive, pink (std)		1000
___	**11-1027**	No. 400E Locomotive, state green (std)		1000
___	**11-1028**	No. 400E Locomotive, black, brass trim (std)		1000
___	**11-1029**	No. 6 NYC Locomotive (std)		900
___	**11-1030**	No. 6 General Locomotive (std)		900
___	**11-1031**	No. 6 Texas Locomotive (std)		950
___	**11-1038**	No. 6 B&O Locomotive (std)		900
___	**11-1039**	No. 6 Long Island Locomotive (std)		900
___	**11-1040**	No. 6 Strasburg Locomotive (std)		900
___	**11-1041**	No. 6 PRR Locomotive (std)		900
___	**11-1042**	Great Northern Steam Locomotive (std)		1000
___	**11-1043**	Lehigh Valley Steam Locomotive (std)		1000
___	**11-1045**	PRR Steam Locomotive (std)		1000
___	**11-2003**	No. 8E Electric Locomotive, olive green (std)		500
___	**11-2004**	No. 8E Electric Locomotive, dark olive green (std)		500
___	**11-2005**	No. 8E Electric Locomotive, orange (std)		500
___	**11-2006**	No. 8E Electric Locomotive, red/cream (std)		500
___	**11-2007**	American Flyer Presidential Passenger Set (std)		1800
___	**11-2008**	AF No. 4689 Presidential Locomotive, blue (std)		800
___	**11-2009**	Big Brute Electric Engine, zinc chromate		1500
___	**11-2010**	Big Brute Electric Engine, green		1500

Lionel Corporation Tinplate		Exc	Mint
11-2015	Super 381 Electric Engine, state green (std)		1300 ___
11-2016	Super 381 MILW Electric Engine (std)		1300 ___
11-2017	No. 408E Electric Locomotive (std)		900 ___
11-2018	No. 408E Electric Locomotive, Mojave		900 ___
11-2019	No. 408E Electric Locomotive, pink		900 ___
11-2020	No. 9 Electric Locomotive, green		600 ___
11-2021	No. 9 Electric Locomotive, orange		600 ___
11-2022	No. 9 Electric Locomotive, gray, nickel trim		600 ___
11-2023	No. 9 Electric Locomotive, dark green		600 ___
11-2024	No. 8 Trolley (std)		530 ___
11-2025	No. 9 Trolley (std)		650 ___
11-2026	No. 8 Christmas Trolley (std)		570 ___
11-2027	No. 381E Electric Locomotive, blue (std)		900 ___
11-2028	No. 381E Electric Locomotive, brown (std)		900 ___
11-2029	No. 381E Great Northern Electric Locomotive (std)		900 ___
11-2031	No. 4689 President's Locomotive, red (std)		900 ___
11-2033	Big Brute Electric Locomotive, brown (std)		1950 ___
11-2034	Big Brute Electric Locomotive, orange (std)		1950 ___
11-2038	Super 381 MILW Electric Locomotive (std)		1300 ___
11-2039	Super 381 PRR Electric Locomotive (std)		1300 ___
11-2040	Super 381 Electric Locomotive, two-tone brown (std)		1300 ___
11-2041	Super 381 New Haven Electric Locomotive (std)		1300 ___
11-5001	No. 384 Locomotive Passenger Set, black, brass trim		600 ___
11-5002	No. 384 Locomotive Christmas Freight Set (std)		600 ___
11-5003	No. 384 Locomotive LV Passenger Set (std)		600 ___
11-5004	No. 384 Locomotive NYC Freight Set		600 ___
11-5006	No. 384E Locomotive Girl's Passenger Set		600 ___
11-5007	No. 386 Freight Set (std)		600 ___
11-5008	No. 340E Coal Freight Set (std)		663 ___
11-5009	No. 342E Baby State Passenger Set (std)		600 ___
11-5010	No. 384E Blue Comet Passenger Set (std)		600 ___
11-5011	No. 386 Christmas Freight Set (std)		600 ___
11-5012	No. 342E Passenger Set (std)		1300 ___
11-5013	No. 318E Christmas Freight Set (std)		600 ___
11-5014	No. 384E PRR Steam Passenger Set (std)		600 ___
11-5501	No. 263E Steam Christmas Freight Set		600 ___
11-5502	No. 263E Steam B&O Freight Set		600 ___
11-5505	No. 249E Christmas Steam Passenger Set		500 ___
11-5506	No. 299 Freight Set		450 ___
11-5507	No. 269E Distant Control Freight Set		500 ___
11-5508	Celebration Passenger Set		480 ___
11-5509	No. 269E Christmas Distant Control Freight Set		500 ___
11-5510	No. 269E Distant Control Freight Set		500 ___
11-6001	No. 263E Locomotive, black, brass trim		430 ___
11-6002	No. 263E Locomotive, blue		430 ___
11-6003	No. 277W Remote Control Work Train		680 ___

	Lionel Corporation Tinplate		Exc	Mint
___	11-6004	Blue Comet Distant Control Passenger Set		650
___	11-6005	No. 275W Distant Control Freight Set		600
___	11-6006	UP Streamliner Passenger Set, silver		800
___	11-6007	UP Streamliner Passenger Set, yellow		800
___	11-6008	No. 249E Steam Passenger Set, black, brass trim		600
___	11-6009	No. 249E Steam Passenger Set, blue		600
___	11-6010	No. 249E Steam Passenger Set, gray, nickel trim		600
___	11-6012	No. 260E Locomotive, black, brass trim		430
___	11-6013	No. 255E Locomotive, gray, nickel trim		430
___	11-6014	No. 255E Lionel Lines Locomotive		430
___	11-6015	No. 279E Distant Control Passenger Set		750
___	11-6016	No. 295E Distant Control Passenger Set		750
___	11-6017	Hiawatha Distance Control Streamliner Set		900
___	11-6018	Hiawatha Passenger Train Set		900
___	11-6019	Hiawatha Distance Control Freight Set		900
___	11-6020	UP City of Denver Passenger Set, green		590
___	11-6021	UP City of Denver Passenger Set, yellow/brown		700
___	11-6022	No. 262E Locomotive, black, brass trim		300
___	11-6023	No. 262E Locomotive, black, nickel trim		300
___	11-6024	No. 260E Locomotive, black, brass trim		450
___	11-6025	No. 214 Armored Motor Car Set		400
___	11-6028	No. 256 Electric Locomotive, orange		450
___	11-6029	No. 214 Armored Motor Car Set		400
___	11-6030	No. 295E Distant Control Passenger Set		750
___	11-6031	No. 279E NYC Distance Control Passenger Set		700
___	11-6033	No. 265E Commodore Vanderbilt Locomotive		430
___	11-6036	No. 263E Baby Blue Comet Locomotive		460
___	11-6037	Girls Freight Set		830
___	11-6038	No. 284E Distant Control Freight Set		700
___	11-6039	No. 616 Flying Yankee Passenger Set, black/chrome		590
___	11-6040	No. 616 Flying Yankee Passenger Set, red/chrome		590
___	11-6041	No. 616 Flying Yankee Passenger Set, green/chrome		590
___	11-6046	No. 279E Distant Control Passenger Set		700
___	11-6047	No. 264 Red Comet Locomotive		460
___	11-6048	No. 263E Baby Blue Comet Locomotive, brass trim		500
___	11-6050	No. 256 New Haven Electric Locomotive		500
___	11-6051	No. 256 Great Northern Electric Locomotive		500
___	11-6052	No. 263E Locomotive, black, nickel trim		500
___	11-6053	No. 263E Chessie Locomotive		500
___	11-6054	No. 263E Southern Locomotive		500
___	11-6055	Boys Freight Set		900
___	11-6056	No. 261E LL Locomotive and Tender		350
___	11-6057	No. 216E Locomotive and Tender		350
___	11-6061	No. 256 MILW Electric Locomotive		500
___	11-6062	No. 256 PRR Electric Locomotive		500
___	11-30004	No. 213 Cattle Car, cream/maroon (std)		130

Lionel Corporation Tinplate		Exc	Mint
11-30005	No. 213 Cattle Car, terra-cotta/green (std)		130
11-30006	No. 214 Boxcar, cream/orange (std)		130
11-30007	No. 214 Boxcar, yellow/brown (std)		130
11-30008	No. 214R Refrigerator Car, white/blue (std)		130
11-30009	No. 215 Tank Car, silver, nickel trim (std)		130
11-30010	No. 215 Tank Car, green, brass trim (std)		130
11-30011	No. 215 Tank Car, white (std)		130
11-30012	No. 216 Hopper Car, red (std)		130
11-30013	No. 217 Caboose, orange/maroon (std)		140
11-30014	No. 217 Caboose, red (std)		160
11-30015	No. 513 Cattle Car, green/orange, brass trim (std)		100
11-30016	No. 514 Boxcar, cream/orange (std)		100
11-30017	No. 514R Refrigerator Car, ivory/peacock, brass trim (std)		100
11-30018	No. 515 Tank Car, terra-cotta, brass trim (std)		100
11-30019	No. 516 Hopper Car, red, brass trim (std)		120
11-30020	No. 517 Caboose, pea green/red (std)		120
11-30021	No. 212 Gondola, maroon (std)		110
11-30022	No. 212 Gondola, pea green (std)		110
11-30023	No. 513 Cattle Car, cream/maroon, nickel trim (std)		100
11-30024	No. 514R Refrigerator Car, white/blue, nickel trim (std)		100
11-30025	No. 515 Tank Car, silver, nickel trim (std)		100
11-30026	No. 516 Hopper Car, red, nickel trim (std)		100
11-30027	No. 517 Caboose, red, nickel trim (std)		120
11-30028	No. 520 Floodlight Car, green, nickel trim (std)		130
11-30029	No. 520 Floodlight Car, terra-cotta, brass trim (std)		130
11-30030	No. 514R Christmas Refrigerator Car, (std)		100
11-30031	No. 514 Christmas Boxcar (std)		100
11-30032	No. 515 MTH/Lionel Tank Car (std)		100
11-30033	No. 211 Flatcar, black, brass trim, with wood (std)		120
11-30034	No. 211 Flatcar, black, nickel trim, with wood (std)		120
11-30035	No. 218 Dump Car, Mojave, nickel trim (std)		140
11-30036	No. 218 Dump Car, Mojave, brass trim (std)		140
11-30037	No. 219 Crane Car, white (std)		200
11-30038	No. 219 Crane Car, yellow, nickel trim (std)		200
11-30039	No. 219 Crane Car, yellow (std)		380
11-30042	No. 514 Boxcar, red/black (std)		100
11-30043	No. 512 Gondola, peacock, brass trim (std)		80
11-30044	No. 512 Gondola, green, nickel trim (std)		80
11-30045	No. 514 Boxcar, yellow/brown (std)		100
11-30046	No. 511 Flatcar, black, brass trim, with wood (std)		100
11-30047	No. 511 Flatcar, black, nickel trim, with wood (std)		100
11-30048	No. 216 Hopper Car, dark green (std)		130
11-30050	No. 219 Crane Car, white, brass trim (std)		380
11-30051	No. 514R NYC Refrigerator Car (std)		100
11-30055	No. 212 Gondola, gray (std)		110
11-30056	No. 213 Cattle Car, Mojave/maroon (std)		130

	Lionel Corporation Tinplate		Exc	Mint
____	**11-30057**	No. 213 Cattle Car, terra-cotta/maroon (std)		130
____	**11-30058**	No. 214 Boxcar, terra-cotta/black, brass trim (std)		130
____	**11-30059**	No. 214R Refrigerator Car, white/peacock, brass trim (std)		130
____	**11-30060**	No. 214R Refrigerator Car, ivory/peacock, brass trim (std)		130
____	**11-30061**	No. 215 Tank Car, silver, brass trim (std)		130
____	**11-30062**	No. 215 Tank Car, silver, nickel trim (std)		130
____	**11-30063**	No. 217 Caboose, olive green (std)		140
____	**11-30064**	No. 217 Lionel Lines Caboose (std)		140
____	**11-30065**	No. 217 Caboose, pea green/red (std)		140
____	**11-30066**	No. 217 Caboose, red/peacock (std)		160
____	**11-30067**	No. 218 Dump Car, gray (std)		140
____	**11-30068**	No. 218 Dump Car, pea green (std)		140
____	**11-30069**	No. 218 Dump Car, peacock (std)		140
____	**11-30070**	No. 219 Crane Car, peacock/dark green (std)		200
____	**11-30071**	No. 219 Lionel Lines Crane Car (std)		380
____	**11-30072**	No. 220 Floodlight Car, green, nickel trim (std)		140
____	**11-30073**	No. 220 Floodlight Car, terra-cotta, brass trim (std)		140
____	**11-30074**	No. 513 Cattle Car, orange/pea green (std)		100
____	**11-30075**	No. 514 Christmas Boxcar (std)		100
____	**11-30076**	No. 514R Refrigerator Car, ivory/blue (std)		100
____	**11-30077**	No. 515 Tank Car, cream (std)		100
____	**11-30078**	No. 515 Tank Car, ivory (std)		100
____	**11-30079**	No. 515 Tank Car, orange (std)		100
____	**11-30080**	No. 516 Christmas Hopper Car (std)		120
____	**11-30081**	No. 516 Hopper Car, red (std)		120
____	**11-30082**	No. 517 Caboose, red/black (std)		120
____	**11-30083**	No. 520 Floodlight Car, green, nickel trim (std)		130
____	**11-30087**	No. 516 Hopper Car, red, brass trim (std)		100
____	**11-30088**	AF 4018 Automobile Car, white/blue		150
____	**11-30089**	AF 4020 Stock Car, blue		150
____	**11-30090**	AF 4006 Hopper Car, red		150
____	**11-30091**	AF 4017 Sand Car, green		150
____	**11-30092**	AF 4010 Tank Car, cream/blue		188
____	**11-30093**	AF 4022 Machine Car, orange		110
____	**11-30094**	AF 4021 Caboose, red		160
____	**11-30095**	AF 4018 Automobile Car, orange/maroon		130
____	**11-30096**	AF 4022 Machine Car, blue		110
____	**11-30097**	AF 4022 Machine Car, orange/green		110
____	**11-30098**	AF 4010 Tank Car, blue		190
____	**11-30099**	AF 4017 Sand Car, maroon		130
____	**11-30100**	AF 4006 Hopper Car, green		130
____	**11-30101**	AF 4020 Stock Car, cream/maroon		130
____	**11-30102**	AF 4021 Caboose, red/maroon		140
____	**11-30103**	AF 4021 Caboose, cream/red		140
____	**11-30104**	No. 215 Tank Car (std)		130
____	**11-30105**	No. 214R Refrigerator Car (std)		130

Lionel Corporation Tinplate		Exc	Mint
11-30107	No. 214R Altoona 36 Lager Refrigerator Car (std)		130 ___
11-30108	No. 214R Budweiser Refrigerator Car (std)		140 ___
11-30109	No. 214R Burp-oh Beer Refrigerator Car (std)		130 ___
11-30110	No. 214R Hood's Dairy Refrigerator Car (std)		130 ___
11-30111	No. 214R Old Reading Refrigerator Car (std)		130 ___
11-30112	No. 214R Palisades Park Refrigerator Car (std)		130 ___
11-30113	No. 214 Circus Boxcar (std)		130 ___
11-30114	No. 214 M&M's Christmas Boxcar (std)		140 ___
11-30115	No. 215 Budweiser Tank Car (std)		140 ___
11-30116	No. 215 Freedomland Tank Car (std)		130 ___
11-30117	No. 215 Gulf Tank Car (std)		130 ___
11-30118	No. 215 Tropicana Tank Car (std)		130 ___
11-30119	No. 513 UP Cattle Car (std)		100 ___
11-30120	No. 513 WM Cattle Car (std)		100 ___
11-30121	No. 514 B&O Boxcar (std)		100 ___
11-30122	No. 514 State of Maine Boxcar (std)		120 ___
11-30123	No. 514R PFE Refrigerator Car (std)		100 ___
11-30124	No. 514R Tropicana Refrigerator Car (std)		120 ___
11-30125	No. 515 Anheuser Busch Tank Car (std)		110 ___
11-30126	No. 515 Hooker Chemicals Tank Car (std)		100 ___
11-30127	No. 516 Blue Coal Hopper Car (std)		100 ___
11-30128	No. 516 Waddell Coal Hopper Car (std)		120 ___
11-30129	No. 517 Pennsylvania Caboose (std)		120 ___
11-30130	No. 517 Santa Fe Caboose (std)		140 ___
11-30131	No. 215 Lionel Lines Tank Car (std)		130 ___
11-30134	No. 515 Christmas Tank Car (std)		100 ___
11-30136	No. 214 Christmas Boxcar (std)		150 ___
11-30137	No. 214 UP Boxcar (std)		150 ___
11-30138	No. 214R Horlacher's Brewing Refrigerator Car (std)		150 ___
11-30139	No. 214R Coors Refrigerator Car (std)		140 ___
11-30140	No. 215 Keystone Gasoline Tank Car (std)		150 ___
11-30141	No. 215 Texaco Tank Car (std)		150 ___
11-30142	No. 216 Peabody Hopper Car (std)		130 ___
11-30143	No. 216 Pennsylvania Power & Light Hopper Car (std)		130 ___
11-30144	No. 213 Cattle Car (std)		130 ___
11-30146	No. 217 Jersey Central Caboose (std)		140 ___
11-30147	No. 214 Jersey Central Boxcar (std)		130 ___
11-30148	No. 214 U.S. Army Boxcar (std)		130 ___
11-30149	No. 215 MTH/Lionel Tank Car		130 ___
11-30150	No. 212 Lionel Lines Gondola (std)		130 ___
11-30151	No. 212 Circus Gondola (std)		240 ___
11-30152	No. 212 NYC Gondola (std)		130 ___
11-30153	No. 214 MKT Boxcar (std)		150 ___
11-30154	No. 214 NYC Boxcar (std)		150 ___
11-30155	No. 215 C&O Tank Car (std)		150 ___
11-30156	No. 215 Shell Tank Car (std)		150 ___

	Lionel Corporation Tinplate		Exc	Mint
___	11-30157	No. 216 Hopper Car, red, brass trim (std)		150
___	11-30158	No. 216 LV Hopper Car (std)		150
___	11-30159	No. 217 Pennsylvania Caboose (std)		160
___	11-30160	No. 219 B&O Crane Car (std)		220
___	11-30161	No. 219 Crane Car, ivory/red (std)		400
___	11-30162	No. 219 Lionel Lines Crane Car (std)		220
___	11-30163	No. 219 Crane Car, red/silver (std)		400
___	11-30164	No. 514R Christmas Refrigerator Car (std)		120
___	11-30168	No. 515 PRR Tank Car (std)		120
___	11-30169	No. 515 Texaco Tank Car (std)		120
___	11-30170	No. 515 Esso Tank Car (std)		120
___	11-30180	No. 219 Crane Car, black/cream (std)		220
___	11-30182	No. 217 NYC Illuminated Caboose (std)		160
___	11-30185	No. 212 Gondola, pea green (std)		150
___	11-30193	No. 514R Altoona Brewing Refrigerator Car (std)		120
___	11-30194	No. 514R PFE Refrigerator Car (std)		120
___	11-30195	No. 514R REA Refrigerator Car (std)		120
___	11-30196	No. 514R Robin Hood Beer Refrigerator Car (std)		120
___	11-30197	No. 514 UP Boxcar (std)		120
___	11-30198	No. 514 Santa Fe Boxcar (std)		120
___	11-30199	No. 514 PRR Boxcar (std)		120
___	11-30200	No. 514 B&O Boxcar (std)		120
___	11-30201	No. 215-3 Shell 3-D Tank Car (std)		150
___	11-30202	No. 215-3 Mazda Lamps 3-D Tank Car (std)		150
___	11-30203	No. 215-3 Celanese Chemicals 3-D Tank Car (std)		150
___	11-30204	No. 215-3 Clark Oil 3-D Tank Car (std)		150
___	11-30205	No. 215-2 Sterling Fuels 2-D Tank Car (std)		150
___	11-30206	No. 215-2 Philadelphia Quartz 2-D Tank Car (std)		150
___	11-30207	No. 215-2 Cookís Paints 2-D Tank Car (std)		150
___	11-30208	No. 215-2 Hercules 2-D Tank Car (std)		150
___	11-30209	No. 216-1 PRR Covered Hopper (std)		150
___	11-30210	No. 216-1 P&LE Covered Hopper (std)		150
___	11-30211	No. 216-1 Jack Frost Covered Hopper (std)		150
___	11-30212	No. 216-1 GE Lamps Covered Hopper (std)		150
___	11-30213	No. 212-1 PRR Covered Gondola Car (std)		150
___	11-30214	No. 212-1 Covered Gondola Car (std)		150
___	11-30215	No. 212-1 NYC Covered Gondola Car (std)		150
___	11-30216	No. 212-1 GN Covered Gondola Car (std)		150
___	11-30217	No. 211 Flatcar with wheel load (std)		150
___	11-30218	No. 211 Altoona Shops Flatcar with wheel load (std)		150
___	11-30219	No. 211 Baldwin Flatcar with wheel load (std)		150
___	11-30220	No. 211 Lima Flatcar with wheel load (std)		150
___	11-30221	No. 217-1 Chessie Bay Window Caboose (std)		160
___	11-30222	No. 217-1 UP Bay Window Caboose (std)		160
___	11-30223	No. 217-1 NYC Bay Window Caboose (std)		160
___	11-30224	No. 217-1 Long Island Bay Window Caboose (std)		160

Lionel Corporation Tinplate		Exc	Mint
11-30225	PRR Automobile Car (std)		150 ___
11-30227	Shell Tank Car (std)		150 ___
11-30230	Waddell Coal Hopper (std)		150 ___
11-30232	PRR Caboose (std)		160 ___
11-40001	Presidential Passenger Set, blue (std)		1200 ___
11-40002	No. 339 Pullman Car, green (std)		150 ___
11-40003	No. 332 Mail/Baggage Car, green (std)		150 ___
11-40004	No. 332 LV Ithaca Baggage Car		150 ___
11-40005	No. 339 LV Easton Passenger Coach		150 ___
11-40007	300 Series 3-Car Passenger Set, blue/silver (std)		450 ___
11-40009	3-Car State Passenger Set, green (std)		1200 ___
11-40010	Pennsylvania State Baggage Car, green (std)		400 ___
11-40011	Illinois State Coach, green (std)		400 ___
11-40012	Solarium State Car, green (std)		400 ___
11-40013	MILW 3-Car State Passenger Set (std)		1200 ___
11-40014	MILW State Baggage Car (std)		538 ___
11-40015	MILW State Passenger Coach (std)		500 ___
11-40016	MILW Solarium State Car (std)		513 ___
11-40017	3-Car Showroom Passenger Set, green (std)		1500 ___
11-40018	Showroom Passenger Coach, green (std)		500 ___
11-40019	3-Car Showroom Passenger Set, zinc chromate (std)		1500 ___
11-40020	Showroom Passenger Coach, zinc chromate (std)		500 ___
11-40021	3-Car Blue Comet Passenger Set (std)		1100 ___
11-40022	No. 432 Olbers Blue Comet Baggage Car (std)		403 ___
11-40023	No. 419 Tuttle Blue Comet Passenger Coach (std)		380 ___
11-40024	No. 4343 Diner Car		180 ___
11-40025	339 Series Passenger Car, pink		130 ___
11-40026	332 Series Baggage Car, pink		130 ___
11-40027	309 Series 3-Car State Passenger Set, brown (std)		1200 ___
11-40028	Pennsylvania State Baggage Car, brown (std)		400 ___
11-40029	Illinois State Passenger Coach, brown (std)		400 ___
11-40030	Solarium State Car, brown (std)		400 ___
11-40031	State 3-Car Passenger Set, blue (std)		1200 ___
11-40032	Pennsylvania State Baggage Car, blue (std)		400 ___
11-40033	Illinois State Passenger Coach, blue (std)		400 ___
11-40034	Solarium State Car, blue (std)		400 ___
11-40035	309 Series 3-Car Passenger Set, blue (std)		400 ___
11-40036	309 Series 3-Car Passenger Set, green (std)		400 ___
11-40037	309 Series 3-Car Passenger Set, red (std)		400 ___
11-40038	No. 309 Passenger Coach (std)		140 ___
11-40039	No. 310 Baggage Car (std)		140 ___
11-40040	3-Car Blue Comet Passenger Set, nickel trim (std)		1100 ___
11-40041	No. 432 Blue Comet Baggage Car, nickel trim (std)		380 ___
11-40042	No. 423 Blue Comet Passenger Coach, nickel trim (std)		380 ___
11-40043	3-Car Stephen Girard Set, brass trim		600 ___
11-40044	No. 4427 Stephen Girard Baggage Car, brass trim		200 ___

	Lionel Corporation Tinplate		Exc	Mint
___	11-40045	No. 427 Stephen Girard Passenger Coach, brass trim		200
___	11-40046	3-Car Stephen Girard Set, nickel trim		600
___	11-40047	No. 4427 Stephen Girard Baggage Car, nickel trim		200
___	11-40048	No. 427 Stephen Girard Passenger Coach, nickel trim		200
___	11-40049	No. 418 3-Car Passenger Set, green, brass trim (std)		600
___	11-40050	No. 418 Diner, green, brass trim (std)		200
___	11-40051	No. 418 3-Car Passenger Set, orange, brass trim (std)		600
___	11-40052	No. 418 Diner, orange brass trim (std)		200
___	11-40053	No. 418 3-Car Passenger Set, Mojave, brass trim (std)		600
___	11-40054	No. 418 Diner, Mojave, brass trim (std)		200
___	11-40055	No. 418 3-Car Passenger Set, pink, brass trim (std)		600
___	11-40056	No. 418 Diner, pink, brass trim (std)		200
___	11-40057	Lionel 3-Car Pullman Passenger Set (std)		700
___	11-40058	Pennsylvania 3-Car Pullman Passenger Set (std)		700
___	11-40059	No. 332 Baggage Car (std)		140
___	11-40060	No. 339 Passenger Coach (std)		140
___	11-40061	Great Northern State 3-Car Passenger Set (std)		1200
___	11-40062	Great Northern State Baggage Car (std)		430
___	11-40063	Great Northern State Passenger Coach (std)		430
___	11-40064	Great Northern State Solarium Car (std)		430
___	11-40065	Presidential 3-Car Passenger Set (std)		1200
___	11-40066	Presidential Baggage Car (std)		430
___	11-40067	Presidential Passenger Coach (std)		430
___	11-40068	Red Comet 3-Car Passenger Set (std)		1140
___	11-40069	Red Comet Baggage Car (std)		400
___	11-40070	Red Comet Passenger Coach (std)		400
___	11-40072	President's Passenger Set, red (std)		1300
___	11-40073	No. 310 Baggage Car (std)		140
___	11-40074	No. 309 Passenger Coach (std)		140
___	11-40076	Green Comet 3-Car Passenger Set (std)		1140
___	11-40077	NYC 3-Car Passenger Set, brown (std)		700
___	11-40078	General 3-Car Pullman Passenger Set (std)		700
___	11-40079	Green Comet Baggage Car (std)		400
___	11-40080	Green Comet Passenger Coach (std)		400
___	11-40081	Showroom 3-Car Passenger Set, brown (std)		1600
___	11-40082	Showroom Passenger Coach, brown (std)		540
___	11-40083	Showroom 3-Car Passenger Set, orange (std)		2050
___	11-40084	Showroom Passenger Coach, orange (std)		540
___	11-40095	3-car B&O Pullman Passenger Set (std)		700
___	11-40096	3-car Long Island Pullman Passenger Set (std)		700
___	11-40097	3-car Strasburg Pullman Passenger Set (std)		700
___	11-40098	3-car PRR Pullman Passenger Set (std)		700
___	11-40099	3-car MILW State Passenger Set (std)		1550
___	11-40100	MILW State Solarium Car (std)		450
___	11-40101	MILW State Passenger Coach (std)		475
___	11-40102	MILW State Baggage Car (std)		475

Lionel Corporation Tinplate		Exc	Mint
11-40103	3-car PRR State Passenger Set (std)		1200 ___
11-40104	PRR State Solarium Car (std)		400 ___
11-40105	PRR State Passenger Coach (std)		400 ___
11-40106	PRR State Baggage Car (std)		400 ___
11-40107	3-car State Passenger Set, two-tone brown (std)		1200 ___
11-40108	State Solarium Car, two-tone brown (std)		400 ___
11-40109	State Passenger Coach, two-tone brown (std)		400 ___
11-40110	State Baggage Car, two-tone brown (std)		400 ___
11-40111	3-car Great Northern Presidential Set (std)		1200 ___
11-40112	Great Northern Presidential Diner (std)		400 ___
11-40113	3-car Lehigh Valley Presidential Set (std)		1200 ___
11-40114	Lehigh Valley Presidential Diner (std)		400 ___
11-40115	3-car New Haven State Passenger Set (std)		1200 ___
11-40116	New Haven State Solarium Car (std)		400 ___
11-40117	New Haven State Passenger Coach (std)		400 ___
11-40118	New Haven State Baggage Car (std)		400 ___
11-60033	No. 607 Christmas Coach Passenger		90 ___
11-70002	No. 2814 Boxcar, cream/orange		80 ___
11-70003	No. 2814R Refrigerator Car, white/brown		80 ___
11-70004	No. 2814R Christmas Refrigerator Car		80 ___
11-70005	No. 2814R Refrigerator Car, Ivory/peacock		80 ___
11-70006	No. 2815 Tank Car, silver		90 ___
11-70007	No. 2815 Tank Car, orange, nickel trim		80 ___
11-70008	No. 2817 Caboose, red/green		90 ___
11-70009	No. 2815 Christmas Tank Car		80 ___
11-70010	No. 2813 Cattle Car, cream/maroon		80 ___
11-70011	No. 2812 Gondola, apple green		80 ___
11-70012	No. 2811 Flatcar, silver		70 ___
11-70013	No. 2816 Hopper Car, red		90 ___
11-70014	No. 2816 Hopper Car, olive green		80 ___
11-70015	No. 2820 Floodlight Car, terra-cotta		90 ___
11-70016	No. 2815 Sunoco Tank Car		80 ___
11-70017	No. 2810 Crane Car, terra-cotta/maroon		180 ___
11-70018	No. 2811 Flatcar, maroon		70 ___
11-70019	No. 2814R MTH/Lionel Refrigerator Car		90 ___
11-70024	No. 2814 Christmas Boxcar		80 ___
11-70025	No. 2814 Boxcar, cream/orange		80 ___
11-70026	No. 2814 Boxcar, orange/brown		80 ___
11-70027	No. 2814 Boxcar, white brown		80 ___
11-70028	No. 2816 Christmas Hopper Car		80 ___
11-70029	No. 2817 Caboose, red/brown		90 ___
11-70030	No. 2812 Gondola, dark orange		70 ___
11-70031	No. 813 Cattle Car, brown		80 ___
11-70032	No. 2816 Hopper Car, black		80 ___
11-70033	No. 2820 Floodlight Car, light green		90 ___
11-70034	No. 2814R Refrigerator Car, white/brown		80 ___

Lionel Corporation Tinplate			Exc	Mint
___	**11-70035**	No. 2651 Flatcar, green		60
___	**11-70036**	No. 2652 Gondola, red		60
___	**11-70037**	No. 2653 Hopper Car, black		60
___	**11-70038**	No. 2654 Shell Tank Car, yellow		60
___	**11-70039**	No. 2655 Boxcar, yellow/brown		60
___	**11-70040**	No. 2656 Cattle Car, red/brown		60
___	**11-70041**	No. 2657 Caboose, red/maroon		60
___	**11-70042**	No. 659 Dump Car, green		60
___	**11-70043**	No. 659 Dump Car, orange		60
___	**11-70045**	No. 2814 Boxcar, yellow/brown		90
___	**11-70046**	No. 2817 Caboose, red		100
___	**11-70047**	No. 2814 Christmas Boxcar		80
___	**11-70048**	No. 2815 Christmas Tank Car		90
___	**11-70049**	No. 2814R Refrigerator Car, silver frame		90
___	**11-70050**	No. 2814R Refrigerator Car, black frame		80
___	**11-70051**	No. 2817 Caboose, red/maroon		90
___	**11-70052**	No. 2654 Shell Tank Car, gray		60
___	**11-70053**	No. 2654 Shell Tank Car, black		60
___	**11-70054**	No. 2653 Hopper Car, green		60
___	**11-70055**	No. 2653 Hopper Car, red		60
___	**11-70056**	No. 2655 Boxcar, yellow/maroon		60
___	**11-70057**	No. 2655 Boxcar, yellow/brown		60
___	**11-70058**	No. 2656 Cattle Car, gray/red		60
___	**11-70059**	No. 2656 Cattle Car, burnt orange		60
___	**11-70060**	No. 659 Dump Car, blue		60
___	**11-70061**	No. 900 Ammunition Car, gray		60
___	**11-70064**	No. 2814R Hoods Dairy Refrigerator Car		80
___	**11-70065**	No. 2814R Isaly's Refrigerator Car		80
___	**11-70066**	No. 2814R Sheffield Farms Refrigerator Car		90
___	**11-70067**	No. 2814R Palisades Park Refrigerator Car		80
___	**11-70068**	No. 2654 UP Tank Car, yellow		60
___	**11-70069**	No. 2654 M&M's Tank Car		70
___	**11-70070**	No. 2654 Baker's Chocolate Tank Car		60
___	**11-70071**	No. 2654 Budweiser Tank Car		70
___	**11-70072**	No. 2655 Delaware & Hudson Boxcar		60
___	**11-70073**	No. 2655 Railbox Boxcar		60
___	**11-70074**	M&M's Christmas Boxcar		70
___	**11-70076**	No. 2654 LL Tank Car, orange/blue		70
___	**11-70078**	No. 900 Ammunition Car, green		60
___	**11-70079**	No. 2820 LL Floodlight Car, black/orange		120
___	**11-70080**	No. 2820 U.S. Army Air Corps Floodlight Car		120
___	**11-70081**	No. 2810 Crane Car, yellow/red		180
___	**11-70082**	No. 2810 Crane Car, white/red		180
___	**11-70083**	No. 2660 Crane Car, cream/red		100
___	**11-70084**	No. 2660 Crane Car, terra-cotta/maroon		100
___	**11-70085**	No. 2660 Crane Car, yellow/red		100

Lionel Corporation Tinplate		Exc	Mint
11-70086	No. 2660 Crane Car, peacock/dark green		100 ___
11-70087	No. 2813 LL Cattle Car, cream/tuscan		90 ___
11-70088	No. 2813 LL Cattle Car, terra cotta/pea green		90 ___
11-70089	No. 2810 B&O Crane Car		180 ___
11-70091	No. 2815 LL Tank Car, cream, orange/blue		80 ___
11-70092	No. 2810 Crane Car, blue		180 ___
11-70095	No. 2820 LL Floodlight Car, black/peacock		120 ___
11-70096	No. 2814 Southern Boxcar		90 ___
11-70097	No. 2814 Chessie Boxcar		90 ___
11-70098	No. 2814 Blue Comet Boxcar, nickel trim		90 ___
11-70098	No. 2814 Blue Comet Boxcar, brass trim		90 ___
11-70102	No. 2654 Mobilgas Tank Car		70 ___
11-70103	No. 2654 Esso Tank Car		70 ___
11-70104	No. 2653 Blue Coal Hopper		70 ___
11-70105	No. 2653 Peabody Hopper		70 ___
11-70106	No. 2655 Altoona Brewing Boxcar		70 ___
11-70107	No. 2655 Hoodís Grade A Milk Boxcar		70 ___
11-70108	No. 2655 LL Boxcar		70 ___
11-70109	No. 2657 LL Caboose, green/red		70 ___
11-70110	No. 2657 LL Caboose, orange/red		70 ___
11-70113	No. 2814 PRR Boxcar		90 ___
11-70114	No. 2814 ATSF Grand Canyon Boxcar		90 ___
11-70115	No. 2814 Long Island Boxcar		90 ___
11-70116	No. 2814 Alaska Boxcar		90 ___
11-70117	No. 2814R M. K. Goetz Brewing Refrigerator Car		90 ___
11-70118	No. 2814R Gerber Refrigerator Car		90 ___
11-70119	No. 2814R Roberts & Oake Meats Refrigerator Car		90 ___
11-70120	No. 2814R Sullivan's Packing Refrigerator Car		90 ___
11-70121	No. 2816 Western Maryland Coal Car		90 ___
11-70122	No. 2816 P&LE Coal Car		90 ___
11-70123	No. 2816 Waddell Mining Coal Car		90 ___
11-70124	No. 2816 Blue Coal Car		90 ___
11-70125	No. 2815 Clark Oil Tank Car		90 ___
11-70126	No. 2815 Celanese Chemicals Tank Car		90 ___
11-70127	No. 2815 Shell Tank Car		90 ___
11-70128	No. 2815 Cook's Paints Tank Car		90 ___
11-70129	No. 2817 C&O Caboose		100 ___
11-70130	No. 2817 Long Island Caboose		100 ___
11-70131	No. 2817 Southern Caboose		100 ___
11-70132	No. 2817 Jersey Central Caboose		100 ___
11-70133	No. 2814R Gerber Refrigerator Car		90 ___
11-70144	No. 2815 Shell Tank Car		90 ___
11-70154	No. 2814 ATSF Grand Canyon Boxcar		90 ___
11-80001	2600 Series 4-Car Blue Comet Passenger Set		430 ___
11-80002	UP Articulated Baggage Car, silver		150 ___
11-80003	UP Articulated Baggage Car, yellow		150 ___

	Lionel Corporation Tinplate		Exc	Mint
___	**11-80004**	UP Articulated Coach, silver		150
___	**11-80005**	UP Articulated Coach, yellow		150
___	**11-80006**	No. 2613 Series Pullman Coach, blue		110
___	**11-80007**	2600 Series 3-Car Passenger Set, red		300
___	**11-80008**	2600 Series 3-Car Passenger Set, green		300
___	**11-80009**	Milwaukee Road Articulated Baggage Car		150
___	**11-80010**	Milwaukee Road Articulated Coach		150
___	**11-80011**	Articulated Streamliner Baggage Car		150
___	**11-80012**	Articulated Streamliner Coach		150
___	**11-80013**	No. 2613 Series Pullman Coach, red		100
___	**11-80014**	No. 2613 Series Pullman Coach, green		100
___	**11-80015**	No. 605 Christmas Baggage Car		90
___	**11-80016**	710 Series 3-Car Passenger Set, blue		350
___	**11-80017**	No. 710 Series Baggage Car, blue		120
___	**11-80018**	No. 710 Series Passenger Coach, blue		120
___	**11-80019**	710 Series 3-Car Passenger Set, orange		350
___	**11-80020**	No. 710 Series Baggage Car, orange		120
___	**11-80021**	No. 710 Series Passenger Coach, orange		120
___	**11-80022**	710 Series 3-Car Passenger Set, red		350
___	**11-80023**	No. 710 Series Baggage Car, red		120
___	**11-80024**	No. 710 Series Passenger Coach, red		120
___	**11-80025**	No. 1695 3-Car Passenger Set, blue/silver		350
___	**11-80026**	No. 1685 Passenger Car, blue/silver		120
___	**11-80027**	1695 Series 3-Car Passenger Set, red/maroon		380
___	**11-80028**	No. 1695 Passenger Coach, red/maroon		130
___	**11-80029**	City of Denver Coach, yellow/green		110
___	**11-80030**	City of Denver Coach, green		110
___	**11-80031**	No. 605 Baggage Car		90
___	**11-80032**	No. 607 Passenger Coach		90
___	**11-80034**	No. 2613 NYC Pullman Car, LCCA 2012 Convention		100
___	**11-80036**	No. 605 Red Comet Baggage Car		90
___	**11-80039**	600 Series 3-Car Red Comet Passenger Set		270
___	**11-80040**	2600 Series 4-Car Blue Comet Passenger Set, brass trim		430
___	**11-80041**	No. 2613 Pullman Coach, brass trim		110
___	**11-80042**	Flying Yankee Chrome Coach		110
___	**11-80047**	710 Series 3-Car NH Passenger Set		400
___	**11-80048**	710 Series 3-Car GN Passenger Set		400
___	**11-80049**	2600 Series 4-Car Chessie Passenger Set		430
___	**11-80050**	2600 Series 4-Car Southern Passenger Set		430
___	**11-80051**	No. 2613 Chessie Pullman Coach		110
___	**11-80052**	No. 2613 Southern Pullman Coach		110
___	**11-80053**	No. 710 NH Baggage Car		140
___	**11-80054**	No. 710 NH Passenger Coach		140
___	**11-80055**	No. 710 GN Baggage Car		140
___	**11-80056**	No. 710 GN Passenger Coach		140
___	**11-80059**	710 Series 3-car MILW Passenger Set		400

Lionel Corporation Tinplate		Exc	Mint
11-80060	No. 713 MILW Baggage Car		140 ___
11-80061	No. 710 MILW Passenger Coach		140 ___
11-80062	710 Series 3-car PRR Passenger Set		400 ___
11-80063	No. 713 PRR Baggage Car		140 ___
11-80064	No. 710 PRR Passenger Coach		140 ___
11-90001	No. 300 Hellgate Bridge, green/cream		500 ___
11-90002	No. 300 Hellgate Bridge, silver/white		500 ___
11-90003	No. 092 Signal Tower, cream/red		70 ___
11-90006	No. 437 Switch Tower		280 ___
11-90007	No. 155 Freight Shed		330 ___
11-90008	No. 116 Passenger Station		400 ___
11-90009	No. 438 Signal Tower		150 ___
11-90010	No. 192 Villa Set		200 ___
11-90011	No. 191 Villa		70 ___
11-90012	No. 54 Street Lamp Set, green		45 ___
11-90013	No. 54 Street Lamp Set, red		45 ___
11-90014	No. 56 Gas Lamp Set, green		35 ___
11-90015	No. 56 Gas Lamp Set, maroon		35 ___
11-90016	No. 57 Corner Lamp Set, black		40 ___
11-90017	No. 57 Corner Lamp Set, red		35 ___
11-90018	No. 58 Lamp Set, single arc, cream		35 ___
11-90019	No. 58 Lamp Set, single arc, dark green		35 ___
11-90020	No. 59 Gooseneck Lamp Set, black		40 ___
11-90021	No. 59 Gooseneck Lamp Set, maroon		40 ___
11-90022	No. 1184 Bungalow (std)		200 ___
11-90023	No. 1184 Bungalow (std)		200 ___
11-90024	No. 1189 Villa (std)		300 ___
11-90025	No. 1191 Villa (std)		300 ___
11-90026	No. 165 Magnetic Crane		300 ___
11-90027	No. 441 Weighing Station (std)		380 ___
11-90028	No. 69 Operating Warning Bell		50 ___
11-90029	No. 78 Automatic Control Signal (std)		70 ___
11-90030	No. 79 Flashing Railroad Signal		70 ___
11-90031	No. 80 Operating Semaphore		70 ___
11-90032	No. 63 Lamp Post Set, aluminum		50 ___
11-90033	No. 87 Railroad Crossing Signal		50 ___
11-90034	No. 92 Floodlight Tower Set		160 ___
11-90035	No. 94 High Tension Tower Set		150 ___
11-90036	No. Automatic Block Signal (std)		70 ___
11-90037	No. 163 Freight Accessory Set, green cart		100 ___
11-90038	No. 163 Freight Accessory Set, orange cart		100 ___
11-90039	No. 208 Tools and Chest, dark gray		80 ___
11-90040	No. 208 Tools and Chest, silver		80 ___
11-90041	No. 550 Miniature Figures		100 ___
11-90042	No. 64 Lamp Post Set, light green		30 ___
11-90043	No. 85 Race Car Set		700 ___

	Lionel Corporation Tinplate		Exc	Mint
___	11-90044	Straight Race Car Track Section		20
___	11-90045	Inside Curve Race Car Track Section		20
___	11-90046	Outside Curve Race Car Track Section		20
___	11-90047	No. 55 Airplane & No. 49 Airport Set with mat		800
___	11-90048	No. 49 Airport Mat		60
___	11-90049	No. 90 Flagpole		50
___	11-90050	No. 205 Merchandise Containers, 3 pieces (std)		130
___	11-90052	No. 442 Diner		160
___	11-90053	No. 43 Runabout Boat, red/white		450
___	11-90054	No. 44 Speed Boat		450
___	11-90055	No. 71 Telegraph Post Set, gray/red		80
___	11-90056	Teardrop Lamp Set, pea green		20
___	11-90057	No. 46 Crossing Gate		40
___	11-90058	Small Oil Drum Set		20
___	11-90060	No. 115 Passenger Station, beige/pea green		300
___	11-90061	No. 115 Passenger Station, cream, orange/blue		300
___	11-90062	No. 134 Lionel City Station with stop		330
___	11-90063	No. 444 Roundhouse Section		500
___	11-90064	No. 200 Turntable, red/black		200
___	11-90065	No. 89 Flagpole, blue base (std)		50
___	11-90066	No. 89 Flagpole, white base (std)		50
___	11-90067	No. 89 American Flag Pole, white base (std)		50
___	11-90068	Operating Industrial Crane		350
___	11-90069	Operating Industrial Crane, TCA 2010 Convention		350
___	11-90070	No. 552 Diner, orange/blue		200
___	11-90071	No. 552 Diner, white/blue		200
___	11-90072	No. 911 Country Estate, cream/red		140
___	11-90073	No. 911 Country Estate, red/green		140
___	11-90074	No. 912 Suburban Home, ivory/peacock		140
___	11-90075	No. 912 Suburban Home, mustard/green		140
___	11-90076	No. 913 Landscaped Bungalow, white/maroon		110
___	11-90077	No. 913 Landscaped Bungalow, light green/peacock		110
___	11-90078	AF No. 2050 Old Glory Flag Pole		100
___	11-90079	No. 43 Runabout Boat, orange/blue		400
___	11-90084	No. 57 Lamp Post Set, Lionel & American Flyer Aves.		40
___	11-90085	No. 57 Lamp Post Set, orange, 21st St. & Fifth Ave.		40
___	11-90086	AF No. 2013 Corner Lamp Set, yellow		40
___	11-90089	No. 436 Power Station, cream		150
___	11-90090	No. 436 Power Station, terra-cotta		150
___	11-90094	No. 438 Signal Tower		160
___	11-90095	No. 116 Passenger Station		400
___	11-90096	No. 1184 Bungalow, gray/green		200
___	11-90097	No. 1184 Bungalow, white/maroon		200
___	11-90098	No. 1189 Villa (std)		300
___	11-90099	No. 1191 Villa (std)		300

Lionel Corporation Tinplate		Exc	Mint
11-90100	No. 442 Diner		160 ___
11-90101	No. 54 Lamp Post Set, pea green		45 ___
11-90102	No. 54 Lamp Post Set, state brown		45 ___
11-90103	No. 58 Lamp Post Set, peacock		35 ___
11-90104	No. 58 Lamp Post Set, orange		35 ___
11-90105	No. 59 Lamp Post Set, dark green		40 ___
11-90106	No. 59 Lamp Post Set, light green		40 ___
11-90107	No. 92 Floodlight Tower Set		170 ___
11-90108	No. 79 Flashing Signal		70 ___
11-90109	No. 69 Warning Signal		50 ___
11-90110	No. 94 High Tension Tower Set		170 ___
11-90111	No. 57 Corner Lamp Set, orange, Lionel		40 ___
11-90112	No. 57 Corner Lamp Set, blue, Lionel		40 ___
11-90113	No. 57 Corner Lamp Set, blue/yellow		40 ___
11-90114	No. 152 Operating Crossing Gate		40 ___
11-90115	No. 153 Operating Block Signal		40 ___
11-90116	No. 154 Highway Flashing Signal		75 ___
11-90117	No. 437 Switch Signal Tower, cream/orange		300 ___
11-90118	No. 437 Switch Signal Tower, terra-cotta/green		300 ___
11-90119	AF No. 4230 Roadside Flashing Signal		100 ___
11-90120	No. 200 Turntable, gray/green		200 ___
11-90121	No. 200 Turntable, orange/blue		200 ___
11-90122	No. 437 Switch Tower		280 ___
11-90123	No. 98 Coal Bunker		180 ___
11-99030	No. 25 Illuminated Track Bumpers (std)		60 ___

Section 5
MODERN TINPLATE

		Exc	Mint
	O Gauge Classics		
____**1-263E**	Lionel Lines Blue Comet 2-4-2 Locomotive		NRS
____**350E**	Lionel Lines Hiawatha 4-4-2 Locomotive	113	200
____**882**	Lionel Lines Combination Car		NRS
____**883**	Lionel Lines Passenger Car		NRS
____**884**	Lionel Lines Observation Car		NRS
____**1612**	Lionel Lines Passenger Car		NRS
____**1613**	Lionel Lines Passenger Car		NRS
____**1614**	Lionel Lines Baggage Car		NRS
____**1615**	Lionel Lines Observation Car		NRS
____**51000**	Milwaukee Road Hiawatha Set, 88 u	314	882
____**51001**	Lionel #44 Freight Special Set, 89	230	600
____**51004**	Blue Comet Set, 91		1600
____**51100**	Lionel Lines Electric Locomotive "44E", 89		NRS
____**51201**	Rail Chief Passenger Cars, set of 4, 90	150	458
____**51202**	Lionel Lines Combination Car "892"		NRS
____**51203**	Lionel Lines Passenger Car "893"		NRS
____**51204**	Lionel Lines Passenger Car "894"		NRS
____**51205**	Lionel Lines Observation Car "895"		NRS
____**51400**	Lionel Lines Boxcar "8814", 89		NRS
____**51500**	Lionel Lines Hopper "8816", 89		NRS
____**51700**	Lionel Lines Caboose "8817", 89		NRS
____**51800**	Lionel Lines Searchlight Car "8820", 89		NRS
	Standard Gauge Classics		
____**1-318E**	Lionel Lines Electric Locomotive	180	600
____**1-4390**	American Flyer West Point Baggage Car		NRS
____**1-4391**	American Flyer Academy Passenger Car		NRS
____**1-4392**	American Flyer Army/Navy Observation Car		NRS
____**5130**	Lionel Lines Flatcar with lumber		NRS
____**5140**	Lionel Lines Reefer		NRS
____**5150**	Lionel Lines Shell Tank Car		NRS
____**5160**	Lionel Lines Caboose		NRS
____**13001**	1-318E Freight Express Train Set, 90-91		960
____**13002**	Fireball Express Set, 90 u		1600
____**13003**	American Flyer Mayflower Passenger Car Set, 92		2000
____**13004**	Milwaukee Road Hiawatha Passenger Set, 01-02		2000
____**13008**	NYC Commodore Vanderbilt Passenger Set, 02	700	1600
____**13100**	Lionel Lines 2-4-2 Locomotive "1-390E", 88 u		610
____**13101**	Lionel Lines 2-4-0 Locomotive "1-384E", 89 u	313	750
____**13102**	Lionel Lines Electric Locomotive "1-381E", 89 u	383	1490
____**13103**	Lionel Lines Blue Comet 4-4-4 Locomotive, 90	425	1350
____**13104**	Lionel Lines "Old #7" 4-4-0 Locomotive, 90		900

MODERN TINPLATE		Exc	Mint
13106	Lionel Lines Fireball Express 2-4-2 Locomotive		NRS ___
13107	Lionel Lines Electric Locomotive "1-408E", 91		990 ___
13108	Lionel Lines 4-4-4 Locomotive "2-400E," Gray, 91		1100 ___
13109	American Flyer Mayflower Electric Locomotive, 92		2500 ___
13200	Lionel Lines Searchlight Car "1520", 89 u	55	155 ___
13300	Lionel Lines Gondola "1512", 89 u		75 ___
13303	Lionel Lines Sunoco Tank Car "1-215", 92		135 ___
13400	Lionel Lines Baggage Car "323", 88 u		173 ___
13401	Lionel Lines Passenger Car "324", 88 u		180 ___
13402	Lionel Lines Observation Car "325", 88 u	35	135 ___
13403	Lionel Lines State Passenger Car Set, 89 u		1100 ___
13404	Lionel Lines California Passenger Car "1412", 90	200	360 ___
13405	Lionel Lines Colorado Passenger Car "1413", 90	200	360 ___
13406	Lionel Lines New York Observation Car "1416", 90	200	360 ___
13407	Lionel Lines Illinois Passenger Car "1414", 90	175	450 ___
13408	Lionel Lines Blue Comet Passenger Car Set, 90	413	1500 ___
13409	Lionel Lines Faye Passenger Car "1420"		NRS ___
13410	Lionel Lines Westphal Passenger Car "1421"		NRS ___
52404	PE Birney Trolley, 06		75 ___
13411	Lionel Lines Tempel Observation Car "1422"		NRS ___
13412	Lionel Lines "Old #7" Passenger Car Set, 90	175	800 ___
13413	Lionel Lines Combination Car "183"		NRS ___
13414	Lionel Lines Passenger Car "184"		NRS ___
13415	Lionel Lines Observation Car "185"		NRS ___
13416	Lionel Lines New Jersey Baggage Car "326"		NRS ___
13417	Lionel Lines Connecticut Passenger Car "327"		NRS ___
13418	Lionel Lines New York Observation Car "328"		NRS ___
13420	Lionel Lines State Passenger Car Set, 91		1300 ___
13421	Lionel Lines California Passenger Car "2412", 90	200	360 ___
13422	Lionel Lines Colorado Passenger Car "2413", 90	200	360 ___
13423	Lionel Lines Illinois Passenger Car "2414", 92 u	200	817 ___
13424	Lionel Lines New York Observation Car "2416", 92	200	360 ___
13425	Lionel Lines Barnard Passenger Car "1423", 91 u		1350 ___
13600	Lionel Lines Cattle Car "1513", 89 u		90 ___
13601	"Season's Greetings" Boxcar, 89 u		105 ___
13602	"Season's Greetings" Boxcar, 90 u		100 ___
13604	"Season's Greetings" Boxcar, 91 u		110 ___
13605	Lionel Lines Boxcar "1-214", 92		155 ___
13700	Lionel Lines Caboose "1517", 89 u		105 ___
13702	Lionel Lines Caboose "1217", 91		115 ___
13800	Lionelville Passenger Station, 88 u		390 ___
13801	Lionelville Station "126", 89 u	55	290 ___
13804	Lionelville Switch Tower "437", 91		400 ___
13900	Electric Rapid Transit Trolley "200", 89 u		290 ___
13901	Electric Rapid Transit Trolley Trailer "201", 89 u		150 ___
51900	Signal Bridge and Control Panel, 89 u		399 ___

Section 6
CLUB CARS AND SPECIAL PRODUCTION

			Exc	Mint
ARTRAIN				
___	**9486**	GTW "I Love Michigan" Boxcar, 87		305
___	**17885**	1-D Tank Car, 90	55	65
___	**17891**	GTW 20th Anniversary Boxcar, 91	70	75
___	**19425**	CSX Flatcar with "Art in Celebration" trailer, 96		80
___	**52013**	Norfolk Southern Flatcar with trailer, 92	160	228
___	**52024**	Conrail Auto Carrier, 93	80	90
___	**52049**	BN Gondola with coil covers, 94	50	56
___	**52097**	Chessie System Reefer, 95		34
___	**52140**	Union Pacific Bunk Car, 97		37
___	**52165**	SP Caboose "6256", 98		60
___	**52197**	Santa Fe GP38 Diesel, 99		243
___	**52227**	"Artistry in Space" Boxcar, 00		75
___	**52255**	30th Anniversary Flatcar with billboard, 01		100
___	**52283**	Paint Vat Car, 02		59
___	**52331**	Flatcar with "America's Railways" trailer, 03		150
___	**52349**	Hometown Art Museum Hopper, purple, 04		35
___	**52350**	"Native Views" 3-bay Hopper, 04		65
___	**52411**	"35 Years" 1-D Tank Car, 06		35
CARNEGIE SCIENCE CENTER				
___	**25085**	Miniature Railroad & Village Boxcar, 09		50
___	**26694**	Carnegie Science Center Flatcar w/Submarine, 12	25	50
___	**26750**	Great Miniature Railroad & Village Boxcar, 99		78
___	**36202**	Great Miniature Railroad 80th Anniversary Boxcar, 00		110
___	**36234**	Great Miniature Railroad & Village Boxcar, 01		50
___	**37098**	Carnegie Science Center Flatcar w/Capsule, 13	25	50
___	**52277**	Carnegie Science Center 10th Anniversary Boxcar, 02		60
___	**52332**	Miniature Railroad & Village Boxcar, 03		58
___	**52362**	Miniature Railroad & Village 50th Anniversary Boxcar, 04		50
___	**52399**	MRR&V Express Boxcar, 05		50
___	**52432**	Miniature Railroad & Village Boxcar, 06		50
___	**52510**	Miniature Railroad & Village Caboose, 08		50
___	**58603**	Carnegie Science Center Boxcar, 11	25	50
CHICAGOLAND RAILROAD CLUB				
___	**18510**	C&NW 25th Anniversary Refrigerator Car, 19		65
___	**52081**	C&NW Boxcar "6464-555", 96	40	68
___	**52101**	BN Maxi-Stack Flatcar "64287" with containers, 97		82
___	**52102**	SF Extended Vision Caboose, red roof, 96		75
___	**52103**	SF Extended Vision Caboose, black roof, 96		75
___	**52120**	Shedd Aquarium Car "3435-557", 98	34	79
___	**52148**	REA/Santa Fe Operating Boxcar, 99	15	70
___	**52170**	SP Operating Boxcar "52170-561", 99		65

CLUB CARS AND SPECIAL PRODUCTION		Exc	Mint
52171	UP Operating Boxcar "52171-561", 99		65 ___
52178	Burlington Operating Boxcar "52178-559", 00		70 ___
52179	ACL Operating Boxcar "52179-560", 00		73 ___
52215	C&NW 3-bay Cylindrical Hopper, 01		60 ___
52216	C&NW Cylindrical Hopper, 02		60 ___
52223	REA/Santa Fe Centennial Operating Boxcar, 00		65 ___
52251	PRR Express Car, green, 01		67 ___
52259	MP GP20 Diesel, traditional, 01		250 ___
52292	PRR Express Car, Tuscan red, 02		50 ___
52327	City of Los Angeles Express Car, 04		65 ___
52328	City of New Haven Express Car, 04		55 ___
52363	City of New Orleans Express Car, 04		55 ___
52364	City of New York Express Car, 04		65 ___
52388	Great Northern Tool Car, 06		48 ___
52389	Great Northern Crew Car, 06		48 ___
52390	Great Northern Welding Caboose, 06		78 ___
52391	Great Northern Racing Crew Car, 06		48 ___
52426	City of San Francisco Express Car, 07		55 ___
52427	Rock Island Rocket Express Car, 07		55 ___
52475	Western Pacific UP Heritage Boxcar, 07		60 ___
2001310	ATSF PS-1 Boxcar, 20		70 ___
2201202	Lumber Jack Lager Refrigerator Car, 22		85 ___
Classic Toy Trains			
52126	10th Anniversary MILW Boxcar "21027", 97		50 ___
69013	30th Anniversary CTT Boxcar, 17		75 ___
Dept. 56			
16270	Heritage Village Boxcar "9796", 96		56 ___
52096	Snow Village Boxcar "9756", 95		85 ___
52139	Square Window Caboose "6256", 97		72 ___
52157	Holly Brothers 3-D Tank Car, 98	6	85 ___
52175	4-6-4 Hudson Locomotive, CC, 99	75	350 ___
52199	4-bay Hopper "6756", 00	20	53 ___
52254	"Happy Holidays" Gondola, 01		35 ___
Eastwood Automobilia			
16275	Radio Flyer Boxcar "16275", 96		50 ___
16757	Johnny Lightning Auto Carrier "3435", 96		90 ___
16985	Flatcar with 2 Ford vans, 97		49 ___
52044	Mogen David Wine Vat Car, 95	21	30 ___
52083	PRR Flatcar "21697" with tanker, 95		41 ___
52130	Flatcar with Hot Wheels tanker, 97		60 ___
Houston Tinplate Operators Society (HTOS)			
8900	Sam Houston Mint Car, 00		120 ___
8901	Miracle Petroleum 1-D Tank Car, 01		100 ___
8902	USS Houston Submarine Car, 02		100 ___

CLUB CARS AND SPECIAL PRODUCTION		Exc	Mint
8903	Railway Express Boxcar, 03		100
8904	Lone Star Bay Window Caboose, 04		100
8999	Lone Star Aquarium Car, mermaid or trout, 99	43	105

INLAND EMPIRE TRAIN COLLECTORS ASSOCIATION (IETCA)

		Exc	Mint
1979	Boxcar, 79		15
1980	SP-type Caboose, 80		14
1981	Quad Hopper, 81		14
1982	3-D Tank Car, 82		14
1983	Refrigerator Car, 83		14
1986	Bunk Car, 86		14
7518	Carson City Mint Car, 84	36	43

LIONEL CENTRAL OPERATING LINES (LCOL)

		Exc	Mint
1981	Boxcar, 81		23
1986	Work Caboose, shell only, 86		14
5724	Pennsylvania Bunk Car, 84	30	39
6508	Canadian Pacific Crane Car, 83		40
6907	NYC Wood-sided Caboose, 97		50
9184	Erie Bay Window Caboose, 82	17	21
9475	D&H "I Love NY" Boxcar, 85		34
16342	CSX Gondola with coil covers, 92		20
17221	NYC Boxcar, 95		30

LIONEL COLLECTORS ASSOCIATION OF CANADA (LCAC)

		Exc	Mint
5710	Canadian Pacific Reefer, 83		215
5714	Michigan Central Reefer, 85	120	150
6100	Ontario Northland Covered Quad Hopper, 82		250
8103	Toronto, Hamilton & Buffalo Boxcar, 81		150
8204	Algoma Central Boxcar, 82		150
8507/08	Canadian National F3 Diesel AA, shells only, 85		400
8912	Canada Southern Operating Hopper, 89		95
9413	Napierville Junction Boxcar, 80		10
9718	Canadian National Boxcar, 79		20
17893	BAOC 1-D Tank Car "914", 91		120
52004	Algoma Central Gondola "9215" with coil covers, 92	70	90
52005	Canadian National F3 Diesel B Unit "9517", 93		30
52006	Canadian Pacific Boxcar "930016" (std O), 93	63	149
52115	Wabash Lake Railway 2-tier Auto Carrier "9519", 98		100
52125	TH&B Gondola 2-pack, 99		90
52245	Northern Alberta Railways Boxcar, 99		160
86009	Canadian National Bunk Car, 86		115
87010	Canadian National Express Reefer, 87		115
88011	Canadian National Caboose (std O), 88		500
830005	Canadian National Boxcar, 83		300
840006	Canadian Wheat Board Covered Quad Hopper, 84		165
900013	Canadian National Flatcar with trailers, 90		225

LIONEL COLLECTORS CLUB OF AMERICA (LCCA)

LCCA National Convention Cars

		Exc	Mint	
6112	Commonwealth Edison Quad Hopper with coal, 83	49	78	___
6323	Virginia Chemicals 1-D Tank Car, 86	47	63	___
6567	Illinois Central Gulf Crane Car "100408", 85	55	63	___
7403	LNAC Boxcar, 84	21	24	___
9118	Corning Covered Quad Hopper, 74	65	92	___
9155	Monsanto 1-D Tank Car, 75	38	47	___
9159	UP Refrigerator Car, 10	50	100	___
9212	Seaboard Coast Line Flatcar with trailers, 76	22	31	___
9259	Southern Bay Window Caboose, 77	11	41	___
9358	Sands of Iowa Covered Quad Hopper, 80	24	33	___
9435	Central of Georgia Boxcar, 81	25	29	___
9460	D&TS Automobile Boxcar, 82	25	34	___
9701	Baltimore & Ohio Automobile Boxcar, 72		170	___
9727	TA&G Boxcar, 73	105	134	___
9728	Union Pacific Stockcar, 78	23	26	___
9733	Airco Boxcar with tank car body, 79	37	50	___
17500	Convention Boxcar 2-pack, 17		120	___
17501	NP PS-1 Boxcar "201706", 17		60	___
17502	GN Mechanical Refrigerator Car "724295", 17		60	___
17510	NP Wood-chip 2-Bay Hopper "724293", 17		85	___
17870	East Camden & Highland Boxcar (std 0), 87	29	33	___
17873	Ashland Oil 3-D Tank Car, 88	55	70	___
17876	Columbia, Newberry & Laurens Boxcar (std 0), 89	32	40	___
17880	D&RGW Wood-sided Caboose (std 0), 90	43	55	___
17887	Conrail Flatcar with Armstrong Tile trailer (std 0), 91	30	49	___
17888	Conrail Flatcar with Ford trailer (std 0), 91	42	80	___
17892	Conrail Flatcar with Armstrong and Ford Trailers (std 0), 91		140	___
17899	NASA Unibody 1-D Tank Car "190" (std 0), 92	47	53	___
27019	Imco PS-2 Covered Hopper, 09		50	___
52023	D&TS 2-bay ACF Hopper "2601" (std 0), 93	27	40	___
52038	Southern Hopper "360794" w/Coal (std 0), 94	36	46	___
52074	Iowa Beef Packers Reefer "197095" (std 0), 95		32	___
52090	Pere Marquette DD Boxcar "71996" (std 0), 96		52	___
52110	CStPM&O Boxcar "71997" (std 0), 97	18	52	___
52151	Amtrak Express Baggage Boxcar "71998" (std 0), 98		64	___
52152	Ben Franklin and Liberty Bell Wood-side Refrigerator Car, 98	65	120	___
52176	Fort Worth & Denver Boxcar "8277" (std 0), 99		55	___
52195	Double-stack Car w/2 containers, 00		100	___
52244	Louisville & Nashville Horse Car "2001", 01		50	___
52266	PRR "Coal Goes To War" Hopper "707025", 02		86	___
52267	PRR "Coal Goes To War" Hopper "707026", 02		92	___
52273	U.S. Navy Flatcar w/Submarine, 02		219	___

CLUB CARS AND SPECIAL PRODUCTION			Exc	Mint
___	52299	Las Vegas Mint Car, 03	23	80
___	52343	MILW Milk Car, orange, 04	43	130
___	52344	MILW Milk Car, blue, 04	50	172
___	52393	MKT Speeder, yellow, nonpowered, 05		20
___	52394	Frisco Speeder, red, powered, 05		25
___	52395	Frisco Flatcar, silver, 05		25
___	52396	Frisco Flatcar w/2 speeders, 05		125
___	52412	UP Auxiliary Power Car, 06		55
___	52455	C&NW UP Heritage Unibody 1-D Tank Car, 07	65	110
___	52491	PS-2 Covered Hopper 2-pack, 08		140
___	52507	NYC Water Tower, 08		83
___	52514	ATSF Mint Car with Gold, 09		275
___	52543	BNSF Mechanical Refrigerator Car, 09		140
___	52559	UP Cylindrical Hopper, 10		100
___	52562	D&RGW Uranium Transport Mint Car, 10		230
___	58045	Chicago Registration Trolley, 18	58	80
___	58046	Chicago Banquet Trolley, 18	60	80
___	58047	Reno Registration Trolley, 19	60	80
___	58060	C&NW UP Heritage Boxcar (std O), 18	75	120
___	58061	C&IM Unibody 1-D Tank Car, 18		100
___	58213	B&M GP7 Diesel "2335," LionChief Plus, 15	135	250
___	58214	B&M GP7 Diesel "2361," non-powered, 15	75	105
___	58217	B&M Smoking Caboose, 15	56	77
___	58251	MEC PS-4 Flatcar w/Trailer, 15	60	85
___	58252	LCCA 45th Anniversary Trailer, 15		35
___	58253	Lionel 115th Anniversary Trailer, 15		35
___	58254	Providence & Worcester PS-4 Flatcar w/Tractor Cabs, 15	75	100
___	58267	KCS Inspection Truck Motorized Unit, 16	56	90
___	58268	KCS Inspection Truck Motorized Unit, 16	55	80
___	58271	MP Katy and Kansas Maxi Stack, set of 2, 16	47	85
___	58272	MKT Maxi-Stack Car and Container, 16	74	110
___	58273	Look-A-Like Container, 16	40	70
___	58515	NS Vulcan Switcher, 12		50
___	58532	Reading Anthracite Blue Coal Mining Set, 17		190
___	58560	Southern "Tennessean" Boxcar, 13	59	90
___	58561	Southern "Pelican" DD Boxcar, 13	39	82
___	58586	South Shore Lines Registration Trolley, 14		95
___	58587	South Shore Line Banquet Trolley, 14		110
___	58589	Boston Electric Banquet Trolley, 15	80	125
___	59003	Lionel Trains ACF 2-Bay Hopper, 13		50
___	59013	Monon Boxcar, 14		29
___	59014	Conway Scenic RR Boxcar, 15	75	100
___	59017	BNSF Boxcar, 16		95
___	72511	Alamo Mint Car, 11	75	150
___	72512	Richard Kughn Car, 10		120
___	75511	Federal Reserve Mint Car, 11		200

CLUB CARS AND SPECIAL PRODUCTION		Exc	Mint
83860	Kansas City Custom Container, 16		20 ___
83861	BNSF Custom Container, 16		20 ___
1901430	SP Daylight Mint Car, 19		120 ___
1901440	Virginia & Truckee Boxcar, 19		90 ___
2001090	50th Anniversary Convention Car 2-pack, 20		300 ___
2001100	50th Anniversary UP Registration Mint Car, 20		75 ___
2001270	50th Anniversary Convention Banquet Boxcar, 20		150 ___
2001281	50th Anniversary Convention Volunteer Boxcar, 20		80 ___
2001282	50th Anniversary Convention Director Boxcar, 20		170 ___
2101270	Scranton Electric City Registration Trolley, 21		125 ___
2101280	Scranton Electric City Banquet Trolley, 21		190 ___
2101520	EL Walking Brakeman Car, 21		115 ___
2101540	Texas Special Walking Brakeman Car, 21		90 ___
2201210	Tennessee Central Mint Car, 22		90 ___
2201220	RJ Corman Flatcar w/Excavator, 22		100 ___
2201230	RJ Corman Gondola w/Coil Covers, 22		80 ___
2201240	Corvette Museum Boxcar, 22	105	200 ___
2201250	Goo Goo Candy Banquet Boxcar, 22		200 ___
2201261	Goo Goo Candy Convention Volunteer Boxcar, 22		175 ___
2201262	Goo Goo Candy Boxcar, 22		225 ___
2301120	Concord Convention Tank Car 2-pack, 23		180 ___
2301121	Southern Heritage Unibody !-D Tank Car, 23		90 ___
2301122	NS Heritage Unibody 1-D Tank Car, 23		90 ___
2301130	NASCAR Racing Mint Car, 23		125 ___
2301140	Aberdeen, Carolina & Western Boxcar, 23		95 ___
2301141	Aberdeen, Carolina & Western Boxcar, 23		95 ___
2301142	Aberdeen, Carollina & Western Boxcar, 23		95 ___
2301150	Concord Convention Registration Boxcar, 23		90 ___
2301200	Lionel Headquarters Tour Boxcar, 23		80 ___
2301250	Aberdeen, Carolina & Western Unibody 1-D Tank Car, 23		150 ___
2301460	Texas Pete Boxcar, 23		110 ___
2301510	Texas Pete Unibody 1-D Tank Car, 23		150 ___
2401190	Krispy Kreme Doughnuts Boxcar, 24		95 ___
2401230	UP Boat Loader, 24		95 ___

■ LCCA Meet Specials

		Exc	Mint
1130	Tender, 76		15 ___
6014-900	Frisco Boxcar (027), 75	17	30 ___
6483	Jersey Central SP-type Caboose, 82	24	28 ___
9016	Chessie System Hopper (027), 79	16	20 ___
9036	Mobilgas 1-D Tank Car (027), 78	20	22 ___
9142	Republic Steel Gondola, green or blue, with canisters, 77	15	23 ___

■ Other LCCA Production

		Exc	Mint
4001	RJ Corman Boxcar, 99		80 ___

CLUB CARS AND SPECIAL PRODUCTION			Exc	Mint
___	4002	RJ Corman Boxcar, 99		40
___	6464-2002	Dick Maddox Retirement Boxcar, 02		100
___	8068	Rock Island GP20 Diesel, 80	85	143
___	9739	D&RGW Boxcar, 78	17	25
___	9771	Norfolk & Western Boxcar, 77		32
___	14154	Water Tower with LCCA plaque, 04		90
___	17174	Great Northern 3-bay Hopper, 03		25
___	17234	Port Huron & Detroit Boxcar, 00		45
___	17377	American Railway Express Reefer "302", 06	25	48
___	17412	Gondola, blue, 02		28
___	17895	LCCA Tractor, 91	13	21
___	17896	Lancaster Lines Tractor, 91	22	30
___	18090	D&RGW 4-6-2 Locomotive and Tender, 90	230	303
___	18483	C&O Ballast Tamper, 07		73
___	18490	UP Ballast Tamper, yellow, 06		125
___	19998	"Seasons Greetings" Boxcar, 03		40
___	26023	Flatcar with bulldozer, 04		53
___	26024	Flatcar with scraper, 04		63
___	26049	Speedboat Willie Flatcar with boat, 05		45
___	26132	UP 1-D Tank Car, 06		27
___	26780	Operating Giraffe Car, green or pink, 05		70
___	26791	UP Chase Gondola, red, 03		32
___	26791	Rio Grande Chase Gondola, black, 06		32
___	26795	Mrs. O'Leary's Dairy Farm Stock Car, 07		100
___	26834	"La Cosa Nostra Railway" Operating Ice Car, 07	25	75
___	29232	Lenny the Lion Hi-Cube, signed by Lenny Dean, 98		63
___	52025	Madison Hardware Tractor and Trailer, 93	13	18
___	52039	"Track 29" Bumper, 94	10	20
___	52055	SOVEX Tractor and Trailer, 94	15	22
___	52056	Southern Tractor and Trailer, 94	17	23
___	52091	Lenox Tractor and Trailer, 95		14
___	52092	Iowa Interstate Tractor and Trailer, 95		20
___	52100	Grand Rapids Station Platform, 98		23
___	52107	On-track Pickup, orange, 96		50
___	52108	On-track Van, blue, 96		35
___	52131	Beechcraft Airplane, blue, 97		25
___	52138	Beechcraft Airplane, orange, 97		25
___	52153	6414 Auto Set, 4-pack, 98	43	72
___	52206	LCCA SD40 Diesel and Extended-Vision Caboose, 00		650
___	52257	"Season's Greetings" Gondola, 01		36
___	52300	Halloween General Train, 04		360
___	52348	Halloween General Sheriff and Outlaw Car, 04		115
___	52405	Halloween General Add-on Cars, 06		160
___	52406	Halloween General Cannon, 08		135

CLUB CARS AND SPECIAL PRODUCTION		Exc	Mint	
52423	Postwar "1608W" NH Alco Diesel Passenger Set, 09	316	510	___
52468	Postwar "2434" Newark Pullman Coach, 09		75	___
52469	Postwar "2432" Clifton Vista-Dome Car, 09		75	___
52581	Texas Special Milk Car, 10		110	___
52582	Gondola with dinosaurs, 12		45	___
58065	2018 Christmas Boxcar, 18	60	90	___
58224	Walking Brakeman Car, 15	55	80	___
58249	2015 Christmas Boxcar, 15	60	90	___
58255	Lionelville Tractor/Trailer, blue, 15	25	40	___
58256	Lionelville Tractor/Trailer, orange, 15	25	40	___
58264	2016 Christmas Boxcar, 16	50	75	___
58269	NP Inspection Truck Motorized Unit, 17	63	100	___
58526	Texas Special NW2 Cow and Calf Switchers, 14		375	___
58527	Lionel Vulcan Switcher, 13		80	___
58536	Texas Special PS4 Flatcar w/Helicopter, 12	77	100	___
58539	Texas Special B-W Caboose, 13		95	___
58549	Texas Special Diamonds Mint Car, 14		75	___
58550	Texas Special Unibody Tank Car, 13	70	95	___
58576	Postwar 3494-550 Monon Operating Boxcar, 14		85	___
58584	Wabash Auto Loader, black, 14		110	___
58585	Wabash Auto Loader, white, 14		110	___
58599	UP Cylindrical Hopper, 11	28	75	___
58613	2014 Christmas Boxcar, 14	62	80	___
59000	Tennessee Valley RR Boxcar, 13		80	___
84609	2017 Christmas Boxcar, 17		40	___
1901420	2019 Christmas Boxcar, 19		125	___
2001110	UP ET44AC Diesel "2020" LionChief Plus 2.0, 20		700	___
2001160	50th Anniversary UP Unibody 1-D Tank Car, 20		75	___
2001300	2020 Christmas Boxcar, 20		60	___
2001330	U.S.A.F. Strategic Air Command Boxcar, 20		130	___
2101320	2021 Christmas Boxcar, 21		85	___
2101530	Salute to First Responders Boxcar, 21	60	85	___
2201290	N&W 2-6-6-4 Class A Locomotive "1222," CC, 22		2100	___
2201470	2022 Christmas Boxcar, 22		80	___
2301050	UP Vision 4-8-8-4 Big Boy Locomotive "4023," CC, 23		2900	___
2301550	2023 Christmas Boxcar, 23		90	___
2401330	LL Triplex Steam Locomotive "2024," CC, 24		2500	___
58538	NYC Flatcar w/Kodak Trailer, 12	95	115	___
22680	NH Yankee Clipper Boxcar, 10	80	110	___

Lionel Operating Train Society (LOTS)

■ LOTS National Convention Cars

303	Stauffer Chemical 1-D Tank Car, 85	85	210	___
3764	Kahn's Brine Tank Refrigerator Car, 81	70	85	___
6111	L&N Covered Quad Hopper, 83	37	42	___

	CLUB CARS AND SPECIAL PRODUCTION		Exc	Mint
____	**6211**	C&O Gondola w/Canisters, 86	60	90
____	**9414**	Cotton Belt Boxcar, 80	39	55
____	**16812**	Grand Trunk ACF 2-Bay Hopper (std O), 96	30	60
____	**16813**	Pennsylvania Power & Light Hopper w/Coal (std O), 97	40	78
____	**17874**	MILW Log Dump Car "59629", 88	90	148
____	**17875**	Port Huron & Detroit Boxcar "1289", 89	40	48
____	**17882**	B&O DD Boxcar "298011" w/ETD, 90	55	65
____	**17890**	CSX Auto Carrier "151161", 91	75	80
____	**19960**	WP Boxcar "1952" (std O), 92	47	66
____	**38356**	Dow Chemical 3-D Tank Car, 87	85	125
____	**52014**	BN TTUX Flatcar Set "637500" w/N&W trailers, 93	165	205
____	**52041**	BN TTUX Flatcar Set "637500" w/Conrail trailers, 94	60	85
____	**52048**	CN Intermodel Laser Service Tractor-Trailer, 94	28	35
____	**52067**	CB&Q Operating Ice Car "50240", 95	30	60
____	**52135**	ATSF Refrigerator Car "22739", 98	30	55
____	**52162**	GM&O DD Boxcar "24580", 99	35	65
____	**52196**	CP Maxi-Stack Flatcar "524115" w/Containers, 00	50	95
____	**52217**	LOTS/LCCA 2000 Convention Billboard, 00	5	10
____	**52234**	WM Well Car /Transformer, 01	30	60
____	**52260**	National Aquarium in Baltimore Car, 01	55	110
____	**52261**	Schlitz Beer Refrigerator Car "92132", 02	30	60
____	**52281**	PRR Operating Boxcar "30129", 03	30	55
____	**52342**	Southern Stockcar "70425" w/Sounds, 04		57
____	**52346**	D&H PS-2 Covered Hopper "12041", 06	35	65
____	**52380**	Virginian Coal Hopper "2605" w/ETD, 05	25	50
____	**52381**	Virginian Coal Hopper "2606", 05	25	50
____	**52425**	SP&S Boxcar (std O), 07	54	90
____	**52474**	NYC Evans Auto Loader w/Studebakers, 08	40	82
____	**52550**	NC&StL Dixieland Boxcar, 09	40	73
____	**52553**	Tennessee Aquarium Car, 09	25	52
____	**52566**	NH State of Maine Double-sheathed Boxcar, 10	30	62
____	**52580**	Robin Hood Beer Double-sheathed Boxcar, 11	40	80
____	**58044**	B&M Operating Welding Flatcar, 18	90	160
____	**58223**	CGW Flatcar w/Edelweiss Beer Trailers, 15	50	90
____	**58228**	CB&Q Zephyr Double-sheathed Boxcar, 15	40	55
____	**58236**	Tucker Automobile Parts DD Boxcar, 15	60	120
____	**58260**	Yuengling Beer Double-sheathed Boxcar, 16	100	150
____	**58508**	Genesee Beer & Ale Double-sheathed Boxcar, 12	35	65
____	**58553**	UP Maxi-Stack Car w/WP Containers, 13	40	75
____	**58575**	H.J. Heinz Double-sheathed Boxcar, 14	35	70
____	**80948**	Michigan Central Boxcar, 82	145	230
____	**83862**	Philadelphia Cradle of Liberty Double-sheathed Boxcar, 16	65	85
____	**83872**	D&RGW Matchless Mine Ore Car "38171", 17		55
____	**83873**	D&RGW Matchless Mine Ore Car "38173", 17		55
____	**121315**	PRR Hi-Cube Boxcar, 84	125	343

CLUB CARS AND SPECIAL PRODUCTION		Exc	Mint	
1901320	L&N Auto Loader w/Corvettes, 19		120	___
2001340	Gorilla Glue Boxcar, 20	120	180	___
2101350	MKT Auto Loader w/Ford Trucks and Thunderbirds, 21		150	___
2401220	ATSF Iron Rail Brewing PS-1 Boxcar, 24		85	___

■ LOTS Meet Specials

52413	Saratoga Brewery Refrigerator Car, 06	30	60	___
52456	Alpenrose Dairy Milk Car, 07	50	95	___
52506	Studebaker Automobile Parts Boxcar, 08	40	75	___
52552	Radioactive Waste Removal Car, 09	45	86	___
58538	NYC Flatcar w/Kodak Express Trailer, 12	90	130	___
58558	Virginia & Truckee Ore Car "34132", 13	30	50	___
58559	Virginia & Truckee Ore Car "34133", 13	30	50	___
58593	Porter Locomotive Works Double-sheathed Boxcar, 15	80	95	___
83869	D&RGW Flatcar w/Celestial Seasoning Maxi-Stack, 17	90	130	___
1801050	Woodstock Brewing Boxcar, 18	90	140	___
1901670	L&N Kentucky Bourbon Trail 3-Bay Covered Hopper, 19	80	125	___
2001450	U.S.A.F. Wright-Patterson Unibody 1-D Tank Car, 20	80	120	___
2301330	Joshua Dairy Farm Flatcar "44232" w/Milk Container, 23	45	65	___
2401240	CPKC Sunflower Oil Unibody 1-D Tank Car, 24		77	___

■ Other LOTS Production

1223	Seattle & North Coast Hi-Cube Boxcar, 86	300	400	___
18890	UP Alco RS-3 Diesel "8805", 89	120	145	___
52042	BN TTUX Flatcar "637500" w/CN trailer, 94	50	60	___
52129	Lighted Billboard with Angela Trotta Thomas art, 97	15	28	___
52280	"More Precious than Gold" Mint Car, 02	45	90	___
52309	Patriotic 1-D Tank Car, 03	35	68	___
52347	ATSF EMD SD80MAC Diesel "2504," CC, 04	170	350	___
52359	Silver Anniversary Ore Car "1979", 04	20	40	___
52360	Silver Anniversary Ore Car "2004", 04	20	40	___
52382	ATSF Warbonnet EV Caboose "2505", 05	165	325	___
52419	Touring Layout Aquarium Car, 056	45	90	___
52477	ATSF Warbonnet Boxcar "2807", 07	125	170	___
52523	ATSF Warbonnet Flatcar w/Trailer, 08	45	88	___
52567	ATSF Warbonnet ACF 2-Bay Hopper "2809", 10	30	58	___
52590	ATSF Warbonnet Mint Car, 11	40	75	___
58535	ATSF Warbonnet Transparent Boxcar, 12	40	75	___
58566	Virginia & Truckee Carson City Mint Car, 13	35	70	___
58594	ATSF Warbonnet Crane Car "35143", 14	150	270	___
58595	ATSF Warbonnet Work Caboose "35144", 14	140	230	___
83863	ATSF Warbonnet Unibody 1-D Tank Car ", 16	140	170	___
83874	ATSF Warbonnet Gondola "38172" w/Coil Covers, 17	80	120	___
1801030	Samuel Adams Lager Beer Boxcar, 18		55	___
1901330	BNSF Warbonnet 3-Bay Hopper "40192", 19		160	___

	CLUB CARS AND SPECIAL PRODUCTION		Exc	Mint
___	**2001350**	CSX Flatcar w/Kroger Trailer, 20		55
___	**2101371**	ATSF Warbonnet Ore Car "42213", 21		60

LIONEL CENTURY CLUB (LCC)

			Exc	Mint
___	**14532**	PRR Sharknose Diesel AA Set, LCC II, 00		690
___	**18053**	2-8-4 Berkshire Locomotive "726", 97	192	705
___	**18057**	6-8-6 PRR S2 Steam Turbine Locomotive "671", 98	250	568
___	**18058**	4-6-4 Hudson Locomotive "773", 97	331	840
___	**18068**	Tender for PRR Steam Turbine Locomotive "773", 99	43	232
___	**18135**	NYC F3 Diesel AA Set, 99	283	650
___	**18178**	NYC F3 Diesel B Unit, 99		230
___	**18314**	PRR GG1 Electric "2332", 97	347	560
___	**18340**	FM Train Master Set, LCC II, 00	175	900
___	**24510**	PRR Sharknose Diesel B Unit, LCC II, 00		200
___	**28069**	NYC 4-8-6 Niagara Locomotive "6024," CC, LCC II, 00		920
___	**29173**	Empire State Express Passenger Car 4-pack, LCC II, 02		372
___	**29178**	Empire State Express Passenger Car 2-pack, LCC II, 02	88	178
___	**29181**	Empire State Express Diner, LCC II, 02	70	195
___	**29204**	Boxcar "1900-2000", 96		331
___	**29226**	Berkshire Boxcar, 97	115	145
___	**29227**	GG1 Boxcar, 98		55
___	**29228**	PRR Turbine Boxcar "671", 99		60
___	**29248**	F3 Boxcar "2333", 99		67
___	**31716**	Niagara Milk Train Set, LCC II, 00		300
___	**31726**	PRR Sharknose Coal Train Set, LCC II, 00		180
___	**31731**	Train Master Freight Train Set, LCC II, 00	103	180
___	**38000**	NYC 4-6-4 Hudson Empire State Locomotive, LCC II, 02	300	990
___	**38106**	NYC F3 Diesel "2333," powered, 99	230	430
___	**38107**	NYC F3 Diesel "2333," non-powered, 99	110	210
___	**39201**	Hudson Boxcar "773", 00		58
___	**39215**	Niagara Boxcar, LCC II, 01		48
___	**39217**	Boxcar, LCC II, 00		60
___	**39218**	Gold Boxcar, LCC II, 00		85
___	**39237**	M-10000 Boxcar, LCC II, 00		70
___	**39246**	PRR Sharknose Boxcar, LCC II, 00		55
___	**39265**	Fairbanks-Morse Train Master Boxcar, LCC II, 00		60
___	**39266**	Empire State Boxcar, LCC II, 00		40
___	**51007**	UP M-10000 4-car Passenger Set, LCC II, 00	600	970
___	**51249**	UP Overland Route Sleeper Car, LCC II, 02	60	150

Lionel Railroader Club (LRRC)

			Exc	Mint
___	**780**	Boxcar, 82	55	67
___	**781**	Flatcar with trailers, 83	40	50
___	**782**	1-D Tank Car, 85	40	43
___	**784**	Covered Quad Hopper, 84	50	60
___	**11183**	Lincoln Funeral Train, 13		800

CLUB CARS AND SPECIAL PRODUCTION		Exc	Mint
11319	PRR Tuscan K4 4-6-2 Pacific Locomotive "5409," CC, 13		900
11320	PRR Tuscan K4 4-6-2 Pacific Locomotive "5436", 13		750
12875	Tractor and Trailer, 94	13	18
12921	Illuminated Station Platform, 95	19	22
14274	Water Tower, 07		20
15034	50th Anniversary Mail Car, 10		50
15035	Holiday Boxcar, 10		50
16800	Ore Car, yellow, 86	60	69
16801	Bunk Car, blue, 88	20	33
16802	Tool Car, 89	24	35
16803	Searchlight Car, 90	23	27
16804	Bay Window Caboose, 91	25	30
16838	Illuminated Station Platform, 09	30	50
16839	Covered Bridge, 11		50
16840	Flagpole, 09	20	40
18680	4-6-4 Hudson Locomotive, 00		300
18684	4-6-2 Pacific Locomotive, 99		220
18818	GP38-2 Diesel, 92	100	117
19399	Christmas Boxcar, 13		60
19437	Flatcar with trailer, 97	11	55
19473	Operating Log Dump Car "3351", 99		38
19685	Western Union Dining Car, 02		47
19695	Western Union 1-D Tank Car, 03		22
19774	Porthole Caboose, 99		49
19775	Stock Car, 99		51
19924	Boxcar, 93	10	22
19930	Quad Hopper with coal, 94	14	20
19935	1-D Tank Car, 95	19	24
19940	Vat Car, 96		32
19953	6464 Boxcar, 97		35
19965	Aquarium Car "3435", 99		56
19966	Gondola "9820" (std O), 98	18	32
19967	Kids Club Animated Gondola, 98	25	32
19978	Gold Membership Boxcar, 99		46
19991	Gold Membership Boxcar, 00		65
19992	Western Union Tool Car "3550", 00		50
19993	Gold Membership Boxcar, 01		65
19994	Western Union Passenger Car "1307", 01		60
19995	25th Anniversary Boxcar (std O), 01		49
22013	Christmas Ornament Keepsake, 13	10	18
24217	Animated Billboard, 08		30
25073	2009 Holiday Boxcar, 09	15	30
25631	Lincoln Train Passenger Car 2-pack, 13		300
25635	Red Passenger Car 3-pack, 12		420
25639	Red Arrow Diner, 12		140

CLUB CARS AND SPECIAL PRODUCTION			Exc	Mint
___	**26089**	Western Union Gondola with handcar, 05		65
___	**26165**	Western Union Refrigerator Car, 04		30
___	**26382**	Flatcar with tractor and tanker, 08		60
___	**26413**	Commemorative 4-bay Hopper, 08		68
___	**26601**	Flatcar w/Pipes, 10		50
___	**26636**	50th Anniversary 6830 Flatcar with submarine, 11		55
___	**26637**	50th Anniversary 6640 USMC Missile Launching Car, 11		65
___	**27058**	ACF 2-Bay Covered Hopper "27058", 09	30	60
___	**27940**	Postwar 6469 Liquified Gas Tank Car, 13		50
___	**27943**	Postwar 6416 Boat Loader, 13		50
___	**27944**	Postwar 3413 Mercury Capsule Launch Car, 13		60
___	**27945**	50th Anniversary 6446-60 LV Covered Quad Hopper, 13		55
___	**28062**	4-6-4 Hudson Locomotive, 00		1150
___	**28571**	GP9 Diesel, CC, 07		250
___	**28665**	Western Union 2-8-4 Berkshire Locomotive "665", 05	63	175
___	**29200**	Lionel Boxcar "9700", 96		38
___	**29313**	50th Anniversary 3409 Helicopter Car, 11		70
___	**29657**	50th Anniversary 6413 Mercury Capsule Car, 12		55
___	**29658**	50th Anniversary 6465 Cities Service 2-D Tank Car, 12		50
___	**29876**	Crane and Boom Car 2-Car Set, CC, 10	450	750
___	**29879**	Crane Car, CC, 10		450
___	**29883**	Boom Car w/RailSounds, 10		300
___	**29931**	Holiday Boxcar, 05		25
___	**29939**	30th Anniversary Boxcar, 06		50
___	**29941**	Holiday Boxcar, 06		25
___	**29946**	Holiday Boxcar, 07		37
___	**29947**	Commemorative Boxcar, 07		30
___	**29957**	Holiday Boxcar, 08		50
___	**29977**	Holiday Boxcar, 11		60
___	**36521**	Western Union Searchlight Caboose, 05		32
___	**36769**	4th of July Lighted Boxcar, 03		70
___	**36841**	Visitor Center 15th Anniversary Lighted Boxcar, 06		70
___	**37968**	Clock Tower with wreath, 11		43
___	**39249**	Holiday Boxcar, 03		30
___	**39264**	Holiday Boxcar, 04		50
___	**39352**	50th Anniversary 6445 Fort Knox Mint Car, 12		70
___	**39353**	50th Anniversary Santa Fe Boxcar, 11		55
___	**39357**	2012 Christmas Boxcar, 12	35	50
___	**39496**	"6475" 50th Anniversary Vat Car, 10		60
___	**58632**	1955 Maintenance of Way Truck, 13		165
___	**81116**	Polar Express Operating Billboard, 14		60
___	**81117**	Polar Express Flatcar with silver bell, 14		45

LIONEL RAILROAD CLUB OF MILWAUKEE				
___	**52116**	MILW Flatcar "194797," black, with tractor and trailer, 97		71
___	**52163**	CMStP&P "Hiawatha" DD Automobile Boxcar, 98	25	63

CLUB CARS AND SPECIAL PRODUCTION		Exc	Mint
52180	MILW Flatcar "194799," tuscan, with trailer, 99	25	70 ___
52228	CMStP&P 1-D Water Tank Car "908309", 00		50 ___
52229	MILW 1-D Diesel Fuel Tank Car "907797", 00		50 ___
52230	1-D Tank Car 2-pack, 00		142 ___
52246	CMStP&P "Olympian" Boxcar "194701", 01	19	61 ___
52265	MILW/Zoological Society Aquarium Car "4701," orange, 02		55 ___
52278	MILW/Zoological Society Aquarium Car "4702," blue, 03		95 ___
52297	MILW Reefer "194703," yellow, 03		67 ___
52298	MILW Flatcar "194704" with orange trailer, 04		115 ___
52337	MILW/Zoological Society Motorized Aquarium Car, 04		90 ___
52368	MILW Flatcar "472004," black, 05		65 ___
52369	MILW Trailer Train Auto Carrier "194705", 05		85 ___
52370	CMStP&P Milk Car "364," tan, 05	57	86 ___
52387	CMStP&P Flatcar "194706," gray, 06	30	59 ___
52400	MILW PS-2 2-bay Hopper "99607," orange, 06		85 ___
52401	MILW PS-2 2-bay Hopper "98809," yellow, 06	33	73 ___
52402	CMStP&P URTX Operating Ice Car "4706", 06	54	85 ___
52428	CMStP&P 0-4-0 Switcher/Caboose Set, 60th Anniversary, 06		275 ___
52429	CMStP&P 0-4-0 Switcher, 06		200 ___
52430	CMStP&P Offset Cupola Caboose, 06	20	65 ___
52458	MILW Stock Car "102721" (std O), 07	24	69 ___
52466	CMStP&P Stock Car "105254" (std O), 07	35	76 ___
52551	MILW "Big M" DD Boxcar "200947," yellow, 09		60 ___
52572	MILW Reiman Aquarium Car, 11		75 ___
52599	MILW 2-bay ACF Hopper, 12		60 ___
58263	Breast Cancer Awareness Boxcar, 16		60 ___
58563	CMStP&P Round-Roof Boxcar, 13	30	73 ___
58591	58591 MILW Flatcar with auto frames, 14, 14		60 ___
2201070	Delafield Brewhaus Beer Wood-side Refrigerator Car, 22		75 ___

LONG ISLAND TOY TRAIN LOCOMOTIVE ENGINEERS			
58520	Entenmann's Vat Car, 12		65 ___
58556	Flatcar with U.S. Navy airplane, 13		70 ___
58562	Entenmann's Quad Hopper, 14		74 ___

NASSAU LIONEL OPERATING ENGINEERS (NLOE)			
8389	Long Island Boxcar, 89	70	100 ___
8390	Long Island Covered Quad Hopper, 90	70	100 ___
8391A	Long Island Bunk Car, 91	70	90 ___
8391B	Long Island Tool Car, 91	70	90 ___
17893	Long Island 1-D Tank Car "8392", 92	80	105 ___
52007	Long Island Alco RS-3 Diesel "1552", 93	120	250 ___
52019	Long Island Boxcar "8393", 93	39	65 ___
52020	Long Island Bay Window Caboose "8393", 93	65	95 ___
52026	Long Island Flatcar "8394" w/Grumman trailer, 94	275	465 ___
52061	Long Island Stern's Pickle Products Vat Car "8395", 95		200 ___

	CLUB CARS AND SPECIAL PRODUCTION		Exc	Mint
___	52072	Grumman Tractor, 94	40	75
___	52076	Long Island Observation"9683", 96	175	350
___	52112	Long Island Ronkonkoma Vista Dome "9783", 97	150	300
___	52122	Meenan Oil 1-D Tank Car "8397" (std O), 97	30	60
___	52123	Long Island Hicksville Diner "9883", 98	150	300
___	52144	Long Island Flatcar "8398" w/Grumman van, 99	50	94
___	52145	Long Island Jamaica Coach "99831", 99	150	300
___	52145	Long Island Penn Station Coach "99832", 99	150	300
___	52166	Long Island Flatcar "8399" w/Grumman trailer, 98	40	77
___	52173	Long Island EMD F3 Diesel A-A Set "2000/2001", 00		260
___	52174	U.S. Mail RPO Aluminum Baggage Car, 00		220
___	52186	Grucci Fireworks Boxcar "2000", 00	35	72
___	52209	Long Island World's Fair Sleeper/Roomette, 01		80
___	52232	Central RR of Long Island Boxcar "8301", 01	30	60
___	52235	Long Island World's Fair Vista Dome, 02		80
___	52256	New York & Atlantic Boxcar "8302", 02	30	58
___	52263	Long Island World's Fair Combination Car, 02		80
___	52296	Long Island Flatcar w/Republic tank truck, 03	40	78
___	52329	New York & Atlantic Caboose, 04	40	80
___	52341	Long Island Flatcar w/Pan Am trailer, 05	45	85
___	52365	Long Island Flatcar w/Lilco transformer, 05	70	135
___	52420	Long Island 80th Anniversary Boxcar, 06	25	45
___	52480	Long Island Flatcar w/Pipes, 08	25	50
___	52489	Long Island Flatcar w/P.C. Richard & Son trailer, 07	35	67
___	52555	Martha Clara Vineyards Vat Car, 09	30	58
___	52568	Long Island Flatcar w/NY Islanders Trailer, 10	30	62
___	52586	Flatcar w/Cradle of Aviation Museum Trailer, 11	25	52
___	52592	Petland Discounts Aquarium Car, 11	35	70
___	58212	Cross Harbor Round-roof Boxcar "8315", 15	45	90
___	58239	Long Island GLa Hopper 2-pack, 16	90	160
___	58240	Long Island GLa Hopper, Tuscan, 16	40	80
___	58241	Long Island GLa Hopper, Black, 16	40	80
___	58266	Nathan's Famous 100th Anniversary Refrigerator Car, 16	95	120
___	58500	Nassau County Firefighters Museum Tank Car, 12	30	55
___	58517	Long Island Alco C-420 Diesel, CC, 12	275	485
___	58567	Nathan's Famous Steel-side Refrigerator Car "83131", 13	40	74
___	58568	Nathan's Famous Steel-side Refrigerator Car "83132", 13	40	74
___	58573	Long island PS-1 Boxcar "8312", 14		125
___	58574	Long Island Flatcar "8313" w/Tractor and Trailer, 13	50	150
___	58581	Long Island Double-sheathed Boxcar "8314", 14	100	170
___	83870	Long Island PS-2CD Covered Hopper, 17	60	120
___	1901070	Long Island 50' DD Boxcar "8318", 18		80
___	2001320	Long Island Milk Car "8319", 19		130
___	2001570	Long Island 50' Flatcar "8320" w/Trailers, 20	60	85
___	2101231	Long Island MOW Bunk Car, 21		95

CLUB CARS AND SPECIAL PRODUCTION		Exc	Mint	
2101232	Long Island MOW Tool Car, 21		95	___
2101510	Long Island MOW Kitchen Car w/RailSounds, 21		140	___
2136150	Long Island 4-6-0 Camelback Locomotive "19," CC, 21		200	___
2301270	Long Island Center-Beam Flatcar "8323", 23		65	___
2401280	Long Island Bobber Caboose "22", 24		130	___

NICHOLAS SMITH TRAINS				
19580	Wood-side Refrigerator Car, 09	17	30	___
19582	Wood-side Refrigerator Car, 09	17	30	___
19583	Wood-side Refrigerator Car, 09	17	30	___
19584	Wood-side Refrigerator Car, 09	17	30	___
1933748	Reading FB-2 Diesel, CC, 19		350	___
1933749	Reading FB-2 SuperBass, 19		350	___
1933758	Southern FB-2 Diesesl, CC, 19		350	___
1933759	Southern FB-2 SuperBass, 19		350	___
2133860	LV EMD SW8 Diesel "253," CC, 21		470	___
2133870	PC EMD SW8 Diesel "8623," CC, 21		470	___
2233861	Alaska EMD SD70ACe Diesel "4001," CC, 22		700	___
2233868	Alaska EMD SD70ACe SuperBass "4006", 22		600	___
2333730	L&NE EMD FA/FB/FA Diesels, CC, 23		1450	___
2333731	L&NE EMD FA-2 Diesel "701," CC, 23		600	___
2333732	L&NE EMD FA-2 Diesel "704," CC, 23		600	___
2333739	L&NE EMD FB-2 SuperBass "751", 23		350	___

RAILROAD MUSEUM OF LONG ISLAND				
52416	RMLI 15th Anniversary LIRR Boxcar, 05	120	170	___
52433	Atlantis Marine World Aquarium Car, 06	95	145	___
52453	North Fork Bank Mint Car, 07	50	90	___
52497	LIRR Flatcar w/Entenmann's trailer and tractor, 08	65	110	___
52498	Boeing Fairchild Container Car, 10	40	75	___
52548	Celebrating 175 Years of Railroading Boxcar, 09	50	90	___
52557	Entenmann's Operating Boxcar, 10	50	90	___
52570	Riverhead Building Supply Boxcar, 11	30	60	___
52571	Riverhead Visitor's Center Boxcar, 11	30	60	___
52577	King Kullen Boxcar, 11	30	60	___
52595	J. P. Holland Submarine Car, 12	30	60	___
58054	Mason Candies Dots and Crows Boxcar, 18	35	65	___
58069	Steam Up! LIRR 39 Blue Boy Boxcar, 18	35	65	___
58521	Wonder Bread PS-2 Covered Hopper, 12	30	60	___
58227	World's Fair Crew Car, 15	30	60	___
58259	Steam Union Pacific LIRR 39 Boxcar, 16	35	65	___
58551	Flatcar with White Castle refrigerated trailer, 13	30	60	___
58554	RCA Operating Radar Car, 13	30	60	___
58555	Grown on Long Island Flatcar w/Trailers, 16	40	65	___
58579	World's Fair Exhibit Car, 14	40	70	___
58580	World's Fair Tool Car, 15	40	70	___

CLUB CARS AND SPECIAL PRODUCTION		Exc	Mint
___ 84598	North Fork Potato Chips Boxcar, 17	35	65
___ 2001260	Long Island Duckling Stockcar, 20	40	70
___ 2101100	White Rock Products Boxcar, 21	40	70
___ 2201150	Tribute B60 Baggage Car, 22	40	70

ST. LOUIS LIONEL RAILROAD CLUB

___ 52099	MP Flatcar with St. Louis trailer, 96	65
___ 52104	St. Louis tractor and trailer, 96	20
___ 52117	Wabash Flatcar with REA tractor and trailer, 97	65
___ 52136A	Christmas Tractor and Trailer, 97	100
___ 52136B	Frisco Tractor and Trailer, 98	100
___ 52147	Frisco Campbell TOFC Flatcar, 98	75
___ 52150	Frisco Campbell TOFC Flatcar, 98	130
___ 52167	ATSF Flatcar "831999" with Navajo trailer, 99	75
___ 52190	IC Flatcar with trailers, 00	80
___ 52222	Cotton Belt Flatcar with SP tractor and trailer, 01	50
___ 52224A	SP Flatcar with Navajo tractor and trailer, 01	25
___ 52224B	SP Flatcar with service tractor and trailer, 01	25
___ 52258	UP Flatcar with UP tractor and trailer, 02	55
___ 52290	UP Flatcar with tractor trailer, 03	75
___ 52336	U.S. Army Flatcar with tanker truck, 04	125
___ 52371	NYC Flatcar with Fire Company tanker truck, 05	145
___ 52392	PRR Flatcar with Hood's Milk tanker truck, 06	100
___ 52440	U.S.M.C. Flatcar with tractor and trailer, 07	135
___ 52490	Silver Special Flatcar with USA tractor and trailer, 08	100
___ 52513	Frisco Flatcar with U.S.A.F. trailer, 09	120
___ 52597	U.S. Navy Flatcar w/Trailer, 12	120
___ 58052	Frisco Boxcar, 18	70
___ 58261	Monsanto Boxcar, 15	70
___ 68677	Frisco/Route 66 Flatcar w/Trailer, 13	120
___ 1901310	Anheuser Busch Beer Car, 19	80

TRAIN COLLECTORS ASSOCIATION (TCA)

■ TCA National Convention Cars

___ 511	St. Louis Baggage Car, 81	36	41
___ 2671-1968	TCA Tender, shell only, 68	10	54
___ 5734	REA Refrigerator Car, 85	42	51
___ 6315	Pittsburgh 1-D Tank Car, 72	55	60
___ 6436-1969	Open Quad Hopper, red, 69	45	70
___ 6464-1965	Pittsburgh Boxcar, blue, 65	128	191
___ 6464-1970	Chicago Boxcar, 70	60	93

CLUB CARS AND SPECIAL PRODUCTION		Exc	Mint	
6464-1971	Disneyland Boxcar, 71	210	240	___
6517-1966	Bay Window Caboose, 66	163	268	___
6926	New Orleans Extended Vision Caboose, 86	27	39	___
7205	Denver Combination Car, 82	37	50	___
7206	Louisville Passenger Car, 83	40	55	___
7212	Pittsburgh Passenger Car, 84	41	50	___
7812	Houston Stock Car, 77	12	25	___
8476	4-6-4 Locomotive "5484", 85	255	310	___
9123	Dearborn 3-tier Auto Carrier, 73	25	36	___
9319	"Silver Jubilee" Mint Car, 79	60	130	___
9544	Chicago Observation Car, 80		50	___
9611	Boston Hi-Cube Boxcar, 78	21	26	___
9774	Orlando "Southern Belle" Boxcar, 75	14	35	___
9779	Philadelphia Boxcar "9700-1976", 76	26	34	___
9864	Seattle Refrigerator Car, 74	37	52	___
11737	TCA 40th Anniversary F3 Diesel ABA Set, 93	368	528	___
17879	Valley Forge Dining Car, 89		60	___
17883	New Georgia Passenger Car, 90	52	64	___
17898	Wabash Reefer "21596", 92	41	44	___
19211	Vermont Railway Flatcars (2) with 4 trailers, 08		160	___
21608	"Fang" Snake Exhibition Car, 09	35	50	___
21612	Oil Creek & Titusville Operating Boxcar, 08		90	___
21714	Copper Basin Hopper w/Load, 09		225	___
22609	Old Bay Seasoning Boxcar, 10		75	___
32660	Valley Forge Dining Car, 89		100	___
52008	Bucyrus Erie Crane Car, 93	44	49	___
52035	Yorkrail GP9 Diesel "1750," shell only, 94	44	55	___
52036	TCA 40th Anniversary Bay Window Caboose, 94	35	40	___
52037	Yorkrail GP9 Diesel "1754", 94	125	150	___
52059	Clinchfield Quad Hopper "16413" with coal, 94	85	110	___
52062	Skytop Observation Car, 95	210	360	___
52085	Full Vista Dome Car, 96		115	___
52106	City of Phoenix Diner, 97		100	___
52142	Massachusetts Central Maxi-Stack Flatcar "5100-01", 98		120	___
52143	City of Providence Passenger Car, 98		140	___
52146	Ocean Spray Refrigerator Car, 98		235	___
52155	City of San Francisco Baggage Car, 99		140	___
52191	City of Grand Rapids Aluminum Passenger Car, 00		135	___
52210	Rico Station, 00		29	___
52220	City of Chattanooga Vista Dome Car, 01		140	___
52221	Norfolk Southern Boxcar, 01		50	___
52237	Lionel Gondola, yellow, 01		110	___
52238	Lionel Gondola, red, 01		110	___

	CLUB CARS AND SPECIAL PRODUCTION		Exc	Mint
___	52239	Lionel Gondola, silver, 01		110
___	52240	Lionel Gondola 3-pack, 01	155	330
___	52241	Lionel Gondola, black, 02		15
___	52242	Lionel Gondola, blue, 02		35
___	52250	City of Chicago Combination Car, 02		130
___	52272	Lionel Gondola, gold, 02		80
___	52274	UP City of Los Angeles RPO Car, 03		95
___	52276	California Gold Mint Car, 03		65
___	52333	Harmony Dairy Milk Car, 04		90
___	52338	Lionel 50th Anniversary Mint Car, 04		75
___	52339	50th Anniversary Convention Banquet Car with coin, 04	88	360
___	52340	Train Order Building, 04		90
___	52373	Montana Rail Link 2-car Set, 05		90
___	52374	Montana Rail Link 2-bay Hopper, 05		50
___	52375	Montana Rail Link Flatcar with pulpwood logs, 05		50
___	52376	GN Refrigerator Car, 05		60
___	52403	T&P Stockcar (std O), 06		75
___	52414	Flatcar w/3 snowmobiles, 07		80
___	52415	Denver Operating Sheriff and Outlaw Car, 07	35	75
___	52417	Denver Mint Banquet Car, 07		200
___	52481	Ben & Jerry's Refrigerator Car, 08		95
___	52482	Vermont Ry. Maxi-Stack Car w/4 Containers, 08		165
___	52483	Rutland PS-1 Boxcar "358", 08		50
___	52500	ATSF Grand Canyon Reefer, 09		60
___	52508	Celebrate America Mint Car, 09		95
___	52554	Bethlehem Steel Hot Metal Car, 10		70
___	52573	Sierra RR Stockcar, 11		50
___	52576	Crystal Creamery General American Milk Car, 11		75
___	52584	Phillips Seafood Aquarium Car, 10		100
___	52593	LN PS-1 Boxcar, 12		45
___	52594	Quikrete Cement & Concrete ACF 4-Bay Covered Hopper, 12		85
___	58042	Heinz Pickle Refrigeration Line Boxcar, 18		190
___	58062	Mermaid Oysters Boxcar, 18		$300
___	58067	Manhattan Project Trinity Site Mint Car, 19		275
___	58068	Manhattan Project Mint Car, 19		300
___	58216	NYC Merchants Despatch Transit Steel-sided Refrigerator Car, 15		60
___	58237	Coney Island & Brooklyn RR Trolley, 15		100
___	58238	Bergen County Traction Co. Trolley, 15		100
___	58258	Texas Mexican Ry. Boxcar, 16		70
___	58511	Chick-Fil-A Poultry Dispatch Operating Boxcar, 12		125
___	58516	C&NW PS-1 Boxcar, 13		75
___	58544	St. Louis Refrigeration Co. Refrigerator Car, 13	85	125
___	58547	Cotton Belt Blue Streak Merchandise Boxcar, 13		75
___	58571	Bethlehem Steel PS-1 Boxcar, 14	80	100
	58572	Reading Philadelphia Mint Car, 14	45	80

CLUB CARS AND SPECIAL PRODUCTION		Exc	Mint
84595	Carnegie Steel Boxcar, gray, 17		40 ___
84596	Carnegie Steel Boxcar, brown, 17		40 ___
1901051	Sierra Blanca Brewing Wood-side Refrigerator Car, 19		75 ___
2001060	Jacksonville Naval Air Station Boxcar , 20		50 ___
2001070	Department 56 Convention Boxcar, 20		100 ___
2001581	SAL Flatcar w/Trailer "32211", 20		100 ___
2101130	WP Boxcar "6464-100," reverse colors, 21		70 ___
2201040	Quikrete Cement & Concrete PS-1 Boxcar w/Roof hatch "30328", 22		200 ___
2201090	Mountain Man Moonshine Boxcar, 22		200 ___
2201310	Quikrete Cement & Concrete PS-1 Boxcar "1940", 22		200 ___

■ TCA Museum-Related and Other Cars

		Exc	Mint
1018-1979	Mortgage Burning Hi-Cube Boxcar, 79	32	35 ___
5731	L&N Reefer, 90		95 ___
7780	TCA Museum Boxcar, 80		26 ___
7781	Hafner Boxcar, 81		26 ___
7782	Carlisle & Finch Boxcar, 82		26 ___
7783	Ives Boxcar, 83		26 ___
7784	Voltamp Boxcar, 84		23 ___
7785	Hoge Boxcar, 85		23 ___
9771	Norfolk & Western Boxcar, 77	24	31 ___
16811	Rutland Boxcar "5477096", 96	18	47 ___
19906	"I Love Pennsylvania" Boxcar: President's Car, 94		40 ___
52045	Pennsylvania Dutch Milk Car "61052", 94		90 ___
52051	Baltimore & Ohio Sentinel Boxcar "6464095", 95	36	42 ___
52052	TCA 40th Anniversary Boxcar, 94		90 ___
52063	NYC Pacemaker Boxcar "6464125", 95		345 ___
52064	Missouri Pacific Boxcar "6464150", 95		370 ___
52065	Pennsylvania Dutch Grain Operating Boxcar "9208", 96		100 ___
52118	Rio Grande Boxcar "5477097", 97		53 ___
52119	TCA Museum 20th Anniversary Boxcar, 97		70 ___
52128	Pennsylvania Dutch Pretzels Boxcar, 99		80 ___
52172	L&N "Share the Freedom Boxcar" "5477099", 99		56 ___
52198	Frisco Boxcar "5477000", 00		43 ___
52215	Museum Work Train Gondola with pipes, 03		53 ___
52226	Angela Trotta Thomas Boxcar "2000", 01		100 ___
52243	Museum Work Train 1-D Tank Car, 01		50 ___
52271	Museum Work Train Flatcar with wheel load, 02		20 ___
52289	National Toy Train Museum 25th Anniversary Bullion Car, 02		75 ___
52295	National Toy Train Museum Gondola with pipes, 03		16 ___
52310	Museum Work Train Boxcar, 04		53 ___
52311	TCA 50th Anniversary Train Master 5-Car Freight Set, 04	279	450 ___
52315	TCA 50th Anniversary PRR Train Master and Caboose, 04		400 ___
52320	TCA 50th Anniversary PRR Porthole Caboose, 04		100

CLUB CARS AND SPECIAL PRODUCTION			Exc	Mint
___	52321	SP Train Master Diesel, 04		375
___	52322	MKT 8,000-Gallon 1-D Tank Car Shell, 04		25
___	52323	C&NW PS-5 Gondola Shell, 04		25
___	52324	B&M PS-2 3-Bay Covered Hopper Shell, 04		25
___	52325	SAL PS-1 Boxcar, 04		65
___	52326	SP Smoking Caboose, 04		200
___	52361	National Toy Train Museum 50th Anniversary Boxcar, 04		70
___	52372	Museum Work Train Baggage Car, 05		70
___	52408	N&W Caboose, 06		55
___	52409	Museum Work Train Idler Caboose, 06		68
___	52437	Museum Work Train Crane Car, 07		78
___	58040	U.S. Navy Seabees Boxcar, 18		170
___	58313	TCA 50th Anniversary SP Train Master 5-Car Freight Set, 04		430
___	58314	TCA 50th Anniversary SP Train Master and Caboose, 04		350
___	61052	Penn Dutch Dairy Operating Milk Car, 15		100
___	1901460	Pennsylvania RR Christmas Boxcar "6464-200", 19		150
___	1901700	York Train Meet October 2019 Boxcar, 19		300
___	2101400	WP Boxcar "6464-100," black lettering, 21		120
___	2101480	B&O Sentinel Boxcar "6464-325", 21		165
___	2101570	SP Boxcar "6464-225", 21		165
___	2101600	York TCA Meet Boxcar October 2021, 21		125
___	2201031	ATSF Bicentennial EMD SD45 Diesel "5700," CC, 22		600

■ TCA Bicentennial Special Set

			Exc	Mint
___	1973	Bicentennial Observation Car, 76	34	50
___	1974	Bicentennial Passenger Car, 76	34	50
___	1975	Bicentennial Passenger Car, 76	34	50
___	1976	Bicentennial U36B Diesel, 76	115	165

■ Atlantic Division

			Exc	Mint
___	1980	Atlantic Division Flatcar with trailers, 80	28	34
___	6101	Burlington Northern Covered Quad Hopper, 82	21	34
___	9186	Conrail N5c Caboose, 79	22	30
___	9193	Budweiser Vat Car, 84	80	110
___	9466	Wanamaker Boxcar, 83	105	135
___	9788	Lehigh Valley Boxcar, 78	19	24
___	58564	Tastykake Cupcake Boxcar, 1, 18		90
___	58565	Tastykake Cupcake Boxcar, 2, 18		90
___	58582	Philly Pretzel Billboard Refrigerator Car, 14		65
___	58592	Tastykake Butterscotch Krimpets Hi-Cube Boxcar, 11	80	125
___	84594	Wawa Hoagiefest Boxcar, 17		90
___	1901410	Yuengling Beer Boxcar, 19		95

■ Desert Division

		Exc	Mint
52088	Desert Division 25th Anniversary On-track Step Van, 96		120
52105	Superstition Mountain Operating Gondola "61997", 97		80
52442	Verde Canyon Boxcar, 07		55
52443	Grand Canyon Boxcar, 07		55
58222	AEC Los Alamos Mint Car, 16		165
58226	Cumbres & Toltec Double-sheathed Boxcar, 17		150
84597	Fred Harvey House Boxcar, 17		50
2001150	El Tova Boxcar, 20		110

■ Dixie Division

		Exc	Mint
52127	Dixie Division 10th Anniversary Southern 3-bay Hopper, 98		70
52438	Southern PS-1 Boxcar "27007", 06	40	80
52444	Southern PS-1 Boxcar "27087", 06	40	80

■ Eastern Division

		Exc	Mint
9412	Richmond, Fredericksburg & Potomac Boxcar, 79		26
9740	Chessie System Boxcar w/Trolley Overstamp, 76		23
9771	Norfolk & Western Boxcar, 78		30
9783	B&O Time-Saver Boxcar, 77		30

■ Fort Pitt Division

		Exc	Mint
1984-30X	Heinz Ketchup Boxcar, 84		500

■ Great Lakes Division

		Exc	Mint
1983	Churchill Downs Boxcar, 83		200
1983	Churchill Downs Reefer, 83		250
9740	10th Anniversary Chessie System Boxcar, 76		23
8957	Season's Greetings BN GP20 Diesel, powered, 80		230
8958	Season's Greetings BN GP20 Diesel, non-powered, 80		150
9119	Detroit & Mackinac Covered Quad Hopper, 77	19	22
9272	New Haven Bay Window Caboose, 79	19	22
9401	Great Northern Boxcar, 78		23
9730	Season's Greetings CP Rail Boxcar, 76		27
52000	Detroit-Toledo Division Flatcar with trailer, 92	70	85

■ Great Lakes Division: Detroit-Toledo Chapter

		Exc	Mint
8957	Burlington Northern GP20 Diesel, 80	115	230
8958	Burlington Northern GP20 Diesel Dummy, 80	75	150
9119	Detroit & Mackinac Covered Quad Hopper, 77	19	22
9272	New Haven Bay Window Caboose, 79	19	22
9401	Great Northern Boxcar, 78	10	23

			Exc	Mint
___	**9730**	CP Rail Boxcar, 76	10	27
___	**52000**	Detroit-Toledo Division Flatcar with trailer, 92	70	85

■ Great Lakes Division: Three Rivers Chapter

			Exc	Mint
___	**9113**	Norfolk & Western Quad Hopper, 76	27	30

■ Great Lakes Division: Western Michigan Chapter

			Exc	Mint
___	**9730**	5th Anniversary CP Rail Boxcar, 74		25

■ Lake & Pines Division

			Exc	Mint
___	**52018**	3-M Boxcar, 93		450

■ Lone Star Division

			Exc	Mint
___	**7522**	New Orleans Mint Car with coin, 86		420
___	**52093**	Lone Star Division Boxcar "6464-696", 96		32
___	**52585**	Texas Special Dallas Federal Reserve Mint Car, 11	35	62
___	**58512**	SP Daylight San Francisco Mint Car, 12		65
___	**58552**	Texas Special Mint Car with silver bars, 12	65	95

■ Lone Star Division: North Texas Chapter

			Exc	Mint
___	**9739**	D&RGW Boxcar, 76		20

■ Metropolitan Division (METCA)

			Exc	Mint
___	**10**	CNJ EMD F3 Diesel A Unit Shell, 71	15	25
___	**9272**	NH BW Caboose, 79	21	25
___	**9754**	NYC Pacemaker Boxcar, 76	15	31
___	**52485**	NYC Mint Car w/Copper load, 08	60	120
___	**52486**	PRR Mint Car, green, 09	60	125
___	**52487**	PRR Mint Car, Tuscan, 09	60	125
___	**52488**	NYC Mint Car Lightning Stripe , 10	30	60
___	**52574**	Fort Knox 50th Anniversary Mint Car, 11	50	100
___	**52583**	B&O Mint Car Capitol Dome, 11	50	100
___	**52596**	LIRR Mint Car, 12	50	100
___	**58033**	CNJ Boxcar, 16	100	120
___	**58038**	Charles Chips Boxcar, 17	110	170
___	**58057**	Halloween Boxcar, 18	50	80
___	**58230**	CNJ Madison Hardware Boxcar, 15	180	220
___	**58231**	NY Connecting RR Madison Hardware Boxcar, 15	175	215
___	**58232**	Lionel Lines Madison Hardware Boxcar, 15	210	250
___	**58243**	Entenmann's Gondola w/Load, 16	100	130
___	**58244**	PRR Madison Hardware Boxcar, 15	185	225
___	**58246**	CNJ Blue Comet Banquet Mint Car, 15	150	230
___	**58247**	CNJ Mint Car, 15	200	275
___	**58248**	E-L Banquet Mint Car, 15	235	335
___	**58274**	LV Boxcar, 16	55	80
___	**58280**	REA Christmas Boxcar, 16	50	85

CLUB CARS AND SPECIAL PRODUCTION		Exc	Mint	
58285	Brookside Milk Refrigerator Car, 17	120	180	___
58286	Riverside Milk Refrigerator Car, 17	90	125	___
58501	REA Flatcar w/Trailer, 15	95	125	___
58502	NYC Flatcar w/Trailer, 15	95	125	___
58503	Lionel Showroom Layout Delivery Flatcar w/Trailer, 15	100	150	___
58504	Lionel Flatcar w/Madison Hardware Trailer, 15	200	225	___
58523	CNJ Blue Comet Mint Car, 13	35	70	___
58534	CNJ Mint Car, 13	35	70	___
58569	E-L Mint Car, 14	35	70	___
58598	Entenmann's 1-D Tank Car, 15	165	290	___
83866	Susquehanna Boxcar, 16	50	85	___
1801011	Edison Cement 2-Bay Covered Hopper "1899", 18	25	45	___
1801012	Edison Cement 2-Bay Covered Hopper "1932", 18	25	45	___
1801041	Spirit of Union Pacific Boxcar "1943", 18	80	120	___
1801042	Spirit of Union Pacific Boxcar "9026", 18	80	120	___
1901012	U.S. Army MASH Boxcar, 19	60	100	___
1901191	PC Boxcar "45612", 19	90	120	___
1901200	LIRR Boxcar "2587", 19	90	135	___
1901230	United States Lines Boxcar, 19	90	125	___
1901240	Manufacturers Ry. Boxcar "257", 19	60	85	___
1901250	Public Service Boxcar, 19	80	110	___
1901260	Brooklyn Navy Yard Boxcar, 19	200	250	___
1901301	CP Boxcar, 19	55	80	___
1901302	CN Boxcar "1918", 19	55	80	___
1901303	BC Rail Boxcar, 19	65	100	___
1901354	Coors Beer Wood-side Refrigerator Car "1880", 19	110	150	___
1901370	Conrail FGE Boxcar "3600602", 19	65	100	___
1901380	ATSF Ore Car 6-pack, 19	180	230	___
1901381	ATSF Ore Car, red, 19	30	55	___
1901382	ATSF Ore Car, black, 19	30	55	___
1901383	ATSF Ore Car, brown, 19	30	55	___
1901384	ATSF Ore Car, blue, 19	30	55	___
1901385	ATSF Ore Car, green, 19	30	55	___
1901386	ATSF Ore Car, orange, 19	30	55	___
1901400	Linde Union Carbide Boxcar "2061", 19	80	110	___
1901500	National Bohemian Wood-sided Refrigerator Car, 19	140	200	___
1904190	George Bush 4141 Boxcar, 19	80	125	___
2001021	Budweiser Beer Wood-sided Refrigerator Car "1876", 20		80	___
2001022	Budweiser Beer Wood-sided Refrigerator Car "1951", 20		80	___
2001130	Conrail GG1 "4800," CC, 20		460	___
2001140	PRR GG1 "1776," LionChief Plus 2.0, 20		460	___
2001180	GATX EMD SD38 Locomotive, 20		600	___
2001202	Morristown & Erie Christmas Boxcar, 20		100	___
2001210	BAR State of Maine Potatoes Boxcar, 20		120	___
2001220	Norfolk Naval Shipyard Boxcar, 20		100	___

CLUB CARS AND SPECIAL PRODUCTION			Exc	Mint
___	2001250	Harley & Davidson Bros. Boxcar, 20		120
___	2001370	LIRR Milk Refrigerator Car "3012", 20		100
___	2001380	PRR Milk Refrigerator Car, 20		100
___	2001400	E-L Train Master Diesel "1856," CC, 20		550
___	2001560	No. 60 Lionelville Trolley, red lettering, 20		130
___	2101190	BAR EMD GP7 Diesel "1776," CC, 21		550
___	2101220	Boxcar Brewing Co. Boxcar, 21		100
___	2101230	Entenmann's EMD GP7 Diesel, LionChief 2.0, 21		550
___	2101240	Entenmann's NE-5 Caboose, 21		90
___	2101380	Alaska RR 6464-825 Boxcar, reverse color, 21		300
___	2101381	Alaska RR 6464-825 Boxcar, yellow roof/ends, 21		300
___	2101390	ATSF EMD SD70ACe Diesel "1863," CC, 21		675
___	2101420	Air Force One EMD SD70ACe, CC, 21		650
___	2101440	Renken's Milk & Cream Milk Refrigerator Car, 21		100
___	2101610	Middleton & New Jersey Boxcar, 21		100
___	2133880	We The People 4th of July EMD SD70ACe Diesel, CC, 21		650
___	2201310	D&H Blue Coal Boxcar, 22		100
___	2201330	DL&W Blue Coal Boxcar, 22		100
___	2201350	Freedom Isn't Free Boxcar, 22		100

■ Midwest Division

___	4	C&NW F3 Diesel A Unit, shell only, 77		80
___	5	Midwest Division Covered Quad Hopper, 78		43
___	1287	C&NW Refrigerator Car, 84		NRS
___	1988	IC Boxcar, 88		40
___	7600	Frisco "Spirit of '76" N5c Caboose "00003", 76		38
___	9872	PFE Reefer "00006", 79		410
___	52516	UP Boxcar "6464-5909", 09		90

■ Midwest Division: Museum Express

___	9264	ICG Covered Quad Hopper, 78	22	26
___	9289	C&NW N5c Caboose, 80	37	44
___	9785	Conrail Boxcar, 77		35
___	9786	C&NW Boxcar, 79		20

■ New England Division (NETCA)

___	1203	Boston & Maine NW2 Diesel, shell only, 72		65
___	5710	Canadian Pacific Reefer, 82	38	45
___	5716	Vermont Central Reefer, 83	25	30
___	6124	Delaware & Hudson Covered Quad Hopper, 84	25	30
___	8051	Hood's Milk Boxcar, 86	44	75
___	9181	Boston & Maine N5c Caboose, 77	23	35
___	9400	Conrail Boxcar, Tuscan or blue, 78	23	27
___	9415	Providence & Worcester Boxcar, 79	28	34
___	9423	NYNH&H Boxcar, 80	25	30
___	9445	Vermont Northern Boxcar, 81	29	39

CLUB CARS AND SPECIAL PRODUCTION		Exc	Mint
9753	Maine Central Boxcar, 75	24	34
9768	Boston & Maine Boxcar, 76	32	39
9785	Conrail Boxcar, 78	22	26
16911	B&M Flatcar with trailer, 95		150
22677	B&M Baked Beans Boxcar, 10		45
52001	B&M Quad Hopper with coal, 92	50	75
52016	B&M Gondola with coil covers, 93	55	65
52043	L.L. Bean Boxcar, 94	115	215
52080	B&M Flatcar "91095" with trailer, 95		215
52111	Ben & Jerry's Flatcar with trailer, 96		313
52212	Berkshire Brewing Reefer, 00		155
52236	Moxie Boxcar, 01		160
52270	Jenney Manufacturing Tank Car, 02		150
52306	NH Flatcar with New England Transportation trailer, 03		150
52352	Poland Spring Boxcar, 04		131
52379	CP Rail Flatcar w/W.B. Mason trailer, 05		75
52383	Fisk Tire Boxcar, 05		108
52397	D&H Flatcar w/Vermont Railway trailer, 06		90
52418	Indian Motorcycle Boxcar, 06		190
52434	New England Central Flatcar w/Cabot's trailer, 07		95
52448	Oilzum Tank Car Set of 2, 08		105
52457	Cape Cod Potato Chip Boxcar, 07		93
52484A	Cabot's Reefer, 08	100	250
52484B	Bay State Beer Reefer, 09		90
52589	B&M Flatcar w/Howard Johnson trailer, 11		100
58221	G. Fox & Co. Boxcar, 15	45	90
58522	Grafton & Upton Flatcar with Spag's trailer, 12		90

■ Ozark Division: Gateway Chapter

		Exc	Mint
5700	Oppenheimer Refrigerator Car, 81	55	110
9068	Reading Bobber Caboose, 76		20
9601	Illinois Central Gulf Hi-Cube Boxcar, 77		21
9767	Railbox Boxcar, 78		20
52003	"Meet Me In St. Louis" Flatcar with trailer, 92		520
58510	Frisco Flatcar w/Trailers, 11		100

■ Pacific Northwest Division

		Exc	Mint
52077	Great Northern Hi-Cube Boxcar "9695", 95		460

■ Rocky Mountain Division

		Exc	Mint
1971-1976	Fifth Anniversary Division Refrigerator Car, 76		75
52511	Colorado Yule Marble Co. Depressed-Center Flatcar "3", 08		90
52512	Colorado Yule Marble Co. Depressed-Center Flatcar "6", 08		90

■ Sacramento Sierra Chapter

			Exc	Mint
___	**6401**	Virginian Bay Window Caboose, 84		35
___	**9301**	U.S. Mail Operating Boxcar, 76	26	38
___	**9414**	Cotton Belt Boxcar, 80		35
___	**9427**	Bay Line Boxcar, 81		30
___	**9444**	Louisiana Midland Boxcar, 82		35
___	**9452**	Western Pacific Boxcar, 83		35
___	**9705**	D&RGW Boxcar, 75		38
___	**9723**	Western Pacific Boxcar, 73		29
___	**9726**	Erie-Lackawanna Boxcar, 79		23
___	**9730**	CP Rail Boxcar w/Chapter logo decal, 77		30
___	**9785**	Conrail Boxcar, 78		22

■ Southern Division

			Exc	Mint
___	**1976**	FEC F3 Diesel ABA, shells only, 76		275
___	**1986**	Southern Division Bunk Car, 86		30
___	**6111**	L&N Covered Quad Hopper, 83	20	22
___	**9287**	Southern N5c Caboose, 77	15	22
___	**9352**	Trailer Train Flatcar with circus trailers, 80	29	55
___	**9403**	Seaboard Coast Line Boxcar, 78		18
___	**9405**	Chattahoochie Boxcar, 79		21
___	**9443**	Florida East Coast Boxcar, 81		23
___	**9471**	ACL Boxcar, 84		23
___	**9482**	Norfolk & Southern Boxcar, 85		23
___	**16606**	Southern Searchlight Car, 88	17	24
___	**19942**	Southern Division 30th Anniversary Boxcar, 96		20

■ Western Division

			Exc	Mint
___	**6464-1967**	WP Convention Boxcar	217	280

TOY TRAIN OPERATING MUSEUM (GADSDEN-PACIFIC DIVISION)

			Exc	Mint
___	**17872**	Anaconda Ore Car, 88	60	72
___	**17878**	Magma Ore Car, 89	45	55
___	**17881**	Phelps Dodge Ore Car, 90	36	40
___	**17886**	Cyprus Ore Car, 91	26	31
___	**19961**	Inspiration Consolidated Copper Ore Car, 92	23	30
___	**52011**	Tucson, Cornelia & Gila Bend Ore Car, 93	20	29
___	**52027**	Pinto Valley Mine Ore Car, 94	20	29
___	**52071**	Copper Basin Railway Ore Car, 95		30
___	**52089**	SMARRCO Ore Car, 96		26
___	**52124**	El Paso & Southwestern Ore Car, 97		40
___	**52164**	SP Ore Car, 98		35
___	**52177**	Arizona Southern Ore Car, 99		35
___	**52213**	BHP Copper Ore Car, 00		29
___	**52248**	Tombstone & Western Ore Car, 01		40

CLUB CARS AND SPECIAL PRODUCTION

		Exc	Mint
52279	Dragoon & Northern Ore Car, 02		50 ___
52307	Twin Buttes Ore Car, 03		35 ___
52358	AJO & Southwestern Ore Car, 04		45 ___
52386	Ray & Gila Bend Ore Car, 05		45 ___
52421	Calabasas, Tucson & Northwestern Ore Car, 06		45 ___
52473	Mascot & Western Ore Car, 07		90 ___
52524	Tucson, Globe & Northern Ore Car, 08		42 ___
52558	Port of Tucson Ore Car, 09		45 ___
52579	Rosemont Copper Ore Car, 10		40 ___
52588	ASARCO Ore Car, 11		40 ___
58234	ASARCO Hayden Smelter Ore Car, 15	20	45 ___
58262	UP Ore Car, 16	20	45 ___
58513	Freeport-McMoRan Ore Car, 12		40 ___
58557	San Pedro & Southwestern Ore Car, 13		40 ___
58583	Arizona Eastern Ore Car, 14		42 ___

TOY TRAIN OPERATING SOCIETY (TTOS)

■ TTOS National Convention Cars

		Exc	Mint
1984	Sacramento Northern Boxcar, 84	65	85 ___
1985	Snowbird Covered Quad Hopper, 85	42	55 ___
6017	SP-type Caboose, blue, 68	125	210 ___
6017	SP-type Caboose, brown, 69	200	300 ___
6057	SP-type Caboose, orange, 69	125	210 ___
6076	Santa Fe Hopper (027), 70		103 ___
6167-1967	Hopper, olive drab with gold lettering, 67	25	85 ___
6257	SP-type Caboose, red, 69	125	210 ___
6476-1	LV Hopper, gray, 69	45	73 ___
6582	Portland Flatcar with wood, 86	44	55 ___
9326	Burlington Northern Bay Window Caboose, 82		25 ___
9347	Niagara Falls 3-D Tank Car, 79	38	46 ___
9355	Delaware & Hudson Bay Window Caboose, 82		50 ___
9361	C&NW Bay Window Caboose, 82	47	55 ___
9382	Florida East Coast Bay Window Caboose, 82		70 ___
9512	Summerdale Junction Passenger Car, 74	38	53 ___
9520	Phoenix Combination Car, 75	29	33 ___
9526	Snowbird Observation Car, 76	36	51 ___
9535	Columbus Baggage Car, 77	33	51 ___
9678	Hollywood Hi-Cube Boxcar, 78	25	32 ___
9684	Museum Exhibit Hi-Cube Boxcar, 84		50 ___
9868	Oklahoma City Reefer, 80	36	44 ___
9883	Phoenix Reefer, 83		50 ___
17871	NYC Flatcar "81487" with Kodak and Xerox trailers, 87	185	217 ___
17877	MKT 1-D Tank Car "3739469", 89	55	70 ___
17884	Columbus & Dayton Terminal Boxcar (std O), 90	32	41 ___
17889	SP Flatcar "15791" (std O) with trailer, 91	43	63 ___

CLUB CARS AND SPECIAL PRODUCTION			Exc	Mint
___	19963	Union Equity 3-bay ACF Hopper "86892" (std O), 92	30	38
___	52010	Weyerhaeuser DD Boxcar "838593" (std O), 93	25	42
___	52028	Ford Freight Car 3-pack, 94		100
___	52029	Ford 1-D Tank Car "12" (027), 94	33	40
___	52030	Ford Gondola "4023", 94	23	29
___	52031	Ford Hopper "1458" (027), 94	28	33
___	52057	Western Pacific Boxcar "64641995", 95	45	48
___	52087	New Mexico Central Boxcar "64641996", 96		55
___	52114	NYC Flatcar with Gleason and SASIB trailers, 97		58
___	52149	Conrail Flatcar with Blum coal shovel, 98		60
___	52192	SP Crane and Gondola Set, 00		75
___	52193	SP Gondola "6060", 00		50
___	52194	SP Crane Car "7111", 00		35
___	52231	British Columbia 1-D Tank Car, 01		25
___	52253	San Pedro, Los Angeles & Salt Lake Ry. Boxcar, 02	27	35
___	52288	D&RGW Cookie Boxcar, 03		20
___	52293	D&RGW 1-D Tank Car, 03		40
___	52334	Forest Service/Smokey Bear 60th Anniversary Boxcar, 04		80
___	52335	Forest Service/Smokey Bear 60th Anniversary 1-D Tank Car, 04		80
___	52351	BNSF Icicle Refrigerator Car w/EOT Device, 04	75	150
___	52378	Las Vegas & Tonopah Boxcar, 05		70
___	52410	SP Flatcar with 2 trailers, 06		70
___	52441	Pennsylvania Operating Hopper, 07		60
___	52445	Pennsylvania RR Boxcar, 07		68
___	52545	Erie "6464" Boxcar, 09		50
___	58053	Nevada Southern Generator Car, 17		110
___	58235	Forest Service/Smokey Bear Gondola, 15		70
___	58257	50th Anniversary Mint Car, 16		50
___	58333	Sierra Railroad Sierra Beer Boxcar, 13		70
___	1901480	Arkansas Valley Terminal Ry. Boxcar, 19		75

■ TTOS Division Cars

			Exc	Mint
___	52009	Sacramento Valley Division WP Boxcar, 93	34	44
___	52040	Wolverine Division GTW Flatcar w/Tractor and trailer, 94	42	51
___	52058	Central California Division Santa Fe Boxcar, 95	32	42
___	52086	Canadian Division Pacific Great Eastern Boxcar, 96	15	48
___	52113	Northeastern Division Genesee & Wyoming 3-bay Hopper, 97		34
___	52264	New Mexico Division Durango & Silverton Operating Hopper, 02		55

■ TTOS Southwestern Division

			Exc	Mint
___	19962	Southern Pacific 3-bay ACF Hopper "496035" (std O), 92	50	65
___	52047	Cotton Belt Wood-sided Caboose (std O), smoke, 93-94	60	68
___	52073	Pacific Fruit Express Reefer "459402" (std O), 95		65
___	52098	National Bureau of Standards Boxcar (std O), 96		47
___	52121	Mobilgas Tank Car "238" (std O), 97	40	75
___	52154	Pacific Fruit Express Reefer "459403" (std O), 98		53

CLUB CARS AND SPECIAL PRODUCTION		Exc	Mint
52287	Operating MX Missile Car, 02		55 ___
52385	Ward Kimball Boxcar, 05		55 ___
52431	Operating MX Missile Car, 06		60 ___
52476	Life Savers Tank Car, 07		85 ___
52515	Life Savers Wild Cherry Tank Car, 08		77 ___
52565	Life Savers Pep O Mint Tank Car, 09		60 ___
52569	Life Savers Butter Rum Tank Car, 10		62 ___
52591	Life Savers Wint O Green Tank Car, 11		62 ___
58208	Life Savers Peppermint Tank Car, 14		110 ___
58548	Life Savers Bay-Window Caboose, 13		82 ___

■ Other TTOS Production

		Exc	Mint
1983	Phoenix 3-D Tank Car, 83		100 ___
17894	Southern Pacific Tractor, 91	17	21 ___
27148	BNSF "4427" PS2 Hopper, 06		50 ___
52021	Weyerhaeuser Tractor and Trailer, 93	24	31 ___
52022	Union Pacific Boxcar, 93		400 ___
52032	Ford 1-D Tank Car (027) with Kughn inscription, 94	70	95 ___
52046	ACL Boxcar "16247", 94		110 ___
52053	Carail Boxcar, 94	50	55 ___
52068	Toy Train Parade Contadina Boxcar "16245", 94		55 ___
52078	Southern Pacific SD9 Diesel "5366", 96	90	235 ___
52079	Southern Pacific Bay Window Caboose, 96	45	55 ___
52084	Union Pacific I-Beam Flatcar "16380" with load, 95		155 ___
52201	SP Overnight Merchandise Service Boxcar "6400-201", 00		50 ___
52202	SP Overnight Merchandise Service Boxcar "6400-202", 00		50 ___
52203	SP Overnight Merchandise Service Boxcar "6400-203", 00		45 ___
52204	SP Overnight Merchandise Service Boxcar "6400-204", 00		35 ___
52205	SP Overnight Merchandise Service Boxcar 5-pack, 00		185 ___
52384	Transparent Damage Control Boxcar, 03		71 ___
52451	Pennsylvania "X2454" Boxcar, 07	107	175 ___
52505	Forest Service/Smokey Bear Flatcar with airplane, 08		45 ___
52525	SP "X6454" Boxcar, 08		50 ___
52526	SP "X6454" Boxcar, 08	8	165 ___
52547	C&NW Reefer, 09		84 ___

VIRGINIA TRAIN COLLECTORS (VTC)			
7679	Boxcar, 79		17 ___
7681	N5c Caboose, 81		23 ___
7682	Covered Quad Hopper, 82		26 ___
7683	Virginia Fruit Express Reefer, 83		26 ___
7684	Vitraco 3-D Tank Car, 84		26 ___
7685	Boxcar, 85		27 ___
7686	GP7 Diesel, 86		100 ___
7692-1	Baggage Car (027), 92	35	45 ___
7692-2	Combination Car (027), 92	35	45 ___

	CLUB CARS AND SPECIAL PRODUCTION		Exc	Mint
___	**7692-3**	Dining Car (027), 92	35	45
___	**7692-4**	Passenger Car (027), 92	35	45
___	**7692-5**	Vista Dome Car (027), 92	35	45
___	**7692-6**	Passenger Car (027), 92	35	45
___	**7692-7**	Observation Car (027), 92	35	45
___	**7696**	20th Anniversary Station, 96		65
___	**52002**	Shenandoah Dining Car, 92		65
___	**52060**	Tender "7694" with whistle, 94		70

NOTES

Section 7
BOXES 1945-1969

		Good P-5	Exc P-7
___ **020**	90-Degree Crossover, 45-61	3	8
___ **020X**	45-Degree Crossover	3	8
___ **022**	Switch Controller	2	3
___ **020**	"O" 90 Degree Crossover	4	8
___ **020X**	"O" 45 Degree Crossover	5	9
___ **022**	Remote Control Switches, pair (with both inserts)	4	10
___ **022**	Remote Control Switches, pair (yellow, with both inserts)	5	12
___ **022A**	Remote Control Switches, pair (with both inserts)	9	20
___ **25**	Bumper	2	4
___ **26**	Bumper	2	4
___ **30**	Water Tower	10	28
___ **35**	Boulevard Lamp	3	11
___ **36**	Operating Car Remote Control Set	5	13
___ **37**	Uncoupling Track Set	2	4
___ **38**	Operating Water Tower	22	76
___ **40**	Hookup Wire, 8 reels (dealer box)	30	317
___ **41**	U.S. Army Switcher	12	45
___ **42**	Manual Switches	2	11
___ **42**	Picatinny Arsenal Switcher	23	77
___ **44**	U.S. Army Mobile Launcher	19	91
___ **44**	U.S. Army Mobile Launcher (with orange sleeve)	34	139
___ **45**	U.S. Marines Mobile Launcher	33	99
___ **45/45N**	Automatic Gateman	5	19
___ **48**	Super O Insulated Straight Track, 6 pieces (dealer box)	9	28
___ **49**	Super O Insulated Curved Track, 6 pieces (dealer box)	8	26
___ **50**	Section Gang Car (early classic)	11	28
___ **50**	Section Gang Car (brown corrugated)	5	14
___ **50**	Section Gang Car (orange picture)	12	33
___ **51**	Navy Yard Switcher	17	52
___ **52**	Fire Car	23	60
___ **53**	Rio Grande Snowplow	28	79
___ **54**	Ballast Tamper	12	37
___ **55**	PRR Tie-Jector Car	13	36
___ **56**	Lamp Post	3	12
___ **56**	M&StL Mine Transport	36	120
___ **57**	AEC Switcher	49	193
___ **58**	Lamp Post	6	21
___ **58**	Great Northern Rotary Snow Blower	51	197
___ **59**	Minuteman Switcher	59	206
___ **60**	Lionelville Rapid Transit Trolley (classic)	10	33
___ **60**	Lionelville Rapid Transit Trolley (brown corrugated)	8	26
___ **64**	Highway Lamp Post	6	22
___ **65**	Handcar	27	128

BOXES		Good P-5	Exc P-7	
68	Executive Inspection Car	25	60	___
69	Maintenance Car	24	65	___
70	Yard Light	3	9	___
71	Lamp Post	2	6	___
75	Goose Neck Lamps	3	11	___
76	Boulevard Street Lamps	5	16	___
76	Boulevard Street Lamps (Hillside Checkerboard)	16	53	___
89	Flagpole	5	22	___
91	Circuit Breaker	4	16	___
92	Circuit Breaker		10	___
93	Water Tower	11	31	___
97	Coal Elevator	16	49	___
108	Trestle Set (overstamped)	7	19	___
110	Graduated Trestle Set	1	4	___
111	Elevated Trestle Set	3	9	___
112	Remote Control Switches, pair (Super O)	6	16	___
112LH	Remote Control Super O Switch, left-hand	5	13	___
112RH	Remote Control Super O Switch, right-hand	5	14	___
114	Newsstand with horn	7	23	___
115	Passenger Station (113-1, Star Corp. stamped on box)	25	107	___
118	Newsstand with whistle	7	21	___
122	Lamp Assortment	18	87	___
123	Lamp Assortment	18	87	___
123-60	Replacement Lamp Assortment	5	55	___
125	Whistle Shack	5	14	___
128	Animated Newsstand	9	26	___
130	60-degree Crossing (Super O)	2	5	___
132	Passenger Station	9	23	___
133	Passenger Station	8	21	___
138	Water Tower	10	27	___
140	Automatic Banjo Signal (classic)	4	11	___
142	Manual Switches, pair (Super O)	5	17	___
145	Automatic Gateman (brown corrugated)	7	18	___
145	Automatic Gateman (cellophane), 66	11	37	___
148	Dwarf Trackside Signal	5	16	___
150	Telegraph Pole Set	4	14	___
151	Automatic Semaphore	3	9	___
151	Automatic Semaphore (narrower box, earlier postwar)	6	17	___
151	Automatic Semaphore (blister pack enclosure)	14	57	___
152	Automatic Crossing Gate	3	18	___
153	Automatic Block Control Signal	5	12	___
154	Automatic Highway Signal (cellophane)	5	18	___
154	Automatic Highway Signal (all other boxes)	3	9	___
155	Blinking Light Signal	7	29	___
156	Station Platform	10	30	___
157	Station Platform	7	19	___

	BOXES		Good P-5	Exc P-7
___	**160**	Unloading Bin	20	68
___	**161**	Mail Pickup Set (with liner)	10	35
___	**163**	Single Target Block Signal (white box)	16	47
___	**164**	Log Loader	17	49
___	**167**	Whistle Controller	2	4
___	**175**	Rocket Launcher	18	54
___	**175-50**	Rocket, separate sale	51	147
___	**175-50**	Dealer Display Box, 6 rockets	75	402
___	**182**	Magnetic Crane	19	57
___	**192**	Operating Control Tower	37	137
___	**193**	Industrial Water Tower	11	39
___	**195**	Floodlight Tower	6	20
___	**195**	Floodlight Tower (cellophane)	7	29
___	**195-75**	Floodlight Extension, 8-bulb (classic)	6	26
___	**195-75**	Floodlight Extension, 8-bulb (white box)	9	42
___	**197**	Rotating Radar Antenna	10	34
___	**197-15**	Separate Sale Radar Head	26	79
___	**199**	Microwave Relay Tower	6	28
___	**202**	UP Alco Diesel A Unit	10	39
___	**204**	Santa Fe Alco AA Set (master carton)	65	196
___	**204**	Santa Fe Alco AA Set (P and T boxes)	24	94
___	**204P**	Santa Fe A Unit	15	42
___	**204T**	Santa Fe Diesel Dummy A Unit	18	50
___	**208**	Santa Fe Alco AA Set (master carton)	46	232
___	**208**	Santa Fe Alco AA Set (P and T boxes)	25	91
___	**208P**	Santa Fe Alco A Unit	16	60
___	**208T**	Santa Fe Alco Dummy A Unit	32	76
___	**209**	New Haven Alco AA Set (master carton)	89	360
___	**209**	New Haven Alco AA Set (P and T boxes)	72	262
___	**209P**	New Haven Alco A Unit	23	84
___	**209T**	New Haven Diesel Dummy A Unit	37	128
___	**210**	Texas Special Alco AA Set (P and T boxes)	18	66
___	**210P**	Texas Special Alco A Unit	9	38
___	**210T**	Texas Special Alco Dummy A Unit	21	69
___	**211**	Texas Special Alco AA Set (P and T boxes)	29	100
___	**211P**	Texas Special Alco A Unit (brown corrugated)	14	45
___	**212**	Santa Fe AA Master Carton	23	170
___	**212P**	USMC Alco Diesel A Unit	31	104
___	**212T**	USMC Diesel Dummy A Unit	194	669
___	**214**	Plate Girder Bridge (classic)	3	8
___	**214**	Plate Girder Bridge (Hillside orange picture)	6	19
___	**216**	Burlington Alco Diesel A Unit	26	94
___	**217**	B&M Alco AB Set (C and P boxes)	34	125
___	**217C**	B&M Alco B Unit	15	48
___	**217P**	B&M Alco A Unit	12	43
___	**217-16**	Sleeve for 217 and 218 outer boxes	26	81

BOXES		Good P-5	Exc P-7	
218	Santa Fe Alco AA Set (master carton)	18	89	___
218C	Santa Fe Alco Diesel B Unit	20	76	___
218P	Santa Fe Alco Diesel A Unit	16	60	___
218T	Santa Fe Diesel Dummy A Unit	21	62	___
220	Santa Fe Alco AA Set (P and T boxes)	21	79	___
220T	Santa Fe Alco Dummy A Unit	20	83	___
221	2-6-4 Locomotive	19	64	___
221T	Tender	11	40	___
221W	Whistling Tender	15	47	___
223P	Santa Fe Alco A Unit	15	51	___
224	2-6-2 Locomotive	19	76	___
224	U.S. Navy Alco AB Set (C and P boxes)	37	161	___
224C	U.S. Navy B Unit	40	101	___
224P	U.S. Navy Alco A unit	36	130	___
225	C & O Alco Diesel A Unit	11	42	___
226	B&M Alco Diesel AB Set (C and P boxes)	25	88	___
226C	B&M Alco Diesel B Unit	13	30	___
226P	B&M Alco Diesel A Unit	13	44	___
228P	CN Alco Diesel A Unit	20	70	___
229C	M&StL Alco B Unit	13	45	___
229P	M&StL Alco A Unit (brown corrugated)	12	41	___
230P	C&O Alco A Unit	13	44	___
231P	Rock Island Alco A Unit	12	56	___
233	2-4-2 Scout Locomotive	14	39	___
234W	Whistle Tender	10	33	___
235	2-4-2 Scout Locomotive	21	79	___
236	2-4-2 Scout Locomotive	9	27	___
237	2-4-2 Scout Locomotive	9	28	___
239	2-4-2 Scout Locomotive	18	39	___
238	Engine and Tender Master Carton	15	34	___
243	2-4-2 Scout Locomotive	9	28	___
243W	Tender	8	23	___
244T	Tender (overstamped 1625T box)	17	52	___
245	2-4-2 Scout Locomotive	17	45	___
246	2-4-2 Scout Locomotive	11	35	___
247	2-4-2 Scout Locomotive	11	30	___
247T	Tender	8	25	___
248	2-4-2 Scout Locomotive	10	34	___
249	2-4-2 Scout Locomotive	15	40	___
250	2-4-2 Scout Locomotive	10	27	___
250T	Tender	8	23	___
252	Crossing Gate	2	7	___
253	Block Control Signal	3	9	___
256	Illuminated Freight Station	12	33	___
257	Freight Station with diesel horn	10	28	___
260	Bumper (Hagerstown checkerboard)	4	10	___

BOXES		Good P-5	Exc P-7
___ 260	Bumper (all other boxes)	2	4
___ 262	Highway Crossing Gate	4	19
___ 264	Operating Forklift Platform	18	56
___ 282	Portal Gantry Crane	37	77
___ 299	Code Transmitter Beacon Set	11	37
___ 308	Railroad Sign Set	3	10
___ 309	Yard Sign Set	3	10
___ 310	Billboard Set	2	6
___ 313	Bascule Bridge	33	135
___ 314	Scale Model Girder Bridge	4	12
___ 315	Illuminated Trestle Bridge	21	68
___ 316	Trestle Bridge	7	22
___ 317	Trestle Bridge	6	17
___ 321	Trestle Bridge	5	15
___ 321-100	Trestle Bridge	8	20
___ 332	Arch-Under Trestle Bridge	5	15
___ 334	Operating Dispatching Board	11	44
___ 342	Culvert Loader	24	72
___ 345	Culvert Unloader	23	73
___ 348	Manual Culvert Unloader	21	60
___ 350	Engine Transfer Table	16	63
___ 350-50	Transfer Table Extension	15	48
___ 352	Ice Depot	18	56
___ 353	Trackside Control Signal	5	15
___ 356	Operating Freight Station	9	33
___ 356-35	Baggage Trucks Set	11	35
___ 362	Barrel Loader	7	23
___ 362-78	Wooden Barrels	2	5
___ 364	Conveyor Lumber Loader	8	26
___ 365	Dispatching Station	12	35
___ 375	Turntable	19	61
___ 394	Rotaring Beacon	6	21
___ 394-37	Rotating Beacon Cap	2	6
___ 395	Floodlight Tower	6	21
___ 397	Operating Coal Loader	9	32
___ 397	Operating Coal Loader (separate label on box)	13	44
___ 400	B&O Passenger Rail Diesel Car	18	48
___ 404	B&O Baggage-Mail Rail Diesel Car	30	78
___ 410	Billboard Blinker	4	15
___ 413	Countdown Control Panel	6	17
___ 415	Diesel Fueling Station	12	37
___ 419	Heliport Control Tower	32	120
___ 443	Missile Launching Platform	11	30
___ 445	Switch Tower	8	23
___ 448	Missile Firing Range Set	12	46
___ 450	Operating Signal Bridge	4	15

BOXES		Good P-5	Exc P-7	
452	Overhead Gantry Signal	10	36	___
455	Operating Oil Derrick	18	60	___
456	Coal Ramp	16	44	___
460	Piggyback Transportation Set	14	43	___
460-150	Two Trailers	66	212	___
461	Platform with truck and trailer	11	42	___
462	Derrick Platform Set	41	144	___
464	Lumber Mill	10	37	___
465	Sound Dispatching Station	11	35	___
470	Missile Launching Platform	7	26	___
494	Rotary Beacon (classic)	6	22	___
497	Coaling Station	18	48	___
600	MKT NW2 Switcher	22	64	___
601	Seaboard NW2 Switcher	25	76	___
602	Seaboard NW2 Switcher	30	93	___
610	Erie NW2 Switcher	16	57	___
611	Jersey Central NW2 Switcher (overstamped 621 box)	43	102	___
613	UP NW2 Switcher	27	82	___
614	Alaska NW2 Switcher	44	148	___
616	Santa Fe NW2 Switcher	24	98	___
617	Santa Fe NW2 Switcher	32	100	___
621	Jersey Central NW2 Switcher	21	65	___
622	Santa Fe NW2 Switcher	32	95	___
623	Santa Fe NW2 Switcher	19	73	___
624	C&O NW2 Switcher	26	73	___
625	Lehigh Valley GE 44-ton Switcher	73	259	___
626	B&O GE 44-ton Switcher	44	159	___
628	Northern Pacific GE 44-ton Switcher	20	73	___
629	Burlington GE 44-ton Switcher	43	162	___
634	Santa Fe NW2 Switcher	28	135	___
637	2-6-4 Locomotive	15	48	___
637LTS	2-6-4 Locomotive and Tender (master carton)	47	185	___
646	4-6-4 Locomotive	21	56	___
665	4-6-4 Locomotive	21	52	___
665LTS	4-6-4 Locomotive and Tender (master carton)	70	252	___
671	6-8-6 Steam Turbine Locomotive	24	71	___
671R	6-8-6 Steam Turbine Locomotive	51	138	___
671W	Whistle Tender	18	92	___
671-75	Smoke Lamp, 12 volt	3	8	___
675	2-6-2 Locomotive (classic), 47-49	18	67	___
675	2-6-2 Locomotive (brown corrugated), 52	39	90	___
681	6-8-6 Steam Turbine Locomotive	44	129	___
681LTS	6-8-6 Steam Turbine Locomotive and Tender (master carton)	163	513	___
682	6-8-6 Steam Turbine Locomotive	48	150	___
682LTS	6-8-6 Steam Turbine Locomotive and Tender (master carton)	338	875	___

BOXES		Good P-5	Exc P-7
685	4-6-4 Hudson Locomotive	25	71
685LTS	4-6-4 Hudson Locomotive and Tender (master carton)	155	457
726	2-8-4 Berkshire Locomotive, 46	54	156
726	2-8-4 Berkshire Locomotive (after 1946)	41	119
726RR	2-8-4 Berkshire Locomotive	25	71
736	2-8-4 Berkshire Locomotive, 50	33	97
736	2-8-4 Berkshire Locomotive	28	81
736X	2-8-4 Berkshire Locomotive	31	93
736LTS	2-8-4 Berkshire Locomotive and Tender (master carton)	97	259
736W	Pennsylvania Tender	17	68
746	N&W 4-8-4 Locomotive	62	185
746LTS	N&W 4-8-4 Locomotive and Tender (master carton)	246	668
746W	N&W Whistle Tender	35	148
746WX	N&W Whistle Tender, long stripe	50	136
760	Curved Track	8	24
773	4-6-4 Hudson Locomotive, 50	95	282
773	4-6-4 Hudson Locomotive, 64-66	66	175
773LTS	4-6-4 Hudson Locomotive and Tender (master carton), 50	166	631
773LTS	4-6-4 Hudson and Whistle Tender (master carton), 64-66	96	307
773W	NYC Tender	42	96
810	Milwaukee Road Freight Set	70	400
920-2	Tunnel Portals	6	20
920	Scenic Display Set	13	39
927	Lubricating Kit	2	6
928	Maintenance and Lubricating Kit	5	20
943	Ammo Dump	5	14
951	Farm Set	13	40
952	Figure Set	11	35
953	Figure Set	13	53
957	Farm Building and Animal Set	15	46
959	Barn Set	15	45
960	Barnyard Set	10	47
961	School Set	30	139
963	Frontier Set	17	58
965	Farm Set	14	53
966	Firehouse Set	14	53
969	Construction Set	11	40
970	Ticket Booth	11	50
972	Landscape Tree Assortment	10	35
981	Freight Yard Set	11	36
983	Farm Set	12	41
984	Railroad Set	14	55
986	Farm Set	20	76
987	Town Set		185
1000W	Steam Freight Set	27	90

BOXES		Good P-5	Exc P-7	
1001	Diesel Freight Set	18	65	___
1001	2-4-2 Scout Locomotive	7	33	___
1001T	Tender	4	12	___
1002	Gondola	3	8	___
X1004	PRR Baby Ruth Boxcar	3	8	___
1005	Sunoco 1-D Tank Car	3	8	___
1007	LL SP-type Caboose	3	8	___
1009	Manumatic Track Section	4	11	___
1019	Remote Control Track Set (027)	3	6	___
1024	Manual Switches for 027 Track Set	6	15	___
1024	Manual Switches	3	6	___
1025	Illuminated Bumper (027)	2	5	___
1032	Transformer, 75 watts	2	5	___
1033	Transformer, 90 watts	3	10	___
1034	Transformer, 75 watts	2	19	___
1041	Transformer, 50 watts	2	7	___
1041	Transformer, 60 watts	2	8	___
1043	Transformer, 50 watts	3	9	___
1043-500	Transformer, 50 watts, ivory	33	85	___
1044	Transformer, 90 watts	3	11	___
1045	Operating Watchman	5	19	___
1047	Operating Switchman	23	75	___
1060	2-4-2 Locomotive (brown corrugated)	16	57	___
1107	Steam Freight Set	13	45	___
1109	Steam Freight Set	12	40	___
1110	2-4-2 Locomotive	5	18	___
1112	Scout Set	7	23	___
1113	Scout Set	10	32	___
1117	Scout Steam Freight Set	14	35	___
1119	Scout Set	9	30	___
1120	2-4-2 Scout Locomotive	5	16	___
1121	027 Remote Control Switches, pair	2	7	___
1121LH	027 Remote Control Switch, left-hand	2	6	___
1121RH	027 Remote Control Switch, right-hand	2	6	___
1122	027 Remote Control Switches, pair	2	8	___
1130	2-4-2 Locomotive	6	21	___
1130T	Tender (classic)	4	13	___
1130T	Tender (orange perforated)	11	30	___
1130T-500	Tender, pink, from Girls Set	46	171	___
1232	Transformer, 75 watts, made for export	4	11	___
1407B	Steam Switcher Work Set	57	249	___
1417WS	Steam Work Train Set	28	122	___
1423W	Steam Freight Set	21	97	___
1425B	Steam Switcher Freight Set	50	203	___
1429WS	Steam Freight Set	28	109	___
1431	Steam Freight Set	27	68	___

BOXES		Good P-5	Exc P-7
___ 1432W	027 Steam Passenger Set	50	216
___ 1433W	Steam Freight Set	14	37
___ 1435WS	Steam Freight Set	10	35
___ 1447WS	Turbine Locomotive Set	39	148
___ 1451WS	027 Steam Freight Set	23	95
___ 1453WS	027 Steam Freight Set	19	71
___ 1455WS	Steam Freight Set	23	82
___ 1457B	Santa Fe Freight Set (marked "1457"), 49	39	151
___ 1457B	Santa Fe Freight Set, 50	43	153
___ 1459WS	Steam Freight Set	33	85
___ 1463WS	Steam Freight Set	31	85
___ 1464W	Union Pacific Diesel Passenger Set	119	463
___ 1465	Steam Freight Set	19	66
___ 1467W	Union Pacific Freight Set	40	137
___ 1469WS	Steam Freight Set	23	76
___ 1471	Steam Freight Set	20	68
___ 1471WS	Steam Freight Set	21	71
___ 1473WS	Steam Freight Set	25	81
___ 1475WS	Steam Freight Set	19	80
___ 1479WS	Steam Freight Set	31	118
___ 1481WS	Steam Freight Set	22	75
___ 1483WS	Steam Freight Set	28	94
___ 1485WS	Steam Freight Set	21	65
___ 1500	Steam Freight Set	12	45
___ 1502WS	Steam Freight Set	129	448
___ 11480	Diesel Freight Set	48	163
___ 1503WS	Steam Freight Set	29	70
___ 1505WS	Steam Freight Set	28	89
___ 1507WS	Steam Freight Set	25	78
___ 1511S	Steam Freight Set	18	59
___ 1513S	Steam Freight Set	20	66
___ 1515WS	Steam Freight Set	30	95
___ 1517W	Texas Special Freight Set	44	155
___ 1519WS	Steam Freight Set	44	154
___ 1520W	Texas Special Passenger Set	170	651
___ 1521WS	Steam Work Train Set	64	225
___ 1523	Diesel Freight Set	35	131
___ 1525	Diesel Freight Set	19	63
___ 1527	027 Steam Work Train Set	42	147
___ 1529	Pennsylvania Diesel Freight Set	58	202
___ 1531W	Diesel Freight Set	29	100
___ 1533WS	Steam Freight Set	23	68
___ 1534W	Burlington Diesel Passenger Set	116	382
___ 1535W	Diesel Freight Set	62	215
___ 1536W	Diesel Passenger Set	80	371
___ 1537WS	Steam Freight Set	38	136

BOXES		Good P-5	Exc P-7	
1538WS	Hudson Passenger Set	190	678	___
1539W	Santa Fe Diesel Freight Set	70	226	___
1541WS	Steam Freight Set	48	169	___
1542	Electric Freight Set	12	49	___
1543	Lehigh Valley Freight Set	13	50	___
1547S	Steam Freight Set	17	55	___
1549	Steam Work Train Set	25	83	___
1551W	Diesel Freight Set	10	43	___
1552W	Diesel Passenger Set	65	251	___
1553W	Diesel Freight Set	25	76	___
1555WS	027 Steam Freight Set	22	61	___
1557	Diesel Freight Set	27	80	___
1559W	MILW Diesel Freight Set	28	88	___
1561WS	Steam Freight Set	21	55	___
1562W	Burlington GP7 Diesel Passenger Set	38	132	___
1569	UP Diesel Freight Set	17	59	___
1571	LV Diesel Freight Set	18	62	___
1573	Steam Freight Set	20	64	___
1575	Diesel Freight Set	21	61	___
1577S	Steam Freight Set	32	75	___
1578S	Steam Passenger Set	139	495	___
1579S	Steam Freight Set	22	65	___
1581	Jersey Central Mixed Set	22	77	___
1583WS	Steam Freight Set	19	61	___
1585W	Diesel Freight Set	23	72	___
1586	Diesel Passenger Set	29	100	___
1587S	Girls Train Set	398	1354	___
1589WS	027 Steam Freight Set	33	122	___
1590	Steam Freight Set	16	62	___
1591	USMC Military Set	111	500	___
1593	UP Diesel Work Train Set	28	95	___
1599W	Texas Special Freight Set	27	96	___
1600	Diesel Passenger Set	137	532	___
1601W	Wabash GP7 Diesel Set	46	202	___
1603WS	Steam Freight Set	32	89	___
1605W	Santa Fe Diesel Freight Set	43	160	___
1607WS	Steam Work Train Set	13	44	___
1608W	New Haven Passenger Set	130	715	___
1609W	Steam Freight Set	22	81	___
1611	027 Alaska Diesel Freight Set	55	196	___
1612	027 General Set	30	112	___
1613S	Steam Freight Set	24	84	___
1615	B&M Diesel Freight Set	22	77	___
1615	0-4-0 Locomotive	19	64	___
1615LTS	0-4-0 Locomotive and Tender (master carton)	46	143	___
1615T	Tender	10	42	___

BOXES			Good P-5	Exc P-7
___	1617S	Steam Work Train	63	140
___	1619W	Santa Fe Diesel Freight Set	33	104
___	1621WS	027 Steam Freight Set (brown corrugated)	62	199
___	1621WS	027 Steam Freight Set (suitcase)	31	103
___	1623W	NP Diesel Freight Set	50	180
___	1625	0-4-0 Locomotive	29	108
___	1625T	Tender	26	76
___	1625WS	Steam Freight Set	28	101
___	1626W	Santa Fe Diesel Passenger Set	77	215
___	1626W	Santa Fe Diesel Passenger Set		123
___	1627S	Stream Freight Set	20	41
___	1629WS	C&O Diesel Freight Set	18	72
___	1631WS	027 Steam Freight Set	21	63
___	1633	U.S. Navy Diesel Freight Set	103	339
___	1635WS	Steam Freight Set	33	118
___	1637	Santa Fe Diesel Freight Set	21	73
___	1639WS	Steam Freight Set	16	38
___	1640-100	Presidential Kit	13	50
___	1643	C&O Diesel Freight Set	15	54
___	1645	Diesel Freight Set	28	88
___	1647	U.S. Marines Military Set	35	111
___	1648	Steam Freight Set	10	43
___	1649	Santa Fe Diesel Freight Set	21	72
___	1650	Steam Military Set	28	95
___	1651	Passenger Train Set	36	136
___	1654	2-4-2 Locomotive	8	29
___	1654W	Whistle Tender	14	23
___	1655	2-4-2 Locomotive	13	40
___	1656	0-4-0 Locomotive	26	105
___	1656LTS	4-4-0 Locomotive and Tender (master carton)	53	200
___	1665	0-4-0 Locomotive	37	146
___	1666	2-6-2 Locomotive	14	53
___	1682T	Tender	5	18
___	1800	General Gift Pack	22	102
___	1805	Marine Land Sea and Air Gift Pack	532	1199
___	1809	Western Gift Pack	14	60
___	1862	4-4-0 Civil War General Locomotive	22	80
___	1862T	Tender	13	47
___	1865	Western & Atlantic Coach	10	41
___	1866	Western & Atlantic Mail-Baggage Car	10	41
___	1872	4-4-0 Civil War General Locomotive	33	100
___	1872LTS	4-4-0 Locomotive and Tender (master carton)	100	400
___	1872T	Tender	16	49
___	1875	Western & Atlantic Coach	38	148
___	1875W	Western & Atlantic Coach, whistle	20	94
___	1876	Western & Atlantic Baggage Car	16	65

BOXES		Good P-5	Exc P-7	
1877	Flatcar with fence and horses	14	51	___
2001	Track Make-up Kit (027)	800	2000	___
2002	Track Make-up Kit (027)	600	1400	___
2016	2-6-4 Locomotive	10	34	___
2018	2-6-4 Locomotive	11	34	___
2018-14	Sleeve for Outer Box	6	20	___
2020	6-8-6 Steam Turbine Locomotive	18	68	___
2020W	Tender	12	55	___
2023	Union Pacific Alco AA Set (master carton), 50	31	115	___
2023	Union Pacific Alco AA Set (master carton), 51	30	94	___
2025	2-6-2 or 2-6-4 Locomotive	15	67	___
2026	2-6-2 or 2-6-4 Locomotive	12	48	___
2028	Pennsylvania GP7 Diesel	29	118	___
2029	2-6-4 Locomotive	8	126	___
2031	Rock Island Alco AA Set (master carton), 52	53	163	___
2032	Erie Alco AA Set (master carton)	39	111	___
2033	Uinion Pacific Alco AA Set (master carton)	28	92	___
2034	2-4-2 Scout Locomotive	10	39	___
2035	2-6-4 Locomotive	20	66	___
2036	2-6-4 Locomotive	12	45	___
2036LTS	2-6-4 Locomotive and Tender (master carton)	400	1581	___
2037	2-6-4 Locomotive (brown corrugated)	10	32	___
2037-500	2-6-4 Locomotive, pink, from Girls Set	75	328	___
2046	4-6-4 Locomotive	22	82	___
2046LTS	4-6-4 Locomotive and Tender (master carton)	83	271	___
2046T	Lionel Lines Tender, for export	21	72	___
2046W	Lionel Lines Tender (early classic, with liner)	16	63	___
2046W	Lionel Lines Tender (marked "2046")	21	78	___
2046W	Pennsylvania Tender	30	99	___
2046W-50	Pennsylvania Tender	12	55	___
2055	4-6-4 Locomotive	20	52	___
2055LTS	4-6-4 Locomotive and Tender (master carton)	64	222	___
2056	4-6-4 Locomotive	21	57	___
2065	4-6-4 Locomotive	19	56	___
2103W	Steam Freight Set	25	90	___
2105WS	Steam Freight Set	32	114	___
2113WS	Steam Freight Set	44	182	___
2120WS	Steam Passenger Set	100	565	___
2121WS	Steam Freight Set	34	162	___
2124W	GG1 Passenger Set	180	952	___
2125WS	Steam Freight Set	44	110	___
2126WS	Steam Turbine Passenger Set	78	483	___
2129WS	Steam Freight Set	113	600	___
2136WS	Steam Passenger Set	42	164	___
2139W	GG1 Freight Set	146	669	___
2140WS	Steam Turbine Passenger Set	51	535	___

	BOXES		Good P-5	Exc P-7
___	**2141WS**	Steam Turbine Freight Set	35	165
___	**2145WS**	Steam Freight Set	87	292
___	**2146W**	Berkshire Passenger Set	97	513
___	**2147WS**	Steam Freight Set	53	140
___	**2148WS**	Hudson Passenger Set	450	1666
___	**2149**	Santa Fe Diesel Freight Set	71	311
___	**2151W**	F3 Freight Set	59	300
___	**2153WS**	Steam Freight Set	47	173
___	**2155WS**	Berkshire Freight Set	57	231
___	**2159W**	GG1 Freight Set	107	452
___	**2161W**	Santa Fe Twin Diesel Freight Set	40	161
___	**2163WS**	Steam Freight Set	40	160
___	**2165WS**	Steam Freight Set	40	139
___	**2167WS**	Steam Freight Set	36	147
___	**2171W**	NYC Diesel Freight Set	43	185
___	**2173WS**	Steam Freight Set	47	174
___	**2175W**	Santa Fe Diesel Freight Set	44	173
___	**2177WS**	Steam Freight Set	18	68
___	**2179WS**	Steam Freight Set	26	88
___	**2183WS**	Steam Freight Set	34	113
___	**2185W**	NYC Diesel Freight Set	34	116
___	**2187WS**	Steam Freight Set	20	75
___	**2190W**	Santa Fe Diesel Passenger Set	38	157
___	**2191W**	Santa Fe Diesel Freight Set	37	160
___	**2193W**	NYC Diesel Freight Set	38	124
___	**2201WS**	Steam Freight Set	44	126
___	**2203WS**	Steam Freight Set	43	231
___	**2205WS**	Steam Freight Set	27	98
___	**2207W**	Santa Fe Diesel Freight Set	36	137
___	**2209W**	NYC Diesel Freight Set	41	142
___	**2211WS**	Steam Freight Set	33	134
___	**2213WS**	Steam Freight Set	30	108
___	**2217WS**	Steam Turbine Freight Set	54	201
___	**2219W**	Diesel Freight Set	75	308
___	**2221WS**	Steam Freight Set	32	127
___	**2222WS**	Hudson Passenger Set	123	528
___	**2223W**	Lackawanna FM Freight Set	131	446
___	**2225T**	Tender	18	77
___	**2225WS**	Steam Freight Set	43	170
___	**2226W**	Tender	33	101
___	**2226WX**	Lionel Lines Tender	40	122
___	**2227W**	Santa Fe Diesel Freight Set	62	264
___	**2229W**	NYC Diesel Freight Set	34	125
___	**2231W**	Southern Diesel Freight Set	75	313
___	**2234W**	Santa Fe Passenger Set	135	319
___	**2235W**	Milwaukee Road Diesel Freight Set	41	164

BOXES		Good P-5	Exc P-7	
2237WS	Steam Freight Set	36	142	___
2239W	Illinois Central Freight Set	88	405	___
2240	Wabash F3 AB Set (C and P boxes)	59	217	___
2240	Wabash F3 AB Set (master carton)	129	610	___
2240C	Wabash F3 B Unit	40	143	___
2240P	Wabash F3 A Unit	30	93	___
2241WS	Steam Freight Set	21	84	___
2242	New Haven F3 AB Set (C and P boxes)	91	513	___
2242	New Haven F3 AB Set (master carton)	482	937	___
2242C	New Haven F3 B Unit	78	319	___
2242P	New Haven F3 A Unit	79	301	___
2243	Santa Fe F3 AB Set (C and P boxes)	30	91	___
2243	Santa Fe F3 AB Set (master carton)	40	179	___
2243C	Santa Fe F3 B Unit	22	76	___
2243P	Santa Fe F3 A Unit	22	74	___
2243W	Diesel Freight Set	32	128	___
2244W	Wabash Passenger Set	188	815	___
2245	Texas Special F3 AB Set (C and P boxes)	55	181	___
2245	Texas Special F3 AB Set (master carton)	245	712	___
2245C	Texas Special F3 B Unit	34	119	___
2245P	Texas Special F3 A Unit	22	83	___
2247W	Wabash F3 Diesel Freight Set	67	268	___
2251W	Diesel Freight Set	43	170	___
2254W	Pennsylvania GG1 Passenger Set, 55	246	906	___
2255W	Diesel Work Train Set	43	140	___
2257	SP-type Caboose	5	18	___
2257WS	Steam Freight Set	29	106	___
2259W	New Haven Electric Freight Set	40	144	___
2261WS	Steam Freight Set	28	90	___
2263W	New Haven Freight Set	42	193	___
2265WS	Steam Freight Set	31	104	___
2267W	Diesel Freight Set	51	205	___
2269W	B&O Diesel Freight Set	129	569	___
2270W	Jersey Central Passenger Set	304	1108	___
2271W	Pennsylvania GG1 Freight Set	81	323	___
2273W	Milwaukee Road Diesel Freight Set	128	486	___
2274W	Pennsylvania Passenger Set	191	671	___
2275W	Wabash GP7 Freight Set	49	131	___
2276W	Budd Passenger Set	67	320	___
2277WS	Work Train Set	41	153	___
2285W	Diesel Freight Set	87	243	___
2279W	NH Electric Freight Set	68	215	___
2283W	Steam Freight Set	35	123	___
2289WS	Berkshire Super O Freight Set	53	201	___
2291W	Rio Grande Diesel Freight Set	116	585	___
2292WS	Steam Passenger Set	110	582	___

	BOXES		Good P-5	Exc P-7
___	**2293W**	Pennsylvania GG1 Freight Set	179	858
___	**2295WS**	N&W Steam Freight Set	168	699
___	**2296W**	Canadian Pacific Passenger Set	330	1161
___	**2297WS**	N&W Steam Freight Set	129	689
___	**2321**	Lackawanna FM Train Master Diesel	33	122
___	**2322**	Virginian FM Train Master Diesel	35	158
___	**2328**	Burlington GP7 Diesel	46	126
___	**2329**	Virginian Electric Locomotive	59	235
___	**2330**	Pennsylvania GG1 Electric Locomotive	79	231
___	**2331**	Virginian FM Train Master Diesel	34	135
___	**2332**	Pennsylvania GG1 Electric Locomotive	40	179
___	**2333**	NYC F3 AA Set (master carton)	43	151
___	**2333**	NYC F3 AA Set (P and T boxes)	40	157
___	**2333P**	NYC F3 A Unit (brown corrugated)	21	78
___	**2333**	Santa Fe F3 AA Set (master carton)	51	191
___	**2333**	Santa Fe F3 AA Set (P and T boxes)	33	109
___	**2333T**	Santa Fe F3 Dummy A Unit	25	133
___	**2333P**	Santa Fe F3 A Unit	21	82
___	**2337**	Wabash GP7 Diesel, 58	28	121
___	**2338**	MILW GP7 Diesel (classic)	25	100
___	**2338**	MILW GP7 Diesel (brown corrugated)	16	58
___	**2338X**	MILW GP7 Diesel (brown corrugated marked “2338X”)	25	140
___	**2339**	Wabash GP7 Diesel, 57	32	117
___	**2340-1**	Pennsylvania GG1 Electric, tuscan	136	226
___	**2340-25**	Pennsylvania GG1 Electric, green, gold stripes	34	263
___	**2341**	Jersey Central FM Train Master Diesel	218	868
___	**2343**	Santa Fe F3 AA Set (master carton)	42	155
___	**2343**	Santa Fe F3 AA Set (P and T boxes)	34	121
___	**2343C**	Santa Fe F3 B Unit	23	89
___	**2343P**	Santa Fe F3 A Unit	20	61
___	**2343T**	Santa Fe F3 Dummy Unit	27	88
___	**2344**	NYC F3 AA Set (master carton)	65	255
___	**2344**	NYC F3 AA Set (P and T boxes)	51	191
___	**2344C**	NYC F3 B Unit	30	93
___	**2344P**	NYC F3 A Unit	44	112
___	**2344T**	NYC F3 Dummy Unit	34	155
___	**2345**	Western Pacific F3 AA Set (master carton)	163	634
___	**2345**	Western Pacific F3 AA Set (P and T boxes, brown corrugated)	55	276
___	**2345P**	Western Pacific F3 A Unit	38	140
___	**2345T**	Western Pacific F3 Dummy A Unit	63	199
___	**2346**	B&M GP9 Diesel	33	120
___	**2347**	C&O GP9 Diesel	550	1425
___	**2348**	M&StL GP9 Diesel	33	128
___	**2349**	Northern Pacific GP9 Diesel	57	206
___	**2349-12**	Sleeve for 2349 and 2359 outer boxes	20	83

BOXES		Good P-5	Exc P-7	
2350	New Haven EP-5 Electric Locomotive	25	86	___
2351	Milwaukee Road EP-5 Electric Locomotive	38	141	___
2352	Pennsylvania EP-5 Electric Locomotive	48	184	___
2353	Santa Fe F3 AA Set (master carton)	55	197	___
2353	Santa Fe F3 AA Set (P and T boxes)	42	165	___
2353P	Santa Fe F3 A Unit (brown corrugated)	19	62	___
2353T	Santa Fe F3 Dummy Unit	23	86	___
2354	NYC F3 AA Set (master carton)	51	228	___
2354P	NYC F3 A Unit (brown corrugated)	37	111	___
2354T	NYC F3 Dummy Unit	39	123	___
2355	Western Pacific F3 AA Set (master carton)	106	577	___
2355	Western Pacific F3 AA Set (P and T boxes)	60	240	___
2355P	Western Pacific F3 A Unit	44	171	___
2355T	Western Pacific F3 Dummy A Unit	44	153	___
2356	Southern F3 AA Set (master carton)	87	379	___
2356C	Southern F3 B Unit	56	201	___
2356P	Southern F3 A Unit	33	121	___
2356T	Southern F3 Dummy Unit	59	193	___
2357	SP-type Caboose	4	14	___
2358	Great Northern EP-5 Electric Locomotive	60	218	___
2358-12	Outer Box Sleeve	48	160	___
2359	Boston & Maine GP9 Diesel	23	86	___
2360-10	Pennsylvania GG1 Electric Locomotive, tuscan	113	270	___
2360-25	Pennsylvania GG1 Electric Locomotive, green	43	178	___
2363	Illinois Central F3 AB Set (master carton)	143	552	___
2363	Illinois Central F3 AB Set (C and P boxes)	76	309	___
2363C	Illinois Central F3 B Unit	48	132	___
2363P	Illinois Central F3 A Unit	34	150	___
2365	C&O GP7 Diesel	21	74	___
2367	Wabash F3 AB Diesel Set Master Carton	45	89	___
2367C	Wabash F3 B Unit	48	234	___
2367P	Wabash F3 A Unit	44	160	___
2368	B&O F3 AB Set (master carton)	216	836	___
2368C	B&O F3 B Unit	71	363	___
2368P	B&O F3 A Unit	42	229	___
2373	CP F3 AA Set (P and T boxes)	147	499	___
2373P	CP F3 A Unit	50	214	___
2373T	CP F3 Dummy A Unit	78	229	___
2378	Milwaukee Road F3 AB Set (master carton)	159	684	___
2378C	Milwaukee Road F3 B Unit	76	267	___
2378P	Milwaukee Road F3 A Unit	59	330	___
2379	Denver and Rio Grande F3 AB Set (master carton)	155	613	___
2379C	Rio Grande F3 B Unit	68	199	___
2379P	Rio Grande F3 A Unit	49	161	___
2383	Santa Fe F3 AA Units (master carton)	55	280	___
2383P	Santa Fe F3 A Unit	23	77	___

	BOXES		Good P-5	Exc P-7
___	**2383T**	Santa Fe F3 Dummy Unit	29	91
___	**2400**	Maplewood Pullman Car	14	48
___	**2401**	Hillside Observation Car	14	48
___	**2402**	Chatham Pullman Car	14	49
___	**2403B**	Tender with bell	25	81
___	**2404**	Santa Fe Vista Dome Car	13	38
___	**2405**	Santa Fe Pullman Car	13	38
___	**2406**	Santa Fe Observation Car	13	38
___	**2408**	Santa Fe Vista Dome Car	12	38
___	**2409**	Santa Fe Pullman Car	13	43
___	**2410**	Santa Fe Observation Car	12	43
___	**2411**	Lionel Lines Flatcar	9	32
___	**2412**	Santa Fe Vista Dome Car	15	47
___	**2414**	Santa Fe Pullman Car	15	47
___	**2416**	Santa Fe Observation Car (orange perforated)	14	58
___	**2416**	Santa Fe Observation Car (orange picture)	15	46
___	**2419**	DL&W Work Caboose	11	33
___	**2420**	DL&W Work Caboose with searchlight	21	57
___	**2421**	Maplewood Pullman Car	14	44
___	**2422**	Chatham Pullman Car	14	44
___	**2423**	Hillside Observation Car	15	45
___	**2426W**	Hudson Tender (early classic)	76	257
___	**2426W**	Hudson Tender (middle classic)	66	226
___	**2429**	Livingston Pullman Car	24	69
___	**2430**	Pullman Car, blue	15	44
___	**2431**	Observation Car, blue	15	45
___	**2432**	Clifton Vista Dome Car	13	43
___	**2434**	Newark Pullman Car	12	41
___	**2435**	Elizabeth Pullman Car	20	58
___	**2436**	Mooseheart Observation Car	13	42
___	**2436**	Mooseheart Observation Car (classic)	12	40
___	**2440**	Pullman Car, green	12	43
___	**2441**	Observation Car, green	12	43
___	**2442**	Pullman Car, brown	12	45
___	**2442**	Clifton Vista Dome Car	16	46
___	**2443**	Observation Car, brown	10	43
___	**2444**	Newark Pullman Car	15	47
___	**2445**	Elizabeth Pullman Car	25	89
___	**2446**	Summit Observation Car	13	43
___	**2452**	Pennsylvania Gondola	5	18
___	**2452X**	Pennsylvania Gondola	5	14
___	**X2454**	Pennsylvania Boxcar (marked "Box Car")	11	34
___	**X2454**	Pennsylvania Boxcar (marked "Merchandise Car")	20	62
___	**2456**	Lehigh Valley Hopper	5	18
___	**2457**	Pennsylvania N5-type Caboose	6	29
___	**2458**	Pennsylvania Automobile Boxcar	11	36

BOXES		Good P-5	Exc P-7	
2460	Bucyrus Erie Crane Car (box with toy logo)	20	50	___
2460	Bucyrus Erie Crane Car (box without toy logo)	29	116	___
2461	Transformer Car	15	47	___
2465	Sunoco 2-D Tank Car	4	10	___
2466T	Tender	8	26	___
2466W	Tender	12	36	___
2466WX	Tender	12	41	___
2472	PRR N5-type Caboose	4	18	___
2481	Plainfield Pullman Car	39	154	___
2482	Westfield Pullman Car	39	154	___
2483	Livingston Observation Car	39	154	___
2501W	M&StL Diesel Freight Set	49	225	___
2502W	Budd RDC Set	112	205	___
2503WS	Super O Steam Freight Set	24	93	___
2505W	Super O Electric Freight Set	51	219	___
2507W	New Haven Diesel Freight Set	67	352	___
2509WS	Super O Steam Freight Set	39	190	___
2511W	Pennsylvania Electric Work Set	56	241	___
2513W	Virginian Rectifier Set	73	347	___
2515WS	Super O Steam Freight Set	70	305	___
2517W	Rio Grande Diesel Freight Set	77	372	___
2518W	Pennsylvania Electric Passenger Set	109	491	___
2519W	Virginian Train Master Super O Freight Set	46	390	___
2521	President McKinley Observation Car	21	79	___
2521WS	Super O Steam Freight Set	58	570	___
2522	President Harrison Vista Dome Car	22	81	___
2523	President Garfield Pullman Car	23	82	___
2523W	Santa Fe Super O Freight Set	54	297	___
2525WS	Super O Steam Work Train Set	131	511	___
2526W	Santa Fe Passenger Set	161	371	___
2527	Missile Launcher Set, yellow	18	73	___
2528WS	Super O General Set	39	169	___
2530	REA Baggage Car	26	119	___
2530	REA Baggage Car (orange perforated)	73	290	___
2531	Silver Dawn Observation Car	17	69	___
2531WS	Super O Steam Freight Set	39	137	___
2532	Silver Range Vista Dome Car	17	90	___
2533	Silver Cloud Pullman Car	17	67	___
2533W	Super O GN Electric Freight Set	95	439	___
2534	Silver Bluff Pullman Car	16	49	___
2535WS	Steam Freight Set	45	170	___
2537W	New Haven Freight Set	65	311	___
2541	Alexander Hamilton Observation Car	25	101	___
2541W	Santa Fe Super O Freight Set	129	446	___
2542	Betsy Ross Vista Dome Car	22	79	___
2543	William Penn Pullman Car	21	79	___

BOXES			Good P-5	Exc P-7
___	2543WS	Berkshire Freight Set	99	528
___	2544	Molly Pitcher Pullman Car	21	79
___	2544W	Santa Fe Passenger Set	109	572
___	2545WS	Super O Military Set	168	772
___	2547WS	Super O Steam Freight Set	35	162
___	2549W	Super O Military Set	45	210
___	2550	B&O Baggage-Mail Rail Diesel Car	38	141
___	2551	Banff Park Observation Car	32	113
___	2551W	GN Electric Set	118	515
___	2552	Skyline 500 Vista Dome Car	32	111
___	2553	Blair Manor Pullman Car	52	204
___	2553WS	Berkshire Freight Set	53	272
___	2554	Craig Manor Pullman Car	56	201
___	2555	Sunoco 1-D Tank Car	10	38
___	2555	Sunoco 1-D Tank Car (overstamped 2755 box)	22	73
___	2559	B&O Passenger Rail Diesel Car	39	126
___	2560	Lionel Lines Crane Car	16	48
___	2561	Vista Valley Observation Car	37	117
___	2561	Vista Valley Observation Car (orange perforated)	52	144
___	2562	Regal Pass Observation Car	36	120
___	2562	Regal Pass Observation Car (orange perforated)	50	157
___	2563	Indian Falls Pullman Car	38	134
___	2570	Super O Santa Fe Work Train Set	55	212
___	2572	Boston & Maine Military Set	39	159
___	2574	Santa Fe Military Set	63	273
___	2625	Irvington Pullman Car	42	175
___	2627	Madison Pullman Car	29	113
___	2628	Manhattan Pullman Car	30	112
___	2671T	Pennsylvania Tender, for export	18	59
___	2671W	Pennsylvania Tender	22	72
___	2671WX	Lionel Lines Tender	27	76
___	2755	Sunoco 1-D Tank Car	17	54
___	X2758	PRR Automobile Boxcar	10	34
___	2855	Sunoco 1-D Tank Car	32	118
___	3330	Flatcar with submarine kit	23	69
___	3330-100	Operating Submarine Kit, separate sale	47	159
___	3349	Turbo Missile Launch Car	7	35
___	3356	Operating Horse Car and Corral Set (classic)	17	66
___	3356	Operating Horse Car and Corral Set (orange picture)	19	69
___	3356-2	Horse Car	75	383
___	3356-100	Black Horses (classic)	4	13
___	3356-100	Black Horses (white box)	8	21
___	3356-150	Horse Car Corral	90	538
___	3357	Hydraulic Maintenance Car	11	43
___	3357-27	Trestle Components for Cop and Hobo Car	8	27
___	3359	Lionel Lines Twin-bin Coal Dump Car	12	42

BOXES		Good P-5	Exc P-7	
3360	Operating Burro Crane	19	68	___
3361	Operating Log Dump Car	5	20	___
3361X	Operating Log Dump Car	6	26	___
3362	Helium Tank Unloading Car	13	41	___
3362/3364	Operating Unloading Car (Hagerstown checkerboard)	20	50	___
3364	Log Unloading Car	9	28	___
3366	Circus Car Corral Set	36	140	___
3366-100	White Horses	11	34	___
3370	W&A Outlaw Car	9	34	___
3376	Bronx Zoo Car	12	41	___
3376-160	Bronx Zoo Car, green	16	47	___
3410	Helicopter Car	15	57	___
3413	Mercury Capsule Car	18	65	___
3419	Helicopter Car	18	85	___
3424	Wabash Operating Boxcar	25	56	___
3424-75	Low Bridge Signal (marked "3424-75" or overstamped on 3424-100 box)	61	206	___
3424-100	Low Bridge Signal	5	19	___
3428	U.S. Mail Operating Boxcar	11	42	___
3434	Poultry Dispatch Car	22	63	___
3435	Traveling Aquarium Car	30	112	___
3444	Erie Operating Gondola	10	32	___
3451	Operating Log Dump Car	8	28	___
3454	PRR Operating Merchandise Car	23	82	___
3456	N&W Operating Hopper	13	40	___
3459	LL Operating Coal Dump Car (no toymaker's logo)	18	60	___
3459	LL Operating Coal Dump Car (toymaker's logo)	13	46	___
3461	LL Operating Log Car	9	26	___
3461X	Automatic Lumber Car	10	35	___
3461-25	Lionel Lines Operating Log Car, green	12	45	___
3462	Automatic Milk Car	11	165	___
3462-70	Milk Cans	2	10	___
3464	NYC Operating Boxcar	5	29	___
3464	Santa Fe Operating Boxcar	5	12	___
3469	LL Operating Coal Dump Car	11	39	___
3469X	LL Operating Coal Dump Car	9	22	___
3470	Target Launching Car	13	41	___
3472	Automatic Milk Car	11	36	___
3474	Western Pacific Operating Boxcar	11	43	___
3482	Automatic Milk Car	14	48	___
3484	Pennsylvania Operating Boxcar	11	29	___
3484-25	ATSF Operating Boxcar	10	33	___
3494	NYC Operating Boxcar	12	43	___
3494-150	Missouri Pacific Operating Boxcar	15	46	___
3494-275	State of Maine Operating Boxcar	14	45	___
3494-550	Monon Operating Boxcar	45	180	___

BOXES			Good P-5	Exc P-7
___	3494-625	Soo Operating Boxcar	48	185
___	3509	Satellite Launching Car	12	50
___	3512	Fireman and Ladder Car	19	86
___	3519	Satellite Launching Car	11	39
___	3520	Searchlight Car	10	30
___	3530	GM Generator Car	16	51
___	3530-50	Searchlight with pole and base, separate sale	38	88
___	3535	Security Car with searchlight	13	48
___	3540	Operating Radar Car	21	70
___	3545	Operating TV Monitor Car	23	95
___	3559	Operating Coal Dump Car	11	35
___	3562-1	ATSF Operating Barrel Car	24	142
___	3562-25	ATSF Operating Barrel Car, gray	14	39
___	3562-50	ATSF Operating Barrel Car, yellow	15	50
___	3562-75	ATSF Operating Barrel Car, orange	20	47
___	3619	Helicopter Reconnaissance Car	12	52
___	3620	Searchlight Car with insert	13	38
___	3650	Extension Searchlight Car	11	37
___	3656	Operating Cattle Car	11	36
___	3656	Stockyard with cattle (set box with car box)	14	61
___	3656-9	Cattle (marked "3656" on 4 sides, unnumbered tuck flaps)	6	16
___	3656-9	Cattle (marked "3656" on 4 sides, "3656-44" on 1 tuck flap)	3	10
___	3656-9	Cattle (marked "3656-34" on 4 sides, "3656-44" on 1 tuck flap)	3	10
___	3656-9	Cattle (marked "3656" on 4 sides, "3656-44" on 1 tuck flap, OPS markings)	6	19
___	3656-9	Cattle (unnumbered sides, marked "3656-44" on 1 tuck flap)	7	20
___	3656-9	Cattle (unnumbered sides, marked "3656-34" on 1 tuck flap)	11	29
___	3656-150	Corral Platform, separate sale	135	706
___	3662	Automatic Milk Car (classic), 55	18	100
___	3662	Automatic Milk Car (orange picture), 64	20	65
___	3662	Automatic Milk Car (white box), 66	25	79
___	3665	Minuteman Operating Car	17	47
___	3672	Bosco Operating Milk Car	85	176
___	3820	USMC Operating Submarine Car	24	74
___	3830	Operating Submarine Car	16	46
___	3854	Automatic Merchandise Car	77	453
___	3927	Lionel Lines Track Cleaning Car	8	28
___	4109WS	Electronic Control Set	103	485
___	4357	SP-type Caboose, electronic	29	103
___	4452	PRR Gondola, electronic	23	85
___	4454	Baby Ruth PRR Boxcar, electronic	26	105
___	4457	PRR N5-type Caboose, tintype, electronic	25	93
___	4671W	Tender	46	151

BOXES		Good P-5	Exc P-7	
5160	Viewing Stand	12	52	___
5459	LL Coal Dump Car, electronic	25	113	___
6001T	Tender	3	9	___
6002	NYC Gondola	2	7	___
6004	Baby Ruth PRR Boxcar	3	9	___
6007	Lionel Lines SP-type Caboose	1	6	___
6009	Remote Control Uncoupling Track	2	5	___
6012	Gondola	3	9	___
6014	Boxcar	3	10	___
6014-60	Frisco Boxcar, white (middle classic)	6	18	___
6014-60	Frisco Boxcar, white	5	16	___
6014-85	Bosco or Frisco Boxcar, orange (classic)	7	23	___
6014-85	Boxcar (Hagerstown production)		19	___
6014-100	Airex Boxcar, red	7	20	___
6014-100	Airex Boxcar, red (orange perforated)	11	30	___
6014-150	Wix Boxcar	40	173	___
6014-335	Frisco Boxcar	6	19	___
6014-410	Frisco Boxcar	14	52	___
6015	Sunoco 1-D Tank Car	4	11	___
6017	Lionel Lines SP-type Caboose	2	6	___
6017-1	Caboose	6	16	___
6017-50	U.S. Marine Corps SP-type Caboose (box marked "6017-60")	16	54	___
6017-60	USMC Caboose	5	18	___
6017-85	Lionel Lines SP-type Caboose, gray	11	31	___
6017-100	B&M SP-type Caboose	12	40	___
6017-185	ATSF SP-type Caboose	5	17	___
6017-200	U.S. Navy SP-type Caboose	43	375	___
6017-235	ATSF SP-type Caboose	11	33	___
6019	Remote Control Track	2	5	___
6020W	Tender	9	36	___
6024	Nabisco Shredded Wheat Boxcar	5	24	___
6024-60	RCA Whirlpool Boxcar	17	54	___
6025	Gulf 1-D Tank Car (classic)	5	14	___
6025-60	Gulf 1-D Tank Car	5	19	___
6025-60	Gulf 1-D Tank Car (classic, overstamped 6024 box)	11	35	___
6025-85	Gulf 1-D Tank Car (classic)	9	32	___
6026T	Lionel Lines Tender	8	23	___
6026W	Lionel Lines Tender (classic or picture)	11	35	___
6027	Alaska SP-type Caboose	50	200	___
6029	Remote Control Uncoupling Track (classic)	2	6	___
6029	Remote Control Uncoupling Track (orange picture)	5	13	___
6032	Short Gondola	3	10	___
6034	Boxcar (Hagerstown production)	2	9	___
X6034	Baby Ruth PRR Boxcar	3	10	___
6035	Sunoco 1-D Tank Car	4	10	___

	BOXES		Good P-5	Exc P-7
___	**6037**	Lionel Lines SP-type Caboose	2	6
___	**6050**	Lionel Savings Bank Boxcar	6	23
___	**6050-110**	Swift Boxcar	7	23
___	**6057**	Lionel Lines SP-type Caboose	6	24
___	**6059**	M&StL SP-type Caboose	7	21
___	**6059-50**	M&StL SP-type Caboose (Hagerstown checkerboard)	10	32
___	**6062**	NYC Gondola	5	18
___	**6066T**	Tender	9	23
___	**6110**	2-4-2 Locomotive	7	25
___	**6111-75**	Flatcar with logs	14	46
___	**6111-110**	Flatcar	16	48
___	**6112-1**	Canister Car	10	28
___	**6112-25**	Canister Set	12	38
___	**6112-85**	Short Gondola (marked "Canister Car")	6	22
___	**6112-110**	Gondola Car with Canisters	6	25
___	**6112-135**	Short Gondola (marked "Canister Car")	6	23
___	**6119**	DL&W Work Caboose, red	6	21
___	**6119-25**	DL&W Work Caboose, orange	9	29
___	**6119-50**	DL&W Work Caboose, brown	10	28
___	**6119-75**	DL&W Work Caboose	10	34
___	**6119-100**	DL&W Work Caboose (classic)	8	27
___	**6119-100**	DL&W Work Caboose (picture, perforated, or window)	14	55
___	**6121**	Flatcar with pipes	14	45
___	**6121-60**	Flatcar with pipes	15	56
___	**6121-85**	Flatcar with pipes (classic)	15	55
___	**6130**	ATSF Work Caboose (cellophane)	13	40
___	**6130**	ATSF Work Caboose (Hagerstown checkerboard)	14	44
___	**6130**	ATSF Work Caboose (all other boxes)	6	23
___	**6149**	Remote Control Uncoupling Track, 64-69	2	5
___	**6151**	Flatcar with patrol truck	11	42
___	**6162-60**	Alaska Gondola	37	127
___	**6162-110**	NYC Gondola, blue (orange picture)	10	32
___	**6162-110**	NYC Gondola, red, separate sale (orange picture with label)	20	66
___	**6167-85**	Union Pacific SP-type Caboose	16	53
___	**6175**	Flatcar with rocket	10	36
___	**6220**	Santa Fe NW2 Switcher	22	90
___	**6250**	Seaboard NW2 Switcher	31	123
___	**6257**	SP-type Caboose	4	10
___	**6257X**	SP-type Caboose	14	41
___	**6257-25**	SP-type Caboose	4	11
___	**6257-50**	SP-type Caboose	5	12
___	**6262**	Flatcar with wheel load	9	29
___	**6264**	Flatcar with lumber, separate sale	64	146
___	**6311**	Flatcar with pipes	12	40
___	**6315**	Gulf 1-D Chemical Tank Car (classic)	14	43

BOXES		Good P-5	Exc P-7	
6315	Gulf 1-D Chemical Tank Car (Hagerstown checkerboard)	20	50	___
6315-60	Gulf 1-D Chemical Tank Car (orange picture)	10	37	___
6342	NYC Gondola	20	654	___
6343	Barrel Ramp Car	11	36	___
6346	Alcoa Quad Hopper	12	37	___
6356	NYC Stock Car	11	31	___
6357	SP-type Caboose (classic)	5	15	___
6357	Caboose (orange perforated)	8	20	___
6357	SP-type Caboose (orange perforated, overstamped)	21	71	___
6357-50	ATSF SP-type Caboose	158	504	___
6361	Timber Transport Car	13	40	___
6361	Timber Transport Car (Hagerstown checkerboard)	18	61	___
6362	Truck Car	10	39	___
6376	LL Circus Stock Car	13	43	___
6401	Flatcar, gray	25	89	___
6403B	Tender with bell	23	68	___
6405	Flatcar with piggyback van	8	28	___
6407	Flatcar with rocket	88	498	___
6411	Flatcar with logs	5	20	___
6413	Mercury Capsule Carrying Car	17	57	___
6414	Evans Auto Loader (classic)	21	67	___
6414	Evans Auto Loader (orange picture)	25	88	___
6414	Evans Auto Loader (orange picture, overstamped 6416 box)	31	97	___
6414	Evans Auto Loader (orange perforated), 59	20	80	___
6414	Evans Auto Loader (cellophane), 66	27	126	___
6414-25	Four Automobiles, separate sale	149	559	___
6414-85	Evans Auto Loader (orange picture)	125	414	___
6415	Sunoco 3-D Tank Car (classic)	8	22	___
6415	Sunoco 3-D Tank Car (orange picture)	13	35	___
6415	Sunoco 3-D Tank Car (cellophane)	21	68	___
6415	Sunoco 3-D Tank Car (Hillside checkerboard)	20	49	___
6415	Sunoco 3-D Tank Car (orange picture with label)	29	84	___
6416	Boat Transport Car	36	115	___
6417	PRR N5c Porthole Caboose	4	21	___
6417-25	Lionel Lines N5c Porthole Caboose	7	26	___
6417-50	Lehigh Valley N5c Porthole Caboose	21	75	___
6418	Machinery Car	17	58	___
6419	DL&W Work Caboose	10	32	___
6419-25	DL&W Work Caboose	7	22	___
6419-50	DL&W Work Caboose	10	32	___
6419-100	N&W Work Caboose	27	74	___
6420	DL&W Work Caboose with searchlight	15	41	___
6424	Twin Auto Flatcar	12	38	___
6424-60	Twin Auto Flatcar	15	62	___
6424-85	Twin Auto Flatcar	14	51	___

BOXES			Good P-5	Exc P-7
___	**6424-110**	Twin Auto Flatcar	23	84
___	**6425**	Gulf 3-D Tank Car	10	32
___	**6427**	Lionel Lines N5c Porthole Caboose	8	21
___	**6427-1**	Caboose	9	28
___	**6427-60**	Virginian N5c Porthole Caboose	66	238
___	**6427-500**	PRR N5c Porthole Caboose, sky blue, from Girls Set	46	156
___	**6428**	U.S. Mail Boxcar	12	40
___	**6429**	DL&W Work Caboose	35	134
___	**6430**	Flatcar with trailers	12	43
___	**6431**	Flatcar with vans and tractor (cellophane), 66	47	157
___	**6434**	Poultry Dispatch Stock Car	15	47
___	**6436**	Lehigh Valley Open Quad Hopper, black	11	39
___	**6436-25**	Lehigh Valley Open Quad Hopper, maroon	9	64
___	**6436-110**	Lehigh Valley Open Quad Hopper, red	12	33
___	**6436-500**	Lehigh Valley Open Quad Hopper, lilac, from Girls Set	51	240
___	**6436-1969**	TCA Hopper (Hagerstown checkered)	15	42
___	**6437**	PRR N5c Porthole Caboose	7	21
___	**6440**	Flatcar with vans	13	41
___	**6440**	Green Pullman Car	11	43
___	**6441**	Green Observation Car	11	42
___	**6442**	Brown Pullman Car	11	43
___	**6443**	Brown Observation Car	11	43
___	**6445**	Fort Knox Gold Reserve Car	14	44
___	**6446**	N&W Covered Quad Hopper	10	34
___	**6446**	N&W Covered Quad Hopper (orange picture)	18	63
___	**6446-25**	N&W Covered Quad Hopper	11	37
___	**6446-60**	Lehigh Valley Covered Quad Hopper	62	264
___	**6447**	PRR N5c Porthole Caboose	55	232
___	**6448**	Exploding Target Range Boxcar	9	31
___	**6452**	Pennsylvania Gondola	4	14
___	**X6454**	Santa Fe, NYC, or Baby Ruth Boxcar	8	28
___	**X6454**	PRR Boxcar	7	28
___	**X6454**	PRR Boxcar (classic, overstamped 3464 box)	9	32
___	**X6454**	Southern Pacific Boxcar	8	28
___	**X6454**	Erie Boxcar	7	28
___	**6456**	Lehigh Valley Short Hopper	6	15
___	**6456-25**	LV Short Hopper ("25" rubber-stamped on end flaps)	8	67
___	**6456-75**	Lehigh Valley Short Hopper	36	124
___	**6457**	SP-type Caboose	6	16
___	**6460**	Bucyrus Erie Crane Car	13	44
___	**6460-25**	Bucyrus Erie Crane Car, red cab	16	51
___	**6461**	Transformer Car	10	33
___	**6462**	NYC Gondola, black	3	10
___	**6462-25**	NYC Gondola, green	7	19
___	**6462-75**	NYC Gondola, red	4	13

BOXES		Good P-5	Exc P-7	
6462-100	NYC Gondola, red	15	40	___
6462-125	NYC Gondola, red plastic	5	15	___
6462-500	NYC Gondola, pink, from Girls Set	52	179	___
6463	Rocket Fuel 2-D Tank Car	12	46	___
6464-1	Western Pacific Boxcar	14	44	___
6464-25	Great Northern Boxcar	17	50	___
6464-50	M&StL Boxcar	15	47	___
6464-50	M&StL Boxcar (overstamped with "S" and "Silver")	22	64	___
6464-75	Rock Island Boxcar	13	43	___
6464-100	Western Pacific Boxcar	29	121	___
6464-125	NYC Pacemaker Boxcar	16	54	___
6464-150	Missouri Pacific Boxcar	15	51	___
6464-175	Rock Island Boxcar	15	60	___
6464-175	Rock Island Boxcar (overstamped with "S" and "Silver")	31	117	___
6464-200	Pennsylvania Boxcar	17	64	___
6464-200	Pennsylvania Boxcar (Hagerstown checkerboard)	23	69	___
6464-225	Southern Pacific Boxcar	15	46	___
6464-250	Western Pacific Boxcar (orange picture with label)	43	142	___
6464-250	Western Pacific Blue Feather Boxcar (classic for 6464-100), 54	105	524	___
6464-250	Western Pacific Boxcar (cellophane)	24	79	___
6464-275	State of Maine Boxcar	19	79	___
6464-300	Rutland Boxcar, 55	24	86	___
6464-325	B&O Sentinel Boxcar	64	209	___
6464-350	MKT Boxcar	43	180	___
6464-375	Central of Georgia Boxcar	18	57	___
6464-400	B&O Time-Saver Boxcar	12	41	___
6464-425	New Haven Boxcar (classic)	10	41	___
6464-425	New Haven Boxcar (Hagerstown)	13	42	___
6464-450	Great Northern Boxcar	12	51	___
6464-450	Great Northern Boxcar (cellophane)	17	60	___
6464-475	B&M Boxcar (classic)	13	46	___
6464-475	B&M Boxcar (orange picture)	23	79	___
6464-500	Timken Boxcar	22	80	___
6464-510	NYC Pacemaker Boxcar	75	242	___
6464-515	MKT Boxcar	74	241	___
6464-525	M&StL Boxcar	13	44	___
6464-650	D&RGW Boxcar (cellophane)	20	71	___
6464-700	Santa Fe Boxcar	16	50	___
6464-725	New Haven Boxcar (orange picture, "735" on box)	11	38	___
6464-725	New Haven Boxcar (Hagerstown checkerboard)	20	64	___
6464-825	Alaska Boxcar	60	221	___
6464-900	NYC Boxcar	13	42	___
6464-960	TCA Boxcar, 1965	34	78	___
6465	Gulf 2-D Tank Car, black (classic)	5	14	___
6465	Sunoco 2-D Tank Car (classic, overstamped 2465 box)	5	18	___

BOXES			Good P-5	Exc P-7
___	6465	Sunoco 2-D Tank Car (classic, overstamped 6555 box)	6	20
___	6465-60	Gulf 2-D Tank Car (classic)	5	17
___	6465-60	Sunoco 2-D Tank Car (classic)	3	12
___	6465-85	Lionel Lines 2-D Tank Car (orange perforated)	25	123
___	6465-110	Cities Service 2-D Tank Car (orange perforated)	14	47
___	6465-160	Lionel Lines Tank Car (orange picture)	38	123
___	6466T	Lionel Lines Tender	6	19
___	6466W	Lionel Lines Tender (with liner)	17	43
___	6466WX	Lionel Lines Tender (with liner)	18	46
___	6467	Miscellaneous Car	15	42
___	6468	B&O Auto Boxcar, Tuscan (marked "X")	43	155
___	6468	B&O Auto Boxcar, blue	11	31
___	6468-25	NH Auto Boxcar	13	41
___	6469	Liquified Gas Tank Car	20	124
___	6470	Explosives Boxcar	11	38
___	6472	Refrigerator Car	5	19
___	6473	Horse Transport Car	10	34
___	6473	Horse Transport Car (end flaps half white, half orange)	22	84
___	6475	Pickles Vat Car (orange picture)	20	65
___	6476	Lehigh Valley Short Hopper	6	19
___	6476	Lehigh Valley Short Hopper (orange perforated)	12	39
___	6476-85	Lehigh Valley Short Hopper	15	49
___	6476-135	Lehigh Valley Short Hopper	8	29
___	6476-160	Lehigh Valley Short Hopper (Hagerstown checkerboard)	9	27
___	6477	Miscellaneous Car with pipes	11	39
___	6482	Refrigerator Car	8	30
___	6500	Flatcar with Bonanza airplane	82	290
___	6501	Flatcar with jet boat	25	70
___	6511	Flatcar with pipes	10	31
___	6512	Cherry Picker Car	13	40
___	6517	Lionel Lines Bay Window Caboose	14	41
___	6517-60	Bay Window Caboose (TCA)	30	109
___	6517-75	Erie Bay Window Caboose	65	231
___	6518	Transformer Car	17	48
___	6519	Allis-Chalmers Flatcar (classic)	21	69
___	6519	Allis-Chalmers Flatcar (orange perforated)	30	101
___	6520	Searchlight Car 2 City	13	41
___	6520	Searchlight Car 3 City	32	105
___	6530	Firefighting Instruction Car	17	56
___	6536	M&StL Open Quad Hopper	18	65
___	6544	Missile Firing Car	21	79
___	6555	Sunoco 1-D Tank Car	12	32
___	6556	MKT Stock Car	45	163
___	6557	SP-type Smoking Caboose	30	117
___	6560	Bucyrus Erie Crane Car (Hagerstown checkerboard)	18	59
___	6560	Bucyrus Erie Crane Car (all other boxes)	12	38

BOXES		Good P-5	Exc P-7	
6560-25	Bucyrus Erie Crane Car, 8-wheel (with liner)	17	48	___
6561	Cable Car, 2 reels	10	39	___
6562-1	NYC Gondola, gray	7	23	___
6562-25	NYC Gondola, red	5	25	___
6562-50	NYC Gondola, black	5	18	___
6572	REA Reefer (classic)	13	53	___
6572	REA Reefer (orange picture)	14	41	___
6636	Alaska Open Quad Hopper	15	63	___
6646	Lionel Lines Stock Car	7	22	___
6650	IRBM Rocket Launcher	9	32	___
6654W	Whistle Tender	12	31	___
6656	Stock Car	9	33	___
6657	Rio Grande SP-type Caboose	23	102	___
6660	Boom Car	12	45	___
6670	Derrick Car	14	50	___
6672	Santa Fe Refrigerator Car	10	32	___
6736	Detroit & Mackinac Open Quad Hopper	16	49	___
6800	Flatcar with airplane (classic)	17	51	___
6800	Flatcar with airplane (orange perforated)	19	65	___
6800-60	Airplane, separate sale	68	195	___
6801	Flatcar with brown and white boat	9	33	___
6801-50	Flatcar with yellow and white boat	13	42	___
6801-60	Boat, separate sale	33	104	___
6801-75	Flatcar with blue and white boat	13	43	___
6802	Flatcar with girders (late classic)	8	26	___
6802	Flatcar with girders (orange perforated)	16	52	___
6803	Flatcar with USMC tank and sound truck	29	99	___
6804	Flatcar with USMC trucks	28	95	___
6805	Atomic Energy Disposal Flatcar	22	79	___
6806	Flatcar with USMC trucks	29	98	___
6807	Flatcar with boat	24	88	___
6808	Flatcar with military units	29	98	___
6809	Flatcar with USMC trucks	29	97	___
6810	Flatcar with trailer	8	29	___
6812	Track Maintenance Car	18	58	___
6814	Rescue Caboose	20	65	___
6816	Flatcar with Allis-Chalmers bulldozer	50	186	___
6816-100	Allis-Chalmers bulldozer	120	419	___
6817	Flatcar with Allis-Chalmers motor scraper	67	188	___
6818	Flatcar with transformer	8	26	___
6819	Flatcar with helicopter	10	45	___
6820	Aerial Missile Transport Car with helicopter	64	235	___
6821	Flatcar with crates	7	26	___
6822	Searchlight Car	7	26	___
6823	Flatcar with IRBM missiles	16	62	___

BOXES			Good P-5	Exc P-7
___	6825	Flatcar with arch trestle bridge	7	23
___	6826	Flatcar with Christmas trees	20	63
___	6827	Flatcar with Harnischfeger power shovel	26	95
___	6827-100	Harnischfeger Power Shovel	31	86
___	6828	Flatcar with Harnischfeger crane (cellophane, no crane kit box)	28	83
___	6828	Flatcar with Harnischfeger crane (orange picture, no crane kit box)	20	69
___	6828	Harnischfeger Crane Kit, used with flatcar	14	62
___	6828-100	Harnischfeger Crane, separate sale	42	137
___	6830	Flatcar with submarine	17	56
___	6844	Missile Carrying Car	19	75
___	11001	Steam Freight Set (advance catalog 1962)	7	28
___	11011	Diesel Freight Set	21	75
___	11201	Steam Freight Set	15	55
___	11212	Diesel Freight Set	25	89
___	11222	027 Steam Freight Set	18	56
___	11232	NH Diesel Freight Set	19	67
___	11242	Steam Freight Set	17	59
___	11252	Diesel Space Set	24	74
___	11268	Military Set	30	109
___	11278	Steam Freight Set	17	58
___	11288	Steam Freight Set	28	102
___	11321	Diesel Freight Set	17	34
___	11331	Steam Freight Set	11	40
___	11341	Diesel Freight Set	10	26
___	11375	027 Steam Freight Set	12	48
___	11415	Steam Freight Set (advance catalog 1963)	21	95
___	11420	Steam Freight Set	8	30
___	11430	Steam Freight Set	20	65
___	11440	Diesel Freight Set	16	58
___	11450	Steam Freight Set	20	62
___	11460	Steam Freight Set	11	36
___	11490	Santa Fe Passenger Set	30	113
___	11500	Steam Freight Set	27	96
___	11520	Steam Freight Set	24	78
___	11530	Diesel Freight Set	32	82
___	11540	Steam Freight Set	13	33
___	11550	Steam Freight Set	17	57
___	11560	Texas Special Set	10	37
___	11590	Santa Fe Passenger Set	25	94
___	11710	Steam Freight Set	23	75
___	11750	Steam Freight Set	22	79
___	12710	Steam Freight Set	31	126
___	12730	Santa Fe Diesel Freight Set	44	155
___	12760	Berkshire Freight Set	77	288

BOXES		Good P-5	Exc P-7	
12780	Santa Fe Passenger Set	106	409	___
12800	B&M Diesel Freight Set	23	80	___
12800X	B&M Diesel Freight Set	42	167	___
12820	Virginian Train Master Freight Set	62	243	___
12840	Steam Freight Set	43	319	___
12850	Diesel Freight Set	38	156	___
13008	Super O Introductory Set	20	74	___
13018	Santa Fe Space-age Military Set	158	622	___
13028	Super O Space Set	56	225	___
13048	Super O Steam Freight Set	47	230	___
13058	Santa Fe Space-age Military Set	70	303	___
13088	Santa Fe Passenger Set	212	736	___
13098	Steam Freight Set	67	251	___
13108	Santa Fe Space Set	60	168	___
13118	Berkshire Freight Set	69	287	___
13128	Santa Fe Space-age Military Set	158	587	___
13150	Hudson Freight Set	243	884	___
A	Transformer, 90 watts	4	11	___
CTC	Master Carton		167	___
CO-1	Track Clips, 100	3	8	___
ECU-1	Electronic Control Unit	35	117	___
KW	Transformer, 190 watts	5	19	___
KW	Transformer, 190 watts (yellow)	6	19	___
LTC	Lockon	1	5	___
LW	Transformer, 125 watts	5	15	___
R	Transformer, 110 watts	4	11	___
RCS	Remote Control Track	2	5	___
RW	Transformer, 110 watts	4	14	___
S	Transformer, 80 watts	4	15	___
SW	Transformer, 130 watts	4	13	___
TW	Transformer, 175 watts	4	16	___
UCS	Remote Control Track (O)	2	5	___
UTC	Lockon	3	6	___
VW	Transformer, 150 watts	5	30	___
Z	Transformer, 250 watts	25	83	___
ZW	Transformer, 250 Watts	10	23	___
ZW	Transformer, 275 watts (classic)	10	33	___
ZW	Transformer, 275 watts (orange, with inserts)	11	34	___
ZW	Transformer, 275 watts (yellow, with inserts)	12	38	___
ZW	Transformer, 275 watts (classic)	11	35	___
ZW	Transformer, 275 watts (orange, with inserts)	11	35	___
ZW	Transformer, 275 watts (yellow, with inserts)	13	35	___

Section 8
CATALOGED SETS 1945-1969

			Good	Exc
___	**463W**	Steam Freight Set, 45	506	812
___	**1000W**	027 Steam Freight Set, 55	159	365
___	**1001**	027 Diesel Freight Set, 55	59	238
___	**1105**	027 Diesel Freight Set (1055, 6042, 6044, 6045, 6047), 59		145
___	**1107**	027 Diesel Freight Set (1055, 6042, 6044, 6047), 60	56	120
___	**1111**	027 Scout Freight Set, 48		225
___	**1112**	027 Scout Freight Set, 48	68	250
___	**1113**	027 Scout Freight Set, 50	56	127
___	**1115**	027 Scout Freight Set, 49	73	163
___	**1117**	027 Scout Freight Set, 49	50	172
___	**1119**	027 Freight Scout Set, 51-52	55	160
___	**1123**	027 Steam Freight Set (1060, 1060T, 6042, 6406, 6067), 60-62	50	98
___	**1400**	027 Steam Passenger Set, 46	110	777
___	**1400W**	027 Steam Passenger Set, 46	63	720
___	**1401**	027 Steam Freight Set, 46		120
___	**1401W**	027 Steam Freight Set, 46	60	220
___	**1402**	027 Steam Passenger Set, 46		550
___	**1402W**	027 Steam Passenger Set, 46	125	550
___	**1403**	027 Steam Freight Set, 46	50	515
___	**1403W**	027 Steam Freight Set, 46	250	760
___	**1405**	027 Steam Freight Set, 46		145
___	**1405W**	027 Steam Freight Set, 46		280
___	**1407B**	027 Steam Switcher Set, 46		1933
___	**1409**	027 Steam Freight Set, 46		425
___	**1409W**	027 Steam Freight Set, 46		435
___	**1411W**	027 Steam Freight Set, 46	188	1008
___	**1413WS**	027 Steam Freight Set, 46		350
___	**1415WS**	027 Steam Freight Set, 46		530
___	**1417WS**	027 Steam Work Train Set, 46		720
___	**1419WS**	027 Steam Freight Set, 46		880
___	**1421WS**	027 Steam Freight Set, 46		1100
___	**1423W**	027 Steam Freight Set, 48-49		239
___	**1425B**	027 Steam Switcher Freight Set, 48	267	711
___	**1425B**	027 Steam Switcher Freight Set, 49		825
___	**1426WS**	027 Steam Passenger Set, 48-49	236	779
___	**1427WS**	027 Steam Freight Set, 48	169	294
___	**1429WS**	027 Steam Freight Set, 48	200	530
___	**1430WS**	027 Steam Passenger Set, 48-49		894
___	**1431**	027 Steam Freight Set, 47		235
___	**1431W**	027 Steam Freight Set, 47	55	168
___	**1432**	027 Steam Passenger Set, 47		850
___	**1432W**	027 Steam Passenger Set, 47		795
___	**1433**	027 Steam Freight Set, 47		521
___	**1433W**	027 Steam Freight Set, 47	237	378
___	**1434WS**	027 Steam Passenger Set, 47		555
___	**1435WS**	027 Steam Freight Set, 47		240
___	**1437WS**	027 Steam Freight Set, 47	95	611
___	**1439WS**	027 Steam Freight Set, 47		470
___	**1441WS**	027 Steam Work Train Set, 47		1225
___	**1443WS**	027 Steam Freight Set, 47		400

SETS		Good	Exc	
1445WS	027 Steam Freight Set, 48	163	363	___
1447WS	027 Steam Work Train Set, 48		460	___
1447WS	027 Steam Work Train Set, 49	238	1463	___
1449WS	027 Steam Freight Set, 48		430	___
1451WS	027 Steam Freight Set, 49	75	290	___
1453WS	027 Steam Freight Set, 49		386	___
1455WS	027 Steam Freight Set, 49		335	___
1457B	027 Diesel Freight Set, 49-50		710	___
1459WS	027 Steam Freight Set, 49		1090	___
1461S	027 Steam Freight Set, 50		175	___
1463W	027 Steam Freight Set, 50		268	___
1463WS	027 Freight Set, 51	88	244	___
1464W	027 UP Diesel Passenger Set, 50	447	1570	___
1464W	027 UP Passenger Set, 51		880	___
1464W	027 UP Passenger Set, 52-53	188	804	___
1465	027 Steam Freight Set, 52	75	188	___
1467W	027 UP Diesel Freight Set, 50-51	126	795	___
1467W	027 Erie Diesel Freight Set, 52-53	79	641	___
1469WS	027 Steam Freight Set, 50-51	187	329	___
1471WS	027 Steam Freight Set, 50-51	142	450	___
1473WS	027 Steam Freight Set, 50	110	560	___
1475WS	027 Steam Freight Set, 50	63	735	___
1477S	027 Steam Freight Set, 51-52	158	275	___
1479WS	027 Steam Freight Set, 52	234	396	___
1481WS	027 Steam Freight Set, 51	230	469	___
1483WS	027 Steam Freight Set, 52	527	1023	___
1484WS	027 Steam Passenger Set, 52		705	___
1485WS	027 Steam Freight Set, 52		270	___
1500	027 Steam Freight Set, 53	43	193	___
1500	027 Steam Freight Set, 54		172	___
1501S	027 Steam Freight Set, 53	95	234	___
1502WS	027 Steam Passenger Set, 53	375	1523	___
1503WS	027 Steam Freight Set, 53-54	216	442	___
1505WS	027 Steam Freight Set, 53	407	592	___
1507WS	027 Steam Freight Set, 53	173	558	___
1509WS	027 Steam Freight Set, 53	188	500	___
1511S	027 Steam Freight Set, 53	91	250	___
1513S	027 Steam Freight Set, 54-55	99	248	___
1515WS	027 Steam Freight Set, 54	212	488	___
1516WS	027 Passenger Set, 54	208	650	___
1517W	027 Diesel Freight Set, 54	625	2075	___
1519WS	027 Steam Freight Set, 54		615	___
1520W	027 Texas Special Passenger Set, 54	792	1900	___
1521WS	027 Steam Work Train Set, 54		758	___
1523	027 Diesel Work Train Set, 54	138	671	___
1525	027 Diesel Freight Set, 55		245	___
1527	027 Steam Work Train Set, 55	332	727	___
1529	027 PRR Diesel Freight Set, 55	320	652	___
1531W	027 Diesel Freight Set, 55	288	1094	___
1533WS	027 Steam Freight Set, 55	113	429	___
1534W	027 Diesel Passenger Set, 55	288	1000	___
1535W	027 Diesel Freight Set, 55		1650	___
1536W	027 Texas Special Passenger Set, 55	240	1800	___

	SETS		Good	Exc
___	**1537WS**	027 Steam Freight Set, 55		508
___	**1538WS**	027 Steam Passenger Set, 55		900
___	**1539W**	027 Santa Fe Diesel Freight Set, 55		850
___	**1541WS**	027 Steam Freight Set, 55		600
___	**1542**	027 Electric Freight Set, 56	108	322
___	**1543**	027 Diesel Freight Set, 56	133	255
___	**1545**	027 Diesel Freight Set, 56		265
___	**1547S**	027 Steam Freight Set, 56		125
___	**1549**	027 Steam Work Train Set, 56		980
___	**1551W**	027 Diesel Freight Set, 56		566
___	**1552**	027 Diesel Passenger Set, 56	183	842
___	**1553W**	027 MILW Diesel Freight Set, 56		505
___	**1555WS**	027 Steam Freight Set, 56	266	404
___	**1557W**	027 Diesel Work Train Set, 56	334	466
___	**1559W**	027 MILW Diesel Freight Set, 56		800
___	**1561WS**	027 Steam Freight Set, 56		733
___	**1562W**	027 Diesel Passenger Set, 56	822	2134
___	**1563W**	027 Wabash Diesel Freight Set, 56		1570
___	**1565WS**	027 Steam Freight Set, 56	311	535
___	**1567W**	027 Santa Fe Diesel Freight Set, 56		1200
___	**1569**	027 UP Diesel Freight Set, 57	63	220
___	**1571**	027 LV Diesel Freight Set, 57	195	845
___	**1573**	027 Steam Freight Set, 57	85	212
___	**1575**	027 MP Diesel Freight Set, 57	118	320
___	**1577S**	027 Steam Freight Set, 57	126	235
___	**1578S**	027 Steam Passenger Set, 57	408	775
___	**1579S**	027 Steam Freight Set, 57		260
___	**1581**	027 Jersey Central Diesel Freight Set, 57		495
___	**1583WS**	027 Steam Freight Set, 57	78	268
___	**1585W**	027 Seaboard Diesel Freight Set, 57		493
___	**1586**	027 Santa Fe Diesel Passenger Set, 57	213	670
___	**1587S**	027 Steam Freight Set (Girls Set), 57-58	1288	3706
___	**1589WS**	027 Steam Freight Set, 57	123	500
___	**1590**	027 Steam Freight Set, 58	87	457
___	**1591**	027 Military Set, 58	475	1719
___	**1593**	027 UP Diesel Work Set, 58		590
___	**1595**	027 Military Set, 58		2050
___	**1597S**	027 Steam Freight Set, 58		355
___	**1599**	027 Texas Special Freight Set, 58		529
___	**1600**	027 Burlington Diesel Passenger Set, 58		750
___	**1601W**	027 Wabash Diesel Freight Set, 58		766
___	**1603WS**	027 Steam Freight Set, 58		433
___	**1605W**	027 Santa Fe Diesel Freight Set, 58		945
___	**1607WS**	027 Steam Work Train Set, 58		483
___	**1608W**	027 NH Diesel Passenger Set, 58	825	1865
___	**1609**	027 Steam Freight Set, 59-60	73	177
___	**1611**	027 Alaska Diesel Freight Set, 59	158	494
___	**1612**	027 General Set, 59-60	192	399
___	**1613S**	027 B&O Steam Freight Set, 59		254
___	**1615**	027 B&M Diesel Freight Set, 59	320	613
___	**1617S**	027 Steam Work Train Set, 59		800
___	**1619W**	027 Santa Fe Diesel Freight Set, 59	225	975
___	**1621WS**	027 Steam Freight Set, 59	255	587

SETS		Good	Exc	
1623W	027 NP Diesel Freight Set, 59	800	1958	___
1625WS	027 Steam Freight Set, 59		563	___
1626W	027 Santa Fe Diesel Passenger Set, 59	288	875	___
1627S	027 Steam Freight Set, 60	23	175	___
1629	027 C&O Diesel Freight Set, 60	120	361	___
1631WS	027 Steam Freight Set, 60	192	275	___
1633	027 U.S. Navy Diesel Freight Set, 60	477	1199	___
1635WS	027 Steam Freight Set, 60		400	___
1637W	027 Santa Fe Diesel Freight Set, 60	459	676	___
1639WS	027 Steam Freight Set, 60		1250	___
1640W	027 Santa Fe Diesel Passenger Set, 60	150	750	___
1641	027 Steam Freight Set, 61		175	___
1642	027 Steam Freight Set, 61		225	___
1643	027 C&O Diesel Freight Set, 61		328	___
1644	027 General Set, 61	53	375	___
1645	027 Diesel Freight Set, 61		250	___
1646	027 Steam Freight Set, 61		325	___
1647	027 U.S. Marines Military Set, 61	685	1203	___
1648	027 Steam Freight Set, 61	168	1120	___
1649	027 Santa Fe Diesel Freight Set, 61		538	___
1650	027 Steam Military Set, 61	105	506	___
1651	027 Santa Fe Diesel Passenger Set, 61		671	___
1800	General Gift Pack, 59-60	231	395	___
1805	027 Military Set (Land-Sea and Air Gift Pack), 60	585	3048	___
1809	Western Gift Pack, 61		300	___
1810	Space Age Gift Pack, 61	736	1165	___
2100	Steam Passenger Set, 46		550	___
2100W	Steam Passenger Set, 46	330	640	___
2101	Steam Freight Set, 46		350	___
2101W	Steam Freight Set, 46	99	395	___
2103W	Steam Freight Set, 46		467	___
2105WS	Steam Freight Set, 46		464	___
2110WS	Steam Passenger Set, 46		1875	___
2111WS	Steam Freight Set, 46		895	___
2113WS	Steam Freight Set, 46		4247	___
2114WS	Steam Passenger Set, 46	782	2500	___
2115WS	Steam Work Train Set, 46	422	1288	___
2120S	Steam Passenger Set, 47		500	___
2120WS	Steam Passenger Set, 47		500	___
2121S	Steam Freight Set, 47		400	___
2121WS	Steam Freight Set, 47		405	___
2123WS	Steam Freight Set, 47		645	___
2124W	PRR Electric Passenger Set, 47	936	3200	___
2125WS	Steam Freight Set, 47	238	568	___
2126WS	Steam Passenger Set, 47	463	1950	___
2127WS	Steam Work Train Set, 47		670	___
2129WS	Steam Freight Set, 47		2250	___
2131WS	Steam Work Train Set, 47		1200	___
2133W	Diesel Freight Set, 48		1350	___
2135WS	Steam Freight Set, 48	148	399	___
2135WS	Steam Freight Set, 49	230	670	___
2136WS	Steam Passenger Set, 48		674	___
2136WS	Steam Passenger Set, 49	86	802	___

	SETS		Good	Exc
____	**2137WS**	Steam Freight Set, 48	263	720
____	**2139W**	PRR Electric Freight Set, 49	475	1360
____	**2139W**	PRR Electric Freight Set, 48		1425
____	**2140WS**	Steam Passenger Set, 48-49	225	1600
____	**2141WS**	Steam Freight Set, 48	188	519
____	**2143WS**	Steam Work Train Set, 48		795
____	**2144W**	PRR Electric Passenger Set, 48-49	1163	1903
____	**2145WS**	Steam Freight Set, 48		815
____	**2146WS**	Steam Passenger Set, 48-49	1050	2000
____	**2147WS**	Steam Freight Set, 49	125	454
____	**2148WS**	Hudson Passenger Set, 50	1150	5800
____	**2149B**	Diesel Work Train Set, 49		690
____	**2150WS**	Steam Passenger Set, 50		1000
____	**2151W**	Diesel Freight Set, 49		888
____	**2153WS**	Steam Work Train Set, 49		1010
____	**2155WS**	Steam Freight Set, 49		1053
____	**2159W**	Electric Freight Set, 50	875	2514
____	**2161W**	Santa Fe Diesel Freight Set, 50		1550
____	**2163WS**	Steam Freight Set, 50		550
____	**2163WS**	Steam Freight Set, 51	363	1164
____	**2165WS**	Steam Freight Set, 50		678
____	**2167WS**	Steam Freight Set, 50-51	110	618
____	**2169WS**	Hudson Freight Set, 50	1100	3205
____	**2171W**	NYC Diesel Freight Set, 50		1335
____	**2173WS**	Steam Freight Set, 50	177	947
____	**2173WS**	Steam Freight Set, 51		523
____	**2175W**	Santa Fe Diesel Freight Set, 50	305	836
____	**2175W**	Santa Fe Diesel Freight Set, 51	271	860
____	**2177WS**	Steam Freight Set, 52	118	342
____	**2179WS**	Steam Freight Set, 52	166	564
____	**2183WS**	Steam Freight Set, 52	313	945
____	**2185W**	NYC Diesel Freight Set, 50		960
____	**2185W**	NYC Diesel Freight Set, 51		1018
____	**2187WS**	Steam Freight Set, 52	280	650
____	**2189WS**	Steam Freight Set, 52	165	580
____	**2190W**	Santa Fe Diesel Passenger Set, 52		1900
____	**2190W**	Santa Fe Diesel Passenger Set, 53	235	2010
____	**2191W**	Santa Fe Diesel Freight Set, 52		1355
____	**2193W**	NYC Diesel Freight Set, 52	388	1487
____	**2201WS**	Steam Freight Set, 53	167	1036
____	**2203WS**	Steam Freight Set, 53	338	1135
____	**2205WS**	Steam Freight Set, 53	371	1123
____	**2207W**	Santa Fe Diesel Freight Set, 53	614	1832
____	**2209W**	NYC Diesel Freight Set, 53	714	1433
____	**2211WS**	Steam Freight Set, 53		740
____	**2213WS**	Steam Freight Set, 53	325	1274
____	**2217WS**	Steam Freight Set, 54	629	1075
____	**2219W**	Diesel Freight Set, 54	870	1543
____	**2221WS**	Steam Freight Set, 54		500
____	**2222WS**	Steam Passenger Set, 54	1423	2613
____	**2223W**	Diesel Freight Set, 54	1430	3098
____	**2225WS**	Steam Work Train Set, 54	223	960
____	**2227W**	Santa Fe Diesel Freight Set, 54	777	1614
____	**2229W**	NYC Freight Set, 54	650	1525

SETS		Good	Exc	
2231W	Southern Diesel Freight Set, 54	797	2829	___
2234W	Santa Fe Diesel Passenger Set, 54	248	1990	___
2235W	MILW Diesel Freight Set, 55	188	654	___
2237WS	Steam Freight Set, 55		393	___
2239W	Illinois Central Diesel Freight Set, 55	288	1366	___
2241WS	Steam Freight Set, 55		615	___
2243W	Diesel Freight Set, 55	488	1375	___
2244W	Wabash Diesel Passenger Set, 55	2207	3650	___
2245WS	Steam Freight Set, 55		1150	___
2247W	Wabash Diesel Freight Set, 55	1596	2583	___
2249WS	Steam Freight Set, 55	341	872	___
2251W	Diesel Freight Set, 55	1250	2842	___
2253W	PRR Electric Freight Set, 55	950	2788	___
2254W	PRR Electric Passenger Set, 55	950	5500	___
2255W	Diesel Work Train Set, 56	224	843	___
2257WS	Steam Freight Set, 56	95	925	___
2259W	NH Electric Freight Set, 56	346	871	___
2261WS	Steam Freight Set, 56	285	636	___
2263W	NH Electric Freight Set, 56	162	978	___
2265WS	Steam Freight Set, 56		1003	___
2267W	Diesel Freight Set, 56		2210	___
2269W	B&O Diesel Freight Set, 56		2967	___
2270W	Jersey Central Diesel Passenger Set, 56	877	5730	___
2271W	PRR Electric Freight Set, 56	1272	2332	___
2273W	MILW Diesel Freight Set, 56	2036	4480	___
2274W	PRR Electric Passenger Set, 56	1493	3834	___
2275W	Wabash Diesel Freight Set, 57	115	820	___
2276W	Budd RDC Set, 57	1035	2035	___
2277WS	Steam Work Train Set, 57		585	___
2279W	NH Electric Freight Set, 57	340	837	___
2281W	Santa Fe Diesel Freight Set, 57		1040	___
2283WS	Steam Freight Set, 57		750	___
2285W	Diesel Freight Set, 57	525	2132	___
2287W	MILW Electric Freight Set, 57	600	2650	___
2289WS	Super O Steam Freight Set, 57	277	1850	___
2291W	Super O Rio Grande Diesel Freight Set, 57	1532	2617	___
2292WS	Super O Steam Passenger Set, 57	1000	1982	___
2293W	Super O PRR Electric Freight Set, 57	950	2400	___
2295WS	Super O Steam Freight Set, 57	1050	2157	___
2296W	Super O CP Diesel Passenger Set, 57	870	3080	___
2297WS	Super O Steam Freight Set, 57		2300	___
2501W	Super O Diesel Work Train Set, 58	188	914	___
2502W	Super O Budd RDC Set, 58		2375	___
2503WS	Super O Steam Freight Set, 58	150	715	___
2505W	Super O Electric Freight Set, 58	375	1400	___
2507W	Super O Diesel Freight Set, 58	763	3000	___
2509WS	Super O Steam Freight Set, 58		927	___
2511W	Super O Electric Work Set, 58		1100	___
2513W	Super O Electric Freight Set, 58	1633	3000	___
2515WS	Super O Steam Freight Set, 58		892	___
2517W	Super O Rio Grande Diesel Freight Set, 58	1275	2625	___
2518W	Super O PRR Electric Passenger Set, 58		1850	___
2519W	Super O Diesel Freight Set, 58	1267	3400	___

	SETS		Good	Exc
___	**2521WS**	Super O Steam Freight Set, 58	1000	2409
___	**2523W**	Super O Santa Fe Diesel Freight Set, 58		1300
___	**2525WS**	Super O Steam Work Train Set, 58	1358	3448
___	**2526W**	Super O Santa Fe Diesel Passenger Set, 58	888	4034
___	**2527**	Super O Missile Launcher Set, 59-60	482	861
___	**2528WS**	Super O General Set, 59-61	492	854
___	**2529W**	Super Electric Work Train Set, 59	950	1634
___	**2531WS**	Super O Steam Freight Set, 59	650	1294
___	**2533W**	Super O GN Electric Freight Set, 59		1910
___	**2535WS**	Super O Steam Freight Set, 59		840
___	**2537W**	Super O NH Diesel Freight Set, 59	332	2500
___	**2539WS**	Super O Steam Freight Set, 59		1483
___	**2541W**	Super O Santa Fe Diesel Freight Set, 59	398	2400
___	**2543WS**	Super O Steam Freight Set, 59		1590
___	**2544W**	Super O Santa Fe Diesel Passenger Set, 59-60	1370	2490
___	**2545WS**	Super O Military Set, 59		3000
___	**2547WS**	Super O Steam Freight Set, 60		484
___	**2549W**	Super O Military Set, 60	580	1237
___	**2551W**	Super O GN Electric Freight Set, 60	1150	3392
___	**2553WS**	Super O Steam Freight Set, 60	1077	2672
___	**2555W**	Super O Santa Fe Freight Set with matching HO Set, 60		10000
___	**2570**	Super O Santa Fe Work Train Set, 61	543	875
___	**2571**	Super O Steam Freight Set, 61		520
___	**2572**	Super O B&M Diesel Freight Set, 61		813
___	**2573**	Super O Steam Freight Set, 61	650	1433
___	**2574**	Super O Santa Fe Diesel Freight Set, 61	750	1875
___	**2575**	Super O PRR Electric Freight Set, 61	1250	3300
___	**2576**	Super O Santa Fe Diesel Passenger Set, 61		3065
___	**4109WS**	Electronic Control Set, 46		1493
___	**4110WS**	Electronic Control Set, 48-49	265	2500
___	**11011**	027 Diesel Freight Set, 62		286
___	**11201**	027 Steam Freight Set, 62		129
___	**11212**	027 Santa Fe Diesel Freight Set, 62		375
___	**11222**	027 Steam Freight Set, 62		243
___	**11232**	027 NH Diesel Freight Set, 62		535
___	**11242**	027 Steam Freight Set, 62		167
___	**11252**	027 Texas Special Space Set, 62	190	477
___	**11268**	027 C&O Diesel Freight Set, 62	817	1425
___	**11278**	027 Steam Freight Set, 62		239
___	**11288**	027 Space Set, 62	500	1215
___	**11298**	027 Steam Freight Set, 62	238	565
___	**11308**	027 Santa Fe Diesel Passenger Set, 62		730
___	**11311**	027 Steam Freight Set, 63		232
___	**11321**	027 Rio Grande Diesel Freight Set, 63		400
___	**11331**	027 Steam Freight Set, 63	35	105
___	**11341**	027 Santa Fe Diesel Freight Set, 63		831
___	**11351**	027 Steam Freight Set, 63		190
___	**11361**	027 Texas Special Space Set, 63		750
___	**11375**	027 Steam Freight Set, 63		700
___	**11385**	027 Santa Fe Space Set, 63		2000
___	**11395**	027 Steam Freight Set, 63		600
___	**11405**	027 Santa Fe Diesel Passenger Set, 63		750
___	**11420**	027 Steam Freight Set, 64		200

SETS		Good	Exc	
11430	027 Steam Freight, 64	97	170	___
11440	027 Rio Grande Diesel Freight Set, 64	143	291	___
11450	027 Steam Freight Set, 64	98	298	___
11460	027 Steam Freight Set, 64		150	___
11470	027 Steam Freight Set, 64	81	305	___
11480	027 Diesel Freight Set, 64		619	___
11490	027 Diesel Passenger Set, 64-65		397	___
11500	027 Steam Freight Set, 64		438	___
11500	027 Steam Freight Set, 65		275	___
11500	027 Steam Freight Set, 66	105	275	___
11510	027 Steam Freight Set, 64		300	___
11520	027 Steam Freight Set, 65-66		143	___
11530	027 Santa Fe Diesel Freight, 65-66	113	439	___
11540	027 Steam Freight Set, 65-66		260	___
11550	027 Steam Freight Set, 65-66	60	207	___
11560	027 Texas Special Freight Set, 65-66	132	360	___
11590	027 Santa Fe Diesel Passenger Set, 66		646	___
11600	027 Steam Freight Set, 68	640	1540	___
11710	027 Steam Freight Set, 69	137	176	___
11720	Diesel Freight Set, 69	100	746	___
11730	027 UP Diesel Freight Set, 69		800	___
11740	027 RI Diesel Freight Set, 69	60	310	___
11750	027 Steam Freight Set, 69		360	___
11760	027 Steam Freight Set, 69		355	___
12502	Prairie-Rider Gift Pack, 62		600	___
12512	Enforcer Gift Pack, 62		1100	___
12700	Steam Freight Set, 64		1000	___
12710	Steam Freight Set, 64-66		1182	___
12720	Santa Fe Diesel Freight Set, 64		1500	___
12730	Santa Fe Diesel Freight Set, 64-66	448	1136	___
12740	Santa Fe Diesel Freight Set, 64		1500	___
12760	Steam Freight Set, 64		1100	___
12780	Santa Fe Diesel Passenger, 64-66	1108	4678	___
12800	B&M Diesel Freight Set, 65-66	355	834	___
12820	Diesel Freight Set, 65	509	2304	___
12840	Steam Freight Set, 66	771	1791	___
12850	Diesel Freight Set, 66	425	2400	___
13008	Super O Steam Freight Set, 62		500	___
13018	Super O Santa Fe Diesel Freight Set, 62	646	1200	___
13028	Super O Space Set, 62		1000	___
13036	Super O General Set, 62	490	1160	___
13048	Super O Steam Freight Set, 62	360	941	___
13058	Super O Space Set, 62	800	2048	___
13068	Super O PRR Electric Freight Set, 62		3200	___
13078	Super O PRR Electric Passenger Set, 62		3500	___
13088	Super O Santa Fe Diesel Passenger Set, 62	1250	3300	___
13098	Super O Steam Freight Set, 63		2000	___
13108	Super O Santa Fe Space Set, 63		1000	___
13118	Super O Steam Freight Set, 63		1500	___
13128	Super O Santa Fe Space Set, 63		1750	___
13138	Super O PRR Electric Freight Set, 63		3800	___
13148	Super O Santa Fe Diesel Passenger Set, 63		2500	___
13150	Super O Hudson Steam Freight Set, 64	1538	4450	___

ABBREVIATIONS

Descriptions

AAR	Association of American Railroads (truck type)
AEC	Atomic Energy Commission
AF	American Flyer
CC	Command Control
DD	Double-door
EMD	Electro-Motive Division
ETD	End-of-train device
FARR	Famous American Railroad Series
FF	Fallen Flag Series
FM	Fairbanks-Morse
GE	General Electric
LL	Lionel Lines
MOW	Maintenance-of-way
MU	Multiple unit (commuter cars)
O	Lionel gauge (1¼" between outside rails)
OO	Lionel gauge (¾" between outside rails)
PFE	Pacific Fruit Express
REA	Railway Express Agency
SSS	Service Station Special
std	Standard gauge (2⅛" between outside rails)
std O	Standard O (scale length and dimension)
TMCC	TrainMaster Command Control
USMC	United States Marine Corps
1-D	One dome
2-D	Two dome
3-D	Three dome

Railroad names

ACL	Atlantic Coast Line
ATSF	Atchison, Topeka & Santa Fe
B&A	Boston & Albany
BAR	Bangor & Aroostook
B&LE	Bessemer & Lake Erie
B&M	Boston & Maine
BN	Burlington Northern
BNSF	Burlington Northern Santa Fe
B&O	Baltimore & Ohio
CB&Q	Chicago, Burlington & Quincy
CMStP&P	Chicago, Milwaukee, St. Paul & Pacific (Milwaukee Road)
CN	Canadian National
CGW	Chicago Great Western
CNJ	Central of New Jersey
C&NW	Chicago & North Western
C&O	Chesapeake & Ohio
CP	Canadian Pacific
CRI&P	Chicago, Rock Island & Pacific (Rock Island)
C&S	Colorado & Southern
CUVA	Cuyahoga Valley Railway
D&H	Delaware & Hudson
D&RGW	Denver & Rio Grande Western
DT&I	Detroit, Toledo & Ironton
DM&IR	Duluth, Missabe & Iron Range
E-L	Erie-Lackawanna (Erie-Lack.)
FEC	Florida East Coast
FWD	Fort Worth & Denver
FY&P	Franklin & Pittsylvania
GM&O	Gulf, Mobile & Ohio
GN	Great Northern
GN&W	Genesee & Wyoming
GTW	Grand Trunk Western
IC	Illinois Central
ICG	Illinois Central Gulf
IGN	International-Great Northern
KCS	Kansas City Southern
L&N	Louisville & Nashville
LNE	Lehigh & New England
LV	Lehigh Valley
MEC	Maine Central
MILW	Milwaukee Road
MKT	Missouri-Kansas-Texas (Katy)
MNS	Minnesota, Northfield & Southern
MP	Missouri Pacific
M&StL	Minneapolis & St. Louis
NdeM	Nacionales de Mexico Railway
NH	New Haven
NKP	Nickel Plate Road
NOT&M	New Orleans, Texas & Mexico
NP	Northern Pacific
NS	Norfolk Southern
N&W	Norfolk & Western
NWP	Northwestern Pacific
NYC	New York Central
NYO&W	New York, Ontario & Western
NYNH&H	New York, New Haven & Hartford (New Haven)
OSL	Oregon Short Line
P&LE	Pittsburgh & Lake Erie
PC	Penn Central
PRR	Pennsylvania Railroad
PMKY	Pittsburgh, McKeesport & Youghiogheny
PTM	ST Rail System
RFP	Richmond, Fredericksburg & Potomac
SF	Santa Fe
SLSF	St. Louis-San Francisco (Frisco)
SP	Southern Pacific
SSW	St. Louis Southwestern (Cotton Belt)
T&P	Texas & Pacific
TP&W	Toledo, Peoria & Western
UP	Union Pacific
WM	Western Maryland
WP	Western Pacific

NOTES

NOTES

NOTES

NOTES